Ireland

THE ROUGH GUIDE

There are more than eighty Rough Guide titles covering
destinations from Amsterdam to Zimbabwe

Forthcoming titles include
China • Jamaica • New Zealand • South Africa

Rough Guide Reference Series
Classical Music • The Internet • Jazz • World Music

Rough Guide Phrasebooks
Czech • French • German • Greek • Italian
Mexican Spanish • Polish • Portuguese • Spanish • Thai • Turkish

Rough Guides on the Internet
http://www.roughguides.com/
http://www.hotwired.com/rough

Rough Guide credits

Text editor:	Catherine McHale
Series editor:	Mark Ellingham
Editorial:	Martin Dunford, Jonathan Buckley, Jo Mead, Samantha Cook, Alison Cowan, Amanda Tomlin, Annie Shaw, Lemisse al-Hafidh, Vivienne Heller, Paul Gray
Production:	Susanne Hillen, Andy Hilliard, Judy Pang, Link Hall, Nicola Williamson, Helen Ostick
Cartography:	Melissa Flack and David Callier
Online Editors:	Alan Spicer (UK), Andrew Rosenberg (US)
Finance:	John Fisher, Celia Crowley, Catherine Gillespie
Marketing & Publicity:	Richard Trillo, Simon Carloss (UK), Jean-Marie Kelly, Jeff Kaye (US)
Administration:	Tania Hummel

Many thanks to all the regional and local offices of **Bord Fáilte** and the **Northern Irish Tourist Board** who helped with the research of this book: in particular Petra McGuiness (Kilkenny), Sinead Kenny (Mullingar) and John Walsh (Waterford). Thanks also to the **Youth Hostel Association of Northern Ireland**, **An Óige**, and **Independent Holiday Hostels** for their help and generosity. Continued thanks to all those who have given their help, encouragement and advice on this and previous editions, and especially the following: Ian Hill, Jo O'Donoghue, Marleen dry Konongen, Anne & Frank Greenwood, Niall Shanahan, Maire Molloy, Charles Hueston, Jack & Fidelis, Alice and John and Ben, George Gavan Duffy, Sean of Derrylahan, Elke & Karsten, Jean & Michael, Cillian Rodgers & family, Emma Gervasio, Timothy Chapman, Julian Walton, Con & Siobhan Lynch, Victoria White, Pól O Muirí, Colin Harper, Enda Hughes, Karlin Lillington, Bill Rolston and Kevin McHale. Many thanks also to Margaret Doyle for her thorough proofreading, Mark Lewis and Barbara Johnson for extensive keying, Link Hall and Judy Pang for typesetting and Matt Welton for maps.

Thanks also to readers of the previous editions for their contributions: see p.635 for the roll call.

The publishers and authors have done their best to ensure the accuracy and currency of all the information in *The Rough Guide to Ireland*; however, they can accept no responsibility for any loss, injury, or inconvenience sustained by any traveller as a result of information or advice contained in the guide.

This fourth edition published June 1996 by Rough Guides Ltd, 1 Mercer St, London WC2H 9QJ.
Distributed by the Penguin Group:

Penguin Books Ltd, 27 Wrights Lane, London W8 5TZ
Penguin Books USA Inc., 375 Hudson Street, New York 10014, USA
Penguin Books Australia Ltd, 487 Maroondah Highway, PO Box 257, Ringwood, Victoria 3134, Australia
Penguin Books Canada Ltd, 10 Alcorn Avenue, Toronto, Ontario, Canada M4V 1E4
Penguin Books (NZ) Ltd, 182–190 Wairau Road, Auckland 10, New Zealand

Typeset in Linotron Univers and Century Old Style to an original design by Andrew Oliver.
Printed in the UK by Cox & Wyman, Reading, Berks.

Illustrations in Part One and Part Three by Ed Briant; Basics illustration by Gila.
Contexts illustration by Andrea McMordie.

656pp
includes index
A catalogue record for this book is available from the British Library

ISBN 1-85828-179-2

Ireland

THE ROUGH GUIDE

Written and researched by

Margaret Greenwood and Hildi Hawkins

With additional contributions by

Frances Power, Sarah Foster, Roderick O'Connor, Debbie Almond,
John S. Doyle, Paul Power, Gerry Smyth, Nuala O'Connor,
Hilary Robinson, Luke Dodd, Seán Doran, Joe O'Connor, Killian Robinson,
Tom Joyce and Richard Nairn

THE ROUGH GUIDES

LIST OF MAPS

MAP SYMBOLS

▦▦▦	Motorway	∴	Ruins
═══	Main road	♟	Museum
───	Minor road	♦	Place of interest
·········	Footpath	⚊	Campsite
▬▬▬	Railway	⌒	Cave
─ ─ ─	Ferry route	⚱	Public Gardens
───────	Waterway	⌒	Mountain range
▬▬·▬▬·▬▬	National border	▲	Mountain peak
▬▬▬▬	County border	⌇	Waterfall
▬ ▬ ▬	Chapter division boundary	ⓘ	Tourist office
────	Wall	⊠	Post office
✕	Airport	■	Building
⌂	Country house	⊞	Church
♜	Castle	⁺₊⁺	Cemetery
⌂	Abbey	▨	Park
†	Church	▨	National Park

CONTENTS

Introduction vi

INTRODUCTION

andscape and people are what bring most visitors to Ireland – the Republic and the North. And once there, few are disappointed by the reality of the stock Irish images: the green, rain-hazed loughs and wild, bluff coastlines, the inspired talent for talk and conversation, the easy pace and rhythms of life. What is perhaps more of a surprise is how much variety this very small land packs into its countryside. The limestone terraces of the stark, eerie Burren seem separated from the fertile flatlands of Tipperary by hundreds rather than tens of miles, and the primitive beauty of the West Coast, with its cliffs, coves and strands, seems to belong in another country altogether from the rolling plains of the central cattle-rearing counties.

The greatest attractions of the place are, with a few fine exceptions, rural. Ireland is becoming increasingly integrated with the industrial economies of western Europe, yet the modernization of the country has to date made few marks: the countryside appears startlingly unspoilt and unpopulated. It's a place to explore slowly, roaming through agricultural landscapes scattered with farmhouses, or along the endlessly indented coastline, where the crash of the sea against the cliffs and myriad islands is often the only sound. It is perfect if you want space to walk, bike or (with a bit of bravado) swim; if you want to fish, sail, or spend a week on inland waterways. In town, too, the pleasures are unhurried: evenings over a *Guinness* or two in the snug of a pub, listening to the chat around a blood-orange turf fire.

This said, there are sights enough. In every corner of the island are traces of a culture established long before the coming of Christianity: sites such as **Newgrange** in County Meath or the clifftop fortress of **Dún Aengus** on Inishmore (the biggest of the Aran Islands) are among the most stupendous Neolithic remains in Europe, while in some areas of Sligo almost every hill is capped by an ancient cairn. In the depths of the so-called Dark Ages the Christian communities of Ireland were great centres of learning, and the ruins of **Clonmacnois** in County Offaly, the **Rock of Cashel** in Tipperary and a score of other **monasteries** are evocative of a time when Ireland won its reputation as a land of saints and scholars. Fortifications raised by the chieftains of the Celtic clans and the Anglo-Norman barons bear witness to a period of later turbulence, while the Ascendancy of the Protestant settlers has left its mark in the form of vast mansions and estates.

But the richness of Irish **culture** is not a matter of monuments. Especially in the Irish-speaking *Gaeltacht* areas, you'll be aware of the strength and continuity of the island's oral and musical traditions. **Myth-making** is for the Irish people their most ancient and fascinating entertainment. The ancient classics are full of extraordinary stories – Cúchulainn the unbeatable hero in war, Medb the insatiable heroine in bed, or Fionn Mac Cumhaill (Finn Mac Cool) chasing Diarmuid and Gráinne up and down the country – and tall tales, superstition-stirring and "mouthing off" (boasting) play as large a part in day-to-day life as they did in the era of the *Táin Bó Cuailnge*, Europe's oldest vernacular epic. As a guileless foreigner enquiring about anything from a beautiful lake to a pound of butter, you're ideally placed to trigger the most colourful responses. And the speech of the country – moulded by the rhythms of the ancient tongue – has fired such twentieth-century greats as Yeats, Joyce and Beckett.

Music has always been at the centre of Irish community life. You'll find **traditional** music sessions all around the touristed coasts and in the cities, too – some of it might be of dubious pedigree, but the *Gaeltacht* areas, and others, can be counted on to provide authentic renditions. Side by side with the traditional circuit is a strong **rock** scene, that has spawned U2, Sinéad O'Connor, Hot House Flowers and more recently such as

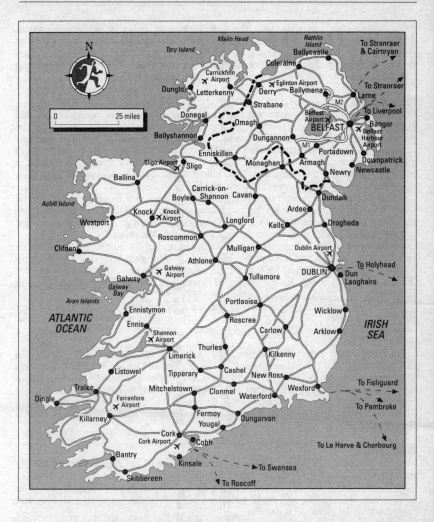

Therapy? and The Cranberries. And ever-present are the country and western performers, fathoming and feeding the old Irish dreams of courting, emigrating and striking it
lucky; there's hardly a dry eye in the house when the guitars are packed away.

The lakes and rivers of Ireland make it an angler's dream, but the **sports** that raise
the greatest enthusiasm amongst the Irish themselves are speedier and more dangerous. Horse racing in Ireland has none of the socially divisive connotations present on
the other side of the Irish Sea, and the country has bred some of the world's finest thor-
oughbreds. Hurling, the oldest team game played in Ireland, requires the most delicate
of ball-skills and the sturdiest of bones. Gaelic football, which commands a larger
following, bears a superficial resemblance to the British version, but allows a wider
range of violent contact. And, in Sean Kelly and Stephen Roche, Ireland has produced
two of the supermen of professional cycling, the cruellest of endurance tests.

No introduction can cope with the complexities of Ireland's **politics**. However, throughout the guide we have addressed the issues wherever they arise, and at the end of the book, in the *Contexts* section, we have included pieces that give a general overview of the current situation. Suffice it to say that, regardless of partisan politics, Irish hospitality is as warm as the brochures say, on both sides of the border.

Where to go

The area that draws most visitors is the **west coast**, where the demonically daunting peninsulas of the northern reaches are immediately contrasted a little inland by the mystical lakes of the **Donegal highlands**. The **midwest coastline** is just as strangely attractive, combining vertiginous cliffs, boulder-strewn wastes, and violent mountains of granite and quartz. In the **south**, the melodramatic peaks of the **Ring of Kerry** fall to lake-pools and seductive seascapes. Less talked about, but no less rewarding in their way, are the gentle sandy coves that **Cork** and **Kerry** share.

In the **north** of the island, the principal draw is the weird basalt geometry of the **Giant's Causeway**, not far from the lush **Glens of Antrim**. To the south of Belfast lies the beautiful walking territory of the softly contoured **Mountains of Mourne**, divided by **Carlingford Lough** from the myth-drenched **Cooley Mountains**.

The **interior** is nowhere as spectacular as the fringes of the island, but the southern heartlands of pastures and low wooded hills, and the wide peat bogs of the very centre are the classic landscapes of Ireland. Of the **inland waterways**, the most alluring are the island-studded **Lough Erne** complex of Fermanagh, and the **River Shannon**, with its string of huge lakes.

Some of the country's wildest scenery lies just offshore: west-coast **Aran** is the best known of the islands, but equally compelling are storm-battered **Tory Island**, to the far northwest, the savage **Skelligs**, off the southwest coast, and sequestered **Scattery**, in the mouth of the Shannon.

For anyone with strictly limited time, one of the best options must be to combine a visit to **Dublin** with the mountains and monastic ruins of **County Wicklow**. Dublin is an extraordinary combination of youthfulness and tradition, a human-scale capital of elegant Georgian squares and vibrant pubs. **Belfast**, in many ways rejuvenated after the ceasefires of 1994, now vies with Dublin in the vitality of its nightlife, while the cities of **Cork**, **Waterford** and, above all, **Galway** have a new-found energy that makes them a pleasure to visit.

When to go

Ireland's **climate**, determined by the pressure-systems of the Atlantic, is notoriously variable, and cannot be relied upon at any time of the year. Each year produces weeks of beautiful weather – the problem lies in predicting when they are likely to arrive. In recent years **late spring** and **early autumn** have proved the sunniest, with May and September as the pleasantest months.

Geographically, the **southeast** is the driest and sunniest part of the country, and the **northwest** is the wettest. But regional variations are not particularly pronounced, the overall climate being characterized by its mildness – the country benefiting from the warming effects of the Gulf Stream. Even in the wetter zones, mornings of rain are frequently followed by afternoons of blue sky and sun – and besides, a downpour on a windswept headland can be exhilarating, and provides as good a pretext as any for a reviving shot of whiskey.

PART ONE

THE

BASICS

GETTING THERE FROM BRITAIN

There are a large number of cheap flights to all parts of the Republic and to Northern Ireland and, unless you need to take a car, flying is often the best-value way of getting there. However, at peak times – Easter, July, August and Christmas – some of the cheaper fares may not apply, or all the cheap seats may be booked. In that case you might want to look at the combined train/ferry or bus/ferry options.

FLIGHTS

Flight time from London **to the Republic** is between an hour (to Dublin) and ninety minutes (to Cork, Carrickfinn, Knock, Shannon, Waterford and Kerry). The main carriers are *Aer Lingus*, which flies from ten UK airports, and its main Irish competitor, *Ryanair*, which flies from seven. **Northern Ireland** is similarly well served: *British Airways* and *British Midland* run frequent daily flights from London to Belfast (1hr 15min), and there are services from eighteen regional airports. You can also fly to Derry from Manchester and Glasgow. Bord Fáilte and the Northern Irish Tourist Board (see p.19 for details) provide information on all available routes – well worth getting before you plan your trip.

In general, there isn't much in the way of seasonal variations or reductions for midweek travel, although the astonishingly complex fare structures are constantly changing, so it's always a good idea to check the latest special deals direct with the airlines or with your local travel

agent. After these, the cheapest fares are the ones usually called **Apex** (Advanced Purchase Excursion) – available year round from most airlines. The conditions governing these tickets vary from airline to airline; however, most require that you stay one Saturday night, allow no changes and offer no refunds if you cancel your flight. In general, it's a good idea to book as far in advance as possible, and especially so if you intend to travel during peak times and/or to one of the regional airports.

Fares from **London to Dublin** with *British Midland* and *Aer Lingus* (from Heathrow) can cost as little as £75; with *British Airways* (from Gatwick) £79; and with *Ryanair* (from Stansted or Luton) £59. Flights from London **to Irish regional airports** are also good value. Tickets for *Aer Lingus's* Heathrow–Cork flights start at £79, Heathrow–Galway at £118. *Manx Airlines* flies Luton–Kerry from £99, and *Ryanair* from Stansted to Knock or Cork from £79.

Aer Lingus operates services from all the main **UK regional airports to Dublin**, from Newcastle, Manchester and Glasgow for as little as £69. *Ryanair* also offers some good fares: from Liverpool or Prestwick from £55; from Manchester or Birmingham from £59. *British Airways Express* (also known by its old name, *Loganair*, and bookable through *British Airways*) flies from Glasgow to Carrickfinn in Co. Donegal from £94.

Flights from **London to Belfast** are also competitively priced. *British Midland* flies from Heathrow to Belfast International from £55 and *British Airways* from £70. From the **north of England**, *British Airways Express* operates flights from Manchester to Belfast International from £89, *McGill Air* flies Newcastle–Belfast City from £89, and *British Airways* Liverpool–Belfast City from £80. **From Scotland**, *British Airways Express* flies Edinburgh–Belfast City from £108 and Glasgow–Belfast City from £57; it also operates flights to **Derry** from Manchester starting at £92, and from Glasgow starting at £80.

If you want to bring a **bike** with you, most airlines will allow you to do so and don't charge (except *Ryanair*, £15 extra each way), as long as you don't exceed your baggage allowance. It makes sense to ask if the airline carries bikes before buying your ticket, to inform them in advance and to check in early – particularly if you

AIRLINES

Aer Lingus, 223 Regent St, London W1R 6LB (☎0171/899 4747).

British Airways, 156 Regent St, London W1R 6LB; other offices in Birmingham, Manchester, Glasgow and Edinburgh (☎0345/222111).

British Airways Express, Glasgow Airport (☎0141/889 1311; and through *British Airways*).

British Midland Airways, Donington Hall, Castle Donington, Derby DE74 2SB (☎0345/554554).

Manx Airlines, Ronald's Way Airport, Ballasalla, Isle of Man (☎0345/256256).

McGill Air, Newcastle International Airport, Newcastle-upon-Tyne NE13 8BT (☎0191/286 2222).

Ryanair, Barkat House, 116–118 Finchley Rd, London NW3 5HT (☎0171/435 7101).

TRAVEL AGENTS

Campus Travel, *London Student Travel*, 52 Grosvenor Gdns, London SW1W 0AG (☎0171/730 3402); other branches in Bristol, Birmingham, Brighton, Cambridge, Edinburgh, Manchester, Oxford and in *YHA* shops and on university campuses all over Britain. Also *USIT* offices in Ireland. *Student/youth travel specialists.*

Council Travel, 28a Poland St, London W1V 3DB (☎0171/437 7767). *Flights and student discounts.*

STA Travel, 86 Old Brompton Rd, London SW7 3LH (☎0171/361 6161); other offices in Bristol, Cambridge, Manchester, Oxford, Leeds, Birmingham, Canterbury, Cardiff, Coventry, Durham, Glasgow, Loughborough, Nottingham, Warwick and Sheffield. *Specialists in low-cost flights and tours for students and under-26s.*

Trailfinders, 42–50 Earls Court Rd, London W8 6FT (☎0171/938 3366); also branches in Manchester, Glasgow, Birmingham, Bristol. *One of the best-informed and most efficient agents.*

are travelling to a small regional airport or during peak times, since carrying bikes is subject to available space.

YOUTH AND STUDENT FARES

Although there are few reductions on offer and the definition of "youth" varies between airlines (anything from under-20 to under-25), it is always worth asking – especially if you want a return period of longer than a month or a one-way ticket only. *Ryanair* offers a good deal to any **student** with an *International Student Identity Card* (*ISIC* – see pp.16–17 for more on special passes): you can buy a confirmed ticket on any of their routes for just £30.

If you are a student or **under 26** it's also worth checking fares through a specialist agency like *STA* or *Campus Travel* (see above for addresses).

FERRIES

Taking the boat from mainland Britain to Ireland is rapidly being outclassed by cheap air travel. However, in recent years ferry companies have responded by upgrading facilities on board, and now journeys are much more comfortable than they used to be. There are also catamaran services on the main routes, Holyhead–Dún Laoghaire, Fishguard–Rosslare and Stranraer–

Belfast, which cut sailing times almost in half (see box opposite for companies, routes and times). If you need a car when you get to Ireland, bringing your own is the best option – car rental in Ireland is among the most expensive in Europe (see "Getting Around"; p.25).

Ferry prices vary enormously depending on the time of year and even the day and hour you travel. Most ferry companies have **peak seasons** of July, August and Christmas and some also operate higher fares on bank holidays. In summer, in particular, car and foot passengers should always book in advance or risk turning up and not getting on the boat. Generally midweek crossings are cheaper throughout the year, and many companies offer special **off-peak deals**. Also bear in mind that prices are higher for the night-time crossings on some routes.

As an indication of **prices**, a return ticket for a car and five passengers on *Irish Ferries'* **Holyhead–Dún Laoghaire** route can cost as little as £168 and as much as £348 at peak times; **Pembroke–Rosslare** is between £148 and £308. *Stena Sealink*'s Holyhead–Dún Laoghaire **catamaran** service for a car and five passengers comes in at between £189 and £398. Ferry fares for individual foot passengers start at around £38 return, rising to £54; catamaran fares are between

£48 and £68. Generally combined bus/ferry or train/ferry tickets (see opposite) are better value.

There's a ten-hour sailing between **Swansea and Cork** operated by *Swansea–Cork Ferries*. Fares for a car and five adults range from £190 to £370; as ever, it's worth looking out for special offers – as little as £145 during off-peak times.

Making the short crossing from **Stranraer to Belfast** (*Stena Sealink*) or **Cairnryan to Larne** (*P&O*) is surprisingly expensive; prices range between £145 and £309 for a car and five passengers. *Seacat Scotland's* faster Stranraer-to-Belfast **catamaran** service costs between £190 and £345 for a car and four people. The one ferry service still operating out of **Liverpool** is *Norse Irish Ferries'* sailing to Belfast. Return fares range between £128 and £180 per car, plus £64–90 per adult. Foot passengers can travel for £90–100 – hefty prices, but a four-course dinner, cabin and full Irish breakfast are included. You must book in advance.

Student reductions on ferries can be considerable – *P&O* give a 50-percent reduction on its Cairnryan–Larne route, and *Stena Sealink* the same on the Stranraer–Belfast crossing. Students can also save up to £12 on a return journey with *Swansea-Cork Ferries*. Savings on fares from Holyhead, Pembroke and Fishguard are generally lower at around £6–8. *Stena Sealink* also offers a 10-percent reduction on all standard fares for members of *Hostelling International* (see p.28).

TRAINS

Prices of combined train/sea tickets vary according to the time of year and time of travel; peak times are July, August, Christmas and bank holidays; throughout the year prices are cheaper Monday to Thursday. The fare from **London to Dublin** ranges from £41 up to £61 return; from Manchester it's £31–46. **London to Belfast** is £53–73 return; **Birmingham to Belfast** is £48–63. Simply book at a mainline station or travel agent.

Anyone **under 26** can get one-third off standard train fares by buying a **Young Person's Railcard** (£16) from your local station or at branches of *Campus Travel* (see opposite).

An **InterRail** pass (£249 for a month) is unlikely to be worth buying when travelling to Ireland; although the pass gives free train travel in the Republic, it doesn't include trains in mainland Britain and gives only a 34-percent reduction in the North. For train passes valid for travel in Ireland only, see "Getting Around", p.21.

BUSES

Getting to Ireland by bus is a slog, but very cheap. *Slattery's* offers an off-peak **London-to-Dublin** city-centre return for £35, rising to £45 at peak times (July, August and Christmas), and operates direct services to the Republic from several English cities: Leeds, Bradford, Birmingham, Manchester, Liverpool, Chester and Holyhead. *Slattery's* only

---

■ FERRY COMPANIES, ROUTES AND TIMES

Irish Ferries (same company as *B&I*), Reliance House, Water St, Liverpool L2 (☎0151/227 3131); 150 New Bond St, London W1Y 0AQ (☎0171/491 8682).
Holyhead–Dún Laoghaire (2 daily; 3hr 45min); Pembroke–Rosslare (2 daily; 4hr 15min).

Norse-Irish Ferries North Brocklebank Dock, Bootle, Merseyside L20 1BY (☎0151/944 1010).
Liverpool–Belfast (1 daily; 11hr).

P&O European Ferries, Cairnryan, Stranraer, Wigtownshire DG9 8RF (☎01581/200276).
Cairnryan–Larne (2–12 daily; 2hr 20min).

Seacat Scotland, Seacat Terminal, West Pier, Stranraer, Wigtownshire DG9 7RE (☎0345/523523).
Stranraer–Belfast (4–5 daily; 1hr 30min).

Stena Sealink Line, Charter House, Park St, Ashford, Kent TN24 8EX (☎01233/647047).
Ferries: Holyhead–Dún Laoghaire (2–4 daily; 3hr 30min); Fishguard–Rosslare (1–2 daily; 3hr 30min); Stranraer–Larne (up to 9 daily; 2hr 20min). Sea Lynx: Holyhead–Dún Laoghaire (4 daily; 1hr 50min); Fishguard–Rosslare (3–4 daily; 1hr 40min).

Swansea Cork Ferries, King's Dock, Swansea, W. Glamorgan (☎01792/456116).
Swansea–Cork (1 daily; 10hr).

■ TRAIN AND BUS COMPANIES

BritRail International, European information line (☎0171/834 2345).

National Express Eurolines, 52 Grosvenor Gdns, London SW1 (☎0171/730 8235).

Slattery's Bus Service, 162 Kentish Town Rd, London NW5 2AG (☎0171/482 1604).

runs buses at night and the outward journey is gruelling: you arrive at Holyhead in the small hours to wait around the ferry terminal until 4am; the return is less of an ordeal as buses connect with the ferry. If you're heading for the **west coast** it's worth buying a direct ticket. Manchester–Galway, for example, starts at £45, and Slattery's also offers services to Cork, Limerick and Tralee, with stops at major towns en route. **Bikes** are carried free subject to available space – unlikely at peak times. *Slattery's* also offers a ten-percent discount to **students**.

The fares for *National Express Eurolines,* which runs both day and night buses on the London-to-Dublin route, start at £29 (day) and £39 (night), rising to £39 and £49 at peak times. It also has departures from the same cities as *Slattery's*, along with services from Sheffield, and in summer from Bristol and Cardiff. Book

these at your local *National Express* station, or through virtually any travel agent.

Getting **to the North** by bus is more expensive: *Euroline's* return journey to Belfast (night travel only) from London, Birmingham or Luton costs £49 and £59.

PACKAGE HOLIDAYS

If you want to avoid the hassle of making your own arrangements, if you are heading for a busy festival or if you are looking for a specific holiday activity (such as angling, cycling, walking or golfing), the numerous **package deals** available from tour operators are worth considering, although you are unlikely to save any money this way. The cheapest packages on offer are the fly/drive and sail/drive deals, which – if you are intending to rent a car – will often be more economical than making separate arrangements.

TOUR OPERATORS

Aer Lingus Holidays, London (☎0181/569 4001); Birmingham (☎0121/631 4680); Manchester (☎0161/839 3357); Glasgow (☎0141/248 4341); flight & car reservations only (☎0181/899 4747). *Dublin city holidays and country weekend breaks with accommodation, ranging from B&Bs to four-star hotels. Good fly/drive deals.*

Celtic Journeys, 111 Whitepark Rd, Ballycastle, Co. Antrim BT54 6LR (☎012657/69651). *Wildlife and walking holidays in the north and west of Ireland.*

Drive Ireland, 311 Tower Building, Water St, Liverpool L3 1AS (☎0151/231 1480). *Combined flight/accommodation/car rental deals – farmhouses, leisure hotels, castles and manor houses.*

Flanagan & Sons World Travel, 115 Radford Rd, Coventry CV6 (☎01203/597000). *Specialists in angling holidays at competitive rates. They also arrange combined ferry/flight and accommodation (town and country houses, farmhouses & self-catering cottages) holidays.*

Golf International, International House, Priestly Way, Staples Corner, London NW2 7AW (☎0181/452 4263). *Upmarket golfing holidays.*

Irish Cycling Safaris, 7 Dartry Park, Dublin 6 (☎01/260 0749). *Well-organized one-week guided*

tours for cyclists of all abilities in prime areas along the west coast from Cork to Donegal, with luggage van and hotel/guesthouse accommodation.

Irish Ferries Holidays, Reliance House, Water St, Liverpool L2 8TP (☎0151/236 8325). *Competitively priced car rental available in its sail/drive and fly/drive packages, with a broad range of accommodation options. Also golfing, fishing and cruising all-in holidays. Under-16s travel free.*

Leisure Breaks, 33 Dovedale Rd, Liverpool L18 5EP (☎0151/734 5200). *Very good range of activity holidays including riding, cycling, horse-drawn caravanning. Also accommodation and ferry deals and fly-drive packages.*

Slattery's, 1 Russel St, Tralee, Co. Kerry (☎66/26277; free phone ☎0-800/515900). *Full range of transport (flight, ferries and bus travel, plus motoring holidays) and accommodation (hotels, country houses and self-catering) deals. Also horse-drawn caravans and rambling with a donkey.*

Stena Line Holidays, *Stena Line Ltd*, Charter House, Park St, Ashford, Kent TN24 8EX (☎01233/647 0222; or call for a brochure on ☎0990 747474). *Full range of ferry and accommodation packages. Under 14s travel free.*

GETTING THERE FROM THE USA AND CANADA

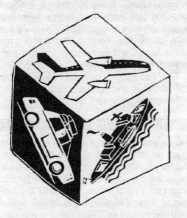

Ireland is easily accessible from the USA by a number of airlines that offer direct flights to the major gateways of Dublin, Shannon and Belfast. From Canada only indirect flights are available. If cost is your main concern, the proliferation of cheap flights from the British Isles, together with the number of train/ferry and bus/ferry options, may also make flying via London worth consideration. Ferries and cheap flights also make Ireland easily accessible as part of a wider European travel itinerary.

SHOPPING FOR TICKETS

Leaving aside discounted tickets, the cheapest way to go is with an **Apex** (Advance Purchase Excursion) ticket, although these carry certain restrictions: you usually have to book – and pay – at least 21 days before departure, spend at least seven days abroad (maximum stay three months), and you tend to get penalized if you change your schedule. There are also winter **Super-Apex** tickets, sometimes known as *Eurosavers* – slightly cheaper than an ordinary Apex, but limiting your stay to between seven and 21 days. Some airlines also issue **Special Apex** tickets to those under 24, often extending the maximum stay to a year. Many airlines offer youth or **student fares** to under 25s; a passport or driving licence is sufficient proof of age, though these tickets are subject to availability and can have

eccentric booking conditions. It's worth remembering that most cheap return fares involve spending at least one Saturday night away and that many will only give a percentage refund if you need to cancel or alter your journey, so make sure you check the restrictions carefully before buying a ticket. Any local travel agent should be able to access up-to-the-minute fares, although in practice they may not have time to research all the possibilities – you might want to call the airlines directly.

Discount outlets, however, can usually do better than any Apex and most student fares. They come in several forms. **Consolidators** buy up large blocks of tickets that airlines don't think they'll be able to sell at their published prices, and sell them at a discount. Besides being cheap, consolidators normally don't impose advance purchase requirements (although in busy times you'll want to book ahead just to be sure of getting a ticket), but they do often charge very stiff fees for date changes. Also, these companies' margins are pretty tiny, so they make their money by dealing in volume – don't expect them to entertain lots of questions. **Discount agents** – such as *STA, Council Travel, Nouvelles Frontières*, or others listed on p.8 – also wheel and deal in blocks of tickets off-loaded by the airlines, but they typically offer a range of other travel-related services such as travel insurance, train passes, youth and student ID cards, car

AIRLINES IN NORTH AMERICA

Air Canada Canada call directory inquiries, ☎1-800/555-1212, for toll-free number; US toll-free number is ☎1-800/776-3000.

Aer Lingus ☎1-800/223-6537.

American Airlines ☎1-800/433-7300.

British Airways US ☎1-800/247-9297; Canada ☎1-800/668-1059.

Canadian Airlines Canada ☎1-800/665-1177; US ☎1-800/426 7000.

Delta Airlines US ☎1-800/241-4141; Canada call directory inquiries, ☎1-800/555-1212, for toll-free number.

United Airlines ☎1-800/538-2929.

Virgin Atlantic Airways ☎1-800/862-8621.

rentals and tours. These agencies tend to be most worthwhile to students and under-26s, who can often benefit from special fares and deals.

Travel clubs are another option for those who travel a lot – most charge you an annual membership fee, which may be worth it for discounts on air tickets, car rental and the like. You should also check the travel section in the Sunday *New York Times*, or your own major local newspaper, for current bargains, and consult a good travel agent.

Be advised also that the pool of travel companies is swimming with sharks – exercise caution with any outfit that sounds shifty or impermanent, and *never* deal with a company that demands cash up front or refuses to accept payment by credit card.

Regardless of where you buy your ticket, the **fare** will depend on **season**. Fares to Ireland (like the rest of Europe) are highest from around early June to mid-September, when everyone wants to travel; they drop during the "shoulder" seasons,

mid-September to early November and mid-April to early June, and you'll get the best deals during the low season, November through mid-April (excluding Christmas). The Christmas–New Year holiday period is a thing unto itself – if you want to travel at this time, book at least two or three months ahead, and be prepared for fares even higher than those in summer.

Note that flying on weekends ordinarily adds $20–60 to the round-trip fare; price ranges quoted in the sections below assume midweek travel.

FLIGHTS FROM THE USA

Aer Lingus, the national airline of Ireland, flies direct out of **Boston** and **New York** to both **Dublin** and **Shannon**. The fares on all these routes are the same: the Apex ticket starts at around $500 in low season, rising to $700 in high season. **From Chicago** the fares are around $700 (low season) and $800 (high). A cheaper option is the promotional fares *Aer Lingus* offers

---

DISCOUNT AGENTS, CONSOLIDATORS AND TRAVEL CLUBS

Air Brokers International, 323 Geary St, Suite 411, San Francisco, CA 94102 (☎1-800/883-3273). *Consolidator.*

Air Courier Association, 191 University Blvd, Suite 300, Denver, CO 80206 (☎303/278-8810). *Courier flight broker.*

Airtech, 584 Broadway, Suite 1007, New York, NY 10012(☎1-800/575 TECH or ☎212/219-7000). *Standby seat broker; also deals in consolidator fares and courier flights.*

Council Travel, 205 E 42nd St, New York, NY 10017 (☎1-800/743-1823), and branches in many other US cities. *Youth/student travel organization. A sister company,* **Council Charter** (☎1-800/223-7402), *specializes in charter flights.*

Educational Travel Center, 438 N Frances St, Madison, WI 53703 (☎1-800/747-5551). *Student/youth discount agent.*

International Student Exchange Flights, 5010 E Shea Blvd, Suite 104A, Scottsdale, AZ 85254 (☎602/951-1177). *Student/youth fares, student IDs.*

Interworld, 800 Douglass Rd, Miami, FL 33134 (☎305/443-4929). *Southeastern US consolidator.*

Moment's Notice, 7301 New Utrecht Ave, Brooklyn, NY 11204 (☎718/234-6295). *Discount travel club.*

New Frontiers/Nouvelles Frontières, 12 E 33rd St, New York, NY 10016 (☎1-800/366-6387); 1001

Sherbrook East, Suite 720, Montréal, PQ H2L 1L3 (☎514/526-8444); others in LA, San Francisco and Québec City. *French discount travel firm.*

Now Voyager, 74 Varick St, Suite 307, New York, NY 10013 (☎212/431-1616). *Courier flight broker and consolidator.*

STA Travel, 48 East 11th St, New York, NY 10003 (☎1-800/777-0112); other branches in the LA, San Francisco and Boston areas. *Worldwide specialist in independent travel.*

TFI Tours International, 34 W 32nd St, New York, NY 10001 (☎1-800/745-8000), and other offices in Las Vegas and Miami. *Consolidator.*

Travac, 989 6th Ave, New York NY 10018 (☎1-800/872-8800). *Consolidator and charter broker.*

Travel CUTS, 187 College St, Toronto, ON M5T 1P7 (☎416/979-2406), and other branches all over Canada. *Specializes in student fares, IDs and other travel services.*

Travelers Advantage, 3033 S Parker Rd, Suite 900, Aurora, CO 80014 (☎1-800/548-1116). *Full-service travel club.*

UniTravel, 1177 N Warson Rd, St Louis, MO 63132 (☎1-800/325-2222). *Consolidator.*

Worldtek Travel, 111 Water St, New Haven, CT 06511 (☎1-800/243-1723). *Discount travel agency.*

throughout the year, including, for example, the Tuesday-to-Tuesday round-trip fare from New York for under $400. These are liable to change, so it's well worth enquiring about the latest promotion when calling. Among agents' deals, *Council Travel* offers round trips from New York in low season, starting at about $400; *STA* has a high-season fare of around $550, with cheap connections from other US cities.

Of the **US airlines** that operate services direct to the Republic, *Delta* flies from **Atlanta** to both Shannon and Dublin. Their Apex fares range from $650 (low season) to $900 (high). If you are connecting from another US city, however, fares can be a good deal more reasonable.

A number of carriers also fly **direct to Belfast**. *Aer Lingus* offers the most flights: three times a week from New York and twice a week from Boston. Low-season fares start at $360, high-season at $700.

With the high volume of transatlantic flights to **London**, you may well find a discounted fare that makes it worthwhile travelling here first. Many airlines offer flights from most of the eastern hub cities – the best deals are generally out of New York and Chicago. The lowest off-peak fare to London from New York with the major carriers – *British Airways*, *American*, *United* and *Virgin*

Atlantic – is around $350, though peak season prices are likely to be at least double this. *Virgin Atlantic* offers by far the best value for money, with excellent in-flight service and entertainment: $348 rising to $678 in high season. The add-on fare to Dublin, Shannon or Belfast is around $100.

From the **West Coast** there's less choice direct to the Republic or the North, and getting to London is again far easier: the big airlines fly at least three times a week (sometimes daily) from Los Angeles, San Francisco and Seattle. *British Airways* has plenty of flights and is competitive, with fares starting at $700 to London. Failing that, take any one of a number of other carriers to New York or Boston and fly from there.

If Ireland is only one stop on a longer journey, you might want to consider buying a **Round The World (RTW)** ticket. Some travel agents can sell you an "off-the-shelf" RTW ticket that will have you touching down in about half a dozen cities (London is easily arranged, but an Irish connection will probably have to be added on separately). Others will have to assemble one for you, which can be more tailored to your needs but is apt to be more expensive (*British Airways* and *Aer Lingus* are your best bets). Figure on $1400 ($1600 in summer) for an RTW ticket including London.

TOUR OPERATORS

Aer Lingus Vacations ☎1-800/223-6537.

American Airways/Fly AAway Vacations ☎1-800/832-8383.

American Express ☎1-800/927-0111.

Brendan Tours ☎1-800/421-8446.

Brian Moore International Tours ☎1-800/982-2299.

British Airways Vacations ☎1-800/247-9297.

Celtic International Tours ☎1-800/833-4373.

CIE Tours International ☎1-800/CIE TOUR.

Collette Tours ☎1-800/832-4656.

Delta Dream Vacations ☎1-800/221-6666.

Destination Ireland ☎1-800/832-1848.

Distinctive Journeys ☎1-800/922-2060.

Irish American International Tours ☎1-800/633-0505.

Irish Links ☎1-800/824-6538.

Isle Inn Tours ☎1-800/237-9376.

Maupintours ☎1-800/255-4266.

Terry Flynn Tours ☎402/571-9319.

Trafalgar Tours ☎1-800/854-0103.

TWA Getaway Vacations ☎1-800/GET-AWAY.

SPECIALIST OPERATORS

All Adventure Travel ☎1-800/537-4025.

Art Horizons International ☎212/969-9140.

Castles, Cottages and Flats ☎617/742-6030.

Classic Bicycle Tours & Treks ☎1-800/777-8090.

Fishing International Hilltop Estate ☎707/542-4242.

Golf International ☎1-800/833-1389.

Irish American Cultural Institute ☎1-800/663-0505.

Irish Festival Tours ☎1-800/441-4277

Jerry Quinlan's Celtic Golf Tours ☎1-800/833-4373.

Owenoak Castle Tours ☎1-800/426-4498.

FLIGHTS FROM CANADA

Aer Lingus does not fly out of **Canada**, but the two major Canadian carriers – **Air Canada** and **Canadian Airlines** – fly indirect (with a change of plane in London) out of Toronto, Montréal and Vancouver to Dublin, Shannon and Belfast. Apex tickets from Toronto and Montréal to Dublin are around Can$750 in low season and Can$1000 in high (add on around $100 for Shannon or Belfast). From Vancouver, expect to pay around Can$1000 to Dublin in low season, Can$1250 in high (add on around Can$150 for Shannon or Belfast).

As is the case from the USA, travelling from Canada to **London** gives you many more options and potential for bargain fares. *British Airways* flies off-peak from Toronto to London for around Can$550, and from Vancouver to London for around Can$750; *Air Canada* is comparable, though its lowest fare from Vancouver is around Can$870. Fares during peak season can go as high as Can$1090 with *Canadian Airlines*. The add-on to the Republic or the North starts at around Can$100. For details of Round the World tickets see p.9.

PACKAGE TOURS AND STUDENT TRAVEL

Package tours may not sound like your kind of travel, but don't dismiss the idea out of hand. It's true that tours arranged in North America tend to be of the everybody-on-the-bus group variety, but many agents can put together very flexible deals, sometimes amounting to no more than a flight

EUROPEAN RAIL PASSES FOR NORTH AMERICAN AND AUSTRALASIAN TRAVELLERS

There are a number of European rail passes that can only be purchased before leaving home, though consider carefully how much travelling you are going to be doing: these all-encompassing passes only really begin to pay for themselves if you intend to see a fair bit of Ireland and the rest of Europe.

The best-known and most flexible is the **Eurail Youthpass** (for under-26s) which costs US$398/A$575 for fifteen days, and there are also one-month and two-month versions; if you're 26 or over you'll have to buy a first-class **Eurail** pass, which costs US$498/A$720 for the fifteen-day option. You stand a better chance of getting your money's worth out of a **Eurail Flexipass**, which is good for a certain number of travel days in a two-month period. This, too, comes in under-26/first-class versions: five days cost US$255/A$370 for under 26s, US$348/A$505 for over 26s, though it also comes in ten-day and fifteen-day formats. These passes can be bought from the agents listed below and also from many regular travel agents, especially youth and student specialists (see listings on p.8 and p.12).

North Americans and Australasians are also eligible to purchase **more specific passes** valid for travel in Ireland only – see "Getting Around", pp.21–2, for details.

RAIL CONTACTS IN NORTH AMERICA

BritRail Travel International, 1500 Broadway, New York, NY 10036 (☎212/575-2667 or ☎1-800/677-8585). *All British train passes, rail-drive and multi country passes.*

CIE Tours International, 108 Ridgedale Ave, Morristown, NJ 07962 (☎1-800/243-7687). *Rail passes.*

CIT Tours, 342 Madison Ave, Suite 207, New York, NY 10173 (☎1-800/223-7987). *Eurail passes.*

Ontario Rail Europe, *2087 Dundas East, Suite 105, Mississauga, Ontario LAX 1M2* (☎416/602-4195).

Rail Europe, 226 Westchester Ave, White Plains, NY 10604 (☎1-800/438 7245). *Official Eurail agent in North America; also sells a wide range of European regional and individual country passes.*

ScanTours, 1535 6th St, Suite 205, Santa Monica, CA 90401 (☎1-800/223 7226). *Eurail and European country passes.*

RAIL CONTACTS IN AUSTRALIA

CIT, 123 Clarence St, Sydney (☎02/9299 4574); offices in Melbourne, Adelaide, Brisbane and Perth (☎09/322 1090). *Comprehensive range of* rail passes. No NZ office – enquiries and reservations via Australian offices.

plus car or train pass and accommodation. If you're planning to travel in moderate or luxury style, and especially if your trip is geared around special interests, a package can work out cheaper than the same arrangements made on arrival. A package can also ensure a worry-free first week while you're finding your feet on a longer tour (of course, you can jump off the itinerary any time you like). Most companies will expect you to book through a local travel agent, and, since it costs the same, you might as well do that.

A variety of short excursions and specialized tours to Ireland are available from a number of organizations, including *Aer Lingus*, which offers a range of **fly-drive packages**. *CIE Tours International* is a good general operator to Ireland

and also sells train passes. Other special-interest operators are listed below.

For students, programmes combining work and study with travel to different destinations including Ireland are available from: *The Council on International Education Exchange*, 205 East 42nd Street, New York, NY 10017 (☎212/661-1414); *The Humanities Institute*, 262 Beacon St, Boston, MA 02116 (☎1-800/754 9991); and *The American Institute of Foreign Study*, College Summer Division, 102 Greenwich Ave, Greenwich, CT 06830. For general information and publications about studying abroad, try contacting the *Institute of International Education*, 809 UN Plaza, New York, NY 10017 (☎212/883-8200).

GETTING THERE FROM AUSTRALIA & NEW ZEALAND

There are no direct scheduled or charter flights to Ireland from Australia or New Zealand; all require a transfer, often at a London terminal. Fares from both Australia and New Zealand are "common rated", so there's no price difference between the main airlines, but they do vary significantly with the seasons. For most major airlines, low season is from mid-January to February 28 and October to November 30, and high from mid-May to August 31 and December 1 to mid-January (shoulder seasons cover the rest of the year). There's no variation in price during the week. The prices quoted below are low-season discounted fares. On top of these you can expect to pay between A$200 and A$400 in shoulder season and A$500 and A$700 in high season.

From **Australia** there are numerous indirect flights to Ireland via Heathrow: *Singapore-British Midland/Aer Lingus* offer several flights a week to **Dublin** and **Belfast** from Sydney, Melbourne, Brisbane and Perth for around A$2150. *KLM* flies to Dublin, Belfast and Cork three times a week from Sydney via Amsterdam (around A$1700). *Malaysian Airlines-British Midland* operate services several times a week to Belfast from Sydney, Melbourne, Brisbane and Perth via Kuala Lumpar (around A$1875), and *British Airways* via Singapore (around A$2250).

From **New Zealand**, indirect flights from Auckland to Dublin are offered by *Singapore Aer Lingus* via Singapore several times a week (around NZ$2600); and via the US, *Air New Zealand-Aer Lingus* fly to Dublin four times a week (around NZ$2300). *Malaysian-British Midland* run services to **Belfast** twice weekly via Kuala Lumpar and Heathrow (around NZ$2240).

In addition to these airlines *Qantas*, *Thai Airways*, *Japan Airlines* and *Cathay Pacific* include free European **side trips** that can be used to get to Ireland from Australia or New Zealand. **Flying to London** is a worthwhile option, if you pick up one of the cheap deals offered by some carriers in low season – for example, A$1400 from Australia with *Malaysian Airlines*. The add-on fare to destinations in Ireland is around A$150/NZ$170.

Numerous **discount agents** (see overleaf) can supply these and other low-price tickets. One of the most reliable operators is *STA*, which can also advise on **visa regulations** for Australian and New Zealand citizens – and for a fee will do all the paperwork for you.

For extended trips, **Round the World** (RTW) tickets, valid for up to a year, are a good option. Six free stopovers are usually offered by participating airlines, with additional stopovers around A/NZ$100. Many routes include London, but for Ireland you'll need to find an airline whose routes allow either backtracking or side trips. Fares start from around A$2400/NZ$2600.

If you are considering a **package holiday**, many agents can put together very flexible deals (amounting to no more than a flight plus car or train pass and accommodation) and special-interests **tours** (such as walking, cycling or staying in historic country houses). See below for details of tour operators.

For information on **European train passes** that you buy before you leave, see the box on p.10.

AIRLINES AND DISCOUNT AGENTS

AIRLINES

Aer Lingus, World Aviation Systems, 64 York St, Sydney (☎02/321 9123); 6th Floor, Trustbank Building, Queen St, Auckland (☎09/308 9098).

Air New Zealand, 5 Elizabeth St, Sydney (☎02/9223 4666); cnr Customs & Queen streets, Auckland (☎09/366 2424).

British Airways, 64 Castlereagh St, Sydney (☎02/9258 3300); 154 Queen St, Auckland (☎09/356 8690).

British Midland, *USAir* (agent in Australia), 140 Arthur St, North Sydney (☎02/9959 3922); *Discover American Marketing* (agent in New Zealand), no address, Auckland (☎09/623 4294).

Cathay Pacific, Level 12, 8 Spring St, Sydney (☎02/931 5500); 11th Floor, Arthur Andersen Tower, 205–209 Queen St, Auckland (☎09/379 0861 or ☎0-800/800 454).

Japan Airlines, Floor 14, Darling Park, 201 Sussex St, Sydney (☎02/9233 1111); Floor 12,

Westpac Tower, 120 Albert St, Auckland (☎09/379 9906).

KLM, Level 6, 5 Elizabeth St, Sydney (☎02/9231 6333 or ☎1-800/505 747). No NZ office.

Malaysian Airlines, 16 Spring St, Sydney (☎02/9364 3500; local call rate ☎13 2627); 12th Floor, The Swanson Centre, 12–26 Swanson St, Auckland (☎09/373 2741).

Qantas, Chifley Square, cnr Hunter & Philip streets, Sydney (☎02/957 0111); Qantas House, 154 Queen St, Auckland (☎09/357 8900).

Singapore Airlines, Singapore Airlines House, 17–19 Bridge St, Sydney (☎02/9236 0144; local call rate ☎13 1011); Lower Ground Floor, West Plaza Building, cnr Customs & Albert streets, Auckland (☎09/379 3209).

Thai Airways, 75–77 Pitt St, Sydney (☎02/844 0999; toll free ☎1-800/221 320); Kensington Swan Building, 22 Fanshawe St, Auckland (☎09/377 3886).

DISCOUNT AGENTS

AUSTRALIA

Anywhere Travel, 345 Anzac Parade, Kingsford, Sydney (☎02/663 0411).

Brisbane Discount Travel, 360 Queen St, Brisbane (☎07/3229 9211).

Flight Centres, Circular Quay, Sydney (☎02/9241 2422); other branches nationwide.

Harvey World Travel, Princess Highway Kogarah, Sydney (☎02/567 099); branches nationwide.

Passport Travel, 320b Glenferrie Rd, Malvern, Melbourne (☎03/9824 7183).

STA Travel, 732 Harris St, Ultimo, Sydney (☎02/9212 1255; toll-free ☎1-800/637 444); other offices in Townsville, state capitals and major universities.

Topdeck Travel, 45 Grenfell St, Adelaide (☎08/8232 7222).

Tymtro Travel, 428 George St, Sydney (☎02/9223 2211).

UTAG Travel Agents, 122 Walker St, North Sydney (☎02/956 8399); branches throughout Australia.

NEW ZEALAND

Budget Travel, Floor 5, Waterhouse Centre, 66 Wyndham St, Auckland (☎09/307 1888); branches throughout New Zealand.

Flight Centres, National Bank Towers, 205–225 Queen St, Auckland (☎09/309 6171); other branches countrywide.

STA Travel, Traveller's Centre, 10 High St, Auckland (☎09/366 6673); offices throughout New Zealand.

Thomas Cook, 96 Anzac Ave, Auckland (☎09/379 3920); other branches nationwide.

TOUR OPERATORS

Adventure World (wholesaler), 73 Walker St, North Sydney (☎02/956 7766; toll free ☎1-800 221 931); 101 Gt South Rd, Remuera, Auckland (☎09/524 5118). *Agents for CIE bus tours, motoring holidays, Dublin city breaks and a range of car-accommodation packages.*

Bluesky, Travel House, 6 Walls Rd, Penrose, New Zealand (☎09/524 5118). *An extensive selection of tours and accommodation packages (from farms to country houses).*

European Travel Office (wholesaler), 122 Rosslyn St, West Melbourne (☎03/9329 8844); 407 Gt South Rd, Penrose, Auckland (☎09/525 3074). *Tours, car rental and accommodation for the independent traveller.*

Mary Lee Eblana, Level 4, 67 Castlereagh St, Sydney (☎02/9232 8144). *A wide selection of Irish accommodation packages and tours.*

Triangle Vacations, 81 Brunswick St, Fortitude Valley, Brisbane (☎07/3216 0855). *Agents for gay-orientated "Our Family Abroad" bus tours (July & Aug only).*

World Travel Holidays, Level 6, 151 Macquarie St, Sydney (☎02/9521 6661). *Republic and Northern Ireland accommodation, bus and cycling tours. Agents for Brendan Tours' "Self-drive Ireland".*

Wiltrans, Level 10, 189 Kent St, Sydney (☎02/9255 0899). *Agents for Maupintour's luxury all-inclusive 15-day bus tours of Ireland, staying in premier hotels and medieval castles.*

VISAS, CUSTOMS REGULATIONS AND TAX

British nationals born in the UK do not need a passport to enter the Republic or the North, but it is useful to carry one in case you use the medical services, and for cashing travellers' cheques. If you don't take a passport, be sure to have some other form of convincing ID. UK passport holders *not* born in Great Britain or Northern Ireland must have a valid passport or national identity document. If you are a British national of Indian, Pakistani, Bangladeshi, Oriental or African descent, it is advisable to take along your passport (or your birth certificate), in spite of the fact that, technically speaking, you don't need one.

In the **Republic** regulations for other EU nationals vary – citizens of Belgium, France, Germany, Liechtenstein, Luxembourg, Switzerland and Norway only need an ID card; those from the remaining EU countries must bring a passport with them. There's no limit on the length of stay for EU nationals. Travellers from the USA, Canada, Australia and New Zealand are simply required to show a passport and can stay for up to three months. After this you'll need to apply to the Department of Justice in Dublin, 72–76 St Stephen's Green, Dublin 2 (residency permits ☎01/678 9711; visas ☎01/678 9466) to stay longer. Travellers from Commonwealth countries should check with the Irish Embassy beforehand since regulations vary; if you are from India, Pakistan and certain African countries you will need a visa.

In the **North**, British regulations apply. This means that citizens of all the countries of Europe (except Albania, Bulgaria, Poland and the former states of the Soviet Union), Canada, Australia and New Zealand can enter Northern Ireland with just a passport, generally for up to three months.

EMBASSIES AND CONSULATES

IRISH

Britain, 17 Grosvenor Place, London SW1X 7HR (☎0171/235 2171).

Australia, 20 Arkana St, Yarralumla, Canberra 2600 ACT (☎062/733 022).

Canada, 30 Albert St, Ottawa K1P 5G4, Ontario (☎613/223 3628).

New Zealand–Honorary Consulate, 2nd Floor Dingwall Building, Queen St, Auckland (☎09/302 2867).

United States, 2234 Massachusetts Ave NW, Washington DC 20008 (☎202/462-3939); 345 Park Ave, 17th Floor, New York, NY 10154 (☎212/319-2555); William McCarthy Building, 535 Boylston St, Boston, MA 02116 (☎617/267-9330); 400 N Michigan Ave, Chicago, IL 60611 (☎312/337-1868); 655 Montgomery St, San Francisco, CA 94111 (☎415/392-4214).

BRITISH

Australia, (High Commission), Commonwealth Ave, Yarralumla, Canberra, ACT 2600 (☎062/6257 1982).

Canada (High Commission), 80 Elgin St, Ottawa, ON K1P 5K7 (☎613/237-1310).

Ireland, 31–33 Merrion Rd, Dublin 4 (☎01/269 5211).

New Zealand (High Commission), 44 Hill St, Wellington (☎04/495-0889).

United States, 3100 Massachusetts Ave NW, Washington, DC 20008 (☎202/462-1340).

Americans can travel in the North for up to six months. Citizens of all other nationalities require a visa, obtainable from the British Consular office in the country of application. For longer stays, apply to the British Embassy (see above).

Travellers coming into the Republic or the North directly from another EU country do not have to make a declaration to **customs** at their place of entry and can effectively bring almost as much wine or beer as they like. However, there are still strict restrictions – details of which are prominently displayed in all duty-free outlets – on tax- or duty-free goods, so you can't invest in a stockpile of cheap cigarettes, wherever you're coming from.

There are import restrictions on a variety of articles and substances, from firearms to furs derived from endangered species, none of which should bother the average tourist. You cannot bring pets into the Republic or the North but you can bring them in for business, as tight quarantine restrictions apply to animals brought from overseas (except mainland Britain).

Throughout Ireland most goods are subject to **Value Added Tax** (VAT) at 17.36 percent in the Republic and 17.5 percent in the North. Visitors from non-EU countries can save a lot of money through the Retail Export Scheme, which allows a refund of VAT on goods to be taken out of the country – though savings will usually be minimal, if anything, for EU nationals, because of their own VAT rates. Note that not all shops participate in this scheme – those doing so display a sign to this effect – and you cannot reclaim VAT charged on hotel bills or other services.

In order to make a claim you have to leave the Republic within two months and the North within three months of purchase. Either have the shop send the goods out of the country for you (in which case no tax is paid) or ask for a special VAT receipt and refund form when you buy. Have the form stamped by customs on your way out of the country, and send the receipt back to the shop for your refund (less commission). Some shops have a slightly different procedure – check at the time of purchase.

COSTS, MONEY AND BANKS

The currency in the Republic is the Irish pound, also known as (but not often called) the *punt*, which is divided into 100 pence as in Britain. Many Irish traders will accept payment in pounds sterling – exchange rates vary, but the pound sterling tends to be worth only a little less than the Irish pound – but for the best rates you should change money either in banks or bureaux de change. The currency in the North is sterling.

It may be a surprise to find that the **Republic** is not a cheap place to travel. The least expensive hostel bed will rarely be less than £5 a night, while bed and breakfast generally works out at £12–15 per person. Reckon on about £5 for a basic, filling meal, and on spending more than you expect on drink, partly because it's expensive and partly because so much social life and entertainment revolves around the pubs. In short, you're likely to spend an absolute minimum of £20 a day, even if you're being very careful, and it's easy to find yourself getting through £30 or more if you plan to live it up in the slightest. As always, if you're travelling in a group you may be able to save some money by sharing rooms and food. Prices for travellers in the **North** are much the same as in the Republic, although basic groceries and consumer goods are cheaper.

Prices quoted in this guide are in punts for the Republic and pounds sterling for Northern Ireland.

If you are planning on visiting a lot of **historic monuments** in the **Republic**, it may be worth buying a **Heritage Card** (£10; children/students £4). This gives you unlimited admittance to sites cared for by the *Office of Public Works* (who run many parks, monuments and gardens) for one year from the date of purchase. Cards can be bought from the first *OPW* site you visit, or in advance from their main office at 51 St Stephen's Green, Dublin 2 (☎01/661 3111 ext 2386). Monuments for which the card is valid are indicated in the *Guide*. In the **North**, the **National Trust** offers a similar deal, but there are a lot fewer sites. If, however, you are also visiting Britain, membership (£24; under-23 £11; family £44) may be worth it (86 Botanic Ave, Belfast BT7 1JR; ☎01232/230018; 36 Queen Anne's Gate, London SW1H 9AS, ☎0171/222 9251).

Throughout this guide, the full entry price for museums, art galleries and other sights has been given. Most places will also offer a **concessionary** price for children, students and those over sixty, which is usually at least a third off the full amount.

CARRYING MONEY

If you have a PIN, the easiest way to draw cash is with a **credit card**. Nearly all towns throughout Ireland have at least one bank with a cash dispenser that will accept *Visa/Barclaycard* and/ or *Mastercard/Access*. Most large department stores, filling stations, hotels and upmarket restaurants in both the Republic and Northern Ireland accept the major credit cards – *Access/ MasterCard*, *Visa/Barclaycard*, although *Diners' Club* and *American Express* are not widely accepted. However, credit cards are less useful in rural areas; smaller establishments all over the country, such as B&Bs, will often accept cash only. Of course, if you are travelling from mainland Britain to the North, you can use your cashpoint card since Northern Irish banks are linked to the major British ones (see overleaf).

Another easy and safe way to carry your money is in **travellers' cheques**, available for a small commission from any major bank. The most commonly accepted travellers' cheques are *American Express*, followed by *Visa* and *Thomas Cook* – most cheques issued by banks will be one of these brands. You'll usually pay commission again when you cash each cheque, or a flat rate – though no commission is payable on *Amex* cheques exchanged at *Amex* branches (main offices are at 116 Grafton St and 14 Upper O'Connell St, Dublin, and 5th Floor, 108–112 Royal Ave, Belfast). Make sure to keep a record of the cheques as you cash them, so you'll be able to get the value of all uncashed cheques refunded immediately if you lose them.

BANKS AND BUREAUX DE CHANGE

Almost everywhere banks are the best places to change money and cheques; outside banking hours you'll have to use a bureau de change, widely found in most city centres and at international airports. Avoid changing money or cheques in hotels, where the rates are normally very poor.

The main high-street **banks** in the **Republic** are *Allied Irish Bank* and *Bank of Ireland*; two smaller clearing banks are *Ulster Bank* and *National Irish Bank*. All are open Mon–Fri 10am–12.30pm and 1.30–3pm; most are also open until 5pm one day a week, usually Thursday. It makes sense to change your money while in the cities since many small country towns are served by sub-offices open only certain days of the week. **Foreign exchange counters** are open at all main **airports**: Dublin daily from 6am to 10.30pm in summer and 6.45am to 9pm in winter; Shannon daily from 6am to 9pm and 7.30am to 5.30pm; Cork daily from 9am to 5.15pm all year; Knock International open all year to service all scheduled flights (located in the tourist office). In Dublin city, there are several outlets where you can change money, including a branch of *Thomas Cook* at 118 Grafton Street.

In the **North**, the main high-street banks are linked with British **banks**: *National Irish Bank* with *Midland*; *Ulster Bank* with *NatWest*; and *Bank of Ireland* with *Barclays*. Main banks in large towns are open Mon–Fri 10am–3.30pm, with late opening till 5pm on Thursday in certain city branches; elsewhere some may close between 12.30pm and 1.30pm. In very small villages the bank may open on only two or three days a week – so, as in the Republic, aim to get your cash in the bigger centres. Belfast International **airport** has a branch of *Thomas Cook*, but there are no **foreign exchange facilities** at Belast City or Derry airports. In Belfast itself, you can change money at the Post Office, 7 Shaftesbury Square, or at *Thomas Cook*, 11 Donegall Place; they also have a branch in Derry at Unit 7, Quayside Strand Road.

EMERGENCIES

If, as a foreign visitor, you run out of money or there is some kind of emergency, the quickest way to get **money sent out** is to contact your bank at home and have them wire the cash to the nearest bank.

For **Americans and Canadians** – or any *Amex* card-holder – one of the quickest ways to get money from home is through *American Express*. The company allows card-holders to draw cash from their checking accounts, up to $1000 every 21 days, as well as offering its own Moneygram Service, through which money can be sent to Europe (fees commensurate with amount of money being sent). Another option is to have cash sent out through *Western Union* (☎1-800/325-6000) to a nearby bank or post office (this service is available to any traveller, not just North Americans). Make sure you know when it's likely to arrive, since you won't be notified by the receiving office. Remember, too, that you'll need some form of identification when you pick up the money. Finally, Americans in dire straits can arrange to have money sent to them via the **State Department**'s *Citizen's Emergency Center* (☎202/647-5225 during business hours, otherwise ☎202/647-7000).

For **Australians and New Zealanders**, your best bet is to take a *Visa* or *Mastercard* with you. Otherwise you have to make arrangements for a possible international money transfer before you leave by nominating a bank and account number in Ireland, entrusting your bank account number with someone at home and paying a fee of A$25/NZ$30.

YOUTH AND STUDENT DISCOUNTS

There are various official and quasi-official youth/student ID cards available that soon pay for themselves in savings.

Full-time students are eligible for the **International Student ID Card** (*ISIC*), which entitles the bearer to special fares on local transport and discounts at museums, theatres and other attractions. For Americans there's also a health benefit, providing up to US$3000 in emergency medical coverage and US$100 a day for sixty days in the hospital, plus a 24-hour hotline to call in the event of a medical, legal or financial emergency. The card, which costs £5 in Britain, £7 in the Republic, US$16 in the US, CAN$15 in Canada and around A/NZ$10 in Australia and New Zealand, is available from branches of *USIT* in Ireland and *Council Travel*, *STA* and *Travel Cuts* around the world.

You only have to be 25 or younger to qualify for the **Go-25 Card**, which costs the same as the *ISIC* and carries the same benefits. It can be purchased through *Council Travel* in the US, *Hostelling International* in Canada (see "Accommodation"), and *STA* in Australia and New Zealand.

STA also sells its own ID card that's good for some discounts, as do various other travel organizations. A university photo ID might open some doors, too.

Also see p.15 for *Heritage* and *National Trust* cards.

HEALTH AND INSURANCE

There are no inoculations required for travellers to Ireland, nor any particular health hazards to beware of beyond those of taking care when travelling in an unknown place. Certainly you're unlikely to suffer sunstroke, and the water is safe almost everywhere. Still, you're as likely to fall ill or have an accident here as anywhere else, so it's as well to make sure you're covered by adequate travel insurance.

A decent policy will cover not just medical costs but also loss or theft of baggage or money; and in real trouble it should get you home. For the peace of mind it offers, it's well worth having. In **Britain** schemes – from around £23 a month for Ireland – are sold by almost every travel agent or bank and by specialist insurance companies. Policies issued by *Campus Travel* or *STA* (see pp.4, 8 and 12 for addresses), *Endsleigh Insurance* (97–107 Southampton Row, London WC1B 4AG; ☎0171/436 4451), *Frizzell Insurance*

(Frizzell House, County Gates, Bournemouth, Dorset BH1 2NF; ☎01202/292 333) or *Columbus Travel Insurance* (17 Devonshire Square, London EC2M 4SQ; ☎0171/375 0011) are all good value. If you are buying a policy from a travel agent, do read the small print to make sure that the cover is adequate and appropriate. You must make sure you keep all medical bills, and, if you have anything stolen, get a copy of the police report when you report the incident – otherwise you won't be able to claim.

NORTH AMERICAN COVER

In the **US and Canada** you should also check the insurance policies you already have carefully before taking out a new one. You may discover that you're covered already for medical and other losses while abroad. Canadians especially are usually covered by their provincial health plans. American holders of official student/youth cards (see above) are entitled to accident cover and hospital in-patient benefits. Students may also find their health coverage extends during vacations, and many bank and charge accounts (particularly *American Express*) include some form of travel cover; insurance is also sometimes included if you pay for your trip with a credit card.

If you do want a specific travel insurance policy, there are several to choose from. The best deals are usually through student/youth travel agencies – *ISIS* policies, for example, cost $48–69 for fifteen days (depending on cover), $80–105 for a month, $149–207 for two months, on up to $510–700 for a year. If you are planning to do any "dangerous sports" (watersports, climbing etc), be sure to ask whether these activities are covered; some policies add a hefty surcharge. One thing to bear in mind is that none of the currently available policies covers theft; they only cover loss while in the custody of an identifiable person – though even then you must make a report to the police and get their written statement.

AUSTRALASIAN COVER

In Australia and New Zealand, travel insurance is offered by airlines and travel agent groups such as *United Travel Agent Group* (UTAG), 122 Walker St, North Sydney (☎02/956 8399); *Australian Federation of Travel Agents Ltd* (AFTA), 144 Pacific Highway, North Sydney (☎02/956 4800); *Ready Plan*, 141 Walker St, Dunenong (☎005/312345) and 10th Floor, 63 Albert St, Auckland (☎09/379 3208). A typical insurance policy for Ireland will cost A$161/NZ$180 for a month and A$226/NZ$254 for two months.

HEALTH CARE

Visitors from **EU countries** are entitled to medical treatment in the **Republic** under the EU Reciprocal Medical Treatment arrangement. EU visitors should collect a form E111 from their Social Security office (or in Britain from any Post Office). Although an E111 is technically not a requirement for people from the UK, in reality it's essential to get the entitlement to free treatment and prescribed medicines. Armed with your E111, check that the doctor or dentist you use is registered with the Health Board Panel, and make it clear you want to be treated under the European Community's social security arrangements. Similarly if you are admitted to hospital, make it clear you want to be treated within the EU Reciprocal Treatment scheme. The only other real problem is that in rural areas you may find yourself miles from the nearest doctor or hospital, and possibly even further from one prepared to treat you under the reciprocal arrangements.

British citizens need no documentation to be treated in the **North**; for non-British EU travellers, the requirements are the same as for the Republic.

Citizens of **non-EU countries** will be charged for all medical services except those administered by accident and emergency units at health service hospitals. Thus a US citizen who has been hit by a car would not be charged if the injuries simply required stitching and setting in the emergency unit, but would if admission to a hospital ward were necessary. Health insurance is therefore extremely advisable for all non-EU nationals.

Citizens of some countries may also enjoy a reciprocal agreement; in Australia, *Medicare* has such an arrangement with Ireland and Britain. Check before you leave. And remember that whatever your legal rights, the local doctor may not necessarily know anything about them.

INFORMATION AND MAPS

stay (booking charge £1–2). It has to be said, though, that they only give details on services which they have approved, thereby excluding some excellent hostels, campsites and private bus services, and they tend to be reluctant to show favouritism among hotels and restaurants, so always go to them for information, not advice. A Bord Fáilte recommendation implies a certain standard of service, however, so if you don't think your approved B&B comes up to scratch, they are the people you should complain to.

There's no shortage of information published on Ireland, much of it free; it's well worth contacting the local office of the Irish Tourist Board (Bord Fáilte) and/or the Northern Ireland Tourist Board before you leave.

Bord Fáilte and NITB offices outside Ireland are listed below. Once **in Ireland**, you'll find some kind of tourist office in nearly all towns with a reasonable number of tourists passing through: either a branch of Bord Fáilte or the NITB, or a locally run information centre, many of which open only for the summer. Most of these are listed in the relevant sections of the guide, and most are extremely helpful, with local maps and leaflets as well as information on where to

MAPS

There's a great variety of **road maps** of Ireland; try the *Michelin* 1:400,000 (no. 405) or the *AA* 1:350,000. The four *Ireland Holiday Maps* – North, West, East and South – at a scale of one mile to one quarter-inch give more contour details and are probably the best general, all-purpose maps on offer. These and others are widely available in Ireland.

For more detail, and for **walking**, the new **Ordnance Survey** *Discovery Series* (1:50,000; a little over 1 mile: 1 inch) are generally the best option, and are now available for Co. Dublin, the Wicklow Mountains and most of the mountainous areas of the west (although not as yet for Connemara and Co. Clare). They are also available for all parts of Northern Ireland. Additionally, there are 1:25,000 maps on offer for certain tourist areas: Lower Lough Erne, Upper Lough Erne

BORD FÁILTE OFFICES ABROAD

Australia, Level 5, 36 Carrington St, Sydney NSW 2000 (☎02/9299 6177).
Britain, 150 New Bond St, London W1Y 0AQ (☎0171/493 3201).
Canada, 160 Bloor St East, Suite 1150, Toronto, Ontario M4W 189 (☎416/929 2777).

New Zealand, Dingwall Building, Queen St, Auckland (☎09/379 3708).
USA, 345 Park Ave, New York, NY 10154 (☎212/418-0800).

NORTHERN IRELAND TOURIST OFFICES ABROAD

Australia, at the same address as the Bord Fáilte office above.
Britain, 12 Lower Regent St, London SW1Y 4PQ (☎0171/355 5040).
Canada, 111 Avenue Rd, Suite 450, Toronto, Ontario M5R 3J8 (☎416/925-6368).

New Zealand, at the same address as the Bord Fáilte office above.
USA, 551 Fifth Ave, Suite 701, New York, NY 10176 (☎212/922-0101).

and Mourne Country. The old *OS* half-inch maps were surveyed in the nineteenth century and can be inaccurate over 1000 feet, so a certain amount of caution is advisable if using them.

For really serious climbing you should always check locally, as tourist boards or bookshops may have something better than the above. If you're in Connemara or the Burren, for example, the locally produced *Folding Landscapes* maps, available in tourist offices and bookstores in Clare and Galway, are excellent. And for the Ulster Way the route guides published by the *Sports Council for Northern Ireland* (House of Sport, Upper Malone Rd, Belfast BT9 5LA; ☎01232/381222) are useful.

MAP OUTLETS

IN BRITAIN

Edinburgh, *HMSO Books*, 71 Lothian Rd, EH3 9AZ (☎0131/228 4181).

Glasgow, *John Smith and Sons*, 57–61 St Vincent St, G2 5TB (☎0141/221 7472).

London, *Daunt Books*, 83 Marylebone High St, W1 (☎0171/224 2295); *National Map Centre*, 22–24 Caxton St, SW1 (☎0171/222 4945); *Stanfords*, 12–14 Long Acre, WC2 (☎0171/836 1321); *The Travellers Bookshop*, 25 Cecil Court, WC2 (☎0171/836 9132).

Maps by **mail or phone order** are available from *Stanfords*.

IN NORTH AMERICA

Chicago, *Rand McNally*, 444 N Michigan Ave, IL 60611 (☎312/321-1751).

Los Angeles area, *Map Link Inc*, 25 E Mason St, Santa Barbara, CA 93101 (☎805/965-4402).

Montréal, *Ulysses Travel Bookshop*, 4176 St-Denis (☎514/289-0993).

New York, *British Travel Bookshop*, 551 5th Ave, NY 10176 (☎212/490-6688), mail order through *BritRail Travel* (☎1-800/677-8585); *The Complete Traveler Bookstore*, 199 Madison Ave, NY 10016 (☎212/685-9007); *Rand McNally*, 150 E 52nd St, NY 10022 (☎212/758-7488); *Traveler's Bookstore*, 22 W 52nd St, NY 10019 (☎212/664-0995).

San Francisco area, *The Complete Traveler Bookstore*, 3207 Filmore St, San Francisco,CA 92123 (☎415/923-1511); *Rand McNally*, 595 Market St, San Francisco, CA 94105 (☎415/777-3131); *Phileas Fogg's Books & Maps*, 87 Stanford Shopping Center, Palo Alto, CA 94304 (☎1-800/233-FOGG in California; ☎1-800/533-FOGG elsewhere); *Sierra Club Bookstore*, 730 Polk St, San Francisco CA 94109 (☎415/923-5500).

Toronto, *Open Air Books and Maps*, 25 Toronto St, M5R 2C1 (☎416/363-0719).

Vancouver, *World Wide Books and Maps*, 1247 Granville St, BC V6Z 1E4 (☎604/687-3320).

Washington, DC, *Rand McNally*, 1201 Connecticut Ave NW, Washington, DC 20036 (☎202/223-6751).

Rand McNally now have 24 stores nationwide. For details of your local branch and direct-mail maps call ☎1-800/333-0136 ext 2111.

IN AUSTRALIA AND NEW ZEALAND

Adelaide, *The Map Shop*, 16a Peel St, SA 5000 (☎08/8231 2033).

Auckland, *Speciality Maps*, 58 Albert St (☎09/307 2217).

Melbourne, *Bowyangs*, 372 Little Bourke St, VIC 3000 (☎03/9670 4383).

Perth, *Perth Map Centre*, 891 Hay St, WA 6000 (☎09/322 5733; ☎08/9322 5733 from Sept 1997).

Sydney, *Travel Bookshop*, 20 Bridge St, NSW 2000 (☎02/9241 3554).

GETTING AROUND

Travel between major centres in the Republic is generally straightforward, with reliable – albeit infrequent and slow – public transport operated by the state-supported train and bus companies *Iarnród Éireann* (*Irish Rail*) and *Bus Éireann*. There are, however, glaring anomalies, and you should never assume that two major, local towns are necessarily going to be connected. It pays to think and plan ahead. Once off the main routes this becomes particularly important since it's quite usual for small towns and villages to be served by a couple of buses a week and no more. Transport in the North is similarly infrequent in rural areas. *Ulsterbus* is generally regular and dependable, as is the (limited) train network.

TRAINS

In the **Republic** *Irish Rail* (*Iarnród Éireann* – ☎01/ 836 6222) operates **trains** to many major cities and towns en route; on direct lines it's by far the fastest way of covering long distances, but the network is by no means comprehensive – Donegal, for instance, has no service at all. In general, train lines fan out from Dublin, with few routes running north–south across the country. So although you can get to the west easily by train, you can't sensibly use the train network to explore the west coast.

Train travel is not particularly cheap, either. Prices are usually cheaper midweek; and, if possible, it's best to buy a return ticket as singles cost nearly as much. As a general example, an off-peak Dublin–Galway single ticket will cost £24, a five-day return £26 and a monthly return £32. It's always worth asking about any special fares that may be on offer; or it may be worth buying a **train pass**. *Irish Rail*'s *Irish Rover* ticket, valid in the Republic

and the North, costs £75 (child £37) for five days out of fifteen, and £100 for fifteen days out of thirty.

Given the limited reach of the rail system, one of the most useful options is the *Irish Explorer Ticket*, a **combined rail and bus pass**, covering all intercity state and private rail and bus lines in the Republic (but no city transportation except *DART*, see p.47), which costs £60 for any five days' travel out of fifteen consecutive days, and £90 for eight out of fifteen days. For **unlimited train and bus travel** in the Republic and the North, an *Emerald Card* costs £105 for eight days out of fifteen, £180 for fifteen days out of thirty (same prices in Northern Ireland). Bear in mind, though, that the nature of travel in Ireland is such that you very rarely stick to your carefully drawn itinerary, and you may not get the value from your pass that you hope for.

The only service **between the Republic and the North** is the Dublin–Belfast express (6 each way daily, 2hr; £14 single, £20 return). Once **in the North**, you'll find only three short train routes, but these are efficient and reasonably cheap: a Belfast–Derry ticket will cost you £5.70 single, £6.50 return. If you are looking for a **train pass** a *Runaround* ticket is valid on all Northern Irish trains for one week and costs around £25.

If you are a **student** in possession of an *ISIC* card, you can buy a *Travelsave* stamp (£7 from any *USIT* office – Dublin, Cork, Galway, Limerick, Maynooth, Waterford, Belfast, Coleraine, Jordanstown and Derry), which entitles you to discounts of 50 percent off standard train fares and 30 percent off bus fares in the Republic. In the North, you'll get a return ticket for the price of a single and single fares for half-price.

The cost of taking **bikes** on trains varies between £2 and £6 per single journey in the Republic. In Northern Ireland it costs a quarter of the single fare.

For **North American** visitors who anticipate covering a lot of ground in Ireland, a rail and bus pass is a wise investment; both the *Irish Explorer* and *Emerald* passes (see above) are also available to buy before you leave for the same time periods and commensurate prices. There is one ticket, however, that you have to buy before you set off: the **Go As You Please Rambler Card**, which combines eight days of bus and train

IRISH TRAINS

0   25 miles

N

To Stranraer
& Cairnryan

Coleraine

Derry

To Stranraer

Antrim

Larne

To Liverpool

BELFAST

Bangor

Lurgan

Lisburn

Portadown

Dundalk

Sligo
Collooney
Ballymote
Carrick-on-Shannon
Dromod

Ballina

Boyle

Castlebar

Achill Island

Ballyhaunis

Castlerea

Longford

Drogheda
Laytown

Westport

Claremorris

Roscommon

Mostrim

Mosney

Balbriggan

Mullingar

Skerries

Woodlawn

Athlone

Moate

Dublin
Connolly

Rush & Lusk

Galway

Ballinasloe

Clara

Dublin Pearse

Athenry

Tullamore

Newbridge

Dun Laoghaire

Galway
Bay

Portarlington

Dublin
Heuston

Bray
Greystones

Aran Islands

Portlaoise

Kildare

ATLANTIC OCEAN

Roscrea

Athy

Wicklow

To Holyhead

Cloughjordan

Ballybrophy

Rathdrum

Nenagh

Carlow

Arklow

IRISH SEA

Birdhill

Templemore

Limerick

Thurles

Muine
Bheag

Gorey

To Fishguard

Limerick Junction

Kilkenny

Rathluirc

Tipperary

Thomastown

Enniscorthy

Tralee

Cahir

Carrick-
on-Suir

Wexford

Rosslare Strand
Rosslare Harbour

Farranfore

Mallow

Clonmel

Waterford

Rosslare Harbour
(Pier)

Killarney

Banteer

Millstreet

Rathmore

Cobh
Junction

Bridgetown
Wellington Bridge
Ballycullane
Campile

To Pembroke

Cork

Cobh

To Swansea

To Le Harve
& Cherbourg

To Roscoff

travel with seven nights' accommodation in your choice of private homes or first-class hotels. The price for the home-stay programme is $345 per person (extra nights for $22); while the hotel pass costs from $455 to $515 per person, depending on the season (additional nights cost $43).

Travellers also taking in Great Britain might benefit from the **BritIreland Pass**, which entitles the holder to five days' unlimited travel within fifteen days ($399 first class, $269 standard) or ten days within a month ($629 first class, $419 standard). The pass, which must be

purchased before departure from North America, is available from *BritRail Travel International* and most travel agents (see p.10 for details of agents selling Irish and British passes).

For **Australians and New Zealanders**, two passes are available from travel agents (see p.10) before you leave: the *Irish Explorer* train-only pass (5 days out of 15 for A$159/NZ$180) and *Emerald Card* train-and-bus pass (8 days out of 15 for A$275/NZ$309; 15 out of 30 for A$470/NZ$528).

For information on **Eurail** passes see "Getting There from North America" p.10.

BUSES

Bus Éireann operates throughout the **Republic**, and its services are reliable, if infrequent. It's possible to travel by bus between all major towns, but routings can be complex, involving several connections, and hence very slow. Fares are generally far lower than the train, especially in midweek – a single, *Boomerang* ticket bought on Tuesday, Wednesday or Thursday gives you the return journey free (if you travel again Tues–Thurs). This system operates on short local journeys too, so it's always worth hanging on to your midweek bus tickets, even if you don't think you'll use them – they remain valid for a month. Occasional special fare offers are also worth looking out for.

Rambler tickets (around £27 for any 3 days out of 8; £65 for any 8 days out of 15; £95 for 15 days out of 30) all give unlimited bus travel throughout the Republic; **students** can get 30-percent reductions on standard fares if they have a *Travelsave* stamp (see p.21). It makes sense to pick up the relevant information for the area you intend to explore before you leave; remote villages may only have a couple of buses a week, so knowing when they are is essential. The current timetables on sale are unreliable and not worth buying, so either ask at a tourist office or call *Bus Éireann* on ☎01/836 6111.

Carrying a **bike** on a bus will cost you £5 single regardless of length of journey, though be warned that the driver is under no obligation to take them and in any case usually only has room for one bike.

Private buses, which operate on many major routes, are often cheaper than *Bus Éireann*, and sometimes faster. Companies, timetables and pick-up points are listed in "Travel Details" at the end of each chapter in this guide. They're very busy at weekends, so it makes sense to book ahead if you can; during the week you can usually pay on the bus. Prices for parts of the journeys are often negotiable, and bikes can be carried if booked with your seat. Some of these companies are unlicensed and have no insurance, so that in the event of an accident you would not be covered: if this bothers you, ask at a tourist office for information on local companies.

If you are backpacking round the Republic you might want to consider travelling on **The Slow Coach** (Round-Ireland-Budget-Bus), which for £89 will pick you up at ferry ports and drop you off at towns, sights (often with free guided tours)

and hostels along an extensive route. Each ticket allows you a full circuit, and you can take as long as you like to complete it. Contact *The Slow Coach* office at First Floor, 6 South William Street, Dublin 2 (☎01/679 2684) or at the *YHA* Hostel, 38 Bolton Gdns, Earls Court, London SW5 0AQ (☎0171/373 7283).

In the **North**, *Ulsterbus* runs regular and reliable services throughout the six counties, particularly to those towns not served by the train network. A *Freedom of Northern Ireland Ticket*, for daily (£9) or weekly (£28) unlimited travel on all scheduled *Ulsterbus* services, is available at the main bus station in Belfast. Students can get a 15-percent discount on certain services with an *ISIC* card.

For details of **joint train and bus passes** see "Trains", p.21.

DRIVING

In order to **drive** in Ireland you must have a current driving licence; foreign nationals will need to supplement this with an international driving permit available from national motoring organizations for a small fee. If you're bringing your own car into the country you should also carry your vehicle registration or ownership document at all times. Furthermore, you must be adequately insured, so be sure to check your existing policy.

Uncongested roads in the **Republic** make driving a very relaxing option. However, it remains (along with Britain) one of the few countries in the world where you drive on the left, a situation that can lead to a few tense days of acclimatization for many overseas drivers. Petrol prices are about 60p per litre; the national **speed limit** is 55mph/88kph, except where posted otherwise. Front-seat occupants must wear seat belts, and motorcyclists and their passengers must wear helmets. In remote areas wandering cattle, unmarked junctions, and appallingly pot-holed minor roads are all potential dangers, particularly for motorbikes. Other hazards to watch out for include drunk drivers late at night, a continuing problem in spite of high accident rates and the beginnings of a police crack-down. Watch out for "passing lanes" or "slow lanes", indicated by a broken yellow line, where you are expected to pull over to the left for the car behind to overtake – they should be used with care as they often have poor surfaces and can suddenly end with little or no warning. Be careful if you

MOTORING ORGANIZATIONS

American Automobile Association, 4100 E Arkanas Ave, Denver, CO 80222 (☎1-800/222-4357). *Most member services apply only in the US and Canada, but the AAA can refer members to the AA and also provide international drivers' licenses.*

Australian Automobile Association, 212 Northbourne Ave, Canberra ACT 2601 (☎61/6247 7311).

Automobile Association, Fanum House, Basingstoke, Hants RG21 2EA (☎01256/20123); 36 Wellington Place, Belfast (☎01232/232131). Emergency number: ☎0-800/887766.

Irish Automobile Association, 23 Suffolk Rd, Dublin (☎01/667 9481); Cork (☎021/276922). Emergency number: ☎1-800/667788.

Canadian Automobile Association. *Each region has its own club – check the phone book for local address and phone number. Benefits are comparable to the AAA's.*

New Zealand Automobile Association, PO Box 1794, Wellington (☎64/473 8738).

Royal Automobile Club, PO Box 100, RAC House, 7 Brighton Rd, South Croydon CR2 6XW (☎0181/686 0088); 79 Chichester St, Belfast (☎01232/232640). Emergency number: ☎0-800/828282.

CAR RENTAL FIRMS

IN IRELAND

Avis Dublin ☎01/677 6971; Belfast ☎01232/240404.

Budget Rent-A-Car Dublin ☎01/837 9611; Belfast ☎01232/230700.

Dan Dooley Dublin ☎01/677 2723.

Europcar Dublin ☎01/668 1777; Belfast ☎01232/450904 or 01232/423444.

Hertz Dublin ☎01/676 7476; Belfast ☎01232/73245.

Holiday Autos Dublin ☎01/454 9090.

Thrifty Rent-A-Car Dublin ☎01/679 9420.

IN BRITAIN

Avis ☎0181/848 8733.

Budget ☎0-800/181181.

Eurodollar ☎01895/233300.

Europcar/InterRent ☎01345/222 525.

Hertz ☎0345/555888.

Holiday Autos ☎0171/491 1111.

IN NORTH AMERICA

Alamo domestic ☎1-800/354-2322; international ☎1-800/522-9696.

Avis domestic ☎1-800/331-1212; international ☎1-800/331-1084.

Budget ☎1-800/527-0700.

Europe By Car ☎1-800/223-1516.

Hertz domestic ☎1-800/654-3131; international ☎1-800/654-3001; in Canada ☎1-800/263-0600.

Holiday Autos ☎1-800/422-7737.

National Car Rental ☎1-800/CAR-RENT.

IN AUSTRALIA

Avis ☎1-800/22 5533.

Budget ☎13 2848.

Hertz ☎13 1918.

Renault Eurodrive ☎02/9299 3344.

IN NEW ZEALAND

Avis ☎09/525 1982.

Budget ☎09/309 6737.

Fly and Drive Holidays ☎09/366 0759.

Hertz ☎09/309 0989.

---

take a car to Dublin – theft and vandalism rates are high, and you're best advised to leave your car in a supervised car park.

Ireland is very slowly converting to metric measures, and on the main roads the new (green) signs are in **kilometres**. In rural areas, however, you'll find mostly the old black-and-white fingerpost signs in miles. Most people continue to think and talk in miles too. There is also such a thing as an "Irish mile" – shorter than the standard imperial measure – though this is rare and found only on very old signposts. **Unleaded petrol** is available everywhere. In all large towns a **disc parking** system is in operation: discs can be bought in newsagents and have to be displayed on the vehicle when parked in a designated area.

Roads in the **North** are in general notably superior to those in the Republic. Driving is on the left and rules of the road are as in Britain:

speed limits are 30–40mph/50–60kph in built up areas, 70mph/110kph on motorways (freeways) and dual carriageways and 60mph/100kph on most other roads. Car seat-belt and motorbike-helmet rules are the same as in the Republic (see p.23). Cars bearing large red "R" (Restricted) plates identify drivers who have passed their driving test within the past twelve months and are meant to keep to low speeds. Despite the end of the IRA ceasefire, security remains low key, but be sensitive to police parking restrictions. A parked car in a control zone is considered a security risk (and likely to be blown up) unless someone is sitting in it. **Petrol prices** in the North are about 55–59p a litre.

In the Republic, the **Irish Automobile Association** (*IAA*) operate 24-hour emergency breakdown services. They also provide many other motoring services, including a reciprocal arrangement for free assistance through many overseas motoring organizations – check the situation with yours before setting out. You can ring the emergency numbers (see opposite) even if you are not a member of the respective organization, although a substantial fee will be charged. In the North, the **Automobile Association** (*AA*) and the **Royal Automobile Club** (*RAC*) both offer the same services as the *IAA*.

CAR RENTAL

Large international **car rental companies** such as *Hertz* have outlets in all major cities, airports and ferry terminals in the **Republic**: they're expensive at around £150–300 a week, and, especially if you're travelling from North America, you'll probably find it cheaper to arrange things in advance. Booking a fly-drive or a train-sail-drive package is one of the cheapest ways to arrange car rental, or if you don't want to be so tied down try an **agency** such as *Holiday Autos*, who will arrange advance booking through a local agent and can usually undercut the big companies considerably.

If you haven't booked, then the smaller local firms can almost always offer better deals than the well-known names. You must produce a full valid driving licence (which you must have held without endorsement for at least two years); most companies will only rent cars to people over 23 years of age, though you might find some that will rent to drivers over 21; it will generally be more expensive if they do. It's advisable to take out a collision damage waiver with your car rental – otherwise expect to be liable for around £1000 damages in the event of an accident. If you intend to drive **across the border**, you should inform your rental company beforehand to check that you are fully insured.

Renting a car in the **North** involves much the same cost and age restrictions as in the Republic. There are fewer outlets, but rental is available in all major cities and at Belfast airport. Again, the cheapest deals are booked ahead, and here too you must inform the car-rental company if you plan to cross the border.

HITCHING

In the **Republic** hitching is commonplace; for locals it's almost as much a normal part of getting around as using the bus and train networks, and for the visitor the human contact makes it one of the best ways to get to know the country. Knowing the shortcomings of public transport, many drivers readily give lifts, and it's not unusual to see single women with babies and the shopping or whole families waiting for a ride. It has to be borne in mind, however, that local people experience no real problems in getting lifts since they usually know just about everybody on the road; visitors can have a less easy time of it.

The chief problem if you plan to hitch extensively is lack of traffic, especially off the main roads, and if you are travelling around one of the tourist-swamped areas of the west, you may find there's a reluctance to pick up foreigners. That said, without transport of your own you are probably going to *have* to hitch if you want to see the best of Ireland's wild, remote places. Just be sure to leave yourself plenty of time.

Though it's probably safer than just about anywhere else in Europe, **women** shouldn't be lulled into naive notions of security. Chances are you'll get lifts easily and have no problems, but it should go without saying that hitching is never entirely risk-free, and you can be unlucky anywhere. If this worries you, simply remember that you don't have to get into a car just because it stops for you.

Hitching a lift in the **North** is rather less straightforward and probably easiest for women who are obviously tourists. Men travelling alone or in pairs can still be viewed with suspicion and may find it impossible to get a lift. Men and women travelling together are at least in with a chance.

CYCLING

If you are lucky enough to get decent weather, cycling is one of the most enjoyable ways to see Ireland, ensuring you're continually in touch with the landscape. Roads are generally empty, though very poor surfaces may well slow you down.

Most airlines carry **bicycles** free as long as you don't exceed your weight allowance; but be sure to check the regulations in advance (charters may be less obliging) and let them know when you book your ticket that you plan to carry a bike. Always deflate the tyres to avoid explosions in the unpressurized hold.

If you don't want to cycle long distances, it's easy and relatively cheap to **rent a bike** in most towns in the **Republic** and at a limited number of places in the **North** (many outlets are listed in the text); you can't take a rented bike across the border. *Raleigh*, who operate a national rental scheme and a choice of drop-off options, are the biggest distributors (£7 per day, £35 per week plus around £30 deposit; collection and delivery

service £6–12; in the North £6.50 a day, £27 a week). Local dealers (including some hostels) are often less expensive. Wherever you rent your bike, it makes sense to check the tyres and brakes immediately and demand a pump and repair kit before you set off. You should also consider the terrain: if you plan on mountain riding, make sure your machine has enough gears to cope. **Cycle helmets** are available for rent at some shops, but if you want to be certain of wearing one, bring your own along.

In tourist spots at high season it's best to collect a bike early in the day (or book it the day before) as supplies frequently run out. If you arrive with your own bike, it's easy enough to carry it across long distances by train, less so by bus (see p.21 and p.23). Finally, a problem you may encounter – for some reason particularly in the west – is that of farmers' dogs chasing and snarling at your wheels. Should you be fortunate enough to be heading downhill at the time, freewheeling silently past cottages and farm entrances is perhaps the only humane way of minimizing the risk of savaged wheels and ankles.

ACCOMMODATION

Ireland offers a wide range of accommodation, from the spartan – camping for free in a farmer's field (usually possible if you ask permission first) – to the sybaritic: many of Ireland's elegant old country houses take bed-and-breakfast guests. There's also a

huge number of hostels, which vary a lot, but all have at least the essentials of a bed and somewhere to cook, and some offer a great deal more. A notch up in price, in more or less the following order, come bed and breakfasts, guesthouses, town houses, country houses, and hotels, all officially graded by the tourist boards on a set formula which, most of the time, gives a fair idea of what to expect. Prices quoted throughout this book, and in the official tourist board guides, are per person per night sharing a double room in high season, or in most hostels in a dormitory: single rates will generally be slightly higher in B&Bs and hotels.

Whatever your budget, remember that in **July and August** accommodation in the cities and big tourist centres gets booked up well in advance, and during **festivals** things get even more hectic. For the really big festivals – like the *Fleadh Cheoil* and the *Cork Jazz Festival* (see p.35 for a full list of events) – there's often an extra accommodation office trying to cope with the overload, but you may still end up sleeping in a different town, or perhaps just revelling your way through to morning. The less famous festivals can be equally difficult for the spontaneous traveller. Since festivals take place all over Ireland throughout the summer, it's worth checking out where and when they are before you head off – simply pick up an events calendar from any major tourist office.

B&B, GUESTHOUSES AND HOTELS

B&Bs in the Republic vary enormously, but most are welcoming, warm and clean, with huge breakfasts including cereal, massive fry-ups of bacon, egg, sausage and tomato, and toast and tea. Afternoon tea can usually be arranged and can be delicious, with home-made scones and soda bread – it will cost you around £3 or £4. Bord Fáilte registered and approved B&Bs are generally pretty good, though it's not an absolute guarantee. Don't assume that non-registered places will be less good – inclusion in the official guide is voluntary, and a fair few simply choose not to bother. Many historic buildings are run as B&Bs, and they too can be surprisingly cheap. Many are managed by extremely good cooks, with some of the best and most inventive examples of new Irish cuisine on the menu.

You can expect to pay from around £12–15 per person sharing (from £10 for non-registered houses) and out of high season you may be able to negotiate the price somewhat. **Bookings** for registered B&Bs can be made through tourist offices (£1–2), or you can do it yourself. Many phone numbers and addresses are given in the text of this guide, but if you want the complete list then buy *The Accommodation Guide* published by Bord Fáilte (£5), which has comprehensive, graded lists of B&Bs, hotels and campsites, or their B&B-only guide which costs £2.50. Alternatively, finding accommodation is simple enough in just about any town or touristy village – simply go into a pub and ask.

In the **North**, B&B accommodation costs much the same as in the Republic but is far less prominent, and you will need to ring ahead if you want to be sure of somewhere to stay during the summer months. Addresses and phone numbers for B&Bs in all of the main centres are given in the *Guide*, and the Northern Ireland Tourist Board's *Where to stay in Northern Ireland* (£3.99) gives extensive, highly detailed lists.

Accommodation in a **farmhouse** or in a cottage can be arranged through the tourist board; for all their simple rooms and turf fires, almost all "Rent-an-Irish-Cottage" cottages cluster in tiny tourist villages, so it's worth checking out exactly what the set-up is if you're after real solitude.

Hotels are generally more expensive, particularly in the cities; however, many of the swanky hotels slash their tariffs at weekends when the business types have gone home. In smaller towns and villages, hotels are not always so pricey and may well be a lively social focus. Virtually all hotels have bars and provide meals to residents and non-residents alike.

HOSTELS

Hostel accommodation in Ireland has grown hugely in breadth and quality recently, and staying in a hostel no longer means subjecting yourself to the rigours of old-fashioned hostelling – although **An Óige** (the official Irish Youth Hostel Association) and the **Youth Hostel Association of Northern Ireland** (*YHANI*) still manage to satisfy more spartan tastes.

Independent hostels – often housed in evocative historic buildings – are generally run along more relaxed lines, making them increasingly attractive alternatives to B&Bs; as well as having traditional dormitory accommodation, a growing number have many private double and family rooms. The majority are classed as **Independent Holiday Hostels** (*IHH*) and are recommended by the Bord Fáilte, but you will also find some excellent (usually small) hostels that don't belong to *An Óige*, YHANI or IHH. All independent hostels are privately owned, and they're all different, each reflecting the character and interests of its owner. Some are on organic farms, some are tucked away in such beautiful countryside that they're worth staying in for the setting alone. Very often the atmosphere is cosy and informal: you can stay in all day if you want, and there are no curfews or chores. On the downside, such is their popularity that some hostels cram people in to the point of discomfort. July and August are particularly bad, especially in the major cities and on the west coast, as are festival times. If you're relying on them it's worth ringing ahead to check what the situation is; or better still use the book-a-bed-ahead scheme. This allows you to book from one *IHH* hostel to another for a nominal charge of 50p; the hostel owner will phone through your booking and on payment of £5.50 will issue you with a ticket that guarantees your bed at the next hostel. Some hostels offer bike rental, some food: details are given in the text. Expect to pay around £5.50–7 for a dormitory bed; £8–12 per person for private rooms where available (more in Dublin). The IHH information office is right next to Busáras in Dublin at **The Backpacker Centre**, 22 Store Street, Dublin 1 (☎01/836 4700, fax ☎01/836 4710) – call in or phone for up-to-date information or a copy of their guide.

An Óige and YHANI hostels are run more traditionally: they are closed during the daytime and enforce evening curfews, at least officially. Thanks to competition from other hostels, you'll find many far more flexible than the rule book would suggest, particularly in out-of-the-way places. Some are worth visiting for the location (which can often make up for the lack of facilities); others, especially in the mountains, may be the only place to stay. In the Republic, **membership** – which includes membership of the umbrella organization, **Hostelling International** (HI), and therefore also membership of YHANI – costs £4 for under 18s and £7.50 for over 18s, and can be obtained by visiting or writing to An Óige's main office in Dublin (see below for details). In Northern Ireland, YHANI membership

(similarly includes membership of HI and therefore An Óige) costs £3.20 for under 18s, £9.30 for over 18s. Visitors from elsewhere in Britain, and foreign nationals, who wish to join the HI once in the Republic or the North can do so. It is worth remembering that if you buy membership before leaving home some transport companies offer discounts; from Britain Stena Sealink offers a 10-percent reduction on fares. If you turn up at an An Óige hostel as a non-member, you will be charged a nightly supplement of £1.25, which accumulates so that after paying six you become a full member.

Hostels are graded according to the quality of facilities, and **prices** in the **Republic** vary accordingly, ranging between £5.50 and £9.50. City hostels are generally more expensive, and prices are at their highest from June to August. It's worth getting a copy of the An Óige Handbook, which clarifies the intricacies of the system, lists every hostel in the association and gives details of YHANI hostels; it's available from the address below. An Óige also offers special accommodation-and-travel deals, which you should check out on arrival – for instance, its combined hostel and train ticket is often very good value. In the **North** charges for an overnight stay include linen: in Belfast the charge is £9.50; elsewhere it's £6.30.

YOUTH HOSTEL ASSOCIATIONS

Australia: Australian Youth Hostels Association, Level 3, 10 Mallett St, Camperdown, NSW (☎02/565 1325). Membership costs A$42 for a year, A$68 for two and A$94 for three; members are entitled to discounts on some air and land travel, travel insurance, car rental, entrance fees to museums and historical sights.

Canada: Hostelling International–Canadian Hostelling Association, Room 400, 205 Catherine St, Ottawa ON K2P 1C3 (☎1-800/663-5777). Annual membership for adults $25, children under 18 free when accompanied by parents; 2-year memberships cost £35.

England and Wales: Youth Hostel Association (YHA), Trevelyan House, 8 St Stephen's Hill, St Albans, Herts AL1 2DY (☎017278/45047). London information office: 14 Southampton St, London WC2E 7HY (☎0171/836 1036). Membership costs £3.20 for under 18s, £9.30 for over 18s. There are 15 other YHA city locations throughout England.

Ireland: An Óige, 61 Mountjoy St, Dublin 7 (☎1/830 4555).

New Zealand: Youth Hostels Association of New Zealand, 36 Customs House, Auckland (☎09/379 4224). Membership costs A$48 for a year, A$76 for two and A$105 for three, with the same discounts as the Australian Association.

Northern Ireland: Youth Hostel Association of Northern Ireland, 22 Donegal Rd, Belfast BT12 5JN (☎01232/324733).

Scotland: Scottish Youth Hostel Association, 7 Glebe Crescent, Stirling FK8 2JA (☎01786/451181). Membership costs £2.50 for under 18s and £6 for over 18s.

USA: Hosteling International–American Youth Hostels (HI–AYH), 773 15th St NW, Suite 840, PO Box 37613, Washington, DC 20013 (☎1-800/444 6111). Annual membership for adults $25, youths (under 19) $10, seniors (55 or over) $15, families $35.

CAMPING

The cheapest way to sleep in Ireland is to **camp rough**, although the distinct possibility of rain, without the facilities of a campsite, may put you off. You'll also find that some of the terrain is very tricky, especially in the areas of bog and rock in Clare, Galway, Mayo and Donegal. There's usually no problem if you ask to camp in a field, and in out-of-the-way places nobody minds where you pitch a tent (the only place you definitely can't camp is in a state forest – but these are usually dark pine woods anyhow). You may find that the farmer will ask you for a pound or two if the field happens to be in a heavily touristed region such as Kerry, and if there's an organized site nearby you'll probably be directed to it, but other than this you can often camp for free. The cost of staying in **organized campsites** varies from about £2.50 to £9 a night depending on the facilities offered, the number of people sharing etc; we've listed sites throughout the *Guide*. It's also worth bearing in mind that most of the **hostels** will let you camp on their land for £3–4 a night, with the use of kitchen facilities and showers.

FOOD AND DRINK

Ireland has no real tradition of eating out, but the range and quality of food has increased monumentally in recent years, especially at the top of the market, and this edition of the *Guide* includes the most luxurious and expensive of eating places, along with more basic establishments. The best of Irish food to be found outside smart restaurants are the super-fresh (although often unimaginative) vegetables, breads and Irish-made cheeses you'll find in the shops, so self-catering is definitely a gastronomic option. If your budget is restricted, the best bet is to fill up with a hearty breakfast and/or a good lunch from a pub or coffee shop in the middle of the day, and then concentrate on drinking in the evening – few pubs serve food at night.

FOOD

Irish food is generally highly meat-orientated, and you don't have to be a vegetarian to find this wearing after a while. For carnivores, meat in Ireland is generally of a good standard – steaks, in particular, are excellent – but after a while you begin to long for some variety in your diet and for something which hasn't been fried.

If you're staying in B&Bs, it's almost impossible to avoid the "traditional" Irish

breakfast of sausages, bacon and eggs, which usually comes accompanied by generous quantities of delicious soda bread. Pub **lunch** staples are usually meat and two veg, with plenty of gravy, although you can usually get freshly made sandwiches (sometimes excellent, but often sliced white bread and processed cheese – and if toasted served in a grill-crisped cellophane wrapper); home-made soups can be very good too. Most larger towns have good, simple **coffee shops** (open daytimes only) where you can get soup, sandwiches, cakes and the omnipresent apple pie as well as slightly more ambitious and filling dishes. In the North, in particular, expect enormous portions of meat and thoroughly overcooked vegetables that will ground you for the rest of the afternoon. It's worth remembering that **hotels** are obliged to offer food to all comers – so you can always find a sandwich and a cup of coffee, at any reasonable hour; you can generally order a plate of sandwiches and a pot of tea in pubs, too.

Many traditional Irish dishes are based on the **potato** and you certainly do get an awful lot of them – often served up in several different forms in the same meal. Potato cakes can be magnificent – a flour and potato dough fried in butter – as can potato soup. **Irish stew** of varying qualities will be available almost everywhere; and **colcannon**, cooked potatoes fried in butter with onions and cabbage, or leeks, can also be very good. Colcannon is a traditional dish for Hallowe'en, as is **barm brack**, a sweet yeast bread with spices and dried fruits.

RESTAURANTS AND ALTERNATIVES

Much is made of Ireland's recent **gastronomic revolution**, with new Irish cuisine, consisting of elegant meals using local produce that are often adaptations of traditional recipes, very much in vogue. Some **guesthouses**, particularly if they're historic buildings, serve very good food, in what can be very grand surroundings, and a growing number of excellent vegetarian and wholefood cafés offer a good budget alternative. There are also some impressive **seafood restaurants**, particularly along the west coast, which serve freshly caught fish and seafood along with home-grown vegetables. Irish **oysters** are famous; the season opens with an oyster festival at Clarinbridge on Galway Bay. **Salmon** and trout can also be fabulous, but be warned that away from the coast fish-farming is the norm.

Catering for yourself, at least some of the time, may be the best option. Produce available in Ireland is usually fresh and excellent, but – aside from in the cities and some tourist towns on the west coast – it is limited in range (you won't find exotic fruits and vegetables, for instance). Irish potatoes, cabbages and carrots are delicious, though surprisingly hard to buy in rural areas, where the population may be too small to support even a grocer's shop. Meat is very good; bread and scones are wonderful; and if you're travelling around the coast, you can often buy seafood cheaply direct from the fishermen. Sometimes you'll come across more unusual things in this way – spider crabs and monkfish, for example – that you would never find in local fish shops; it's all exported. In many places you can gather your own mussels from the rocks – but be sure to check locally in case there's a sewage outlet nearby.

Dairy products, especially cheese, can also be excellent. The past decade has seen an upturn in the Irish cheese business, which now produces many delicious, often unpasteurized cheeses. Look out for the creamy Cashel Blue, St Killian brie, and Gubbeen Farmhouse in west Cork as well as countless more idiosyncratic cheeses from smaller makes, many of whom like to experiment. There's no need to go to a smart restaurant to taste these – you can often find them in grocer's shops.

DRINK

To travel through Ireland without visiting a **pub** would be to miss out on a huge chunk of Irish life, some would say the most important. Especially in rural areas, the pub is far more than just a place to drink. It's the social and conversational heart of any Irish village, and often the political and cultural centre too. If you're after food, advice or company, the pub is almost always the place to head for; and very often they'll also be the venues for local entertainment, especially traditional and not so traditional music (see "Festivals and Entertainment", p.34).

Along with Mass and market day, the pub is the centre of Irish social activity: a cultural cliché, perhaps, but one that wears very well. Talking is an important business here, and drink is the great lubricant of social discourse. That said, it doesn't pay to arrive with too romantic a notion of what this actually means. Away from the cities and the touristed west coast, there are plenty of miserable, dingy bars where the only spark of conviviality is the dull glow of the TV. But in most big towns and cities you'll find bars heaving with life, and out in remote country villages it can be great fun drinking among the shelves of the ancient grocery shops-cum-bars you'll find dotted around.

While women will always be treated with genuine (unreconstructed) civility, it's true to say that the majority of bars are a predominantly male preserve. In the evening, especially, women travellers can expect occasional unwanted attention, though this rarely amounts to anything too unpleasant. Should your first encounters be bad ones, persist – the good nights will come, and will probably rank amongst the most memorable experiences of your trip.

In the Republic, **opening hours** are (in summer) Monday to Saturday 10.30am–11.30pm, on Sunday 12.30–2pm & 4–11.30pm – they close at 11pm in winter, and some pubs, especially in the cities, may close for a couple of hours in the afternoon ("holy hour"); illegal lock-ins remain something of an after-hours institution in rural parts. In the **North** pubs are open Monday to Saturday 11.30am–11pm, on Sunday 12.30–2.30pm and 7–10pm.

WHAT TO DRINK

The classic Irish drink is, of course, **Guinness** ("a Guinness" is a pint; if you want a half of any beer, ask for "a glass") which, as anybody will tell you, is simply not the same as the drink marketed as *Guinness* outside Ireland. For one thing, good *Guinness* has to be kept properly, something non-Irish pubs abroad tend not to do; it has to be poured gradually (the ultimate gaffe in a pub is to ask them to hurry this process); and

even across Ireland you'll taste differences – it's best in Dublin where it's brewed. A proper pint of Irish *Guinness* is a dream, far less heavy than you may be used to, though still a considerable, filling drink. Other local stouts, like *Beamish* and *Murphy's* (a Cork stout, far sweeter and creamier), make for interesting comparison: they all have their faithful adherents.

If you want a pint of English-style **bitter**, then try *Smithwicks*, which is not so different from what you'd get in an English pub. As everywhere, of course, **lager** is also increasingly popular: mostly *Harp* (made by Guinness) or *Heineken*. Whatever your tipple, you're likely to find drinking in Ireland an expensive business at around IR£1.70 a pint.

Irish **whiskeys** – try *Paddy's*, *Powers*, *Jameson's* or, from the North, *Bushmills* – also seem expensive, but in fact the measures are far larger than those you'll get in mainland Britain. If you've come in from the cold you can have your whiskey served warm with cloves and lemon – just ask for a hot whiskey. Asking for Scotch in an Irish pub is frowned on, and in any case anyone here will tell you that the Irish version is infinitely superior.

Non-alcoholic drinks are limited to an uninspiring array of the usual soft drinks and bottled fruit juices, plus Ireland's own, aggressively fizzy, mineral water, which is now available in a number of pleasantly un-sweet, fruity flavours. Unless the bar is extremely busy, you can always get **coffee** (generally served with a dollop of full cream) or **tea**. You can usually get **Irish coffee** too (with whiskey and cream), which is delicious if not very traditional – it was invented at Shannon airport.

COMMUNICATIONS: PHONES, MAIL AND THE MEDIA

In towns throughout Ireland you'll find fully automatic payphones in kiosks; instructions for use are on display, and internal and international calls can easily be made. A local call costs 20p minimum but, as you might imagine, long-distance daytime calls are expensive. International calls are cheapest if dialled direct after 6pm. New cardphones, found in towns all over the country, are by far the most convenient way of making long-distance calls, avoiding the chugging of coins interrupting your call; they're also cheaper than coin-operated phones. Phone cards can be bought at newsagents and post offices – it's worth carrying one with you since cash-operated phones are rare in

remote areas. If you make calls from a hotel or the like, expect a hefty premium charged on top of the normal price.

International dialling codes in the United Kingdom (including Northern Ireland) and Ireland have now been adjusted to follow the European standard – to call Ireland the code is 353, and for Northern Ireland, as part of the UK, it's 44.

There are few **fax bureaux** outside Dublin or Belfast. If you need to use a fax, ask at one of the swankier hotels – they're usually pleased to help and are unlikely to charge you an unreasonable rate.

MAIL

Post to or from the Republic is generally reasonably fast and efficient. If it's something important, it's worth spending the extra for recorded or registered mail. To send a letter within the Republic and to all EU countries costs 32p – postcards are 28p; to North America 52p and 32p. Main post offices are open Monday to Friday 8.30am–5.30pm, Saturday 9am–noon. Post from the North is more efficient. Letters and postcards travel anywhere in the EU for 25p, 41p for most of the rest of the world. Post office hours in the North are Monday to Friday 9am–5.30pm and Saturday 9am–1pm.

THE MEDIA

The most widely read **papers** in the **Republic** are the heavyweight *Irish Times* and the lighter *Irish Independent*. High-quality but remarkably slim papers, they really bring home just how small the population is. *The Times* is the more upmarket, a liberal newspaper with comparatively good foreign news coverage and plenty of feature material on home news and sport. *The Cork Examiner* is another well-regarded national daily (although mainly distributed around Munster), and the *Star* is Ireland's tabloid. Sunday newspapers include *The Times* and *Independent* equivalents, the liberal *Sunday Tribune* and the more sensational *Sunday World*. British newspapers are generally available the same day in Dublin and other cities. Mostly conservative and varying widely in quality, there's a local daily paper in every county; some of the best are *The Kerryman*, *The Donegal Democrat* and *The Kilkenny People*.

OPERATOR SERVICES

In the Republic:

Operator	☎10
Directory Enquiries within Ireland including Northern Ireland	☎1190
International Directory Enquiries	☎1198
International Operator Services	☎114
Telegrams	☎196

In the North:

Operator	☎100
Directory Enquiries	☎192
International Directory Enquiries	☎153
International Operator Services	☎155
Telegrams	☎190/193

In the **North**, all the main British papers are sold. Of the newspapers produced in Northern Ireland, the biggest seller is the evening paper, the *Belfast Telegraph*, which attempts to steer a middle course in terms of Northern Irish politics. The morning papers are the *Irish News*, read by the Nationalist community, and the Loyalist tabloid *News Letter*.

In the **Republic**, RTE (Radio Telefís Éireann) runs two state-sponsored **television** channels: RTE 1 and Network 2. RTE 1 reflects the state broadcasting policy with an emphasis on public information and Irish-language programmes (however, from late 1996, all Irish-language programmes will be on the new station *Teilifís na Gaeilge*). Network 2 is more upbeat, with plenty of chat shows and youth-orientated programmes. Ireland's most popular, long-running (36 years) and often controversial chat show is Gay Byrne's much-loved *The Late Late Show* on Friday evenings; very much a voice box for the

nation, it's probably the best, and most entertaining, indicator of current issues and concerns. In the **North** you get the BBC and Ulster Television, and you can also pick up broadcasts from the Republic. Throughout Ireland the four major English terrestrial TV channels are available on cable, as are satellite channels such as Sky One and Skysport.

RTE also runs three **radio** stations – Radio 1, 2 and FM3. Radio 1 is devoted to middle/high-brow music and cultural and political programmes. RTE 2 is a pop channel, and FM3 is the national Irish-language station, Radio na Gaeltachta, which shares the frequency with classical music programming. Recent deregulation of the radio has resulted in the growth of local radio on the FM airwaves. The quality varies, but you'll find some interesting fare, including all-Irish stations in Connemara and Ring, C. Waterford, that are worth listening to for traditional music, country and western and insights into local issues.

OPENING HOURS AND HOLIDAYS

Business and shop **opening hours**, both North and South, are very similar to Britain's: approximately 9am to 5.30pm, Monday to Saturday, with a smattering of late openings (usually Thursday or Friday) and half days.

In the Republic, however, particularly away from the bigger towns, hours are more approximate, with later opening and closing times. In rural areas you can generally find someone to sell you groceries at any reasonable hour, even if they have to open their shop to do it – and very often

the village shop doubles as the local pub. For banking hours see "Costs, Money and Banks" on p.16. On the main **public holidays** (see below), virtually everything will be closed except the pubs.

There's no pattern to the opening and closing of **museums**, **archeological sites** and the like, though most close altogether for at least one day a week. Wherever possible, hours and prices are listed in the *Guide*. The bigger attractions will normally be open throughout the day, while

PUBLIC HOLIDAYS

IN THE REPUBLIC:	IN THE NORTH:
New Year's Day	New Year's Day
St Patrick's Day, March 17	St Patrick's Day, March 17
Good Friday	Easter Monday
Easter Monday	First Monday in May
First Monday in May	Last Monday in May
First Monday in June	Orange Day, July 12
First Monday in August	Last Monday in August
Last Monday in October	Christmas Day
Christmas Day	December 26
St Stephen's Day, December 26	

smaller places may open only in the afternoon. Many sites away from the main tourist trails – especially houses or castles which are also private homes – are open only during the peak summer months.

Churches, at least if they're still in use, are almost always open, and if they're locked there's usually someone living nearby (often the priest) who will have the keys; otherwise, opening times will follow religious activity fairly closely.

FESTIVALS AND ENTERTAINMENT

A festival in Ireland is never a half-hearted affair. Whatever the pretext for the celebration, it's always also an excuse for serious partying. Well-established ones like the Cork Jazz Festival and the Wexford Opera Festival are big international events, and getting tickets for top performances can be well nigh impossible without advance planning. The very word "festival" seems to act as a magnet for all sorts of musicians, and many events are wonderfully overwhelming – no matter what the size of the town, there's rarely enough room for all that's going on, with music and dancing bursting out of the official venues into surrounding streets and bars. The biggest of the annual happenings are listed here, but pick up a calendar of events at any major tourist office and you'll soon get a picture of the huge range of celebration.

MUSIC

The most enjoyable aspect of Irish festivals – sheer exuberance apart – is probably the **traditional music**. Many festivals (known as *Fleadh* –

pronounced *fla*) are devoted almost exclusively to this: the biggest of them is the *Fleadh Cheoil na hÉireann* (see opposite), which includes the finals of the All Ireland music and dance contests.

However, you don't have to go to a festival to experience this; music in Irish **pubs** is similarly legendary, and again there's a huge range to choose from, only a relatively small proportion of it "traditional". **Country and western**, for example, is extremely popular, and there is a frightening number of middle-of-the-road pop bands lurking in country areas, with regular country and western nights at pubs across Ireland. **Ballads** are another well-developed Irish music form. The term "ballad" is a bit of a catch-all and open to countless interpretations – it's generally some form of dull crooning and essentially middle-aged in spirit. Brace yourself for the worst, and from time to time you'll be very pleasantly surprised.

The cream of pub music, however, has to be the **traditional folk sessions** of fiddles, accordions, *bodhrán* (a drum) and singing. Interest from abroad and the tourist industry have a lot to do with the resurgence of this musical culture – but this hardly matters, since the music can be phenomenal. The west coast (especially around Clare and Galway) has the best of the traditional scene. There's plenty in all the major cities, and pointers as to where to find sessions are given in the text. However, the locations of the best are hard to pin down for long. The thing to do is to ask around and keep your ears open for local tips.

Traditionally Sunday evening was the night for sessions, and in rural areas this is still often the case (a throwback to restrictions on holy days that meant partying on Saturdays had to stop at midnight), but increasingly Friday and Saturday are becoming just as important – and you may find something happening any night of the week. Things generally don't get going till late, and a bar that's still empty at 10pm may be a riot of music by half-past. While it's all extremely

MAJOR ANNUAL FESTIVALS AND EVENTS

Saint Patrick's Day (March 17): celebrations in all the big cities for several days roundabout.

Irish Grand National (April): horse racing at Fairyhouse (Meath).

Cork International Choral Festival (April/May): one of the big ones.

Festival of Music in Great Irish Houses (June): just what it says, at venues around the country.

Irish Derby (June): and other important races at the Curragh (Kildare).

James Joyce Summer School (July): strictly for Joyce buffs; Dublin.

Galway Arts Festival (July): festival of music, theatre and general partying; one of the best.

Galway Races (July/August): another important race meeting, very popular.

Yeats International Summer School (August): this Sligo event has often courted controversy through its exploration of nationalistic themes.

Rose of Tralee International Festival (August): a massive event, centred round a beauty contest.

Fleadh Cheoil na hÉireann (July): the most important of all the traditional music festivals, held in a different town every year.

Kilkenny International Arts Week (August): includes recitals, poetry readings, art exhibitions.

Lisdoonvarna Matchmaking Festival (September): plenty of traditional entertainment accompanies the lonely hearts side of the festivities.

All Ireland Hurling Final (September): the biggest event of the hurling year, in Dublin.

Cork Film and Jazz Festivals (October): actually two separate events, but they often run into one another. The jazz especially is enormously popular.

Wexford Opera Festival (October/November): a large gathering of international renown.

---

convivial and relaxed, if you're a musician yourself and want to join in, then do so tactfully. The first thing to do is sit and listen for a while – to make sure you can play to a high enough standard – and then work out who the leader is and ask. If you're not playing, don't crowd the musicians; the empty seats around them are for others who may join in.

Comhaltas Ceoltóiri Éireann is an organization that exists purely to promote traditional music and culture, and evenings organized by them (not always in bars), though by their nature not spontaneous, are well worth looking out for. They are run by real enthusiasts, and the standard of playing is usually pretty high.

SPECTATOR SPORTS

Ireland has two main indigenous sports, hurling and gaelic football, and both attract huge crowds and passionate support. **Hurling** is a stick game, a precursor of hockey and lacrosse, in which players can knock the ball along the ground, hit it through the air – catching it again by hand or with their broad wooden hurley (*camán*) – or carry it in the hurley. The ball (*solitar*), is made of leather and the size of a baseball; the goalposts are in the shape of an H, as in rugby. Three-point goals are scored by getting the ball under the bar, and one point for over the bar. The game is said

to have originated with the mythical hero Cúchulainn (see p.539), who became a star at the sport at the tender age of five. The hurling **season** begins with local games in the early summer, progressing through county and then province championships to reach its climax in the All Ireland Hurling Final on the first Sunday in September at Croke Park in Dublin (see p.91).

Gaelic football is a fast and aggressive kind of mix of rugby and soccer: the ball is round, as in soccer, but can be kicked, handled and run with, making it more similiar to rugby. The goalposts and scoring are the same as in hurling. The season, which runs from mid-February, is organized like hurling's, culminating in an All Ireland final at Croke Park on the third Sunday in September. Details of fixtures for hurling and gaelic football can be obtained from the **Gaelic Athletic Association** (☎01/836 3222).

Rugby union and soccer are also extremely popular, the latter particularly so in the North. The international **rugby** team is a joint Republic/ Northern Ireland side, with home matches played at Dublin's Lansdowne Road Stadium (see p.92). The main event of the year is the Five Nations Championship, a series of international games against France, England, Scotland and Wales played between January and March. **Soccer** is only played at league level – as in Britain – in the North; although the standard isn't as high. At international level, there are separate teams for the Republic and the North, with home games for both at Lansdowne Road. Since the successes of the 1990 and 1994 World Cups, the Republic's team – then under the managership of Englishman Jack Charlton or "Big Jack" – have gained a high profile and credible international reputation. Not surprisingly, soccer is on the up and up in Ireland and is supported with growing enthusiasm and national pride.

Horse racing unites two Irish passions, horses and betting, and is carried out with a relaxed good humour that you shouldn't miss. Racing is concentrated around the Curragh, a grassy plain in Co. Kildare (see p.115), where the classic flat-race course of the same name is located, along with Punchestown race course and many of Ireland's famous stud farms. The Irish Grand National is run at Fairyhouse in Co. Meath in April, the Irish Derby at the Curragh in June. Flat-racing runs from mid-March to early November, with the winter months being devoted entirely to jump-racing. For details of the fixtures at Dublin's race course, Leopardstown, see p.91.

SECURITY AND THE POLICE

The Republic is one of the safest countries in Europe in which to travel. This said, don't let the friendliness of people as a whole lull you into a general carelessness; like anywhere else visitors are seen as easy targets for petty thieves (particularly in Dublin and the bigger cities) and women especially should always take note of our advice on choosing accommodation. Although the North has opened up a lot in the last few years, there is still a security presence, and you should be careful in certain city areas. Personal security, and crimes against the individual, are not a major worry. You're probably less likely to be robbed or mugged here than in the rest of Britain.

In the Republic, people generally have a healthy indifference to law and red tape, perhaps in part a vestige of pre-Independence days, when any dealings with the police smacked of collusion with the British. The **police** – known as **Garda** or **Gardai** (pronounced "gar-dee") – accordingly have a low profile. In rural areas the low level of crime is such that policing is minimal and, should you need them, you might spend an entire afternoon waiting for the Garda to arrive. If you have any dealings with the Garda at all, the chances are that you'll find them affable enough.

In the **North** the **Royal Ulster Constabulary** (RUC) deal with all general civic policing and are

> The emergency number in both the North and the Republic is ☎999.

the people you should go to if in difficulties. Security at police stations is tight and they're generally covered in barbed wire. You may well find yourself being quizzed about where you are going, what you are doing, and so forth, especially in border areas. Be cooperative and polite and you should have no difficulties. Again, whatever their reputation, you'll find that the RUC are helpful in matters of everyday police activity.

Since the ending of the eighteen-month **IRA ceasefire** in February 1996 – during which time many security measures were dropped and there were no army patrols on the streets – police roadblocks have been re-introduced at certain key border crossings and a significant number of soldiers have been sent back. Despite the setback in the peace process, at the time of writing the North has a considerably more relaxed feel, and it's not thought that a return to full security measures will be necessary.

Obviously politics remains a sensitive subject in the North, and you should use your common sense about what you say to whom; and be careful when moving through particular areas of Belfast and Derry (see p.455 and p.499).

SEXUAL HARASSMENT, PREJUDICE AND RACISM

For women Ireland is wonderfully relaxing: the outlandish sexism of Irish society manifests itself in a male courtesy that can range from the genuine and delightful to the downright insufferable, but you are unlikely to experience any really threatening behaviour. Most uncomfortable situations can be defused by a straightforward, firm response.

This said, don't believe the general view that *nothing* can happen to you. It is worth remembering that outside the cities, communities are very small, and local women you see hitching alone do so in safety because they know and are known by just about everybody on the road. Foreign travellers don't have that added security, and, though it is very unlikely, you could be unlucky. In particular, if you are travelling alone use only the budget accommodation that is listed in this guide or recommended by the tourist office, and don't go with touts at stations. In the case of serious assault, if possible contact a Rape Crisis Centre before going to the police (telephone numbers are given in chapter listings). Attacks are rare and the Garda, though well-meaning, have little experience of handling distressed women.

Black travellers may have a less easy time of it. The Republic of Ireland, and, to an extent, the rural North are fiercely conservative and shamefully intolerant of minority groups. If you are black you may well experience a peculiarly naive brand of ignorant racism. Open comment on the colour of a person's skin isn't uncommon outside the major cities, especially in the remote west, where people simply aren't used to seeing black people. This said, there's no need to anticipate any real malice.

The **gay** community is both the biggest and least visible minority in Ireland. Although part of the UK, Northern Ireland was excluded from the 1967 Act that legalized homosexuality for consenting adults in Britain. This led one individual to take his case to the European Court of Human Rights in 1982, which brought the legal status of gays in Northern Ireland into line with the rest of the UK. In the Republic, homosexuality has been legal since 1990, and a nominally wide-ranging Incitement Against Hatred Act was passed in 1994 specifically prohibiting discrimination against people on the grounds of sexual orientation as well as race. However, public indecency charges are still pursued – such as surveillance and arrest of gays cruising Dublin's Phoenix Park, and censorship laws are used to exclude gay material. Outside the big cities homosexuality is not at all socially accepted, and public displays of affection are out of the question.

TRAVELLERS WITH DISABILITIES

The disabled traveller in Ireland is not well served, and wheelchair users in particular are not likely to find ramps, lifts and wide doors commonly available. With this in mind, it is well worth contacting the National Rehabilitation Board (NRB) in the Republic and the Northern Irish Tourist Board (NITB) for information before you travel.

The NRB publish very useful and comphrensive **survey guides** of **accommodation**, **tourist amenities** and **restaurants/pubs** in the Republic. They also have listings of accessible toilets and provide the keys to them. Another useful publication is their **Dublin: A Guide for People with Disabilities**, which has detailed information on access to transport, toilets, public buildings, accommodation, shops and nightlife etc in the capital (all NRB publications are free). Even if you don't intend staying in Dublin, it's worth getting for its advice on transport to Ireland and how to get the best service from airlines and ferry companies.

Certain **ferry companies** offer good reductions to disabled travellers if you are travelling from mainland Britain. If you are a member of the Disabled Drivers Association (DDA) or the Disabled Drivers Motor Club (DDMC), *Irish Ferries* let your car travel free of charge, although they levy a £55 harbour fee on the return journey; car passengers pay foot passenger rates. *Stena Sealink* allow the car of a disabled driver, who is a member of the DDMC, and passengers to travel between Britain and Ireland at a reduced rate (about 10 percent); certain days may be excluded so check well in advance. The NRB also have a holiday file with information on **activity holi**

days and details of **travel agencies** catering specifically for the disabled. The staff are extremely helpful, and if they don't have what you are looking for they will go out of their way to try and find it for you.

CONTACTS FOR TRAVELLERS WITH DISABILITIES

IN IRELAND

Disability Federation of Ireland, 2 Sandyford Office Park, Sandyford, Dublin 18 (☎01/295 9344).

Irish Wheelchair Association, Blackheath Drive, Clontarf, Dublin 3 (☎01/833 8241).

Mental Health Association of Ireland, Mensane House, 6 Adelaide St, Dún Laoghaire, Co. Dublin (☎01/284 1166).

National Rehabilitation Board, 44 North Great George's Street, Dublin 1 (☎01/874 7503, fax ☎01/874 7490).

Northern Irish Tourist Board, St Anne's Court, 59 North St, Belfast BT1 1NB (☎01232/246609).

IN BRITAIN

Holiday Care Service, 2nd floor, Imperial Building, Victoria Rd, Horley, Surrey RH6 9HW (☎01293/774535). *Information on all aspect of travel.*

Disabled Drivers Association, Ashwellthorpe, Norwich NR16 1EX (☎01508/489449).

Disabled Drivers Motor Club, Cottingham Way, Thrapston, Northamptonshire NN14 4PL (☎01832/734724).

Mobility International, 228 Borough High St, London SE1 1JX (☎0171/403 5688). *Put out a quarterly newsletter that keeps up-to-date with developments in disabled travel.*

Royal Association for Disability and Rehabilitation (RADAR), 250 City Rd, London EC1V 8AF (☎0171/250 3222). *All kinds of information and advice.*

IN NORTH AMERICA

Directions Unlimited, 720 N Bedford Rd, Bedford Hills, NY 10507 (☎1-800/533-5343). *Tour operator specializing in custom tours for people with disabilities.*

Jewish Rehabilitation Hospital, 3205 Place Alton Goldbloom, Montréal, PQ H7V 1R2 (☎514/688-9550, ext 226). *Guidebooks and travel information.*

Mobility International USA, PO Box 10767, Eugene, OR 97440 (Voice and TDD: ☎503/343-1284). *Information and referral services, access guides, tours and exchange programmes. Annual membership $20 (includes quarterly newsletter).*

Society for the Advancement of Travel for the Handicapped (SATH), 347 5th Ave, New York, NY 10016 (☎212/4470-7284). *Non-profit travel-*

industry referral service that passes queries on to its members as appropriate; allow plenty of time for a response.

Travel Information Service, Moss Rehabilitation Hospital, 1200 West Tabor Rd, Philadelphia, PA 19141 (☎215/456-9600). *Telephone information and referral service.*

Twin Peaks Press, Box 129, Vancouver, WA 98666; ☎206/694-2462 or 1-800/637-2256). *Publisher of the Directory of Travel Agencies for the Disabled ($19.95), listing more than 370 agencies worldwide; Travel for the Disabled ($14.95); the Directory of Accessible Van Rentals and Wheelchair Vagabond ($9.95), loaded with personal tips.*

IN AUSTRALASIA

ACROD, PO Box 60, Curtin, ACT 2605 (☎06/682 4333). *Compiles lists of organizations, accommodation, travel agencies and tour operators.*

Barrier Free Travel, 36 Wheatley St, North Bellingen, NSW 2454 (☎066/551733; ☎02/6655

1733 from April 1998). *Fee-based travel access information service.*

Disabled Persons Assembly, PO Box 10,138 The Terrace, Wellington (☎04/472 2626).

In **Northern Ireland**, NITB (also very helpful) publish a guide to accessible accommodation, and their general guide to restaurants throughout the North highlights those with wheelchair ramps and facilities for disabled people (a nominal fee is charged for both publications).

DIRECTORY

CHILDREN Children are generally liked and indulged in Ireland, even if there are few places actually designed to cater for them. Baby supplies are sold everywhere, and children are generally welcome at B&Bs (though few have cots or special facilities), in pubs during the daytime, and almost anywhere else.

CONTRACEPTIVES Throughout Ireland anyone over 18 can buy condoms at pharmacies (though in the Republic, where legal contraception was only recently introduced, you may still find places which don't sell them – or don't approve). The pill is available on prescription only.

ELECTRICITY In the Republic, electricity is 220V AC, in the North 240V AC. Plugs everywhere are British-style three square pins (just occasionally you may still find old round ones). In other words British appliances will work everywhere; North American ones will need both a transformer and a plug adapter; Australian and New Zealand appliances only an adapter.

LAUNDRY You'll find laundries only in the bigger towns and on large caravan/campsites. Hostels, though, will often have a washing machine for residents' use, and at many B&Bs they'll do your washing for you. Elsewhere it's worth taking along a tube of *Travel Wash* – designed to be used in hotel washbasins – which makes a lot less mess than powder.

TOILETS Public toilets are reasonably common in all the big towns, and generally acceptably clean, if no more. Or you can pop into the local pub, and stop for a drink while there. The Irish labels to look out for are *Fír* (Men) and *Mna* (Women).

WORK Although EU citizens are legally allowed to live and work in Ireland, local unemployment is extremely high, and your chances of finding a decent job are slim. The best opportunities for travellers are in seasonal work in resorts, poorly paid cleaning and waiting jobs, or perhaps helping out in a hostel in return for board and pocket money. You'll need to search locally.

PART TWO

THE
GUIDE

N

CH15
ANTRIM
& DERRY

CH13
DONEGAL

CH14
BELFAST

CH17
TYRONE &
FERMANAGH

CH16
DOWN &
ARMAGH

CH11
SLIGO AND
LEITRIM

CH12
CAVAN &
MONAGHAN

CH4
MEATH, LOUTH,
WESTMEATH &
LONGFORD

CH10
GALWAY, MAYO
& ROSCOMMON

CH1
DUBLIN

CH3
LAOIS &
OFFALY

CH2
WICKLOW
& KILDARE

CH9
CLARE

CH6
WATERFORD,
TIPPERARY
& LIMERICK

CH5
WEXFORD,
CARLOW
& KILKENNY

CH8
KERRY

CH7
CORK

CHAPTER ONE

DUBLIN

Emphatically the Republic of Ireland's capital, **DUBLIN** is a focus for the energy of a country now redefining itself as a European nation and has a growing reputation as a cosmopolitan young city. Of roughly one and a half million people in greater Dublin, more than 50 percent are under 25, and the relative prosperity of many of them is making its impact on a rapidly changing city. New shops are everywhere, and restaurants, cafés, bars and clubs are opening in abundance, bringing a unmistakable buzz to the capital, especially at night. The city's emergence from provincialism is, however, only part of the truth, as Dubliners will be quick to tell you. With the continuing drift of population from the land to the capital, Dublin is bulging at the seams, which, of course, brings its problems – spend just a couple of days here and you'll come upon inner-city deprivation as bad as any in Europe. The spirit of Dublin has its contradictions, too, with youthful enterprise set against a leaden traditionalism that won't relinquish its grip for many years yet – the national divorce referendum in 1995 may have gone in favour of reform, but it was a close-run thing. But the collision of the old order and the forward-looking younger generations is an essential part of the appeal of this extrovert and dynamic city.

If you approach Dublin by sea, you'll have an opportunity to appreciate its magnificent physical setting, with the fine sweep of **Dublin Bay** and the weird, conical silhouettes of the Wicklow Mountains providing an exhilarating backdrop to the south. Central Dublin is not big, and it's easy to find your way around. One obvious axis is formed by the river, the **Liffey**, running from west to east and dividing the city into two regions of very distinct character – the **North Side**, poorer and less developed than its neighbour the **South Side** – each of which has a strong allegiance among its inhabitants. The other main axis is the north–south one formed by Grafton and Westmoreland streets south of the river, running into O'Connell Street in the north.

The majority of the famous attractions are south of the river, and, for many visitors, the city's heart lies around the best of what is left of Georgian Dublin – the grand set pieces of **Fitzwilliam** and **Merrion squares**, with their graceful brick houses with ornate, fanlighted doors and immaculately kept central gardens, and the wide but strangely decorous open space of **St Stephen's Green**. The elegant South Side is also the setting for Dublin's august seat of learning, **Trinity College** and its famous library; **Grafton Street**, the city's upmarket shopping area; **Temple Bar**, the in-place for the arts, alternative shopping and socializing; and most of the city's museums and art galleries.

North of the Liffey, the main thoroughfare is **O'Connell Street**, whose main monument, the **General Post Office**, was the scene of violent fighting in the Easter Rising of 1916. Further north, among Georgian squares older and seedier than the ones you'll see on the South Side, are the **Irish Writers' Museum** and the **Hugh Lane Municipal Museum of Art**. West again, and you come to Dublin's biggest open space – indeed, one of the world's largest city parks – **Phoenix Park**, home of both the President's Residence and the **zoo**.

The urban sprawl is in sharp contrast to the countryside around – trains make access easy to the whole curve of Dublin Bay, from the fishing port of **Howth** in the north to the southern suburbs of **Sandycove** with its James Joyce connections, **Dalkey**, made famous by the comic writer Flann O'Brien, and salubrious **Killiney**, now

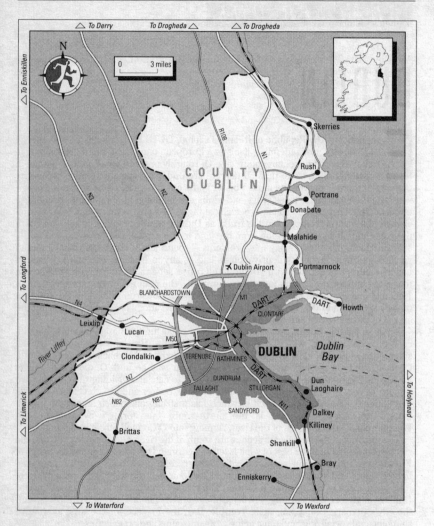

colonized by the rich and famous. And further: Dublin must be one of the world's easiest capitals to get out of, making it a good base for exploring the hills and coastline of Wicklow to the south and the gentler scenery to the north that leads up to the megalithic monuments of the verdant Boyne Valley.

Some history

Dublin celebrated its millennium in 1988, and though there was much argument as to what the anniversary really meant, it does give an indication of the city's antiquity. Although the first evidence of a settlement beside the Liffey is in Ptolemy's celebrated map of 140 AD, which shows a place called *Eblana*, it's as a Viking settlement that

Dublin's history really begins. The Norse raiders sailed up the Liffey and, destroying a small Celtic township, set up a trading post on the south bank of the river at the ford where the royal road from the Hill of Tara in the north crossed the Liffey on its way to Wicklow. The Vikings adopted the Irish name, **Dubh Linn** or Dark Pool, for their settlement, which soon amalgamated with another Celtic settlement, **Baile Átha Cliath** ("town of the hurdles", pronounced *Ballya-aw-kleea*, and still the Irish name for Dublin), on the north bank.

The next wave of invaders were the **Anglo-Normans**. In the twelfth century, the opportunistic Strongbow and a band of Welsh knights were sent over by Henry II in response to the beleaguered King of Leinster Dermot McMurrough's request for help to regain his throne – in return he gave an oath of fealty. The invasion was successful, and the English king, concerned that Strongbow and his Welsh adventurers were becoming too powerful, fixed a court at Dublin. The city was thereby established as the centre of British influence in Ireland and set the precedent for the annual social and political **Seasons**, which were to shape Dublin's role and character for the next seven centuries.

Because most of the early city was built of wood, only the two cathedrals, part of the Castle and one or two churches have survived from before the seventeenth century. What you see today, in both plan and buildings, dates essentially from the **Georgian** period. By this time, soldiers in the service of the English monarchs, who had been rewarded with confiscated land, had begun to derive income from their new estates. As they began to replace their original fortified houses with something more fashionable, they wished also to participate in the country's burgeoning economic and political life, which was centred on Dublin. Their town houses (along with those of the growing business and professional classes), and the grandeur of the public buildings erected during this period, embodied the new confidence of the British ruling class: a group that was, however, starting to regard itself not as British, but as Irish.

In the second half of the eighteenth century the wealth of this **Anglo-Irish class** was reflected in a rich cultural life – Handel's *Messiah*, for instance, was first performed in Ireland, and the legacy of architecture, furniture and silverware, though now much diminished, speaks for itself. Growing political freedom was to culminate in the **parliament of 1782** in which Henry Grattan made a famous **Declaration of Rights**, modelled on the recent American example, which came very close to declaring Irish (by which he meant Protestant Anglo-Irish) independence. A severely limited and precarious enterprise, the Irish bid for self-government was to collapse very soon, with the abortive uprising of 1798 and the Act of Union which followed in 1801.

The **Act of Union** may have shorn Dublin of its independent political power, but the city remained the centre of British administration, in the shape of the Vice Regent, and the Seasons continued to revolve around the Viceroy's Lodge (now the President's Residence) in Phoenix Park. Along with the rest of Ireland, Dublin entered a long economic decline and became the stage for much of the agitation that eventually led to independence. In 1829 the Catholic lawyer (and Kerryman) **Daniel O'Connell** secured an important advance by achieving limited Catholic emancipation, allowing Catholics to play some part in the administration and politics of their capital city and, in a signal victory, was elected Lord Mayor of Dublin. Dublin was also the centre of the **Gaelic League**, which, founded by Douglas Hyde in 1893, encouraged the formation of an Irish national consciousness through efforts to restore the native language and culture. This paved the way for the **Celtic literary revival** under W.B. Yeats and Lady Gregory and the establishment, in 1904, of the *Abbey Theatre*.

Poverty and violence were the other side of the political coin, and the early years of the **twentieth century** saw the fight for the establishment of trade unionism in Ireland. In 1913 this came to a head in the Great Lock-Out, when forcibly unemployed workers and their families died of hunger and cold. Open violence hit the streets during Easter Week of 1916 in the uprising that was the main event in the long **struggle for Irish**

independence. The prominent battles were fought in and around the centre of Dublin, and the insurgents made the General Post Office their headquarters (see p. 77). The city's streets were the scene of violence once more during the brief Civil War that broke out after the creation of the Irish Free State in 1921, when supporters and opponents of the partition of Ireland fought it out across the Liffey, and the Four Courts, one of Dublin's great Georgian buildings, went up in flames after being bombed by opponents of the Anglo-Irish Treaty.

The history of Dublin since independence has been the history of the capital of a young-old nation endeavouring to leave behind its colonial past. It's to this, as well as the appalling condition of many of the old tenements, that the **destruction of much of the Georgian city** can be attributed. Today areas of the inner-city, especially on the North Side, remain fractured and decaying, despite the decanting of people from the tenements to – as it turned out rather inadequately planned – suburban estates during the 1960s and 1970s, and more recent corporate plans to attract investment and build new housing rather than the previous high-rises. On the South Side Georgian streets have been replaced in many places by modern offices – you can see how human civic planning has given way to corporate exhibitionism.

One of the outstanding successes of recent years is the new development at Temple Bar (see p.67), which has done much to enhance the image and atmosphere of the city. Indeed Dublin now has a new feel to it, a sense that the legacy of its colonial relationship with Britain has finally been put to one side, as the capital, with the rest of the Republic, looks increasingly to Europe, and America, rather than across the Irish Sea.

Arrival, information and transport

Buses from out of town, the airport included, will drop you at or close by the Central Bus Station, or **Busáras** (☎874 6301), in Store Street, behind the Custom House. Right by the river, this is dead central for almost anywhere in the city and is one of the few places you can leave **luggage** during the day (£1.10–1.50). Coming in from the airport, six miles north of the centre, you can take the official airport bus for £2.50, or a scheduled city bus (#41A or #41C) will do the same job for £1.10. Either takes around half an hour to reach the bus station; a taxi will cost you around £10. If you arrive by **ferry**, you'll come in at one of two harbours: **Dún Laoghaire** (pronounced *Learey*; for *Stena Sealink* services), six miles out, is on the efficient **DART** (Dublin Area Rapid Transport) city train network, which will whisk you into town in about twenty minutes; **Dublin Port** (*Irish Ferries/B&I*), nearer in, is served by local bus #53, although this can be a rare bird – a taxi may be necessary. For information on leaving the city see "Listings".

Information

The obvious first stop for information is **Dublin Tourism**'s main office at Suffolk Street (July–August Mon–Sat 9.30am–8.30pm, Sun 11am–5.30pm; Sept–June Mon–Sat 9am–6pm, except Tues 9.30am–6pm; ☎605 7700): other branches are at Dublin Airport (8am–10pm; ☎844 5977), the port at Dún Laoghaire (open times vary according to ferry times, minimum hours 9am–8pm; ☎284 6361) and at Dublin Port (June–Aug for ferry arrivals). **Bord Fáilte** have a much smaller office at Baggot Street Bridge (9am–5.15pm; ☎676 5871). There's a Northern Ireland Tourist Information office in *Clery's* department store on O'Connell St (☎878 6055). The main Dublin Tourism office is always incredibly busy, but it has much of the most frequently needed information

The telephone code for Dublin and around is ☎01.

posted on the walls and has a vast collection of literature and maps (not all of it free). There's a room-booking service, which costs £1 for accommodation in Dublin and £3 for anywhere else. Since the staff aren't allowed to make recommendations all you're paying for is a phone call: if you're planning to stay in bed and breakfasts or hotels most of the time – and you find you need more information than we can supply – you can buy one of their **accommodation guides** and do the phoning yourself.

More practical, but always in a state of total chaos, is the **USIT office** on Aston Quay, just opposite O'Connell Bridge (Mon–Fri 9am–5.30pm, Sat 10am–1pm; ☎677 8117). *USIT* not only books bed and breakfasts during the summer but also has its own hostel and a travel agency offering student discounts on ferries and flights. Go here for *Travelsave* stamps (see p.21), *ISIC* cards, and information on everything that's going on in Dublin.

For **listings of Dublin** events, the best source is the fortnightly magazine *In Dublin*, which you can pick up from any newsagent for £1.50. An inferior alternative is the *Dublin Event Guide*, free from the tourist office. The *Irish Times* and *Evening Herald* have theatre and cinema listings daily – the *Irish Times* does a good weekly overview in its Saturday edition.

City transport

It's customary to say that the way to get to know Dublin is to walk. It's true that the city's size makes this a practical possibility, but equally true that walking the city streets can quickly become a tiring slog. Luckily there's an extensive, and reasonably priced, **local bus network** that makes it easy to hop on a bus whenever you want. Buses start running between 6am and 6.30am, and the last city-centre buses leave town around 11.30pm. Maximum fare on the bus system is £1.10. A one-day bus-only **pass** costs £3.30; an *Explorer Ticket*, a one-day bus-and-train pass (including DART) costs £4.50; a four-day version of the latter is still better value at £10. Passes are available from most newsagents. Finding your way around the bus system may prove more of a problem, although most stops do now have timetables and routes for the buses that stop there. If you don't know which stop to go to in the first place, though, either ask a bus inspector – there usually seems to be one around, dispensing directions – or invest in a bus timetable, which includes a Dublin bus map, for £1.20 from **Dublin Bus**, 59 Upper O'Connell Street (Mon–Fri 9am–5pm, Sat 9am–1pm; ☎873 4222 for city buses, ☎836 6111 for provincial services). Or you can do what most locals seem to: pop into the nearest newsagent when you're lost, look up the route, and put the book back on the shelf. *Dublin Bus* also runs city tours and cheap trips outside Dublin to places the regular services don't visit, so it's worth enquiring about these.

The other useful city transportation service is the **DART**, the Dublin Area Rapid Transport system (☎836 3333), which links Howth to the north of the city with Bray to the south in County Wicklow, via such places as Sandycove. DART services are quick, efficient and easy to use, and the stretch that runs along Dublin Bay from Dalkey to Killiney gives you such an amazing view that it's worth taking the train just to see it. It's not expensive – maximum single fare is £1.50 – but if you're considering taking more than one or two trips, it's worth buying an *Explorer Ticket* (see above). The DART runs from 6.55am to 11.30pm.

Although, if you're lucky, you may be able to flag one down, **taxis** in Dublin don't generally cruise the streets. Instead they wait at ranks in central locations, such as outside the *Shelbourne Hotel* on St Stephen's Green, Dame Street (opposite the main gate of Trinity College), Abbey Street (on the right-hand side going up O'Connell Street from the bridge), or close to *Jury's Hotel and Towers* in Ballsbridge. If you want to order a taxi by phone, ring *National Radio Cabs* (☎677 2222; 24hr) or *City Cabs* (☎872 7272), who run a fleet of **wheelchair-accessible** black cabs.

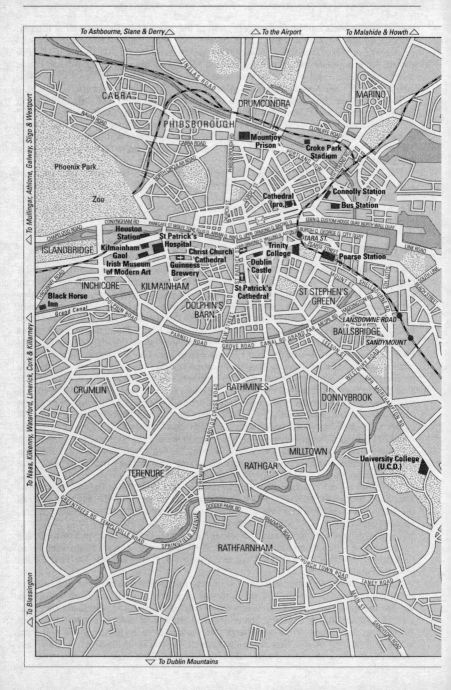

To Ashbourne, Slane & Derry △
△ To the Airport
To Malahide & Howth △

△ To Mullingar, Athlone, Galway, Sligo & Westport

To Naas, Kilkenny, Waterford, Limerick, Cork & Killarney △

△ To Blessington

▽ To Dublin Mountains

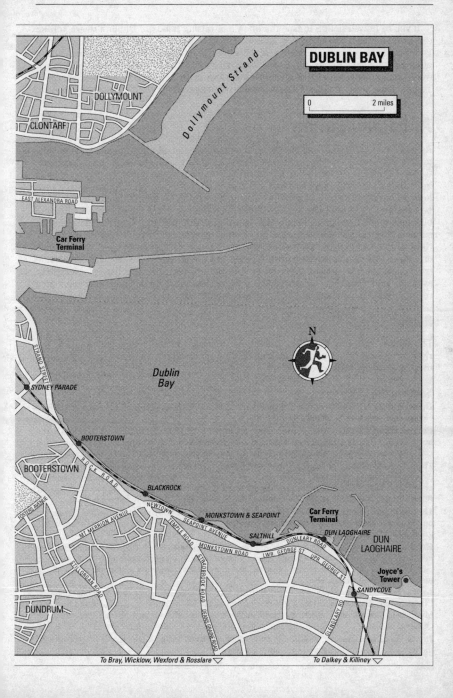

DUBLIN BAY

0   2 miles

DOLLYMOUNT

CLONTARF

Dollymount Strand

EAST ALEXANDRA ROAD

Car Ferry
Terminal

N

Dublin
Bay

STRAND STREET

SYDNEY PARADE

BOOTERSTOWN

BOOTERSTOWN

ROCK ROAD

BLACKROCK

NEWTOWN

FOSTERS AVENUE

MONKSTOWN & SEAPOINT

SEAPOINT AVENUE

MT MERRION AVENUE

TEMPLE ROAD

Car Ferry
Terminal

SALTHILL

DUN LAOGHAIRE

DUN
LAOGHAIRE

MONKSTOWN ROAD

STRADBROOK ROAD

DUNLEARY ROAD

LWR. GEORGE ST

UPR. GEORGE ST

STILLORGAN ROAD

Joyce's
Tower

SANDYCOVE

DUNDRUM

JEANS GRANE ROAD

GLENGEARY RD

To Bray, Wicklow, Wexford & Rosslare ▽   To Dalkey & Killiney ▽

If you're brave enough to face the often hair-raising habits of Dublin drivers, a **bike** can make a useful way of getting around. Try *Rent-A-Bike* at 58 Lower Gardiner Street (☎872 5399: £6 per day, £30 per week, £30 deposit), or *Raleigh Rent-a-Bike*, whose main office is at Raleigh House, Kylemore Road, Dublin 10 (☎626 1333: £7 per day, £30 per week, credit card deposit). For more on cycling in Dublin, *Square Wheel Cycleworks*, Temple Lane South (☎679/0838), is a workers' co-operative cyclists' information centre.

Accommodation

As you'd expect, Dublin has plenty of accommodation in all price ranges, from hostels to five-star hotels, so finding somewhere to stay really shouldn't be a problem. Generally prices are cheaper on the North Side and anywhere out of the centre. **Hotels** in Dublin are mostly expensive and sometimes no more comfortable than good guest-houses, but if you're travelling out of season, it's worth checking reductions, which can be considerable. Also many swanky hotels drop their tariffs at the weekends when the business types have gone home. **B&Bs** are plentiful, and of a high standard, in the suburbs, but central **B&Bs** tend to be grimy or overpriced. If you're determined to be right at the heart of the action and you are on a fairly limited budget, various well-organized official and private **youth hostels** are the cheapest option; most have some private rooms. The tourist office in Suffolk Street (see p.46) has lists of everything available and should know where there are vacancies at peak times; however, they recommend that you book ahead for all accommodation.

Hotels

The limited range of **hotels** in Dublin, concentrated in the centre and south of the river, are pricy; but, if you are looking for luxury, Georgian elegance, and good food, there are several to choose from.

South of the Liffey

Buswell's, 23-27 Molesworth St (☎676 4013, fax ☎676 2090). Comfortable, well-run hotel in a Georgian terrace near St Stephen's Green. ⑨.

Central Hotel, 1–5 Exchequer St (☎679 7302, fax ☎679 7303). Recently refurbished and close to the lively Temple Bar area. Bright pink walls and colourful modern Irish art save it from overpowering tastefulness; excellent breakfasts and a good restaurant serving some organically grown food. ⑧.

The Clarence Hotel, Wellington Quay (☎662 3066, fax ☎662 3077). Overlooking the Liffey and close to Temple Bar, the hotel is now run by rock band U2. The new, trendy crowd is served by phlegmatic staff still sporting old green hotel uniforms. (At the time of writing it was closed for refurbishment and due to re-open in summer 1996.) For details of the nightclub see p.88. ⑧.

The Georgian House, 20–21 Lower Baggot St (☎661 8832, fax ☎661 8834). One of the few period buildings in Dublin where you can actually stay, five minutes' walk from St Stephen's Green, with a good seafood restaurant. ⑦.

Harding Hotel, Copper Alley, Christchurch (☎679 6500, fax ☎679 6504). Right by Temple Bar, this newly built *USIT* hotel offers en-suite rooms, many of which accommodate up to 3 people, at a competitive flat rate (single rooms, however, are more costly); there's a restaurant with a varied menu serving food all day. ④–⑦.

Jury's Hotel, Christchurch Place (☎874 0225, fax ☎874 5239). Ugly new building opposite Christchurch; the interior is less hideous. Close to St Patrick's Cathedral, Guinness and the Irish Museum of Modern Art. Flat rate for rooms makes it a good option for anyone travelling with small children. ⑤.

Jury's Hotel and Towers, Ballsbridge (☎660 5000, fax ☎660 5540). A popular meeting place with modern and comfortable bars and a lively atmosphere. ⑧.

Throughout this book, accommodation prices have been graded according to the cost per person per night in high season; with hotels and many hostels this represents half the cost of a double room, whereas with the more basic hostels it represents the cost of a single dormitory bed. The prices signified by our grades are as follows:

① Up to £6	③ £10–14	⑤ £20–26	⑦ £36–45
② £6–10	④ £14–20	⑥ £26–36	⑧ Over £45

Lansdowne, 27 Pembroke Rd, Ballsbridge (☎668 2522, fax ☎668 5585). Popular with the rugby and more recently football crowds because of the proximity of Lansdowne Road Stadium, this comfortable hotel is two miles from the city centre in leafy surroundings. ⑧.

Mont Clare, Merrion Square, (☎661 6799, fax ☎661 5663). Charming, recently renovated hotel in the heart of Georgian Dublin, within walking distance of the centre. ⑧.

Shelbourne Hotel, St Stephen's Green (☎676 6471, fax ☎661 6006). Widely acknowledged to be Dublin's best hotel, and an old-money society watering hole. Elegantly furnished period interiors and a buzzing social life, plus an excellent restaurant and bar. Be prepared to pay, though. ⑧.

Wellington Hotel, Wellington Quay, Temple Bar (☎677 9315, fax ☎677 9387). Small new budget option in the centre of Temple Bar. If you have children, the room rate makes it a particularly worthwhile option. ⑤.

North of the Liffey

Gresham, Upper O'Connell St (☎874 6881, fax ☎878 7175). Traditionally regarded as Dublin's second-best hotel (after the *Shelbourne*), and considerably flashier. ⑧.

Maple Hotel, 75 Lower Gardiner St (☎874 0225; fax ☎874 5239). Comfortable, small, central hotel – handy for the airport and Busáras – with budget rates. ⑥.

Othello House, 74 Lower Gardiner St (☎874 0442, fax ☎874 3460). A good budget option, just off O'Connell St – a small hotel with 16 rooms. ④.

Wynn's Hotel, 38-39 Lower Abbey St (☎874 5131, fax ☎874 1556). An old-fashioned, dusty place mainly frequented by people up from the country. Close to the *Abbey Theatre*. ⑦.

Bed and breakfast

Bed and breakfast places abound, with the cheapest dives clustered around Connolly Station on the North Side. In the south there are more salubrious, and more expensive, guesthouses in the Ballsbridge area, still within easy walking distance of the centre. The best balance between price and quality, though, generally involves staying further out in the suburbs. Given the relatively small scale of the city and the excellent public transport, these places are definitely the better option.

Centre

If you're determined to find something **central**, start from O'Connell Street and head north towards Mountjoy Square; Gardiner Street, in particular, has a high density of B&Bs.

Elmar Hotel, 34 Lower Gardiner St (☎874 1246). Small but adequate rooms, handy for Busáras and the bus to the airport. ④.

Leitrim House, 34 Blessington St (☎830 8728). Perhaps the best value in the centre. ④.

Mrs M McMahon, *Sinclair House*, 3 Hardwicke St, off North Frederick St (☎878 8412). Convenient location just north of Parnell Square. ④.

Trinity College, Dublin 2 (☎702 1177). Although not cheap, this must be one of the most atmospheric places to stay. From June to Sept you can rent out single en-suite rooms, double apartments (with a lounge but shared bathroom), or 4–5 people en-suite apartments. ④–⑥.

Ballsbridge

Directly south of the centre, about two miles out, the better-heeled inner suburb of **Ballsbridge** (on bus routes #5, #6, #6A and #7) has high-standard B&Bs on offer.

Mrs Bridget Brady, *Northumberland Lodge*, 68 Northumberland Rd (☎660 5270). A spacious Victorian house in pleasant suburban street. ⑤.

Mrs O'Donoghue, 41 Northumberland Rd (☎668 1105). Comfortable and friendly, this large Victorian guesthouse has quite a few non-tourist guests. ⑤.

Mrs Doran, *Wesley House*, 113 Angelsey Rd (☎668 1201). Pricier option with comfort to match. ⑦.

Mr & Mrs Dunne, *Aaronmore*, 1c Sandymount Ave (☎668 7972). Quiet location, near the DART stop for Sandymount. ⑤.

Mrs Sheila Matthews, *Elva*, 5 Pembroke Park (☎668 3500). Convenient location at the centre-of-town end of Ballsbridge. ⑤.

Mrs Teresa Muldoon, *Oaklodge*, 4 Pembroke Park, Ballsbridge (☎660 6096). Across the road from *Mrs Matthews'*; within walking distance of the city centre. ④.

Sandymount

Sandymount (buses #1, #2, #3 and #6, and a short walk from DART stations Sandymount and Sydney Parade) is slightly further out again, but the attraction here is that you're near the sea; it's also fairly handy for the ferry.

Mrs M. Bermingham, 8 Dromard Terrace (☎668 3861). Old-fashioned comfort; television in the living room for evenings when the city gets too much. ③.

Mrs R. Casey, *Villa Jude*, 2 Church Ave (☎668 4982). Quiet rooms and an excellent breakfast. TVs in all rooms. ③.

Kane's B&B, 49 Beach Rd (☎660 2969). Standard B&B, right on the seashore. ④.

Mrs M. Smyth, 21 Sandymount Rd (☎668 3602). Quiet location close to the seafront. ④.

Mrs E. Trehy's, 110 Ringsend Park (☎668 9477). One of the cheapest in the area (but no breakfast provided). ③.

Northwest

Glasnevin (to the north and west of the centre), **Cabra** (on the northern fringes of Phoenix Park) and **Castlenock** (to the west of the park) are all reasonable places to stay and not too far from the centre.

Mrs E. Delahunty, *Marymount*, 137 New Cabra Rd, Cabra (☎868 0026). Just a 20min walk from the centre, with TVs in all the rooms. ④.

Mrs M. Lambert, 8 Ballymun Rd, Glasnevin (☎837 6125). A little over two miles from the centre; showers 50p. ③.

Mrs Mary McKay, *Deerpark House*, Castlenock Rd, nr. Phoenix Park gates (☎820 7466). To the west of the park, beside Castlenock riding school, this comfortable B&B has en-suite rooms, most with TVs. ④.

Northeast

Northeast, in **Clontarf**, you're into suburbia again, but you'll be close to the sea. Here rates are generally reasonable, with lots of places to choose from, particularly along the Clontarf Road, which runs right by the seafront. The only drawback to staying here is that Clontarf buses terminate around Talbot Street in the north of the city, so getting to the South Side can be time consuming. Inland from Clontarf, **Drumcondra**, although less salubrious than its neighbour, is well served by bus routes (#11, #13 and #16, as well as airport buses) and has a similarly high number of places to stay.

Mrs Maureen Black, 35 Ormond Rd, Drumcondra (☎837 0299). Standard B&B with four double rooms, two of which are en-suite. ④.

Mrs C. Canavan, 81 Kincora Rd, off Vernon Ave, Clontarf (☎833 1007). An easy walk from the wildlife preserve on North Bull Island. ④.

Mrs Carmel Drain, *Bayview*, 265 Clontarf Rd (☎833 9870). Fine views of Dublin and the Wicklow Mountains, and a palm tree in the front garden. ④.

Mrs R. Gibbons, *Joyville,* 24 Alphonsus Rd, Drumcondra (☎830 3221). Just a mile from the centre, with one double room, three singles and shared bathroom. ④.

Carmel Geoghegan, *The White House,* 125 Clontarf Rd (☎833 3196). Close to Dublin Bay and on the #30 bus route. ③.

Kathleen Hurney, 69 Hollybank Rd, Drumcondra (☎837 7907). Comfortable en-suite rooms with TVs, and near the bus stop for easy access to the centre of town. ④.

Mrs C. Kehoe, 13 St Patrick's Rd, off Whitworth Rd, Drumcondra (☎830 6934). Handy for Mountjoy Prison and the Royal Canal. ③.

Hostels

As well as the official **An Óige** hostel, Dublin has a variety of less formal and often more enjoyable independent hostels, many of which are part of **Independent Holiday Hostels** (*IHH*; see p.27 for more details).

Abraham House, 82–83 Lower Gardiner St (*IHH*; ☎855 0600). This well-equipped North-Side hostel is handy for the airport and Busárus. Friendly and clean, there's a self-catering kitchen, a launderette, bureau de change, free hot showers and no curfew; although breakfast isn't included in the price. There's also a secure car park. Open year around. ②.

Avalon House, 55 Aungier St (*IHH*; ☎475 0001, fax ☎475 0303). Impressive red-brick Victorian ex-medical school close to St Stephen's Green. Friendly café; comfortable, well-designed privacy-preserving dorms and some smaller rooms. No curfew, co-ed bathrooms; open all year. ②.

Cardijn House, 15 Talbot St, above *Tiffany's Shoe Shop* (*IHH*; ☎874 1720). Also known as **"Goin' My Way"**. Closes from 10am to 5pm, although the coffee bar stays open; midnight curfew. Includes breakfast and sheet rental. Closed Dec 20–Jan 4. ①.

Dublin International Youth Hostel, 61 Mountjoy St (*An Óige*; ☎830 1766, fax ☎830 1600). This ex-convent hostel is extremely well set-up and open all year. You'll need an *An Óige* or *HI* membership card to use it. ③.

Dunsinea House, Ashtown (☎838 3252; bus #37, #38 or #39 from Abbey St to the *Halfway House* pub nearby). Some way out, but welcoming and open all year round. ①.

Globetrotters Tourist Hotel, 46 Lower Gardiner St (*IHH*; ☎874 0592, fax ☎878 8787). Comfortable upper-crust hostel open all year, close to Busárus and on the airport bus route. Includes continental breakfast. ③.

Isaac's, 2–5 Frenchman's Lane, just round the corner from Busáras (*IHH*; ☎874 9321, fax ☎874 1574). Otherwise known as the *Dublin Tourist Hostel, Isaac's* is housed in an eighteenth-century wine warehouse. It offers a mix of accommodation, from dormitory bunks to single and double rooms, plus kitchen and a good restaurant with plenty of choice for vegetarians. There's live music some evenings, with jazz on Sun. Open all year; room lockout is from 11am–5pm; no curfew. Blankets cost 50p, sheets £1. ②.

Kinlay House, 2–12 Lord Edward St (*IHH*; ☎679 6644, fax ☎679 7437). This *USIT* hostel is close to the trendy Temple Bar area. A relaxed and friendly place, it offers 4–6 bedded rooms, some doubles and laundry and kitchen facilities. There's no curfew and it can be noisy at night. Breakfast is included in the price. Open all year round. ②.

Morehampton House, 78 Morehampton Rd (☎668 8866, fax ☎668 8794). A few miles out of the centre in Donnybrook, a spacious Victorian house with hostel accommodation in 4–8-bedded rooms. Open all year except Christmas Day. ②.

Student Care Accommodation, 114 Lower Baggot St (☎661 6516 or ☎661 9860). Great location among the bars of Baggot Street, not far from St Stephen's Green. Next door, the new **The Baggot University Centre** offers the same high standard of hostel accommodation (same phone and fax). The price at both includes bed linen, towels and breakfast. Both open June 1 to Sept 30. ②.

Trinity Hall, Dartry Rd, Rathmines (☎497 1772). During the summer vacation (mid-June to Sept) you can stay in student accommodation here; students in possession of an *ISIC* card may get a price reduction. On bus routes #4 and #14A, 3 miles out of the centre. ④–⑤.

UCD Village, Belfield (☎269 7111, fax ☎269 7704). A complex of modern self-catering apartments about 3 miles south of the centre (take bus #46), with 3 or 4 single bedrooms, a kitchen, dining area and shower room; available during student vacations (mid-June to mid-Sept). ④.

The Young Traveller, St Mary's Place, just north of Parnell Square (☎830 5000, fax ☎830 5317). Luxurious and sociable accommodation in small, 4-bed rooms in what used to be a school run by the Christian Brothers. It also has a restaurant and washing machine. No curfew or daytime lockout. Includes continental breakfast. Open all year. ②.

Camping

There's no central **campsite** in Dublin, but several on the outskirts, including two south of Dún Laoghaire.

Cromlech, three miles south of Dún Laoghaire, close to the pretty seaside village of Dalkey, on the DART line (☎282 6882 or ☎282 4783; bus #46 from Dublin or #46A from Dún Laoghaire). Relatively luxurious caravan and camping site; mid-April to mid-Sept. £4 per tent, 50p per person.

Donabate, on the North Side, a few miles beyond Swords (☎845 0038; bus #33B from Eden Quay). Fairly basic site with only limited space for tents, so phone in advance. £4 per tent.

Shankill, close to the DART stop at Shankill (☎282 0011; take bus #45, #45A, #46 or #84). South of Dún Laoghaire by the sea, within reach of secluded beaches. £6 per tent, plus 50p per person.

The city

Although almost all of Dublin's cinemas, two of its most important theatres, the Gate and the Abbey, and one of its busiest shopping areas are on the North Side around O'Connell Street, the majority of the city's historic monuments, including its ancient centre, are south of the river. As you'll probably be spending most of your time on the South Side – also the hub of the newer, more upmarket centres for shopping and socializing – Trinity College, linked to St Stephen's Green by the pedestrianized shopping street, Grafton Street, seems as good a place as any to start.

College Green and Trinity College

In some ways the topography of Dublin has stayed remarkably constant since the city was founded, when the Vikings sited their Haugen or Thengmote, the central meeting place and burial ground, on what is now **College Green**. Formerly known as Hoggen Green, it remained the centre of administrative power in Ireland until the Act of Union.

Trinity College

In comparison to the mighty facade of the *Bank of Ireland* opposite, the modest portico of **Trinity College** seems almost domestic in scale. Founded in 1591 by Queen Elizabeth I, it played a major role in the development of an **Anglo-Irish tradition**, with leading families often sending their sons to be educated here rather than in England. The statues outside represent Edmund Burke and Oliver Goldsmith, two of Trinity's most famous graduates. The philosopher and statesman Burke (1729–97) adopted an interesting position, simultaneously defending Ireland's independence and insisting on its role as an integral part of the British Empire (see p.119); Goldsmith (1728–94) was a noted wit and poet (see p.182). Other illustrious alumni include Jonathan Swift, author of *Gulliver's Travels* and many other satirical works (see p.72), and Wolfe Tone, leader of the United Irishmen and prime mover of the 1798 uprising, as well as Bram Stoker, of *Dracula* fame, the playwright J.M. Synge and playwright and novelist Samuel Beckett.

Until recently, Trinity's Anglo-Irish connections gave it a strong **Protestant bias**. At its foundation, the college offered free education to Catholics who were prepared to change their religion, and right up to 1966 – long after the rule on religion had been dropped by the college itself – Catholics had to get a special dispensation to study at Trinity or risk excommunication. Nowadays, roughly 70 percent of the student population is Catholic, and Trinity is just one of Dublin's universities; University College

Dublin is based just south of Donnybrook and forms part of the National University of Ireland; Dublin City University is in Glasnevin.

Simply as an architectural set piece, Trinity takes some beating. It served as an English university in the film *Educating Rita* – bizarre but understandable, given that it looks the way a great university should. Its cream stone college buildings are ranged around cobbled quadrangles in a grander version of the arrangement at Oxford and Cambridge (the cobbles apparently have to be relaid every seven years as the land, reclaimed from the sea, subsides).

Just inside the entrance, the **Chapel** is reflected on the right by the **Theatre** or examination hall, whose elegant, stuccoed interior is sometimes used for concerts (check the notice boards in the main entrance). Both were designed by Sir William Chambers, a Scottish Neoclassical architect who never visited Ireland. Beyond the chapel on the left is the **Dining Hall**, also used for exams, built by the German architect Richard Cassels in 1743. The bell tower, or **Campanile**, in the middle of the square, was put up in 1853 and is believed to mark the site of the priory which long predated the university. A startling element of colour is introduced by the red brick of the **Rubrics**, student accommodation dating from 1712 and one of Trinity's oldest surviving buildings.

THE LIBRARY AND THE BOOK OF KELLS

The other early survivor is the famous **Library** (Mon–Sat 9.30am–5pm, June–Sept also Sun 9.30am–5pm; £3), which is meant to receive a free copy of every book published in Britain and Ireland and also contains a famous collection of priceless Irish manuscripts, above all the celebrated *Book of Kells*. Some 200,000 of the total collection of three million books are held here in the old library: the rest is stored off site, where over half a mile of new shelving is needed every year to accommodate new volumes. It's a long – 209ft in all – tall, aristocratic room, flooded with light, with books housed on two storeys of shelves. As designed by Thomas Burgh in the early eighteenth century, the library originally had just one floor, but in 1859 the roof was raised and the upper bookcases were added.

Trinity's **illuminated manuscripts** are derived from the Celtic ecclesiastical tradition of Saint Columba, which embraced not only Ireland but also Scotland and the north of England and had a strong influence on monastic institutions in mainland Europe. There's still some debate over whether the most famous of the manuscripts, the eighth-century **Book of Kells**, was really copied and illuminated in Ireland at all; the location may have been Scotland – maybe Iona, Saint Columba's first Scottish port of call – or even Lindisfarne in northern England; at all events, the book was taken to the monastery of Kells in County Meath for safekeeping during the Viking raids of the ninth century, and, after a chequered history – during which it spent some time buried underground and some thirty of its pages disappeared, it was brought to Dublin in the seventeenth century. Totalling 680 pages, the *Book of Kells* consists of the four gospels of the New Testament, written in Latin. The book was rebound in the 1950s into four separate volumes, of which two are on show at any one time: one open at a completely illuminated page, the other at a text page, itself not exactly unadorned, with patterns and fantastic animals intertwined with the capitals.

Famous as the *Book of Kells* is, the *Book of Durrow* is in many ways equally interesting. It is the first of the great Irish illuminated manuscripts, dating from between 650 and 680, and has, unusually, a whole page (known as the carpet page, for obvious reasons) given over to ornament. It's noticeable in all these early manuscripts that the depictions of the human form make no attempt at realism – Saint Matthew in the *Book of Durrow*, for instance, is apparently wrapped in a poncho, with no hands. The important thing is the pattern, which is derived from metalwork (as in the amazing Ardagh Chalice and Tara Brooch, which you can see in the National Museum close by). The

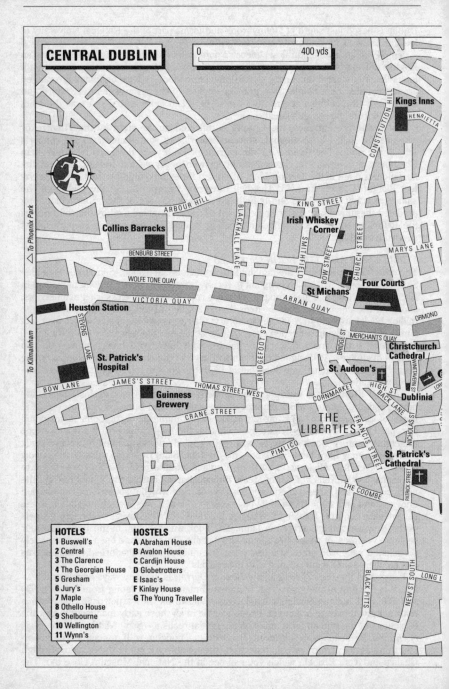

CENTRAL DUBLIN

0   400 yds

Kings Inns

HENRIETTA

CONSTITUTION HILL

ARBOUR HILL

KING STREET

Collins Barracks

BLACKHALL PLACE

Irish Whiskey Corner

SMITHFIELD

BOW STREET

CHURCH STREET

MARYS LANE

BENBURB STREET

WOLFE TONE QUAY

St Michans

Four Courts

VICTORIA QUAY

ARRAN QUAY

ORMOND

Heuston Station

STEVENS LANE

MERCHANTS QUAY

BRIDGE ST

Christchurch Cathedral

WINETAVERN ST

St. Patrick's Hospital

BRIDGEFOOT ST

St. Audoen's

HIGH ST

BLACK LANE

Dublinia

BOW LANE

JAMES'S STREET

THOMAS STREET WEST

CORNMARKET

NICHOLAS ST

Guinness Brewery

CRANE STREET

THE LIBERTIES

FRANCIS STREET

St. Patrick's Cathedral

PIMLICO

PATRICK STREET

THE COOMBE

BLACK PITTS

NEW ST SOUTH

LONG L

To Phoenix Park

To Kilmainham

HOTELS	HOSTELS
1 Buswell's	**A** Abraham House
2 Central	**B** Avalon House
3 The Clarence	**C** Cardijn House
4 The Georgian House	**D** Globetrotters
5 Gresham	**E** Isaac's
6 Jury's	**F** Kinlay House
7 Maple	**G** The Young Traveller
8 Othello House	
9 Shelbourne	
10 Wellington	
11 Wynn's	

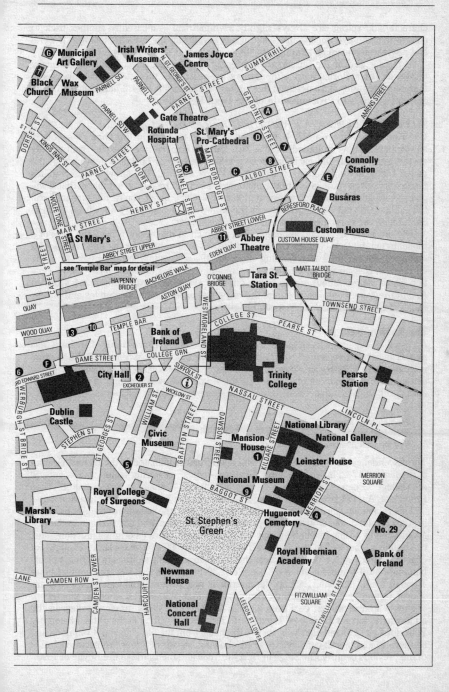

6 Municipal Art Gallery
Irish Writers' Museum
James Joyce Centre
Black Church
Wax Museum
PARNELL SQ.
PARNELL SQ. E
N. GT GEORGE'S ST.
SUMMERHILL
PARNELL STREET
PARNELL SQ. W
DORSET ST
KINGS INNS ST
Gate Theatre
Rotunda Hospital
St Mary's Pro-Cathedral
PARNELL STREET
MOORE ST
O'CONNELL STREET
MARLBOROUGH ST
GARDINER STREET
A
D
7
5
C
8
TALBOT STREET
AMIENS STREET
Connolly Station
E
Busáras
BERESFORD PLACE
HENRY ST
MARY STREET
WOLFE TONE ST
MARY STREET
St Mary's
ABBEY STREET UPPER
ABBEY STREET LOWER
11
Abbey Theatre
EDEN QUAY
Custom House
CUSTOM HOUSE QUAY
CAPEL STREET
see 'Temple Bar' map for detail
HA'PENNY BRIDGE
BACHELORS WALK
ASTON QUAY
O'CONNEL BRIDGE
Tara St. Station
MATT TALBOT BRIDGE
TOWNSEND STREET
QUAY
WOOD QUAY
3 **10**
TEMPLE BAR
COLLEGE ST
WESTMORELAND ST
PEARSE ST
Bank of Ireland
DAME STREET
COLLEGE GRN
SUFFOLK ST
2
i
WICKLOW ST
Trinity College
Pearse Station
LINCOLN PL
6 **F**
RD EDWARD STREET
City Hall
EXCHEQUER ST
NASSAU STREET
National Library
National Gallery
WERBURGH ST
BRIDE ST
Dublin Castle
STEPHEN ST
GT GEORGES ST
WILLIAM STREET
GRAFTON STREET
DAWSON STREET
Civic Museum
Mansion House
1
KILDARE STREET
Leinster House
MERRION SQUARE
5
National Museum
9
BAGGOT ST
MERRION ST
Huguenot Cemetery
4
No. 29
Marsh's Library
Royal College of Surgeons
St. Stephen's Green
Royal Hibernian Academy
Bank of Ireland
LANE
CAMDEN ROW
CAMDEN ST TOWER
HARCOURT ST
Newman House
National Concert Hall
LEESON ST LOWER
FITZWILLIAM SQUARE
FITZWILLIAM ST EAST

characteristic spirals are always slightly asymmetrical – apparently another trick to ensure that the eye doesn't tire – and it's believed that the ornamentation in general had a symbolic meaning, although its full significance is now unknown.

At the far end of the library are two early Irish **harps**, one of them traditionally known as Brian Boru's harp, although it's been dated to the fifteenth century, some four centuries after Boru defeated the Vikings at Clontarf in 1014. There's also an original copy of the 1916 **Proclamation of the Irish Republic**.

THE DUBLIN EXPERIENCE AND THE DOUGLAS HYDE GALLERY

Unfortunately, you are unlikely to be left in peace to drink in the library's scholarly atmosphere. A new multimedia show, **The Dublin Experience**, has put Trinity firmly on the tourist trail, and each day sees a steady stream of busloads deposited at the gates. Using a combination of archive and new material, the show traces Dublin's history and gives some guide to the main events of Irish history. It's unlikely that it will give, as it claims, a "complete orientation to the city", but if you're footsore and still have money in your pocket, tickets for the shows (June–Sept every hour from 10am to 5pm; £5.50) are combined with admission to the library.

The old parts of Trinity, although all very much in use, tend to have the look of a museum exhibit. For contact with student life, it's best to head for the **arts and social sciences block**, an award-winning piece of 1960s concrete brutalism by the side entrance in Nassau Street. There's a theatre and coffee bar here and plenty of information, in term-time, about what's going on. **The Douglas Hyde Gallery of Modern Art**, in the same complex, is one of the city's few experimental art venues and always worth checking out (it also has a good bookshop).

The Bank of Ireland

Across the busy traffic interchange from the college, the massive **Bank of Ireland** has played an even more central role in the history of Anglo-Irish Ascendancy. When originally begun in 1729 by Sir Edward Lovett Pearce, it was envisaged as a suitably grand setting for the parliament of a nation, as the Anglo-Irish were coming to regard themselves, although Jonathan Swift, for one, had some typically tart opinions as to its worth:

As I stroll the city, oft I
Spy a building large and lofty
Not a bow-shot from the college
Half the globe from sense and knowledge.

The Ascendancy's efforts to achieve self-government culminated in the famous Grattan parliament of 1782, in which **Henry Grattan** – whose gesturing statue stands outside on College Green – uttered the celebrated phrase, "Ireland is now a nation". The Protestant, Anglo-Irish parliament endorsed the country's independence unanimously.

This rebellious spirit was, however, short-lived; with the passing of the Act of Union in 1801, Ireland lost both its independence as a nation and its parliament (which acquiesced by voting itself obediently out of existence). With its original function gone, the building was sold to the *Bank of Ireland* for £40,000 two years later. Though not exactly geared up for coach parties, the bank does admit sightseers during normal banking hours (Mon–Fri 10am–12.30pm & 1.30–3pm; Thurs closes 5pm; guided tours Tues 10.30am, 11.30am, 1.45pm). Its interior is magnificently old-fashioned – you are shown around by ushers wearing costumes seemingly unchanged since the nineteenth century – and in winter, coal fires glow in the entrance hall's massive grates. In the atmospheric former **House of Lords**, with its coffered ceiling and eighteenth-century Waterford glass chandelier, you can see the mace from the old House of Commons and some early eighteenth-century tapestries showing two of the great Protestant victories of the previous century, the Siege of Derry of 1689 and the Battle of the Boyne of 1690.

Grafton Street to the National Museum

The streets that surround pedestrianized **Grafton Street** frame Dublin's quality shopping area. Boasting no fewer than two shopping malls – the converted Georgian *Powerscourt Town House* and an extraordinary 1980s confection on the corner of St Stephen's Green, exhibiting a confusion of cultural references that have been variously described as French, Indian, Renaissance and Georgian – it's a totally different Dublin from that which you'll find on the North Side: chic, sophisticated and expensive.

Grafton Street

Grafton Street itself is unabashedly commercial, but it's a pleasant enough place to while away some time – here as in most metropolises, shopping is a way of life, and people come here as much to see and be seen as to buy (also see the "Shopping" list). Cafés and restaurants of all sorts abound; shops are middle-of-the-road and upward. Dublin's leading **department store**, *Brown Thomas*, is a classy location for some retail therapy, while *Powerscourt Town House* is similarly upmarket and set back a little on Clarendon Street. As well as simply wandering in and out of its retail palaces, you can also take in the street life. Since its pedestrianization, Grafton Street has become the centre of Dublin's burgeoning **street theatre**, and this is one of the few places where you'll find **buskers**, including a poetry busker who claims to be able to recite any (Irish) poem on request and often throws in works of his own, too.

Unmissable in Grafton Street, even if you have no other business in the area, is **Bewley's coffee house** (daily 7–1am; Thurs–Sat until 2am). In its dark wood and marble-tabled interior, *Bewley's* does all-day tea, coffee and food ranging from meals to cakes and sticky buns, along with the best potato soup in the universe. It's an extraordinary atmosphere and unbeatable value – a great place to sit and watch people, read a book or write your novel (no one will try to hurry you, even if you've only bought a cup of tea). A testament to the vigour of the café tradition in the city, *Bewley's* is a place where everyone goes – you'll see a range of people from students and old ladies to high-powered businessmen. On the top floor, a small **museum** traces the history of this Dublin institution. Founded in the 1840s by the Quaker Bewley family, it became a workers' co-operative in 1971 and subsequently almost folded in 1986, provoking a national crisis until the government stepped in and offered to help before a buyer was secured. There are two other central branches of *Bewley's*, each with a slightly different character: in Westmoreland Street, which has wonderful Art Nouveau fireplaces (daily 7.30am–9pm), and South Great George's Street, a smaller and more subdued incarnation (Mon–Sat 6.45am–6pm).

Close to Grafton Street is the **Dublin Civic Museum** at 58 South William Street (Tues–Sat 10am–6pm, Sun 11am–2pm; free), a tiny establishment that is probably strictly for museum and history buffs. The display consists of a garbled but oddly intriguing collection of artefacts relating to the history of the city from Viking times to the present. You can see, among other things, the head of the statue of Lord Nelson that used to stand outside the General Post Office in O'Connell Street and was blown up by the IRA in 1966, one of the original 1916 proclamations of the Republic of Ireland, and fascinating minutiae such as timetables detailing the excruciatingly slow progress of that state-of-the-art mode of transport, the canal-boat, across Ireland in the late eighteenth and early nineteenth centuries.

Dawson Street

Dawson Street, just east of Grafton Street, is altogether quieter than its neighbour, and is home of some of Dublin's better **bookshops** (see p.90) as well as a number of august institutions. Chief among these is the **Mansion House**, a delicate building of 1710 weighed down by heavy Victorian wrought iron. This has been the official residence of the Lord Mayor since 1715 and was also where the *Dáil Éireann*, the Irish parliament, met in 1919 to ratify the independence proclamation of 1916. The Mansion House isn't generally open to the public, but in any case there's not a great deal to be seen inside.

Next door, the decorous red-brick house containing the **Royal Irish Academy** is also closed to the public. One of the great learned institutions of Europe, it publishes books of Irish interest and has a weighty collection of Irish manuscripts. Next door again, **St Anne's** (Church of Ireland) church has an amazingly ornate Italianate facade which is a real surprise when you catch sight of it along Anne Street. Inside, behind the altar, are wooden shelves that were originally designed to take loaves of bread for distribution among the poor of the parish under the provisions of a 1720s bequest. On Thursday lunchtimes, St Anne's hosts a series of recitals and other cultural activities – check *In Dublin* for details.

Kildare Street: Leinster House

Moving east again, and marking the point where what's left of the Georgian city begins, **Kildare Street** is the really monumental part of the Grafton, Dawson, Kildare trio. The most imposing building is undoubtedly **Leinster House**, built in 1745 as the Duke of Leinster's town house. At that time, the fashionable area of Dublin was north of the river, and there were those who mocked him for building a town house in the south on what was then a green-field site. The Kildare Street facade, facing the town, is built to look like a town house; the other side, looking out on to what is now Merrion Square, resembles a country house.

Today, this is one of the most important buildings in Dublin, housing the Irish parliament – the **Dáil Éireann**, or House of Representatives, and the **Seanad Éireann**, or Senate – as well as the National Museum and National Library. The Dáil (pronounced *Doil*) has 166 representatives – *Teachtaí Dála*, usually shortened to TDs – elected by direct proportional vote, representing 41 constituencies. The Senate is proposed on a vocational basis, with six members elected by the universities and eleven nominated by the *Taoiseach* (pronounced *Tee-shuck*), or Prime Minister. General elections take place at least every five years; presidential elections, which are also direct, are held every seven years. Mary Robinson, elected in 1990 as Ireland's first woman president, has breathed welcome new life into this formerly symbolic role by speaking out for women and the political left in a country whose politics, although beginning to change, are still essentially defined by conservative parochial ideals.

National Library and National Museum

Whether or not the massive twin rotundas, housing the entrances of the National Library on the left and the National Museum on the right, do anything to complement the Georgian elegance of Leinster House is debatable; they were added in 1890. The **National Library** (Mon 10am–9pm, Tues & Wed 2–9pm, Thurs & Fri 10am–5pm, Sat 10am–1pm; free) is, however, worth visiting for its associations alone: it seems that every major Irish writer from Joyce onwards used it at some time, and the Reading Room is also the scene of Stephen Dedalus's great literary debate in *Ulysses*. The Library has a good collection of first editions and works of Irish writers, including Swift, Goldsmith, Yeats, Shaw, Joyce and Beckett. It's also often used for temporary exhibitions on Irish books and authors.

The **National Museum** (Tues–Sat 10am–5pm, Sun 2–5pm; free) is the place to go to see the treasures of ancient Ireland, as well as a small collection of artefacts – mainly silver, glass and ceramics – from Dublin's eighteenth-century heyday. It is national policy to gather treasures found all around the country in this one museum, so the place is a real treasure-trove of wonderful objects. The really venerable exhibits, dating from the Irish **Bronze** and **Iron ages**, bear eloquent testimony to the ancient high culture of Ireland: there's jewellery ranging from the eighth to the first centuries BC, mainly the twisted gold bars known as *torcs*, cloak-fasteners and collars, and the beaten gold *lunulae* that are characteristic of the period.

The **medieval** antiquities are still more spectacular and include the Tara Brooch and the Ardagh Chalice, found in county Limerick in 1868, both of which date from the eighth century. The twelfth-century cross of Cong, an ornate reliquary of wood, bronze and silver, is said to contain a fragment of the True Cross; and there's also an eleventh-century shrine, made of gold wire, that houses a bell said to have belonged to Saint Patrick. The **Tara Brooch** is regarded as perhaps the greatest piece of Irish metal-work, and it's thought that the patterns of manuscript illuminations such as the *Book of Kells*, which you can see in Trinity College Library, may be derived from this rich craft tradition. Remarkably, the Tara Brooch is decorated both on the front and the back, where the intricate filigree work could be seen only by the wearer – the brooch is displayed above a mirror so that you can see both sides.

One of the more recent finds is the **Derrynaflan Hoard**, a testament to the Irish enthusiasm for metal-detecting. This collection of eighth- and ninth-century silver objects, including a chalice and a paten, was discovered in February 1980 in County Tipperary by amateur treasure-hunters using a metal detector that one of them had got for Christmas.

To discover more about the Viking tradition, go round the corner into Merrion Row (past the *Shelbourne Hotel*) for the **National Museum Annexe**, which exhibits the results of digs at the Christchurch Place, Winetavern and Wood Quay sites around Christchurch, carried out between 1962 and 1981. The complexity of the culture (Norse invaders first arrived in 795) is evident in artefacts such as eleventh-century combs and carrying cases carved from bones and antlers, scales for weighing precious metals together with accurate lead weights, and iron swords.

Right at the top of Kildare Street, at the point where it intersects with Nassau Street, the fussy, Venetian-inspired red-brick building on the corner used to house one of the major institutions of Anglo-Irish Dublin, the **Kildare Street Club** – the carved billiard-playing monkeys on the pillars hint toward the past use of the building as a gentlemen's playground. The place now houses the **Genealogical Office**, where you can trace the history of Irish names (call ☎661 4877 for details), the Heraldry Museum and the Alliance Française. The **Heraldry Museum** gives a general account of the development of its subject in Ireland and Europe (Mon–Fri 10am–12.30pm & 2.30–4.30pm).

St Stephen's Green

Walk to the bottom of Kildare Street and you'll emerge on the northwest side of **St Stephen's Green**, the focus of central Dublin's city planning. It's an oddly decorous expanse, neat and tidy with little bandstands and pergolas, laid out as a public park in 1880 by Lord Ardilaun (Sir Arthur Edward Guinness). It was an open common until 1663, and the final buildings ringing it went up in the eighteenth century; unfortunately, very few of these have survived, and their replacements speak eloquently to the failure of 1960s planning regulations.

The **gardens**, with their ornamental pond, can be a pleasant place to while away some time on a sunny day, but in terms of architecture, or even city life, there's not a lot to see. The statue in memory of Wolfe Tone, backed by slabs of granite, is nick-named "Tone-henge".

The north side of the square – known in the eighteenth century as the "Beaux Walk" for the dandies and glitterati who used to promenade there – is dominated by the **Shelbourne Hotel**. Fittingly, the *Shelbourne* – which boasts that it has "the best address in Dublin" – continues to be a focus for the upper echelons of the city's social life. It's worth bearing in mind that, as with all Irish hotels, you can wander in for a drink and something to eat in the lobby at any time of day, even if you're not staying. The *Shelbourne's* afternoon teas (from 3pm) are wonderful; but the airy, chandeliered lobby and the *Horseshoe* bar come into their own in the early evening, when the hotel is a great place for both celebrity spotting and watching the parade of young Dubliners who are there to be seen. The *Shelbourne* is too well bred to pass comment on jeans and trainers in the lobby, but you'll feel out of place if you penetrate to the excellent (but expensive) restaurant (see p.85) unless you dress up a bit.

Just past the hotel, to the left of a shuttered garden, lies the **Huguenot Graveyard**, which dates from 1693. The Huguenots – French Protestants who fled persecution under Louis XIV, after the repeal of the Edict of Nantes in 1685 took away the religious privileges they had previously enjoyed – enriched cultural life all over Europe with their craftsmanship (their silverwork was particularly valued). Ireland was no exception, and this quiet burial place, with its understated French headstones, seems a particularly fitting tribute to their quietly industrious way of life. Call the **Huguenot Society** (☎669 2852) for more information about the graveyard; for more on the Huguenots in Dublin see p.73.

Linked to the east side of the Green by Hume Street is **Ely Place**, where you can see some of the best-preserved Georgian domestic buildings in Dublin. The sober exteriors conceal some extraordinary flights of fancy: no. 8, for instance, has an amazing staircase with elaborate stuccowork telling the story of the labours of Hercules. Unfortunately, though, it isn't open to the public.

The Catholic University of Ireland: Newman House

University College, Dublin's second-oldest university (after Trinity), is now at Belfield in the suburb of Donnybrook, but the first premises of its predecessor, the **Catholic University of Ireland**, are at nos. 85–86 on the south side of the Green and are now being restored to something approaching their original appearance (the phased restoration scheme is due for completion in 1999). The aim of the foundation was to provide a Catholic answer to the great academic traditions of Oxford and Cambridge, but, despite the appointment of John Henry Newman (who had famously converted from High-church Anglicanism) as its rector, the new university was initially denied official recognition in Britain. Eventually, in 1853, it was successfully established as a University College. The poet and Jesuit priest Gerard Manley Hopkins (1844–89) had a chair here; the 1916 Republican leader Pádraig Pearse, prime minister Éamon de Valera and James Joyce are among its more famous graduates.

The original, newly restored university buildings, collectively known as **Newman House** (June–Sept Tues–Fri 10am–4pm, Sat 12–4.30pm; £1), provide an unparalleled opportunity to get a taste of what the Georgian town houses of St Stephen's Green must have originally been like. **No. 85** is a small, early **Georgian villa** built about 1738 for Hugh Montgomery, a wealthy Ulster landowner and member of parliament for County Fermanagh. This was one of the first town houses built by Richard Castle, or Cassels, the fashionable German country-house architect (who also designed Leinster House, and later the Dining Hall at Trinity College), and shows his mastery of the more intimate scale of urban building.

Inside, this remarkable interior is worth visiting just to see the **Apollo Room**, with its stucco reliefs of the nine muses made by the brilliant Swiss stuccadores Paolo and Filippo Lanfranchini. Upstairs on the first floor, a fine double-cube room with ceiling reliefs celebrating the subjects of good government and prudent economy awaits restoration. The Lanfranchinis boasted that their work was so good that it didn't need colour, so the ghastly colour scheme imposed in the 1940s is completely wrong, destroying the delicacy of the mouldings (compare the simple grey of the restored Apollo room). Notice also the extraordinarily ham-fisted additions made by the nineteenth-century Jesuits, who decided that the ceiling showed far too many naked female bodies and helpfully added what look like fur suits to protect the morals of their students.

In 1765 the small villa was joined by a bigger town house, which is still undergoing restoration. The original house was then extended with an additional room at the back, later to become the physics theatre, where James Joyce lectured to the "L & H" (the "Literary and Historical Society") and which features in his *Portrait of the Artist as a Young Man*. The **new house** was built by Richard "Burnchapel" Whaley, a virulent anti-Catholic who swore never to let a Papist across his threshold and earned his sobriquet by burning chapels in County Wicklow. His son, "Jerusalem" Whaley, was a founder of the Hellfire Club. Legend tells that he threw a crucifix through the front window on Maundy Thursday, and ever afterwards on the same day its image is still to be seen there. The newer house is characterized by lighter, airier plasterwork (the main staircase, decorated with musical instruments and flowers, is particularly beautiful) and is to be restored to its mid-nineteenth-century appearance, with some of the interventions made by the university prelates.

Next door, **University Church** is an amazingly prolix Byzantine fantasy of 1854–56, with an interior decorated with coloured marble – more familiar from the cloud-burst patterns on country bungalows – quarried in Armagh, Offaly and Kilkenny as well as at the better-known quarries of the far west, Mayo and Connemara; it's now a chic location for Dublin weddings.

West of the Green

Harcourt Street, leading off from the southwest corner of St Stephen's Green, is a graceful Georgian street that has survived relatively unscathed. There's nothing much to do here (though there is a good Celtic bookshop), but it's worth strolling down a little way to admire the graceful proportions and elegant town planning.

On the west side of the Green is the **Royal College of Surgeons**, which during the events of Easter week in 1916 was held by the Irish Citizen Army with Constance Markiewicz as second-in-command; the facade is still pocked with stray bullet-marks. The most recent interruption to the skyline of St Stephen's Green is the shopping mall on the corner with Grafton Street, its white wrought-iron detailing intended, presumably, to echo the Georgian balconies of Merrion and Fitzwilliam squares. In the few years since it was built, its flashy architecture has made its peace extraordinarily well with its surroundings, something perhaps not so surprising, given that the famous good taste of Georgian building conceals much the same kind of boom-time, get-rich-quick expansionism.

The Shaw birthplace

A short walk up Harcourt Street, which leaves St Stephen's Green at its southwest corner, will bring you to Harrington Street. Turn right, then left into Synge Street, a modest street of patchy Georgian houses, for the **birthplace of George Bernard Shaw** (May–Oct Mon–Sat 11.30am–6pm; £2). For playwright Shaw (see overleaf) this house, where he lived until he was ten, was not exactly a cause for celebration; Shaw remembered that "neither our hearts nor our imaginations were in it" and recalled the "loveless" atmosphere: you certainly get a vivid impression of the claustrophobic surroundings of the house and its tiny, neat garden. The terse inscription on the facade, "Bernard Shaw, author of many plays", is as Shaw wished.

GEORGE BERNARD SHAW

Born in Dublin in 1856, **George Bernard Shaw** was technically a member of the privileged Ascendancy, but his father's failed attempt, after leaving the civil service, to make money as a grain merchant, meant that Shaw grew up in an atmosphere of genteel poverty and, by the age of sixteen, was earning his living in a land agency. When his mother left his father for her singing teacher and took her two daughters with her to London, Shaw soon joined them and set about the process of educating himself. Subsidized by his mother's meagre income as a music teacher, he spent his afternoons in the British Museum's reading room and his evenings writing novels. He also became a vegetarian, a socialist, and a public speaker of some note.

Shaw's novels were unsuccessful, but his plays were a different matter entirely: in a way that perhaps underlined the flamboyant young man's wholehearted involvement with his new London environment, he was acclaimed the most important British playwright since the eighteenth century. However, Shaw recognized his foreignness as being a big part of his success: "the position of foreigner with complete command of the same language has great advantages. I can take an objective view of England, which no Englishman can." In the 1890s, influenced by the new drama represented by Ibsen, he began to write plays hinged on moral and social questions rather than romantic or personal interests. In play after play – his best-known dramas include *Man and Superman, Caesar and Cleopatra, Major Barbara, St Joan*, and, of course, *Pygmalion*, from which the musical *My Fair Lady* was adapted – he expounds a progressive view of humanity. For Shaw, the "life-force" is evolving toward an ever-higher level, and his plays successfully mix the accompanying moral fervour with high social comedy. As well as a dramatist, he was an active pamphleteer, critic, journalist and essayist, on subjects ranging from politics and economics to music. Shaw was awarded the Nobel prize for literature – which he refused – in 1925, after the ecstatic reception of *St Joan*. In his old age, he was famous almost as much for his dandified persona as his work. He died in 1950.

Merrion Square and Georgian Dublin

Merrion Square, Fitzwilliam Square and the streets immediately around them form the heart of what's left of **Georgian Dublin**. Representing the latest of the city's Georgian architecture – decrepit Mountjoy Square and Parnell Square, north of the river, are almost all that's left of the earlier Georgian city – their worn, red-brick facades are a brilliant example of confident, relaxed urban planning. The overall layout, in terms of squares and linking streets, may be formal, but there's a huge variation of detail. Height, windows, wrought-iron balconies, ornate doorways, are all different, but the result is a graceful meeting of form and function that's immensely beguiling.

The apogee of the Georgian area, imbued with an atmosphere of grandeur and repose, **Merrion Square**, which was built around 1770, has been home to a lot of well-known people – Daniel O'Connell, the Wildes and W.B. Yeats as well as, less predictably, the Nobel prize-winning physicist Erwin Schrödinger, who lived here between 1940 and 1956. However, it hasn't always been an area only devoted to gracious living: during the Famine, between 1845 and 1849, the park in the centre of the square was the site of soup kitchens to which the starving and destitute flocked. Today, the buildings are mainly occupied by offices, but the square still retains a residential feel, and a hard core of people still live here. The park railings are used on Saturdays and Sundays by artists flogging their wares; the area is also a centre for most of Dublin's private galleries.

Looking along the south side of the square, you experience one of the set pieces of Dublin's architecture: the hard outlines – pepperpot tower, Ionic columns and pediment – of **St Stephen's Church** (1825). If you want to know more about Ireland's architectural heritage, Georgian in particular, call at the **Irish Architectural Archive** at no. 63 (Mon–Fri 10am–1pm & 2–5pm). The house is a particularly tatty one, but it will give you some idea of what the interiors of these elegant buildings are like.

The National Gallery and the Natural History Museum

At the northeast of the square, alongside the back of Leinster House – its country-house facade – is Ireland's **National Gallery** (Mon–Sat 10am–6pm, until 9pm on Thurs; Sun 2–5pm; guided tours Sat 3pm, Sun 3pm & 4pm; free). It's a place that has a real feeling of activity, mainly because of all the people dropping in to eat at the excellent restaurant (see "Cafés and restaurants"), and as a gallery it's also a delight. The collection is not huge, though there are more than 2000 paintings on show, but the intimacy of its scale gives it a particular charm.

The gallery is divided into three sections. The **Dargan Wing** – named after the nineteenth-century railway magnate and benefactor William Dargan, who organized the 1853 Dublin Industrial Exhibition here and used the proceeds to start the gallery – houses the collections of **European art** from the Renaissance to the eighteenth century. Among the artists represented are Fra Angelico, Titian, Tintoretto and Rembrandt. There's also a sumptuous, recently rediscovered Caravaggio, *The Taking of Christ* (1602), which hung on the dining-room wall of the Jesuit community on Leeson Street for many years before it was identified. Once they realized the artistic and financial worth of the painting, the Jesuits lent it to the gallery for safe-keeping and public view.

The **Milltown Rooms** house Irish art and a small British collection; they were built at the turn of the century to display the collection of Russborough House, which was donated to the gallery in 1902. **British art** on show includes work by Hogarth, Reynolds, Gainsborough, Turner and Landseer. The **Irish section**, inevitably, is heavy on the art of the Anglo-Irish, and you can trace in the paintings the pattern of their history from the formal portraits of the early seventeenth century to the beginnings of interest in the life of ordinary people, which is to say the native Irish. Some of these pictures seem shockingly sentimental – one, by Edwin Hayes, is a calmly beautiful depiction of an emigrant ship at sunset in Dublin Harbour. Exotica, in the shape of such subjects as Indians and Mandarins, also make their appearance, presumably through the involvement of the Anglo-Irish in British military and trading activities. Later paintings include walls of chaotic colour by Jack B. Yeats, brother of the poet.

For anyone who's travelled around Ireland before arriving in Dublin, some of the most fascinating items have to be the gallery's **topographical paintings**. These landscapes of estates, commissioned by their owners, show much more than a true portrayal of what was actually there: rather they're aspirational portraits, images of how their owners wanted them to be. There's an amazingly evocative painting of the estates at Lucan in County Dublin, and a group of depictions of Ballinrobe in County Mayo – a place that today, though it exudes a tantalizing sense of past glory, gives no indication of the pleasure gardens depicted in these paintings.

The **Modern Wing** (due to re-open after extensive refurbishment in summer 1996), contains **twentieth-century British and European art**, including paintings by Degas, Delacroix, Millet, Monet and Pissaro. If the Irish paintings seem poorly represented in the modern period, it's because the late nineteenth and twentieth centuries are well represented in the Irish Museum of Modern Art in the Royal Hospital Kilmainham (see p.74) and the Municipal Art Gallery in Parnell Square (see p.78).

Flanking Leinster House on the opposite side of the National Gallery is the **Natural History Museum** (Tues–Sat 10am–5pm, Sun 2–5pm; free), which has been dubbed the "Dead Zoo" by one Dublin writer (the "live" version being in Phoenix Park, see p.81). A wonderful illustration of intact Victorian architecture, it's also a kind of museum of a Victorian museum – the place has hardly changed since it opened in 1857. Plenty of stuffed animals and skeletons, including a giant Chinese panda, rhinoceroses, two whale skeletons and three examples of the Irish giant elk, which died out some 10,000 years ago.

No. 29 Lower Fitzwilliam Street

At the opposite end of Merrion Square, at **no. 29 Lower Fitzwilliam Street**, is what's billed as a "faithfully re-created Georgian family home" (Tues–Sat 10am–5pm, Sun 2–5pm; free). Re-created is the word – the house fell down and has been rebuilt, brick by brick, by the Electricity Board, whose offices adjoin it at the back. Considering that the Electricity Supply Board was responsible, in the 1960s, for knocking down 26 Georgian houses and destroying the longest unbroken row of period houses then surviving, this act of homage is perhaps the least that could be demanded of it. If you want a postmodern take on the Georgian, this is it, furnished in a notional style of between 1790 and 1820. Viewing the house is an extraordinary experience, a bit like being an alien on a visit to earth. There's little feeling that you'd have anything in common with the people who once lived here: rather you're told that these creatures "only drank wine and beer" and that the women "did nothing but write letters to themselves". Georgian life is turned into a cabinet of curiosities, a weird kind of sideshow which does, admittedly, have its fascination. For an idea of "real" eighteenth-century Dublin life, Newman House (see p.62) is far superior; but if you have a taste for kitsch, you may find some grotesque humour at no. 29.

Fitzwilliam Square, south of Merrion Square along Fitzwilliam Street, is another elegant example of a late Georgian square – it was built between 1791 and 1825 – with some of the city's finest Georgian doors and fanlights. The dwindling number of residents still hold keys to the central garden.

Baggot Street and the Grand Canal

Crossing over Fitzwilliam Street, **Baggot Street** – with its multitude of lively pubs – starts out Georgian, but the street plan is pretty soon broken by the great black metal-and-glass bulk of the *Bank of Ireland* building, enlivened only by a few brightly coloured metal constructivist sculptures. Just afterwards, you reach the Grand Canal, one of Dublin's two constructed waterways: the Royal Canal runs through the north of the city. True Dubliners, or "Jackeens", are said to be those born between the two waterways.

The **Grand Canal** was the earlier and more successful of the two: started in 1756 and reaching the Shannon by 1803 (the Royal Canal was begun in 1790), it carried passengers and freight between Dublin, the midland towns and the Shannon right up to the 1960s, despite competition from the railways. Its total length, including stretches of the rivers Barrow and Shannon, was 340 miles. The potential for tourism in re-opening the canals has only recently been realized; consequently some patches are clean, free-flowing and beautiful while around the bend the vista is a picture of economic decline. Perhaps the best stretch of the canal to visit is the section around Baggot Street Bridge, where the water is fringed by trees. Baggot Street and a Dublin institution, the late, lamented **Parson's bookshop**, were haunts of many of Dublin's celebrated writers in the 1950s, including the poet Patrick Kavanagh and the playwright Brendan Behan. Kavanagh lived in a flat nearby in Pembroke Road and produced a "journal of literature and politics", entitled *Kavanagh's Weekly* and written largely by himself (with a few contributions from Behan and Myles na Gopaleen, aka Flann O'Brien). It ran to a total of thirteen issues before folding, with pieces about anything and everything – professional marriage makers, visits to the bookies, weeks when nothing happens.

The Grand Canal reaches the River Liffey at Ringsend (about a mile northeast of Baggot Street Bridge), through its original locks, constructed in 1796. You can find out more about the history and use of all of Ireland's canals and waterways at the **Waterways visitors centre**, a little upstream from the Grand Canal Dock.

Ballsbridge

If you walk for just over half a mile west of Baggot Street Bridge (buses from the centre of town: #5, #6, #6A, #7A, #8, #10, #46 & #46A) you'll get to **Ballsbridge**, a respectable, essentially Victorian suburb with some pleasant guesthouses (see "Accommodation", p.52) as well as many of the foreign embassies and smarter hotels – and, for soccer fans, the essential Lansdowne Road Stadium.

The showgrounds of the **Royal Dublin Society** (off the main Pembroke/Merrion Road) – the first of its kind in Europe, founded in 1731 years ago to promote improvements in agriculture, stock breeding and veterinary medicine – are also here. The Society was highly instrumental in the development of Dublin as a modern metropolis, and encouraged the foundation of the National Museum, the National Library, the National Gallery and the Botanic Gardens. If you're in town for the Spring Show in May, don't pass it by; the Dublin Horse Show (usually in August) is even more impressive – its international showjumping draws the horsey elite (human and equine) from both Ireland and Britain. Details and tickets from the Royal Dublin Society, PO Box 121, Ballsbridge, Dublin 4 (☎669 2386).

Further south, the **Chester Beatty Library and Gallery of Oriental Art** at 20 Shrewsbury Road (Tues–Fri 10am–5pm, Sat 2–5pm) is a collection of biblical papyruses, Persian and Turkish paintings, Korans, Chinese jade books and Japanese and European wood-block prints, some of them going back 4500 years. It's a testament to one man's tenacity: Sir Alfred Chester Beatty (1875–1968), who began his career mining in the Wild West, made his first million at forty and developed a fascination with exotic art through spending his winters in Africa to ease the symptoms of silicosis. He settled in Dublin in 1950 and bequeathed this collection to the Irish nation, along with some important paintings of the Barbizon school which are shown in the National Gallery.

West of College Green: Temple Bar

Staying south of the river, the main thoroughfare west from College Green is **Dame Street**. Immediately north, the area between the modern Central Bank and the Liffey is known as **Temple Bar**. Bought up in the 1960s by *CIE* (formerly the state transport company), which wanted to build a new central bus terminal to replace the one on the other side of the river, it suffered for many years from a benign sort of planning blight: even after the bus station idea was abandoned in the 1980s, shops, studios and offices in the area continued to be rented out on short leases, and as a result the streets are full of restaurants, second-hand bookshops, art galleries and bric-a-brac stores, plus, among other cultural institutions, the admirable Project Arts Centre. The place is often compared with Covent Garden in London or Les Halles in Paris. In the late 1980s, the subsequently discredited Haughey government poured funds into the area, and the result is intense gentrification in the form of cobbling and olde-worlde street lights.

Until the dissolution of the monasteries in 1537, the land on which Temple Bar stands was the property of the Augustinian order. Originally built on marshy land reclaimed from the Liffey, Temple Bar owes its name not to the friars, as you might expect, but to a seventeenth-century owner, Sir William Temple. During the eighteenth century, the place was a centre for Dublin's low life, in the shape of brothels and pubs (the pubs are still there), while in the nineteenth century it attracted the small businesses and tradesmen who gave it its character.

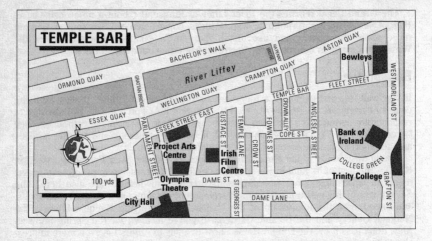

Today, there's sometimes friction between the artists and craftspeople who gave Temple Bar its "alternative" cachet and official plans to capitalize on them: Temple Bar Properties, the umbrella organization charged with the "development" of the area, has more than £30 million of government money to spend on arts projects including centres for children, photography and multimedia, but doesn't always remember to consult the artists. All the same, Temple Bar still remains one of the liveliest and most interesting parts of town and a place worth spending some time in, especially in the evenings. U2's new hotel, *The Clarence*, is here, and a selection of the hippest clubs (*The Blue Note, IFC*; see p.88) and music venues (*Olympia*; see p.87) in town; for movies, eating, or people-spotting try the bar at the super-cool *Irish Film Centre* (see p.86). You can bone up on the more official side of Temple Bar life at the **Temple Bar information centre**, Eustace Street (☎671 5717), which publishes a *Temple Bar Guide* with a useful map; or consult *In Dublin* for a more general guide to what's on.

The **Project Arts Centre**, in East Essex Street, is where you're most likely to find experimental or politically sensitive theatre; the innovative Rough Magic Theatre Company performs regularly, and writers such as Jim Sheridan, Joe O'Connor, Declan Hughes and Gerry Stembridge have given premieres here. It also runs late-night music spots at weekends, and there's a gallery space, which organizes temporary exhibitions. Also worth a visit is the **Dublin Resource Centre** in Crow Street, a bookshop with plenty of material to provide an alternative, radical view of Irish politics and history, attached to an old-fashioned (Sixties/Seventies-style) vegetarian co-operative, the *Well-Fed Café*. Just off the other side of Dame Street, the **Andrews Lane Theatre** is a small and fun late-night theatre that's also a leading place for new Irish writing.

The **Irish Film Centre**, 6 Eustace Street, is a coolly minimalist conversion of an old Quaker meeting house. Entry is through a long corridor lit from beneath your feet, where you feel you're making a symbolic passage between reality and the surreal world of celluloid. Inside, you meet with a courtyard with a film bookshop, and an excellent restaurant and bar, plus two screens where can catch an interesting repertory of art-house movies: there are seasons of world cinema and gay cinema, children's film festivals and other seasons of special-interest films. The National Film Archive and Film Base, an independent co-operative of Irish film-makers, is housed here. A worthwhile introduction to Irish film is screened every afternoon.

The elegant, arching pedestrian bridge that leads from Temple Bar to the north bank of the Liffey is known as the **Ha'penny Bridge**, from the toll which was charged until early this century. Close by, on the north side of the river, is The Winding Stair (40 Lower Ormond Quay), a kind of northerly outpost of the anarchic spirit of Temple Bar as it used to be before the money-men arrived: an excellent second-hand bookshop with plenty of good remaindered paperbacks, and a café where you can sit and stare peacefully through the grimy windows while the Liffey oozes past the Ha'penny Bridge.

Dublin Castle and around

Dublin Castle (Mon–Fri 10am–12.15pm & 2–5pm, Sat & Sun 2–5pm; £1.50) is just a short walk along Dame Street. Outside its gates are the lime-green headquarters of the Sick and Indigent Roomkeepers Society, founded in 1790 and still going strong; the building has recently been bought by a conservationist who intends to preserve the facade while converting the inside into a family home.

Once inside the castle precinct, you're confronted with a real pig's breakfast of architectural styles: an ugly modern tax office stands to your left, an over-precise Gothic fantasy of a church of 1803 adorns the ridge straight ahead, and to your right is the worn red brick of the castle itself.

The castle dates from King John's first Dublin court of 1207, so it's a surprise to find that today it has the appearance of a graceful eighteenth-century building, with only the massive stone **Record Tower** giving the game away – although, in the nineteenth, this too was heavily rebuilt. Originally there were four such towers (the base of the Bermingham Tower, to the southwest, also survives), and the castle was a real fortified building; but it later became more an administrative rather than a military centre. The simplicity of the inner courtyard, all warm old red brick and stone facing, with a little clock tower on one side, is evocative of the grace and elegance with which, by the eighteenth century, the British had learned to cloak their hegemony over the country. As the heart of British power – the castle continued as the Viceroy's seat after the Act of Union at the beginning of the nineteenth century – the place stands as a symbol of 700 years of British power in Ireland.

Sometimes, however, the intended symbolism is subverted by Dublin humour: the figure of Justice that stands at the top of the **Bedford Tower**, on the north side of the yard, turns her back to the city – which shows, it was said, just how much justice Dubliners could expect from the English. Further, the scales she holds used to tilt when it rained; to ensure even-handedness, the problem was solved by drilling holes in the scale-pans.

The castle hosted the European Parliament in 1990, and massive amounts of EU funds were spent on refurbishing it in honour of the occasion. The **State Apartments** are now used by the president to entertain foreign dignitaries (so at times they will be closed to visitors) and there's a great deal of pomp and circumstance. It's these, including the **State Drawing Room** and the **Throne Room**, that you'll see on the official tour. The grandeur of the furnishings takes a bit of adjusting to – for instance, all the rooms have Donegal hand-tufted carpets mirroring the eighteenth-century stuccowork, which may be superb examples of craftsmanship but really are quiet revolting. This opulence must always have been in stark contrast to the surrounding reality of the city: the high wall that you'll notice at the end of the castle's garden is said to have been built to shield the delicate sensibilities of Queen Victoria from the appalling condition of the slums on St Stephen Street.

Given the anonymous grandeur of the interior, it's sometimes difficult to appreciate the age and interest of some of the buildings that go to make up the compound. Excavations for the new conference centre built in 1990 revealed perhaps the most interesting part of the tour, the **Undercroft**. Here you can see remains of an earlier

Viking fort, part of the original thirteenth-century moat plus the base of the Powder Tower, a section of the old city wall and the steps that used to lead down to the Liffey.

Wood Quay

Directly down towards the Liffey from the castle is **Wood Quay**, site of the Viking and Norman settlements that have yielded amazing quantities of archeological finds (on show in the National Museum Annexe). The excavations were never completed and there's undoubtedly more to be discovered on the site, but despite a lot of argument the corporation of Dublin was able to go ahead and put up two massive Civic Offices, known to one and all as "The Bunkers", destroying what may have been the most important early Viking archeological site in Europe.

St Werburgh's Church

Going westwards, the historical mosaic becomes both increasingly rich and increasingly chaotic. Werburgh Street (left as you come out of the castle, and then left again) was the site of Dublin's first theatre; today, it's home of *Leo Burdock's*, the legendary fish-and-chip shop (see p.83) as well as **St Werburgh's Church**. Reputedly, by origin, the oldest church in Dublin, its plain exterior, with peeling paint in motley shades of grey, conceals a flamboyant and elegant 1759 interior built in the height of Georgian style, which is well worth seeing. Unfortunately, as with a lot of Dublin's Church of Ireland churches, you'd better resign yourself to the fact that it nearly always seems to be closed (this one is open by arrangement; Mon–Fri 10am–4pm; ☎478 3710). Lord Edward Fitzgerald, one of the leaders of the 1798 rebellion (see p.370), is buried in the vault; Major Henry Sirr, who captured him for the British, is interred in the churchyard. Also John Field, the early nineteenth-century Irish composer and pianist who is credited with having invented the nocturne, later developed by Chopin, was baptized here.

The cathedrals

The area west of Dublin Castle is the site of the **original Viking settlement** and represents the most ancient part of the city: the old Tholsel, or town hall, used to stand here, as did the original Four Courts. Today, this historic place is remarkable for its strange combination of urban desolation (haphazardly built housing and shops with bag ladies, drunks and beggars on the streets) and urban renewal (generous tax concessions are ensuring that there's plenty of new building), and the massive, over-restored grey bulks of not one but two **cathedrals**. Both date originally from the twelfth century – Christchurch from 1172 and St Patrick's, designed to supersede it, from 1190. The reason why both have survived appears to be that one (Christchurch) stood inside the city walls, the other outside. Both cathedrals remain dedicated to the Church of Ireland, their huge bulks once a symbol of the dominance of the British – but now manifestations of what is very much a minority religious denomination.

Christchurch Cathedral and around

Christchurch (daily 10am–5pm: 50p donation) stands isolated by the traffic system. Like St Patrick's, it suffered at the hands of Victorian restorers, but is still very much a resonant historic site. Dublin's first (wooden) cathedral was founded here by Sitric Silkenbeard, first Christian king of the Dublin Norsemen, in 1038; that church was demolished by the Norman Richard de Clare – Strongbow – who built the new stone cathedral in 1172. This building didn't fare very well, either: it was built on inadequate foundations on a peat bog, and the south wall fell down in 1562. The building you see now is the result of an 1870s restoration; even the flying buttresses are a figment of the imagination of its architect, G.E. Street.

Despite all this, the building remains a monument to that first serious British incursion into Ireland, in the twelfth century. Strongbow himself is interred here (or part of him, most likely his bowels), underneath an effigy which quite possibly depicts an Earl of Drogheda.

Like many of Dublin's larger monuments, Christchurch keeps packing 'em in with multimedia evocations of history: styling itself "a bridge to the medieval past", **Dublinia** (April–Sept daily 10am–5pm; Feb–March Mon–Sat 10am–4.30pm; last admission one hour before closing; £4, includes admission to Christchurch) offers a series of presentations of medieval Dublin, including Strongbow's arrival, a full-size reconstruction of a merchant's house and a grotesque depiction of the Black Death. The Viking and Norman artefacts dug up at nearby Wood Quay are also on display here.

Close by, the augustly monumental **St Audoen's church** (2.30–5pm), the oldest of Dublin's parish churches, was founded by the Normans. Today, it's a strange hybrid: the original church, part of which dates from the twelfth century, is now a Protestant church; but it is grafted on to a much larger, nineteenth-century, Catholic one. The arch beside the church, dating back to 1215, is the only surviving gate from the old city walls.

Not all is as old as it seems hereabouts; for all its air of authenticity, the pub, *Mother Redcap's* (a little further west on Back Lane, off High Street), is a modern creation amid the open spaces left by the clearance of the inner-city slums. Nearby, however, the **Tailors' Guild Hall** (1706) is the city's last surviving guildhall, with an assembly room that includes an eighteenth-century musicians' gallery where Wolfe Tone and Napper Tandy spoke to the revolutionary "Back Lane Parliament" in the run-up to the 1798 uprising. Tailors' Hall is now the headquarters of *An Taisce* (pronounced *On Tashka*), a pioneering conservation organization. The restoration of the building was carried out in conjunction with the Irish Georgian Society, and the two groups join forces to lobby the government to devote more funds to caring for Ireland's architectural heritage. With the setting up of a National Heritage Committee in 1988, funded from the National Lottery, that aim came one step closer to fulfilment.

St Patrick's Cathedral

South down Patrick Street from the Guild Hall, **St Patrick's Cathedral** (Mon–Fri 9am–6pm, Sat 9am–5pm, Sun 10am–3pm; £1; bus #50, #50A, #54, #54A, #56A) is now the national cathedral of the Church of Ireland, and is a much more elegant place inside than the grey tank-like exterior leads you to expect. Legend has it that St Patrick baptized converts within its grounds; but its most famous association is with the writer Jonathan Swift, who was dean of St Patrick's in the eighteenth century (see overleaf).

At the west end of the church is an old **wooden door** with a roughly hewn aperture, formerly the chapter door of the south transept. Anecdote claims this to have brought a new phrase into the English language when, in 1492, the feuding earls of Kildare and Ormonde met here. Ormonde's supporters were barricaded inside the cathedral; Kildare, eager to end the struggle, cut a hole in the door and put his arm through it, inviting Ormonde to shake hands. He did, peace was restored, and the phrase "chancing your arm" was born.

There are plenty of interesting tombs and memorials in the cathedral. One of the most elaborate, at the west end of the church, is a seventeenth-century **monument to the Boyle family**, earls of Cork, teeming with painted figures of family members. The tomb originally stood beside the altar; but a year after being installed in 1632, it was moved, when Thomas Wentworth, Earl of Strafford and the British Viceroy in Dublin, objected that churchgoers were forced to pray "crouching to an Earl of Cork and his lady... or to those sea nymphs his daughters, with coronets upon their heads, their hair dishevelled, down upon their shoulders." This was not the end of the argument, and it was the Earl of Cork who won: he later had Wentworth executed. Robert

JONATHAN SWIFT

Best known for his satires, including the classic *Gulliver's Travels*, **Jonathan Swift** (1667–1745) was born at Hoey's Court, close to St Werburgh's Church. He could read by the age of three, and at fifteen got a place at Trinity College. On graduating, he worked for the diplomat Sir William Temple, after whom Temple Bar is named, and subsequently for the Church of England. He was appointed Dean of St Patrick's in 1713, where he remained until his death.

Swift began publishing political pamphlets in 1704, and was forced to return to Ireland, after spending some time in London, because his pen had made him enemies among the Whigs. Over the next couple of decades, both his commitment to Ireland and his social conscience grew. He was among those who advocated Irish economic independence: in 1720 his *Proposal for the Universal Use of Irish Manufactures*, published anonymously, suggested that the Irish burn everything English except its coal. More notorious is his *A Modest Proposal* of 1729, a bitter satire in which he suggested that the Irish could solve their problems by selling their babies to the English for food.

Swift's presence is everywhere in the cathedral, giving hints of both his often vitriolic interventions in Dublin's public life and his own mysterious and contorted private life. Immediately to the right of the entrance are memorials to both him and Esther Johnson (1681–1728), the "Stella" with whom he had a passionate, though apparently platonic, relationship. Stella was the daughter of Sir William Temple's housekeeper; in 1701, after Temple's death, Swift brought her to Dublin and lived near her for the rest of her life.

Elsewhere in the church there's a tribute from the sharp-quilled English poet Alexander Pope:

> *Let Ireland tell how Wit upheld her cause,*
> *Her Trade supported and supplied her Laws*
> *And leave on Swift this grateful verse engraved*
> *"The rights a Court attack'd a Poet sav'd."*

The two men were good friends and used to plan sharing a home in retirement (the correspondence is an interesting one, particularly for the gentle light it casts on Pope).

The **north pulpit** contains Swift's writing table, chair, portrait and death mask. He died at 78 after years of agony from an ailment, unidentified at the time, whose symptoms – giddiness and deafness – terrified him with the possibility that he might be going mad. (It's thought that his malady was Méunière's disease, a degenerative disease of the middle ear that was finally identified in 1861.) He left money to build a hospital for the insane – Swift's Hospital, now St Patrick's, close to the Royal Hospital Kilmainham – which, opening in 1757, was one of the first psychiatric institutions in the world.

Swift's epitaph, which he wrote himself, appears in simple gold lettering on a plain black slab:

> *Here is laid the body of*
> *Jonathan Swift, Doctor of Divinity,*
> *Dean of this Cathedral Church,*
> *Where fierce indignation can no longer*
> *Rend the heart*
> *Go, traveller, and imitate, if you can*
> *This earnest and dedicated*
> *Champion of liberty.*

Boyle (who, as the only son, has pride of place in a niche of his own in the centre of the lowest tier) went on to become a scientist who established the important relationship, still known as Boyle's Law, between the pressure, volume and temperature of a gas.

At the east end of the church a series of three **Elizabethan brasses** tells the plaintive stories of some of the early English settlers in Ireland. There's a small, plain monument in the north transept to one Alexander McGeek, a servant of Swift, erected by the dean in what was clearly an unusual gesture – all the other tablets are to people of property. A message from one William Taylour strikes a chilling note:

> *As You are, so were Wee*
> *And as Wee are, so shall You be.*

Finally, near the entrance, it comes as a surprise, among all the relics of the Anglo-Irish, to find an inscription in Irish: to Douglas Hyde, founder of the Gaelic League, first president of Ireland and son of a Church of Ireland clergyman.

Archbishop Marsh's Library

Just outside the main entrance is a compact Georgian building, faced in brick at the front but, tactfully, in the same unrelenting grey stone as the cathedral on the side that faces the church. This is **Archbishop Marsh's Library** (Mon & Wed–Fri 10am–12.45pm & 2–5pm, Sat 10.30am–12.45pm; £1), Ireland's first public library, built in 1701 (by Sir William Robinson, who also designed the Royal Hospital Kilmainham) and given to the city by the wonderfully named Archbishop Narcissus Marsh. Inside, the tiny reading cubicles and the dark carved bookcases carrying huge leather-bound tomes – some 25,000 of them, most dating from the sixteenth to the eighteenth centuries; the earliest a Latin manuscript of 1400 – can hardly have changed since the library was built. The library was peppered with bullets during the 1916 rising, and some of the seventeenth-century volumes are marked by British Army bullets intended for the nearby *Jacob's* factory, which was a rebel stronghold. The single most important collection in the library is that of one Edward Stillingfleet, Archbishop of Worcestor. His 10,000 books were bought for £2,500 and include works from some of the earliest English printers, including Berthelet, Daye and Fawkes. Archbishop Marsh – of whom Swift remarked that "no man will be either glad or sorry at his death" (the dean believed that it was Marsh's fault he had not risen higher in his ecclesiastical career) – was responsible for the preparation of the first translation of the Old Testament into Irish, and two of the volumes survive in the library. The chains that once protected the books from theft are long gone, but three lock-in cages for readers of rare books survive – however, today readers sit in the main office under the watchful eye of the librarian.

The Liberties, the Guinness brewery and Kilmainham

Heading westwards along High Street, you'll enter **The Liberties**, an area spreading out to the south which was once outside the legal jurisdiction of the city and settled by French Huguenot refugees escaping religious persecution in their own country. They set up home, and poplin- and silk-weaving industries, in the southern part of The Liberties known as the Coombe (there is now a street named after it). The 10,000 Huguenots who arrived between 1650 and the early eighteenth century had a great civilizing effect on what was then a small and underdeveloped city; they founded a horticultural society and encouraged the wine trade. The Liberties have maintained the characteristics of self-sufficiency that the Huguenots brought with them, and there are families able to trace their local roots back for many generations. In the nineteenth century, local rivalries frequently erupted into violence between the Liberty Boys, the tailors and weavers of the Coombe, and the Ormond Boys, butchers who lived in Ormond Market (to the north of the Liffey at Ormond Quay).

Today, this colourful history is not immediately obvious to the visitor. The Liberties are a hotch-potch of busy streets full of barrows and bargain- and betting-shops. Government tax incentives and low property prices have encouraged speculators to build blocks of high-security luxury apartments, which sit oddly among the urban jumble. Francis Street, a mix of swish antique shops and dereliction, now boasts a great deli, *The Gallic Kitchen*.

The main road leading west of Christchurch (High Street leading to Jame's Street), interspersed with grim corporate housing and deserted factories, is dominated by the **Guinness brewery** – a setting out of Fritz Lang's *Metropolis*, with huge dark chimneys belching smoke, tiny figures hurrying along grimy balconies and the smell of malt heavy in the air. For all the seediness of its surroundings, however, Guinness is one of Ireland's biggest commercial successes. Founded in 1759, the St James's Gate brewery covers 64 acres and has the distinction of being the world's largest single beer-exporting company, exporting some 300 million pints a year; 2.5 million pints are brewed here every day, more than half the total amount of beer drunk in Ireland. Unfortunately you can't go round it, but the former *Guinness Hop Store* in Crane Street houses an exhibition centre (Mon–Fri 10am–4pm; £2; buses #21A, #78, #78A & #78B from outside the *Virgin Megastore* opposite O'Connell Bridge). You may feel ripped off at having to pay for what is essentially a souvenir shop, but you can at least taste what is arguably the best *Guinness* in Dublin – arguably because the honours traditionally went to *Mulligan's* in Poolbeg Street (northeast of College Green near George's Quay, see p.86), which still has its supporters. In addition, the upper floors of the airy, four-storey building are given over to exhibitions of contemporary art and offer fine views over Dublin.

The Royal Hospital Kilmainham and the Irish Museum of Modern Art

If you get off the bus (including the #21A, #78, #78B, #79 and #90) where Bow Lane joins James's Street, you'll walk past Swift's Hospital, now known as St Patrick's, on your way to the **Royal Hospital Kilmainham** (just five minutes walk further west). The hospital was extensively and well restored between 1980 and 1984, and the result is that Ireland's first Classical building – its date is 1680 – is a joy to look at, from the outside at least. The name doesn't imply a medical institution of any kind: it was built as a home for wounded army pensioners, like Chelsea Hospital in London or Les Invalides in Paris. The plan is simple: a colonnaded building around a central courtyard, erected with cool restraint so that the sober stone arcading creates a lovely, unadorned rhythm.

The use of the hospital to house the **Irish Museum of Modern Art** (Tues–Sat 10am–5.30pm; free), which opened in 1991, has caused a great deal of controversy, not least because the re-conversion has eaten up funds that might have been better used elsewhere. Almost half the inside has been depersonalized and painted white to provide gallery space of the correct, "modern" kind in a conversion which has led one commentator to quote the Flann O'Brien story about a man born at the age of 25 with a consciousness but no history: the clean white spaces, and the art hung in them, certainly betray no awareness of the hospital's past.

More critically, the museum has been seen as an effort on behalf of the Irish government – and, behind it, the figure of the then prime minister, Charles Haughey, who some felt cut an unlikely figure as a patron of the arts – to "buy into" the modernist tradition in art. However, the record of the director, Declan McGonagle, in commissioning and exhibiting radical and interesting art at the Orchard Gallery in Derry (see p.507), does make him someone to watch. There is no permanent exhibition in the museum (consult *In Dublin* for current exhibitions), which so far owns few works of its own, but instead a regularly changing collection of works mainly borrowed from European collections, hung alongside Irish ones. Whatever else, it is always stimulating; and there's an excellent restaurant in the basement under the north wing.

Kilmainham Gaol

Outside the hospital, a small formal garden runs down to the Liffey, and a long, tree-lined avenue leads out to the front gates, beyond which looms the grim mass of **Kilmainham Gaol** (May–Sept daily 10am–6pm; Oct–April Mon–Fri 1–4pm, Sun 1–6pm; £2; Heritage Card). Built in 1792, the jail was completed just in time to hold a succession of Nationalist agitators, from the United Irishmen of 1798, through Young

Irelanders, Fenians and Land Leaguers (including Parnell and Davitt) in 1883, to the leading insurgents of the 1916 Easter Rising – Pádraig Pearse and James Connolly were executed in the prison yard. Eamon de Valera, subsequently three times prime minister and later president, was the very last prisoner to be incarcerated here; he was released in July 1924.

The complex is a grim monument to the dark side of the Republican struggle, with tiny cells, covered walkways and stone exercise yards. Not all the prisoners were political: an indication of the severity of punishments is given by a document recording a sentence of seven years' transportation for stealing a piece of printed calico. The guided tours (included in admission price) give an emotionally coloured impression of the place, climaxing in the low lighting of the chapel, where, on May 4, 1916, Joseph Plunkett, one of the leaders of the 1916 uprising, was married by candlelight to Grace Gifford while twenty British soldiers stood to attention, bayonets fixed. They were married at 1.30am; he was executed at 3.30am, after just ten minutes in his wife's company. Until the executions of the sixteen leaders of the Easter Rising, the insurrection commanded little popular support in Dublin. The rebels had held notable buildings, among them the General Post Office (see overleaf) and the *Jacob's* factory, for five days until British artillery pounded them into submission. It was only after James Connolly, already almost mortally wounded, was executed at Kilmainham (he had to be tied to a chair so they could shoot him) that a wave of support gathered behind the Nationalist cause – leading, ultimately, to the withdrawal of British troops, the division of Ireland, and civil war.

The North Side: O'Connell Street and around

Crossing over O'Connell Bridge you reach the North Side's main thoroughfare and once the most grandiose of Dublin streets. However, before wandering up what is still the city's busiest, although less salubrious, centre for shopping, it's worth taking a detour eastwards along Eden Quay to the famous *Abbey Theatre* and the elegant Custom House.

The Abbey Theatre

Not far along Eden Quay, turn left up Marlborough Street to the **Abbey Theatre** on the corner of Lower Abbey St. Ireland's national theatre, it was opened in 1904 (nearly 20 years before independence), with co-founders and Celtic literature revivalists W.B. Yeats and Lady Gregory as its first directors. *The Abbey* soon gained worldwide prestige for its productions of Irish playwrights such as Yeats, J.M. Synge and Sean O'Casey. At home, it also caused great controversy – even riots. Indicative of how much the theatre in Ireland has always been a platform for political dialogue, Synge's *Playboy of the Western World*, and much more directly O'Casey's *The Plough and the Stars* (1926), which questioned the motivations of the by-now haloed martyrs of 1916, so undercut and discredited the romanticized vision of Ireland that Yeats had helped to create – and the Nationalists had encouraged – that Dubliners took to the streets to protest. Today the new *Abbey* (its predecessor was destroyed in a fire in 1951) holds two theatres, the main one devoted to the Irish classics and new work by such as Brian Friel and Frank McGuinness, while the **Peacock Theatre** downstairs often shows new experimental drama; there's also a vegetarian restaurant, *Midday's* (see p.83). For details of what's on, see *In Dublin*.

The Custom House

It's easy enough to overlook the **Custom House**, lying in the shadow of the metal railway viaduct that runs parallel to O'Connell Bridge, east along the river. But, as one of the great Georgian masterpieces built by James Gandon, it's an impressive reminder of the city's eighteenth-century splendour. It is principally Gandon's public buildings that put Dublin ahead of other great, and better-preserved, Georgian cities such as Bath and Edinburgh. The Custom House was the first of them, completed in 1791 (the Four Courts, although started in 1786, were not completed until 1802, and the King's Inns were designed in 1795). It burned for five days after it was set alight by Republicans in 1921, but was thoroughly restored (and has just been refurbished again) and now houses government offices.

The best **view** of the building is from the other side of Matt Talbot Bridge, from where you can admire the long, regular loggia, portico and dome, all reflected in the muddy waters of the Liffey. This elegance conceals a story of personal ambition and dirty tricks. The building was originally planned by John Beresford, chief commissioner of revenue, and his friend Luke Gardiner. A large stone in the bed of the Liffey was preventing some boats from reaching the old customs point, further upstream, and this was ostensibly the argument for building a new one; but Beresford and Gardiner's prime reason for backing the scheme was that it served their own purposes to shift the commercial centre of the city east from Capel Street to the area where O'Connell Street now stands. Their plans were opposed through parliamentary petitions, personal complaints, even violence, and the hostile party was delighted to discover that the site for the new building was the muddy banks of the Liffey where, they thought, it would be impossible to build foundations. Gandon, however, confounded the scheme's critics by building the foundations on a layer of pine planks – which seems to have done the job.

O'Connell Street

Most things of historical interest on **O'Connell Street** – now lined by fast-food restaurants, shops, cinemas and modern offices – have long since been submerged under the tide of neon lights and plate glass, but one major exception is the **General Post Office** (GPO), which stands at the corner of Henry Street. It was opened in 1818, and its fame stems from the fact that almost a century later it became the rebel headquarters in one of the most significant battles in the fight for independence (see opposite). The entire building, with the exception of the facade, was destroyed in the fighting; it was later restored and re-opened in 1929. From the street you can still see the scars left by bullets: inside (Mon–Sat 8am–8pm, Sun 10.30am–6.30pm) the reconstructed marbled halls are also worth a look.

O'Connell Street itself is reputedly one of Europe's widest, and there's a paved stretch down the middle with a series of **statues**. Until 1966 one of them, directly in front of the GPO, depicted Nelson on top of a column; it was blown up by IRA sympathizers in March 1966 (you can inspect the statue's head in the Civic Museum see p.59). Millennium year saw a notoriously expensive new addition to the gallery: an angular recumbent woman bathed by a fountain, quickly nicknamed "the floozie in the jacuzzi", or "the whore in the sewer" (this rhymes in a Dublin accent).

Beside the GPO, Henry Street leads to **Moore Street Market**, where you'll find some of the disappearing street life that people are apt to get misty-eyed about. Truth is that the same activities continue to flourish in the less romantic settings of the *Ilac* shopping centre, round the corner, or in the new mall on St Stephen's Green; that doesn't alter the fact that Moore Street's brightly coloured stalls and banter are a lot of fun. A little further up, a turning to the right, Cathedral Street, leads to the Greek Revival **St Mary's Pro-Cathedral** (1816–25), Dublin's most important Catholic church. Due to fears that the originally planned position on O'Connell Street would incite anti-Catholic feeling among the English, the cathedral is hidden away here. Consequently, getting a good view of its six Doric columns – based on the Temple of Theseus in Athens – is nigh on impossible. Inside, every Sunday at 11am, you can hear the famous Palestina Choir, started in 1902; John McCormack, the respected and popular tenor, began his career here in 1904.

THE EASTER RISING

The **Easter Rising** of 1916, which resulted in pitched battles in the streets of Dublin, is remembered as one of the key events leading to Irish self-government.

In fact, at the time, it seemed to most Nationalists a botched and inconclusive event. Leaders of the **Irish Volunteers**, a Nationalist group that had been founded in 1913, secretly planned a nationwide uprising for Easter Sunday 1916. The insurrection was to be staged with the help of a shipment of arms from Germany which were to be picked up by Sir Roger Casement (a British official who became an fervent Nationalist supporter; see p.489). Things began to go wrong almost immediately: the arms arrived a day too early, and the British apprehended Casement and hanged him.

So secret had the preparations for the uprising been that the Irish Volunteers' leader, Eoin MacNeill, knew nothing of them. A week before Easter, the extremist plotters, led by **Pádraig Pearse**, showed MacNeill a forged order, purporting to come from the British authorities at Dublin Castle, for the suppression of the Irish Volunteers. MacNeill consented to give the order for the uprising. Then, the day before it was due to happen, he learned that the document was a forgery, and placed advertisements in the Sunday papers cancelling the insurrection.

Pearse and his allies, however, pressed ahead, in Dublin only, the following day – Easter Monday. They took, among other public buildings, the General Post Office (GPO) in O'Connell Street, and Pearse walked out onto the steps of the GPO to read the historic **Proclamation of the Irish Republic** (see p.576). Fighting continued for five days before being put down by the British authorities.

It was not the rising itself, but the British reaction to it, that was significant for the Republicans. The authorities executed a total of fifteen leaders of the rebellion, including Pearse and another patriot, James Connolly, at Kilmainham Gaol (see p.75). The result was to turn these men, in the eyes of the public, into martyrs to the Nationalist cause. When, a year later, the British attempted to introduce conscription to the trenches of the First World War, the public mood turned sharply away from accommodation with the ruling powers – and toward independence, which was finally achieved in 1921.

The final statue at the top of O'Connell Street commemorates the nineteenth-century politician Charles Stewart Parnell (see p.111), quoting his famous words, "No man has a right to fix the boundary to the march of a nation. No man has a right to say to his country, Thus far shalt thou go and no futher...."

Parnell Square to Mountoy Square

At the top of O'Connell Street, behind Parnell's statue in the square named for him, stands the **Rotunda Maternity Hospital**, dated 1752. This was the very first purpose-built maternity hospital in Europe: the barber-surgeon Bartholomew Mosse funded the enterprise by organizing events including fancy dress balls, recitals and concerts – one of these was the first performance of Handel's *Messiah*, which took place on April 15, 1742. There's a superb chapel with a stucco ceiling by Bartholomew Cramillion. The Rotunda Room itself houses *The Ambassador* cinema (see p.88). Part of the remainder of the building is still a maternity hospital, while another section – the old Assembly Rooms – houses the **Gate Theatre**, which was opened by the legendary actor Micheál MacLiammóir and Hilton Edwards in 1929.

Behind the Rotunda, bordering on Parnell Square, is all that remains of the pleasure gardens, yet another of Dr Mosse's successful fund-raising ventures. This little open space is now a **Garden of Remembrance** for all those who died in the independence struggle, with a sculpture by Oisin Kelly of the *Children of Lir* (see p.176).

Parnell Square, originally called Rutland Square, was one of the first of Dublin's Georgian squares and still has its plain, bright, red-brick houses, broken by the grey stone mass of the **Hugh Lane Municipal Art Gallery** (Tues–Sat 9.30am–6pm, Sun 11am–5pm; free; buses passing include #10, #11, #13, #16 & #22). This was originally the town house of the Earl of Charlemont, built for him by the Scottish architect Sir William Chambers in 1762 and the focus of fashionable Dublin – the north side of the square was known as Palace Row – before the city centre moved south of the river. Chambers was also the architect of the delightful Casino, built to embellish the aesthetic Lord Charlemont's country house a few miles away at Marino (see p.95).

The house works well in its revised role as an art gallery, with plenty of good lighting and an intimate scale that complements the pictures. The gallery was set up in 1908 with funds donated by Sir Hugh Lane (nephew of Lady Gregory of *Abbey Theatre* fame), who died when the *Lusitania* was torpedoed in 1915. He left his collection – centred round the French Impressionists – to "the nation", and with Ireland's independence the problem arose of which of the two nations he might have meant. In 1960 the two governments agreed to exchange halves of the collection every five years, but in 1982 the British government put in a claim for the lot; the matter has recently been settled, with half the collection permanently in residence at Hugh Lane. All the same, it makes interesting viewing, with work from the pre-Raphaelites onwards added to by more modern Irish painters such as Jack B. Yeats and Paul Henry; of particular note is a stained glass window by Harry Clarke, who was also responsible for the *Birds of Paradise* window in the Westmoreland Street *Bewley's*. There are sometimes free recitals on Sunday lunchtimes (see *In Dublin* for details), and downstairs there's a good-value café/restaurant.

Two doors down, at nos. 18 to 19, a pair of modest Georgian houses are the home of the new **Dublin Writers' Museum** (Mon–Sat 10am–5pm, Sun 11.30am–6pm; £2.60, or £3.95 including Shaw's birthplace), a sometimes uneasy combination of tourist crowd-puller and serious literary venue that celebrates Ireland's greatest exploits, literature and writers, many of whom found themselves forced into exile: Joyce, Beckett, O'Casey…. There's plenty of material to draw on: apart from its three Nobel laureates – George Bernard Shaw, W. B. Yeats and Samuel Beckett – Dublin nurtured a host of other writers, including Joseph Sheridan le Fanu, Jonathan Swift, Sean O'Casey, Brendan Behan and, of course, James Joyce. The exhibits are on the dull side – there's a predictable range of memorabilia, including Brendan Behan's typewriter – but they are slightly enlivened if you opt to use the free audio guide. The exhibition begins with a reference to early Irish poetry and the English poet Edmund Spenser's *Faerie Queen*, weaves rapidly through Jonathan Swift's *Modest Proposal* of 1729 and the romantic fiction of the mid-nineteenth century to Oscar Wilde (who, on being asked by a United States customs officer if he had anything to declare, replied "Only my genius"), and the playwright G. B. Shaw. Joyce shares a cabinet with Sean O'Casey – this really is a whistle-stop tour – and the exhibits wind up with material on Samuel Beckett, Brendan Behan and the comic writer Flann O'Brien. Upstairs is a fine 1760s library with rather oppressive colour added in the nineteenth century, now somewhat sententiously dubbed the Gallery of Writers. There's a good bookshop with an intelligent selection of books, including contemporary authors, plus a café with a modest selection of salads – go to the café at the Hugh Lane Gallery, a couple of doors up, if you're feeling hungrier.

Next door is the **Living Writers' Centre**, with work rooms, a couple of apartments and a lecture room, and an ongoing programme of literary lectures and seminars. Ring the museum for further details (☎872 2077).

Mountjoy Square

As you head northeast toward Mountjoy Square, the streets are full of rotting Georgian and Victorian tenements (lots of cheap dives here – see p.51). Appropriately enough given the presence of the new Writers' Museum, the area also has plenty of **literary associations**: Belvedere College in Great Denmark Street is where James Joyce went to school; Sean O'Casey wrote all his plays for the *Abbey Theatre* – *The Shadow of a*

JAMES JOYCE

Author of *Ulysses* (1922), the ultimate celebration of his native city, **James Joyce** – who spent most of his adult life in voluntary exile from Ireland – was born in 1882. After an impoverished childhood, he went to University College, a place of learning then staffed by Jesuit priests, where he led a dissolute life and began to experiment with writing short pieces of prose which he called "epiphanies". In 1904 he started writing the short stories that were eventually published as *Dubliners*. On 10 June of that year, Joyce met Nora Barnacle, and, on their next meeting, 16 June, he fell in love with her; it's on this day that the entire epic narrative of *Ulysses* is set. They finally got married some 27 years later.

With the exception of two brief visits to Dublin in 1909, when he attempted to set up a chain of cinemas, and a final visit in 1912, Joyce never again lived in Ireland. All the great works, including *A Portrait of the Artist as a Young Man* (1916) and his late masterpiece, *Finnegan's Wake* (1939), were written in various European capitals – Zurich, Paris – where Joyce and his family eked out a penurious existence supported mostly by donations from rich patrons. At the time of Joyce's death in 1941, *Ulysses* was banned in Ireland, condemned as a pornographic book; it wasn't published in the Rebublic until the 1960s.

Joyce once remarked that he was "more interested in the street names of Dublin than in the riddle of the universe", and boasted that Dublin could be rebuilt from scratch using the information contained in his books. The **Bloomsday** pilgrimage – on June 16 every year people from all over the world meet in Dublin to retrace the action of the novel – starts at the Martello Tower at Sandycove (see p.93) and then progresses through the streets of Dublin, taking in lunch at *Davy Byrne's* pub (see p.85), where Leopold Bloom's lunch of a glass of burgundy and a gorgonzola-and-mustard sandwich is served, then the National Library, the *Ormonde Hotel* (Ormond Quay, north Dublin) and all the other locations made iconic by this great novel.

For serious Joyceans, the **James Joyce Centre** at 35 North Great Georges Street (Tues–Sat 10am–4.30pm, Sun 12–4.30pm; £2; ☎873 1984), not far from the Irish Writers' Centre, has a museum with documents of his life and work, and an excellent bookshop. It also has information on lectures, walking tours, and Bloomsday events.

Gunman, Juno and the Paycock, The Plough and the Stars and *The Silver Tassie* – at 422 North Circular Road (a few streets north of the square), and Brendan Behan grew up nearby at 14 Russell Street.

Mountjoy Square itself is Dublin's earliest Georgian square, now in an advanced state of decay. Although there are some signs of revitalization, there's little left of the elegance described by Thomas Cromwell in his *Excursions through Ireland* in 1820: "Taste and opulence have united to embellish; the streets in the vicinity are all built on a regular plan; the houses are lofty and elegant; and neither hotels, shops, nor ware-houses, obtruding upon the scene, the whole possesses an air of dignified retirement – the tranquillity of ease, affluence and leisure. The inhabitants of this parish are indeed almost exclusively of the upper ranks. . . ."

The King's Inns, the Four Courts and St Michan's

Leaving Parnell Square at the northwest, you come to Dublin's – indeed, the nation's – **Wax Museum** (Mon–Sat 12–5.30pm; £3.50) at the corner of Granby Row and Dorset Street. If you like that sort of thing, and if you have children to entertain, it's a good way of whiling away a wet afternoon: there are more than 300 exhibits of Irish and international interest. In addition to a chamber of horrors, plentiful rock stars, and a curious representation of Leonardo da Vinci's *The Last Supper*, there are topical inclu-sions such as Jack Charlton, the much-loved former national football team manager, and the popular country and western singer Garth Brookes, who topped a recent survey in the museum for the likeness people most wanted to see.

Across Dorset Street, the **Black Church** (or St Mary's Chapel of Ease) in St Mary's Place is a sinister, brooding building with spiky finials, next to the excellent *Young Traveller* hostel (see p.54). Legend has it that St Mary's and other similar massive Protestant churches built during the 1820s were designed so that they could be turned into defensive positions should the Catholics attack.

As you walk down Dorset Street and into Bolton Street, everything speaks of urban deprivation: rubbish blowing in the gutters, broken glass, barred shop windows. Henrietta Street, dowdy as it is now, comes as a surprise: one of the first sites of really big houses in Dublin, it has two (nos. 9 and 10, at the far end) by Sir Edward Lovett Pearce. These adjoin the impressive **King's Inns**, designed by James Gandon, architect of the Four Courts and the Custom House, but sadly not open to the public.

The Four Courts

Making your way south from the King's Inns to the Four Courts (about a ten-minute walk), you're assailed by more blighted urban landscapes. If you walk down **Capel Street**, once one of Dublin's most fashionable addresses, you'll see few signs of modishness now – it's full of cut-price furniture stores and pawnbrokers. More streets full of rubbish and rotting vegetables from the early-morning fruit and vegetable market in Mary's Lane do nothing to prepare you for a solid example of Georgian architecture and urban planning: the **Four Courts** (Mon–Fri 9.30am–5pm), designed by Gandon between 1786 and 1802 as the seat of the High Court of Justice of Ireland and a sort of chambers for barristers.

From the outside the Four Courts have a grim perfection. Inside, the courts – Exchequer, Common Pleas, King's Bench and Chancery – radiate from a circular central hall. The building was completely gutted during the civil war but has been thoroughly restored.

Saint Michan's Church

Though it doesn't look much now – only the tower and a few other fragments are original – **St Michan's Church** (Mon–Fri 10am–12.45pm & 2–4.45pm, Sat 10am–12.45pm; £1.50), founded in 1095, is the oldest building on the North Side. Turn right up Church Street just west of the Four Courts and you'll find the church a short walk along near the junction with St Mary's Lane. The reason it's on the tourist trail is that the crypt's combination of dry air and constant temperature, together with methane gas secreted by rotting vegetation beneath the church, keeps corpses in a state of unnatural, **mummified preservation**: some of the "best" are on display, with skin, fingernails and hair all clearly identifiable, sometimes after 300 years. Depending on the mood of the guide, different crypts are opened, and among the dead are a nun, a crusader and a thief – this last identified as such because of a missing hand, amputated as penance for an earlier offence. None of the bodies was originally stored in the church, and how this odd collection of corpses got here is still a mystery. St Michan's also boasts an early eighteenth-century organ, still with its original gilding on the case, which Handel played and admired during a visit to Dublin.

Towards Phoenix Park

As you head west from St Michan's towards Phoenix Park, the street scene remains desolate. A large area is taken up by the decaying remains of Jameson's distillery, closed in 1972: enormous walls with weeds growing from the top and gaping, broken windows. The **Irish Whiskey Corner** (Bow Street Distillery) is an unexpected patch of neatness – a well-kept little courtyard leads to a whiskey museum (daily tours at 3.30pm; £2.50), converted from an old warehouse. There's an audiovisual show on the history and manufacture of Irish whiskey, working models of the distilling process and artefacts associated with it and, best of all, at the end of the tour you're invited to conduct a comparative tasting of five different kinds of Irish whiskey with Scotch and bourbon.

Smithfield Horse Sales and Collins Barracks

The cobbled expanse of **Smithfield**, just west of Bow Street, seems like an opening without a purpose unless you're there on the first Sunday of a month, when it's the scene of horse sales. There's nothing remotely glamorous about it, but the event does possess a certain fascination. Apparently an entirely male activity, it consists of a load of horse boxes carrying filthy ponies, and deals being struck through the ritual of spitting into the palm and clapping the hands together. Many of the buyers and sellers are travellers, once known as itinerants, and before that gypsies: people who speak their own secret language, *shelta*. In fact, *shelta* has nothing to do with Romany (the most common theory is that the travellers are of purely Irish origin, and took to the roads at the time of the Famine), but the travellers do share with gypsies an impressive knowledge of horses. After the sales you'll see ragged ponies being ridden away bareback towards the grim northern suburbs, where impromptu pony races are held. A few roads west of Smithfield stand **Collins Barracks**, a series of imposing grey stone buildings formerly known as the Royal Barracks. Founded in 1704, their chief claim to fame is as the oldest continuously occupied purpose-built barracks in the world. They are currently being revamped to house the National Museum's decorative arts collection, and are scheduled to open in summer 1996.

Phoenix Park

If you have walked through the urban confusion of the North Side, the open spaces of Phoenix Park, Dublin's playground – which begins a few minutes walk west of Collins Barracks – come as a welcome relief. A series of pillars stand across the road and suddenly you're surrounded by grand clipped hedges and tended flowerbeds in what is one of the largest city parks in the world – it's more than twice the size of London's Hampstead Heath or New York's Central Park, for example. The name is a corruption of the Irish *fionn uisce*, or clear water; the park originated as priory lands, which were seized after the Reformation in the seventeenth century and made into a royal deer park. The Viceroy's Lodge – now *Áras an Uachtaráin*, the President's Residence – is here, as well as a 205-foot obelisk erected in 1817 in tribute to the **Duke of Wellington**. Wellington was born in Dublin, but was less than proud of his roots – when reminded that he was Irish by birth, the duke replied tersely, "Being born in a stable doesn't make one a horse."

The park was also the scene of two politically significant **murders** in the late spring of 1882, when two officials of the British parliament, Lord Frederick Cavendish, the chief secretary, and T.H. Burke, the under-secretary, were killed by an obscure organization known as "The Invincibles". At first it seemed that the motivation for the crime – longstanding bitterness over the landlord-and-tenant relationship in post-Famine Ireland – was directly connected with the Anglo-Irish politician Charles Stuart Parnell's ongoing agitation for reform on behalf of the Irish tenancy (see p.111). It seemed to Parnell that he would have to withdraw from public life due to the implication – however ill-founded – that he was connected with these murders, but his obvious sincerity in denouncing them, and the effect that the event had on British policy regarding the tenancy issue, was in fact to make his position in Ireland stronger than ever.

Phoenix Park also contains Dublin's **zoo** (Mon–Sat 9.30am–6pm, Sun 11am–6pm; adults £5.50; at the southeast corner of the park; buses #10, #25, #26), the second oldest in Europe – it was opened in 1830. Its claim to fame used to be that this is where the *MGM* lion was bred; the zoo now has a programme for breeding endangered species for subsequent release into the wild.

The old duelling grounds, or Fifteen Acres, are also to be found here – now the venue for gaelic football, cricket, soccer and, occasionally, polo – as well as a race-course where a flea market is held every Sunday from noon onwards. The quality of what's available can vary tremendously, and there seems no way of knowing what it will be like until the day.

Cafés and restaurants

Dublin may not be the gastronomic capital of the world, but there's plenty of choice – nearly all of it south of the Liffey – for both lunchtime and evening eating. **Café society** has reached Dublin in a big way in recent years, providing a new range of chic and trendy locations – in and around Grafton Street and Temple Bar – for all-day eating and drinking, and on Sundays many more places open up for sustaining brunches. At least once, you should experience one of the three *Bewley's* coffee houses. Try the table-service section on the second floor of the Grafton Street branch for elegance and potted palms at much the same prices. At lunchtime, Dublin's many **pubs** traditionally offer the best value: you can usually get soup and sandwiches and often much more substantial, traditional meals. The cheapest **fast-food** outlets – everything from *Pizzaland* and *Wimpy* to cheap Chinese and the ubiquitous kebab houses – are centred around O'Connell Street, but are generally, with one or two exceptions such as *Beshoff Ocean Foods*, pretty unpleasant.

In the evening there's no shortage of **restaurants** either; although on the North Side, places where you'll want to spend any time are thin on the ground. The spectrum of cuisines on offer is impressively wide, ranging from Egyptian, Lebanese, Russian and Cajun to the more familiar dishes from France, Italy and China. There are several restaurants offering **traditional Irish** fare, a number of good **seafood** places and plenty of **vegetarian** options. The cheaper, livelier restaurants are concentrated around the Temple Bar area, between Dame Street and the Liffey, while more expensive establishments are scattered throughout the city, with a concentration around St Stephen's Green.

Cafés

Beshoff Ocean Foods, 14 Westmoreland St & 7 Upper O'Connell St. Superior fish and chips, with bistro-type decor. Daily 11–3am.

Bewley's, 78 Grafton St (daily 7–1am, Thurs–Sat till 2am), 12 Westmoreland St (daily 7.30am–9pm) & 13 South Great George's St (Mon–Sat 6.45am–6pm). A Dublin institution, serving everything from drinks to sticky buns and full meals, and its delicious, renowned potato soup, in an elegant ambience.

Café Java, 5 South Anne St. Good for breakfasts and coffees. Mon–Fri 7.45am–6pm, Sat 9am–5pm, Sun 10am–5pm.

Café Kylemore, 1 O'Connell St, at the junction with North Earl St. A North Side cross between *Bewley's* and a Parisian brasserie, all brass and bentwood chairs, this serves good, plain basics – chips with almost everything – and has a drinks licence. Open Mon–Sat 8am–9pm, Sun 12–8pm.

Cornucopia Wholefoods, 21 Wicklow St (☎677 7583). Vegetarian shop and café. For anyone who has pigged out on one traditional Irish breakfast too many, *Cornucopia* offers a vegetarian alternative, including vegetarian sausages, between 8 and 11am. Café open daily until 9pm.

Cyber Café, Dame St. Very West Coast, the place to link in to the Internet in cool surroundings, primary colours, organic snacks; open till late.

The Globe, 11 South Great George's St. A bar by night (see p.86), this is a buzzing café by day, serving cappuccinos and herbal teas.

Harveys, 14 Moira House, Trinity St. Good-value breakfast and excellent coffee; Mon–Sat 8am–7pm, Sun 11am–5pm.

Image Gallery, 25 East Essex St, Temple Bar. Photographic gallery plus café, opposite the Irish Design Centre. Cappuccino, espresso, light snacks. Sells a range of interesting photographic postcards which it will mail for you. Fri & Sat until 11pm.

Juice, South Great George's St. Imaginative macrobiotic food, mix of oriental and Californian; a chic vegetarian eating place for the '90s, not a sweaty sandal in sight. Juices, lassis, smoothies from £1.50, lunch £2.25 upwards. Daily 8am–11 pm.

Marks Bros, 7 South Great George's St. A vibrant café with a good choice of eats. Open Mon–Sat 10am–5pm.

Odessa, 13/14 Dame Court. Exotic snacks and outré decor make this one of the trendiest new cafés; downstairs is good for gossipping in big squashy sofas. Noon–midnight daily; breakfast served noon–4pm.

Well Fed Café, *Dublin Resource Centre*, 6 Crow St, Temple Bar. Truly excellent old-fashioned radical vegetarian cooking, run by a workers' co-operative, seasoned with the almost forgotten smell (for Sixties/Seventies survivors) of patchouli oil. Good, small bookshop in the front of the café has a fine selection of alternative/feminist/politically radical books. Daily 10am–8.30pm.

Winding Stair Café, 40 Lower Ormond Quay. This vast second-hand book emporium also has a café serving soup, salads, sandwiches and cakes. Sit by the window and watch the Liffey ooze by. Open to 6pm only.

Budget (under £10)

Bad Ass Café, 9 Crown Alley, Temple Bar (☎671 2596). Once the hippest of Dublin's pizza joints. Sinead O'Connor was waitressing here when she cut her first disc with Ton Ton Macoute; now distinctly unhip for adults, but great fun for kids. Daily 11am–11pm.

Blazing Salads II, *Powerscourt Townhouse Centre*, Clarendon St (☎671 9552). Marvellous vegetarian food, despite the excruciating pun, in this Georgian town house turned shopping centre. Open Mon–Sat 9am–6pm.

Coffee Bean, 4 Nassau St (☎668 4626). Above the *Runner Bean*, a vegetable shop which is doing pioneering work selling exotica such as chillies, avocados and garlic in a country of cabbage, carrots and potatoes. The cooking is subtle and excellent, making good use of the vegetables downstairs, with a selection of vegetarian dishes as well as plenty of choice for serious carnivores. There's a good panorama over the wall into Trinity College. Daily 12–11pm.

Gresham Hotel, 20–22 O'Connell St. North of the Liffey, Dublin's second-best hotel serves drinks and excellent sandwiches all day in the elegant lobby. Daily 11am–11pm.

Kilkenny Design Centre Restaurant, 6 Nassau St; on the first floor. Great place for lunch but always packed, so be prepared to queue. Open Mon–Sat 9am–5pm.

La Paloma, 17B Temple Bar (☎677 7392). Saturated yellows and hot pinks offer a suitably un-Irish backdrop for good, cheap tapas (£2.50 each; noon–7pm), with a pricier evening menu. Open daily; last orders at midnight.

Leo Burdock's, 2 Werburgh St. Dublin's legendary fish-and-chip shop, now modestly wondering whether its fish and chips are the best not only in Dublin, but maybe in the world. Carry-out only; Mon–Fri 12.30–11pm, Sat 2–11pm.

Midday's, self-service restaurant in the *Peacock Theatre*, Lower Abbey St. A pioneer of vegetarian/wholefood cooking in Dublin. Open Mon–Sat 10am–5pm.

Omar Khayyam, 51 Wellington Quay (☎677 5758). Egyptian and vegetarian restaurant offering a three-course lunch for £4.95. Open until midnight daily, with a belly dancer on Fri and Sat nights.

Pasta Fresca, Chatham St (☎879 2402). Ireland's first fresh pasta shop. Its restaurant consists of a few tables and chairs in the window, always busy at lunchtime, so get there early. Closes at 7pm.

Il Pasticcio, 12 Fownes St. Cosy Italian restaurant, pasta from £4.50, great deserts and salads. Open Mon–Sat till 11pm, Sun 10pm.

Da Pino, 38 Parliament St (☎671 9308). Marvellous fresh pasta and huge pizzas at low prices. Daily 12–11.30pm.

Pizzeria Italiana, 123 Temple Bar (☎677 8528). Minuscule; great garlic bread, pasta and pizza at tiny prices. If there's a wait for a table, you're encouraged to adjourn to the pub opposite – the waitress will come and fetch you. Also takeaway from a hatch down the sidestreet. Daily 12–11pm.

South Street Pizzeria, South Great George's St (☎475 2273). Great pizzas from £4.25 in a relaxed and friendly atmosphere. Daily 12–8pm.

The Turks Head, 27–30 Parliament St (☎679 2606). Still bearing the name of the original 1760s "chop house", this restaurant now boasts an astonishing, sub-Gaudí interior and serves Cal-Ital food. Last orders 1.45am daily; the bar downstairs is open 11pm–2am every night.

Moderate (£10–15)

Ayumi-Ya Japanese Steakhouse, 132 Lower Baggot St (☎622 0233). Authentic Japanese food at affordable prices. Bento boxes available, and plenty of slurpy noodles. Mon–Sat 12.30–2.30pm, 6–11.30pm.

The Cedar Tree, 11 St Andrew's St (☎677 2121). Good Lebanese food served in a cavernous basement. Dazzling array of mezze dishes, with plenty of choice for vegetarians. Open Mon–Sat 5.30–11.45pm, Sun until 11.30pm.

Elephant and Castle, 18 Temple Bar (☎679 3121). Cross between a diner and a brasserie: busy and elegant place – would be equally at home in New York – to pop in for anything from a drink to dinner. Unpretentious; ketchup bottles on the tables. Best place by far for Sun brunch, but make sure you book. Open Mon–Thurs 8am–11.30pm, Fri till midnight, Sat 10.30am to midnight, Sun noon to 11.30pm.

Fitzer's, 51 Dawson St (☎660 1644). Cool, airy café/restaurant serving a Californian-style, new-wave menu of soulful food; plenty of pasta, salads, seafood and char-grills, or you can just drop in for a coffee. Outdoor seating on busy Dawson St. Good choice of vegetarian dishes. Open Mon–Sat 8am–11pm.

Gallagher's Boxty House, 20 Temple Bar (☎677 2762). A *boxty* is an Irish potato pancake cooked on a griddle, offered with a variety of meat and vegetable stuffings. Filling, if bland, food in a pleasant and friendly atmosphere. Known familiarly as GBH and somewhat looked down on by Dubliners, who probably regard its menu as strictly tourist fodder. Daily 12–11.30pm.

The Irish Film Centre, 6 Eustace St, Temple Bar (☎677 8788). Coolly minimalist designer bar and restaurant in what used to be a Quaker meeting house. Serves delicious food – including highly sinful cakes and pastries – all day. Plenty of vegetarian choice on an eclectic menu; vegetable pâtés, burgers, chicken, jambalaya with bananas all recommended. Open according to programme.

Little Lisbon, 3 Fownes St, Temple Bar (☎671 1274). Somewhat uneven cooking from Portugal. Early evening "happy hour". You can bring your own wine. Daily 10am–11pm, Sat until 1am.

Milano, 61 Dawson St (☎677 8611). First venture of the British *Pizza Express* chain in Ireland – swish surroundings with the familiar and affordable range of pizzas. Daily 6.30–11pm.

101 Talbot, 101–102 Talbot St (☎874 5011). One of the very few good restaurants north of the Liffey, this spacious dining room, close to the *Abbey Theatre*, is worth visiting for its excellent, eclectic menu and relaxed conviviality. Pasta bar open daily 12–11pm; main restaurant Mon–Sat lunch 12–3pm, dinner 6–11pm.

Tante Zoe's, 1 Crow St, Temple Bar (☎679 4407). Cajun/Creole restaurant with good food at decent prices. Very popular, so book. Daily noon to midnight.

Tosca, 20 Suffolk St (☎679 6744). Excellent new-wave Italian cooking in a cool halogen-lit interior guarantees this restaurant's continuing fashionability. Separate lunch and evening menus, piles of newspapers for slow browsing. Daily 12–3.30pm & 5.30pm to midnight, Fri & Sat until 1am.

Trocadero, 3 St Andrew St (☎677 5545 or ☎679 2385). Looks like an obnoxiously rich sort of trattoria, but in fact is pleasant, friendly and has excellent food. It's one of Dublin's oldest Italian restaurants, and the walls are hung with plaudits in the form of signed photographs of visiting showbiz luminaries. Early-bird menu for £9.75, but the place really comes into its own late at night when it fills up with theatre folk. Daily 6pm–12.15am.

Wildebeest, 7 Johnson's Court, a narrow lane off Grafton St close to *Bewley's* (☎671 2276). An elegant self-service restaurant – oil-cloth on the tables, plenty of newspapers to read – which does salads and hot dishes (vegetarian included) at lunch and dinner. Good for late-night snacks (open to 11pm) and drinks. Live music Wed–Sat.

Expensive (over £15)

Cooke's Café, 14 South William St (☎679 0535). Accomplished cooking in cool, terracotta surroundings. Very fashionable, very new wave. *Upstairs at Cooke's* now offers a cheaper way of sampling this delicious food, with main courses from £4.50, plus a range of delicious salads and breads. Mon–Sat 10am–5pm, Sun 11am–4pm.

Lord Edward Seafood Restaurant, 23 Christchurch Place (☎454 2420). Around the corner from *Leo Burdock's*, the legendary chippie, the *Lord Edward* represents the other end of the scale. Located above a very ordinary pub, it's been going for decades and is a Dublin tradition with a terrific reputation for simple cooking using the very freshest fish. Set lunch from £5, set dinner around £25. Open Mon–Sat 12.30–3pm & 6–10.45pm.

The Old Dublin, 90–91 Francis St (☎454 2028). Superb, if unlikely sounding, Russo-Irish food amid the dusty junk shops and markets of The Liberties area; borscht, gravad lax (*The Old Dublin's* definition of Russia seems to include most of Scandinavia), coupled with hearty Irish meat and veg. Cheap menu early evenings. Booking advisable. Open Mon–Sat 12.30–2pm & 6–10.30pm; no Sat lunch.

Shelbourne Hotel, St Stephen's Green (☎676 6471). Prime location and loads of cachet. You can have a drink in the lobby even if you're not staying, and the restaurant, now called *No. 27, The Green* (which, like the lobby, faces out on to St Stephen's Green) is excellent, though not cheap. Still, it's good value by international standards, with classily presented, French-inspired cuisine which includes vegetarian dishes. Open Mon–Sat 6.30–10.30pm, Sun till 10pm.

The Unicorn, off Merrion Row in an unpromising little courtyard that leads off to the right a few paces down from St Stephen's Green (☎676 2182). Plain, no-nonsense interior and an extensive Italian menu including pasta and pizzas as well as the standard meat-and-sauce dishes. With *Doheny and Nesbitt's* pub (see below), across Lower Baggot St, it forms a focus for the more intellectual side of Dublin life, frequented by journalists, economists, campaigners and musicians. Daily 12–3pm & 6–11pm.

Pubs and music

Pubs are an integral part of Dublin's social life and an essential part of any visit. Guidebooks are apt to write as if there's a great mystery about them, or as if they're somehow dangerous places where you shouldn't venture alone, and certainly not without a recommendation from this or that authority. Neither is true, and the charm of most of Dublin's older pubs derives from the fact that they're simple, no-nonsense places, the better ones unchanged for decades, where you can get a good pint of *Guinness* and the people are friendly. There are over 800 pubs and bars in the city, so what follows doesn't try to be anything like a comprehensive, or even a representative, guide. Instead it's a small – and very personal – selection of Dublin's traditional pubs and new drinking places, with some indication of where you're likely to find music and other entertainment.

The **music scene** is volatile, though, so if you're after something in particular – jazz, folk, traditional – the best place to check is yet again the listings magazine *In Dublin*. *Hot Press*, the national music paper, is another useful source of information. For traditional music, contact the traditional music society, *Comhaltas Ceoltóirí Éireann* (also known as *Cultúrlann*) at 32 Belgrave Square, Monkstown (☎280 0295). Their offices are, in any case, worth a visit almost any night for their programmes of traditional music and theatre.

Two general points of **etiquette**: pubs in Dublin tend to be fairly male preserves, but if you're a woman don't be put off – you're unlikely to be made to feel uncomfortable, even if you're alone. And many Dublin pubs have snugs, or small private rooms, which can be the cosiest places to drink if you're in a group. There's nothing exclusive about these – just go in and stake your claim if you find one empty – and drinks cost the same as in the main bar.

Pubs and bars

Café en Seine, 40 Dawson St. Cavernously lively and hip new café/bar with extraordinary Celtic/Art Nouveau murals. Good place to drop in for a cappuccino or espresso during the day.

Davy Byrne's, 21 Duke St, off Grafton St (☎677 5217). Here, in *Ulysses*, Leopold Bloom stopped to eat a gorgonzola sandwich and quaff a glass of burgundy; and here, on Bloomsday (16 June) every year, numerous pilgrims stop to do exactly the same thing. Now decked out in tasteful shades of lemon and grey, *Davy Byrne's* no longer looks exactly Joycean.

Doheny and Nesbitt, 5 Lower Baggot St. Archetypal Dublin pub – the tiny, atmospheric, smoke-filled room looks as if it has hardly changed since the beginning of the century. Always packed, cosy snugs. Upstairs is a slightly less hectic lounge if you can't stand the pace. Much frequented by *Irish Times* hacks.

Flannery's, 44 Temple Bar. Gathering place of the Temple Bar crowd; young, friendly and unhurried.

The Globe and Hogans, 11 South Great George's St. Meccas for the terminally hip, these are big, airy bars that share much the same clientele. *The Globe* is a café by day (see p.82). Close to *Avalon House*, one of Dublin's best budget hostels (see p.53).

The Irish Film Centre, 6 Eustace St, Temple Bar. This designer bar is one of *the* places to see and be seen. Open according to programme (also see p.84).

Kehoe's, 9 Anne St South, off Grafton St. Wonderful snugs if you want to curl up in comparative privacy to sip your pint.

The Long Hall, 51 South Great George's St. Victorian pub with an astonishing array of antiques on show.

McDaid's, 3 Harry St. A literary pub, this is where Brendan Behan used to drown his talent in *Guinness* – there's a photograph of him with a tiny typewriter wedged between two glasses of the black stuff, one full, one empty.

Mulligan's, 8 Poolbeg St. *Mulligan's* traditionally served the best *Guinness* in Dublin; many people now acknowledge that honour to have passed to Guinness's own visitor centre, but *Mulligan's* still has its partisans.

Neary's, 1 Chatham St. Announcing its presence with a pair of arms in flowing sleeves holding lighted glass orbs, inside *Neary's* is no less exalted in tone: plenty of bevelled glass and shiny wood, plus Liberty print curtains to demonstrate a sense of style to suit the stars from the *Gaiety Theatre*, opposite, who like to frequent it after shows.

The Oak, 81 Dame St. Tastefully decorated pub on the edge of Temple Bar; small, quiet and relaxed.

The Palace, 21 Fleet St. Wood-and-glass interior, crowded and friendly pub much loved by Dubliners.

Thomas Read's, 79 Dame St. Trendy new pub with good food at lunchtime and a good house in the evenings.

Ryan's, Parkgate St, across the river from Heuston Station. Another pub famous for its cosy, wood-lined snugs; considered the finest Victorian pub in Dublin.

Stag's Head, 1 Dame Court, a tiny turning off Dame St almost opposite the Central Bank. Hard to find – a mosaic set in the pavement on Dame St alerts you to the tiny alleyway it's located in – but worth it when you get there: inside it's all mahogany, stained glass and mirrors. Good pub lunches, too, and friendly atmosphere.

Toners Victorian Bar, 139 Lower Baggot St. Dark, cosy pub with a refreshingly plain interior. Snugs, with glazed partitions, for making and breaking confidences.

Music pubs and venues

An Béal Bocht, 58 Charlemont St (☎475 5614). Traditional location for traditional music; most nights. Also puts on traditional theatre in Irish on Wed nights.

Bad Bob's Backstage Bar, East Essex St, Temple Bar (☎677 5842). Still Dublin's central late-night music venue, known to one and all as the "Backside Bar". Traditional and contemporary music.

The Baggot Inn, 143 Lower Baggot St (☎676 1430). Ageing rock clientele congregates to hear rock music nightly. U2 were here in the early 1980s.

The Brazen Head, 20 Lower Bridge St (☎679 5156). Claims to be the oldest bar in the city – there's been an inn here since 1198, although the present building dates from the seventeenth century (a group of United Irishmen were arrested here during the 1798 rebellion). A recent refurbishment has apparently left the ancient strata of nicotine on the anaglypta totally untouched. Traditional music every night.

The Ferryman, 35 Sir John Rogerson Quay (☎671 7053). A walk along the South Quay, or a short #3 bus ride toward Ringsend. This is the place where serious musicians go.

Hughes's, 19 Chancery St, North Side ☎872 6540). Traditional music and set dancing nightly.

International Bar, 23 Wicklow St (☎677 9250). Very spacious, if smoky; a Dublin institution. Good music pub, mostly rock bands. Comedy club upstairs on Wed nights.

The Mean Fiddler, 26 Wexford St (☎475 8555). A seriously cool interior and a good line-up of live acts have made this newly opened venue a strong competitor with *Whelans* (see opposite), next door.

The Merchant, Lower Bridge St, opposite the *Brazen Head*. Traditional music most nights with impromptu sessions in between.

Mother Redcap's Tavern, Back Lane, off High St (☎453 8306). Traditional and country music – Ireland's other folk tradition – in an old shoe factory in one of the oldest parts of Dublin. A pint of *Guinness* here, fried fish and a poke of chips from *Leo Burdock's* famous fish-and-chip shop around the corner (see p.83), and your night's made. Big-name billing on Fri and Sat nights for a £6 cover charge.

The Norseman, 29 Essex St, Temple Bar (☎671 5135). Beloved of film-makers and artists, a crowded and smoky bar with live traditional music some evenings.

O'Donoghue's, 15 Merrion Row (☎676 2807). The place where the Dubliners began their career; very popular and packed. Get there for 9–9.30pm, when new bands perform nightly.

The Olympia, 74 Dame St, off Temple Bar (☎677 7744). When the evening performance ends in this tinselly ex-music hall on Fri & Sat nights, the theatre closes down for half an hour; at 11.30pm the doors open and the late-night music spot, *Midnight at the Olympia*, begins. As a music venue it's a strange place – you sit in plush theatre seats and dance in the aisles – but it's unbeatable for its line-up of both up-and-coming and established performers. Bar stays open until 2am.

Slattery's, 129 Capel St (☎672 7971). Dublin's best-known venue for traditional music, with set dancing and ballads as regular features; also rock and blues in upstairs bar.

Whelans, 25 Wexford St (☎478 0766). Very lively pub with bands and bar extensions most nights; an eclectic line-up of acts, sometimes Irish traditional or "world music".

Theatre and cinema

As seems fitting for a city with Dublin's rich literary past, **theatre** flourishes. The traditional diet of Irish classics at the "establishment" theatres is now spiced by experimental or fringe programmes at newer, smaller venues; tickets are cheap – averaging £7–8 – and drama is accessible, and popular.

Dublin has a large number of **cinemas** – almost all of them on and around O'Connell Street – showing mainstream films. All Dublin's cinemas operate an enlightened policy of cheap seats before 5pm (6.30pm in some cases), seven days a week. The peculiarities of the film distribution system mean that new movies are often released earlier in Ireland than in Britain. There are two art-houses cinemas, both showing a changing repertoire of film.

You'll find details of all theatre performances and cinema programmes in the fortnightly listings magazine, *In Dublin*.

Theatre

Abbey Theatre, Lower Abbey St, just off O'Connell St (☎878 7222). The grim concrete building housing the famous *Abbey Theatre* gives little away about its illustrious past (see p.75). On its rebuilding in 1952, however, Patrick Kavanagh was scathing, writing in his eponymous *Kavanagh's Weekly*: "The *Abbey Theatre* is the opposite of what it set out to be. The *Abbey Theatre* was never much good. The life it portrayed was not Irish, but a convention invented by Synge mainly." The theatre is still known for its productions of older Irish plays (by playwrights such as Boucicaut and Richard Brinsley Sheridan), but does encourage younger writers. One of the most acclaimed productions of the 1990s was Brian Friel's *Dancing at Lughnasa*. In addition to the main auditorium, the building houses the smaller *Peacock Theatre*, which sometimes has more experimental shows.

Andrews Lane Theatre, Andrews Lane (☎679 5720). Theatre and studio, just off Dame St in what appears to be the middle of a car park, concentrating on the latest Irish writing. One of Dublin's new performance spaces, under the same management as the remarkable *Gate Theatre* (see below).

Gaiety Theatre, South King St (☎677 1717). Dublin's oldest theatre stages a mix of musical comedy, revues, occasional opera, and, every now and then, something really worth seeing.

Gate Theatre, Cavendish Row, next to the Rotunda (☎874 4045 or ☎674 6042). Another of Dublin's literary institutions, it stages more modern Irish plays and can be lively and atmospheric.

New Eblana Theatre, in the basement of Busáras (☎679 8404). Tends to concentrate on slightly more "popular" billings.

Olympia Theatre, Dame St (☎677 8962 or ☎677 8147). Formerly *Dan Lowry's Music Hall*, and that's exactly how it looks: raffish, down-at-heel, with an air of faded, once tinselly glamour. It now puts on (no surprises) vaudeville, comedy, ballet and drama, sometimes packing in two completely different shows in one evening with a late-night music spot to round things off.

Project Arts Centre, East Sussex St, Temple Bar (☎671 2321). This is where you're most likely to find experimental or politically sensitive work. There's also a gallery space that runs temporary exhibitions, which are well worth checking out, and occasional late-night music sessions.

Cinemas

Irish Film Centre, 6 Eustace St, Temple Bar (☎679 5744). Art-house cinema with two screens and an excellent restaurant (see p.84), as well as a film-related bookshop and dance-club IFC nights on Fri & Sat (see below). Films include new, low-budget Irish work plus seasons of world, gay and children's cinema; a worthwhile survey of Irish film-making is shown every afternoon.

Light House Cinema, 107 Fleet St (☎873 0438). Tiny cinema with two screens showing art-house films; mostly continental European.

Mainstream cinemas include: **The Ambassador**, 1 Parnell Square (☎872 7000; 1 screen); **The Savoy**, O'Connell St Upper (☎874 6000; 5 screens); **Screen**, D'Olier St (☎671 4988; 3 screens); and **Virgin**, Parnell St (☎872 8400; 9 screens).

Clubs and discos

Clubs are by nature volatile, so you should check the latest *In Dublin* listings to see which club nights are still in operation. There are two distinct club scenes in Dublin. The first (and the one listed here) is an eclectic collection – including the new, much talked-about chic clubs – scattered around the city centre, many of which offer special interest and theme nights. Most are hard to get into – that's part of their cachet – and expensive at the weekends (also see "Gay Life" opposite).

The second, and distinctly less appealing, is based in and around Leeson Street, southeast of St Stephens's Green. The clubs here do, however, serve a purpose: a string of basement places busy after everything else has shut, these are the clubs to hit at two or three in the morning if you're really desperate to go on partying. Most have no entry fee but very expensive drinks – they're at their dubious best Thursday to Sunday from around 1am till dawn.

Blue Note Club, Bedford Lane, Temple Bar (☎671 9354). Acid jazz and rare grooves for the younger crowd that missed this music first time around.

Dazed, 13th floor above *McGraths*, O'Connell St (☎878 7505). Excellent Wed-night indie rock, ambient and hip-hop on two floors. Cheap beer.

Furnace, Aston Place, Aston Quay (☎671 0433). Gig venue and club run by the Union of Students in Ireland, but open to all.

Gaiety Theatre, South King St (☎677 1717). *Velure* – a mainly jazz, funk and soul night; Sat only.

IFC, 6 Eustace St, Temple Bar (☎679 17170). Theme nights include comedy, readings and multimedia experiences in *Cybernia* on Sun night.

The Kitchen, *The Clarence Hotel*, 6–8 Wellington Quay, Temple Bar (☎677 6178). With a moated dance floor, the U2-inspired club is a good mix of serious and more relaxed clubbers. Open all week.

Lillie's Bordello, Adam Court, Grafton St (☎679 9204). This was the coolest place in town but has now become a victim of its own exclusivity. Older clubbers; meeting place for the social climbers of Dublin. Tiny dance floor.

Major Tom's, South King's St (☎478 3266). Late-night bar and diner, loud, with rock-and-roll memorabilia.

POD, 35 Harcourt St (☎478 0166). The music played in this tunnel-like interior beneath the arches of Harcourt St station is acoustically damaging, but this is *the* club to check out.

Ri-Ra, *Central Hotel*, 1–5 Exchequer St (☎677 4835). One of the coolest: good mix of music styles and clientele in comfortable surroundings.

River Club at the *Ha'penny Theatre*, Merchants Hall, Temple Bar (☎677 2382). Relaxed atmosphere in elegant building.

The System, 21 South Ann St (☎677 4402). Dublin's latest venue for happy house and techno.

The Temple of Sound, Ormonde Quay (☎872 1811). Young crowd seriously into dancing.

Gay life

Although Ireland's celebrated gays include Oscar Wilde, Somerville and Ross, Eva Gore-Booth and Brendan Behan, prejudice remains considerable. In 1988 the European Court of Human Rights decreed that Ireland's anti-gay law contravened the European Convention on Human Rights, and in 1990 the law was repealed and the age of consent lowered to seventeen. The result, half a decade on, is that, despite the hegemony of the Catholic Church, gay voices are increasingly making themselves heard in public debate, and Dublin now has a visible gay scene. Ring Gay Switchboard Dublin (daily 8–10pm, except Sat 3.30–6pm; ☎872 1055) or Lesbian Line (Thurs 7–9pm; ☎661 3777) for more details, or check the freebie *Gay Community News* – which you can pick up at the Temple Bar information centre or *Books Upstairs* – for what's on.

Gay and mixed meeting places include *Bewley's* cafés, *Marks Bros* and the *Well Fed Café* (see pp.82–83). A lot of mainstream venues have themed nights and gay events, and many of the city-centre pubs have a very mixed clientele. More specifically gay places include:

The George Bar and Bistro, 89 South Great George's St (☎478 2983). Three bars in total: the *Loft* disco, a trendy bar with music and a quiet bar. Wed–Sun there's also *The Block*, a lively and vibrant club; open until 2.30am.

Hogans (*The Globe and Hogans;* see p.86), 11 South Great George's St. Busy and stylish mixed crowd.

Shaft, 22 Ely Place. Free except on Sat, with many special events. Almost exclusively gay club.

Strictly Handbag, at *The Kitchen*, *The Clarence Hotel*, 6–8 Wellington Quay (☎677 6178). Mon night is the very popular gay/mixed night.

Shopping

Around Grafton Street and O'Connell Street, the business of buying and selling rates second only to pub life for vigour, humour and sheer panache. Although many of the store chains – *Next, Marks & Spencers, Waterstones* – will be familiar to British visitors, the importance of seeing and being seen, and above all of conversation, makes shopping a spectator and participant sport of a high order. The **O'Connell Street** area represents the more ordinary, high-street end of the market, with cut-price shops, chain stores, and a boisterous street market concentrated on nearby Henry Street. *Clery's*, the august department store, and *Eason's* bookstore are two of the highlights; the *Ilac* centre, behind Moore Street, is probably the nadir.

South of the river are the smarter outlets and the tourist shops, as well as the kaleidoscopic and rapidly changing range of "alternative" boutiques that characterizes the fashionable **Temple Bar** area (the place to go for club gear and street fashions). Pedestrianized **Grafton Street** contains Dublin's swankiest department store, *Brown Thomas*. Just off Grafton St, the 200-year-old *Powerscourt Town House* has been converted into a covered mall, with plenty of expensive clothes shops.

As a visitor, you'll find it difficult to escape the range of shops touting "typically" **Irish goods** aimed at tourists, mainly wool, ceramics and crystal. You may well come away with the impression that these are universally depressing and overpriced, but there are some exceptions, and you can occasionally pick up some real bargains.

Antiques

Sullivan Antiques, 43 Francis Street in The Liberties, is one of the best established antique shops specializing in *objet d'art* and furniture. Shops in Molesworth Street – including *Alexander Antiques* at no. 16, which has a wide range of antique clocks, pictures and period furniture – South Anne Street and Kildare Street are all worth a browse.

Bookstores

General bookstores include *Eason's*, 40–42 Lower O'Connell Street (beside the GPO); *Waterstones* at 7 Dawson Street; and *Hodges Figgis,* nearby at 56–58 Dawson Street, which has a particularly extensive stock of **Irish books**, a good remainder bookshop downstairs and a pleasant café on the first floor. *Books Upstairs*, 36 College Green (just outside the gates of Trinity College), is still Dublin's major alternative bookshop and has a good selection including feminist and gay fiction, women's studies, poetry and cinema, and magazines and reviews. For **second-hand** books try *Fred Hanna's*, 29 Nassau Street; *Greenes*, 16 Clare Street, an academic topsy-turvy second-hand book-shop that can be worth a look; and *The Winding Stair*, 40 Ormond Quay, which is an excellent and pleasantly shabby second-hand bookstore with an unhurried café where you can peruse your finds, before or after purchase.

Clothes

Brown Thomas, Grafton Street, offers smart **designer** wear from Irish labels such as Paul Costelloe, Louise Kennedy and John Rocha; while the *Irish Fashion Design Centre* (*Powerscourt Town House*), Clarendon Street, has a changing range of stalls by young designers who work mainly in natural materials such as linen, silk and wool. For **second-hand** clothes, *Flip* at 4 Fownes Street specializes in Americana, jackets, shirts and jeans; at *Eager Beaver*, The Crown Alley, you can find a wider range of good-quality used clothing. You could also try the *George's St Market Arcade*, off South Great George's Street, which has a range of stalls selling second-hand clothing (plus jewel-lery and records).

Irish goods

Kilkenny Design Centre, 6 Nassau Street, originally set up by the government to promote good design, is now privately run and stocks high-quality Irish goods: clothes (mainly linen and knitware), crystal and ceramics, which come significantly reduced in price at sale-time. *The Blarney Woollen Mills,* College Park House, Nassau Street, offers a more traditional range of Irish crystal and china, plus the obligatory woolly pullovers and linen blouses; again, some bargains if you are prepared to sift. *House of Ireland*, also in Nassau Street, has fancy Irish crystal ranging from Belleek to Waterford, as well as the sweetly sentimental Lladro ceramics. At 41 Lower Ormond Quay, *The Dublin Woollen Company* sells a huge range of cut-price Irish knitwear, tweeds and lace. *Weir and Sons*, 96 Grafton Street, has antique silver and jewellery plus a good selection of Irish crystal. If you are keen on **genealogy**, *Clans of Ireland*, 2 Kildare Street, is able to trace the location and significance of most Irish family names.

Music

Claddagh Records, 2 Cecilia Street, Temple Bar, stocks a good range of **traditional** Irish and "world music". Also in Temple Bar, *Comet Records*, 5 Cope Street, sells new indie CDs and **second-hand** records, and dispenses useful information on current bands and where to see them; *Freebird*, 1 Eden Quay, specializes in second-hand indie music. Both *HMV*, 65 Grafton Street, and *Virgin Megastore*, 14 Aston Quay, offer main-stream sounds.

Listings

Airlines *Aer Lingus,* 41 Upper O'Connell St & 42 Grafton St (☎844 4777); *British Airways,* 60 Dawson St (☎1 800 626742); *British Midland,* Merrion Centre (☎283 8833; Dublin Airport ☎677 4422); *Ryanair,* 3 Dawson St (☎677 4422).

Banks Banking hours are Mon–Fri 10am–4pm, except Thurs when they stay open until 5pm. Main high-street banks are the *Allied Irish* and *Bank of Ireland*; branches throughout the city centre.

Car rental *Budget,* 29 Lower Abbey St (☎878 7814 or ☎874 7816); *Dan Dooley Rent-a-Car,* 5 Lyon House, Cathal Brugha St (☎872 0777); *Kenning Car Hire,* 42 Westland Row (☎677 2723); *Thrifty Rent-a-Car,* 14 Duke St (☎679 9420); plus all the usual desks at the airport.

Counselling *Samaritans,* 112 Marlborough St (☎872 7700); *Well Woman's Centre,* 73 Lower Leeson St (☎661 0083); *Rape Crisis Centre,* 70 Lower Leeson St (☎661 4564 or ☎661 4911).

Departures Buses to the **airport** set off from Eden Quay (not all of them go into the airport compound, so check with the driver), or there's a service that goes round all the major hotels collecting airport passengers (check times with *Dublin Bus* – ☎873 4222). For the ferries, take the DART service to Dún Laoghaire; or a bus to Dublin Port from Eden Quay. Buses to **all parts of the country** (*Bus Éireann*) leave from Busáras or the streets immediately around (Eden Quay/Abbey St/Talbot St); enquiries all handled at the information office located at 59 Upper O'Connell St, opposite the main tourist information office (Mon–Fri 9am–5pm, Sat 9am–1pm; ☎836 6111). Officially approved private buses are generally cheaper: ask to see the bus information file at the tourist office or go to *Funtrek,* 32 Bachelor's Walk by O'Connell Bridge (☎873 3633 or ☎873 3244). Unofficial buses may be cheaper still; they leave from various points around the city, especially on Fri & Sun evenings. Check the *Evening Herald* for advertisements – weekend buses generally need advance booking. **Trains** to the limited parts of Ireland served by the national train system leave from Heuston Station (still sometimes known by its old name of Kingsbridge) on the South Side (Cork, Waterford, Limerick, Killarney, Tralee, Athlone, Galway, Westport, Ballina, Claremorris) or Connolly Station (aka Amiens St Station) on the North Side (Belfast, Derry, Portadown, Dundalk, Sligo, Arklow, Wexford, Rosslare Harbour). Mainline commuter trains serving coastal towns north and south of Dublin call at Connolly, Tara St and Pearse St stations. For train information call ☎836 6222.

Embassies *Australia,* Fitzwilton House, Wilton Terrace (☎676 1517); *Britain,* 31–33 Merrion Rd (☎269 5211); *Canada,* 65 St Stephen's Green (☎478 1988); *Denmark,* 121 St Stephen's Green (☎475 6404); *France,* 36 Ailesbury Rd (☎269 4777); *Netherlands,* 160 Merrion Rd (☎269 3444); *Norway,* 34 Molesworth St (☎662 1800); *Sweden,* Sun Alliance House, Dawson St (☎671 5822); *United States,* 42 Elgin Rd, Ballsbridge (☎668 8777).

Exchange *Thomas Cook,* 118 Grafton St, give a fair rate; although the best exchange rates are given by banks (see above).

Ferry companies *Irish Ferries,* 16 Westmoreland St (☎661 0511); *Stena Sealink,* 15 Westmoreland St (☎280 8844).

Gaelic football All the major games of the season are played at Croke Park (☎831 2099). The season runs from mid-February, culminating in the All Ireland finals on the third Sun in September. Prices reflect the status of the match, with stand tickets ranging from £12 to £16 for semi-finals and £19 to £30 for finals (terrraces £7 to £10). For more on gaelic football see "Spectator sports" in *Basics.*

Gay Switchboard *National Gay and Lesbian Federation* (☎871 0939). For gay health information try *Gay Health Action* (☎671 0895). Also see "Gay life" p.89.

Horse racing You shouldn't leave Dublin without experiencing Irish horseracing (and betting). Many of the bigger races are run out in County Kildare (see p.115), but check for more local events at Leopardstown (☎289 3994); its major jump-race festival is held on the four days after Christmas, while its most important flat races are the Heinz 57 Phoenix Stakes (mid-Aug) and the Guinness Champion Stakes (mid-Sept). *Dublin Bus* (see above for details) run a special service to Leopardstown on race days. Tickets range from £6 to £8, with an extra £3 to £5 for admission to the enclosure.

Hospitals South Side: *Meath Hospital,* Heytesbury St (☎453 655); North Side: *Mater Misericordiae Hospital,* Eccles St (☎830 1122).

Hurling As with gaelic football (see above for ticket prices) the important games are played at Croke Park; the season which begins in early summer finishes with the All Ireland final on the first Sat in September. For more on hurling see "Spectator sports" in *Basics.*

Laundry *Exel Launderette*, 12 Main St, Donnybrook (☎269 7172); *Nova Launderette*, 2 Belvedere St, just off Dorset St; *Powder Launderette*, 42a South Richmond St (☎478 2655); *Shirley's*, 141 Rathmines Rd (☎962 2228).

Left luggage There are left luggage offices at Busáras (Mon–Sat 8am–8pm, Sun 10am–6pm), Heuston Station (Mon–Sat 7.15am–8.35pm, Sun 8am–3pm & 5–9pm) and Connolly Station (Mon–Sat 7.40am–9.30pm, Sun 9.15am–1pm & 5–9pm).

Legal advice *Free Legal Advice Centre*, administration office, 49 South William St (☎679 4239).

Pharmacy *O'Connell's*, 55 Lower O'Connell St (☎873 0427), is open till 10pm daily.

Phones At least half of Dublin's public phones now operate on CallCards, available from newsagents, garages etc. International pay phones are available in the GPO.

Police The main metropolitan Garda station is in Harcourt St, just off St Stephen's Green (☎873 2222). In an emergency dial ☎999.

Post office *General Post Office*, O'Connell St (☎705 7000). Open Mon–Sat 8am–8pm, Sun 10.30am–6.30pm.

Rugby The big games – the Five Nations Championship matches held between January and March – are played at the Lansdowne Road Stadium in Ballsbridge (☎668 9300); stand tickets are from £16 to £25, for the terraces £10.

Travel agents *USIT*, 19–21 Aston Quay, O'Connell Bridge (☎679 8833), are experts in student/youth travel; *Thomas Cook*, 118 Grafton St (☎677 1721), offers good general services; *CIE Tours*, 35 Lower Abbey St (☎830 0777), is the biggest internal tour operator, if you want a bus trip around Ireland.

The outskirts

Even without going as far as the Wicklow Mountains, whose unlikely, conical outlines you encounter every time you look to the south, there are a number of rewarding **trips beyond the city centre** which are well worth making time for. The best of these are out along Dublin Bay, using the frequent DART services. These trains will take you southwards to **Sandycove** – a mile beyond **Dún Laoghaire** – and the James Joyce Tower; to the pretty village of **Dalkey**, with its incongruously continental atmosphere; and to the magnificent views across Dublin Bay between Dalkey and **Killiney**. Although the journey north on the DART is nothing like as spectacular as the southward trip – once the industrial city ends, it gives way to suburbia, and it's only when you get as far as **Sutton** (a much sought-after address) that you even see the sea – it takes you to the popular seaside resort of **Howth** (the DART terminus at the northern end of Dublin Bay), with its rugged hill and long views south. Further out, **Malahide** and its castle and the charming villages of **Donabate** and **Skerries** are accessible both by commuter train and bus. For the worthwhile stops closer in to the city – **Glasnevin**, **Marino** and **Dollymount Strand** – it's easier to take the bus.

The outskirts of Dublin have now become a retreat for a host of film, sport and pop stars. A trip to Killiney, in particular, will transport you to the Irish equivalent of Beverly Hills. Pop stars George Michael, Jim Kerr, Lisa Stansfield, and racing car driver Damon Hill live alongside indigenous talents such as singers Bono and Chris De Burgh, writers Maeve Binchy and Hugh Leonard, and novelist and film director Neil Jordan.

Dún Laoghaire and Sandycove

Taking the DART south out of Dublin, you very quickly have the feeling that you're leaving the grime of the city far behind. Almost immediately, the track starts to run along the coast, past **Booterstown Marsh**, a designated bird sanctuary protected against a proposed motorway development, and out to **DÚN LAOGHAIRE**, where the *Stena Sealink* car ferries come in from Britain. At this distance, Dún Laoghaire manages to retain some of its flavour as a superior kind of Victorian resort, full of wide tree-lined avenues, promenades and wedding-cake architecture. Its port is still the base for Irish lightships and the biggest Irish centre for yachting (call the National Sailing School for details; ☎280 6654). This aspect of its history is chronicled in the **National Maritime Museum**, Haigh Terrace (☎280 0969), housed in the Mariners' church and containing, among other things, a longboat sent by the French in support of the United Irishmen, two years before the 1798 rebellion.

A mile south of Dún Laoghaire, **SANDYCOVE**'s Martello Tower (see box above) is its main claim to fame: James Joyce spent some time here with his friend Oliver St John Gogarty, whom he later transformed into Buck Mulligan in *Ulysses*. Although for some reason not signposted from the station, it's not hard to find. Turn right down the street into what appears to be the centre of this sleepy suburb, then left at the lights for the seafront. On your right you'll see the tower, next to an extraordinary bit of 1930s modern seaside building – "Geragh", a house built for his family by the late Michael Scott, architect of Busáras and some of the small, and still vanishing, number of Dublin's other modernist buildings.

On the seaward side of the tower is the **Forty Foot Pool** (named not for its size but because the 40th Regiment of Foot of the British army used to be stationed in a battery above it), for many years a men-only swimming hole where nude bathing was the rule. Now that women are allowed – although you seldom see them – it's strictly "togs required – by order", as the notice says. The hardier swimmers use this rocky, natural swimming pool all year round. Sandycove is also good for canoeing, wind-surfing and water-skiing. For all watersports, check *Oceantec*, 10–11 Marine Terrace (☎280 1083), a diving equipment shop that will also arrange local diving.

Practicalities

Dún Laoghaire is a compact town, and everything you need is in easy walking distance. Although probably not the first place you'd choose to base yourself, it is, of course, handy for the ferry terminal, has a certain solidly Victorian charm, and the swift train connection (takes just 20 minutes) makes it perfectly possible to explore central Dublin from here. The DART station is on Crofton Road, not far from the ferry terminal, and opposite the **tourist information** office (☎280 6984) on St Michael's Wharf. Of the

places to stay, top of the range and reflecting Dún Loaghaire's slightly faded identity as a seaside resort is the *Royal Marine Hotel*, Royal Marine Road (☎284 1600, fax ☎280 1089; ⑧). For B&B you could try Mrs Gorby's *Innisfree*, 31 Northumberland Avenue, a couple of minutes walk from the seafront (☎280 5598; ④), where the rooms are large and all with private bathrooms; or, not far away to the southeast of town, Mrs Murphy's comfortable *Rosmeen House*, 13 Rosmeen Gardens (☎280 7613; ④). In Sandycove, the *Sandycove Guesthouse*, 6 Newtownsmith Seafront (☎284 1600; ⑤), is a relatively luxurious option. A fairly rough-and-tumble **independent hostel**, *The Old School House*, Eblana Avenue (*IHH*; ☎280 8777, fax ☎284 2266; ②), is open all year and has two-, four- and five-bedded rooms, a laundry, a coffee shop, and no curfew.

There's a healthy selection of **restaurants** to choose from, mostly on or just off the main thoroughfare, George's Street, running parallel to the seafront. *La Pizza* on George's Street or the *Ritz Café* (traditional fish and chips) on nearby Patrick Street make good day-time places. In the evening, *Krishna Indian Restaurant* on the first floor of 47 George's Street (☎284 4604) has a good reputation. If you want to go more upmarket, *Restaurant na Mara*, 1 Harbour Road (☎280 6767), offers premier seafood with prices to match, or try the similarly expensive *La Vie en Rose* (☎280 9870) on Marine Parade, between Dún Laoghaire and Sandycove, which serves old-fashioned French cuisine to a high standard.

Dalkey and Killiney

Further south along the coast lies the little town of **DALKEY**. Immortalized, if that's the word, in Flann O'Brien's satirical *The Dalkey Archive*, Dalkey (pronounced *Dawkey*) is nowadays a charming little seaside town, and nothing much besides. Its origins as a walled medieval settlement and important landing place for travellers from England are evident, though, especially in the massive Archibold's Castle which dominates the main street. There are narrow lanes with fine, bourgeois residences and, back in the main street, a really excellent new and second-hand bookshop, with plenty of recent review copies. John Dowland, the melancholy Elizabethan lutenist and composer, may have been born here, and George Bernard Shaw certainly lived at Torca Cottage on Dalkey Hill: he later claimed to be "a product of Dalkey's outlook". When the sun is shining, Dalkey has an almost Mediterranean holiday atmosphere, and it's thoroughly pleasant just to stroll about and drink it all in.

In the summer you can rent a boat to take you out to Dalkey Island, where you'll find a bird sanctuary, another in the series of Martello towers that were built to defend the coast from Napoleonic attack, and the ruins of the early Irish St Begnet's Church. A curious ritual involving the "King of Dalkey", complete with crown and sword, is still occasionally enacted here: originating in the eighteenth century, it started out as a student joke, but became increasingly political until it was stamped out by Lord Clare in 1797. If you are here around lunchtime, *Finnegans*, Sorrento Road (☎285 8505), has a great seafood menu (12–3pm), freshly caught from nearby Coliemore Harbour, served in a beautiful mahogany lounge bar. If you miss lunch, you can dine on the excellent *Guinness*.

Dublin Bay, views and fishing

From Dalkey Hill a ridge leads to the public park laid out atop **KILLINEY HILL** (pronounced *Kill-eye-nee*), with terrific views of Dublin Bay and the Wicklow Mountains. The stretch south from Dalkey Head is as beautiful a piece of scenery as you'll come across anywhere. As good a way as any to see it is from the DART line (if you walk, you're restricted to the road until you round Sorrento Point, so you're probably better off taking the train to Killiney): as you come out of Dalkey hilltop tunnel you're overwhelmed by the sweep of the bay, the blue sea on one side and on the other the weird bulk of the Sugarloaf mountain.

The entire coastline from Dún Laoghaire to Bray is good for **fishing**. Off Dalkey Island the dominant catches are conger, tope, pollock, skate and coalfish; further out, on the Burford and Kish banks, turbot, brill, dab and plaice are common. Fishing from the rocks and piers at Dún Laoghaire is free, and you can rent boats at Bullock and Coliemore harbours.

Glasnevin, Marino and Dollymount Strand

The suburb of **GLASNEVIN**, a couple of miles north of O'Connell Street (take bus #13 or #19, #19A, or from Abbey St Middle #34 or #34A), has two attractions to recommend it. The **National Botanic Gardens** (March–Oct Mon–Sat 9am–6pm, Sun 11am–6pm; Nov–Feb 10am–4.30pm, Sun 11am–4.30pm), founded in 1795, is a quiet open space with a couple of large greenhouses dating from the mid-nineteenth century – their designer, Richard Turner, also constructed the glasshouse at Belfast's Botanic Gardens and the magnificent Palm House at Kew Gardens in London. Ireland's mild climate makes it an excellent place for growing exotic species – witness all those palm trees you see in front gardens along the seafront – and the Botanic Gardens were the first place in the world to raise orchids from seed, in 1844, and the first place in Europe to grow pampas grass and the giant lily successfully.

Close by is **Prospect Cemetery**, started as a burial place for Roman Catholics in 1832, and a jungle of patriotic iconography – shamrocks, high crosses, harps – still eerily surveyed by the watch-towers in the walls, from which sentries would endeavour to deter body-snatchers in the nineteenth century. The Prospect's famous dead include: the politicians Daniel O'Connell (see p.307), who died in 1847 but whose body was brought here in 1869; Charles Stewart Parnell (see p.111); Sir Roger Casement, who was executed as a traitor by the British government in 1916; the independence fighter Michael Collins; and the poet Gerard Manley Hopkins.

Marino

MARINO, just off the Malahide Road three miles north of the city centre (#20A or #24 bus from Eden Quay), is the home of the eighteenth-century Casino, one of the most delightful pieces of Neoclassical lightheartedness you could hope to see anywhere. The bus will let you off next to some playing fields, from where the Casino, exuberantly decorated with urns and swags of carved drapery, is clearly visible to the left.

Needless to say, the **Casino** (mid-June to Sept daily 9.30am–6.30pm; Oct daily 10am–5pm; Nov & May to mid-June Sun & Wed only 12–6pm; closed Dec–April; last admission 45 minutes before closing; £2; Heritage Card) has nothing to do with gambling. Commissioned by Lord Charlemont (whose town house in Parnell Square is now the home of the Municipal Art Gallery), it was designed in the 1750s by Sir William Chambers, the leading Neoclassical architect of the day, to accompany a villa which would in turn house some of the priceless works of art he had brought home from his grand tour of Europe. Marino House – the building of which spared no expense, and is said to have crippled Lord Charlemont's estate – was demolished long ago, but the Casino, restored in 1984, survives in perfect condition, crowded with witty and unlikely architectural features: the urns, for example, conceal chimneys.

As you go back into town, try to sit upstairs on the left-hand side of the bus. As it turns from the Malahide Road into Fairview, you can see Marino Crescent, an elegant row of Georgian town houses, once nicknamed "Ffolliot's revenge" after a painter who built the crescent out of spite to block the view from Marino House to the sea. Ffolliot's final twist of the knife in the flesh of the aesthetic Lord Charlemont was to make the backs of the houses, which faced Marino House, an unsightly jumble of chimneys, ill-placed windows and sheds.

Dollymount Strand

Immediately north of Dublin Harbour, **DOLLYMOUNT STRAND**, or Bull Island (bus #30 will take you out here, up the Clontarf Road), is one of the seaside areas most readily accessible to Dubliners. Designated, like Booterstown Marsh (in the south bay), a UNESCO Biosphere Reserve, Dollymount Strand is a spit of low sand dunes linked to the shore by a turn-of-the-century wooden bridge. Apart from holidaying Dubliners, it's host to thousands of overwintering wildfowl and wading birds and provides a stopping-off point for Arctic migrants. Birds are not the only interesting wildlife of Dollymount Strand: just a couple of miles from the centre of Dublin, there are foxes, shrews, badgers and rabbits, as well as a wide range of grass and plant species. You can find out more at the new **interpretative centre**, where the causeway road meets the island.

Howth

HOWTH (the name derives from the Danish *hoved*, or "head", and is pronounced to rhyme with both) lies at the northernmost point of both Dublin Bay and the DART line. Arriving in Howth, turn right out of the DART station for the castle, left for the village, abbey and cliff walks. You can also get here on the #31 bus, which passes not far from Marino on its way out.

Howth Head is a natural vantage point giving views right across Dublin Bay to the Wicklow Mountains and at times, so they claim, even as far as the distant Mountains of Mourne in the north and those of Wales across the Irish Sea. Not surprisingly, it has been a strategic military point for centuries, and its history involves a long line of fearful incumbents on the lookout for raiders. The legendary copper-mining Parthalons and Firbolg were the first to come, later conquered by the Gaelic chieftain Criomthain, whose grave is reputedly marked by a cairn on the summit. The Gaels, in turn, were ousted by the Vikings in the eighth century, and they were overthrown by the technologically and strategically superior Normans, led by Sir Almeric Tristram. His descendants, bearing the surname St Lawrence, continue to live at Howth Castle today.

Howth is a popular day-trip destination for Dubliners, and it has the happy and bracing air of a seaside resort, even off-season. There's a **harbour** on the north side, dating from the days when it, rather than Dún Laoghaire, was the main packet station for Dublin. At the jetty at the end of the West Pier you can see the footprint of King George IV, who landed here in 1821 instead of at Dún Laoghaire (which was expecting to rename itself Kingstown in honour of the event; he made up for it later by going home that way). It was from the same jetty, in July 1914, that the Irish Volunteers succeeded in landing 900 rifles and 25,000 rounds of ammunition from Erskine Childers's yacht *Asgard*, which you can see at Kilmainham Gaol. The harbour, full of working boats, is nowadays sited alongside a marina crowded with less practical craft. You can fish from the harbour pier; and, if you're in Howth on a Thursday evening, it's worth staying to see the spectacle when the herring boats come in. *Michael Wright*, on the quay, sells freshly caught fish and seafood from his shop all week.

Opposite the harbour, the rock-encrusted island is **Ireland's Eye**. A bird sanctuary, this uninhabited expanse of scrub grass and ferns sports yet another Martello tower and the ruins of a sixth-century monastic church, St Nessan's. In summer, you can cross by boat (*Frank Doyle & Sons*; ☎831 4200; return trip £3) to explore the island.

Much of the interior of Howth Head is built up, but a **footpath** runs all the way round the coast. There are impressive cliffs and amazing views – south past the mouth of the Liffey to the Wicklow Mountains and beyond, north to the flatlands of the Boyne. To get to the cliffs, either carry straight on along the shore road, or take the #31B bus up to the summit and cut down from there.

Howth village itself is a slow, suburban place full of steep streets and sudden views. Its one monument, on a quiet site overlooking Ireland's Eye, is the ruined **Howth**

Abbey, the first church founded by Sigtrygg, Norse king of Dublin, in 1042. In one of the later phases of a chequered history, it was used by smugglers for storing contraband. The abbey is kept locked, but you can get the keys from Mrs O'Rourke at 13 Church Street, opposite: inside you'll see the fifteenth-century tomb of Christopher St Lawrence and his wife. Just below the abbey is the *Abbey Tavern*: bare, stone-walled, with stark wood furniture, turf fires and gas lighting. The air of authenticity can seem overdone, but it's worth visiting, as long as you don't mind the tourist bus-trip approach to Irish wit and music (see below for details of the restaurant).

To get to **Howth Castle**, backtrack a few hundred yards along the road to Dublin and turn left. The castle itself isn't open to the public, but you pass it on the way to the unlovely and expensive *Deer Park Hotel*, and there's a small **transport museum** (daily 2–6pm; ☎847 5623 to check). It's an impressive building, even from the outside – a true, battlemented castle, partly ruined, partly inhabited – and one that architects from Francis Bindon to Edwin Lutyens have had a hand in restoring. The gardens are famous for their azaleas and rhododendrons in May and June.

Practicalities

Since it's served by the DART (the station is on the north side of town near the harbour), Howth can make a good **place to stay** if you want to spend your evenings recovering from the excitements of the teeming capital; the *St Lawrence Hotel*, overlooking the harbour in Harbour Road (☎832 2643, fax ☎839 0346; ⑤), will keep you in the midst of what action Howth has. For B&B, Mrs Margaret Campbell's *Highfield* (☎832 3936; ③), on the Thormanby Road, makes a secluded choice, or try Mrs Hobbs's *Hazelwood* (☎839 1391; ③), in the Thormanby Woods estate off Thormanby Road. The *Abbey Tavern* **restaurant** specializes in fish (best to book; ☎839 0307), and music in the evenings from around 9pm, for which there's a £3 cover charge. The other good eating place, if you've money to burn, is the excellent *King Sitric's Tavern*, East Pier (☎633 5235) again worth booking. For a less expensive, but still luxurious, alternative, try *Adrian's*, at 8 Abbey Street (☎839 1696), serving food that manages to be both sophisticated and hearty in friendly, elegant surroundings, while making the most of Howth's abundant fresh fish.

Malahide

The easiest way to get to **MALAHIDE** from the centre of town is to take the suburban train service from Connolly Station (you can also take the #42 bus from Talbot St or the #47 bus from Marino Casino). Either way, **Malahide Castle** makes for a enjoyable day out (April–Oct Mon–Fri 10am–5pm, Sat 11am–6pm, Sun 11.30am–6pm; Nov–March Mon–Fri 10am–5pm, Sat & Sun 2–6pm; park open daily June 10am–9pm, July–Aug 10am–8pm, Oct 10am–7pm, Nov–Jan 10am–5pm, Feb–March 10am–6pm; adults £2.50; recorded guided tour available). When the last Lord Talbot died in 1973, his family home was taken over by the state. Much of the grounds has since been given over to playing fields but, unpromising as these look, the castle itself is terrific.

Dating in parts from 1174, when a marauding Norman, Richard Talbot, seized the lands and made it his fortress, the castle has been added to haphazardly over the ensuing centuries to make it look just how you think a castle ought to: turrets, Gothic windows, battlements and all. As well as being satisfyingly picturesque, what's fascinating about Malahide Castle is that you can follow its progress from a simple defensive tower – the first room you see inside, with amazing black carved panelling, is within the original square tower – to the addition of embellishments such as battlemented walls and turrets and, later still, its transformation into a country house, all fortifications now strictly decorative, with a mock-Gothic entrance.

Inside, a remarkably successful attempt has been made to show the best Irish furniture and pictures in good period settings: much of what you see is on loan from the National Portrait Gallery of Ireland. In case you're in need of refreshment, there's also an excellent tea room. It's indicative of the complex history of the Anglo-Irish that the rich and powerful Anglo-Norman Talbot family didn't actually turn Protestant until the eighteenth century. The castle even passed out of the hands of the family for ten years during the Cromwellian wars, but they managed to get it back. In the dining room is a large picture of the Battle of the Boyne; as Catholics, the Talbots fought not for Prince William but on the losing side. It's said that of the fourteen members of the family who sat down to breakfast in the dining room before setting out to fight, not one returned alive. For miniature-train buffs, Malahide also has the **Fry Model Railway**, a working O-gauge layout (same hours as castle; closed 1–2pm; £2.10; ☎845 2858).

Malahide village, which must once have been little more than a crossroads at the gates of the castle, has long since outgrown its estate village status. It's a delight, one of those places where there's nothing much to write about, but which for some reason is really pleasant to be in: just a few grandish houses, some more modest colour-washed ones, the most spick-and-span train station you've ever seen and quiet streets sloping gently down to the golden strand and wild sea beyond. In fact, with its easy train connections with Dublin, Malahide makes a possible, stress-reduced, base for exploring the capital.

Practicalities
There's a **tourist information office** (Mon–Fri 10am–1pm, 2–5pm; ☎845 0490) in the smart new marina development. If you want **to stay**, top choice is the *Grand Hotel* (☎845 0000, fax ☎845 0987; ⑦), with cheaper options including the *Grove Hotel* (☎845 2208; ⑥) and the many B&Bs that cluster around the Coast Road – try Mrs Noreen Handley's *Aishling* at 59 Biscayne (☎845 2292; ④). Malahide has a good range of **restaurants**, from ethnic to pizza parlour – and the excellent *Costa Café* in New Street for daytime eating – plus a few more special places, some of which offer reduced prices for early diners. *Roche's Bistro* (☎845 2777), a couple of doors up from the *Costa Café*, offers elegant food with some startling juxtapositions of flavours; *Bon Appetit* (☎845 0314), tucked away in St James Terrace, close to the seafront, has a more standard menu rich in seafood, and the more laid-back *Old Street Wine Bar* (☎845 1882) is a relaxed, pub-like place to hang out in over long lunches or dinners – excellent food with no shortage of genuine choice for vegetarians. **Yachting** culture is unavoidable in Malahide; if you find the lure of the sea irresistible, ring the marina office (☎845 4129) or *Fingal Maritime* (☎845 1979).

Donabate and Skerries

A stop northward from Malahide on the commuter train (or the #33 bus from Dublin) is **DONABATE**, another trim town, worth visiting for **Newbridge House** (April–Oct Tues–Fri 10am–5pm, Sat 11am–7pm, Sun 2–6pm; closed 1–2pm; Nov–March Sat & Sun 2–5pm; £2.25; ☎843 6534), signposted from the station, at the end of a twenty-minute ramble through woodlands, or a car journey from the main road. Built in 1737 for the Cobbe family, who came to Ireland in 1717 and rose rapidly through the Church of Ireland, it's a solid Georgian mansion whose main draw is the extraordinary **Museum of Curiosities**, a rare and marvellous family museum, started in 1790 and almost intact. Decorated with elegant representations of the "labours of China", it includes everything from exotic weapons and fish to an African chief's umbrella and the mummified ear of an Egyptian bull. The house remained unelectrified until the 1960s, when it was wired up for the filming of *The Spy Who Came in from the Cold*, which starred Richard Burton and Clare Bloom. There's a cosy **coffee shop** with soup and cakes, and the courtyards have been converted into a traditional farm with wandering goats and publicity-shy pigs.

SKERRIES, on the coast a few miles further north on the rail line, is close enough to Dublin to have a prosperous suburban hinterland; but the long main street, and the brightly painted huddle of houses on the spit of land that forms the harbour, preserve the romantic air of a remote fishing village. Atmospheric when it basks in the westering sun, and yet more so when the rain lashes down, this is a place to hole up and write your masterpiece – and, if your publisher's advance is big enough, to enjoy the **seafood** at the *Red Bank Restaurant* (☎849 1005) in Church Street. You can **stay** at the noisy, down-at-heel *Pier Hotel* (☎849 1708; ③), or at one of a number of B&Bs, such as Mrs Chrissie Halpin's *Seafield*, 24 Harbour Road (☎849 0932; ③).

travel details

Trains

Dublin Connolly to: Arklow (4 daily; 1hr 45min); Belfast (6 daily; 2hr 15min); Derry (5 daily; 5hr); Dundalk (9 daily; 1–1hr 25min); Portadown (6 daily; 1hr 50min); Rosslare (3 daily; 2hr 50min); Sligo (3 daily; 3hr 15min); Wexford (3 daily; 2hr 30min).

Dublin Heuston to: Athlone (7 daily; 1hr 40min); Ballina (3 daily; 3hr 40min); Claremorris (3 daily; 3hr); Cork (9 daily; 3hr); Galway (4 daily; 3hr); Killarney (4 daily; 3hr 30min); Limerick (11 daily; 2hr 15min); Tralee (4 daily; 4hr); Waterford (4 daily; 2hr 30min); Westport (3 daily; 3hr 40min).

Buses

Dublin to: Belfast (6 daily; 3hr); Cork (4 daily; 4hr 25min); Derry (4 daily; 4hr 25min); Donegal (4 daily; 4hr 15 min); Galway (9 daily; 3hr 45min); Limerick (6 daily; 3hr 30min); Waterford (6 daily; 2hr 45min); Westport (3 daily; 5hr).

Private buses

Scores of private companies connect Dublin with the rest of the country. Routes are too numerous to detail here – we've listed the most useful under the "Travel details" section of the relevant chapters. Major companies include *Funtrek*, 32 Bachelors Walk, O'Connell Bridge, Dublin (☎873 3633 or ☎873 3244).

CHAPTER TWO

WICKLOW AND KILDARE

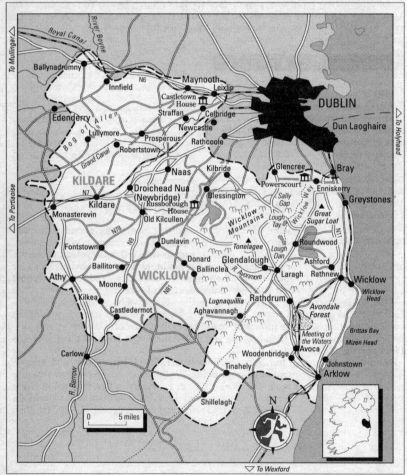

To Mullingar ◁

Royal Canal

River Boyne

Ballynadrumny

Innfield · N6 · Maynooth · Leixlip

Castletown House

Straffan · Celbridge

Edenderry

Lullymore

Bog of Allen

Newcastle

Prosperous · Rathcoole

Robertstown

Grand Canal

KILDARE

Naas · Kilbride

Droichead Nua (Newbridge) · Blessington

Kildare · Russborough House

Monasterevin

Old Kilcullen

◁ To Portlaoise

N7

N78

Fontstown

N9

Dunlavin

Ballitore

WICKLOW

N81

Athy

Moone

Kilkea

Castledermot

Carlow

R. Barrow

Donard · Ballinclea · R. Avonmore

Glendalough

Lugnaquillia

Aghavannagh

Rathdrum

Woodenbridge

Tinahely

Shillelagh

DUBLIN

Dun Laoghaire

To Holyhead ▷

Glencree · Bray

Powerscourt

Enniskerry

Sally Gap

Wicklow Way

Greystones

Wicklow Mountains

Lough Tay

Great Sugar Loaf

Tonelagee · Lough Dan

Roundwood

Ashford

Laragh · Rathnew

Wicklow

Wicklow Head

Avondale Forest

Brittas Bay

Mizen Head

Meeting of the Waters · Avoca

Johnstown

Arklow

0   5 miles

N

△ To Wexford

K ildare and Wicklow, both easily accessible from Dublin, provide a welcome respite from the capital's urban bustle. As central counties of the Pale region, each is heavily resonant with the presence of the Anglo-Irish, yet scenically they are in complete contrast. **County Wicklow** has some of the wildest, most spectacular mountain scenery in Ireland, as well as some impressive monuments: the early Celtic monastery of **Glendalough** and the Neoclassical splendours of the great houses of **Russborough** and the ruined **Powerscourt**.

County Kildare's charms are more understated: a gently undulating landscape of farming land punctuated only by the great horse-racing plain of the **Curragh**, where the National Stud and Japanese Gardens are well worth making time to see. Here, too, there are signs of the shifting patterns of settlement and land ownership – Celtic high crosses and pedimented buildings – written into the landscape for you to read as you travel.

Their proximity to Dublin makes **transport** very easy in both counties. The Dublin inner-city railway network, or DART, will take you southwards as far as the dull seaside resort of Bray on the Wicklow coast; the main line continues to the much more enticing towns of Wicklow and Arklow. The major tourist locations inland in County Wicklow are well served by buses. Wicklow, Arklow and Bray also provide good bases for exploration of the interior of the county in terms of both public transport and bike rental. In County Kildare the major N7 road and the railway line to Limerick offer ready access to most sites. The scenic beauties of Wicklow attract a lot of visitors, principally Dubliners, and the positive spin-off is that **accommodation** is no problem – there are plenty of youth hostels and cheap B&Bs, with many developing along the long-distance walking route, the Wicklow Way, as well as an increasing number of grander country houses and some excellent restaurants. Kildare is less visited, although here too a few pioneers are beginning to offer good food and accommodation in beautiful surroundings; but generally you'll find yourself relying on the standard B&B trade.

COUNTY WICKLOW

Get on a bus in central Dublin, and in half an hour or so you can be deep into **County Wicklow**, high in the mountains among gorse, heather, bracken and bent grass, breathing in clear air with no one in sight. It's great **walking** and **cycling** country – particularly challenging for mountain bikers; the **Wicklow Way** is an obvious focus for hiking – with plenty of golden sandy **beaches**, too (and some rather stuffy **resort towns** closer to Dublin, best avoided). On a short trip to Ireland, you could do a lot worse than simply combine Dublin with a few days in the wilds of Wicklow; it's also a place to get to grips with two of the dominant themes of Irish history, sometimes strangely superimposed: the **monastic tradition** in the shape of one of its most important and charismatic sites, Glendalough; and that of the **Anglo-Irish**, at the great seats of Russborough and Powerscourt.

Wherever you go, apart from a few obvious centres like Wicklow town and Arklow, you're struck by the **sparseness of population**. It's the same story as everywhere else in Ireland, and Wicklow is far from being the most painful sufferer: first the Great Famine of 1845–49, and then the gradual drift of the rural population to the towns. In 1841 the population of Wicklow was 126,431; the Famine reduced it to 100,000, then

---

ACCOMMODATION PRICES

Throughout this book, accommodation prices have been graded according to the cost per person per night in high season; with hotels and many hostels this represents half the cost of a double room, whereas with the more basic hostels it represents the cost of a single dormitory bed. The prices signified by our grades are as follows:

① Up to £6	③ £10–14	⑤ £20–26	⑦ £36–45
② £6–10	④ £14–20	⑥ £26–36	⑧ Over £45

steady seepage of the population brought it to a low of 58,473 by 1961. Since then it has recovered to around 90,000, partly through the development of commuter towns, as first the railway, then the suburban DART service have penetrated further into the county.

Heading out from Dublin you could follow the **coast**, but a far more attractive option is to head for the hills, where **Enniskerry** and **Powerscourt** make an obvious first stop.

The Wicklow Mountains

The **Wicklow Mountains**, so clearly viewed from Dublin, are really round-topped hills, ground down by the Ice Ages, with the occasional freakish shape like the Great Sugarloaf Mountain, where a granite layer has arrested the weathering. Despite their relatively modest height – Lugnaquilla, the highest peak, only just tops 3000ft – they're wild and uninhabited, with little traffic even at the main passes. Given this, and their proximity to Dublin, it's hardly surprising that the Wicklow Mountains were traditionally bandit territory, and that the last insurgents of the land agitation that spread all over Ireland following the French invasion of County Mayo in 1798 hid out here; the mountains were virtually inaccessible until after the ensuing uprisings, when the army built a road to enable them to patrol effectively. This you can still follow, from Rathfarnham in the Dublin suburbs to Aghavannagh, high in the mountains: the **Wicklow Way** partly follows the road, too.

Enniskerry and Powerscourt House

ENNISKERRY, the estate village of **Powerscourt House**, is famously picturesque, and there are people who travel to Ireland just to see it, and go no further. That's just about understandable, for it is indeed picture-book pretty, with a sloping triangular "square" and plenty of day-trippers from Dublin always in attendance to admire it. But what's more interesting is that the town's reason for existing is its relationship with the great house, just a mile or so to the west. It was here, in the heart of the Pale, that the Anglo-Irish were at their most confident and relaxed. This is a bold statement of a theme repeated all over Ireland: big houses with adjoining tied villages. But in Powerscourt's case, the estate stands as a sort of metaphor for the passing of the power of the Ascendancy. For Powerscourt is an estate without a heart, the shell of a house designed in 1740 by the German architect Richard Cassels (later anglicized to Castle), and burnt out in 1974 on the eve of a big party to celebrate the completion of an extensive programme of renovation. Although the Irish Georgian Society has announced plans to restore it, the house remains a ruin, surrounded by magnificently showy gardens. Typical of the scale that Powerscourt is built on, the avenue leading up to the house is nearly a mile long – the estate itself covers some 14,000 acres.

The **gardens** (March–Oct daily 9.30am–5.30pm; £2.50; waterfall March–Oct daily 9.30am–7pm, Nov–Feb daily 10.30am–dusk) are essentially mid-Victorian in character and, if you enjoy the municipal park-like formal school of gardening, well worth seeing. The Wicklow Mountains to the south and east give shelter from the wind and rain, and there are some rare plants and curiosities including a pets' cemetery and the obligatory Japanese garden. The Edwardian craze for Japanese gardening had a major impact on Ireland, perhaps because the mild climate was highly suited to growing the right kind of plants. It is also visible at Russborough, about fifteen miles away on the other side of the Wicklow Mountains, and in its most unbridled and eccentric form at the National Stud not far away in County Kildare (see p.116).

The really spectacular aspect of the landscaping is the view across a massive 250-yard terrace to the unlikely cones of the **Great and Little Sugarloaf mountains**, one of many instances in Ireland where landscape and landscaping are miraculously blended.

At Powerscourt, the designer of the upper terraces was one Daniel Roberton, an all-too-human individual with a relaxed approach to his job. Roberton had himself trundled about in a wheelbarrow, clutching a bottle of sherry; when this was exhausted his creative powers waned and he finished work for the day. A four-mile walk (signposted) through the grounds will bring you to the **waterfall**, at 400ft the highest in Ireland or Britain, and another place where the landscape seems almost too good to be true.

To get to Enniskerry and Powerscourt, take the #44 bus from the Quays in Dublin (every 25min) or the DART train to Bray and then #85 bus (every 40min). The *Powerscourt Arms Hotel*, beside the town square, offers comfortable, central **accommodation** (☎01/282 8903; ⑤); *Harvest Home*, off the square, has good **food**, including vegetarian options, at cheap prices.

Glencree

The village of **GLENCREE**, sitting about five miles west of Powerscourt House, and with its eponymous valley leading southeast to the Wicklow Way, is a quiet place with wonderful views of the Sugarloaf Mountains. The *An Óige* **youth hostel** in Glencree, *Stone House* (open all year; ☎01/286 4037; ①), is a solid, pedimented stone building dating from the construction of the military road in 1798 (the barrack buildings opposite now house the Glencree Reconciliation Centre, which attempts to promote dialogue between young people of the north and south). There's another official hostel, *Lackan House*, at Knockree (open all year; ☎01/286 4036; ①), halfway up the valley and closer to Powerscourt, but it's many degrees less prepossessing than the one in the village; you have to book for both through the main Dublin office (☎01/830 4555, fax ☎01/830 5808).

Glencree was once famous for its **oak woods**, but the small one behind the hostel was actually planted in 1988, in sad commemoration of the fact that broadleaved woodlands now cover barely one percent of the country. Further down the valley a dense conifer plantation has been designated a place for walks, with the misleading name of Old Boley Wood.

Above the youth hostel, dark, sinister terrain ascends southwards as you follow the military road to one of the two main mountain passes, the **Sally Gap**. Close to the source of the Liffey, it has been heavily invaded by Dubliners seeking peat – a further depredation inflicted upon the landscape. The most spectacular route on from here is to continue along the military road down from the Sally Gap to Glendalough, which runs over rough country until it joins the Glenmacnass river – at this point there's an extraordinary, extended waterfall. The other road (R579) takes you past Lough Tay and Lough Dan as it winds its way down to Sraghmore.

Dramatic, inaccessible **Lough Tay** – whose scree sides plunge straight into the water – is owned by Garech a'Brún, a member of the Guinness family who is also the man behind *Claddagh Records* in Dublin (see p.90). Although **Lough Dan** has gentler woodlands, visitors are made to feel unwelcome by numerous signs warning against trespassing on private land and barring access to the lake. Even avoiding such areas, though, there's still plenty of good, boggy walking and some spectacular views.

Roundwood

Coming down to Glendalough, you pass through **ROUNDWOOD** (one of the stops for *St Kevin's Bus Service*, see overleaf), which makes a good centre for exploring the surrounding uplands and the area around the vast expanses of the Vartry Reservoir. There are some serviceable **B&Bs** – *Mrs Nancy O'Brien* (☎01/281 8195; ③), *Mrs Mary Malone* (☎01/281 8168; ③), both open May–September, or *Ms Grainne Foy* (☎01/281 8429; ③). There is also a **campsite** (April–Sept; ☎01/281 8163); but on the whole the best bet is probably to head on down to the crossroads at Laragh, which has plenty of accommodation of all sorts (see p.106) and where any of the three roads out leads on

THE WICKLOW WAY

Glencree is one of the better places to pick up the **Wicklow Way**, Ireland's first officially designated long-distance walk. Following a series of sheep tracks, forest firebreaks and bog roads, above 1600ft for most of the way, the walk leads from Marlay Park in the Dublin suburbs up into the Dublin mountains, skirts the end of Glencree, cuts across the bleak, boggy hillside below Djouce Mountain, and pushes on to Glendalough and Aghavannagh; it finally ends up 82 miles later at Clonegal on the Wexford border. It's not particularly well organized – one of its chief attractions for many hikers – but the whole route can be walked comfortably in ten to twelve days.

If you want to do this, **Marlay Park** is accessible via the #47B or #48A bus from Dublin city centre. If you're short of time, the best part to walk is probably the three-day section between Enniskerry and Glendalough; the path reaches its highest point at White Hill (2073ft), from which you can get a view of the mountains of North Wales on a fine day. Take the #44 bus from Dublin Quays to Enniskerry, and pick up *St Kevin's Bus Service* at Glendalough for the return journey.

Low as they are, the Wicklow Mountains are notoriously treacherous, and even if you're planning on spending no more than a day **walking**, you should make sure you have the *Ordnance Survey*'s Wicklow Way map, plus the tourist board's information sheet on the Wicklow Way (no. 30); if you can pick up a copy of *An Óige*'s excellent *A Walking Guide for Hostellers* (no. 4), so much the better. Ireland's infamously unreliable ordnance maps are currently being updated, and you can pick up the Wicklow section in the tourist office in Wicklow or at the Wicklow Mountains National Park information centre in Glendalough (see opposite). Bad weather can close in rapidly, making the going dangerous and frightening if you're far from a road or house. All the customary warnings about mountain walking apply; and if you don't have any great experience of map reading, you'd do best to follow the yellow way-marking arrows. Trail walking – and indeed the whole idea of walking for pleasure – is fairly new in Ireland; consequently, the paths are far less crowded than their counterparts in, say, Britain.

There are four *An Óige* **hostels** along the way – Glencree (see p.103), Glendalough, Glenmalure and Aghavannagh (see p.106) – plus plenty of other places to stay around Glendalough, so accommodation shouldn't be a problem, although it may be wise to book ahead in high summer. For these hostels and the one at Ballinclea – not actually on the Wicklow Way but in the locale – you book through the main *An Óige* office in Dublin (☎01/830 4555, fax ☎01/830 5808). By a stroke of great imagination, two of the hostels – Glencree and Aghavannagh – are housed in the great stone barracks complexes built to serve the military road built after 1798, and you can feel the resonances of those grim times.

to more impressively lonely scenery. For eating in Roundwood, *Christine's Country Kitchen* does good home cooking during the day; *Kavanagh's Vartry House* serves up some appetizing dishes; while the restaurant at *The Roundwood Inn* (☎01/281 8107), appearances notwithstanding, offers excellent food and is a relaxed mecca for Dubliners at weekend lunchtimes.

Glendalough

GLENDALOUGH – the valley of the two lakes – is one of the standard and very popular bus tours out of Dublin. Nonetheless, besides being one of the most important, and well preserved, monastic sites in Ireland, it has an amazing, quite tangible quality of peace and spirituality (mid-June to Aug daily 9am–6.30pm; mid-May to mid-June & Sept daily 10am–6pm; mid-March to mid-May & Oct daily 10am–5pm; Nov to mid-March Tues–Sun 10am–4.30pm; ☎0404/45325; £2; Heritage Card). **Transport** to Glendalough from Dublin is easy – use the *St Kevin's Bus Service* (£5 one-way, £8 return; ☎01/281 8119), which leaves from the Royal College of Surgeons on St Stephen's Green at

11.30am every day (second service Mon–Sat at 6pm, Sun 7pm; bus back Mon–Sat 4.15pm, Sun 5.30pm). The bus passes through Bray, where you can pick up the train if you're heading south.

Glendalough is amply equipped to receive its many sightseers, with acres of car parking and a huge, modern **visitor centre** (same hours as site). This is genuinely helpful, with an excellent exhibition and a video show that sets Glendalough in the context of the monastic ruins elsewhere in Ireland – worth seeing, particularly if you're not visiting any others. The admission charge includes the video show, exhibition and the guided tour of the site itself.

The monastery

The **monastery** at Glendalough was founded by Saint Kevin, a member of the royal house of Leinster, during the sixth century. As a centre of the Celtic Church, it became famous throughout Europe for its learning, and despite being sacked by the Vikings in the ninth and tenth centuries and by the English in the fourteenth century, it was patiently restored each time, and monastic life continued tenaciously until the sixteenth century.

The **cathedral**, dating from the tenth and twelfth centuries (it was built in two phases), has an impressively ornamental east window, while **St Kevin's Cross** is a massive slab of granite, carved in the eighth century, in the Celtic form of a cross superimposed on a wheel. It may have been left unfinished, since the "halo" formed by the wheel has not been pierced. In the **round tower**, the doorway is ten feet above the ground. The traditional explanation, and the one that the guide will undoubtedly tell you, is that this design was adopted so that monks could pull up the ladder in times of trouble, turning the tower into an inaccessible treasury and refuge; however, more recent thinking suggests that the reason may be structural. The twelfth-century **Priest's House**, partially reconstructed 700 years later, got its name from being used as a burial place for local priests during the suppression of Catholicism. The carving above the door, so worn as to be indecipherable, possibly shows Saint Kevin between two ecclesiastical figures.

Glendalough's most famous building is **St Kevin's Church**, a solid, barrel-vaulted stone oratory, also known as St Kevin's Kitchen. Although it may well date from Saint Kevin's time, the round-tower belfry is an eleventh-century addition, and the structure has clearly been altered many times.

The lakes and surrounding attractions

All these buildings are clustered between the visitor centre and the **Lower Lake**, and you'll be shown all of them unless it's raining hard, in which case the tour gets truncated. But the real delights of Glendalough lie beyond what you get to see on the tour. As you climb above the monastery complex, landscape and architecture combine in a particularly magical way, and you could spend days walking the footpaths that crisscross the upper valley, drinking it all in. The scenery is at its most spectacular at the **Upper Lake**, where wooded cliffs and a waterfall plunge vertically into the water. Also here is the Wicklow Mountains National Park **information point** (mid-June to mid-Sept daily 10am–6.30pm), where you can get details of some of the many **local walks**.

There are plenty more antiquities connected with the monastic life among the cliffs around the upper lake, many of them formerly pilgrim shrines. The site of Saint Kevin's original church, the **Temple-na-Skellig**, is on a platform approached by a flight of stone steps, accessible only by boat. **St Kevin's Bed** is a rocky ledge high up the cliff, where it's said the holy man used to sleep in an attempt to escape from the unwelcome advances of a young girl. Eventually she found his hiding place and, waking up one morning to find her beside him, he reacted with the misogyny characteristic of the early Church fathers – and pushed her into the lake.

Practicalities

Accommodation in **Glendalough** is plentiful. The site itself is surrounded by the usual tourist detritus, plus the solid *Glendalough Hotel* (☎0404/45135; ⑥). For a grand-stand view of the entire area, you should try *Brockagh Heights* guesthouse (☎0404/45243; ③). The *An Óige* hostel, *The Lodge*, is right by the lower lake (open all year; ☎0404/45342; ②), but is full of school parties in the summer holidays. Most of the plea-santer accommodation is clustered a mile to the east around **LARAGH**. Just north of the crossroads is *Mitchell's Schoolhouse* (☎0404/45302; ⑤), in a picturesque stone build-ing, whose restaurant is the gastronomic high point of the area. A short distance out of town towards Rathdrum (on the R755) is *Derrybawn House* (☎0404/45134; ④, dinner £17), an elegant late eighteenth-century house tucked into the hillside in extensive, wooded grounds. For B&B, closer to the Laragh crossroads, in a crook in the Wicklow Way, is the *Glendalough River House* (☎0404/45156; ③). This converted mill building, which used to house a hostel, is now a factory outlet where you can pick up hand-loomed and hand-knitted **woollens** at reasonable prices. A few miles south on the R755, through the lush Vale of Clara, there's more B&B at *Doire Coille* (☎0404/45131; ③).

Finally, if you need guidance on how to exploit the **sporting opportunities** of the area, you could check out the rock-climbing, mountaineering, canoeing and kayaking courses offered by the *Tiglin Adventure Centre* (☎0404/40169), about eight miles east of Glendalough near Ashford. There's also an *An Óige* **hostel** here (see p.109).

Glenmalure and the Glen of Imaal

Northwest of Glendalough, the main road takes you over the **Wicklow Gap**, whence there's a tolerably tough climb up to the top of **Tonelagee** (2677ft). South and west, the country rises, becoming wilder and more desolate, dominated by **Lugnaquilla**, the highest mountain in the Wicklow range. In this direction you can head southwest along the military road towards **Aghavannagh** and stay in the *An Óige* hostel (March–Nov; ☎0402/36366; ②), a massively grand and remote barracks building on a hill with views all round; experienced walkers and map-readers have the option of trekking to the head of Glendalough and down into the next glen.

Either way, you'll arrive in dark and lonely **GLENMALURE**, half of which is off limits as an army firing range. Perhaps appropriately, Glenmalure was the scene of a decisive victory by the Wicklow Irish under Fiach MacHugh O'Byrne over the English under Elizabeth I. One of the 1798 barracks, now ruined, stands at the point where the military road hits the glen. It's a symbol of decay that somehow sets the tone for the entire valley, with its enclosed, mysterious feel and steep scree sides which scarcely afford a foothold to the heather. The road eventually peters out in a car park, but a track continues past a weir up to the *An Óige* **youth hostel** (July–Aug & Sat nights throughout the year; no phone; ①), which stands at the head of the valley just above the point where the river rushes over a weir. With no other buildings in sight, it's a beautiful and unspoilt setting.

Past the hostel, the trail forks right for Glendalough and left, over the Table Mountain, for the Glen of Imaal.

By comparison with Glenmalure, the **Glen of Imaal** is almost inviting. Again, it's dominated by the impressive head of Lugnaquilla and, likewise, half of it is reserved as an army shooting range. Altogether, it's as wild and desolate as you could wish for, though more open and lighter than Glenmalure. There's an *An Óige* **youth hostel** at **BALLINCLEA** (March–Nov; ☎045/404657; ①).

At **DERRYNAMUCK**, on the southeast side of the valley, stands a cottage where Michael O'Dwyer, one of the last insurgents of 1798, took refuge when trapped by the British, and escaped because Samuel McAllister drew the enemy's fire and died in his place. Now run as a **folk museum**, the cottage is unmarked on most maps, the excep-tion being the *Ordnance Survey* Kildare-Wicklow sheet.

If you need some time out, **Chrysalis** (☎045/54713), a holistic centre in **DONARD**, is worth a visit. The secluded, restored eighteenth-century rectory and grounds, near the western end of the Glen of Imaal, accommodates personal growth courses at weekends, but midweek breaks (on Tues, Wed and Thurs) from April to September are also available on a **B&B** basis (③); vegetarian and vegan meals are served. Self-catering breaks are offered throughout the winter in a wooden chalet in the grounds (single room ⑤). To get to *Chrysalis* from Dublin take the bus (9am & 6pm) which will be met if prior warning is given.

Russborough House

The third of Wicklow's great cultural landmarks is in west Wicklow: **Russborough House** (June–Aug daily 10.30am–5.30pm; April, May, Sept & Oct Sun 10.30am–5.30pm; 45-min tour of main rooms and paintings £2.50; outside official opening hours, ring ☎045/65239) and its impressive art collection. Designed, like Powerscourt, by the German architect Richard Castle (with the assistance of Francis Bindon), Russborough is one of the jewels of the Pale. A classic Palladian structure whose central block is linked to two wings with curving arms, its design was subsequently repeated throughout Ireland, as a result of Castle's influence and its own suitability as a kind of glorified farmhouse.

In Russborough's case, it's very glorified indeed. The house was constructed for Joseph Leeson, son of a rich Dublin brewer and MP for Rathcormack in the days of the semi-independent Irish parliament: he was created **Lord Russborough** in 1756. Russborough epitomizes the great flowering of Anglo-Irish confidence before the Act of Union deprived Ireland of its parliament, much of its trade and its high society (thereafter, the rich Anglo-Irish spent much of the year in London). No expense was spared. Not only were the fashionable architects of the day employed, but the plasterers, the Francini brothers, were also of the best. The plaster ovals in the drawing room, for instance, were made to order to fit the four Joseph Vernet marine paintings that still occupy them, and the over-the-top plasterwork on the stairs has been described as representing the ravings of a lunatic, and an Irish lunatic at that.

The **lake** in front of Russborough provides the house with an idiomatically eighteenth-century prospect. The impression is a false one, however – it's actually a thoroughly twentieth-century reservoir, created by damming the Liffey, which provides Dublin with twenty million gallons of water a day.

The art collection

Impressive though it is, the chief reason why Russborough is so firmly on the tourist trail is its collection of **paintings**. The German entrepreneur Alfred Beit (1853–1906) was a co-founder with Cecil Rhodes of the De Beer Diamond Mining Company, and he poured the fortune he derived from that enterprise into amassing works of art. His nephew, Sir Alfred Beit, acquired Russborough in 1952, which explains why such an extraordinary collection of famous pictures is kept in this obscure corner of County Wicklow. Whatever you may feel about their irrelevance to the site or the source of the wealth that made the acquisitions possible, there are some marvellous paintings by Goya, Murillo, Velazquez, Gainsborough, Rubens and Frans Hals, to name a handful.

Russborough has been burgled twice: in 1974, when Bridget Rose Dugdale stole sixteen paintings to raise money for the IRA – although her booty, worth £18 million, was recovered undamaged from a farmhouse in County Cork a week later; and in May 1986 – some of the paintings taken in the second heist have since been retrieved in The Netherlands. Nowadays security is tight, and visitors are herded around the house in groups, with little chance to study the paintings – or anything else – in detail. You could take a second tour, but a better way to get a more leisurely look would be to visit during the **Festival of Irish Music in Great Irish Houses** in June (☎045/65239).

Practicalities

Getting to Russborough is no problem – **BLESSINGTON**, the pleasant coaching town it adjoins, is forty minutes from central Dublin on the Waterford **bus**. There's a central **tourist office** (June–Aug Mon–Thurs 9.30am–1pm & 2–5pm; open to 7pm on Fri; ☎045/65850), which has information on possibilities for outdoor pursuits. A wide range of these – including canoeing, sail-boarding, pony-trekking and hill-walking – is available at the *Blessington Lakes Leisure Pursuits Centre* (☎045/65092), signposted from the centre of town. Blessington's marvellous **location** – close to the shining waters of the Blessington lakes and, beyond them, the spectacular heights of the Wicklow Mountains – should make it a good base for exploration – but unfortunately, with the exception of an overpriced hotel and a half-hearted restaurant, there's nowhere to **eat** or **sleep**. A few miles out of town, there's an *An Óige* **hostel**, on the wooded shores of the lake (March–Nov & weekends throughout the year; ☎045/867266; book through the Dublin office, see p.28; ①).

The Wicklow coast

If you are travelling south from Dublin and along the **Wicklow coast**, the N11 will get you to Bray, the first major town; from then on the coastal road offers more picturesque sights down to Rathnew, where you join the main road again. By train, the DART service from the capital runs as far as Bray – very much a dormitory suburb; to get to Wicklow town or Arklow, catch the Wexford train. Alternatively you could take the Wexford bus, which also runs to Wicklow town but then takes you on a scenic detour inland via the heavily wooded Vale of Avoca to Arklow; from Wicklow buses leave at 10.30am, 11.10am, 12.10pm, 5.10pm and 7pm, and the journey takes just under an hour.

Bray

BRAY, originally a Victorian resort developed when the railway was extended south of Dún Laoghaire in the 1850s, provides a grotty welcome for the hordes of visitors from Dublin at the weekends. With a seafront full of dingy hotels, video arcades, B&Bs and fast-food shops, Bray – once genteel – has lost most of its charm. Its chief claim to fame is that James Joyce lived here from 1889 to 1891, and its chief visitor attraction, if that's your thing, is the *National Aquarium* (April–Sept daily 10am–6pm, Oct–March Tues–Fri 10am–1pm & 2–5pm, Sat & Sun 10am–5pm; £3; ☎01/286 4688). Perhaps the best thing to do here is to walk round **Bray Head**, a knob of rock pushing into the sea, where a massive cross erected to mark the holy year of 1950 serves as a reminder that you are now in Catholic Europe. There are a few secluded coves in the shadow of the Head where you can **swim**.

Outside Bray, **Killruddery House** and its **garden** are worth seeing (May, June & Sept 1–5pm; £2.50, garden only £1), reached by bus #84 leaving from Main Street. Laid out in the seventeenth century, Killruddery has one of the earliest surviving gardens in Ireland and has been home of the Brabazon family since 1618. The house was remodelled by Richard and William Morrison in the 1820s.

The **tourist office** is in the town hall (open all year Mon–Fri 10am–1pm & 2–5pm, Sat till 4pm; ☎01/286 7128). **Bicycle rental** in Bray is available from *Raleigh Rent-a-bike* (☎01/286 3357), and horse riding is possible through *Brennanstown Riding School*. On the whole though, it's better to push on down the coast through Greystones and on to Wicklow, the county town.

Wicklow

There's nothing much to **WICKLOW**, but it is the first place that wholly escapes the influence of Dublin as you go down the coast, and should you find yourself with time on your hands, it's a pleasant, ramshackle town with plenty of entertainment, one or two good, cheap places to eat, a couple of smarter places on the fringes of the town, and walking and swimming, too. It has none of the presence you might expect of a county town and comes across as a happily disorganized kind of place, full of people chatting on pavements, cars parked on double yellow lines and solidly built little houses in bright marine pastels. Restoration is underway of the old jail, originally built in 1702 to hold prisoners under the repressive penal laws, and it is expected that the finished building will house the county heritage centre, including a genealogical research section.

Just outside town on the seaward side, a knoll encrusted with some knobbly piles of stone constitutes all that's left of **Black Castle**, one of the fortifications built by the Fitzgeralds in return for lands granted them by Strongbow after the Anglo-Norman invasion of 1169 – and all but demolished by the O'Byrnes and O'Tooles in 1301. **Wicklow Head**, unlike Bray, really is spectacular, and you can walk all the way round (there are two tiny swimming beaches, sunny in the mornings) accompanied by exhilarating views of the open sea and, northwards, the weird silhouettes of the Great and Little Sugarloaf mountains. There's also sociable – if unglamorous – swimming with the harbour breakwater closer to the centre of town in summer. Wicklow – along with Arklow and Bray – provides a convenient point of entry to the hinterland; a fledgling private mini-bus service is now running (9am–6pm every 1hr 30min; £6 return, £4 single) to Glendalough (via Avondale), but check first with the Wicklow tourist office.

Practicalities

The **tourist office** is in the central square (June–Sept Mon–Sat 9am–6pm; Oct–May Mon–Fri 9.30am–1pm & 2–5pm; ☎0404/69117). If you **want to stay**, B&Bs are in good supply – try, for example, the *Bridge Tavern* (☎0404/67718; ③), or Mrs Gormond's *Thomond House* in St Patrick's Road Upper (☎0404/67940; ③). For a bit more comfort in the centre of town, try the slightly tatty but friendly *Bayview Hotel* in the Mall (☎0404/67383; ④). The rather dour independent **hostel** is on the quayside at *Marine House* (☎0404/69213; ②, also does bicycle rental); otherwise, the nearest hostel accommodation is the *An Óige* one at Tiglin, six miles away near Ashford (open all year; ☎0404/40259; ①); to book contact the main office in Dublin (see p.28). There's **camping** on the beach at Silver Strand, a little over two miles south of town (☎0404/67615). For **food and drink** there are plenty of pubs – *Philip Healy's* is a genial, old-fashioned drinking place, while *Leinster Lodge* does music nights, as does the bar of the *Bayview*. There's a useful cheap pizza/steak restaurant on Main Street, the *Pizza del Forno*, which stays open until 11.30pm in summer, now in competition with a more metropolitan new arrival at the *Opera House*, decorated in fashionable terracotta tones.

Just outside town are a trio of **hotel/restaurants** to hide away in if you're feeling self-indulgent. *The Old Rectory* (April–Oct; ☎0404/67048; ⑦) is a delicate pink mansion up a lane off the Dublin Road, only five minutes walk from the town centre; while the more luxurious *Tinakilly House* (☎0404/69274; rooms starting at £63 per person sharing) is a Victorian pile further up the road just outside Rathnew – both offering tranquil settings and the best of new Irish cuisine. *Hunter's Hotel* at Rathnew (☎0404/40106; ⑦) is a good, old-fashioned hostelry where the nineteenth-century politician Charles Stewart Parnell used to stay. It's worth visiting just for a drink in the bar and a stroll in the gardens sloping down to the River Vartry.

Brittas Bay and Mount Usher Gardens

Heading south towards Arklow on the R750, there's a string of white sand **beaches**. The one at **Brittas Bay**, just north of Mizen Head (beloved of the fishing forecasts), is particularly good – don't be put off by the caravan site. In summer, you can buy great seafood there, particularly crab.

Horticultural enthusiasts should also know about **Mount Usher Gardens** (mid-March to Oct Mon–Sat 10.30am–6pm, Sun 11am–6pm; £2), a few miles inland near Ashford, where rare trees, shrubs and flowers grow in profusion in a narrow strip next to the road. For others, the gardens' main attraction may be the miniature suspension bridges where you can see engineering principles at work as they sway and bounce under your weight.

Arklow

ARKLOW has all the vitality you might have expected to find in Wicklow. Built on a site sloping gently towards the sea at the mouth of the Avoca river, it has a long and prosperous history, based on fishing, shipbuilding and the export of copper ore, pyrites and even gold, mined further up the valley. Evidence of continued riches in relatively recent times can be seen in the elegant Art Deco cinema at the top of the main street.

Arklow is no longer a major port, but shipbuilding continues to be a dominant factor – *Gypsy Moth IV*, Sir Francis Chichester's prize-winning transatlantic yacht, moored permanently at London's Greenwich, was built at John Tyrrell's yard here. For a grip on the past, stop off at the **Maritime Museum** (daily 10am–5pm; £1): turn left at the top of the main street. A happily haphazard collection of local finds, it claims a history for Arklow going back to Ptolemy's celebrated second-century map. It also emerges that Arklow was a major centre for arms-smuggling during the upheavals of 1798. The museum houses such curiosities as a whale's tooth and eardrum and a model ship made with 10,700 matchsticks. Arklow's **beach**, white sand like the rest of this part of the coast, is sandwiched between the docks and a gravel extraction plant – you may prefer to head north to Brittas Bay.

Practicalities

The **tourist office** (June–Aug Mon–Sat 9am–6pm; Sept–May Mon–Fri 9.30am–1pm & 2–5pm; ☎0404/69117) is located in a portacabin next to the courthouse in the centre of town. **Accommodation** should be easy enough to find, with plenty of B&Bs – try Mrs Crotty's *Vale View*, Coolgreany Road (☎0402/32622; ④), or Mrs Hayes's *Tara*, Gorey Road (☎0402/39333; ④). *Christy's Conservatory* **restaurant** caters for vegetarians, with tasty, reasonably priced meals. If you're picnicking, stock up with sandwich supplies from the *Stone Oven Bakery* at 65 Lower Main Street, where Egon Friedrich, a German baker, sells delicious sourdough bread, sausage rolls and strudels. There are lots of **pubs** – an ID system operates at all of them so be prepared to be questioned if you look under 18 – most of which seem to have some kind of entertainment on offer, including traditional Irish music, discos and the odd pub quiz. The *Ormonde* on Main Street shows recent-release **films**.

Avondale and the Vale of Avoca

The Wexford-to-Dublin bus heads north from Arklow twice a day (8am and 1pm) inland through the **Vale of Avoca**. Designated "scenic", the vale draws scores of bus parties, but don't be put off; its beauty – once you leave the fertilizer plant behind – is genuinely rewarding, with thickly wooded slopes on either side of the river, culminating in the **Meeting of the Waters**, the confluence of the Avonmore and Avonbeg rivers.

The Meeting has attracted its fair share of coffee shops, and there's a pleasant pub, but for really excellent daytime **food**, among other things, you're better advised to stop a mile or so downstream at the pleasantly unassuming village of **AVOCA** and its hand-weaving mill. The weavers are housed in a group of whitewashed buildings with steep grey roofs, where the fly-shuttle looms that caused mass unemployment when they were introduced in 1723 are presented as picturesquely traditional. Avoca has abandoned its old range of cloaks, kilts and deerstalker hats in bright, heathery pinks and purples for a more appealing range of woollens and knitwear; there's also a good, cheap lunch room selling sandwiches, soup and cakes. For pleasant **accommodation** try *Riverview House* (☎0402/35181; ③), perched above the opposite bank of the rushing river.

A few miles upriver towards Rathdrum is the **Avondale Forest Park**, where you can see **Parnell's house** (daily 11am–6pm; admission to park £1; house £2.50) at **AVONDALE**. One of Ireland's most influential and important politicians, **Charles Stewart Parnell**, born in Avondale in 1846, was hailed as the "the uncrowned king of Ireland" until his career – and his campaign for home rule – was brought to an end by the scandal of his love for a married woman. A successful businessman – Parnell ran his own local lead mine – he was elected to parliament in 1875. Later, under his leadership, the **Irish Home Rule Party** brought the government down, and Parnell persuaded Gladstone's Liberals to support the idea of home rule for Ireland. Although the first Home Rule Bill was defeated in 1886, prospects seemed bright for its eventual success – but scandal intervened. In 1881 Parnell had met, and fallen in love with, the estranged wife of one Captain O'Shea. Parnell and Kitty O'Shea set up house together and had three children. In 1889 the hitherto complaisant Captain O'Shea sued for divorce. Longing to marry Kitty, Parnell refused to defend himself – and the British press destroyed his good name. It was, effectively, the end of Parnell's political career. He died, two years later, in the arms of Kitty O'Shea, to whom he had been married for four months.

The **house**, designed in 1779 by the celebrated English architect John Wyatt, is a modest, box-like building. Inside, there's a delicate, Wedgwood-like blue dining room with plasterwork by the famous Lanfranchini brothers, a striking vermilion library (Parnell's favourite room), and, in the entrance hall, an elegant minstrels' gallery from where Parnell, a nervous orator, usesd to practise his political speeches.

The Avondale estate has been in the possession of the Irish Forestry Board since 1904, and the grounds are used for silvicultural experiments. As a result, they're filled with rare tree species. A Land League museum is planned for some of the outbuildings. There's a coffee shop, and plenty of picnic tables.

COUNTY KILDARE

County Kildare, in the heart of the Pale, forms part of the hinterland of Dublin. Although it lacks the spectacle of Wicklow to the capital's south, or the extraordinary range of ancient monuments of the lush Boyne Valley to the north, it has a quiet charm of its own. The **landscape** is a calm one of rolling farmland for the most part, with open grasslands and rough pasturage, just touching the drab stretches of the monotonous Bog of Allen in the northwest. This is ancient countryside, marked by a string of **Celtic crosses** at Moone, Old Kilcullen and Castledermot; but you're also constantly made aware that you're in Pale country – with big stone estate walls bordering many of the fields and Georgian proportions in the buildings noticeable features of the landscape, as well as more obvious attractions such as the magnificent **Castletown House** with its model village at Celbridge; the **Grand Canal**, which traverses the county and has a walkable towpath; and the pin-neat **National Stud** at Kildare town and its extraordinarily extravagant Japanese Garden.

Because of its proximity to Dublin, there's no problem about transport in County Kildare. The main **buses** to Limerick ply up and down the N7 trunk road, with the **rail** line running close beside it for most of the way. **Accommodation** is less easy – you're reliant on B&Bs, many of them the more expensive kind, catering for business travellers rather than individual tourists.

Maynooth and Castletown House

Both Maynooth – due west of Dublin on the N6 – and Celbridge (for Castletown House) are firmly on the daytrippers trail from Dublin, so you're unlikely to be on your own here. There really isn't all that much to detain you in **MAYNOOTH** (pronounced *Ma-nooth*, with the stress on the second syllable), pretty though it is. Its main claim to fame is its seminary, **St Patrick's College**, which in addition to training priests now houses two universities. For fans of Victoriana, the square is by Pugin in Gothic Revival style. The ruins beside the entrance to the college are those of the thirteenth-century **Maynooth Castle**, one of the two main strongholds of the Anglo-Norman Fitzgerald family who ruled Kildare and, effectively, most of Ireland from the thirteenth century until the coming of the Tudor monarchs (their other castle is at Kilkea, in the south of the county; see p.119). Maynooth's formal town planning is made sense of by Carton House, a Georgian gem by Richard Castle which lies at the other end of the main street; although its grand avenue looks promising, you can't visit the house at present (however, its owner plans a luxury hotel and golf course, so this may change).

Castletown House

Few places give a better impression of the immense scale on which the Anglo-Irish imagination was able to work than **Castletown House** (April–Sept Mon–Fri 10am–6pm, Sun 2–6pm; Oct Mon–Fri 10am–5pm; Nov–March Sun 2–5pm; £2.50; outside official opening times in winter, ring ☎01/628 8252), designed in 1722 for the Speaker of the Irish House of Commons, William Conolly, by the Italian Alessandro Galilei. You enter the grounds through the village of Celbridge, planned to lend importance to the house itself. This exhibits the strictest Classicism: the front facade, facing out over the Liffey, gives little away except for a rigidly repeated succession of windows. It's the only thing about the house that is restrained, though, for Castletown, from the very beginning, was built for show.

William Conolly, who commissioned it, was a publican's son from Donegal who – like many others – owed his success to the changed conditions after the Battle of the Boyne and made his fortune by dealing in forfeited estates. Member for Donegal in the Irish parliament since 1692, he was a staunch supporter of the Hanoverian cause and was unanimously elected Speaker of the Irish House of Commons in 1715. In 1717 the ambassador at Florence noted Conolly's intention to bring to Ireland "the best architect in Europe", a move of some significance to national self-esteem. A letter to the famous metaphysician, Bishop Berkeley, states: "I am glad for the honour of my country that Mr Conolly has undertaken so magnificent a pile of building. . . . Since this house will be the finest Ireland ever saw, and by your description fit for a Prince, I would have it as it were the epitome of the Kingdom, and all the natural rarities she affords should have a place there." Although plans for the house were magnificent, work proceeded in a haphazard way. The cellar vaults, begun before the design of the house was finalized, still bear little relation to what's above ground; and the house interior remained unfinished – lacking, for instance, a main staircase – until the end of the long life of William's wife, who preferred building **follies**.

The fruits of old Mrs Conolly's imagination are most obvious in the **grounds**, where one folly, 140ft of what appears to be a monument to chimney-sweeping, closes the vista to the north, while the **Wonderful Barn** forms a focus for the view to the east. Both projects were set up to provide relief work for estate workers hard hit by the famine-ridden winter of 1739, and Mrs Conolly's sister, for one, disapproved: "My sister is building an obleix to answer a vistow from the bake of Castletown house," she wrote of the folly. "It will cost her three or four hundred pounds at least, but I believe more. I really wonder how she can dow so much and live as she duse." Incidentally, it seems that the ground on which the obelisk stands did not belong to Castletown, not that this bothered Mrs Conolly. The Wonderful Barn is currently occupied by *Focus Point*, a charity working with homeless people. You can be given access to the staircase that snakes around the barn's belly and up to its top by ringing ☎01/624 5448.

The **interior** decoration was the inspiration of Lady Louisa Lennox, who married into the Conolly family in 1759 at the age of fifteen. The newlyweds might have lived in London (Louisa's brother-in-law described her as wanting "to buy every house she sees"), but the fact that Louisa's elder sister, Lady Emily Kildare, had settled at Carton, close by at Maynooth, decided matters. (The life of the Lennox sisters is vividly chronicled, through their letters and diaries, in Stella Tillyard's novel *Aristocrats*, published by Vintage in 1995.) Although little of the furniture at Castletown is original to the house, you can see some of the results of Louisa's efforts. It was she who, with her sister Lady Sarah Bunbury, created the print room on the ground floor, commissioned the Lanfranchini brothers to produce the hall's extraordinary plasterwork and ordered the long gallery at the back of the house, which she considered "the most comfortable room you ever saw, and quite warm; supper at one end, the company at the other, and I am writing in one of the piers at a distance from them all". Apparently, she ordered the magnificent Murano glass chandeliers on a journey to Venice, but when they arrived they were found to clash with the room's blue, Pompeiian-style decor: it was too late to redecorate, so both decor and chandeliers are still there.

The Irish Georgian Society

Given this personal, idiosyncratic stamp on Castletown, it seems a shame that no one lives here any more. In 1967 the house was bought by Desmond Guinness, a founder of the **Irish Georgian Society**. Established in 1958 with the aim of preserving Ireland's magnificent Georgian heritage, the society is regarded with suspicion or amusement in some quarters. It has strong Anglo-Irish leanings and shows some degree of eccentricity (the English chapter teams up with the Silver Ghost Club to cruise around the countryside in antique Rolls Royces), but it's done sterling work in, for example, providing small but vital grants that have enabled buildings to be saved; enquiries to the *Irish Georgian Society*, Leixlip Castle, Leixlip, County Kildare (☎01/824 4211). Castletown House itself was taken over by the Office of Public Works (OPW) in 1994. As we go to press, much of the house is under conservation; the OPW is big on interpretation of the nation's heritage, of which the Anglo-Irish element forms a recently acknowledged part, so be prepared for some changes in the way the place is presented.

Accommodation with a suitably Georgian flavour is to be found for a reasonable price about three miles south in **NEWCASTLE** at *Ringwood*, an eighteenth-century house in 65 acres of rolling farmland, and open May to October (☎01/628 8220; ④).

Straffan and the Steam Museum

About three miles southwest of Castletown, housed in a neat Victorian church that's been brought stone by stone from Dublin, the **Straffan Steam Museum** (Easter–Sept Tues–Sun 11am–6pm; Oct–Easter 2pm–dusk; £3; ☎01/627 3155) offers a benign view of the driving force behind the Industrial Revolution. There are miniature models of steam trains and four – amazingly quiet – working steam engines, plus a series of wall panels offering a rather rose-tinted account of how steam advanced the way forward to our modern world. They also reflect Ireland's uneven industrialization – in 1838 the north had more steam horsepower than the rest of Ireland put together. There's a coffee shop, and there are plans to start up a small steam railway in the grounds. The local Big House, **Kildare House**, has recently opened up as an extremely swish country house **hotel** (☎01/662 7333; ⑧) – well worth visiting for an example of unreconstructed high living.

Kildare town and the Curragh

If you are heading from Dublin to **Kildare town** and **the Curragh**, the N7, the main Dublin–Limerick road, is a relatively swift but rather dull drive; additionally, there's a new stretch of motorway, the M7, which runs from before Naas for about ten miles, rejoining the N11 near Kildare town (from Maynooth, take minor roads southwards and join the N7 at Naas). A road sign advertises **NAAS** (pronounced *Nace*) as "a nice place to shop", and there's probably not a great deal more to be said. *Nás na Rí* (Naas of the Kings), once the centre of the extensive kingdom of the Uí Dunlainge and their successors, the Uí Faelain, now seems little more than a battered parade of shops. Its one great attraction is **Punchestown Racecourse**, whose main meeting is the three-day steeplechasing festival in late April, when the racecourse itself is greatly celebrated for its flowering gorse.

NEWBRIDGE, a nineteenth-century town which grew up around the British barracks there (now re-Irishized as *Droichead Nua*), is similarly unmemorable, except for its traffic jams. But after Newbridge the road heads over the grassy, unfenced stretches of the Curragh, and you're into racing country proper.

Kildare town

KILDARE town is a delight: a solid, respectable little place around a sloping triangular square, with none of that feeling of depopulation that becomes so familiar in other parts of Ireland. The town is dominated by the massive, squat Church of Ireland **Cathedral of St Brigid**, who founded a religious house here in 490. The present structure dates originally from the thirteenth century, though the north transept and choir were burned to the ground in the Confederate War of 1641, and the Victorian reconstruction of 1875 is pseudo-medieval. Its round tower, probably twelfth century, has a particularly elaborate doorway twelve feet up, and it's hoped that the bizarre nineteenth-century battlements that have been removed can be replaced with something more in sympathy with the original style. For £1 you can climb it and get a good view of the rolling farmland to the south and the Bay of Allen to the north.

The **tourist office** (March–Oct Mon–Sat 10am–1pm & 2–6pm; ☎045/22696) is sited in the nineteenth-century waterworks building right in the middle of the main square. **Accommodation** is limited; there's a hotel, the *Curragh Lodge* (☎045/22144; ⑤), with a reasonably good, though not cheap, Chinese restaurant attached, *The Kingsland*; or for B&B try Mrs O'Connell's *Freemont*, Tully Road (☎045/21604; ③). *Nolan's*, in the square and close to the cathedral, is an old bar with cosy snugs and regular music nights. In the old cinema, there's a chi-chi steak bar that wouldn't be out of place in the metropolis, named after Silken Thomas, a member of the ruling Fitzgerald family, whom the growing powers of the Tudor monarchy provoked into rebellion in 1536. The uprising was unsuccessful, and a bloody massacre followed at Maynooth, later known, ironically, as "the pardon of Maynooth".

The Curragh and the National Stud

The real reason for spending time in the county town, however, is **racing**. **The Curragh**, just south of Kildare, is the centre of the Irish racing world, with the race-course itself and dozens of studs. In early morning you can see strings of slim race-horses exercising on the 6000 acres of grassland. Breeding and training them is one of Ireland's major money-spinners, and much of it is centred on the Curragh. For an idea of the scale of the operation, Goff's Kildare Paddocks at Kill, which sells over half of all Irish-bred horses, has an annual turnover of around £IR20 million. At Kill you can rent a staider kind of steed, at the *Old Mill Riding Centre* (☎045/77053).

Security considerations mean that none of the working stud farms are open to the public. The best place to see the perfectionism that attends the breeding and training of these valuable pieces of horseflesh is the **National Stud** (Easter–Oct Mon–Sat 10.30am–12.30pm & 2–5pm, Sun 2–5.30pm; £4 for Stud and Japanese Garden; ☎045/21617), just outside Kildare, signposted from the centre of town. You can easily walk out from the town, though the entrance is not the obvious one through the main gates that you pass on the road from Dublin – instead follow the signs from the centre for the Stud and the Japanese Garden. You can pay to see just the Stud, or buy a joint ticket including the garden. This is well worth it even if you're not interested in horticulture: far more than a collection of rare plants, it's also an extraordinary legacy of Anglo-Irish eccentricity.

The National Stud itself consists of neat white buildings set in green lawns as close-cropped and well groomed as a Derby-winner's coat: a spick-and-span monument to the greater glory and perfectability of horses. Established in 1900 by Colonel William Hall Walker, who believed that horoscopes affected horses' form, the stud enjoyed an marvellous record of success, and in 1915 was bequeathed to the British Crown, which rewarded Walker by creating him Lord Wavertree. When transferred to the Irish state in 1943, it became the National Stud.

Colonel Hall Walker's belief in the stars is reflected in the **stallion boxes**, built in the 1960s according to his astrological principles, with lantern roofs allowing moon and stars to exert their influence on the occupants. There's a brass plaque on each door giving the stallion's name and details of his racing career. The National Stud's **museum** is an enjoyably chaotic account of the history of horses and horse racing which contains, among other bizarre exhibits, the skeleton of the 1960s champion race-horse, Arkle.

The Japanese Garden

Adjacent to the stud is the rather bizarre **Japanese Garden**, which was laid out on a drained bog (between 1906 and 1910) by Colonel Hall Walker and two Japanese gardeners. Part of the Edwardian craze for all things Japanese, they're planned to represent the "life of man" – man, emphatically, it has to be said, rather than woman. In a weird kind of enumerated metaphysical joyride, you're led from birth to death via the Tunnel of Ignorance (no. 3) and the Parting of Ways (no. 6), where you're invited to choose between a life of philandering bachelorhood or marriage. Choosing marriage, you step across stepping stones to the Island of Joy and Wonder (no. 7) and meet your wife at the engagement bridge (no. 8; easily confused with the Red Bridge of Life, no. 17) and so on. Finally you pass through the Gateway to Eternity (no. 20), and it's time to go.

The Bog of Allen

The Bog of Allen, which has figured in Irish history and legend since prehistoric times, marks the beginning of a great belt of bogland that stretches westward across the country to the Shannon and beyond. **LULLYMORE**, at the foot of the Hill of Allen, site of the legendary Finn MacCool's palace, offers a good opportunity to get to grips with the life of the bogs, past and present. The place – its name means "great dairy pasture" – is an island in the bog where Saint Patrick appointed Eve, an early convert, to run a training college for monks; the heritage centre has a reconstruction of a turf-walled monastic dwelling.

Although it's already open to the public, **Peatland Information Centre** (Mon–Fri 9.30am–5pm, Sat & Sun 2–6pm; £2), housed in the eighteenth-century stable block of Lullymore House, is still in the throes of becoming a comprehensive introduction to Irish bogs. When complete, it will include exhibitions on conservation, energy production, plant and animal life, together with a history of the area and the estate itself. Bear in mind, though, that the project is supported by both *Bórd na Móna* (the Irish Peat Board) and the Electricity Supply Board, whose attitudes to bogland conservation may not necessarily coincide with your own.

ALL ABOUT BOGS

Ten thousand years ago, after the last Ice Age, the melting glaciers and ice sheets left central Ireland covered by shallow lakes. As time went by the lake and lakeside vegetation grew and died and partly decomposed, in a continuing cycle that changed these lakes to fens, and eventually into domed bogs. Ireland now has the finest range of peatlands in Europe.

At one time there were 770,000 acres of raised bog in Ireland; by 1974 there were 160,500; and by 1985 there were just 50,000 acres left. They continue to disappear at a rate of 7500 acres per year. It is only recently that the Irish have awoken to the great natural importance of the boglands. Not only are they home to rare plants, from mosses to bilberries, but they provide a habitat for birds. The bog gases also act as preservatives, and the bogs of Ireland have yielded archeological evidence of botanical and human history up to 9000 years ago in the form of pollens and plant remains, gold and silver artefacts, dug-out canoes and human bodies.

To see a raised bog of international importance, go to **Mongan Bog** in County Offaly. Part of the Clonmacnoise Heritage Zone, it's situated on the banks of the Shannon. And if the bog bug really bites, head for the **Peatland Information Centre** in Lullymore (see above), where you can buy a copy of the Irish Peatland Conservation Council's *Guide to Irish Peatlands*.

Canal country

Monuments to eighteenth-century confidence in Irish trade, which was to be dashed by the Act of Union, the **Royal and Grand canals** flow from Dublin through County Kildare and on into the Irish heartland (see map overleaf). While Ireland had experienced a minor industrial revolution in the mid- to late-eighteenth century, when mines, mills, workshops and canals were created, the Act of Union precluded further development. By walking along the **towpaths**, or cruising on the Grand Canal, you can see how industrialization affected – and failed to affect – the eighteenth-century landscape. **Grand Canal cruises** are based at Tullamore in County Offaly (*Celtic Canal Cruisers*; ☎0506/21861); from here you can head on to the Shannon, or join the River Barrow, which meets the Grand Canal at Robertsbridge and is navigable all the way down to Waterford.

The **Grand Canal** was a monumentally ambitious project, running from Dublin to Robertstown, where it forks. The southern branch joins the River Barrow at Athy, effectively extending the waterway as far south as Waterford, while the western branch runs up to Tullamore in County Offaly and on to join the great natural waterway of the Shannon at Shannon Harbour. As late as 1837 the Grand Canal was carrying over 100,000 passengers a year; it continued to be used for freight right up to 1959. The **Royal Canal** runs past Maynooth and Mullingar before joining the Shannon, many tortuous meanderings later, at Cloondara, north of Lough Rea, for access to the northwest. With the recent re-opening of the Shannon-Erne Waterway (see p.410), these southern waterways are linked once more with the Fermanagh Lakes in the North, as they were in the nineteenth century.

Robertstown and Monasterevin

Two locations are particularly evocative of canal life. **ROBERTSTOWN**, due north of Kildare, where the ways divide – the canal arrived here in 1785 – is no more than a village, yet it boasts a canal stop complete with a grand, pedimented canalside hotel (now pebbledashed and painted bright orange). This is occasionally used for candlelit dinners and is also a centre for canoe training and canal barge trips; for more information call ☎045/70005.

At **MONASTEREVIN**, west of Kildare along the N7, there's a truly magnificent example of eighteenth-century state-of-the-art technology. Here the Grand Canal crosses the River Barrow on an aqueduct (in eighteenth-century terms, the equivalent of a motorway flyover), with superseding technologies upstream (a railway bridge) and downstream (the N7 Dublin–Limerick trunk road). Otherwise, Monasterevin follows the set pattern of an Irish Pale town: a big house, in this case **Moore Abbey** (once the home of the Irish tenor John McCormack), a church and the town itself, a street of eighteenth-century houses on one side of the road only, their gardens sloping down to the River Barrow on the other. The houses get steadily grander and more derelict, going towards the canal; almost at the end of the terrace, next to one that's about to collapse, *Carlow House* offers **B&B** (④). Reasonably priced **food** is available from the *Royal Chinese Restaurant* on the main Dublin Road.

South Kildare: ancient remains

It's a mistake to think of County Kildare as a relatively modern landscape, or to see in it only the legacies of the Anglo-Normans and Anglo-Irish. South of Naas on the Carlow Road (N9), three **high crosses** set in the green, rolling farmland attest that settlements and cultural history here are much, much older. **OLD KILCULLEN**, off the road in a field, is the site of an early Celtic monastery with the remains of eighth-

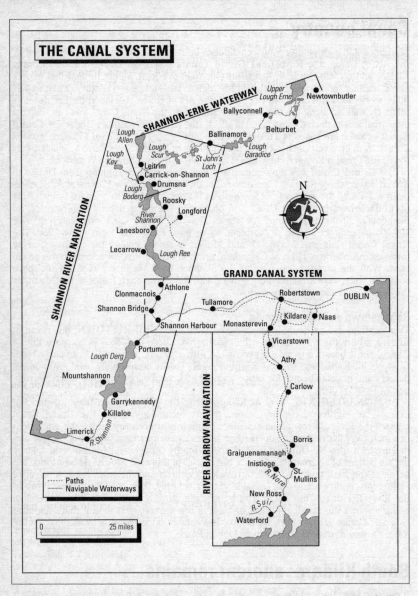

THE CANAL SYSTEM

SHANNON-ERNE WATERWAY

Upper Lough Erne
Newtownbutler
Ballyconnell
Belturbet
Ballinamore
Lough Garadice
Lough Allen
Lough Scur
St John's Loch
Lough Key
Leitrim
Carrick-on-Shannon
Drumsna
Lough Boderg
Roosky
River Shannon
Longford
Lanesboro
Lecarrow
Lough Ree

N

SHANNON RIVER NAVIGATION

GRAND CANAL SYSTEM

Clonmacnois
Athlone
Tullamore
Robertstown
DUBLIN
Shannon Bridge
Kildare
Naas
Shannon Harbour
Monasterevin
Portumna
Vicarstown
Lough Derg
Athy
Mountshannon
Carlow
Garrykennedy
Killaloe
Limerick
R. Shannon
Borris
Graiguenamanagh
Inistioge
R. Nore
St. Mullins
New Ross
R. Suir
Waterford

RIVER BARROW NAVIGATION

----- Paths
·········· Navigable Waterways

0   25 miles

century crosses and an evocative round tower damaged during the 1798 rebellion. Further south along the Carlow Road, there are more monuments to Ireland's ancient heritage at Moone and Castledermot, then, taking the R418 northwestwards, at Kilkea; but first it's well worth taking a short detour west before Moone to the village of Ballitore (about seven miles south of Old Kilcullen).

Ballitore

BALLITORE is an old Quaker village where the eighteenth-century Anglo-Irish political philosopher **Edmund Burke** (1729–97) was educated in the school run by Quaker Abraham Shackleton – a good example of the religious toleration that it seems the British government was prepared to grant anyone but Catholics. Born in Dublin of a Catholic mother and Protestant father, Burke went on to attend Trinity College, and, moving to London in 1750, he kept company with some of the leading figures of the time, among them Oliver Goldsmith (also a Trinity graduate), Samuel Johnson and Joshua Reynolds. His most important works are *A Philosophical Enquiry into the Origin of Ideas of the Sublime and the Beautiful,* an essay in aesthetic theory that is still studied by art historians, and *Reflections on the Revolution in France,* published the year after the event in 1790, in which he argued strongly against Jacobinism and for counter-revolutionary conservatism.

A **museum** (Mon–Sat 11am–6pm) above the village library, which is housed in the old Friends Meeting House, gives a vivid picture of what Quaker life was like here: each member of the industrious community plied a trade, and their sober, business-like approach made Ballitore a model village by comparison with the general squalor and poverty of surrounding places. But the dominant impression given by the copper-plate handwritten letters on show is the sheer boredom of life in a place where any stranger was cause for excitement. The *Cottage Biography* (on sale at the museum) of one of Ballitore's nineteenth-century residents, Mary Leadbeater, preserves more of the same stultifying atmosphere. Up towards the main road is the walled **Quaker graveyard,** whose plain, dignified tombstones seem suitable monuments to the qualities of the dead. If Ballitore's peaceful simplicity takes hold, you can stay at *Griesmount* (☎0507/23158; ④), a fine yellow Georgian house a little way from the village centre.

Signposted from the centre of the village is **Crookstown Mill** (April–Sept 10am–7pm; Oct–March 10am–4pm; £2). Built in the 1840s and still functioning, it contributed to an independence from the potato that, along with the industries introduced by the Quakers, meant that there was strikingly little emigration or starvation here during the Famine.

A mile or so further south is the **Irish Pewtermill** (☎0507/24164); although you can see pewter being worked, the place is primarily a retail experience – fine if you're into the Claddagh rings and ancestral crest-type of export Irishry.

From Moone to Kilkea

Back on the N9, the small village of **MOONE** (three miles from Ballitore) once formed a link in the chain of monasteries founded by Saint Columba, and the garden of Moone Abbey contains the ruins of a fourteenth-century Franciscan friary and a ninth-century cross. The *Moone High Cross Inn* (☎0507/24112; ③) is a friendly, rambling old pub; it serves a good range of bar food, plus a more ambitious menu in the **restaurant**.

Five or so miles further south at **CASTLEDERMOT** there's more to see: two tenth-century granite high crosses, plus a bizarre twelfth-century Romanesque doorway standing by itself in front of an ugly modern church and a truncated round tower. Castledermot also has a thirteenth-century Augustinian abbey, an example of how the European monastic orders muscled in on the indigenous Irish church. Its substantial remains give a completely different feel to what might otherwise be merely a roadside stop; get the keys from the caretaker, who lives next door. There's a scattering of coffee shops; or, for evening meals and accommodation, try *Doyle's School House* **B&B** (☎0503/44282; ④).

Kilkea Castle, the Fitzgeralds' second Kildare stronghold (after Maynooth), stands a couple of miles up the Athy Road (R418) from Castledermot. It's impressive looking, though largely a sham – originally built in 1180, it was modified in the seventeenth century, and most of it is a mid-nineteenth-century restoration. Massively refurbished again in the 1980s, it's now a luxury **hotel** (☎0503/45156; ⑨) with a leisure centre and sauna which you can use even if you're not staying there. There's a more reasonable **B&B** option at *Kilkea Lodge Farm* (☎0503/45112; ⑤), a modest stone-built farmhouse with a riding centre attached, and it does dinner for £15–20.

Athy

On the border with County Laois, close to the point where the Grand Canal meets the River Barrow, sits **ATHY** (rhymes with *sty*, emphasis on the last syllable), one of those places where a bucketful of imagination is required to envisage it as it once was: prosperity has turned a formerly handsome Georgian town with a fine main square into something much more ramshackle. A massive riverside factory sits oddly with the Georgian fanlights and a hideous modern church: the latter is apparently supposed to make reference to a dolmen, although the Sydney Opera House seems a stronger influence. Athy's designation as a heritage town, however, is bringing its historical resonances to life. By the riverside stands the square tower of the fifteenth-century **White's Castle**, built by Sir John Talbot, Viceroy of Ireland, to protect the ford across the River Barrow and the inhabitants of the Pale from the dispossessed Irish beyond. Across from the town hall, the fanciful neo-Jacobean courthouse, built in 1862, is to house a **heritage centre** (ring the public library for details; ☎0507/31424).

Also in the courthouse is the **tourist information office** (July & Aug Mon–Sat 10am–5pm; Sept–June Mon–Fri 10am–5pm; ☎0507/31859). Aside from some leisurely **strolls** along the Grand Canal, however, the town's unlikely to detain you for too long – except to **eat** or **stay** at *Tonlegee House* (☎0507/31473; ⑥; dinner £20), a restaurant with rooms in a solidly built mansion that surveys the countryside just beyond Athy's suburban sprawl. It's signposted off the Kilkenny Road.

travel details

Trains

Arklow to: Dublin (4 daily; 1hr 20min).
Bray to: Dublin Connolly (4 daily; 25min).
Kildare to: Dublin Heuston (20 daily; 30min).

Wicklow to: Dublin (4 daily; 50min).

Bus Éireann

Kildare to: Dublin (15 daily; 1hr 20min).

CHAPTER THREE

LAOIS AND OFFALY

f you've come to Ireland for the scenery, or the wild remote places, or the romance of the far west, then the central counties of **Laois** and **Offaly** probably don't hold a great deal to entice you. But this quiet and unremarkable part of the country between Dublin and the Shannon is an excellent place to get to know another Ireland, one not yet much hyped by the tourist authorities. Its gentle, green farming land bears the marks of a complex pattern of settlement: the Celtic Church, Viking invaders, the arrival of the Anglo-Normans and, very strongly in these twin counties, the planted settlements with which the British sought to keep their base in the Pale secure. It's a subtle, detailed landscape, which the destruction of Ireland's foreign trade by the Act of Union in 1801 ensured remained virtually untouched by the industrial revolution.

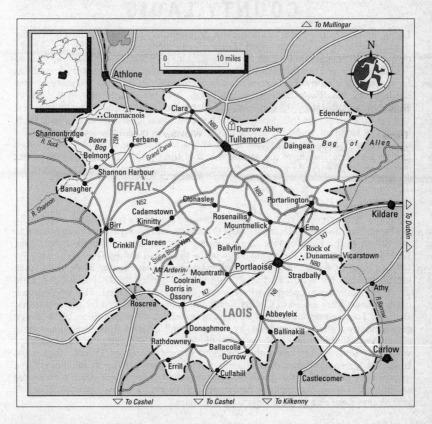

Transport in Laois and Offaly is easy – the main N7 trunk road and the main railway line to Limerick slice straight through Laois, while the industrial centre of Tullamore makes an obvious transport centre, both road and rail, for Offaly. There's an increasing number of **accommodation** possibilities – some comfortable, mid-price hotels and even the odd hostel – but, with the exception of the Celtic monastery at Clonmacnois, the area remains lightly touristed, and it's wise to plan overnight stops in advance.

COUNTY LAOIS

Laois, or *Leix* in the more old-fashioned orthography – neither spelling gives any useful clue as to its pronunciation: *Leash* – is in many ways Ireland's least-known county. Most people know it only for the maximum security jail at Portlaoise, or as an ill-defined area you go through on the way to Limerick. While most Irish counties have a strong identity, Laois seems oddly accidental. To the east it's more or less bordered by the **River Barrow**; to the north, it forms a large part of the **Slieve Bloom** mountain range (though some of that is in County Offaly); but to the west and south there seems little sense in the borders. Laois smarts from an image problem that's summed up by the adage that its landscape is like the local accent – flat and boring. That unjust reputation seems at last to be fading, and the cheap rentals and proximity to Dublin of the southern half of the county are beginning to attract **artists** and **craftspeople** who've had enough of the big-money cultural politics of the capital.

Some history

Until the mid-sixteenth century, Laois remained under its **traditional chiefs**, the O'Mores, FitzPatricks, O'Dempseys and O'Dunnes, and posed an increasing threat to the British in the Pale. In 1556, a new county was carved out of these tribal lands, settled (or "planted", in the terminology of the time) and named Queen's County (to Offaly's King's County). A new town, **Maryborough**, named after Mary Tudor, was established at what is now Portlaoise. None of this quelled the O'Mores, but eventually transplantation succeeded where mere plantation had failed. The troublesome clans of Laois were exiled to County Kerry and Laois was left free for the colonizers. Because Laois came under British control so early, there are none of the huge estates that were later dished out, by Cromwell and Charles II, to loyal followers in the far west. Rather, there are smaller landholdings and planned towns, interspersed with some settlements of dissenting religious groups – Quakers, French Huguenots. Ironically, given the treatment Ireland's Catholics were getting at the time, these groups were able to find the freedom of worship they desired here. All this makes for an intimate – if unspectacular – landscape, epitomizing a history of colonialism as real as anywhere else in the former British Empire.

Portlaoise and around

PORTLAOISE is best known for its top-security **jail**, which leaps into the news whenever there's an argument about extradition of a prisoner to the North, and the mental hospital – they're both on the same street, known to locals as Nuts 'n' Bolts Road. The prison was founded in 1547, when the O'Mores held the fortress of Dunamase to the south, as a fortification under the name of Fort Protector. In 1556 the town was planted and renamed Maryborough. Today it's seedy and depressed; the main road bypasses it entirely and, unless you arrive by train and can't avoid it, you're probably well advised to do the same. It does, however, have a useful **tourist office** (May–Sept Mon–Sat 10am–6pm; open sporadically at other times; ☎0502/21178). If you find yourself needing to stay, there's a comfortable **hotel**, *The Regency* (☎0502/21305; ④) on Main Street; *Brad's Alley* coffee shop, almost opposite, does good daytime **food**. For **drinking**, you could head a few miles out of town on the Dublin Road to the thatched *Treacy's*, supposedly the oldest family-run pub in Ireland (founded in 1780), which still fulfils its traditional role serving travellers on the long haul from Dublin to the west.

What is well worth seeing, though, is the **Rock of Dunamase**, two or three miles east on the Stradbally Road (N80). An extraordinary, knobbly mound encrusted with layer upon layer of fortifications, it's a great place for gazing out, beyond the flat surrounding countryside, to the Slieve Bloom hills to the north and the Wicklow Mountains in the east. There are suggestions that Dunamase was known to Ptolemy under the name of *Dunum*, and Celtic *Dun Masc* was valuable enough to be plundered by the Vikings in 845. Today, the hill is crowned by a **ruined castle** of the twelfth-century king of Leinster, Dermot MacMurrough. He invited Strongbow to Ireland and married his daughter, Aoife, to him, including Dunamase in her dowry. Explicable only in terms of the complex history of the Anglo-Normans, Dunamase eventually passed from Strongbow – Henry II's right-hand man – to the Mortimers and the O'Mores, bitter opponents of the English. It was finally blown up by Cromwell's troops in 1650. The earthworks 500 yards to the east of the fortress are still known as Cromwell's lines.

STRADBALLY (literally "street-town"), a few miles further west, is notable chiefly for the **narrow-gauge railway** at Stradbally Hall. A nineteenth-century steam locomotive, formerly used in the Guinness brewery in Dublin, runs six times a year; there's also a **traction engine museum** (pick up keys at *Dunne's* bar, Court Square or 27 Church Avenue) in the town – strictly for steam buffs – and a **steam engine rally** on the first weekend in August. You can **stay** in solid comfort at *Tullamoy House*, a stone-built nineteenth-century farmhouse set in its own parkland three miles out of town (May–Oct; ☎0507/27111; ③).

Once a busy halt on the Grand Canal, **VICARSTOWN**, north of Stradbally on the R427 (about ten miles from Portlaoise) is now just a few houses and some crumbling stone warehouses clustered round a hump-backed bridge, although it's showing new signs of life as a result of the increased use of the canal (see the map on p.118). It's chiefly remarkable for the spirited **traditional music** sessions on Monday nights in *Turley's* bar (aka *The Anchor Inn*) – be there by nine and sit tight. You can **stay** on the other side of the water at *Crean's*, offically known as *The Vicarstown Inn* (☎0502/25189; ④).

The South: Abbeyleix and Durrow

The south of County Laois consists of lush farmland, dotted with estate towns and villages. The largest of these is **ABBEYLEIX** (about ten miles from Portlaoise on the N8), named after a Cistercian abbey founded here by a member of the O'More family in 1183. In one of those periodic bursts of enthusiasm that seem to be a mark of the Ascendancy, Abbeyleix was entirely remodelled by Viscount de Vesci in the eighteenth century and relocated on the coach road away from the old village to the southwest. The place has been designated a heritage town, so no doubt there'll be more information (and accommodation) available before long.

Unfortunately, the attractive pedimented eighteenth-century **Abbeyleix House** (designed by James Wyatt) isn't open to the public, and the gardens are open just two Sundays a year. The best way to see them is to go **riding** with the estate's school, *Parkland Trekking* (☎0502/31400), which will take you through the grounds. In the village, the famous *Morrissey's Bar* is an enormous grocer's shop and pub combined which probably hasn't changed in fifty years, with pew seats and a brazier and old advertisements for beer and tobacco that seem to have been forgotten by time. It's a great place to sit and soak up the atmosphere. There are a couple of small **B&Bs** in Abbeyleix itself; try Ms Peverell's *Olde Manse* on Lower Main Steet (☎0502/31423; ③) or the newly refurbished *Hibernian Hotel* (☎0502/31252; ④), a couple of doors up. A mile out of town, just past the gates of Abbeyleix House, you can stay in the solidly handsome *Norefield House* (☎0502/31059; ④). *Quinn's Tea and Coffee Room* does cheap and delicious soup, sandwiches and home baking.

About three miles southeast in **BALLINAKILL**, itself a pretty Georgian village on a sloping main street, just north of the town the gardens of **Heywood House** (ring ☎0502/33334 for opening times) are worth a look for their re-creation of a distant Italianate idyll. The house was burned down early this century, but the gardens, with planting by the English garden designer Gertrude Jeckyll and architecture – complete with gazebos and sunken terraces – by Sir Edwin Lutyens, architect to the Empire, are currently being restored. You can stay in a modest example of Georgian architecture, *The Glebe*, which is run as a B&B by Mrs Dowling (☎0502/33368; ④).

DURROW, back on the N8 (about six miles south of Abbeyleix), is yet another planned estate town, grouped around a green adjoining **Castle Durrow**, which is, its medievalized gateway notwithstanding, the first great Palladian house to be built in this area (1716). It's now a convent, but you can walk up the drive and see it. The town was owned by the Duke of Ormond, who for reasons of his own had it adopted by County Kilkenny; it took an act of parliament to get it returned to what was then Queen's County in 1834. If you hit an **auction** day, *Sheppard's* the auctioneers (☎0502/36123) is diverting – not only for the hushed excitement of an Irish auction, but also for the quality of the furniture: generally both more solidly made and more fanciful than its English equivalent. The *Castle Arms* (☎0502/36118; ⑤), facing the green, is about the only place to **stay**; sturdy **home cooking** can be found at the *Copper Kettle*, two doors up. Comfortable independent **hostel** accommodation (self-catering or breakfast for £2 and dinner for around £10) is available in a converted grain loft on a working farm at **BALLACOLLA** (*IHH*, open all year; ☎0502/34032; ②), about two miles northwest of Durrow on the R434 and a good base for exploring the surrounding countryside.

The very **southwest** corner of County Laois is quiet farming land punctuated by small villages such as Cullahill, Rathdowney and Erill, full of neat colour-washed houses. About eight miles west of Durrow (take the R434 then the R433), **RATHDOWNEY** is altogether a more metropolitan sort of place, with a raffish pride that gives it a continental flavour. The *Central* bar on the main square does B&B (☎0505/46567; ②), plus breakfast, tea and dinner. Mrs Carroll runs a B&B at *River House* (☎0505/44120; ④) in Erill, four miles west along the R433.

Just north of Rathdowney, **DONAGHMORE**'s **Workhouse and Agricultural Museum** (daily 2–5pm; £2) gives some idea of the less picturesque aspects of the area's past. The austere building, formerly the parish workhouse (at some distance from the village itself) is evocative of the lives of the poor – its very size indicates the scale of the problem of rural poverty, even if the exhibits themselves, a selection of mainly agricultural machinery, seem a bit random. Families were frequently broken up on admission and no one was allowed to leave the premises; on average two of the 800 inmates died every week, to be buried in the mass grave behind the workhouse.

The buildings functioned as a workhouse between 1853 and 1886, and the museum exhibits take up the story again with a series of documents relating to the Donaghmore Co-operative, which was founded in 1927. Unfortunately, many of them – one of the cases has an order for sandwiches at a hotel in Birr – are of little more than local interest. The museum practises a strenuous self-censorship over the intervening period, during which the buildings were used as a British army barracks, at one stage housing the notorious Black and Tans – something the authorities deem as wiser not to address.

The village itself – three pubs, a Protestant church and a mill – is a clear statement of the inability of these little settlements to ride out the economic turbulence of the nineteenth century.

Slieve Bloom and North Laois

North Laois is dominated by the **Slieve Bloom** (pronounced *Shlieve Bloom*) **Mountains**, which bring some welcome variation to this flat county. Although the highest point, the Alderin Mountain (in the south half of the range, beyond the Glendine Gap, near the border with Offaly) only reaches to 1735ft, they're ruggedly desolate enough to give a taste of real wilderness, even if you follow the **Slieve Bloom Way**. The Way, little over 31 miles in length, takes you round a complete circuit of the mountains across moorland, woods and bog, along part of one of the old high roads to Tara and through the bed of a pre-Ice Age river valley. Along the way dense conifer plantations attempt to survive, with a little help from the taxpayer, way above the natural tree line. If your time is limited and you have a car, the best place to start is probably at the northern end of the range at **Glen Barrow's** car park (three miles west of Rosenallis). Skirting the mountains, the road from Mountmellick (R422), as it passes through Clonaslee and Cadamstown (strictly speaking in Co. Offaly), offers easy access to some pleasant walking, particularly at Cadamstown. Here a waterfall's icy waters are used for bathing by hardy locals, with the tweely named *My Little Tea and Craft Shop* (actually the front room of a cottage) open for a revitalizing feed afterwards. If you don't have a car, you can catch the Dublin–Portumna **bus** at Birr or Portarlington and start walking at Kinnitty, a couple of miles south of Cadamstown, a delightful upland village, which has an excellent pub. The old custom of walking to the summit of Arderin has recently been revived; if you're here on the last Sunday in July, ask around.

Unfortunately, **accommodation** is limited in this neck of the woods; you'll either have to base yourself in Birr (see p.132) or head for the Slieve Bloom's southeastern foothills. Here, in **COOLRAIN**, the *Village Inn* – also good for traditional music – has rooms (☎0502/35126; ③), and *High Pine Farm* at Annaghmore (☎0509/37029; ③) can make a good base for walking. If you feel like a real treat, there's **Roundwood House**, just outside **Mountrath**, a mid-eighteenth-century Palladian mansion nowadays run as a guesthouse. Originally built by a Quaker who had made his fortune in America, it's a doll's house of a building decorated in vibrantly authentic Georgian colours, with a double-height hall boasting a Chinese Chippendale-style staircase. It's a relaxed, unceremonious sort of place that seems devoted to the virtues of good food, conversation and alcohol: you are likely to find yourself sitting by the turf fire after an excellent dinner, arguing endlessly with other guests about anything and everything (☎0502/32120; ⑥); dinner £20.

Mountmellick, Portarlington and Emo

Mountmellick and Portarlington are typical of the few little settlements that grew up independently of the great houses, and both were communities of outsiders.

MOUNTMELLICK (about six miles north of Portlaoise on the N80) was founded in the seventeenth century by Quakers and still has a spacious eighteenth-century feel to it. You need imagination to see the houses as the elegant buildings they must once have been, but Mountmellick in its heyday was undoubtedly both cultured and prosperous – it had 27 industries, including brewing, distilling, soap- and glue-making and iron foundries.

It was also famous for **Mountmellick work**, white-on-white embroidery that used the forms of flowers and plans to create elegant designs. Local women are setting up a co-operative to revive the art of Mountmellick work, and it's planned to hold residential and day courses in this calm old Quaker craft. The Mountmellick Embroidery Group is based at Codd's Mill, a little way out of town on the Portlaoise Road, which also houses Mountmellick's embryonic **tourist information centre** (daily 9am–5.30pm; ☎0502/24525) and a small exhibition about the town's Quaker heritage.

Six miles northeast of Mountmellick (take the R423), **PORTARLINGTON** was founded in 1667 by Sir Henry Bennett, Lord Arlington (for whom Arlington, Virginia, is also named), and settled by a group of Huguenot refugees here in the late seventeenth century; they built elegant Georgian houses with spacious orchards and gardens, which once grew exotic fruit such as peaches and apricots (particularly fine mansions are to be seen in Patrick Street). Some of the inscriptions on the tombstones of St Michael's Church, still known as the French Church, are in French, and surnames such as Champ and Le Blanc survive.

The town's elegant Huguenot menfolk used to sit outside the Tholsel, or Market House, in Market Square, sipping that exotic new beverage, tea, from porcelain cups. This idyll had its darker side: a channel was dug to encircle the town, already surrounded on three sides by the River Owenmass, with water to protect it from the displaced Irish, who had gone to live in the bogs. Today, the town's heritage is celebrated in a French week – complete with snail-eating competition – in July.

The **People's Museum** (Sun 11.30am–1pm & 3–5.30pm; free) in the Catholic Club on Main Street has exhibits ranging from 4000-year-old axe-heads to twentieth-century artefacts. North of the town, the *Bord na Mona* (the Irish Peat Board) power station is busy burning away the bogland's unrenewable resources.

One of the few really big estates in County Laois is **Emo Court**; take the R419 from Portarlington (or if approaching from Portlaoise it's just off the N7 at New Inn). Designed by James Gandon for Lord Arlington around 1790 (but finished, not entirely according to Gandon's plans, only in the mid-nineteenth century), it's a massive domed building which has been impressively restored by its present owner after years of neglect when it was run as a Jesuit seminary. The house is now administered by the Office of Public Works, and you can wander through the extensive **grounds** during daylight hours; the **house** itself is open for guided tours (mid-June to mid-Sept Fri–Mon 1–6pm; £2; Heritage Card). The nearby **Coolbanagher Church** is a modest and graceful building by Gandon; unfortunately, it's almost always locked.

If the charms of Laois's quiet landscape take hold of you, you can discover more in John Feehan's excellent topographical survey, *Laois: an environmental history* – a good example of the new breed of local history that integrates both the natural and the human-made past.

COUNTY OFFALY

From the Bog of Allen in the east to Boora Bog in the west, **County Offaly** is dominated by bog and peat. It's a low-lying region bounded to the northwest by the meandering Shannon and its flood plain, and it's only in the south that the land rises at all into the foothills of the Slieve Bloom range. The **Bog of Allen**, vast, black and desolate, has been intensively exploited for peat; only real bog freaks will find much of interest there. **Boora Bog** is entirely different – smaller and less unremittingly flat and bare, it's the site of an archeological find that proves that there was human life here 9000 years ago. Western County Offaly is also the location of **Clonmacnois**, the greatest monastery of early Celtic Ireland, on the great, watery flood-plain of the Shannon.

The Bog of Allen only really becomes overpowering after Edenderry, which traditionally marked the edge of the Pale. But even here, after miles of dark bogland, it's a distinct relief to reach somewhere with lots of people and an air of prosperity: Edenderry's single wide street is lined with cheerfully painted houses. Pushing on along the Dublin–Portumna bus route towards Tullamore, you pass through Daingean, formerly Philipstown, the provincial capital in the days when Offaly was known as King's County (both county and capital were planted in Mary Tudor's reign and named after her husband, Philip II of Spain).

Tullamore

Coming from either direction, the Bog of Allen to the east or Boora Bog to the west, the bright lights and solid buildings of **TULLAMORE**, astride the Grand Canal, seem welcoming. Its Victorian ambience makes the town look more English than Irish, a result of moving the capital from Philipstown to Tullamore in 1834, following decades in which the British pushed the boundaries of King's County ever further westwards. Apart from the shops and a certain amount of nightlife, there are really only two reasons to come to Tullamore. One is to pay homage to **Irish Mist**, a truly delicious whiskey liqueur, although unfortunately the factory, right in the middle of town, isn't open to the public and doesn't give away free samples.

The other reason is **Charleville Forest Castle** (June–Sept Wed–Sun 1–4pm; April–May Sat & Sun 2–5pm; Oct–March by appointment on ☎0506/21279; £2.50), an extraordinary Georgian-Gothic mansion ("perhaps the first deliberately formed asymmetrical house in Ireland", wrote Dan Cruickshank in the excellent *Guide to the Georgian Buildings of Britain and Ireland*), built in 1779 to the designs of Francis Johnston. The surrounding estate is wonderfully spooky, with a Gothic element suggestive of a horror movie – castellated turrets, shady trees and clinging ivy – while the house in the centre of the estate, surrounded by a second wall topped by urns, is a secretive place ready-made for diabolical activities. With its splendid old trees, leafy walks and even a grotto, the place has everything you could wish for. To get there, take the Birr road out of Tullamore (the N52): Charleville's gates are on the right as you leave the town – about ten minutes' walk.

Practicalities

Tullamore's **tourist office** (June–Aug Mon–Fri 10am–5pm; ☎0506/52617) is on Bury Quay, a little way down the Rahan road and turn right. If you want to **stay**, there are numerous B&Bs roundabout, such as *Oakfield House*, Rahan Road (☎0506/21385; ④), as well as the comfortable *Phoenix Arms* on Bridge Street (☎0506/21066; ⑥) – also a good place to **eat**.

The town's location on the Grand Canal (see the map on p.118) can make it a good starting-point for exploring either the Shannon or Barrow rivers by **boat** – it's linked to both by the Grand Canal – although if you're headed for the Shannon, it's worth considering basing yourself among the quieter charms of Banagher (see p.130); cruisers can be rented from *Celtic Canal Cruisers* (☎0506/21861). **Bike rental** is available from *Buckley Cycles*, Brewery Lane (£6.50 per day, £27 per week; ☎0902/81606), which is a participant in the *Raleigh Rent-a-Bike* scheme.

Durrow Abbey

Four miles north of Tullamore on the N52, beyond some handsome wrought-iron gates to the left of the road, lies the site of **Durrow Abbey** (daily 9am–1pm), one of the monasteries founded by the energetic Saint Colmcille (better known as Saint Columba), and the place where the *Book of Durrow* – an illuminated late seventh-century copy of the Gospels, now exhibited in Trinity College Library, Dublin – was made.

A long avenue brings you to a typically Irish juxtaposition: a grand Georgian mansion next to a medieval church, which stands on the site of the monastery. A notice at the main gates gives directions to the high cross and tombstones; behind you is the formality of the avenue, ahead the well-tended grounds of the house. Inside the church walls everything is different – the disused churchyard, the masonry strangled with ivy, gravestones leaning crazily on uneven ground as if the earth has opened and disgorged their contents . . . an eerie place, where Durrow's high cross and tombstones seem to represent sweet reason.

The Shannon: Clonmacnois to Banagher

Western Offaly is dominated by the bog and the **Shannon**, one virtually impassable, the other for centuries a means of communication; there's a huge range of ancient sites along the river. Exploring the *esker* ridges (raised paths above the bog) of this drowsy, bog-and-water landscape has a quiet appeal if you hit good weather. It's excellent **cycling** country, and while there may not be much the untrained eye can identify most of the time, the romantic ruins that dot the landscape offer plenty of food for the imagination, and following roads that have for centuries been the only passages through the bog has a resonance of its own.

Although the monastery at **Clonmacnois** has made it onto the bus-tour itinerary, these visitors generally climb straight back on board and head for the west, and in general the area remains pleasantly unfashionable and untouristed. That said, there's an increasing range and number of places to **stay** in the area as the Shannon-based tourist industry expands, with the best base located in the relaxed Georgian town of **Banagher**, basking on the banks of the river. Alternatively, you could stay in the busier town of **Birr**, further south, with its elegant Georgian architecture and impressive Big House (see p.132).

Clonmacnois

Of all the ancient sites along the Shannon, **CLONMACNOIS**, early Celtic Ireland's foremost monastery, in the northwest of the county, is by far the most important. Approaching from Shannonbridge to the south, the first evidence of its whereabouts is a stone wall leaning precariously towards the Shannon. This is actually a remnant of a thirteenth-century Norman **castle**, built to protect the river crossing, which has leaned ever since its wooden foundations were destroyed by fire, and has nothing whatever to do with the monastery.

When you first see the **monastic complex** (daily June–Sept 9am–7pm; mid-March to May & Sept–Oct 10am–6pm; Nov to mid-March 10am–5pm; £1.50; Heritage Card) – a huddle of wind- and rain-swept buildings on an open plain in a bend in the Shannon, which can seem almost dwarfed by the sheer volume of non-stop tourist traffic that its gleaming new visitor centre processes – it seems hard to believe that this was a settlement of any importance. Yet this was not just a monastery, but a **royal city** and burial place for the kings of Connacht and Tara, including the last high king of Ireland, Rory O'Conor, buried here in 1198. It stood at what was then the busy junction of *Escir*

Riada, the great road from Dublin to the west, and the Shannon; and as the book-shrines, croziers and other richly decorated artefacts on show in the National Museum in Dublin testify, it was also an artistic centre of the highest order. The twelfth-century *Book of the Dun Cow*, now in the Royal Irish Academy Library in Dublin, is only one of many treasures made here.

Founded by **Saint Kieran** around 548, the monastery was largely protected by its isolation; surrounded by bog, Clonmacnois could only be reached by boat or by one road that ran along what are still called *eskers*. It withstood Irish, Viking and Norman attacks, but in 1552 the English garrison at Athlone looted the monastery and left it beyond recovery. However, plenty remains: a cathedral, eight churches, two round towers, high crosses, grave slabs and a thirteenth-century ring fort.

The admission fee to the complex entitles you to an audio-visual presentation and a guided tour, as well as access to the interpretative centre, exhibition (and cosy coffee shop). Clonmacnois is still a pilgrimage site – Saint Kieran's festival is in September – and the video is a rather romantic hagiography, detailing the saint's peregrinations through ancient Ireland before he settled at Clonmacnois. More important is the **exhibition**; all the site's carved crosses – it has the richest collection in Ireland – have been moved inside to protect them from County Offaly's incessant wind and rain.

The early tenth-century **Great Cross**, over twelve feet high, is unusual in that it includes a secular scene; it is believed to commemorate King Flann and Abbot Coman; the carvings represent the monastery's foundation and scenes from the passion story. The **South Cross**, dating from the ninth century, is decorated with flower and animal motifs.

The buildings

Seeing any significant differences between these small, gaunt, grey buildings takes a trained eye. The **cathedral**, scarcely bigger than its companions, was built in 904 by King Flann and Abbot Coman Conailleach and rebuilt in the fourteenth century by Tomultach MacDermot; the sandstone pillars of the west doorway may have been incorporated from the earlier church.

Not everything at Clonmacnois, however, is as simple as it seems: to the right of the cathedral, **Teampall** (Temple) **Doolin** carries the elaborate coat of arms of Edmund Dowling of Clondarane, who restored the building in 1689; **Teampall Hurpan**, adjacent, was actually added in its entirety in the seventeenth century. **Teampall Kieran**, on the other side of the cathedral, is the reputed burial place of the founding saint, as well as allegedly the place where he built the first church on the site; the ruined **Teampall Kelly** is probably twelfth century.

Away from the main group of buildings is **O'Rourke's tower**, a round tower 60ft high, erected just after the cathedral and blasted by lightning in 1134. On the outer boundary of the site, by the Shannon, are the **Teampall Finghin**, with another round tower dating from 1124, and the **Teampall Conor**, which was founded early in the eleventh century by Cathal O'Connor and used as a parish church from around 1790.

The **Church of the Nunnery**, away from the main enclosure, is signposted but difficult to find, and most people lose heart before they reach it. Follow the path across the site and bear left along the lane. The church is a little further along on the right, two lovely Romanesque arches in a field by the Shannon, exuding a feeling of peace. It's hard to imagine Clonmacnois ever feeling crowded, but if your arrival does happen to coincide with a bus party, this is the place to come.

The **boats** you'll see moored at Clonmacnois, incidentally, are all private; to rent a craft, you'll have to go downstream to Banagher or Athlone.

The Clonmacnois **tourist office** is next to the monastery (June–July 9am–7pm; March–May & Aug–Oct 10am–6pm; ; ☎0906/74134). There's B&B **accommodation** a mile from Clonmacnois on the Shannonbridge Road at *Kajon House* (☎0905/74191; ③);

you can also **camp** there. One of the best places to stay, however, is a picturesque nineteenth-century cottage – white-painted, with red windows and a peat roof – restored and rented out by the Claffeys (☎0905/74149; ③).

About five miles east of Clonmacnois, just off the main N62 Athlone–Roscrea road, the An Dún Transport and Heritage Museum (daily 10am–6pm; £2) has a small collection of lovingly tended vintage cars, plus agricultural vehicles and an odd assortment of butter churns, televisions and typewriters. There's also a pleasant coffee shop.

Shannonbridge and Shannon Harbour

From Clonmacnois, the road to Shannonbridge skirts the Boora Bog. **SHANNONBRIDGE** has a set of traffic lights, but only because the sixteen-span bridge across the river is so narrow. Upstream, the wetlands of the Shannon open up; downstream a power station signifies the exploitation of the boglands. This is the point where counties Offaly, Roscommon and Galway meet and the River Suck joins the Shannon: hence the strategically placed and massive artillery fortification dating from Napoleonic times. There are a couple of **B&Bs** here including *Racha House* (☎0905/ 74249; ③) and *Laurel Lodge* (☎0905/74189; ④), a mile out of town towards Banagher, which rent out bikes and boats. The *Shannonside Diner* does snacks and light meals; there's a music pub – *Killeen's Tavern* – on the main street.

Just outside the town on the Tullamore Road (the R357), at *Bord na Mona*'s (the Irish Peat Board) Blackwater power-generating plant, you can explore the bog on the **Clonmacnois and West Offaly Railway**, which will take you on a five-mile circular tour on narrow gauge through the Blackwater Bog. Unlike Clara Bog (see opposite), Blackwater Bog is being exploited hell-for-leather; you can't miss the power station with its thin chimneys belching brown smoke into the air – the irony of touring the bog under the auspices of the organization that's itself helping to destroy it won't be lost on anyone. "A few hundred years from now", says the publicity material, suavely, the bog "will be an integrated tapestry of fields, woodlands and wetlands. The landscape never stands still." The tour, which lasts some 45 minutes, leaves every hour on the hour (April–Oct 10am–5pm; £3, families £8.50) and is preceded by a 35-minute video on the flora and fauna you're about to see.

Also nearby, and of particular interest if you have children to entertain, is the Ashbrook Open Farm and Agricultural Museum (April–Sept 10am–7pm; adults £2, children £1.50, family £7), with plenty of farm animals, donkeys, rare birds and farm implements.

About five miles further south (take the R357 and turn at Clonony), **SHANNON HARBOUR** – a few buildings and the ivy-covered *Grand Hotel* – is where the River Brosna and the Grand Canal meet the Shannon after their journey right across Ireland. As you walk down to the junction, there comes a magical point where the entire landscape seems to become water. **Clonony Castle**, a mile or two further inland, is a ruined sixteenth-century tower house with a nineteenth-century reconstructed barn, scene of a private colonization attempt, in the seventeenth century, by an entrepreneurial German, Matthew de Renzi.

Banagher and around

Another couple of miles downstream, **BANAGHER** consists of one long street sloping down to the Shannon, fortified on the Connacht side by a Martello tower. With the construction of a new marina, it's rapidly turning itself into a relaxed and elegant touring centre for the Irish Midlands. Anthony Trollope was posted here as a Post Office surveyor in 1841, and wrote his first book, *The Macdermots of Ballycloran*, in Banagher; Charlotte Brontë spent her honeymoon here. There's a wayward local variant on

Classical architecture: two houses on the main street have pepperpot towers, inside which everything curves – doors, fanlights, pediments, the lot. One of these, dated around 1760, has been transformed into an excellent **hostel**, *Crank House* (*IHH*, open all year; ☎0509/51458; ②), which has no curfew but does have a coffee shop (daily 8am–8pm), art gallery and **tourist information office** (March–Oct Mon–Fri 9.30am–8pm, Sat & Sun 9.30am–5pm). There's B&B **accommodation** across the road at the *Old Forge* (☎0509/51504; ④) and a comfortable friendly hotel, *The Brosna Lodge* (☎0509/51350; ④), with rooms at practically B&B prices.

The range of **eating** and **drinking** places reflects the extra visitors the town is getting. For daytime eating, *The Water's Edge* offers coffee and snacks – and a fine view of how the other half lives on the pitch 'n' putt course on the opposite bank. *The Vine House* **restaurant** and music bar, close to the river, has a courtyard garden and elegantly hearty menu with an emphasis on seafood (main courses around £8.75). *The Brosna Lodge*'s restaurant, *Snipes*, has a good menu at around the same price. There's a handful of **bars** – the *Shannon Hotel* often has music and also has a pleasant garden where you can sit outside in good weather. *J.J. Hough's*, on Main Street, is a good old singing pub. You can **rent bikes** from *K. Donegan* in the main street (☎0509/51178), **canoes** from *Shannon Adventure Canoeing Holidays* (☎0509/51411), and **boats** to cruise up the Shannon from *Silverline Cruisers* (☎0509/61112) and *Carrick-Craft* (☎0509/51189). A Clare Class cruiser, which will sleep up to eight, costs between £800 and £1400 per week, although smaller boats are available from £235. For real luxury, this is one of the points where you can pick up the *Shannon Princess*, an old Dutch barge that plies the river between Killaloe and Lanesborough, offering the services of a first-class hotel, including cordon bleu cooking (☎088/514809).

Croghan Castle, two miles out of town and signposted from the centre, is a massive Norman tower house with Georgian additions, inside an equally massive enclosure (May–Sept Wed–Sat 2–6.50pm; £3, families £7.50; outside opening hours ☎0509/51650). Inhabited continuously for more than 800 years, it packs a wealth of history, starting with a seventh-century monastery founded by St Cronan on the site. For £40 a night, you can also **stay** there and eat breakfast in the magnificent dining hall, warmed in winter by a massive fire. The Thompsons, who own Croghan, also have another castle, **Emmell Castle**, thirteen miles to the south, which you can rent. A sixteenth-century keep with a Georgian house attached, it sleeps seven and costs £400–490 a week and £300 for a three-day weekend. When visiting the castle, you can also take in Lusmagh Pet Farm (summer daily 2–6pm; £2, families £5) for some therapeutic patting of pigs, geese, ostriches and sheep.

Close to the castle, and also signposted, is **Victoria Lock**, understandably something of a local beauty spot, where the Shannon runs into two separate channels. Trollope's biographer, James Pope-Hennessy, found the vegetation "so rich and wild, so tangled and impenetrable", that he was moved to compare it, in unreflective colonial tones, to Jamaica or Dominica. It's certainly a beautiful place; beneath the lock, released from artificial constraints, the river spills over once more across its flood-plain – the feeling is one of privation followed by liberation.

Clara Bog

Banagher also provides a good base for exploring **Clara Bog**, a large (665 hectares) and relatively unspoiled tract of raised bog. *Bord na Mona* planned to develop it for industrial-scale peat-cutting and began draining the eastern section in the early 1980s, but in 1987 public pressure resulted in its takeover by the Office of Public Works. In the bog you can find rare species of lichen, moss and the specialized plants that can survive in the intensely acid environment – including, in the hollows and pools, the carnivorous sundews and bladderworts that like to supplement their diet with unwary insects. Check the Banagher tourist office for more details.

Birr

BIRR is a perfect example of a middling-sized town planned round a great house – in this case, Birr Castle, home of the Parsons family (Birr used to be known as Parsonstown), later elevated to the Earls of Rosse. Here, eighteenth-century urban planning has resulted in a truly delightful Georgian town, with wide, airy streets and finely detailed, fan-lit houses. Surprisingly, it's not a prissy place but instead feels slightly seedy, down-at-heel and full of life, but with Birr's recent designation as a heritage town this relaxed feel may well evaporate. One of the many places to be billed as the centre point of Ireland, Birr makes a good base for exploring the wetlands of the Shannon and the Slieve Bloom Mountains in County Laois.

Habitation at Birr dates back to the sixth century, when there was a monastery here; an Anglo-Norman castle was succeeded by an Irish stronghold of the O'Carrolls and then, after the place was granted to Sir Laurence Parsons in 1619, an English garrison town. The development of the Georgian town dates from the time of another Laurence, who succeeded to the title in 1740 and immediately began to "improve" the town, fired by the architectural enthusiasm he'd gained on his Grand Tour.

The town

Birr is now a heritage town, and there are plans to open one of its Georgian houses on John's Mall to the public, followed perhaps by a pub, school and shop, which may help penetrate behind the town's elegant facade to the reality of eighteenth-century life.

Already open is the local **heritage centre** on the refined John's Mall (Mon–Sat 2.30–5.30pm, Sun 3–5pm; £1), housed in an impeccably elegant miniature Greek temple, which will fill you in on the town's architectural and social background. In the grounds is a small standing stone, mentioned by Giraldus Cambrensis in the twelfth century as the "navel of Ireland" and used in the early nineteenth century, when it had temporarily migrated to County Clare, for secret celebrations of the Mass.

The Earls of Rosse still live at **Birr Castle**, and their house isn't open to the public, except occasionally to very rich paying guests (contact *Elegant Ireland*, 15 Harcourt St, Dublin, ☎01/475 1665 or ☎475 1012); you can visit the **grounds** (daily 9am–1pm & 2–6pm or dusk; £3). Laid out in the 1830s and 1840s by the second earl, they contain rare plants from all over the world as well as an enormous artificial lake and a really charming suspension bridge over the river. It's a pleasant place to while away a sunny day – the grounds are shut at lunchtime, but the keepers are perfectly happy to lock you in.

Much more remarkable, and Birr's real claim to fame, is the shell of the **Rosse telescope**. In 1845, the third earl built what was then, and remained for three-quarters of a century, the largest telescope in the world – a reflector with a diameter of 72 inches. The instrument was used by the fourth earl (1840–1908) to make the first accurate measurement of the temperature of the moon and to catalogue the spiral nebulae. The walls that held the telescope – at 54ft long, it was too cumbersome to be rotated through more than one plane – are still in place, built in the same stone and battlemented style as the house; unfortunately the telescope itself has been dismantled. The housing is being rebuilt, and there are perhaps quixotic plans to retrieve the telescope mirror from the Science Museum in London. The current exhibition gives some information about the casting of the lens, no mean feat in those days, but on the whole the exhibition drastically underplays an extraordinary episode in the history of modern science. The third and fourth earls were not the only scientists of the family: the latter's youngest brother, Charles, invented the steam turbine, while his mother, in the 1850s, was an early photographer; and Mary Ward, a friend of the family, was a talented microscopist. In 1869 she also became the first motor fatality in Ireland when she was run over in the grounds by an experimental, steam-powered car.

The castle also runs changing **summer exhibitions** on subjects connected with life there, such as cooking or scientific activities, and is planning a science centre to celebrate the achievements of Irish scientists through the ages.

Practicalities

The **tourist office** is in the heritage centre on John's Mall (daily 10am–5.30pm May–Sept; ☎0509/20110). One of the best places to **stay** in Birr is also one of the cheapest: *Spinner's Town House* (☎0509/21673; ③–④). Carved out of old warehouse buildings grouped around a courtyard, it offers hostel or twin-bedded accommodation in cosy rooms with bare wooden floors and thick cotton bedspreads; amazingly, the price includes a delicious cooked breakfast with freshly squeezed orange juice and croissants. There's a small theatre and space for art exhibitions, and plans for a video library of Irish films, music and books – come for a day and you may well stay a week. The planned bistro will serve a menu that will be welcome to the urbanite: soup, salads, bruschetta, filled ciabatta rolls. *Dooly's Hotel* in Emmet Square, recently refurbished and extremely pleasant (☎0509/20032; ⑤), is one of the focal points for the town's **social life**. *Dooly's* is where the Galway Hunt acquired the nickname of the Galway Blazers after a hunt in 1809, when their over-enthusiastic celebrations resulted in the gutting of the building by fire. Up another notch in comfort, and perfection for anyone with an expensive taste in interiors, is *Tullanisk*, Birr Castle's Dower House (☎0509/20572; ⑥), which also does a delicious dinner at £18. Set in its own parkland a couple of miles out of town on the Banagher Road (R439), *Tullanisk* dates from around 1790 and boasts a huge bay window in the drawing room through which you can contemplate the deer munching the grass.

Back in town, for daytime **eating** *The Castle Kitchen* (☎0509/20985), opposite the castle gates, is a good coffee shop. *The Stables* (☎0509/20263; also B&B, ④), close by on Oxmantown Mall, serves sturdy, dinner-party food; *Kong Lam* (☎0509/21253) in Bridge Street is a surprisingly good Chinese restaurant. *The Thatch* (☎0509/20682), a bar and restaurant a little way south out of town at Crinkill, serves good, if mega-rich, special-occasion food in friendly surroundings. There are also some fascinating photographs of the precise military architecture of the old British army barracks, blown up in 1922. An alternative is the *Riverbank Restaurant and Coffee Shop*, which overlooks the Little Brosna river and the old stone bridge that will take you over into County Tipperary. *Craughwell's*, in Castle Street (just down from *Spinner's Town House*), is a friendly **pub** which often has music and barbecues; *Kelly's* has a beer garden, or you can sit ouside on the street and watch the world go by.

Excursions

A mile out on the Roscrea Road (the N62), if you're thinking of doing some **walking**, is the Slieve Bloom Interpretive Centre (daily 10am–6pm), which offers some rather dry background on the hills' flora and fauna, land use, architecture and legend. It's also the *Birr Outdoor Education Centre* (☎0509/20029), which runs courses in canoeing, windsurfing, rock-climbing and so on. For **horseriding**, ring the *Birr Riding Centre* (☎0509/20551). You can rent **bikes** from *P. Dolan & Sons* on Main Street (☎0509/20006) for £6.50 per day or £27 per week.

Finally, a little excursion for ghostbusters. A few miles southeast of town beyond **Clareen**, as the land rises towards the Slieve Bloom Mountains, the fifteenth-century **Leap Castle** fortifies the valley between Leinster and Munster. Before it was destroyed in 1922, it enjoyed the sinister reputation of being the most haunted house in Ireland, and was particularly famous for an unusual, smelly ghost, which was described both by Yeats and his contemporary Oliver St John Gogarty.

travel details

Trains
Portlaoise to: Cork (9 daily; 2hr); Dublin (8 daily; 1hr); Limerick Junction (13 daily; 1hr).

Bus Éireann
Portlaoise to: Abbeyleix (2 daily; 20min); Dublin (6 daily; 2hr); Durrow (1 daily; 30min).

Private buses
Pierce Kavanagh Coaches (☎056/31213) serve Durrow, Abbeyleix and Portlaoise on their daily Thurles–Dublin route.

CHAPTER FOUR

MEATH, LOUTH, WESTMEATH AND LONGFORD

Stretching from the borders of County Dublin to the frontier with the North, and from the coast to the heart of Ireland, these four counties epitomize green and rural Ireland yet provide a total contrast to the west of the country. It's a region neglected by most visitors, whose impression is one of monotonously similar countryside. Pass through at speed, as most people do, and you'll probably share that impression. But if you slow down and target a small area for more detailed exploration, you'll discover far more. In the east there's a wealth of remains of an exceptionally long, rich history, including the great ritual landscapes flanking the River Boyne, and one or two great beaches on the coast. Further west, you're into the lush, green, agricultural heart of Ireland; it's not spectacular country, but as dense in historical resonance as anywhere else, and largely untouristed, with a slow pace and plain style of living that have a steady charm of their own.

In practical terms, you'll find it easy enough to get about, with most of the sites conveniently strung along major roads well served by public transport. Accommodation is less easy, with only a handful of hostels throughout the four counties, and B&Bs only in the major centres. Still, if you base yourself strategically you'll find that a surprising amount can be seen in a short time.

County Louth, the smallest of southern Ireland's 26 counties – and along with Meath part of the area known as the Pale – stretches northwards along the coast. Here you'll find the only two towns of any real size in this chapter, **Drogheda** and **Dundalk**. Inland, hilly drumlin country hardens in the northeast to real mountains. Here, on the **Cooley Peninsula**, lies the most exciting part of the coast between Dublin and the border. The peninsula is also the setting of one of the richest and oldest legendary tales of Irish literature, the **Táin Bó Cúailnge** (Cattle Raid of Cooley).

Until the mid-sixteenth century **County Meath** (*Midhe*, middle) was combined with Westmeath, making it Ireland's fifth and most powerful province. Although it does touch the coast (with a couple of excellent beaches), this is primarily an inland county, whose exceptionally rich farmland unfurls lazily around its major river, the **Boyne**, and its tributaries. To discover the place you simply follow these waterways – above all the Boyne itself and the **Blackwater** – as thousands of years of civilization have done before. Along its rivers, Meath can boast by far the richest bounty of historical remains in Ireland. This history starts in the Stone Age, with some of the oldest buildings in the world at **Brú Na Bóinne** and **Sliabh Na Caillighe**, and other important Neolithic remains still being discovered. Celtic Ireland was ruled from **Tara**, in Meath, and from Uisneach in Westmeath. Christian Ireland has left a wealth of early monastic remains,

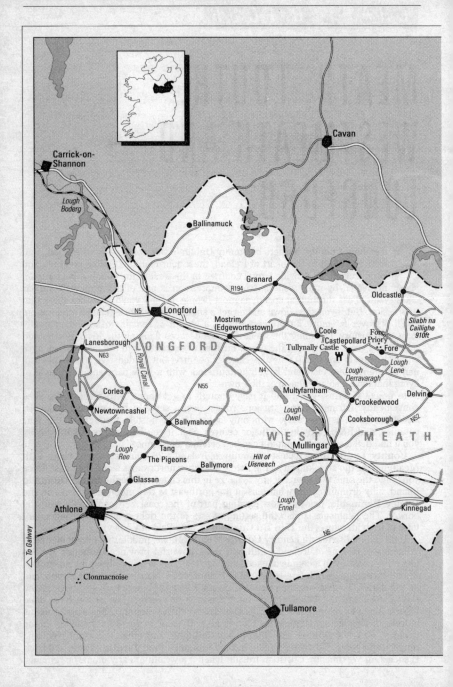

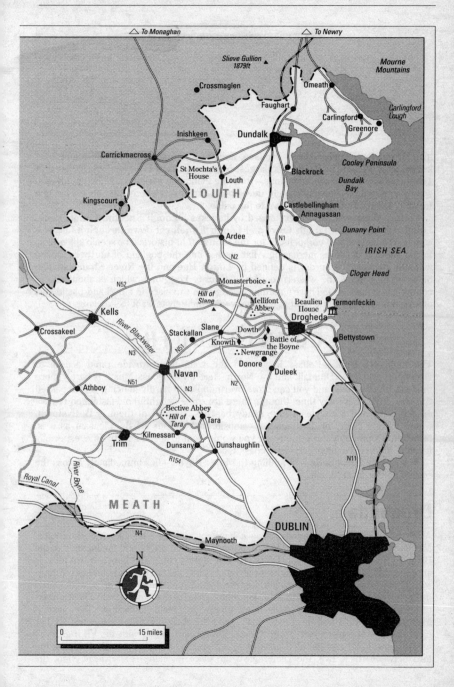

△ To Monaghan △ To Newry

Slieve Gullion
1879ft

Mourne
Mountains

Crossmaglen

Omeath

Carlingford
Lough

Faughart

Carlingford

Greenore

Inishkeen

Dundalk

Carrickmacross

St Mochta's
House

Louth

Blackrock

Cooley Peninsula

Dundalk
Bay

L O U T H

Kingscourt

Castlebellingham

Annagassan

Dunany Point

Ardee

N1

IRISH SEA

N2

Cloger Head

N52

Monasterboice

Hill of
Slane

Beaulieu
House

Termonfeckin

Kells

River Blackwater

Mellifont
Abbey

Drogheda

Crossakeel

Stackallan

Slane

Dowth

Battle of
the Boyne

Bettystown

N51

Knowth

N3

Newgrange

Navan

Donore

Duleek

Athboy

N51

N3

N2

Bective Abbey
Hill of
Tara

Tara

Trim

Kilmessan

Dunsany

Dunshaughlin

R154

Royal Canal

River Boyne

M E A T H

N11

DUBLIN

N4

Maynooth

N

0   15 miles

magnificent tenth-century **high crosses**, and the celebrated illuminated manuscript known as the **Book of Kells**. The largest Norman fortress in Ireland can be seen at **Trim**, and later castles and mansions – from the Plantation period when the county was wholly confiscated and extensively developed – are everywhere, though only a few (notably **Dunsany Castle**) are open to the public.

County Westmeath is characterized by its lakes – **Lough Sheelin**, **Lough Lene**, **Lough Derravaragh**, **Lough Owel** and **Lough Ennell** cut down through its heart – which go a long way to compensate for the falling off in historical or scenic splendour. In the south it becomes increasingly flat, easing into the bogland of northern Offaly, while in the west the border is defined by **Lough Ree** and the **River Shannon**. The Shannon also forms the western border of **County Longford**, which is about all the county has going for it. There's nothing wrong with the place in a dull and placid sort of way, but placid and dull is what it is, and you're unlikely to want to stay long.

COUNTY LOUTH

The main N1 Dublin–Belfast Road, and the train line, provide rapid access to Drogheda, and on to Dundalk and the North. Here on the coast, Meath is barely more than ten miles across, and you can cross over into Louth hardly noticing you've passed through. If you have any time, though, there are some delightful old-fashioned resorts on the coast and a couple of fine, sandy beaches. Biggest of them is **Bettystown**, where there's plenty of dark sand, a campsite and various B&Bs. Pleasant as it is, however, it's probably not somewhere you would want to spend a lot of time, especially if you're going to be seeing the west coast, too.

Pressing on, **Drogheda** – straddling the River Boyne – lies immediately across the county border from Meath.

Drogheda

Aside from its obvious advantages as a base for visiting sites like Monasterboice, Mellifont, and, nearby in County Meath, Newgrange (see p.155) and the location of the Battle of the Boyne (see p.153), **DROGHEDA**, tightly contained between two hills, is an enjoyable place in its own right: easily accessible and surprisingly unused to tourism. The precise grey stone of which the town is built, combined with its post-industrial decay, give it a slightly forbidding air, but it has a vitality that suits it well. The architectural legacy of successive civilizations forms the main attraction. The ancient **Millmount mound** and the Boyne itself echo the early habitation you'll see further upstream, but the history of Drogheda as a town really began with the **Vikings**, who arrived in 911 AD and founded a separate settlement on each bank. By bridging the ford between these two, the Danes gave the place its name – *Droichead Átha*, the

Bridge of the Ford. By the fourteenth century, the walled town was one of the most important in the country, where the parliament would meet from time to time: remnants of **medieval** walls and abbeys lie like splinters throughout the town. As ever, though, most of what you see is from the **eighteenth century** or later, reflecting the sober style of the Protestant bourgeoisie after the horrific slaughter of Drogheda's defenders and inhabitants by Cromwell. The important surviving buildings of this age – the Tholsel, Courthouse and St Peter's Church – have mellowed romantically and stand among the **nineteenth-century** flowering of triumphal churches, celebrating the relaxation of the persecuting stranglehold on Catholicism, and the riverside warehouses and huge rail viaduct that welcomed the industrial boom years. More recent development, with riverside laneways and suburban housing estates, has affected the flavour of the place very little: the past somehow seems stronger here than the present.

Arrival, information and accommodation

Drogheda is a pretty easy place to find your way around. The **Bus Éireann** depot is on New Street, on the south bank of the river, and the **train** station is also on the south side, a short way east of town just off the Dublin Road. **Taxis** line up on Lawrence Street. The town is small enough not to need them for local trips, but you could arrange a lightning **tour** around the sights of Newgrange, Mellifont and Monasterboice for around £30 – though you'd have to be in a real hurry to want to see it all this way. A cheaper way to do this would be with the bus operated by the *Harpur House Hostel* (see below), which offers regular half-day tours of the Boyne Valley (£10), worthwhile if you can spare a few hours.

There's a **tourist information office** at the bus station on New Street (June to mid-Sept Mon–Sat 10am–6pm; ☎041/37070), where they'll have details of other local tours. If you want to stay, **B&B** is available at *Mrs Caffrey*, 69 Maple Drive (☎041/32244; ③), or the more upmarket *Rosnaree Park* on the Dublin Road (☎041/37673, fax ☎041/33116; ⑤). The forty-bed *Harpur House Tourist Hostel* is on William Street (☎041/32736; ②; private rooms available, ③) and offers breakfast at £3 and no curfew. If you want to **rent a bike** to explore on your own try *P.J. Carolan*, 77 Trinity Street (£6 per day, £30 per week, £30 deposit; ☎041/38242).

The town

The Meath side of town, south of the river, is probably the best place to start exploring Drogheda. Atop the southern hill, Millmount's **Martello tower** offers an excellent overview, both in a literal sense and through the excellent display in the local museum sited here. The tower (key from the museum) was severely damaged by bombardment during the 1922 Civil War (there's a large picture of the attack in the museum), but in any event it is the earthen mound on which it stands that gives the place its real importance. The strategic value of the site was recognized from the earliest times: in mythology the mound is the burial place of **Amergin**, the poet warrior, one of the sons of **Mil** of the Milesians who are reckoned to be the ancestors of the Gaels. He arrived in Ireland from northern Spain around 1498 BC and later defeated the *Tuatha Dé Danann* at Tailtiu (Telltown). Another belief is that the mound houses a passage grave. However, the tumulus has never been excavated to find out which story – if either – is true. Not surprisingly, the Normans chose the same strategic eminence for their motte in the twelfth century, and later a castle was built, standing until 1808 when it was replaced by the tower and military barracks you see today. The quickest way up here on foot is via the narrow flight of steps by *Dina's* corner shop, directly opposite **St Mary's Bridge**. This is near enough the spot where the original bridge was built by the Danes.

Millmount Museum

The eighteenth-century houses in the barracks' square now shelter various arts and crafts enterprises and, above all, **Millmount Museum** (April–Oct Tues–Sat 10am–6pm, Sun 2–6pm; Nov–March Wed, Sat & Sun 2–5pm; £1), one of Ireland's finest town museums, in the best chaotic style of the genre. Within a glass cabinet in the **foyer** hangs a topographical quilt showing much of Ireland's east coast – note the two thousand or so grains of French knots that depict the sandy shores. Next to this is a quilted cummerbund of the Georgian houses in Fair Street, very pleasing and precise in its eighteenth-century detail. When you get out into the town you'll find that the area depicted (Fair Street, along with William, Lower and Upper Magdalene streets and Rope Walk) is still rich in period buildings and architectural detail.

The **Guilds Room** follows, hung with three large drapes (the only surviving Guilds' banners left in the country) celebrating the broguemakers', carpenters' and weavers' trades. The broguemakers' banner – in effect an early advertisement – is particularly wonderful. It depicts Saint Patrick, who in legend rid the country of snakes, standing with his foot on a serpent: even the saint needs some protection, however, so he is sturdily shod in a pair of good Irish brogues. King Charles I also has a bit part, hiding up an oak tree to symbolize both the use of oak for tanning the leather and the security offered by a good pair of shoes (Charles escaped from Cromwell's troops in 1651 by hiding in an oak tree). The carpenters' and weavers' banners are more straightforward, the former depicting compasses and blades, the latter with shuttles clasped in leopards' mouths. In the next room there's a similar theme, with the trade banners of fishermen, labourers and bricklayers. The bricklayers' shows the **barbican at St Lawrence Gate** as their proudest achievement. This, again, is something worth seeing once you get out into the town: still standing, perfectly preserved, with two round towers flanking a portcullis entry and retaining wall. It is the most significant part of the town walls to have survived (part of the West Gate also exists, and a buttress and embrasure can be seen just south of the gate), and arguably the finest such surviving structure anywhere in Ireland.

Heading down the museum stairs you come to a series of displays of a more domestic and industrial nature. The last heavy manufacturing industry left Drogheda in 1986; the exhibits record the sources of its former prosperity, linen and alcohol – at one time the town had sixteen distilleries and fourteen breweries. Next to a case charting the history of the linen trade and a painting of the ship that used to ply between Drogheda and the English coast is a vessel from a much earlier period in the town's long history: a **Boyne coracle**, a recent example of the type of circular fishing boat in use from prehistoric times right up to the middle of this century. This one has a framework of hazel twigs and a leather hide taken from a prize bull in 1943.

There's also a fully equipped **period kitchen**, pantry and scullery. Among the artefacts displayed are an 1860 vacuum cleaner (a man would wind the suction mechanism from outside the house), a tailor's hen and goose irons (clothes irons named for their various shapes and sizes), which would be heated in the fire (hence the phrase "too many irons in the fire"), a settle bed (preferred by the Irish peasant because it would be next to the warmth of the dying embers and could sleep two adults lengthways and four or five children acrossways) and a vast array of other everyday miscellany, including an eccentric collection of geological samples gathered by a Drogheda resident whose wife finally insisted he should give them to the museum. On the **top floor** are a small picture gallery and some rooms devoted to the Foresters and Hibernian societies, both nineteenth-century benevolent institutions set up to provide sickness benefits, burial expenses and the like for the poor. Perhaps ironically, given Drogheda's manufacturing history, the temperance movement was strong here, and one of the banners carries the exhortation: "Hibernia be thou sober."

The north side

Standing on the Millmount hill, you can enjoy an unimpeded **panorama** of Drogheda, with the bulk of the town climbing up the northern hill-slope opposite. From this standpoint, it's clearly apparent how the tight-fitting street pattern of the medieval town gave scant breathing space for the overcrowding of succeeding centuries. The backs of the houses stagger down to the River Boyne in a colourless wash of daubed mortar, their windows staring blankly back at you. On top of the hill opposite, the fifteenth-century **Magdalene Tower** was once the belfry tower of an extensive Dominican friary, founded in 1224 by Lucas De Netterville, Archbishop of Armagh. The tower rises above a Gothic arch where the transept and nave would have met; inside, a spiral staircase reaches up into its two storeys, but since it is railed off from public access it's probably seen to best advantage from a distance. In March 1395 **Richard II**, King of England, received within the priory the submission of the Ulster Chiefs; and later Thomas, Earl of Desmond, a former Lord Chief Justice, was found guilty of treason and beheaded here in 1467 (with him expired his Act of Parliament for a university in Drogheda).

Lower down, the spire that leaps out from the centre of town belongs to the heavily Gothic-styled nineteenth-century **St Peter's Roman Catholic Church** on West Street, the town's main thoroughfare. It's an imposing building (not to be confused with the eighteenth-century Church of Ireland St Peter's on Magdalene Street) with a grand double flight of steps, but it's the presence of a martyr's head, on view in a tabernacle-like box that forms part of a small shrine down the left-hand aisle, that transforms the place into a centre of pilgrimage. The severed head is a searing reminder of the days of religious persecution. It once belonged to **Oliver Plunkett**, archbishop of Armagh and primate of all Ireland in the seventeenth century, when Drogheda was the principal seat in Ireland. On July 1, 1681, Plunkett was executed in London for treason: as the Lord Chief Justice of England explained, "the bottom of your treason was your setting up your false religion, than which there is not anything more displeasing to God". His head and mutilated members were snatched from the fire but were not brought back to Ireland until 1721, a time when persecution had somewhat subsided. Plunkett was canonized in 1975, after miracles were performed in his name in southern Italy.

East of the church, towards the docks, the back alleys and stone warehouses are relics of the short-lived industrial revolution and of the local brewing and milling trades. A few are being done up by a new breed of entrepreneur, but as many are empty and crumbling. The docks themselves seem mostly lifeless and deserted, too, and the Boyne's funereal pace does little to enliven a depleted commercial shipping fleet where once sixty Viking ships are said to have rested at anchor. There is, however, one very bright spot down here in the form of **Mrs Carbery's pub**, as appealing as any in Ireland. This has been a local, family-run institution for over a century, and in the evening or early morning (it opens at 7.30am to cater for the dockers and the men off the boats) the faint orange glow from the lanterns or fire inside makes a welcome landmark and sign of life.

Beaulieu House

Further downstream, the **viaduct** carrying trains on the Dublin–Belfast line spans what is effectively a 200ft-deep gorge. It's an impressive feat of nineteenth-century engineering by Sir John MacNeill, and you can examine it at closer quarters if you feel like extending your visit to *Carbery's* into stroll a mile or so east along the Baltray Road. Beyond the viaduct and cement works you reach some pleasant woodland. Part of this belongs to **Beaulieu House**, a private domain that claims to have been Ireland's first unfortified mansion, built during 1660–65 after Cromwell's departure, when the land was confiscated from Oliver Plunkett and given to Sir Henry Tichbourne, whose descendants reside there today. The house has a hipped roof in the artisan style and an almost perfectly preserved interior. Most rewarding of all is a mouth-wateringly indulgent picture gallery, with a collection ranging from contemporary portraits of William and Mary on tall canvases by the court painter Van der Wyck to an intense collection of early twentieth-century Irish art. Unfortunately the house is strictly private, but the owners do open their doors to tours by the Drogheda Historical Society, so it's worth checking at the museum to see if your visit coincides with one of these.

Eating, drinking and entertainment

Weavers on Dominick Street is an excellent pub for a cheap lunch, always crowded; *Go Bananas*, a few doors down, serves similar **food** and is also good value. The *Buttergate Restaurant* in Millmount Square (Tues–Sun 12.30–2.30pm, also Thurs–Sat 7–11pm; ☎041/37407) is much more expensive, but worth it for fine French cuisine. At the other end of the scale, *King's Cafe* (popular with truckers), a short way out on the Collon Road, will serve up four courses for around £3.50. *The Swan House* on West Street is a good Chinese restaurant, with cheap takeaway and sit-down meals; while *La Pizzeria*, a new Italian restaurant on Peter Street, is proving very popular with locals (Thurs–Tues 6–11pm; ☎014/34208).

As far as entertainment goes, check out the **pubs**, many of which are rich in character. *Carbery's* on the North Strand is probably the best-known gathering place on this part of the east coast, especially for the traditional sessions on Tuesday nights (from 9pm) and Sunday lunchtimes (12.30–2.30pm). To get a seat on Sunday make sure you're there by noon. *Clarkes*, on the corner of Fair and Peter streets, is quiet and old-fashioned during the week, popular with the local literary set, but on Saturday nights is a fashionable meeting place. *Peter Matthews* on Lawrence Street (known locally as *McPhail's*) is frequented by a younger crowd and has lots of toffee-brown woodwork, partitions and cubicles, and a back room for music. *McHugh's*, just up from here on Lawrence Street, is a friendly place with traditional music on Thursday nights. Less traditional venues include *Reds* on Dominick Street, formerly the *Horse and Hounds*, now a disco-bar, *Branagan's* on Lower Magdalene Street (hot snacks 12.30–2.30pm & 5–11pm), and the recently opened *Squires* on West Street.

Entertainment outside the pubs is limited. The best bet is to check out what's happening at the *Droichead Arts Centre* in Bellscourt Lane off West Street, which regularly hosts plays, poetry readings and exhibitions. There are also two **theatres**, both amateur and neither very exciting – *Duke Theatre*, Duke Street (☎041/36122), and the *Parochial Theatre* – and a **cinema** in the Abbey shopping centre. There's also an occasional **disco** at *Lucianos* in the *Boyne Valley Hotel* (☎041/37737), and at *The Place* in the *Rosnaree Park*, each a couple of miles out of town.

Mellifont and Monasterboice

Not far north from Drogheda, in the south of County Louth, lie two of the great historical sites which characterize this part of the country: the monasteries of Mellifont and Monasterboice. Both are easily reached from Drogheda and can be visited on your way to or from the sites of the lower Boyne Valley.

To get to Mellifont from Drogheda (about five miles), turn off the road to Collon at Monleek Cross; alternatively turn off the Slane–Collon Road at the signpost. There is no direct bus service to Mellifont, but *Mullens* taxis (☎041/33377) will bring you for £7 each way. Monasterboice can be reached from the main N1 Dublin–Belfast Road, or by continuing up the Drogheda–Collon Road and following the signs to the right.

Mellifont Abbey

Mellifont (daily May to mid-June 10am–5pm; mid-June to mid-Sept 9.30am–6.30pm; mid-Sept to Oct 10am–5pm; last admission 45min before closing; £1.50; Heritage Card) was, in medieval times, one of the most important monasteries in Ireland, the Motherhouse of the Cistercian Order and a building of exceptional beauty and grandeur. The ruins you see today in no way do justice to this former glory, but they're pretty impressive even so.

At its foundation in 1142 – the inspiration of Saint Malachy, Archbishop of Armagh, who did much to bring the early Irish Church closer to Rome – Mellifont was the first **Cistercian monastery** in Ireland. Malachy's friend Saint Bernard, then abbot of the Cistercian monastery at Clairvaux, did much to inspire the work, and sent nine of his own monks to form the basis of the new community. The abbey took fifteen years to build, and you can gauge something of its original size and former glory by imagining the gargantuan pillars that once rose, finishing high among a riotous sprouting of arches and vaulted ceilings, from the broad stumps remaining today. For nearly 400 years Mellifont flourished, at its peak presiding over as many as 38 other Cistercian monasteries throughout the country, until in 1539 all of them were suppressed by Henry VIII.

One hundred and fifty monks fled from Mellifont, and the buildings were handed over to Edward Moore, ancestor of the Earls of Drogheda, who converted the place into a fortified mansion. In 1603 the last of the great Irish chieftains, **Hugh O'Neill**, was starved into submission here before eventually escaping to the Continent in the Flight of the Earls. Mellifont, meanwhile, went into gradual decline. It was attacked by Cromwellian forces, and then used as William's headquarters during the Battle of the Boyne, before eventually falling so far as to be pressed into service as a pigsty in the nineteenth century.

The ruins

Today the remains rarely rise above shoulder height, with the striking exception of the Romanesque octagonal **lavabo**, built around 1200, whose basins and water jets provided washing facilities for the monks.

The rest of the ruins can be easily identified on the map provided, their ground plan almost perfectly intact. You enter through the **north transept**, which originally had five chapels, three in its eastern and two in its western aisle. Two of the three on the eastern side had apsidal ends, an unusual feature in medieval Ireland, seen here presumably because of the French influence on the builders. The chancel area, or **presbytery**, has the remains of an ornate arch and **sedilia** where the priests celebrating Mass would sit. The entire **nave** would have been paved in red and blue tiles, some inscribed with the words "Ave Maria" and others decorated with the fleur-de-lis emblem; the **pillars**, too, would originally have been painted in brilliant colours and topped with flowery capitals. At the river end of the nave is a **crypt** – an unusual position which served to level the site on which the church was built. The **chapter house**, beyond the south transept, was once the venue for the daily meetings of the monks. It now houses a collection of medieval **glazed tiles**, moved here from around the site for safety.

Behind the lavabo is the **south range**, where the refectory would have been, and back towards the road you'll find the **gatehouse**, the only surviving part of a high defensive wall that once completely ringed the monastic buildings. Also within the grounds are another ruined church up on the slope (converted to a Protestant one in 1542) and a building that was converted by *An Óige* into a youth hostel. This is now permanently closed, a shame since the setting is delightful, with the River Mattock gliding through gently wooded country, and it used to make a great base from which to move out to the other places of interest nearby – Monasterboice and the Brú Na Bóinne complex.

Monasterboice

Monasterboice (*Mainistir Buite* or Buite's monastery) is a tiny enclosure, but it contains two of the finest high crosses (both dating from the tenth century) and one of the best round towers in the country – the site is open to all during daylight hours. As you enter, the squat cross nearer to you is reckoned the finer of the two, and certainly its high-relief carving has worn the centuries better. It is known as **Muiredach's Cross** after the inscription in Irish at the base of the stem – *Or do Muiredach i Chros*, "A prayer for Muiredach by whom this cross was made". The boldly ornate stone picture panels retell biblical stories and were designed to educate and inspire the largely illiterate populace. Some of the subjects are ambivalent and open to a certain amount of conjecture (William Wilde, father of Oscar, argued that many relate as strongly to events associated with Monasterboice as with the Bible), but most have been fairly convincingly identified.

The story begins at the bottom of the **east face** of the cross, nearest the wall, with **Eve tempting Adam** on the left and **Cain slaying Abel** on the right. Above this,

David and Goliath share a panel with **King Saul** and David's son **Jonathan**. The next panel up shows **Moses striking the rock** with his staff to conjure water while the Israelites wait with parched throats, and above this, the **Wise Men** bear gifts to the Virgin Mary and baby Jesus. The centrepiece of the wheel is the scene of the **Last Judgement**, with the multitudes risen from the dead begging for entry to Heaven, their hands holding one another in good will and the trumpets playing loudly. Below Christ's foot the Archangel Michael is seen driving a staff through Satan's head after weighing the balance of good and evil in one individual's favour. At the very top, saints Anthony and Paul are seen breaking bread.

The **west face** of the cross is largely devoted to the **life of Christ**. At the bottom is his arrest in the Garden of Gethsemane, with Roman soldiers and the treacherous kiss of Judas. This is followed by three figures clutching books – thought to represent the dispelling of the **doubts of Saint Thomas**. The third panel shows the **Risen Christ** returned to meet Saint Peter and Saint Paul, their faces bowed in shame at ever having doubted the truth. The hub of the wheel shows the **Crucifixion**, with soldiers below, angels above and evil humanity to the sides. This is surmounted by **Moses** descending from Mount Sinai with the ten commandments. The flanks of the cross are also decorated. On the **north side** are saints Anthony and Paul again, Christ's scourging at the pillar, and the **Hand of God** (under the arm of the cross) warning mankind. On the **south side** is the Flight of the Israelites from Egypt and also possibly Pontius Pilate washing his hands. All this is capped at the top as if under the roof of the church and surrounded with abstract or uninterpreted embellishment.

The West Cross

The **West Cross**, the taller of the two, is made up of three separate stone sections, all of them much more worn. The east face shows **David** killing the lion, then **Abraham** ready to sacrifice his son Isaac, with the ram which became the last-minute substitute. Above this is the worship of the **golden calf**, with Moses coming down from Mount Sinai to catch his people red-handed in idolatry. The panel shows them trembling for forgiveness. The other three panels, before Christ seated in Heaven at the end of the world in the centre of the wheel, are hard to identify, though on the right arm of the wheel you can see the upside-down Satan being speared again by Saint Michael. The **west face** begins with the **Resurrection**, and the **Baptism of Christ** is shown on the second panel. The four three-figure panels before the wheel are again hard to identify, although the central figure looks a strong candidate for Christ. Again the **Crucifixion** dominates the wheel, with Christ tied to the Cross by rope; the left arm shows him being blindfolded and ridiculed, while the right arm has Judas's kiss of betrayal.

The round tower and two churches

Behind the West Cross stands possibly the tallest **round tower** in Ireland, 110ft tall even without its conical peak. Round towers were adopted between the ninth and eleventh centuries by monks throughout the country as a defence against constant Viking attack. They needed no keystone that enemies could pull out for speedy demolition; their height created a perfect look-out post; and the entrance would be several feet from the ground, allowing a ladder to be drawn in when under attack. The only drawback was that if a lighted arrow were to pierce the inner floorboards the whole column would act as a chimney, guaranteeing a blazing inferno. Sadly, you can't go into the tower, which has been closed for safety reasons.

Finally within the enclosure are two thirteenth-century **churches**, the north and the south church. They probably had no real connection with the monastic settlement, which had almost certainly ceased to function by then, and there's little of great interest within their ruined walls.

North to Dundalk

The main reason to head northwards into County Louth, apart from reaching the border, is to get to the mountains of the **Cooley Peninsula**. You have three routes to choose from. The main Drogheda–Belfast Road, the N1, is the fastest, speeding directly towards the border and passing Monasterboice early on, but with little other reason to stop. An alternative inland route to take is to head towards Collon, taking in Mellifont Abbey, and from there continue to Ardee and Louth town (for **St Mochta's House**) and ultimately on to Dundalk or into County Monaghan. Both these routes give excellent, unhindered cross-country views of County Louth, especially of the drumlins rising inland towards counties Cavan and Monaghan. The third option, to take the bay road out of Drogheda and **follow the coast** north, is the most scenic and the one to choose if you want to dawdle along the way or if you're cycling. In the early stages, there's little point diverting to Baltray: instead, carry straight on for **Termonfeckin**.

Termonfeckin

TERMONFECKIN is a placid country village lying in a wooded dip half a mile from the shore. The village has a small tower house **castle** and a tenth-century **high cross** in the graveyard of St Feckin's Church. The castle (keys from Patrick Duff in the bungalow across the cul-de-sac) dates basically from the fifteenth and sixteenth centuries and has as its most unusual feature a corbelled roof – notably less well constructed than the 4000-year-older one at Newgrange. For **accommodation**, try Mrs Kitty McElvoy at *Highfield House* (May–Sept ☎041/22172; ④), where you can have a hearty breakfast for £3. You can get good **food** here at *The Triple House* restaurant, whose Italian/French menu offers five courses for £14.95, or four courses for £9.95 before 7.30pm (four-course Sun lunch £9.95 from 12.30pm to 2.30pm, otherwise open daily 6.30–9.30pm; Sept–May closed Mon; ☎041/22616). If you're neither hungry nor in a hurry, then take a stroll into the reception area to see three highly individual computer-print collages by the Irish artist Robert Ballagh – *The Ambidextrous Paradigm*, *The Global Embrace* and *The Plough and the Stars*.

Clogherhead and Castlebellingham

CLOGHERHEAD is a far busier place – not difficult to achieve: it's a glum beach resort with ancient mobile homes and windswept beach cabins and a few bars aimed squarely at the holiday trade; their briny names, *The Lobster Inn* for example, give the game away. From here the road to **PORT ORIEL** takes you to **Clogher Head** (one mile) and a tiny fishing harbour tucked hard into the coast's rockface – good mackerel fishing off the pier in summer. It's only beyond here, as you approach **ANNAGASSAN**, that the signposts designating the scenic route begin to earn their keep, with the mountains of Cooley and Mourne, one range south of the border, the other north, spectacularly silhouetted against the sky. It's an enthrallingly unimpeded view of the best that lies ahead in counties Louth and Down. *The Glyde Inn* in Annagassan has food (of sorts) and is a nice reclusive spot to take time out for "a small drop of medicine". There's little else to see around the village, although local archeological explorations are provoking controversy as they lay bare what is claimed to have been the first permanent Norse settlement in Ireland, predating even Dublin. Continuing northwards across the hump-backed stone bridge, you've a watercolourist's idyll of rowing boats laid out along the bulging ramparts of the canalized river as it meets the sea.

A couple of miles further on, you'll rejoin the N1 at **CASTLEBELLINGHAM**. Despite the main Dublin–Belfast Road blundering right through the middle, Castlebellingham remains a pretty village. It's a strange clash of ancient and modern, from which you can take refuge down by the mill, now converted into a restaurant. This has a turning gable-end water wheel and a run of several man-made weirs on the River Glyde up the back through woodland alongside a sugary, castellated hotel (good two-course bar lunches), the *Bellingham Castle*, also the only place to stay in Castlebellingham, should the temptation of the hotel's *Knight Club* prove overwhelming (☎042/72176; ⑤): contrived, but pretty nevertheless. Moving northwards again the next significant turning off the N1 (right) takes you to **BLACKROCK** and later allows you to bypass most of Dundalk. Blackrock itself (the *Claremount Arms* has good Saturday-night traditional sessions involving the *uilleann* pipes) is an overstretched ribbon of Victorian seaside villas along a mudflat beach. It does, though, offer a handsomely crystalline view across **Dundalk Bay** and on to the Cooley Peninsula, by now looming really close.

Ardee

The inland route is far less travelled, and there's less to see along it. Without transport of your own you'll have difficulty getting anywhere, unless you're prepared for some very leisurely hitching. Nonetheless, it has its rewards, mostly in just this lack of traffic or population; a rural tranquillity unrivalled even in the west. Almost exactly halfway between Drogheda and Dundalk, **ARDEE** (*Baile Átha Fhirdia* or Ferdia's Ford) recalls the tragic legendary duel between Cúchulainn the defender of Ulster and his foster-brother Ferdia, a battle brought about through the trickery of Medb, Queen of Connacht.*

> Ferdia: *"Attack then if we must.*
> *Before sunset and nightfall*
> *I'll fight you at Bairche*
> *in bloody battle.*
> *Men of Ulster will cry out:*
> *'Death has seized you!'*
> *The terrible sight*
> *will pierce you through."*
>
> Cúchulainn: *"You have reached your doom,*
> *your hour is come.*
> *My sword will slash*
> *and not softly.*
> *When we meet you will fall*
> *at a hero's hands.*
> *Never again*
> *will you lead men."*

These taunting jibes threw down the gauntlet for their fight to the death, in which eventually Ferdia was fatally wounded by the *gae bolga*, a weapon summoned from the *Tuatha Dé Danann*, God Lug, by Cúchulainn during the fight in the stream. Ardee is named after the ford where this great battle was fought.

Today, Ardee reeks far more strongly of the Plantation era, with fortified buildings along the main street and a memorial **statue** to a landlord erected by his thankful

---

*Although Medb (pronounced *Maeve*) is always referred to as queen, she was more likely a goddess of Tara. The duel is only one episode in Europe's earliest vernacular epic, the *Táin Bó Cúailnge* or Cattle Raid of Cooley, but makes a glorious 38 pages of reading in Thomas Kinsella's translation, *The Táin*, published in Ireland by the Dolmen Press and well worth getting hold of.

tenants in 1861. The thirteenth-century **castle** on the main street (key in the house on the right) is now used as a courthouse and inside bears no intimation of its original purpose. It stands here mainly because the town was at the northern edge of the Pale, and from here the Anglo-Irish made forays into Ulster, or were themselves periodically forced onto the defensive. If you **stay**, there's a handful of B&Bs – try Linda Connolly's at the *Red House* (☎041/53523; ⑤).

An interesting short diversion from Ardee takes you to the so-called **Jumping Church** at Kildemock. To get there head east from the junction at the southern end of Ardee's main street and turn right after about a quarter of a mile – the small, ruined church lies a further mile down this road. It gets its name from its end wall having shifted three feet from its foundations, which, according to local lore, it did to exclude the grave of an excommunicated person. Less romantic accounts tell of a severe storm taking place in 1715 at around the time the wall jumped, but either way it's a remarkable sight, with the wall shorn clear of its foundations yet still standing (albeit at a 35-degree angle). In the graveyard are simple, foot-high stone markers, some of the earliest graveslabs for the poor.

Louth Village

Ardee is a major road junction, and moving on you could head northeast to Dundalk, northwest to Carrickmacross or west to Kells. If you want to go on heading north, however, a more interesting route is along the minor roads to **LOUTH VILLAGE**: keep on the left fork at the northern end of Ardee and take an immediate right towards Tallanstown, where you'll need to turn right again for Louth. It's not much in itself (and certainly doesn't seem to deserve sharing a name with the county), but it does have one thing well worth seeing in **St Mochta's Church** – turn left towards Carrickmacross and immediately right onto the Inniskeen Road.

According to legend the church was built in a night to give shelter to its founder, **Saint Mochta**, who died in 534. Originally part of a monastery, and dating probably from the late twelfth century, it has a high, vaulted roof, beautifully crafted, reached by a constricted stairway. In its early years it was plundered many times; these days they obviously feel safer, since the church is left open to any passing visitor. The fourteenth-century **Louth Abbey** is accessible through the graveyard back up the road, from where, if you look west, you'll notice a motte on the nearby hill.

Dundalk

DUNDALK has a reputation as a tough border town, but the atmosphere has lightened somewhat since the 1994 ceasefires. Starting life in legendary prehistory as a fort guarding a gap in the mountains to the north (*Dún Dealga,* the Fortress of Dealga), it became in turn a Celtic, Norse, Anglo-Norman, Jacobean and finally Williamite stronghold. This hard tradition seems still to hang over the town, and it never seems a place where you – or for that matter the locals – can feel fully at ease (having said that, the town has some excellent pubs; see "Practicalities" opposite).

As far as sights go, the outstanding one is the nineteenth-century Neoclassical **Courthouse**, whose open Doric portico leads in to an airy, classically proportioned interior. In the plaza outside, the *Guardian Angel* or motherland statue is unequivocally dedicated to "the martyrs in the cause of liberty who fought and died in the struggle against English Tyranny and foreign rule in Ireland" – a far cry from the monument of gratitude in Ardee. **St Patrick's Cathedral** in Francis Street is also worth a look while you're here: its cornucopia of embellished towers, turrets and crenellated walls is a reasonably successful imitation of King's College Chapel, Cambridge. Inside are some rich mosaics using gold pieces in abundance to depict biblical stories.

Louth County Museum (Tues–Sat 10.30am–5.30pm; Sun 2–6 pm; £2), in a warehouse on Jocelyn Street (next to the tourist office), uses a variety of artefacts and documents to tell the stories of local industries, from coopering to cigarettes. The museum is an uneasy mix of high-tech display and poorly labelled exhibits, but there is a wealth of material here. During the 1960s, Henkel bomber cockpits were sent over to Dundalk to be made into bubble cars – you'll find a 1966 model on the first-floor landing. The top two floors house travelling art exhibitions.

Should you wish to see that rare thing, a well-designed and well-maintained Irish Modernist building, head for the 1970 *Carrolls* tobacco factory, designed by Scott Tallon Walker. A mile south of Dundalk on the Dublin Road (N1), it is fronted by a striking sculpture by Gerda Froemmel reflected in an artficial lake, and contains an impressive collection of modern Irish art.

Practicalities

The regional **tourist information office**, which also hosts touring art exhibitions, is in a restored tobacco warehouse on Jocelyn Street (Mon–Fri 9.30am–1pm & 2–5.30pm; July & Aug also open Sat; ☎042/35484); they can provide information on **B&Bs**, of which there are plenty should you need to stay. **Eating** well and cheaply is not a Dundalk speciality, but there are plenty of fast-food places around the centre of town which will do if you're starving. Slightly better fare can be had at *McKeowns Pub* on Clanbrassil Street or, more upmarket, at *La Cantina*, off Park Street (evenings only). **Bikes** can be rented at the *Cycle Centre*, opposite the shopping complex (£6.50 per day, £27 per week; 9am–6pm, open till 9pm Thurs & Fri; ☎042/37159).

Pubs that are well worth visiting include *Toal's* on Crowe Street, a sawdust-on-flagstone hide-out where the men have what looks like designer stubble but which here is probably for real: there's good traditional music (Thurs, Fri & Sat). *McManus's* pub near the library in Seatown is self-described as "simply a great pub" – there are old-fashioned snugs to drink in, excellent-value soup and sandwiches, guitar folk music on a Sunday night and more bluesy stuff on Monday. *McArdles* on Anne Street hosts *Ceolteóirí* every Thursday night, or if rock is more to your taste, try the *Tara* on Park Street. The Council Arts Office in the Market Square (Mon–Fri 9am–5pm; ☎042/32276) provides up-to-the-minute details of music and theatre.

Faughert

From Dundalk, **the border** lies just eight miles on up the N1, and Newry only five miles beyond that. Opposite the turning for the Cooley Peninsula, a couple of miles outside Dundalk, is a lesser road that leads a short distance inland to **FAUGHERT**. A small place of little modern interest, Faughert nevertheless has several older associations worth mentioning as you pass. **Cúchulainn** was born at Castletown Hill on the edge of the plain of *Muirthemne*, which stretches away towards Armagh in the north, and in the legendary account he was sent a false offer of peace by Medb asking him to meet her at Faughert. Instead, fourteen of Medb's most skilful followers awaited him: fourteen javelins were hurled at him simultaneously but Cúchulainn guarded himself so that his skin, and even his armour, was untouched. Then he turned on them and killed every one of the "Fourteen at Focherd".

Faughert is also said to be the birthplace of **Saint Brigid**, patron of Ireland, whose four-armed rush-cross is so common on the walls of rural Irish households. In the local churchyard you can see her holy well and pillar-stone, as well as the grave of **Edward Bruce**, who was defeated here in 1318 after being sent to Ireland by his brother (Robert the Bruce) to divert the English away from the Anglo-Scottish border. There is a stone nearby which in legend was used for his decapitation.

The Cooley Peninsula

You come to **Cooley** for the raw beauty of its mountains, to walk and to experience a life where the twentieth century intrudes only rarely. Indeed, when you get up among the bare hilltops the peninsula's links with legend seem at least as strong as its grip on modern reality. For above all this is country associated with the **Táin Bó Cúailnge**, and in the mountains many of the episodes of the great epic were played out. Its plot (set around the first century AD) concerns the Brown Bull of Cooley (*Donn Cúailnge*) which is coveted by Medb, Queen of Connacht, in her envy of her husband Ailill's White Bull (*Finnbenach*). In their efforts to capture the bull, Medb and Ailill, who come from the west, effectively declare war on the east in general, and Ulster in particular. All the men of Ulster – save one, Cúchulainn – are struck by a curse which immobilizes them through most of the tale, leaving our hero to face the might of Medb's troops alone. The action consists largely of his (often gory) feats, but the text is also rich in topography and placenames, many of them still clearly identifiable.

A single road runs around the peninsula, leaving the N1 to trace the southern slopes of the Cooley Mountains and then cutting across country to Greenore and Carlingford on the north shore. It is here, facing the Mountains of Mourne across **Carlingford Lough**, that the most beautiful scenes lie, with forested slopes plunging steeply towards the lough. The southern slopes are gentler and lazier, making a far more sedate progress to the water's edge. The exact location of the border, visible on the map as a dotted line bisecting the lough, has been in dispute since 1922. Once, it was continually patrolled by British Army helicopters; now, a gunboat riding at anchor is all you are likely to see.

Before you reach any of this, however, only about a mile down the peninsula road, there's a short and rewarding detour. From the back of the *Ballymascanlon Hotel*, a footpath leads to the **Proleek Dolmen**, whose massive capstone balances with far more elegance than its 46 tons ought to allow. If you see smaller stones on top they're recent additions, flung there by visitors who hope to have a wish granted. On the path just before the dolmen, a Bronze Age wedge-shaped **gallery grave** can be seen: both of these monuments may become harder to visit if, as local rumour has it, they are incorporated into holes five and six of a new golf course.

Omeath

Aside from being the more scenic, the peninsula's north shore is also the best place to base yourself for **hill walking** and the easiest for finding food and a bed. Here at **OMEATH**, the lough has narrowed dramatically, so that the sedate towns of Warrenpoint and Rostrevor on the Mourne Mountain slopes across the border seem only a handshake away. In summer there's a handy passenger **ferry service**, which also takes bikes, between Omeath and Warrenpoint (July & Aug daily till about 6pm, tides permitting; £1.50 return; 5min). Staying in the Republic, you can rent **jaunting cars** for short trips out of town; they run mostly to the open-air **stations of the cross** at the Rosminian Fathers' School down the road. As a village, Omeath, with its widely scattered dwellings, is far from typical of the east coast – it was until recent years the last remaining *Gaeltacht* village of any significance in this part of the country.

Omeath's luxury accommodation option is *Omeath Park* (☎042/75116; ⑥), half a mile out on the other side of town at the end of a long driveway up the hillside. Right up towards the border, there's an *An Óige* **hostel** (open all year; ☎042/75142; ①) a mile or so south of town, a few yards off the main road behind the *Ranch Pub and Restaurant* (☎042/75142; ①). The youth hostel has two separate houses, one for lounging and eating, the other divided into dormitories with some basic washing facilities. As ever you can't check in before 5pm, but the sitting area is always open to drop off your stuff and to get shelter if it's raining.

Around the crossroads that mark the centre of town are grouped a few **grocery stores** and **pubs**, the only facilities apart from the hostel that the place offers. One of Ireland's best young flautists, Des Wilkinson, lives in Omeath, so look out for his regular Friday-night sessions in one or other of the pubs. *Davey's Lounge*, a few miles up the road towards the border, is another pub to check out.

Carlingford

CARLINGFORD, a former fishing village five miles or so back down the lough, makes a considerable contrast to Omeath, both for its neatly ordered network of narrow, whitewashed, terraced streets, often with naive murals, at the foot of the Sliabh Foye Mountain, and in its development as an upmarket resort. Although the latter may take a trained eye to detect – it's discernable perhaps mainly as a sprinkling of craft shops – the place retains real charm as well as some excellent places to eat and drink. There's an **oyster festival** here around the middle of August, though it's now over-run by lager-swilling bus tours from the North, and – one of the less brilliant ideas to encourage tourists – a **leprechaun hunt** for a prize of £500 (£10 entry fee) on Easter Monday.

Carlingford is also an historic place. Saint Patrick is said to have landed here briefly on his way to introduce Christianity to Ireland (he finally ended his journey further north, in County Down), and the settlement is ancient enough to have been raided by the Vikings. But the oldest visible remain is the D-shaped ruin of **King John's Castle**, down by the main road on the water's edge. King John is said to have visited in 1210, and the Anglo-Norman castle, guarding the entrance to the lough, may be even older than that. It has its counterpart across the lough at Greencastle. The village in general retains a distinctly medieval feel, and there are a couple of solid fifteenth-century buildings: the **Mint**, in a narrow street off the square, is a fortified town house with an impressive gate tower; **Taafe's Castle**, which stood on the shore when it was built but is now some way from it, is impressively crenellated and fortified but sadly not open to the public. The best and safest **beaches** in the area are at Gyles Quay and Shelling Hill.

Practicalities

If you want to **stay**, try B&B at the *Viewpoint* on Omeath Road, whose modern, motel-like flatlets enjoy good views from a little way up the hill (☎042/73149; ④); *McKevitt's Village*, Market Square (☎042/73116; ⑤), for a little more luxury; *Jordan's* on Newry Street (☎042/73223; ⑥) for a real treat; or the *Carlingford Holiday Hostel*, Tholsel Street (*IHH*, open Feb–Nov; ☎042/73100; ②). This is part of the new **Carlingford Adventure Centre**, in converted warehouses around the Mint, where they also organize group tours and adventure holidays involving canoeing, wind-surfing and hill-walking: you can join in these activities, which cost from £13 per half-day.

Jordan's pub-cum-bistro is easily the best of the places to **eat and drink** in Carlingford. The menu includes some perhaps over-sophisticated variations (mango sauce) on excellent local ingredients, but the food, especially the fish, is good and excellent value (blow-out five-course gourmet dinner £21; bar food from £4; Sun lunch £12.50; open year-round 12.30–2.30pm, summer 6–10pm, winter 7–9.30pm; ☎042/73223); you'll need to book, weekends especially. There's a small room at the back of the pub which sometimes acts as a pre-dinner theatre. *O'Hare's* (aka *PJ's*), on the corner near the Mint, is an old grocery store and bar and the most entertaining place to drink – its publican has a considerable local reputation as a raconteur of tall tales; they also serve pub grub and oysters in season, which here seems to mean most of the year round. Nearby *McKevitt's Village* serves more substantial food, including filling bar meals from around £5. *Ghan House*, a fine Georgian mansion down near the crab-clawed pier, is yet another place where you can get a meal and a drop to drink.

LEGENDARY WALKS

You can walk almost anywhere in the mountains behind Carlingford and Omeath, and once you're up there the heather-tuffeted ground on top offers some of the most beautiful hill-walking imaginable, stained with episodes from the *Táin Bó Cúailnge*. It's at its best in the afternoon, with the light bringing out the colours of the Mourne Mountains across the water – in the morning the sun tends to get in your eyes. The road up behind the youth hostel in Omeath (see p.150) offers the best approach, switchbacking its way into the hills with the climb ever increasing the drama of the fjord below. At about 1200ft there's a car park where a map table marks out the major sights, and there's a long spiel on the formation of the lough: a valley gouged out by a glacier which was flooded at the end of the last Ice Age.

With a little imagination, it's not hard to translate the gaps, boulders and fording points of rivers up here into the scenes of Cúchulainn's epic battles. And some of the places are clearly identified. From **Trumpet Hill** (*Ochaine*) he slew a hundred men of Medb's army with his sling on three successive nights as they rested in a plain to the west. This forced Ailill, fearing that his entire force would be destroyed, to offer up champions in single combat. Between Ochaine and the sea Cúchulainn slew the first of these warriors, **Nadcranntail**, by letting his spear fly high into the air so that it dropped down onto Nadcranntail's skull and pinned him to the ground. Then he sprang onto the rim of Nadcranntail's shield and struck his head off and then struck again through the neck right down to the navel so that he fell in four sections to the ground.

From **Slievenaglogh** (*Sliab Cuinciu*) Cúchulainn swore to hurl a sling stone at Medb's head – no easy task as she never moved without her army in front holding a barrel-shaped shelter of shields over their heads. Then one of Medb's bondmaids, Lochu, went to fetch water and, thinking it was Medb herself, he loosed two stones, killing her on the plain in the place known as *Réid Locha*, Lochu's level ground. In fact, when he had the chance, Cúchulainn couldn't bring himself to kill Medb. During the final battle an earthy episode is inserted in which Medb suddenly gets a gush of blood that makes her need to urinate. Fergus, her chief warrior and lover, is furious at her bad timing and takes his place in the army of shields raised to protect her while she relieves herself, creating three great channels known as *Fual Medba*, Medb's foul place. Finding her in this delicate position, Cúchulainn was too honourable to kill her from behind (though he seems happy enough to kill everyone else whenever and wherever he can).

Fual Medba is not clearly identified, but you can find the scene of an earlier episode, the **Black Cauldron** (*Dubchoire*), where Medb divides her armies to search for the white bull, which has last been seen here: it's a recess north of the Glenngat Valley (the valley above Ballymackellet). When the spoils are brought back and the cattle have to be driven over the mountain at the source of the Big River (the River Cronn), Fergus decides that they will have to cut a gap in the hills to get the cattle. This is the *Bernas Bo Ulad*, today known as **Windy Gap**. It's also the point in the story where Fergus and Medb hang back behind the army to make love, and where Ailill, aware of their trysts, sent a spy to take Fergus's sword, thus acquiring proof of his unguarded weakness and providing the basis of a phallic joke which recurs throughout the story.

Windy Gap is also the setting of a far later tale, the tragic legend behind the **Long Woman's Grave**, marked by a pile of stones at the roadside. The story concerns two sons at their father's deathbed: the elder promised to give his younger brother a fair share of the estate, saying he would take him up to a high place in the mountains and give him all he could see. He kept his word, but the place where they stood was Windy Gap, where if you look around you see nothing but the immediate hills rising on all sides. The younger son instead became a trader, and on one trip wooed a Spanish beauty to whom he gave the same promise, tempting her hand in marriage. When he brought her home and took her up to the Windy Gap to show her his estate she dropped dead on the spot from shock. Thus the Long Woman's Grave for the tall Spanish beauty is explained.

COUNTY MEATH

The River Boyne has a name redolent of Irish history, for it was on its northern banks that one of the battles which shaped the nation's destiny was fought. If you travel up the river, however, this is not what most occupies your attention. For in the early stages, following the N51 to Navan, is the area known as the **Brú Na Bóinne** complex, with some of Europe's finest prehistoric remains. The whole Boyne Valley, in fact, has been heavily populated from the earliest times, and traces of virtually every period of Irish history can be found here.

However, before exploring the sites along the northern shore of the Boyne – and especially as there is no river crossing between Drogheda and Slane – you might want to take in two secondary diversions south of the river, easily reached from Drogheda (or if you're heading up the N2 from Dublin).

Donore and Duleek

A couple of miles southwest of Drogheda, **DONORE**'s chief interest, apart from having been King James's base at the time of the Battle of the Boyne, lies in its **ten-pound castle**. In 1429 Henry VI promised a grant of £10 to every one of his subjects who, in the next ten years, built a castle 20ft long, 16ft wide and 40ft high within the counties of Meath, Louth, Kildare and Dublin, the area known as the **Pale**. The three-storey castle here is built almost exactly to these measurements, though unfortunately it seems to be permanently locked up.

DULEEK (*An Damh Liag*, the stone church), a few miles further south, on the River Nanny, is an historic little place of considerably more interest. The south-of-the-

---

THE BATTLE OF THE BOYNE

For all the significance attached to it now (including big Protestant celebrations in the North on July 12), the **Battle of the Boyne** was just one skirmish – and arguably not the decisive one – in the "War of the Kings" between James II of Ireland and William of Orange, King of England. It took place at Oldgrange, less than five miles from Drogheda, on July 1, 1690 (the change of date came with the switch to the Gregorian calendar in the eighteenth century). The deposed James II, retreating southwards, took up defensive positions on the south bank of the river, with some 25,000 men (including 7000 well-equipped French troops, but largely Irish irregulars) holding the last major line of defence on the road to Dublin. William's forces – around 36,000 – occupied a rise on the north bank from where they forced a crossing of the river and put their enemies to flight. In terms of losses, the battle was a minor one – some 1500 Jacobites and 500 of William's men – and James's forces were to regroup and fight on for another year. But in political terms it was highly significant and can legitimately be seen as a turning point. In the complexities of European struggle, the Protestant William was supported by the pope and the Catholic king of Spain, both fearful of the burgeoning power of James's ally, the French King Louis XIV. Although the victory on the battlefield was small, the news gave heart to William's supporters in Europe while making Louis fearful of extending further aid to the Jacobite cause. At the same time, it gave William a breathing space to establish his control back home: in the long run, Protestant ascendancy was assured.

The location of the **battlefield** is directly opposite the turn-off from the N51 to Tullyallen, a couple of miles out of Drogheda. Here a stepped path leads to a viewing point on the site occupied by William's troops before the battle. It's only a slight elevation, but it nevertheless commands a broad swath of the valley and it's not too hard to conjure up a picture of the armies battling it out in front of you. A panoramic plan marks out the various positions of the opposing forces.

Boyne equivalent of Kells, it was founded by Saint Patrick who settled Saint Ciaran here to build the first stone church in Ireland and found a monastic settlement; it was also an early bishopric. Much later, the Jacobite forces withdrew to Duleek after the Battle of the Boyne and spent the night here, while James himself fled to Dublin and then on to France. The ruined **St Mary's Priory** you see today was probably founded in the twelfth century, and was abandoned after Henry VIII's dissolution of the monasteries: there are some fine tombs in the roofless building, and nearby a squat, tenth-century **high cross**. In the town square is a **wayside cross** of a different nature, erected by Genet de Bathe in 1601 as a memorial to William, one of her husbands, and one of the finest examples of a type of cross that crops up all over the place.

If you want to **stay** in this area there's good, reasonably priced B&B accommodation and home-produced food at the historic house of *Annesbrook*, a short, well-signposted distance out of town (May–Sept; contact Mrs Kate Sweetman, ☎041/23293; ⑤). William Thackeray in his *Irish Sketchbook* (1842) wrote uninspiringly about *Annesbrook*, but its most striking asset, the Ionic pedimented portico, has an interesting tale attached. The stately entrance is said to have been hastily affixed onto the box-shaped house when its owner was told to expect a visit from George IV, the first king to arrive from England after the departure of William and James. The portico was felt a necessary addition to bring the house up to the standards expected by royalty. The north wing, housing a Gothic dining room, was also built in the king's honour, but he preferred to dine in the garden.

Brú Na Bóinne

The area known as **Brú Na Bóinne** comprises a landscape made up of a group of forty or so related prehistoric monuments caught within a curve of the river between Tullyallen and Slane. The three most important of them, Dowth, Knowth and Newgrange, are what is known as **passage graves** – high round mounds raised over stone burial chambers. They predate the pyramids by several centuries, and although there's no comparison in terms of size or architecture, there are certain parallels. Just as the fertility of the Nile floodplain helped create the great Egyptian culture, so the lands of the River Boyne and its watershed have been proved to have had some of the richest soil in Europe (and considerably higher temperatures than today) around 3000 BC. On the banks flourished what seems to have been the most advanced Neolithic civilization in Europe. Physically, the tombs' size and solidity are what impress most; beyond the massive, bare stones there's not much to be seen, but there's plenty of scope to try and disentangle the various theories about these structures, to work out who built them, where they came from and where they went.

Dowth

Dowth is the first of the great sites if you're heading upstream, reached by taking the first left off the N51 after the battlesite, a minor road which trails the north bank of the river. Just before you reach the cairn you'll see the tower of **Dowth Castle** on the left, adjoining a rambling red-brick Victorian mansion, now converted into a Buddhist centre. John Boyle O'Reilly, a Fenian patriot transported to Australia, who later became editor and part-owner of the *Boston Pilot*, was born in the castle in 1844. At the back of the neighbouring ruined church there's a monument to him that forms the heart of a small **commemorative festival** every year on the Sunday closest to August 10.

The **Dowth mound** itself – roughly 50ft high and 200ft in diameter – is closed for conservation work at the time of writing, but you can wander about and see the outside. The signs of earlier excavations and of pillaging (in the nineteenth century some of the stones were removed for road-making) are immediately apparent, having left a crater in the top of the mound and a large chunk burrowed out of the side. Around 100 **kerbstones**, perhaps half of which can be seen today, originally marked the edge of the tumulus. Inside are two **passage tombs** and an early Christian chamber. The passages are similar in construction to those at Newgrange (see below), as is the decoration of the standing stones which form the walls of the passage, and the ten-foot-high corbelled roof. One distinction between the two sites, however, are the **sill stones** placed across the passage floor and at the entrance to the chamber.

The name Dowth derives from the Irish for "darkness", and the main chamber faces west to the setting sun (the minor chamber looks southwest, directly towards Newgrange). In myth, the site was built when the Druid Bresal, attempting to build a tower that would reach heaven, contracted all the men of Erin for a single day. His sister worked a spell so that the sun would not set until the mound was built, but the two then committed incest, destroying the magic and causing the sun to set: thereafter the sister declared "Dubad (darkness) shall be the name of that place forever". Today, as the sun sets at the winter solstice, its rays enter the tomb (at about 3pm), lighting up the tall stone slab at the back and then moving across to illuminate a recess in which is a decorated stone precisely angled to catch this moment, before finally sinking below the horizon.

If you want to **stay** close to the site with its fine views over the Boyne Valley, the *Glebe House* offers **B&B** (☎041/36101; ④), as well as afternoon tea.

Newgrange

The second of the tombs, **Newgrange** (daily June–Sept 9.30am–7pm; Oct 10am–5pm; Nov–Feb 10am–4.30pm; March & April 10am–5pm; May 9.30am–6pm; £3; Heritage Card), is far more visited, so much so in fact that long queues can build up at peak times. It's hardly surprising that the authorities have been unable to resist the temptation to open the place up as a heritage moneyspinner: as you approach the tomb, a roadside protest placard announces: "Newgrange to close after 5000 years. Disneygrange opening soon."

The plan is to build a heritage centre on the opposite bank of the Boyne, complete with a replica of Newgrange; with daily visitor numbers sometimes exceeding a thousand, there's concern that the monument can't take it. Local opposition is not so much aesthetic or environmental, however, as commercial: the new centre would mean that visitors would be brought in from Drogheda, with only scholars crossing the river or visiting the original site, and local business would suffer. The Office of Public Works, which is in charge of the project at the Burren in County Clare (see p.316), has brought a change in the law whereby it must seek planning permission at both sites. The project's at a stalemate.

To get to Newgrange follow the road directly on from Dowth and take a left at the T-junction. You're led around the monument in a guided tour about 25 minutes long (the closing times above are the *end* of the last tour), and if you want to avoid a long wait and a large group you should try not to come between noon and 4pm at peak times or especially on Sunday during the holidays. One or two of the most popular dates are booked up months in advance, above all the winter solstice when you've no chance at all of getting in to see the phenomenon described overleaf (it is effectively reserved for local dignitaries). You may be lucky, though, if you come a couple of days before or after the solstice, when the effect is almost as good – cloud cover permitting. To book ahead, which is essential for large groups at any time, call the Newgrange office (☎041/24488), or write to The Director, Office of Public Works, National Parks and Monuments Branch, 51 St Stephen's Green, Dublin 2.

At the entrance to the site there's a **museum and interpretative centre** where aspects of Newgrange and other nearby prehistoric sites are more fully explored, and there's also a seasonal **tourist office** (April–Nov, same hours as site; ☎041/24274). In the farmhouse just down from the entrance is a welcome **coffee shop** (same hours as site; ☎041/24119), with an open fire, but don't get your hopes up – you're more than likely to find yourself completely crowded out by shrieking bus parties. There's also a **working farm** (same hours as site; £2) where you can hug the more appealing of the animals should you feel the need.

The site

The **Newgrange tumulus** has an average diameter of around 338ft and is some 30ft high at its centre point. It has been so completely restored that at first sight it reminds you of a grounded Fifties sci-fi flying saucer. But once you get over the initial shock, the sparklingly new appearance of it all serves only to heighten the wonder. The quartzite retaining wall is glisteningly white and gives some hint (not revealed at other sites where everything is grey and moss-covered) of the power this particular stone must have had for the builders. The nearest natural source is in the Wicklow Mountains, south of Dublin. You'll notice that the wall is bossed with small, round granite stones, the purpose of which no one knows. Speculation is not helped by the fact that they are probably not in their original positions: during the most extensive of the renovations (1962–75) the original photographs were lost and their placement was therefore a matter of educated guess. Other non-original features worth noting are that the front and most ornate kerbstone was originally placed by the entrance tunnel (it was moved to prevent damage by visitors); that the entrance tunnel itself was closed by a standing slab; and that the concave wall at the entrance is designed to accommodate 100,000-odd tourists each year – originally the wall would have continued directly up to the sides of the spirally decorated kerbstone. It is also believed that an obelisk once stood at the top of the mound, to mark it out from afar.

The outer ring of **standing stones**, of which only twelve uprights now remain, was a feature unique among passage grave tombs, and it may have been the addition of a later civilization. None of the standing stones is decorated, and many show signs of being eroded by water, which suggests that they may have been hauled up here from the river. There is an inner ring of 97 **kerbstones** all placed on their sides and touching each other, engineered one supposes as a support for the layers of sod, loose stones, shale and boulder clay (20,000 tons of it) that were laid over the chambers.

Perhaps the most important feature of Newgrange – again unique – is the **roof-box** several feet in from the tunnel mouth. This contains a slit through which, at the **winter solstice**, the light of the rising sun begins to penetrate as soon as its full disc appears above the horizon. The rays edge their way slowly up the passage tunnel and, narrowed into a single shaft, eventually find the back of the cruciform chamber. In minutes the chamber becomes radiant with a glow of orange light which fades just as suddenly as it has blazed. The sun actually rises at about 8.20am above a hill known as the Red Mountain: it reaches the chamber a couple of minutes before 9am, and fifteen minutes later the whole thing is over. The guided tour includes a "re-creation" of the phenomenon which involves a flash of orange electric light: if you prefer to rely on your imagination, keep your eyes shut through this performance.

The rest you'll be effectively guided through on the tour. The entry passage, about three feet wide, leads into the **central chamber** where the finest of the work is. Its corbelled roof creates a space some 20ft high, and on the stones everywhere are carved superbly intricate decorations, apparently abstract but perhaps (see opposite) with some more precise meaning. On the way out, beware the last roof-slab – on which most tall people will graze their heads even after this warning.

Myth and supposition

The name Newgrange derives from "new granary", simply because that was its function at one stage in its history. This hardly seems an adequate description for one of the most important Stone Age sites in Europe, however, and an alternative derivation ("the Cave of Gráinne") is considerably more satisfying, if less accurate. The site has many associations with **myth**. First among these concern the **Tuatha Dé Danann**, the first Irish gods who descended from the sky and inhabited the land before the Celts. Dagda (the Irish Zeus, chief of the gods) gained possession of the mound by making love to Boand (the white cow goddess who later deliberately drowned herself at the source of the Boyne so as to invest the river with her divinity), first tricking her husband Elcmar by sending him on an errand for a day which took him nine months. From their union **Oengus** was born and called *ac ind Oc* (The Youthful Son). In ancient literature Newgrange is *Brugh Mac ind Oc*, the Brugh of Oengus. Oengus also appears later in the **Fenian Cycle** as the succourer of Diarmuid and Gráinne, carrying the fatally wounded body of Diarmuid to Newgrange "to put aerial life into him so that he will talk to me every day". Other legends make the local mounds the tombs of the Kings of Tara; radio-carbon dating, pinpointing the third millennium BC, disproves this fairly convincingly.

What does emerge is just how little concrete information there is on the people who created Newgrange. Perhaps the most tempting of the more off-beat **theories** regarding the meaning of the monuments is that of the American Martin Brennan in his book *Stars and Stones* (Thames and Hudson, 1983). He claims that the scrollwork, lozenges and lines on the stones, which most archeologists see as abstract decoration, perhaps with religious significance, are in fact all part of a single incredibly involved **astronomical chart** which includes not only Newgrange itself, but the rest of the Brú Na Bóinne complex and even sites as far-flung as Loughcrew (see p.163) and those in the Curlew Mountains in south Sligo. In his book he claims that the scrollwork all relates to a calibration system based on the diameter of the earth. Brennan insists that the Newgrange monument is not only the largest but also the oldest such system in the world: predating and far outranking in sophistication the instruments of the Greek astronomers. It is not a theory you are likely to find espoused by your guide, but it does have its convincing aspects. In the end, though, you have to ask why, if they were so sophisticated, is this the only evidence that survives?

Knowth

To reach **Knowth**, carry on up the road from Newgrange and take a left, whereupon you'll see a makeshift wooden watchtower overlooking the site. Major excavations have been going on here since 1962, but recently about a third of the complex has been opened to the public (May to mid-June 10am–5pm; mid-June to mid-Sept 9.30am–6.30pm; mid-Sept to Oct 10am–5pm; £2; Heritage Card). Though there's less to see for visitors, the discoveries at Knowth have already surpassed what was excavated at Newgrange, perhaps because, unlike Newgrange, the site was continuously inhabited until the fourteenth century, and archeologists have been able to explore four distinct phases of settlement – although the use of earth-moving equipment is apt to provoke suspicion that what's going on here is less archeology and more wholesale reinvention.

Several periods of occupation by different cultures have been identified, from the **Neolithic**, when the original passage tombs were built (3000–2000 BC), through occupation by the Beaker people (2000–1800 BC), so called because of a distinctive beaker left with each of their dead, a late **Celtic** settlement in the early centuries AD, early **Christian** occupation (eighth to twelfth centuries) and finally **Norman** usage (twelfth and thirteenth centuries) that brought an extensive settlement and a glut of *souterrains* (underground passages and chambers), some bored into the Neolithic mound itself. The main passage tomb is about twice the size of that at Newgrange – with a tunnel over 100ft long leading to the central chamber – and even more richly decorated. At Knowth there is also, so far uniquely, a second, smaller passage tomb within the main tumulus, and up to seventeen **satellite tumuli.** Both main tombs are aligned east–west. In construction the mound is basically the same as Newgrange, with a cruciform chamber, high corbelled roof and richly decorated stones, but here there is also evidence of settlement around the mound. Probably the two were created by two distinct communities of the same culture: a supposition backed by carbon dating that places the Knowth mound some 500 years earlier than Newgrange. At Knowth alone, about 250 decorated stones have been found: over half of all known Irish passage grave art. The most recent discovery is a series of large post-holes arranged in a circle, suggesting the existence of some form of wood-henge.

Slane

SLANE itself, set on a steep hillside running down to the Boyne a mile or so west of Knowth, is a beautiful little place which packs a surprising amount of interest. The scene is set at the village centre, where four three-storey eighteenth-century houses stand at the four corners of a crossroads, each virtually identical (with arched entrance court-yards to the side) and composed of a lovely, rough-cut grey limestone. There's a good yarn about these, concerning the four spinster sisters said to have built them, which may be recounted to you locally. It's not true, but you can't help feeling it ought to be.

Down by the river, the Georgian theme is continued in the fine **mill**, built in 1766, across the road from which stands a large Gothic gate to Slane Castle, whose lands stretch out westward along the river. There's a **Transport Museum** (daily June–Sept) on the river bank as well, with around fifty cars on display.

Slane Castle suffered an enormous fire in the spring of 1992 and is strictly out of bounds to the public. Some restoration work is underway, but money is short and the place is unlikely to open to the public again for several years. During the reconstruction period, the owners have appealed to tourists not to enter the grounds at all, for their own safety. Approximately once a year, however, the castle does open its gates to half of young Ireland for massive, open-air rock concerts promoted by the entrepreneurial Lord Henry Mountcharles, who has a warm relationship with Ireland's rock business – including U2, who recorded *The Joshua Tree* in one of the rooms at Slane. On Friday and Saturday nights the tiny castle **nightclub** used to open up in the basement, and with luck, it may start up again (ring ☎041/24207). On a more traditional level, the castle is the seat of the **Conyngham family** and is a classically ordered mass of mock battlements and turrets with a neo-Gothic library. The best architects of the day – Wyatt, Johnston and Gandon – were involved in the design, and the grounds were laid out by Capability Brown. Inside, there's a substantial art collection and many mementos of King George IV, who is said to have spent the last years of his life involved in a heady liaison with the Marchioness Conyngham: some claim that this relationship accounts for the exceptionally fast, straight road between Slane and Dublin. Further out in the castle grounds, and not for public consumption beyond a glimpse from the river towpath, is **St Erc's Hermitage**. Lord Mountcharles recently gave this to the nation, but it will be some time before it opens to the public.

The Hill of Slane

Walking north from the crossroads, uphill, you can climb to the top of the **Hill of Slane**, where **Saint Patrick** lit his Paschal Fire in 433 AD, announcing the arrival of Christianity. This was in direct defiance of Laoghaire, High King of Tara, who had ordered no fire-making until Tara's own hillside was set alight. Fortunately for Saint Patrick, Laoghaire was promptly converted, welcoming the new religion throughout the country. The summit commands magnificent views of the whole Boyne Valley. Near the top, the ruined **Friary Church** (1512) and separate college building are worth investigating. The church has a well-preserved **tower**, with a very narrow and steep flight of sixty-odd steps: if you make it up you're rewarded with a broad panorama of the eastern counties, though Slane itself is all but hidden from view. In the graveyard there is a very unusual early Christian tomb with gable-shaped end-slabs. This is supposed to be the final resting place of **Saint Erc**, Patrick's greatest friend and servant whom he made Bishop of Slane. The **college** was built to house the four priests, four lay-brothers and four choristers there to serve the church; assorted pieces of carved stonework can be found if you mooch round its ruins.

Practicalities

If you're looking for somewhere to **stay** in Slane, the best option is probably a newly converted Georgian house by the canal walk, tucked in behind the mill, which offers both B&B and basic hostel-type accommodation; there's accommodation also at the *Conyngham Arms Hotel* (☎041/24155; ⑤) and a couple of other B&Bs including *Castle Hill House* at 2 Castle Hill (☎041/24696; ③); or try *Boyneview* (☎041/24121; ③), one of a row of stone cottages overlooking both the river and the grandiose entrance lodge of the castle. You'll find reasonably priced **food** at the *Conyngham Arms* (pub lunches and evening meals) or at the *Roadhouse Restaurant* a few miles from Slane out on the Dublin Road (going south take the right turn just before *McKeever's Esso Garage*). There's a good **swimming** spot on the Boyne below the weir, but check first with locals as the river currents can be strong in places. You can get to Slane by *Expressway* bus from Dublin – at least two services a day – for £7.20 return.

East to the Ledwidge Museum

A short way east, a mile or so out of Slane, is the **Francis Ledwidge Museum** (daily 10am–1pm, 2–7pm; in winter on Wed only till 5.30pm; £1; if closed get the key from the small printing firm further down the road on the left-hand side). This stone-built labourer's cottage was the birthplace, in 1887, of the local poet Francis Ledwidge, who died on a battlefield in Flanders on July 31, 1917. Ledwidge was untypically pastoral for an Irish poet, and perhaps for this reason comparatively little known. His poems were written on the small scale, and the museum reflects this: a modest, almost spartan house with the poetry daintily hung in miniature picture frames. The lines inscribed on a stone plaque outside the cottage were written when Ledwidge heard of the death of his Irish poet friend Thomas MacDonagh, who was executed by the British for his involvement with the Easter Rising of 1916: it's an echo of MacDonagh's own poetic translation of Cathal Buidhe's *Mac Giolla Ghunna* (The Yellow Bittern):

> He shall not hear the bittern cry
> In the wild sky, where he is lain,
> Nor voices of the sweeter birds
> Above the wailing of the rain

There's a fine parallel to this in the poet Seamus Heaney's *In Memoriam Francis Ledwidge*:

> I think of you in your Tommy's uniform,
> A haunted Catholic face, pallid and brave,
> Ghosting the trenches with a bloom of hawthorn
> Or silence cored from a Boyne passage-grave.

Upstream to Navan

In its course upstream to Navan, the **Boyne** runs past the grounds of several great houses. You can't visit any of them, but if you follow the river – a distance of some eight miles from Slane to Navan – you get a real sense of an all but vanished world. The old towpath switches sides from time to time, with no obvious means of crossing: the solution to this apparent mystery is that the horse would step onto the barge and be poled across to the other side. It is just about possible to walk all the way if you're prepared to crash out your own path some of the time, but it's a great deal easier to walk as far as you can from this end, then travel to Navan by road and do the same from the other end. After Slane Castle itself, on the opposite side of the river, comes **Beauparc House**, the mid-eighteenth-century mansion also owned by Lord Mountcharles.

A little further on you pass the remains of **Dunmoe Castle** (signposted off the N51, but accessible from there only by a nightmarish potholed lane), high on the northern bank. All that remains are two sides of a four-storey castle which was square in shape with large rounded turrets at the four corners. Inside you can still see parts of the vaulted ceilings of the lower storeys. Better than the crumbling structure, though, are the views it commands: in the river a diagonally dividing weir breaks the water into a stretch of rapids and another of calm, while on the opposite bank, there's a delightful red-brick mansion with a stretch of garden steps worthy of Versailles breaking through the wooded thickets to reach the river. Finally, shortly before Navan and right by the side of the main road, you pass the **Domhnach Mór** (Great Church), site of a superbly preserved round tower above whose arched doorway is carved a relief figure of Christ.

Navan

At **NAVAN** the **River Blackwater** meets the Boyne. It's an historic crossroads – important in the days when the waterways were the chief means of transport – and also a modern one. The N3 comes up from Dublin to follow the course of the Blackwater to Kells and to the Loughcrew Mountains in the northwestern corner of Meath; the N51 arrives from Drogheda to continue into Westmeath, its interest diminishing rapidly as you go; and to the south you can take the N3 to Tara (see p.165), Dunsany and then go eastwards on minor roads to Bective Abbey and Trim (see p.169).

Although it offers access to a lot of places, Navan itself has little to detain you. There's no tourist information office at present, but one is due to open. There are a couple of hotels here and a number of fairly simple B&Bs not far away, should you wish to **stay**, such as *Tower View*, on the Slane Road at Donaghmore (✆046/23358; ③); for a bit more style and seclusion, try *Swynnerton Lodge*, half a mile out on the Slane Road (✆046/21371; ④). You'll find a good cheap **lunch** at *Susie's Cookhouse*, centrally placed on the Market Square, or at *Bon Appetit*, on the square at the corner of Ludlow Street, and there's a nice quiet **pub** nearby, the *Bermingham Bar* opposite the cinema on Ludlow Street. *Peter Kavanagh's* on Trimgate Street is another good, old-fashioned pub, and there are **traditional music** sessions every Wednesday and poetry readings once a month in the *Lantern*, Watergate Street. *Molloys* on Bridge Street, opposite the infirmary, hosts traditional-music sessions on a Thursday.

Athlumney Castle

One local sight worth going out of your way for is **Athlumney Castle**, about a mile's walk from the centre of town – head over the bridge, then turn first right following the signs. Just as you come up to the ruin, veer right into **Loreto Convent** (once the castle's outbuildings) where you can pick up the keys. In the convent grounds you should immediately spot the twelfth-century motte (now surrounded by a ring of trees) that would have had a *Bretesche*, or wooden tower, built on it. This was purely defensive, and the owner would actually have lived closer to the river.

The castle you see now is a fifteenth-century tower house to which a Jacobean manor house was added in the early seventeenth century. The **Tower House** has four floors in excellent condition, the first of which has a secret chamber down the stairs in the wall. The last occupant of the mansion was Sir Lancelot Dowdall, a Catholic who on hearing of the defeat of James II decided to set his home alight rather than see it fall into the hands of William's army. According to the story, he crossed the river and stood all night watching it burn before heading into permanent exile. The interior shows large gaping fireplaces and a horseshoe stone-oven on the bottom floor which would have been the area of the kitchens (the heat from which would rise to warm up the living quarters above). It once had a gabled roof within which the servants were housed, and it still has many impressive mullioned windows as well as a magnificent oriel window overlooking the modern road.

If you head back to the bridge you can take the steps down to the **ramparts**, then follow the canalside all the way to Stackallen, though a certain amount of building work may disrupt your way to begin with. A mile or so northeast of Navan on the Slane Road is a fine 100ft-high round tower at Donaghmore. This stands on an early Christian site, reputedly founded by Saint Patrick.

Kells and around

Following the Blackwater upstream from Navan, Kells is the obvious place to make for, ten miles up the N3 Dublin–Cavan Road. En route, you'll pass the site of the **Tailteann games** (on the hill above Teltown House), a little over halfway. Here games and ancient assemblies sacred to the god **Lugh** took place in the first days of August (the Irish for the month of August is *Lúnasa*, or *Lughnasa*).* As late as the twelfth century the games were still being recorded, and right up to the eighteenth century a smaller celebration took place, in which locals rode their horses across the river for the benefit of the sacred qualities of its waters. Christianity eventually put paid to most of the rituals, but there is still talk of what was known as the **Teltown marriages**, where young couples would join hands through a hole in a wooden door, live together for a year and a day, and then be free to part if they so wished. Today only a very few earthworks remain, and certainly if you have visited Tara, or intend doing so, there's little to be gained in stopping here.

Kells

KELLS itself (*Ceanannus Mór*) is a place of history and monastic antiquities – several high crosses, an eleventh-century oratory, a round tower and an ancient square bell tower – but it is most famous for what is not here, the magnificent illuminated manuscript known as the **Book of Kells**, now housed in Trinity College, Dublin. The **monastery** was founded by Saint Columba in the sixth century, and from about 807 it became the leading Columban monastery in Ireland, when the monks from the original foundation on the Scottish island of Iona fled here from repeated Viking raids. It is probable that the Book of Kells was actually made on Iona and that they brought it with them when they moved. The new home was little safer than the original one and was attacked time and again by Danes and later the Normans: in the twelfth century the

---

*Old Irish literature not untypically begs to differ and describes the place rather as a pagan cemetery named after the goddess Tailtiu.

monastic order's headquarters moved on to Derry, and by the time of the Dissolution there was little left to suppress. So most of what you actually see is eighteenth century or later, and although the town's layout still etches out the concentric ridges of the early monastery's plan, it's a surprisingly characterless place. Nonetheless, the little that survives is well worth making the effort to see.

When you arrive, head for the spire of the **bell tower** that stands within the grounds of the modern church where most of the relics are to be seen. In the church itself (if it's not open the key can be got from the gate-lodge outside working hours, otherwise search for the priest) there's a facsimile copy of the Book of Kells, and up in the gallery you'll find a small exhibition of blown-up photos of some of its pages. The **Round Tower** in the churchyard is known to have been here before 1076, for in that year Murchadh Mac Flainn, who was claiming the High Kingship, was murdered within the tower. It's a little under 100ft high, with five windows near the top, and missing only its roof.

Near the tower is the **South High Cross**, the best and probably the oldest of the crosses in Kells, carved as ever with scenes from the Bible. Here you'll see, on the south face, Adam and Eve and Cain and Abel; then the three children in the fiery furnace; then Daniel in the lions' den. On the left arm of the wheel Abraham is about to sacrifice Isaac, and on the right are saints Paul and Anthony in the desert; at the top is David with his harp and the miracle of the loaves and fishes. There are two other complete crosses in the churchyard, and the stem of a fourth (behind the church back-entrance door) with the inscription *Oroit do Artgal*, A Prayer for Artgal. This has several identifiable panels. The near side shows the baptism of Christ, the marriage feast at Cana, David with his harp again, the presentation in the Temple, and others too worn to make out. On the other side are a self-conscious Adam and Eve, Noah's ark, and others hard to identify accurately. There are sculptured stones embedded in the walls of the bell tower.

St Colmcille's House, probably built by the Columban community, can be found just outside the churchyard walls at the north end – coming out of the main gates take a sharp left uphill, but first obtain the keys from the chocolate-brown house just after the stop sign. It's a beautifully preserved building – thick-walled and high-roofed – and peculiarly in character with the terrace of nineteenth-century workers' houses alongside which it stands. A modern entrance has been broken in at ground level, when originally the door would have been about eight feet off the ground in the west wall (reached, for security, by a removable ladder); you can still see the intended way in round to the left from where you enter now. Inside is a space about 19ft by 16ft, where you emerge into a vaulted room that would have once had two levels (with the present ground floor as a basement). Above were three tiny attic rooms, reached now by a metal ladder, which were probably where the residents slept and also a hideout in times of trouble. Underground tunnels link the oratory and the Round Tower, supposedly running beneath *O'Rourke's* pub on Castle Street.

In the central **market square** there's another fine **high cross**, discoloured by traffic fumes, said to have been placed here by Jonathan Swift. In 1798 it served as the gallows from which local rebels were hanged. Yet again, it is liberally festooned with fine stone carving. The base shows horsemen and animals in a battle scene; on the west face are the adoration of the Magi, the marriage at Cana and the miracle of the loaves and fishes, all surrounding the Crucifixion in the centre of the wheel; on the east are Christ in the tomb, Goliath, Adam and Eve, and Cain and Abel, with Daniel in the lions' den occupying centre stage.

Practicalities

Buses pick up outside *O'Rourke's* lounge in Castle Street – an *Expressway* bus from Dublin is £8 return; Kells has no tourist office. For **accommodation**, the *Headfort Arms* hotel (☎046/40063; ⑥) at the beginning of the Dublin Road is a reasonable choice. Kells's independent **hostel** (*IHH*, open all year; ☎046/40100; ②) is part of

Monaghan's pub, at the top of Garrick Street, a steep street of pastel-coloured flat-fronted houses that leads out of the centre of town. You'll get very tasty **food** during the day at *Penny's Place*, a café/lunch room at the bottom end of Market Street (closes 6pm), but in the evenings there's not much choice outside the pubs. *Magee's* on Farrell Street serves fine snacks, but otherwise good **pubs** are surprisingly scarce. One that's definitely worth a visit, however, is *O'Shaughnessy's* on Church Street (running along the bottom of the church plot), which has Irish ballads and old-time music on Friday, Saturday and Sunday nights at 9pm. The song *The Isle of Inishfree* was actually written there by D. Farley, the former owner who was also once superintendent at Dublin Castle.

The Castlekeeran crosses

From Kells the N3 follows the Blackwater northwest into County Cavan. A considerably more interesting route takes the Oldcastle Road or R163 (the one that passes alongside the round tower) towards the Loughcrew cairns (see below*)*. Only a mile out of Kells a very worthwhile short detour takes you up a winding road to the right that leads, after about another mile, to the **Castlekeeran crosses**. Entry is signposted through the yard of a creamy-orange farmhouse and across a field which will take you into the old monastery enclosure.

Hardly anything of the monastery known as **Díseart Chiaráin**, the Hermitage of Ciaran, has survived, although you can pick out a partially earth-covered arch. The high crosses here, three of them plus a fourth in the middle of the river, are older than those at Monasterboice and Kells and far simpler. But their greatest charm lies in the fact that you'll probably be quite alone as you contemplate their history. The only decoration on the crosses are some simple fringing patterns and boss protruberances in the "armpits" and tops and wheel centres. The story of the cross in the River Blackwater tells how Saint Columba was caught red-handed by Saint Ciaran as he carried the cross off to his own monastery. In his shame he dropped the cross where he stood and fled back to Kells.

There is also an **early Christian grave slab** in the graveyard, and a very good example of an **Ogham stone**. Ogham was an early Irish script which was widely used from around the fourth to the seventh century AD, after which it was very gradually replaced by Latin script. Even at the height of its popularity Ogham co-existed with Latin writing: it was used primarily on stones and monuments such as this, while Latin script was found in manuscripts. It is thought that the script was once used for secret communication, part of a signalling or gesture system for magical or cryptic purposes; it can also be found in parts of Devon, Wales and Scotland. As late as the nineteenth century some isolated peasant communities still used Ogham script if they needed to write anything down – it had the advantage that no one from outside would be able to interpret it. On stones like this, the edge is used to help define the characters. Five strokes above the line give you five letters; five below another five letters. Five strokes that cross the line make five more letters and five oblique strokes five more: to these a few less obvious symbols are added to make up the alphabet. The inscription here apparently reads *covagni maqi mucoi luguni*, but although the letters can be made out nobody seems to know what these words actually mean.

Sliabh Na Caillighe

SLIABH NA CAILLIGHE, the Mountain of the Sorceress (910ft), is the highest part of the **Loughcrew Mountains**, whose two-mile east–west stretch virtually cuts off the furthest tip of County Meath. From the top there's a wonderfully disparate view, with the Cavan lakelands in one direction and the undulating flow of earthy Meath in the other, blending in the far distance into the mountains of Wicklow and Slieve Bloom. Three major groupings of **Neolithic cairns** were constructed on these summits, no doubt chosen to be seen from afar. The first group (coming from the east) is known as the **Patrickstown Cairns** and has been so thoroughly despoiled, largely for building material in the nineteenth century, that no significant trace remains. The other two summits have one major cairn each: **Cairn T on Carnbane East** and **Cairn L on Carnbane West**. Each of these has a handful of satellite mounds, though these represent only a fraction of what must once have been here. The sites are not easy to get to – you'll need transport and still face a hefty walk at the end – but they are well worth the effort. Little known as they are, the Loughcrew cairns are almost as impressive as the Newgrange mounds (certainly when you take into account the sheer number) and you'll almost certainly be free to explore them entirely alone, and with as much time as you want. Bring a torch if you want to appreciate what lies inside.

The Oldcastle Road runs beneath the northern flank of the mountains, and about four and a half miles before Oldcastle you'll see a broken signpost pointing off to the left, to *Sliabh Na Caillighe*. Follow this road for a mile and then take the right turn (signposted) that clearly heads towards the hill complex. In the first bungalow on the right you will be able to get the loan of keys from John Balfe (buy a leaflet plan off him for 20p, and to be sure of finding someone in – or if you want to be there for sunrise – ring ahead to arrange to pick up the keys, ☎049/41256). These open the iron grilles on the few major cairns on top of the hills; the minor ones have either been deroofed or are left open. Alternatively, Sarah Keogh gives guided tours of the cairns in English, Irish, French and German; call to make an appointment (June–Sept ☎046/43635; £3). She also runs tours of the Seven Wonders at Fore (see p.176; a ticket for both, £5).

Carnbane West

Half a mile up the road – a steep climb – you'll come to a small clearing where a stile leads into a field: this path heads to the **Carnbane West** grouping. On your way across you'll notice **Cairn M** off to your left on a high peak – except for its astronomical involvement with Cairn L, this hasn't much of interest and it's not really worth the hike. **Cairn L**, with its wide ring of kerbstones, should be obvious to you immediately. It was most recently explored by Martin Brennan in 1980, after years of relative neglect by archeologists; it is his astronomical theories which are in part set out below: they are far from being generally accepted, but in the absence of other explorations they do at least attempt to answer some of the questions about the sites.

Cairn L has an asymmetrical chamber unique among the Loughcrew cairns, with a white **standing stone**, over six feet high, positioned at the back right. It is probable that the mound was built as a majestic housing for this one special stone. According to Brennan its function is found in the rising sun on the cross-quarter days November 8 and February 4 (the days halfway between the solstices and the equinoxes). On these days a flash of light enters the tomb from the rising sun at about 7.40am and catches the top of the standing stone. The lower edge of the light is formed by the shadow of Cairn M, and other standing slabs in L further shape it so that the ray marks out only the standing stone. If you have a torch, then study the decorated slab by the basin to the left of the stone, facing away from the entrance. There are many designs carved into the various stones, but at the bottom of this one, according to Brennan, you can see a pictorial representation of this astronomical event.

Brennan sees **Cairn H** as a warning of the November cross-quarter day. The rising sun begins to penetrate its chamber from mid-October onwards, with the backstone being touched come November, and then from about the third onwards the sun leaves Cairn H and moves on to Cairns M and L for November 8. **Cairn F**, with several examples of decorative grooves, kicks off another alignment series. The sun begins to enter in late April, ready to mark another cross-quarter day on May 6, when the rays of the setting sun centre on **Cairn S**. Cairn S is also aligned for the final cross-quarter day, August 8. By August 16 they enter F again, and from there move on to **Cairn I** to warn of the autumn equinox. If Brennan's theories are correct (critics tend to claim that if you look long enough, and pick enough times and days, you can prove almost anything this way), then cairns I, T, F and S form the longest such sequence of alignments known.

Carnbane East

To get to **Carnbane East**, return to the hill road and carry on until you reach a large car-parking space where a path leads up the hill to the mounds. If you lose the path, which is vague at times, just keep climbing steeply, steering left if there's any doubt: towards the top follow the barbed wire round and enter by the kissing gate which will put you on the threshold of Cairn T. At Carnbane East Brennan sees three mounds functioning as solar dials. **Cairn T** deals with the spring and autumn equinoxes (March 23 and Sept 22). In its cruciform chamber is a large backstone liberally patterned with chevrons, ferns, petals and moon and sun signs. At the spring equinox a shaped patch of light passes across a passage stone and various of the other designs to focus on the large radial sun sign in the centre of this stone. At the autumn equinox the sun makes a more leisurely progress, rising at about 7.11am, and strikes the backstone just over half an hour later. Once again it crosses the sunwheel emblem. Of the satellite mounds, neither of which has a roof any more, **Cairn S** is said to mark the cross-quarter days on May 6 and August 8, while **Cairn U** is synchronized with Cairn L to mark November 8 and February 4. Cairn S has lots of sun emblems, while Cairn U has a variety of more unusual (and less identifiable) markings. Whatever you make of Brennan's theories in the end, he has at least opened an important new area of exploration; and in the undeniable light of Newgrange's connection with the equinox there are few people any more who would contend that these structures were simply tombs and nothing more.

Oldcastle

OLDCASTLE is a mild-natured, genially ramshackle eighteenth-century town, built around a crossroads. Set in sheep country, it was once the largest yarn market in Ireland, but no longer seems to have much significance. You can eat and sleep here – there's a **B&B** (☎049/41437; ③) out on the main road, below the cairns, a good **lunch** in the *Naper Arms Hotel* in the square, and traditional music at weekends in the *Céilí House Bar* – but there's not much else to do. Three miles out of town (take the Castlepollard Road and turn left at the garage) is the family church of the (Oliver) Plunketts. Their estate was given by Cromwell to one of his soldiers, named Naper, in payment of salary arrears. You can **stay** in the present-day Charlie Naper's *Loughcrew House* (☎049/41356; ⑤).

In terms of interest, you're better off heading on to Castlepollard, ten miles south in County Westmeath (p.175), from where you can explore the Fore Valley, Tullynally Castle and the sights around Lough Derravaragh.

Tara and around

South from Navan down the Dublin–Navan Road, there's a trio of places well worth seeing; the first is one of the most famous historic and mythical sites in Ireland, **Tara** and its eponymous hill. Moving south again is **Dunsany Castle**, where you'll find an interesting art collection. Not far west of the castle, the remains of **Bective Abbey** are beautifully located on the River Boyne and make a pleasant stop on the way to Trim (the R161 from Navan to Trim is just by the abbey).

Tara

TARA, the home of the High Kings of Ireland and source of so many of the great tales, looks nowadays like nothing so much as a neatly kept nine-hole golf course: a gently undulating swath of green marked out by archeological plaques. To re-create the palace, whose wood-and-wattle structures have entirely disappeared, leaving only scars in the earth, takes a fair degree of imagination. But it's an effort worth making, for this was a great royal residence, already thriving before the Trojan Wars and still flourishing as late as the tenth century AD. The origins of the site are lost in prehistory, but it probably originally had a religious significance, gradually growing from the base of a local priest-king to become the seat of the High Kings. Its heyday came in the years following the reign of the legendary Cormac Mac Art* in the third century AD – when five great highways converged here: this was a ritual, rather than a residential, centre – and by the time of the confrontation of Saint Patrick with King Laoghaire in the fifth century, its power was already declining. The title of High King was not, on the whole, a hereditary one: rather the kings were chosen, or won power on the battlefield. So they were not necessarily local – or even permanently based here – but all evoked the spirit of Tara as the basis of their power.

In later history, there was a minor battle at the site during the 1798 revolution, and in the mid-nineteenth century **Daniel O'Connell** held a mass "Monster" meeting – said to have attracted as many as a million people (a quarter of Ireland's population today) – as part of his campaign against union with Britain.

You'll find the **site** signposted just off the N3; from the car park it appears as a wild meadow on a table-top hill, no more than 300ft above the surrounding countryside (just beside the car park is the *Banquet Hall Café*, open daily 9.30am–6/7pm). There is a plan of the place near the entrance, which will help you to identify the various mounds. The path to the site leads through the yard of the old Church of Ireland church, which is now used as a **visitor centre** (May to mid-June 9.30am–5pm; mid-June to mid-Sept 9.30am–6.30pm; mid-Sept to Oct 10am–5pm; last admission 45min before closing; £1), with a romantic but reasonably sophisticated audio-visual show that gives some background to Tara's history and also, more valuable, shows a number of aerial views that do a lot to make sense of the design. The **church** itself, dated 1822, is a modest grey building typical of the Anglican churches found all over Ireland; somehow it seems fitting that it should find a role participating in the re-enhancement of a more ancient landscape that its builders once attempted to dominate. The church's only remarkable feature is a bright stained-glass window by the well-known Dublin artist Evie Hone, which was installed in 1935 to commemorate the 1500th anniversary of the visit of Saint Patrick to the site and thus the coming of Christianity to Ireland. Saint Patrick challenged the then High King at Tara, Laoghaire, by lighting his paschal (Easter) flame on the nearby Hill of Slane in response to the holy fire at Tara – thereby demonstrating the ritual sympathies of the

---

*One of the more frequently recounted stories concerning Cormac is about his death. After years of heroism he died, the victim of a druid's curse, in a singularly unheroic manner, choking on a salmon bone (salmon being the Celtic symbol of wisdom). The curse had been laid after he began proclaiming his belief in a new god who would soon be arriving in Ireland (a belief borne out by the arrival of Saint Patrick). In defiance of the king's stated wishes, his body was taken to be buried at Newgrange; but when the funeral procession reached the Boyne, the tides came to the king's defence, and in the end his body had to be laid to rest on the south side of the river, at Ros Na Rí.

new religion with the old. Once you are on top of what is actually very rich pasture, the power of the setting immediately becomes clear, with endless views that take in whole counties and their patchwork fields, and a huge sky.

The Banquet Hall

Teach Miodhchuarta – once known as the Banquet Hall – is on the northern hill slope and consists of two parallel banks between which runs a long sunken corridor. Its length is about 750ft and the breadth 90ft. An account of it in the medieval book known as the *Dinnshenchas* reads:

> *The ruins of this house are situated thus: the lower part to the north and the higher part to the south; and walls are raised about it to the east and to the west. The northern side of it is enclosed and small; the lie of it is north and south. It is in the form of a long house, with twelve doors upon it, or fourteen, seven to the west, and seven to the east. It is said that it was here the Feis Teamhrach was held, which seems true; because as many men would fit in it as would form the choice part of the men of Ireland. And this was the great house of a thousand soldiers.*

Easy as it is to imagine the five ancient highways thronged with people on their way to crowd the hall for the great *Feis*, all this is now known to be fantasy. There was no banqueting hall, and the meaning of the banks remains unclear; they may perhaps have been part of a ceremonial entrance to the site.

Gráinne's Fort and the Sloping Trenches

Northwest of the hall is a smaller group of earthworks, the first of which is **Ráth Gráinne** (Gráinne's Fort). It is surrounded by a fosse and bank and has a low mound at its centre, probably once a burial mound or maybe a house site. From here the tragic love tale of the *Pursuit of Diarmuid and Gráinne* began its journey, although, as a much later invention, it wasn't originally associated with the mound. Gráinne was the daughter of Cormac Mac Art, who had arranged to marry her to his aged commander-in-chief, Finn Mac Cool. Instead she fell in love with Diarmuid, one of Mac Cool's young warriors, and the two of them fled together, relentlessly pursued by Finn Mac Cool. Their various hiding places lie strewn throughout Ireland, marking practically every geological oddity in the country.

Further west lie the **Claoin-Fhearta**, or Sloping Trenches, created, according to the legend, when Cormac Mac Art as a youth in disguise corrected the judgements of the then king, Lugaid MacCon. (Mac Art was also something of an Irish Solomon figure.) The consequence of his justice was that half the house where the false judgements had been given slipped down the hill, creating the sloping trenches. The southern part of the trenches witnessed the murder of the princesses of Tara, some thirty of them in a massacre whose total casualties were said to have been 3000, by Dúnlaing, King of Leinster, in 222 AD.

The major mounds

South of the Banquet Hall lies the main group of mounds, and first of all the **Rath of the Synods**. This is so called because of the various church synods said to have been held here by saints Patrick, Brendan, Ruadhan and Adamnan, although little archeological evidence has been found relating to this function. Two gold torques (flat strips of gold soldered and twisted together rope-like into a necklace) were found here in 1810. Much of the rath, however, which appears to have originally been a ring fort defended by three concentric banks, has been destroyed over the years: partly by the graveyard which encroaches on it, but more especially by a group of British Israelites who earlier this century rooted around trying to find the Ark of the Covenant. More serious archeologists have discovered four stages in the rath's construction: in the centre was a flat-topped mound known locally as the **King's Chair**. There were timber palisades on the banks, and in the middle a house where five burnt bodies were found, along with Roman artefacts which suggest trading links between Tara and the Romans in Britain or Gaul.

The **Mound of the Hostages** (*Dumha na nGiall*) is the most prominent of the mounds and also the most ancient. It contained a passage grave to which entrance is now barred, though you can look in to see the markings on the upright slab at the threshold. About forty Bronze Age cremated burials were found inside, many in large urns which were then inverted over the remains. Eating vessels and knives were found with them, and an elaborate necklace of amber, jet, bronze and faience round the neck of a fifteen-year-old boy, the only body not cremated. A wealth of goods from the passage grave culture (carbon dated 2000 BC) were also discovered, making it the most comprehensive find rescued from any tumulus in Ireland. The mound, once again, is associated with Cormac Mac Art: here he is said to have imprisoned hostages taken from Connacht, who subsequently died within the chamber.

The **Ráth na Ríogh** (Royal Enclosure), immediately to the south, is a large area surrounded by a bank and ditch, within which are two earthworks, the **Forradh** (Royal Seat) and **Teach Cormaic** (Cormac's House). Both, though they're not contemporary, are typical ring forts, with a central raised area for a rectangular house – Cormac's has two protective fosses and banks, the Royal Seat only one. In the centre of Cormac's House are a grotesque, lichen-scabbed **statue of Saint Patrick**, entirely inappropriate to the site, and the **Lia Fáil** (Stone of Destiny), a standing stone moved from elsewhere on the site and re-erected here in memory of those who died in 1798. It is marked with a cross and the letters RIP. According to one tradition this stone was the original Jacob's pillow, brought to Ireland by the Milesians from the Island of Fal. It is also said to be the stone used in the inauguration of the High Kings, which would roar three times to signify its approval of the coronation.

The final remaining rath on the site is named after High King Laoghaire, who made the historic meeting with Patrick when he lit his challenging fire on the Hill of Slane.

For accommodation at Tara, there's a modern bungalow B&B, *Seamróg*, right next to the site (☎ 046/25296; ③).

Dunsany

Dunsany Castle (July to mid-Sept Mon–Sat 9am–1pm) is only a few miles south of Tara, just outside the village of Dunsany. This is still a private residence, owned by the Plunkett family (under the title Lord Dunsany) who have lived here since the sixteenth century. The Lord Dunsany who died in 1957 established an unlikely dual reputation as an author; he wrote witty sketches of London clubland and also bizarre dream-fantasy tales that influenced such American writers as H.P. Lovecraft. It's worth going to the trouble of arranging a visit, for this is one of the finest, most thriving examples of an Irish castle you're likely to see, and packed with a wealth of art.

The castle was originally built in the twelfth century by Hugh de Lacy, another of his fortresses defending the Anglo-Norman possessions around Dublin. It has been much altered and added to since, but it's still a magnificent building, with grounds to match. Among the family relics kept here – and quite apart from the superb private art collection and the furniture that you'll see on the tour – are the ring and other reminders of Patrick Sarsfield, second-in-command of the Jacobite forces in Ireland and successful defender of Limerick for over a year, and possessions and a portrait of Saint Oliver Plunkett, who was hanged in London for treason (his offence: being Catholic). The Dunsanys, in fact, seem to have made a habit of being on the wrong side in Ireland's conflicts, and it's remarkable that they have held on here so long.

Neighbouring **Killeen Castle** belonged to another branch of the Plunkett family (when the estate was divided, the boundaries were supposedly set by a race; the wives of the inheritors ran from their castles, and the border was set where they met), and during the long years of Catholic suppression it was kept in trust for them by the (converted) Protestant Dunsanys.

In the grounds of Dunsany Castle is a fifteenth-century **church** built by and for the family on the site of a still older one – however, you'll need permission to visit. There are some fine family tombs in here and a beautiful carved fifteenth-century font, with representations of the Twelve Apostles and the Crucifixion.

Bective Abbey

West along the minor roads from Tara or Dunsany is **Bective Abbey**. A beautiful example of medieval Cistercian architecture, it is also set in flawlessly idyllic surroundings by an old bridge over the river. The abbey was once a considerable power in the land, and its abbot held a peer's seat in the English Parliament – one of only fifteen granted to the whole of the Pale. At this time the Church as a whole owned as much as a third of the county of Meath. The buildings you see date from a variety of different periods, sometimes bewilderingly so, but its basics are clearly identifiable.

Of the original abbey, founded in 1146 by **Murcha O Maelechlainn**, King of Meath, nothing at all survives. In the late twelfth century, the abbey was completely rebuilt, perhaps in time to accept the disinterred body of **Hugh de Lacy** in 1195 (see below). By 1228 it was decided that Bective should sever its ties with Mellifont and go under direct rule from Clairvaux in France. Of this second abbey you can still see the **chapter house** with its central column, part of the **west range** and fragments of the cruciform **church**. In the fifteenth century, this church was shortened on the west side, its aisles were removed, new south and west ranges were built inside the lines of the old cloister and a smaller cloister erected. Both the south and west sides of this latest cloister remain. The **tower** at the entrance over the porch is in excellent shape, and you can also see the layout of the fortified mansion that was built after the abbey's dissolution in 1543.

Trim

Nine miles south of Navan, **TRIM** marks the final real glory, a medieval one this time, to stand on the banks of the Boyne. The town can boast the remains of the largest Anglo-Norman castle in Ireland, ruins of various abbeys and a host of other medieval remains. Yet it remains surprisingly little visited and somewhat downbeat in atmosphere. Nonetheless, it's worth stopping here, with plenty to see in and around the town.

The obvious place to start exploring is the **castle** itself – used as a location for Mel Gibson's 1995 film *Braveheart* – right in the centre of town and approached either from the riverside walk or via the gate at the end of a modern causeway off Castle Street. Inside you're free to wander at will. The first castle on the site was a motte-and-bailey construction put up by **Hugh de Lacy** in 1173 after he had been granted the lordship of Meath by Henry II. Within a year this was attacked by Rory O'Connor, King of Connacht, and destroyed. A new castle was begun in the late 1190s, too late for Hugh de Lacy who, in the meantime, had been beheaded with an axe by an Irish labourer in Durrow. It was this second attempt that eventually grew to become the finest, and largest, Anglo-Norman castle seen in Ireland.

The stronghold became known as **King John's Castle** after John spent a day or two in Trim in 1210 – though in fact he didn't even lodge there – but it has stronger associations with Richard II, who incarcerated his ward Prince Henry of Lancaster (later Henry

IV) here for a time. In look and feel this is very much an English medieval castle, with a 486-yard **curtain wall** enclosing some three acres, ten D-shaped **towers**, various **sally gates** (small openings in the wall for surprise sorties) and, most impressive of all, a massive, square, 70ft-high **keep** with its walls running at a thickness of a solid eleven feet. The keep is named after Geoffrey de Joinville who, along with Walter de Lacy, was responsible for its construction in 1220–25. De Joinville spent many years on the Crusades (his brother Jean was the companion and biographer of Saint Louis, King of France), and finally became a monk in the Dominican "Black Friary" which he built at the northern end of Trim (currently undergoing excavation). One unusual, and not altogether successful, feature of the keep was the addition of a side chamber on each face (three out of four survive): an experiment not repeated elsewhere as it greatly increased the number of places which could be attacked, and hence which had to be defended. Here, though, it hardly mattered given the solidity of the outer wall. Hardly anything is left inside the keep, but you can make out the outlines of two great halls and, above these, the main bedrooms. The entrance door was in the east tower on the second floor.

Outside, the curtain wall runs round only three sides of the keep – on the fourth, the deep-running river was relied on as adequate cover. As you walk around, take in especially the **Dublin gate**, with its well-preserved barbican and two drawbridges, and the impressive section of the wall between here and the river, near the end of which is an underground chamber thought to have been used as a **mint** in the fifteenth century.

Across the river

On the opposite bank of the river from the keep stands **Talbot's Castle**, a beautiful three-storey fortified manor house. It was built in 1415 by the Lord Lieutenant of Ireland, Sir John Talbot, on the site of an Augustinian abbey; remains of the earlier building are incorporated into the lower floors of the castle. Queen Elizabeth I formulated a plan to convert it into Ireland's first university, but instead it was established as a Latin school whose most famous scholar was Arthur Wesley, later (having changed his name to Wellesley) the Duke of Wellington. Wellington entered parliament as MP for Trim and, despite his contempt for his Irish roots, was responsible as prime minister for passing the Act of Catholic Emancipation.

Behind Talbot's Castle rises the **Yellow Steeple**, so called because of the glint of its stone in the sunset. This is the only surviving part of **St Mary's Abbey**, and its ruined state owes more to Cromwell's attack in 1642 than the ravages of time. The abbey itself once housed **"Our Lady of Trim"**, venerated by pilgrims for the miraculous cures it performed. The wooden statue was burnt in front of Commander Croot, Cromwell's general, as he lay recuperating from wounds received in the attack on Trim. An artist's impression of this lost treasure can be seen at the roadside by the junction of the Dublin Road and New Dublin Road. Near the Yellow Steeple, **Sheep Gate** is the only remaining piece of the fourteenth-century town walls.

Also on this side of the river, and easiest reached from Trim Castle by heading out of Dublin Gate, along the Dublin Road and across the river by the sign, are the ruins of thirteenth-century **St Patrick's Cathedral** and its cemetery. The cathedral burned down over five hundred years ago, but its remains preserve a surprising amount that is worth seeing, especially in the cloister. The wall also acts as a soundpost to create a natural echo that is eerily brilliant in its clarity and closeness. In the cemetery, look out for the famous tomb of the **Jealous Man and Woman**, Sir Lucas Dillon and his wife Lady Jane Bathe. Their stone effigies are in Elizabethan costume and a sword rests between them. The rusty pins you'll see left in the stone tresses are thanksgiving offerings to the rainwater caught here that is reckoned to cure warts.

Taking the next left turn off the Dublin Road, about a mile out of town, will take you to the ruins of Newtown, to which Simon de Rochfort, first Norman bishop of Meath, moved his seat in 1210. The cathedral he built here was the biggest in Ireland. Close by is **Crutched Friary** (key from the tourist information office), yet another fine medieval ruin. This was a hospital run by the so-called Crutched (or Crossed) Friars, the Fratres Cruciferi, whose habits were marked with a cross on recognition of the fact that they had tended the Crusaders. Next to it is a gorgeous old **Norman bridge**, reckoned to be the second oldest in Ireland, and still very much in use (*Marcy Regan's*, at the other end of the bridge, similarly claims to be the **second oldest pub** in the land!). In the 1950s the film *Captain Lightfoot* used the bridge as a location, and its star, Rock Hudson, is said to have spent much of his time in the pub.

Practicalities

The **tourist office** is in a glisteningly refurbished Georgian building next to the town's Heritage Centre in Mill Street close to the river (May–Sept; ☎046/37111). For **B&B** try *Brogan's* in the High Street (☎046/31237; ③), also a bar, or *Ms O'Brien's* (☎046/31745; ③). More upmarket accommodation can be found at the *Station House* (☎046/25239; ⑥), an old cattle-loading bay station six miles or so to the east in Kilmessan, which is almost equidistant from Tara, Bective and Dunsany. If you're hungry, you can get excellent wholefood snacks from the *Salad Bowl Delicatessen* on Market Street, or more substantial **meals** at *Brogan's*, which does a four-course lunch for £4.50, as well as a range of hefty bar snacks. **Pubs** are as plentiful as ever, but one you should definitely sample is *Marcy Regan's* (see above), a tiny, ancient place painted in brilliant lemon and viridian, the proud colours of Meath's football and hurley teams: remember not to order a pint for the pub is too old to cope with draught.

Around Trim

A couple of miles south of Trim is **LARACOR**, the place where Jonathan Swift lived during his association with Esther "Stella" Johnson and where he was rector (with very little rectitude) from 1699 to 1714. No trace of him, however, remains. Two miles further is **Dangan Castle**, the family home of the Duke of Wellington, now no more than a shell and again with little trace of its past. Ambrosio O'Higgins, father of Bernardo O'Higgins, liberator of Chile, was born here.

Perhaps a more interesting excursion is to the Irish-speaking community at **RATHCAIRN**, near Athboy, eight miles northwest of Trim, where traditional Irish entertainment may well be taking place. The community was uprooted from Connemara by the Land Commission between 1935 and 1940 and replanted here in Meath as a *Gaeltacht*. The population is about 350 and increasing, a unique statistic as most Irish-speaking peoples in their natural habitats are rapidly decreasing in numbers. Not far away, in a field beside the Athboy–Navan Road, is the **Rathmore Church and Cross** (*An Ráth Mhór Teampall agus Cros*). The church was built by the Plunkett family in the fifteenth century, a fine example of the flowering of Irish-Norman culture, with its sympathy towards the native Irish, before the arrival of the Tudor English in the following century, and is full of interesting stone carvings which are worth leaving the road to take a look at. There's an octagonal shaft from a baptismal font, a violated Norman sarcophagus in the fortified tower, a decorated altar stone, the stalk of an ancient cross and other stonework. Note the corbelled roof in the other tower, now trapped as a pigeon-cote.

WESTMEATH AND LONGFORD

As you head west, leaving the Boyne Valley behind, historical interest diminishes rapidly. The attraction of Westmeath lies mainly in its lakes, although in the northeast, around **Castlepollard**, there is an area which deserves more exploration. **Athlone**, in the far west, is an important meeting of the ways near the very heart of Ireland and is a centre for Shannon cruising but, again, it preserves little of interest in itself. Longford, if you visit at all, you'll see only briefly as you pass through on your way to the northwest coast.

The main route into the counties is the N4, following the Royal Canal, and the borders of counties Meath and Kildare, out from Dublin to **Mullingar** and then **Longford town**. As the road enters Westmeath the N6 turns off, to cut across the south of the county to Athlone. If you're coming from Meath, roads from Navan and from Kells converge at Delvin, to run on together towards Mullingar; if you're up by Oldcastle in northwestern Meath, you can cut directly across the border to the most interesting part of Westmeath, the Fore Valley and Castlepollard.

Mullingar and around

MULLINGAR, the chief town of Westmeath, is a raucous, wheeling-and-dealing provincial capital, constantly choked with traffic, that pretty much sums up the things you don't come to Ireland for. It's the centre of a rich cattle-rearing area, and its inhabitants are rural, but the speed and noise of everything is continually wound up by its being a big trading centre on a short lead from Dublin. The first ever **Fleadh Cheoil** (Festival of Music) was held in Mullingar in the late 1960s, but it fell so far short of local expectations that the town has never asked for it back. In short, you're unlikely to fall in love at first sight with Mullingar, but with perseverance you should be able to find a few positive moments before moving on – and there are a couple of good museums.

The first of these, on the corner of the main street at the turn-off to Tullamore, is the **Market House Museum** (May–Sept Mon–Sat 11.30am–1pm & 2–5pm, at other times ring Paddy Raleigh, ☎044/48152; 50p). Run by local enthusiasts, it doesn't have any one item of outstanding interest (and if it had, it would no doubt be whipped off to the Dublin Museum), but it does have a modest charm in the peculiar wealth of local items on display. There's also the usual quota of Iron Age implements, quernstones and weaponry, together with a potted history of the celebrated local eccentric, Adolphus Cooke (see opposite).

A second museum is attached to Mullingar's **cathedral**, an uninspiring Neoclassical structure whose tapering twin towers – which look like melting candles – you'll be able to spot in the south of town. Inside, behind the side altars of St Patrick and St Anne, are two well-known mosaics by the Russian artist Boris Anrep. To get into the **Ecclesiastical Museum** – whose contents include many wooden penal crosses and the vestments of Saint Oliver Plunkett – ask for the key at the parochial house, on the right.

The Military Museum

Best of all, however, is the **Military Museum** (currently under renovation and due to re-open in late 1996; ☎044/48391) at the Columb Barracks; going southwards, turn right after the bridge over the canal, then swing left and it's 200 yards up on the left, easily walkable. The collection, in the **Old Guard Room**, has a surprisingly broad range of interest. There's all the weaponry you'd expect, of course, with plenty of World War I and II firearms, and uniforms and flags from all over the world. But more intriguing are the sections devoted to the **old IRA**, with various local bands' uniforms and the tunic of Dan Hogan, Chief of Staff after 1929, who was shot by the FBI in 1941. There's also the uniform of Giles Vandeleur, whose role in World War II was portrayed by Michael Caine in the film *A Bridge Too Far*, and a pistol said to be that of **Michael Collins**, who was Chief of Staff throughout the War of Independence and the Civil War – though it's well known that Collins rarely carried a weapon.

More miscellaneous items on display include long, canoe-like boats of bog-blackened oak dredged up from the surrounding lakelands; first thought to be of Viking origin, they have been carbon dated well into the first millennium AD. Similar boats are still being dredged up today, especially in Lough Derravaragh, but are as quickly being wrapped up again in peat and resunk in the middle of the lake. One of the stranger curios is the **military cycling handbook** that was in use until at least 1964. The book instructs the young cadet as to where to put his left foot and where his right and, with even more disciplinary stringency, orders him not to twist the handlebars without the officer's permission. All of this is arranged (or not arranged) amid a fair degree of chaos, though there's usually someone to show you around and attempt to make sense of it all.

Practicalities

The **tourist office** is up a driveway on your right as you enter town on the Dublin Road (June–Sept Mon–Fri 9am–6pm, Sat 10am–6pm; Oct–May Mon–Fri 9.30am–1pm & 2–5.30pm; ☎044/48650). If you want to **stay** in Mullingar, there are plenty of places to choose from. The best central **B&B** is Gladys Buckley's *Grove House*, Grove Avenue (☎044/41974; ③); *Hilltop* (☎044/48958; ④), a mile or so out on the Navan Road, is also good; or you can **camp** at the *Lough Ennell Caravan and Camping Park* (£7 per person and tent; ☎044/48101), three miles out on the Tullamore Road. Good **food** is served in the *Greville Arms* on central Pearse Street (where they also offer slightly more luxurious accommodation; ☎044/48563; ⑤); a wax effigy of James Joyce stands in the foyer, a reminder of a mention of Mullingar somewhere in *Stephen Hero*. There's no shortage of other eating places of all descriptions; try *Canton Casey's* café/wine bar on Pearse Street, next to the Market House, for filling portions of spag bol, nachos and baked potatoes at rock-bottom prices (from £2.95); or *Oscar's* Italian restaurant, 28 Oliver Plunkett Street (pastas from £5.50). Congenial drinking places include *Hughes's* on Main Street, *Caffrey's* on Mount Street, with traditional music sessions, and the more upmarket *Danny Byrne's*, Pearse Street, with good food as well.

Mullingar is on the main Dublin–Sligo railway line, with **trains** accordingly (☎044/48274); **buses** go to Dublin, Sligo, Athlone and Galway.

Around Mullingar

There are a number of minor attractions out from Mullingar; the best of them is **Lough Ennell**, which offers a relaxing mix of aquatic activities and nearby the impressive **Belvedere House and Gardens**.

Cooksborough

COOKSBOROUGH, a hamlet of a few houses strung together about eight miles east of Mullingar on the Delvin Road (N52), might tempt you as a detour before heading south or west. What you're looking for is a tomb in the shape of a beehive in the graveyard. Neither Cooksborough nor the tomb is signposted but you can find it by looking out for the sign to the *Bee Hive Nite Club*: about thirty yards past this, in the direction of Delvin, enter by an old gate and cross the field to a church and graveyard smothered in bramble, weed and grass. The tomb, which looks like a stone missile warhead poking out of its silo, is that of **Adolphus Cooke** and his nurse Mary Kelly. A famous local eccentric, Cooke was convinced that he would be reincarnated as a bee and he was making sure he was prepared for the event. During his life he was similarly convinced that one of the turkeys scratching around in his yard was his father reincarnated. He also had the windows of his house made into the shape of spoon-backed chairs, in order to reflect the furniture within. There's more information on Adolphus Cooke in the Market House Museum in Mullingar.

Lough Ennell and Belvedere House

Lough Ennell, with its low-lying, rushy shoreline, is not an especially dramatic expanse of water, but it is an easy place to go bathing, boating or fishing, especially if you base yourself at the holiday camp, immediately outside Mullingar, or in any of the B&Bs that cluster around the lough – one secluded and rather stately establishment close to the water is *Lynnbury*, a few miles out on the Tullamore Road (☎044/48432; ④). If you do stay here, it's well worth making the short trip to **Belvedere House and Gardens** (May–Sept Mon–Fri noon–4.30pm, Sat, Sun & bank hols noon–6pm; £1), further out on the Tullamore Road just before the turning to the campsite. You're not meant to cut across the fields from the campsite – the way lies across private land – but it does save a lot of walking.

The house was built by **Lord Belfield**, the first Earl of Belvedere, in 1740, and conceived by him as a fishing villa. Much of Belfield's life seems to have been spent feuding with his younger brothers, George and Arthur. In 1736 he married the sixteen-year-old Mary Molesworth, daughter of the third Viscount Molesworth. Within a few years of building Belvedere House he accused her of having an affair with Arthur, and virtually imprisoned her for 31 years at another of his houses. She was eventually released by her son on his father's death in 1774, still protesting her innocence. Meanwhile Arthur had fled to Yorkshire, but when he returned to Ireland in 1759 the earl sued him for adultery and Arthur, unable to pay, spent the rest of his life in jail. An argument with his other brother was responsible for one of the first sights you'll come across in the gardens south of the house, the **Jealous Wall**. This folly is said to be Ireland's largest purpose-built ruin, and was built to block the view of Tudenham House, where George lived, from the earl's own home. Considerable expense went into the construction, including the employment of an Italian architect to design the authentic-looking Gothic facade.

The interior of the **house** is still in the process of renovation, a job which shortage of funds looks certain to make a long one. However, the **rococo plasterwork** of the drawing and dining room ceilings is well worth ducking inside to snatch a look at for a few moments, as is the curved balustrade **staircase** in the entrance recess. Otherwise, the **gardens** are the main attraction. In front of the house three terraces run down to the lake's shore and, behind, woodland stretches along the northeast shore of Lough Ennell. There's also the aforementioned Jealous Wall to see, and a walled garden, gazebo, ice house and stables, where there is a **coffee shop** for refreshments.

Further south at **KILBEGGAN**, and heavily advertised for miles around, is **Locke's Distillery Museum** (April–Oct 9am–6pm, Sun 10am–6pm; Nov–March by appointment only; ☎0506/32134; £2). Although the mill-wheel is still working, the entrance fee may seem a bit steep for what's effectively just a look at the equipment used for making the whiskey, with nothing to slake your thirst at the end of the tour (although the air's still suffused with a tantalizingly malty smell). The building that looks like a small coal-tip is actually a whiskey warehouse reputedly modelled on a Syrian palace.

If you need to break your journey on the haul back to Dublin on the N6, you could head for **TYRRELLSPASS** – a tiny cluster of high Georgian and vernacular buildings around a green – just to bask in its delicious prettiness. The *Village Hotel* (☎044/23171; ⑤), right on the green, is the place to stay. The impressive tower house at the other end of town houses a **museum** and a café that does a range of bar-type lunches for around £4. **St Sinian's**, a Gothic Revival church on The Crescent, has some elaborate Beldevere tombs. One of the simplest commemorates Jane, a countess "gifted with a masculine understanding".

Northern Westmeath

A good portion of the interest of Westmeath lies in the northeast, around the Fore Valley, Lough Lene and Lough Derravaragh. Certainly this is the most beautiful part of the county by some way. It's easily approached from Meath, from the area of Oldcastle and the Loughcrew cairns, or from Mullingar. Coming from Mullingar you'll pass through **CROOKEDWOOD**, near the scenic lower end of **Lough Derravaragh**, set among steep wooded hills that stand out immediately in such flat country. There are two main attractions here: a **restaurant**, *Crookedwood House* (Tues–Sat dinner from £18.50, Sun lunch £12; ☎044/72165), which is far better than you would normally hope to find in such an obscure location, and **St Munna's Church**. This beautifully restored fifteenth-century tower-fortified church lies a mile and a half up the road that turns off to the right by the pub; fifty yards before is a butterscotch-coloured bungalow on the left belonging to Seamus O'Simon, who has the key. From the church you can spot a motte on the hill slope, behind which is the Georgian house whose rustic cellar contains the restaurant already mentioned.

Castlepollard and Tullynally Castle

Towards the northern end of Lough Derravaragh, **CASTLEPOLLARD** is the most convenient base from which to explore the whole area, handily placed right in the middle of all the attractions. It's not the most exciting of villages, although it clearly sets great store by its picturesqueness, with a vast triangular green surrounded by carefully tended eighteenth- and nineteenth-century dwellings. Many of the visitors are here for the fishing – mainly roach, pike and trout – on Lake Derravaragh, and consequently there are a number of **B&Bs**, of which the *Pollard Arms* is probably the most attractive.

The biggest draw in the immediate vicinity is **Tullynally Castle** (castle daily mid-June to mid Aug 2–6pm; £2.50; gardens May–Sept; £2; ☎044/61159), whose entrance can be found a half-mile from Castlepollard down the road to Granard (alongside the gable of the *Derravaragh Inn*). From the gatehouse a drive leads across another half-mile of rolling parkland to the castle itself. The home of ten generations of the Anglo-Irish Pakenham family – the Earls of Longford – it's one of the largest and most romantic of castles in Ireland, a vast conglomeration of architectural styles (largely Gothic Revival) with four towers and a long stretch of battlements.

Three hundred years ago the castle was no more than a tower house set amidst the ancient oakwoods which grow around Lough Derravaragh. The park was first laid out, very much along the lines you see today, in 1760 by the first Earl of Longford. His wife founded the family **library** of more than 8000 volumes, which will be in one room on your tour. Their son returned from the French wars to greatly expand the castle to the Gothic designs of **Francis Johnston**, whose work crops up throughout Ireland. The second earl's other claim to fame is to have refused his daughter Kitty's hand in marriage to the young man later to become the Duke of Wellington – they eventually married regardless. One of Kitty's brothers, Edward, fought as Commander-in-Chief of the British Army in America in 1814, and died leading his troops in the attack on New Orleans. His body was sent home pickled in a barrel of rum. In 1840 the third earl added a further 600ft of battlements, a servants' hall for forty, and an immense **Victorian kitchen** which will also make up part of your tour. Later Pakenhams have been less militarily inclined than their forebears: one, Charles Pakenham, forsook the army in the nineteenth century to found the Irish Passionist order of priests; and the present Lord Longford is well known in Britain for his liberal writings and involvement in prison reform.

In the grounds in front of the castle, a **Garden Walk** leads to a spacious demesne on the left, and the flower garden, River Sham pond and walled gardens off to the right. Passing further to the right, between two stone sphinxes, is the **kitchen garden**, one of the largest in the country and still resplendent with its row of Irish yews. Slightly further afield, the most rewarding walk of all is a forest path which takes you around the perimeter of the spearhead-shaped demesne, with excellent views back onto the castle.

THE CHILDREN OF LIR

You'll find continually throughout Ireland that physically atmospheric places are the setting for ancient tales or myths, and Lough Derravaragh is no exception. In this case the legend is that of the **Children of Lir** (*oidheadh cloinne Lir*), one of the most tragic of all Irish fables.

Lir had married the daughter of Bodb Derg, King of Connacht. Her name was Aebh and she bore him twins, Fionula and Aodh, and then two more children, Fiachra and Conn. Aebh died and Lir then married her sister, Aoife, who very quickly became jealous of Lir's love for her sister's children. She took them to Lough Derravaragh, and with the help of a druid changed them into swans, condemned to spend 300 years on Derravaragh, another 300 years on the Sea of Moyle, the waters between Ireland and Scotland, and a final 300 on Inis Glóire off Erris Head, County Mayo. In a last-minute pang of remorse she granted them one mercy: that they could have human voices and make the most beautiful music for all humans to hear. When Lir learned of what had happened, in a rage he changed Aoife into an ugly grey vulture. Meanwhile the sons of Bodb Derg, Fergus and Aed, set out to search for the Children of Lir with a host of the Tuátha Dé Danann. They eventually found them suffering on the Sea of Moyle, but were helpless to save them from the spell. Left to their destiny the children flew towards Inis Glóire, stopping on the way to search for their father's palace on the plains of Armagh, but finding that only earth mounds remained as they were now 600 years on in their own lives. At the end of the allotted span they died, finally returning to a very aged human form for their last few breaths, and were buried at the onset of the Christian era on Inis Glóire.

The Fore Valley

East of Castlepollard towards the Meath border, the **Fore Valley** is an area of exceptional natural beauty. It's easy hiking country with a wealth of small-scale interest, especially in the **Seven Wonders of Fore**. There are moves afoot to convert these into some kind of tourist trail, but so far there are few visitors, and the local tradition, strengthened by an early Christian legacy in stone, still seems close to the surface. The wonders are all based on ordinary things which you can find in the valley, and in this perhaps lies the lasting strength of their reputation. They are: the water that will not boil; the wood that will not burn; the monastery built on a quaking sod; the mill without a race; the miraculous emplacement of the lintel stone above the door of St Fechin's Church; the water that flows uphill; and the Anchorite's Cell in the Greville-Nugent family vault.

The village of **FORE** sits at the eastern end of the valley and is the best place to start, discovering the wonders as you walk west. There's a tiny ancient cross on the tiny village green, once part of a stations of the cross, and a couple of pubs are worth visiting. You'll need to pop into the *Seven Wonders* anyway to pick up the key for the **Anchorite's Cell**: the *Abbey* next door has seven old murals depicting the wonders, worth contemplating over a pint. There's usually plenty of ready advice in here for anyone planning to head down the valley; for a guided tour contact Sarah Keogh (see p.164 for details).

If you want to base yourself here for some gentle rambling, there's B&B **accommodation** available nearby at *Hounslow House* (April–Oct ☎044/61144; ③), which is well signposted.

The Seven Wonders

On the valley plain you'll immediately spot the ruined Benedictine priory built on reclaimed bogland (the third wonder), and en route to it you'll pass the first two. The **wood that will not burn** consists of a dead branch of a tree, landscaped into a viewing spot as part of the creation of the tourist trail (from the picture in the *Abbey* pub you'll remember it looking more lively than this); the idea of piercing its bark with coins is also a recent invention. The **well of unboilable water** is handily close by.

The **priory** itself was founded by the De Lacys around 1200, and its remains are the most substantial reminder of the Benedictine Order left in Ireland. It was fortified in the fifteenth century; the towers also served as living quarters. There's a plan in the cloister of the various periods' additions, and some subtly sensitive restoration has been undertaken so that although it's very much a ruin, there's a strong monastic feel to the walls and halls. If you intend to ascend the **tower** at the chancel end, beware that its spiral staircase seems to wind around the diameter of a dinner plate and above all that the steps finish in midair; it should certainly not be attempted in poor light.

On the far hillside from here, the lower of the two buildings is the tenth-century **St Fechin's Church**, which marks the site of the original monastery founded in 630 by Saint Fechin himself, at one time housing over 300 monks. Note the rare Greek cross on the massive **lintel stone** (which weighs over two tons and was only moved by the miraculous intervention of the saint, hence wonder five), resting on two boulder-sized jambs. Within the ruin is a very weatherbeaten font to your left, a cross slab pinned next to the wall in the chancel at the far end (the chancel was a thirteenth-century addition) and a few other stone slabs, the engravings on which are not clear. From here a ridged path takes you up to the tiny, fortified church known as the **Anchorite's Cell** (wonder seven), decoratively hugged by a low-lying, castellated perimeter wall. The most famous hermit who lived here was Patrick Beaglan, who broke his neck trying to climb out of the window in 1616, thereby fulfilling his vow to stay in the cell till his death. The Romanesque doorway leads into a barrel-vaulted, sandstone interior.

The **water that flows uphill** (wonder six) refers to another of Saint Fechin's miracles; and the river flowing out of Lough Lene up at the head of the valley does look as if it's flowing upwards. The **mill without a race** (wonder four) is not so easy to trace.

The heart of Ireland: Uisneach to Athlone

As you head west from Mullingar towards Athlone on the R390, you're approaching the middle of Ireland, a spot traditionally identified as the **Hill of Uisneach**. About a mile before Killare (ten miles or so from Mullingar) there are two signposts pointing off the road up to the hill. Follow the second, more westerly one, climb the hill steeply, veering a little to the left, and after crossing a few fields you'll come to the **Catstone** (so called because it resembles the poise of a pouncing cat). More historically known as the *Ail na Mearainn* (the Stone of Divisions), it's a massive boulder (now fragmented a little) set into a circular indentation in the hillside. The stone was said to mark the very centre of Ireland and the division of the five provinces of old. A further and longer walk up the slope will bring you to the summit of a flat-topped hill, barely 250ft above the neighbouring land yet able, on a clear day, to command a view of parts of twenty of the 32 counties of Ireland.

Here, it is recorded, stood the palace of **King Tuathal Techtmar** in the second century AD, and here some claim that the High Kings of Ireland ruled for the two centuries preceding the arrival of Saint Patrick in 433 AD, when the seat moved back to Tara. On the hill there are two spurs with traces of earthworks, but these are neither easy to find nor to make out if you do, so it's probably easier to accept the history without evidence. Excavations were made here in the late 1920s, but came up with surprisingly little. No pottery was found, nor any significant trace of permanent occupation. Instead there were great **beds of ashes** which suggested that the place was used for elaborate feasts and ceremonials rather than for defence or peaceful habitation. This accords with the tales of the great pagan festival of *Bealtaine* (Bel's Fire) that was said to be held here in the opening days of the month of May, when vast fires were lit and cattle sacrificed. It was both a religious festival and a market, where traders from the Mediterranean would arrive with their silks and spices in exchange for Irish tools and materials. *Bealtaine*, incidentally, is now the Irish word for the month of May.

As you continue towards Athlone, look out for the tenth-century **Twyford Cross** on a hillside to the left about four miles before you arrive. It was re-erected here after being found sunk in a bog.

Athlone and around

The Hill of Uisneach may be the traditional centre of Ireland, but the busy, apparently thriving, town of **ATHLONE** is a more convincing modern contender. Here, east meets west and north meets south at the midpoint of the River Shannon. This position is its greatest asset, with access by boat upstream to the islands and shores of **Lough Ree** (see p.180), and downstream to the magnificent early Christian site of **Clonmacnois** (see p.128). Either of these trips can easily be done in an afternoon: ask for details at the tourist information office (see p.180).

Not surprisingly, perhaps, given its position, Athlone has quite a history attached, and at least one important legend. The name *Áth Luain*, the **Ford of Luan**, came from (or may perhaps have inspired) the **Snám Dá Én** (Swim of Two Birds), a tale that tells of Estiu, wife of Nár. She had a lover called Buide who used to come and visit her in the form of a bird with his foster-brother Luan. The magic of their song lulled all around to sleep, allowing the lovers to enjoy their trysts undisturbed. Nár, however, questioned a druid about the coming of the birds and on learning the secret he set out for the place on the Shannon (near Clonmacnois) where Buide and Luan could be found and shot both of them with one cast of his sling. Buide was killed instantly, but Luan managed to fly as far north as the ford that marks Athlone today, where he dropped dead from the sky. An alternative derivation of the name comes from the *Táin*, which describes how the remains of the white bull (*Finnbennach*) were deposited throughout the countryside as he died. His loins were left at a place that came to be known as *Áth Luain*, the Ford of the Loins.

In straight historical terms, this ford of the Shannon has always been strategically important. The first castle was erected in 1129 by Toirdelbach Ó Conchobhair, King of Connacht, and replaced in 1210 by the **Norman castle** which, in essence, still stands today. It saw action many times, above all in the seventeenth century in the Cromwellian Wars and the Jacobite invasion. The former put a swift end to the predominantly Catholic nature of the town, placing most of the land and political power in the hands of Protestants. The later battles of 1690–91 saw probably the most vicious fighting in the **War of the Kings**, as the Williamites captured first the Leinster part of town and, after 12,000 cannonballs had reduced much of it to rubble, the Connacht side. In some ways Athlone has still to recover.

The town

The few really distinguished old buildings that survive – the castle apart – can be found off Church Street in the **Court Devenish** area. Finest of them is **Court Devenish House**, a seventeenth-century Jacobean mansion now resting ruined in private grounds. Nearby the ruins of the likewise seventeenth-century **abbey** offer perhaps the most peaceful spot in town. There's an intriguing corridor of tombstones leading off the Abbey Road into its graveyard.

The one place really worth visiting, if only briefly, is the **castle museum** by Market Square (April–Oct 10am–6pm; rest of year by arrangement, ☎0902/72107; £2.50), housed in the two storeys of the circular keep. On the upper storey is a section devoted to **folk history**, an Aladdin's cave of rustic implements used in threshing, seeding,

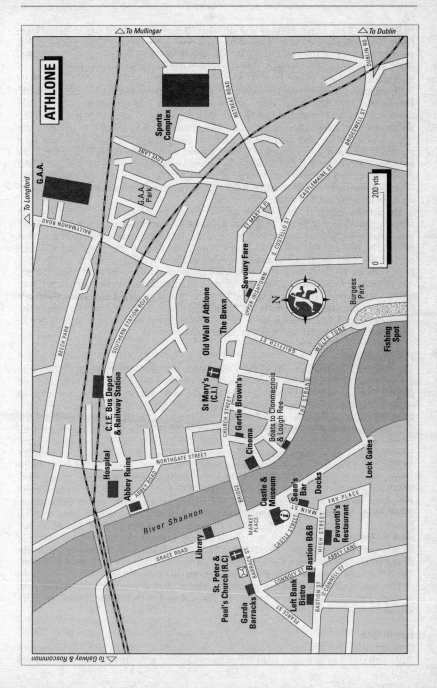

ropemaking, harnessing, milking and the like. There's a beautiful article on milking, telling how a few squirts were always dropped first on the grass for the fairies and at the end the sign of the cross made on the teat to bless its consumption. You'll also come across a pair of pony boots that were used when rolling the lawn, to prevent any hoof marks.

Downstairs is a more regular collection on local history, and the ever-present Stone, Bronze and Iron Age finds. There are two **Sheila na Gig** sculptures, nude female figures generally represented face on with their legs splayed and hands placed behind the thighs, the fingers opening the vulva. The sculptures were thought to be either the symbol of a fertility cult or used to ward off the evil eye, though quite how they managed the latter is not explained. Most appear in the walls (usually near the main entrance door) of castles, and occasionally churches, built between 1200 and 1600. To a lesser extent they are also found in round towers and on standing stones, bridges etc. They are also known in other parts of the British Isles, and even France, but the majority of them by far are in Ireland.

On a quite different level there's an old 78rpm gramophone on which you can request your choice of the recordings of **John McCormack**. McCormack (1884–1945) was a native of Athlone and arguably one of the best lyric tenors the world has ever heard. The gramophone was McCormack's own, travelling all over the world with him so that he could use it to test out the quality of his new releases. He is said to have been born in the Bawn area, the old market quarter up behind Devenish Gate Street, and in 1928 he was rewarded for his work for Catholic charities by being made a Count of the Papal Court. The one song that even the youngest generations in Ireland are able to associate with his voice is his *Panis Angelicus* – the record may be among the pile. Before you leave, look out for an early Christian grave slab with carvings as beautifully ornate as any high cross that you're likely to have seen.

Practicalities

The **tourist information office** (May–Sept Mon–Sat 9am–6pm; ☎0902/94630) is in the castle in Market Square. Boats of all sizes can be rented locally. Much good rod **fishing** can also be done in Athlone, just past the weir, where you'll often see a line of anglers – rent rod and reel from the *Strand Tackle Shop* in the Strand (£3 per day). **Bike rental**, is available from *Hardiman's*, 48 Connaught Street (☎0902/78669).

If you plan to stay in Athlone, by far the nicest **B&B** is *The Bastion*, above a trendy clothes shop on Bastion Street (☎0902/94954; ③); *Villa St John* in Roscommon Road (☎0902/92490; ③) is good value, or try *Bogganfin House*, Roscommon Road (☎0902/94255; ③), or *Cluain Inis* in Galway Road (☎0902/94202; ③). Your best bet for lunch or afternoon tea is *Savoury Fare* on Mardyke Street (Mon–Sat), where everything from Turkish flatbread to cheesecake is home-made. The *Left Bank Bistro* on Bastion Street (Mon–Sat; ☎0902/94446), café by day and restaurant by night, serves imaginative, flavoursome Mediterranean dishes at low prices. *Pavarotti's* Italian restaurant on High Street has a cosy wine bar (Thurs–Sun 11pm–2am); and there's good lunchtime bar food at *Gertie Brown's*. This apart, the best **pub** is probably *Sean's Bar*, tucked in behind the castle and easily identified by its four Ionic columns. It has popular **traditional music** sessions on a Tuesday (pipes and violin), Thursday (violins) and Sunday. You'll find both the **post office** and a **launderette** on Pearse Street.

The **bus** and **train stations** are on Southern Station Road (off Church Street); buses to Dublin, Galway, Cork, Mullingar, Cavan; trains to Dublin and Galway (☎0902/72651).

Lough Ree

If you're taking a trip out to Lough Ree, the islands to ask for are **Inchclearaun** (although this may better be approached from a more northerly point on the lake) and

Inchbofin. Both islands, especially Inchclearaun, have churches and early Christian grave slabs. Inchclearaun (Inis Clothrand) took its name from Clothru, who was murdered by her sister Medb so that she could wed and bed Clothru's husband Ailill and rule Connacht from the island. Medb, goddess of war and fertility, is the most famous of all the legendary and historical characters and a source of continual argument as to which branch of study (legend or history) she truly belongs to. Her life was to end in the waters by the island when Clothru's son Furbaide hurled a piece of cheese from his sling that entered Medb's forehead and struck her dead while she was bathing, thus avenging the murder of his mother.

Goldsmith country

The N55 rushes north from Athlone into **Goldsmith country**, so called after its geographical associations with the works of the eighteenth-century poet, playwright and novelist, Oliver Goldsmith (see overleaf). It's pretty, small-scale countryside, gently rolling and ready-made for cycling through landscaped villages and along aromatic hedge-lined lanes that run off the N55 down to various small boating points on Lough Ree (Killinure, Kileenmore, Muckanagh).

Glassan and around

Ironically enough, **GLASSAN** – identified as "Sweet Auburn", the subject of Goldsmith's celebrated anti-enclosure poem *The Deserted Village* and described as "the village of the roses" – owes its orderly layout of creamy-grey pebbledash cottages to enclosure: it was built by the neighbouring Waterstown estate to provide accommodation for the artisans needed to tend the massive estate with its ten-acre formal garden. The estate was divided by the Land Commission in the 1920s; the house, designed by the eighteenth-century architect Richard Castle, was sold for scrap. As you head north towards Ballitore, there's a profusion of brown "Goldsmith country" signs. Only the front and end walls of Goldsmith's childhood home, the parsonage at **Lissoy**, remain, and still less of the school he attended, or of the "busy mill" that may be the one mentioned in the poem. **Forgney Church**, where Goldsmith's father worked as curate until 1730, was rebuilt in 1810 and is usually locked. Goldsmith's supposed birthplace at **Pallas** has a rather spooky shrine erected by members of the Oliver Goldsmith Society in 1974: a larger-than-life statue of the writer enclosed behind bars in a sort of grotto-prison, as if his poetic spirit is too dangerous to be let out into the world. One wonders what Goldsmith's mocking soul would have made of such funereal pomposity.

Glassan is probably the best **place to stay** to explore this part of Lough Ree and Goldsmith country. At present, there's little to see of the Goldsmith collection, but an interpretative centre is planned to open in the old school building. There's a scattering of B&Bs – try *Carraun View* in the village (☎0902/85391; ③); and the good, rather elaborate *Village Restaurant* (☎0902/85001), a *Village Inn* and a craft shop that also does teas and sandwiches – in short, a whole range of creature comforts you're unlikely to find further north. Heading back down the road to Athlone you'll find the excellent *Wineport* restaurant on the shores of Lough Ree (open daily from noon in summer, eves only off-season; lunch from £5, dinner from £12.50; ☎0902/85466).

From Glassan, you could do worse than follow the way-marked **Lough Ree tour**, especially if you're cycling. Leaving the village, this takes you down winding lanes for **PORTLICK**, the "local Killarney", set in romantically wooded country and farmland sloping down to the loughside, but without the crowds of Kerry. Portlick's fifteenth-century castle gazes wistfully across the lake, gothically crumbling but still inhabited.

At **KILLINURE**, where there's a spanking new marina, you can rent boats to take you out to the islands of Inchmore or Inchbofin from the local pub *Manto's*, down the road at Killeenmore, which also does B&B (☎0902/85204; ④), with camping and self-catering apartments also available. The *Wineport Sailing Centre*, signposted from the village (☎0902/85466), rents out boats and has a loughside restaurant.

TUBBERCLAIR, a mile up the road, offers one of the better panoramic views towards the east of the county. A little further (exactly eight miles from Ballymahon) is the site of the "never failing brook, the busy mill", nowadays no more than a bubbling rivulet, but still easy to identify. The original millstone is now said to be the lintel-stone at the *Three Jolly Pigeons* pub, a quarter of a mile up the road, where the school once stood.

Ballymahon to Lanesborough

Halfway up Lough Ree, Goldsmith Country seeps into **County Longford** through Ballymahon (where his mother lived) and across to Pallas (near Abbeyshrule) where he was born. **BALLYMAHON** is a pretty dull village with an imposingly wide main street, and not somewhere to hang around – aside from a multiplicity of seedy bars, there's nowhere at all to get a meal.

Heading north from Ballymahon to Lanesborough on the N63, you'll pass **CORLEA**. On the edge of the Bog of Allen, it's worth stopping here for the **Corlea Interpretive Centre** (daily May–Sept 9.30am–6.30pm; for winter hours, call the OPW on ☎01/661 3111 ext. 2386; last admission 45min before closing; £2.50), a low, mustard-coloured cruciform building, aligned with a buried *togher*, a trackway of oak planks discovered by turf cutters in 1985. Some of this has been excavated and preserved in an air-

---

OLIVER GOLDSMITH

Best known for his prose, including the comedy *She Stoops to Conquer* and the novel *The Vicar of Wakefield*, **Oliver Goldsmith** (1728–74) was probably born in Pallas, ten miles north of Glassan in County Longford, the son of a Church of Ireland parson; when he was two, he and his family moved to the parsonage at Lisson, just a couple of miles north of Glassan. Goldsmith was also active as a poet, and in travelling through this depopulated landscape, his epic anti-enclosure poem, *The Deserted Village*, helps conjure up the reality of the short-lived heyday of the Anglo-Irish society of which he was a part:

> *Sweet was the sound, when oft at evening's close*
> *Up yonder hill the village murmur rose;*
> *There, as I passed with careless steps and slow,*
> *The mingling notes came softened from below.*

> *But now the sounds of population fail,*
> *No cheerful murmurs fluctuate in the gale,*
> *No busy steps the grassgrown foot-way tread,*
> *For all the bloomy flush of life is fled.*

The poem is a protest against an oppression of the rural poor all over the British Isles, and not just Ireland; whether it can really be traced to Glassan village is uncertain, but its mood of nostalgic regret for a golden childhood past undoubtedly gives it some points of contact with the local landscape. The treasure-hunt for locations mentioned in the poem, all signposted and almost all in ruins, can prove oddly evocative of an absent population – removed not by enclosure but by much more recent economic pressures. The poem also points out some of the internal contradictions of the self-confident Georgian building mania: Goldsmith's lament is for a landscape that disappeared with the building of the great Georgian houses – many of which, like Waterstown at Glassan itself, have now disappeared.

A Goldsmith summer school is held in the area each June. Details from Sean Ryan (☎043/41030 or ☎46493).

conditioned chamber, while the rest still lies beneath the bog. The bog dates from 147 BC, and its construction and the way of life in the bog is examined in a number of displays, while the guided tour includes a walk outside in the bog and a video of the archeological dig.

Alternatively, if you turn off the main road north of Ballymahon (before Corlea) and follow the more minor roads up the lough to the rather nondescript **Newtowncashel**, you'll pass the workshop of the bogwood sculptor Michael Casey, whose raw material is timber many thousands of years old. The wood is dug out of the bog and left for a few years to dry out. On the road north from Newtowncashel to Lanesborough stands **Rakish Paddy's Pub**, worth a visit above all on a Tuesday night for its traditional session: look in for a drink anytime, though, and you can see the three superb modern metal sculptures (by John Mahan) of a seated fiddler, boy and girl dancers and a wooden-flute player evidently playing the well-known reel called Rakish Paddy.

LANESBOROUGH itself, at the head of Lough Ree, is another place to stop off for the boating or fishing (the last bungalow before the bridge has boats for hire) but for no other reason.

Longford

Inland, County Longford doesn't improve, and as far as tourism goes the county is a desert, the half-hearted attempts to promote Goldsmith country notwithstanding. Along with large parts of southern Sligo and Leitrim, Longford has been hard hit by very recent emigration, leaving even the grandest looking houses and mansions deserted by the roadsides. However, if yours is an endlessly indulgent holiday and you have transport of your own, then there are a few things you can catch on your way through. **LONGFORD** itself is a market town that has little to offer beyond convenience as a base. There's a **tourist office** (Easter–Aug Mon–Fri 10am–1pm & 2–6pm; Sept–Easter Mon–Fri 9.30am–1pm & 2–5.30pm; ☎043/46566) for local information, and if you've time to spare an **ecclesiastical museum** in nineteenth-century St Mel's Cathedral (Mon & Wed 11am–1pm, Sat 1–3pm, Sun 4–6pm). **Accommodation** is plentiful, including the *Longford Arms* on Main Street (☎043/46296; ⑥), which does good food, and numerous B&Bs, especially on Dublin Road, such as *Mrs O'Donnell's* (☎043/41569; ③).

Carriglas Manor
Chief of the surrounding attractions is **Carriglas Manor** (June–Sept Mon, Tues & Fri 1.30–5pm, Aug until 6pm, 40min tours on the hour beginning 2pm; Sun 2–6pm, tours 2pm, 3pm, 4pm, 5pm; £4). Situated just three miles out of Longford on the R194 to Granard, it's the seat of the descendants of Huguenot Lefroys. As you go up the avenue, the stables with their classically pedimented and rusticated archways (designed by James Gandon of O'Connell Bridge and Dublin Custom House repute) are on the left. They now house a **costume museum** and tearoom. The yard and buildings are being restored at the moment, but you're free to wander around it and the parkland, within the hours listed above. The costumes in the museum date mainly from the mid-eighteenth century and were found mouldering in trunks in the castle. The castle's architecture is perhaps best described as Tudor-Gothic Revival, and extremely handsome it is, too. It was built in 1837 by Chief Justice Thomas Lefroy, possibly the model for Darcy in *Pride and Prejudice*, as at one stage he enjoyed a romantic liaison with Jane Austen.

The **tour** of the building is directed by the present Lefroys, who are attempting to restore the place to its former majesty. It takes in the dining room, with its set of 1825 Waterford glasses and original ironstone china; the drawing room with its Dutch furniture, one cabinet of which contains an original tea and breakfast set of 1799; a fastidiously well-stocked library; and family portraiture on virtually every wall. All this is explained and expanded on in detail by the present occupier. Carriglas Manor also does **B&B** (☎043/45165; ⑧), with dinner at £22.50.

Granard and Edgeworthstown

Continuing on this same road you'll reach **GRANARD**, about fifteen miles from Longford. A famous **harp festival**, originating in 1781, took place here and was revived in 1981. Nowadays it spreads over the second weekend of August, starting on the Friday afternoon with competitions, street entertainment, *seisiúns* and *ceilis*. Lessons on the harp can be arranged on the spot and usually start on the Friday morning. Two **campsites** are set up for visitors, or you can stay at *Houricans Hotel* on Main Street (☎043/86041; ④). The biggest Norman **motte** in Ireland is sited at Granard, with yet another statue of Saint Patrick on top. The site is said to date back to 5 AD, and to Cairbre, eldest son of Niall of the Nine Hostages.

Finally, it's worth noting a couple of Longford's other literary connections, centred on Mostrim or **EDGEWORTHSTOWN** (about ten miles southeast of Longford town; take the N4), which takes its name from the family name of Maria Edgeworth (1767–1849), who, in her day, was an extremely famous author. *Castle Rackrent*, perhaps her most famous book, was written just before the Act of Union of 1801. Although its caricatures of both the Irish and Anglo-Irish can veer uncomfortably close to stage Irishry, it's a hilariously ironic and oddly prophetic insight into a chaotic Anglo-Irish lifestyle that was disappearing even as she wrote. The town now is little more than a crossroads and **Edgeworthstown House** is used as a nursing home. Maria's father, Richard, was a keen inventor, and the house once boasted central heating and a water pump which dispensed coins to beggars in return for a stint at the handle. The Edgeworth family vault can be seen in the graveyard of St John's Church, on the N4 south to Mullingar. Oscar Wilde's sister Isola is also buried here, and one of his most touching poems, *Requiescat*, was written in her memory:

> *Tread lightly, she is near*
> *Under the snow,*
> *Speak gently, she can hear*
> *The daisies grow.*
>
> *All her bright golden hair*
> *Tarnished with rust,*
> *She that was young and fair*
> *Fallen to dust.*
>
> *Lily-like, white as snow,*
> *She hardly knew*
> *She was a woman, so*
> *Sweetly she grew.*
>
> *Coffin-board, heavy stone,*
> *Lie on her breast,*
> *I vex my heart alone,*
> *She is at rest.*
>
> *Peace, peace, she cannot hear*
> *Lyre or sonnet,*
> *All my life's buried here,*
> *Heap earth upon it.*

travel details

Trains
Athlone to: Dublin Heuston (11 daily; 1hr 25min); Galway (4 daily; 1hr 10min); Westport (3 daily; 2hr).

Longford to: Dublin Connolly (4 daily; 2hr 10min); Sligo (3 daily; 1hr 20min).

Mullingar to: Dublin Connolly (4 daily; 1hr 10min); Sligo (3 daily; 2hr 10min).

Bus Éireann
Athlone to: Dublin (13 daily; 2hr); Galway (9 daily; 1hr 45min); Sligo (2 daily; 2hr 30min); Westport (4 daily; 2hr 45min).

Longford to: Dublin (3 daily; 2hr 10min).

Mullingar to: Dublin (10 daily; 1hr 30min); Sligo (3 daily; 2hr 30min).

Private Buses
North Galway Club: Galway–Dublin service calls at Athlone. See Galway chapter "Travel Details".

Funtrek: Sligo–Dublin bus calls at Longford. See Sligo chapter "Travel Details".

CHAPTER FIVE

WEXFORD, CARLOW AND KILKENNY

I f you're in the southeast at all, the chances are that you've come to Ireland via Rosslare Harbour; it's not the most obvious of areas to visit, especially if this is your first time in the country. There are none of the wild wastes of rock, bog and water, nor the accompanying abandoned cottages that tell of famine, eviction and emigration, so appealing to romantic tastes. It is, however, Ireland's sunniest and driest corner, and what the region does have to offer – whether you're spending a couple of days passing through, or if you simply haven't the time for more distant wanderings – is worth savouring. On the whole, the region's attractions are frustratingly widely scattered, but its medieval and Anglo-Norman history is richly concentrated in the ancient city of **Kilkenny** – the region's only heavily touristed town – and the lush countryside around it shelters some powerful medieval ruins. **Wexford town**'s conviviality makes up for its disappointingly scant traces of a vigorous Viking and Norman past; **Carlow town**, sadly, doesn't. While the extreme east is dull and low-lying, and the Blackstairs Mountains open and empty, the southeast is characterized overall by a quality of rich cultivation, as much to do with its history as its natural fertility.

Inland the region is shaped by three majestic **rivers**: the Nore, the Barrow and the Slaney, and by the empty Blackstairs Mountains which form a rough natural boundary between the counties of Wexford and Carlow. The rivers roll through rich, lush pastures and pretty wooded valleys, past medieval Christian ruins and little towns and villages, whose history belongs to the trade these waterways brought inland. This landscape is at its prettiest in the hills and valleys of the Nore and Barrow, just north of New Ross, and south of Kilkenny town, perfect countryside for leisurely **cycling** and easy **walking** – an option made all the more attractive by the hostels at New Ross and Kilkenny. The signposted **South Leinster Way** meanders through the heart of this countryside to some of the choicest spots, before heading northeast to the less intimate country of Carlow and the Blackstairs Mountains.

Head for the coast and, to the east, superb sandy **beaches** stretch practically the entire length of County Wexford. While the south coast is less suitable for swimming, its sand banks, shallow lagoons and silted rivers offer great opportunities for **wildlife**

ACCOMMODATION PRICES

Throughout this book, accommodation prices have been graded according to the cost per person per night in high season; with hotels and many hostels this represents half the cost of a double room, whereas with the more basic hostels it represents the cost of a single dormitory bed. The prices signified by our grades are as follows:

① Up to £6	③ £10–14	⑤ £20–26	⑦ £36–45
② £6–10	④ £14–20	⑥ £26–36	⑧ Over £45

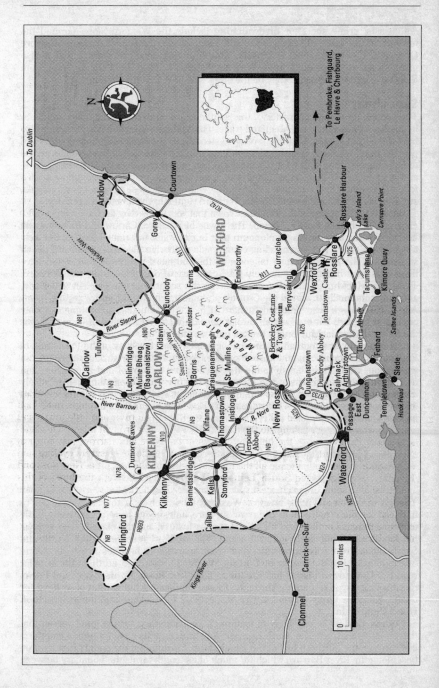

enthusiasts: prime spots for **birdwatching** include the Wexford Slobs (around the town itself), the lakes of Lady's Island and Tacumshane, the Saltee Islands off Kilmore Quay and the Hook Head Peninsula. This low-lying southern coastal region also provides an excellent quick route west to Waterford, since there's a car ferry from Ballyhack across to Passage East on the other side of Waterford Harbour.

Some history

The settled, developed character of this southeastern corner of Ireland owes much to its history of invasion, settlement and trade. The Vikings wrought havoc, but they also built the port of Wexford, which developed steadily, all the while assimilating ideas and peoples from overseas, ensuring the continual cultural influence of Europe. The arrival of mercenaries from Wales, for instance, was common throughout the medieval period, and after Henry II had consolidated the Anglo-Norman victories, Strongbow settled fellow Welshmen in the region: a dialect descended from these people, known as *yola*, survived in the far southeast of County Wexford right into the nineteenth century.

But it was the power of the English Crown that was to have by far the greatest influence on the character of the region. The towns of Wexford, Carlow and Kilkenny still bear the marks of their **Anglo-Norman** past in city walls and ruined castles; the well-tended farmland of rich surrounding countryside similarly reflects centuries of English settlement. The Anglo-Norman takeover of the southeast was swift, and would have been total were it not for the fiercely Gaelic enclave of counties Carlow and Wexford. There the MacMurrough Kavanaghs became the scourge of the English in Ireland, and they continually thwarted the Crown's attempts to control the entire region. It was Art MacMurrough who defeated Richard II in battles which lost the king not only control of Ireland, but his English throne, too. Only after the arrival of Cromwell was the power of the MacMurroughs broken once and for all.

Colonization was thereafter pursued vigorously: the proximity of the Pale – and of England itself – meant that the Crown's influence was always far stronger here than in the remote west. The English found this area easier to control and administer, and during the growing unrest of the eighteenth century the region remained relatively tranquil. Surprisingly then, by far the most significant uprisings of the **Insurrection of 1798** took place in counties Wexford and Carlow. For nationalists the bloodshed and heroics of that summer form the region's most fêted history and legend.

COUNTIES WEXFORD AND CARLOW

Though the ancient Viking town of **Wexford** bills itself as a tourist centre, you're unlikely to spend more than a day or so here unless you have a car. Sadly, little evidence remains of the town's long and stormy history, and the place is most enjoyable for its small but lively cultural scene. The wildfowl reserves of the North and South Slobs are easily accessible, and some marvellous beaches are to be found nearby, stretching the length of **County Wexford**'s shoreline north to the popular resort of **Courtown**. Inland, historic towns like **New Ross**, **Enniscorthy** and **Ferns** merit a visit if you're passing through. To see the best of the south coast, head for quaint **Kilmore Quay**, or rent a bike and explore the isolated and intriguing **Hook Head Peninsula**.

County Carlow is less likely to feature on your itinerary, for the good reason that there's little to attract. The South Leinster Way trudges at its most lonesome and desolate through the northern half of the **Blackstairs Mountains**; the county is at its prettiest along the River Barrow, which for much of its length forms the boundary between

Carlow and Kilkenny. **Carlow town**, situated on the Dublin-to-Kilkenny train route, barely warrants attention.

Wexford town

Apart from the Viking legacy of narrow, quirky lanes, **WEXFORD** town retains few traces of its past, and only the quays suggest that it was once an important trading centre. In fact, the harbour, in business from the ninth century, has now silted up, and Wexford has lost its trade to its old rival Waterford. That's not to say, though, that the town's history stopped with the fall of the Vikings. Settled by the Normans in the twelfth century, it became an English garrison town, brutally taken by Cromwell in 1649, who had 1500 Wexford citizens put to death. In the 1798 Insurrection, the town saw brave rebel fighting against the English Crown (backed by a mainly Protestant yeomanry), which was fearful that the port might be used as a landing place by the French. The rising lasted longer in Wexford than in most places, but the rebels were finally put down and the Crown was quick to exact retribution. Wexford, though, plays down its contribution to Republicanism and has emerged as a positive, forward-looking place, proud of its ethnic and religious mix. It is internationally famous for its prestigious **Opera Festival**, while a more mainstream draw are the town's estimated 93 **bars**, reason enough to give Wexford at least a night.

Arrival, information and accommodation

If you're **arriving** by *Bus Éireann* or by train, you'll be dropped at the **train station**, at the north end of the quays and just past the bridge over the estuary – which, if you crossed, would take you out to the campsite, the wildfowl reserve (see p.191) and the beaches of the county's east coast. The *Ardcavan Coach Company*'s **buses** to and from Dublin stop at The Crescent (see "Travel Details" at the end of the chapter), just beside the **tourist office** (April–Sept daily 9am–6pm; Oct–March Mon–Fri 9am–1pm & 2–5.15pm; ☎053/23111). If you need to rent a **bike**, try *Dave Allen Cycles*, 84 South Main Street (☎053/22516; £6 per day, £28 per week), *Hayes*, 108 South Main Street (☎053/22462), or *The Bike Shop*, 9 Selskar Street (☎053/22514).

There are a handful of **B&Bs** right in town. Along Westgate is Mrs Allen's *Westgate House* (☎053/24428; ③), *Bilrene*, 91 John Street (☎053/24190; ③), and *John's Gate Street House* (☎053/41124; ④). There are others along North Main Street, and some bars along Commercial Quay also offer B&B accommodation, such as *The Wavecrest* at no. 17 (☎053/22849; ④). Best of the possibilities further out is the thirteenth-century *Killiane Castle* (☎053/58898; ④) on the Rosslare Road, a B&B with style. Bear in mind that rooms are at a premium during the Opera Festival (see overleaf).

You can **camp** at the municipal site, immediately over the bridge from Commercial Quay (Easter to mid-Sept; ☎053/44378) – and there's a **swimming pool** next to the campsite. The nearest **hostel** is at Rosslare Harbour (see p.192); a day-return ticket by bus or train costs around £3. *My Beautiful Laundrette* is in Peter Square.

The town

Set on the south side of the broad, featureless Slaney estuary, Wexford town sits behind its **quays**, which drag on relentlessly. The only relief is **The Crescent**, where a statue of John Barry, a local who founded the American Navy during their War of Independence, strides against the buffeting wind with cloak billowing. Parallel to the quays runs Wexford's lengthy **Main Street**, a narrow and winding route that gives some idea of the medieval town's layout. Once you've seen it, there is little else left to explore. A monument to the fighting of 1798 briefly draws your attention to the **Bull Ring** (part of Main Street), also scene of a massacre by Cromwell that left all but 400 of the population dead. A lane up behind *Macken's* off-licence, most famous as being both pub and undertakers, leads to the Cornmarket and the parallel streets of the small town centre.

The **Westgate**, built around 1300, is the sole survivor of the medieval walled city's original five gates, and is now designated as **West Gate Heritage Tower**; here you can watch a short film of the town's history (£2.50) and potter around a craft shop. Nearby are the remains of **Selskar Abbey**, wrecked by Cromwell, where Henry II spent an entire Lent in penitence for the murder of Thomas à Becket in Canterbury Cathedral.

Food, drink and entertainment

There's no shortage of places to get a decent **meal** in Wexford. *Michael's Restaurant*, 94 North Main Street, and *Nangles*, 22 North Main Street, both offer good-value meals daily till around midnight, along with *Robertino's* at 19 South Main Street, with an evening Italian menu. For vegetarian meals, try the café in the *Wexford Arts Centre*. For something a little more stylish there's the lovely, intimate *La Riva Restaurant*, Crescent Quay (☎053/24330), with main courses from £5.50. Some of the best cheap food is to be found in pubs and bars; *The Wren's Nest*, Custom House Quay, offers reliable, reasonably priced pub meals, as does *The Centenary Stores*, Charlotte Street; *Tim's Tavern*, 51 South Main Street, serves hot food throughout the day, as does *Asples*, on The Crescent, where you'll also hear a jazz session on Sunday mornings.

Beside these, the town has a vast selection of plain-drinking **pubs** and **bars**, many featuring **live music** on one or more days of the week. Start your explorations at *The Centenary Stores*, Charlotte Street, a lively, young spot with traditional Irish music (Wed nights & Sun mornings) and local blues band (Mon nights); *Ó Faoláins*, at 11–12 Moncke Street, has traditional music (Thurs evenings & Sun mornings), plus occasional jazz on Wednesdays. *The Thomas Moore Tavern*, Cornmarket, is known for being a music pub, although sessions here are sporadic – frequent set-dancing sessions are held here during the winter. Other spots for traditional music include *The Wren's Nest*, Custom House Quay, (Tues & Thurs), *Tommy Roche's*, in the Bull Ring (Thurs & Sat), and *Tim's Tavern* (Wed, Sat & Sun). You can find ballad and pop sessions at *Mooney's*, 12 Commercial Quay, every Friday night. *The Talbot Hotel* bar has occasional jazz and traditional sessions, while *White's Hotel* offers traditional and folk interspersed with mellow evenings of classical piano and guitar music. If all these fail to satisfy, the *Goal Bar*, South Main Street, guarantees anything from rock and country and western to traditional seven nights a week. And if you just want a drink try *The Crown Bar*, Moncke Street – this is the oldest pub in the city, run by the family for the last 150 years, and chock-full of ancient firearms.

Opera and theatre

October's **Opera Festival** is an international drawcard, usually featuring rarely performed works by renowned composers; information on ticket availability and programmes from the festival office on High Street (☎053/22400). This annual festival attracts a range of other performers, too, and you'll find traditional music, blues and jazz in the bars, along with poetry readings and exhibitions. Even out of festival time Wexford has a lively cultural life, largely generated by a couple of **theatre venues** – *The Theatre Royal* on High Street (☎053/22240 or 22144) and *The Wexford Arts Centre* (☎053/23764), in Cornmarket, housed in an eighteenth-century market house and town hall. The latter has a healthy turnover of exhibitions and hosts performance artists, dance groups, drama and music.

Around Wexford town

Within a few miles of Wexford are plenty of attractions to justify staying around for a few days. Some, like the **wildfowl reserves** at the endearingly named North and South Slobs, are of specialist interest. Others, though, could claim anyone's time – not least the excellent **sandy beaches** as near as Curracloe, five miles to the north, or the resort town of **Rosslare** to the south.

Birdwatching in the North and South Slobs

The mud flats sheltered behind the sea walls of the Slaney estuary, known as the **North and South Slobs**, are home to the **Wexford Wildfowl Reserve**. The Slobs are the main wintering grounds for half the world's population of Greenland white-fronted geese, Bewick's swans, pintails and blacktailed godwits; you can also see spotted redshanks, gulls and terns. At the reserve there's a wildfowl collection, a research station, hides, lookout towers and identification charts, all freely accessible, and at the North Slobs a new **visitor centre** (daily mid-April to Sept 9am–6pm, Oct to mid-April 10am–5pm; free).

To reach the North Slobs, take the Dublin Road (the N11) out of Wexford over the bridge, and it's signposted on the right after about two miles; for the South Slobs take the Rosslare Road (the N25) out of Wexford for two miles, turn left at the *Farmer's Kitchen* pub, and take the second turn on the left. Either of these is a considerable walk, but it's easy enough to hitch to the turn-offs, or a short, pleasant bike ride.

Ferrycarrig

Just two and a half miles inland from Wexford, the **Irish National Heritage Park** at **FERRYCARRIG** (March–Oct daily 10am–7pm, last admission 5pm; £3) plots 9000 years of social change through full-scale models of settlements, homesteads and burial places, from the Stone Age through to Norman times. It's a great place to clarify your knowledge of Ireland's ancient history, and helps make sense of the numerous archeological remains dotted throughout the country. The park is also being developed as a nature reserve, and the environment has been carefully nurtured to provide the appropriate settings. It works well, so that as you walk through the Mesolithic campsite, the shaggy lichen-covering on the hazel trees, the mud and the reeds all help evoke a primeval bog, while the Viking shipyard nestles convincingly on the estuary's banks. Access by public bus is only possible on Fridays; ask at the tourist office about tours from Wexford, or rent a bike.

Johnstown Castle

Four miles southwest of Wexford, off the Rosslare Road, the **Irish Agricultural Museum** (June–Aug Mon–Fri 9am–5pm, Sat & Sun 2–5pm; April, May & Sept to mid-Nov closed 12.30–1.30pm; winter closed Sat & Sun; £1.75; gardens only £1.50) is set in the gardens of **Johnstown Castle**, a Gothic Revival castellated mansion. The museum, which is signposted *Research Centre*, has good, clear displays on all aspects of rural life, encompassing domestic objects, farming machinery, carts and carriages, reconstructed workshops, and much on dairy farming. In addition, the **grounds** have mounds of rhododendrons, ornamental lakes, hot houses, dark woodland and walled gardens – all very spruce and well maintained. Again, mini-tours can be arranged from Wexford tourist office.

The beaches

The southeast has more sunshine than any other part of Ireland, and as the entire coastline of the county to the north of Wexford town is made up of safe and sandy **beaches**, the region is a popular spot in summer for families and caravanners.

From **CURRACLOE**, five miles northeast of town (take the R742), superb, sandy dunes stretch away into the far distance, and though the little villages roundabout are overloaded in July and August, the sands themselves aren't. If you want to stay in the area, try *O'Gorman's Caravan and Camping Park* (April–Sept; ☎053/37110 or 37221). Camping on the dunes is discouraged. If you don't have your own transport, then you'll have to rely on the *Bus Éireann* **buses** from Wexford to Curracloe, which run highly infrequently.

Roughly six miles southeast of Wexford is the huge sandy beach at **ROSSLARE**, the county's other main seaside resort, not to be confused with Rosslare Harbour, another five miles further south. Right on the edge of the beach, the best hotel in the southeast, *Kelly's* (☎053/32114; ⑦), has excellent sporting facilities, outdoor hot tubs, and an impressive collection of modern Irish art.

Rosslare Harbour

ROSSLARE HARBOUR is served by ferries from Cherbourg and Le Havre in France, and Fishguard and Pembroke Dock in South Wales. At Rosslare Harbour terminal there's a **tourist office** (☎053/33622), which opens during June, July and August for all incoming sailings, and in winter for afternoon and evening sailings only; if you are driving, you might use Rosslare Kilrane tourist office just over a mile from the ferry along the N25 (☎053/33232). St Martin's Road, the village's main street, is the area for **accommodation** possibilities: the pleasant and friendly *Killara*, Cawdor Street (☎053/33559; ③), and *Rock Villa*, St Martin's Road (☎053/33212; ③), are just two of the many. The *An Óige* **hostel** is also nearby in Goulding Street (open all year; rent-a-bike drop-off scheme; ☎053/33399, fax ☎33624); ②), and there's also a supermarket. You can **camp** down in the dunes by the beach, or in the small secluded garden of *Foley's* at 3 Coastguard Station, signposted off St Martin's Road. For more facilities, try *The Holiday Inn Caravan and Camping Park* at Kilrane (☎053/31168), three miles from the port.

ROSSLARE HARBOUR TRAVEL INFORMATION

Note that you have to pay £5 **tax** to leave the country on tickets bought in Ireland.

Ardcavan Coach Company (☎053/22561). Buses to Dublin.

Bus Éireann (☎053/33114). For local and national bus services, with direct links to Cork, Limerick and Galway in summer, see "Travel Details" at the end of this chapter.

Funtrek (☎01/873 0852). Buses to Dublin.

Irish Ferries (☎053/33158). Services to Pembroke Dock (4hr 30min), Cherbourg (twice weekly, winter weekly; 18hr) and Le Havre (5 weekly, winter twice weekly; 22 hr).

Irish Rail, Rosslare Harbour (☎053/33114).

Stena Sealink Line (☎053/33115). Sailings to Fishguard (four daily all year; 3hr 30min). *Hostelling International Card* holders eligible for reductions of ten percent; *InterRail* ticket holders get a 50-percent reduction; student fares (about £6–8 off) available to holders of *International Student Identity Cards*; bikes carried free. A single to Fishguard costs £28; boat and train to London £66.

The south coast

In the southeast corner of Ireland, the sea has made inroads into an otherwise flat region, forming small lagoons popular with wind-surfers, at **TACUMSHANE** and **LADY'S ISLAND**, both venues for bird enthusiasts. Lady's Island itself sits mid-lagoon at the end of a causeway and has been a place of religious devotion for centuries: an annual pilgrimage is still made here on August 15. On the island are the remains of an Augustinian priory and a Norman castle, both built in the thirteenth century, but the spirit of the place has been destroyed by a large, modern church building that has been tacked onto the side. There are few amenities for travellers in the area, but the *Lobster Pot* bar and restaurant at **CARNE** is a great exception, serving delicious seafood meals. There are **campsites** at both Carne and Lady's Island, but nowhere else to stay.

Kilmore Quay and the Saltee Islands

KILMORE QUAY comes as a real surprise after the largely dull countryside which precedes it. A small, unspoilt fishing and holiday village of thatched cottages and white-washed walls, it's prettily situated around a stone harbour wall, looking out at the nearby Saltee Islands. County Wexford's **Maritime Museum** is housed in an old lightship in the harbour (June–Sept daily noon–6pm; £1). There's also a fine sandy beach.

Kilmore Quay hosts a **seafood festival**, usually in the second week of July – a fine excuse to eat plenty of seafood, whatever your budget. The best seafood restaurant is *The Silver Fox*, with lunch from £4.50 (noon–3pm & 7–9.30pm; ☎053/29888). The village also has a handful of good **bars**, including *Kehoe's*, which has singalongs, and *The Wooden House*, with a disco during the summer months. Both pubs do bar **food**, and *Walkers*, down by the harbour, is one of the best fish-and-chip shops in Ireland.

Kilmore Quay is also point of departure for visiting the uninhabited **Saltee Islands**, one of Ireland's most important bird sanctuaries, especially for puffins, razorbills, cormorants, shags, gannets, kittiwakes and auks. In the nesting period of late spring and early summer, there are thousands of them; by the end of July they've all left – so time your trip carefully. Boat trips may be available during the summer – contact Declan Bates (☎053/29684) or Dick Hayes (☎053/29704), who organizes deep-sea angling trips at around £15 per day.

You can **camp** among the dunes at Kilmore Quay; about a mile outside the village, the *Kilturk Independent Hostel* (*IHH*, May to early Oct; tel/fax ☎053/29883; ①) is an airy bohemian place (bike rental, £4), and there are also a couple of **B&Bs** – the cute thatched *Curlew Cottage* (☎053/29772; ③) and *Tranquil Sea* (☎053/29658; ③), both a short walk from the harbour.

The Hook Head Peninsula

Heading west from Kilmore Quay, the R736/R733 will take you to the **Hook Head Peninsula**, which forms the eastern side of Waterford Harbour. Only when you reach the peninsula does the flat coastline begin to undulate and the scenery become more attractive. The first town you'll encounter is **Arthurstown** – probably the best base for exploring the area – and **Ballyhack**, where you can catch the time-saving ferry across the Barrow estuary from Waterford Harbour.

Arthurstown and Tintern Abbey

ARTHURSTOWN, on the estuary near the neck of the peninsula, has a tiny sandy spot you can swim from, a nice pub that serves seafood, a post office, a shop and several good B&Bs. *Clogheen* (☎051/389110; ③) is the cheapest, *Arthur's Rest* (☎051/389192; ④) is extremely comfortable, while *Glendine House* (☎051/389258 or 362276; ④) is beautifully spacious and can arrange sailing, scuba diving, **camping** and **bike rental** (£5). There's also an *An Óige* **hostel** (June–Sept; ☎051/389411; ②) in the old Coastguard Station – ring ahead to book.

About five miles east of Arthurstown (take the R733), near the muddy Bannow Bay, scene of the first Norman landing in 1169, is **Tintern Abbey** (free access), built in 1200 by William Marshall, Earl of Pembroke. Another fine Cistercian edifice, it owes its existence in this unprepossessing spot to a vow made by the earl while he was caught in a storm off the south coast. Praying that he might be saved, he promised to build an abbey wherever his boat came ashore. The presbytery is based on the foundation's more famous namesake in Wales.

Ballyhack and Dunbrody Abbey

Just a mile to the north of Arthurstown is the village of **BALLYHACK**, which has a useful year-round **car ferry** service running regularly across the harbour to Passage East in County Waterford. The crossing takes just ten minutes (see p.216). Setting off the picturesque scene is **Ballyhack Castle**, a fine five-storey, sixteenth-century tower house in the process of being restored. You can climb about halfway up the tower and enjoy a strong sense of its stout proportions (April–June & Sept Wed–Sun noon–6pm; July & Aug daily 10am–6pm; winter Sat & Sun variable hours; £1; at other times collect the key from the house next to the pub). Ballyhack village also boasts a very good seafood **restaurant**, the *Neptune* (☎051/389284), and a small **B&B**, *Riverdale*, beside the ferry (☎051/389424; ④).

The magnificent ruin of **Dunbrody Abbey**, to the northeast of town off the R733, stands open to all at the widening of the Barrow estuary. A thirteenth-century Cistercian foundation, it was altered in the sixteenth century after the Dissolution of the Monasteries, when the large central tower and adjacent buildings were added. There's free parking at the new so-called visitor centre (April–Sept only; £1), but the admission ticket only buys access to a tearoom and a skimpy maze that needs a good twenty years' growth. The "museum" is non-existent.

Duncannon to Slade

Unfortunately, the pretty, wooded coastline south of Ballyhack, down to Duncannon, is privately owned, and you can't walk along it. **DUNCANNON** itself is a holiday town, pleasant enough, and with a rocky coast to the south that protects its big, sandy beach. Up on the headland, eerie **Duncannon Fort** (summer daily 11am–5.30pm, £1) dates back to 1586, when the Spanish Armada was expected to attack. Constantly added to since then, one of its grislier sights is the reputed dungeon of the Croppy Boy, tortured hero of a well-known rebel song. Facilities in Duncannon are minimal: if you're going to **stay**, try the *Hook Trekking Centre*, one mile from Duncannon on the Hook Road (☎051/389166; ③), which does B&B; the pony trekking itself operates only in June, July and August for £9 an hour, with reduced B&B rates for riders. Back in Duncannon, there's also a caravan site, but better if you're **camping** is to sleep amidst the dunes, or ask to use a local field. A couple of bars do sandwiches and burgers, and *The Moorings Restaurant* (☎051/389242; summer daily 11am–9.30pm) serves fresh salads, snacks and evening **meals**.

From Duncannon, you can walk wherever you like southwards, but a bike is the ideal way to get down to the very **end of the peninsula**. Little sandy bays lie concealed behind low cliffs, and there are lovely views across to the broad and beautiful Waterford coastline. Although the Hook Head Peninsula promotes itself as a tourist area, the caravans and kids mostly keep to the areas around Duncannon and Fethard to the east, and there are plenty of isolated spots to be found. (If you want to take a break, try the very pretty **teashop** at Saltmills, 3 miles north of Fethard.) A couple of particularly fine, sandy beaches are **Booley Strand**, two miles south of Duncannon, and beyond that the smaller **Dollar Bay**.

Beyond these, six miles from Duncannon, **Loftus Hall** sits at the end of a long drive behind an ostentatious gateway. It's said that the hall was built for a princess whom the owner was to bring home as his bride, and that the princess never arrived. There's something quite eerie about all this decorative splendour in such a desolate spot: the grandiose Italian staircase, for instance, is made up of 49 different shades of wood and cost the monumental sum of £5000 in 1822. Although the house is not geared up for tourists, the owner may show you around the ground floor in return for a £2 donation to the Lifeboat Fund.

At the peninsula's tip the shoreline is rockier, the limestone rich with fossils, and the land, flat and desolate, just slips away into the sea. The extremity is marked by a **light-house**, said to be the oldest in Europe – the first on this site was built in the twelfth century. This part of Hook Head is favoured by ornithologists who come to watch the bird migrations, and if you're lucky you can sometimes spot seals. Crashing spray and blow-holes make it a dangerous and dramatic place in a storm – and you certainly shouldn't swim here at any time. You can **camp** near the lighthouse, though be careful not to pitch your tent by the blowholes on the other side of the lane. The nearest **shop** is three and a half miles away at the *Texaco* petrol station at the Fethard–Duncannon junction. Taking the Duncannon Road, *The Templars Inn* in Templetown, about three miles from the tip, has a **restaurant** and bar food. Just outside Fethard, the ivyclad *Innyard House* (☎051/397126; ④) is hidden away behind a walled garden, where you can dine outdoors on Fridays or Saturdays, or drop in for Sunday lunch (5 courses for £8.50; booking essential).

Tucked away on the east flank of the peninsula, the evocatively crumbling harbour of **SLADE** is a quiet, beautiful place: fishing boats cluster around its quays and slip-ways, stacked lobster pots lean against a fifteenth-century castle, and the whole place is built from stone a nutty brown colour, rich, rusty and warm. There's a tiny shop (July & Aug only), and if you want to look around the castle, take the lane that runs along-side it and ask at the farm.

New Ross

First impressions of **NEW ROSS** (21 miles west of Wexford on the N25) are not encouraging: a glamourless old port of grubby wharf buildings. However, the place isn't without character, thanks mostly to the river that has long given access to the heart of the Wexford and Kilkenny countryside, and the clutter of narrow lanes that do much to preserve the human scale of the place. Should you find yourself with time to spare in New Ross, it's worth climbing the steep back alleys to the top of town for views over the river and hills and exploring the ruins of New Ross's thirteenth-century **abbey** (beside St Mary's Church), with its graceful, early English windows and some carved, medieval tombstones in the chancel.

Today the river can be enjoyed from the *Galley Cruising Restaurant*, which runs **river trips** up the Barrow and Nore as far as Inistioge and St Mullins (see pp.203 and 204), and along the Suir to Waterford. Lunch (for around £11), afternoon tea (£5) or dinner (£17) is part of the package, and cruises operate from mid-May to late September; advance booking is advisable (☎051/21723).

New Ross has a **tourist office** (June–Sept Mon–Sat 9am–8pm; Sun 2–6pm; ☎051/21857), currently housed in the Kennedy Centre (though it may move), while *Bus Éireann* **buses** to local towns and the Hook Head Peninsula leave from the quays, outside the *Mariner's Inn*. If you are looking for **accommodation**, the *Hotel New Ross*, 1 North Street (☎051/21457; ⑤), is right in the centre of town; and there are also a fair number of B&Bs roundabout. *Rossmore*, Priory Street (☎051/21685; ③), is probably the cheapest. One of the best places to stay, however, is the very friendly *MacMurrough Farm Hostel* (*IHH*, open all year; ☎051/21383; ①), a comfy cottage hostel in a beautiful setting a couple of miles out of town; if you're cycling, it makes a good base from which to explore the Nore and Barrow river valleys (see pp.202-3). Ask for directions to *Kelly's* BP petrol station on the ring road; the hostel is signposted down the lane alongside.

If you want to **eat**, *The Crusty Kitchen* (Mon–Sat till 6pm) serves cheap light lunches. South Street has several coffee shops, and the *M&J Restaurant* (Mon–Fri till 9pm, Sat till 7pm) serves big fry-ups; there are also a couple of places serving decent bar food every day till around 9.30pm: *Katie Pat's* and *John V's*, both on the Quays. There's a young crowd at *Spider O'Brien's* **pub** on South Street, and traditional sessions at *John V's* (Thurs) and the *Mariner's* (Tues and Fri).

Around New Ross
Four miles north of New Ross along the Enniscorthy Road, take a right turn sign-posted for the **Berkeley Costume and Toy Museum** (May–Sept Thurs–Sun tours 11.30am, 3pm, 5pm; other times by appointment, ☎051/21361; £3). This private collection of textiles, dolls and toys, dating back to the 1720s, is enthusiastically explained by the owners, allowing the rare experience of seeing Georgian and Victorian dress without glass cases or artificial light. Wedding dresses from three generations of one family, restyled court dresses and French dolls as ambassadors of fashion afford glimpses of social history and how styles were transmitted throughout Ireland from Britain and Europe.

The **arboretum**, five miles south of New Ross, known as the *J.F. Kennedy Memorial Park* (May–Aug 10am–8pm; April & Sept 10am–6.30pm; Oct–March 10am–5pm; £2, family ticket £5; Heritage Card), contains a collection of around 5000 species of trees and shrubs. Kennedy's great-grandfather was born close by in Dunganstown, so the place is often frequented by Americans in search of presidential roots. If you have transport, the road south of here will take you to the coast and the Hook Head Peninsula.

Enniscorthy, Ferns and Courtown

At the likeable market town of **ENNISCORTHY** (14 miles north of Wexford on the N11) is the **County Museum** (April–Sept Mon–Sat 10am–6pm, Sun 2–5.30pm; Oct, Nov, Feb & March daily 2–5.30pm; Dec & Jan Sun only, 2–5pm; £2). Focusing on the events of 1798 and 1916, the museum is housed in the Norman castle that dominates the town, overlooking the Slaney. The museum is also crammed with a wonderful mixture of local objects, from an ogham stone to a sedan chair. One gloomy portrait bears the plaintive label, "Information Please". Across the river, covered in mustard and yellow gorse, lies **Vinegar Hill**, the site of the rebels' main encampment during the 1798 Insurrection – and the scene of their final slaughter by Crown forces. If you're around in summer, Enniscorthy has the enjoyable "Strawberry Fair", usually held the first or second week in July.

The higher countryside to the north and west of Enniscorthy is bald and spartan. There's little in the way of sights on this side of the Blackstairs Mountains, though if you're heading north, **FERNS** – seven miles from Enniscorthy – would make a good lunch stop. One-time seat of the kings of Leinster, it's now a little scrap of a village, top-heavy with history; it was here that Dermot MacMurrough was attacked by Tiernán O'Rourke – whose wife he had abducted fourteen years earlier. MacMurrough sought help from Henry II in France, who lent him Richard Fitzherbert de Clare (**Strongbow**), and thus an adultery led to the Norman invasion of Ireland. An abbey was founded in Ferns in the sixth century, and you can see its remains in **St Edan**'s churchyard and the adjacent field. Most impressive, though, are the ruins of the thirteenth-century **castle**, with its pair of towers – which you can climb – and two curtain walls. When you're feeling peckish, the *Celtic Arms* in the village does daily set meals. If you're heading for the coast, *The 64* bar and *Honeypot* coffee shop in Gorey, five miles east of Ferns, are good places to eat.

Quite the nicest family seaside town in the area is **COURTOWN**, around 25 miles north of Wexford (turn off the N11 onto the R742 at Gorey) and plumb in the middle of another excellent, long stretch of sand. Three miles south at Poulshone is the tiny, family-run *Anchorage Hostel* (May–Oct; ☎055/25335; ②), with a nearby shop and a delightful beach just five minutes' walk away.

County Carlow

Northwest of Wexford, tiny **County Carlow** shares little of the appeal of its close neighbours. Much of the terrain is unenticing agricultural land, and none of the few small towns retains much of its history, though the county capital does sport a ruined Norman castle. The most attractive fringes of the county – along the River Barrow and in the Blackstairs Mountains – are covered in the "County Kilkenny" section below, being more approachable from that direction.

Carlow town

For centuries, the town of **CARLOW** was an Anglo-Norman stronghold at the edge of an otherwise fiercely Gaelic county. As such, it has a bloody history, with its most terrible battle during the Insurrection of 1798, when over 600 rebels were slaughtered. Today there's nothing to suggest its former frontier status, and this small, busy town is distinguished only by a fine Classical courthouse with a portico modelled on the Parthenon, and an elegant Regency Gothic cathedral – one of the first Catholic churches to be built after Catholic Emancipation in 1829. The remains of the once proud Norman **castle** now lie neglected within the grounds of *Corcoran & Co*; if you want to poke around, ask at the factory. Otherwise, there's plenty on local military, religious and folk history in the **museum**, housed in the Town Hall (Tues–Sat 9.30am–5.30pm, Sun 2.30–5.30pm; £1).

You can get more local information, including a free map and historical guide, from Carlow's **tourist office** in Cathedral Close, on the corner of Tullow Street and College Street (April–Aug 10am–1pm & 2–5.30pm; Sept–March 9.30am–1pm & 2–5.30pm; ☎0503/31554). There's a **train** link north to Kildare and Dublin, and south to Kilkenny, Thomastown and Waterford. **Bike rental** is available during the summer from *A.E. Coleman* in Dublin Street (☎0503/31273).

If you want to **stay**, B&Bs include Mrs Farrell's *Westlow*, Green Lane (☎0503/43964; ③), or *Redsetter House*, 14 Dublin Street (☎0503/41848; ④), and there are several more out along the Kilkenny Road. To go **drinking** with a young crowd try *Scragg's Alley*, *The Buzz's* or *Tully's* (something of a bikers' hang-out), all along Tullow Street and all serving bar food; if you want to **eat** with a more mature crowd try *The Little Owl*, Dublin Street.

Two miles out of town on the R726 road is arguably County Carlow's most impressive sight: the **Browneshill dolmen**. It's enormous, possibly the largest Neolithic stone formation in Europe, but you must ask the farmer for permission to view it.

COUNTY KILKENNY

County Kilkenny offers the finest of the southeast's countryside. Mostly it's intensely pretty, rich farmland, especially to the north of New Ross around the confluence of the Nore and the Barrow rivers. Medieval ruins are spattered all over the county, but they reach their richest concentration in ancient **Kilkenny** city – a quaint but really bustling favourite. The delightful surroundings make it ideal for biking around the river valleys and their medieval ruins, most notably **Kells Priory** and **Jerpoint Abbey**. The **cycling** is easy: off the main roads there's little traffic, and the minor roads that stay close to the rivers are especially scenic. Alternatively, the heart of this rich, historical farmland can be crossed **on foot**. As they head south, the Nore and Barrow rivers flow through gentle valleys of mixed woodland: the **South Leinster Way** provides unstrenuous walking, passing through pretty riverside villages – **Inistioge**, **Graiguenamanagh**, and nearby **Borris** and **St Mullins** – before heading north towards the Blackstairs Mountains. Immediate access from Kilkenny is by local bus or by taking the train as far as Thomastown and walking. Alternatively, you could see the region from the **cruises** that operate from the river port of New Ross (see p.195).

Kilkenny

KILKENNY is Ireland's finest medieval city. Above the broad sweep of the River Nore sits the castle, while a pretty, humpbacked stone bridge leads up into narrow, cheerful streets laced with carefully maintained buildings. Kilkenny's earliest settlement was a monastery founded by Saint Canice in the sixth century, but all that remains from those days is the round tower which stands alongside the cathedral. The city's layout today owes more to its medieval history. Following continual skirmishes between local clans, the arrival of the **Normans** in 1169 saw the building of a fort by Strongbow on the site of today's castle. His son-in-law, William Marshall, consolidated Norman power in Kilkenny, maintaining the fortified city and keeping the indigenous Irish in an area of less substantial housing, beyond its walls – of which only the name "Irishtown" remains. In 1391, the Butler family acquired Kilkenny Castle and so ensured the city's loyalty to the English Crown.

In the mid-seventeenth century, Kilkenny virtually became the capital of Ireland, with the founding of a parliament in 1641 known as the **Confederation of Kilkenny** (see "Historical Framework" in *Contexts*). This attempt to unite resistance to the English persecution of Catholics was powerful for a while, though its effectiveness had greatly diminished by the time Cromwell arrived – in his usual destructive fashion – in 1650. Kilkenny never recovered its former prosperity and importance. The disgrace of the Butler family in 1715, coupled with English attacks upon the rights of Catholics through the Penal Laws, saw the city decline still further, though the towering mill buildings on the river banks are evidence of a considerable industrial history.

Enough medieval buildings remain to attest to Kilkenny's former importance, however, and in a place brimming with civic pride, there's been a tasteful push towards making the town a major tourist attraction. Kilkenny is sometimes known as "the marble city" because of the limestone mined locally, which develops a deep black shine when polished. Echoing this, the town's bar and shop signs all gleam with black and brown lacquer, the names cut in deeply bevelled, stout gold lettering.

> The telephone code for Kilkenny city is ☎056.

Arrival, information and accommodation

The **bus** (☎64933) and **train stations** (☎22024) lie on the north road out of the city, at the top of John Street: note that in Irish the city is called *Cill Chainnigh*, and this is what it says on the front of buses; all **local buses** go from The Parade outside Kilkenny Castle.

The **tourist office** in Rose Inn Street (April–Sept Mon–Sat 9am–6pm, Sun 11am–1pm & 2–5pm; Oct–March Tues–Sat 9am–12.45pm & 2–5.15pm; ☎51500) is a worthwhile first stop, with free maps of the city and plenty of other information.

Kilkenny is well served by **B&Bs**, although in the summer the city can get crowded, and during festival week in August (see p.201) you'll need to book in advance. There are a couple above pubs on Parliament Street – *Fennelly's* (☎61796; ④) and *The Pumphouse* (☎63924; ③) – and another in James Street, just off here – *Mrs Dempsey's* at no. 26 (☎21954; ③). Follow Parliament Street towards the cathedral, turn left at the traffic lights and you are in Dean Street, where there are yet more central alternatives: *Church View* at no. 6, above a coffee shop (☎61734; ④), and *Kilkenny Bed & Breakfast*, Dean Street (☎64040; ③). If you are driving you might consider staying out along the Waterford Road at Mrs Flannery's at *Ashleigh* (☎22809; ③) or Mrs Flanagan's at *Burwood* (June–Sept; ☎62266; ③); or *Lackan House*, out on the Dublin Road, which offers luxurious B&B (☎61085; ⑥).

The new *Kilkenny Tourist Hostel* is in a great spot in the town centre, at 35 Parliament Street (*IHH*, open all year; ☎63541; ②); it has a bright airy kitchen and is run by a friendly crowd. The *An Óige* **hostel**, *Foulksrath Castle*, Jenkinstown (March–Oct; ☎67674; ①), is eight miles north of town along the N77, but the setting – a sixteenth-century fort in lush meadows – makes up for the inconvenience. *Buggy's* buses (☎41264) run from Kilkenny Castle to Jenkinstown (Mon–Sat 11.30am & 5.30pm); for the return journey buses depart from the hostel to town (Mon–Sat 8.10am & 2.50pm). A minibus service has just started, which also does trips to local sights – check with the hostel for details.

The city

Kilkenny is focused on the hill and its castle. Climbing **Rose Inn Street** from the river brings you to the tourist office (see opposite), housed in the sixteenth-century **Shee Alms House**, one of the very few Tudor almshouses to be found in Ireland. A **walking tour** of the city leaves from here six times a day (£2.50). At the top of Rose Inn Street to the left is the broad stretch known as **The Parade**, which leads up to the castle. Formerly used for military and civic ceremonies, it now serves as a bus park in summer. To the right, the High Street soon becomes the busy main thoroughfare of **Parliament Street**, then continues through Irishtown towards the cathedral. Crooked and intriguing, little medieval slips and alleyways duck off it, while there's more substantial interest in the eighteenth-century **Tholsel**, with its stone pillars and arches. This was once the centre of the city's financial dealings, and is now the town hall.

Of all the surviving buildings from the prosperous Tudor commercial period, **Rothe House** (April–Oct Mon–Sat 10.30am–5pm, Sun 3–5pm; Nov & Dec Mon–Sat 1–5pm, Sun 3–5pm; Jan–March Sat & Sun 3–5pm; £1.50) on Parliament Street is the finest. Home to the Kilkenny Archeological Society **museum**, and a newly opened **costume gallery** of waistcoats, bonnets and gowns from the eighteenth century onwards, the building itself is a unique example of an Irish Tudor merchant's home dating back to 1594, and comprises three separate houses linked by interconnecting courtyards. There is also a genealogical research centre here for those wanting to trace their roots locally.

Kilkenny Castle

It's the **castle** (April–May daily 10am–5pm; June–Sept daily 10am–7pm; Oct–March Mon–Tues 10.30am–12.45pm & 2–5pm, Sun 11am–12.45pm & 2–5pm; guided tours only; £3), an imposing building standing high and square over the river, that really defines Kilkenny. Dating originally from the twelfth century, it was much added to in the seventeenth and nineteenth centuries. While the furnishings and paintings suggest a civilized wealth and domesticity, the scale and grandeur of the rooms, with their deeply recessed windows and robust fireplaces, signify a much cruder political power. The biggest surprise is the flimsy wooden hammer-beam roof of the **picture gallery**, covered with the folksy, pre-Raphaelite decoration of John Hungerford Pollen – plenty of gold and burnt umber plant life smudging its way across the ceiling. The newly renovated bedrooms of the west wing have recently re-opened and house an exhibition of nineteenth-century furniture.

Also within the castle is the **Butler Gallery**, housing an exhibition of modern art. You can take a break in the **tearoom** (May–Sept, closing 5.30pm) in the castle's former kitchen – you don't have to pay the castle entrance fee to visit either the Butler Gallery or the tearoom. The eighteenth-century stables, opposite the castle, have been converted into *The Design Centre*, an outlet for high-quality Irish crafts.

The cathedral, round tower and churches

The other must in Kilkenny is **St Canice's Cathedral** (Mon–Sat 9am–1pm & 2–6pm, Sun 2–6pm). It was built in the thirteenth century, and the purity and unity of its architecture lends it a grandeur beyond its actual size. Rich in carvings, it has an exemplary selection of sixteenth-century monuments, many in black Kilkenny marble, the most striking being effigies of the Butler family.

The **Round Tower** (50p) next to the church is all that remains of the early monastic settlement reputedly founded by Saint Canice in the sixth century; there are superb views from the top – ask anyone working in the church or churchyard for access (if you want to climb the tower during June, July and August be there before 6pm; arrangements are more flexible at other times).

Kilkenny is littered with the remains of other medieval churches. The **Black Abbey**, founded by Dominicans in 1225, has been carefully restored and contains some unusual carvings and sepulchral slabs. On the other side of town, **St John's Priory** has only a roofless chancel, a fine seven-light window and a medieval tomb. Thirteenth-century **St Francis's Abbey** stands in ruins by the river.

Eating, drinking and music

There are plenty of good choices for **food** in Kilkenny, in a multitude of pubs and restaurants. A couple of good Italian places are the budget-priced and tremendously popular *Italian Connection*, Parliament Street (☎64225), and *Ristorante Rinuccini* opposite the castle (☎51288), which is much more pricy during the evenings but manages a broodingly sensual atmosphere. *Emerald Gardens* Chinese restaurant, Parliament Street (☎61812), has a good reputation. If you want a more medieval atmosphere try *Alice's* restaurant (☎21064; daily till 9pm), with main courses from £6; *Lautrec's*, 9 St Kieran Street (12.30–3pm & 5.30pm–1am, Sun evenings only; ☎62720), is the best bistro/wine bar in town. The finest restaurant of all is out on the Dublin Road at *Lackan House* (dinner £22 Tues–Sat; ☎61085).

For cheaper eating, *M.L. Dore* delicatessen and restaurant, 65 High Street, serves great-value hot dinners and varied salads under £4 (daily 8am–10pm); *Crottys*, at no. 92 (Mon–Sat till 5.30pm), also offers good-value hot lunches and excellent pastries and cappuccinos. Lunches at the *Kilkenny Design Centre* (till 5pm) are similarly reasonably priced, and the tearoom in Kilkenny Castle (see above) is worth visiting for the setting and the cakes. Arguably the best **chip shop** in town is the one up beyond the campsite in Patrick Street. There's good **pub food** on offer, too: the best is *Edward Langton's*, John Street (daily till 10pm); otherwise, try *Kyteler's Inn*, St Kieran Street (Mon–Sat till 6pm, Sun till 2pm), *The Caisleàn Uí Cuain*, Patrick Street, or the *Arch Bar* and *Shem's*, both in John Street. If you need picnic supplies, call in at *Shortis Wong* deli, John Street, for delicious bread, cheese and sandwiches.

Bars are as alluring in Kilkenny as anywhere in Ireland, and you won't be hard pushed to find **music** here either, though it will be a matter of luck as to what you get. The *Caisleàn Uí Cuain* is one of the youngest and liveliest; *John Cleere's* bar in

Parliament Street has traditional Irish and folk music on Mondays, plus a tiny theatre where they occasionally lay on drama and comedy; and *The Pumphouse*, also in Parliament Street, has bands virtually every night during summer and on Fridays and Saturdays during winter – a mix of blues, rock, folk and traditional. *The Watergate Theatre* (see below) sometimes runs evenings of Irish music, dance and storytelling – ask at the tourist board for details, and expect a cover charge; *Maggie's*, St Kieran Street, has traditional music on a Tuesday during summer. In John Street there's *The Arch Bar*, which encourages young rock, folk and blues bands (look out for posters around town), and *Teach Ósta Uí hAogaín* at no. 45, near the train station, has traditional music on Thursday nights. There are plenty more **traditional bars** around town; two favourites in High Street are *Jim Holland's* and *The Marble City Bar*. If you want to **disco** try *Nero's*, St Kieran Street (Thurs–Sun, £5 charge).

Entertainment – Arts Week

Other **entertainment** is fairly easy to come by in summer. *The Kilkenny People*, published on Wednesday, lists what's on in the city and the surrounding villages; and it is worth checking out the *Watergate Theatre*, Parliament Street (☎61674). One event to try to coincide with is the **Arts Week** festival, held one of the last two weeks in August. The emphasis is on classical music, but alongside this are literary readings, art exhibitions and jazz and folk sessions. All in all it's well worth catching, though you'll need to reserve accommodation some time in advance. A new festival at the beginning of June, *The Cat Laughs*, brings together comedians from all over the world.

Listings

Bank *Allied Irish Bank*, 3 High St; *M.L. Dore* restaurant, 65 High St (☎63374), will cash travellers' cheques, personal cheques and currency, and operates *Western Union* till 10pm daily.

Bike rental and repairs *Bikes 'n Beds*, 49 John St, offer guided bike tours from £2.50 as well as bike hire at £6 per day; *J.J. Wall*, Maudlin St (☎21236), is £7 per day, £30 per week, £30 deposit – a *Raleigh* drop-off point; *Kilkenny Rent-A-Bike*, Lower Patrick St (☎51399).

Books For Irish-interest books, maps and guides, try *The Book Centre* in the High St – they also have a wide selection of foreign newspapers.

Camping supplies *Kilkenny Camping and Watersports*, Kilkenny Arcade (upstairs), High St (☎64025).

Laundry *Bretts*, Michael St (☎63200).

Pharmacy *Michael O'Connell*, High St.

Police ☎22222.

Post office High St (Mon–Sat 9am–5.30pm, Wed opens 9.30am).

Swimming pool Michael St (☎21380 or 61631 ext. 222 for opening times).

Travel agent *Mannings Travel*, High St (closed for lunch 1–2pm; ☎22950).

Walking tours Leave six times a day outside the Shee Arms House, £2.50; details from tourist office.

The Dunmore Caves

If you ask about places of interest, the tourist office will doubtless direct you to the **Dunmore Caves** (mid-March to mid-June Tues–Sat 10am–4.15pm, Sun 2–4.15pm; mid-June to mid-Sept daily 10am–6.15pm; mid-Sept to mid-March Sat & Sun only 10am–4.15pm; £2), situated seven miles north of Kilkenny (take the N77 then the N78) on an isolated limestone outcrop of the Castlecomer plateau. In 1967 Viking coins and the skeletons of 46 women and children were found among the stalactites and stalagmites. It's thought that the Vikings attacked the native Irish, and the women and children hid in the caves for protection. The plan obviously failed, but the fact that the skeletons showed no broken bones suggests that the victims starved to death or were lost, or that the Vikings tried to smoke them out.

To reach the caves, rent a bike in Kilkenny, hitch out on the Castlecomer Road past the train station, or take *Buggy's* bus from The Parade at 12.30pm (Mon–Sat), returning at 3.40pm; it's a one-mile walk to the caves from the bus stop.

The Nore and Barrow rivers

Two rivers, the Nore and the Barrow, flowing magnificently through rich countryside, have long been of immense importance to the southeast. Formerly they were the chief means of communication, bringing prosperity to the heart of the region: the Nore brought trade to medieval Kilkenny, the Barrow to Carlow. Today they are treasured for their considerable beauty and are a real treat for fishers. The surrounding countryside is as pretty as you'll find anywhere, perfectly enjoyed on bike or on foot – the *South Leinster Way* dips down into some of the choicest spots. Plan a leisurely route, and you can meander your way through picturesque ancient villages and take in exceptional medieval ruins.

The Nore Valley

The **Nore Valley** is deservedly renowned for its beauty, the river rolling through lush countryside, past old villages and some engaging ruins. It is perhaps at its finest as it broadens to the south of Kilkenny, where, along the tributary King's River eight miles south of the city (take the R697 or the N10 and turn off at Stonyford), sits medieval **KELLS**. Set amidst lush pastureland, the tiny village is an unexpected sight: its broad bridge is majestically out of scale, an ancient stone water mill stands on the river bank, and the encompassing deep hollow is flecked with mallows, marsh marigolds, docks and irises. Hard by, the magnificent ruin of **Kells Priory** – founded in 1193 – sits like a perfect scale model of a medieval walled city, a clean iron-grey against the surrounding green fields. The ruins consist of a complete curtain wall with square towers and fortified gatehouse, and the remnants of the fourteenth- and fifteenth-century church form one of the most impressive and largest medieval sites in Ireland. This town has nothing to do with the Book of Kells, which is associated with Kells in County Meath, though ironically enough the remains at that far more famous site are considerably less exciting than these.

Signposted from Kells, two miles south, are **Kilkree Round Tower** – just one of the many round towers scattered around this part of the country – and the nearby **high cross**, decorated with much-eroded biblical carvings. Alternatively, you can take the road east out of Kells and past Stonyford to placid **Jerpoint Abbey** (mid-April to mid-June Tues–Sun 10am–1pm & 2–5pm; mid-June to end Sept daily 9.30am–6.30pm; end Sept to mid-Oct 10am–1pm & 2–5pm; rest of the year, collect the key from the caretaker at the fourth house on the left; £2, Heritage Card). The abbey follows a typical Cistercian-Gothic layout around an elegant, cloistered garden, and is built of warm, oat-coloured stone, generally visited for its tombs and twelfth-century carvings – especially the animated figures in the cloister.

If you want to **camp**, *Nore Valley Park* (☎056/27229), about two miles along the Stonyford Road from Bennettsbridge, is a neat, family-geared site with animals for kids to look at.

Thomastown and Inistioge

A mile north of Jerpoint is **THOMASTOWN**. Formerly a medieval walled town of some importance, it's now simply a picturesque country town on the Kilkenny–Waterford train line. Minimal ruins of the walls, a castle and a thirteenth-century church (with some weathered effigies) remain, and in the Catholic church you'll find the high altar from Jerpoint. If you want to stop over, the *Bridge Brook Arms* (☎056/24152; ④) does **B&B**. For a little more you can stay in a restored medieval tower, *The Tower House* on Low Street (☎056/24500 or 24234; ④). *The Watergarden* tearoom run by the local Camphill Community makes a refreshing place for a break, and there are plenty of places doing **pub lunches**. *Rapid Express Club Coaches* operate a cheap **bus** to Dublin and Waterford three times a day, picking up at *K. Mullins'* shop by the bridge (☎056/31106 for timetable).

If you're heading north, it's worth visiting the **restored garden** not far from Kilfane (May–Sept Tues–Sun 2–6pm, or by appointment with Susan Mosse, ☎056/24558; £3; teas on Sun), a steep glen, complete with *cottage orné*, waterfall and hermit's grotto, that is an unusual Irish example of the Romantic craze for constructing "wild" landscapes in the back garden. To get to the garden, turn right two miles north of Thomastown on the N9 (before you get to Kilfane), then right again, following the signposts. In **KILFANE** itself, a ruined church holds the fourteenth-century **Cantwell Effigy**, an impressive piece of stone carving of a knight in full armour.

INISTIOGE, a few miles southeast of Thomastown on the R700, boasts a tree-lined square beside a fine stone bridge. The village is dotted with crumbling stonework, and little eighteenth- and nineteenth-century houses climb the steep lane that twists away from its centre. The grounds of the local estate, **Woodstock**, are open to the public if you fancy a stroll overlooking the neighbouring countryside, but the house itself was burnt down in 1922 after it had been occupied by the Black and Tans (see *Contexts*). For **accommodation**, the beautifully situated *Kookaburra House* B&B is on Rock Road (☎056/58519; ③) – head over the bridge towards New Ross, turn left, and follow the lane for just under a mile. There's no pub grub available in the village, but the *Old Schoolhouse Café* serves tea, homemade cakes and local salmon (May–Sept daily 11am–6.30pm; March & April Sat & Sun only). *The Motte* restaurant offers an adventurous menu for around £18.50, and reputedly keeps an exceptionally good red house wine (☎056/58655; booking essential); the *Guinness* at *The Castle Inn* gets a similarly good press.

The Barrow Valley

For **walking**, the stretch of **South Leinster Way** northeast from Inistioge is particularly pretty and offers a couple of pleasant places to rest up. The dusty little market town of **GRAIGUENAMANAGH** (you can also reach here by road from Inistioge and Thomastown) stands in a lovely spot beside the **River Barrow**, with herons fishing in the rushing weir. The town's great age is indicated by the central **Duiske Abbey** which dominates Graiguenamanagh. Founded in 1204, it was the largest Cistercian abbey in Ireland, and although much has been altered and added outside (including a nineteenth-century clock tower and pebble-dashed walls), the thirteenth-century interior has been lovingly preserved. Besides some original fleur-de-lys tiling and a fine effigy of a knight in chain mail, most impressive is the superb Romanesque processional doorway to the right of the organ – heavily decorated and one of the best to have survived the Reformation. In the churchyard, near the steps outside the south transept, stand a couple of ninth-century stone crosses, and a sixth-century font from Ullard stands outside the north wall of the chancel. The **Abbey Centre** nearby (daily 10am–1pm & 2–6pm; winter Mon–Fri only) displays interesting contemporary religious art exhibitions.

If you need **B&B** in Graiguenamanagh you can try the plush *Waterside* (☎0503/24246 or 24737; dormitory ③, B&B ④), a beautifully restored stone building overlooking the river, or *The Anchor Bar* (☎0503/24207; ③). The pub also serves **food** all day every day (Sun till 2pm). The *Waterside* has an expensive restaurant; while *The Old Bakehouse* (daily 10am–6pm; ☎0503/24700), just opposite the abbey, has a more extensive menu of similar fare.

St Mullins

Five miles south down the towpath (also on the R729), **ST MULLINS** is tucked away from the river among wooded hills, with the open heights of the Blackstairs Mountains beyond. Strolling through the village, you'll come across the scant remains of a monastery, founded in 696AD by Saint Moling, Bishop of Ferns and Glendalough, and alongside them in the churchyard are the base of a round tower and a very worn stone cross. Down beside the stream, at the back of the ruins, a path leads to St Moling's Well, while near the centre of the village stands a defensive earthwork, looking like a sturdy pudding just shaken from its bowl. You might want a break here, too: *Teaċ Moling* down by the river (follow the steep lane down beside the church) is one of the prettiest places to stop and **eat** round these parts, offering anything from soups and sandwiches through to dinner (with plenty of salmon from the river), and it's all reasonably priced (Easter–Oct; ☎051/24665; daily till 7.30pm); alternatively *Blanchfield's* **pub** does less imaginative soup and sandwiches anytime. *Teaċ Moling* also offers **B&B** (☎051/24665; ④), or you can **camp** on the village green. The nearest shop is at Glynn, one and a half miles away.

Borris and Mount Leinster

Following the South Leinster Way north from Graiguenamanagh, along the Barrow, you'll reach tiny **BORRIS**, just over the border in County Carlow. It's not especially attractive aside from its fresh air and one broad (fast) main road, the R729, that sweeps down towards a striking backdrop formed by the ash-mottled Blackstairs Mountains, but it's as good a place as any to stop in the area. *Mrs Susan Breen* in Church Street does **B&B** (☎0503/73231; ④). You can **camp** by the disused train line, getting provisions from *O'Shea's* bar and shop. *Kiernan's* petrol station (☎0503/73211) is open for cheap **bike rental** (Mon–Sat until 9pm; £4 a day, £24 a week).

The Green Drake Inn serves snacks and lunches every day till 6pm, and more expensive **meals** until 9.30pm. Considering its size, there's a lot going on in Borris, with live **music** several nights of the week, mostly in the singalongs and ballads category: try *The Green Drake Inn*, *O'Connors* or *O'Shea's*. This last doubles up as a hardware shop so you can sup your pint leaning on a bacon slicer, keeping a weather-eye on the hacksaws and sink plungers dangling from the ceiling.

East of Borris, the South Leinster Way leaves the intimate landscape of the valleys, crossing the open farmland of south Carlow and eventually skirting the bleak height of **Mount Leinster**. The way finally descends to the lonely cluster of houses which is Kildavin, six miles or so from Mount Leinster on the main Carlow–Enniscorthy Road.

travel details

Trains

Kilkenny to: Carlow (4 daily; 35min); Dublin (4 daily; 1hr 40min).

Rosslare Harbour to: Dublin (3 daily; 3hr 10min).

Wexford to: Dublin (3 daily; 2hr 30min); Rosslare Pier (3 daily; 30min).

Bus Éireann

Kilkenny to: Dublin (9 daily; 2hr 5min).

Rosslare Harbour to: Cork (2–6 daily; 2hr 55min); Dublin (4–6 daily; 3hr 10min); Limerick (3–4 daily; 4hr).

Wexford to: Dublin (5 daily; 2hr 45min); Kilkenny (summer only 1 daily; 1hr 40min); Rosslare Harbour (6 daily; 20min).

Private buses

Kavanagh's buses serve **Urlingford** daily (☎056/31106 or 31272) on the Thurles–Dublin route, handy if you then want to hitch to **Cashel**.

Waterford Travel Club (☎051/77177) serve **Thomastown**, **Gowran** and **Carlow** on their daily Waterford–Dublin route.

Funtrek (☎01/873 0852) run a daily service **from Wexford to Dublin**, leaving from The Crescent (Mon–Sat 8am, Sun 6.30pm & 8pm); also serving Arklow, Gorey and Rosslare. **Departs Rosslare** half an hour earlier.

Ardcavan Coach Company (☎053/22561) operate a service **from Rosslare**, outside the chapel (Mon–Sat 7.30am, Sun 7.30pm) and **from Wexford to Dublin**, leaving from The Crescent (Mon 6am & 8am, Tues–Sat 8am, Fri 2pm, Sun 6pm & 8pm). Returns from Dublin daily (*Gresham Hotel*, O'Connell St, Mon–Thurs & Sat 6pm;

Kildare St, Fri 4.30pm, 6pm & 8pm; Sun departs *Penny's*, O'Connell St at 9pm & 10.15pm; £6 day return, £8 monthly return).

Kavanagh's (☎056/31106) run a **Cashel–Kilkenny** service, Mon–Sat departs Cashel 7.25am, 2.02pm; Kilkenny Parade 11.15am, 5.45pm.

New Princess Coach Services (☎01/679 1549 or ☎056/31555) depart Dublin (*Gresham Hotel*, O'Connell St) twice daily for **Kilkenny** and **Clonmel**.

Quantabus (☎01/729644 or ☎056/31534) depart Dublin (George's Quay) Mon–Sat 6pm for **New Ross**, **Arthurstown** and **Ballyhack**. Depart **New Ross** for Dublin Mon–Sat 7.45am, Sun 6pm; £6 single, £7 return.

Quantas buses depart New Ross (*L&N* supermarket) daily 8am for **Dublin**, returning from Dublin (Tara St, beside the DART) 5.30pm.

CHAPTER SIX

WATERFORD, TIPPERARY AND LIMERICK

T
he route from Waterford through Tipperary to Limerick is the quickest way
from the southeast, and the arrival points of the ferries, to the centre of western
Ireland. Yet it's the south, rather than the west, that has all the real appeal.
Both Tipperary, and to a certain extent Limerick, conceal pockets of scenic
splendour and can be a delight.

Waterford, whose coastline stretches west from the expanse of Waterford Harbour
towards Cork, combines many of the attractions of the south. Rolling green hills spread
down to a fine shore of cliffs interspersed with expansive bays and secluded beaches.
There's plenty of history around the county where **Lismore** and **Ardmore** preserve
extensive early Christian remains, and **Waterford city** itself has been an important port
since the Viking invasions. Nowadays the city preserves an ancient heart, but it's also a
thriving modern commercial centre, young and enjoyably lively to visit. Inland, rich farming country is contained by mountain ranges that offer excellent opportunities for easy,
scenic walking – and occasionally for more challenging exercise, above all the **Munster
Way** in the northwest, by which you can cross to Tipperary. All of this is contained within
a relatively small area, and if you wanted further confirmation that Waterford combines a
little of everything, it even has its own tiny *Gaeltacht* area, around **Ring** (An Rinn).

Straddling the border with County Tipperary, the **Knockmealdown Mountains**
offer similarly attractive walking, as do the **Galtees**, and the landscape reaches its
most sumptuous in the velvety slopes around the **Glen of Aherlow**. Scenery aside,
Tipperary's farming towns have little to offer the visitor. At the very heart of the county,
though, is a site of outstanding interest – the **Rock of Cashel**. A spectacular natural
formation topped with Christian buildings from virtually every period, it's effectively a
primer in the development of Irish ecclesiastical architecture. The historic sites at
Cahir and **Carrick-on-Suir** are also well worth taking in.

In **Limerick** you've arrived in the west of Ireland, but the county still has relatively
little to tempt you. Industrial and depressed, **Limerick city** has a luckless reputation.
Nonetheless, recent efforts do seem to be teasing out strands of elegance and interest
in its weather-worn Georgian streets and Norman castle. This said, it still can't

compare in terms of enjoyment with the other big towns of the south and west. Inland, the county continues the rich pasture of Tipperary, and perhaps its greatest attraction is the exceptional number of medieval **castles** and towers that dot the landscape; immaculately preserved **Castle Matrix** in the west is one of the finest anywhere. There's also an extremely important Neolithic site at **Lough Gur**, in the heart of the county, and at **Adare** a famously quaint village. In the end, though, Limerick is somewhere you go through to get to counties Clare or Kerry.

COUNTY WATERFORD

Photographs rarely do justice to the beauty of **Waterford**. Its strengths lie in a broad grandeur of scale and richness of colour, dark greens and ruddy sandstone reds. In the **south**, grand hills rise gradually from coast and valley, their slopes cloaked with plantations of fir trees. The smoothly sculpted **coastline** is of bold proportions, low cliffs giving views over large, open bays. The mountains in the **north** lose the prettiness of their wooded valleys as they rise – not dramatically, but describing gradual, open heights, offering long walks with stupendous views over the plains of Tipperary. Central to the county, Waterford's **river valleys** are luxuriant and fertile, the finest being that of the **Blackwater**, which rolls through rich farmland with a real majesty. Here, it's obvious why the county was so attractive to foreign invaders – Viking, Norman and English. The influence of wealthy colonists is clear, their opulence reflected in remnants of stately, elegant estates.

The county and the city of Waterford developed quite separately. The city was initially a Viking settlement that became a Norman stronghold and thrived as an independent city-state with a major share of Ireland's European trade. While the city prospered as a mercantile centre, the surrounding county lived off farming and fishing, retaining much of its Celtic identity. The Vikings and Normans were not the first newcomers to leave their mark: the area of **Old Parish** around Ardmore gets its name as the arrival point of Saint Declan in the first half of the fifth century, supposedly the very first of Ireland's proselytizing Christians, preceding Saint Patrick. The region's early Christian foundations became influential across the country, the most important being that at **Lismore**, founded in 636. It flourished first as a centre of ecclesiastical learning, and later as a secular power rivalling that of Waterford city itself.

Today the distinctions between urban and rural remain marked. Alongside thriving, modern Waterford city, pockets of ancient cultures and histories survive, such as the tiny Irish-speaking community of **Ring** and the historic ecclesiastical foundations of **Ardmore** and **Lismore**. An air of prosperity pervades the county as a whole, in farmland enriched by centuries of cultivation and in the renewed commercial importance of the historic port of Waterford city. The coast offers sandy beaches, a handful of quaint fishing harbours and some great seascapes. It's easily accessible, too – notably good main roads serve city and county, good for long-distance **cycling** and **hitching**.

Waterford

WATERFORD's appearance from the river is deceptively grim: the bare and open stretch of water with the ugly grey wharves and cranes of the working port holds no suggestion of the lively city pulsating behind its dull quays. This is the commercial capital of the southeast; and yet it retains buildings from Viking and Norman times, and from the eighteenth century, all periods of past eminence. The web of narrow streets that grew up as the focus for commercial activity in the city's earliest days holds the modern city together in compact dynamism. While Waterford has had the modern

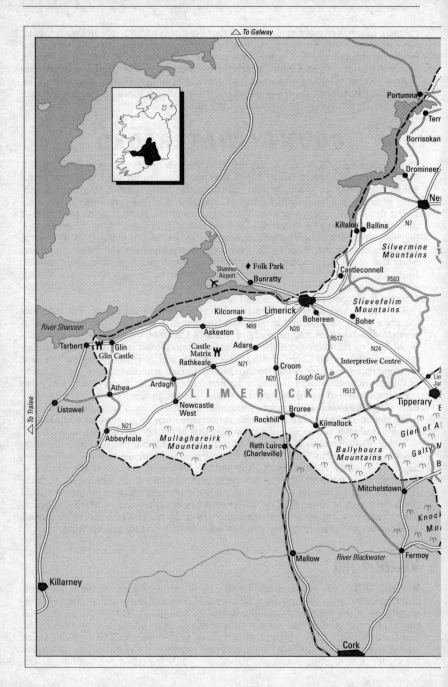

△ To Galway

Portumna
Terr
Borrisokan
Dromineer
Ne
Killaloe Ballina
N7
Silvermine Mountains
T
Castleconnell
R503
Shannon Airport
◆ Folk Park
Bunratty
Slievefelim Mountains
Kilcornan
Limerick
Bohereen
Boher
Askeaton
N69
N20
River Shannon
R512
Tarbert
Glin
Glin Castle
Castle Matrix
Adare
N24
Interpretive Centre
Rathkeale
N21
Croom
Lim
Jur
N20
Lough Gur
Athea
Ardagh
L I M E R I C K
R513
Tipperary
E
△ To Tralee
Listowel
Newcastle West
Bruree
Rockhill
Kilmallock
Glen of A
N21
Galty
Abbeyfeale
Mullaghareirk Mountains
Rath Luirc (Charleville)
Ballyhoura Mountains
B
Mitchelstown
Knoc
Mou
Killarney
Mallow
River Blackwater
Fermoy
Cork

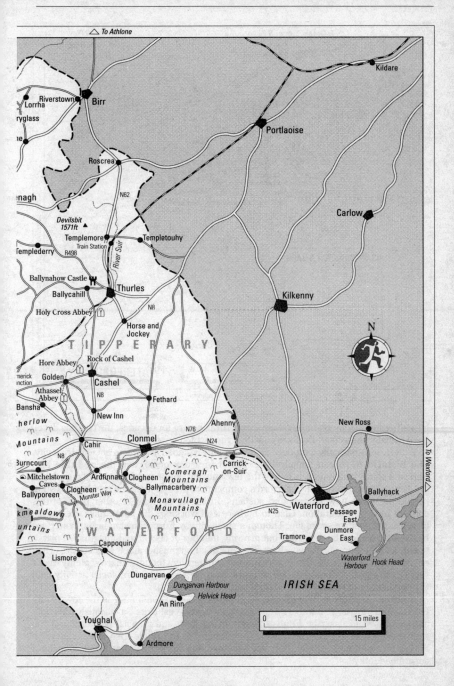

To Clonmel, Kilkenny & Dublin

To New Ross & Wexford

Train & Bus Stations

River Suir

Clock Tower

Holy Trinity Cathedral

Heritage Centre

Chamber of Commerce

The French Church

Christ Church Cathedral

City Hall

Reginald's Tower

Peoples Park

To Waterford Airport, Dunmore East & Passage East

ACCOMMODATION & BARS
1 Dooleys Hotel
2 Egan's Pub
3 Geoff's Pub
4 Granville Hotel
5 O'Connell House
6 Opus 1 Restaurant
7 Portree Guest House
8 The Pulpit Pub
9 Viking House Hostel

0   400yds

WATERFORD CITY

To Cork, Fermoy, Tramore & Dungarven

infrastructure of a mercantile, rather than a rural, centre for decades, the city has developed socially and economically even within the last ten years.

Waterford is basically a modern European port wrapped around an ancient Irish city. The **historic town** can happily be explored in a day or so, and the **nightlife** also warrants some sampling. It is one of the few buoyant commercial centres of any size in the Republic, and a sign of Waterford's comparative prosperity is the number of young people the place now attracts and sustains, in strong contrast to other parts of this country bled by emigration. Glad to be here and working, the youth have created an increasingly positive social life. Though a small city by European standards, Waterford has some excellent bars, a small but growing number of decent and imaginative places to eat, and the burgeoning youth/rock scene of an optimistic, albeit small-scale, urban environment. Alongside the city's vigorous modernity, though, there's plenty that's traditional, most obviously the place of the **pub** as a focal point of social activity, and the persistence of **music** as an integral part of city life.

A further measure of Waterford's social and economic confidence is the town's attitude towards the large numbers of people known as "West Brits", a curiously affectionate term used to describe English people living here and a social peculiarity of the southeast. Either recently arrived or, if remnants of the Anglo-Irish Ascendancy, no longer representing a threat, they are accepted and have integrated while keeping a separate identity.

Some history

The deep, navigable **River Suir** has been the source of the city's importance since the tenth century. Waterford has an excellent harbour; deep inland, and therefore easily defended, it was also perfectly positioned for the internal trading routes of the Barrow and the Nore rivers, reaching into the heart of the southeast's rich farmland. Reliable recorded history of the city starts with the **Viking** settlement founded in the tenth century. The layout of the city (so similar to that other Viking town, Wexford) retains its Viking roots, the very long quays and adjacent narrow lanes forming the trading centre. Waterford was the most important Viking settlement in Ireland, and its inhabitants were so feared that even the bellicose Celtic Déisí had to pay them tribute – failure to pay *Airgead Sróine* (Nose Money) resulted in having your nose chopped off. Reginald's (originally Ranguald's) Tower dates from this time, as do some of the remains of the city walls. Nearby, two well-preserved stone arches inside the *Reginald Grill Bar* were in fact "sallyports", through which ships entered the fortified city from what is now The Mall but was then water.

The next wave of invaders to leave their mark were the **Anglo-Normans** in the twelfth century. When the King of Leinster, Dermot MacMurrough, made his bid for the High Kingship of Ireland, he knew Waterford was strategically vital for control of the southwest. In 1170, he called on his Welsh Anglo-Norman allies, the most important of these being the Earl of Pembroke, or **Strongbow**, to attack the city. The city walls and towers were formidably strong, but on the third day of attack, August 25, the Normans discovered a weak point, made a breach and flooded in, taking the city with scenes of bloodcurdling violence. Strongbow received his reward: Dermot MacMurrough's daughter Aoife's hand in marriage, and her inheritance. The wedding celebrations took place in Reginald's Tower; the marriage was the first such alliance between a Norman earl and an Irish king, a crucial and symbolic historical event.

The following year, surprised at the Welsh-Norman lords' success, **Henry II** arrived with an awesome display of naval strength (400 ships) and gave the Waterford Normans a charter offering protection – his way of ensuring allegiance to the English crown. Subsequent English monarchs maintained this allegiance, and in 1210 King John arrived with a huge army and enlarged the city with new fortifications. The best-preserved towers of these **Norman walls** are at Railway Square, Castle Street, Stephen Street and Jenkins Lane. During the thirteenth century, the city was the unspoken capital of Ireland. It reaped further royal favour through its part in bringing to ground two would-be usurpers threatening Henry VII: first Lambert Simnel in 1487, then Perkin Warbeck eight years later.

Waterford flourished as an important European port into the sixteenth and seventeenth centuries, **trading** with England, France, Spain and Portugal, and Newfoundland during the eighteenth and early nineteenth centuries, as well as maintaining its inland commerce. It was the only city in Ireland to withstand **Cromwell**, though his forces returned under the command of General Ireton, who took the city without the usual scenes of carnage, giving its citizens honourable terms. The city's importance in trade continued into the eighteenth century, and there's plenty of architectural evidence, both ecclesiastical and secular, of this period's prosperity. The name Waterford is nowadays most famous for its **crystal**, first produced in 1783. The factory closed in 1851 but re-opened in 1951 and is now one of the city's major employers.

The telephone code for Waterford city is ☎051.

Arrival, information and accommodation

Roads from the north and the east converge on the river at the **train** (☎73401) and **bus** (☎79000) **stations**; the city lies over the bridge to the south. Regular daily **trains** connect Waterford to Clonmel, Tipperary, Limerick, Wexford, Kilkenny and Dublin. *Rapid Express Club Travel* (see "Travel Details" at the end of this chapter) operates a cheap **bus service** to Dublin and Tramore. Buses leave from outside the *Bank of Ireland*, Parnell Street. There are scheduled **flights** to London daily from **Waterford Regional Airport**, Killowen (☎75589). There's no bus to the airport: a taxi will cost you around £8–10.

The **tourist office** is at 41 Merchants Quay (April & Sept Mon–Sat 9am–5.15pm; May & June 9am–6pm; July & Aug Mon–Sat 9am–7pm, Sun 10am–5pm; Oct–March Mon–Fri 9am–1pm & 2–5.15pm; ☎75788), roughly midway between the bridge and the nineteenth-century clock tower. It has a comprehensive list of Waterford's **hotels and B&Bs**. The cheaper establishments are concentrated along Parnell Street, The Mall and O'Connell Street: you'll find the best of the central possibilities recommended below.

An excellent new **independent hostel** has just opened – *Viking House*, Coffee House Lane, Greyfriars (*IHH*, open all year; ☎53827, fax ☎71730; ②). If this turns out to be full, and you're contemplating staying in any other hostel accommodation in Waterford, we strongly advise you to talk to the tourist office before booking your bed. There's no **campsite** within walking distance of the city.

Hotels and B&B

Beechwood, 7 Cathedral Square (☎76677). Standard B&B; open March–Nov. ③.

Derrynane House, 19 The Mall (☎75179). Good, plain B&B; open March–Aug. ③.

Dooley's, 30 The Quay (☎73531, fax ☎70262). Fine central location for this upmarket hotel. ⑥.

Foxmount Farm, Passage East Rd (☎74308). Four miles from town, off the Dunmore Rd, this farmhouse B&B also does excellent evening meals. ④.

The Granville Hotel, The Quay (☎55111, fax ☎70307). Swish, well-run hotel in good location. ⑦.

Mrs O'Brien's, 2 New St (☎75764). Another good B&B. ③.

O'Connell House, O'Connell St (☎74175). Welcoming and central. ③.

Portree Guest House, Mary St (☎74574). Friendly, comfy and clean. ③.

The city

Waterford is centred on a lovely wedge of Georgiana, between the eighteenth-century shops and houses of **O'Connell** and **George** streets, which run behind the modern quays, and the decaying splendour of **Parnell Street** and **The Mall** with their fine doorways and fanlights. These last converge on **Reginald's Tower**, and the angle the two thoroughfares describe is arced by the extensive remains of Viking and Norman city walls. The area immediately behind the quays is still the city's commercial centre. Continue from **Barronstrand Street** through all its changes of name down to where **John Street** meets Parnell Street, and you find a great concentration of fast-food joints and bars. The area of lanes between The Mall and **Parade Quay** contain some of the city's nicest juxtapositions of medieval and eighteenth-century architecture.

Reginald's Tower and the French Church

Waterford's most historic building is **Reginald's Tower**, a large cylindrical late twelfth-century tower, its design similar to the Scottish *broch*, with a concealed stairway built within its massive wall; the original Viking tower which stood here was built in 1003. It houses the city's **museum** (April–May Mon–Fri 10am–1pm & 2–6pm, Sat 10am–1pm; June–Oct Mon–Fri 10am–8pm, Sat 10am–1pm & 2–5pm; winter contact City Hall in The Mall; £1), which has an impressive collection of royal charters that make quite clear the central role Waterford's allegiance to the English crown played in the city's history. The collection includes the Charter Roll of Richard II (1399), a fabulous transcript of earlier charters.

Wander up Bailey's New Street just behind Reginald's Tower and you immediately come to Waterford's other important medieval building, the **French Church**, or Greyfriars. Founded by Franciscans in 1240, the church served as an almshouse in the sixteenth century, and from 1693 to 1815 was used as a place of worship by French Huguenot refugees, whom the city sheltered in their exile from persecution at home. It's now a solid, roofless ruin with a complete tower and fine east triple-lancet window. Stones at the base of the outer windows have comic carved figures, and the church has some interesting carved slabs, including that of Sir Neal O'Neill, who accompanied James II in his flight from the Battle of the Boyne; you can borrow keys from the house directly opposite.

Heritage Centre and the cathedral
Just off to the right of Bailey's New Street, in Greyfriars Street, the **Waterford Heritage Centre** is housed in a small, old church (hours same as Reginald's Tower; £1). This is arguably Ireland's most exciting new museum: in 1987–88 extensive excavations of a large portion of the city's old Viking and Norman centre (prior to building development) resulted in finds of quite exceptional quality and variety, dating largely from the early eleventh century. The Heritage Centre displays the best of these, including leather footwear, antler combs, intricately wrought brooches, lathe-turned wooden bowls, weaponry and ceramic vessels. The collection should grow as conservation work continues, and even now it's worth inspecting.

Further up Bailey's New Street, you enter Waterford's next significant period of church building at the Church of Ireland **Christ Church Cathedral** (May–Oct Mon–Fri 10am–1pm & 2–4.30pm, though this does vary). Rebuilt in the 1770s by John Roberts, who did much work in Waterford for both Catholics and Protestants, it's a nicely proportioned building in soothing cream and grey, with a fine steeple and a spacious interior with an elaborate stucco ceiling. The monuments inside the cathedral are worth a look, in particular that of James Rice (1482), a gruesome effigy of a corpse in an advanced state of decay, with various creatures crawling in and out of the carcass.

Roberts was also responsible for **Holy Trinity Cathedral** in Barron Strand Street. Originally built in 1793, this was greatly altered during the nineteenth century to become the curving, heavy extravaganza it is today. It's a swirling exercise in decoration, hung with Waterford chandeliers and striving for maximum opulence. The city's history of religious tolerance is reflected not only in the shared architect of both Catholic and Protestant cathedrals, but also in the little church of **St Patrick's**, tucked up a lane off Great George's Street. Built in the mid-eighteenth century, it remained a Catholic church throughout Penal times and as such is unique. It seems that mercantile strength gave Waterford considerable cultural independence, and Catholics were allowed to hold services here – in stark contrast to the suppression that went on in the rest of the country. Funding came from the sons of Waterford merchants who settled in Spain during the eighteenth century, and dark and dolorous paintings hang either side of the altar, revealing a heavy Spanish influence.

City Hall, Georgian architecture and Waterford crystal
Christ Church apart, it's in the city's secular architecture that the best of the eighteenth century is realized. Christ Church Cathedral looks down over The Mall where the **City Hall** (built in 1788 by John Roberts) has a spacious entrance hall that was once used as a meeting place and merchants' exchange. It's now the council building, but if you are interested in Waterford crystal ask at the desk to see pieces from the original glassworks, including a huge **chandelier**. By far the finest eighteenth-century architectural detail in the city, though, is the oval staircase inside the lilac-coloured **Chamber of Commerce** in George Street (open office hours). Once again the work of John Roberts (1785), it's a beautiful cantilevered staircase with fine decorative stucco-

work. Georgian housing continues down O'Connell Street, where you'll also find the *Garter Lane Arts Centre*, at numbers 5 and 22a (see opposite).

If you want to follow up on Waterford Crystal (which is of course for sale all over town), the **Waterford Crystal Glass Factory** offers tours (April–Oct daily 8.30am–4pm; Nov–March Mon–Fri 9am–3.15pm; £2.50) around its glass-cutting and blowing workshops. This is interesting if you've never seen the process before, and a fair way to work up an appetite on a wet day, but not the "absolute must" the publicity tends to suggest. Tours take about forty minutes and in high season it's advisable to book in advance; the tourist office will do this for you free of charge, or you can do it yourself on ☎73311. Buses to the factory leave from beside the clock tower on the quays: ask the driver to put you off at the factory, which is located about a mile from the city centre, on the N25 to Cork.

River cruises

If you want to escape the city for a while, *Galley River Cruises'* **trips to New Ross** offer a unique view of the countryside. The cruise includes lunch, afternoon tea or evening meal (June–Aug, £5–17; book at tourist office or phone on ☎21723 or ☎73752). Alternatively, enquire at the tourist office about *Viking Cruises*.

Eating, drinking and entertainment

Finding something to **eat** is unlikely to prove a problem. There are plenty of **fast-food** joints down Michael Street and John Street, or for more substantial fare try the *Pantry*, behind *Chapman's Deli* on The Quay (Mon–Sat 8am–6pm: meals from £3.20). *Haricot's* on O'Connell Street (Mon–Fri 9am–8pm, Sat 9.30am–5.45pm) is a cosy and reasonably priced wholefood restaurant also catering well for vegetarians. **Pizza** and **pasta** are plentiful; *Gino's*, the Applemarket (daily noon–midnight), is cheery and serviceable, with pizzas from £2.50 and home-made Italian ice cream. *The Happy Garden*, 53 High Street, is the best **Chinese** restaurant in town, with meals from around £5.95. *Loughman's* coffee shop and restaurant, opposite the cathedral on Barronstrand Street, serves substantial breakfasts and meals throughout the day till 9pm. Best of all, though, is *Opus 1*, serving fresh, zappy bistro food at low prices (lunch Mon–Sat; dinner Tues–Sat) tucked away on Olaf Street, near Viking House.

For **pub food**, *Egans* in Broad Street (Mon–Sat noon–2.30pm) serves delicious home-made bread, soup and cooked lunches for around £4.50, as does *The Metropole*, Bridge Street; *Geoff's* bar on John Street has good sandwiches.

Drinking and the music scene

Waterford has some wonderful **bars**, and there is a steadily growing **music scene** here. John Street has two of the city's favourite watering holes – *Geoff's* and *The Pulpit* – both lively, young places with a good social mix, and useful for keying into what's happening in the city. *The Olde Rogue*, across the street on Applemarket, has a good mixed crowd and is another useful place to check out what music is on locally. In Michael Street, *The Old Stand* is a lively young bar, while *Barrs* on Mayors Walk is also young and friendly, and a good bet for women who don't want to be hassled. This pub has occasional **blues/jazz** sessions on a Monday. *Rourke's*, O'Connell Street, is another upbeat bar frequented by a young crowd with blues, rock and indie bands on occasional Sunday nights (£1, till 11.30pm); *M. Walsh's*, 11 Great George's Street, is a wonderful old bar-cum-shop of the type more usually found out in the country.

For **traditional music** there are a few regular spots: *T. & H. Doolans*, Great George's Street; *Mullanes*, Newgate Street, a singing pub; and *The Metropole*, Bridge Street (Mon). Out of town there's *Meade's Bar* at Halfwayhouse (☎73187), four miles down the road to Cheekpoint, with very good sessions on Wednesdays and at weekends. There is not a great deal of **jazz** in Waterford, but you could try *The Reginald*, next to Reginald's Tower.

If you are looking for **clubs**, *Preachers*, behind *The Pulpit* (opposite), is arguably the liveliest – and most bizarre – of Waterford's late-night options: indie and dance music (Wed–Sun £3–5, women free on Thursdays). *Metroland* is a pricier, straighter kind of disco, though there is no cover charge for the pop bands in the lounge next door. As everywhere, most of the hotels have discos at weekends. *The Bridge Hotel* on The Quay is a bit of a meat market, probably at its best at weekends, but it's also where big-name bands play.

Finally, Waterford's music scene would not be the same without the *Freewheelers*, a local bikers' club. They may look like Hell's Angels, but they're more interested in their bikes than in violence. It's well worth checking out gigs organized by them – usually in *O'Shea's* out at Tramore, for which they arrange buses so people don't have to drink and drive. They also organize a **custom and classic bike** weekend at Whitsun, which involves lots of bands, bonfires and camping. For further information about any of their events, ask those who display *Freewheeler* posters on their premises, or call in at *The Hog's Head* on the quays, something of a bikers' lair.

Arts and theatre

The *Garter Lane Arts Centre* (Tues–Sat 11am–6pm; ☎77153), with two locations at 5 and 22a O'Connell Street, has painting and sculpture exhibitions, a theatre and a good current events notice board. It's the place to catch a performance by *Red Kettle Theatre Company* (☎79688) and by a varied programme of touring companies. Waterford's other theatre is the *Theatre Royal*, on The Mall (☎74402), which stages the city's **Light Opera Festival** in October. The Regional Technical College on the main Cork Road is used for **classical music** recitals, generally advertised in the tourist office.

Listings

Bike Rental *Wright's Cycle Depot*, Henrietta St, off Parade Quay (☎74411). Bike rental, repairs and parts.

Dental emergencies South Eastern Health Board (Mon–Fri 9am–5pm; ☎76111). Ask to be put through to Newgate St Dental Clinic.

Hospital Waterford Regional Hospital, Ardkeen, Dunmore Rd (☎73321). Medical and dental emergencies out of office hours.

Laundry *Washed Ashore*, The Quay (Mon–Fri 8am–9pm, Sat 8.30am–6.30pm).

Rape Crisis Centre ☎73362 or PO Box 57, GPO, Waterford.

Shopping There's shopping until 9pm every Friday; the Applemarket is a general market held on Fridays and Saturdays.

Travel agents *USIT Youth and Student Travel Office*, 36–37 George St (☎72601). *Harvey Travel Ltd*, Gladstone St (☎72048 or ☎72784), is the agent for *Slattery* and *Funtrek*.

The Waterford coast

Waterford's coastline offers good sandy beaches and some breathtaking coastal walks. The open grandeur of bays like Dungarvan is offset by the intimacy of hidden fishing ports and pockets of ancient history at Ring and Ardmore. The best of the **beaches** are at **Dunmore East**, **Tramore**, **Annestown**, **Bunmahon** and **Ardmore**. Major seaside towns are connected to Waterford by regular bus services, but the choicest spots are best walked, cycled or slowly hitched to; using *Bus Éireann* to get to these involves a manipulation of the timetable verging on the miraculous.

Passage East and Ballyhack

Immediately east of Waterford city, at the neck of its long harbour, the pretty ferry village of **PASSAGE EAST** nestles under craggy hills, the estuary slopes aflame with wild gorse. The ferry here connects with Ballyhack in County Wexford (*Passage East Car Ferry* ☎051/ 382488, continuous services Mon–Sat 7.20am–8pm & Sun 9.30am–8pm; summer until 10pm; crossing time 10min; car and passengers £3.50 single, £5.50 return, pedestrians £1 return) – a particularly useful route east for cyclists, especially if you're making for Rosslare or want to stay with the coast. *The Farleigh Pub* in Passage East does a great range of **bar food** during the summer and sandwiches anytime of year. Across the water, less than a mile from Ballyhack, there's an *An Óige* **hostel** at Arthurstown (June–Sept; ☎051/389411; ②). Ballyhack should be as pretty as its Waterford counterpart but isn't, despite the fact that the village is dominated by a fine sixteenth-century tower house. It has one miserable bar and a very good seafood restaurant, *The Neptune*.

Dunmore East

Further around the Waterford coast, **DUNMORE EAST** settles snugly between small, chunky sandstone cliffs topped by masses of rambling golden gorse. The main street follows a higgledy-piggledy contour from the safe, sandy cove beside which the east village sits, towards a busy harbour full of the rippled reflections of brightly coloured fishing boats and cradled by the crooked finger of the harbour wall. From here, the ruddy sandstone cliffs make bold ribs around the coast. This is still a very active fishing harbour, but has also cashed in on its undeniable picturesqueness, with self-consciously new thatched houses sneaking in alongside the originals.

Quaint as it is, Dunmore East has become very much a playground for affluent Waterford people, and there are three large **hotels** to cater for them – the best being the *Haven* (☎051/383150; ⑤); at least this means there are plenty of facilities. You can get decent **pub food** at *The Ocean Hotel* (☎051/383136; ⑤) and the conservative *Candlelight Inn* (☎051/383215; ⑥); both have very middle-of-the-road singalongs by way of entertainment. *The Ship* (☎051/383141) restaurant and bar serves mostly sailors, visiting and local, and the food is excellent. The handiest reasonably priced **B&Bs** are Mrs Butler's *Church Villa* (☎051/383390; ④) and *Copper Beech*, Dock Road (☎051/ 383187; ④). If you are looking for a **hostel**, the new *Dunmore Harbour Hostel* (*IHH*, open all year; ☎051/383218, fax ☎383728; ②) is approved by the tourist board and also does B&B (③). For **camping**, there's *Strand Caravan Park* (June to mid-Sept; ☎051/ 383174). The **supermarket** is on Dock Road, and there's an *Allied Irish* **bank** with a Banklink machine always available. Dunmore East is the home of *Waterford Harbour Sailing Club* (☎051/383230), where an experienced sailor might get some crewing; and of the *Adventure Centre* (☎051/383783), which organizes canoeing and wind-surfing. Locals flock to McAlpin's *Suir Inn* at **CHECKPOINT**, a tiny fishing village (follow the signs off the Dunmore Road) for great **seafood** and fine *Guinness* (April–June Tues–Sat 6–10pm; July–Aug Mon–Sat 6–10pm; Sept & Oct Tues–Sat 6–10pm; Nov–March Wed–Sat 6–10pm; ☎051/382220).

Tramore to Dungarvan

Nine miles west of Dunmore East, **TRAMORE** caters for a different type of holidaymaker and a different kind of bank balance. It's a busy, popular seaside resort serving families from Waterford and Cork, and has plenty of amusements, caravans and B&Bs and a huge sandy beach. Hilary O'Sullivan's *Cliff House* on Cliff Road (☎051/381497; ④) is a friendly, comfy **B&B**. If you want **hostel** accommodation, *The Monkey Puzzle* on Upper Branch Road (*IHH*, open all year; ☎051/386754; ②) is tourist-board approved, and *The Cliff Accommodation* on Church Road (☎051/381363; ②) also has private rooms. *O'Shea's* is probably the liveliest **bar** in Tramore, very popular, with rock or blues every weekend; a good alternative watering-hole is the bar of *The Victoria Hotel*.

DUNGARVAN is the major coastal town of County Waterford, and its setting is magnificent. There's a wonderful view over the grand, broad bay as you descend to the town, the open heights around topped by pine forests that seem to have been poured on like thick syrup. The town itself is modern, with all the amenities that go along with that, as well as a fine beach at Clonea; again, a brand-new tourist-board–approved **hostel**, the *Dungarvan Holiday Hostel*, on Youghal Road, offers budget accommodation (*IHH*, open all year; ☎058/44340, fax ☎052/36141; ②). *An Bialann* on the square serves home-cooked food till 8.30pm on weekdays, and 7pm on Sundays. Of more interest and charm are the small communities along the coast to the west.

The An Rinn Gaeltacht

AN RINN, or Ring, is a pocket of Irish tradition hidden away on the modern Waterford coast. It's a tiny **Irish-speaking community** of about 1500 that has somehow survived in what is otherwise one of Ireland's more developed counties, all the more remarkable given the "West Brit" flavour of much of the county's coast. The language survives healthily, as do other traditions, notably music and set dancing.

It's quite tricky to find – signposts to An Rinn on the R674 (off the N25) are minimal – and hard to recognize when you do: like many *Gaeltacht* villages Ring consists of a community of farms and a handful of **bars** spread over a wide area, with no real centre. This can be frustrating if you don't have transport, as you have to rely on hitching to and from some of the best bars. *Mooney's* is the first pub on the way into Ring if you are travelling from Dungarvan and is a great spot for traditional music, and the owners will let you camp in their field; another good place to get your bearings is *Tigh an Cheoil* (☎058/46470), a bar down by the pier with traditional sessions on Thursdays, Saturdays and Sundays throughout the year, and at other times during the summer. The owners will put you in touch with whatever's going on in the area. Other bars for **traditional music** are *Murrays*, just over a mile away at Helvick, *The Marine Bar*, six miles west of Dungarvan on the N25, *The Seanachie*, signposted off the N25, and *John Paul Walsh's* bar, Old Parish – enquire locally for directions. Ask permission at *Murray's* bar to **camp** in the fields nearby.

Ring has some very pleasant **B&Bs**. Breda Maher's welcoming, well-run *Aisling*, Gurtnadiha, Ring (closed end June to mid-Aug; ☎058/46134; ③), is in a fabulous spot overlooking Dungarvan Harbour, or call Liam and Breda Maher at *Helvick View*, Ring (☎058/46297; ④).

There's nothing specific at Ring beyond the way of life. When the tide's out, you can walk a few miles along the shoreline west of the pier towards Dungarvan, and out along a sand spit. When the tide's in, a walk along the cliffs at **Helvick Head** gives splendid views of sculpted coastal cliffs and of the mountains inland.

Ardmore

ARDMORE is delightful, combining ancient history with a setting full of character. The fifth century saw the arrival here of Saint Declan, at least thirty years before Saint Patrick, and the surrounding area of **Old Parish** is so called because it's supposedly the oldest parish in Ireland. At Ardmore, a medieval **cathedral** and **round tower** stand on the site of the saint's original monastic foundation, commanding stunning views over Ardmore Bay. The long, low twelfth-century cathedral has massive buttresses, its stoutly rounded doors and windows confirming the proud – albeit roofless – Romanesque solidity of the building, while the slender round tower, tall and fine with a conical roof, stands alongside in poignant contrast. There are stones with early *ogham* inscriptions inside the cathedral, but the most exceptional carvings are on the west external wall. Romanesque arcading, originally from an earlier building, has been set here beneath the window, with boldly carved scenes showing the weighing of souls, the fall of man, the judgement of Solomon and the adoration of the Magi: truly impressive, and unique in quality and design. **Saint Declan's Oratory**, supposedly his burial site, also stands in the graveyard. Earth from the saint's grave is believed to protect them from disease.

The village down below – busy with people in summer – consists of a pleasant row of cottages, a few pubs, a shop and a couple of excellent sandy beaches. There's a small **hotel**, *Cliff House* (☎024/94106; ⑥), with good bar food, the **B&B** *Byron Lodge* (☎024/94157; ③), and a **caravan** and **camping** site. The welcoming *Paddy Mac's* pub does good bar food, and traditional sessions are held on Thursday nights and Sunday afternoons. A hostel is due to open shortly. Myth has it that when Saint Declan arrived here from Wales, his bell and vestments were magically carried by the large stone that now sits on the beach. This would explain why the boulder is completely different geologically from the surrounding land – though the Ice Age seems a more likely, if comparatively mundane, explanation. Another improbable tale is that crawling under the stone cures rheumatism. It looks unlikely that a fit person could squirm under it, let alone an invalid.

Walking through the village to the east, up the hill and to the path past the *Cliff House Hotel*, you come to the ancient **Saint Declan's Well** and a steeply gabled **oratory**. It's a moving spot, with fresh water springing beside three primitive stone crosses where pilgrims used to wash, and a stone chair. From here, there's a fine walk around the headland along rocky cliffs for five miles or so, as far as Whiting Bay; alternatively the waymarked path takes you over three miles and brings you back down by the round tower. In the future there should be more walking opportunities, as plans are afoot to open a new walking route, St Declan's Way, linking Cashel and Ardmore.

The Blackwater Valley and the Munster Way

Typical of the outstanding beauty of the inland county is the stretch of the **Blackwater Valley** around Cappoquin, where the river makes a sharp westward turn towards County Cork, describing as it goes the southerly limit of the Knockmealdown Mountains (also see p.223). **CAPPOQUIN** itself is prettily situated on a wooded hillside overlooking the river. Despite this beautiful location, the village seems strangely neglected, and there's little attempt to cater for visitors beyond a few B&Bs used mainly by a handful of fishermen at holiday times: if you want to **stay**, Mrs Flynn's *Riverview House* (☎058/54073; ③) is a friendly, central option. *Fawlty's* bar, Mill Street, occasionally does music, and serves lunches. The bar is so called due to the similarities between the owner and Basil Fawlty – though this one has considerably more charm. You'll get good home-cooked food at *The Saddlers* (Mon–Sat 7.30am–6pm), including marvellous breads baked in *Barrons'* Victorian ovens next door. *Richmond House* (☎058/54278; ⑤), on the way to Lismore, is the place for a more extravagant meal (dinner from about £20) and also does B&B. There's **music** every Saturday night at the *Central Bar*.

Although there's little to detain you in the village, the surrounding countryside is lovely. Walk half a mile east, take the right fork by the statue of the Virgin, and you come to the **Glenshelane River walk**. This follows the river through its deep valley banked by pine trees and, after about three miles, brings you to **Mount Melleray**, a Cistercian monastery that welcomes visitors in search of solitude. The trail eventually opens out to more level country, affording great views of the Knockmealdowns and the Galtee Mountains of Tipperary. In all, the walk's a taster for the varied terrain of the major long-distance walk in this part of the country, the Munster Way (see p.220).

Lismore

Set in the lovely broad plain of the Blackwater Valley three miles west of Cappoquin, **LISMORE** is a gem of ecclesiastical history. Roads approach the town between the river and gentle slopes of mixed woodland – especially beautiful in spring and autumn. The setting is dominated by the hugely romantic towers and battlements of **Lismore Castle**, whose pale, white-grey stone, set with mullioned windows, rises magnificently on the hill from glorious woodlands and sumptuous **gardens** (summer daily except Sat 1.45–4.45pm; £2), though hardly worth the steep entrance fee. The castle itself is a successful mid-nineteenth-century imitation of a Tudor castle, remodelled by Joseph Paxton (designer of London's Crystal Palace) around the remains of the medieval fort that originally stood here. The castle's long occupation by the Anglo-Irish aristocracy (and less permanent colonists, including Sir Walter Raleigh) explains why so much of the layout of the parkland and farmland around here is reminiscent of wealthy English shires. The whole setting is strongly evocative of Lismore's former power and glory – even though this building in fact has nothing to do with that era.

In 635 AD Saint Carthage founded a monastic complex for both monks and nuns in Lismore, and the place so flourished as a centre of learning that in the next century, under the influence of great teachers such as Saint Colman, it became an important university city. This growth continued into the twelfth century, despite 300 years of sporadic pillage by first Vikings then Normans. Lismore held great political as well as religious power, and the rivalry between the Sees of Lismore and Waterford, which epitomizes the split histories of Waterford city and county, was only resolved in 1363 when the two were united.

Invaders continued to attack the city, and in the late sixteenth century the medieval cathedral was almost totally destroyed by Queen Elizabeth's army. Its site is now occupied by the Church of Ireland **Saint Carthage's Cathedral**. Although built in 1633, its overall appearance is early nineteenth-century neo-Gothic, the tower and ribbed spire having been added in 1827 by James Pain and the windows of the nave reshaped at the same time. It's a lovely building, sitting in a cobbled churchyard of ancient yews and pollarded limes. Inside is some interesting stonework, including the McGrath family tomb (1548), which has carvings of the apostles, mystical beasts and skulls. The chunky carving of a bishop holding an open book set in the back wall is probably from the ninth-century monastic settlement. In the south transept, just on your left as you enter, there's some striking stained glass by Burne-Jones, the English pre-Raphaelite.

There's not much sign of this rich history in Lismore's current economically depressed existence, but it does somehow seem to preserve a quiet reverence about itself. It's recent designation as a **heritage town** has done something to shake this though, resulting in a disappointing audio-visual show housed in the old courthouse.

Practicalities

The tourist office is in the heritage centre in the courthouse (April & May Mon–Sat 10am–5.30pm, Sun noon–5.30pm; June–Aug Mon–Sat 9.30am–6pm, Sun noon–5.30pm; Sept Mon–Sat 10am–5.30pm, Sun noon–5.30pm; Oct Sun noon–5.30pm; ☎058/54855). If you want to stay in Lismore, you'll find **B&B** in the centre of town at *Alana* (☎058/54106; ③) in Chapel Street, just up behind the tourist office; *Mrs Cashman's*, South Mall (☎058/54114; ③); *Ballyrafter House Hotel*, a quarter of a mile along the Vee Road (☎058/54002; ⑤); or Mrs J. Power's *Beechcroft*, Deerpark Road, half a mile out of town (☎058/54273; ④). A new **hostel** in converted Georgian coach-houses behind a farm at *Kilmorna House* (☎058/54315; ②), is positively luxurious; a family room is available, and breakfasts and evening meals are served on request. For free **camping** in town go down over the bridge and to the left through the gate; there's a fabulous spot beneath the castle.

Options for **eating** are pretty limited: along the main street are *Eamonn's Place*, for good bar food daily and dinner (Tues–Sat) from £4.75, and *The Ballyrafter*, which serves excellent cheap, simple lunches. Away from bars, *The Celtic Kitchen* is open for coffee and snacks all day. Lismore has some fascinating ancient **bars** and grocery stores, a delight to explore in themselves, though there's not much beyond this trip into the past by way of food or entertainment. Try *Foleys*, *O'Briens*, or *Maddens*, proud of its history as the "local" for castle guests, such as Fred Astaire. For **music**, try *Rosie's West End Bar*, *Eamonn's Place* or *The Red House*, at any of which you might catch traditional, country and western, and ballad sessions on summer weekends.

The Munster Way

The road north from Lismore towards Cahir is typical of this area's gorgeous river valleys, stuffed with rhododendrons, bracken, beech trees and oaks, and dripping feathery pines. Spongy mosses cover walls, and young ferns spring out of them. About three miles along the road you can pick up the **Munster Way**, which heads for higher ground and more open spaces scattered with sheep and fir trees. The path goes through the Knockmealdowns, round the huge peat-covered mound of Sugarloaf Hill and after five miles leads to a viewing spot known as **The Vee**. From its steep, heathery V-shaped sides there's a tremendous view of the perfectly flat vale below with its patches of fields and of the town of Cahir at the foot of the Galtee Mountains. If you want to stop off at this point you can follow the road down to Clogheen and hitch to the independent **hostel** at Cahir, County Tipperary (see p.225), or the *An Óige* hostel of *Mountain Lodge*, Burncourt, Cahir (see p.224).

From here the Way descends to Clonmel in County Tipperary, around seventeen miles further, taking in the scenic wooded **Nire Valley**. Mrs Ryan's *Clonanar Guesthouse* (☎052/36141; ⑤) at **BALLYMACARBERY** is a good base for walking or fishing, as the Ryan family are expert at both. You can rent rods and waders, and get advice, during the fishing season. There is plenty of traditional music to be found in the pubs of the Nire Valley: *Melody's* bar in Ballymacarbery has regular sessions (Tues, Wed). Further along the Way, east of Clonmel (and about seven miles from Ballymacarbery), a good **hostel** is *Powers the Pot* at Harneys Cross (May–Sept; ☎052/23085; ①), which can provide breakfast and excellent dinners and has a very welcome cosy bar; camping is also available, as are private rooms (②). At 1200ft this claims to be the highest house in the country, and it's on the threshold of excellent hill-walking country.

The Munster Way is clearly signposted all the way to Carrick-on-Suir in Tipperary. The walk involves long distances rather than steep, dramatic inclines, and for most of the way you're within a mile or so of habitation. Nevertheless, solitary walkers should bear in mind that much of the route is out of sight of the lowlands, and distress signals won't be noticed. The relevant Bord Fáilte Information Sheet, giving route guidelines for this section of the way, is *Carrick-on-Suir–the Vee*, Information Sheet No. 26J.

COUNTY TIPPERARY

Tipperary is the largest of Ireland's inland counties, and also the richest. The county's wealth comes from the central **Golden Vale**, a flat limestone plain shared with eastern Limerick that's prime beef and dairy cattle territory. This enormous stretch of farming land is abutted on most borders by crops of mountain ranges, the most beautiful of which are the **Comeragh** and **Galtee mountains** and the **Glen of Aherlow**. These are all in the south of the county, and it's this area, without doubt, that packs in the most excitement. The curling course of the **Suir**, Tipperary's principal river, sweeps up most of what there is to see. But for many, Tipperary's attractions hang on one site alone. The **Rock of Cashel** is the county's most dramatic feature by far, its limestone sides rising cliff-like 200ft above the level ground, crowned with the high walls and towers of some splendid medieval ecclesiastical architecture.

Tipperary often has a vaguely familiar ring, thanks to the World War I marching song *It's a long way to Tipperary*. The county was actually picked for the song simply for the rhythmic beat of its name, which dashes the romance somewhat. In fact, Tipperary isn't particularly far from anywhere in southern Ireland, and this is probably its greatest advantage: you can catch the few worthwhile sights on your way through, and still be on the south or west coast within a few hours.

Carrick-on-Suir

Tucked in Tipperary's southeast corner, at the foot of the mountain slopes of neighbouring County Waterford, **CARRICK-ON-SUIR** may well be the first place you see in Tipperary, a slight country town raised a cut above the rest by what is perhaps Ireland's most beautiful **Elizabethan mansion**: similar examples abound in England but were always a rarity here. Set at the very eastern end of the main street, the mansion was built by Thomas, tenth Earl of Ormond ("Black Tom"), in anticipation of a visit from Queen Elizabeth I – and tributes to her are incorporated in the decoration throughout: above all in a fresco over the entrance way and in the superb stuccowork of the long gallery. A stunning mansion, with mullioned windows running the length of the building, it's the only major example in Ireland of a completely unfortified dwelling to date from the sixteenth century. It adjoins the remains of an earlier castle built in 1309; the two rectangular towers currently undergoing renovation date from the mid-fifteenth century. There's a collection of magnificent royal charters here, too: the oldest dates from 1661 and granted James Butler the title of Duke of Ormond. A claim is still disputed among historians that Anne Boleyn was born here. The guided tour, available on request, is well worth taking (mid-June to Sept daily 9.30am–6.30pm; ☎051/640787; £2, Heritage Card).

Regardless of the mansion's splendours, it's as the birthplace of the champion cyclist **Sean Kelly** that the town is most proud of itself – and the tiny main square at the west end of the main street has been renamed in his honour.

Tourist information (June–Sept daily 10am–5pm; ☎051/640200) can be found in the Heritage Centre. If you need to **stay**, *Fatima House*, John Street (☎051/640298; ③), is probably the cheapest **B&B**; or try *Orchard House* in Sean Kelly Square (☎051/641390; ④). Cyclists heading for the **hostel** outside Clonmel (see below) are better off leaving the main road at Carrick-on-Suir and heading across country via Rathgormuck. There are are a few places serving good **bar food**: *Luigi's* and *The Carraig Hotel*, in Main Street (daily till 9.30pm), and *The Park Inn*, New Street. Alternatively, you can find fast food in Main Street at the *Central Grill* or *The Europa*.

Five miles north of Carrick, **AHENNY** has two beautiful high crosses in its graveyard. They're thought to be eighth century, and are excellent examples of the transitional style between the early Christian plain shaft crosses and the highly ornate didactic crosses of Monasterboice and Kells.

Clonmel

CLONMEL, thirteen miles upstream, is far and away Tipperary's prettiest centre. It's a strangely genteel kind of place and retains something of its flavour as an early coaching town. It was the birthplace in 1713 of Laurence Sterne, philosopher and literary comic genius of the age of the stage, and it's not at all difficult to imagine Shandyesque shenanigans in the fine Georgian inns around about. A hundred years later Clonmel became the principal base for *Bianconi,* the most successful coach business in the country. Bianconi came from Lombardy in Italy and ran his so-called *Bians* from what is now *Hearn's Hotel* on Parnell Street; if you are here on July 6, expect to find costumed street celebrations of his achievements.

The town is a beautiful place to breeze through: you can't miss Clonmel's finest building, the sorely dilapidated **Main Guard** sagging at the eastern end of O'Connell Street. The oldest public Classical building in Ireland, predating Dublin's Royal Hospital, is now undergoing full renovation. The facade visible today was built by James Butler, first Duke of Ormond, as a courthouse for the Palatinate of the County of Tipperary, and it bears two panels showing coats of arms dated 1675.

Off to the left of the Main Guard runs Gladstone Street; to the right Sarsfield Street runs down to the river, and it's worth wandering here through the town's preserved backstreets and quayside mills. Other examples of period architecture include the nineteenth-century **St Mary's Roman Catholic Church**, with ziggurat tower and portico, in Irishtown, out past the imitation West Gate; the Greek-Revival–styled **Wesleyan Church** on Wolfe Tone Street; and the **Old St Mary's** Church of Ireland church with its octagonal tower and tower house. All of these are impressive from the outside; none offer much if you venture in. The **museum** in Parnell Street (Tues–Sat 10am–1pm & 2–5pm) records local history in a collection of maps, newspapers, postcards and Bianconi prints, and also has a small gallery of fine paintings.

Practicalities

Clonmel's **tourist information** point is in the Chamber of Commerce building on Nelson Street down by the quays (Mon–Fri 9.30am–5.30pm; July & Aug also Sat same hours; Oct–April closed 1–2pm; ☎052/22960). There are plenty of **B&Bs** in the area, but few in the centre of town: try *Jervis*, 3 Jervis Place, Parnell Street (☎052/25327; ③), or *Larkins Guest House*, Gladstone Street (☎052/22005; ③). Heading out towards Cahir you will spot *Hilldale*, Marlfield Road (☎052/21078; ③), just up a left-hand fork about three-quarters of a mile out of town; further up the lane are *Benuala* (☎052/22158; ③) and *Hillcourt* (☎052/21029; ④). Breda Moran's welcoming farmhouse B&B, *Ballyboy House*, at **CLOGHEEN** (☎052/65297; ③), is worth the extra journey (5 miles south on the R671; not to be confused with the town of the same name further west). The nearest **hostel** is *Powers the Pot* at Harneys Cross, five and a half miles up the slopes of the Comeragh Mountains in County Waterford (see p.220).

There's no shortage of places to **eat** in Clonmel. For great pizzas head for *Tom Skinny's*, Gladstone Street (noon–midnight, later at weekends); for a more formal evening atmosphere there are a couple of Italian restaurants: *Bianconi's*, Sarsfield Street (☎052/22952), and *La Scala*, just off Gladstone Street. Great-value wholefood and vegetarian lunches can be had at *The Bees Nees Bistro*, Abbey Street, off behind the Main Guard (Mon–Sat till 6pm). *Niamh's* deli and coffee shop, Mitchell Street (till 6pm), is a good alternative. For budget hot lunches, try *The Gallery Coffee Dock*, hidden away above *The Nest*, Mitchell Street (Mon–Sat 9.30am–6pm), or *Café Marie*, upstairs in the shopping mall opposite the museum (Mon–Sat 9am–6pm); for good **pub grub** try *Tierney's*, O'Connell Street (daily till 9.30pm, Sun 8.30pm), the carvery in *Hearn's Hotel*, Parnell Street, or *Mulcahy's*, Gladstone Street.

There's no shortage of decent **pubs**, too: if you want **music**, try *Kitty O'Donnell's* near the station for occasional traditional sessions at weekends, or *Carey's*, Irishtown (through the Westgate towards Cahir). *Brendan Dunne's*, the Mall, and *Lonergan's*, O'Connell Street, have sessions on Thursdays and Mondays respectively. Alternatively *Chawke's*, Gladstone Street, and *Phil Carroll's* "antique bar", Parnell Street, are both full of character.

Clonmel is the capital of Irish **greyhound racing**, and you can see the sport on Monday and Thursday nights at the local stadium; the surrounding countryside is also famous for racehorse breeding. **Fishing** off the quay is free, otherwise you can get a day's trout licence (£5) from Niall Carroll at *Powers the Pot* (☎052/23085) or

Kavanagh's Sports Shop, O'Connell Street. The river is said to be very good for the late run of the salmon in early September, and trout stocks have risen recently.

Fethard

Leaving Clonmel, you could either head southwest to the plain between the Knockmealdown and Galtee mountains (see below); or north for Cashel, in which case the route via **FETHARD** is the most rewarding. A touchingly plain place to travel through, and rarely sought out by tourists, Fethard has a number of forgotten medieval remains, set at the back of the town towards the river. One of these is a ruined **Templar's Castle**, access to which is through the *Castle Inn* (contact the publican, Mr Keogh). Other remains of old friaries and Iron Age raths can be found in the surrounding land. There's also a **Folk Farm and Transport Museum** at the beginning of the Cashel Road (May–Sept Mon–Sat 10am–6pm, Sun 1.30–6pm). If you want to eat, *P.J. Lonegan's* home-cooked **lunches** are worth stopping off for; if you want to drink, try *McCarthy's*.

The Knockmealdown and Galtee mountains

Of the mountain ranges in southern Tipperary, the **Galtees** make up one of the most scenic inland ranges in the country and are well worth discovering. The **Knockmealdowns** are less interesting but offer easier hill-walking. The valley plain between the two, which runs for about ten miles east of Mitchelstown (itself over the border in County Cork, see p.246), is not much in itself – but if you base yourself plumb in the centre, you're well placed to walk either range. Starting from Clonmel you've a choice of two routes west: the main roads via Cahir, or the lesser R665, which cuts straight across to Mitchelstown.

Cahir

You're unlikely to miss **CAHIR**. The town sits on a major crossroads, its rectangular-shaped central area radiating routes from each corner: to Clonmel, Cork, Cashel and Tipperary itself. The **castle** (daily April to mid-June & mid-Sept to Oct 10am–6pm; mid-June to mid-Sept 9am–7.30pm; Nov–March 10am–1pm & 2–4.30pm; last admission 40min before closing; £2, Heritage Card), set on a rocky islet in the River Suir, beside the road to Cork, is Cahir's outstanding attraction (even the name Cahir means "fort"). In essence the building is Anglo-Norman, dating originally from the thirteenth and fifteenth centuries, though the virgin appearance of the outer shell is deceptive, with a good deal of the brickwork going on into the eighteenth and nineteenth centuries. The Irish chieftain Conor O'Brien was the first to build a fortress on the rock; but it was the Anglo-Norman Butlers, the Earls of Ormond, who made this into one of the most powerful castles in the country. The Earl of Essex showered the castle with artillery fire in 1599; but it had a quiet time of the Cromwellian and Williamite invasions, and receded towards ruin until rejuvenated, along with other town buildings, by the Earl of Glengall in the mid-nineteenth century. In modern times, the interior has been uniformly whitewashed and spartanly furnished.

Entrance to the castle is along the side rampart, bringing you into the confined space of the **middle ward**, dominated by the three-storey thirteenth-century **keep**. The keep itself consists of vaulted chambers, a portcullis and a round tower containing a prison, accessible through a trap door. Down to the left, you pass through a gateway topped by machicolations, musket loops to either side, where sixteenth-century invaders could have been bombarded with missiles or boiling oil. Beyond is the much larger **outer ward** and, at its far end, the cottage built by the Earl of Glengall. The cottage now houses a **video theatre** where a twenty-minute film enthuses rhapsodically on the antiquities of southern Tipperary.

In the **inner ward**, two corner towers overlook the road to Cork. The larger was probably designed to be independently defensible once the keep had fallen, and it dates from a mixture of periods – straight, thirteenth-century stone stairs; fifteenth- to sixteenth-century stone vaulting over the ground-floor main room; and nineteenth-century renovation work in the Great Hall, whose stepped battlements reflect sixteenth-century style. The smaller, square tower at the other end of the ward and the curtain wall date from the nineteenth century, though with medieval bases. Just to the left of this second tower, steps lead to the bottom of the well tower, where the castle could safeguard its water supply during a siege. The informative **guided tour** of the castle is well worth taking.

One further building worth seeing is the **Swiss Cottage** (April Tues–Sun 10am–1pm, 2–4.15pm; May–Sept daily 10am–5.15pm; Oct, Nov & mid–end March Tues–Sun 10am–1pm & 2–3.45pm; £2, Heritage Card), about a mile out of Cahir on the Clonmel Road. This *cottage orné*, probably designed by John Nash, was built in 1810 to provide the Earls of Glengall with a lodge of romanticized – and fashionable – rustic simplicity from which to enjoy their hunting, shooting and fishing. With its thatched roof and ornate timberwork it certainly looks the part, and its status as a unique period piece makes it a popular attraction.

Practicalities

The **tourist information office** (April–Sept Mon–Sat 9.30am–6pm; July–Aug Sun 11am–5pm; ☎052/41453) is in the car park beside the castle. From the castle you can see

---

ACCOMMODATION IN THE MOUNTAINS

There are several very good **hostels** in the region. Nearest to Clonmel, up in the Comeragh Mountains in County Waterford, is *Powers the Pot* (see p.220 for hostel and B&B accommodation along the Munster Way). The owner will pick up hostellers from Clonmel by arrangement; otherwise follow the hostel's signpost leaving Clonmel over the bridge straight through the roundabout and on up the R678 (the golf club road).

Accessible from Cahir in low-lying farmland is the pretty *Kilcoran Farm Hostel* (IHH, open all year; ☎052/41906, fax ☎42630; ②), which usually has fresh produce for sale: it is clean, basic and something of a rustic idyll. To get there from Cahir follow the N8 towards Mitchelstown for about four miles; take the lane on the left opposite the *Tops* petrol station and it's about another (winding) mile, tucked by the laneside on the right; alternatively, phone for a lift from Cahir. Closer to town is the The *Lisakyle Hostel* (see opposite).

Two more **hostels**, both *An Óige*, are conveniently set in the Galtee Mountains and the Glen of Aherlow on the northern edge of the range, deliberately distanced a short day's trek apart. The intervening terrain has its fair share of tarns, cliffs and wooded forests. The *Mountain Lodge Hostel* (March–Sept; ☎052/67277; ①) is a spacious Alpine-style old shooting lodge, eight miles along the Mitchelstown Road from Cahir, then up a right turn, climbing for a mile by the river into the mountain. The *Ballydavid Wood Hostel* (March–Nov; ☎062/54148; ②) is in the Glen of Aherlow six miles out of Cahir. Try and arrive in daylight for this one, for although meticulously signposted, the route has enough twists and turns to get you lost.

There is a particularly picturesque **campsite** and **B&B** just off the R663 west of Bansha and just north of the Glen of Aherlow: *Ballinacourty House* (Easter–Sept; ☎062/56230; ③). Seventeenth- and eighteenth-century haylofts have been converted to conceal bedrooms, a wine bar and a **restaurant** (daily snacks, dinner from around £6), which all look out over an extremely pretty, cobbled courtyard; campers meanwhile enjoy fine mountain views.

If you are driving through the area it's also worth stopping for a drink on the terrace of the *Aherlow House Hotel* (☎062/56153; ⑥), where you can have soup and sandwiches from £3.50 and Sunday lunch for £9.50, both accompanied by superb views of the Galtee Mountains.

another castellated mansion on the hill further along the Cork Road: the *Carrigeen Castle* (☎052/41370; ④) was once the town prison but now offers **B&B** for little more than many others around town. The *Lisakyle Hostel* (*IHH*, open all year; ☎052/41963; ①), one mile out of Cahir beyond the Swiss Cottage, is basic, though the owners are friendly; camping is available. Alternatively the *Kilcoran Farm Hostel* (see "Accommodation in the mountains" opposite), four miles out of town, is worth staying at.

For **food**, the coffee shop above the *Crock of Gold* provides sandwiches, scones and lunches. *Roma's Café*, on the Dublin side of the square, has normal café fare and the cheapest prices in town; and the *Italian Connection* (☎052/42152) is open every day till 11pm for fresh pasta, pizzas and Irish food. For good pub lunches try the *Galtee Inn* on the square. **Traditional music** is minimal and not of a high standard but sometimes takes place at *Morrissey's*, opposite the castle and the *Forge Tavern*, beyond the bridges. The liveliest **pub** on the square is the *Stop Inn*, while *Black Toms* on the Tipperary Road is another lively pub to pop into: strictly sawdust floor and very macho – even rough – but animated, with ballads and rebel songs playing on the tape recorder.

Bus Éireann **buses** to Waterford and Dublin leave from outside the *Crock of Gold*, across from the castle, and those to Cork and Limerick leave from outside the tourist office; there's a timetable posted in the window.

Ardfinnan to the Mitchelstown Caves

Along the minor road from Clonmel to Mitchelstown, you pass through **ARDFINNAN**, where a beautiful fourteen-arched stone bridge crosses the Suir and a private castle stands on the overlooking hillside. Follow along the foot of the Knockmealdowns for several miles and you'll come to Clogheen, where there's the best turn-off route into the mountains, towards the terrific scenic point known as the **Vee** (see p.220). Powerfully telescopic views over Waterford and Tipperary stretch out from beside the lough in the mountain gap, revealing how uncompromisingly flat Tipperary is, hemmed in by its opposing and distant sets of mountain ranges. Two shepherds' shelters are set up here, with half the back wall missing so that the shepherds could always keep an eye on the sheep on the hill behind.

Back on the R665, you'll come next to **BALLYPOREEN**, a wide-streeted crossroads turned ghost town, whose moment of glory came on June 3, 1984, when **Ronald Reagan** made a prodigal return – his great-grandfather was supposedly born here in 1810. You can read all about it and look at photos of the visit in a specially built centre at the crossroads, opposite the *Ronald Reagan* pub.

Eight miles from Mitchelstown itself, the massive pre-glacial underworld of the **Mitchelstown Caves** – signposted north from Ballyporeen down the interlacing lanes of the valley, or south off the N8 – are, aside from walking, the main attraction in the area. By far the most extensive and complicated cave system in Ireland (a couple of miles in all), they have remained, considering their scale, very uncommercialized. The whole underground system was discovered in 1833, when a labourer lost his crowbar down a crevice, though there are records from much earlier of one cave being used as a hiding place, most famously to shelter the Earl of Desmond after his unsuccessful rebellion in 1601.

The opening to the system is a cleft in the hill behind the house of the curator, Jackie English, whose harnessing of legend and folklore to match every calcite formation makes for an imaginative **tour**. Oisín, Niamh of the long golden hair, the cave of the Tír Na nÓg, the Tower of Babel and even the Shroud of Turin are all visualized in a range of colours washed down from the minerals in the limestone above – brown from the iron oxide, blue from the copper sulphate, black from the manganese and grey from the lead and zinc. The caves were formed by the incessant action of rainwater on the limestone over millions of years, and the fantastical stone formations grew out of the calcium carbonate (dissolved limestone) deposited by the dripping water, hardening as it evaporated into gigantic encrustations of stalactites and stalagmites. The temperature in the caves is around 54°F – this can feel chilly in summer, so bring a sweater, and a musical instrument, too, if you fancy toying with the acoustics. The tours only take in a few of the major caves but are nonetheless worth taking.

Cashel

Just eleven miles north of Cahir en route to Dublin, **CASHEL** is an obvious next stop. The town has grown around, and is completely dominated by, the spectacular **Rock of Cashel**. No tourist bus will bypass the site – so an early-morning or late-afternoon visit will make an important difference to your first impressions.

In deep contrast to the ecclesiastical splendour of the Rock is the tiny **Bothàn Scóir** – a unique one-roomed peasant dwelling that simply has to be seen. For antiquarian booklovers the **GPA Bolton Library** is a must, as is **Cashel Folk Village**, for anyone interested in the old IRA.

If you want to stay, there are several central **B&Bs**: *Abbey House*, 1 Dominic Street opposite St Dominic's Friary (☎062/61104; ④), Mary and Pat Duane's welcoming *Maryville*, Bankplace (☎062/61098; ④), and *Copperfield House* (☎062/61075; ④). Cashel now also has two of the best **hostels** in the country. One is *O'Brien's Farmhouse Hostel* (☎062/61003; ②), which boasts private rooms, camping and a wet-weather area. It is housed in a beautifully converted stone barn: to find it, walk to the bottom end of Main Street and turn right at the junction following the Dundrum Road – it's less than a mile. Just off Main Street is *Cashel Holiday Hostel*, 6 John Street (*IHH*, open all year; ☎062/62330, fax ☎62445; ②), with doubles available and **bike rental** (see below): it's cunningly decorated, very comfortable and possibly the only hostel in Ireland to have extra-long bunks for tall folk!

There are plenty of places to **eat**; try *Bailey's* licensed restaurant (☎062/61937; lunch around £4, dinner £10), *Hannigan's* or *Spearman's* (☎062/61143; daily for lunch from £4, dinner from £6). If you feel like splashing out, *Chez Hans* (☎062/61177; Tues–Sat 6.30–9.30pm) offers virtuoso dinners from £22 in the unlikely setting of a former Wesleyan chapel. There are several coffee shops serving home baking, most of them in Main Street. *The Bakehouse* (daily till 8pm in summer) is great value with decent hot meals from around £2.50. For pub food try *Kearney's Castle Hotel*, *Reilly's* (Mon–Sat lunch only) or *Hannigan's* home cooking (Mon–Sat lunch and evenings), the latter in Ladyswell Street, the top end of the main road.

If you are looking for **music pubs** try *Feehan's*, in the very centre of town, or cosy *Dowling's*, at the bottom end of the main street. **Cycle** parts and repairs are available at *Burke's*, in the centre, and **bike rental** from the hostel in John Street (£6 per day, £30 per week; drop-off scheme). The **tourist information office** (Easter–Sept Mon–Sat 10am–6pm; ☎062/61333) sits in the market house in the middle of the main street. If you want to go **pony trekking**, Claire Maher, seven miles away at Killough (☎0504/41291), offers woodland treks for £10 – and will arrange lifts from Cashel for small groups.

The Rock of Cashel

Approached from the north or west, the **Rock of Cashel** (mid-June to mid-Sept daily 9am–7.30pm; mid-March to mid-June daily 9.30am–5.30pm; mid-Sept to mid-March Mon–Sat 9.30am–4.30pm, Sun 2–5pm; last admission 45min before closing; £2.50, Heritage Card) appears as a spectacular mirage of fairytale turrets, crenellations and walls rising bolt upright from the vast encircling plain. It's a tour operator's dream: on one piece of freak limestone outcrop stands the most beautiful and complete Romanesque church in the country, a gargantuan medieval cathedral, a castle tower house, an eleventh-century round tower, a unique early high cross and an exquisite fifteenth-century Hall of Vicars – medieval Irish architecture wrapped up in a morning's investigation. Two more medieval priories lie at its feet.

In **legend** the Rock was formed when the Devil, flying overhead with a large stone in his mouth, suddenly caught sight of Saint Patrick standing ready to found his new church on the site, and in his shock dropped the rock (in the northeast of the county, a striking gap in a mountain range is known as the "Devil's Bit"). The Rock is also the place where Saint Patrick is supposed to have picked a shamrock in order to explain the doctrine of the Trinity – God the Father, Christ the Son and the Holy Ghost as three beings of the one stem – since which time the shamrock became Ireland's unofficial emblem.

The Hall of the Vicars

Approaching the Rock from Cashel town, you come first to the **Hall of the Vicars**, built in the fifteenth century to cater for eight vicar *meistersingers*, who assisted in the cathedral services but were later dispensed with due to jealousy of the power and land their privileged office entailed. The upper floor of the building is divided between the main hall, with screens and a minstrels' gallery, and what would have been the dormitories. The ground floor, a vaulted undercroft, today contains the original **Saint Patrick's Cross**, a unique type of high cross. It once stood outside, where there's now a replica. Tradition has it that the cross's huge plinth was the coronation stone of the High Kings of Munster, the most famous of whom was Brian Boru, killed in his tent by a fleeing Viking at the Battle of Clontarf. The cross is simpler than other high crosses, with a carving of Christ on one side and Saint Patrick on the other. It has an upright supporting its left arm and is without the usual ring-wheel in the centre. It may be that originally the upright and its missing counterpart represented the two thieves crucified with Jesus, and it is also possible that it was never intended as a freestanding cross in the first place, but for erection on a wall.

Cormac's Chapel

Cormac's Chapel (built 1127–34) is the earliest and most beautiful of Ireland's surviving Romanesque churches, and the intricacies of its decoration are as spectacular as they are unique. The architecture has clear continental influences – the twin square **towers**, for example, were probably engineered by monks sent from Regensburg, Germany. The **tympana**, or panels, above the grandiose north door (more than likely the original entrance, now leading blindly into the flank of the cathedral) and south door (today's entrance), are also rare in Irish church architecture. Above the north door is depicted a curious carved scene of a large beast ensnaring a smaller one, itself on the point of being speared by a macho centaur in a Norman helmet. The north door is set in six orders of pillars, creating a tunnel-vaulted **porch**, which is sheltered by an outer stone roof porch. Each arch is crowned with capitals, human heads, fantastic beasts, flutings and scallops.

The small size of the chapel is particularly Irish, as are the lack of aisles and the steeply pitched stone roof – you'll find similar-looking buildings at Glendalough and Kells, though Cormac's Chapel is larger than these. Inside are a nave and a chancel with a small recess in the east wall. The wall opposite you as you walk in has a tall triple arcade, in the centre of which is a large round-headed **window** that would once have lit up the whole interior, illuminating all the painted colour – of which a little remains up at the altar and just above the chancel arch. The **sarcophagus** at the foot of this wall, although fragmented, has an exquisite Scandinavian *Urnes* design of interlacing serpents and ribbon decoration. It's said to have been the tomb of King Cormac, and is certainly old enough to be so.

The cathedral and round tower

The **Cathedral** was begun a century or so after Cormac's chapel. Although Anglo-Norman in conception, with Gothic arches and lancet windows, it's a purely Irish-built endeavour, without help from abroad. A graceful limestone building, it features a series of tall, high-set lancet **windows**, and also some good examples of quatrefoil, or four-petalled, windows, especially above the lancets in the choir space. You'll notice that some of the lancets have been shortened – probably as a measure of fortification. The **choir** is longer than the nave and both are without aisles. The nave was shortened to make room for the **castle tower**, built most obviously for refuge, and also as an archiepiscopal residence. A wooden-floored hall would once have been above the nave (the corbels are still apparent), accessible from the castle tower.

The **central tower**, at the meeting of the transepts, is also on a grand scale and, typically, did not appear until the fourteenth century. It's supported by four Gothic arches rising from very wide piers, their shafts sweeping beautifully into the concave bottom. Access to the tower is by winding stairs from the south transept (may not be open to the public, so ask). **Passages** also ran through the nave and choir walls, supposedly for the outcasts or lepers of the community, so that they could watch the holy ceremonies without being seen themselves. The **transepts** have shallow chapel altars with some tomb and *piscina* niches. In the north transept, panels from sixteenth-century altar-tombs survive – one with an intricately carved retinue of saints, the others more broken but just as dextrously beautiful.

The **Round Tower** is the earliest building on the rock. Its tapering features have led to suggestions that it's as early as tenth century, though the officially accepted date is early twelfth century. It's not a typical tower; the entrance door was originally twelve feet above the ground, and various levels of windows ensnare viewpoints in all directions.

Around the Rock

From the grounds of the Rock you can look down at **Hore Abbey** on the plain below, and it's an easy enough walk down, over the fields and jumping the road wall. But there's little to be gained in doing this, beyond escaping the sightseers – you can see just as well from the Rock. The thirteenth-century abbey was the last Cistercian daughter monastery of Mellifont to be completed before the Reformation, and was probably built by those working on the cathedral on the Rock. Originally a Benedictine foundation, it converted after its abbot had a wild dream that his Benedictine monks were plotting to cut his head off; he expelled them and donned the Cistercian habit in 1269. There's yet another abbey ruin, **Saint Dominic's**, down the south side of the Rock in the town, but this has even less to offer in terms of things to see.

A path known as the **Bishop's Walk** leads from the Rock's rampart entrance down through the back garden of the **Palace Hotel** (closed indefinitely). The *Palace* was built in Queen Anne style by Archbishop Theophilus Bolton in 1730 as a mansion for the archbishops of Cashel (hence the Bishop's Walk to the Rock). It has a simple, red-brick front and a cut stone rear. Cashel owes much thanks to this particular archbishop; it was he who saw the value of Cormac's Chapel and put his wealth into its restoration at a time when the Rock's antiquities were degenerating rapidly towards irrevocable ruin. A further legacy is the **GPA Bolton Library** (view by appointment with the Dean; ☎062/61232 or 71332; £2.50), out on the road opposite the hotel and set in the grounds of the slender-spired eighteenth-century St John's Protestant Cathedral. Its manuscripts (from as early as the twelfth century), rare maps and wealth of literary treasures were principally his bequest when he died in 1744. A selection of the books and maps are on display, changing bi-monthly and well worth viewing.

It's worth the effort of visiting the **Bothán Scóir**: walk up the street past the tourist office, turn first right and look out for a tiny cottage about half a mile up on your right.

If there's no one there, ask for Albert Carrie at 6 Ard Mhuire, the first cul-de-sac on the right as you head back down the hill towards town. The Bothán Scóir is a one-roomed peasant dwelling dating from around 1600, the only one of its kind in Ireland. *Bothán* means "hut", *scóir* is "score", referring to the score notched up on a tallystick as the peasant worked the 180 days of the year demanded by the landlord in payment for rent of the cottage and a patch of land. The soot-black thatch, the chimney-less roof, the half-door and the jamb wall – layer after layer of authentic detail tell a history of systematic oppression and thorough misery. All this is wonderfully articulated by Albert – a man with an inspiring passion for the history of the common people; it proves a wholly memorable experience.

If you have the time to delve further into Cashel's social history, **Cashel Folk Village** (daily 9.30am–7.30pm; craft demonstrations Sun 2–6pm; £2), in a lane behind the tourist office, is crammed with interest, including a gruesome traditional butcher's shop guaranteed to turn you vegetarian and a fascinating museum of Republican history.

Golden

Having seen the Rock of Cashel, most people head out of Tipperary for the west, and frankly this isn't a bad idea – the north of the county has little to distract you. Leaving Cashel on the N74, you come after a few miles to **GOLDEN**, where **Athassel Abbey** sits on the banks of the Suir. It was once the largest medieval priory in Ireland, and its ruins even today are fairly extensive – though not dramatic enough to seriously draw you off your route. The west door is the most impressive feature, and the peacefulness of the surroundings the most rewarding. The plain immediately encircling the abbey was once the site of the town, but it was razed to the ground twice during the fourteenth century – enough to obliterate it forever.

Tipperary town

A few miles further on, twelve miles from Cashel and less than five from the border of Limerick, the county's honorary namesake, **TIPPERARY** town, is tucked by the northern side of the Glen of Aherlow. Like many of these namesake county towns, Tipperary is much less important than it sounds. If you've already visited Clonmel, it will come as something of a shock – compared to Clonmel's yuppy prosperity, Tipperary feels out of another century altogether. The town has bold statues sculpted in granite here and there, most notably one to its literary local son, Charles J. Kickham, entitled *Poet, Novelist but above all Patriot.*

You might want to stop over briefly for one of the monthly meetings at the **racecourse**, or to take in an intriguing small **museum** (Mon–Sat 9.30am–10pm) hidden away in the foyer of the town swimming pool, by the Cashel Road exit. A tiny store of memorabilia, it exhibits photos, letters and weaponry from the warring years of 1919–23, especially relating to the old IRA. Tipperary was a particularly hot spot during the Anglo-Irish and Civil War strife, especially through its most remembered son, **Seán Tracey**, whose battalion fired the first shots of the Anglo-Irish War (1919–21). There are letters he wrote to his family from prison, some talking about the honour the British had bestowed on him by taking the trouble to get him captured, others of a more domestic nature. A violin belonging to **Joseph Mary Plunkett** (one of the poets executed in the 1916 uprising) hangs beside revolvers, pistols and land mines. Most striking of all, perhaps, are the photographs of the young officers shown clenching their revolvers, either posturing a rebel's stance of defiance or slightly abashed, with innocent-looking smiles.

Practicalities

The **tourist information office** is on James's Street (April–Sept Mon–Fri 9.30am–6pm, Sat 9.30am–1pm; Nov–March Mon–Fri 9.30am–5pm, Sat 9.30am–1pm; ☎062/51457). If you plan to **stay**, *Central Accommodation*, 45 Main Street (☎062/51117; ③), is a B&B run by a very friendly family; if they are full, try *The Brown Trout* (☎062/51912; ④). Those on a more generous purse can head six miles out of town to *Aherlow House* (☎062/56153; ⑤), a fine hotel situated in stunning mountain scenery, or can **camp** at *Ballinacourty House* (see p.224).

The *Brown Trout* **restaurant** is open every day and serves lunches from £3.50 and dinner from £7. Several pubs also serve good food: *Kickham House* (Mon–Sat noon–3pm) and *Nellie O'Brien's* (daily noon–10pm), both on Main Street, and *O'Donovan's* at the top of O'Brien Street. *The Basement* coffee house, Kickham Place (behind the statue), is cheap and cheerful, and serves till 8.30pm in the summer (Wed–Sat). There are plenty of **bars** in town: *Corney's Pub*, Davitt Street, has traditional music every night; *Nellie O'Brien's* has sessions from Thursday to Sunday; and the *Kickham* has occasional sessions. *The Underground* on James's Street is a great cavernous bar for live rock bands.

Thurles and around

Upstream from Cashel, both the Suir itself and the attractions along its banks wane. The river passes through the larger towns of Thurles and Templemore, though its source in the Devil's Bit Mountain falls short of the major town in the northeast, Roscrea. All three centres have train connections.

THURLES is of very little interest in itself, but **Holy Cross Abbey**, just four miles south, sits beside a fat stretch of the Suir and is well worth a visit if you're passing by. Founded in 1180, restored significantly in the fifteenth century and then left derelict for 400 years, the abbey was totally restored between 1971 and 1985 and is now a thriving parish church as well as a tourist attraction. You really need to see photographs of the period before restoration to appreciate its significance; these suggest that every other ruin you've seen could as easily be converted. Holy Cross always had singular importance as a centre of pilgrimage, claiming to possess a splinter of the wood from the **True Cross**, Christ's cross on Calvary. The splinter relic was reckoned to have been given to Murtagh O'Brien, King of Munster, by Pope Paschal II in 1110. At the turn of the seventeenth century both O'Donnell and O'Neill, the Ulster chiefs, stopped off to venerate this relic on their way to Kinsale to meet the French – no doubt hoping they'd be rewarded with a victory over Elizabeth I.

The **interior** of the church is fully restored, though here there's been no particular attempt at period accuracy; virtually every wall and pillar has been whitewashed, and all the pews have been varnished. The incongruities are, in a sense, inherent in the major fifteenth-century renovations that stripped the site of its medieval character and left a confused mix of revelation and awe for today. Nevertheless, it's rewarding to see the stone ribbing of the vaulted roofs and most particularly the undamaged fifteenth-century **sedilia** in the chancel area, the finest in the country. The sedilia, recessed stone seats for the celebrants of the Mass, is of a hard limestone shaped into cusped arches and crowned with crockets, showing decorative friezework as well as the English royal crest and the escutcheon of the Earls of Ormond. In the transept to the left of the nave, you'll find one of Ireland's rare medieval **frescoes**, this one showing a Norman hunting scene painted in browns, reds and greens. The exterior of the church has a startling full-length slate roof, which reaches down to the cloister pillars. There's a **tourist information centre**, a coffee shop and a religious crafts shop within the abbey complex.

Ballynahow Castle

If you're cycling or driving north towards Thurles you might also think of taking in **Ballynahow Castle**, a circular castle tower built by the Purcell family in the sixteenth century. To get there from Holy Cross, take the road directly opposite the Protestant church, not the Thurles route (even though the signpost says so). From Thurles itself, it's out on the Nenagh Road, right at the *Jet Petrol* station, and after another mile the castle stands next to a farmhouse – *Ballynahow Castle Farm* (☎0504/21297; ④), where you can pick up the key, or stay in **B&B** accommodation from April to October. The castle is distinguished by its circular plan; inside, entering the lowest of its five storeys is like walking into an igloo, with the corbelled roof curving round almost to the floor. There are many little rooms hidden within the walls and, although undecorated and entirely bare (and quite dark), most of it is in an excellent state of preservation and strongly atmospheric.

Templemore and Cranagh Castle

TEMPLEMORE is even less interesting than Thurles, but it does happen to be within easy reach of one of the more historical of listed hostels, **Cranagh Castle** – though it's not particularly easy to get to, and hard to find even when you do get there. From Templemore, head first for Templetuohy, five miles away. Once there, turn right through the village and at the first bend on the other side of town head straight on, off the main road; the castle lies about a mile and a half further on, through a narrow gateway edged by two stone pillars, its rusty white gates peeled back. Coming up the Thurles–Templemore Road from the south, take the turn-off for Loughmore (signposted as "Loughmoe", a few miles before Templemore), where you'll find the ruin of a four-storeyed tower house. Head straight on from here in the direction of Templetuohy, and the gateway into *Cranagh Castle* is on the left-hand side. There's no sign on the gate.

The **hostel** (☎0504/53104; ①) occupies parts of the eighteenth-century mansion house attached to the circular Purcell tower house – the family live in the basement. A wide wooden stairway leads to the dorm rooms on the second and third floors, which are extremely spacious, with single beds and left-over period furnishings. Outside, the yard is full of the sounds of an old-fashioned farm: geese, cocks, cows and the gallop of horses first thing in the morning. The produce here is all organic, and there's wonderful fresh milk and bread, though not at all cheap. If you're interested in the working of the farm, then ask about the courses on organic farming that are run off-season. If you can take the silence, it can be a very relaxing place to take time out (though smokers are discouraged) – in low season their motto "hard to find and hard to leave" takes on an eerie twist once you've stayed here. If you're on a bike, the **Devil's Bit Mountain** is within easy reach and is reckoned worth the climb for the views.

Roscrea

ROSCREA sits on a low hillock between the Slieve Bloom Mountains to the northeast and the Devil's Bit to the southwest. It's a charming place, with streets running down the hill slopes and a certain conscious lack of worldliness. However, where the rest of Ireland has secluded river sites and spacious countryside for its abbey ruins, Roscrea has the main Dublin–Limerick Road running raucously through the middle of **St Cronan's Monastery**. On one side of the road is the round tower, with a garage shed built into the side of it and the top third removed by the British in 1798. Immediately opposite, virtually on the pavement, is the west gable of St Cronan's church, its yellow sandstone carved out in a twelfth-century Romanesque style reminiscent of Cormac's

Chapel in Cashel. The rest of the church was pulled down in the nineteenth century and the stone used as building material elsewhere. **Saint Cronan's Cross**, just to the right of the gable, must have been a beauty once, but now it's severely weatherbeaten and hacked. Up by the centre of the town is a large, sturdy-looking **Gate Tower Castle** from the thirteenth century. Backed by a polygonal curtain wall, it now houses a **Heritage Centre** (June–Sept daily 9.30am–5.45pm; £2.50). An imposing eighteenth-century town house now used for office purposes stands at the centre of the medieval plot. As both the cross and the castle are on the Dublin–Limerick route, you'd get a reasonable view staring out of a bus window in slow traffic.

Nenagh and Lough Derg

Once again, in comparison with the south of the county, the northwest lacks significant attractions. The remaining crumbs of interest rest on the shores of **Lough Derg**, not far from the sole town of any size, Nenagh. There are no hostels on this east side of the lake but there is one across the water at Mountshannon in County Clare (see p.312).

NENAGH is usually jam-packed with heavy traffic trying to plough its way through. It has one singular historical remain, a colossal round **castle keep** (or donjon) with walls 20ft thick, its five storeys reaching a height of 100ft and topped with nineteenth-century castellations. Totally gutted within, this final retreat tower was originally one of five round towers which, linked by a curtain wall, formed a Norman stronghold. Founded by Theobald Walter, a cousin of Thomas à Becket, the tower was occupied by the Butlers, then captured in turn by the O'Carrols of Eile, Cromwell, went back to James II and then to and fro between Ginckel (King William's chief general) and O'Carrol in the Williamite war. And there the fighting stopped until many centuries later when a farmer, wanting to get rid of a nest of sparrows that were feeding on his crops, stuck some gunpowder in the walls of the donjon and blew another hole in the fortress. A few reinforced concrete steps help you to get near the top, but there's little to be seen.

Across the road from the donjon, the Nenagh **heritage centre** (£1) is set in the old jail, now a Convent of Mercy school. Housed in the octagonal Governor's House, up the driveway, the museum has a display room housing temporary exhibitions, a mock-up of an old schoolroom with a four-foot mannequin nun (very liberal with her mascara), and a re-created old post office/bar/telephone exchange. In the basement are the usual agricultural items and a realistic but clinical-looking forge. Back at the entrance arch, the cells of the jail have their original hefty iron cell doors, and you can also see the former exercise yard, tiny and cluttered.

Tourist information is on Connolly Street (early May to early Sept Mon–Sat 9.30am–1pm & 2–5.30pm; ☎067/31610). There's the reasonably priced **B&B** *Sun View*, Ciamaltha Road (☎067/31064; ③), quite close to the bus and train stations, and you can get fairly good snack **food** at the *Foodhall* on Pearse Street. At the northern end of this road, the *JKC Shopping Arcade* provides more substantial lunch venues, or try the *Pantry* on Abbey Street.

Lough Derg

Along the shores of **Lough Derg** are a number of small villages, none of them really worth making a special trip to visit (unless you're after the fishing), but which may be worth calling at if you're cruising on the lake. **DROMINEER** is a small and pictu-resque yachting harbour, with a tiny castle ruin on its pier; there's food (and drink) at the *Whiskey Still Pub*. **KILGARVAN** has a good antiques shop next to the *Brocka-on-the-water* restaurant. **TERRYGLASS**, where *Paddy's Pub* has a nice interior and bar food, offers little else besides a crafts shop in the old church and a good B&B nearby – the Heenans' *Tir na Fiuise* (☎067/22041; ④).

COUNTY LIMERICK

To an even greater extent than Tipperary, everyone passes through **County Limerick**, and hardly anyone stays. Once here, you're tantalizingly close to the much more rewarding counties of Cork, Kerry and Clare, and frankly you're not likely to linger. Still, what interest there is lies close to the roads to Cork, Killarney and Tralee, three main routes that run southwards from Limerick city in the northeastern corner. You should try to see at least one of two places: **Castle Matrix**, an authentic, lavishly restored and renovated tower house on the Killarney route, and **Lough Gur**, a Mesolithic-to-Neolithic lake and hill enclave of preternatural beauty. Both can be reached easily no matter what transport you're using.

For **cyclists**, Limerick's terrain is more variable than it's usually given credit for. In its western-to-southwestern corner, the upland bears a likeness to barren stretches of Donegal, whereas the northern estuary stretch is indeed only a slightly bumpy flatland. The centre and east bow in contour towards the eastern frontier of the Tipperary Golden Vale's rich dairy land, but not without gently rising mounds for hills and broadish trickles for rivers. More so than any other county, the land in Limerick is dotted with an array of **tower castles**, some inhabited but most in ruins or no more than stumps.

Historically, Limerick's most notable period arrived with the Norman strongholds, the most dominant family being the Fitzgeralds (or **Geraldines**), also known as the Earls of Desmond – virtually all of Limerick's significant ruins were once this clan's power bases. They quickly became Gaelicized and ruled as independent monarchs, pulling very much away from English rule. The inevitable confrontation with Britain came to a head at the end of the sixteenth century, when in 1571 the Geraldine uprising against Elizabeth I sparked off a savage war, which brought about their downfall and destroyed in its wake much of the province of Munster.

SPORT IN LIMERICK: THE GARRYOWEN

Even more than most of Ireland, Limerick seems obsessed with sport; horse racing, hurling, gaelic football, soccer and rugby are all avidly followed, and hurling and rugby have particularly strong local traditions. In rugby, the region has passed into immortality with the invention of the **Garryowen** – named after the district of Limerick city which lent its name to one of Ireland's finest rugby clubs. The move, a high kick upfield pursued by a charging team who hope to hit the opposition as they catch the ball, the equivalent of Rugby League's "up-and-under", is said to have been invented here in the 1920s.

Limerick city

Squarely on the path of all the major routes across the country, and situated pretty much at the head of the Shannon estuary, **LIMERICK CITY** seems a logical place to make for, but it's a disappointment. Though it's the Republic's third city, and heavily industrialized, it somehow falls significantly short of being a metropolis, but also lacks the attractions of a typically relaxed western seaboard town. It's also probably the most Catholic of all Irish cities, its churches seemingly crowded every minute of the day.

Like Derry in the north, Limerick also seems tainted by 300-year-old wars, carrying a stigma that it has still to shrug off. Modern unemployment and economic hard times have also left their mark. It doesn't always seem a friendly town, and certain areas can feel positively intimidating at night. However, recent efforts to clean up Limerick's image are starting to pay off: regeneration, most obvious around Arthur's Quay and King John's Castle, has blown fresh gusts of optimism into most quarters of the city, and while you are unlikely to spend long here, it can be rewarding to explore what the place does have to offer.

The city you see now is predominantly Georgian, but nevertheless Limerick has three distinct historical sectors: **Englishtown**, the oldest part of the city, built on an island in the Shannon, and focus of renewed interest; **Irishtown**, which began to take shape in the thirteenth and fourteenth centuries; and **Newtown Pery**, the modern centre, an infuriating, battered mix of beautiful Georgian terraces and garish fast-food joints.

Some history

Limerick's history has to be spelt out. Even today, the town is only too aware of spectres from its past. This lowest fording point of the Shannon was first exploited by the **Vikings**, who in the tenth century sailed up the Shannon to *Inis Sibhton* (now Kingstown in Englishtown), an island by the eastern bank formed by a narrow by-pass from the main stream now known as Abbey river. Here they established a port, and for a hundred years war after war raged between them and the native Irish. The Vikings were frequently defeated and were finally crushed nationally in 1014 at the Battle of Clontarf, at the hands of Brian Boru, the High King of Ireland. Limerick itself was attacked soon after and burned to the ground. Most of the Vikings didn't actually leave, but from then on they were gradually assimilated into the Gaelic population. The fate of Limerick itself didn't improve much, however, as over the next hundred years the Irish fought amongst themselves, burning the town to the ground again and again.

Some kind of stability was established with the arrival of the **Normans** at the end of the twelfth century. They expanded and fortified the town; King John arriving in 1210 to inaugurate King John's Castle, one of his finest. High walls were built that were now to keep the Gaels out, and because of this exile the first suburb across the Abbey river began to grow into **Irishtown**. There was trouble again with the visits of Edward Bruce in the fourteenth century; but the real emasculation of the city began with the onslaught of Cromwell's forces under the command of his son-in-law, Ireton, in the late 1640s. It was concluded when the city rallied to the **Jacobite** cause in 1689.

Once James II had lost the Battle of the Boyne in 1690, most of his supporters surrendered quickly – except for the ones at Limerick. As the Williamites advanced, the Jacobite forces within Limerick castle resolved to fight it out under the command of their Irish champion **Patrick Sarsfield**, Earl of Lucan and second in overall command of the Jacobean army. Although the walls of a medieval castle had little hope of withstanding seventeenth-century artillery (one of James's French generals declared that they would not stand up to a bombardment of apples), Sarsfield gained time by sneaking out, with five hundred of his troops, for a surprise night attack on William's supply train. He succeeded in totally destroying the munitions, while William sat waiting for them in front of the castle walls. However, when the Williamites returned the following year, Sarsfield could finally hold out no longer, and he surrendered on October 3, 1691, to the terms of a **treaty** that's so sore an historical point that it's still stuck in the minds of most Limerick people today.

The treaty terms were divided into military and civil articles. Militarily, Jacobeans were allowed to sail to France, which most of them did, along with Sarsfield himself (he died on the battlefield at Landon in Belgium, two years later); the civil agreement promised Catholics the religious and property rights they'd once had under Charles II. Within a couple of months the English reneged on this part of the treaty, and instead enforced extreme **anti-Catholic measures**. There followed civil unrest on such a scale that the city gates were locked every night for the next sixty years, and the betrayal has never been forgotten – it alone may explain the roots of today's element of Republican support in the city. The concordat was supposedly signed upon the **Treaty Stone** that rests on a plinth at the western end of Thomond Bridge. For many years, although this was used as a stepping stone for mounting horses, small pieces continued to be gouged out as souvenirs; one fragment set into a ring is said to have fetched £1000 in the USA.

It was not a promising start for the modern city, and there are those who claim that festering resentment has stunted Limerick's growth ever since. Being also lumbered with a geographical setting that gives it the Irish name *luimneach* ("a barren spot of land") has not helped. One redeeming factor has to lie in its humour; how else could its corporate motto read *An ancient city well studied in the arts of war*.

> The telephone code for Limerick city is ☎061.

Arrival, information and accommodation

Limerick is the nearest big city to **Shannon Airport** (☎61444; see p.304) – ten miles away off the Ennis Road. Airport buses (£4) run approximately every 30min in the morning, hourly in the afternoon and irregularly after 6pm; a taxi costs around £15. The **train** (☎315555) and **bus** (☎313333) **stations** are next door to each other on Parnell Street in Newtown Pery.

The new, well-informed **tourist information office** (June–Aug daily 9am–6.30pm; April, May, Sept & Oct Mon–Sat 9.30am–5.30pm; Nov–March Mon–Fri 9.30am–5.30pm, Sat 9.30am–1pm; ☎317522) is at Arthur's Quay, near where the river branches merge and you cross over into Englishtown: easiest found by following O'Connell Street north to the Custom House. Their city map has useful information and phone numbers; you can buy **parking discs** from most local newsagents and shops displaying a green and yellow disc. **Walking tours** of the city are organized by the tourist office in summer.

For **bike rental** try *Emerald Cycles*, 1 Patrick Street (☎416983; £7 per day, £30 per week; *Raleigh* drop-off scheme); or *Rent-A-Bike*, Barrington Street (☎411090; £7 per day, £30 per week).

Accommodation

The area around the train and bus stations is fairly unkempt, but the *Railway Hotel* opposite (☎44250; ④) is comfortable and convenient. A few rather more expensive hotels can be found nearby in and around Glentworth and Henry streets – head down Davis Street, then right and left into Glentworth Street, which crosses first O'Connell Street (the main commercial thoroughfare) and then Henry Street further down towards the Shannon. Try, for example, the *Glentworth Hotel* on Glentworth Street (☎413822, fax ☎413073; ⑤) or the *Royal George* on O'Connell Street (☎414566, fax ☎317171; ⑥).

Newtown Pery also has several decent **B&Bs** in Davis Street, which runs straight ahead from the stations, including *Boylan's* at no. 22 (☎418916; ③) and *Hibernian House* at no. 32 (☎417382; ③). There's an easy-going *An Óige* **youth hostel** not far away in Pery Square on the far side of People's Park (open all year; ☎314672, fax ☎314572; ②); turn left from the stations to find People's Park. The *Limerick Holiday Hostel*, Barrington House, George's Quay (☎415222; ①), is an excellent, large independent hostel, with private rooms available: it's further away, but a much more pleasant place to stay; you'll find it across the river from *The Granary*, not far from St Mary's Cathedral. *Clyde House* budget accommodation, Alphonsus Street, offers self-catering (②) and B&B (③) as well as hostel facilities (☎314357, fax ☎314234).

Other **B&Bs** are some way out, above all across the river on the Ennis Road: try *Parkview* (☎451505; ④), *Clifton House* (☎454361; ④), or *Trelawne House* (☎454063; ④). Most of the big hotels are out on Ennis Road, too. The nearest **campsite** is at Currahchase Forest Park, sixteen miles west (see p.239).

The City

The sometimes incongruous blend of old and new in Limerick is testimony to a city discovering itself after years of neglect. Renovations and new building programmes stand alongside buildings – and indeed whole districts – that seem barely touched by the last fifty years. The best **views** of the city are to be had walking along the banks of the Shannon, especially around Arthur's Quay and the City Hall, or alternatively from the top of King John's Castle. Although virtually all the sights are in the old parts, Englishtown and Irishtown, the modern centre of the city is **Newtown Pery** – where the shops, pubs and restaurants congregate – an area of broad parallel streets scattered with fine Georgian buildings. O'Connell Street is the chief artery of this part of the city, and it's worth wandering down here, checking out the side streets with their characterful pubs and shops. Getting around the centre is easiest on foot.

Englishtown

Englishtown, which still has the narrow curving streets of its medieval origins, if few of the buildings, is the oldest part of the city, north of the modern centre. Crossing Matthew Bridge, the first things you'll see are St Mary's Cathedral ahead of you and the City Hall to your left. If you look down to the embankment of **George's Quay** on the right, your eye should just catch two very fine but armless torsos, metal-sculpted and set upon tall plinths facing one another some forty paces apart. This twentieth-century grotesquerie of war from within and without takes you by surprise – it's an unusually strong statement for Limerick.

The Church of Ireland **St Mary's Cathedral** (June–Sept Mon–Sat 9am–1pm & 2.30–5pm; Oct–May Mon–Sat 9am–1pm; free) was built at the end of the twelfth century, but only the Romanesque doorway facing the Courthouse, the nave and parts of the transepts remain from this period. The chancel, windows and the rest of the transepts date from the fifteenth century. The cathedral's unique feature is its **misericords**, the only set in Ireland: these are choir seats of lovely black oak with reptilian animals – cockatrice, griffins, sphinx and wild boar – carved in bold relief. The area around St Mary's has had a very successful face-lift. As you leave the cathedral, walk down to the Courthouse and stroll around City Hall – a brand-new affair of glass and pink tubing – to appreciate the rushing river and Limerick's buoyant new civic pride. Although it's just a local council building, it's worth using the City Hall's café: light and airy, it's a much nicer spot to take a break than inside the castle.

Further into Englishtown, next to Thomond Bridge, is **King John's Castle** (mid-April to Oct daily 9.30am–5.30pm, last admission 4.30pm; Nov to mid-April Sun noon–4pm, last admission 3pm), built in the early thirteenth century, and retaining much of its medieval structure. You may well be put off by the newly built entrance hall, a senseless addition of overwhelming vacuity, negating any sense of power as you approach what is in fact one of the most impressive Anglo-Norman castles in Ireland. The castle was originally a five-sided fortress with four stout round towers; but these were shortened at a much later stage to accommodate artillery positions – though one was actually replaced as a bastion in 1611. Inside, instruments of medieval siege warfare enliven the castle yard, or you can climb the battlements for superb views; there's an interesting twenty-minute **film** of the history of Limerick, and a much more detailed history of the Normans in Ireland in the "stand-and-read" **interpretative centre**. Beneath all of this are the foundations of pre-Norman dwellings – the finds of recent excavations. Despite all this, the castle is probably most impressive from the outside, staring up at the cliff-like immensity of its walls alongside Thomond Bridge.

The **treaty stone** stands on the far side of Thomond Bridge, on Clancy Strand on the west bank of the Shannon. In recent years it has been moved – only about twenty yards – and sandblasted clean. This, if you want to read symbolic significance into it, can be seen as an attempt to loosen a burden that was preventing the city from developing.

Irishtown

Back across Matthew Bridge you're in **Irishtown**, much of it now given over to grey council housing. Perhaps the brightest spark here is the **Custom House**, an eighteenth-century structure of harmonious Classical balance, due to house the **Hunt Museum** in late 1996; until then the museum will remain at the university (see below). A good ten-minute walk from here, the city **museum** is in St John's Square (Tues–Sat 10am–1pm & 2.15–5pm; free), housed in a fine Georgian end-house close to St John's Cathedral. It displays currency going as far back as the Viking period, guild regalia, historic maps showing the old walled towns of Englishtown and Irishtown, memorabilia of various Fenian uprisings (notably a Pádraig Pearse letter from the 1916 insurrection), and Stone, Iron and especially Bronze Age implements. Many of the Mesolithic items (c.7000–4000 BC) are from the Lough Gur area, and it's worth looking at the excavation photographs of this site before you visit it.

St John's Cathedral, a nineteenth-century Gothic Revival monstrosity which boasts the tallest spire in the country (at 280ft), is the seat of the Catholic diocese. Its two chief treasures are a fifteenth-century mitre and carved crozier, made by Bishop Cornelius O'Dea. Inside, there's a sombre atmosphere appropriate to this most Catholic of cities; outside is a memorial to Patrick Sarsfield, unsuccessful Jacobite defender of the city. A short way north of the cathedral, on Lelia Street, you can see the best surviving section of the fifteenth-century **city walls**, built to guard the approaches from the North Munster territory of the O'Briens, with its Gaelic traditions, language and culture.

The Hunt Museum

The most interesting museum in Limerick, the **Hunt Museum** (Mon–Sat 10am–5pm; £1.60), is housed in Limerick University some way from the centre. To get there, head out on the Dublin Road. After a few miles, take a left turn immediately after a *Maxol* petrol station for Plassey, follow the road round for another third of a mile, then turn left through the white-gated entrance, to the reception at the three flag poles, and ask for the museum. This is one of the best-conceived museums around, with art objects (mainly Irish antiquities but also European) of consistently high interest, beautifully presented and extensively documented. The museum owes much to the originator of the collection, John Hunt, who was also the enlightened creator of the Craggaunowen habitation project in County Clare (see p.308). Many of the objects here date from the Bronze Age: highlights include the **Antrim Cross**, one of Ireland's most important examples of ninth-century early Christian metalwork and thought to be a precursor of the high cross designs at Monasterboice and Kells. There are also a late Bronze Age shield, cauldron and bucket, wholly intact, and a thirteenth-century Limoges enamelled chasse. While on campus you can also take in the small but absorbing **National Self-Portrait Collection** and the **Watercolour Society of Ireland Collection**. These will remain here after the Hunt Museum relocates to the Custom House in the city centre.

Eating, drinking and entertainment

A welcome symptom of Limerick's regeneration is the rate at which good new cafés and pubs are appearing. The list overleaf will give you some useful starting points. **Bars** there are in abundance, and in recent years Limerick has revived its reputation as a **musical** centre – particularly for contemporary and rock music. Again, a selection of bars and places to hear music can be found below. The *Belltable* and the *City Gallery*, listed below, are good places to make contact with the Irish arts scene, and are worthy of a visit if you've more than half a day in the city.

Cafés and restaurants

Bella Italia, 22 Thomas St (☎418872). Huge delicious helpings of fresh pasta and sauces from £3–4, to eat in or take away. Mon–Sat till 6pm.

Belltable Arts Centre, 69 O'Connell St. Good café downstairs with home-cooked lunches and snacks. Daytime only.

Doc's in *The Granary*, Bank Place (opposite George's Quay). Busy young bar with a four-course lunch for £4; open Mon–Fri.

Freddy's Bistro, Theatre Lane (☎418749), down an alley off Lower Glentworth St, near the *Belltable Arts Centre*. Relaxing and affordable place with good food – not only pizza. Tues–Sun 5.30pm till late.

George Bistro Restaurant, *Royal George Hotel*, O'Connell St (☎414566). Restaurant with vegetarian choices.

Green Onions Caffe, 3 Ellen St (☎400710). Adventurous but affordable, daily till 10pm.

The Grove, Cecil St. Health-food shop that does tasty takeaways.

Henry Cecil, Lower Cecil St. Steaks, grills, burgers from £6.

Java's, 5 Catherine St. Delicious breakfasts and lunches, and the best coffee in Limerick. Mon–Sat 8am–4pm, Sun noon–4pm.

Lavazza Le Bistro, Steamboat Quay (☎319800). Dinner (Mon–Sat) in classy surroundings; main courses from £4.95.

The Tea and Coffee Counter, Thomas St. Pleasant coffee shop serving lunches for under £3; open till 5.30pm.

The Vintage Club, Ellen St. Pub/restaurant good for quick meals and sandwiches; decent wine selection, too. Lunches and evening meals around £5; open till 11pm.

Bars and music venues

Butch McKenzies, Catherine St (near People's Park and next to *Lane Antiques*). Wild West theme bar playing nothing but American rock, country and rhythm and blues.

Charlie Chaplin's, Chapel St. New, very trendy bar off Cruises St.

Doc's (see above). Upbeat bar in brick-vaulted granary courtyard; live rock and pop bands (Tues, Weds, Thurs, Sun); discos as advertised (rave, rap, hiphop; Thurs–Sun, £3).

Henry Cecil (see above). Lively bar, mixed young crowd; live music four nights a week; regular disco upstairs.

James Gleeson, *The White House Bar*, 52 O'Connell St. Ancient ale house, full of character (and characters); packed, but warm and friendly.

The Locke, George's Quay. Traditional music on Sun, Mon & Tues; pleasant place to sit outside on fine evenings.

Micky Martins, Augustinian Lane, off Thomas St. Friendly bar, great music; somewhat studenty.

Nancy Blake's, Upper Denmark St (☎416443). Pub with traditional music Sun–Wed; pleasant beer garden.

The Old Quarter, Cruises St. Airy new bar with good daytime food.

The Outback, literally at the back of *Nancy Blake's*; great venue for live blues and rock bands.

Saints and Scholars, 7 Robert St (☎417616). New music venue with rave disco Thurs–Sun. Also food.

Tait's Tavern, 54 Parnell St (☎418133). Occasional traditional music.

Tom Collins, Cecil St. Quieter bar, popular with local arty types.

The Vintage Club, Ellen St (see above). Traditional music Wed & Fri.

Willie Sexton's, Upper O'Connell St. Bar for rugby enthusiasts; big sports events screened. No music.

Arts centres and galleries

Belltable Arts Centre, 69 O'Connell St (☎319866). Interesting mix, usually including a summer season of Irish plays in July & Aug, with films on Sundays. Also some gallery space, exhibiting community and national artists (10am–8pm).

City Gallery of Art, Pery Square (Mon–Wed & Fri 10am–1pm & 2–6pm, Thurs 2–7pm, Sat 10am–1pm; free). Situated in the People's Park, emphasizes international contemporary art, with a lesser focus on Irish work.

The Clare Glens

The **Clare Glens** on the Limerick–Tipperary border is a beautiful area of flowing falls, parts of which you can swim in: it makes a great day's excursion for cyclists. Head for Moroe (sometimes spelt Murroe), east of the city; Clare Glens is two miles north of this. A circular ride of some twenty miles could take this in, along with Glenstal Abbey and the village of **CASTLECONNELL**, a well-known Irish music and Irish-language centre in a scenic setting on the banks of the Shannon some seven miles from Limerick. **Currahchase Forest Park**, sixteen miles west of the city, has a well-equipped campground, the *Currahchase Caravan and Camping* (☎061/396349), picnic site, arboretum and the ruins of the home of poet Aubrey de Vere. To the south, it's not much further to Lough Gur (see below) and Adare (p.242).

Lough Gur and around

Leaving Limerick city in the direction of Cork the main route is the N20, a fast and efficient but rather dull route south. If you have time to stop along the way, the smaller R512 road has considerably more to offer – above all Lough Gur, site of a wealth of Neolithic finds and one of County Limerick's chief attractions.

Lough Gur

Seventeen miles south of Limerick city, **Lough Gur** looks as though its waters have been accidentally spilt onto the Limerick soil. It's the only significant lake in the country, and comes as a rare treat in the midst of an otherwise lustreless terrain. The area that surrounds the lake has been an extremely rich source of archeological finds – though what exists now is often an extremely frugal sketch of what took place 5000 years ago. The lake is C-shaped, with a marshy area to the east that would complete the full circle.

In the middle of this circle is a small rise known as **Knockadoon**, whose slopes are studded with faint remains of earthworks showing ring forts and hut foundations dating from 3500 to 1000 BC. The length of its less secure marshy side is naturally forested and guarded at either end by two medieval tower houses, Bouchier's Castle and Black Castle. Mary Carbery's nineteenth-century book, *The Farm by Lough Gur*, gives a vivid contemporary account of life by the lough – the farm still stands up the road from the Neolithic huts known as the Spectacles.

Lough Gur must have been the perfect setting for a **Neolithic settlement**. The lake provided fish, and the gentle hillsides produced berries, nuts and trappings for animal hunting, as well as protection from the elements – and detection. When the lake was partly drained in the middle of the nineteenth century, and its level dropped by three yards, prehistoric artefacts were found in such quantities that stories tell of whole cartloads being hauled away. This may not be such an exaggeration; visit museums across the world today, and you'll discover some find from Lough Gur on display. The most famous discovery was a bronze shield from 700 BC, perfect in its concentric rings of bosses, but for a hacking in two places by the reedcutter who discovered it. The finds here pair well with the Neolithic discoveries made in Meath; this was once a Neolithic living commune, where the *Brú Na Bóinne* site is concerned with ritual and burial. Today there's abundant **birdlife** on the lake; the grazing cattle, antlered goats and lack of modern buildings give you a strong intimation of the life of 5000 years ago.

The Interpretative centre and stone circle

The simplest approach to Lough Gur is to come off the R512 at Holycross. Follow the road to the northernmost section of the lake, keeping an eye out for a wedge-shaped **gallery grave**. The grave, typically, shows a long gallery space where the bodies of eight adults and four children from around 2000 BC were found. The gallery has parallel double walls of stone slabs filled in with rubble and what's called a septal slab at its back. The road then circles on round the marsh to an **interpretative centre** (mid-May to Sept daily 10am–6pm; £1.80). Housed in replica Neolithic huts, this attempts to give some idea of what life was like for the early inhabitants. From here the chief attractions on **Knockadoon** are easily accessible on foot.

A quarter of a mile north of the Holycross turn-off, the first thing you'll have seen is a gargantuan **stone circle** close to the main road, the most substantial of the area's prehistoric remains. Possibly the grandest example in the country, it has a ring of standing stones (*orthostats*) marking out an almost perfect circle. A posthole was found at the centre which must have held a stake, from which, with a length of cord attached, the circle could be struck. Some of the stones are massive and are bolstered within their earth sockets by smaller boulders, which were then covered. Flints, arrowheads, blades and bowls were found within the enclosure, but little has been learned about the site's exact function. A circle of this size clearly demanded a good deal of social organization and a strong sense of purpose; the obvious conclusion is that this was a great centre for religious rituals, and frustratingly little else can be said.

The castles and Knockadoon

If you're walking, an alternative approach to Knockadoon is across the stone causeway that leads from near the gallery grave to **Black Castle**. Possibly thirteenth century, the castle is now weighed down by a swarthy camouflage of nettles, brambles and trees. It was once quite extensive, with a high curtain wall and square towers, and acted as a principal seat for the Earls of Desmond. The pathway north to Bouchier's Castle has three **Neolithic hut** remains at various degrees up the hill slope. If you're intent on seeing them, you'll have to forage around among the wooded thickets. A 1681 map shows the Knockadoon Peninsula as an island with a drawbridge sticking out of **Bouchier's Castle**. It's a typical fifteenth-century Desmond tower house of five storeys; but it's still privately owned and can't yet be visited (in any case, there's a better example at Castle Matrix; see p.242).

Turning westwards from the Black Castle towards the lakeshore, you'll see various ring forts and hut traces on the bare grassy slopes. It's not much, but even this scant evidence is enough to conjure up a thriving Stone Age community on **Knockadoon**. Rather than continue round along the bank of the lake, it's best to take this opportunity to cross back along the hilltop centre, where from a point known as **M**, you can get penetrating views into Kerry and Cork, with Limerick spreading towards them in a swath of low hills. **Crock** and **Bolin islands** in the lake are both *crannógs* which the mainland has now caught up with. They were built by laying down a ring of boulders, then the inner space was filled with earth and brushwood. **Garret Island** is a natural island with some stone remains of another Desmond castle.

Kilmallock

Eight miles further down the main road from Lough Gur, **KILMALLOCK** has some good Norman remains: a tower castle, a town gate, a Dominican friary and a medieval stone mansion on the main street. **St John's Tower Castle** stands in the middle of the street and was the town citadel (get the key at the bungalow across the road), but there's little to see here. Turn instead down the lane opposite and you'll find a tiny

museum (Mon–Fri 1.30–5pm, free; otherwise contact T. Bohan, Lord Edward St) which won't take a minute to get through, unless you lend an ear to the home-made audiovisual history of the town. One interesting fact that crops up, and which goes a long way to explaining the prestigious-looking fortifications and friary bases, is that at the end of the sixteenth century Kilmallock had a population of 2000, compared to Dublin's 5000. Kilmallock's importance was swift to decline – its population today is only 1500.

Bruree

Four miles west of Kilmallock, **BRUREE** was the childhood home of **Eamon De Valera**, familiarly known as the "big man" or "Dev" to a population for whom he's been the most influential political instigator since the birth of the Free State in 1922. He founded the *Fianna Fáil* (Soldiers of Destiny) party in 1926, acted as premier of Ireland in 1932–48, 1951–54 and 1957–59, and assumed the honorary role of president from 1959 to 1973. This makes up a sizeable chunk of the Republic's history, and his grip on the nation has left an ambivalent attitude to his worth and integrity.

De Valera was the only leader of the 1916 Easter Rising to survive. His initial death sentence was commuted to imprisonment because of his American dual nationality – he was born in New York, and at this time the British were sensitive to American neutrality in World War I. He escaped from prison in England and was unconstitutionally elected the first president of the Irish Republic in 1919; his almost miraculous survival had marked him out as the man to lead Ireland out of seven hundred years of British domination. The Republic immediately declared war on Britain, and when two years of struggle forced the British to negotiate, De Valera's was the leading rebel voice against the signing of the Anglo-Irish Treaty in 1921. He wanted to hold out for an all-Ireland Free State, rather than accept only 26 counties out of 32, as was laid down in the Treaty. This stance divided the Irish and provoked the Civil War of 1921–23. The one war he succeeded in keeping the Irish out of was World War II, at the end of which he had the gall to send official commiserations to the Reichstag on Hitler's death, so profound was the bitterness of his battle with the British.

De Valera was brought up just outside Bruree in a small **cottage**, which has now been turned into a modest memorial of the family's household possessions, including a bulky trunk that was used for their return from exile in New York. The cottage is signposted nearly a mile down the road to the right at the eastern end of Bruree village (key from next house on the right, 150 yards further down the road). At the western end of Bruree village itself is the old schoolhouse, which has been turned into a **museum** and **heritage centre** (July & Aug Mon–Fri 10am–5pm, Sat & Sun noon–6pm; Sept–June Mon–Fri 10am–5pm, Sat & Sun 2–5pm; ☎063/90900; £2), stocked with memorabilia of the ex-premier and president, plus a few rural items of general interest.

South and west of Limerick

The road southwest to Killarney is by far the most interesting route out of Limerick, catching the prim English beauty of thatched cottages in **Adare** and, much more importantly, taking in **Castle Matrix**, a Desmond tower house that has been brilliantly restored and gives a unique insight into life as it might have been lived in these castles. The road west to Tralee, the N69, is the least interesting of the three major routes across County Limerick. It runs parallel to the Shannon estuary but mostly through flat alluvial land, without the compensation of having the waters alongside except for the last few miles into Glin.

Adare

Famously picturesque **ADARE** has cultivated nearly as many antiques shops as pubs. In peak season, it will more than likely be infested with tourists snapping the wayside cottages that sit in a neat row, their purposefully quaint deep-brown thatch hanging in low fringes. The cottages represent the nineteenth-century ideal of romanticized rusticity, as realized by the third Earl of Dunraven (1812–71), landlord and master of Adare Manor and an eternal improver of circumstances for his tenants. Given that Adare is now probably regarded as the prettiest (and, it must be added, prissiest) village in Ireland, it's hard to believe that before the earl's improvements it was one of the grottiest. The cottages today feature a **tourist information office** (mid-April to Oct; ☎061/396255), an antiques shop and an upmarket **restaurant**, *The Mustard Seed* (dinner from £25; imaginative vegetarian dishes; ☎061/396451).

Adare Manor House, to the north of the village, is a huge, near fanatical assembly of castellations and turrets in limestone, built by the earl to Gothic Revival designs in 1832. This castle has only recently passed into private hands as a grand hotel, the *Adare Manor* (☎061/396566), at over £90 a night – it costs even to walk into the grounds. The River Maigue flows by the estate a little further up, at the head of the village, and although an exciting-looking triumvirate of **medieval buildings** beckons, a golf course steers its course next to all of them, inhibiting any snooping around you might want to do. You're meant to declare your intentions at the clubhouse (entrance a little further up the road) but you could probably slip from ruin to ruin without being noticed. It may not be worth the effort anyhow, for the **Desmond Castle** – interesting to explore as it looks – is completely bricked up and deemed unsafe. The fifteenth-century **Friary** appears far better preserved, but it was extensively restored as late as the mid-nineteenth century. All of these are perhaps easiest viewed from the bridge.

Back in the village there are ecclesiastical sites, too, starting with an **Augustinian Priory** just by the bridge. Beautifully conserved, this still serves as the local Church of Ireland church, its interior as close as any to the old medieval model. The **Trinitarian Abbey**, halfway down the main street, was founded in 1230 for the Trinitarian Canons of the Order of the Redemption of Captives, and is the only house of this order in Ireland. Today, it's Adare's Catholic church, with one of its turrets at the back a deserted columbarium. If you're thinking of staying over in Adare – there are a couple of **B&Bs** in the village and plenty more in the immediate surrounds – *Bill Chawke's* and *Collin's Bar* both have traditional sessions one evening a week all year round.

Rathkeale and Castle Matrix

About eight miles on from Adare, **RATHKEALE** was once an important Geraldine town, and the main source of interest here is their one-time stronghold, **Castle Matrix** (mid-May to mid-Sept daily 11am–5pm; other times by arrangement; ☎069/64284; £2). To get there, turn right at the south end of the exceptionally long main street, just after the bridge: the castle lies half a mile down the road, on the right. Castle Matrix is a fifteenth-century tower house built by the seventh Earl of Desmond, and would inevitably have met with the same ruinous fate as virtually all the other 427 tower houses that once existed in Limerick, or the 2700 that once stood throughout the country – but for the brilliant restoration work of current owner Seán O'Driscoll, an Irish-American military enthusiast. With his army expertise, he understood the design of the fortifications and realized that measurements needed to be within an inch for the battlements on the parapets to be effective (in contrast, the ornamental battlements at somewhere like Bunratty in County Clare wouldn't have lasted long in a fifteenth-century siege).

Tower houses flourished between the fifteenth and seventeenth centuries, especially in these southern counties. They provided a robust enough mini-fortress for the shift in the times; Anglo-Norman confidence was increasing, resulting in an expansion of settlements. The big Irish estates were being broken up due to the fall of the old Gaelic chiefs, and more towns were cropping up, with land being cultivated in hitherto uninhabited areas. Tower houses took on a uniform plan, usually of four or five floors, the top floor being the living quarters, the bottom windowless and usually used for storage. Castle Matrix has a tiny chapel re-created on its top floor and a medieval bedroom on another floor. It's stocked with exciting *objets d'art*, including a jewel-encrusted nineteenth-century Gaelic harp made by Fall of Belfast; an ebony writing bureau imported by the Southwells from China and finally donated back to Matrix some years ago, now sitting in the Oriental Room; documents referring to the Wild Geese (Irish officers who fled to the Continent at the beginning of the seventeenth century); and the most remarkable item of all to return home – the original deed of the Southwells (the Earls of Desmond), which Seán O'Driscoll came across accidentally in London's Portobello Road.

The castle derived its name from the *matres*, a Celtic sanctuary, on which it stands. The scattering of destroyed cashels and raths in the surrounding area give substance to the idea of an ancient sanctuary here. An annexe of the castle offers luxury **B&B** (☎069/64284; ⑤); gourmet banquets are also held at the request of groups. Alternatively, *Rathkeale House Hotel* offers food and accommodation for those living slightly less high on the hog (☎069/64322; ④).

Newcastle West

Between Rathkeale and Newcastle West a signpost points to **Ardagh**, the ring fort where the wonderful Ardagh Chalice was found in 1868 (it's now in the Dublin National Museum). The site here is unimpressive, however, and it's not worth dragging yourself off the main road.

NEWCASTLE WEST should make the last, if very brief, stop on your way out of Limerick, to look at the almost perfectly preserved **Desmond Banqueting Hall**. The hall is on the main square and very little fuss is made of it; but it's part of a scattered and hidden complex of ruined buildings – a keep, a peel tower, a bastion and curtain wall. Even though this was once the principal seat of the Fitzgeralds, the town hasn't harnessed its history to its advantage. The hall is in a near perfect state of preservation, and ready for an inspired restoration. At present, apart from a marriage fireplace said to have been imported from Egypt, it's all bare. You can get the key from what used to be the old gatehouse, down the drive at the immediate right of the hall grounds. Again, there are several small **B&Bs** – try, for example, Mrs Kennedy on Bishop Street (☎069/62050; ③); you can also get food and rooms at the *River Room Hotel* (☎069/62244; ④).

There's another excellently preserved but entirely deserted tower house, **Glenquin Castle**, signposted left several miles off the Newcastle–Abbeyfeale Road by a petrol station (head for Killeady). It has very good views of the countryside, but the effort to get here is really only worthwhile if you have a car.

West of Limerick

The first sign of interest you'll spot is **Carrigogunnell Castle** – no more than a well-worn ruin, overgrown with shrubs and trees, but with striking views across the estuary's waist. It's probably not worth leaving the main road; catch sight of it as the road passes Clarina, from where the ruin cuts a dramatic appearance atop its rocky outcrop.

The road passes a few more tower houses on the right and the **Currahchase Forest Park** (see p.239) on the left before reaching **ASKEATON**. Here, there's an Anglo-Norman **friary** next to the River Deel, just off the main road at its second entry to Askeaton from the east. The friary was founded by the fourth Earl of Desmond, Gerald the Poet, in 1389. It now seems particularly hidden away, and has one of the loveliest cloisters you'll come across and some excellent window tracery. From the dormitory above, you can pick out the towering remains of the **castle**, penned in towards the centre of the town. This is worth no more than a quick scout around (keys from Billy Casey at the house by the entrance gate); there's a large banqueting hall, very similar to the better example in Newcastle West, its vaulted ground-floor chambers remaining just within the walls. A very dodgy-looking fifteenth-century end tower stands upon a rock in the centre of what was once an island in the River Deel. The castle's present decay does little to suggest its one-time Anglo-Norman prominence, when it flourished in the hands of the Earls of Desmond, until their fall to the Earl of Essex during the sixteenth century.

FOYNES is a moderately busy seaport, with a **museum** (April–Oct daily 10am–6pm, last admission 5.30pm; Nov–March by appointment on ☎069/65416; £2.50) which celebrates the town's past as an aviation centre of flying boats. In the late 1930s and early 1940s, Foynes, as Limerick's only seaport, was the terminus for a transatlantic flying-boat service. Moving on, the afforested hillsides that now appear mark a pleasant route along the estuary as far as Glin on the Limerick–Kerry border.

travel details

Trains

Limerick to: Cahir (2 daily; 1hr 15min); Carrick-on-Suir (2 daily; 1hr 45min); Clonmel (2 daily; 1hr 30min); Dublin (8 daily; 2hr 35min); Rosslare Harbour (2 daily; 3hr 20min); Tipperary (2 daily; 50min).

Limerick Junction to: Cork (6 daily; 1hr 10min).

Waterford to: Dublin (4 daily; 2hr 30min); Limerick (2 daily; 3hr).

Bus Éireann

Limerick to: Cahir (5 daily; 1hr 10min); Cork (8 daily; 1hr 50min); Dublin (14 daily; 3hr 15min); Shannon Airport (frequent service; 45min; passenger enquiries ☎061/474311); Tipperary (11 daily; 50min); Waterford (5 daily; 2hr 25min).

Waterford to: Dublin (8 daily; 3hr 30min).

Private buses

Pierce Kavanagh Coaches (☎01/873 0671) leave **from Dublin**, Liberty Hall on Fridays at 5.30pm for Cashel (8pm), Cahir (8.15pm) and Mitchelstown (9pm), continuing on to Cork and Bantry. A return service **from Bantry** leaves on Sundays at 3.30pm for Cork (5.05pm), Mitchelstown, Cahir, Cashel and Dublin. Another service runs **from Thurles**, Liberty Square (Mon–Sat 8.45am) for Dublin, and **from Dublin**, *Burger King*, O'Connell St (Mon–Sat 6pm) to Thurles.

Funtrek (☎01/873 0852) runs daily services **from Limerick**, Roscrea and Nenagh to Dublin, and **from Waterford** to Dublin.

Rapid Express Club Travel, 32 Michael Street, Waterford (☎051/72149 and ☎01/6791549), has at least five buses daily from Tramore to Waterford and on to Dublin (leaving *Manahan's* shop, Tramore, approx. 30min before leaving Waterford). Mon–Sat depart Waterford (from *Bank of Ireland*, Parnell Street) 6am, 8.30am, 11am, 1.45pm, 4pm, 5.30pm & 8.30pm; Sun 9.30am. For the return journey depart Dublin (Custom House Quay) 7.15am, 9am, 11.15am, 1.45pm, 4.15pm, 6pm & 8.30pm. Prices from as little as £8 return. Bikes carried free if there's room.

CHAPTER SEVEN

COUNTY CORK

C ork, Ireland's largest county, is the perfect place to ease yourself gently into the exhilarations of Ireland's west coast. **Cork city** is the south's self-proclaimed cultural capital and manages to be at one and the same time a relaxed and a spirited place. There are no spectacular sights, but Cork has to be one of Ireland's most pleasurable and accessible cities. Always a port, and with an island at its core, Cork nestles well inland on the estuary of the **River Lee**, which sustains the city with that same clear, soothing atmosphere that characterizes most of the county, and in particular its coast and rivers. In the east of the county maritime history is still more richly distilled, in the small ports of **Cobh, Youghal** and – most of all – **Kinsale**, all suggestive of a prosperity that Ireland could have had were it not for the strangulation of its overseas trade by Britain. On the other side of this coin are the riches of the Anglo-Irish legacy: the Neoclassical perfection of **Fota House** near Cobh, and the outrageously sumptuous art treasures of **Bantry House** in the west.

Every county of Ireland's wild west coast has its devotees, and Cork is certainly no exception. The place elicits strong reaction from locals and visitors alike, and its rivalry with neighbouring Kerry is legendary. Critics like to call the scenery of **West Cork** tame or mild – even genteel – since it can only occasionally match the sheer wild physicality of coasts further north. But this quality probably has as much to do with the people and the relative mildness of the climate – blessed by the continual influence of the Gulf Stream – as with landscape.

In the main the charms of the Cork countryside are those of a gently rural backwater, but as you head west along a fabulously indented coastline of hidden bays and coves to the wild peninsulas of the extreme southwest, or through the ravine of Gougane Barra high above **Glengarriff** and **Bantry Bay**, the soft contours of a comfortable and easy prettiness slip away to reveal beauty of a more elemental kind. There's not as much of this as you might find in, say, Kerry, but in the **Caha Mountains** careering north from Bantry Bay, the scintillating cliffs of **Mizen Head** or the seascapes of **Sherkin** and **Clear Island**, teeming with birdlife, Cork has scenery as exciting and dramatic as you'll find anywhere.

Public transport around the county is fairly plentiful. **Bus Éireann** covers the whole of Cork except for the north side of Mizen Head. Major towns have daily connections – though there's only one bus a week along Sheep's Head and one linking Kenmare with Castletownbere. Small towns and villages off the main roads are served less frequently, so if you are relying on public transport it's worth taking details of times and days of services you are likely to want while in a major bus station. Ask about return fares – often they are as cheap as single tickets if used on certain days. On certain routes private buses provide the only transport: see "Travel Details" at the end of this chapter for details. The intricate landscape of West Cork, in particular, is best explored at a slow pace, making it an ideal country for touring by **bike** or **hitching**. If you are travelling by car the N71 is the main coastal road, but it's much more rewarding to meander off along the minor roads through remoter areas, past sandy coves and small communities.

If you have a tent, you can **camp** almost anywhere along the coast if you ask permission first, though the Beara Peninsula and the Caha Mountains are very rocky. The few official campsites are listed in the text.

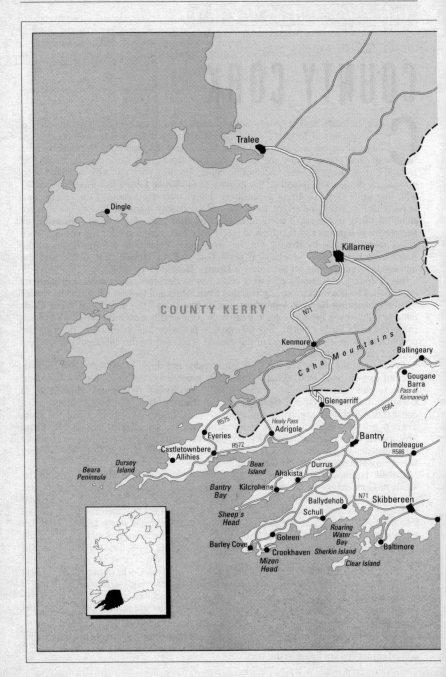

Tralee

Dingle

Killarney

COUNTY KERRY

N71

Kenmore

Caha Mountains

Ballingeary

Gougane
Barra
Pass of
Keimaneigh

Glengarriff

R584

R575

Healy Pass

Adrigole

Bantry

Eyeries

R572

Drimoleague

R586

Castletownbere
Allihies

Durrus

Beara
Peninsula

Dursey
Island

Bear
Island

Ahakista

Kilcrohane

N71

Skibbereen

Bantry
Bay

Ballydehob

Schull

Sheep's
Head

Roaring
Water
Bay

Barley Cove

Goleen

Baltimore

Crookhaven

Sherkin Island

Mizen
Head

Clear Island

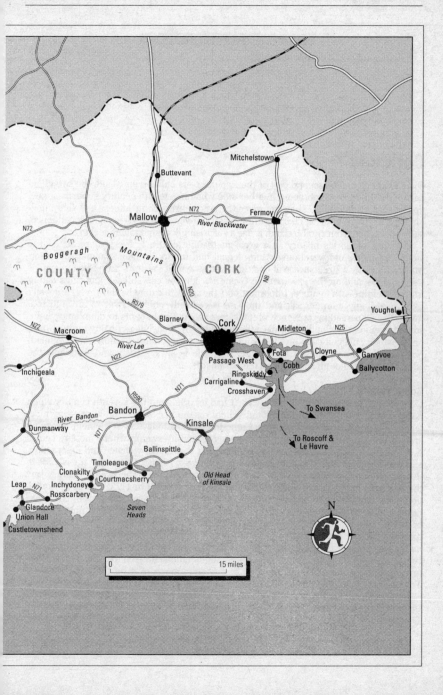

Cork city

Old **CORK** city – the second city of the Republic – is built on an island, the two channels of the River Lee embracing it either side while nineteenth-century suburbs sprawl
up the surrounding hills. The river gives the city centre a compactness and sharp definition. It's a place of great charm, with a history of vigorous intellectual independence,
and approached from rural Ireland, it has a surprisingly cosmopolitan feel to it.

Evidence of Cork's history as a great mercantile centre is everywhere, with grey
stone quaysides, old warehouses and elegant and quirky bridges spanning the river.
Many of the city's streets were at one time waterways: St Patrick's Street had quays for
sailing ships, and on the pavement in Grand Parade you can still see moorings dating
from the eighteenth century. Important port though Cork may be, however, it doesn't
feel overridingly commercial, and the Lee is certainly not the river of an industrial
town. The all-pervading presence of its waters reflects and seems to double any light,
so that even on the cloudiest of days there is a balmy, translucent quality to the atmosphere which effects a calm on the visitor. Cork is a welcoming, friendly place. While it
has the vibrancy to enliven and excite, the pace is always Irish, and somehow the
island breathes enough space for all temperaments.

Some history

Cork (*Corcaigh*, meaning "marshy place") had its origins in the seventh century when
Saint Finbarr founded an abbey and school on the site where the impressive nineteenth-century Gothic St Finbarr's Cathedral stands today. A settlement grew up
around the monastic foundation, overlooking a marshy swamp where the city centre
now stands. In 820 the **Vikings** arrived, bringing their usual violence and destruction,
and wrecked both abbey and town. They built a new settlement on one of the islands in
the marshes and eventually integrated with the native Celts. The twelfth century saw
the **Norman** invasion and Cork, like other ports, was taken in 1172. The new acquisition was fortified with massive stone walls, which survived Cromwell but were
destroyed by Williamite forces at the **Siege of Cork** in 1690. From this time the city
began to take on the shape recognizable today. **Expansion** saw the reclamation of
marshes and the development of canals within the city, and waterborne **trade** brought
increasing prosperity. Evidence of this wealth survives in the form of fine eighteenth-
century bow-fronted houses and the ostentatious nineteenth-century church architecture decorating the city – sharp, grey and Gothic, much of it by the Pain brothers.
Traces of the great dairy trade of that period can still be seen in the Shandon area.

More recently, Cork saw much violence and suffered greatly during the Anglo-Irish and
Civil wars: the city's part in **Republican** history is well documented in the local museum.
The Black and Tans reigned here with particular terror, destroying much of the town by fire,

The telephone code for Cork city is ☎021.

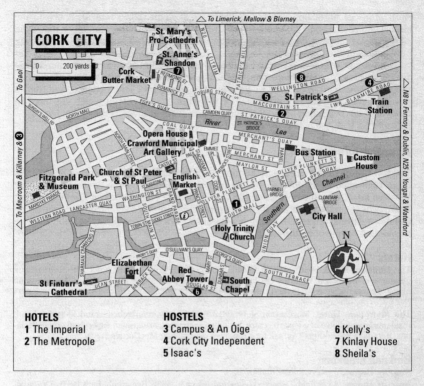

To Limerick, Mallow & Blarney

CORK CITY

0   200 yards

To Gaol

To Macroom & Killarney

To Macroom & Killarney

N8 to Fermoy & Dublin, N25 to Youghal & Waterford

St. Mary's
Pro-Cathedral
St. Anne's
Shandon
Cork
Butter Market
Opera House
Crawford Municipal
Art Gallery
Fitzgerald Park
& Museum
Church of St Peter
& St Paul
English
Market
St Finbarr's
Cathedral
Elizabethan
Fort
Red
Abbey Tower
South
Chapel
Holy Trinity
Church
St. Patrick's
Train
Station
Bus Station
Custom
House
City Hall

N

HOTELS
1 The Imperial
2 The Metropole

HOSTELS
3 Campus & An Óige
4 Cork City Independent
5 Isaac's

6 Kelly's
7 Kinlay House
8 Sheila's

and were responsible for the murder of Thomas MacCurtain, the mayor of Cork, in 1920. Cork's next mayor, Terence MacSwiney, was jailed as a Republican and died in Brixton prison after a hunger strike of 74 days. He was a popular hero, and his hunger strike remains one of the longest achieved in the history of the IRA. One of his colleagues in Cork prison, Joseph Murphy, achieved the longest fast on record, going 76 days without food.

As part of the Republic, Cork has continued to develop – as a port, a university town and a cultural centre – and to assert its independence of Dublin.

Arrival and information

One of the joys of Cork is the fact that its scale is human: most of what it has to offer can be explored on foot. **Buses** to the suburbs and outlying towns and villages all go from the **Bus Éireann station** at Parnell Place alongside Merchant's Quay (☎508188), and most of these also pick up from the more central St Patrick's Street. The *Bus Éireann* station also operates an extensive nationwide bus service, while the **train station** (☎506766; *Travel Centre* ☎504888) is less than a mile out of the city centre on the Lower Glanmire Road. **Private buses** (see "Travel Details" at the end of the chapter) operate from various central points, mostly along St Patrick's Street and from outside *Mulligan's*, Parnell Place. If you arrive by **ferry** you'll be at Ringaskiddy, some ten miles out, from where you can catch a connecting bus into the centre. Coming in by **plane** you can easily pick up a bus for the twenty-minute journey into town: a shuttle service from the airport operates every 45 minutes (April–Sept till 8.45pm; Sept–

April Mon–Sat till 6.30pm, Sun till 3.30pm; £2.50 single, £3.50 return). A taxi to the airport will cost around £5, to the ferryport £10. If you're **driving** remember that, as in all the major cities, a disc parking system is in operation: discs can be bought from newsagents or the tourist office.

The **tourist office** is on Grand Parade (July–Aug Mon–Sat 9am–7pm, Sun 10am–1pm; Oct–May Mon–Sat 9am–6pm; ☎273251), with the usual wide variety of information. They will book rooms for £1 for a local phone call, £2 long distance, and there's plenty of choice. Cork is a great city for **festivals**, the biggest of which are the **film festival** at the beginning of October and the **jazz festival** towards the end of October – for more on both see p.256.

Accommodation

The few **hotels** in the city are at the top end of the market; the mid-range, however, is more than adequately covered by the numerous **B&Bs**, mainly concentrated along Western Road, near the university, and at the opposite end of town on Lower Glanmire Road, near the railway station. If you are planning your stay to coincide with one of the October festivals, advance booking is advisable. Cork also has plenty of good **hostels** as well as a couple of **campsites**.

Hotels

The Imperial Hotel, South Mall (☎274040; fax ☎274040). Cork's oldest hotel. The foyer retains glimmers of the grand Victorian era in chandeliers and portraiture; the bedrooms are a curious blend of conservative restraint and early 1970s design statements. Worth checking out their lower-rate offers out of season. ⑧.

The Metropole Hotel, MacCurtain St (☎508122). Pleasantly refurbished grand Victorian hotel; residents have full use of a leisure centre, including gym, pool, saunas and supervised creche facilities. If traffic noise bothers you, ask for a room not overlooking MacCurtain St. ⑦.

Bed and breakfast

Antoine House, Western Rd (☎273494). ④.

Auburn House, 3 Garfield Terrace, Wellington Rd (☎508555). Beautifully kept B&B, TVs in all rooms. Pricy singles. ④.

The Blarney Stone, 1 Carriglee Terrace, Western Rd (☎270083). ④.

Clare D'Arcy, 7 Sydney Place, Wellington Rd (☎504658). Worth paying a little more to stay in this beautiful Georgian town house. ⑤.

Clon Ross, 85 Lower Glanmire Rd (☎502602). TVs in all rooms. ④.

Kent House, 47 Lower Glanmire Rd (☎504260). ③–④.

Oakland, 51 Lower Glanmire Rd (☎500578). ④.

Tara House, 52 Lower Glanmire Rd (☎500294). ④.

Westbourne House, 2 Westbourne Villas, Western Rd (☎276153). ④.

York House, York St, off MacCurtain St (☎501055). Cheap and very cheerful. ③.

Self-catering apartments

Dean's Hall, Crosses Green, nr St Finbarr's Cathedral (☎312623; fax ☎316523). Student accommodation let as self-catering apartments. Central, clean, well-equipped 4-6–person apartments. Open from the end of June to mid-Sept. ③.

North Quay Place, Pope's Quay, near Shandon (☎551300). Clean, comfortable and efficiently run, with full cooking facilities and TVs. Apartment rates the same for 4, 5 or 6 people, with reductions for longer stays. ②–③.

Hostels

An Óige Hostel, 1–2 Redclyffe, Western Rd (☎543289, fax ☎343715). Just before the *Campus Hostel*, predictably a bit more formal. Open all year. ②.

Campus Hostel, 3 Woodland View, Western Rd (*IHH*; ☎343531). Tiny, friendly, hostel; pick up a #8 bus from the station along Western Rd. Open all year. ②.

Cork City Independent Hostel, 100 Lower Glanmire Rd (☎509089). Handily situated about 100 yards from the train station. Rainbow-coloured hippy hostel, friendly; beds have seen better days. Bikes £5 per day. Open all year. ②.

Isaac's, 48 MacCurtain St (*IHH*; ☎500011, fax ☎506355). Certainly the plushest in town, but if you are intending to cook your own food, the kitchen facilities become pretty cramped during high season; inconvenient daytime lock-out of all dormitory accommodation, too. Bike rental £7 per day; credit cards accepted. Twin/double and family rooms also available. Open all year. ①.

Kelly's Hostel, 25 Summerhill South, off Douglas St (☎315612). Small, friendly and colourful hostel. Cable TV dominates the common room. Laundry facilities. Dorm, twin and 3-bedded rooms available. Open all year. ②.

Kinlay House, Shandon (*IHH*; ☎508966, fax ☎506927). Very clean and efficiently run *USIT* hostel, with laundry facilities. Price includes breakfast. Also singles and twin rooms. Bike rental £6 per day. Open all year. ②.

Sheila's Cork Tourist Hostel, Belgrave Place, Wellington Rd (*IHH*; ☎505562, fax ☎500940). A central, friendly and well-run hostel with good cooking facilities, a garden to the rear, breakfast for £1.50, sauna £2, bike rental £6 per day. *Western Union* agent. Open all year. ②.

Campsites

Bienvenue Caravan and Camping Park (☎312711). Near the airport – the Airport/Kinsale bus stops 600 yards from the site, or follow the signposts to Kinsale and airport, and then the signs from the airport gates. £6 per tent plus £1 per adult. Campsite may increase charges at festival times. Open May–Sept.

Cork City Caravan and Camping Park (☎961866). The nearest to the centre of town, with a **launderette** on the site. Pick up a #14 bus from St Patrick St or South Main St (every 20min) and the driver will put you down outside the site; last bus out of town runs at 11.15pm. To walk or cycle, climb Barrack St beside Sullivan's Quay, follow it for about half a mile, then take Lough Rd on the left. £5 per tent plus £1 per adult. Campsite may increase charges at festival times. Open late May to mid-Sept, plus jazz weekend.

The city

Cork has no really spectacular sights, but it's a fine place to wander: around the quays, through the narrow lanes, into the markets, up to Shandon. The ambience and sense of place are enjoyable in themselves, and for those with a taste for it there's plenty of nineteenth-century Gothic church architecture punctuating the river banks, and evocative remnants of a great mercantile past. Exploration on foot is rewarding – the city's medieval core is embedded in its central narrow lanes, and the meshing of its history can be felt embodied in its buildings, reflected in the constant flow of the Lee. But don't go expecting to be astounded. Enjoying Cork city is to do with tuning in to the pace and life of the place.

The island

The **city centre** is essentially the island, with its quaysides, pretty bridges, alleyways and lanes, plus that segment to the north of the River Lee that has MacCurtain Street as its central thoroughfare, and the lanes leading up to Shandon. **St Patrick's Street** and **Grand Parade** form the modern commercial heart, with a healthy smattering of the modish amenities generally associated with much larger European cities. Not that you are ever engulfed by commercialism; aggressive multinationals barely dominate, and major chainstores exist alongside modest traditional businesses. It is in such immediate contrasts that the charms of the city lie. A hundred yards from the elegant shopfronts of St Patrick's Street you'll find **Coal Quay Market** in Cornmarket Street – a flea market, worth investigating if you are fascinated by the shabby side of a damp, rural life in its unchanged nineteenth-century setting. A minute's walk from Coal Quay

Market down **Paul Street** brings still more variety in the bijou environs of French Church Street and Carey's Lane, busy with new restaurants, pavement cafés, artists' studios and period clothes shops.

The eastern, downstream, end of the island is the more clearly defined: many of its quays are still in use, and it's here that you best get a sense of the old port city. Trips out into **Cork harbour** are available during the summer months – ask at the tourist office. In the west the island peters out in a predominantly residential area. Heading in this direction, though, you can follow the signs off Western Road for **Fitzgerald Park**, home of the **Cork Public Museum** (Mon–Fri 11am–1pm & 2.15–5pm, Sun 3–5pm; June–Aug Mon–Fri closes 6pm; free, Sun 50p), about a mile out of the city centre, easily combined with a trip to Cork Gaol (see below). Primarily a museum of Republican history, it has an excellent commentary on the part played by nationally significant local characters and events in the Republican movement. There are exhibits of local archeological and geological finds, too, and a section on the history of the dairy trade.

Shandon

North of the River Lee is the area known as **Shandon**, a sadly neglected reminder of Cork's eighteenth-century status as the most important port in Europe for dairy products. To get there head up John Redmond Street, or simply aim for the giant fish atop the church tower. The most striking survival is the **Cork Butter Exchange**, stout nineteenth-century Classical buildings recently given over to select craft workshops. The old **butter market** itself sits like a generously proportioned butter tub in a cobbled square, recently renovated to house the *Firkin Crane Theatre*. Despite the air of dereliction, this part of town is worth a visit for the pleasant Georgian church of **St Anne's Shandon** (1750), easily distinguishable from all over Cork city by its weather vane – an eleven-foot salmon. For £1 you can view the not particularly remarkable interior of St Anne's, and the old books. For a much more worthwhile £1.50 you can climb the **tower** (June–Aug Mon–Sat 9.30am–5pm; winter Mon–Sat 10am–4pm), two of its sides finished in red sandstone, two in white limestone, for excellent views, and ring the famous bells – a good stock of sheet tunes is provided.

To the west of here is an area known as Sunday's Well, and **Cork City Gaol** (March–Oct daily 9.30am–6pm, Nov–Feb daily tours 10.30am & 2.30pm, Sat & Sun 10am–5pm; last admission 1hr before closing; £3). It's a good 25 minutes' walk from the city centre, up the hill from North Mall. A lively taped tour (English, French or German) takes you through the prison, focusing on social history in a way that is both engaging and enlightening. It's occasionally threaded with characters of national importance, all vividly brought to life by a dramatic audiovisual finale. There's a pleasant walk from here to Fitzgerald Park: turn right as you leave the prison, left, right and then left down a flight of steps and over the Shaky Bridge.

The stark precision of nineteenth-century Gothic which is repeated time and again in the city's churches may not be to everyone's taste, but here it undeniably gives the city a rhythmic architectural cohesion. Both Pugin and Pain are very much in evidence, Pugin in the brilliant Revivalist essay of the Church of St Peter and St Paul on Friar Mathew Quay, with its handsome lantern spire, and in St Patrick's Church on Lower Glanmire Road. Best of all is William Burges's **St Finbarr's Cathedral** (built 1867–79): obsessively detailed, its impressive French Gothic spire providing a grand silhouette on the southwesterly shoulder of the city.

Eating

Cork doesn't have a wide range of cuisines for you to choose from – the main influence is Mediterranean – but it does have a high standard of food on offer, with several cafés and restaurants serving dishes made from organic local produce, plenty of seafood and vegetarian options. Alongside the more conventional eating places, **The English Market** (see overleaf) is a wonderful place to share in the city's enthusiasm for all things culinary.

Cafés and budget places

Le Chateau, 93 Patrick St. Worth heading for if you want bar food on Sun.

Ciao Italy, Caroline St, off Oliver Plunkett St. Cheery atmosphere, cheap pizzas.

The Crawford Municipal Art Gallery, Emmet Place. An affordable offshoot of the famous *Ballymaloe House* restaurant near Cloyne.

The Farm Gate Café, upstairs in The English Market, Princes St. Great for affordable lunches and teas; listen to the pianist and watch the market below. Lots of Mediterranean salads, savory tarts, and plenty of seafood. The emphasis is on using fresh, local produce, and, in line with tradition, they also serve tripe and drisheen (a kind of black pudding) daily. Open Mon–Sat 8.30am–5.30pm.

The Gingerbread House, Paul St. Great café for soaking up the Paul St scene. Tasty baguettes, tartlets, soups and coffees. Open Mon–Sat 8.15am–10pm.

Harlequin Café, 26 Paul St. Cheap and fairly wholesome café, though not all as homemade as its appearance might suggest. A nice spot to sit and watch the world drift past or read the café papers. Open 10am–6pm.

Luciano's, 8 MacCurtain St. Swarthy café; great pizzas.

Café Mexicana, Carey's Lane. Enchilladas, tacos, tortillas, all from around £7.

Nash 19, 19 Princes St. No-nonsense, self-service café serving good-value sandwiches and gorgeous gateaux. Open Mon–Sat 8am–5pm.

The Other Side, South Main St. Off shoot of *The Quay Co-op*; cheap vegetarian café. Open Mon–Sat 10am–6.30pm.

Café Paradiso, 16 Lancaster Quay; Western Rd (opposite *Jury's Hotel*). Relaxed, informal and generally considered the best vegetarian/vegan food in town: gleefully high fat. Lunches from £4.50, dinner main course from £8. Open Tues–Sat from 10.30am to last orders at 10.30pm.

The Quay Co-op, 24 Sullivan's Quay. Delicious, large vegetarian and vegan meals, soups, puddings and teas, all in surroundings of wonderfully faded elegance. Meals from £3.50; dearer in the evenings. Mon–Sat 9.30am–6pm & 6.30–10.30pm, Sun 6–10.30pm.

Tribes, Tuckey St. Smoky coffee bar for trendy diehards. Over 30 strains of coffee, and many herbal teas. Till 4pm daily.

The Triskel Arts Centre, Tobin St, off South Main St. Home-made bread, soups and salads; hot vegetarian and non-vegetarian dishes from £4; tasty and good value. Mon 11am–3pm, Tues–Fri 10.30am–5.30pm, Sat 11am–5pm.

Restaurants and winebars

Bully's, 40 Paul St. Wine bar serving pizzas, fresh pasta and fish (from around £5); popular with families. Mon–Sat noon–11.30pm, Sun 5–11pm.

The Half Moon Wine Bar, 15 Lavitt's Quay (behind the Opera House). Good food very reasonably priced, and late bar.

Halpins, 14–15 Cook St. Self-service delicatessen restaurant, serving salads, seafoods, quiches and cakes; from £4 during the day; evening menu of steaks, curries etc £5–14. Open Mon–Sat 9am–midnight; Sun 12.30–11pm.

Isaac's Restaurant, MacCurtain St (☎503805). Deservingly popular restaurant. Light, delicious food with a good range of salads, fresh breads, cheeses, seafood and past. Caters well for vegetarians, with a high emphasis on local and organic produce. Lunch from £5, dinner main courses £6.50–9. Open Mon–Sat 10am–10.30pm, Sun 6.30–9pm.

The Ivory Tower, The Exchange Buildings, 35 Princes St (☎274665). The place to go to treat yourself: adventurous menu specializing in wild and organic food. Exquisite. They also sell croissants, patés, charcuterie, etc. Lunches Mon–Sat 12–3.30pm, £4–5; dinner Tues–Sat 6.30–11pm with a 3-course menu from £15.

Paddy Garibaldi's, Carey's Lane. Friendly café-restaurant for burgers and pizzas; from around £4, evenings from £6. Daily noon–midnight.

THE ENGLISH MARKET

The **English Market** is an absolute must for all edible goodies and the ideal place to pick up fresh provisions. Lodged between Ground Parade and Princes Street, with entrances off both, its name originates from a charter granted by James I in 1610. Here the cosmopolitian nestles shoulder to shoulder with the decidedly unpretentious; there are stalls specializing in the finest olive oils and cheeses jostling for space among the rakes of tripe and bacon. Stands to look for include:

De Crepe Pit, all you could wish for, from crepes with goat's cheese and basil through to chocolate truffle.

Fish stalls, between them the fish stalls can probably offer you anything you care to name: oysters, mussels, shrimps, lobster and crab, turbot, brill and ray.

Iago, made-to-order sandwiches from a huge range of cheeses, salamis and wine by the glass. They also make fresh pasta before your eyes.

The Olive Stall, a fabulous array of olives, pickles, preserves, vinegars and olive oils – with plenty of encouragement to sample as you buy – plus olive soaps.

On the Pig's Back, patés, terrines, mousses and saucisson all bursting with flavour; produced by a French enthusiast using free-range meat.

Pierre's, 17–18 French Church St (☎278107). Young person's restaurant with casual, pavement café atmosphere. Mon–Wed 3-course set lunch £5; set-dinner menu £9; à la carte 6–11pm.

Pizza Pomodoro, Cook St. Cheap pizzas in quiet, candlelit restaurant.

Proby's Bistro, Proby's Quay, Crosses Green, nr St Finbarr's Cathedral (☎316531). Slightly formal bistro; eclectic menu with strong American and Mediterranean influences. Mon–Sat lunch main courses £5–6 and dinner £9–12. Open for US and Irish breakfasts during the summer till 11am.

Pubs, nightlife and the arts

There are plenty of good watering holes in the city, and if all you want is a drink, you won't need a guide to find somewhere – though a couple of the city's older bars mentioned below are worth seeking for their atmosphere. Many bars have **music**, traditional or otherwise, and the following list should give some good pointers on where to find the best of this. Cork abounds with disco-type **clubs** around the city centre, easy enough to stumble upon late at night. Some of the (slightly) more interesting are given here; many also have live entertainment. As with any large city, though, venues and session nights change: pick up *In Cork* for detailed what's-on information and look for fliers in cafés such as *The Quay Co-op* and *The Other Side,* and in *The Phoenix* pub. Wherever you end up, this is not a difficult town to enjoy yourself in.

Pubs and music

An Bodhrán, 42 Oliver Plunkett St. Chance midweek sessions of traditional music.

An Bróg, 78 Oliver Plunkett St. Popular young bar, with unplugged indie, rock, alternative folk.

An Cuilegg, 26 South Main St. Down-to-earth bar with traditional Irish (Sun), rock (Tues), acoustic folk, blues, rock or traditional (Wed).

An Siol Broin, MacCurtain St. Young, lively crowd; indie and dance music.

An Spailpín Fánach, 28 South Main St. Traditional Irish music every night except Sat; bar lunches Mon–Fri 12–3pm.

The Corner House, Coburg St. Popular, young bar with a mixture of mainly acoustic country, bluegrass, folk and Irish music. Most nights, though less likely at weekends during the summer.

The Donkey's Ears, Union Quay. Mainly reggae with leanings towards funky house and hip hop. A good place to pick up club concessions.

Elroy's, behind *Westimer*, Sullivan's Quay. Live bands, chart and country music. Also see "Clubs" opposite.

Gable's, Douglas St. Handy for *Kelly's Hostel,* with traditional music on Tues.

Isaac Bells, St Patrick's Quay (behind the *Metropole Hotel*). Very popular, lively bar playing reggae (Mon & Thurs), traditional Irish or folk (Wed), blues afternoons (Sun in winter); chart and house music (Fri).

Loafers, 26 Douglas St. Friendly bar with pleasant beer garden, attracts a bohemian clientele; probably the most relaxed place for gays to drink in the city.

The Lobby, Union Quay. A good spot to catch live music: traditional Irish sessions (Tues & Fri) and bluegrass (Mon); the upstairs bar, for which there is a cover charge, has just about any kind of music – rock, folk, pop, traditional – throughout the week.

The Long Valley, Winthrop St. Something of a one off and a locals' favourite; the place also does good substantial sandwiches.

The Metropole Hotel, MacCurtain St. Hotel bar generally catering for tour buses, but the focal point for the jazz festival.

The Mutton Lane Inn, Mutton Lane, off Patrick St. Convivial, old, traditional city-centre bar.

Nancy Spain's, Barrack St. Upbeat bar with plenty of live music – rock, indie bands on Fri, plus "world music". Also see "Clubs" below.

The Oyster Tavern, 4 Market Lane, off St Patrick's St. Old-fashioned atmosphere – all brass and polished wood.

The Phoenix, Union Quay. Traditional, blues and folk (Tues, Thurs & Sun); the bar upstairs attracts a younger crowd into heavy metal.

The Vineyard, Market Lane, off Patrick St. Quaint old bar; spacious enough to think as you drink.

Clubs

City Limits, Coburg St. Mixed crowd at this fun and unpretentious club, with salsa, acid jazz, "world music" disco (Thurs; £3–4), and **comedy** from 9pm followed by dancing till 2am (Fri & Sat; £5) – anything from Ska to Blondie, James Brown to Sinatra; Sun there's a mellower mix.

Elroy's, behind *Westimer*, Sullivan's Quay. At the Fri & Sat's discos neat dress is the norm; till 2am. Also a live music venue; see opposite.

The Forum, Grand Parade. Indie music, plus occasional gigs; look for fliers around town. Tues–Sun; £3–5.

Gorby's, above *Brannagan's*, 74 Oliver Plunkett St. This is a popular club with indie and pop music.

The Half Moon Club, in the back of the Opera House. Small, bluesy nightclub with a sane, theatrical crowd; a jazz-based band (Thurs), blues, rock, R&B (Fri & Sat); £5. Open midnight–2am.

Nancy Spain's, Barrack St. Sat is club night (also see above); mainly house music (£4–5). Look out for fliers around town. Open till 2am.

Sir Henry's, South Main St. Dance, indie and house music; occasional gigs. Wed–Sun; £3–6.

Art, theatre, film and festivals

The latest hub of artistic activity in Cork is the **Triskel Arts Centre**, found down the narrow and dingy Tobin Street, off South Main Street (☎272022). It has changing exhibitions of contemporary art, a film theatre, a continuous programme of performance art, poetry reading, contemporary music, and a very good wholefood café. It is also an excellent source of information about what's on – Triskel will know about any theatre or music performances in the city. Alternatively, ask at the tourist office or consult the *Cork Examiner*.

Considering the amount of painting and sculpture generated around the country, Cork city is poorly served in terms of the visual arts. **Fine art** has a high profile in cafés, restaurants and private houses, but good galleries are in short supply. Worth a visit, however, is the Crawford Municipal Gallery in Emmet Place (Mon–Sat 10am–5pm), which has a permanent collection of Irish and European painting and usually an interesting contemporary exhibition. The Cork Arts Society, 5 Father Matthew Quay, off South Mall, is a good commercial gallery, with exhibitions of contemporary works. The Blackcombe Galleries, 44A MacCurtain Street (above the antiques shop), is a pleasant space, showing eighteen contemporary exhibitions per year.

The **Cork Opera House** (☎276357), in Emmet Place, offers a full programme of drama, concerts both classical and popular, ballet, opera, review and variety, though very rarely anything at all out of the mainstream. Classical concerts are also held at **Triskel**, the **School of Music**, on Union Quay, or the **City Hall**, Anglesea Street. **The Everyman Palace**, MacCurtain Street (☎501673), and **Cork Arts Theatre (CATs)**, in Knapps Square, off Camden Quay, both offer a range of local small-scale productions; as does *The Firkin Crane*, Shandon (☎507487), which also stages evenings of traditional music and dance during the summer months.

Cork has a very popular **international jazz festival**, one of the last two weekends in October. With music bursting out of every doorway, you don't need to go and see the big names to enjoy yourself if you are short of cash. It's a great time to be in the city, though accommodation is scarce. There's also an important **film festival** at the beginning of October, with films screened at Triskel and the Opera House. The International Choral Festival is held the first weekend in May, and there is a folk festival during September: ask at the tourist office for exact dates of all festivals.

Listings

Airlines *Aer Lingus*, 38 Patrick St (☎274331); *Ryanair* (☎313000); *British Airways* (☎1 800/626747).

Airport Cork airport is 5 miles along the Kinsale Rd (flight information ☎313131).

Banks Branches of the *Allied Irish Bank* in Patrick St, North Main St, Bridge St and Western Rd.

Bike rental *CycleScene*, 396 Blarney St (☎301183); *The Cycle Repair Centre*, 6 Kyle St (☎276255), or from the campsite; *Kilgrews Ltd*, 30 North Main St (☎273458); *Rent a bike*, 48 MacCurtain St (next to *Isaac's*).

Bookshops *Collins*, Carey's Lane; *Eason's*, Patrick St; *Keogh's Books*, 6 MacCurtain St (old, rare and second-hand); *Liam Russell*, Oliver Plunkett St; *Mercier Bookshop*, 4 Bridge St; *The Other Side*, South Main St – gay bookshop and drop-in centre; *Waterstones*, Patrick St.

Bureau de change At the tourist office and at *Sheila's Hostel*.

Buses *Bus Éireann* station, Parnell Place, alongside Merchant's Quay (☎508188) for local and inter-city buses. Several private bus companies also operate from Cork: see "Travel Details" at the end of this chapter.

Camping equipment *The Tent Shop*, Rutland St, off South Terrace, offers camping gear for sale or rent; *Matthews*, Academy St, for equipment and Gaz.

Car rental *Car Rental Ireland*, Monahan Rd (☎962277); *Eurodollar Rent a Car*, Cork airport (☎344884), city office: Carrigrohane Rd (☎344884); *Great Island Car Rentals*, 47 MacCurtain St (☎503536 or ☎ 811609).

Ferries to France operate from Ringaskiddy, about ten miles from Cork. *Brittany Ferries*, 42 Grand Parade (☎277801), sail during summer to Roscoff twice a week and to St Malo once a week; *Irish Ferries*, 9 Bridge St (☎504333), operate services to Roscoff and Le Havre (both once a week). *Swansea–Cork Ferries*, 52 South Mall (☎271166), operate a 10-hour crossing, around 6 days a week according to season, usually not on Tues. *Stena Sealink*, for Rosslare–Fishguard and Dún Laoghaire–Holyhead, are based at the tourist office (☎272965).

Gay information and advice lines *Gay and Lesbian News*, Munster edition, available at *The Other Side*; *Lesbian Line* Thurs 8–10pm and *Gay Information Cork* Wed 7–9pm & Sat 3–5pm on ☎271087.

Hospital Cork University Hospital (☎546400).

Hurling and gaelic football For fixtures phone ☎385876 or ☎963311.

Laundry MacCurtain St, next door to the *Everyman Palace* theatre, Mon–Sat from 9am to last wash at 8pm.

Music *The Living Tradition*, 40 MacCurtain St (☎502040). A great range of Irish music: CD, cassette, sheet music, plus *bodhráns* and tin whistles; also "world music".

Pharmacy *Phelan's Late Night Pharmacy*, 9 Patrick St (☎272511); *Denis O'Leary*, 8 Grand Parade (☎274563).

Rape Crisis Centre 26 MacCurtain St (☎968086).

Swimming pool Douglas Swimming Pool, Douglas Rd (☎293073), in Churchfield on the north side of the city.

Taxis *Tele Cabs* ☎505050 or ☎505533.

Trains The station is on Lower Glanmire Rd, about a mile from the centre; *Irish Rail*'s travel centre is right in the centre at 65 Patrick St (☎506766 or ☎504888 for all information).

Travel agents *USIT* have two offices in Cork: at 10–11 Market Parade (☎270900), and *UCC Student Travel*, near The Boole Library, University College.

East of Cork

There are a couple of good, short day-trips around the harbour that will allow you to get back in time to take advantage of Cork's nightlife: **Fota** has wild animals and eighteenth-century Classicism; and **Cobh** boasts fine water sports. On the way further east to the quaint port of **Youghal** – with its colourful maritime history and scenic location – there are a string of places worth a brief stop, including **Middleton**, the home of *Jameson* whiskey, and some pleasant beaches at **Ballycotton** and **Garryvoe**.

Fota and Cobh

A visit to Fota House Wildlife Park and the pretty harbour town of Cobh can be managed in a day on a return train ticket from Cork. Going by train really is the best option, taking you across the mudflats of an estuary teeming with birdlife. Both are situated on islands in the mouth of Cork harbour. **Fota Wildlife Park** (April–Oct Mon–Sat 10am–5pm, Sun 11am–5pm; £3.50, families £13.50) is a small, pleasant park with apes, cheetahs, giraffes, red pandas and zebras, among others, all wandering about the landscaped eighteenth-century estate of Fota House.

The **house** is no longer open to the public, though this situation may change. Originally an eighteenth-century hunting lodge, it was much enlarged in 1820. The building is one of Classical unity: Doric columns and plastered stonework outside are in complete harmony with the perfect Neoclassical interiors. Access to the estate's **arboretum** is free though – it's one of the most important in Europe, with a great variety of rare and exotic flowering shrubs and trees.

Cobh

Rejoining the train from Fota takes you out to the extremely pretty little town of **COBH**. Cobh (pronounced *Cove*) is held in a quaint cup of land with steep, narrow streets climbing the hill to the Pugin cathedral. One of the most enjoyable of these neo-Gothic monsters, it dominates the town, giving marvellous views out across the great curve of the bay to Spike Island. Thanks to its fine natural harbour, Cobh has long been an important port: it served as an assembly point for ships during the Napoleonic wars and was a major departure point for steamers carrying emigrants to America and convicts to Australia. The first-ever transatlantic steamer sailed from here in 1838, and the *Titanic* called in on her ill-fated voyage, too; a monument to the victims of the *Lusitania* disaster stands in Casement Square. Cobh's dramatic maritime history is now retold at the The Queenstown Story (March–Oct daily 10am–6pm; £3.50), one of the best of Ireland's new heritage centres. Today the port is still used by a substantial fishing fleet. From September to February, when it is awash with fishermen, the town's character changes completely.

First and foremost, though, Cobh is a holiday resort, itself an historic function. Ireland's first yacht club was established here in 1720, and from 1830 on the town was a popular health resort, imitative of English Regency resorts like Brighton, a style reflected in its architecture. The main square is flanked by brightly painted Victorian town houses, and the place has a robust cheerfulness – though none of the cosmopolitan flavour of harbours further west. It attracts Irish holidaying families and offers pitch and putt,

---

> ### CORK COAST ROUTE
>
> If you want to head west from Cobh along the coast, or you want to cut around twenty minutes' driving time off your return to Cork city, you can take a five-minute ferry from Carrigaloe, a couple of miles north of Cobh as you head back up towards the N25.
>
> *Cross River Ferries* services start at 7.15am from Carrigaloe and run about every ten minutes till 12.20am. Car £3 return, £2 single; adult 60p, 40p; bikes carried free.

tennis, swimming and a stony beach. At the **International Sailing Centre** on East Beach (☎021/811237) you can rent sailing dinghies (£12 per hour, £35 per day), canoes (£4 per hour) and wind-surfing boards – the centre also has accommodation available for long-term use. There's a **regatta** weekend in mid-August, and for enthusiasts, the third week in July sees the exciting **Ford Yacht Week** across the harbour in Crosshaven (alternate summers); best observation points are reckoned to be Ringabella, Fennel's Bay, Myrtleville or Roche's Point. Any other time in the summer you can at least take a **harbour boat trip** (*Marine Transport Services*, Atlantic Quay; ☎021/811485; £3).

Cobh **tourist office** (March to mid-Oct Mon–Fri 9.30am–5.30pm, Sat & Sun 11am–5.30pm; mid-Oct to Feb Mon–Fri 9.30am–5.30pm, Sat 2.30–5.30pm; ☎021/813301), housed in the old yacht club, an Italianate nineteenth-century building in the town centre, has maps and local information – it also hosts art exhibitions in conjunction with The Crawford Municipal Gallery in Cork city. If you want to stay, **B&Bs** include *Westbourne House*, Westbourne Place, Main Street (☎021/811391; ③); *Atlantic*, 8 West Beach (☎021/811489; ④), *Ardeen*, 3 Harbour Hill (☎021/811803; ④); and *The New European*, 1 East Beach (☎021/811122; ③). There's a brand new **hostel** at **CROSSHAVEN**: *The Grand* (☎021/832272; ②) overlooks Cork harbour from the west, and it's particularly handy for the Ringaskiddy ferries. We have not visited it yet, but by all accounts it is beautifully appointed, and it has a bureau de change.

Middleton to Garryvoe beach

MIDDLETON, about ten miles east of Cork, is a cheery market town and home of *Jameson* Irish whiskey. The **Jameson Heritage Centre** (May–Oct daily 10am–6pm, last admission 4pm; £3.50) tour is a highly polished promotional affair, taking you through the distillery and culminating in a whiskey-tasting session. Middleton is home, too, of *The Farm Gate*, Coolbawn (☎021/632771), a deli and restaurant with a relaxed approach to enjoying the fruits of the earth, serving and selling free-range poultry and fresh local produce, with lunches for £4–7 and dinners (Fri and Sat only) for £10–18. For accommodation try the **hostel** *An Stoir* (☎021/633105; ②), a newly converted mill.

Four miles to the south is the sleepy, historic village of **CLOYNE**. Its interest lies in its history, not in anything that exists today, as there's not much to see here. One of Ireland's earliest Christian foundations, the monastery of Saint Colman, was established here in the sixth century. In medieval times the village continued to be of religious importance with the establishment of the See of Cloyne, a diocese which extended well into County Limerick. Reminders of this era, though, are few. There's a fine tenth-century **round tower**, from whose top, 100ft up, there are superb views (key from Cathedral House; £1), and you can also visit **St Colman's Cathedral**, a large building of warm, mottled stone originally built in 1250 but disappointingly restored in the nineteenth century. Inside are the grand and grim seventeenth-century Fitzgerald of Imokelly tomb and the alabaster tomb of George Berkley, the famous philosopher who was bishop here from 1734 to 1753. An Egyptian *tau* cross and the St Anthony's cross on the cathedral doorway are faint traces of earlier Mediterranean influences. Off the Cloyne–Ballycotton Road, *Ballymaloe House* (☎021/652531) is an exceptional **restaurant,** one of the most famous in Ireland; a meal here will cost you from around £25. In Cloyne itself, *Dorgan's* bar has a mix of traditional, rock and folk **music** on Monday nights.

Although the beaches on this stretch of coast are unspectacular and have nothing like the charm of the west, five miles on from Cloyne, **BALLYCOTTON** is a pleasant enough spot, with a little quayside, fine cliff walks for miles to the west, and a beach half a mile away. If you want to stay, there's fine guesthouse **accommodation** at *Spanish Point Restaurant* (tel/fax ☎021/646177; dinner £18; ④). Bright and airy, it's in a terrific spot and has a beautiful conservatory–dining room overlooking Ballycotton Bay. *The Cliffstop Café* (summer only Tues–Sun noon–8pm, till 9pm weekends) is worth the steep climb to the west of the village for good pizzas, seafood and salads (from £3.50), and views over the rock-island lighthouse. Not far away to the north are the holiday villages of Shanagarry and **GARRYVOE**. Garryvoe **beach** is very long and sandy, but it's beset by caravans advancing upon the shore and very busy during high season. To the east of here the bay is flat and of interest only to bird watchers, its reed-infested estuary now a protected bird sanctuary. Here a river sidles its way, smooth and khaki, through the mudflats to the sea.

Youghal

YOUGHAL (pronounced *Yawl*) is an ancient port at the mouth of the River Blackwater, where the counties of Cork and Waterford meet. In a small way it combines the richness of the Blackwater towns with the prettiness of Kinsale and Cobh. A picturesque holiday town, Youghal has real character, with a colourful history and some fine architecture to remember it by.

Youghal's walls were first built by the Norman settlers who established the town, but those which stand today were erected by Edward I in 1275. From medieval times the town prospered as one of Ireland's leading ports, trading with the Continent – particularly France – and with England. Political disturbances and trade restrictions imposed on Irish ports by the English Crown, however, meant the town's growth began to slow in the mid-sixteenth century. It fell into the hands of the Earl of Desmond, and in 1579 the "Rebel" Earl (rebelling against Elizabeth I) sacked and burned the place. After Desmond's death, Youghal was part of the 40,000 acres granted to Walter Raleigh during the Munster Plantations, with which Elizabeth hoped to control Ireland. Raleigh, though, had little interest in Ireland, and spent most of his time composing poetry in an attempt to curry favour with the queen. In this he was abetted by Edmund Spenser, another local colonist, author of *The Faerie Queen*. Spenser proved to be capable of both great poetry and of barbarism in his dealings with the Irish: they eventually repaid him by burning down his castle, Kilcolman, near Buttevant. Raleigh himself spent little time in Youghal, selling his land to Richard Boyle, the "Great" Earl of Cork (and father of the scientist), who then greatly developed the town as he did all his newly acquired land.

When Cromwell reached New Ross in 1649, the English garrison at Youghal went over to the Parliamentarian side, and so the town escaped destruction. Nonetheless, the importance of the port continued to diminish through the seventeenth century. Still, the decline was only relative to its former stature, and there is enough fine eighteenth-century architecture to make it clear that a small but affluent class of merchants still prospered. Today Youghal is a quiet seaside resort, and the history preserved in its buildings continues to suggest prosperity earned through centuries of vigorous commerce, and offers an insight into the privileged lives of the early colonists.

The town

Youghal's most famous landmark is the **clock tower**, which bridges the long, curvy main street: a superbly proportioned Georgian structure of warm, plum-coloured stone.

A century ago it was used as a prison, more recently it served as a museum, but it's now closed indefinitely. Steps leading off the tower climb the steep hill through little lanes to the top of the town, where the walls and turrets of the old defences still define the shape of the compact harbour.

The most charming buildings lie, in the main, on the landward side of North Main Street and in the lanes that run behind it. On Main Street itself the **Red House**, built in 1710, is a fine example of domestic architecture, clearly showing the Dutch influence of the original merchant owner. Here, too, are seventeenth-century almshouses, built by Richard Boyle to house Protestant widows. Lanes off to the west of this end of Main Street lead to the Elizabethan **Myrtle Grove**, known as "Raleigh's House". One of the oldest unfortified houses in Ireland, its elaborately carved fireplaces and creaky panelled rooms evoke a fascinating past; yet equally interesting is the history of the family who live here today and their collection of nineteenth-century botanical illustrations and treasures from the East. Access is by arrangement; contact the local tourist office.

Alongside you'll find the **Collegiate Church of St Mary's**, a large, simple, thirteenth-century building, one of the few of such age still in use in Ireland. The building has been greatly altered over the centuries, but still has interesting medieval tombs and effigies. Particularly notable are the thirteenth-century monuments in the south transept (entrance is by a little door to the left as you walk up towards the church, or by the main door when open). Wrecked when the town was sacked by Desmond's men in 1579, they were later restored by Boyle, with the addition of effigies in seventeenth-century costume. Heading out of town towards Waterford, you pass the ruins of North Abbey, a thirteenth-century Dominican priory of which little remains.

On the east side of North Main Street is **Tyntes Castle**, a fifteenth-century tower house that is now sadly dilapidated (and, by the look of it, rapidly deteriorating). Edmund Spenser's widow married Robert Tynte, who lived here. Lanes off this side of the street lead to the **quayside**. Here it's all very quaint: warehouse buildings warm with the patina of age surround the harbour; yucca palms decorate the walkways, and the cultivated fields of Waterford across the water look very near.

There is an interesting **walking tour** of the town (June–Aug Mon–Sat at 11am and 3pm; £2.50) which starts at an exhibition in the tourist office and lasts around ninety minutes. Signposted from here too is **Fox's Lane Museum** (summer Mon–Sat 10am–1pm & 2–6pm, Sun 2–6pm; £2), which displays with illuminating clarity and imagination a collection of domestic gadgetry – everything from sausage makers to petrol-fuelled irons and cucumber straighteners – all mapping the dogged march of progress from the nineteenth century.

Practicalities

The **tourist office** is on Market Square (June–Sept daily 9.30am–7pm; Oct–May Mon–Fri 9.30am–5.30pm; ☎024/92390), just behind the harbour, and there's plenty of **accommodation** nearby. *The Devonshire Arms Hotel*, Pearse Square (☎024/92827; ⑦), and *Aherne's* 163 North Main Street (☎024/92424, fax ☎93633; ⑧), both in the town centre, and *The Hilltop Hotel* (☎024/92911, fax ☎93503; ⑥), a mile and a half along the Cork Road, are the most expensive options. At the other end of the scale is *Hillside*, 6 Strand Street (☎024/92468; ②), which doesn't include breakfast. If you want **B&B** or midpriced hotels, there are plenty along the main streets and around the quayside – try *Avonmore House*, South Abbey (☎024/92617; ④), or *Roseville*, New Catherine Street (☎024/92571; ④). Other options include *Ferry View*, The Mall (☎024/93414; ③), and *Attracta*, South Abbey (☎024/92062; ④). There are plenty more out on the Cork Road: *Carriglea* (☎024/92520; ④), less than two miles out of town, is particularly friendly. The International Busking Festival during the first weekend in August offers £2,000 prize money – and suddenly **camping space** is available everywhere. To the west of town, sandy (European Blue Flag) **beaches** stretch for miles. There's a **laundry** on North Main Street.

There's no shortage of places to **eat** in Youghal. *The Coffee Shop,* North Main Street, just near the clock tower, serves good-value meals from £3 (till 7.30pm in summer); *The Old Well* next door offers filling meals till 9pm daily. Also on this side of town, *The Paddock* at 140 North Main Street is a relaxed café with fine cakes, open sandwiches and an imaginative steak-and-seafood dinner menu (till 10.30pm daily during summer). The renowned *Aherne's Seafood Restaurant* (☎024/92424; dinner around £24, bar meals around £5–£10) is further up Main Street. For decent, well-priced **bar food** try *The Devonshire Arms Hotel* and *The Walter Raleigh,* both at the west end of the town centre.

You'll find **music** in Youghal's **bars** most nights during the summer, and at the weekends throughout the year. *The Nook* and *The Blackwater Inn,* both on Main Street, are good for traditional music and ballads; *The Spinning Wheel* has rock bands and discos; and, a mile and a half along the Cork Road, *The Hilltop Hotel* has a mix of ballads, traditional, classical and, on Sunday mornings, jazz.

Every town selects which portion of its history it wishes to celebrate, and in Youghal the Raleigh connection takes first place. Thus the town celebrates music and potatoes in its **Walter Raleigh Potato Festival**, usually early July. A close second is the use of the town as a location for the film of *Moby Dick;* memorabilia and photographs from the making of the film are found in the bar of the same name by the quays.

Inland Cork

Although most people head straight for the coast, **inland Cork**, aside from providing a quick route west, does have its merits, and, unless you yearn for the sea, it's just as beautiful. The main tourist attraction is the famous historic town of **Blarney**, close to the scenic Lee Valley; it makes a pleasurable stop on your way westwards or an easy day-trip from Cork city. Further inland, the **Boggeragh Mountains** and the route from Macroom to Bantry are perfect for gentle walking.

Blarney

BLARNEY is an easy six miles from Cork city; buses leave the bus station every half hour. The town itself functions chiefly as a tourist service centre – it is perhaps the only place in Ireland where you see not *Mná* and *Fir*, not Ladies and Gents, but "Rest Room". Naturally there are plenty of places to eat here: try *The Muskerry Arms* or the bar of *Christy's Hotel* for pub food. One surprise is the **Blarney Woollen Mills**, one of Blarney's original industries, now doing very nicely out of the castle's visitors. It has a couple of shops here, and the smaller of the two is one of the best places in Ireland for woolly bargains. Alongside is a **tourist office** (daily April–Sept 9am–7pm, Oct–March till 5pm), and you can **rent bikes** from *McGrath Cycles* on Stoneview (☎021/385658) for some easy and scenic cycling from Blarney up the Lee Valley.

If you can manage to divorce the **castle** (Mon–Sat May & Sept 9am–6.30pm, Sun 9.30am–5.30pm; June–Aug closes 7pm; Oct–April 9am–sundown; £3, students £2, combined ticket with house and gardens £5) from the whole "Blarney phenomenon", it actually is a fine stronghold, built in 1446 by Dermot McCarthy, King of Munster. The **Blarney Stone** has been kissed by visitors for over a hundred years, the legend being that to do so gives you the gift of eloquent and persuasive speech. The most famous story of how the legend came about tells of one McCarthy – King of Munster and Lord of Blarney – who, supposedly loyal to the colonizing Queen Elizabeth I, never actually got around to fulfilling any of the agreements between them, always sidetracking her emissaries with drinking, dancing and sweet talk. He was said to be able to talk "the noose off his head". In her frustration the queen is said to have eventually cried out "Blarney, Blarney, what he says he does not mean. It is the usual Blarney." And so the word entered the English language.

The stone itself is a four foot by one foot limestone block set in the battlements 83ft above the ground, so kissing it requires a head for heights. If you want to, you'll have to join the queue in the castle keep from which you can watch everyone else (one at a time) being dangled backwards by the shins over the battlements aided by two strong men. This also gives you time to consider whether or not you really want to join in. According to a less challenging legend, the stone is half of the Stone of Scone, given to Cormac McCarthy by Robert the Bruce in gratitude for the support of 4000 men at the Battle of Bannockburn (the rest is at Westminster Abbey in London). Views from the top of the castle are superb.

In the castle grounds, **Rock Close** is a nineteenth-century folly, a rock garden supposedly built around druidic remains. It is a pity that myths authentic or not, are such big business around here, because without the hype, these ancient yews and oaks could create a potent atmosphere. **Blarney House** (June to mid-Sept Mon–Sat noon–5.30pm; house and gardens £2.50; combined ticket with castle £4), nearby, is a nineteenth-century Scots Baronial mansion. Inside, it's oppressively lush and Victorian, despite some fine eighteenth- and nineteenth-century satinwood furnishings and Waterford chandeliers.

Macroom

The secondary roads west of Cork city run up the Lee Valley, through scenic countryside and a number of small villages. Chief of these is **MACROOM**, a focus for tourists and music enthusiasts heading for Killarney. It's on a main road and is a relatively easy hitch through the mountains. The **Boggeragh Mountains** to the north of the Lee Valley appear as high, rolling moorland, unspectacular compared with other ranges in Cork and Kerry but particularly rich in archeological remains: stone circles, standing stones, wedge tombs and ring forts. A leaflet, *Antiquities of the Boggeragh Mountains*, is available from the tourist office in Cork city – of great value in locating these sites. The Bantry Road from Macroom is far quieter, leading into the mountains and one of the county's last remaining *Gaeltacht* regions. There's a small, friendly **hostel**, *Tigh Barra* (*IHH*, mid-March to Sept; ☎026/47016; ①), which also offers **camping**, about a mile and a half west of the tiny village of **BALLINGEARY**; beyond here the road passes through the dramatic glacial valley of Gougane Barra and down to Bantry Bay (see p.274).

Dunmanway

Alternatively, taking the road south of Cork city to Bandon and then west to **DUNMANWAY** brings you to very promising country of deserted hills and lakes. Dunmanway is a plain country town, but just outside it the **hostel**, *Shiplake House Mountain Hostel* (*IHH*, open all year; ☎023/45750, fax ☎45750; ①), is in a beautiful setting and also has gypsy caravans for couples and families (②), **camping** and delicious vegetarian food. To find it take the Castle Road next to the *Market Diner* out of town, follow it for two and a half miles in the direction of Coolkelure (the road to Kealkill) and turn right at the hostel sign. *Bus Éireann* run at least two daily buses from Cork to Dunmanway, and a bus from Dunmanway to Bantry and Glengarriff. A **private bus** runs a Dunmanway–Cork return trip at weekends; phone the hostel for details of times.

Kinsale

KINSALE has retained much of the flavour of its rich maritime history and has much in common with the formerly affluent ports of Youghal, Cork and Cobh. The eighteen-mile road from Cork city travels through gentle rolling farmland and alongside an estuary. This easy, meandering coast is a favourite for fishing and bird watching, so alive with birdlife that it's rewarding even for the uninitiated. At Kinsale the harbour is broad, and cormorants and shags skim across its gentle waters. A tongue of land curls from the west into the centre of the harbour, protecting the town from harsh winds, and on this promontory are the ivy-clad ruins of Jamesfort, a ruddy castle built by the English James I.

With its pretty harbour, busy with yachts, and its reputation as the gourmet centre of the southwest, Kinsale is an extremely successful tourist town. For the most part development has been tasteful, though the pace of change is swift and a garish scar of pastel-coloured apartments rippling along the hillside illustrates the threat commercialism poses to Kinsale's historic character. Still, despite the crowds and the cars, there is plenty of interest in the life, landscape and history to keep you here.

Some history
Originally a fishing town, Kindale's sheltered harbour has made it a key place of strategic importance in Irish, and English, history. The town received its first royal charter from Edward III in 1333, but it was of little importance up until the **Battle of Kinsale** in 1601, a disastrous defeat for the Irish which signalled the end of the Gaelic aristocracy as a power for the English to reckon with. A Spanish fleet stood in the bay ready to support the Irish cause against Elizabethan forces, but was unable to make useful contact with O'Neill and O'Donnell attacking from the north. So the battle was lost, and although resistance to English rule continued, six years later came "the flight of the Earls" – when the Irish nobility fled to the Continent, giving up the fight for their own lands.

It was also at Kinsale that **James II** landed with French support in an attempt to regain his throne in 1689, and it was later the port of his final departure from Ireland after the Battle of the Boyne. The town was an important naval base for the English Crown in the seventeenth and eighteenth centuries, and the sixteenth-century tower house in Cork Street – Desmond Castle – became known as "The French Prison" when it was used to hold as many as 600 French prisoners during the Napoleonic wars.

It was off the Old Head of Kinsale that the ocean liner, the **Lusitania**, en route to Liverpool from New York, was torpedoed by a German submarine in 1915, killing 1198 people. It remains a controversial incident: Germany claimed there was ammunition on board; the US said it contained only civilians. Whatever the truuth, it has been seen as a catalyst for America's entry into World War I.

The town
The town's history is recorded in the **museum** (most afternoons; 50p), bang in the centre of town above the old market (1600) with its Dutch-style facade (1704). It's a friendly and intriguing jumble of stuff, including memorabilia from the *Lusitania* disaster; sixteenth-century royal charters and maps; local craftwork; personal effects of the eighteenth-century giant of Kinsale; and a variety of bizarre local inventions that never got further than the local museum. Here, too, is the musty old courthouse that had remained much the same from the eighteenth century up until 1915, when the inquest into the sinking of the *Lusitania* was held here and Kinsale suddenly became the focus of the world's press; after the inquest it was decided that the courtroom should be left as a memorial.

Desmond Castle (mid-April to mid-June Tues–Sun 10am–5pm; mid-June to mid-Sept daily 9am–6pm; mid-Sept to Oct Mon–Sat 9am–5pm, Sun 10am–5pm; £1, Heritage Card) has little to see beyond its simple, sturdy structure, although the tour is worth taking since the guides are instructive and entertaining. Nearby **St Multose Church** has traces of a medieval structure, and in the church porch are the town stocks from the eighteenth century.

Beyond the town's centre, **James' Fort** (1601) is fun to clamber over, but if your time is limited, head instead for **Charles' Fort** (1677), two miles out of town at Summercove (mid-April to mid-June & mid-Sept to mid-Oct Mon–Sat 9am–5pm, Sun 9.30am–5.30pm; mid-June to mid-Sept daily 9am–6pm; £2, Heritage Card). The outer walls of this fort, barely touched by weather or gunfire, seem pretty innocuous, but they conceal a formidable war machine. Within is an awesome system of barracks, ramparts and bastions, impressive testimony to the complexity and precision of seventeenth-century military science. The barracks were occupied until 1922, when the British left and handed the fort over to the Irish government. Today they remain largely intact, with only the barracks' missing roofs to give the place an eerily deserted feel. There are free guided tours every hour.

Practicalities

The **tourist office** is next to the bus depot and cinema (March–Nov Mon–Sat 9.30am–6pm; July & Aug Mon–Sat 9am–7pm, Sun 11am–5pm; May & June Mon–Sat 10am–6pm; ☎021/772234), in the centre of town; when it's closed tourist information is readily available at *Peter Barry's*, opposite *The Spaniards* pub in Scilly, on the eastern coast road out of town. As always, the tourist office can help out with **accommodation**: booking ahead is strongly advised during July, August and the gourmet festival. In the town centre are the unmissable *Yello Gallery Café*, 43 Main Street (☎021/772393; ③); *The Little Skillet*, 47 Main Street (☎021/774202; ④); and *Pier House*, Pier Road (☎021/774475; ⑧). *O'Donovan's*, Guardwell Street (☎021/772428; ④), and *Ivy House*, Long Quay (☎021/774563; ④), are other central options. *The Lighthouse* (☎021/772734; ⑤), found a steep walk up the hill behind the museum, is a flurry of antique lace.

For **hostel** accommodation, a short walk from the town centre is *Dempsey's Hostel*, Eastern Road (*IHH*, open all year; ☎012/772124; ①), just up the road to Cork. A smarter budget option is *Castlepark Marina Centre* (☎021/774959, fax ☎774958; ②), less than a couple of miles west out of town: cross over the new bridge and take a sharp left. Clean, comfortable and well run, with basic cooking facilities, it's in a beautiful spot looking out across the harbour to Kinsale. There's a pub, *The Dock*, next door, and a lovely sandy beach two minutes' walk away where you can rent windsurfs, sailing dinghies and canoes at very reasonable prices (contact the Outdoor Education Centre ☎021/772896). You can **camp** at *Dempsey's Hostel* or at Ballinspittle (see below). **Bike rental** is available at *Mylie Murphy's*, Pearce Street (☎021/772703; £5 per day, £28 per week).

Kinsale is a well-known gourmet centre – it even has a **gourmet festival** which starts the first Thursday in October (book well ahead), crowded with the affluent well-fed – and has numerous expensive **restaurants**: one of the best is *The Blue Haven* in Pearse Street (☎021/772209), where there's a good-value lunchtime menu. Pick up details of others in the free *Kinsale Good Food Circle* listings available at the tourist office. For more everyday food and drink, the town is also famous for its **pubs**, many of which serve delicious seafood – oysters are the local speciality. For picnics and self-catering *Kinsale Gourmet Store*, Short Quay (across from the tourist office), has a wonderful array of oils, relishes, seafood and local cheeses. For **music** try *The Shankee, The Lord Kinsale* or *The Tap Tavern* in the centre of town, or stroll out to *The Spaniards* in Scilly, a mile away. *Acton's Hotel* has jazz at Sunday lunchtimes, and *The Grey Hound* is a quaint old bar – its interior originally came from England.

Ballinspittle

Seven miles southwest of Kinsale is the tiny village of **BALLINSPITTLE**, which has found fame in recent years for popular sightings of its miraculous moving statues. The peninsula to the south, the Old Head of Kinsale, guarantees superb cliff walks, and at the neck of this peninsula are the remains of a fifteenth-century De Courcy castle. The

BLOW-INS AND ARTISTS

The potential of the beautiful, unspoilt and remote West Cork countryside was first widely perceived over twenty years ago, when the area was subject to a significant social upheaval with the immigration of large numbers of northern Europeans. "Blow-ins", as they're referred to, are people who have come to the area and have somehow managed to create an alternative lifestyle for themselves. Most of them are German, Belgian or Dutch and came here for a number of reasons: to escape political systems they abhorred at home; to distance themselves from nuclear issues; to escape pollution, overcrowding and stress; or to key into the perceived creative energies, and the romantic mysticism, generated by the West Coast.

This influx of outsiders began in the 1960s at a time when there was plenty of money to be earned in the major cities of western Europe, and since then there has been a process of natural selection. Those who don't make a total commitment to the lifestyle no longer find it so easy to nip back to developed Europe, to earn swift cash with which to subsidize their romantic idyll. Consequently those who are still here are either survivors, or rich at home, too. Missing the irony, many visitors consider them an intrusion, making the experience somehow less "Irish", less authentic. In fact the presence of "blow-ins" is positively beneficial to the budget traveller. While they may have originally settled with a vision of living off organic farming, craftwork and home-grown entertainment, the harsh realities of subsistence have borne a real resourcefulness, the most useful sign of which is the mushrooming of **independent hostels**. Many of these are tucked away in delightfully secret places the owner has discovered and now chooses to share with visitors, and they're often worth visiting purely for the setting or the very special personal atmosphere that's been created. Another spin-off from the "blow-in" phenomenon is the high incidence of **wholefood** shops in tiny towns; welcome indeed in an area where traditional grocery shops are poor at providing anything that doesn't come in a tin.

Finally, West Cork has attracted a large number of people who have come here to be artists, some of whom have succeeded. A local **arts centre** may be nothing more than a shed, but it can hold surprises, so look out for them. Some of the work is folksy and boring, but you may also stumble across exciting work of refreshing originality. What adds to these centres' appeal is the deeper understanding of the land they can offer: the best work has been inspired by, and so reflects, the colours and textures of the landscape.

Garrettstown House Holiday Park **campsite** (Easter to early Sept; ☎021/778156 or ☎775286; gas cylinders on sale, washing facilities) is clearly signposted from the centre of the village.

The Seven Heads Peninsula

The stretch of coast from Timoleague to Clonakilty is known as the **Seven Heads Peninsula**. It's a pretty, indented shoreline, good for walking and bird watching. The spruce village of **TIMOLEAGUE** sits inland on the muddy estuary of the Ardigeen river, dominated by the extensive remains of a **Franciscan abbey** which was sacked in 1649. The much advertised **Castle Gardens** include a beautiful walled garden, but the ruins of Timoleague Castle itself are negligible and not worth the entrance fee. Timoleague is only a small place, but it can boast a handful of good bars promising music: *Pad Joes*, *Charlie Madden's* and *Dillon's*; this last is a cross between a bar and a French café with a very varied menu, reasonably priced (mid-March to Oct). The nearby **hostel**, *Lettercollum House* (mid-March to late Oct; tel/fax ☎023/46251; ①), is a friendly place, worth visiting for the food alone: seafood, lamb and vegetarian dishes, locally produced and lovingly prepared. Meals for hostellers cost around £8–£13;

those not staying at the hostel are advised to phone and book for the restaurant in advance (£17–20). You can **rent bikes** at the hostel, which makes it a perfect point from which to explore the Seven Heads Peninsula. There's also good **camping** around two miles out of Timoleague along the R600 towards Clonakilty at *Sexton's Camping* (☎023/46347).

At the broad mouth of the estuary, the village of **COURTMACSHERRY** is currently being developed as a safe, quiet family resort. It's certainly tranquil – when asked what happens here one local reckoned "the tide comes in and the tide goes out again". That's slightly exaggerated – if you're feeling rich you can go deep-sea angling or shark fishing (*Courtmacsherry Sea Angling Centre*; ☎023/46427), and horse riding can be arranged through the *Courtmacsherry Hotel* (☎023/46198); in the evenings you may find a singsong round the piano at the *Lifeboat Inn* or *Anchor Bar*. *Dunworley Cottage Restaurant* (☎023/40314) is noted for its organic food – expect to pay around £18 for dinner. If you're looking for **B&B**, nearby *Sea Court* (June–Aug; ☎023/50151; ⑤), a few miles south at **BUTLERSTOWN**, is an eighteenth-century mansion of some interest, furnished with antiques.

Clonakilty

The busy little town of **CLONAKILTY**, birthplace of the Republican leader Michael Collins, has a growing reputation as a **traditional music** centre, thanks to the enthusiasm of local people; it's also home to the much respected, innovative **street theatre** group *Craic Na Coillte*, so any of the town's festivals are worth taking in. A **country and western festival** is usually held over the last weekend in August; expect accommodation to be tight. The traditional **Clonakilty Festival** (late June/early July) includes pub talent, debating contests and street entertainment.

The local **pub scene** is also very lively, attracting a lot of young people. There are plenty of excellent old bars: for music *De Barra's* on Pearse Street is probably the most popular place, with traditional or rock music more or less every night all year round. *Shanley's* in Connolly Street has MOR pop and 1960s sessions (7 nights a week in summer, 5 in winter); *The Kitty Stone Tavern*, Main Street, has contemporary folk on a Thursday; and *Teach Beag* (behind *O'Donovan's Hotel*) has traditional music every night during the summer, and at weekends throught the year. *Fiddler's Green*, Clarke Street, is always popular with a younger crowd, though there's rarely live music. The club in *Emmett Hotel*, Emmett Square, and *O'Donovan's Hotel* both have music during July and August. *O'Donovan's* is also a good place to pick up what's-on information, and they have a mini-museum of local history upstairs, with a 130-year-old polyphon – a gigantic antique jukebox – still in operation.

Pubs and festivals aside, the recently excavated Lisnagun Christian **ringfort** might appeal, especially if you have young children in tow. It's the only one in Ireland to be reconstructed in its original site, with defensive walls, a thatched central house, souterrains, replica weapons, utensils and clothing – all of which create a vivid picture of tenth-century life. Your ticket includes entrance to a small animal park nearby, where you can encounter fowl, rabbit and reindeer (daily 10am–5pm; £2, children £1). Clonakilty also makes a good base from which to explore the crazily indented coastline roundabout, especially enjoyable by bike. The best **beach** is at Inchydoney, three miles to the south: formerly an island, it's now linked to the mainland by a causeway. Just over a mile north of town are the remains of the Templebryan **stone circle** – four of the original nine stones still stand, along with a central white quartzite pillar; to find it head out of town up MacCurtain Hill.

There's a **tourist office** in the town centre (July & Aug Mon–Sat closed 1–2pm; ☎023/33226). For upmarket accommodation, *Strand House Guest House* (☎023/33498; ⑤) – ask at the *Súgán* restaurant – and *O'Donovan's Hotel* (tel/fax ☎023/33250; ⑤) are both central. There are also plenty of **B&Bs**. *Nordar*, Western Road (☎023/33655; ④), and *Wytchwod,* off Emmet Square (☎023/33525; ③ & ④), are both at the west end of town, and the latter also has purpose-built hostel accommodation (②). At the east end of town are *Bay View,* Old Timologue Road (☎023/33539; ④), and *Desert House* (☎023/33331; ④). Or you could try Mrs A. O'Driscoll's *Aisling,* Clogheen Road (☎023/33491; ③). **Camping** is available a mere 500 yards' stagger from the pubs at Dorothy Jennings' *Desert House,* near the shore (May–Sept; ☎023/33331); head east out of the village and turn right at the roundabout. For **bike rental** try *MTM Cycles,* Ashe Street (☎023/33584), or *Tom Sheehy,* Aston Square (☎023/33362).

The town has several decent **places to eat:** for light lunches try *An Chistin,* next door to *De Barra's; O'Donovan's Hotel* serves meals till 9pm daily; *Fionnuala's,* 30 Ashe Street, is a cheap and cosy Italian restaurant. Nearby *The Druid's Table* has an imaginative menu of seafood, lamb and vegetarian dishes (light lunches from £3.50, dinner around £12; till 11pm, closed Mon). If you just want a takeaway, head for *The Rossa Grill.*

Skibbereen and around

SKIBBEREEN, a cheerful place, smartly painted and set on the River Illen in a landscape of low wooded hills and pasture, is the main service and administrative centre for the south of West Cork. This traditional role is still remarkably alive: on Wednesdays the cattle market still operates, drawing crowds from the surrounding country, and every Friday afternoon there's the regular country market. For travellers, it's a good place to stock up or to stop over – there are plenty of supermarkets and liqueur stores, a smattering of health-food shops and delis, plenty of pubs. The **West Cork Arts Centre** on North Street (Mon–Sat winter 12.30–5pm; summer 11am–6pm) is worth checking out. It hosts monthly exhibitions which can be first-rate, stages occasional music and dance performances, and has a reference and slide library through which you can locate local artists.

The **tourist office** (mid-June to mid-Sept Mon–Sat 9am–7pm, Oct–May Mon–Fri 9.15am–1pm & 2.15–5.30pm; ☎028/21766) is also along North Street and will help with accommodation. If you feel like splashing out, there's the *Liss Ard Lake Lodge* (☎028/22365; ⑧) out of town on the road to Castletownshend. A masterpiece of understatement, it's a nineteenth-century house refurbished in a minimalist style. It's in a choice spot too, overlooking a glassy lake. Residents have access to the *Liss Ard Experience* (see overleaf), and non-residents also can eat in the excellent restaurant (dinner around £24). For **B&Bs** try *Ilenvoy House* (☎028/22751; ⑤) or *The Ivanhoe* (☎028/21749; ④), both in North Street, *Illenside,* 18 Bridge Street (☎028/21605; ③), or Mrs Calnan's *Riverside* (☎028/33577; ③). *Mont Bretia* (☎028/33663; ④), four miles out of town, is developing a reputation for relaxed accommodation, offering vegetarian food, breakfast till noon, free bike loans, and a gay- and lesbian-friendly environment. There's a new **hostel**, *The Russagh Mill Hostel,* a mile out on the Castletownshend Road, before the *Liss Ard Lodge* (☎028/22451 or ☎22988; laundry and drying room; ②). Mick Murphy, the hostel manager, is happy to talk to visitors about his Everest climb in 1993, and leads hillwalking, canoeing and sail-boarding activities most days (£8–10 per day). You can get **Bus Eireann information** from *O'Cahalales* in Bridge St, and rent **bikes** from *N.W. Roycroft and Son* in Ilen Street (☎028/21235; £7.50 per day, £30 per week).

For good **pub food** try *The Wine Vaults* (till 8pm) or *Bernard's* (till 9pm), both in Main Street, *McCarthy's* on Bridge Street, or, for seafood, *The Windmill Tavern* on North Street. *The Stove* café, Main Street, does good budget meals; while *Ann O'Donovan's* on Bridge Street is good for coffee and snacks. Skibbereen has a handful of interesting **bars**: *McCarthy's* is a popular tourist spot and *Baby Hannah's* is a lively young place, both on Bridge Street. For **music** try *The Wine Vaults* (Thurs–Sun R&B, traditional and folk), or *Seanogs,* Market Street (folk and ballads at weekends).

East to Rosscarbery

The coastline east of Skibbereen is a beautiful stretch of little bays and creeks, sandy coves and tidal loughs. There are tiny lagoons here and there, isolated along the shore from the main body of the sea, providing placid contrast to the furling white ocean spray. Each place has its own special charms – Castletownshend, Union Hall, Leap, Glandore, Rosscarbery. If you take the main N71 you're never far from these places, with easy access by a couple of miles' walk or a short hitch.

About a mile or so out along the Castletownshend Road (ask locally for directions) is the **Liss Ard Experience**, a New Age garden where the emphasis is very much on conservation (Mon–Sun 10am–8pm, till 5pm winter; £5). The original landscaped garden had been left unmanaged since 1924; consequently wild flora and fauna have found their own balance, and the area has been developed in such a way as to allow the natural order to hold sway. Discrete pathways lead to natural "chambers" of vegetation, the idea being to encourage secluded contemplation and a deeper awareness of the environment. The real highlight at *Liss Ard*, however, is the **Sky Garden**, the work of contemporary American artist James Turell. When finished it will have five key "monuments": a pyramid, a crater, a mound, a sky walk and a grotto, which you will be led towards along narrow pathways. At the moment only the crater is finished: a huge elliptical grassy bowl with a stark stone slab at its centre for two people to lie on and view. Using light and landscape, the artist creates space and plays with our powers of sensory perception – the result is a profoundly powerful experience, awe inspiring in its stillness. Irreverent as it may sound, sunglasses are advisable on bright days, and in wet weather viewing is impossible (tours daily at noon, 2pm & 4pm; £5; combined ticket for main and Sky gardens, £7).

Carrying on southwards from *Liss Ard*, on a ridge overlooking Castletownshend is the **Knockdrum stone ring fort**, outside of which is a large rock with megalithic cup and ring marks. Pretty **Castletownshend** itself was the home of Edith Somerville of Somerville and Ross fame, authors of the "Irish RM" stories. Their graves are to be found in St Barrahane's churchyard. Further along the coast, on the minor R597 road between Rosscarbery and Glandore, is the single recumbent stone of the fine **Drombeg stone circle**, which marks the position of the midwinter sunset; it probably dates from the early Bronze Age. Nearby is a **Fulacht Fiadh** of the same era: a stone trough used for cooking that would be filled with spring water and heated by throwing in hot stones from a fire.

If you are planning on staying in the area, **LEAP** is the main town and holds the biggest surprise: *Connolly's* bar (☎028/33215), with arguably the best **live music** in West Cork and a great range of bands all year round: rock, traditional, bluegrass – just about anything that's on in the county will be on here. There are a couple of **B&Bs** in the village: *Highfield* (☎028/33273; ④) and *Riverside* (☎028/33577; ③). For **camping** try *The Meadow* a mile or so southeast just outside **Glandore** (☎028/33280; wet weather room and laundry facilities); or *O'Riordan's Caravan Park* (☎023/48216 or ☎541825) in **ROSSCARBERY**, just over five miles east of Leap. *The Pier House Bistro* (Tues–Sun 6–9pm) in Glandore has an excellent reputation (main courses £6–11). There's a pleasant **B&B** here too, *Bay View* (☎028/33115; ④). The nearest **hostel** is at Cahergah in **Union Hall**. *Maria's Schoolhouse* (*IHH*, March–Sept; ☎028/33002; ②) is a bright and cheery place, with comfy armchairs, log fires and a laundry; it also serves vegetarian and non-vegetarian meals, and can arrange **bike rental**, diving and canoeing. They will pick up backpackers from Leap.

Southwest to Baltimore

Less than four miles southwest of Skibbereen along the Baltimore Road, the **Creagh Gardens** (10am–6pm; £2) offer a very different horticultural experience to that of *Liss Ard*, and are a delightful place to unwind. They are ostensibly fairly traditional – with woodland glades, lawns running down to the estuary and a Regency walled kitchen garden – but the late owner's desire to create a garden based on the richness of tone and colour found in Rousseau's jungle paintings was less conventional and is achieved here by a dense, textured build-up of lush vegetation and exotic palms. If you head back a little way up the road and take the turning on your right, you'll soon find **Lough Hyne** (pronounced *Ine*), a land-locked salt lake, linked to the ocean only by a very slender channel down which the receding tide returns to the sea. The lough, surrounded by hillsides dripping with lush, moist greenery, is a unique phenomenon, of great interest to marine biologists. From the head of the lake steep slopes, easily climbed, rise to panoramic views: eastwards along the coast to Kinsale; west across the length of the Mizen Peninsula; and out across to Sherkin and Clear islands.

Baltimore and the islands

The approach to Baltimore takes you through a landscape that is disarmingly low-key. Instead of some dramatic climax at this, the most southerly point of all Ireland, the land seems simply to be fading away: rocky terrain and scrawny vegetation accompany the windy, listless estuary, untidy with lumps of land that seem to have been tossed at random towards the sea. The whole ragged effect is as if the country is running out of substance; the landmass, already moth-bitten, is now fraying, too. But as the ocean comes into full view this tailing off is put into spectacular context: the whole weight of Ireland is behind you, while ahead are dots, wracks and scraps of islands, petering out across the great open expanse of water to Sherkin and Clear islands.

FERRIES

Baltimore–Sherkin Island (£4 return) June–Sept depart Baltimore daily 10.30am, noon, 2pm, 4pm, 5.30pm, 7pm & 8.30pm; returning from Sherkin roughly a quarter of an hour after these times. Winter 1–3 daily: ask at *Bushe's* bar or telephone ☎028/20125, eves ☎20218.

Baltimore–Clear Island (£8 return) July & Aug depart Baltimore daily 11am, 2.15pm & 7pm; returning at 9am, noon & 6pm: June & Sept depart Baltimore daily 2.15pm & 7pm; returning 9am & 6pm; Sun return 12pm & 6pm. Oct–May daily depart Baltimore 2.15pm, depart Clear 9am ☎028/

39159. If you stay at the youth hostel on the island, you get a £1 refund on your ferry ticket, so ask the warden to stamp it.

Baltimore–Schull (£6 single, bikes free) June–Aug, daily except Tues & Sat, depart Baltimore 11.15am, 4pm; depart Schull 12.15pm & 5pm; ☎028/39153.

Schull–Clear Island (£8 return, £4 single) June and first week Sept depart Schull daily 2.30pm, return from Clear Island 5.30pm; July & Aug depart Schull 10am, 2.30pm & 4.30pm; return from Clear Island 11am, 3.30pm & 5.30pm; ☎028/28138.

Baltimore

BALTIMORE, a delightful harbour village overlooked by a sixteenth-century O'Driscoll stronghold, is the last significant mainland settlement. Combining traditional fishing activities with tourism, it's also the departure point for ferries to Sherkin, Clear Island and Schull (see above): for most people this is the chief reason to come. During the last two weeks of July and the first weekend in August the yachting crowd descend en masse for the **regatta**: there are a few pricy restaurants to cater for them. If you're staying, there's **B&B** accommodation at *Island View* (☎028/20124; ③) and *The Algiers Inn* (☎028/20145; ④); *Bushe's* bar has good accommodation with continental breakfast (☎028/20119; ③), and they also have **showers** for people camping or sailing.

Rolf's **independent hostel** is cheerful and friendly, a real favourite (*IHH*, open all year; book ahead in July and August; ☎028/20289; ②), and also rents bikes for £6 per day and sells organic produce. Tasty meals are available in the hostel common room (£2–10) or in the *Opus* **restaurant** alongside, where vegetarians are well catered for, produce is fresh, and Malaysian food is their speciality. *The Life-Boat Restaurant*, overlooking the quays, serves budget meals and you can get great seafood and steaks all day at *Casey's Cabin* (music on Sat & Sun nights), about a mile towards Skibbereen. *Declan McCarthy's* bar by the harbour also serves seafood and has traditional, folk and ballad sessions several nights a week in summer; it also cashes cheques and **changes money**. Contact *Baltimore Diving and Watersports Centre* (☎028/20300) if you fancy scuba diving (£28 for 3hr) or canoeing (£15, 3hr). As well as the scheduled *Bus Éireann*, there is a private service that operates from the harbour to Skibbereen around 10–10.30am – check the exact schedule locally.

Sherkin Island

Tiny **SHERKIN ISLAND** is a delightfully pretty place: the considerable remains of a fifteenth-century Franciscan friary nestle down by the quayside, and little fuschia-spattered lanes lead across the island to fine sandy beaches in the west. There are the remains of an O'Driscoll stronghold, too, and the annual O'Driscoll clan gathering in June is a hectic five-day event spread between Sherkin, Clear Island and Baltimore. For a community of only some ninety people, the island has a great **pub scene**, with sessions at *The Jolly Roger* attracting crowds from the mainland. If there's a band booked and you are staying in Baltimore, there's usually a late-night ferry laid on to take everybody home.

The place can get busy with day-trippers at bank holidays and in July and August. If you want to stay there are a few places that do **B&B**: *Cuina* (☎028/20384; ④) and *Island House* (☎028/20314; ④) – all closed in winter. If you want to **camp**, ask locally. If these are all full, it's worth asking at the pub for alternatives – they've a very helpful source of local information. *The Jolly Roger* does bar food during the summer: at other times you can buy supplies at the post office.

Clear Island

CLEAR ISLAND (*Oileán Chléire*) offers rather more to do, but it would be worth visiting for the ferry trip alone, though it can be a topsy-turvy, stomach-churning ride. There's an important ornithology station here, and on the 45-minute ride out to the island, it's obvious that the place is paradise for **wildlife** enthusiasts. The bay is alive with seabirds – guillemots, cormorants, auks and storm petrels – and with luck you may see seals and, in warm weather, basking sharks. With even more luck you might find your boat raced by a playful dolphin or two, dodging around the bows and leaping out of the ocean to crash back down right alongside the ferry.

The hilly, rocky island seems to have been pinched in the middle where two inlets, North Harbour and South Harbour, almost meet. In the south, steep and inaccessible cliffs rise from the water; the North Harbour is perfectly sheltered. Roads climb up from here through hills covered in the coarse grass that seems to spread over everything, including old walls and houses long derelict. Sea pinks cling to rocky outcrops, and honeysuckle clambers wherever it can. The island's high points give spectacular views back across the archipelago to the mainland.

The **bird observatory** at North Harbour has been here since 1959 and has complete records going back to that time. When it was set up, by an amateur group, this station was a pioneer of the constant observation of seabirds, and its work has done much for the knowledge of migratory patterns. Clear Island is one of the most important places for seabirds in Ireland, including some genuine rarities – especially plentiful are storm petrels, shearwaters, black guillemots and choughs. There is **hostel**-style accommodation here (book in advance), available for ornithologists, too, but likely to be full in late spring and in September and October. If you are new to bird watching, but fancy learning more, call in and see what's happening, though be warned that midsummer is not the best time.

Clear Island is also an isolated remnant of the *Gaeltacht*, where Irish is still spoken by about 130 islanders. During the summer Irish youth are sent here to practise the language. The island has a **festival** of drama, music, art and dance, *Féile Shamhna Chléire*, usually held on the bank holiday weekend in late October. The **Heritage Centre** (daily June–Aug 3.30–5.30pm, and by arrangement – call at the house opposite; £1), a steep, well-signposted walk from North Harbour, is a tiny museum of the domestic, fishing and seafaring history of the island. The island prides itself on being the birthplace of Saint Kieran, who supposedly preceded Saint Patrick by thirty years, but the holy well and stone that are attributed to him stand in a sadly unromantic spot by the road at North Harbour. The best of Clear Island's historic ruins is **Dún an Óir** ("Fort of Gold"), an O'Driscoll fort, impressive on a high, narrow splinter of rock which is now an island at high tide – sadly inaccessible, though you can see it as you walk down the hill from the Heritage Centre, or from the 200ft cliffs to the south.

There are a number of **B&Bs**: try Mary Uí Drisceóil, *Cluain Mara*, North Harbour (☎028/39153; ④), or Eleanor Uí Drisceóil, *Fáilte*, Glen East, up by the lighthouse (☎028/39135; ④). The *An Óige* **hostel** is at South Harbour (Easter–Oct; ☎028/39144; ②). **Camping** is available a short walk from the ferry (June–end Sept). Wherever you intend to stay, it makes sense during the summer to arrange accommodation before sailing. The island has two pubs, *Cotters Bar* and *The Club*; this last has some excellent **music** sessions going on into the small hours (mostly July–Aug), and *Chistin Cléire* directly beneath it is the island's one **café** (May–Sept daily 10am–8.30pm; weekends in Oct). There's an excellent **shop** beside North Harbour, though bring your own *Gaz* if you're camping.

Mizen Head

The Mizen Head Peninsula is a beautiful, remote finger of land poking its way west, offering superb sandy beaches and cliff scenery, getting wilder the further west you go. It's an area rich in **archeological sites**, from Bronze Age wedge graves contemporary with the first copper mining of Mount Gabriel, through Iron Age and early Christian ring forts, down to medieval castles – pick up a copy of the leaflet *Antiquities of the Mizen Peninsula* from the tourist office in Cork city if you want to locate these sites. Great care should be taken at the Mizen cliffs, as the land ends abruptly and without warning.

Most spectacular of the coastal scenery is at **Mizen Head** itself – sheer, vertiginous cliffs, with an offshore lighthouse linked by a little suspension bridge, which is now accessible if you visit the *Mizen Vision* heritage centre. Standing at this exhilarating spot it takes little effort to imagine the great number of ships that have been wrecked in Dunlough Bay to the north. A walk round to **Three Castles Head** brings in sight the curtain wall and two turrets of an O'Mahoney stronghold, one of twelve that were built along this peninsula in the fifteenth century. The setting makes this one truly spectacular. The whole of the peninsula's wild and empty northern coast, in fact, is one of sheer cliffs and stupendous views – an impossible route for hitching, but great for those with transport.

The south coast of the peninsula is more travelled, with small towns at Ballydehob, Schull and Crookhaven, and lovely sandy **beaches**. The best of these is the long and sandy strand at Barleycove, whose rolling breakers make it a favourite with windsurfers. Nearby is the busy little holiday resort of Crookhaven, with a large **caravan** and camping park on the Goleen–Crookhaven Road; unless you want the facilities, though, there is no real need to use this – there are plenty of remote spots where you can pitch a tent for free. At Goleen is the delightful *Heron Cove* (☎028/35225), a restaurant where if you don't want a full meal you can still enjoy chowder, cakes and creek life. The only public transport along the peninsula is run by *Bus Éireann* as far as Crookhaven.

Ballydehob

BALLYDEHOB, a town of gaily coloured streets at the neck of the peninsula, was once known as the hippy capital of the west because it was said to have more "blow-ins" than locals. Heavily colonized in the 1960s, it still has traces of their influence, like health food and artists, and remains a liberal place compared to others of its size. For all this it's a sleepy town with just a handful of craft and antique shops worth exploring. If you want to **stay**, *dunan oir* (☎028/37272; ④) is a pleasant option, and the *Ballydehob Inn* (☎028/37139; ④) is similarly friendly. There's a **campsite** just a couple of hundred yards down the Durrus Road (price includes hot water and showers). *Annie's Restaurant* (☎028/37292; book for dinner, £21) is renowned for its seafood, and the same people serve affordable lunches during the day at *The Bookshop Café*. There are some interesting old bars – Julie and Nell run *Levis*, a bar-grocery store (opposite *Annie's*); *Coughlan's* has country, ballad and occasional traditional sessions (Wed, Fri & Sun).

Ballydehob's nearest **beach** is three miles away at Audley Cove: a pebbly cove, secluded and personal, with lovely views of the islands.

Schull

SCHULL, as well as being the place to catch the **ferry** for Clear Island (see p.269), is perhaps the most obvious place to stay on the peninsula, a place with plenty of cheery amenities aimed at holidaying families and the unpretentious yachting fraternity. An attractive, seaside market town, Schull's sheltered, bulb-shaped harbour looks out over Carbery's Hundred Islands, while Mount Gabriel rises to 1339ft to the north, offering wonderful views. To make this walk from Schull (nine miles there and back) head up Gap Road past the convent and you'll find a clear track all the way. From the top you can continue around the north side of the mountain, to return through Rathcool and Glaun. The domes at the summit of Mount Gabriel are aircraft-tracking stations. As you walk, beware of unguarded mine shafts: this rough and rocky land was heavily mined for copper in the nineteenth century, and is still dotted with Cornish-style mining chimneys.

Schull is at its liveliest during its **sailing events**. The international sailing festival for children is usually held the second week in July, when the town is awash with nautical teenagers, and the yachting set proper swamp the town for the regatta held in Calves week (following the August bank holiday weekend, usually the first week of the month). At these times accommodation can be difficult, and phoning ahead is advisable.

PRACTICALITIES

If you want **B&B** try *O'Regan's*, Main Street (☎028/28334; ③), *Hillside* (☎028/28248; ④), the extremely pleasant *Old Bank House* (☎028/28306; ④) or *Adele's* (☎028/28459; ③). Five minutes' walk from the village centre is *Schull's Backpackers' Lodge* (*IHH*, open all year; tel/fax ☎028/28681; ②), a lovely wooden **hostel** surrounded by trees, where you can also rent bikes and **camp**. There are **ferries** from Schull to Baltimore (see p.269) and *Karycraft* (☎028/28138 or ☎28278) **cruises** around Roaring Water Bay (July & Aug Mon & Fri 7pm, 90min; £5) or the Fastnet Rock (July & Aug Tues & Thurs 7pm, 2hr 30min; £10). If you fancy a spot of **sailing** yourself *Schull Watersports Centre*, The Pier (☎028/28554 or ☎28351), organizes sea-angling trips, dinghy rental

(£25 a half day), wind-surfing (£10 per half-day) and diving for the experienced only. It also offers hot showers (£1). For canoeing try *Argonauts* (☎027/70692), wet suits provided. If you want to go **horse riding**, there's *The Colla House Hotel* on Colla Road (☎028/28105). **Bike rental** is also available from Alan Murphy at *The Black Sheep* (☎028/28203).

As for **eating**, *Adele's Coffee Shop* in Main Street does excellent home-made cakes, soups, salads and fresh pasta. *The Courtyard* serves seafood and vegetarian meals and has a good deli selling fresh bread from its brick-built steam oven, local cheeses, oils and pickles. For **bar food** try *The Courtyard* or the *Bunratty Inn*. The pubs have **music** year round (Thurs–Sat and during the week in July & Aug). Between them *The Bunratty Inn* and *The Courtyard* offer traditional, jazz, folk and swing; and *The Galley* and *Arundel's* both have traditional (Thurs), as does *An Tigin* (Sat). *The Courtyard* also has set dancing (Tues). There are a bank and post office in town, and two good **bookshops**, *Mizen Books*, in Main Street (☎028/28414), and *Fuschia Books* (second-hand), good for rainy afternoons.

Sheep's Head

The peninsula north of Mizen, **Sheep's Head**, has an ancient feel to it: barren land almost entirely devoid of people. There are only a couple of tiny villages here, and traffic is sparse – the sole weekly bus runs on Saturday – so don't try to hitch if you're going to need to return in a hurry. It's a changing landscape, where surges of harsh granite rise from sweet green fields, fuschias and honeysuckle scramble over greystone walls, gorse and heather colour wild heathland, and at every twist of the road plantlife, rock and water fall together to describe some new magic ideal. There are also fabulous panoramic views over County Cork, the Beara Peninsula, and County Kerry from the top of **Seefin**, Sheep's Head's highest hill (1136ft).

DURRUS has a handful of pubs, shops and the pleasant *Dunbeacon campsite* (☎027/61246; wet-weather hut), three miles down the Crookhaven Road. West towards Sheep's Head, minuscule **AHAKISTA** has a narrow slip of sandy beach backed by a showering of trees. *Arundel's* bar here is a quiet old place to stop off for tea and sandwiches, and there are snacks, too, at *The Ahakista Bar*, along with a gorgeous lush beer garden that runs down to the water's edge. For directions to the only place selling basic provisions, ask at either bar. One and a half miles beyond the bars is *Reenmore* **B&B** (☎027/67051; ④). At **KILCROMANE** there's a post office, a bar serving sandwiches, and *Dunmahon* B&B (☎027/67092; ⑤). A summer **café** (May–Sept) serving teas and salmon sandwiches is right at the end of the peninsula. Whichever way you drive down to the Sheep's Head the scenery is superb. The north coast looks down on the magnificent Bantry Bay, backed by the wild Caha Mountains, and offers cyclists a wonderful scenic descent towards Bantry.

Bantry

The beauty of **BANTRY** is its setting at the head of ever-turbulent Bantry Bay, which stretches thirty miles from the town to the ocean. The deep, churning blue waters of the bay, backed by the dramatic heights of the Beara's Caha Mountains and cowering, usually, under a notoriously changeable sky, form as dramatic a backdrop as any in Ireland. The town itself sits around a long square focused at the head of the bay, with a slaty Regency Gothic church and a statue of Saint Brendan staring out to sea. In the immediate surrounds are lush wooded slopes – a safe haven indulged between the ravages of the sea and the wilds of the rocky mountains. It's also a place of history and character – a commercial harbour, fishing port and market town, where the traditional market is still held on the first Friday of every month.

Some history

For centuries **Bantry Bay** attracted attempts from abroad to overthrow English rule. Once inside its shelter, ships were protected from attack by the rugged mountains of the peninsulas on either side.

In 1689, a French fleet sailed up the bay to assist James II, but was forced to return after an indecisive battle with Williamite forces. A century later, in 1796, Wolfe Tone arrived with another French fleet – and this time with revolutionary ideals – to try to overthrow the Protestant Anglo-Irish. Channel storms, however, had already reduced the fleet from 43 ships to 16 by the time it arrived, and the remaining vessels spent six days in the bay unable to land, even though, as Tone said, "we were close enough to toss a biscuit on shore". After this failure they were forced to turn back. Richard White, a local landowner, was rewarded for his loyalty to the English Crown at the time of the invasion by being made Baron Bantry.

Arrival, information and accommodation

Bus Éireann **buses**, connecting with Cork, Skibbereen, Glengarriff, Killarney and the Mizen Head Peninsula, leave from outside *Lynch's Bar* (information inside), towards the harbour from the tourist office. For details of private bus services, see "Travel Details". The **tourist office** lies on Wolfe Tone Square, known as The Square (June–Sept; ☎027/50229). **Bike rental** is available along the Glengarriff Road, to the right just before the turning for the industrial estate (☎027/50278; £6 per day).

Finding somewhere to **stay** in Bantry should present few problems. If you feel like splashing out on a night or two of real luxury, you can enjoy bed and breakfast at the aristocratic **Bantry House** (☎027/50047; ⑧). **B&Bs** abound: *Bay View House*, The Square (☎027/50403; ③), is worth it just to try out the famous antique shower; *The Cosy Cabin*, Barrack Street (☎027/50687; ③), has accommodation above the bar; and there are plenty of others out along the Glengarriff Road – *Sunville* (☎027/50175; ④), Mrs Kramer's *The Mill*, Newtown (☎027/50278; ④), or *Doire Liath* (☎027/50223; ④). Friendly, welcoming *Bantry Independent Hostel*, Bishop Lucey Place (*IHH*, mid-March to Oct; ☎027/51050; ①), is a short signposted walk from The Square. Budget accommodation is also available on The Square at *Harbour View Independent Hostel* (open all year; ☎027/51140; ①). The nearest **campsite** is at Ballylickey, four miles from Bantry along the Glengarriff Road: the *Eagle Point Caravan and Camping Park* (May–Sept; ☎027/50630) is a superbly situated site right on the edge of the bay; you can swim from their pebbly beach and there are excellent wild mountain walks roundabout – ask the owners to point you in the right direction. It's well worth calling in at *Manning's Emporium* nearby, an excellent deli with a huge range of Irish cheeses.

The town

The baron's home, **Bantry House** (daily 9am–6pm, summer closes 8pm most evenings; £3), nowadays provides an elegant vision of the rarefied life led by the Anglo-Irish aristocracy. Sumptuously decorated and packed with art treasures, it deserves some time. Much of the furniture is French Napoleonic, and there are Gobelin tapestries and Aubusson carpets; but what makes this house such a gem is the sheer variety of artefacts that have been collected, many of them during the second earl's European wanderings in the nineteenth century. The setting is superb: ordered landscaped gardens look down over the bay, calmly asserting the harmony of the aristocratic order, unruffled by the ruggedness of the surroundings. The **Bantry 1796 French Armada Exhibition Centre** (April–Oct daily 10am–6pm, other times by arrangement; £2.50, students £1.50; combined ticket including Bantry House £4.50, students £3, family £9; ☎027/51796), housed in one of the courtyards, gives a blow-by-blow account of Wolfe Tone's failed mission and displays artefacts recovered from the wreck of the frigate *La Surveillante,* scuttled on Whiddy Island in 1797 and excavated in 1982, though you would need to be an enthusiast to enjoy the centre.

Another side of the past is remembered with relish by the ladies who run the **Bantry Museum**, behind the fire station on Wolfe Tone Square (June–Sept Tues & Thurs 10.30am–1pm, Wed & Fri 3–5.30pm; 50p). The museum is the collection of the local history society – domestic paraphernalia, old newspapers and everyday trivia of every sort – which the curators willingly demonstrate with an entertaining blend of history and gossip. The modern **library**, at the top of Bridge Street, was built in 1974 and, at first glance, looks like some sort of spaceship, though the design was in fact inspired by a prehistoric dolmen: as adventurous a piece of modern architecture as you'll find in the west of Ireland, it's let down by a white facade that already seems thoroughly tacky.

One final thing worth going out of your way to see is the fine, early Christian **Kilnaruane Pillar Stone** just out of town. Its worn carvings depict four men rowing, an apostle and the cross. Follow the main road south out of town and take the first turning on the left past the *Westlodge Hotel*: the stone is in a field 500 yards further on the right.

Eating, drinking and entertainment

There are a handful of places to **eat** in Bantry: *O'Connor's* (☎027/50221) on The Square is highly popular for seafood – lunches from around £5, dearer in the evenings; *Kearney's Kitchen*, Barrack Street, serves tasty snacks and lunches all day until 9pm (6pm in winter); *Ó Síocháin*, in Bridge Street, is a cheery café serving hearty lunches and seafood platters during the summer months till 9.30pm. *The 5A* in Barrack Street is more of a hippy hang-out and similarly popular, the original vegetarian greasy spoon, serving soups, vege-burgers and delicious homemade cakes. If you want **pub food**, a handful of places around The Square are good value; try *The Wolfe Tone Tavern* or the massive lunches in *The Snug* (both till 8.30pm during the summer), or *The Bantry Bay Hotel*.

Regular **pubs** are plentiful as ever: the *Anchor Bar* is a convivial place to start, with a good, friendly mix of locals and visitors, as is *The Clinic*, Main Street. Bantry is a small town, and entertainment is a matter of getting involved in whatever's going on. You're as likely to enjoy a handful of **rock music** sessions in the bars as anything else: try *The Bantry Bay* (Fri–Sun); *Caill an Ceann*, an engagingly unpretentious spot for traditional, folk and rock (most evenings July & Aug); *The Wolfe Tone Tavern*, which has country, blues and traditional (4 nights a week in summer, winter weekends); *Vickery's*, rather low key, but with folk on a Monday night. For discos try *The Bantry Bay* or, on a Sunday, *The Westlodge Hotel,* a couple of miles along the main road to Skibbereen.

There's a **mussel festival** over the second weekend in May promising music, late bars and plenty of seafood. One local sport worth looking out for is **bowling**, a West Cork game played around Bantry on Sundays. A 28lb iron ball is thrown along country roads, and the winner of the game is the man (it's generally only men who play) who moves the ball over a prescribed distance (usually two and a half miles) with the fewest throws. Undoubtedly a fair amount of betting goes on too. If you come across handfuls of grass that have been dropped along a lane at intervals, it generally means a game has been or is being played along that route – clumps of grass are used as markers.

Glengarriff and the mountains

Heading on from Bantry you're spoilt for choice: whichever way you travel, the scenery is magnificent. Heading **east**, the road to Dunmanway and its fine independent hostel (p.262) takes you through fabulous empty mountains, while the Pass of Keimaneigh further north leads through a steep, rocky ravine up to the Ballingeary hostel (p.262), **Gougane Barra** and a corrie lake, the source of the River Lee. An island on this lake was the site of Saint Finbarr's hermitage before he founded his monastery at Cork city downstream. The remains on the island are, however, eighteenth century. It's an area famous for its beauty, popular for day-trips, and there's a bar that does teas and sandwiches beside the lake. Gougane Barra also has a forest park with nature trails (£1).

Glengarriff

Cradled between the Caha Mountains and Bantry Bay, **GLENGARRIFF** is an oasis of greenery. South-facing and sheltered by rugged mountains, it has a peculiarly gentle climate; oak and holly woodlands hug the shoreline while occasional palms flourish in hotel gardens. This picturesque juxtaposition has been exploited since the nineteenth century, when sensitive Victorians became alerted to the beneficial effects of the uniquely mild atmosphere in this pocket of lushness. Unfortunately, recent exploitation has resulted in a barrage of billboarding; ads for gift shops and boat trips have destroyed virtually all of the village's former character. When a bus tour meets Glengarriff nowadays, it's difficult to say which is the victim.

Despite the commercialism, Glengarriff is a great place to stay if you want to explore some of Cork and Kerry's most wildly beautiful countryside. The surrounding mountains are wonderfully wild; huge areas of barren rock show odd patches of scrawny, rough vegetation, and then the occasional seam of brilliant deciduous woods. There is a real exhilaration up here as you watch the constantly changing patterns of weather over the mountains and the bay, with squalls of rain and pools of sunlight bowling across the landscape. Pick up a leaflet of suggested walks at the **tourist office** (mid–June to mid–Sept) in front of the *Eccles Hotel*. They will also supply local **B&B** information. There are a couple of **independent hostels** on the road towards Bantry: *O'Mahoney's*, three minutes walk from the centre (also camping; ☎027/63033; ①) and, about a mile out, *St Anthony's* (May–Sept; ☎027/63109; ②). Both are pretty basic, and neither is purpose built. (Ask at the tourist office for details of a new hostel due to open summer 1996.) *O'Shea's* **campsite** (mid-March to mid-Oct; ☎027/63140) is a beautiful little site, about a mile out of Glengarriff on the Castletownbere Road (R572). **Bike rental** is available at *Jem Creations*, Ladybird House (☎027/63113).

As for **bars**, *Johnny Barry's* is extremely touristy, but both *The Blue Loo* (blues, folk, country most nights during July & Aug) and *Bernard Harrington's* bar (pop bands) are lively spots.

Garinish Island

Walking down the street in Glengarriff you'll inevitably be hassled sooner or later by a stage-Irish boatman trying to sell you a ticket for **Garinish Island**. The island trip is quite something, although massively overpriced. In 1910, the owner of Garinish conceived a plan to turn his island – then bare rock – into a floating oasis of exotic plantlife. All the topsoil had to be imported and the resultant growth delicately nurtured for years. The end product is undeniably impressive: flowers and shrubs from all over the world flourish here, and through much of the year the place is ablaze with colour, in vibrant contrast to the desolate mountains of the Beara a stone's throw across the water. If you decide to take the ten-minute trip out there past basking seals, be warned that the price you pay the boatmen (£5) does not include admission to the island (daily June–Sept 10am–5pm; £2.50, Heritage Card).

The Beara Peninsula

The **Beara Peninsula**, barren and remote, seems to have an energy all of its own, bounding in great ribs of rock thirty miles out into the ocean. It is a fine place for tough cycling and energetic hiking, though you need to be prepared: the weather is notoriously changeable, and careful planning of routes, particularly the descent, is vital. Alternatively, you could try *The Beara Way*, a signposted, long-distance walk (125 miles) following old roads and tracks, stretching from Glengarriff west along the southern side of the peninsula to Dursey Island, along the north side to Kenmare and back down to Glengarriff (route guides available locally). Everywhere along the peninsula you are accompanied by fine views of the mountains and the sea, and there are occasional sandy beaches on either side; take local advice before swimming, as currents can be treacherous.

In practical terms, there are enough good **hostels** to make lengthy exploration a viable proposition, but it's worth bearing in mind that a sparse population means there's little traffic of any sort – don't rely on being able to hitch back if you're in a hurry. If you're planning to **camp**, be aware that though there is no shortage of open land, a lot of it is very rocky. **Private buses** – the only public transport – connect the Beara communities with Glengarriff, Bantry and Cork several days a week. See "Travel Details" at the end of the chapter. **Bus Éireann** connects Castletownbere with Kenmore.

Adrigole

The first settlement along the coast, about fifteen miles west of Glengarriff, is **ADRIGOLE**, a string of houses stretching over a couple of miles with no real centre. You are most likely to be here if you've walked along the **Beara Way** from Glengarriff. Just to the west of the junction for the Healy Pass is a shop and a pub; three miles to the east is a simple **B&B**, *Beachmount* (May–Oct; ☎027/60075; ③). It's all wild and wonderful walking country. **Hungry Hill** rises to 2251ft, a good climb rewarded by fabulous views, hidden lakes and waterfalls, while the steep road through the **Healy Pass** leads north to Lauragh, County Kerry, where there is an *An Óige* hostel at Glanmore Lake (May–Oct; ☎064/83181; ①).

Castletownbere

Beara communities have always relied heavily on fishing; **CASTLETOWNBERE**, the peninsula's main town, is no exception. Set on Ireland's second largest natural harbour, it's periodically awash with Spanish and Portuguese sailors. To serve them there's a handful of cafés, well-stocked shops, a chip shop and some enjoyable pubs (see below).

The town serves as a useful base from which to walk or cycle or to catch a ferry for **Bere Island**, which shelters the harbour: seven ferries a day during July and August, and by arrangement at other times (☎027/75009; car £15 return, foot £3). The **stone circle** a mile from town is worth seeing; a coastal walk from Castletownbere takes you to the ruins of **Dunboy Castle** (where an Irish and Spanish force was besieged and overcome by the English in 1602) and **Puxley's Castle**, the eerie, dilapidated shell of a Victorian Gothic mansion. This was the home of the Puxley family, who made their money out of copper-mining; their story, and that of the mines, was used by Daphne du Maurier in her novel *Hungry Hill*. The castle itself was burnt down by the IRA in the 1920s, but its setting is idyllic: a placid inlet behind Castletownbere harbour fringed by rich woodlands, with stunning views of the wild mountains – expect to be charged 50p to enter the grounds.

There's a useful **tourist information** hut by the ferry terminal. If you want to stay in Castletownbere, there are several **B&Bs**: one pleasant options at the west end of town is *Mountain View* (☎027/70424; ④), hung with some interesting paintings by Allihies artists. You can **camp** in the grounds of Puxley Castle for around £3 per tent, though there are no toilet facilities; you can go **horse riding** here, too. You can also camp at nearby *Beara Hostel*, two miles west of Castletownbere on the road towards Allihies (open all year; ☎027/70184; ①). It's a clean **hostel** with a rather crisp atmosphere, laundry facilities and bike rental (£7 per day). Alternatively you can **rent bikes** from the *Super Valu* supermarket (£7 per day, £35 per week). There is a **laundry** at West End, Castletownbere. For **food**, *Jack Patrick's* café on Main Street is pleasant; *Lynch's* bar is a very friendly place and serves exquiste seafood sandwiches. Provisions are available at all hours from *MacCarthy's* shop-cum-bar. Should you feel the need, there are regular Saturday **discos** at *The Beara Bay Hotel*.

On to Dursey Island

Moving on from Castletownbere you can head down to the remote, tiny villages at the end of the peninsula, a few houses, a shop and a pub being the typical set-up. This extreme of the peninsula saw some development in the nineteenth century when copper was mined, but little remains beyond the unguarded shafts; beware of these if you're walking. Signposted to the left off the road around five miles west of Castletownbere (then about another half a mile on) is the remote *Garranes Farmhouse Hostel* (☎027/73147; ①), clinging to a beautiful, ravaged coastline. The **hostel** is next to the Buddhist *Dzogchen Beara Retreat Centre*, and hostellers are welcome to join meditation classes. Phoning ahead is advised since the hostel can be full of people on retreat at any time of the year. Note that the nearest shop is Cahermore post office over two miles away, which stocks basic provisions; the nearest pub is six miles away.

Tiny **ALLIHIES**, formerly a major mining centre, nowadays has simply four pubs, a shop, a sandy beach and a handful of places to stay. For **B&B** try *Sea View* (☎027/73004; ③ & ④) in the main street, or *Sea Haven Lodge* (☎027/73225; ④) in a fabulous spot overlooking the beach. There are a couple of **hostels**: the comfy, central *Bonnie Braes* (*IHH*, mid-March to Sept; ☎027/73107; ②) is a delightful place and has a good bookshelf, but needs booking ahead in the summer (bike rental for £6); the *An Óige* hostel (June–Sept; ☎027/73014; ①) is about a mile from the centre and is rather more basic, though adequate nonetheless and beautifully secluded. You can **camp** by the beach – either rough or on a small site.

Perhaps the quietest of the islands to be visited off West Cork is **Dursey Island**, situated at the very tip of the peninsula and fringed by high cliffs. Dursey's attractions include fabulous views, solitude and the thrill of taking a very dodgy-looking cable car across the narrow and treacherous sound. You can walk up its hills for endless views westward over the ocean, with three great lumps of rock in the foreground: the Cow, the Calf and the Bull. For a day-trip, you need to get to the very end of the R572 in the morning. The cable car has no regular schedule, but during July and August you can usually get to the island between 9.30am and 11am, 2.30pm and 5pm, and between 7pm and 8pm daily; there's usually a late trip around 11pm. There is a **B&B** near the cable car station: *Windy Point House*, Garrish (☎027/73017; ③), which also serves tea and snacks. If you want to stop over you'll need to pitch a tent, as Dursey Island has just a few houses – which claim to be the most westerly habitation in Europe, and no pub or shop.

Heading along the northside of the Beara Peninsula towards Kenmare, the fine scenery continues, with peerless views of the Kerry mountains. **EYERIES** is a brightly painted village with some pleasant pubs and the friendly little *Ard Na Mara* **hostel** (☎027/74271; ②), a spacious bungalow in a beautiful spot overlooking the sea, where you can also camp – to find it walk around half a mile along the road east from the pubs and it's signposted off to the left. Phoning ahead is strongly advised. There is a **B&B** in the village at *Coulagh Bay House* (☎027/74013; ④), high on the main road.

travel details

Trains

Cork to: Cobh (19 daily; 25min); Fota (19 daily; 15min); Rosslare Harbour (summer Mon–Sat 2 daily; 6hr 20min); Dublin (6–9 daily, 3hr).

Bus Éireann

Cork to: Cork airport April–Sept from 7am (Sun 8am) hourly, after 8am every 45min till 8.25pm; reduced winter service; Dublin (4 daily; 4hr 45min– 5hr 15min); Limerick (6 daily; 2hr).

Private buses

Bantry–Dublin *Pierce Kavanagh Coaches* (☎01/ 873 0671). Departs Bantry (Courthouse) 3.30pm Sun, calling at Dunmanway, Cork (*Chateau Bar*, Patrick Street) 5.05pm, Cahir, Cashel, Dublin (Eden Quay) 9.30pm. Departs Dublin (Liberty Hall) 5.30pm Fri, calling at Cashel, Cahir, Cork (*Roches Stores*, Patrick Street) 10pm, Dunmanway, Bantry 11.30pm.

Bantry–Glengarriff–Castletownbere *O'Donohue's* (☎027/70007). Mon· Castletownbere 7am & 4.30pm, calling at Glengarriff 7.45am and 5.20pm, arrives Bantry 8.15am & 5.50pm. Return from Bantry 11.25am & 8.20pm, Glengarriff 11.55am & 8.50pm, arrives Castletownbere 1pm & 9.45pm. Schedule may change so phone for confirmation. Tues, Fri & Sat:

Castletownbere 10.30am, calling at Glengarriff 11.20am, arrives Bantry 11.50am. Return from Bantry 3.45pm, Glengarriff 4.15pm, arrives Castletownbere 5pm.

Castletownbere–Cork *O'Donoghue's* (☎027/ 70007). Depart Castletownbere Thurs only 7.30am, Glengarriff 8.15am, Bantry 8.45am, arrive Cork 10.30am. Return from Cork (*Mulligan's*, Parnell Place) 6pm, Bantry 7.45pm, Glengarriff 8.25pm, arrive Castletownbere 9.15pm.

Harrington's Buses (☎027/74003) Depart Castletownbere Mon, Tues, Wed, Fri (& Sat in summer) at 8am to arrive in **Cork** 9.45am; Sun at 5pm to arrive in Cork 7.30pm. Services depart **from Cork** (*Mulligan's*, Parnell Place) at 6pm on the same days, to arrive in Castletownbere at 8.30pm; Sun departure at 8pm.

Other private companies serving the Beara from Cork include *Peter O'Sullivan* (☎027/74168), whose buses run every day except Thurs.

Ferries

Cork–Swansea (3–7 days a week according to season; 10hr). *Brittany Ferries* (to Roscoff 2 per week, 14 hr; St Malo 1 per week, 18hr, summer only).

CHAPTER EIGHT

COUNTY KERRY

f you've come to Ireland for the scenery, mountains, sea and the remoteness, you'll find them all in **County Kerry**: miles and miles of mountain-moorland where the heather and the bracken are broken only by the occasional lake; smooth hills whose fragrant, tussocky grass is covered with sea pinks, speedwells, thrift and red campion, and that fragment into jagged rocks as they reach the sea. The ocean looks enormous, and you can stand in the sunshine and watch a storm coming in for miles before you have to run for cover. The only catch is that a good part of the county is very much on the tourist trail.

The plus side of Kerry's long tradition of welcoming tourists is that it's very easy country to travel in, with plenty of accommodation and food in all price brackets. And, during the summer at least, transport is pretty good – though with some notable exceptions.

Broadly speaking, Kerry divides into four areas: the Dingle Peninsula; the Iveragh Peninsula, encircled by the Ring of Kerry, with Killarney in its hinterland; the Kenmare River, bordered to the north and south by the Iveragh and Beara peninsulas; and northern Kerry, from Tralee to the Shannon. Each section is quite distinct and has its partisans. By far the most visited area – indeed the most visited in the whole of Ireland – is **Killarney and the Ring of Kerry**. Deservedly famous for the beauty of the adjacent lakes and mountains, this region is, predictably, geared up for tourism, and the principal roads and sights are often overburdened with visitors. Luckily, however, the real wilds are never far away, and whether you head for the mountains or the sea you can soon lose yourself and feel remote from modern civilization. The **Dingle Peninsula** is on a smaller scale than Iveragh, but equally magical: peppered with monastic remains, it has a contemplative atmosphere that makes you understand why people talk about the mystic quality of the west. Around **Kenmare** things are different again, with a tamed feeling about the scenery; one half of the Beara Peninsula belongs to more cultivated, genteel County Cork. To the **north**, flat, fertile farming land makes for less exciting scenery, but in contrast to the rest of the county there are many signs of a long-established Anglo-Norman presence.

Killarney and around

Although **KILLARNEY** has been commercialized to saturation point and has little in the way of architectural interest, the real reason for coming here is without doubt the

---

ACCOMMODATION PRICES

Throughout this book, accommodation prices have been graded according to the cost per person per night in high season; with hotels and many hostels this represents half the cost of a double room, whereas with the more basic hostels it represents the cost of a single dormitory bed. The prices signified by our grades are as follows:

① Up to £6	③ £10–14	⑤ £20–26	⑦ £36–45
② £6–10	④ £14–20	⑥ £26–36	⑧ Over £45

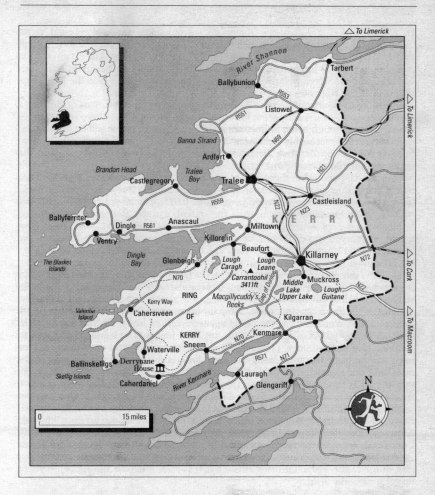

surrounding landscape. Its three spectacular **lakes**, Lough Leane (the Lower Lake), Muckross Lake (the Middle Lake) and the Upper Lake, are only the appetizer. Behind them loom **Macgillycuddy's Reeks**, which have a grandeur out of all proportion to their height: rarely exceeding 3000ft, they're still the highest mountains in Ireland. Much of this is contained within the huge **Killarney National Park**.

Arrival, information and accommodation

Killarney's train and bus **station** is pretty central, off East Avenue Road; it's obvious where to go. Although there's plentiful accommodation of all sorts, it is very crowded in high season and it's worth calling the **tourist office**, on the main street by the town hall (July & Aug Mon–Sat 9am–8pm, Sun 10am–6pm; June & Sept Mon–Sat 9am–6pm; Oct–May Mon–Fri 9.15am–5.30pm, Sat 9.15am–1pm; ☎064/31633) to make advance bookings. Even if you're not planning to bike round the Ring of Kerry, **cycling** is a great way of seeing Killarney's immediate surroundings, and makes good sense because local transport is almost non-existent. *O'Callaghan Brothers*, College Street (☎064/31175), are the local participants in the *Raleigh* scheme; bikes can also be rented from *O'Neill's* in Plunkett Street (☎064/31970). **Banks** and the **post office** can be found on New Street. Killarney's **laundry** (Mon–Sat 9am–8pm) is in the little shopping mall off the High Street.

One thing the tourist office can't do is make specific recommendations of **B&Bs** – a shame since price and quality seem to vary a lot here. Nonetheless, there are dozens to choose from, although being in Ireland's main tourist centre prices will be higher than elsewhere. A few reasonable central options are *Lisaden*, Countess Grove, off Countess Road (☎064/32006; ③), *Arch House*, East Avenue Road (☎064/32184; ③), and the *Orchard* in the High Street (③).

Over the last two years there has been a **hostel**-building epidemic, and there are now a staggering nine to choose from in and around Killarney. In Killarney itself, there's the *Súgán Kitchen Hostel* on Lewis Road (*IHH*, open all year; ☎064/33104, fax ☎33914; ②), a few minutes' walk from the station, and the *Bunrower House Hostel*, formerly *Loch Lein Hostel* (*IHH*, March–Oct; tel/fax ☎064/33914; ②), near Ross Castle, where you can camp in a beautiful garden; bookings and free bus from the *Súgán*; both do bike rental for £5 a day. The *Súgán* also has a wholefood bistro serving great food (three courses for around £6.50 for residents; more expensive for visitors). The *Four Winds Hostel* at 43 New Street (*IHH*, open all year; ☎064/33094; ②) is extrovert and noisy; their minibus sometimes touts for business at the train station. Turn left outside the tourist office, left at the crossroads, and it's a few minutes' walk down on your right. They do bike rental, including mountain bikes, from £5 a day. Worth a try is the newly opened *Neptune Hostel* off New Street (*IHH*, open all year; ☎064/35255, fax ☎32310; ②). This hostel is welcoming, manages to combine size and intimacy, provides masses of information and does discounts for most tours around the area. Along the same lines is the comfortable *Railway Hostel* near the Franciscan church (☎064/35299; ②). The *An Óige* hostel (☎064/31240, fax ☎34300; ②) is three miles out along the Killorglin Road, at Aghadoe; there is a free shuttle service to and from the bus and train station, and bike rental at £5 a day, but booking is essential in July and August. Six miles out of town, the beautifully situated *Peacock Farm Hostel* at Muckross (April–Sept; ☎064/33557; ①) can arrange lifts from Killarney. The *Park Hostel* (*IHH*, open all year; ☎064/32119; ②) is up the hill off Cork Road, opposite the petrol station. A big new hostel off Park Road, *Atlas House* (☎064/36144, fax ☎36533; ②), is tourist board approved and has private rooms. You can **camp** at the *Fossa Caravan Park* (☎064/31497), just past the Aghadoe youth hostel west of the town.

The town

The town is essentially one main street and a couple of side roads, full of souvenir shops, cafés, pubs, restaurants and B&Bs. Pony traps and jaunting cars line up against walls while their weather-beaten owners talk visitors into extortionate trips through the surrounding country. It's all done with bags of charm, true to Killarney's long tradition of profitably hosting the visiting masses ever since its discovery as a resort in the mid-eighteenth century.

The town's Irish name (*Cill Áirne*, Church of the Sloe) doesn't imply a settlement of any great antiquity, and the Cromwellian Survey of 1654 found no town or village of that name. By 1756, however, a burgeoning **tourist trade**, soon fed by the growing Romantic attraction to lakes and mountains, had created Killarney: "A new street with a large commodious inn was designed to be built here, for the curiosities of the neigh-

KILLARNEY'S FLORA AND FAUNA

It was the last Ice Age that formed the Killarney **landscape**. Glaciation has left its mark on the contorted limestone valleys of the Lower and Middle lakes, and the nearby Devil's Punch Bowl and Horses' Glen show other signs: huge rocks smoothed to sucked-sweet shapes, and improbably teetering boulders. The lower slopes of the mountains are covered with what is often virgin **forest**, a joy to see in a country that has cut down almost all its trees. Almost everything seems to thrive in the local combination of high rainfall and humidity, and in the woods you'll find a rich mix of trees dominated by oak, but with bilberry, woodrush and woodsorrel plus mosses, liverworts and lichens, sensitive organisms whose continued survival testifies to the clean air here.

As elsewhere in the west of Ireland, the Killarney area's **vegetation** includes a number of plants generally found in quite different parts of Europe. The famous arbutus, or strawberry tree – so called from its bright-red (and non-edible) fruit – for example, generally grows only in Mediterranean countries and Brittany. Some saxifrages and the greater butterwort, with its fleshy purple flowers and sickly green leaf rosettes, are otherwise found only in northwest Spain and Portugal (see p.317 for more on the west's strange flora).

bouring lake have of late drawn great numbers of curious travellers to visit it," said a contemporary survey. The local landowner, Lord Kenmare, quickly spotted commercial opportunities and granted free leases for new inns and houses, building four major roads to connect his creation with the outside world.

That said, the town doesn't look particularly planned, and the only building of any distinction is the high Gothic Revival **cathedral**, built by Augustus Pugin in 1855. A particularly florid Victorian interpretation of medieval architecture, the cathedral inspires respect or derision, but is worth seeing either way. During the Famine, when building work ceased for five years, the covered area served as a hospital for victims of starvation and disease.

Eating, drinking and entertainment

Places to **eat and drink** are so thick on the ground in Killarney that it seems pointless to list them. Nevertheless, one of the best is *Bricín* (Mon–Sat 10am–10pm; lunch £4, dinner from £10) above a craft shop on High Street, serving home-cooked food all day; or try *Paddy's Restaurant*, High Street (daily 12.30–9.30pm; lunch £4, dinner from £15; ☎064/36600). Slightly pricier, *The Kiwi's Restaurant* (opens 6pm; ☎064/34694), St Anthony's Place, off College Street, does good fish and vegetarian dishes; *An Taelann* in Bridewell Lane is also great for vegetarian meals. Evening **entertainment** is everywhere as you walk along the streets: the widely publicized "traditional" Irish music can seem pretty spurious when you are surrounded by bus loads of other tourists, but it sounds great in places like *Jimmy O'Brien's* (near the Priory), the *Súgán Kitchen* (part of the hostel, also serves good food) or *The Laurels* (for Ireland's other folk tradition, country and western). *Tattler Jack's* is an ordinary pub with lively atmosphere. The *Strawberry Tree* on College Street attracts a young crowd, and also runs a late bar, *Rudy's*.

In May, July and October there's **racing** at Killarney's race course on Ross Road which, like any Irish race meeting, is well worth a detour. The tourist office can give details of **gaelic football** matches; Killarney is a top team and feelings run high. If you're heading for Killarney in the spring, check out the **Pan-Celtic Week**, a gathering of artists and film-makers from Ireland, Scotland, Wales, Cornwall and Brittany; details from the tourist office.

Knockreer Estate and Lough Leane

Oddly enough, given its origins as a tourist town, Killarney turns its back on the grand scenery to the west and south, hunching itself inwards so that you'd hardly guess at the delights that await you. But the gates of the old Kenmare Estate – now known as the **KNOCKREER ESTATE** – are just over the road from the cathedral, and a short walk through the grounds takes you to the banks of Lough Leane. The Browne family, Earls of Kenmare, were unusual among the Irish peerage in that they never renounced their Catholic faith. Given lands confiscated from the O'Donoghues in the seventeenth century, they were subject in the eighteenth century to the penal laws which decreed that every Catholic landowner had to divide his property among his male heirs. The Brownes' estate remained intact quite simply because there was only one son in each generation.

At **LOUGH LEANE**, the scenery is magnificent: tall wooded hills plunge into the water, with the mountain peaks rising behind to the highest, **Carrauntoohil** (3411ft). Ireland's last wild wolf was killed here in 1700, and when the weather's bad (as it often is) there's a satisfying similarity to early Romantic engravings. The main path through the Knockreer Estate leads to the restored fourteenth-century tower of **Ross Castle**, the last place in Munster to succumb to Cromwell's forces in 1652. The story is that General Ludlow, having learned of a tradition that Ross Castle would never be taken from land, brought prefabricated ships from Kenmare and sailed them up from Castlemaine, whereupon the defenders – whom nothing else had budged – immediately surrendered. Near the water you can make out copper workings, last used during the Napoleonic Wars and thought to date back four thousand years.

From Ross Castle you can **tour the lake** in large glassed-over boats like the *bateaux-mouches* that ply the Seine in Paris; but these don't make stops, and an alternative is to get a fisherman to take you out in a little craft with an outboard motor, or rent one yourself. This way, you can land on and explore the island of Inisfallen. (If you're navigating yourself, look for a limestone outcrop in the water. Inisfallen is the island to the left, about a mile out.)

Inisfallen

Of the thirty-odd small islands that dot Lough Leane, **INISFALLEN** is the biggest and the most enchanting, particularly if there's no one else on it (which can easily happen as you watch the *bateaux mouches* grind by). The monastery founded here in the seventh century was an important scholastic centre for a thousand years. Brian Boru, the eleventh-century High King and victor over the Vikings at Clontarf in 1014, was allegedly educated here, and the twelfth-century *Annals of Inisfallen*, now in Oxford's Bodleian Library, are an important source document for early Irish history. Wandering round the island is a delight: heavily wooded, it's also scattered with monastic buildings – nothing from the original seventh-century foundation, but there's a small Romanesque church and an extremely ruined twelfth-century Augustinian priory. Eighteenth-century tourists were clearly awake to Inisfallen's charms: Lord Kenmare used to give parties for his influential friends here, and the gap in the wall of the Romanesque church is where he installed a bay window when the building was converted into a banqueting house. The picturesque ruin you see now is the result of further tinkering, around 1840.

Muckross Estate and the lakes

The road from Killarney to the **MUCKROSS ESTATE** passes through unlovely territory dominated by huge modern hotels, and though jaunting cars from the centre of Killarney will take you out to Muckross (cars are prohibited on the Muckross Estate), it's more fun to rent a bike. Take the earliest turning right into the park that's available, to escape the busy main road. The first place to head for is **Muckross Abbey**, not only for the ruin itself – one of the best preserved in Ireland, part Norman, part Gothic, though sadly despoiled by Cromwell's troops – but also for its calm, contemplative location, and the fact that it, like Ross Castle, hints at something predating Killarney's tourist history. Founded as a Franciscan institution by Macarthy Mor in the mid-fifteenth century, it was suppressed by Henry VIII; the friars returned again, but were finally driven out by Cromwell's army in 1652.

Back at the main road, signposts direct you to **Muckross House**, a solid, nineteenth-century neo-Elizabethan mansion designed by the Scottish architect William Burn. The **museum** (July–Aug daily 9am–7pm; mid-March to June, Sept & Oct daily 9am–6pm; Nov to mid-March Tues–Sun 11am–5pm; £3), while no great shakes, has a section on Kerry folk life where craftspeople (blacksmiths, weavers, potters) demonstrate their trades – but only at peak times. The excellent **tea shop** provides a good refuge from the rain, but the **gardens** – well known for their rhododendrons and azaleas – are the place to be when the weather is fine.

The estate gives access to well-trodden paths along the shores of the **Middle Lake**, and it's here that you can see one of Killarney's celebrated beauty spots, the **Meeting of the Waters**. Actually a parting, but highly picturesque nonetheless, it has a profusion of indigenous and flowering subtropical plants – eucalyptus, magnolia, bamboo and an arbutus, or strawberry tree, on the left of the Old Weir Bridge. Close by is the massive shoulder of Torc Mountain, shrugging off the spectacular 60ft **Torc Waterfall**. There's a not terribly informative **visitor centre** by the car park for the waterfall; but the climb up the side of the mountain is worth doing, if only for the view across to Macgillycuddy's Reeks. On a good day, the Slievemish Mountains on the far side of Dingle Bay are visible.

About two miles south, the **Upper Lake** is beautiful, too, but still firmly on the tourist trail, with the main road running along one side up to **Ladies' View**, where many queue up to admire the scenery – which is, in fact, truly amazing, including the Gap of Dunloe and the wild and desolate Black Valley beyond the lake.

The Gap of Dunloe

Although the **Gap of Dunloe** – a narrow defile formed by glacial overflow that cuts the mountains in two – is one of Killarney's prime tourist attractions, it's possible to find a modicum of solitude if you're willing to use your legs. **Jaunting cars** continually run here from Killarney's centre, a fact which, as the jarveys tout loudly for business, you're not likely to miss. One version of the trip, combining jaunting cars with a bus ride, sets off from the tourist office at 10.30am, transferring you to a pony and trap for the Gap itself, before returning to town at 5.15pm. Apart from being highly overpriced, this entails being stuck in the traffic jam of bored ponies pulling traps up the Gap. The other option is to **walk**, ignoring the offers of rides that will assail you for the first half-mile or so. If you peg out before the four miles are up, it's possible to haggle for a lift – the whole trip generally costs about £13 for the car, plus £8 for the pony.

Kate Kearney's Cottage, at the foot of the road leading up to the Gap – a confusion of shops and sweating horses – is the last place for food and water before Lord Brandon's Cottage, seven miles away over the other side of the Black Valley. The best time to walk is late afternoon, when the jaunting cars have gone home and the light is at its most magical. The road – closed to motor traffic – winds its way up the desolate valley between high rock cliffs and waterfalls (Macgillycuddy's Reeks to your right, and the Purple Mountain, so called because in late summer it's covered in purple heather), past a chain of icy loughs and tarns, up to the top, where you find yourself in what feels like one of the remotest places in the world: the **Black Valley**.

Named after its entire population perished during the potato famine, and now inhabited by a mere handful of families, the Black Valley makes you begin to feel that you've

THE KERRY WAY

The **Kerry Way** is part of a long-distance footpath that goes through the Macgillycuddy Reeks then right around the Iveragh Peninsula through Glenbeigh, Cahersiveen, Waterville, Caherdaniel and Kenmare – a sort of walkers' Ring of Kerry. More than most of Ireland's long-distance footpaths, it's resonant of the culture, as well as the nature, of the area and consists largely of green roads, many of them old drovers' roads or "butter roads" (along which butter was transported) and routes between Kerry's ancient Christian settlements. It's also one of the best ways of starting to explore the spectacular uplands of **Macgillycuddy's Reeks**.

The Kerry Way starts inauspiciously in **Killarney**, threads down through the Muckross Estate and alongside the Upper Lake – road walking, most of it – before heading up to meet the Black Valley (see p.285). From the Black Valley, it heads on towards **Cloghernoosh** via a stony path that becomes a green road. After the footbridge over the stream running out of Curraghmore Lake, there's a stretch of bridleway, and from here on you're among the peaks, with exhilarating views of Carrauntoohil to the north.

Next, the footpath follows the Lack Road, zigzagging up to a saddle point at the top, then skirting the side of **Lough Acoose** before reaching the **Glencar Valley** (and the first tourist accommodation since the Black Valley). No longer traversing really high ground, the rest of the way into Glenbeigh is less exciting, although the stretch on **Seefin Mountain** above Caragh Lake is still spectacular. From here the Way runs around the peninsula and eventually leads back to Killarney.

All the usual **precautions** need to be taken seriously in a region where gales blowing in off the Atlantic can make the weather change rapidly. Bring waterproofs, walking boots, food and a good map: the one-inch *Map of Killarney District*, covering most of the walk, is useful, while the half-inch *Dingle Bay Ordnance Survey Map* details most of the first leg, up to the Black Valley.

You should really fix up **accommodation** beforehand. There's an *An Óige* hostel in the **Black Valley** (see below); and an independent hostel, *Mountain Lodge* (Easter–Sept; ☎066/60173; ③), a little further on in the **Bridia Valley**, which does meals and sleeps just eight. It's roughly eight hours' walk from Killarney; hitching isn't recommended, since the nearest road seeing any traffic is eight miles from the start of the valley. Check it's open before you set off as it's currently changing ownership and may be closed. Next stop is the *Climbers' Inn*, hidden among woodlands at **GLENCAR** (☎066/60104; ①); meals are available in the bar, decorated with a church pulpit, and there's a shop, bunkhouse accommodation and excellent advice on local walks and climbs. For accommodation in **GLENBEIGH** see opposite. Nine miles from Killarney, the *Mountain Rest Lodge* (☎064/44272; ②), Carnahone, **BEAUFORT**, is close to the main approach to Carrauntoohil. If you do plan to scale Ireland's highest mountain, you should really get some local advice first. Try John Walsh at the *Climber's Inn*, Glencar, or phone Eileen Daly of Killarney Mountaineering Club on ☎064/32638.

left mass tourism behind. The fact that it was the very last valley in Ireland to get electricity is some measure of its isolation, and there are no pubs or shops here. There is, however, a **hostel** run by *An Óige* (open all year; ☎064/34712; ②), which has ponies and boats for rental and sells supplies at strictly limited times. Moving on, you can either carry on down to the Upper Lake (Lord Brandon's Cottage, food, boat rental and the quick way back to Killarney) or pick up the Kerry Way.

The Ring of Kerry

The 110-mile **Ring of Kerry**, which encircles the Iveragh Peninsula, can be driven around in a day, and most tourists view its spectacular scenery without ever leaving their bus or car. Consequently, anyone straying from the road or waiting until the buses knock off in the afternoon will be left to experience the long, slow twilights of the Atlantic seaboard in perfect seclusion. Part of the excitement of travelling round the Kerry coast comes from the clarity with which its physical outline stands out against the vast grey expanse of the Atlantic. Every gully, bay, channel and island is as distinct as it is on the map, giving a powerful sense of place amidst the isolation.

If you really are limited to a **day's exploration** of the wild coastal scenery, it could be worth heading for Dingle, the next peninsula north, instead: its intimacy of scale means you can see a lot more without having to rely upon buses or cars. **Cycling** the Ring itself takes three days (not counting any diversions), and a bike will let you get on to the largely deserted mountain roads; just be sure your machine has lots of gears, and you have plenty of energy – the combination of gradients and strong winds can be gruelling. You can pick up a useful **map** showing quiet cycling roads at the tourist office in Killarney for 50p. Public transport doesn't serve the entire circuit – the **buses** from Killarney only go as far as Cahersiveen (twice daily in July and August, once daily otherwise) – but during summer flotillas of tourist buses ply the Ring. Most of them leave from opposite the tourist office, where you can get details, and for an extra charge will drop you off somewhere along the way and pick you up the next day. Hitching is unreliable; while you're likely to get a lift from anyone who passes, traffic simply may not exist away from the main roads.

Killorglin to Glenbeigh

By travelling the Ring of Kerry **anticlockwise**, you get a gradual introduction to the wild grandeur of the coastline scenery, with the Dingle Peninsula and the dim shapes of the Blasket Islands visible in the distance.

The first stop on the way out from Killarney is the pleasantly unexceptional hillside town of **KILLORGLIN**, whose main claim to fame is the **Puck Fair**, held over three days in mid-August, a bacchanalian event with a wild goat captured and enthroned, plenty of dancing and drinking, plus a cattle, sheep and horse fair. These rituals honour the wild goats which, stampeding through the town, warned residents of the approach of Cromwell's army. The fair's pagan origins date back to the Celtic festival of Lughnasa, three days of feasting and ritual sacrifices to celebrate the beginning of harvest. If you want to **stay**, try the *Laune Valley Farm Hostel* (*IHH*, open all year; ☎066/61488; ②), which has camping facilities and serves meals. The *Bianconi Inn* does very good **bar food**, and *Nick's Restaurant* (☎066/61219; dinner £20–22) offers a more expensive cuisine. If you're feeling energetic, the *Cappanalea Outdoor Education Centre* (groups collected from Killorglin or Killarney by arrangement; ☎066/69244) organizes a wide range of adventure sports (£17 per day, children £10) – turn left off the main street at the *Bianconi*, then follow the weather-beaten wooden signs.

Next comes **GLENBEIGH**, where almost everything is given over to tourism; despite plenty of accommodation, the town illustrates the disadvantages of sticking rigidly to the Ring – however, there are wonderful views all along the coastline and across to Dingle. For **accommodation**, try the *Glenbeigh Hotel* (☎066/68333; ⑤), the *Village House* B&B (☎066/68128, ③), or the *Hillside House Hostel* (☎066/68228; ①), which has private rooms and showers (50p). By taking the road up past **Caragh Lake**, you'll find some of Kerry's best mountain scenery, full of deep silences and the magical slanting light of the west. If you're on a relaxed budget and are looking for comparative luxury, you could stay at the *Glendalough House*, a mid-nineteenth-century country house on the shores of Caragh Lake (☎066/69156; ⑥). Alternatively, you could carry on up to the three small lakes of **Coomnacronia**, **Coomaglaslaw** and **Coomasaharn** (good trout fishing, but you'll need a licence).

SOUTH KERRY AND THE FIANNA

Many legends of the **Fianna**, a band of warriors led by **Finn Mac Cool** who served the High King in the third century, are set in South Kerry. One of them tells of how, near Killarney, Niamh, a golden-haired beauty on a white horse, persuaded Finn's son Oisin to come away to her kingdom. Where the magical wave Tonn Toime roars between Inch and Rossbeigh, they galloped out across the sea to *Tír na nÓg*, the Land of Eternal Youth. After a blissful three hundred years, Oisin borrowed Niamh's magical horse to visit his homeland, with a warning not to dismount. Unable to find any of the Fianna in Kerry, he rode north to Dublin and found a band of puny men trying to shift a boulder. Leaning down to help, he broke a girth and landed on the ground a very old man. Before he died, Saint Patrick persuaded him to convert to Christianity.

The lack of trees that contributes to the feeling of austerity in this area was not an original feature of the landscape; Sir William Petty, Cromwell's surveyor general, had an iron mine at Blackstones and felled the forests to fuel a smelter.

Cahersiveen

At **Kells Bay** the road veers inland for **CAHERSIVEEN**, giving you an opportunity to take a detour. On the way you'll pass *Caitín Beatear*'s pub, beside which is the clean and bright newly built *Kells Ring of Kerry Hostel* (☎066/77614; ①). Any of the turnings right will lead eventually to the sea, past bright fuchsia hedges, with little or no traffic. "One wonders, in this place, why anyone is left in Dublin, or London, or Paris, when it would be better one would think, to live in a tent, or a hut, with this magnificent sea and sky, and to breathe this wonderful air, which is like wine in one's teeth," wrote J. M. Synge of the Kerry landscape; and here, for the first time, you begin to understand how the Ring inspires such hyperbole.

Cahersiveen (*Cathair Saidhbhín*; pronounced *Caher-sigh-veen*, stress on the last syllable) was said by Daniel O'Connell, its most famous son, to be the only town established in Ireland after the Act of Union. It is a long, narrow street of a town and the main shopping centre for the western part of the peninsula, giving itself over cheerfully to the tourist trade in summer. A laid-back, unremarkable place, it has more relaxed attitudes to shopping hours than anywhere else on the peninsula, and there are plenty of friendly bars – try *Teach Chulann*, or the *Skellig Rock Bar*. Worth having a look at is the community-funded **Barracks Heritage Centre** (June–Sept Mon–Sat 10am–6pm, Sun 1–6pm; ☎066/72955; £2.50), which contains a concise history of the town and a gallery of paintings and sculptures by local artists. The **tourist office** is also in the Heritage Centre. Not far from here is the magnificent Daniel O'Connell Memorial Church (June–Sept daily 10am–7pm). For **B&B** try Mrs O'Donoghue at *Ocean View Farmhouse* (☎066/72261; ③), half a mile out of town; Mrs Mahony, *Castleview*, Valentia Road (☎066/72252; ②); or Mrs Landers, *San Antoine*, Valentia Road (☎066/72521; ③). Alternatively there are two independent **hostels**, *Sive Hostel*, 15 East End (*IHH*, open all year; ☎066/72717; ①), with camping facilities; and the friendly *Mortimer's*, West Main Street (☎066/72338; ②).

Beyond Cahersiveen, the main road takes the bulk of the traffic inland again towards Waterville, giving you an opportunity to explore the quiet lanes that lead out to Valentia Island and the peninsula's end. The *An Óige* **hostel** at Ballinskelligs (see p.291) makes a good base for exploring the area, as do the **holiday cottages** which abound here. These tend to get booked up ahead, so if you want to be sure of a place you'll need to book early in the year – they're administered by Bord Fáilte (see *Basics* for details) – but you can check availability on the spot with the Killarney tourist office. Staying here, the slow life works its spell; and you can buy fish direct from the boats at **REENARD POINT**, where, weather permitting, the regular **ferries** for Valentia Island depart (£1; £2 with a bike; ask at Cahersiveen post office for details), and boats for the Skelligs (the latter must be booked, and trips cost £20; see p.290). It is also possible to sail to Dingle (see "Dingle town", p.297). The minor road linking Ballinskelligs and Portmagee has better views, and less traffic, than the main Ring Road.

Valentia Island

VALENTIA, an island now linked to the mainland by bridge, is Europe's most westerly harbour, and standing at Bray Head on the island's tip, there's nothing but ocean between you and Newfoundland, 1900 miles away. Valentia's significance is out of all proportion to its size: the first ever transatlantic telegraph cable was laid from here in 1857 – though permanent contact wasn't established until 1866 – and for years it had better communications with New York than with Dublin.

In contrast to the endless vistas west, the island itself is small, and consequently every scrap of land has been cultivated, forming a rolling patchwork of fields stitched with dry slate walls. Valentia's position in the Gulf Stream gives it a mild, balmy climate, and the abundance of fuchsias grown by the inhabitants in local hedgerows enhances its domesticated atmosphere. It's a homely, tame place to stay, though from July onwards the peace is disturbed by tourists.

Arrival and accommodation

Access by **ferry** is from Reenard Point (see above) to Knightstown, or via the Maurice O'Neill Bridge, at the south end of the island, thirteen miles from the main coast road and a difficult hitch. Once on the island there's no public transport at all. Accommodation is at a premium during the summer season, when most **B&Bs** in Knightstown and Portmagee raise their prices; a couple to try are *Mrs O'Sullivan's,* Glenveen Heights, Knightstown Road (☎066/76241; ③), and Mrs Lynch's *Harbour Grove Farmhouse*, Portmagee (☎066/77116; ③). The *An Óige* **hostel** has space for forty at the Coastguard Station in Knightstown for members only, and services are spartan (June–Sept; ☎066/76154; ①). The independent hostel on the harbour front, the *Royal and Pier Hostel* (☎066/76144; ①), is rather big and unfriendly, but never short of space and also offers camping. Midway between the bridge and Knightstown at Chapeltown, there's the independent *Ring Lyne Hostel* (☎066/76103; ①), which also does B&B (③) and camping.

The island

KNIGHTSTOWN is the focal village on the island and, facing Cahersiveen across the Portmagee Channel, affords fine panoramic views of the Kerry mountains. A pretty harbour front with sprucely painted fishers cottages is dominated by the Victorian *Royal and Pier Hotel*; now damply dilapidated and something of a white elephant, it's currently being run as an independent hostel (see above). Tolerating rather than encouraging tourists, Knightstown is deeply old-fashioned, and if there are more than three in your group, you could feel something of an intruder. About a thousand houses cluster around a slate church hidden within a dark rookery. The main street has a few well-stocked shops, a post office offering a good selection of Irish literature and free maps of the island, and a couple of **bars**. Uninspiring by day, these come to life after 10pm several nights a week, when locals playing accordions and pipes accompany vigorous Irish dancing, the faces of the participants (average age sixty-plus) showing serious concentration in this wild pastime.

From Knightstown, take the Kilmore Road down towards the lighthouse, where there's a fine view of Valentia's empty harbour, the Beginish Islands and tiny **Church**

Island. This mere rock supports the ruins of an eighth-century cell, once inhabited by a solitary monk, a soulmate of the brotherhood on the nearby Skellig Islands, whose only company was the seabirds. On a clear day you can also make out the sheer cliffs of the Blasket Islands beyond the Dingle Peninsula to the north.

Continuing west, the foreshore is an imposing clutter of megalithic slabs hurled together by the waves, with deep, limpid pools left by the winter storms. A couple of miles further on, a wonderful swimming cove combines intimacy with the grandiose, sheltered by lush, deciduous woods, with the whole of Kerry as its scenic backdrop. This appears to be part of the grounds of **Glanleam House**, former seat of the local magnate, the Knight of Kerry, attached to which are incongruously exotic gardens, but it's actually a public beach.

The fervour with which locals urge you to visit the **Grotto** is misplaced. A gaping slate cavern, it boasts a crude, municipal bath-blue statue of the Virgin (erected 1954) perched 200ft up, amidst monotonously dripping icy water. Nevertheless, this is the highest point on the island and a good walk for a clear day. But more exciting by far is the cliff scenery to the northwest, some of the most spectacular of the Kerry coast.

The Skellig Islands

From Valentia you get a tantalizing view across a broad strip of sea to the **Skellig Islands** (*Na Sceilig*), apparently no more than two massive rocks. Little Skellig is a bird sanctuary, home to 40,000 gannets, and landing isn't permitted, but you can visit Great Skellig, or Skellig Michael as it's also called, and climb up to the ancient monastic site at the summit.

To get there, enquire at local shops in Knightstown or Portmagee about **boat trips**, or call the Lavelles (☎066/76124), *Casey Boats* (☎066/77125) or Brendan or David Walsh (☎066/79147); the trips are dear at around £20 but, if the weather's good, make a fascinating and dramatic voyage. The boats run between Easter and September, and sometimes can be delayed by bad weather: September 1991 saw a party of civil servants stranded on Skellig Michael for three days. Once at sea, boats are followed by wheeling seagulls and, if you're lucky, puffins, too. Oddly staid little birds that look like miniature flying businessmen, they come from the nature reserve of Puffin Island, further north. You'll also pass the huge, jagged arch of rock that forms **Little Skellig**, where gannets with six-foot wingspans career overhead or make headlong dives into the sea for fish.

Skellig Michael looms sheer from the ocean, a gargantuan slaty mass with no visible route to the summit. From the tiny landing stage, however, you can see steps cut into the cliff face, formerly a treacherous monks' path. Nowadays there's also a road leading to Christ's Saddle, the only patch of green on this inhospitable island. From here, a path leads on to the arched stone remains of **St Fionan's Abbey** (560 AD). Amongst the ruins are six complete beehive cells – drystone huts that have survived centuries of foul weather. The island is dedicated to Saint Michael, guardian against the powers of darkness and patron of high places, who helped Saint Patrick drive the last of the venomous serpents over the 700ft cliffs to perish in the sea. Contrasted with Valentia, it's a wild, cruel place, an awesome sanctuary of devotion, even if the monks didn't remain here all year round to feel the violence of the elements. The Viking invasion of the island in the ninth century lived long in folk memory, inspiring a Skellig monk to write:

Bitter and wild is the wind tonight
Tossing the tresses of the sea to white
On such a night as this I feel at ease
Fierce Northmen only course the quiet seas.

An amenity you may wish to avoid is the dire **Skellig Heritage Centre** (£3, or £15 including cruise round, but not landing on, the islands), a "major, weather-independent tourist attraction" at Portmagee. On a wet day the interpretative centre – with information about Celtic monastic life, lighthouses and lighthouse-keeping, seabirds and aquatic life – could be a pleasant refuge (and a "comprehensively stocked retail area" offers an opportunity for shopping therapy), but it's all too easy to see this as another example of theme-park Ireland.

Waterville and around

WATERVILLE may be touristy, but it does it with a lot of grace. Popular as a Victorian and Edwardian resort and angling centre, it still has an air of consequence that sits oddly with the wild Atlantic views. Its few bars and hotels aside, the town is chiefly notable as the best base on the Ring for exploring the coast and the mountainous country inland. If you want to stay, cheaper **B&Bs** include Mrs Murphy's *Ashling House*, Main Street (☎066/74247; ③), and the very friendly Mrs McAuliffe's *Lake Rise*, Lake Road (☎066/74278; ③). The **hostel** at *Waterville Leisure Hostel* (May to late Sept; tel/fax ☎066/74644; ②) can supply information about surfing, mountaineering and riding in the vicinity. *Pat's Place* (☎066/74383; ①) is a much friendlier establishment, and also organizes walking holidays. Probably the nicest, though, is the small, cosy *Peter's Place Hostel* (no phone; ①), whose jovial owner may rustle you up a meal, and there are camping facilities.

From Waterville, it's a long haul by bike or on foot up to the **Coomakista Pass**, but the effort is well worth it for the breathtaking views over the mouth of the Kenmare River, all greys and blues, the three rocks called the Bull, the Cow and the Calf, and beyond them the Beara Peninsula – most spectacular when the weather's good; when it rains you can see the squalls being driven in across the ocean. However, you can't hope to avoid lots of other tourists here.

The stretch of coast between Valentia and Waterville is wild and almost deserted, apart from a scattering of farms and fishing villages. Sweet-smelling, tussocky grass dotted with wild flowers is raked by Atlantic winds, ending in abrupt cliffs or sandy beaches – a beguiling landscape where you can wander for days. The *An Óige* **hostel** (May–Sept; ☎066/79229; ①) in **BALLINSKELLIGS** (*Baile an Sceilg*) makes a good base and sells supplies. Monks from the Skellig Islands retreated to Ballinskelligs Abbey in the thirteenth century; today the town is largely Irish-speaking and is the focus of the Kerry *Gaeltacht*, in the summer being busy with schoolchildren and students learning Irish.

WATERVILLE IN LEGEND: NOAH'S CHILDREN IN IRELAND

Waterville and Ballinskelligs Bay form the setting for one of the more wayward Irish legends. When the biblical flood was imminent, so the story goes, Noah's son **Bith** and his daughter **Cessair** found that there was no room for them in the ark. So they and their retinue set sail for Ireland which, Cessair was advised, was uninhabited, free of monsters, reptiles and sin, and would therefore escape the flood. However, although 49 women survived to land along with Cessair in 2958 BC, only two men besides Bith made it. The three men divided the women between them, but when Bith and Ladra, the pilot, died, Fintan, the last man, was overwhelmed and, to his eternal shame, ran away – upon which Cessair, who loved him, died of sorrow.

Derrynane to Sneem

Tucked away on a little promontory of its own between the Ring of Kerry and the sea is **DERRYNANE** (pronounced *Derrynaan*), home of the family of **Daniel O'Connell**, the Catholic lawyer and politician who negotiated limited Catholic emancipation in 1829. You can visit his house, and Derrynane itself is a pleasant place, with wide, flat sand beaches, two miles of dunes, good swimming and rocks glistening black with delicious mussels. Although fun in the daytime, like everywhere along this western seaboard it's most atmospheric at sunset, when the long twilight lingers; the Gaels believed that sunset and sunrise were points of transition (like stiles and gates) where it was possible to slip from the real world into the faerie one, and here you can see their point.

The **Derrynane House** (May–Sept Mon–Sat 9am–6pm, Sun 11am–7pm; Oct & April Tues–Sun 1–5pm; £2, Heritage Card), remodelled by Daniel O'Connell himself, is absolutely simple – a square slate tower and roughly elegant rooms with the slanting sea-light a constant presence. The O'Connells were an old Gaelic family who'd made their money trading and smuggling – the west of Ireland had a long tradition of trade with Europe in wine, spices and silks. Daniel O'Connell's uncle bequeathed him a fortune, giving him the financial independence necessary to devote himself to politics. Discrimination against Catholics was widespread and closely experienced by Daniel: another uncle was shot dead because he would not give up his fine horse, as the law demanded of Catholics.

The immediate area has plenty of ancient forts and standing stones. On the way to Castlecove, there's a sign on the left for **Staigue Fort**; after two-and-a-half miles up a rough lane, you'll come to a very well-preserved ring fort, possibly created as early as 1000 BC, and probably a residence of the Kings of Munster. Local **B&B** options include the *Scarriff Inn* (☎066/75132; ④) and *Mrs Sullivan* (☎066/75124; ④). The nearest **hostel** (with another fort 300 yards away) lies at **CAHERDANIEL** (*Cathair Dónall*), just outside Derrynane Park on a bend in the road overlooking the sea; the gorgeous *Carrigbeg* **hostel** (*IHH*, open all year; ☎066/75229; ①) serves a breakfast of muesli and brown bread, making a welcome relief from the ubiquitous bacon and eggs. In addition there is a hostel in Caherdaniel itself, the *Caherdaniel Village Hostel* (Feb–Nov; ☎066/75277; ①), but it is run in a very military fashion, with a curfew, and is pretty unfriendly. The best **restaurant** in the area, *Loaves and Fishes* (Easter–Oct Tues–Sun; ☎066/75273; dinner £18–22), is clearly signposted off the main road through the village. As the road winds onwards towards Sneem, there's good swimming, particularly at White Strand, past hedgerows blossoming with both fuchsia and hydrangea.

SNEEM (*An tSnaidhm*) is spectacularly set against the mountains, dominated by the 2245ft Knockmoyle; but the village has lost something by selling out to tourism. Sneem's houses are washed in different colours – reputedly so that drunken residents can find their way home – and their picture-book prettiness juxtaposed against tourist shops and cafés has a touch of the surreal. Good local fishing is advertised by the salmon-shaped weathercock on the Protestant church. You'll probably want to push on to more interesting Kenmare, but if you do decide to **stay** here, you could try Mrs Hussey at *Avonlea House* (☎064/45221; ③), Mrs O'Sullivan at *Woodvale House* (☎064/45181; ③) or Mrs Drummond's *Rockville House* (☎064/45135; ③).

The approach to Kenmare along the estuary is unexciting, seemingly more in character with the Beara Peninsula opposite than with wild Iveragh, and you'll have a more scenic journey back to Killarney if you take the mountain road direct from Sneem. The two routes join up again at the spectacular **Moll's Gap**, north of Kenmare.

Kenmare and around

With its unlikely shops – delicatessens, designer boutiques and arty second-hand clothes shops – **KENMARE** feels like a foreign enclave, and you're more likely to hear English or German tones here than Irish. Neatly organized on an X-plan (laid out by the first Marquess of Lansdowne in 1775), the town is pleasantly cosmopolitan: besides the resident foreigners, it's the natural crossing-over point for everyone travelling up from Cork.

Kenmare was founded by **Sir William Petty**, Cromwell's surveyor general, to serve his mining works beside the River Finnihy. Petty was extremely active in (and benefited greatly from) the dealings in confiscated properties that went on after the Cromwellian wars. Many soldiers were paid by the impecunious government in land, but not all of them wanted to settle in Ireland and so sold their land to dealers – such as Petty. His acquisition of land all over Ireland, including roughly a quarter of Kerry, was surely helped by his commission to survey the country on behalf of the government, when he investigated two-thirds of the Irish counties in the amazingly short period of fifteen months. Petty's other achievements were no less remarkable: a professor of medicine at Oxford at 27, he was also a professor of music and founder member of the Royal Society in London; an early statistician, economist and demographer; and politically astute enough to get yet more land and a knighthood out of Charles II, even though he had earlier served Cromwell faithfully. In Kerry, he laid the foundations of the mining and smelting industries, encouraged fishing, and founded the enormous Lansdowne estate which once surrounded the town; many of its buildings still remain today.

Evidence of a much more ancient settlement is the fifteen-stone **stone circle** just outside the centre of town on the banks of the river; go up by the right of the market house that faces the park, and past some estate houses. Then walk up the lane at the cul-de-sac sign, and a few yards after it meets another lane coming in from the left you'll find the circle, behind a high ditch.

Practicalities

The **tourist office** is on The Square (April–Oct; ☎064/41233). Kenmare's famous *Park Hotel*, at the top of Main Street (☎064/41200), provides doubles at a massive £94–136; it's worth investigating though, if only for a drink. There are plenty of **B&Bs**, both in and just outside town; check vacancies at the tourist office. Some that are worth a try are: Mrs Hickey's *Sunville* on the Cork Road (☎064/41169; ③), Mrs Falvey's *Bay View Farm* on the Ring of Kerry Road at Templenoe (☎064/41383; ③), or Mrs Hayes' *Ceann Mara*, at Killowen on the outskirts of town (☎064/41220; ③), who also serves organically grown food. Kenmare has one independent **hostel**, the *Fáilte* in Shelbourne Street (*IHH*, open all year; ☎064/41083; ②). As for **meals**, *The Pantry*, 30 Henry Street, has a stock of wholefoods and health foods, plus organic vegetables and a wonderful range of unpasteurized cheeses. An excellent, though not cheap, Italian-Irish restaurant, with good seafood and vegetarian options, *An Leath Phingin*, 35 Main Street (daily 6–10pm; closed Nov; ☎064/41559), is an old house with stone walls, wooden tables and a turf fire (burning even in June). Also in Main Street, *d'Arcy's* (April–Oct daily 5–10.30pm; Nov–March Fri–Sun 7–10.30pm; ☎064/41589; dinner around £15) specializes in fish and vegetable dishes. Slightly less pricy is *Packie's* (Mon–Sat 5.30–10pm; ☎064/41508), a lively bistro on Henry Street with dinner from £12. **Bike rental** is available from the *Fáilte* hostel, *Finnegans* on Henry Street or *Whites* on the Killarney Road.

The Beara Peninsula

Cross the river from Kenmare and you're on the **Beara Peninsula**, which Kerry shares with Cork. Beara has its followers, but after the wildness of the rest of Kerry, it can at first seem over-lush and polite, with more of the flavour of Cork. Even along the River Kenmare, though, the scenery is attractive enough and curiously, once you actually cross into County Cork, the Beara becomes far wilder (see p.276).

Turn right after the bridge, and the road runs through heavily wooded country alongside the Kenmare estuary, with a signpost to the left for **Inchiquin Lake** a few miles later. Following this, you soon quit the luxuriant vegetation as the bumpy road ascends rapidly to the lake, giving exhilarating views of the countryside left behind. A waterfall tumbles down from a second lake, and on the far side of Inchiquin Lake is

Uragh Wood, one of the last surviving remnants of the ancient sessile oakwoods that once covered most of Ireland. The entire valley is packed with **plants**: large-flowered butterwort covers the meadows in spring, and you can find Irish spurge, saxifrage, arbutus and other flora specific to the southwest. At the lake itself, the surrounding hills seem to act as some kind of intensifier focused on a tiny stone circle by the side of the water – bringing to mind the theory that these prehistoric monuments indicate earth forces. There's salmon, sea trout and brown trout fishing in both lakes, but, as always, check the licence position before you start.

Lauragh

Following the main road for **LAURAGH**, you're still in the enormous estate once owned by Petty. The gardens at **Derreen House**, for a long time one of the Irish residences of Petty's descendant, the Marquess of Lansdowne, are open to the public and stocked with plants that clearly luxuriate in the mild sea climate, including such exotica as tree ferns and bamboo, plus rhododendrons and camellias. Yet despite its magnificence, it doesn't compare with the wild and windswept grassy uplands. Head westwards from Lauragh and you're soon over the border into Cork; south, the road climbs spectacularly above Glanmore Lake to the Healy Pass – again, the county border – giving amazing views in both directions. There's a fairly basic *An Óige* **hostel** here (April–Sept; ☎064/83181; ①).

Dingle Peninsula

In common with the rest of the far west, particularly the Irish-speaking areas, the **Dingle Peninsula** has almost fallen victim to its own romance. It's as if it has been telling stories about itself for so long that it has come to believe them: the remoteness and beauty, the hard life and poverty and – above all in the **Irish-speaking** or *Gaeltacht* areas – the language have all lent fuel to easy romanticizing, creating the modern chocolate-box, almost mythologized picture of the west. In Dingle's case, the myth is strengthened by its location on the extreme western seaboard of Europe, its numerous early Christian remains, the wealth of Irish literature created on the now uninhabited Blasket Islands – and the fact that *Ryan's Daughter* and parts of *Far and Away*, starring Tom Cruise, were filmed here. Concern about the peninsula's reputation for fey otherworldliness is such that the local paper has found it necessary to assure Irish visitors that there are actually real nightspots here.

But Dingle really scores with its **landscape** and antiquities. The former is spectacular, dominated by the **Beenoskee Mountain** (2627ft), while west of Dingle town lies an Irish-speaking region, strongly resonant of its history. Dingle also has probably the greatest concentration of Celtic monastic, and older, **ruins** outside the Aran Islands. Ring forts, beehive huts, oratories and stone crosses are more prevalent here than almost anywhere else in Ireland (a useful map of the local antiquities can be had from Dingle tourist office for 50p); and the vigour of the Christian culture that set out from here to evangelize and educate the rest of Europe is almost palpable.*

---

*This culture is vividly brought to life in Penguin's *A Celtic Miscellany*, a collection of epigrams, nature poems, satires and love poems, whose translations remain true to a virile Irish idiom rather than the traditionally romantic Celtic twilight mode. "Pleasant to me is the glittering of the sun today upon these margins, because it flickers so," some ninth-century scribe noted in the margin of an illuminated manuscript. "Whether morning, whether evening, whether by land or by sea, though I know I shall die, alas, I know not when," runs a more sombre epigram, also of the ninth century; and a tiny example of the nature poetry of the same time goes, "Winter has come with scarcity, lakes have flooded their sides, frost crumbles the leaves, the merry wave begins to mutter." Dingle's *An Cafe Liteartha* has copies.

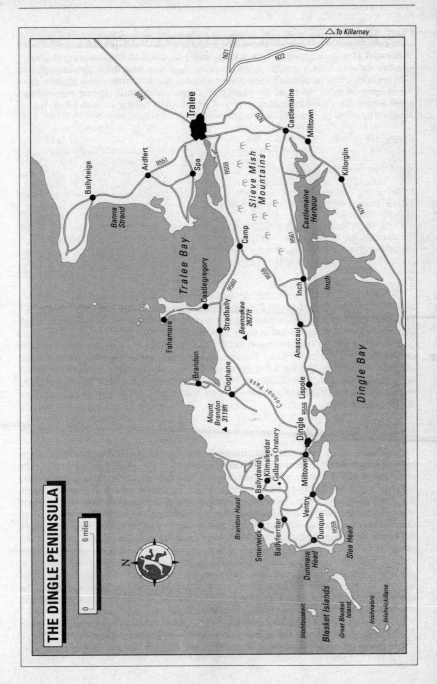

THE DINGLE PENINSULA

0 — 6 miles

N

△ To Killarney

N21
N22
N69
N9

Tralee

Castlemaine
Milltown

Ballyheige

Ardfert
R551

Spa
R559

N70

Slieve Mish Mountains

Killorglin

Banna Strand

Camp

Castlemaine Harbour

Tralee Bay

Castlegregory

R561

R560

R558

Fahamore

Stradbally

Beenoskee 2627ft

Inch

Inch

Dingle Bay

Brandon

Cloghane

Anascaul

Connor Pass

Lispole

Mount Brandon 3119ft

Dingle
R559

Brandon Head

Ballydavid
Kilmalkedar
Gallarus Oratory

Milltown

Ventry

Smerwick
Ballyferriter

Dunmore Head

Dunquin
R559

Slea Head

Inishtooskert

Blasket Islands

Great Blasket Island

Inishnabro

Inishvickillane

HORSE-DRAWN CARAVAN HOLIDAYS ON THE DINGLE PENINSULA

The ultimate Irish tourism cliché it may be, but a **horse-drawn caravan holiday** is a great way to unwind and to absorb the breathtaking beauty of the Dingle Peninsula. What's more, you're likely to have a very sociable time – the caravan's theatricality provoking plenty of conversation. You can also expect to develop a strong relationship with your horse – one way or another.

Slattery's Travel, 1 Russell Street, Tralee (☎066/29122; freephone ☎0800/387691 for brochure) rent out caravans for three-day weekends (£120, low season only) and week-long breaks (£200 low season, £500 high season); additional costs include £7 per night stopover fee, £4 per day insurance and £10 per week horsefeed. *Slattery's* will tell you no previous experience of handling horses is necessary, but it certainly helps – as do height and brute strength. Before setting off, however, friendly stable-workers take you through the basics of catching, harnessing, driving, watering and feeding your horse. *Slattery's* also supply a map of the peninsula with a range of routes and stopover sites; most sites are fields alongside pubs, so you can have a drink beneath the stars and still keep an eye on the children.

Caravans have one double bed, a small single, and a couple of extra fold-down bunks – with bedding. In theory there's room for five people, though in fact any more than three adults may well find it a bit cramped, and if there are more of you, it's a good idea to have a small tent. The caravans also come equipped with a small stove and cooking utensils.

On a fine day it can be exhilarating, with views out as far as the monastic settlement on Great Skellig, off the Iveragh Peninsula; but it's more exciting still in the **rain**, when the cloud shifts down over the land and you find yourself in a white mist through which the dim shapes of oratories and beehive huts loom mysteriously.

A great nightlife is not the reason to visit this region. True, there are plenty of pubs in **Dingle town** – a small place reputed to have 52 – and lots of traditional music, perhaps even a *ceili*. The town has been fortunate in only realizing its tourist potential in the past few years; while Killarney is stuck with its tacky souvenir shops and pubs, Dingle has done an altogether more elegant job, mixing traditional places and new seafood restaurants.

Inch and Anascaul

Though most of the peninsula's delights are to the west of Dingle town, there are a few notable stopping points on your way to Dingle town from the east. There's a break in the shoreline at **INCH**, where a long, narrow sand-bar pushes out into Dingle Bay – good bucket-and-spade territory when the weather's fine. In the eighteenth century the beach was used by wreckers who, on stormy nights, would tie a lantern to a horse's head and leave the horse grazing; mariners mistaking the bobbing light for another ship steered their vessels aground on the strand. Inch also provides somewhere to **stay**: high above the bay at Inch Heights, *Lios Dana*, the *Natural Living and Healing Centre* (☎066/58189; phone ahead), has a B&B (④) and serves macrobiotic, vegan and vegetarian food. Anne Hyland, who also owns *The Country Kitchen* in Anascaul (see below), runs classes in relaxation, yoga, art and shiatsu here. There are a couple of **B&Bs**, as well as a choice of **hostels**: the *Inch Hostel* (☎066/55181; ①), where camping is also possible, and, by far the nicest place to stay, the *Bog View Hostel* (IHH, May–Oct; ☎066/58125, fax ☎23870; ②), situated mid-way between Camp and Anascaul (or three miles north of Inch).

Soon the road turns inland for **ANASCAUL** (*Abhainn an Scáil*), where *The Country Kitchen*'s good vegetarian and vegan food is worth seeking out. The village itself is a single street of brightly painted houses, pleasant enough but with a curiously safe, inland feel considering the proximity of the wild Atlantic coast. Two pubs here have famous associations: the magician *Dan Foley's* shocking-pink bar, familiar from a host of postcards, and the *South Pole Inn*, so named by local man Tom Crean, a veteran of Scott's Antarctic expedition. There are two **B&Bs**: Mrs O'Connor's *Four Winds* (☎066/57168; ③) and Mrs Flahive's *Lake View*, Ballintarmon (☎066/57122; ③). In addition there's a **hostel**, *Fuchsia Lodge* (*IHH*, open all year; ☎066/57150, fax ☎57402; ②), where it is also possible to camp. Head northwards, along a string of increasingly rough tracks, and you'll reach **Anascaul Lake**, overshadowed by the scree slopes of Stradbally Mountain: a secret-seeming place, despite the "Scenic Car Park" sign, with plenty of wilder country beyond.

Dingle town

DINGLE (*An Daingean*) doesn't offer a huge amount to see, but the town is a pleasant place to stay, devoted to fishing and tourism, and certainly makes the best base for exploring the peninsula. Though crammed with pubs, little restaurants and B&Bs, Dingle somehow never feels too crowded, and even if you don't like the way the place has geared itself up for tourism, you'll be glad when the weather's bad – which it often is – that there are plenty of places to hole up.

Arrival and accommodation

Getting to Dingle is easy. From June to September, a daily **bus** leaves from outside Killarney's train station at 10.30am and 1.30pm; there's a more frequent year-round service from Tralee. For getting around the town and surrounding countryside, buses for Dunquin and Slea Head leave Dingle at 12.30pm and 3.10pm every day except Sunday in summer, with additional services at 8.50am and 5.45pm on Mondays and Thursdays all year. **Bikes** can be rented from *Moriarty's* in Main Street (☎066/51316), which has mountain bikes: useful on the punishing Conor Pass. *Paddy's* and *Fios Feasa*, both in Dykegate Street, rent out bikes from around £5 a day. Recently introduced are **sailings** to Cahersiveen, the Skelligs and Valentia Island by *Fionan Ferries Ltd* (☎066/76124).

The **tourist office** in Main Street (July–Aug Mon–Sat 9.30am–7pm; June & Sept 9.30am–6pm; ☎066/51188) has an accommodation service. For standard old-fashioned **hotel** comfort, try *Benners Hotel* on Main Street (☎066/51638; ⑥). The handiest places to look for a central **B&B** are Dykegate Street, where there are several – try *Mrs Connor's* (☎066/51598; ④) – or Strand Street, where *Tig Uí Mhurcú* (☎066/51754; ④) is comfortable and friendly. *Doyle's* excellent restaurant (see overleaf) also takes guests (mid-March to mid-Nov; ☎066/51174, fax 51816; ⑥). Dingle now boasts at least seven **hostels**, of which we recommend: *Lovett's Hostel* (☎066/51903; ①), opposite *Moran's* garage on the other side of town; more central but smaller is the *Marine Hostel* (☎066/51065; ①), with a camping site, by the Quay. By far the nicest are the *Rainbow Hostel* set about a mile west out of town (☎066/51044; ①), with camping, bike rental and tours available, and the *Ballintaggart House Hostel* on Racecourse Road (*IHH*, open all year; ☎066/51454, fax ☎51385; ②), one mile east of Dingle, with camping and its own resident ghost. If these are all full, you could try the *Seacrest Hostel* in **LISPOLE**, a few miles east, overlooking cliffs and beach (*IHH*, March–Oct; tel/fax ☎066/51390; ①), with a shop and camping space.

The town

Essentially just a few streets by the side of Dingle Bay, the town has a hugely impressive natural **harbour** where the boats come in and **Fungi the dolphin** likes to play; half-tame Fungi is one of Dingle's main tourist attractions. It may sound silly, but there are people who talk of their meetings with this solitary, 663lb maritime mammal in the terms of a religious conversion, and others travel hundreds of miles just to see him (enquire at the tourist office about boats).

The solidity of the town's colour-washed houses suggests this was a place of some consequence, and Dingle was indeed Kerry's leading port in the fourteenth and fifteenth centuries. It later became a centre for smuggling, and at one stage during the eighteenth century (when the revenue from smuggling was at its height) even minted its own coinage. Contemporary reports describe the stone houses with balconies and oval windows, imparting a Spanish feel to the town. In the nineteenth century, Dingle was the focus of a uniquely successful attempt to woo the Kerry Catholics from their faith, when in 1831 the Protestant curate T. Goodman began preaching in Irish, establishing schools on the peninsula and building houses as inducements for converts; these still stand at the edge of town.

Eating, drinking and entertainment

All of Dingle's **restaurants**, from the cheapest to decidedly expense-account places, serve excellent fresh seafood, landed just a few hundred yards away. *Doyle's Seafood* in John Street (evenings only; ☎066/51174) is the best-known restaurant locally and pioneered haute cuisine in Dingle. The often miraculous dishes are expensive, but worth it; you can get three courses for £14 between 6pm and 7pm. Delicious vegetarian evening meals are available at *Sméara Dubha*, just outside town on the road to Ventry (mid-May to mid-Sept daily 6–10pm; ☎066/51465). *Greaney's*, on the corner of Dykegate and Strand streets, does good cheap lunches and dinners, and *Cul an Tí* is a good vegetarian option behind *Dick Mac's* pub. *Máire de Barra*'s pub on Strand Street, and *Adams* on Main Street, do hearty pub food. For daytime, and for getting away from the weather if it rains, there's no better place than Dingle's truly excellent bookshop-café, *An Cafe Liteartha*, off Main Street. You can browse through the shelves (politics and local-interest sections are especially good), tuck into home baking and soups, read the papers and listen to conversation in Irish and English.

Life in the evenings is centred on Dingle's many pubs, which between them offer **traditional music sessions** on just about any night you choose. *Dick Mac's*, opposite the church, *An Droichead Beag* at the bottom of Main Street, and *O'Flaherty's* in Bridge Street are good places to start, with music most nights or advice on where to find it somewhere else. *Mrs Nelligan's Pub* on Lower Main Street also has traditional music in a slightly more staid setting, or try *Murphys* or the *Star Inn*, in Strand Street, for Friday or Saturday night revels with **dancing**. **Special events** here include the mid-July cultural festival, *Dúchas An Daingin*, the compulsive Dingle Races in early August, and the Dingle Regatta later in the month; see the tourist office for details.

Ventry and ancient monuments

The first town of interest west of Dingle is **VENTRY** (*Ceann Trá*), once the main port of the peninsula and another fine natural harbour: a wide curve of sandy beach supporting a few houses, shops and a pub. Beyond it looms the enormous, gnarled shoulder of **Mount Eagle**, dropping almost sheer to the sea with only a precarious ledge for the road. It's in these inhospitable surroundings on the stretch out to Slea Head that the main concentration of **ancient monuments** can be found. What follows here can only be an introduction to the major sites; the minor ones alone could take weeks to explore. A good local **map**, such as the one available at the tourist office, is essential, while several excellent guides to the peninsula exist for real enthusiasts (available at bookshops in Dingle town).

First off there's the spectacular **Dún Beag** (dating from the eighth or ninth century AD), a scramble down from the road towards the ocean about four miles out from Ventry (entry £1). A promontory fort, its defences include four earthen rings, with an underground escape route, or souterrain, by the main entrance. It's a magical location, overlooking the open sea and the Iveragh Peninsula, the drama of its setting only increased by the fact that some of the building has fallen off into the sea.

Between Dún Beag and **Slea Head**, the hillside above the road is studded with stone beehive huts, cave dwellings, souterrains, forts, churches, standing stones and crosses – over five hundred in all. The beehive huts can be deceptive – they were still being built and used for storing farm tools and produce until the late nineteenth century, so not all of them are as old as they look. But once you're standing among genuinely ancient buildings like the signposted **Fahan group** (entry £1) and looking south over a landscape that's remained essentially unchanged for centuries, the Iveragh Peninsula and the two Skellig Islands (see p.290) in the distance (if not hidden by clouds), you get a strong sense of past lives, with their unimaginable hopes and aspirations. If you're travelling with children, they may enjoy **The Enchanted Forest** (daily summer 10am–6pm; spring & autumn noon–5pm; winter 1–4pm; £2, children £1) just past the shrine at Slea Head, "a merry, magical, miniature fairyland where bears and dolls celebrate the seasons"; there's a café downstairs serving bear-shaped scones.

The Blasket Islands

At Slea Head, the view opens up to include the desolate, splintered masses of the **Blasket Islands** (*Na Blascaodaí*), uninhabited since 1953. The weather in Blasket Sound can be treacherous – two of the Armada's ships were shattered to matchwood when they came bowling round the Head in September 1588 – but inhospitable as they seem, the islands were once the home of thriving communities. The astonishing body of **Irish literature** that emerged from these tiny islands (Maurice O'Sullivan's *Twenty Years A-Growing*, Peig Sayers's *Peig* and Tomas O'Crohan's *Island Cross-Talk*) gives a vivid picture of the life of the islanders which, although remote, was anything but unsophisticated. Ironically, these literary works describe life among people who could neither read nor write; but their oral tradition emerges as far from primitive. Locals are less than enamoured of the new interpretative centre, **Ionad an Bhlascaoíd Mhóir**, at Dunquin (daily Easter–June & Sept 10am–6pm; July & Aug 10am–7pm; £2.50), but you may find it a welcome refuge on misty days.

In the summer, boats bound for **Great Blasket** (*An Blascaod Mór*) leave the pier just south of Dunquin every hour between 10am and 6pm for around £8 return (May–Sept in good weather; ☎066/56188). Whether or not you choose to stay over, Great Blasket's delights are simple ones: sitting on the beaches and staring out to sea, tramping the many footpaths that criss-cross the island, or trying to spot a seal. If you're staying, the island offers an amazing view of the sun sinking into the ocean.

At present free camping is available, but plans are afoot to designate the island a national park, so check with the Dingle tourist office; as there's no shop on the island, you'll need to bring supplies. At the **café** (noon–5pm), you can order good, cheap dinners for around £5.

There's an *An Óige* hostel on the mainland a little further on at **DUNQUIN** (*Dún Chaoin*), with plenty of beds (open all year; ☎066/56145, fax ☎56355; ②); or **B&B** in the local *Kruger's* pub (☎066/56121; ③), where you may also come across some live **music**. The best place for daytime eating is the *Dunquin Pottery Café* (10am–8pm), with a spectacular view out across the Blaskets and, behind, a mass of mountain laced with a network of stone dykes. *Tig Áine* (☎066/56214), further on at An Ghráig, is good for seafood and salads.

Ballyferriter and Ballydavid

A couple of miles further round the headland, largely Irish-speaking **BALLYFERRITER** (*Baile an Fheirtearaigh*) can be bleak out of season, but in summer there are several cafés, plus a museum in the old schoolhouse, **Músaem Chorca Dhuibhne** (summer daily 10am–5.30pm; winter Mon–Fri 10am–noon & 2–4pm; £1.50). *Tig an Tobair* (☎066/ 56404) is the best **restaurant** but it closes at about 6pm. The village is still reeling from the scandal of topless dancers in *Tigh Pheig*, now under new management and serving very good bar food daily until 9pm in summer. The little northward lanes will lead you to impressive 500ft hilltop walling at Sybil Head and the Three Sisters rock (with the Norman ruins of Castle Sybil, built within an older promontory fort); or to Smerwick Harbour and **Dún an Óir**. In September 1580 at Dún an Óir (the Golden Fort), a band of Italian, Spanish, English and Irish supporters of the rebellion in Munster, backed by papal funds in support of Catholic Ireland against Protestant England, were defeated by the English. The rebels were massacred – men, women and children – as a warning to others; the poet Edmund Spenser participated in the indiscriminate slaughter.

In Ballyferriter, the *Granville Hotel* (☎066/56116; ⑤) offers comfortable rooms and has special rates for longer stays; there are also several B&Bs and the *An Cat Dubh* (The Black Cat) **hostel** just up the road from Smerwick Harbour (☎066/56286; ①), which has a grocery shop attached. Just outside Ballyferriter towards Ballydavid is a comfortable independent **hostel**, *Tigh an Phoist* (*IHH*, March–Oct; ☎066/55109; ②), on the strand at Murreagh (*An Mhuiríoch*).

At the other end of Smerwick Harbour lies **BALLYDAVID** (*Baile na nGall*), backed by the mass of Mount Brandon and within easy reach of the cliffs at Ballydavid Head. **Brandon Creek**, just east of Ballydavid Head, is one of a number of contenders for Saint Brendan's sixth-century departure point, when he sailed off to discover the Islands of Paradise in the Western Ocean and, arguably, America. If you wish to **stay** here there are a few B&Bs and a campsite, as well as the *Ballydavid Hostel* (☎066/ 55143 or ☎55300; ②). Over two miles south of the village, B&B at Mary úi Choibhani's *Ard na Carraige* (☎066/55295; ③) comes recommended, or there's the O'Gormain's *Caife na Mara*, Glaise Bheag (☎066/55162; ③).

Riasc, the Gallarus Oratory and Kilmalkedar

A short way out of Ballyferriter – keep left on the main road, turn right over the bridge by a petrol pump, then right again – is the monastic site of **Riasc**. Recent excavation has revealed walls and foundations a few feet high, and the ruins evoke the early Christian monastery, dating from the tenth century.

The single most impressive early Christian monument on the Dingle Peninsula, however, is the **Gallarus Oratory**, a little further east. The most perfectly preserved of around twenty such oratories in Ireland, it looks almost too good to be true, though apparently it hasn't undergone any great restoration programmes. Though the oratory can't be dated with any great certainty, it's thought to have been built between the ninth and twelfth centuries (Christian architectural activity dates from the late sixth or early seventh century, but it wasn't until the ninth century that churches began to be built of stone rather than wood), and to represent a transition between the round beehive huts elsewhere on the peninsula and the later rectangular churches. The problem with this construction (and the reason why so many similar buildings have fallen down) is that the long sides tend to cave in – if you look carefully at the Gallarus Oratory, you can see it's beginning to happen here, too.

The next architectural stage can be seen a mile to the north in the rectangular church at **KILMALKEDAR**. Its nave dates from the mid-twelfth century, and the corbelled stone roof was a direct improvement on the structure at Gallarus. The site marks the beginning of the Saint's Road, dedicated to **Saint Brendan**, patron saint of Kerry, which leads to the top of Mount Brandon – the route taken by pilgrims to Saint Brendan's shrine. If you want to follow this tough but historically resonant route up the mountainside, it's marked on the half-inch *Ordnance Survey* map. Alternatively, there's a marked route from the west beginning between Cloghane and Brandon.

The Conor Pass

The interior of the Dingle Peninsula is dominated by two **mountains**, Mount Brandon and Stradbally Mountain, separated by the steep **Conor Pass**. This mountainous terrain is excellent walking country; not only are there countless relics of the Celtic church and earlier to explore, but the area is dotted by a series of lakes that give the tussocky landscape some focus. There's a hostel at the foot of the pass on the northern side, the *Connor Pass Hostel* (*IHH*, mid-March to Oct; ☎066/39179; ②) in **STRADBALLY**. You'll find good sandy **beaches** for swimming at Stradbally and **CASTLEGREGORY**, where *Fitzgerald's Euro Hostel* (☎066/39133; ①) is a friendly place, well situated over a pub and shop, and with private rooms; or try *Lynch's Hostel* (☎066/39128; ①), which also has private rooms available. For home-cooked food, there's *O'Riordan's Café* on the Conor Pass Road from Tralee (R559/560), just before the turning for Castlegregory.

Tralee and around

TRALEE (*Trá Lí*) is, in many ways, an ideal base to explore the Dingle and Ring of Kerry. Of late it has had quite a facelift, and chief among its new attractions is the excellent **Kerry County Museum** in the Ashe Memorial Hall (daily mid-March to July 10am–6pm; August 10am–7pm; Sept & Oct 10am–6pm; Nov & Dec 2–5pm; £3.50), which uses interactive media and lifesize models in tracing Irish history back to 5000 BC. Other attractions include the **Tralee–Blennerville Steam Railway** (daily May–Oct; £2.50), which is part of the famous Tralee–Dingle line (1891–1953), and the largest working windmill in Ireland and Britain, the **Blennerville Windmill** (daily April–Oct 10am–6pm), which has its own exhibition, craft workshops and the usual tourist trinkets.

Tralee is a point of orientation rather than somewhere to stay, and the helpful **tourist office** (July–Aug Mon–Sat 9am–7pm, Sun 9am–6pm; May, June & Sept Mon–Sat 9am–6pm; Oct–April Tues–Sat 9am–5pm; ☎066/21288) is also in the Ashe Memorial Hall. Tralee now has five **hostels** (as well as innumerable B&Bs). The friendly and cosy *Lisnagree Hostel* (☎066/27133; ①) is out towards the general hospital; alternatively, *Finnegan's Hostel* on Denny Street near the tourist office (*IHH*, open all year; tel/fax ☎066/27610; ②) makes an excellent base, and has bikes for rental. Other hostels are *Sean Ógs* off Ashe Street (☎066/27199; ②), the ramshackle *Drive In* hostel (☎066/21272; ①), which has camping space, and if you want to stay out of town, try the *Drumtacker* hostel off the Listowel Road (☎066/25631; ①), also with camping space, about a mile and a half out.

You can rent **bikes** in Tralee (though if you're headed for Dingle, it's a tough ride over the Conor Pass) from *J. Caball Himself* at Staughtons Row (☎066/21654); *Tralee Gas Supplies* in Strand Street also do mountain bikes (☎066/22018). Both are part of the *Raleigh* rent-a-bike scheme.

Finding a cheap place to **eat** in Tralee isn't a problem – the town is full of them. *Roots*, on Boherboy, serves terrific organic vegetarian meals, which you can also take away (Mon & Tues 11am–3pm, Wed–Fri also 7–9pm; lunch £3.90, dinner £6.50). *Brat's Place*, Milk Market Lane (Mon–Sat 12.30–3pm), also does very good vegetarian food (lunch from £4). There are plenty of **pubs**, too; try *Kirby's Brogue Inn* in Rock Street for jazz and traditional music, *Bally's Corner* on Ashe Street for lunch and traditional music most nights, *Jack's Pub* on the Square with music on Wednesdays, or *Val O'Shea's* on Bridge Street. If you want to master **set dancing**, the *Oyster Tavern* holds classes each Wednesday night.

The **Folk Theatre of Ireland** has its home at the *Siamsa Tíre Theatre* beside the tourist office, though their excellent performances don't draw the same crowds as the **Rose of Tralee International Festival**. Held in the last week of August, with much accompanying merriment, this is a beauty contest in which women, including foreigners who can demonstrate some credible Irish connection, compete for the dubious honour of being Rose of Tralee; details are available from the Festival Office in Lower Castle Street (☎066/21322).

Ardfert and Banna Strand

More worthy of your time than anything in Tralee itself is the ruined thirteenth-century cathedral at **ARDFERT**, five miles to the northwest. In a landscape littered with ruined ring forts, castles and churches, Ardfert was the site of a **monastery** founded by Saint Brendan in the seventh century, and later became the centre of the Anglo-Norman church in Kerry. As well as some interesting monastic remains, there's a **Franciscan friary** and two smaller fifteenth-century **churches**.

It's also worth taking the road out to **BANNA STRAND** for the spectacular view over Tralee Bay, and its association with Sir Roger Casement, to whom there's a monument. In April 1916, on the eve of the Easter Uprising, Casement was captured by local police as he attempted to land at Banna Strand from a German submarine. He was tried and executed for high treason in 1916, and his body was returned from England to Ireland in 1965 to be reinterred with full military honours (for more on Casement see p.489). If you're driving, you can carry on round the cliffs of **Kerry Head** for more great vistas – south over Tralee Bay, north across the mouth of the Shannon.

Castleisland and Crag Cave

If getting to Limerick in a hurry is your main preoccupation, the faster route (the N21) runs east inland via Newcastle West. On this road **CASTLEISLAND** offers shops, and places to stop for a drink or a bite to eat. Nearby **Crag Cave** (daily July & Aug 10am–7pm; March–June, Sept & Oct 10am–6pm; £3) is an impressive limestone cave system extending a couple of miles underground. If you're passing, the thirty-minute guided tour is enjoyable, with plenty of weirdly sculpted stalactites and stalagmites to keep you amused.

North Kerry

This coastal road aside, **North Kerry** is unexciting – undulating farmland rolling up to the Shannon. The main road from Tralee heads up through **LISTOWEL**, a workaday Irish town that does, however, have a degree of literary distinction. In June it hosts a week-long **festival** of writers' workshops and meetings: Brian MacMahon, a local schoolteacher, is a strong proponent of the vigorous Irish short story tradition (try *The Sound of Hooves*, a volume of Kerry stories available locally). The time when Listowel – and surrounding places as far away as Tarbert and Ballybunion – really come to life, however, is for the annual **Listowel races**, in the third week of September, when farming people from far and wide, their harvest in, take time off to eat, drink and lose money on the horses. Further information can be had from the **tourist office** (May–Sept Mon–Sat 10am–6pm, Sun 11am–3pm; ☎068/22590). There's plenty of **accommodation** here, ranging from the comfort of the *Listowel Arms* (☎068/21500; ⑥) to simpler B&Bs such as *The North County House*, 67 Church Street (☎068/21238; ③), or Mrs Walsh's *Fairhill*, Cahirdown on the Tarbert Road (☎068/21561; ③).

From Listowel the main road continues to **TARBERT** on the Shannon estuary, and from there trails the river inland (through County Limerick) towards Limerick and Shannon Airport. Immediately north of the town, the **car ferry** across the estuary provides a useful short cut into County Clare; there's no other river crossing west of Limerick (April–Sept Mon–Sat 7am–9.30pm, Sun 9am–9.30pm; Oct–March Mon–Sat 7am–7.30pm, Sun 10am–7.30pm; sailings every 60min on the half-hour, return from Killimer on the hour; £6 single car, £9 return, £2 bikes; ☎065/53124).

Turning westwards at Listowel, **BALLYBUNION** lies about ten miles away on the coast at the mouth of the Shannon. It does have a kind of charm – it's the sort of sleepy resort that most people remember with a mixture of affection and horror from childhood holidays, and there are good sandy beaches – but unless you're beguiled by nostalgia you're unlikely to want to stay long. If you do, in addition to the complement of cheerful tat, pubs and amusement arcades, there are two golf courses, the caves under the cliffs and the seaweed baths to occupy you. One of the cliff caves, the **Seven Sisters cave**, is named after the seven daughters of a local chieftain, who tried to elope with seven Norsemen he was holding prisoner. When the plan was discovered, their father had them thrown through the roof of the cave.

Perhaps the town's most intriguing feature is its **seaweed baths**. In Ballybunion, great store is set by the restorative powers of seaweed: every year local people would take to the sea at the end of the summer, to ease joints aching from the exertions of the harvest, and there are two bathing houses – dating back to the 1920s – perched above Ladies' Strand. *Collins'* and *Dalys'* seaweed baths both consist of a series of private bathrooms, supplied with hot salt water from a constantly stoked boiler and seaweed gathered from the Black Rocks beyond the headland each morning. After your soothing, slithery soak you can take a tray of restorative tea and apple tart onto the beach.

B&Bs in this holiday resort tend to be expensive (and full) in summer. A couple worth trying are *Invergordon*, Cliff Road (☎068/27246; ③), and *Doon House*, Doon Road (☎068/27411; ④), but you'll save a long walk around the *No Vacancy* signs by checking out possibilities first at the **tourist office**, which operates in season out of a mobile caravan: check at the local post office for details of its whereabouts. Cheap accommodation is available in Ballybunion at *O'Flaherty's Hostel*, East End (☎068/27684; ②), or if you seek somewhere quieter visit **BALLHEIGUE**, further down the coast, and stay at the *Breaker's Hostel*, Cliff Road (☎066/33242; ①).

If you've time to spare on your onward journey, you can allow yourself to be beguiled by the flatlands of the **Shannon estuary**, whose quiet plains are bathed in the oblique light of the west and dotted with monasteries and castles. The ruined fifteenth-century **Carrigafoyle Castle** rises miraculously from the water, joined to the land by a causeway; close by, a road separates two sheets of water, the land it's built on long since submerged.

travel details

Trains
Killarney to: Cork (5 daily; 1hr 45min); Dublin (4 daily; 3hr); Tralee (5 daily; 35min).

Bus Éireann
Killarney to: Tralee (10 daily; 35min).

Tralee to: Cork (5 daily; 2hr 30min); Dingle (summer 13 daily, winter 7 daily); Limerick (summer 13 daily, winter 10 daily; 2hr 20min).

Private buses
Funtrek (☎01/873 0852) runs one bus daily, two on Friday and Sunday, from Tralee, outside the *Brandon Hotel*, to Adare, Newcastlewest, Listowel, Killarney and Dublin.

O'Sheas Tours (☎066/27111) from Tralee to Dingle, Ring of Kerry and Killarney.

CHAPTER NINE

COUNTY CLARE

P hysically, **County Clare** is clearly defined, with Galway Bay and the Shannon estuary to the north and south, massive Lough Derg forming its eastern boundary, and the Atlantic to the west. Strangely, although plenty of people visit, the county is sometimes glossed over by travellers as simply land between the magnificent scenery of Kerry and Galway. It's true that it doesn't have the scenic splendour of either of these, and for many, the north of the county is too bleak to be attractive. Nonetheless, Clare has a subtle flavour that, once tasted, can be addictive.

Clare is known as the "banner county" – originally because of the part played by its men in the battle of Ramilles – more recently for its courageous political history, particularly in the fight for Catholic emancipation. It's known as the "singing county", too, for its strong musical traditions that are still very much alive and constitute a major reason for coming here (see p.318). Both titles – the strong and the gentle – suggest something of the character of the place and are echoed in the contrasts of the landscape.

The **Burren** heights in the north are startlingly stark and barren, while **Ennis**, the county's capital, is surrounded by low, rolling farmland. Fabulous cliff scenery stretches for miles round Clare's southern extreme at **Loop Head** and is spectacularly sheer at the **Cliffs of Moher**, further north.

In between are sandy beaches and small seaside towns and villages. In the east, **Lough Derg** offers panoramic views across to the mountains of Tipperary from the slopes of the Slieve Bernagh and Slieve Aughtie mountains, and the opportunity for watersports.

This varied countryside holds plenty of specialist interest. The Burren is a major attraction for geology and botany enthusiasts, and is also rich in ring forts, dolmens and cairns in the north. The legacy of later communities is found throughout the county, in the thickly sprinkled medieval monastic remains and the tower houses of the O'Brien and MacNamara clans.

SHANNON AIRPORT

Arriving at **Shannon International Airport** – where Irish coffee was invented to placate stranded passengers – you're most likely to want to head for **Limerick**, barely fifteen miles away, for bus and train connections to just about anywhere in the country. **Ennis**, a similar distance, is also easily accessible and a pleasant place to stop over if you're exhausted, plan to head north or want to spend some time in County Clare. *Bus Éireann* **buses** (☎061/474311) run to both towns: around 16 daily to Limerick (45min); slightly less frequently to Ennis (both cost £3.50 single). A **taxi** (☎061/471538) to either place will cost about £15.

The airport **tourist information office** (daily May–Oct 6am–7pm; Nov–April 6.30am–5.30pm; ☎061/471664 or ☎471604) is extremely helpful and will book accommodation for you for the usual charge. There's a *Bus Éireann* and *Irish Rail* information point (April–Sept) right next to the tourist office, and an **airport information desk**, open to serve all flights – if there's no one there, pick up the phone and dial 0. The airport **bank** is open every day from 6am until 5.30pm – though it sometimes closes early.

If all you want to do is find a bed for the night, the nearest **B&Bs** are a little over two miles away at Shannon town: try *Mrs Sheridan*, 24 Dún an Óir, Tullyglass (☎061/362282; ③), or *Mrs Lohan*, 35 Tullyglass Crescent (☎061/364268; ④); marginally further away is *Mrs Moloney*, 21 Coill Mhara (☎061/364185; ③).

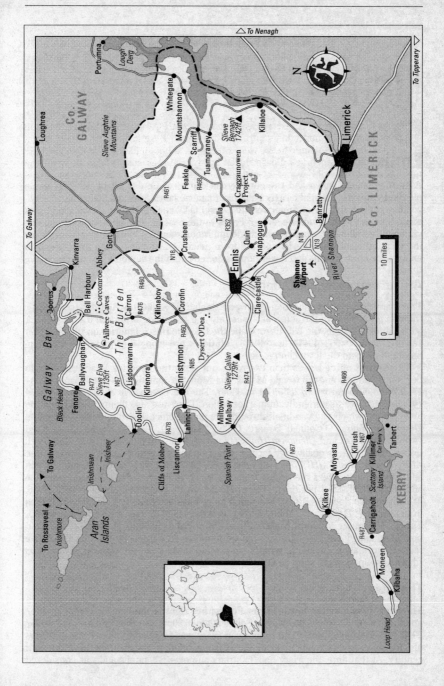

Ennis

A bustling market town and the commercial capital of County Clare, **ENNIS** has a pleasantly inconsequential air. Its handful of central lanes lace together a nineteenth-century cathedral, a stout monument to Daniel O'Connell and a medieval friary. You could probably walk from one side of Ennis to the other in half an hour, and you can certainly see all it has to offer in a single afternoon – but it's worth staying longer for the plentiful traditional music, and the town makes an excellent base from which to explore the church ruins and tower houses dotted about the surrounding countryside.

Arrival and accommodation

There are direct bus connections between Ennis and **Shannon Airport** (see p.304), thirteen miles away in the south of the county and the major airport on the west coast, with flights to Dublin, the UK, Europe and the US. The **bus** (enquiries on ☎065/24177) and the **train** (☎065/40444 or ☎40411) **stations** are alongside one another, a ten-minute walk from the town centre.

The **tourist office** is less than two miles out along the Limerick Road (mid-May to Sept daily 9am–6pm; April to mid-May & Oct Mon–Sat 9am–6pm; Nov to March Mon–Fri 9.30am–5.15pm; ☎065/28366 or ☎28308). The *Old Ground Hotel*, O'Connell Street (☎065/28127; ⑧), is a friendly, upmarket option. There are also plenty of **B&Bs** in the town centre, which you can book through the tourist office. Good possibilities include *Derrynane House*, O'Connell Square (☎065/28464; ④), *Ardlea House*, Clare Road (☎065/20256; ④), and *Glenomra House,* Limerick Road (☎065/20531; ④); all are well priced and excellent quality. By far the nicest budget accommodation in Ennis is the *Abbey Tourist Hostel* (*IHH*, open all year; ☎065/22620, fax ☎21423; ①), beautifully run and situated just across the bridge from the friary; it also has double rooms available and rents bikes (£5–7 per day). *Walnut House* hostel, O'Connell Street (☎065/28956; ①), which also does B&B (②), is a much more basic alternative. You can **rent bikes** from *Michael Tierney*, 17 Abbey Street (☎065/29433; £7 per day, £30 per week). There's a **laundry** in Lower Market Street (Mon–Sat 9am–6pm). A good second-hand bookshop called *The Book Gallery* can be found at 68 Parnell Street. For alternative tourist information, including **what's on** around town, head for *Upstairs, Downstairs* (daily 9am–9pm), a gift shop on O'Connell Square.

The town

The finest monument in town, **Ennis Friary**, lies right in the historic centre (guide/information service daily late May to Sept 9.30am–6.30pm; at other times phone ☎065/29100; £1, Heritage Card). The Franciscan friary was founded by the O'Briens, Kings of Thomond, in 1242, but most of the existing building dates from the fourteenth century. At that time, the friary had 350 friars and over 600 pupils and was considered the finest educational institution in Ireland for the clergy and upper classes. In parts it remains striking: graceful lancet windows fill the east end of the chancel, while adjacent convent buildings include cloister ruins and a stoutly barrel-vaulted chapter house. There is much good sculpture, too: look out for the small square carving on the jamb of the arch between the nave and transept, which shows a half-length figure of Christ with his hands bound; the relief of Saint Francis with cross-staff and stigmata at the east end of the nave; and the carved corbels beneath the south tower showing the Virgin and Child and an archbishop. The real sculptural highlight, however, is the fifteenth-century **MacMahon tomb** (now incorporated in the Creagh Tomb), which has fine alabaster carvings of the Passion.

Despite the beauty of the friary, Ennis today seems more proud of its later history, as capital of the unyielding "banner county" and a bastion of Nationalism. A monument to **Daniel O'Connell** solidly dominates the old, narrow streets that meet in **O'Connell Square**. In 1828, County Clare returned O'Connell to Westminster by such a huge majority that he had to be allowed to take his seat, despite the fact that he was a Catholic, which should have barred him at the time; he went on to force through parliament the Catholic Emancipation Act. It was in Ennis, too, that **Parnell** made his famous speech advocating the boycott in the land agitations of the late nineteenth century. **De Valera** was TD for the county from 1917 to 1959 (and *Taoiseach* for much of that time) and is remembered in a memorial outside the Classical courthouse, and in the **De Valera Library Museum** on Harmony Row (Mon & Thurs 11am–5.30pm; Tues, Wed & Fri 11am–8pm; free), a small, local museum covering a history of national importance. Exhibits include an interesting collection of letters and telegrams: from Daniel O'Connell seeking support in the forthcoming election; from De Valera while in prison expecting to be executed; from the Black and Tans threatening retribution for the kidnapping of two constables, and so on. The museum also houses a collection of weapons used by the Royal Irish Constabulary and the IRA, and hosts changing exhibitions by modern Irish artists.

As for other things to search out, the town's status as a city demands that it has a **cathedral**, and a nineteenth-century building with a sharp spire stands icy and grey at the far end of O'Connell Street, at odds with this friendly town. More interesting is to wander the ancient lanes that run from O'Connell Street to the **old market place**, where a Saturday vegetable and livestock market is held.

Eating, drinking and entertainment

There isn't an abundance of good eating places in Ennis, but *The Prince Dragon,* Lower Market Street, is considered the best Chinese **restaurant**, and for excellent takeaway pizzas try *Numero Uno*, Barrack Street (till midnight). There are also a number of pubs offering decent **bar food**: in O'Connell Street try *Brogan's* or *The Derrynane*; in Abbey Street *Cruise's* or, more upmarket, *The Cloister*. The latter caters fairly well for vegetarians. Away from the bars, *Bewley's Coffee Shop*, in Bank Place, off O'Connell Square, serves cheap light lunches and excellent coffee. If you're on a tight budget, *The Sherwood Inn* (daily till 6pm, Thurs & Fri till 9pm) in *Quinnsworth* in the new shopping centre (follow the lane beside *The Queen's Hotel*) is probably the best place for a hearty breakfast or lunch for around £4.

Clare is famous for **traditional music**, and if you want to be certain not to miss out, pick up a copy of the *Shannon Region Traditional Irish Music Pubs* list at a tourist office. Ennis has two music festivals, the **Fleadh Nua** over the last weekend in May and the **Guinness Traditional Music Festival**, a major event, usually held over the second weekend in November. The town, in fact, is particularly well served any time of the year: perhaps the best place to start is *Cois na hAbhann*, less than half a mile out on the Gort Road (☎065/34158), a centre for local traditional music enthusiasts. Throughout the summer they have *Oíche Ceili* and *Seisiún* evenings – both evenings of song and dance, though the latter is a more structured entertainment (around £3: set-dancing sessions on Wed year round). These sessions also move around the county, so it's worth watching out for them in smaller towns roundabout.

Ennis itself, for such a small town, has a surprising number of **bars** with traditional, cajun and rock sessions. For **traditional music** try *Brogan's*, O'Connell Street (summer Mon & Tues); *Kerin's*, Lifford, a short walk along Newbridge Road (summer Mon & Fri); *P.J. Kelly's* in Carmody Street (Sat & Sun); *Cruise's*, Abbey Street (summer most nights); *Ciaran's*, Francis Street (all year round Thurs–Sun plus Mon in summer); and *Lucas*, Parnell Street, a great little bar with traditional music in the old bar (Fri) and a pop/rock jukebox to the rear. Two of the liveliest young bars are *Brandon's*, O'Connell Street, and *Brannagan's*, Mill Road (off the bottom of Parnell Street), both of which have a good rock, folk and cajun mix. For the big-name Irish bands and traditional music check out *Kearney's Bar* on Newbridge Road, or *Roslevan Arms* out of town along the Tulla Road. Obviously the crowd depends on the band, and it's really a matter of luck, but Ennis is so small you are unlikely to be hunting for long. For **clubs** try *Central Park* (above *Brannagan's*) or *The Sanctuary* (behind *Cruise's*).

Around Ennis

Ennis sits in a low-lying strip of land that runs from a deep inlet of the Shannon river right up to South Galway. To the east of the town are lush fields edged by white-grey walls and clumps of wild flowers: pinks, purples and yellows of willow herb and ragwort, the strong white horns of bindweed, and even the occasional orchid. Further out, the land breaks into little lakes and rivers before becoming gently hilly to meet the Slieve Bernagh Mountains. This gentle farmland makes for easy cycling, and your trip can be punctuated by village pubs and plenty of church ruins and castles.

Quin, Knappogue and Craggaunowen

One of the most pleasant rides east of Ennis is to **Quin Abbey**, the area's best-preserved Franciscan friary, founded in 1433. The main church building is graceful, its slender tower rising clear over the high, open archway between chancel and nave and making a distinct outline against the green of the surrounding pastures. Climb up a floor to the first storey and you can look down on the abbey's complete cloister that has not only the usual arches but also slim buttresses. For all the uplifting beauty of the tower, the abbey seems to have been built on a human scale, to function as a place in which to live and worship rather than to impress and dominate.

On the other hand, the massy walls of **Knappogue Castle** emanate an awesome sense of power. Leave Quin and continue two miles south on the L31 to reach this huge sixteenth-century tower house (Easter to late Oct daily 9.30am–5pm, last admission 4.30pm; £2.50). It was originally built by the Macnamaras, but they lost it to Cromwell, who then used it as his HQ – thereby, no doubt, saving it from the major damage he inflicted elsewhere. At the Restoration, the Macnamaras managed to regain ownership of the castle and hung on to it until 1800. It's been beautifully restored, and inside are boldly carved sixteenth-century oak fireplaces and stout oak furniture. At odds with the overall flavour of Knappogue, the nineteenth-century domestic additions are furnished as if eighteenth-century rooms, beautifully appointed with Irish Chippendale furniture and Waterford crystal. The main body of the castle is used for medieval banquets.

The Craggaunowen Project
The second left turning, two miles south of Knappogue, brings you to the **Craggaunowen Project**, tucked on the edge of a reedy lake under a wooded hillside

(May–Sept daily 10am to last admission 5pm; £3.50). This is based around another fortified tower house, the ground floor of which houses a collection of sixteenth-century European wood carvings. The project itself aims to re-create a sense of Ireland's ancient history, with reconstructions of earlier forms of homes and farm-steads; a ring fort and a *crannóg*, or artificial islands, for example. Young workers experiment with old craft techniques, using replicas of wooden lathes, kilns and other traditional devices, and double up as guides if asked.

The most adventurous and certainly the most famous of the working replicas here is Tim Severin's **Brendan**, a leather-hulled boat in which he and four crew successfully sailed across the Atlantic in 1976, to prove that the legend of Saint Brendan could be true. Saint Brendan's story – he was supposedly the first European to reach America – is recorded in a ninth-century manuscript, and the design of the *Brendan* is based on its descriptions, along with the features of *curraghs* still used off Ireland's west coast. The result is a remarkable vessel of oak-tanned oxhides stretched over an ash-wood frame. Craggaunowen also has an actual **Iron Age road**, excavated at Corlea Bog, County Longford and moved to this site. Made of large oak planks placed across runners of birch or alder, it must have formed part of an important route across difficult bog. For refreshment, there's also a nice **tea shop** here, which serves delicious home-made cakes.

Eight miles beyond Craggaunowen, the village of **CRATLOE** is renowned for its oak-wooded hills overlooking the Shannon and Fergus estuaries and is a particularly lovely spot for walking.

Bunratty

Bunratty Castle (daily 9.30am to last admission 4.15pm; Folk Park June–Aug until 7pm; £4.50) stands on what was once an island on the north bank of the Shannon, now handily situated on the N18 Limerick–Ennis Road. The Vikings of Limerick recognized the site's strategic importance for protecting trade, and so they fortified it – you can still see the moat. The first castle on the site was built by Normans, but they lost control and, in 1460, the Macnamaras built the castle that stands today. It's exceptionally impressive: the fine rectangular keep has been perfectly restored and now houses a large collection of furni-ture, tapestries, paintings and ornate carvings from all over Europe, spanning the four-teenth to the seventeenth centuries. In the castle grounds, **Bunratty Folk Park** is a complete reconstruction of a nineteenth-century village. Although extremely touristy, both castle and folk village are well worth taking time over, and you can break up your visit in the excellent tearoom or the pub within the Folk Park. The nearby *Durty Nellies* is a favourite tourist bar, regularly overrun by bus parties.

Dysert O'Dea and Corofin

Alternative routes from Ennis can take you north through low-lying country fretted with rush-bordered lakes. Seven miles north is **Dysert O'Dea**: take the Ennistymon Road out of Ennis, then after two miles take the right fork for Corofin, and it's up a road to the left. Dysert O'Dea is the site of the ancient monastic foundation of Saint Tola (d. 737) and was the scene of an important battle in 1318 when the O'Briens defeated the de Clares of Bunratty, thus preventing the Anglo-Norman takeover of Clare. There are the remains of a twelfth- to thirteenth-century Romanesque church with a richly carved south doorway and grotesque carvings of animal heads and human faces. Nearby is the base of a round tower and the twelfth-century White Cross of Tola, with carvings of Christ and a bishop in high relief, Daniel in the lion's den, as well as intricate pattern-ing. The **O'Dea Castle** nearby is a museum (May–Sept daily 10am–6pm; £1.80) and archeology centre.

The Clare Heritage Centre (☎065/37955) has a genealogy service for those with origins in the county, holding details of over half a million people – McMahon, Macnamara, Moloney and O'Brien being the most common names. If you want to research your roots in detail, write to the centre a few months *before* your trip (they get especially busy here in July and August) and find out as much as possible before you visit (names, dates, marriages, deaths, location, occupation, parish etc). The more prepared you are, the more detailed the research the centre can do. An initial search costs around £40–60, a full one £100–130. Alternatively, the new library here is freely available: a morning spent poring over records will probably convince you just why it's worth paying a trained genealogist to do it for you.

COROFIN lies at the heart of the abundance of little lakes that wriggle their way north of here, their banks dotted with ruined O'Brien strongholds. The area offers good fishing and tranquil cycling, disturbed only by the wind scything its way through squeaky bullrushes, reeds and yellow water irises. The new friendly, family-run *Corofin Village Hostel* (*IHH*, open all year; ☎065/37683, fax ☎37239; ②) is very clean and warm, with laundry facilities, camping and bike rental (£5 per day). There is little to the village beyond a handful of houses, but there is a *Teach Cheoil* (music house) in the main street where traditional music is dished up with tea and brown bread in a pleasantly relaxed atmosphere (July & Aug Thurs nights; ☎065/27955). The village also boasts the **Clare Heritage Centre** (March–Oct daily 10am–6pm; Oct–March Mon–Fri 9am–5pm; geneaology service open year round, see above), which portrays the traumatic period of Irish history between 1800 and 1860 and fills in the horrors that the Bunratty Folk Park omits: famine, disease, emigration and the issue of land tenure.

Lough Derg

The west bank of **Lough Derg** is a seam of beautiful countryside set between bald, boggy mountains and the great expanse of the lake. It forms the county's eastern boundary and, isolated by the empty heights of the Slieve Bernagh and the Slieve Aughtie mountains, has a different character from the rest of Clare. The waterway's wealth of fish and bird life, and the quaint villages on either shore, have long made Lough Derg popular with a wealthy Lough-cruising set, whose exclusive brand of tourism means villages are fairly conservative and well kept. The hunting, shooting and fishing crowds are well catered for and tend to dominate the character of local pubs; but there are also pockets renowned for their traditional music sessions, attracting predominantly local crowds.

The main road north varies the scene, at times clinging to the lakeshore, at others gaining higher ground and panoramic views over the lough, its islands and the mountains of Tipperary. It connects the historic, picturesque towns of Portumna in County Galway, at the head of the Lough, and Killaloe at its southerly tip, and laces together a handful of choice little villages.

Access to the area is via Limerick or Portumna. *Bus Éireann* runs at least one **bus** (Mon–Sat) from Limerick to Killaloe, Tuamgraney and Scarriff. For timetable information, phone Limerick ☎061/313333. Journeys along the shore north of Scarriff involve **hitching** or **cycling**, though this isn't such a good idea in the Slieve Bernagh and Slieve Aughtie mountains to the west. Here roads are empty, making hitching difficult, and deceptively steep and unsheltered, making cycling tough. You can **rent bikes** from *Guerins* in Mountshannon (see p.312).

Killaloe

At **KILLALOE**, the Shannon narrows again after the Lough for the final stretch of this great river's journey to the sea. An old stone bridge still spans the waters at this traditional crossing point. The old part of Killaloe focuses on **St Flannan's Cathedral**, and the narrow lanes that run up the steep slopes to the west suggest the town's ancient origins. The cathedral itself is a plain thirteenth-century building, impressive in its solid simplicity, with a low square tower and straight, strong buttresses. Just inside the entrance is a heavily decorated Romanesque doorway from an earlier church, and alongside it the huge **Thorgrim Stone**, unique in its *ogham* and *runic* inscriptions (*ogham* is a form of the Latin alphabet associated with early Christianity; the *runic* forms are Scandinavian in origin), which is probably the memorial of a Viking convert. In the churchyard the stout Romanesque **St Flannan's Oratory** dates from the twelfth century and is complete with barrel-vaulted roof. Well signposted just over a mile north of town on the western shore of Lough Derg, **Beal Boru** is an earthen fort and possibly the site of Brian Boru's palace "Kincora", which was either here or in Killaloe itself. The best way to spend your time in Killaloe, though, is to get out onto the water; see below for details of cruises and boat rental.

Practicalities

The **tourist information office** is in Lock House on The Bridge (May to mid-Sept daily 10am–6pm; ☎061/376866) and is very helpful with accommodation. If you want to **stay**, several B&Bs offer an alternative to the luxury of the *Lakeside Hotel* (☎061/376122; ⑦): try Mrs Keogh's *Lakeside House* (☎061/376292; ④) or *Canter Lodge Cloonfadda*, about a mile from town (☎061/376954; ④). For **camping** beside the lake, the *Lough Derg Holiday Park* (May–Sept; ☎061/376329) is just three miles north of Killaloe along the Scarriff Road. For lough **cruises** (£5) or dinghy rental call ☎061/376364; for **boats** with outboard engines call in at *Whelen's Foodstore* (both dinghies and boats cost £10 an hr, £30 a day). You can rent out wind-surfers, canoes and wetsuits from *Shannonside Activity and Sailing Centre* (☎061/376622). The centre, situated two miles out along the Scarriff Road, also runs reasonably priced residential courses.

There are a couple of pubs serving decent **food** over on the Tipperary side of the bridge: *Molly's* and the somewhat pricier *Gooser's*; the *Simply Delicious* café nearby is just that, serving very cheap meals (daily till around 5.30pm). Over on the County Clare side of the bridge *The Dalcassian* also serves bar food. Most pubs have some kind of **music** at weekends during the summer – usually a traditional/country mix: try *The Sean Achaoi* (Fri year round) or *Crotty's Courtyard Bar*, both in Bridge Street. The *Anchor Inn* has traditional set dancing (Wed year round); over the bridge in Tipperary, *Molly's* has music (Mon).

The West Bank

The villages along the scenic road north are all very small. Wealthy tourists into hunting, shooting and fishing tend to stay in fancy hotels, and amenities for other visitors are sparse – even campsites here cost above the average rate.

SCARRIFF is a little farming town set high in rough, open country overlooking the lough. It's a handy place to pick up provisions. There's a *Bank of Ireland* here and a couple of pubs doing bar food, *Ryan's* and *McNamara's*. **FEAKLE**, about six miles to the west, is another small village buts holds a major **traditional music festival** (usually the weekend after the August bank holiday); throughout the year, there are often very good midweek sessions in *Pepper's* bar (also Sun in summer). **Accommodation** can be problematic: unless you bring a tent and ask at a farm your choices are limited to *The Smyth Village Hotel* (☎061/924002; ⑤) or *Laccaroe House* (☎061/924150; ④), about a mile away.

The best spot to stay right by the lake, Killaloe and Portumna aside, is **MOUNTSHANNON** (about five miles north of Scarriff). It's among the prettiest of the villages and has a couple of cosy pubs-cum-grocery shops with music in the summer, a restaurant as well as the upmarket *Mountshannon Hotel* (☎061/927162; ⑥) and a couple of small B&Bs – try *Derg Lodge* (☎061/927180; ③). The *Lakeside Watersport Hostel and Caravan and Camping Park* (☎061/927225) is a great place for **watersports**: canoeing, wind-surfing, sailing and motor boat rental are all very reasonably priced, and there is no need to book. They also have a couple of mobile homes available at hostel prices if you get rained out. You can **rent bikes** at *Guerins* grocery shop, and there's a safe swimming area at the lakeshore. From Mountshannon, too, you can take a boat to **Holy Island**, where there are ruins of a monastic settlement dating from the seventh to the thirteenth centuries.

North of Mountshannon, the beauty of the scenery fades as the main road leaves the lakeshore and the mountains to the west become less dramatic. **WHITEGATE** is tiny and dominated by a handful of bars. For traditional music sessions try *The Maple Bar* (Fri & Sun during summer).

Southwest Clare

The southwest of the county has glorious sandy beaches, stunning cliff scenery and a couple of popular family holiday resorts. Inland doesn't look so promising. Southwest from Ennis the country flattens out and becomes scrubby and barren: bog, marsh, the odd bit of cotton grass here, the occasional lump of thistles there, with only sporadic pockets of cultivated land. The bald flank of Slievecallan is to the north and the outline of the Kerry hills to the south across the Shannon.

Kilrush and Scattery Island

At present, the best reason to stop in **KILRUSH** is for a trip across the broad Shannon estuary to Scattery Island (see opposite); the town itself boasts traditional **Horse Fairs** in June, October and November, but the character of the place is changing. What was a muddy, tidal harbour is now a fine marina, the main thrust of the town's bid for the upmarket tourist trade, and in the **market square**, a statue of the Maid of Éireann (see opposite) looks resolutely down the broad main street to the quayside where it's all still yet to happen. The old market house is now a **heritage centre** (May–Sept Mon–Sat 10am–1pm & 2–5.30pm, Sun noon–3.30pm; £2), for the most part a stand-and-read display telling the eighteenth- and nineteenth-century economic and social history of the town. In Toler Street, just off the main street, the spacious **Saint Senan's Catholic church** is worth looking in for the Harry Clarke stained glass windows.

The **tourist office** is in the town hall in the main square (June to mid-Sept Mon–Sat 10am–1pm & 2–6pm, Sun noon–4pm ☎065/51577). There's no shortage of **B&Bs** in the town centre: *Crotty's* (☎065/54154, ④), Frances Street (the main street that leads down to the marina), is reasonably priced. Turn left at the bottom of Frances Street and a short walk brings you to Mrs M. O'Mahony's *Ferry Lodge*, Cappa Road (☎065/51291; ③), which is friendly and relatively palatial. *Katie O'Conner's Hostel*, Frances Street (☎065/51133; ②), is a decent place. For **camping**, *Aylevarroo Caravan and Camping Park* (mid-May to early Sept; ☎065/51102), on the N67 Killimer Road, is less than two miles from Kilrush – though primarily for caravans. There are two **banks**, *Allied Irish Bank* and *Bank of Ireland*, which are both on Frances Street. *Bus Éireann* information for **buses** to Ennis and around the coast throughout the year, and to Galway and Cork during the summer, is available from the tourist office. *Gleesons*, Henry Street, **rent bikes** (☎065/

THE MANCHESTER MARTYRS

Statues of the Maid of Éireann, commemorating the **Manchester Martyrs**, are scattered around Ireland. In Manchester in 1867, a band of Fenians blew open the back of a Black Maria in an attempt to rescue some of their leaders, who had been arrested after an armed uprising. A police sergeant was killed in the explosion, and three Fenians were hanged as a result. The executions provoked demonstrations throughout England and Ireland, since many considered the sergeant's death to have been an accident and the trials rigged: these monuments are testimony to the strength of those feelings.

51127; £7 per day, £30 per week) and stock camping *Gaz*. Access to Scattery Island is by small boat (£3.50), and trips are restricted by tides; enquire at the **Scattery Island Centre** down by the marina (daily May–Sept 9.30am–6.30pm; ☎065/52139), where an exhibition tells of Scattery's monastic history. For trips to the island at other times, and for details of **dolphin-watching** trips, phone ☎065/51327 or ☎52031.

Local hotels and pubs have been assiduously upgraded to prepare for the new clientele floating in at the marina, which means that you can currently get good-quality **food** at reasonable prices. In Henry Street, just off the square, the friendly *Ryan's Deli* serves burgers, pizza and tacos, and there's good pub food at *Kelly's* and *The Haven Arms,* both on Henry Street, and at *Crotty's* on Frances Street. For coffee and cakes there's *The Quayside* on Frances Street. In the evenings there are a couple of restaurants: *The Saddle Room* in Vaudeleur Street (☎065/51258) and upstairs in *Kelly's.* Kilrush is quite a quiet town, but *Crotty's* is a great old bar, with **traditional sessions** (Tues & Thurs). *O'Looney's,* John Street (just off the square), has rock music (Fri) and folk (Sat). Other spots for traditional music include *The Percy Frence Bar,* Moore Street (summer Wed, Fri & Sun), and *The Way Inn,* Vaudeleur Street (Sun year round).

Scattery Island

SCATTERY ISLAND was last inhabited in the late 1970s, and as you land the quay before you is dotted with overgrown derelict cottages. Walking up the lanes, spongy with moss and bracken, you disturb the burrows the island is now riddled with, and rabbits pop out madly all over the place. Saint Senan founded a **monastery** here in the sixth century, and at one time there were seven monastic settlements. The community suffered greatly from Viking raids, but there are still the remains of several churches dating from between the ninth and the fifteenth centuries.

Wherever you wander on Scattery, you get the feeling of stepping back into a timeless past, a mythical world protected by its isolation in the Shannon estuary. But Scattery's most impressive feature has to be the **round tower**, perfect in form, the stone made a warm mustardy yellow by the lichen that covers it. Unusually for a round tower, the doorway here is at ground level, as opposed to the more typical high-up entrances reached by a ladder that could be withdrawn to make the tower impregnable.

Killimer

If you have children in tow it's well worth calling at *Fortfield Farm*, **KILLIMER**, just a mile before the ferry terminal (see overleaf) if you're travelling from Kilrush. It's a small **farm zoo** (May–Sept Mon–Sat 10am–6pm, Sun 2–6pm; £2, children £1, family £6) with llamas, red deer, pot-bellied pigs, numerous breeds of rabbits and other domesticated rare animals. It's run by a friendly crowd who encourage children to handle the animals. The farm also does **B&B** (☎065/51457; ③ & ④); if you are staying there access to the zoo is free.

THE FERRY TO KERRY

If you're **cycling or driving on to Kerry**, you can cut out many miles and the mental congestion of Limerick city by heading for Killimer, five miles from Kilrush, and taking the **car ferry** to Tarbert (April–Sept Mon–Sat 7am–9pm, Sun 9am–9pm; Oct–March Mon–Sat 7am–7pm, Sun 10am–7pm; sailings every 60min on the hour, return from Tarbert on the half-hour; £7 single car, £10 return, £2 bikes; ☎065/53124).

Kilkee and around

KILKEE, over on the Atlantic coast, is a small, busy, seaside holiday town with all the amenities you'd expect: cheap cafés, restaurants, amusements and nightlife. Popular with the bucket-and-spade brigade, the town comes as a healthy piece of normality if the offbeat romanticism of the west coast has become too much. There's a magnificent beach, a torc of golden sand set in dramatic cliff scenery. The beach's westerly tip meets an apron of laminated rock strata known as the Duggerna Rocks, which protects it from the ravages of the Atlantic. Here, when the tide is out, deep, clear pollock holes form, filled with colourful marine life.

The area is a favourite for scuba diving and snorkelling, but even without equipment, exploration is rewarding. There are exhilarating walks for miles along the cliffs both to the north and, more spectacularly, to the south round **Loop Head**, where you can walk for sixteen miles along the cliff's edge past stack rocks, puffing holes (where the sea spouts up through crevices in the rock) and the natural Bridges of Ross. The other good way to see this peninsula is by **bike**; you can rent them at *Williams Pharmacy*, Circular Road (☎065/56041).

In the little church at **MONEEN**, near Kilbaha at the tip of the peninsula, is the nineteenth-century curiosity known as **The Little Arc**. In penal times, Catholics were forced to be both ingenious and secret in the practise of their faith. Here they were not allowed to worship on land, and so built a little hut on wheels which was kept on the beach and wheeled down below the high-water mark between tides, beyond the legal grasp of the local Protestant landowner. The priest would then say Mass in it while the congregation knelt around it on the beach. If you want to break your explorations of the Loop Head there are a couple of pubs at tiny Cross; but better by far is the unspoilt fishing village of **CARRIGAHOLT**, which has a slither of beach beside the quays, a ruined castle overlooking the harbour and some very welcoming pubs; *The Long Duck* has good **pub food**. It's also an excellent area for **dolphin spotting**; for trips out phone *Dolphin Watch* (☎088/584711; 2hr £8).

Practicalities

The **tourist office** in The Square (June–Aug daily 10am–1pm & 2–6pm; ☎065/56112) offers very useful help with accommodation; Kilkee is a popular resort and often booked out in August. Near here in O'Connell Street, *Kincora* (☎065/56107; ④) and *Bay View* (☎065/56058; ④) are good bets for **B&B**. *Inis Fail*, right on the seafront, is very reasonable (☎065/56184; ③). Alternatively, you could try *Dunearn House* (☎065/56152; ④) at the end of town. The cheapest decent accommodation is at *Kilkee Hostel*, O'Curry Street (*IHH*, Feb–Nov; ☎065/56209; ②), a friendly, family-run **hostel** right in the centre of town, which offers **bike rental** and also runs a **bureau de change**. There are two **campsites**: *Cunninghams Caravan and Camping Park* (Easter weekend & May to mid-Sept; ☎065/451009) is reached as you approach town from Kilrush by taking the first left after the *Texaco* station; the other site, far less attractive, is just up the Kilrush Road from the main square. The *Bank of Ireland* and the *Allied Irish Bank* are in O'Curry Street. As for **sport**, the choice is pitch and putt at the west end, golf at the new eighteen-hole championship golf course, scuba diving (*Killkee Diving and Watersports Centre* ☎065/56707) or pony trekking (☎065/56635). **Bus Éireann services**, departing from outside *Kett's* pub just along the Lahinch Road, link Kilkee with Ennis and other towns along the coast.

There are a handful of good **places to eat** lodged in amongst the bars and chippies. *The Strand Restaurant* (☎065/56177) on the seafront is a popular spot for seafood (evening menu around £15); for **bar food** try *Myles' Creek*, O'Curry Street, or *Kett's*. For pasta, steaks, pizzas and a good atmosphere try *Purtill's*, or *The Pantry* for home baking, both in O'Curry Street. Kilkee has no shortage of **pubs**: *O'Mara's*, O'Curry Street, is a great old bar, with traditional, folk and singalongs and a lively local crowd; *Fitzpatrick's*, Chapel Street, also has traditional music sessions. For a younger crowd try *Myles' Creek* (rock and pop five nights a week), or *The Strand*, on the seafront, a regular bar with a mix of ballads, traditional, blues and rock music.

Milltown Malbay and Spanish Point

The coastline north of Kilkee is one of fine cliffs and sandy beaches, though not all of them are accessible. **MILLTOWN MALBAY**, eighteen miles north of Kilkee, is a Victorian resort, strangely situated some way inland. The place comes alive for the Willie Clancy Summer School held here (usually the first or second week in July), when it's packed with traditional music enthusiasts from all over the world. If you want **B&B** *The Station House* (☎065/84008; ③) is a very good value. Two and a half miles away is **SPANISH POINT**, so called because it was here that survivors from wrecked Armada ships swam ashore, only to be executed by the High Sheriff of Clare. It's a holiday spot for nuns, and appropriately enough there's a very quiet **campsite**, *Lahiff's Caravan and Camping Park* (May–Sept; ☎065/84006), and an excellent sandy swimming beach.

To the east of Spanish Point, **Slieve Callan** rises beside the main road to Ennis. Taking this road you pass Knocknalassa, where there's an impressive wedge-shaped gallery grave, known as *Diarmuid and Gráinne's Bed* (after the Irish version of the Tristan and Isolde story). It's quite tricky to find: five miles along the road from Milltown Malbay you will pass a house with a newly thatched little barn alongside; the grave is about half a mile further east from here, tucked out of sight behind a hummocky rise to the left of the road. Follow the cows – it's worth seeing.

Ennistymon and Lahinch

ENNISTYMON, about ten miles north of Milltown Malbay, is an old market town (Tuesday is market day) with low shop-fronts, a pretty nineteenth-century Gothic church and some great old bars tucked away in the most unlikely of places. The town has a life, albeit a leisurely one, regardless of tourism, and its people enjoy **traditional music** and ballads in the **bars** year round: try *The Archway Bar*, *Phil's Bar*, *Daly's Bar*, *Eugene's*, *The Falls Hotel* or *Cooley's House*, all on Main Street. The church at the end of the main street has been converted into a *teach ceoil* (*ceili* house) where you can catch evenings of traditional music: it's run by local enthusiasts so expect standards to be high (entrance around £3). The traditional singing festival is scheduled for the first weekend in June; there's also a traditional music festival in the third weekend in July.

Ennistymon's setting is surprisingly green; nip down behind the *Archway Bar* and the **Cascades Walk** takes you alongside the River Cullenagh as it rushes over slabs of rock through the heart of the little town. Lodged at the side of these falls is a basic hydroelectric power station housed in a shed providing electricity for the *Falls Hotel* – a resourceful piece of alternative technology. Ennistymon's eighteenth-century church stands on a hill above the town, from where you can see the blue river snaking its way out of the woods and beyond to the sea at Liscannor.

There are several reasonably central **B&Bs**, including the very welcoming *Station House* (☎065/71149; ④) and *The Matchmakers' Rest* (☎065/71699; ④) above *The Súgán Chair* restaurant on Main Street. The cheapest place to stay is *The White House Hostel* (May–Oct; ☎065/26793; ①), up behind *Phil's Bar*. The bunks are archaic, but at least the kitchen is reasonably clean – collect the key from *Eugene's* bar.

Two miles or so east of Ennistymon, **LAHINCH** is a busy family holiday resort with a fabulous broad sandy beach, ideal for surfing. Not far along the coast are two natural waterspouts. The town pitches itself at a conservative market, its two golf courses hosting major golf competitions in July and August; for a round, try the *Lahinch Golf Club* (☎065/81003). While there's good **music**, both country and traditional, to be had in the bars, there's not a great deal to attract you to Lahinch – it's characterless and very much a seasonal town that shuts down in winter. Nonetheless, *O'Looney's* is a lively place, favoured by the surf crowd, and *Galvin's* has traditional music. The **tourist office** is beside the church (June–Sept daily 10am–7pm), and, if you do want to stay, they are very helpful with B&B addresses. The new **hostel**, *Lahinch*, also next door to the church (*IHH*, open all year; ☎065/81040, fax ☎81704; ②), is very clean and pleasant, with laundry facilities. You can **camp** at *Lahinch Camping and Caravan Park* (May–Sept; ☎065/81424), an orderly family site that has a **laundry** for service washes, **bike rental** (£7 per day) and a wet-weather shelter. For **seafood**, good vegetarian options and fine views the *Barrtra* **restaurant** (☎065/81280; lunch £5–6, dinner £16–19) is signposted off the road two miles south of Lahinch.

The Burren

The Burren (*Boireann*, or "rocky land") is a huge plateau of limestone and shale that covers over a hundred square miles of northwest Clare, a highland shaped by a series of cliffs, terraces and expanses of limestone pavement, with little to punctuate the view. Bleak and grey, the northern reaches of the Burren can come as a shock to anyone associating Ireland with all things lush and verdant. It's an extraordinary landscape of stark rock, fading lower green fields, and above all the sky and the ocean. Its cliffs and terraces lurch towards the sea like huge steps of wind-pocked pumice. Bone white in sunshine, in the rain it becomes darkened and metallic, the cliffs and canyons blurred by mists. A harsh place, barely capable of sustaining human habitation, it was aptly summed up in the words of Cromwell's surveyor Ludlow: "savage land, yielding neither water enough to drown a man, nor a tree to hang him, nor soil enough to bury". There are no sweet rolling fields here, but stick with it and its fascination emerges – cruel and barren as it is, there's a raw beauty about the place and an exceptional combination of light, rock and water.

In recent centuries, the Burren has supported a sparse population, living, like most of the west of Ireland, in harsh poverty. It was to this land, west of the Shannon, that Cromwell drove the dispossessed Irish Catholics after his campaign of terror. Few could survive for long in such country. The area's lack of appeal to centuries of speculators and colonizers greedy to cream the fat off Ireland's lusher pastures has meant that evidence of many of the Burren's earlier inhabitants has remained. The place buzzes with the **prehistoric and historic past**, having over sixty Stone Age (3000–2000 BC) burial monuments, the most common types being wedge-shaped tombs, cairns and dolmens; over 400 Iron Age ring forts (500 BC–500 AD), which were defensive dwellings; and numerous Christian churches, monasteries, round towers and high crosses.

You can **get to the area** by taking a *Bus Éireann* connection from stations at Galway or Limerick. There's a direct **bus** service from Limerick and Galway to Doolin and in

GEOLOGY AND FLORA

The Burren has an austerity of almost mythical dimensions, suggesting ancient privations. The pavementing that stretches before you is a floor of grey rock, split by long parallel grooves known as *grykes*. Throughout the Burren, rainwater seeps through the highly porous rock and gouges away at the many underground potholes, caves and tunnels. The only visible **river** is the Caher at Fanore, but there are a multitude of underground waterways, and there are **lakes**, known as *turloughs*, that are peculiar to this landscape; they appear only after heavy rainfall, when the underground systems fill up, and vanish once again after a few dry days.

The panorama is bleak, but close up, **wild flowers** burst from the grooves in specks and splashes of brilliant colour. A botanist's delight and enigma, the Burren supports an astounding variety of **flora**, with Arctic, Alpine and Mediterranean plants growing alongside each other. The best time to see the flowers is late spring, when the strong blue, five-petalled spring gentians flourish. Here, too, are mountain avens, various saxifrages and maidenhair fern. Later in summer, the magenta bloody cranesbill and a fantastic variety of orchids (considered rare elsewhere) bloom: bee orchids, fly orchids and the lesser butterfly. More common flowers look stunning by sheer force of quantity: bright yellow birdsfoot trefoil and hoary rockrose, and milkwort. Obviously flowers must not be picked.

Nobody knows exactly how these plants came to be here, nor why they remain. It has been suggested that some of the Mediterranean flowers were here since Ireland had a far hotter climate, but how they survived is a source of speculation: it may be the peculiar conditions of moist warm air coming in from the sea, the Gulf Stream ensuring a mild, frostless climate, and very effective drainage through the porous limestone. It's also thought that the bare rock absorbs heat all summer and stores it, so that the Burren land is appreciably warmer in wintertime than areas of a different geology. There's more on the Burren's geology in the **Burren Display Centre** in Kilfenora: proposals to open a new interpretative centre in the heart of the Burren continue to cause great controversy, with conservationists around the world joining the protests against it.

summer at least one bus a day from Limerick passes through Ennistymon and Lisdoonvarna, and at least one a day connects Galway with Lisdoonvarna. To see the Burren's archeological and ecclesiastical sites, it's best to go by car or bike (bike rental is available in the main centres of Doolin, Lisdoonvarna, Ballyvaughan and Kinvarra); to get to know its landscape and flowers, go on foot. For either of these, the excellent Tim Robinson **map** *The Burren* (available in tourist offices, good bookshops or directly from him at Roundstone, County Galway) is usefully detailed and will make finding sites easy. There are two north–south routes across the Burren that are of particular **archeological interest**; these run from Bell Harbour to Killinaboy and from Ballyvaughan to Leamaneh. If you're doing a lot of **walking**, a compass is a good idea as there's a shortage of easy landmarks. You're allowed to walk more or less where you want: a good start might be to follow the Burren Way, signposted from Liscannor to Ballyvaughan. The big disadvantage if you have a car or bike is that this isn't a circular walk.

Liscannor and the Cliffs of Moher

LISCANNOR is a useful coastal base – and an alternative to the busier tourist centre of Doolin further north – for exploring Clare's most famous tourist spot, the Cliffs of Moher. The village has a few nice bars, a caravan site which accepts tents, supermarket, post office, tea shop and a fairly basic **hostel**. *The Village Hostel* (*IHH*, open all year; ☎065/81385, fax ☎81417; ①) is right next to the bars. For **B&B**, try *The Anchor Inn* (☎065/81548; ③) or *Cois na Mara* (☎065/81527; ④). The sandy stretches south towards Lahinch, towards the mouth of the river, are unsafe due to quicksand.

Circling north round the Burren from Liscannor, you arrive almost immediately at the **Cliffs of Moher**. At their highest, they tower 660ft above the Atlantic, and standing on the headlands that jut over the sheer, ravaged cliffs with their great bands of shale and sandstone, you can feel the huge destructive power of the waves. At points the battering of the water has left jagged stack rocks standing, continually lashed by white spume. Erosion is constant: during a storm some years ago a section of the cliff fell, taking its picnic table with it. The cliffs have to be seen – ideally on a summer evening, when the setting sun is full on them – but be prepared for the oppressively commercial **visitor centre**, where readily changed money and travellers' cheques are quickly spent on coffee, cakes and souvenirs. Be prepared, too, for the professional Irish "characters", ready to sell you any baloney you're willing to buy, and the swarms of tourists newly armed with piercing tin whistles. Do see the cliffs, though – you can soon walk away from the crowds in either direction, after checking there are no bulls in the field to the north. The cliffs actually stretch for five miles, from Hag's Head, just west of Liscannor, to a point beyond **O'Brien's Tower** – a superfluous viewing point with telescope – some four miles south of Doolin.

Doolin

The village of **DOOLIN** itself – marked as "Fisherstreet" on some maps – has become *the* music mecca of the "singing county", and in fact of Ireland's west. By the time you get here, you'll no doubt already have met a good few traditional music enthusiasts on their way from across northern Europe, and there are extra buses laid on to bring them here (see below).

Without the music, Doolin would be a forlorn and desolate place, lodged beside a treacherous sandy beach at the tail end of the coast that climaxes with the Cliffs of Moher. Bold shelves of limestone pavement step into the sea by the pier, from which a **ferry** now runs to **Inisheer** and **Inishmore** (mid-April to late Sept 1–6 daily; single £7.50 & £10, return £15 & £20 respectively; ☎065/74455) and to **Inishmaan** by arrangement; single £15, return £18. Day-trips are only available to Inisheer and Inishmore. It is also possible to sail from Doolin to all three islands and then on to Galway or return to Doolin (£20; bikes £2). See p.340 for more on the Aran Islands.

Music may be its *raison d'être*, but the village is now ruthlessly geared to providing **accommodation** for as many visitors as it's possible to squeeze into the place's three pubs, B&Bs, 100 hostel beds and the couple of campsites. For **B&B**, *Seacrest* (☎065/74458; ④), towards the pier, has wild, blustery views of the coast, or try *Atlantic View* (☎065/74189; ③). There are several smart new B&Bs behind *O'Connor's* pub: *Fisherman's Rest* (☎065/74673; ③ & ④), *Cuckoo's Nest* (☎065/74774; ④) and *Lane Lodge* (☎065/74747; ③). Other good options include *The Horseshoe* (☎065/74006; ④), *O'Connor's* (☎065/74314; ③) and, just near the *Aille River Hostel* (see below), two good budget options: *The Blue Dolphin* (☎065/74692; ③) and *Doolin Cottage* (book through the hostel nearby; ③). Despite their number, the **hostels** do get packed in July and August, so ringing ahead is essential (if they're full, try the ones in Liscannor or Lisdoonvarna, both five miles away, or Ennistymon, eight miles away). Doolin's hostels include *The Rainbow Hostel* (*IHH*, open all year; ☎065/74415; ②), with camping space; the friendly, laid-back *Aille River Hostel* (*IHH*, early March to early Nov; ☎065/74260; ②), also with camping; or *Paddy Moloney's Doolin Holiday Hostel* and *Fisherstreet Hostel* (both *IHH*, open all year; ☎065/74006, ②), with tennis court, laundry facilities and bike rental (£5.50 per day). Another option is to go for one of the **special package deals** available through **Bus Éireann**. These combine transport from Galway, Limerick or Dublin, one night's stay (or more) in *Paddy Moloney's Doolin Holiday Hostel* plus a bus journey to anywhere else in the country (☎065/74006 for details). *Bus Éireann* also runs extra services to Doolin in summer – see "Travel Details" at the end of the chapter – and *West Clare Shuttle* operates a Galway–Doolin door-to-door service, picking up at all hostels (£5). There's **camping** down by the pier at *Nagle's* (May to late Sept; ☎065/74458) – a great spot to absorb the drama of the landscape – and at *Riverside Camping* (Easter–Oct). *Doolin Café* (see below) also **rents bikes** (£6 per day, £35 per week) and does repairs.

The thatched *Ivy Cottage* (☎065/74244) is a cosy **restaurant** with good food reasonably priced. *O'Connor's* does good-value bar meals; while the time-honoured *Doolin Café* is the epitome of laid-back west coast style with wholesome food and plenty of books and papers to browse through (daily till 9.30pm, closed 2–6pm). Apart from *O'Connor's* pub, Doolin's two other **bars** – *McGann's* and *McDermott's* – are around half a mile inland, and are both lively. Whatever day you arrive in summer, traditional music will be playing in all of them – though while the music will be fine, the "pub experience" might pall, as you can find yourself sitting amidst an audience rapt in reverential silence, awed at just being there or overwhelmed by huge swaths of tourists.

Fanore to Bell Harbour

North of Doolin, the coast remains spectacular but bleak and empty. The first place to stop is **FANORE**, where you can **stay** in the cosy *Bridge Hostel* (March to end Oct; ☎065/76134; ①), which also does camping; it only has eighteen beds, so in July and August it's best to ring ahead. Breakfasts and evening meals are available (£1.50–2.50), with a vegetarian option. There are excellent Burren walks easily accessible from here, and the owners will gladly point you in the right direction.

Beyond, the scenic coast road to Black Head and Ballyvaughan is well worth taking. **BALLYVAUGHAN** is an attractive village with a quay of neat grey blocks, beautifully poised between Galway Bay and the Burren. Its significance as a trading centre has dwindled into tourism, but it makes a calm haven from which to explore the Burren hills. There's a **tourist office** (daily mid-May to Oct 9am–8.30pm; ☎065/77105), and a cluster of shops, and a rent-an-Irish-cottage scheme (book well in advance through Bord Fáilte). For **B&B**, try *Gentian Villa* (☎065/77042; ④). **Free camping** is possible down by the shore just beyond *Monk's* bar, which also does **bike rental** (May–Sept; ☎065/77059; £7 per day, £30 per week). **Sea trips** on Galway hookers, traditional sailing boats, are available locally (☎091/37539; £6 per hr). For **food**, *Whitehorn Restaurant & Crafts*, on the road towards Kinvarra, is worth visiting in itself for its style and setting – lunches, teas and cakes are all affordable, and there's an evening tourist menu for £13 (☎065/77044). *Monk's* bar does good seafood, while the home-cooked dinners at *Hyland's Bar* cater for hearty appetites. *The Tea Junction* café-restaurant serves fresh pizza and baguettes; and the excellent *An Féar Gorta* tearooms down by the quays offers great soups, cakes and salmon sandwiches. For **music** try *Monk's* bar (Fri all year, other nights in summer), *Hyland's* or *O'Brien's* – where there's also set dancing.

From Ballyvaughan, interesting routes strike south through the heart of the Burren (see p.317). A couple of sites of interest within three miles of Ballyvaughan are Newtown Castle and the Aillwee Caves, both signposted off the Lisdoonvarna Road. Newly restored, **Newtown Castle** is a sixteenth-century fortified tower house. It's a simple defensive building, but the guided tour is interesting, telling of the medieval law and bardic schools of the surrounding area (Easter–Oct daily 10am–6pm; tour £2 – though there need to be a few of you for it to run). The well-lit tour through the two-million-year-old **Aillwee Caves** (daily mid-March to early Nov 10am–5.30pm, July & Aug till 6.30pm; £3.95) will take you past amazing caverns of stalagmites and stalactites and spectacular rock formations. However, these caves are privately owned and massively promoted, and the tour is very fast: the experience does not induce the wonder it should.

All along this coast, east of Ballyvaughan, where the Burren borders Galway Bay, short stretches of well-tended farmland reach from the foot of the hills to the shoreline, and water glints through gaps in the high stone walls, while way over Galway Bay the muted cobalt mountains of Connemara are hazy in the distance. There's a wealth of **birdlife** along these shores: cormorants, guillemots, terns, herons, grebes, fulmars, mallards, teals and swans, as well as sea-otters and seals. Heading towards Galway on the coast road, you pass through **BELL HARBOUR** (*Beulaclugga*), at the southern tip of Muckinish Bay, where the road towards Killinaboy sets off, soon passing the placid **Corcomroe Abbey** signposted on your left. A twelfth-century Cistercian foundation, its considerable remains are beautifully set in a secluded valley.

Kinvarra and Doorus

Approaching the Burren from Galway you come straight to some of the best spots: tiny villages on the northerly edge of the plateau – and actually in County Galway – little settlements between glinting inlets and the eerie white Burren hills. These offer magical views across the wide expanse of Galway Bay, where changes in the broad sky are reflected in the bay's surface, and the shimmering silver and turquoise light bounces off the white-grey Burren rock.

Set in the southeasterly inlet of Galway Bay, **KINVARRA** is a fishing village with a stone quayside that's almost too pretty; water laps the shore while swans drift to the side of Dunguaire Castle. This quaintness has been recognized, and for such a small place there are disproportionate amenities: a smattering of coffee shops, an expensive restaurant, a supermarket and some good bars. None of these sets the little village off-balance, though, and the only environmental aberration is a bizarre development of modern thatched two-storey houses with Victorian gas lamps. There's enough variety in the area to warrant a reasonable stay between the rigours of Burren-walking and Galway city-life. The informative *Kinvarra: A Ramblers Map and Guide*, by Anne Korff and Jeff O'Connell, is worth buying if you intend to explore the immediate countryside; it's available in local shops and at **Dunguaire Castle**. The castle (mid-April to Sept daily 9.30am–5.30pm; £2.25), on the edge of the village, was built in 1520 and is a well-restored tower house, one of several used by Shannon Development for medieval banquets. These "castles" were in fact fortified houses, very much a fashion for wealthy landowners from 1450 to 1650, and found in their greatest concentration in East Clare, East Limerick and South Galway. If you've not yet been in one, this is a particularly good example, as the guide delivers a vigorous interpretation of both local history and the political sense of the old building.

Accommodation is provided by B&Bs at *Kinvara House* (☎091/37118; ③) and *Cois Cuain* (☎091/37119; ④), or the cheerful *Johnston's Hostel*, Main Street (June to end Sept; ☎091/37164; ①), in a beautiful spot by the quays (also camping). **Bikes** can be rented from the hostel (£3 per day) or *McMahon's* filling station (£5 a day). Kinvarra's early spring **festival** is the *Fleadh na gCuach* (the cuckoo *Fleadh*), held over the spring bank holiday weekend at the end of April. The *Crumniú na mBád* is held here usually in the second weekend in August and involves, along with singing and dancing, the racing of Galway's traditional fishing vessels (Galway hookers). The **hookers** come in four sizes – *Bád Mór* (Big Boat) and *Leath Bhád* (Half Boat), at around 40ft and 30ft, then the *Gleoiteog* (28ft) and the tiny *Púcán*.

Doorus

In addition to all its other attractions, this part of South Galway is closely associated with the poetry of the **literary revival group** of Yeats, Lady Gregory, A.E. and Douglas Hyde; it was in what is now the *An Óige* hostel in **DOORUS** (out on the peninsula northwest of Kinvarra) that the idea of a national theatre was first discussed – later to become the Abbey Theatre in Dublin. The hostel was then the home of Count Florimond de Basterot, who entertained and encouraged the group (and also the likes of Guy de Maupassant and Paul Bourget). Given the political implications of the Irish literary revival, it's perhaps ironic that Count Florimond's cash came from French estates which his fleeing aristocratic ancestors had somehow hung on to, despite the Revolution.

Doorus is on a small peninsula of the same name that was an island until the eighteenth century. The **village** has only a pub and a shop, and you can stay at the welcoming *An Óige* **hostel** (☎091/37512; ②), although August is very busy, so ring ahead; you can also **camp** down by the beach – ask at the farm. The gentle waters to the south are pleasant, tidal backwaters that contrast sharply with the wide sweep of Traught beach to the north, which is stony but safe for swimming and surfing – there's a lifeguard on duty in summer. The beach at Parkmore, to the northeast, however, is dangerous. Along this coast, mussels are free for the picking – ask a local for the good spots. You can walk the wriggling coastline from Doorus down to Aughinish or back to Kinvarra, or cycle out to the Martello tower at Finavarra and around the inlet of Muckinish Bay towards Bell Harbour.

Lisdoonvarna and the heart of the Burren

"LISDOONVARNA – for the crack and the women": the radio ad sets the tone for what the spa town of Lisdoonvarna's famous month-long **matchmaking festival** has become. Traditionally, after the harvest, farmers come down from the hills to spend their hard-earned cash and look for a wife in a September festival of singing, dancing and drinking. Today tradition wears a sad and sleazy face: it's a hugely promoted festival, and the bars – in particular *The Hydro, The Matchmakers Arms* of *The Imperial Hotel* and *The King Thomond* – heave with middle-aged money-spinners and the bewildered and lonely, nervously cracking dirty jokes, drinking, singing and leering at any women brave enough to venture in. Between the crooning balladeers and the fortune-tellers' caravans the place bubbles with decades of repression and disappointment – a sad, archaic curiosity, fascinating in its own way. If you are here in September and want to drink with a younger crowd, try *The Roadside Tavern*.

There is, however, another side to Lisdoonvarna, best enjoyed in spring and early summer, since the place serves as one of the handiest spots from which to explore the Burren. It remains a popular **spa** town, too: the spring waters here contain magnesia, iodine and iron, and reputedly have restorative qualities. The town's principal sulphur spring is in the *Spa Wells Health Centre* (daily 10am–6pm; ☎065/74023), where you can take the waters in the pumphouse, or have a sulphur bath, a sauna, a shower or a massage. Generally full of elderly holiday-makers, the centre offers an invigorating afternoon for weary cyclists and walkers. The whirlwind tour of *The Burren Smokehouse* (daily 10am–7pm; ☎065/74432), right in the centre of town, will fill you in on all there is to know about traditional methods of smoking fish: frankly, there's not much to it, but it's worth taking for the banter and the sliver of smoked salmon thrown in to tempt you to buy more.

The **tourist office** (June–Sept; ☎065/74062) is helpful with accommodation – especially useful in August and September, when getting a bed for the night can be difficult. For **B&B** try the extremely friendly *Sunny Bank,* Kincora Road (☎065/74185; ③); *St Joseph's,* Main Street (☎065/74076; ③) is another good option. There's a very pleasant **hostel**, too: *The Burren Holiday Hostel* in Kincora House, right in the centre (*IHH*, open all year; ☎065/74300, fax ☎74490; ②). **Bike rental** is available at the hostel and at *Burke's* (☎065/74022). If you want to eat, plenty of pubs serve **food**; especially good is *The Roadside Tavern* (till 8.30pm). All of the pubs have **music** most nights during July and August, some of it pretty mixed, but good starting points include *The Roadside Tavern, The Royal Spa* and *Meg Maguire's*.

If you're heading north, the Ballyvaughan Road leads you through a brief area of dank forestry and out onto the **corkscrew hill**, a famous winding descent with fabulous views between grey hills to the broad expanse of Galway Bay – a visual treat and an especially exhilarating release for cyclists after the long steady climb.

Kilfenora

The tiny village of **KILFENORA**, about four miles south of Lisdoonvarna, is a great spot for **traditional music**: *Linnane's* has sessions most nights during the summer, as does *Vaughn's*, where there's also music on Mondays and set dancing on Thursdays year round, and good bar food. Kilfenora's music **festival**, held over the October bank holiday weekend, is a wonderful and strictly traditional event. The village is also home to the much-publicized **Burren Display Centre** (mid-March to Oct daily 10am–5pm; July & Aug till 7pm; May & Sept till 6pm; June; £2). The centre explains clearly the basic geography and geology of the Burren (in English, French and German), with the aid of a landscape model and a film; it's instructive rather than entertaining. The centre has a very good **tearoom**.

Next door is **Kilfenora Cathedral**, certainly worth a visit for its high crosses. The finest of these is the twelfth-century **Doorty Cross**, showing three bishops and what is probably Christ's entry into Jerusalem, with beautiful Celtic patterning. Nearby in the churchyard are remains of two other twelfth-century high crosses, one near the north-west corner, one opposite the church door. Wander through the gateway behind the church to see a fourth cross, with a decorated Crucifixion, in the field to the west. The cathedral itself was built in 1190 and altered in the fifteenth century: it has a roofless chancel with a finely carved triple-light east window and two effigies of bishops, possibly fourteenth century.

Brigid & Tony's **B&B** (☎065/88148; ③), next door to *Nagle's*, is very welcoming and a good value; or try *The Village*, Main Street (☎065/88040; ③). If you want to **camp** in the village ask at *Dermot Hogan's* shop; the site is the very public patch of green opposite (no showers).

Killinaboy and routes north

Heading east from Kilfenora you pass **Leamaneh Castle**, a fifteenth-century O'Brien stronghold, adjoining which is a four-storey building with mullioned and transomed windows (c.1640). If you turn off north here, the R480 towards Ballyvaughan runs through an area littered with ancient remains. The most impressive of these are around **Caher Connell**, a well-preserved ring fort. Barely half a mile beyond this is Poulabrone **Megalithic tomb**, the most famous of the Burren's portal dolmens, dating from 2500 BC, and two miles further is Gleninsheen, a wedge-shaped tomb of similar vintage a short walk from the road.

Continuing east from Leamaneh Castle you reach **KILLINABOY**, where a ruined eleventh- to fourteenth-century church has a striking *Sheila na gig* over the doorway: a carving of a naked woman with grotesquely exaggerated genitalia (*sheila* is the Irish equivalent of "Julia", and *gig* means "breast") which was probably some kind of fertility symbol. They're more usually found above castle doorways, and it may be that its siting here was intended as a warning against the sins of the flesh. From Killinaboy the road continues to Corofin (p.310).

Another road heads north from **Killinaboy** to **Bell Harbour**. There are many gallery graves around the early part of this road, climbing towards Carron, and you also pass through a limestone valley with several ring forts, the most impressive of which is **Caher Commaun**, a ninth-century triple cliff fort to the east of the road. Finally, near Bell Harbour are the remains of Corcomroe Abbey (see p.320).

travel details

Trains
Ennis to: Dublin (1–2daily; 3hr 5min), Limerick (1–2daily; 50min).

Bus Éireann
Doolin to Dublin (2–3 daily via either Limerick or Galway; 6hr 30min); Galway (June–Oct 12 daily; 1hr 25min); Limerick (June–Oct 3 daily; 1hr 40min–2hr 20min).

Ennis to: Cork (3 daily; 3hr); Dublin (6 daily; 4hr–4hr 30min); Galway (6 daily; 1hr 15min); Limerick (20 daily; 1hr); Shannon Airport (15 daily; 45min).

Shannon Airport to: Limerick (16 daily; 45min).

CHAPTER TEN

GALWAY, MAYO AND ROSCOMMON

Galway, Mayo and Roscommon mark a distinct change in the west of Ireland scene. Coming from the south, **County Galway** may at first seem a continuation of what has gone before in Clare and Kerry. And Galway city is in some ways the west coast town par excellence – an exceptionally enjoyable, free-spirited sort of place, and a gathering point for young travellers. But once you get beyond the city things start to change. The landscape is dramatically harsher and far less populous, and there are fewer visitors, too.

Lough Corrib, which divides Galway in two, delineates another dramatic split in the landscape of the county, this time between east and west, inland and coast. To the east of the lake lies tame, fertile land which people have farmed for centuries, while to the west lies **Connemara**, a magnificently wild terrain of wind and rock and water. The **Aran Islands**, in the mouth of Galway Bay, resemble Connemara both in their elemental beauty and in their culture; the Galway *Gaeltacht* – areas where Irish is still spoken – comprises the islands, Iar-Chonnacht and some scattered communities in north Connemara and Joyce country. While it can't compete with the rest of the county, **east Galway**'s medieval monastic sites are well worth taking in as you pass through. Again, **Galway city** straddles the divide. A bridging point both physically and culturally, it's a fishing port, an historic city and now the focus of an energetic social and artistic scene.

If you carry on up the coast you'll enter **County Mayo**, where the landscape softens somewhat but is still relatively free of tourists. The pilgrimage centre of **Knock** and the attractions of historic towns like **Westport** aside, it's the coast which is once again the main draw. Physically, it's as exciting and rugged as any in the Republic, and far less exploited, though the downside is that facilities for travellers are relatively thin on the ground. An exception is **Achill**, the largest Irish offshore island and popular holiday resort, which provides both some of the most spectacular cliffs and some practical necessities for travellers. **County Roscommon** is entirely landlocked and less visited still. There are few real excitements, and the land is for the most part flat and low lying; nevertheless, the fine detail of this landscape, scattered with small lakes and large houses, has a slow charm. There are places that merit a look as you pass through, and in the extreme north, around **Lough Key**, there's some very attractive scenery indeed.

ACCOMMODATION PRICES

Throughout this book, accommodation prices have been graded according to the cost per person per night in high season; with hotels and many hostels this represents half the cost of a double room, whereas with the more basic hostels it represents the cost of a single dormitory bed. The prices signified by our grades are as follows:

① Up to £6	③ £10–14	⑤ £20–26	⑦ £36–45
② £6–10	④ £14–20	⑥ £26–36	⑧ Over £45

COUNTY GALWAY

County Galway splits into clearly identifiable areas, each with strong distinctive characteristics. **Galway city** is the great social magnet of the region, a lively place to visit any time of the year. **Connemara** – a term loosely applied to encompass the west of the county – has the best of the scenery, with vast open expanses of bog, exhilarating mountains and superb white-sand beaches. Equally appealing, the **Aran Islands** combine raw landscape with some of the most exciting pre-Christian sites in Europe – and considerable legends. The east of the county is far less compelling; flat and less inspiring, it nonetheless does hold medieval ruins of interest. The area around south Galway Bay, nestling between the **Burren** and the water, at times has some of the tantalizing mercurial quality of north Clare.

Galway city

The city of **GALWAY**, folk capital of the west, has a vibrancy and surly hedonism that make it unique. People come here with energies primed for enjoyment – the drink, the music, the "crack" – and it can be a difficult place to leave. University College Galway guarantees a high proportion of young people in term time, maintained in summer by the attractions of the city's festivals. This youthful **energy** is an important part of Galway's identity. Galway has become a playground for disaffected Dubliners, and folksy young Europeans return each year with an almost religious devotion. The city commands a vigorous loyalty: try criticizing the place and you're liable to find yourself in a fight.

Again in contrast to many other Irish cities, Galway is experiencing a surge of economic **growth**. Constant renovation is in progress in the small and crowded city centre, and during the summer it has the energy of a boom town, with an expanding number of shops and restaurants to cater for the increase in fashionable visitors and students. The downside of this is the huge amount of property development galloping ahead in the city centre, threatening to knock all character out of the place. For the time being, at least, Galway retains its human scale.

Prosperity allows a vigorous independence from Dublin, mirrored in the artistic dynamism of the city. It's a focus for the traditional **music** of Galway and Clare – Galway's status as an old fishing town on the mythical west coast adding a certain potency – and there's strong interest in drama. The new theatre here reflects a renewed sense of civic and artistic optimism. At no time is the energy of Galway more evident than during its **festivals**, especially the Galway Arts Festival during the last two weeks in July, when practitioners of theatre, music, poetry and the visual arts create a rich cultural jamboree. It's a great time to be in the city, but be prepared for a squeeze on accommodation. The festival is swiftly followed by the **Galway Races** (the week before the Irish bank holiday – which usually makes it the first week in August), when accommodation is again at a premium. At the end of September, the Galway Oyster Festival completes the annual round.

Some history

Galway originated as a crossing point on the River Corrib, giving an access to Connemara denied further north by the lough. It was seized by the **Norman** family of De Burgos in the thirteenth century and developed as a strong Anglo-Norman colony, ruled by an oligarchy of fourteen families. They maintained control despite continual attacks by the bellicose Connacht clans, the most ferocious of whom were the O'Flaherties. To the O'Flahertie motto "Fortuna Favet Fortibus" (Fortune Favours the

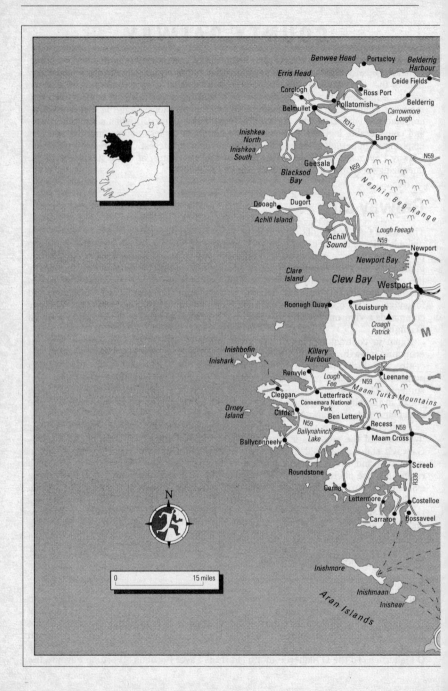

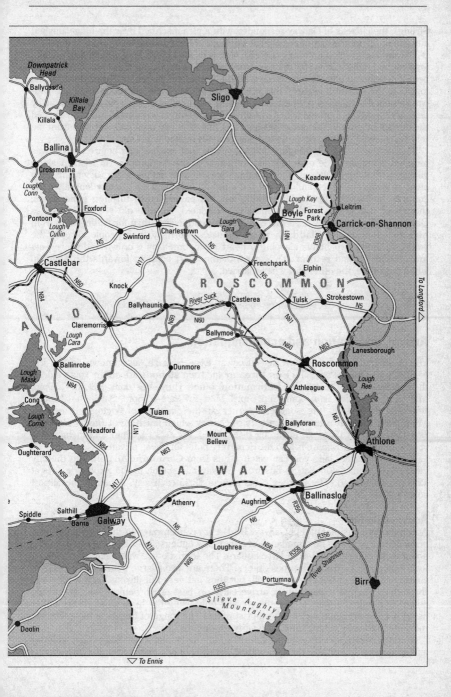

Strong), the citizens of Galway responded with a plea inscribed over the long-vanished city gates: "From the fury of the O'Flaherties, good Lord deliver us."

Galway was granted a charter and **city status** in 1484 by Richard III and was proudly loyal to the English Crown for the next two hundred years. During this time the city prospered, developing a flourishing trade with the Continent, especially Spain. However, its loyalty to the monarch ensured that when Cromwellian forces arrived in 1652 the place was besieged without mercy for ninety days. It was Cromwell who coined the originally derisory term "the fourteen tribes of Galway"; this didn't worry the Irish, who returned the disdain by proudly adopting the name as a title. The city went into a decline from the mid-seventeenth century onwards and only recently started to revive.

The history of the **Claddagh**, a fishing village that existed long before Galway was founded alongside it, is quite distinct from that of the city proper. An Irish-speaking village of thatched cottages, the Claddagh was fiercely independent, having its own laws, customs and chief, and it remained a proud, close-knit community long after the cottages had gone. Boat-building skills are still passed down through generations, though of course this work has massively declined, and the old vessels known as Galway hookers are now used more by boating enthusiasts than for fishing. It is from here that the famous **Claddagh ring** originates, worn by Irish people all over the world. It shows two hands clasping a heart surmounted by a crown and represents love, friendship and respect. It's worn with the heart pointing towards the fingertip when betrothed, the other way when married.

The telephone code for Galway city is ☎091.

Arrival, information and accommodation

You're almost bound to arrive in Galway at **Eyre Square**, also known as the J.F. Kennedy Memorial Park. The **Bus Éireann** and train **stations** are off the south side of the square, while the **tourist information office** (July–Aug daily 8.30am–7.30pm; May–June Mon–Sat 9am–6pm; Sept–April Mon–Fri 9am–5.45pm, Sat 9am–12.45pm; ☎563081) is just off the southern corner at the junction of Victoria Place and Merchant's Road. It runs walking tours of Galway which finish off at *Busker Browne's Bar* (Mon–Sat 12.45pm, £5 including drink; Wed, Fri & Sat 5.45pm, £12 including 3-course meal). Eyre Square is also the departure point for cheap private buses.

If you arrive by plane you can catch a bus from **Carnmore Airport** into the city centre at 1.25pm (Mon–Sat); a bus from Galway bus station to the airport departs at 12.50pm (Mon–Sat). The journey costs around £2.25 each way. A taxi to the airport costs around £7.

Accommodation

Accommodation is plentiful in Galway. **B&Bs** are concentrated in the centre and eastern side of town, with an abundance of smart new options along Father Griffin Road – about eight minutes walk from Eyre Square. The tourist office will make your booking for a £1 fee – not a bad idea at peak times. There are also a large number of **hostels** in Galway and east of the city in Salthill, but they get very full during festival time and throughout August – ring ahead, arrive early or, best of all, book ahead. We would advise ignoring the touts at the station, and only using the hostels which are either listed here or are approved by the tourist office. The range of **hotels** is more limited: most are in the city centre and all are fairly expensive.

You can **camp** at *Ballyloughane Caravan Park* on Dublin Road (May–Sept; ☎55338) and at several in Salthill, the pleasantest being *Hunter's Silver Strand Caravan and*

Camping Park, about four miles west on the coast road (Easter–Sept; ☎92452 or ☎92040). Camping is also available at *Glenavon House B&B*, 109 Upper Salthill.

Hotels and B&Bs

Atlanta Hotel, Dominick St (☎562241). Pleasant hotel, not far from Eyre Square. ⑥.

Crookhaven, 96 Father Griffin Rd (☎589019). ④.

Great Southern Hotel, Eyre Square (☎564041). Rambling Victorian establishment, taking up one side of the square, with a rooftop pool and spacious rooms. ⑨.

Inishmore, 109 Father Griffin Rd (☎582639). ④.

Joan Sullivan's, 46 Prospect Hill (☎566324). A friendly option just off Eyre Square. ④.

Jury's Galway Inn, Quay St (☎566444). This hotel offers a good deal: rooms for two adults plus two children sharing for £53, without breakfast. ⑤.

Lisduff, 102 Father Griffin Rd (☎588760). ④.

Skeffington Arms Hotel, Eyre Square (☎563173). An attractive cheaper alternative to the *Great Southern*. ⑦.

The Swallow, 98 Father Griffin Rd (☎589073). ④.

Villa Maria, 94 Father Griffin Rd (☎589033). ④.

The Western, Prospect Hill (☎562834). Another comfortable central B&B. ④.

Hostels

Arch View Hostel, 1 Upper Dominick St (☎586661). Decent, well-run hostel. Open all year. ②.

Corrib Villa, 4 Waterside (*IHH*; ☎562892). Not the crispest linen around, but a clean hostel with big rooms, a decent kitchen and common room. Open all year. ②.

Galway City Hostel, 25–27 Dominick St (*IHH*; ☎566367, fax ☎564581). Homely, if a bit down at heel. Doubles available; 3.30am curfew. Open all year. ②.

Galway Hostel, Frenchville Lane, Eyre Square (☎566959). Opposite the station. A good, friendly budget option, with twin and 4-bedded rooms available. Open all year. ②.

Grand Holiday Hostel, The Promenade, Salthill (*IHH*; tel/fax ☎521150). Very pleasant: clean, comfortable, family run, and right on the prom. Twins and doubles available; bike rental (£6) and laundry facilities. Suitable for families. Open mid-Jan to mid-Dec. ②.

Great Western House, Frenchville Lane, Eyre Square (☎561139). Also opposite the station, a very smart, comfortable hostel, with disabled access. Four-bedded, twin, double and family rooms available; plus laundry, bike shed, TV rooms, sauna. Takes credit cards. No curfew; open all year. ②.

Kinlay House, Merchants Rd, Eyre Square, opposite the tourist office (*IHH*; ☎565244). New, purpose-built hostel, with double rooms available; clean, efficiently run. Price includes continental breakfast, bed linen and towel. No curfew; open all year. ②.

Mary Ryan's, 4 Beechmont Rd, Highfield Park (☎523303). Very popular small hostel a little way from the centre. Mostly small 2- or 3-bedded rooms. Take #2 bus from Eyre Square to Taylor's Hill Convent, cross the road and walk up the lane into the estate; it's to your right. Summer only. ②.

Quay Street House, 10 Quay St (*IHH*; ☎568644). A pleasant place; light and airy rooms – also 4-bedded and twin/double – well-equipped kitchen and laundry. Price includes bed linen. Will take credit-card bookings and is open all year. ②.

The Salmon Weir Hostel, St Vincent's Ave, Woodquay (☎561133 or ☎522653). Another friendly, comfortable hostel. But it's small, and their idiosyncratic reservation system can make it difficult to book ahead. Twin and doubles available; laundry, bike shed, 3am curfew. Open all year. ②.

Stella Maris Hostel, 151 Upper Salthill (tel/fax ☎521950). Although an *IHH* member, the place is pretty basic. Still, the rooms are clean enough, some have balconies with fabulous views over Galway Bay. Worth considering if you're caught without a bed for the night. Open all year. ②.

West End Hostel, 20 Upper Dominick St (☎583636). A hosteller's hostel, with busy kitchen and a sense of roughing it. Laundry service; 3am curfew; open all year. ②.

Woodquay Hostel, 23–24 Woodquay (☎562618). Efficiently run hostel, with double rooms available. Take a bus from Eyre Square. ②.

The city

Galway's centre is defined by the **River Corrib**. Issuing from the lough, it thunders under the Salmon Weir Bridge and wraps itself round the full body of the city, meeting the lively **Shop and Quay streets** areas at Wolfe Tone Bridge, where it flows into the bay. The quaint old shops and bars that give Galway its villagey appeal are being squeezed on all sides by ugly postmodern facades and bone-headed business development; the area around the bridge has to be one of the most architecturally abused spots in Ireland. Still, Galway is a robust city and somehow its charm pulls through. Over the bridge is the Claddagh, and about a mile and a half west of that is **Salthill**, Galway's commercial seaside town. The **CLADDAGH** now appears as a small area of modest housing, strangely flanked by a crusting of luxury apartments, but it's worth getting to know for some of its excellent bars and cheap eats. From any of the bridges you can wander beside the pleasant walkways of river and canals, checking out the industrial archeology, watching salmon make their way upstream, anglers fly-fishing in the centre of the city and cormorants diving for eels, while gawky herons splash through watery suburban back gardens. At the harbour, a walk out around the stone pier places the city in its impressive setting, with a level coastline stretching to the west and the eerie Burren hills washed and etched in half-tones across the bay.

Eyre Square is an almost inevitable starting point. This small park, set in the middle of a traffic interchange, is one of the places to which everyone seems to gravitate, the other being the Shop and Quay streets area. It's used as a performance space during festivals, and outdoor sessions can start up here at any time, the relaxed atmosphere lending itself to improvisation. Visually, though, the place is a mess. A sentimental statue of the writer Pádraic Ó Conaire, a seventeenth-century doorway, a couple of cannon from the Crimean War and a clutter of disused flagpoles all detract from what should form the focus of the square: Eamonn O'Donnell's splendid sculpture, whose arcs of rusted metal and gushing white fountains evoke the sails of the Galway hookers and the city's nautical history. The distinctive **town houses** of the merchant class – remnants of which are lightly littered around the city – also hark back to the prosperity of maritime Galway and its sense of civic dignity, with their finely carved doorways, windows and stone slabs bearing armorial carving. The **Browne doorway** in Eyre Square is one such monument, a bay window and doorway with the coats of arms of the Browne and Lynch families, dated 1627. Before you leave the square, it's worth calling into the **Eyre Square Centre**, as the building of this shopping mall in the late 1980s revealed impressive sections of medieval city walls, and these are now preserved within the new complex.

Just about the finest medieval town house in Ireland is **Lynch's Castle** in Shop Street (leading off from the southwest of the square), now housing the *Allied Irish Bank*. The Lynchs were Galway's most prominent family for three hundred years. A local story relates that in 1493 James Lynch Fitzstephen, mayor of the town, found his own son guilty of the jealous murder of a Spanish visitor, and that such was the popularity of the lad that no one in the town would take on the job of hangman – so the boy's father did it himself. The house, dating from the fifteenth century, has a smooth stone facade decorated with carved panels, medieval gargoyles and a lion devouring another animal. Step inside for a detailed history of the building and its heraldry. The similarly styled **Lynch's Window** is on Market Street (further down Shop Street and to the right) just outside the **Collegiate Church of St Nicholas**. The largest medieval church in Ireland, it was built in 1320 and enlarged in the next two centuries. The building – dedicated to Saint Nicholas of Myra, patron saint of sailors – is also decorated with finely chiselled carvings and gargoyles. Continuing south along Market Street, and turning off into Bowling Green Lane, you'll find a gift shop that was formerly the home of **Nora Barnacle**, wife of James Joyce (Mon–Sat; £1).

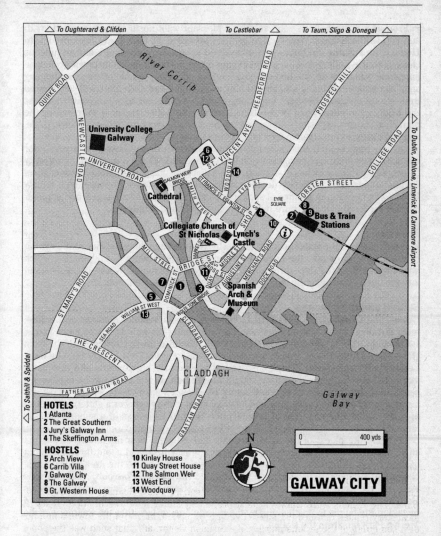

To Oughterard & Clifden △   To Castlebar △   To Taum, Sligo & Donegal △

△ To Dublin, Athlone, Limerick & Carnmore Airport

△ To Salthill & Spiddal

River Corrib

QUIRKE ROAD

NEWCASTLE ROAD

UNIVERSITY ROAD

NEWCASTLE ROAD

University College Galway

HEADFORD ROAD

PROSPECT HILL

COLLEGE ROAD

SALMON WEIR BRIDGE

SMITH STREET

ST FRANCIS ST

ST VINCENT AVE

WOODQUAY

EGLINTON ST

FORSTER STREET

Cathedral

6
12

14

EYRE ST

EYRE SQUARE

SHOP ST

4

2 **9** **Bus & Train Stations**

10

i

Collegiate Church of St Nicholas

Lynch's Castle

MILL STREET

BRIDGE ST

MARKET STREET

MIDDLE ST

AUGUSTINE ST

ST MARY'S ROAD

DOMINICK ST

7

1

3

11

Spanish Arch & Museum

MERCHANTS ROAD

DOCK ROAD

5

WILLIAM ST WEST

13

SEA ROAD

NEW TONE BRIDGE

CLADDAGH QUAY

THE CRESCENT

FATHER GRIFFIN ROAD

GRATTAN ROAD

CLADDAGH ROAD

CLADDAGH

Galway Bay

HOTELS
1 Atlanta
2 The Great Southern
3 Jury's Galway Inn
4 The Skeffington Arms

HOSTELS
5 Arch View
6 Carrib Villa
7 Galway City
8 The Galway
9 Gt. Western House

10 Kinlay House
11 Quay Street House
12 The Salmon Weir
13 West End
14 Woodquay

N

0 ——— 400 yds

GALWAY CITY

For arguably the best sense of medieval Galway make your way through the punters and the pints up to the top floor of **Busker Browne's Bar**, Cross Street (a short walk south from Nora Barnacle's house). The upper room was the meeting place of the tribes of Galway, and the building has served as a barracks and a Dominican convent.

Down by the harbour stands the **Spanish Arch**; more evocative in name than in reality, it's a sixteenth-century structure that was used to protect galleons unloading wine and rum. Behind it is a fine piece of medieval wall, and next door is the uninspiring **Galway Museum** (daily May–Sept 10am–1pm & 2.15–5.15pm; 60p), where the only things of real interest are old photographs of the Claddagh and a few examples of sixteenth- and seventeenth-century stone carving from around the city.

From the Spanish Arch you can take a pleasant walk north along a riverside path and across the Salmon Weir Bridge to the **Cathedral of Our Lady Assumed into Heaven and Saint Nicholas**. Commissioned about thirty years ago and in hideous contrast to the Collegiate College, its copper dome seeps green stains down grotesque limestone walls. Inside, the horrors continue in a senseless jumble of stone, mahogany and Connemara marble. It's so remarkably awful that it demands attention, and viewed from a long distance its sheer bulk does achieve a grandeur of sorts. Nearby, across the bridge, the clean lines of the Neoclassical courthouse are now mirrored in the municipal theatre opposite – an assured symbol of contemporary Galway's civic pride, and surprisingly conservative for a post-colonial nation.

On the road behind the cathedral is **University College Galway**, a mock-Tudor imitation of an Oxbridge college, which was opened in 1849 at a time when the majority of people in Connacht were starving. The university has the dubious distinction of having conferred an honorary degree on Ronald Reagan. More importantly, it is now UNESCO's base for an archive of spoken material in all Celtic languages, and summer courses for foreign students are held annually in July and August.

The river

If a restful trip on the water appeals, at nearby **Woodquay** you can either rent a rowing boat (May–Sept) or take the Lough Corrib river cruise (2.30pm & 4.30pm; £5), which goes five miles up the river through flat countryside punctuated by derelict castles, out into the open expanse of the lough. Both are reasonably pleasant options.

Salthill and the beaches

Beyond the Claddagh lies **SALTHILL**, Galway's seaside resort, complete with amusement arcades, discos, seasonal cafés and a fairground – as well as scores more hotels, B&Bs and a couple of **hostels** (see pp.328–29). Salthill's **tourist office** is on the front (June Mon–Sat 9am–6pm, July & Aug daily 9am–8.15pm; ☎563081 ext 48/49). The huge **Leisureland** amusement complex is used as a venue for big concerts and also has a swimming pool (summer daily 8am–10pm). **Lower Salthill** has a long promenade with a series of unspectacular but safe and sandy beaches. Even on a hot summer's day it's never so busy as to be oppressive, and its great asset is the view over a glittering expanse of water to the Burren. West of here, **Upper Salthill** is a mess of a suburb that sits around its golf course, despoiled by huge billboards and caravan parks.

Probably the nicest of the sandy beaches immediately west of Galway City is the small one at **Silver Strand**, nestling beneath a grassy headland about three miles out of the centre. Here, in a small inlet backed by a copse, is also the area's pleasantest **campsite**, signposted *Hunters* (see pp.328–29). *The Twelve Pins* pub, around a mile west of the site, is renowned for seafood. Galway's other special beach is **Ballyloughrun**, east of the city; this, too, has a campsite alongside and can be reached by taking the public footpath along by the railway line, or by either the Renmore or the Merlyn Park bus from the station.

Eating, drinking and entertainment

You'll find a good range of food on offer in Galway – from hot dogs to cajun and Thai – with some particulary upmarket Continental **restaurants** and great seafood. For daytime eating, there are plenty of cafés and bars offering good-value meals and snacks.

If the "crack" has eluded you so far on your travels, Galway is where you're going to find it. The **bars** are the social lungs of this town, and even the most abstemious travellers are going to find themselves sucked in. **Traditional music** is performed in many of them; some of it will be depressingly over-amplified, but you can hit a great session on any day of the week and at almost any time of the day during the summer months. The bars of Shop and Quay streets are especially good, as are those over the bridge around Dominick Street. You can't really go far wrong; those listed below are popular in the main with a young crowd, but there are plenty more well worth exploring. Look out for *The Edge,* Galway's free listings magazine, and the *Galway Advertiser* (out Thurs).

There are numerous **clubs** and **discos** in Galway and Salthill – the latter easy enough to walk back from, though not advisable if you are on your own. As ever, clubs change frequently; to find out what's on look out for flyers round town, and for concessions being handed out in bars. Note, too, that clubs can stop serving at 1.30am, and generally wind down at around 2am. The **gay scene** moves around, so call the information line (see "Listings", p.335) for up-to-the-minute information, and look out, too, for Liberation posters. Gay clubbing usually happens on Sundays.

Eating

The Brasserie, Middle St (☎561610). Pizza, tacos and ribs. Mon–Sat 12.30–10pm.

The Bridge Mills Restaurant, O'Brien's Bridge (☎566231). Relaxed licensed restaurant and coffee shop in beautifully restored mill, complete with working mill wheel. Home-made cakes, chowders, sandwiches and lunches (£5); evening menu £8–15. Organic produce; vegetarian dishes always available. Till 10.30pm in summer.

Busker Browne's Bar, Cross St. Original rough medieval stonework, pitched Gothic roof and floor upon floor of alcoves for comfy eating and drinking (see "Bars and music" overleaf). Bar serves salads and open sandwiches – crab, salmon and oysters. Till 7pm.

Cafe du Journal, Quay St. Squeeze through a blur of smoke and ideology for a caffeine-heads' nirvana. Numerous blends served: Italian, Spanish and cajun. Also omelettes, croissants, desserts, and newspapers to read. Till 10.30pm.

Couch Potatas, Upper Abbeygate St. Or 101 ways to serve a potato, with all manner of sauces and stuffings – and a good selection for vegetarians.

Eddie Rocket's, Eglinton St. American diner, offering hot dogs, chicken wings, shakes and burgers. Very vinyl. Handy for late-night munchies. Till 3am.

Fat Freddy's, Quay St. Great atmosphere, great pizzas; one of the cheapest places to get an evening meal.

Food For Thought, in the tourist office and also in Lower Abbeygate St. Cheap wholefood and vegetarian snacks, light meals and takeaways.

Galway Bakery Company, 7 Williamsgate St. Coffee shop and restaurant serving good-value breakfasts, lunches, dinners; highly child-friendly. Till 10pm.

The Home Plate, Mary St. Café serving tasty pitta, pasta, Thai meals, and a clutch of vegetarian options. Around £3.50–4.50. Mon–Sat till 8pm.

The Hungry Grass, Cross St. Wholesome sandwiches amidst the hustle and bustle. Good-value and highly popular café.

Java's, 17 Upper Abbeygate St. Excellent coffee shop serving a dozen blends, plus scones, salads, croissants. Daily till 4am. Also see "Bars and music" overleaf.

The Kebab House, 4 Dominick St. Takeaway offering delicious, sizeable helpings. Daily noon–3am.

Le Wine Bar, Spanish Arch (☎561114). Authentic French wine bar and charcuterie. Wines from small vineyards sold by the glass or bottle; affordable light meals from an imaginative menu – where else in Ireland could you savour sea urchin soup or smoked eels on toast? Food till 11pm daily, wine till later.

Macken's, The Cornstore, Middle St. Self-service café: an excellent spot for a multitude of breakfasts, lunches and afternoon teas.

MacSwiggans, Eyre St. Good lunchtime pub grub for around £5–6; and a lively, popular young hang-out in the evenings.

McDonagh's Seafood Bar, 22 Quay St (☎565001). A must for seafood; nip in for a thick and creamy chowder, or stay for a full meal – nobody minds what you order, you get the feeling that someone actually wants to feed you. Also excellent English-style fish and chips. Daily till 12.30am.

Nimmo's, Long Walk, Spanish Arch (☎563565). *Nimmo's* serves an imaginative Continental menu with plenty of seafood and organic produce (lunch around £5; eves from £15). Closed Mon eve.

The Round Table, 6 High St. Dishes up huge traditional lunches around midday – roasts, pies and gravy etc, in a wholly unpretentious setting. £3.50–4.50.

Sev'nth Heaven, Courthouse Lane, Quay St (☎563838). Popular restaurant/bar serving cajun, Tex-Mex, Italian and vegetarian food. Delicious 3-course lunch £5. Daily noon–midnight. Regular late-night blues, country and folk music 3-4 nights a week.

Strawberry Fields, Cross St. Gum-pink diner for the sweet-toothed – waffles and home-made ice cream; locals reckon their Salthill outfit is even better.

Bars and music

An Púcán, Forster St. Popular with boozy, tub-thumping tourists. Can be fun.

Aras na Gael, 45 Dominick St. Irish traditional music and folk theatre run and frequented by Irish-speaking enthusiasts. Admission is usually free, though during the summer it has special programmes costing £3.

The Blue Note, Sea Rd. Highly laid-back and groovy bar: acid jazz and jazz.

Busker Browne's Bar, Cross St. Frighteningly popular. Traditional Irish music three nights a week during summer; jazz on a Sun lunchtime.

Calico Jack's, Sea Rd. Another great place for traditional Irish sessions.

The Crane, Sea Rd. Busy bar with great traditional sessions.

Java's, 17 Upper Abbeygate St. Mellow jazz fusion, folk and traditional. Till 4am; £1 cover charge.

The King's Head, Shop St. Diddle and stomping, traditional music. Lunchtime comedy and theatre.

Mick Taylors, Dominick St. Traditional bar – and values. You might catch the occasional session.

Monroe's, Dominick St. Good for live bands: rock, blues, cajun, washboards – more or less anything that can pass for rhythm. Seven nights a week plus Sun lunchtime.

Naughtons, 17 Cross St. Popular with locals and visitors alike. Good traditional sessions.

The Quays, Quay St. Traditional bar; not the greatest spot to drink all night, but worth calling in for a heritage pint early evening. Usually heaving by 9.30pm. Live music.

Roísin Dubh, 9 Upper Dominick St. Lively bar with folk, traditional, cajun or world music nightly.

Sally Long's, 33 Upper Abbeygate St. Bikers' pub – rock, metal. Live bands Fri & Sat. Worth a look for Last Supper mural of rock heroes.

Clubs and discos

Baywatch, Salthill. Fairly standard laser nightclub.

Bentley's, Prospect Hill. Pub until midnight, disco afterwards; if you're in before 11pm you won't pay an admission charge. A shirts-and-drinkers' disco.

The Castle, Salthill. Dance music, house and hip hop; ravey atmosphere.

Central Park, Upper Abbeygate St. Bit of a cattle market; commercial dance and chart music.

GPO, Eglinton St. One of Galway's best. Young, trendy crowd; acid jazz, funk, ska and soul – all highly danceable – plus live bands. Look out for the Fri night **comedy club**, *The Funny Baie* – acts from 9pm; your £4 entrance sees you through to the club later.

Oasis, Salthill. Techno club.

Vagabond's, Salthill. Popular, busy but relaxed, studenty club with two dance floors. Soul, blues, reggae (Thurs); grunge (Fri); dance music and more grunge downstairs (Sat); indie bands (Sun).

Warwick Hotel, Salthill. Older studenty venue – upper 20s. No dress hang-ups. Danceable, offbeat soul.

The arts

Galway is experiencing a real growth in artistic activity, and it's at its most vibrant during **The Galway Arts Festival** (last two weeks in July; check with the tourist office for details of the Festival Box Office location). There's plenty to detain you year round too: Galway's the home of the versatile **Druid Theatre Company** (☎568617), in Chapel Lane, off Quay Street; a relatively young company, it produces six new plays a year – many of them new Irish works – and undertakes extensive tours. If you're lucky enough to be in Galway city when they're on, book a ticket in advance, as they play to packed houses.

Look out, too, for **The Punchbag Theatre Company**, based in the city down by the quays (☎565422), committed to performing new Irish plays along with the classics and hosting touring companies, live bands, readings and comedy. **An Taibhdhearc na Gaillimhe** in Middle Street (☎562024) is an Irish-language theatre that puts on an annual summer show of traditional singing, music and drama. The **Galway Arts Centre**, Nun's Island, off Mill Street, is used as a performance space for dance, theatre and music; bookings, information and visual arts exhibitions at 47 Dominick St (☎565886). It's also a good place to find out what's going on in the arts locally. Look out too for Galway's brand-new municipal theatre.

There are a couple of **commercial art galleries**, too: *The Bridge Mills Gallery*, O'Brien's Bridge, and *The Kenny Gallery*, Middle Street. One of the most exciting recent developments in Galway is the **Design Concourse Ireland** (☎566016), down a lane off Cross Street, just near *Busker Browne's*. Housed in a beautifully restored medieval town house, it's a permanent exhibition centre promoting quality manufacture and design – mainly domestic – from both the Republic and the North. There's a quiet library café where you can examine the portfolios of the designers on show. Dating from the sixteenth and seventeenth centuries, the building once housed a theatre owned by Humanity Dick (see p.351), and it is said that Wolfe Tone performed here.

Galway is now home to the **Irish Film Board**, and the city's film festival is a part of the Arts Festival; during the rest of the year cinema is pretty unappealing.

Listings

Airport Carnmore Airport (flight enquiries ☎55569); *Aer Árann* at Connemara Regional Airport, Inverin (☎593034).

Bike rental *Europa Bicycles*, Earls Island (☎563355) opposite the cathedral; £3 a day, £5 for 24 hours, £30 deposit; *Rent-a-bike-Ireland* from *Great Western Hostel*, Frenchman's Lane (☎561139; £6 a day, £30 a week; one-way rental £5 extra).

Bookshops *Charlie Byrne's*, The Cornstore, 4 Middle St (☎561766), is a good second-hand bookstore (July & Aug Sun till 7pm); *Eason's*, Shop St, is a major general bookstore with foreign newspapers; *Hawkins House*, Churchyard Lane, includes comprehensive feminist and Irish-language sections; *Needful Things,* Cathedral Buildings, Middle St (☎565882), has sci-fi, horror, fantasy and cult writers.

Buses *Bus Éireann* (enquiries ☎562000) runs 7–8 buses to Dublin daily (3hr 45min) from as little as £6 single, £8 return – check in advance for special deals. Bikes are carried subject to space – £5 extra each journey. *CityLink* (☎564163 or ☎564164 & ☎01/626 6888) also runs a Galway–Dublin service from £5 return. *Feda O'Donnell Coaches* (☎761656 or ☎075/48114) operates services to Sligo, Donegal and Letterkenny. *Nestor Travel* (☎797144 & ☎01/832 0094) runs services to Dublin and Dublin Airport from £5 return – depending on the times you travel, bikes are free.

Camping equipment *Great Outdoors*, Eglinton St (☎562869); *Radar Stores*, Mainguard St (☎568810).

Family planning clinic (☎562992).

Gay and lesbian line (☎566134); lesbians Wed 8–10pm; gay men Tues & Thurs 8–10pm.

Horse riding *Clonboo Riding School*, Clonboo Cross, Corrundulla (near Annaghdown; ☎591362).

Hospital University College Hospital, Newcastle Rd (casualty ☎563081).

Laundry *The Launderette*, Sea Rd (Mon–Sat 9am–6pm); *Old Malte Laundrette*, Old Malte Arcade, High St (Mon–Sat 8.30am–6pm), does service wash only.

Left luggage *Quay Street House Hostel*, 10 Quay St, 50p per bag, or at the station for £1.

Library Galway County Library, Hynes Building, St Augustine St.

Market For more than just fruit and vegetables, try the Sat market around St Nicholas's Church; stalls sell everything from handmade cheeses to sculptured bog oak. There's also a junk and antiques market beneath the medieval walls inside the Eyre Square Centre (Fri & Sat).

Music *Mulligan*, 5 Middle St (☎564961). Traditional, world music, reggae, country, folk and blues on tape, vinyl and CD.

Parking Free in front of the cathedral; elsewhere, buy a disc from a newsagent (20p per hr).

Police, Mill St (☎563161).

Rape Crisis Centre 15a Mary St (☎564983).

Sailing *Galway Sailing Club*, Rinville, Oranmore, five miles from the city (☎594527).

Taxi *MGM* (☎757888); taxi ranks at Eyre Square and Victoria Place.

Train Enquiries ☎561444 or ☎564222. Galway–Dublin (4 daily) from £13 single, from £19 return; Galway–Killarney (2–3 daily) £19 single.

Travel agents *USIT*, at the New Science Building on the university campus (Mon–Fri 10am–5pm; ☎524601), is the best agent for youth and student travel; *Corrib Travel*, in the centre of town in Cathedral Building, Lower Abbeygate Street (☎563879 or ☎568318), deals with *Slattery's*, *Supabus*, student flights and youth fares.

Wind-surfing At Rusheen Bay (☎557486 or ☎525295).

East Galway

East Galway cannot rival the spectacular landscapes of west Galway or County Clare, nor their romantic isolation. Nonetheless, to hurry through east Galway without seeing what the place does have to offer would be a mistake. A lot of the land here is low lying and easily cultivatable, attributes which made it attractive to earlier settlers. They've left not only a network of roads and villages, but also a wealth of historic remains, particularly medieval monastic sites. The east of the county has nothing like the strong culture of the west, but towards the south, the musical traditions of County Clare wash over the county boundaries and form an important part of the region's culture. And while the landscape is never exciting, some of it is very pleasant, notably the lakesides of **Lough Derg** at **Portumna** and the delightful southern shore of **Galway Bay**, which becomes particularly special where the heights of the Burren of County Clare become a part of the scene.

In contrast to Connemara, transport in east Galway is easy. Galway-to-Dublin **trains** call at Athenry and Ballinasloe (for train information phone Athenry ☎091/544020 or Ballinasloe ☎0905/42105), and there are *Bus Éireann* services to surrounding towns. *North Galway Club* runs a Dublin-to-Galway bus that picks up in Tuam, Athlone and Ballinasloe. **Hitching** is relatively easy, too, since the area is well served by busy main roads. There is plenty of accommodation throughout the area, in the form of B&Bs and independent and *An Óige* hostels.

Galway Bay and the south

The countryside of the south of the county, around the southern shores of Galway Bay and on towards Clare, is some of the prettiest in Galway, and was greatly loved by Yeats, Lady Gregory and others associated with the Gaelic League. The main N18 road round the bay from the city is a busy one, passing through the villages of Galway's **"oyster country"** – Oranmore, Clarinbridge and Kilcolgan (where the main road leaves the water to head south towards Ennis) – and bringing plenty of visitors, particularly during the **Oyster Festival** over the second weekend in September. The most famous of the oyster pubs are *Paddy Burke's Oyster Tavern* at **CLARINBRIDGE** and *Moran's of the Weir*, in a beautiful waterside setting at **KILCOLGAN**. Two miles south of Kilcolgan, off the Kinvarra Road, stands **Drumacoo Church**, a fine stone building of about 1200, with a Regency Gothic chapel of iron alongside, rusting and derelict.

The villages of Doorus, Aughinish and Kinvarra, on the south shore of Galway Bay, are covered in the section on the Burren in County Clare (see pp.320–21) as you're more likely to be visiting them from that direction.

Sticking with the Ennis Road, you'll find **Coole Park** (mid-June to end Aug daily 9.30am–6.30pm; mid-April to mid-June & Sept Tues–Sun 10am–5pm; £2, Heritage

Card), the old demesne of the house of Lady Gregory, much visited by Yeats, and the subject of some of his most famous poetry, two miles to the north of Gort. All that remains of the house itself are some crumbling walls and a stable yard, but the grounds and the lake are now a particularly beautiful forest park. Sadly, its **autograph tree**, bearing the graffiti of George Bernard Shaw, Sean O'Casey, Augustus John and others, has been incarcerated in railings and barbed wire to stop the less famous getting in on the act. A pleasant tearoom has been opened by the stables. A mile and a half northeast of Coole, **Thoor Ballylee** (Easter–Sept daily 10am–6pm; £2.50) is signposted off the N18. This is a sixteenth-century tower house which Yeats bought in 1916, renovated and made his home off and on over the next ten years. A short film tells the story of his life, rare and first editions are on show and readings of his verse are relayed into the spartan rooms of the tower – all best enjoyed if you can avoid clashing with a bus party. Alongside is a very cosy tearoom.

Four miles southwest of Gort, just off the Corofin Road, are the remains of **Kilmacduagh**, a monastic settlement founded by Saint Colman Mac Duagh around 632. The sheer quantity of buildings – dating from the eleventh to the thirteenth centuries – is more impressive than any particular architectural detail: a cathedral, four churches, the Glebe House and a round tower 115ft high, all on one site. And the setting, against the shimmering, distant Burren slopes, lends something magical to the ancient grey stone.

Portumna

PORTUMNA, on the north shore of Lough Derg, is a traditional market town and Shannon crossing point, happy to be cashing in on the upmarket tourism that drifts its way on the lough cruisers, yet still retaining a friendly and unpretentious character. Close to the shore is the freely accessible ruin of **Portumna Priory**, for the most part a fifteenth-century Dominican building, though its delicately arched cloisters are built around the remains of a much earlier Cistercian foundation. Nearby **Portumna Castle** (Mon–Sat 9.30am–6.30pm; £1), a fine, early seventeenth-century mansion with Jacobean gables (something of a rarity in Ireland), is currently undergoing renovation. Nobody minds if you take a look via the fields to the rear. The castle's estate is a wildlife sanctuary with a large herd of fallow deer.

There's a **tourist office** here during the summer months and several good **B&Bs** in the centre: try Mrs Ryan's *Auvergne Lodge*, Dominick Street (☎0509/41138; ④), or Mrs Finlay's *Cnoc Rua*, St Brendan's Road (☎0509/41197; ③). It's easy **camping** country, too – just ask a farmer – and in the summer there are **public showers** down by the lough jetty (July and Aug only). Swimming is relatively safe on the lake, but not on the river. For **bike rental** and repairs, *Tony Cunningham's* on Dominick Street (☎0509/41070; £5 per day) is the place to go. The *Bank of Ireland* is on Clonfert Avenue, and the post office is on Abbey Street. There's also a **laundry** – *Frank's* in Brendan Street.

There are two very friendly places to **eat**, both in the main street: *Peter's Restaurant*, a fast-food place that will rustle up whatever you fancy, and *Clonwyn House*, which does traditional cooked meals any day any time. Although small, Portumna has an astounding 21 **pubs**, and there's no shortage of ballad sessions. The *Corner House* offers regular nights hosted by owner John Horan, and you can catch a traditional *ceili* at *Clonwyn House* on Sunday nights, when the old folk come in to do their set dancing.

Clonfert Cathedral

About four miles north is **Clonfert Cathedral**, on the site where a Benedictine monastery was founded around 560 by Saint Brendan. In subsequent centuries the monastery was pillaged, but towards the end of the twelfth century the church was rebuilt and dedicated to Saint Brendan. There's a superb Romanesque doorway made up of six arches, each a perfect semicircle and richly carved with heavily stylized plants and animals. The capitals are Romanesque cubes carved with crazy, bold animal heads. The Bishop's Palace beyond the cathedral – now derelict as a result of an accidental fire – was the home of Sir Oswald Mosley after his release from prison in 1949.

East to Ballinasloe

Chances are you'll see **ATHENRY**, if at all, from a train. The place is more renowned for the song *The Fields of Athenry* – which you're unlikely to have got this far without hearing – than as a tourist centre. Still, if you've time to kill between connections, it's worth nipping out of the station to take a look at its remains of Anglo-Norman power – so much a feature of east Galway and so conspicuously absent further west. The town was founded by the de Berminghams, and large portions of its Norman town walls have survived, along with a tower gate, five flanking towers and a market cross. On the edge of town stands a bold thirteenth-century **castle**, again built by the de Berminghams; its stout, three-storey keep is still impressively intact, though the castle is closed to the public. If you're looking for **B&B**, try *Miss Gardener's*, Old Church Street (☎091/544464; ③), or *The Dunclarin Arms* (☎091/544035; ③).

Loughrea
LOUGHREA, on the main road to Ballinasloe, is like Portumna (see p.337) in that it's a lakeside market town. But it's much smaller, and tiny Lough Rea can't compare with the beauty of Lough Derg for a setting. In the thirteenth century, Richard de Burgo founded a **Carmelite monastery** here, and it still stands in an excellent state of preservation. The town also has a late nineteenth-century **cathedral**, whose interior demonstrates the development of the modern Dublin School of Stained Glass – an acquired taste. Much earlier religious art is on display next door in the **Loughrea Museum** (by appointment only; ☎091/541212). This small museum includes episcopal vestments and carved crucifixes from the seventeenth century, beautifully simple silver and gold chalices from as early as 1500, penal crosses and a few rare wood carvings from the twelfth and thirteenth centuries. The Kilcorban *Virgin and Child* is the earliest of only three such carvings that have been found in Ireland.

In a field two miles to the north of Loughrea, near Bullaun, stands the **Turoe Stone**. A superb, rounded pillar-stone, this is decorated with the bold swirls of Celtic La Tène art, a style found more typically in Brittany. The finest of its kind in Ireland, it dates from the third or second century BC and was probably a phallic fertility stone, used in pagan rituals. For **B&B** in Loughrea, try Mrs Pauline Burke's *Four Seasons*, Athenry Road (☎091/541414; ③).

Aughrim and Kilconnell Friary
Tiny **AUGHRIM**, on the road just short of Ballinasloe, makes a good base from which to explore some of the ecclesiastical remains of the area. In 1691, Aughrim was the scene of a key battle of the Williamite War in which the Irish and French forces were defeated; a small **museum** in the local primary school has finds connected with the battle. *Hynes* **hostel** (☎0905/73734; ①) is attached to the local pub, which has music at weekends during the summer. The hostel does camping and has 21 beds – it's worth ringing ahead in July and August if you want to sleep inside; during Ballinasloe's horse fair (see opposite), it's booked up way in advance.

Four miles to the northwest are the very beautiful remains of **Kilconnell Friary**, a Franciscan foundation built near the site of the sixth-century church of St Conall, which gives the place its name. The friary held out successfully against Cromwellian attack in 1651. The ruins are extensive, with additions to the early fourteenth-century building showing that there was increased monastic activity here in the later Middle

Ages. There's a very pretty arcaded cloister, and in the north wall of the nave are two splendid canopied wall-tombs.

Ballinasloe

Galway's eastern boundary is one of water: Lough Derg, the Shannon and the River Suck. The tourist-geared villages are again catering mainly for the fishing fraternity, but there is enough of historic interest to warrant leisurely exploration. **BALLINASLOE** is the main town in east Galway. Important as a crossing point of the River Suck since 1124 when Turlough O'Conor, King of Connacht, built a castle here, the remains that can be seen today date mainly from the fourteenth century. You're only really likely to be here if you've come for the famous **horse fair**, which starts on the first weekend in October and lasts for eight days. The largest of the ancient fairs left in the country, drawing horse dealers from all over Ireland and England, it gives a fascinating glimpse of a slowly dying way of life. The bartering is very much a game, though a serious one. Generally, both parties know the value of the beast in question but enjoy the bartering ritual anyway, with its possibilities of outdoing an opponent. The logic seems to be that if you're not up to the bartering, you don't deserve the right price for the animal. This system of exchange is threatened by EU regulations which insist that animals be sold by weight, a sorry demise for an ancient tradition.

If you intend to visit the fair, you'll have to book accommodation well in advance. The **tourist office** (July–Aug Mon–Sat 10am–6pm; ☎0905/42131) can give more information on accommodation around the region and make bookings. The main **hotel** in town is *Hayden's* in Dunlo Street (☎0905/42347; ⑤); for **B&B** try Mrs Molloy's *Ashling*, Old Mount Pleasant Avenue (☎0905/42457; ③), Mrs Lynagh's *Oban*, Athlone Road (☎0905/42365; ③) or Mrs Burton's *Woodlands* (☎0905/43123; ③), on Dublin Road half a mile out. **Bike rental** is available from *P. Clarke & Sons*, Dunlo Street (☎0905/42417; £1 per day).

The countryside to the south of Ballinasloe makes a dull setting for a fine piece of ecclesiastical architecture, well worth taking in if you're staying in the area or heading south towards Portumna and Lough Derg. From the road five miles south of town, **Clontuskert Abbey** looks impressive in this open countryside, like some iron-grey battleship adrift on the flat and muddy approaches to the Suck. The church is the only sizeable remnant of the abbey complex, with a perpendicular west door of 1471, carved with figures of the saints.

The east shore of Lough Corrib

The east shore of Lough Corrib provides a gentle route between County Mayo and Galway city, less dramatic than the Connemara roads. The lake shore and the many rivers are popular with fishermen (for trout and salmon in summer, pike in winter), and visitors with no taste for field sports have a number of medieval ruins to admire.

Two miles north of Headford, virtually on the border of County Mayo, is **Ross Errilly** (or "Ross Abbey"), the biggest and best-preserved Franciscan abbey in Ireland. It was founded in the mid-fourteenth century, but the bulk of the buildings belong to the fifteenth – the Franciscan Order's greatest period of expansion. The church buildings themselves are impressive, with a battlemented slender tower (typical of Franciscan abbeys) and well-preserved windows, and there's a wonderful tiny cloister, but it's the adjacent domestic buildings and the picture they give of the everyday life of the order that are perhaps the most interesting. Stand in the cloister with your back to the church and you'll see the refectory ahead and to the right, with the reader's window-side desk up in the far northeast corner. Straight ahead is a second cloister (this one without arcading) and behind that the bakehouse. To the northwest of this second courtyard lies the kitchen, where you can see a water-tank used for holding fish and an oven which reaches into the little mill-room to the rear.

Five miles south of Headford, a detour off the main road leads you right down to the lough shore and the ruined Franciscan friary of **Annaghdown** – far less impressive than Ross Errilly – and a nearby Norman castle. It was at this site, after all his voyaging and preaching, that Saint Brendan finally died, nursed by his sister, who was head of Annaghdown nunnery. The road loops back to rejoin the main Galway Road. Seventeenth-century *Gregg Castle* at Corandulla (☎091/591434; ⑤) is an unusual B&B: a place of beautiful faded splendour. Everything is geared towards relaxation (with breakfast till noon) and conviviality: the owners are garrulous traditional musicians and enjoy evenings with guests around the log fire in the Great Hall. Self-catering is also available.

Tuam and around

Northeast County Galway is served chiefly by the small market town of **TUAM**. There's little here to detain you, but should you wish to sniff out the scant remnants of the town's former importance, have a look inside the Church of Ireland **cathedral** on Galway Road. It's primarily a nineteenth-century building, but survivals from the twelfth-century chancel include a magnificent Romanesque arch, showing strong signs of Scandinavian influence, and the accompanying east window. The shaft of an ornamented high cross is set in the wall near the west door. It's a great shame that so little remains of medieval Tuam; a monastery was founded here in the sixth century by Saint Iarlath, a disciple of Saint Enda of Inishmore, and in the medieval period Tuam became not only an archiepiscopal seat but also the power centre of the O'Conors of Connacht. The high cross in the town square dates from the twelfth century: it's highly decorated but actually a bit of a patchwork, as the head and the shaft don't really belong together. The **tourist office** is in the Mill Museum (July–Aug Mon–Sat 10am–6pm; ☎093/24463) and can book **accommodation**. Should you need to stop over, the *Imperial Hotel* (☎093/24188; ④), in the central square, offers rooms and food. There's no shortage of **B&Bs**: try Mrs Clarke, *Chessington House*, Ballygaddy Road (☎093/24584; ③), or Mrs O'Connor's *Kilmore House*, Galway Road, Kilmore (☎093/28118; ③), half a mile out of town.

Dunmore and Knockmoy abbeys

Yet more medieval ruins are dotted roundabout: if you're heading through Dunmore in the northeast of the county, there's **Dunmore Abbey**, an Augustinian priory of 1425, and just to the west of the town, a Norman castle built by the de Berminghams. Alternatively, seven miles south of Tuam off the N63 Galway–Roscommon road, **Knockmoy Abbey** is a Cistercian foundation of 1190 – though the central tower is probably a fifteenth-century addition. The most remarkable feature of the abbey is on the north wall of the chancel, where you'll see one of Ireland's few surviving medieval frescoes. Extremely faint (only the black outlines retain their original colour), it depicts the legend of the Three Dead Kings and the Three Live Kings. Under the dead kings an inscription reads "We have been as you are, you shall be as we are"; the live kings are out hawking. Underneath this is a picture of Christ holding his hand up in blessing and a barely visible angel with scales.

The Aran Islands

The **Aran Islands** – **Inishmore**, **Inishmaan** and **Inisheer** – lying about thirty miles out across the mouth of Galway Bay, have exerted a fascination over visitors for over a hundred years. Their geology creates one of the most distinctive landscapes in Ireland, the limestone pavement giving the islands a stark character akin to the Burren of

TRANSPORT TO THE ISLANDS

Several **ferry companies** operate between Galway and the Aran Islands, but they are rivals and won't let you mix your journeys between services on one ticket; there are also services from Doolin, County Clare (see p.318). A return to any of the islands costs in the region of £12–20, and it's usually possible to buy tickets on the boat. With any of these ferry services it's a good idea to check on the times of return journeys with the skipper, especially if you are going to Inishmaan or Inisheer as services can be unreliable – during winter, you're at the mercy of the weather, and there's a chance you'll get cut off from the mainland. If you are planning on travelling between the islands check the schedule closely as doing so can be more complicated and time consuming than you might at first imagine. If you intend to drive to **Rossaveal** (signposted *Ros an Mhil*) and pick up a ferry from there, bear in mind you will be charged £2–3 per day, £10–15 per week respectively to park a car or van.

Island Ferries, Victoria Place, Eyre Square, Galway (or *Aran Island Ferries*; ☎091/561767 or ☎572273 eves), behind the *Allied Irish Bank*, serve the islands all year round from Rossaveal, with bus connections from Galway city. A return, including the bus from Galway to Inishmore, costs £15; to Inisheer or Inishmaan £18; students and hostellers staying at *Mainistir House Hostel* on Inishmore £13, family ticket £30 from Rossaveal (plus the bus fare from Galway), bikes carried free. B&B booked free of charge. Round trips taking in all three islands negotiable.

Aran Ferries (☎091/568903) are based at the Galway tourist office. Their service direct from Galway city (late May to early Oct; £15 return) takes just 90 minutes. Departures from Rossaveal for Inishmore are at 10.30am, 1.30pm and 6pm (operates April–Sept, £12 return, £6 single); a connecting bus leaves the tourist office an hour before the boat departs (bus journey costs £3 each way). Reductions of £2 are available for students and interailers. **Package deals** from Galway are available and well worth considering: return ferry and hostel £12–15 (at *Aran Islands Hostel* or *Dún Aengus Hostel* on Inishmore; see p.343).

O'Brien Shipping, tourist office, Galway (☎091/567283 or ☎567676), operate from County Clare.

Galway to Inishmore (1 daily year round), to Inishmaan and Inisheer (4 days weekly). Fare £16 return; to all three islands by arrangement. Student reductions of £2–4; bikes free.

Doolin Ferry Co (☎065/74455, evenings ☎065/74189) sail mid-April to end Sept from Doolin (County Clare) to Inisheer (1–6 daily); and to Inishmore (2 daily). They will also arrange a Doolin–Aran–Galway ticket £20. Return prices are Doolin–Inisheer £15, Doolin–Inishmore £20, Doolin–Inishmaan £18 (phone confirmation is strongly advised). A trip to all three islands, returning to Doolin, is £20. Bikes £2 return.

Aer Árann (☎091/593034) are based at a new airstrip at Inverin, west beyond Spiddal. They offer **flights** to all three of the islands: at least three flights daily throughout the year and during the summer months a non-stop shuttle service seven days a week. A connecting bus from Galway city meets all flights. The return fare is £35, students £29, bookable at the *Aer Árann* desk in the tourist office, where it is also worth asking about **fly/sail** deals. It is not possible to take a bicycle on the plane. Island airport numbers are: Inishmore ☎099/61109 or ☎61131; Inishmaan ☎099/73020; Inisheer ☎099/75039.

This spectacular setting contains a wealth of pre-Christian and early Christian remains and some of the finest archeological sites in Europe. And it's not only works in stone that have survived out here: the islands are Irish-speaking, and up until the early part of this century a primitive way of life persisted, a result of the isolation enforced by the Atlantic.

The most detailed **map** of the islands is produced by Tim Robinson of Roundstone, available on Inishmore and at bookshops and tourist offices in the Galway and Clare area. In fact the Aran Islands are quite easy to explore and the map isn't essential for finding the major sites. It is, however, of great value to those interested in detailed archeology and in Irish placenames. Although it's possible to do a **day-trip** from Galway to Inishmore, and from Doolin (County Clare) to Inisheer, you really need two full days to see the main sites of Inishmore alone, and an overnight stay on Inisheer gives a priceless dimension to a visit. On Inishmaan, staying the night is the only way to experience its bewitching silence – and to be guaranteed of a return journey. For more detailed information on transport to the islands see below.

Some history

The Aran Islands abound with evidence of their **early inhabitants**: the earliest ring forts possibly date from the Iron Age (c.400 BC–500 AD), though recent research suggests that some of the larger structures may be even earlier, perhaps Late Bronze Age (c.700 BC). The next group of people to figure are the **Christians**, who came here to study at the foundation of Saint Enda in the fifth century and went on to found Iona, Clonmacnoise and Kilmacduagh. However, the earliest surviving ecclesiastical remains date from the eighth century.

As Galway's trade grew, so the strategic importance of the islands increased, and in **medieval** times control of them was disputed between the O'Flaherties of Connacht and the O'Briens of Munster, the latter generally maintaining the upper hand. In 1565, Queen Elizabeth resolved the dispute by granting the islands to an Englishman on condition he kept soldiers there to guarantee the Crown's interests. In the mid-seventeenth century the islands lost their political usefulness; the Cromwellian soldiers garrisoned there simply transferred to the new regime after the Restoration and became absorbed into the islands' traditional way of life.

After the decline of English interest and influence, the islands fell into poverty, aggravated in the nineteenth century by rack-renting. That rents should be levied on this barren rock suggests a cruel avarice, and not surprisingly, Aranmen were active in the **Land League** agitations: acts of defiance included walking the landlord's cattle blindfolded over the Dún Aengus cliff edge. Despite this link with the general political movement on the mainland and the islands' use as a refuge for Nationalists during the War of Independence, it is their isolation that has allowed the continuation of a unique, ancient culture. Ironically, this very isolation has been a source of interest for outsiders in the twentieth century.

THE GAELIC REVIVAL

With the burgeoning fascination for all things Gaelic from the 1890s onwards, the Aran Islands, along with the Blaskets, became the subject of great sociological and linguistic enquiry, the most famous of their literary visitors being J.M. Synge. His writings brought the islands to the attention of other intellectuals involved in the **Gaelic Revival**, and the notion of a surviving community of pure Gaels provided fuel for the Nationalist movement. Ironically, this notion may have been misconceived. The distinct physical type found on Aran – the dark skin, large brow and Roman nose – is, some argue, the legacy of the Cromwellian soldiers who were left on the islands.

In 1934 Robert Flaherty made his classic documentary *Man of Aran*, which recorded the ancient and disappearing culture he found here. (The film can be seen during the summer in Halla Rónáin, Kilronan.) While the **folklore and traditions** recorded in the film have obviously declined, *currachs* – light wood-framed boats covered formerly with hide, now with tar-coated canvas – are still used for fishing and for getting ashore on the smaller islands when the ferry can't pull in, and you may even witness, as in the film, a man fishing with a simple line off the edge of a 200ft cliff. Fishing and farming are still very much a way of life on Inishmaan, while tourism is the major earner on Inishmore and Inisheer. This means that, though their purpose will change, knowledge of these customs will not vanish, and tourism may even help ensure the language survives, as Irish provides the islanders with a curtain of privacy against the visitors.

Inishmore (Inis Mór)

Although there's some truth behind the attitude that does down **Inishmore** as the most tourist orientated and least "authentic" of the Aran Islands, its wealth of dramatic ancient sites overrides such considerations. Increased numbers of minibuses and bicycles can make the main road west along the island pretty hectic in high season, and it's worth taking the low road along the north shore if you want to escape the crowds.

It's a long strip of an island, a great tilted plateau of limestone, with a scattering of **villages** along the sheltered northerly coast. The land slants up to the southern edge, where tremendous **cliffs** rip along the entire length of the island. Walking anywhere on this high southern side, you can see the geological affinity with the Burren of County Clare, and visualize the time when these islands were part of a barrier enclosing what is now Galway Bay. As far as the eye can see is a tremendous patterning of stone, some of it the bare formation of the land (the pavementing of grey rock split in bold parallel grooves), some the form of dry-stone walls that might be contemporary, or might be pre-Christian. The textures blur so that it's impossible to make sense of planes and distances, the only certainties being the stark outline of the cliffs' edges and the constant pounding of the waves below. Across the water in contrast are the Connemara mountains, coloured pink and golden and slatey blue in the evening sun. Up the bay is Galway, now an insignificant speck, and around to the southeast, appearing as just a silvery ridge, are the Cliffs of Moher.

Getting around and accommodation

The best way to **get about** Inishmore is by a combination of cycling and walking. *Aran Bicycle Hire* is beside the pier in Kilronan, where the ferry docks (£4–5 per day, £20 per week); *Costello's Bike Hire* (☎099/61241; May–Oct; £4 per day) is opposite the *American Bar* further up the lane; and *Mullin & Burke* is situated by the *Aran Islands Hostel*. **Pony buggies** will take you on a round tour for about £20 for a group of four, and **minibuses** ply the length of the island constantly. Expect to pay around £5. If you have limited time you can take the public minibus up the island through the villages that stretch over seven miles to the west – Mainistir, Eochaill, Kilmurvey, Eoghannacht and Bún Gabhla – and walk back from any point. The bus leaves Kilronan grocery shop, up behind the hostel, every two hours between 9am and 5pm (£2 single). The village of Killeany, a mile and a half to the south of Kilronan, has to be either walked or cycled to.

If you're looking for **places to stay** there are three **hostels** on Inishmore. *Aran Islands Hostel*, Kilronan (April–Oct; ☎099/61255; ①), is very near the pier, handy if you want to spend the night in the pub below, noisy if you don't. *Dún Aengus Hostel* (①) is out at Kilmurvey – both of these can *only* be used if you have travelled on an *Aran Ferries* boat (bookable through the tourist office in Galway; combined ferry plus one hostel night £12–15; extra nights £5). *Mainistir House Hostel* at Mainistir (☎099/61169; ②) has deals with *Island Ferries* (see p.341), but will accommodate you however you have arrived. The nightly rate includes bed linen and an "alternative" continental breakfast, and there are laundry facilities. The sitting and dining areas are a cut above average hostel standards, it's all non-smoking, and there is good, vaguely vegetarian food available (also open to non-resident bookings). Check the time of the evening meal if you want to be sure to eat here.

B&Bs can be booked through the **tourist office** (June to mid-Sept daily 10am–6pm), a couple of minutes' walk from the pier in Kilronan, although there will be a small service charge. Try Mrs Gill, *Ard Éinne*, Killeany (☎099/61126; ③), and *St*

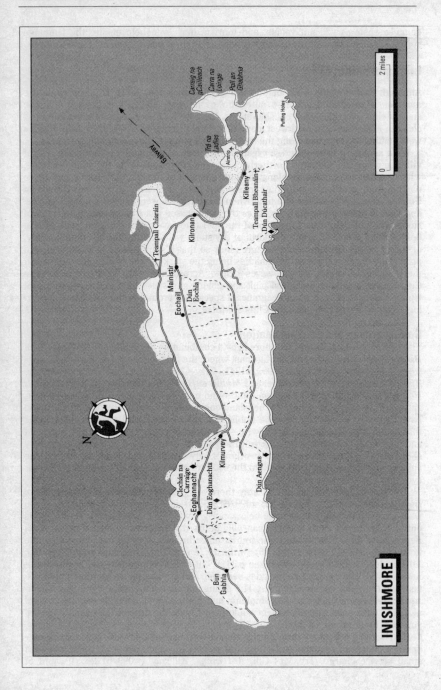

INISHMORE

2 miles

Carraig na gCailleach
Carra na Loinge
Poll an Ghabhna

Puffing Holes

Trá na Ladies
Kilronan
Killeany
Teampall Bheanáin
Dún Dúcathair

Galway

Teampall Chiaráin

Mainistir
Eochaill
Dún Eochla

Kilmurvey
Clochán na Carraige
Eoghannacht
Dún Eoghanachta
Dún Aengus

Bun Gabhla

Brendans House, Kilronan (☎099/61149; ③). *Dormer House*, Kilronan (☎099/61125; ④), is a good central option, and in the summer there are others. There is a basic **campsite** (no showers) an easy walk from Kilronan: take the lane heading west out of the village and turn right in front of *Joe Watty's* pub. Alternatively, it's just about possible to pitch a tent down by the idyllic beach at Kilmurvey, a lovely sweep of white sand looking out over to the Connemara mountain range; anywhere else is either bare rock or a treasured piece of cultivatable land. Should you stumble across a likely spot, finding the owner and asking permission is essential.

The island's **supermarket** houses a small off-licence and newsagents; it is in the lane behind *Aran Islands Hostel*, and there's a second shop by *Joe Watty's* bar. Kilronan has a **post office**, with a public phone (and cardphone) outside, and the *Bank of Ireland* opens here Wednesdays (10.15am–12.30pm & 1.30–3pm), plus additional Thursdays in July and August. You can also **change money** at the tourist office, the post office and *Carraig Donn*, a craft shop selling hand-knitted Aran sweaters by the pier at Kilronan (April–Oct daily) – this last will also advance cash on credit cards. Should the weather break, *Snámara Crafts* has a good selection of Irish books.

The island

Inishmore's villages are strung along the main road that runs the length of the northern shore, the hub of activity being **KILRONAN**, where the ferry lands. There are some great sandy **beaches**: the one at **KILMURVEY** (four miles west of Kilronan) is safe and sheltered, with fabulous views of the Connemara mountains, or you could take the main road to its eastern extreme and then walk north to get to the safe beaches from Carraig na gCailleach, through Carra na Loinge, down to Poll an Ghabhna. Tucked closer to **KILLEANY**, three quarters of a mile to the south, is Cockle Strand, safe for swimming; little over a mile further on, near the airstrip, is Tra na Ladies, which looks nice but where you can get caught by tides or sinking sand. You can **walk** just about anywhere so long as it doesn't look like someone's garden, but be careful when walking on the south of the island in poor visibility, as the cliffs are sheer and sudden.

DÚN AENGUS AND THE FORTS

The most spectacular of Aran's prehistoric sites is Inishmore's fort of **Dún Aengus** (signposted from Kilmurvey, three-quarters of a mile), a massive semicircular ring fort of three concentric enclosures lodged on the edge of cliffs that plunge 300ft into the Atlantic. The inner citadel is a 20ft-high, 18ft-wide solid construction of precise blocks of grey stone, their symmetry echoing the almost geometric regularity of the land's limestone pavementing and the bands of rock that form the cliffs. Standing on the ramparts you can see clearly the *chevaux-de-frise* outside the middle wall, a field bristling with lurching rocks like jagged teeth, designed to slow down any attack.

The place is tremendously evocative, and it's easy to understand how superstitions have survived on the islands long after their disappearance on the mainland. Visible west of the cliffs of Inishmore under certain meteorological conditions is the outline of what looks like a mountainous island. This is a mirage, a mythical island called *Hy Brasil* that features in ancient Aran stories as the island of the blessed, visited by saints and heroes. Until the sixteenth century *Hy Brasil* was actually marked on maps.

Dún Eoghanachta is a huge drum of a fort, a perfect circle of stone settled in a lonely field with the Connemara mountains as a scenic backdrop. Its walls are 16ft thick, and inner steps give access to the parapets. Inside are the foundations of the ancient drystone huts known as *clocháns*. The stronghold is accessible by tiny lanes from Dún Aengus if you've a detailed map; otherwise retrace your steps to Kilmurvey and follow the road west for just over a mile, where it's (poorly) signposted off to the left.

Dún Dúcathair (the Black Fort) is especially worth visiting for its dramatic location. It's a promontory fort, and what remains is a massive stone wall straddling an ever-shrinking headland precariously placed between cliffs. The eastern gateway fell into the sea early in the last century, leaving the entrance a perilous twelve inches from the sheer drop. Inside are the curved remains of four *clocháns*. It's about a two-mile walk from Kilronan – head south out of the village for three-quarters of a mile, take a turning to the right (signposted to "Cliff House") and follow the lane to the cliffs. If on a bike be warned: the lane becomes extremely rocky, making cycling impossible. Once at the cliff edge you can see the fort on the second promontory to your left.

The **dating** of these forts is tricky: Dún Aengus and Dún Dúcathair have long been considered to date from the first century BC, though recent excavations of the middle enclosure have found pottery fragments from the Late Bronze Age, suggesting a much earlier date of 700 BC. Dún Eoghanachta and **Dún Eochla** (just south off the road to the west of Mainistir) could have been constructed at any time between the first and seventh centuries AD, or possibly earlier. The massive buttresses of Dún Eochla are nineteenth-century additions, but the forts have generally been kept in exceptional condition.

CHURCH SITES AND CLOCHÁNS

From the fifth century onwards, the Aran Islands were a centre of monastic learning, the most important of the eremitical settlements being that of Saint Enda (Eanna). At the **seven churches**, just east of **EOGHANNACHT**, there are ancient slabs commemorating seven Romans who died here, testifying to the far-reaching influence of Aran's monastic teaching. The site is in fact that of two churches and several domestic buildings, dating from the eighth to the thirteenth centuries. Here **Saint Brendan's grave** is adorned by an early cross with interlaced patterns and, on the west side, part of a Crucifixion carving. There are also parts of three high crosses, possibly eleventh century, and in the southeast corner of the graveyard, alongside the slabs of the Romans, lie several ninth-century slabs incised with crosses and inscriptions.

The most interesting of the ecclesiastical sites on Inishmore, however, is **Teampall Chiaráin**. Take the low road from **MAINISTIR** (opposite *Joe Watty's* pub), follow the lane parallel to the shoreline, and you'll come to it, a simple twelfth-century church on an old monastic site. Alongside is **Saint Kieran's Well**, a long U-shaped spring backed by huge blocks of plant-covered stone. It's very pagan-looking – such wells often held sacred significance in pre-Christian times, and were adopted and renamed with the arrival of Christianity. Similarly, some of the tall stones that stand around the site look pre-Christian, even though they have crosses inscribed on them. The one by the east gable has a hole in it that may have held part of a sundial, and nowadays people sometimes pass handkerchiefs through it for luck.

Teampall Bheanáin, on the hill behind Killeany, is a pre-Romanesque oratory of around the sixth or seventh century, dedicated to Saint Benen. It's distinguished by its very steep gable ends and by its unusual north–south orientation. In all probability, it used to form part of the great early monastic site that existed at Killeany.

The finest of Aran's *clocháns* is **Clochán na Carraige**, just north of Kilmurvey. This 19ft-long dry-stone hut has a corbelled roof whose arrangement is probably an early Christian design. There are fifty lesser examples of such huts on Inishmore.

Eating, drinking and entertainment

Not surprisingly, **seafood** is the great speciality on the island. *Dún Aonghasa* in Kilronan (Easter–Oct; ☎099/61104) has probably the most varied menu and is good value for anything from light snacks up to full meals. *Dormer House* in Kilronan has an extensive and reasonable menu, with seafood and steak a speciality. And there are a couple of self-service places in Kilronan: *An tSean chéibh* (lunch from £5, dinner from

£7) and *Aran Fisherman* (lunches from £4.50). Kilronan also has a fast-food restaurant (summer daily until 10pm, later if there is a *ceili* on). *Joe Watty's* bar is good for soups and stews (summer until 8pm), and *Pota Stair* in the Heritage Centre serves home-made soups and cakes. Non-residents are welcome for evening meals, too, at *Mainistir House Hostel* (£7, see p.343).

You can punctuate your cycling or walking with lunch, tea or snacks at *Man of Aran Cottages* in Kilmurvey, used as a set in the eponymous film (June–Sept daily 11.30am–7.45pm). The film, made in 1934, is shown during the summer in Halla Rónáin, Kilronan (3pm, 5.30pm & 8pm; £2.50). *Ionad Árann* (April–Oct daily 10am–7pm; £2) offers a rather more sober introduction to the island's history, geography and geology.

The **pub** beneath the hostel in Kilronan is convivial enough, but it's still a good idea to wander away from here to sample some of the island's other bars: *The American Bar*, *Joe Watty's* further west, *John Dirrane's* at the top of the road as it slopes down to the beach at Kilmurvey, or *Tigh Fitz* bar in Killeany. In addition to this there are **ceilis** in Kilronan parish hall (June–Sept Fri, Sat & Sun; winter Sat; £3) and a **disco** on Thursday nights.

Inishmaan (Inis Meáin)

Coming from Inishmore you are immediately struck by how much greener **Inishmaan** is. Brambles and ferns shoot from walls, and bindweed clings to the limestone terraces. Here the stone walls are a warm brown and seem almost to glow with yellow moss. They're remarkably high – up to six feet – and form a stone maze that chequers off tiny fields of lush grass and clover. Yet despite this verdancy, the island still feels dour and desolate. Farming here is at subsistence level; farm buildings and cottages are grubby and dull, and soggy thatches sag over low doorways. The only sudden splashes of colour are from tiny cultivated gardens – the bright reds, pinks and oranges of geraniums, gladioli and carnations.

The island is shaped something like an oyster shell. It rises in clear levels from the soft dunes of the north, through stages of flat naked rock, up to minuscule green pastures, then again up a craggy band of limestone (along which sit the main villages of the island), eventually levelling out on higher ground to meet the crinkled blowhole-pitted southerly edge. Inishmaan is the least visited, least touched by tourism of the three islands, though it has had visitors since the turn of the century. J.M. Synge stayed here for four summers from 1898, recording the life and language of the people. His play *Riders to the Sea* – which influenced Lorca's *Blood Wedding* – is set here, and his book *The Aran Islands* provides a fascinating insight into the way of life he found. **Synge's Chair**, a sheltered place on the westerly cliffs overlooking St Gregory's Sound, was his favourite contemplative spot. Traces of the **culture** he discovered remain. Some of the women still wear traditional brightly coloured shawls; Irish is the main language, though English is understood; and the islanders get on with what they've always done: farming and fishing. There's no hostility to visitors, but tourism isn't the islanders' concern. If you want to be impressed or entertained, you'll have to look elsewhere.

Forts and churches

One of the most impressive of the Aran forts is Inishmaan's **Dún Conchúir**, loosely dated between the first and seventh centuries AD. Its massive oval wall is almost intact and commands great views of the island, being built on the side of a limestone valley. (In myth, Conchúir was the brother of Aengus of the Firbolg.) To the east, the smaller **Dún Fearbhaí** stands above the village of Baile an Mhothair and looks out over the little eighth-century **Cill Cheannannach** by the shore. In this context, the interior of the island's modern church, just below Dún Conchúir, comes as a shock: garish, stylized windows of virulent turquoise and purple from the workshop of Harry Clarke. As you step outside, the old magic reasserts itself, with the island's ancient graves and wells.

Practicalities

Inishmaan's indifference to tourism means that amenities for visitors are minimal. The three **shops** in the main street of the central village have limited provisions: tinned foods, bread and milk. The **pub** is central, too, serving snacks throughout the day during July and August (till 7.30pm); lunches (£4) and evening meals (around £15) are available at *An Dún*, a seasonal café and restaurant just below Dún Conchúir (summer only; ☎099/73068). There are few other going commercial concerns on the island: *Cniotáil Inis Meáin*, the knitwear factory, produces beautifully simple designs in alpaca, linen and wool; it's home, too, to the **museum**, a fascinating photographic archive of island history, largely documented in Irish, and there's a pleasant tearoom. **B&Bs** are cheaper than on the mainland, though if you have an evening meal it may nearly double the price. If you arrive on spec, ask at the pub for some friendly information beforehand; the phone number is ☎099/73003. If you want to book ahead, try *Mrs A. Faherty* (☎099/73012; ③) or *Máire Bu Uí Mhaolchiaráin* near the church (☎099/73016; ③), with free camping (campers' breakfast £2.50) and organized guided walks arranged by Maureen Conneely for £1. Other advanced-booking accommodation information is available on ☎099/73010. Most farmers will let you **camp**, but remember to ask them – all land belongs to somebody here; it's also worth making sure that the knitwear factory is out of ear-shot before pitching your tent. There is no chemist or doctor on the island, and **emergencies** are dealt with by a nurse (☎099/73005). A **public phone** is located outside the post office and in the pub, and the *Bank of Ireland* operates on the second Tuesday of every month.

Inisheer (Inis Oírr)

Inisheer, at just under two miles across, is the smallest of the Aran Islands. Tourism has a key role here; Inisheer doesn't have the archeological wealth of Inishmore, or the wild solitude of Inishmaan, but the introduction of regular day-trip ferry services from Doolin promises a constant, if small, flow of visitors. This new service also now makes for a handy route from County Clare to Connemara. Of course tourism threatens the very stuff of its attraction – the purity of traditions and a romantic isolation – but for the moment Inisheer retains its old character, and for some it's a favourite place.

A great plug of rock dominates the island, its rough, pale-grey stone dripping with greenery. At the top the fifteenth-century **O'Brien's castle** stands inside an ancient ring fort. Set around it are low fields, a small community of pubs and houses, and wind-swept sand dunes. Half buried in sand just south of the beach is the ancient **church of Saint Kevin**; still in use in the last century, it is now used only to commemorate him as the patron saint of the island every June 14.

Practicalities

The **tourist information office** (June–Sept daily 10am–7pm), in a hut by the pier, will give you a map and a list of **B&Bs**, all of which cost around £12. You should have little trouble finding accommodation unless you arrive in the first weekend of August or at

Whit weekend, which are usually booked up well ahead. The *Bru* **hostel** (*IHH*, open all year; ☎099/75024; ②) is new and comfortable, with meals and family rooms available. There's a second hostel up behind the post office – look out for a small single-storey house with *Rory* carved on the gate. Enquire at the post office or call ☎099/70577. *Rory's* also provides meals. The only **camping** is on the official site.

There are a handful of places to get cooked **food** on Inisheer: *Radharc na Mara* (June–Sept until 9pm) does breakfasts and lunches (£3–4) and evening meals (£7–8), and the *Óstán Inis Oírr* (*Hotel Inisheer*; Easter to mid-Sept; ☎099/75020) does bar meals for non-residents, from 9am to 9pm, with evening meals from £7.50–12. *Fisherman's Cottage* restaurant (May–Sept; ☎099/75073) uses organic produce, catches its own seafood and caters well for vegetarians (lunches around £5, dinner including wine £17). Both the hotel bar, *Tigh Ruairí*, and *Tigh Ned* bar have **music** any time of the week during the summer. There is no bank on the island, but the hotel has a bureau de change.

Connemara

Dominated by two mountain ranges, **Connemara** is exceptionally beautiful. The **Twelve Bens** and **Maam Turks** glower over vast open areas of bog wilderness, while to the southwest the land breaks up into myriad tiny islands linked by causeways, slipping out into the ocean. The whole area has superb beaches, huge sweeps of opalescent white sand washed by clear blue water. Chance upon good weather here and you feel you've hit paradise; even on the hottest of days the beaches are never crowded.

This is country you visit for its scenery rather than its history. There is little evidence of medieval power in Connemara, either ecclesiastical or secular, beyond a few castles along the shore of Lough Corrib and the occasional one further west. The great exception is the profusion of **monastic remains** dotted over the little islands off the west coast. Mainland settlements up until the nineteenth century were widely scattered, and the area has always been sparsely populated, due to the poverty of the land. There's never been much to attract marauders or colonizers, and any incursions have involved a battle against the terrain as much as against the people. It's easy to see how such a land would remain under the control of clans like the O'Flaherties for centuries, while gentler landscapes bowed to the pressure of foreign rule. In the famine years the area suffered some of the worst of the misery, and a thinly peopled land was depopulated further as people chose to escape starvation by emigration.

Continued economic deprivation and isolation have meant that an ancient rural way of life has continued for far longer here, so Connemara is still Irish-speaking, the largest of the *Gaeltacht* areas. A *Gaeltacht* summer school is held in **Spiddal**, and **Casla** (Costelloe) is the home of *Raidió na Gaeltachta* radio station (556m. MW, broadcasting 8am–7.30pm). English is spoken, too, however, and the only difficulty for the visitor is that the signs on the roads, and on some buses, are often in Irish only.

For all its beauty, the dramatic mountain landscape of west Galway is surprisingly undeveloped in terms of tourism, owing in part to the infamous Irish weather and in part to the fact that walking has not been the popular recreation in Ireland that it is in other, more urbanized European countries. If you're in search of solitude, you won't have to go far to find it.

Practicalities
Bus Éireann services link all villages on major routes between Galway, Oughterard, Roundstone, Clifden and Cong. They are reliable, although infrequent, often with only one service daily, occasionally even less frequently. Timetables can be picked up in Galway bus station (☎091/562000).

Hostels and **B&Bs** are both in reasonably good supply throughout Connemara, and you can **camp** more or less anywhere, bearing in mind that a lot of the area is bog and therefore very wet. Away from towns and villages, you may have trouble getting hold of water; very irritating when in the middle of a bog! *Gaz* canisters are available in Galway city, at *Keogh's* in Oughterard, *Michael Ferron's* in Roundstone, *Peter Veldon's* in Letterfrack, and in Clifden at *The Twelve Bens, Stanley's* and *Miller's*. Bord Fáilte-approved **campsites** are listed in the text.

If you intend to go **walking** bear in mind that the mountains here are potentially **dangerous**. There is no organized mountain-rescue service such as you get in European countries that are more developed for mountain sports. The *Ordnance Survey* 1:126,720 maps are based on surveying done in 1837 and are inaccurate, especially above 1000ft. If you are doing any serious walking it is worth getting either the *Connemara Map and Guide Booklet* or *The Mountains of Connemara*, a map and guide to eighteen walks, including the Western Way. Both are produced by *Folding Landscapes* of Roundstone, Connemara, County Galway, and can be obtained in tourist offices in the west of Ireland or by post. **Bike rental** is available at Clifden, Galway, Roundstone and at several hostels (mentioned in the text).

Most of Connemara's more beautiful **beaches** are safe for swimming, including Clifden, Lettergesh, Dog's Bay, Gurteen Bay, Renvyle, Ardmore, Mannin Bay, Aillebrack, Omey, Letterfrack and Spiddal. It is, however, a very varied coast, so if in doubt, ask about safety locally.

Finally, being the *Gaeltacht*, **signposts** are often in Irish, as are names on buses (even Galway is sometimes *Gaillimh*); where common these are added in parentheses in the course of the guide. Variations in the Irish spellings are common – sometimes the "An" is omitted.

Iar-Chonnacht

Draw a large triangle between Maam Cross, Rossaveal and Galway and you've defined the area known as **Iar-Chonnacht**, an open and bleak moorland of bog. Occasional white-splotched boulders lie naked on the peat that stretches to the skyline; any grass that survives is coarse and wind-bitten, and, but for small pockets of forestation, the bog has no trees. It's difficult, wet walking country, but numerous lanes and *boreens* lead to tiny loughs set in the granite hollows of the hills – good for fishing for brown trout, sea trout or salmon. The moorland reaches its highest point near Lough Lettercraffoe on the **Rossaveal-to-Oughterard Road**, giving fine views down onto **Lough Corrib**, whose green and wooded shores are a vivid foil to the barren west.

To Oughterard and around

If you're heading for the dramatic **walking country** of the mountains, or if you plan to base yourself at Clifden, the road to take from Galway is the N59 through Oughterard. It makes the easiest hitch and most pleasant cycle ride from Galway, avoiding the boring strip development down to Spiddal and taking you instead along the shore of island-flecked **Lough Corrib**, past crumbling ruins. These include the main sixteenth-century O'Flaherty fortress of **Aughnanure Castle**, two miles south of Oughterard (May–Sept daily 9.30am–6.30pm, last admission 40min before closing; £2). A six-storey tower house standing on a rock island surrounded by a fast-flowing stream, Aughnanure was one of the strongest fortresses in the country at the time of Cromwell's blockade of Galway during 1652–54.

OUGHTERARD itself is a small town serving fishing-based tourism, from where you can rent boats on the lough or take a trip to the uninhabited island of **Inchagoill** (boat trip around £6; ☎091/82644); it's a magical place, with a couple of evocative ruined churches: St Patrick's and the twelfth-century *Teampall na Naomh* (Church of the Saints), which has interesting carvings and a superb Romanesque doorway. Approached from the east, Oughterard can beguile you into thinking that Connemara is going to be a populated, thriving, developed place, but arriving from the west, it seems a lush, green oasis, the beech trees that line the banks of the river sumptuous and luxuriant after the barren wilds of the bog. If you want to stop over there are plenty of **B&Bs**: try *Ms Small*, Camp Street (☎091/82475; ③), or Mrs McKiernan's *Hill Top Lodge*, Claremont (☎091/82137; ③). The very helpful **tourist office** will direct you to others. *Lough Corrib Hostel* in Camp Street (☎091/82866; ①) also has camping and bike rental (£6 per day); it's a very pleasant alternative – make sure you arrive before 9.30pm.

Oughterard is the starting point of the **Western Way** (approximately 31 miles), which follows the lough shore northwest, heads through the Maumturks a couple of miles north of Maum and winds up in Leenane. Alternatively, if you want a quick route north, there's a ferry (£8 return; same number as for boat trips above) to Cong in County Mayo twice daily during summer.

The main N59 road then takes you through the hamlets of **MAAM CROSS** (*Crois Mám*), where there's a craft shop, petrol station and a pub which serves rather uninspiring **food** all day, and **RECESS**, where all you will find is *Joyce's* bar and shop. Five miles further west, close in under the rugged peaks of the Twelve Bens, is *Ben Lettery An Óige* hostel, *Binn Leitrí*, Ballinafad (Easter–Sept; ☎095/34636; ①), a cosy haven run by friendly wardens, with a well-stocked shop; its location makes it one of the best spots from which to strike off into the mountains. The nearby castle of **Ballynahinch** was once the home of the land-owning Martin family and is now a hotel with a bar – and food – open to non-residents (☎095/31006; ⑧). On Ballynahinch lake are the remains of an old O'Flahertie castle, known as Martin's Prison after the use it was put to by Ballynahinch's most famous son, Dick Martin – aka **Humanity Dick** (1754– 1834). The story behind the name is that Richard Martin, originally dubbed "Hairtrigger Dick" because of his duelling prowess, spent his adult life campaigning for animal rights, and any tenant he caught causing suffering to animals was thrown into jail in the castle. Dick was known to have fought duels on behalf of threatened animals, and when asked why he did so replied: "Sir, an ox cannot hold a pistol." More constructively, he pushed various acts through parliament protecting farm animals from maltreatment and was instrumental in founding the RSPCA.

West around the coast

The **coast road** is the alternative route west from Galway, passing through the *Gaeltacht* villages of Barna (*Bearna*) and **SPIDDAL** (*An Spidéal*). The *Spiddal Craft Centre* is a collection of workshops showing high-quality sculpture, ceramics, weaving and jewellery. Spiddal itself can be surprisingly lively for such a tiny, drive-through town. You can catch good sessions in the pubs here; it also has a small beach. If you want **B&B**, there's plenty of choice – try Mrs Concannon's *Dún Lios*, Park West (☎091/83165; ③). Travellers looking for budget accommodation here are **strongly** advised to check with the tourist office in Clifden or Galway before booking in at independent hostels in the area. Alternatively, use the cheerful *Bru Spideal* hostel in the centre of the village (☎091/83638; ②), which is owned by *Aran Ferries* and can arrange trips to the islands. Also you can try the drab *An Óige* hostel, *Indreabhán*, at nearby Inverin (☎091/593154; ②).

Beyond **ROSSAVEAL** (*Ros an Mhil*), another departure point for the Aran Islands, the land breaks up into little chains of low-lying islands, linked to one another by natural causeways. These islets, more gentle than the main body of Connemara, make a perfect place to get lost: meandering around the inlets and gullies you experience a happy disorientation.

CARRAROE (*An Cheathrú Rua*) has a strangely suburban feel to it, but the boulder-strewn coast looks across to the Aran Islands, and the beach is made up of tiny fragments of coralline seaweed. *Réalt na Maidne* (☎091/595193; ④) offers a bar, a restaurant and **B&B**. *Carraroe Caravan and Camping Park* is situated half a mile from the village (April–Sept; ☎091/595266). Near Rosmuc, a speck of a hamlet, is the cottage of the Republican and poet **Pádraig Pearse** (mid-June to mid-Sept daily 9.30am–6.30pm; £1, Heritage Card), who signed the 1916 proclamation and was subsequently executed. The cottage is where he wrote short stories, plays and *O'Donovan's Funeral Oration*. At Carna you can wander out onto Mweenish Island and look out to Saint Mac Dara's Island, where the remains of a monastery still stand. Such was the former reverence for the saint that fishermen would dip their sails three times when passing the island. A three-day festival, *Féile Mhic Dara*, is still held in July in Carna. There is a grim budget **hostel** here, too: *Carna Hostel* (☎095/32240; ①). Five miles north of Carna on the R340 is a pretty campsite.

Roundstone

The next place of interest along the coast is **ROUNDSTONE** (*Cloch na Rón*), a fishing village at the foot of the Errisbeg Mountain. Curving its back to the Atlantic, the quaint stone harbour looks across its sheltered waters to the magnificent Twelve Bens of Connemara. Fishing is the main source of income, along with an unobtrusive tourism that makes the most of the unique prettiness of the setting and the glorious beach at Gurteen Bay, one and a quarter miles away to the west. A huge sweep of white sand with lucid blue water, this is really very seductive. There's a **campsite**, the *Gurteen Caravan Site* beside the beach (March–Sept; ☎095/35882), with laundry facilities, a shop and a tennis court. An Industrial Development Authority complex is discreetly tucked away to the west of Roundstone, where you can wander around the various studios and see *bodhráns* (traditional instruments) being made, buy flutes, whistles and harps, and visit pottery workshops.

It's an easy couple of hours' walk from Roundstone up to the top of **Errisbeg** – follow the fuchsia-flooded lane up the side of *O'Dowd's* bar and then the track ahead. The views are panoramic: the frilly coast of isthmuses and islets runs out to the south, while the plain of bog to the north is vast and open, punctuated only by the irregular glinting surfaces of dozens of little lakes, like sinister jellied eyes on the stark face of the landscape. It's through this wilderness that the **bog road** runs, the source of such superstition that some local people will not travel along it at night. Around the turn of the century, two old women, who lived in the road's only dwelling, robbed and murdered a traveller who'd taken refuge with them, and the road is considered to be haunted. From Errisbeg the view across the bog to the Connemara mountain ranges is tremendous. To the west, extensive beaches of white sand scoop their way north – Gurteen, Dog's Bay, Ballyconneely, Bunowen and the coral strand of Mannin Bay – each one echoing the beauty of the last.

There are several places for **B&B** – try Pádraic and Carmel Faherty, *Connolly's Bar* (☎095/35863; ④); Patricia Keane, *Heather Glen* (☎095/35837; ④); Mrs C. Lowry, *St Josephs* (☎095/35865; ④); or the friendly *Wits End* (☎095/35951; ③). You can buy *Camping Gaz* bottles and **rent bikes** from *Michael Ferron's* shop (£7 per day, £25 per week). **Pony trekking** is available at *Derrada West Pony Trekking Centre*, Toombeola, Roundstone (☎095/31022; £8 per hour). As far as **food and drink** go, there's good pub grub at *O'Dowd's Bar*, and also in their *Seafood Restaurant* (☎095/35809); or you might try *Ryan's Bar*. Other popular bars are *Connolly's Vaughan's Lounge* in the *Roundstone House Hotel* and *The Hilltop* bar, which has music every night (traditional on Fri & Sat) during the summer.

Clifden

Because of the dramatic grandeur of the Connemara mountains and the romantic pull of Galway, you expect **CLIFDEN** (*Clochán*) – known as the capital of Connemara – to be something special. In fact it's a very small place with only two significant streets. Its great asset is its position, perched high above the deep sides of the boulder-strewn estuary of the River Owenglin. The circling jumble of the Twelve Bens provides a magnificent scenic backdrop, and the broad streets seem consciously to open out, to take in the fresh air of the mountains and the Atlantic. Gimlet spires of matching nineteenth-century churches pierce the sky, giving Clifden a sharp, distinctive skyline.

Clifden seems to be trying hard to cultivate the cosmopolitan atmosphere of Galway. Lots of European tourists come here, but, aiming to serve all tastes, the town somehow misses the mark. Bars have loud disco music blaring out onto the streets – exactly the kind of thing most Gaelophile Europeans have come to get away from. It attracts a fair number of young Dubliners, too, revving up the life of this otherwise quiet, rural town. The place is at its most interesting when it's busy being Irish: during the annual **Connemara Pony Show**, for example, on the third Thursday in August (entrance £3). This is for the sale and judging of Connemara ponies, tough, hardy animals that are well suited to a harsh bog and mountain existence, yet renowned for their docile temperament. There's also a community festival in the last week of September.

Arrival and accommodation

Clifden is an obvious base if you're hostelling or camping, despite its limitations, and even though the Connemara mountains *look* magnificent from here, they're not at all accessible without transport of one kind or another. *Bus Éireann* **buses** leave from Market Street, with three buses to Galway daily in the summer and one a day for the rest of the year. The **tourist office** is in Market Street (July–Aug Mon–Sat 9am–6pm, Sun 10am–5pm; mid-May to mid-Sept Mon–Sat 10am–6pm; ☎095/21163).

There's plenty of hotel and B&B **accommodation** in the centre of Clifden, though everything can be very busy in July and August. *Hillview House*, Church Hill (☎095/21836; ③), and *The White Heather Guest House*, The Square (☎095/21085; ③), are both good budget options. Others include: *Kingstown House*, Bridge Street (☎095/21470; ④), *Ben View House*, Bridge Street (☎095/21256; ④), and *Benbawn House*, Westport Road (☎095/21462; ④). A couple of central pubs offer rather more upmarket rooms: *Barry's* on Main Street (☎095/21287; ⑤) or *Alcock & Brown* (☎095/21206; ⑤). At the other end of the scale there are several **hostels** in the centre of town: *Leo's* on the Beach Road (*IHH*, open all year; ☎095/21429; ①) is a friendly place with cosy turf fires, private rooms (②) and the best campsite for miles. *The Clifden Town Hostel*, Market Street (☎095/21076; ②), with family rooms (②) as well as bike rental (£5 per day), is smart and comfy. *Brookside Hostel*, 300 yards down the hill from the tourist office (☎095/21812; ②), is similarly well run, has family rooms and looks out over a field of Connemara ponies, and *Ard-Ri Bayview Hostel* (☎095/21866; ①) offers a view of the bay.

There are plenty of places for **bike rental**: try *John Mannion*, Bridge Street(☎095/21160; they also stock *Gaz*). Clifden's **laundry** is in Main Square. **Pony trekking** is organized at *Errislannan Manor* (☎095/21134; closed Sun; £10 per hour), about a mile beyond the Alcock and Brown Memorial, south of Clifden on the L102. **Wind-surfing** is available at the boat club, Coast Road. **Dinghy sailing** can be arranged through *Clifden Boat Club* (☎095/21711; £120 for a week course) – the setting is superb. *The Island House*, Market Street (☎095/21379), organizes **guided walks** (4–5hr; around £10–20), focusing on the archeology and natural history of Connemara, an excellent way to explore the countryside, especially if you're travelling alone or don't have your own transport.

Eating and drinking

As for **food and drink**, there's no problem getting provisions in Clifden, and the town's two main streets harbour plenty of places to eat. For coffee and home-baked cakes, try either *Cullen's*, Market Street, or *Kelly's*, Church Hill (just off The Square) – which also has a good bookshop. For light lunches and bar food, there's *The Marconi Bar*, *E.J. King's*, *Barry's Hotel* or *Mannion's*. Several places serve evening meals from around £7: *Mitchell's*, *The Derryclare* and *E.J. King's*. *The Old Skillet*, *D'Arcy Inn* and *Dorris Restaurant* are good value with evening meals for around £10 and light lunches during the day. The friendly, upmarket *Crannmer Restaurant* (☎095/21174; from 6pm) is tucked away off Church Hill. Seafood is their speciality, and if you can't afford a full meal (£13–30), you're welcome to enjoy a starter or a dessert along with the fine views from the terrace.

There are plenty of decent **bars** in Clifden, and several places where you'll find music: for traditional sounds, try *Tom King's*, *Lowry's* or *Barry's Hotel* during the summer, *Mannion's* or *Griffin's* at any time of year. Loud and lively *E.J. King's* on The Square is the likeliest spot for rock and roll and modern folk.

Around Clifden

Clifden offers easy access to some beautiful scenery. To get to the **Twelve Bens** (see opposite) you will need to cycle, hitch or skilfully manipulate the bus service. For more spontaneous walking, take the westward **coast road** out of Clifden (past *Leo's* hostel) to a fine, sandy beach and a path that follows the shore of Clifden Bay. The shell of a nineteenth-century Gothic castellated mansion that you pass on the way was the home of John D'Arcy, who founded the town. Running north from beside the hostels, the **sky road** takes you to more desolate countryside and the long thin inlet of Streamstown Bay. Stick to the road and you'll eventually come down to the little village of Claddaghduff, where at low tide you can walk across to **Omey Island**. There are excellent beaches here. In the bay three miles north is the little village of **CLEGGAN**, where you'll find a comfy **hostel**, *The Master's House* (☎095/44746; ①), which also has private rooms (②), meals, camping, laundry and bike rental and the ferry for the island of **Inishbofin** (see below).

To the immediate south of Clifden, there's equally pleasant country. A 14ft aeroplane wing carved in limestone sticks out of the bog four miles from Clifden on the **Ballyconneely Road**, as a melodramatic memorial to the landing of **Alcock and Brown** at the end of their pioneering non-stop transatlantic flight in June 1919. Beyond this is the coral strand of Mannin Bay, excellent for swimming, as is that at Doonlonghan.

Inishbofin

The island of **INISHBOFIN** is a mellow, balmy place, quite different from the mainland. It's more fertile, with sheltered sandy beaches, and there's a general softness to its contours. The only jagged features are the cliffs to the west (the *stags*), a fine vantage point for viewing seals basking on the shore. Even the high, heathery moorland soon gently descends to the placid **Lough Boffin**, rimmed with rustling water iris and bullrushes. The lough is the scene of the island's most durable **myth**, a story that explains how it got its name. Several versions of the tale exist, but the basic elements are constant. For eons the island lay shrouded in mist under the spell of an enchantment, but one day two lost fishermen came upon it and lit a fire by the shore, thus breaking the spell. As the mist cleared, they saw an old woman driving a white cow along the strand. She hit it with a stick and was instantly turned to rock. Taking her for a witch, the men hit her and they too immediately turned to rock: *Inis Bó Finne* means "Island of the White Cow".

You can visit Inishbofin on a day-trip from Clifden, even without a car. Take the bus to **CLEGGAN** (summer Tues & Fri 8am, returning 7.50pm; check with driver). A private bus leaves the square at 10am daily in summer. **Ferry** tickets are available at *King's* store, Cleggan, or Clifden tourist information office for sailings on *The Queen* (£10 return, students £8; April–Sept), departing Cleggan 11.30am & 6.45pm, with an extra sailing at 2pm during July & Aug; departing Inishbofin April–Sept 9.30am & 5pm, July & Aug an extra 1pm sailing. In winter there's a boat approximately once a week (☎095/44642). Sailing times on the *Dún Aengus*, booked at *Spar* in Cleggan, seem to be fairly variable.

The known **history** of the island starts in the seventh century, when Saint Colman arrived here from Iona after a quarrel with Rome over the method of calculating the date of Easter. No remains exist of the monastery he founded, but ruins of a thirteenth-century church stand on the original site in a sheltered vale beside the lake in the east. Later the island was taken over by the O'Flaherties, and then Grace O'Malley is supposed to have fortified the place for her fleet. Coming into the island's long protected harbour you'll see the remains of a sixteenth-century castle, low on the hummocky terrain. It was taken and strengthened yet further by Cromwell, who used Inishbofin – and other west coast islands – as a kind of concentration camp for clerics. The most chilling reminder of his barbarity is the rock visible in the harbour at low tide. Known as **Bishop's Rock**, it was here that Cromwell chained one unfortunate ecclesiastic, then let his troops watch the tide come slowly in and drown him.

Practicalities

Both *Day's Bofin House* (☎095/45861; ④) and *Doonmore Hotel* (☎095/45806; ④) have restaurants open to non-residents, and also serve good **bar food** (Easter–Sept). If you want to book **B&B**, try *Regina King* (☎095/45833; ③), *Fiona Lowell* (☎095/45817; ③) or *Lena Schofield* (☎095/45812; ③). The *Inishbofin Island Hostel* (IHH, April–Sept; ☎095/45855; ①) is an extremely friendly place. *Miko's* **pub** is very friendly and has **music sessions** any time of the week during the summer season and at weekends in winter. There's an island shop, with the usual limitations on supplies, and *Miko's* pub will change travellers' cheques.

You can **camp** on any of the open common land. A particularly good spot is at the east end of the island at Rusheen beach, from where you're treated to the glorious sight of the Connemara mountains lurching into the sea. The only places that are dangerous for swimming are at Tra Geall, just beneath Doonmore, opposite the island of Inishark in the west.

The Connemara National Park

The **Connemara National Park** typifies the scenic splendour of west Galway. Its chief functions are to promote the area's natural beauty while conserving this area of bog, heath and granite mountains. The park includes part of the famous **Twelve Bens** range – Benbaun, Bencullagh, Benbrack and Muckanaght – all of which are for experienced walkers only. Less threatening are the spectacular Polldark River gorge and Glanmore Valley, and the multifaceted granite Diamond Hill – though problems of soil erosion here have led the park to discourage a walk to the top: ask at the visitor centre for the current state of play.

The park's **visitor centre** (May–Sept daily 9.30am–6pm; £2, Heritage Card), near Letterfrack, is a good source of information on the fauna, flora and geology of the area; there's an exhibition on ten thousand years of Connemara, which takes in peatland and the changing landscape. It's also the focus for the bogland conservation work that's going on in the area, and the herbarium here is worth looking at if you're interested in botany. The staff can suggest safe hiking routes of varying length and difficulty, and you can leave details of your own route and intended time of return – an invaluable service in this potentially hazardous landscape. The centre has kitchen facilities available for walkers, an indoor "picnic" area and a new tearoom. In July and August a botanist leads a guided walk of about two and a half hours, currently leaving at 10.30am on Monday, Wednesday and Friday, though it's wise to ring and check the schedule. As well as offering facilities to outsiders, the centre is doing much to raise local awareness of the value of the area as a tourist amenity – particularly important in view of the current threat of goldmining in the area.

Letterfrack

LETTERFRACK itself is an orderly nineteenth-century Quaker village in a rugged setting. The village is tiny, but there's good food (especially wholefood and cheeses), and occasionally music, at *Veldon's* and discos in *The Bard's Den* (Fri & Sat). There's also a post office, phone, shop and bureau de change and the lovely rambling independent *Old Monastery* hostel (*IHH*, open all year; tel/fax ☎095/41132; ②), with camping, bike rental and great food; it makes a perfect base for walking in the national park. Bog Week (the weekend leading up to the first Monday in June) and Sea Week (the weekend leading up to the last Monday in October) see Letterfrack at its liveliest, when a heady mix of conservationists and musicians descend upon the place for field trips, conferences and sessions.

Two miles east of here, the towers of **Kylemore Abbey** sit in a rhododendron-filled hollow against lush deciduous slopes. Its white castellated outline, perfectly reflected in the reed-punctured lake, has made it the subject of many a postcard: Kylemore is in fact a nineteenth-century neo-Gothic building. It's home to Irish Benedictine nuns and houses a girls' boarding school, but the library and entrance hall are freely accessible, and there's an exhibition telling the history of Kylemore (Easter–Oct daily 10am–6pm; £1.50). A stroll through the woods leads to the Gothic church, a small-scale copy of Norwich Cathedral built in 1868. The abbey also has a major heritage shop and restaurant. **Renvyle House**, some eight miles northwest of Kylemore Abbey, is of immense interest in Irish literary and political history. At one time it was visited by the great Edwardian comic twosome Somerville and Ross, authors of *Stories of an Irish R.M.*, but the house's most famous owner was Oliver St John Gogarty, the distinguished surgeon, writer and wit. An associate of the Gaelic League, he attended the literary evenings of Yeats, Moore and AE (George Russell), and is immortalized as "stately plump Buck Mulligan" in Joyce's *Ulysses*. Renvyle House is now a hotel (June–Sept; ☎095/43511 or ☎43444; ⑧) offering facilities such as horse riding, wind-surfing and a swimming pool to non-residents. About a mile west of the hotel is a ruined O'Flahertie castle, superbly overlooking the sea. The coast road to the east offers magnificent scenery, a great route for the **hostel** at Killary Harbour, if you are cycling, and some lovely beaches.

Killary Harbour and around

Inland, the N59 route to **KILLARY HARBOUR** is faster and similarly beautiful. The lightly wooded shore around Ballinakill Harbour provides a brief luxuriant interlude before the landscape of wild bog and granite reasserts itself with ever increasing austerity. The *An Óige* **hostel** at Killary (March–Sept; ☎095/43417; ①), where Wittgenstein finished writing his *Philosophical Investigations* in 1948, has a deeply ponderous setting at the mouth of Ireland's only fjord, a cold dark tongue of water which cuts eight miles into the barren mountains. The hostel is five miles of extremely difficult hitching off the N59, so be prepared to walk. There's a shop at the hostel open evenings; otherwise you have to go to Lettergesh shop and post office. From the hostel walk south, past the adventure centre (see below), then take the right turn before the crest of the hill, and keep on for about one and a quarter miles; the shop is the first big house on the left, with a phone box outside. There are good sandy beaches in the vicinity.

The *Little Killary Adventure Centre*, Salruck, Renvyle (☎095/43411), runs courses in mountain walking, climbing, sailing, canoeing, sailboarding, archery and orienteering. Courses are generally booked well in advance, though it is often possible to join a course for part of a week or weekend. Further north, **LEENANE** is most famous as a location for shooting *The Field*, and stills from the film hang on the walls of *Gaynor's Bar*. It's also a finishing (or starting) point for the Western Way. *Leenane Cultural Centre* (April–Sept; £2) explores the history of wool, with spinning and weaving demonstrations and a collection of various sheep outside – if you've an interest, it's very enjoyable, and there's a good tea shop, too. For **B&B**, Mrs Hamilton's *Bayview House* (☎095/42240; ④) and Mrs Hoult's *Hillcrest House*, Clifden Road (☎095/42244; ③), are both reasonable options. If you're heading towards Cong in County Mayo (p.374), the desolate road takes you through Maum and on past *Cornamona Hostel* on the shores of Lough Corrib (*IHH*, April–Oct; ☎092/48002; ①), just nine miles from Cong.

COUNTY MAYO

Often seen as simply a passage between scenic Galway and literary Yeats country, **Mayo** is little visited – though it's hard to see why. Like Galway to the south and Sligo to the north, it has a landscape of high cliffs, lonely mountains and bright fuchsia hedges; in the wild, boggy area to the northwest are the vestiges of a *Gaeltacht*; and on Lough Conn there's some of the best fishing in Ireland. The Georgian town of **Westport**, an elegantly urban playground for travellers needing a break from the dazzling lights and landscapes of the wild west, is the only place that's really on the international tourist trail. **Achill Island**, the biggest of the Irish offshore islands and a traditional Irish family holiday resort, has an oddly fly-blown air that won't suit everyone. Some of the most exciting country, however, is the little-travelled northwest. The new interpretative centre at **Ceide** holds the key to understanding a landscape that's hardly changed for millennia. The area is easily accessible: the railway will take you right out to Westport, and there's an international airport at **Knock** (with cheap flights designed for pilgrims to the shrine of the Virgin Mary). Furthermore the whole of the county is magical cycling country. Mayo is bound to become busier, but for the moment it remains wonderfully empty.

The Barony of Murrisk and Clare Island

If you're travelling by road, you'll probably enter Mayo from Galway, via the spectacular scenery of **Killary Harbour**, part of the lobe of land between the Galway border and Westport that's known as the **Barony of Murrisk**. This is country as rugged and remote as anything you'll find in the west, and two ranges of hills, the Mweelrea Mountains and the Sheefry Hills, provide terrain for energetic walking, mountaineering, riding, fishing and canoeing.

Delphi and Louisburgh

The road due north from Killary threads along a narrow valley which opens up, briefly, for a famous salmon and sea-trout lough-fishery with the unlikely name of **DELPHI** (in the local pronunciation, *Delph-eye*). The story behind the name involves the first

Marquess of Sligo, whose seat, misleadingly, was at Westport. The flamboyant Marquess, a friend of Lord Byron, was caught in the sway of romantic Hellenism and in 1811 set sail for Greece to search for antiquities. He swam the Hellespont with Byron and rode with him overland to Corinth; but when he got to Delphi, he suffered a bout of homesickness, finding that it reminded him of nothing so much as his fishery at home in County Mayo. After numerous adventures, and some pillaging of ancient sites, the Marquess returned home to reminisce. Nowadays, there's an **adventure centre** at Delphi (☎095/42307), offering supervised instruction in anything from wind-surfing and canoeing to abseiling and mountaineering. More important for people of a more sedentary disposition, there's also a **hostel** (②) and a comfortable, glassed-in coffee-shop where you can sit and gaze out as the cloud creeps down the slopes of Mweelrea and Ben Gorm. **Pony trekking** is based at the *Drumindoo Stud* (☎098/66195). Luxurious **accommodation**, plus a taste of the area's history, can be had at the *Delphi Lodge* (Jan–Oct; ☎095/42211; ⑧; excellent dinners), an 1830s sporting lodge by the lake, built for the Marquess of Sligo in a surprisingly austere, and predictably Hellenistic, style.

Take the right turn at the southern end of the lough, and the road climbs high into the **Sheefry Hills**, giving some of the best access for walking. A mile past the village of **DRUMMIN**, three-quarters of a mile up a track, is one of the best places to **stay** in these parts: the *Derryann* vegetarian B&B (☎098/26885; ③). Housed in a stone-built cottage, it offers an amazing range of breakfasts for veggie sybarites (or anyone else who's had one Irish breakfast too many): mushroom and pine-nut crêpes, eggs Florentine, French toast with maple syrup – but no evening meals, although they will produce snacks or sandwiches; the **pub** in the village does a limited range of pub food. There's a **tourist information office**, close to the crossroads (June–Sept daily 9.30am–6.30pm; ☎098/66394).

North of Delphi, the road runs alongside sombre **Doo Lough**, also known as the Black Lake, and over desolate moorland before reaching **LOUISBURGH** (*Lewisburg*). This is one of the few instances where a town this side of the Atlantic has been named after one on the other: it was renamed after Henry Browne, uncle of the first Marquess of Sligo, had taken part in the capture of Louisburgh, Nova Scotia, in 1758. Louisburgh is essentially little more than a crossroads, but its planned buildings give it an incongruous air of importance, and it's a pleasant enough place to stay. A new **interpretative centre** (June–Aug Mon–Sat 10am–6pm, Sun 11am–5pm; £2.25) provides useful information about the historical background to the scenery. Like all of this stretch of the coast, Louisburgh is associated with the pirate queen, **Grace O'Malley** (see p.363). It also suffered heavily during the 1845–49 Famine: there's a harrowing tale about the march of six hundred starving locals in 1849 to Delphi Lodge to beg, unsuccessfully, for famine relief; many of them, weak and ill clothed, died on the return journey amid the uncompromising scenery of Doo Lough. This event is commemorated annually in the Great Famine Walk (enquire at the heritage centre for details).

Louisburgh makes a good base for exploring the sandy **beaches** that run along the north coast as far as Murrisk Abbey. There's a **tourist information** centre close to the main crossroads (June–Aug Mon–Sat 10am–1pm; ☎098/66410), which has details of local **walking** and **water sports**. It has some good **self-catering accommodation** (details on ☎098/66260) and a number of **hotels** including the reasonably priced *Durkan's* in Chapel Street (☎098/66140; ③), which also does good food. Just outside Louisburgh, at **OLD HEAD** (on the Westport Road), there's a **campsite** with showers and laundry (June–Aug; ☎098/66021). Old Head has a good **beach**, and for greater comfort you can stay in the *Old Head House* hotel (☎098/66021; ⑤), which can also arrange adventure sports in the area. Another fine beach is the **Silver Strand**, claimed grandiosely in the local tourist leaflets to be second only to Florida's Key West; it is, incidentally, the site of a mass Famine burial. You can reach it by turning southwest at the crossroads just outside Louisburgh on the Killary Road along lanes that pick their way through rolling country rich in megalithic monuments, with a clear view out to Clare Island, Inishmore and the smaller islets; it has a couple of **B&Bs** – *Silver Strand House* (☎098/68730; ③) is homely and comfortable and offers evening meals of local seafood. Not far away at **KILLADOON**, there's a hotel with equally spectacular sunset views, called the *Killadoon Beach Hotel* (☎098/68605; ③).

Clare Island

Follow the road from Louisburgh west along the strand to the land's tip, and you reach **Roonagh Quay**, where a boat leaves three times a day for **CLARE ISLAND**. (The bus from Westport runs at least twice a day and will drop you two miles away in Louisburgh.) The crossing takes 25 minutes; boats leave Roonagh at 10.45 am and 5.45pm, Clare Island at 9.45am and 4.45pm; in July and August there's an extra service leaving Clare Island at 1.15pm and returning to the mainland at 1.45pm (☎098/25045; fares are £10 return, £6 for students). Although it's tiny – only fifteen or so square miles – Clare Island rises to a height of 1522ft in a massive shoulder of land that dominates everything around. There's not much here besides the hills, some ruins and some unfrequented sandy beaches, but there's plenty of walking, and you can go pony trekking, or water-ski, sailboard or fish.

The island is famed above all as the stronghold of Grace O'Malley (see p.363). Her massive castle is at the eastern end of the island; also at the eastern end of the island, she – or a close relative – is buried in a tomb on the north side of the ruined thirteenth-century Cistercian abbey halfway along the south coast of the island.

You can **stay** overnight on Clare Island, at the *Bay View Hotel* (☎098/26307; ④), which also organizes local watersports.

Croagh Patrick and Murrisk Abbey

The land between Louisburgh and Westport is dominated by the strange, perfectly conical silhouette of **Croagh** (pronounced *Croak*) **Patrick**, which at 2513ft is by far the highest mountain in the immediate area. The sandy beaches of the shore peter out at Bertra Strand, just short of Murrisk and the ruins of **Murrisk Abbey**, a house of Augustinian canons set up on the shore of Clew Bay by the O'Malley family in 1457, less than a hundred years before Henry VIII's dissolution of the monasteries.

Looking out over the hummocky islets of the bay, the abbey is the best starting point if you want to climb the mountain. On the landward side, a little saint's head carved in the wall peers glumly up the slope – it's a very tough **climb**. Still, there's a surprise when you get to the top. The summit isn't conical, as it looks from the bottom, but forms a flat plateau, with a little chapel and a breathtaking view: on a good day you can see right from the Twelve Bens in the south to the mountains of Achill Island in the north, the Nephin Beg east of the island and on to the Slieve League in Donegal.

ST PATRICK AND THE SNAKE

In 441, **Saint Patrick** spent the forty days of Lent on Croagh Patrick in prayer and fasting, and it's from here that he is supposed to have sent the reptiles of Ireland crawling to their doom. Just to the south of the summit is the **precipice of Lugnanarrib**, where he stood, ringing his bell, then repeatedly hurled it over the edge, each time taking with it a stream of toads, snakes and other creepy-crawlies. Luckily he didn't have to go down to the bottom to get his bell back – helpful spirits did the job for him. There's a pilgrimage to the top of Croagh Patrick, which is carried out by some 60,000 people, some of them in bare feet, every year on the last Sunday of July.

A fine place to stop for **refreshments** after a climb, barefoot or not, up the mountain is *Glosh House*, a restaurant overlooking the sea and specializing in seafood and vegetarian dishes. It also does Irish breakfasts and sustaining afternoon teas.

Westport and around

"The islands in the bay which was of gold colour, look like so many dolphins and whales basking there," wrote the English novelist W.M. Thackeray on a visit to Westport in 1842. Set in a picturesque eighteenth-century landscape on the shores of Clew Bay, **WESTPORT** is a comfortable, relaxed town, still recognizably Georgian – it was planned by the architects Richard Castle and James Wyatt – with a leafy mall, octagonal square, a canalized river and one of Ireland's great stately homes, Westport House. For the past ten years, it has capitalized on its fine architecture and busy urban buzz to offer visitors some elegant town living in the midst of the wild scenery of the remote west. During summer, the place is tremendously lively, with Irish, British, French and German visitors returning annually to re-sample its charms, and a couple of excellent festivals.

In its heyday the town was extremely prosperous, fattened by the trade in linen and cotton cloth and yarn. However, like many places throughout Ireland, Westport was hit hard by the Act of Union of 1801. Although local landowners like the first Marquess of Sligo supported the Act in the belief that it would be of economic benefit, the reverse was in fact true: Irish hand looms were no competition for the new spinning jennies in Britain's industrial towns, the national linen and cotton industries declined, and Westport's economy was ruined. Mass unemployment forced a choice between reverting to subsistence farming or starting a new life in America.

Its quiet Georgian beauties and its lively modern streetlife apart, the reason Westport is on the tourist trail nowadays is **Westport House** (Mon–Sat 10.30am–6.30pm, Sun 2–6pm; house £6, zoo £3.50, both £8), a mile or so out of town towards Clew Bay. Built on the site of one of the castles of the sixteenth-century pirate queen Grace O'Malley (a direct ancestor of the current owner; see p.363), Westport House was beautifully designed in 1730 by the ubiquitous Richard Castle, with later additions by Thomas Ivory and James Wyatt. This was one of the first Irish houses opened to the public – and it's had a go at any and every way of making money. There's a zoo park in the grounds and horse-drawn caravans for rental, while the dungeons (which belong to an earlier house) have everything from a trace-your-ancestor service to ghostly sound-effects; the loos are billed, with some welcome self-irony, "Westport House Toilet Centre". On the plus side, though, the delicate response of the house to its luminous surroundings of land, light and water is undimmed and wonderful if you can ignore the commerce – and feel like shelling out the swingeing admission fee.

Inside the house there's a *Holy Family* by Rubens, a violin which used to belong to J. M. Synge and, on the first floor, a room with lovely Chinese wallpapers dating from 1780. A lot of the mahogany in the house was brought back from Jamaica by the first marquess, who was instrumental in freeing slaves during his time as governor there. On the walls of the staircase, a series of paintings of local views by James Arthur O'Connor, commissioned by the second marquess in 1818 and 1819, shows an idyllic nineteenth-century landscape, an overweeningly romantic version of the dramatic scenery at Delphi; bustling activity as sailing boats are unloaded at Westport Quay. This was wishful thinking – Westport in the 1810s was already overshadowed by the changes in the relationship with England, and by 1825 was finished as an industrial centre.

Further out on The Quay, the Clew Bay Heritage Centre (Mon–Fri 10am–6pm, Sat–Sun 2–6pm; £1) – an engaging but chaotic jumble of old coins, agricultural implements, typewriters, ration books and other detritus – fails to live up to its grandiose title.

Information and accommodation

The **tourist office** in the Mall (June–Sept Mon–Fri 9am–6pm, Sat 10am–7pm; Oct–May Mon–Fri 9am–5.15pm; ☎098/25711) can also help with accommodation. Although you may be put off by the olde-worlde pretensions of the *Olde Railway Hotel* (☎098/25166; ⑤), its location, facing the canalized river on the leafy Mall, could hardly be better; they'll also fix up canoeing, hill-climbing, pony trekking and golf. There are also dozens of **B&Bs**: try Mrs Sheridan at *Altamont House*, Ballinrobe Road (☎098/25266; ③), Mrs Reidy's *Clooneen House*, Castlebar Street (☎098/25361; ③), or Mrs Kelly's *Dún na Mara*, Castlebar Street (☎098/25205; ③).

For cheap accommodation, you've a choice of one *An Óige* and two independent **hostels**. The newest and most central, the independent *Old Mill Hostel* (*IHH*, open all year; ☎098/27045, fax ☎094/21745; ②), converted from part of an eighteenth-century complex of mills and warehouses, is on James Street, up from the Octagon. Alternatively, there's the roughly stone-built *Granary*, past *Ryan's Hotel* on Quay Road, just before the road forks (☎098/25903; ①). The large *An Óige* hostel *Club Atlantic* (mid-March to Oct; ☎098/26644, fax ☎25229; ②) is clean and comfortable: it's opposite the train station on Altamont Street and very close to Fair Green, where buses stop. Currently it's the location for a well-researched **exhibition** on Croagh Patrick, well worth going to if you're heading westward toward the holy mountain itself (daily 2–5pm; £1.50). If you want to pitch a **tent**, *Parklands Caravan and Camping Park* (May–Aug; ☎098/25141) is on the Westport Estate; there's more camping further out at Old Head. Out at The Quay, the *Helm* bar has rooms (☎098/26194; ③); make sure to ask for one facing the bay. A terrace of newly built **self-catering cottages** on the quayside blends in very effectively with the eighteenth-century architecture around it (☎098/25511). A new **hotel** is scheduled to open in a refurbished warehouse building, but its name and price are as yet unknown.

Eating

There are plenty of places to **eat**. *Circe's* truly excellent café/wine bar on Bridge Street serves delicious breakfasts, lunches and dinners of mostly organic produce for both vegetarians and non-vegetarians in relaxed surroundings (Mon–Sat 10am–10pm, Sun 6pm–10pm; ☎098/27096). Don't be put off by the down-home decor – plastic garden furniture and kitchen utensils – of *The Cork*, just off the Octagon (☎098/26929; evenings only), or excruciatingly named dishes – "Blah Blah Black Sheep", "Chic Chic"; along with *Circe's*, this is one of the best restaurants in town. The *Continental Café and Healthfood Shop*, High Street (☎098/26679), offers a different intepretation of healthy food: fired eggs (free range), baked beans (organic) and frankfurters (unspecified) in an old-fashioned New Age environment (open until 6pm). Two budget options, serving sustaining salads and soups, are *McCormack's* (open only till 6pm) and *The Crockery Pot* (open till 9pm), both in Bridge Street. Other good places are *Anthony Hoban's* pub on James Street (☎098/25020), with value-for-money home-cooked meals in the evening; or the more expensive *Carvery and Seafood Bar* in the *Olde Railway Hotel* (daily 12.30–3pm & 6.30–10pm). Out at The Quay, *Quay Cottage* (☎098/26412), at the entrance to Westport House, serves enormous salmon salads and plenty of vegetarian food – great value for lunch but pricier in the evenings; nearby *Moorings Restaurant* (☎098/25874; booking essential) is good, too.

If you're self-catering, you can find some excellent local produce, much of it organic, at the **Thursday market** (also Fri & Sat in summer) at the Octagon. *Bourke's Wine and Cheese Shop* in Bridge Street is another good stopping-off point, for salmon, preserves, bread and the best selection of wine in town.

Festivals, nightlife and entertainment

If you want to see Westport at its liveliest, try to make it for the **Westport Street Festival**, in the second week of July, with free street concerts and general carousal.

The season stretches from then until the **Arts Festival** at the end of September. Even if you don't coincide with a festival, you'll find plenty to do. There are two main centres of activity: the town centre and the fast-developing complex of shops, pubs and restaurants around The Quay by the entrance to Westport House. In the centre, the best **music pubs** are on Bridge Street, where *The West* is hugely popular (arrive early and stay put) and *Matt Molloy's Bar*, owned by the eponymous flautist of The Chieftains, features occasional musical celebrities. The best **dancing** takes place at the *Castlecourt Hotel*, Castlebar Street (Fri & Sat till 1.30am; £5 admission includes bar meal). Out at **The Quay**, the waterside complex of refurbished buildings is guaranteed to be humming until late on any summer evening. *The Towers*, overlooking Clew Bay, is a musical pub with excellent seafood. The *Asgard* bar/restaurant (☎098/25319) is also worth a look, while up the drive to Westport House you'll find the *Wagon Wheel Bar*, always crowded and featuring Brendan Shine every Tuesday in season.

For a rather quieter evening of Irish culture, look out for theatrical events at the **Wyatt Theatre**, in the Town Hall on the Octagon, where there are good amateur productions of Irish drama.

Daytime activities, sightseeing apart, are plentiful. If you're lucky with the weather the best **beaches** are at Bertra, six miles out on the Louisburgh Road, and Mulrany, 18 miles away on the Achill Road. **Cycling** from Westport is rewarding, if strenuous – there are hills in almost all directions except towards Newport: bike rental is from *J.P. Breheny & Sons*, Castlebar Street (☎098/25020). **Walking** in the nearby Sheefry Hills or Dartry Mountains can be spectacular – pick up Paul Simms and Tony Wyatt's *Northwest Walks* at the tourist office or in any of the local bookshops. **Horse riding**, which will let you get right off the road, is available half a mile out of town on the Castlebar Road at the *Drummindoo Equitation Centre* (☎098/25616) and also at Westport House. The **sea angling** in Clew Bay is magnificent, and there are also good opportunities for salmon and trout fishing in nearby lakes and rivers – details from the *Sea Angling Centre* in town. **Sailing** in sheltered waters can be arranged through the Mayo Sailing Club in Rosmoney – good facilities and teaching for newcomers.

Newport and around

The road north out of Westport, bordered by bright fuchsia hedges, follows the shore of Clew Bay to **NEWPORT**, a neat, trim little eighteenth-century town unashamedly devoted to tourism and a serviceable base for both the sea and the Nephin Beg Mountains. Newport's main boast is that one of Grace Kelly's ancestors once lived in nearby Drimurla. It's also a centre for sea angling; if you go in the evening to the swanky *Newport House Hotel*, you'll see massive sea trout – caught by guests earlier in the day – laid out for the less energetic to admire.

About two miles outside Newport and signposted off the road to Achill is **Burrishoole Abbey**, a Dominican priory in a peaceful setting, lapped by the waters of the bay – at high tide you have to hop across a stepping stone to get in. Founded in the fifteenth century by Richard Burke – second husband of the pirate queen Grace O'Malley and unfortunately nicknamed "Iron Dick" – who spent the last years of his life here. The abbey has some cloisters still surviving and stands as a symbol of the spread of religious life under the "more Irish than the Irish" Normans. Another mile or so along the Achill Road, the turning labelled "Carrickanowley Castle" brings you to **Rockfleet Castle**, a perfect fifteenth- or sixteenth-century tower house that stands with its feet in a quiet outlet of Clew Bay – you'll get your feet wet stepping up to the door at high tide. An English attack on it was quelled by Grace O'Malley, who subsequently lived here.

Tourist **information** can be had from the stand at *Darac Crafts* in the Main Street (☎098/41116). If you want to **stay** in Newport, there's the upmarket *Newport House*

Hotel (☎098/41222; ⑤), or for B&B try *De Bille House*, a handsome stone building on the main street (☎098/41195; ③), which also runs a pleasant coffee shop; its generously sized rooms are a good option for families. The house is named after a Danish sea-captain who was shipwrecked en route for the Danish West Indian Isles in 1782; he and his crew were rescued, but subsequently died of a fever. You can still see the house in which he was nursed in the back yard. Hostel-style accommodation is available at the *Skerdagh Outdoor Centre*, three miles northeast of Newport on the R317, which also arranges bicycle rental, rock climbing, orienteering, hill-walking and canoeing (June–Aug, but group bookings taken at other times; ☎098/41500). There's **self-catering** accommodation at Loch Morchan at Kilbride, just outside Newport (☎098/41221). **Eating** can be a problem after 9pm: good, basic food is available from *Kelly's Kitchen* on the main street or *The Black Oak Inn* across the bridge. **Drinking** itself is best done at *Cowley's Singing Lounge* or at the *Angler's Rest*, which also does traditional music and good food.

Five miles away, high among the powerful outlines of the Nephin Beg Mountains – take the Achill Road and follow the signs – is the *An Óige* **hostel**, *Traenlaur Lodge* at Logh Feeagh (Easter–Sept; ☎096/13272; ①), a hefty climb but well worth it to stay in an unparalleled location at the head of this upland lake – and a perfect base for **walking** in the area (see pp.366–67 for details of the long-distance Bangor trail). For **horse riding** and pony trekking the contact is ☎098/36126; permits for **fishing** are available from the *Newport House Hotel*.

The road northwest towards Achill runs, for the most part, too far inland for the glories of Clew Bay to be visible; but it's always worth making detours down the lanes that lead to the water's edge. There's a **hostel** at Mulranny, just off the main road ten miles before you reach Achill Sound: the *Erris Gateway Hostel* (☎096/36124; ②).

GRACE O'MALLEY, THE PIRATE QUEEN

There came to me also a most famous feminine sea captain called Granny Ny Mally and offered her services unto me, wheresoever I would command her, with three galleys and 200 fighting men, either in Scotland or in Ireland. She brought with her her husband, for she was as well by sea as by land well more than Mrs Mate with him…. This was a notorious woman in all the coasts of Ireland.

Sir Henry Sidney, Lord Deputy of Ireland, 1577

Grace O'Malley, or Gráinne Ní Mháille (c.1530–1600; often corrupted to **Granuaile**), was the daughter of Owen O'Malley, chief of the west coast islands. Through fearless and none-too-scrupulous warfare and piracy, she made herself queen of the Clew Bay area when she died. She effectively controlled the vigorous trade between Galway and the Continent, as well as running a lucrative business importing Scottish mercenaries for chieftains' wars against Elizabeth I and their cattle-rustling and plundering. She earned her place in Irish legend by being one of the few Irish chiefs to stand up to the English.

In 1575, she visited the St Lawrences of Howth Castle near Dublin (see p.97), expecting to be made welcome in the Irish fashion. When, instead, she was told that the family was eating and that she would have to wait, she responded by abducting the family's heir. When she met Elizabeth I in London in 1593, she insisted on being treated as her regal equal. However, always a canny tactician, Grace switched sides when she realized she couldn't beat the English, and her son was created first Viscount Mayo. Continually mentioned in sixteenth-century dispatches, her exploits included dissolving her Celtic secular marriage to her second husband, Sir Richard Burke of Mayo, by slamming the castle door in his face and then stealing all his castles. At a time when the old Gaelic world was crumbling around her, Grace ensured the continuation of her own dynasty and something of the old culture.

Achill Island

More than with most places in the west, you need good weather for **ACHILL ISLAND**. Although it's the part of County Mayo most developed for tourism, this means no more than a few hotels, B&Bs and hostels, and if it rains there's simply nothing to do but pack up and head for Westport or Sligo. The scattered houses can sometimes give the place an oddly prosaic, almost suburban feel; but against this, there's the magnificence of the mountains and cliffs, and in good weather, Achill can be magical, especially for campers who can live at the water's edge. The island's sandy beaches never seem overcrowded, although they attract plenty of (mostly Irish) tourists in high summer. Inland, the bogs and mountains are dotted with ancient relics – standing stones, stone circles and dolmens. The largest of the Irish islands (although it's connected to the mainland by a road bridge), Achill was Irish-speaking until very recently. Tourism here seems to have had an almost entirely beneficial effect, economically at least: before its arrival, islanders subsisted to a very great extent on remittances sent home by emigrant relatives.

Achill Sound

The bridge that crosses to the island will bring you first to **ACHILL SOUND**. There's a small **tourist office**, on the mainland side at *Alice's Harbour Inn* (July & Aug Mon–Sat 10am–6pm; ☎098/45384), and a number of souvenir shops. These can be discou-

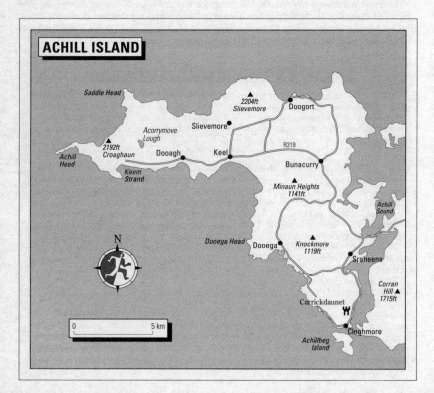

ACHILL ISLAND

raging, but it's best to ignore them – they're in no way typical of what's to come. More useful are a post office and **bike rental** (£6 per day) over the bridge at *Óstán gob A'choire*, aka *Achill Sound Hotel* (☎098/45245; ④). Achill Sound really isn't the best base for exploring the island, but if you decide to go no further, it's worth pressing on a few hundred yards for an excellent independent **hostel**, the *Wild Haven* (☎098/45392; ①), which does offer the comforts of warm duvets and an open fire. Nearby, there's a little café, *An Bolg Lán*, that serves good home baking and sandwiches.

The island

A combination of walking and cycling is the most pleasurable way to get to know Achill, although the island can be fairly strenuous going (hitching is a viable alternative, especially in season when the island is full of visitors).

The road that encircles the island has now been signposted as the "Atlantic drive". After a left turn, you'll follow a narrow inlet of the sea for three miles, before coming to **KILDOWNET**, where the well-preserved tower of the fifteenth-century **Carrickdaunet Castle**, once owned by the redoubtable Grace O'Malley, gazes out at the mainland (keys from the house next door). There are also the ruins of a twelfth-century church. As you round the corner of the island, the view of the ocean opens up, and the massive shoulder of **Minaun**, Achill's third highest mountain, appears.

At **DOOEGA**, there's B&B at *Lavelle's* bar (☎098/45116; ③) and a tiny art gallery and natural history museum. Here, the road turns inland across heathery moorland for Keel and Dugort, which make the best bases for exploring the island.

Keel and Dooagh

At **KEEL**, there's a wonderful two-mile sandy **beach**, which ends at the twin village of Dooagh. At the Keel end of the strand are the fantastic Cathedral Rocks, eroded into a series of caves and pillars by the wind and water. They are backed by the **Minaun**, at 1532ft another mountain worth climbing for the view. A turning off the road into Keel will take you close up to the summit.

West along the strand at **DOOAGH**, one road leads on over the side of the Croghaun to the golden sands and, on a good day, sparkling turquoise waters of **Keem Strand**. Often deserted, it's a rewarding place to make for, with its impressive views over Clew Bay, but if you're on a bike, be warned: it's tough going (and the sheer drop on the seaward side is vertigo inducing). A turning off the Keem Road will take you up to **Acorrymore Lough** – surrounded by scree slopes, and now dammed to supply water locally. It's a bleak, rather than poetic, spot and is the best ascent of **Croghaun**, the island's second highest mountain and just a whisker lower than Slievemore at 2195ft – its seaward side boasts spectacularly high cliffs, the island's highest. This is decidedly tough hill-walking country, so you need to be reasonably experienced even to think of attempting it. Once at the top, however, you're rewarded with a magnificent view of the Belmullet Peninsula and the scattered islands, while mountains rise spectacularly in the southeast.

If you want to **stay**, at Keel there's the *Wayfarer Hostel*, which is right on the strand (*IHH*, mid-March to mid-Oct; ☎098/43266, fax ☎47253; ①), as is the **campsite** (June–Sept; ☎098/43211). Dooagh's *Achill Head Hotel* (☎098/43108; ④) has a nightclub and could make a more lively base. The best places for eating and drinking are in Dooagh; here the *Beehive* is a relaxed crafts and coffee shop, and you can get fresh seafood **dinners** at the pleasantly run-down *Seafood Chalet Restaurant*, which serves main courses for around £7. The culinary star of the area – indeed, the island – is *The Boley House* (6–9pm; ☎098/43147), with modest home cooking using super-fresh ingredients (signposted from the eastern end of the village). You can rent **bikes** at *O'Malley's Island Sports* in Dooagh (☎098/43125); for **music**, try the nearby *Village Inn* or the *The Mihaun*.

Dugort

DUGORT, decidedly less fly-blown than Keel or Dooagh, though without their magnificent open views of the Atlantic, may make a more comfortable base. Follow the signs
for the Deserted Village, and take the Atlantic Drive for Dugort. Half a mile out of Keel,
a signposted footpath leads to a mini megalithic tomb set in the hillside where the
gorse meets the heather – well worth the climb, if only for the view. A couple of miles
further on, some ruined buildings and scattered gravestones are all that's left of a
village known simply as **The Settlement**. It was founded in 1834 by a Protestant vicar,
the Reverend E. Nangle, who bought up sixty percent of the island and built schools
and a printing press in an ultimately unsuccessful effort to evangelize the islanders.
Towering to the north is **Slievemore**, Achill's highest mountain at 2205ft – a massive
pile of quartzite and mica. Here on its southern slopes stands a **dolmen** with a stone
circle at each end and a *booley* village of huts formerly used during summer pasturing –
a reminder of a much newer, but equally extinct, transhumant way of life. At the foot of
Slievemore, on the seaward side, are the **Seal Caves**, burrowing way back under the
mountain; you can visit them by boat from the tiny pier at Dugort.

  If you want to get away from the seaside holiday atmosphere, you can **stay** on the
southern slopes of the mountain at *McDowell's Hotel* (April–Sept; ☎098/472051; ④),
which does excellent food, including vegetarian, and runs frequent traditional music
sessions, or, closer to Dugort, at the *Slievemore Hotel* (☎098/43224; ④). Two miles east
of Dugort, *Atoka House*, at Valley Crossroads, is a comfortable **B&B** (☎098/47229; ③)
with a good, cheap restaurant attached. A few hundred yards away and signposted is
the *Valley House Hostel* (April–Nov; ☎098/47204; ①), a handsome, crumbling edifice
that was once home to the woman whose story is told in J.M. Synge's *The Playboy of the
Western World* – her rejected suitor burned down a barn and tossed her onto the
flames. The place now has four-bed rooms and the luxury of a bar. Dugort has two
campsites: the *Seal Caves Caravan and Camping Park* (April–Sept; ☎098/43262) and
Lavele's Golden Strand Caravan and Camping Park (April–Sept; ☎098/47232).

  The flatlands between Achill and Belmullet are currently being reafforested with
thick conifer plantations, but are less than exciting.

North Mayo

Predominantly bogland, **north Mayo** – and especially the northwest – is an area that can
seem forbidding in bad weather, but when the sun shines and suffuses everything in a
hazy glow, you can forgive all. The most interesting sights are the **Céide Fields**, where
prehistoric field patterns have been uncovered beneath nearly seven feet of bog, offering
a startling view of the unchanging nature of human habitation here over five millennia;
and the historically resonant town of **Killala**, scene of the 1798 French invasion.

Bangor, the walking trail and Erris

About 25 miles north from Achill, **BANGOR** is pleasant enough, although its land-
locked location makes it less exciting than the seaside places nearby. The local **tourist
information office** (April–Sept daily 10am–5pm) is on the Achill Road. There's a
hostel a little way out of town at *Owenmore Riverlodge* (☎097/83497; ①), and the pleasantest B&B is probably the newly renovated *Old School Lodge* (☎097/83532; ③),
where you can also rent self-catering accommodation; or try the B&B at *Doherty's Bar*.
The *Kiltane Tavern* serves fresh and smoked local wild salmon.

  Bangor marks the start of a spectacular long-distance hike, the **Bangor Trail**, an
ancient route that runs southeast through the **Nephin Beg Mountains** to Newport. As
R.L. Praeger, who walked the route in 1937 wrote:

> *Where else even in Ireland will you find this hundred square miles which is homeless and roadless – nothing but brown heather rising as far as you can see... into high bare hills breaking down here and there in rocky scarps, with the Atlantic winds singing along their slopes?*

It is indeed lonely country, with the legacy of the Famine everywhere visible, but the desolation of the landscape can be exhilarating. A detailed, though expensive, guide to the trail is available at £6.95 from local tourist information offices.

If you are heading northwest from Bangor to Belmullet along the main road (the R313), you'll pass through the northern side of the district of **Erris**. As a whole it's a bleak area, where you'll see scenes of mass destruction of the bog as Bord na Mona extracts peat on an industrial scale to fuel Bellacorrick Peat Power Station. Should you want to explore further south, take the Srahmore Road from Bangor to **GAOTH SÁILE** (Geesala), a village of a few houses and – improbably for a Irish-speaking place – a bar called the *High Chaparral*; it also has a comfortable **hostel**, the *Ostan Synge* (May–Sept; ①), with large, balconied rooms looking south to Achill.

Belmullet and the peninsula

BELMULLET (*Béál à mhuirthead*, "mouth of the Mullet") is a functional little village, its streets perpetually mired from the mud of the bogs. Like most Irish towns, it's a planned settlement, founded as late as 1825 by the local landlord, William Carter, to "create a home market for produce that did not previously exist nearer than thirty miles by land". Its success was such that it eclipsed the older landlord village of Binghamstown (*An Geata Mór*), on the peninsula, which was deserted by the late nineteenth century. The attraction of the place lies not so much in its physical charms as in a kind of unpretentious unhurriedness – life goes on, shops stay open until late, and the sun arches slowly toward the horizon over the wide western sea. You can **stay** in the *Western Strands Hotel* (☎097/81096; ③), which has basic rooms, and there are numerous B&Bs; try *Mill House* in American Street (☎097/81181; ④). There are plenty of bars and fast-food joints, so take your pick; the liveliest **bar** is probably the one at the *Western Strands*, where you'll also get a good cheap dinner. *Leneghan's*, next to the hotel, has *Comhaltas* (traditional music) sessions on the third Friday of the month; so does the *Anchor Bar*, which serves local seafood.

A flat slab of land that seems tacked on to the mainland almost as an afterthought, **Belmullet Peninsula** is sparsely populated, but the houses are scattered in the characteristically Irish way (town-dwelling, as well as Ireland's town-planning, was largely an Anglo-Irish invention). Along with this pattern of habitation, you'll also see field-systems not much different from the Stone Age ones uncovered at Céide (see overleaf).

The seaward side of the peninsula is raked by Atlantic winds to the extent that almost no vegetation can survive. The landward side, overlooking Blacksod Bay, at the southern tip of the peninsula, is much more sheltered and has some good **beaches**, notably at Elly Bay halfway down. To the east and north the land rises; although the cliffs are not hugely spectacular, there's some rewarding walking. The peninsula is one of the locations where the legendary Children of Lír (see p.176) were condemned to spend their last three hundred years; they are buried, according to legend, on Inishglora, a tiny island off the west coast. The peninsula is rich in historical remains, too: there are promontory **forts** at Doonamo, Doonaneanir and Portnafrankach. The one at Doonamo, on an impressive clifftop site, encloses three *clocháns* and a circular fort. Under the waters of Blacksod Bay lies **La Rata**, the largest of three Spanish Armada galleons that sank in 1588.

In calm weather, Matthew and Josephine Geraghty run boat trips out to the islands of **Inis Gé** (Inishkea North and South) for £10 return (☎097/85741) from Belmullet; Millicent Sweeney at Blacksod is an alternative (☎097/85661). You can arrange **riding** at the *Durham Riding Centre* near Blacksod (☎097/85811). An **adventure centre** at Elly Bay, *10° West* (☎097/82111), can arrange canoeing, wind-surfing, sailing and cycling; it also offers weekend courses with accommodation (June–Aug).

Northeast along the coast to Downpatrick Head

East of Belmullet, the country becomes much wilder: surveyed by the ice-polished shapes of the mountains, it's rough, boggy terrain where many of the remoter villages are still Irish-speaking.

Deep in this fjord-like country, at **POLLATOMISH**, there are a handful of houses and two pubs. *Mrs B. McGrath* does **B&B** (April–Sept; ☎097/84626; ③), and there's an *An Óige* **hostel** housed in an old rectory (Easter–Sept; ☎097/84511; ①); they never turn away anyone out of season, but phone ahead to confirm. The hostel also does meals. The independent hostel close by at *Kilcommon Lodge* (☎097/84621; ①) also does B&B and meals. *McGrath's* bar has set dancing on Wednesday nights.

From here single-track roads lead up to Benwee Head; at almost 820ft, this massive cliff has great views of the Donegal cliffs to the northeast and the **Stags of Broadhaven**, a series of seven 300ft rocks, which stand a mile and a half off the coast. **PORTACLOY**, where there's a deply indented bay edged with golden sand, makes a good starting point for walking on the headland; there's a B&B high up on the hill facing the headland. The **Hackett and Turpin** factory shop is on the road to Rinroe Point at Ceathrú Thaidgh (Carrowteige), the other obvious setting-off point for Benwee Head and an unlikely – not to be missed – outpost of the fashion industry. Here local women work on six handlooms to produce designer knitwear in linen, silk and wool at amazingly low prices. The road descends through intricate interlockings of land and sea to golden beaches and the tiny harbour at Rinroe itself.

Further east, near Porturlin, the waves have carved the rocks into weird, contorted shapes, including the **Arches**, a 30ft opening in the cliff which the brave – or foolhardy – attempt to row through in good weather at low tide.

At **Downpatrick Head**, there are some puffing holes that send up tall plumes of water in rough weather, and a detached stack of rock with a fort perched on it; a plaque commemorates those who were killed in the aftermath of the 1798 uprisings. There's a profusion of rare birds and grand views over to Céide Fields and the wild country to the west, eastwards to the Sligo mountains and north across the wide, empty sea.

Céide Fields

In terms of understanding the landscape, the most important site on this stretch of coast is the prehistoric farm that covers some 24 square miles of boggy moorland between Belderrig and Ballycastle. Although signposted from the road, the Belderrig site offers little enlightenment to the untrained eye: for that, carry on another five miles to the main site at **Céide Fields** – pronounced *Cajun* without the *n* – (June–Sept daily 9.30am–6.30pm; Oct 10am–1pm & 2–5pm; Nov–May call ☎01/661 3111, ext 2366; £1.50). As Seamus Heaney's poem *Belderg* observes:

> *They just kept turning up*
> *and were thought of as foreign*
> *one-eyed and benign, they lie about his house*
> *quernstones out of a bog*

Under nearly seven feet of blanket bog, archeologists have unearthed the stone walls of a Neolithic farm system and apparently solved the riddle of how the builders of the great megalithic tombs that run across the northern part of Ireland lived. They were, it seems, farming people who joined the original fishers and hunters of Ireland around 5000 years ago and seem to have lived in harmony with them, and each other: the pattern of settlement is dispersed and shows no defensive features. The fields run longitudinally with the slope of the land and appear to have been used for pasture – as in contemporary Ireland, where the largest single contribution to the national economy still comes from grass-raised livestock.

The faint marks left by these ancient farmers don't look like much to the untrained eye, and the Céide Fields centre is, inevitably, heavy on interpretation. Based in a pyramidal building that will soon – when the heather planted on its slopes takes root – begin to merge with the surrounding landscape, it includes an exhibition, a viewing platform at the pyramid's apex, an audiovisual theatre (with a romantically voice-overed show giving some of the area's geological background) and an excellent, if pricy, café (small portion of lasagne £3.25). The entrance fee also includes a guided tour, usually by one of the archeological workers on the dig. The pyramid shape of the building seems mad in this context – it may be intended to indicate the age of the site (*older* than the Egyptian pyramids, in fact), but you can't help feeling it's got more to do with contemporary museum fashions and the famous pyramid at the Paris Louvre than with the mystery and rhythms of the Mayo landscape.

Ballycastle

BALLYCASTLE, just east of the Céide Fields, in the wide valley of the River Ballinglen, is a tranquil village of just one broad, sloping street, with good swimming beaches. Don't leave without checking out the **Ballinglen Arts Foundation**: two Philadelphia art dealers have settled here and bring "mid-career" artists here to paint, with the proviso that they leave some of the work they produce in Ballycastle. The results are to be seen in the courtroom and the old schoolhouse, which is used for studio space (☎096/43184).

The **tourist information office**, which will be able to offer detailed advice on walking nearby, is based just below the church (Mon–Sat 10.30am–5pm, Sun 1–4pm; closed for long lunches). There are a handful of relaxed **bars** – try the tiny *Lavell's* or *Barlett's* pub – and one or two **B&Bs**: try *Hilltop House* (③) on the road out to Downpatrick Head. Heading up towards Céide Fields, the brilliantly painted *Doonfeeny House* (☎096/43092; ③) offers a restaurant (with local seafood), bar and B&B accommodation, plus equally dazzling views out to sea.

Killala and around

KILLALA, overlooking Killala Bay as the coast curves back round towards Ballina, is a must, both for the magnificent local scenery and for its historical connections. Scene of one of the most significant events in Irish history – the unsuccessful French invasion organized by Wolfe Tone in 1798 (see overleaf) – it's a pleasantly run-down seaside town, so small it's difficult to believe it's a bishopric, with lovely wild sea coasts and some good roads for cycling. As far as sights go, the highlights are an attractive quayside and a fine round tower, but it's the historic atmosphere that's the real attraction here. Killala's a convivial place with a disproportionate number of **pubs** – *An Gránuaile* and *The Village Inn* are two of the most traditional. Music is available at *The Anchor Bar*, as is local seafood. There's a tea shop down on the strand with fine views out to sea. A mile or so north there's a good, sheltered, sandy beach for swimming at Ross Point (signposted from the Ballycastle Road).

If you want to **stay**, there are just a couple of **B&Bs** – try Mrs Carey's *Rathoma House* (☎096/32035; ③), four miles out of town, or Michael Caplice's *Avondale*, Pier Road (☎096/32229; ③) – and an *An Óige* **hostel** in an old stone house near the centre of town (☎096/32172; ②). The **tourist office** (very part time) is in the hideous community centre next door. Most local newsagents sell Bishop Stock's *Narrative* of the events of 1798 – a surprisingly sympathetic account of the uprising.

THE FRENCH INVASION

On August 22, 1798, three warships flying British colours anchored at Kilcummin, near Killala. The Protestant Bishop Stock, relieved that they were apparently English and not the rumoured French invasion fleet, sent his two sons and the port surveyor to pay their respects. They were immediately taken prisoner; the **invasion** had begun. After a brief resistance, Killala yielded to the French, and at sunset that evening a French soldier climbed to the top of the Bishop's Palace and replaced the British flag with a green flag with a harp in the centre, bearing the words *Erin go Bragh* (Ireland for Ever).

Wolfe Tone, the inspirational leader of the United Irishmen, had been working since his exile from Ireland in 1794 to secure foreign aid for his planned insurrection against the British. However, by the time the first French expedition of 1100 men under General Humbert reached Killala, rebellion had already been all but crushed. Not only was there a military mismatch between the French professional soldiers and the few poorly armed Irish novices who joined them, but there were also ideological clashes. The French had expected that liberation from British rule would appeal to Catholics and Protestants alike, and were further confused to find the Irish volunteers greeting them in the name of the Blessed Virgin and apparently having no idea of the significance of the French Revolution.

The rest of the story is sadly predictable. With some heroic fighting, the Franco-Irish army took Killala, Ballina and Castlebar, but on September 8, near the village of Ballinamuck in County Longford, seriously depleted in both numbers and weapons, it was defeated by the united armies of Lord Cornwallis and General Lake. The French were taken prisoner and returned to France; the Irish rebels were hanged. At Rath Lackan, there's a statue to the first French soldier who fell in the 1798 struggle, as well as a wide bay with golden sands looking over to the Sligo mountains.

A month later, sailing with another French force from Brest, Wolfe Tone was himself captured – along with the French fleet – off the coast of Donegal. He was subsequently courtmartialled and condemned to death. Despite his insistence that he should be treated with military honour, and therefore shot, he was sentenced to hang. Before that could be carried out, he cut his throat with a pocketknife and died after seven days of agony. He came to personify the tradition of both revolutionary violence and religious tolerance (he was a Protestant) in the cause of an independent Ireland.

The events of 1798 led directly to the Act of Union with Britain three years later, while the land agitation that spread throughout the country laid the foundations for land reform, Catholic emancipation and, eventually, the long process that led to Irish independence.

Ballina to Castlebar

The interior of County Mayo can't match the splendour of its sea coasts, and unless you're keen on fishing or walking, you're unlikely to spend much time here. Like all of Ireland's less touristed areas, however, it has a charm of its own if you stick with it. A region of rough moorland – the foothills of the Nephin Beg and Ox ranges – it's strewn with lakes, giving way in the east to flatter, more fertile country. It's dotted, too, with market towns, each with its own distinctive architecture and character.

The road from Killala to Ballina runs through flat farm country. The minor road that runs closer to the Moy estuary is more interesting, with two abbeys on the estuary, **Moyne** and **Rosserk**, both of them founded in the fifteenth century. Rosserk, with a tower at the water's edge, is the bigger and more poetic of the two – and considered the best Franciscan building in the country – but both have good cloisters. Look out for the sixteenth-century graffiti on the wall at Moyne; the place was burned down by Sir Richard Bingham, the English governor of Connacht, in 1590.

Ballina

The busy town of **BALLINA**, clustered around two graceful bridges on the River Moy, makes a good place to stock up on provisions and information. The elegant Victorian and Edwardian pub- and shop-fronts testify to a long history of vigorous trading, and this tradition continues in the rebuilding and energetic business activity that's evident everywhere. Stock up on smoked salmon at *Clarke's Salmon Smokery* on O'Rahilly Street, which also displays an impressive range of fresh, whole fish in its windows. *Keehane's* in Arran Street is a reasonable bookshop, and the West of Ireland **cycling club** is based at *American House* on Station Road (☎096/21350). You can enquire about cycle rental for the ride up through Killala (see p.369) and on along the spectacular cliffy coastline around Downpatrick Head (see p.368).

The **tourist office** (April–Sept Mon–Sat 10am–1pm & 2–5.15pm; ☎096/70848) is between the bridges on the side of the river away from town. If you want to **stay** and indulge in some real splendour, with a touch of Gothic-horror excess, try *Belleek Castle* (☎096/71750; ⑥). Take Pearse Street eastward from the centre, and follow the signs; a left turn will bring you through an imposing stone gateway and to a long drive through dark forest to a neo-Jacobean mansion in forbidding grey stone. For more affordable accommodation the *Bartra House Hotel* (☎096/22200; ⑤) is a cheerful and friendly place; while the *Salmon Weir Hostel* (*IHH*, open all year; ☎096/71903; ②), built on the site of an old timber and grain mill on the banks of the River Moy, is an imaginative piece of industrial rehab – the car park is graced with a series of Firoic columns. There are also plenty of B&Bs in town.

When **eating**, make sure you try the famous Moy salmon. The *River Bar Inn*, on the right bank of the Moy, a little down-river from town, does good seafood. *The Broken Jub* (☎096/72379) – named after John Banville's play – a roomy bar and restaurant at the top of Pearse Street, offers a fine selection of carvery meals from about £4. The *Old Bond Store Restaurant and Crafts Shop* in Dillon Terrace, another refurbishment, makes a good stop for daytime meals.

Crossmolina and Lough Conn

Five or so miles southwest, relaxed, raffish **CROSSMOLINA**, at the top of Lough Conn, has a place to stay that's a sight in itself. Not far south on the lakeshore, *Enniscoe House* (☎096/31112; ⑦), a delicate pink Georgian mansion that does B&B, is a good example of easygoing Georgian attitudes to architecture. Originally built in the mid-eighteenth century as a three-storey house, it was extended in the 1790s (and damaged in 1798 when the French army marched down the back avenue) to include a grand facade overlooking Lough Conn. The result inside is two completely different structures whose floor levels and room sizes don't correspond at all. There's a heritage centre here, mainly agricultural artefacts, with demonstrations of traditional crafts, and a family history research centre that will help you look up your north Mayo ancestors (Mon–Thurs Mon–Fri 9am–4.30pm, Sat & Sun June–Oct only 2–6pm; £1).

There is a **tourist information centre** in town (May–Oct Mon–Fri 10am–1.30pm & 2–5pm, Sat 10.30am–1pm & 2–4.30pm; no phone); and the *Dolphin Hotel* (☎096/31270; ③) makes for a comfortable run-down alternative to the *Enniscoe*. You can get good daytime **meals** in the *Tea Room*, and there are plenty of **bars**, most with **music** a couple of nights during the week – *McMorrow's* has traditional sessions on Friday nights, and also sells fishing tackle for anglers bound for the nearby lough.

The main attraction of **Lough Conn** is for fishermen: the lake itself is rich in trout, and the River Moy is a delight for salmon anglers. If this is your thing then the place to stay would be the marvellously eccentric *Mount Falcon Castle* (☎096/21172; ⑦), run by the indomitable Constance Aldridge a few miles out of Ballina, which has its own fishing. If you're staying elsewhere you'll need to check the position on licences locally.

However, the area has plenty of scenic and historical interest to sustain non-anglers. The moorland hills that border the lake are good for gentle **walking**; for a taste of the Nephin Beg wilderness and some more demanding hikes (see p.363) head south from Crossmolina down the west side of the lough and take a right at Lahardaun. The lakesides themselves are scattered with abbeys, castles and megaliths, as well as some hidden sandy beaches.

Pontoon and Foxford

Continuing south along the R315 for Foxford, through rough, peaty terrain strewn with boulders, you reach **PONTOON**, on the neck of land that separates Lough Conn from Lough Cullin. The village is a good base for exploring both the lakes' shores and the foothills of the Nephin Beg Mountains to the northwest and the Ox Mountains to the northeast. For **accommodation**, try *Healy's Hotel* (☎094/56443; ⑥), a no-nonsense anglers' **hotel** and former coaching inn on the lakeside, where the restaurant specializes in home-cooked Irish food using local produce, or *Cooltra Lodge* (June to mid-Sept; ☎094/56640; ①), a **hostel** that also has good watery views.

   FOXFORD, a couple of miles east, is a trim village in the lee of the Ox Mountains which owed its late nineteenth-century survival to the **Foxford Woollen Mill** (Mon–Sat 10am–6pm; £2.85, includes tour of present-day factory), which now has an elaborate audiovisual presentation to tell its story. There's a gift shop and, upstairs, a pleasant tea shop; rooms are let to local artists and craftspeople. After the 1840s Famine, the potato crop failed again in the 1870s, resulting in evictions and abject poverty for the people of the town and the peat-cutting districts around. Most families led a precarious existence, relying on their own potato crop and, in the absence of significant cash employment in Foxford, the meagre earnings the men were able to bring back from summers working on big farms in Scotland. Such conditions led to demands for land reform – the Land League was founded in 1879 by Michael Davitt, also the bringer of trade unionism to Ireland, whose cottage at **STRADE**, between Foxford and Castlebar, you can also visit (Tues–Sat 2–6pm; 50p). The mill at Foxford was founded in 1890 by a far-sighted nun called Marrough Bernard, who called it Providence. At a time when more professionally run mills were failing – so unused were her workers to ideas of productivity that she had to bribe them with cash prizes – the success of the mill could certainly be called providential. Its profits were used to fund schools and a diverse range of cultural activities, of which one, the Foxford Mill brass band, still survives.

   The **tourist accommodation office**, in one of the mill buildings (Mon–Sat 11am–5pm, Sun noon–6pm; ☎094/56488), has useful details of walking and fishing in the area; the *North Mayo Angling Advice Centre*, where you can buy licences, is also in the town. There are a few **B&Bs** in Foxford – try *Mrs M. Gannon* on Providence Road (☎094/56101; ③), but on the whole you're probably better off among the scenic beauties of Pontoon. *Hennigan's* pub has traditional music and ballad nights.

Castlebar and around

CASTLEBAR, although it's the county town of Mayo, offers little reason to hang around. The tree-bordered green is attractive, and the main street has all the facilities you might need conveniently gathered together, but since the demise of the annual rock festival there seems to be little going on. Historically, it's notable for a Franco-Irish victory in 1798, at which General Humbert's army routed a stronger force commanded by General Lake – the event has gone down in history as the "Castlebar Races" because of the speed of the British retreat. The **tourist information office** (Mon–Sat 9.30am–6pm; ☎094/21207) is in the Old Linen Hall – which was the venue for a celebratory dinner after the rout of the British in 1798 – and, with information about the whole of north Mayo, is more than usually useful if you're planning an extended stay; it's particularly strong on walking. In the same building is the *Linen*

Hall Arts Centre, which puts on sometimes imaginative shows (including plenty for children); and, if your body is cyring out for cappuccinos, you can buy them in the attached café.

Should you need to **stay**, there's plenty to choose from. There's the swanky *Breaffy House* (☎094/22033; ⑤), a Victorian pile out on the Claremont Road, with hideous modern extensions; or back in town, the friendly and comfortable *Imperial Hotel* (☎094/21961; ⑤), which is ideally situated on the green. **B&Bs** are mainly concentrated on the Westport Road, where you could try *Nephin House* (☎094/23840; ③) or *Millhill House* (☎094/24279; ③). In the centre of town, in Thomas Street, is an independent **hostel**, *Hughes House* (IHH, June–Sept; ☎094/23877, fax ☎23877; ②). There's a sprinkling of Indian and Chinese **restaurants**, or you could try the unexpectedly appetizing food at the *Imperial*. *Café Rouge* in New Antrim Street does a good range of home cooking for daytime eating (10am–6pm). For cheerful fast food, go to *Chipadora* in Thomas Street – done out, diner-style, in ice-cream pastel colours. *McCarthy's Bar* in Main Street has snugs and **traditional music**. *Johnnie McHale's*, opposite the *Welcome Inn* in Upper Chapel Street, is a great old Castlebar music pub, as is the *Irish House* in Thomas Street. *Moran's*, off the green in Spencer Street, has music on Thursday nights.

Seven miles south of Castlebar on the Ballinrobe Road (N84) is **Ballintubber Abbey**. Founded in 1216 by Cathal O'Connor, King of Connacht, it's an important site and ought to be atmospheric. Sadly that's not the case. It's been grossly over-restored, and around the church the Stations of the Cross form a kind of ghastly theme park in stone, including representations of an empty tomb, an inexplicable dolmen and some human figures whose overall impression is vaguely pornographic. The excavations, however, did uncover a hospice for pilgrims on their way to climb the holy mountain of Croagh Patrick and part of the cloisters, which have been re-erected. Grace O'Malley's son, Tioad na Long, is buried here. **Tóchar Phádraig**, the 22-mile pilgrim route to Croagh Patrick, has been re-opened but for now can only be walked when conducted by a pilgrim guide (☎094/21207).

Southeast of Ballintubber Abbey, on the shores of Lough Carra, you can explore the **Doon Archeological Nature Peninsula** (10am–6pm June–Sept; £3). With things to see from standing stones to Norman castles, and a Famine grave, the place opens up the complex human history of this seemingly little-populated area.

About five miles southeast along the N60, **Balla**, a single wide street of pastel-coloured houses, has a short round tower, off the main square, that may be a twelfth-century "fake". The hamlet of **Mayo**, lost in a maze of unsignposted lanes, has only an abrupt right-angle bend in the road to mark the ghostly presence of the Augustinian abbey that gave the place enough importance to make it the county town.

Knock to Cong

East Mayo is dominated by the devotional shrine at Knock, easier to visit since the opening of an international **airport** at nearby Charlestown in 1986. However, if you're not a believer or religious kitsch isn't a strong-enough draw, you're best off heading south to the more engaging and historically rich town of Cong.

Knock

Ever since an apparition of the Virgin Mary, accompanied by Saint Joseph and Saint John, was seen on the gable of the parish church of **KNOCK** in 1879, it has been a place of pilgrimage. As a passer-by in Ireland, it's surprisingly easy to forget the all-pervasive influence of the Catholic Church, but at Knock you're brought slap up against it. Whatever you may believe about the possible authenticity of the apparitions,

Knock rates for Catholics, along with Lourdes in France and Fatima in Portugal, as one of the leading modern miraculous confirmations of their faith. A massive and ugly church with a capacity of twenty thousand was opened nearby in 1976, and the pope visited the shrine in 1979.

When Monsignor Horan, a local priest, first hatched the plan for the new airport it seemed a crazy and profligate idea, and there were years of bitter controversy over this apparent waste of public funds. In fact it has proved remarkably successful, and as well as bringing in pilgrims to see the shrine, the airport has had the effect of opening up the northwest of Ireland for travellers – to the extent that Mayo is in reach of London for weekend breaks, and house prices in the county are booming as wealthy inhabitants of southeast England buy their second homes. The Lourdes-to-Knock run is also used by fishers from the southwest of France to reach west Ireland's lake fisheries.

The **airport** (situated three miles from Charlestown at the junction of the N17 and N5) is open from 9am to 6pm daily, serving many UK airports including Luton, Stansted and Coventry. An *Aer Lingus* shuttle service to Dublin connects with major international flights. There's a **tourist information office** in the airport, open to greet arriving flights (winter closed Tues & Thurs; ☎094/67247), and another in Knock itself (May–Sept daily 10am–6pm; ☎094/88193); ask them for details of transport – most of the time you seem to have to rely on taxis to Charlestown (a major crossroads where you can pick up buses and there are a number of B&Bs) or Knock.

As a **place**, Knock is nothing much to look at. The scene of the apparitions has been glassed in to form a **chapel**, and pilgrims can be seen there praying at all hours. Other than that, and the religious tat shops (whose main line is plastic bottles to take your holy water away in), there's also a **Museum of Folk Life** (10am–7pm; £1.50). If you need a place to **stay**, there's no problem finding somewhere. There are a couple of hotels, such as the *Belmont* (☎094/88122; ⑥), and numerous B&Bs: try Mrs Carney's *Burren*, Kiltimagh Road (☎094/88362; ③), or *Mervue*, overlooking the shrine (☎094/88127; ③).

Ballinrobe to Cong

BALLINROBE is probably worth visiting only if you're here in the third week of July, for the **Ballinrobe Races**. This is Irish racing as you've imagined it, with a great atmosphere at a picturesque and compact course; there's excellent viewing and it's all very relaxed and amateur. For accommodation, there are a couple of **B&Bs** – book early for race week – try Mrs Anne Mahon's *Riverside House* in the Cornmarket (☎092/41674; ②).

South of Ballinrobe, on the R334 around Neale, is clustered a sequence of monuments, ancient and not-so-ancient. They range from a series of stone circles, nearer Cong, to a cross and another of the mysterious monuments that abound in Ireland, a massive stone-stepped **pyramid**, with an inscription, almost indecipherable, including the name George Browne and some worn Roman numerals, dating it somewhere in the eighteenth century. The Brownes are the family who occupy Westport House; but the reason for the pyramid remains obscure.

Cong and around

CONG lies on the narrow spit of land that divides Lough Mask from Lough Corrib at the point where the dramatically mountainous country of Connemara to the west gives way to the flat and fertile farmland that makes up the east of County Mayo. A picture-book pretty village that caters for plenty of tourists, it's also the site of the ruined **Cong Abbey**, which was founded in 1128 for the Augustinians by Turlough O'Connor, King of Ireland (though it's probably built on a seventh-century monastic site). The door-ways represent the transition between the quite different styles of Romanesque and

Gothic. The cloisters look just a little bit too good to be true: they were partially rebuilt in 1860. At its height, Cong Abbey had a population of some 3000, and the practicalities of feeding such multitudes can be glimpsed in the remains of the refectory and kitchen by the river, where a fishing house over the water contains a fish trap beneath the floor. The **Cross of Cong**, a twelfth-century ornamented Celtic cross originally made in County Roscommon for the abbey, gives an indication of the wealth and status of the foundation – it's now on show at the National Museum in Dublin. From the abbey there's a pleasant wander through woods down to the river and the lough, although this runs through the grounds of the local big house, **Ashford Castle**, now a luxury hotel (see below), which charges for admission to its lands (£2).

It's also worth taking a look at the **canal**. In the 1840s attempts were made, as a famine relief project, to dig a canal between Lough Corrib and Lough Mask. The river that links the two, though you can get to it at various points, including the Pigeon Hole, a mile or so north of Cong, runs underground through porous limestone for most of its length. This might have been an indication of what would happen to the canal: the porosity of the rock meant that the water just drained away, and Cong is left with a dry canal, complete with locks.

The town is obsessed with *The Quiet Man*, a film that much of the rest of the world may have forgotten but which, shot here in 1956 and starring John Wayne and Maureen O'Hara, is well remembered here. It's shown nightly at the eponymous *Quiet Man* independent hostel (see below).

Practicalities

An unofficial **tourist information office** in Abbey Street (June–Sept daily 9am–6pm) gives out a free leaflet, *Get to Know Cong*. Undoubtedly the swishest place to **stay** – Ronald Reagan did – is *Ashford Castle*, which stands at the point where the river meets Lough Corrib, and has been converted into a luxury hotel (☎092/46003; ⑧). Although its history goes back to the thirteenth century, what you see now is essentially a Victorian castellated reconstruction. Two spruce hotels offer comfortable rooms: pastel green *Danagher's* (☎092/46494; ⑤), by the Abbey, and terracotta red *Ryan's*, on the main street (☎092/46243; ④). Among the numerous **B&Bs**, try Mr Connolly's *The White House* (☎092/46243; ③) and the *Rising of the Waters Inn* (☎092/46316; ③), which has simple rooms and good bar food. *The Quiet Man* independent **hostel** (*IHH*, May–Sept; ☎092/46089, fax ☎46448; ②) is centrally located on Abbey Street, and the *An Óige* **hostel** (☎092/46089, fax ☎46448; ②) is on Quay Road, signposted from the centre of town. Both hostels rent **bikes**, as does *O'Connor's Garage* on Main Street. There's more hostel accommodation and **camping** seven miles to the east in **Cross** (*IHH*, open all year; ☎092/46203; ①). You can pitch your tent for nothing on the island of Inchágoill (one of literally hundreds). The Corrib Queen does a tour from Ashford Castle pier, taking in Oughterard, on the Galway shore of the lough (☎092/46029; return £10). The island is the site of two early Christian churches as well as the Stone of Lugha, the tombstone of Saint Patrick's nephew, which bears the earliest Christian inscriptions in Ireland.

For **eating** in Cong, the place to treat yourself is *Echoes* (☎092/46059), with plenty of fish dishes, and lots of organic vegetables and herbs. The hotels do good bar food, and the *Quiet Man Coffee Shop* is a friendly place with good home baking.

Loughmask House

Loughmask House (not open to the public), on the shores of Lough Mask a couple of miles due north of Cong, was the home of the notorious **Charles Boycott**, a retired captain of the British army and land agent to Lord Erne. His behaviour towards the tenant farmers during the Land League unrest of the 1880s – particularly acute in Mayo, where the League originated and many of the "congested areas" were located –

made him one of the victims of Parnell's "moral Coventry" policy, subsequently known as "boycotting". As Parnell himself put it in a meeting in Ennis in 1880:

> *You must show what you think of him on the roadside when you meet him, you must show him in the streets of the town, you must show him at the shop counter . . . even in the house of worship, by leaving him severely alone, by putting him into a sort of moral Coventry, by isolating him from the rest of his kind as if he were a leper of old, you must show him your detestation of the crime he has committed.*

COUNTY ROSCOMMON

Roscommon has the unjust reputation of being the most boring county in Ireland. A long sliver of land running from south to north, it's the only county in Connacht without any sea coast, though it is bounded for almost its entire western border by the upper reaches of the Shannon. Although most of the county is either bog or good grassland pasture, the **Curlew Mountains** on the Sligo and Leitrim border rise high and wild. Chances are you'll be approaching the county from the south, which is not its best aspect: the most worthwhile places are **Boyle**, in the far north, for its access to the Curlew Mountains, and **Strokestown** in the east, with its remarkable Georgian mansion and Famine Museum.

Roscommon town and around

More or less in the centre of the county, there's nothing much to **ROSCOMMON**, but it's an oddly pleasant town to spend time and soak up the atmosphere. Its solid tone is set by heavy stone buildings – among them the *Bank of Ireland*, once the courthouse, and the **county jail**, now housing a collection of shops, its serrated top giving the town a characteristic silhouette, identifiable for miles around. The jail was the scene of all public hangings in the county and used to have a woman executioner called Lady Betty, whose own sentence for murder was revoked on condition that she did her gruesome job for free.

Roscommon boasts two impressive ruins: on the Boyle Road out of town, the enormous and well-preserved **Roscommon Castle** was built by the Normans in 1269, burnt down by the Irish four years later and rebuilt in 1280. Remodelling clearly continued for some time – there are some incongruously refined windows among the massive walls. The other ruin, in the lower part of the town, is the **abbey**. Roscommon takes its name from a Celtic saint, Saint Coman, who was the first bishop here and under whom the see became well known as a seat of learning, having close ties with the more famous abbey at Clonmacnois in County Offaly. The priory ruin, however, is Dominican, dating from 1253. Amazingly enough, despite the religious persecution that followed the Reformation and the Plantations, the Dominicans managed to hang on well into the nineteenth century, the last two incumbents, parish priests of Fuerty and Athleague, dying in 1830 and 1872 respectively.

The church in the centre of town houses a slightly higgledy-piggledy **museum** of local history (mid-June to mid-Aug daily 10am–5.30pm; free), the kind of place that museologists are beginning to regard as an endangered species. The building's striking Star of David window was put there by its nineteenth-century Welsh builders in honour of their patron saint.

Practicalities

The **tourist information office** is in the church (mid-June to mid-Aug daily 10am–6pm; ☎0903/26342), which houses the museum. For **accommodation** in Roscommon, there's the central *Royal Hotel* on Castle Street (☎0903/26317; ⑤), one of those fine, upstanding inns that still exist in rural Irish towns: comfortable and good fun, with plenty of locals in the bar. Otherwise, you've a sprinkling of B&Bs to choose between. These include Mrs O'Grady's *The Villa* (☎0903/26048; ③) and Mrs Campbell's *Westway*, on the Galway Road (☎0903/26927; ③), or Mrs Dolan's *Munsboro House*, a mile out on the Sligo Road (☎0903/26375; ④). *Gleeson's* is a restaurant and B&B (☎0903/26954; ③) situated in what used to be the manse of the Presbyterian church opposite the old courthouse (all three with squeaky clean stonework). For **eating**, the restaurant side of *Gleeson's* (8am–9pm) does everything from breakfast to dinner, with delicious home baking; you can sit outside in good weather. There's also a reasonable Chinese, the *China Palace* (☎0903/26337), a little further down the hill on Main Street, above the *Lyons Den* bar.

Strokestown

In the east of the county, on the N5 from Longford, **STROKESTOWN** is a gem of a planned town whose main reason for existence is Strokestown Park House, once the centre of the second biggest estate in Roscommon after Rockingham. The enormously wide main street – reputedly the result of an ambition on the part of an early owner to have the widest street in Europe – ends abruptly in a castellated wall with three Gothic arches, behind which lies Strokestown Park House.

The **Country Heritage Centre** (May–Sept Tues–Fri 9.30am–1pm & 2–3.30pm, Sat & Sun 2–6pm; £2) is located in the elegant St John's church, designed in 1819 in imitation of a medieval chapter house by the fashionable English architect John Nash (who never visited Ireland). There's material on the Ireland of the Heroes, with a focus on the Rathcrogan monuments (see p.379) and the epic *Tain Bo Chailgne*, but check what's currently on show before you pay up; the admission fee may seem a lot for an exhibition of the local football team. There are plans to turn the place into an interpretative centre for Strokestown itself, to complement the Famine Museum (see overleaf).

Accommodation is thin on the ground in Strokestown. Try B&B at the *Percy French* (☎078/33300; ③) or with Mrs Cox, two miles out of town at *Church View House* (☎078/33047; ③).

Strokestown Park House

Strokestown Park House is a graceful Georgian residence designed by Richard Castle on a plan – a central block with two side wings linked by curved arms – whose adaptability as a sort of glorified farmhouse ensures that it turns up again and again throughout Ireland. Sold by the family of the original owners to the local garage in 1979, the house has never gone through an auction and therefore retains everything from furniture to papers relating to the Famine and 1930s school exercise books.

The **house** makes a good place to get to grips with the Anglo-Irish tradition. Its story is a fairly typical one. Originally a massive 27,000 acres, the estate was granted to one Nicholas Mahon in reward for his support of the House of Stuart during the English Civil War. The original building, finished around 1696, was fortified but not particularly grand; only one room of it survives, the stillroom in the cellar. As the family became richer and more secure, it made more grandiose additions, and the current house dates essentially from the 1730s, with some early nineteenth-century alterations. In the mid-nineteenth century Major Denis Mahon, who was a particularly nasty piece of work, is believed to have been one of the first landowners to charter less-than-seaworthy vessels (the notorious **coffin ships**) to take evicted tenants to America during the Famine. His activities were reported and censured in contemporary newspapers both in Ireland and abroad. In 1847 he was shot dead on his own estate.

To give a measure of the inter-connectedness of Anglo-Irish society even in compara-tively recent times, the lady who sold the house to the garage, the redoubtable Mrs Olive Hales Pakenham-Mahon, married the heir to the Rockingham Estate in 1914, thus uniting the two biggest estates in Roscommon, though the land empire set up by this dynastic marriage ceased to exist very soon afterwards, as did the marriage: the Rockingham heir was killed at the front in the first few days of fighting of World War I. Also in the house, in one of the upstairs bedrooms, is a painting of horses and stooks of corn by Woodbrook's Phoebe Kirkwood (see p.382).

The interior of the house gives off a feeling of very comfortable living, but not extraordinary opulence; there's a relaxed living room, and a spacious library and dining room, while upstairs you can see the old schoolroom, complete with desks, blackboard and school-books. One of its really extraordinary features is a gallery that runs the length of the kitchen, allowing the lady of the house to watch what was happening there without having to venture in; on Monday mornings she would drop the week's menu down from above.

The **Irish Famine Museum** in the stableyards of the Strokestown Estate provides a provocative interpretation of the house and its history and explores wider issues of Famine migration, emigration and oppression in a historical context, aiming, in particu-lar, to break the traumatic silence that surrounds the subject. In 1945, a century after the terrible events, the Irish Folklore Commission noted:

> *I am sorry that this is such a meagre account of what was a dreadful period; but there seems to be very little information or interest left in the minds of the old people about that time. Indeed, it seems there was a sort of conspiracy of silence on the part of their moth-ers and fathers about it all.*

Informed by a sense of outrage at the attitudes, on the part of the British government and landlords, that allowed this terrible disaster to happen, the exhibition follows the harrowing story of the Famine, juxtaposing it with images of Ascendancy luxury and of present-day famine and emigration. In 1841, Ireland was the most densely populated country in Europe, with a vigorous trading and commercial life. The exhibition shows the tragic results of over-reliance on the potato, which had been introduced into the country in the early eighteenth century; by the 1840s, it was the staple diet of the popu-lation. Blight arrived in Ireland in October 1845. In a letter to the British Secretary of the Treasury, a contemporary eyewitness surveyed the devastation:

> *On the 27th of last month I passed from Cork to Dublin and this doomed plant bloomed in all the luxuriance of abundant harvest. Returning on the third instant I beheld with sorrow one wide waste of putrefying vegetation. In many places the wretched people were seated on the fences of their decaying gardens, wringing their hands and wailing bitterly the destruction that has left them foodless.*

The exhibition traces the poverty and hard-heartedness of the Whig government's lais-sez-faire economic response to the crisis. Its callousness in the face of human suffering on a massive scale – as well as its attitude to Irish ways of life – is indicated by Trevelyan's response, as the famine deepened:

> *The great evil with which we have to contend is not the physical evil of famine but the moral evil of the selfish, perverse and turbulent character of the [Irish] people.*

The government resolved to make no official intervention to hinder the operation of private enterprise: relief food imports were stopped. Between 1841 and 1851, about 1.4 million Irish people died and another 1.4 million people emigrated – figures almost entirely attributable to the Famine.

The house and museum – plus a walled garden with a spectacular herbaceous border – are geared for group visits, but it can still be a thought-provoking experience, particularly if you arrive between bus-loads (May–Sept Wed–Sun noon–5pm; house £3; museum £2.70; garden £2).

West from Strokestown

Heading west from Strokestown, there are a number of historical attractions that may divert you on your way to Mayo, including an extensive ancient Irish settlement near Tulsk, and Clonalis House, at Castlerea, the home of one of Ireland's oldest Gaelic families.

Elphin

The trim village of **ELPHIN**, about four miles northwest of Strokestown, has been the seat of a bishopric for 1500 years, ever since Saint Patrick founded a church on this spot. The **cathedral**, rather unconvincingly restored in part in 1982, contains the tombs both of early bishops and of members of the Goldsmith family – Oliver's birthplace is disputed between here and Pallas in County Longford, which has been doing its rather feeble best to cash in on the Goldsmith connection (see p.182). Even his famous poem *The Deserted Village* may describe County Roscommon rather than County Longford (and the English claim it's about the *English* enclosures); at any rate, he went to school here.

Tulsk and Rathcroghan

> *Paganism has been destroyed though it was splendid and far flung . . . their old cities are deserts without worship.*
>
> Oengus the Culdee, early Christian poet

Centred roughly on the village of **TULSK** on main N5 is a collection of some seventy megalithic monuments that mark one of the great centres of ancient Ireland, plus more than eighty ring forts. Unlike the monuments of, say, County Sligo, they're unmarked and largely unexcavated – most of them are no more to look at than grassy shapes in the fields – and access is generally free and unrestricted. According to legend, the most important of them, the long-barrow of Rathcroghan itself, was built by Eochard Fedleach, King of Connacht and father of Medb – who herself took power by killing her pregnant sister Clothro, who had inherited the title from their father.

In the absence of signposting, the area's monuments are difficult to identify, even using the detailed map in *The Heritage Guide to Rathcroghan* (available from tourist offices; £1.95). **Rathcroghan** – or Cruachan – itself lies just beyond the first crossroads on the N5 northwest of Tulsk and is signposted. It's a ring-barrow, traditionally the inauguration place of the kings of Connacht; close by are a cluster of standing stones, cairns and ring-barrows with legendary associations with Medb.

MEDB AND EARTH MAGIC

Medb's prodigious appetite for men – she was reported to have thirty lovers a day, "each man in another man's shadow" – reflects her non-historical career as a spiritual symbol: her name links her with the sanskrit *madhu*, a sort of demon, and with Shakespeare's Queen Mab, Queen of the Fairies. She's now enjoying a renaissance in a reincarnation as Gaia, the spirit of earth.

Clothro's unborn child, in one of the gruesome details beloved of those legends, was cut from her womb with a sword and himself grew up to become a warrior. Medb took as a lover the great Cuchulainn of the epic poem *Tain Bo Cuailgne*.

For the rest, it's probably best to rely on inspired guesswork when moving among these unexcavated monuments, knowing that, in this ancient landscape, anything you identify is likely to be at least as old as you think.

Frenchpark

Carrying on along the N5, at **FRENCHPARK**, the **Douglas Hyde Interpretive Centre** (May–Sept Tues–Fri 2–5pm, Sat & Sun 2–6pm; donation suggested) is housed in an old Church of Ireland church. Hyde (1860–1949), one of the founders of the Gaelic League in 1893 and the leading exponent of the importance of the Irish language and culture in the Nationalist movement, was – like his approximate contemporaries, the poet W.B. Yeats and the playwright J.M. Synge – of Anglo-Irish background. The son of the rector of Tibohine, he was sent home from boarding school when he contracted measles, and was brought up here among Irish-speakers, and later did much to record the rich vernacular tradition, as well as writing in the language – he collaborated with Lady Gregory on a number of Irish-language plays. Hyde's aim was to unite all classes in an Irish Ireland, through the Irish language; but such political naivety was bound to end in disappointment. His unhappiness with the Gaelic League's espousal of revolutionary violence led him to resign from it; eventually, however, he returned to political life when he served as the first president of Ireland. With the founding in Dublin of popular new Irish-speaking primary schools in recent years, there is some sign that Hyde's legacy, which had sometimes seemed a conservative and retrograde form of nationalism, may still be of importance. Hyde is buried in the graveyard of this simple church.

Castlerea

CASTLEREA in the west, Roscommon's third most important town after Roscommon and Boyle, is an unprepossessing place, and the only real reason for going there is to visit **Clonalis House** (June to mid-Sept Mon–Fri 11am–5.30pm, Sun 2–6pm; at other times, ring ☎0907/20014; £1.50), just outside the town to the west. Clonalis is the ancestral home of the O'Conor clan, which claims to be Europe's oldest family; it is, in fact, one of the few ancient Gaelic families – the O'Conors were traditional Kings of Connacht and last High Kings of Ireland, and can trace their family back to one Feredach the Just in 75 AD – although an even more fanciful family tree preserved in the house goes back to the fifteenth century BC. If you're expecting the house itself to be ancient, however, you're in for a disappointment – it's a Victorian pile, even if an engagingly Italianate one, of 1878. Unlike most noble Irish families, the O'Conors always remained Catholic and, although their royal past allowed them to hang on to some of their ancestral lands, they weren't in a position to flaunt their wealth – much of it derived from astute marriages to rich heiresses – until the late nineteenth century.

The house, still very much lived in, is a fascinating jumble of furniture, paintings – many of them portraits charting the family's colourful history at home and abroad – and mementos. There's a modest chapel displaying a penal chalice, which unscrews into three parts to make it easy to hide. The manuscript room contains the oldest surviving judgement under the ancient Irish Brehon law system, as well as a number of letters from Douglas Hyde (see above). Pride of place, however, goes to the harp of the blind harpist Turlough O'Carolan (1670–1738; see p.404), who numbered the then O'Conor Don among his patrons. There's a tearoom and craft shop – and you can also **stay** in the house (May–Sept; ⑦).

The house aside, there's no need to linger in Castlerea apart perhaps to visit *Hell's Kitchen*, an antiques-packed pub on the main street on the corner of the Boyle Road, describing itself as "the only national museum with a licence".

Boyle

It's disparagingly said that County Roscommon doesn't have any towns. It does, and **BOYLE**, although not the county town, is a fine, upstanding example. It's not a place marked out by particular charm or beauty, but there's enough here to keep you entertained for a one-night stopover, if you're not hurrying to cross the Curlew Mountains into Sligo. Boyle grew up around the greatest estate in County Roscommon, **Rockingham**, and although what remained of the estate was disbanded long ago and the house – in what is now the Lough Key Forest Park – was burned down in 1957, the town is still marked by their ghostly presence.

In Boyle itself, the most charismatic building is the Cistercian monastery, **Boyle Abbey** (June to mid-Sept daily 9.30am–6.30pm; out of season, keys available from Abbey House, next door; £1, Heritage Card), consecrated in 1220 and one of the early results of the arrival of foreign monastic orders in Ireland during the medieval pan-European upsurge in spiritual life. In 1142 a group of monks sent to Ireland by the redoubtable Cistercian abbot Saint Bernard of Clairvaux, at the instigation of Saint Malachy, established the great abbey of Mellifont in County Louth. Clonmacnois, the important Celtic monastery on the banks of the Shannon in County Offaly, was quickly abandoned, and within twenty years monks from Mellifont had settled at a site beside the River Boyle here at Mainistir na Buaille.

The abbey is small and compact, in very pale stone, well enough preserved to let you see how the monks must have lived. You still go in through the gatehouse (a sixteenth- or seventeenth-century addition), and there's a wonderful twelfth-century church. During the sixty-odd years it took to build the place, the Gothic style arrived in the west of Ireland; in a remarkably playful relaxation of their famous austerity, the Cistercian monks allowed themselves to build Romanesque arches down one side, and the new Gothic down the other. Look out, too, for the fantastically ornate (at least, for Cistercians) column capitals.

Boyle's big house may be gone, but the earlier residence of the King family, **King House** (May–Sept Tues–Sun 10am–6pm; April & Oct Sat & Sun only; £3), in the centre of town, has recently been restored and opened to the public with a range of high-tech exhibitions. An imposing stone mansion built around 1730, King House, with its pleasure grounds across the river, was home to the family for fifty years before they moved to Rockingham, and it represents the heyday of what was aptly known as the Ascendancy. The original Sir John King, a Staffordshire man, had been granted his land for "reducing the Irish to obedience", achieved in part through violent subjugation and by the enforcement of the notorious anti-Catholic Penal Laws. For the King family, establishing themselves in Ireland was a process of determined and successful social climbing: inheriting a baronetcy in 1755, by 1768 Edward King had ensured his elevation to Earl of Kingston.

One section of the exhibition deals with the Famine and recounts a familiar story: Robert King, Viscount Lordon, although not an absentee landlord, did – like many other landlords, after the removal of the corn tariffs flooded the Irish market with cheap grain – find it economic to evict his tenants, transport them to America and use the land for cattle grazing. Other accounts detail the Kings' colourful family history – an eighteenth-century crime of passion and a very public nineteenth-century divorce – and there's a section on the house's use as a base from 1775 for the Connacht Rangers. This details their service to the British Army in such conflicts as the Crimean and Boer wars and World War I, culminating in their mutiny at Jullandar in the Punjab in 1920 in protest at the atrocities being perpetrated by the Black and Tans back home in Ireland. Boyle's civic art collection, with some interesting modern pieces, is housed on the ground floor of the building, and there's a pleasant coffee shop, much frequented by locals at lunchtime.

At the other end of town, down the driveway that leads from beside the bridge, **Frybrook House** (daily June–Sept 2–6pm; £2.50; B&B ④; ☎079/62170) offers a view of more modest eighteenth-century living – as well as a great place to **stay**. Built around 1752, the house belonged to Henry Fry, an English Quaker (the family may be related to the Cadbury Frys of confectionery fame), who came to Boyle at the invitation of the Earl of Kingston to establish a weaving community in the town. The house has recently been extensively restored and, although only three pieces of the original furniture remain, it has been sympathetically decorated with items from the same period.

Practicalities

The **tourist information office** is at the entrance to King House in Patrick Street (June–Sept 10am–5pm; ☎079/62145), near the bridge; as well as the usual services, it can give you details of the Boyle Arts Festival, well worth catching for its ambitious programme of concerts, theatre, poetry readings, lectures and exhibitions if you're in town in late July/early August (or call ☎079/63085). *Abbey House* is a pleasant place to **stay**, wedged between the rushing river and the abbey (Feb–Nov; ☎079/62385; ③), and there are plenty of other B&Bs and a few hotels. The 250-year-old *Royal* (☎079/62016; ④) is a solid country inn where the river rushes by your window. A little outside the town at Knockvicar is *Riversdale House* (see below for details).

You can **rent bikes** (this makes a good starting point for touring the lakelands of northern and southern Sligo) from *Brendan Sheerin*, on Main Street. **Horse riding** is available at the *Curlew Trekking Centre* (☎079/62764). Places to **eat** are thin on the ground: the restaurant at the *Royal* serves indifferent food at extraordinarily high prices, but has a good coffee shop for daytime eating; and there's a useful Chinese restaurant, *Chung's*, by the bridge. For really good food, plus accommodation, head out on the Sligo Road to *Cromleach Lodge* (☎071/65155; ④), up in the Curlew Mountains.

Lough Key Forest Park and Woodbrook

The road west out of Boyle towards the **Lough Key Forest Park**, part of the old Rockingham Estate, leads through the gate of the grounds, itself a Gothic fancy, and past a castellated lodge. The park has been thoroughly and relentlessly amenitized, with a hideous wood-and-glass restaurant at the side of the lake and masses of tarmacked car-parking on the former site of the great house. The latter was designed, in an elegant if fanciful Classical style, by the English architect John Nash, who was also responsible for the Classical mansions in London's Regent's Park. Yet the stable block, church, icehouse and temple – the graces of an eighteenth-century estate – as well as the spine-chilling subterranean passages used to keep the servants out of sight, give an impression of what it must have been like. With boats for rental and plenty of ring forts to explore, it's a pleasant enough place to spend a sunny day.

You can gaze out, too, at the islands on the lake; in a disused castle on one of them W.B. Yeats planned, after his Innisfree days, to base an Irish cult devoted to the occult principles of Theosophy and the Order of the Golden Dawn – the idea was to aid the Nationalist cause by trapping the hidden forces of the land. The **circuit** of the lake is well worth doing, particularly the west side, where the road rises to give you a panoramic view. A possible stop on the way is B&B **accommodation** at *Riversdale House* (☎079/67012; ④), where the River Boyle flows out of the lough – a compact Georgian lodge on a working farm that was once home to Maureen O'Sullivan – where you can also have dinner (£12).

A little further out of Boyle on the Carrick-on-Shannon Road, **Woodbrook** is another old Anglo-Irish house. It's not open to the public, and the reason for mentioning it is that it's the subject of a remarkable book, *Woodbrook*, written by an Englishman, David Thompson, who worked there for most of the 1930s as tutor to the Kirkwood family's two young daughters, one of whom – Phoebe – was a well-known painter. Sometimes naive, sometimes sentimental, it's strong in its evocation of place and in its documentation of the passing of Anglo-Irish culture.

The very north of the county, hilly terrain where farmland gives way to the moors and lakes of the **Arigna Mountains**, is a good introduction to the more spectacular landscape over the county border in Sligo. You can break your journey in the twin villages of **Ballyfarnon** and **Keadue** and, outside Keadue by the ruins of the sixth-century **Killoran Abbey**, visit the grave of the famous blind harpist Turlough O'Carolan (see p.404).

travel details

Trains

Galway to: Athenry (4 daily; 15min); Athlone (4 daily; 1hr); Dublin (4 daily; 2hr 30min–3hr); Portarlington (3 daily; 2hr).

Westport to: Castlebar (3 daily; 14min); Castlerea (3 daily; 1hr 10min); Dublin (3 daily; 3hr 30min); Roscommon (3 daily; 1hr 30min).

Bus Éireann

Galway to: Clifden (2–5 daily; 1hr 45min–2hr 20min); Cork (5 daily; 4hr); Doolin (3 daily; 1hr 30min); Dublin (5–7 daily, 3hr 30min); Limerick (9 daily; 2hr).

Private buses

North Galway Club (☎093/55492) departs **from Galway**, Kiltartan House, Forster Street, daily for Dublin (Mon–Sat 8am). Departs **from Tuam** Cathedral daily for Dublin (same hours as above). Departs **from Dublin**, Ormond Quay, for Galway (Mon–Sat 6pm) and Tuam. There are summer connections to Dublin Airport.

Feda O'Donnell Coaches (☎075/761655 or ☎48114) depart **from Galway** Cathedral to Letterkenny (Mon–Thurs 4pm, Fri 11.30am, 5.30pm, Sat 10am & 4pm, Sun 8pm), serving many towns along the way including Knock, Sligo and Donegal town, and continuing **to Gweedore**. Depart **from Letterkenny** (Mon–Thurs 9am & 4.30pm, Fri 9am, 12.30pm & 4.30pm, Sun 3.30pm).

Nestor's (☎091/797144 or ☎01/832 0049) from Galway *Imperial* to Dublin airport and city (daily 8am). Dublin–Galway departs Tara Street Station 6pm daily.

CHAPTER ELEVEN

SLIGO AND LEITRIM

Counties Sligo and Leitrim pair up well, offering a distinctively luscious and gentle scenery that contrasts with the wilder streaks of Donegal and Mayo, yet equally far removed from the dullness of Longford and Cavan to the east. **Leitrim**, one of the most neglected counties in the country, is an area of lakelets and low mounds, and presents a singularly withdrawn face to the outside world. **Sligo**, also phenomenally underrated, is the more enticing of the two, containing the beautiful mountains of **Benbulben** and **Knocknarea** and the enchanting **Gill** and **Glencar** loughs, as well as an array of standing stones and other megalithic monuments as dramatic as any in Ireland. Much of the terrain is gently undulating farm land, allowing long cross-country views to the higher outcrops in the county's far corners: the **Ox Mountains** range to the west, the **Bricklieve** to the south and the **Dartry** to the north. And at **Streedagh** and **Mullaghmore** you'll find some of the country's finest beaches.

COUNTY SLIGO

Sligo has the greatest concentration of megalithic monuments in Ireland, as well as some of the wildest and most remote country. Especially poetic testaments to the ancient fusion of landscape and human presence are the extensive Neolithic cemetery at **Carrowmore**, to the west of Sligo town, and the large prehistoric village at **Carrowkeel**, on top of the Bricklieve Mountains. The pimple on top of Knocknarea is an unexcavated burial mound known locally as Maeve's Lump: legend has it that Queen Medb – Sligo's guardian spirit – is buried there, standing upright and still facing her enemies. The wealth and variety of legends covering the terrain of Sligo and Antrim have no rival, and the modern literary associations are no less strong, as this landscape and its culture inspired the great Irish poet **W.B. Yeats**. His poetry is saturated with the atmosphere of Sligo, and his presence still makes itself felt: above all at places such as the island of **Innisfree** on Lough Gill and **Lissadell House**, north of Sligo.

Sligo town

SLIGO, with a population of about 18,000, is, after Derry, the biggest town in the north-west of Ireland and a real focal point for the surrounding area. This engaging place,

---

ACCOMMODATION PRICES

Throughout this book, accommodation prices have been graded according to the cost per person per night in high season; with hotels and many hostels this represents half the cost of a double room, whereas with the more basic hostels it represents the cost of a single dormitory bed. The prices signified by our grades are as follows:

① Up to £6	③ £10–14	⑤ £20–26	⑦ £36–45
② £6–10	④ £14–20	⑥ £26–36	⑧ Over £45

overshadowed by the presence of the Knocknarea and Benbulben mountains, manages to be relaxed and busy at the same time, with a fair dash of the Irish New Age spirit that suffuses much of the country. If you've been too long in the wildernesses, you can soak up something of a city atmosphere; the annual Yeats summer school and arts festival, both of which take place in August, are indications of Sligo's vitality. If the beauty of the landscape has inspired you to read its literature, *Keohane's* bookshop in Castle Street is one of the best in the west.

The first recorded mention of Sligo dates from 807 AD, when the town was sacked by the Vikings, and by the thirteenth century it had become the gateway between Connacht and Ulster, with a castle (since destroyed) on what is now Castle Street. The Middle Ages was a period of sporadic violence, most notably between the Anglo-Norman Maurice Fitzgerald and the O'Connells. Thanks to its strong defences, Sligo was the last of the western garrisons to surrender to Williamite forces after the Battle of the Boyne.

The town suffered during the nineteenth-century **Famine**, when its population fell by a third through death and emigration, but by the end of the last century things had picked up to the extent that it was described in guidebooks as "a progressive and busy centre". The upswing has continued to the present day, and in summer the streets are always crowded with visitors – but if you have a chance to look at the photos of old Sligo hanging in the County Museum on Stephen Street, you'll appreciate how remarkably constant the look of the town has been. The tightly packed and narrow **back streets** make it feel a little like Latin Quarter Paris, with grocery stores and bars on the street corners open late into the evening. Apart from the Dominican Abbey there's not much left in the way of sites that recall the town's long history, but the old-fashioned market town atmosphere and the equally atmospheric old pubs make it an ideal base for exploring the surrounding countryside and sights.

Arrival, information and accommodation

Buses and **trains** both arrive at the station, handily placed on the western edge of town in easy walking distance of almost everything. Sligo's **tourist office**, on Temple Street (July & Aug Mon–Sat 9am–8pm, Sun 10am–2pm; Sept–June Mon–Fri 9am–5pm; ☎071/61201), is the headquarters for Sligo, Leitrim, Monaghan, Cavan and Donegal – a wide brief which means it often has little hard information to give out. They do, however, offer car rental, money exhange and an **accommodation** booking service. To find out what's happening in town get hold of a copy of the weekly *Sligo Champion* (published Wed), which lists music in pubs and other entertainment, or the freebie *The Buzz*, both available at *Keohane's* bookshop.

If you're staying in Sligo town itself **B&B** is probably the best option. Try *Renaté Central House*, 9 Upper John Street (☎071/62014; ④), or *Crúis C'n Lán* (The Full Jug), Connolly Street (☎071/62857; ③), a friendly place with a bar and cheap pub meals. There are also dozens on Strandhill Road, heading away from town from the station. Moving upmarket, try the *Bonne Chère* hotel, 44 High Street (☎071/42014; ⑤). For really luxurious living, your best bet is to head out of town to *Glebe House* or *Markree Castle*, a few miles south at Collooney (see p. 399). There are also three independent **hostels**, *White House Hostel* on Markiewicz Road (*IHH*, open all year; ☎071/45160, fax ☎44456; ②), pleasant and hip, with breakfast included in the price, but very crowded in summer, and the *Yeats County Hostel* on Lord Edward Street (①), very handy for the railway station but with little else to recommend it. Finally the *Eden Hill* hostel is on Pearse Road in the south of town (*IHH*, open all year; ☎071/44113, fax ☎43204; ②), and has a range of facilities, including laundry, bike rental and camping.

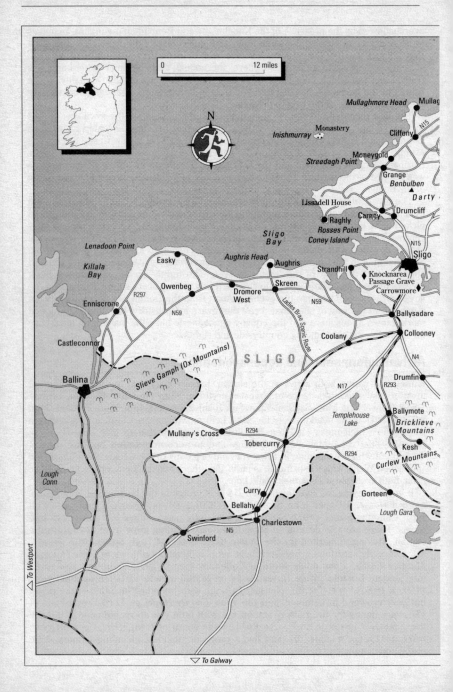

0   12 miles

N

Mullaghmore Head   Mullag

Inishmurray   Monastery

Cliffony

N15

Streedagh Point   Moneygold

Grange

Benbulben   *Darty*

Lissadell House   Drumcliff

Raghly   Carney

Rosses Point   *Sligo*
Coney Island

Sligo Bay   N15

Aughris Head   Aughris   Strandhill   Knocknarea
    Passage Grave
Lenadoon Point   Easky   Skreen   Carrowmore

Killala Bay   Owenbeg   Dromore West   Ballysadare

R297   N59   Coolany   Collooney

Enniscrone   N59   N4

Castleconnor   *Ladies Brae Scenic Route*   Drumfin

Slieve Gamph (Ox Mountains)   S L I G O   R293

Ballina   N17   Ballymote

    Templehouse Lake   *Bricklieve Mountains*

Mullany's Cross   R294   Kesh

Tobercurry   R294   *Curlew Mountains*

Lough Conn   Gorteen

Curry   *Lough Gara*

Bellahy   Charlestown

Swinford   N5

To Westport

To Galway

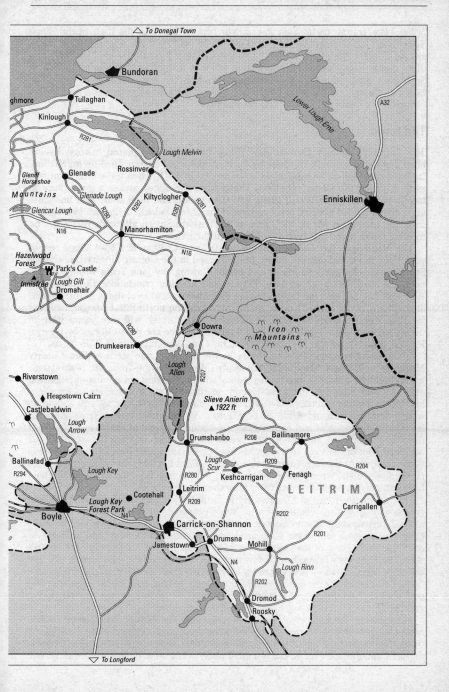

△ To Donegal Town

Bundoran

ghmore
Tullaghan
Kinlough
R281
Lough Melvin
Rossinver
Glenade
Gleniff
Horseshoe
Glenade Lough
Kiltyclogher
Mountains
R282
R283
R281
Enniskillen
Glencar Lough
R280
N16
Manorhamilton
Hazelwood
Forest
Park's Castle
N16
Innisfrae
Lough Gill
Dromahair
R280
Dowra
Iron
Mountains
Drumkeeran
Lough
Allen
R207
Riverstown
Heapstown Cairn
Slieve Anierin
▲ 1922 ft
Castlebaldwin
Lough
Arrow
Drumshanbo
R208
Ballinamore
Ballinafad
Lough Key
Lough
Scur
R209
R204
R294
R280
Keshcarrigan
Fenagh
Boyle
Lough Key
Forest Park
Cootehall
Leitrim
R209
LEITRIM
R202
Carrigallen
N4
Carrick-on-Shannon
Jamestown
Drumsna
R201
Mohill
N4
Lough Rinn
R202
Dromod
Roosky

▽ To Longford

For **bike rental**, try *Raleigh Rent-a-Bike* (☎071/67560), at the back of the *Silver Swan Hotel*, or *Conway Brothers*, 6 High Street (☎071/61370). For **minibus tours** around Lough Gill and other north Sligo areas contact John Houze (☎071/42747); the tours depart from the tourist information office at 9.30am and 1.30pm from June to September (£4–5); there are also **walking tours** from the tourist office in summer. For **boats** on the river and around Lough Gill – one of the best ways to spend time here – contact Peter Henry at *The Blue Lagoon*, Riverside.

The town

The thirteenth-century **Dominican Abbey** has had a chequered history, having been destroyed a couple of times by both accident and design since its foundation. Its life as a religious foundation came to an end in 1641, when the whole town was sacked during the Ulster rebellion. These days, the abbey makes a good place to have a picnic as its walls still stand, and the chancel and high altar, with fine carvings, are in a good state of preservation. If the abbey is locked you can get the key from the caretaker, Mr A. McGuinn, at 6 Charlotte Street, although you won't be missing much if you just take a look through the gates.

The **Municipal Art Gallery** (July–Aug 10.30am–12.30pm & 2.30–4.30pm; rest of year Tues & Fri 10.30am–12.30pm; free), housed in the County Library on Stephen Street, possesses many paintings and pencil drawings by Jack Yeats, brother of the poet. His work has a strong local flavour, and his later efforts like *The Graveyard Wall* and *The Sea and the Lighthouse* are especially potent evocations of the life and atmosphere of the area. If you're going to be heading north into Donegal, look out for Paul Henry's *Early Morning in Donegal Lough*, which will give you a taste of things to come. Also worth more than a passing glance are the paintings by George Russell, better known as AE, the mystical poet and contemporary of W.B. Yeats.

In the same compound as the library by the entrance gate are the **Sligo County Museum** and **Yeats Memorial Museum** (Mon–Fri 10am–5pm, Sat 10am–1pm), which together comprise two rooms. Along with interesting old photos of Sligo, the more unusual items in the local history section include a sequence of excellent nineteenth-century sketches of the monastic ruins on Inishmurray and a double-weight hundred-year-old firkin of bog butter. Memorabilia in the Yeats museum include photographs of and commentary on his funeral, lots of letters and photos of the man himself and the Nobel Prize medal awarded him in 1923. Before you head out, read a bit of the long article on Michael Coleman, one of Ireland's most famous fiddle players. At the beginning of the century, Fritz Kreisler, one of the greatest of classical violinists, wrote that even he could not attempt the kind of music Michael Coleman played, even if he practised for a thousand years.

Just down the road, at Douglas Hyde Bridge, the **Yeats Memorial Building** (☎071/42693) is the headquarters of the Yeats Society and venue for August's Yeats International Summer School. Inaugurated about thirty years back, the gathering has become something of an academic institution, attracting scholars from all over the world, and of late has also gained something of a reputation for controversy. At *Keohane's* **bookshop**, a few minutes walk away in Castle Street, you can also pick up as much of Yeats's poetry as you can carry, as well as Richard Ellman's classic biography, *Yeats: The Man and the Mask* – written only eight years after the poet's death, when many of the important people in his life were still alive, and a good read.

For a taste of the northwest's energetic arts scene, **The Model Arts Centre** on The Mall (☎071/41405) is housed in an imposing nineteenth-century stone building. It hosts changing art exhibitions, mainly of local artists, runs a busy schedule of literary, dramatic and musical events, and is a good place to tune in to the more alternative side

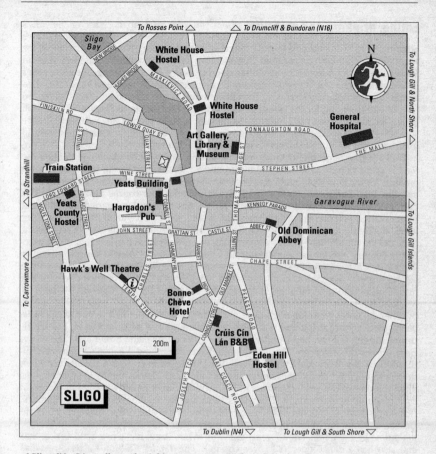

Map of Sligo Town showing:
To Rosses Point △ To Drumcliff & Bundoran (N16) △
N
To Lough Gill & North Shore ▷
Sligo Bay
White House Hostel
NEW BRIDGE
HIGHS BRIDGE
MARKIEVICZ ROAD
FINISKLIN RD
UNION ST
LOWER QUAY ST
QUAY STREET
WHITE HOUSE Hostel
CONNAUGHTON ROAD
General Hospital
THE MALL
Art Gallery, Library & Museum
BRIDGE ST
STEPHEN STREET
WINE STREET
Train Station
To Strandhill ◁
LORD EDWARD STREET
ADELAIDE STREET
O'CONNELL STREET
Yeats Building
Yeats County Hostel
Hargadon's Pub
WOLFE TONE STREET
JOHN STREET
GRATTAN ST
CASTLE ST
THOMAS ST
ABBEY ST
Old Dominican Abbey
KENNEDY PARADE
Garavogue River
To Lough Gill Islands ▷
HARMONY HILL
MARKET ST
TEELING ST
To Carrowmore ◁
CHAPEL STREET
Hawk's Well Theatre
CHARLES STREET
HIGH ST
OLD MARKET ST
PEARSE ROAD
Bonne Chève Hotel
TEMPLE STREET
CONNOLLY STREET
Crúis Cín Lán B&B
0 200m
MALL COACH ROAD
ST. JOSEPH'S TCE
Eden Hill Hostel
SLIGO
To Dublin (N4) ▽ To Lough Gill & South Shore ▽

of Sligo life. It's well worth picking up a copy of the admirable *Force 10* magazine here, full of poetry, prose and reportage by local writers.

By far the most entertaining historical set piece in Sligo is **Hargadon's Pub** on O'Connell Street. An exclusively male establishment until about ten years ago, it's a fine old pub for talking, with dark recesses and shut-off rooms, and shelves of nineteenth-century earthenware stout jugs. Note the little swivel windows at the far end of the serving bar, where the whiskey could be slipped through with little fuss by either drinker or landlord.

Another place of great interest is an old butcher's shop turned sculpture studio, **Michael Quirke's** on Wine Street. A butcher for 27 years, Michael Quirke began in the 1980s to sculpt the figures of Irish mythology in windfallen wood. Every feature of these small carvings bears the mark of his encyclopedic knowledge of every legend or myth ever dreamed up about Ireland – if you get a chance to listen to him, it could well be one of the most inspiring moments of your stay. So far his work isn't too expensive (£30 upwards), but it's getting increasingly popular. For souvenirs of a more traditional kind, *Dooney's* in O'Connell Street sells excellent Irish tweed and knitwear at well below Dublin prices – which is still far from cheap.

Eating, drinking and nightlife

Sligo has a high-standard, if limited range, of eating places with plenty of choices for vegetarians. *Gullivers* on Grattan Street has a busy atmosphere and serves good American-style food from £5 (open till midnight). *Bistro Biancioni*, opposite *Hargadon's* in O'Connell Street, is a newish pizza and pasta **restaurant** with an elegant decor to match its upmarket aspirations. Excellent lunches are served at *The Cellars*, 30 O'Connell Street, but for the ultimate Sligo food experience, go to *Truffles*, 11 The Mall (Tues–Sat 5–10.30pm; ☎071/44226). Nominally a pizza restaurant – though they're advertised as New Age pizzas – this gastronomic haven inclines toward a new-world interpretation, with plenty of foccaccia and sun-dried tomatoes.

Every pub in Sligo seems to serve a **bar lunch**, and with so much competition the food is great value – a decent meal for around £2.50. Away from the pubs, *Fortes Café* on Markiewicz Road does main courses from about £2 and three-course meals from £3, and the *Ritz Restaurant*, 35 O'Connell Street, offers a four-course lunch for £5. The *Cottage Coffee Shop*, upstairs at 4 Castle Street, has a cheap and varied hot and cold menu with vegetarian specials; *Lyons Café* at the top of O'Connell Street is another good, if slightly tatty, café serving meals or drinks throughout the day. *Cosgrove's*, a delicatessen on Market Square, is something of a tourist attraction in itself, with a nine-teenth-century interior and a craft shop attached. You can get **picnic supplies** here, or from *Kate's Kitchen* on Market Street. *T'r na n-g* in Grattan Street is a wholefood store selling organic vegetables, salad stuffs and a delicious selection of Irish cheeses. For bread, cakes and delectable puddings to take out, head for *The Gourmet Parlour*, 24 Market Street.

When it comes to **pubs**, Sligo does well. *Hargadon's* (see p.389) is one of the most enjoyable places to drink and talk, with several snugs and no distractions. For **traditional music**, the two best regular spots are *T.D.s* on Adelaide Street and the *Leitrim Bar*, across the river on The Mall: both have something happening most nights throughout the year. *MacLynn's* on Old Market Street is cosy and usually crowded; there's an open fire in the bar and traditional folk music almost nightly in summer, less often the rest of the year. *Hennigan's Pub* on Wine Street is fairly seedy but has pop/rock once a week, usually Thursdays, and mainly traditional stuff on Sundays. *Comhaltas* have traditional sessions on Wednesdays in the *Silver Swan Hotel*, Hyde Bridge, a venue for other types of music most other nights and an excellent Sunday lunchtime jazz session. The *Clarence Hotel* on Wine Street has a live band (Fri & Sat) and also has a dance floor (£3 cover charge). The *Trades Club* on Castle Street has good traditional sessions from 9.45pm every Tuesday, sometimes with a brilliant young violinist and, from time to time, Lord Templemore on spoons – arrive early to ensure getting in (the entrance is an ordinary house door and is easy to miss).

The big **nightclub** in town is still *Toffs* at the *Embassy Lounge*, Riverside; *Zanadus* on Teeling Street also has **discos** (Wed & Fri–Sun 11pm–1.30am; £4 including food). *The Blue Lagoon*, Riverside, has traditional music (Mon & Tues) and discos (Thurs & Sat). The *Hawk's Well Theatre* on Temple Street (below the tourist office) often has a reasonable programme of **plays**, both modern and classic, particularly during the **Yeats International Summer School** and the **Sligo Arts Festival** in late August (which includes a national fiddling festival); the *Gaiety Cinema* on Wine Street has four screens showing a variety of **films**.

Lough Gill

The 24-mile circuit of **Lough Gill**, a broad lake with luscious woodland covering the small hills that rise off its indented banks, makes a great day-trip by bike from Sligo –

THE LEGENDS OF LOUGH GILL

A place of such natural beauty inevitably features in legend: Lough Gill's story tells of a warrior called Romra who had a daughter named Gille ("beauty" in Irish). One day Gille was seen bathing by Omra, a friend of Romra. Omra was captivated by the girl, and she wasn't altogether indifferent to him; but when Romra got to hear about it, a fight ensued in which Omra was killed and Romra received wounds from which he later died. Grief-stricken, Gille drowned herself, and from the tears of her doubly grief-stricken nurse-maid Lough Gill(e) was formed. According to another tale, the silver bell from the Dominican Abbey in Sligo lies at the bottom of the lake. Only those free from sin can hear its pealing.

or you could break the journey midway in Dromahair and allow yourself more time to explore. There are also plenty of shorter walks, and this is one of the most enjoyable ways to spend time around Sligo. To **walk** to the lake – a little over an hour away from town – set off from Bridge Street along Riverside on the south bank of the Garavogue, until you come after about a mile to **Doorly Park**. Follow the path through the park alongside the river until it rejoins the road, which leads eventually to a lakeside jetty. Here the entire length of Lough Gill is spread out before you.

If you have transport, the northern shore is much the more interesting and is reached from town by taking The Mall past the hospital, turning onto the R286 at the garage and then following signposts for the **Hazelwood Estate** on the right. A left turn off the road leading into the estate grounds will bring you after half a mile to **Half Moon Bay**, where there's a picnic site and a pleasant lakeside walk. Wooden sculptures by various artists are ranged in the woods around – the most stunning is a set piece of chariot and horses, set in its own artificial dell.

Back on the R286, a left turn soon after the road forks for the "Lough Gill Loop" will take you up to the Deerpark Forest, where a magnificent megalithic **court tomb** surveys the wild country. Ten minutes of walking on an unpaved road brings you to the top of **Cashelgal Mountain**, where you'll find both the tomb and an unparalleled view of the surrounding country.

At the Leitrim end of the lake, the road begins to skirt the shore on its approach to **Parke's Castle** (daily 11am–6.30pm; £1.50, Heritage Card), a romantic-looking seventeenth-century fortress only yards from the water. The castle, built by one Robert Parke in the 1620s, is an evocative example of an early planter building and of the talents displayed by the Office of Public Works for conjuring heritage sites out of virtually nothing. The foundations discovered in the courtyard of the present castle are thought to be those of the moated tower-house of the Irish chieftain Brian O'Rourke, prince of Breffni. In 1588 O'Rourke sheltered a Spaniard from the wrecked Armada; arraigned for high treason, he was executed at Tyburn in 1591. It seems that Parke used the simplest (and cheapest) method of making a home for himself, by utilizing the outer walls of O'Rourke's castle (and probably completing the demolition of the tower in the process). The reconstruction is clearly a fairly creative one, but it works well as a focus for the surrounding topography. The entrance ticket also admits you to the **audiovisual show** which, as a quick introduction to the area's built environment, is also worth seeing.

The *Wild Rose* **water bus** plies between Doorly Park in Sligo and Parke's Castle (daily 10.30am, 1.30pm, 4.30pm & 6.30pm), with tours of the lough's main island Innisfree from Parke's Castle fitted in between these times (12.30pm, 3.30pm & 6.30pm; ☎071/64266, or enquire at the *Blue Lagoon*, Sligo); from June to September a shuttle bus service will pick you up at *Adelaide Bar*, Wine Street, Sligo, and take you out to Parke's Castle for the Innisfree tour.

From the east end of the lough, a signposted road leads to the modern uninspiring **Newtown Manor** church; but the journey, a steep climb through the high wild moorland behind the lake, is exhilarating. The main road winds on through lush woodland to Dromahair, where, at the end of a short walk on the other side of the rushing River Bonet, lies **Creevelea Friary**, its ruined east window turned away from the harsh outlines of the mountains and towards the friendly valley below. The Franciscan friary, founded in 1508, was the last to be built in Ireland before Henry VIII's dissolution of the monasteries. It still has some fine sculptures in the cloister arcade: look out for Saint Francis with the stigmata, and another of him preaching to the birds from a pulpit. The place was still used for burials until a few years ago – some of the tombstones date from the 1970s. You can **stay** at *Stanford's Village Inn* (☎071/64140; ③), which also offers self-catering accommodation, or at the *Breffni Centre* opposite (☎071/64199; ③).

Continuing from Dromahair, the road climbs to offer breathtaking views of the mountains opposite. A signposted lane shortly after the Sligo county sign will lead you down to the lakeside where you can gaze out at Yeats's tiny "Lake Isle of Innisfree" and breathe in the tranquillity:

> *I will arise and go now, and go to Innisfree*
> *And a small cabin build there, of clay and wattles made*
> *Nine bean-rows will I have there, and a hive for the honey-bee,*
> *And live alone in the bee-loud glade*
>
> *And I shall have some peace there, for peace comes dropping slow,*
> *Dropping from the veils of the morning to where the cricket sings;*
> *There midnight's all a glimmer, and noon a purple glow,*
> *And evening full of the linnet's wings.*
>
> *I will arise and go now, for always night and day*
> *I hear lake water lapping with low sounds by the shore*
> *While I stand on the roadway, or on the pavements grey,*
> *I hear it in the deep heart's core.*

Inismor, Innisfree's sister island, was the site of the medieval school of poets to the O'Rourke's; unfortunately, the priceless library of manuscripts was destroyed by fire. Continuing back towards Sligo, the road winds gently through woods with occasional views of the lough. At **Dooney Rock**, a brief stroll through woodlands brings you to a secluded shore where you can view the island opposite and consider swimming over.

The south road back into Sligo passes **Cairns Hill Forest Park**. From the car park a path leads to the top of Cairns Hill, with a view across to a second cairn on the peak of Belvoir Hill. These are reckoned to be the tombs of Romra and Omra, though another legend makes them out to be the breasts of a monstrous hag, with Lough Gill as her navel.

North of Sligo town

Leaving Sligo along the coast to the north, almost immediately there's the option of a short detour to **ROSSES POINT** (bus #286), via the promontory that forms the north side of Sligo Bay. This (or Strandhill, see p.397) is the place to go for a day at the beach, a perfect picture-postcard scene, with the streaks of Coney and Oyster islands guarding the entrance to the bay and the distinctive beauty of Knocknarea and Benbulben standing behind. A sea marker called the *Metal Man* marks the deepest part of the channel for Sligo-bound boats; placed there in 1822, it was called by Yeats the "Rosses Point man who never told a lie". The tip of the headland, **Deadman's Point** (now an upper-crust recreation centre), took its name from a sailor who was buried at sea here with a loaf of bread thoughtfully provided by his comrades – they weren't sure whether he was really dead but wanted to despatch him quickly so they could make port before the tide turned. There are a few small **hotels** like the *Yeats Country Hotel* (☎071/77211; ⑥), which gazes straight out across the Atlantic, and lots of **B&Bs**, too: try *Oyster View* (☎071/77201; ③), with an unimpressive view of Knocknarea Mountain. For seafood, head for *The Moorings Restaurant*, in the village at Rosses Point.

Drumcliff, Benbulben and Glencar Lough

Sticking to the main N15 road out of Sligo you'll bypass this small peninsula, reaching water again at **DRUMCLIFF** (bus #290 or #291 from Sligo), an early monastic site probably better known as the last resting place of **W.B. Yeats**. His grave is in the grounds of an austere nineteenth-century Protestant church, within sight of the nearby Benbulben Mountain, as the poet wished. You could easily miss the grave of W.B. and his wife, George, and the simple headstone bearing the epitaph from Yeats's last poem:

> *Cast a cold eye*
> *On life, on death.*
> *Horseman, pass by!*

In 575, Saint Columba founded a **monastery** here, and you can still see the remnants of a round tower to the left of the road and a tenth-century high cross – the only one in the county – on the right. The east face of the cross has carvings of Adam and Eve, Cain killing Abel and Daniel in the lion's den; the west face shows scenes from the New Testament, including the Presentation in the Temple and the Crucifixion. Local excavations have turned up a wealth of Iron and Bronze Age remains, too. There's a good **teashop**, with home baking, next to the church (closed in winter) – a welcome refuge on a rainy day.

At 1730ft, **Benbulben** is one of the most dramatic mountains in the country, and its profile changes constantly as you round it. According to the Fionn Mac Cumhaill legend, it was here that Diarmuid, the ill-fated young warrior, was killed by the wild boar, its bristles puncturing his heel – his one vulnerable point. Access to the slopes is easy, but you need to take care as there are a lot of dangerous clefts into which the unsuspecting walker can all too easily plunge – especially as it's invariably shrouded in mist. There are **hostel** facilities at the *Yeats Tavern* in Drumcliff (☎071/63117; ①), about a hundred yards past the church. It's part of the roadside pub, and although it's handy for drinks and basic eating, you won't want to spend more than one night there. There's also **B&B** at *Castletown House* (☎071/63204; ③), a short distance along the Glencar Road, and numerous others nearby.

Just to the east of Drumcliff, and equally well reached from the T17 road to Manorhamilton, is **Glencar Lough** (bus #125 or #283 from Sligo), squeezed between Benbulben and the range of hills known as the **Sleeping Warrior**, a secluded lakelet with good salmon and trout fishing, if you're lucky. Follow the road round the northern edge of the lake passing the recently reopened barium mine sheds on the left, until you see the "Waterfall" signpost. From the nearby car park a path leads up to the 50ft-high waterfall, especially impressive after heavy rain. There are more waterfalls, visible from the road, in the upper reaches of the valley, although none is quite as romantic as this one. For an even better mountain walk continue along the road to the eastern end of the lake, where a track rises steeply northwards to the **Swiss Valley**, a deep rift in the mountain crowned with silver fir.

Cooldrumman and Lissadell House

Beyond Drumcliff the first left turn off the main road (signposted "Lissadell") runs to Carney village, to the north of which is an area known as **Cooldrumman**, where the

Battle of the Book took place. This battle followed the refusal of Saint Columba to hand over a psalm book copied from the original owned by Saint Finian of Moville, in defiance of the High King, who ruled that just as a calf belongs to its cow so every copy belongs to the owner of the book from which it is made. Columba won the battle at a cost of 3000 lives; repenting the bloodshed he had caused, he then went into exile on the Scottish island of Iona.

In Carney a signpost to the left indicates the way to **Lissadell House** (June to mid-Sept Mon–Sat 10.30am–noon & 2–4.30pm; £2; bus #290 or #291 from Sligo), an austere nineteenth-century Greek Revival mansion, whose popularity is mainly due to its Yeats associations. This was the home of the Gore-Booth family, which produced several generations of artists, travellers and fighters for Irish freedom. During the Famine Sir Robert Gore-Booth, who built Lissadell, mortgaged the place to feed the local people and doled out rations from the hall. His grand-daughters, Eva Gore-Booth and Constance Markiewicz, were friends of Yeats and took part in the 1916 Rising. Constance was condemned to death by the British for her participation but was pardoned and went on to become the first British female MP and then Minister of Labour in the Dáil's first cabinet.

Inside, the house seems in many ways like the archetype of the decaying Anglo-Irish home: despite the fact that the Gore-Booths still live there, the place hasn't been decorated since 1908, and problems with a leaking roof mean that a valuable Italian Baroque tapestry hangs in the hall festooned with strips of tea-bag paper, intended to hold it together until better times. The roof's now been fixed, however, and the house, bathed in Sligo's luminous marine light, still has an intimacy that makes it easy to imagine how it looked when Yeats used to visit in 1894:

Light of evening Lissadell
Great windows, open to the south,
Two girls in silk kimonos, both
Beautiful, one a gazelle

From *In Memory of Eva Gore-Booth and Constance Markiewicz*

During that year, Yeats was in the throes of his unrequited love for Maude Gonne, and much of his time at Lissadell was spent confessing his problems to the gazelle-like Eva, to whom he also briefly considered declaring his love.

It was not only Constance and Eva who espoused radical ideas: their brother, Jocelyn, was drummed out of his club in Sligo for his practical encouragement of the early co-operative movement. He was also one of the first landlords to start selling off land to tenants, retaining no more than 3000 acres of the original 31,000 to run a thriving market garden.

Among the more eccentric decorative features of the interior are a series of elongated mural portraits of Jocelyn and family retainers and a self-portrait in the dining room, all by Constance's husband Count Casimir Markiewicz. They came into being only because bad weather kept the count from shooting during Christmas 1908. One of the rooms has Constance's name scratched on a window, and a photograph shows her playing Joan of Arc in her husband's theatre company: an appropriate role for a woman whose life was soon to turn so completely to politics and propaganda.

The house went through a difficult period after World War II, when the family lost control of the estate to the government: Sligo newspapers were keenly aware of the irony of the Gore-Booth sisters, nieces of Constance – one of the founders of the Irish Free State – being pursued by the police as they protested against the state's inept administration of the property. The experience has left the family with a distrust of government intervention, even in the form of funding, and although plans for restoration are afoot, Lissadell is likely to retain its air of elegant decay for some time.

Walks around Lissadell: Ellen's Pub

The area around Lissadell has some lovely **walks** and reputedly the warmest patch of sea on the Sligo coast. Also worth seeking out is *Ellen's Pub* at Ballyconnell (☎071/ 63761), whose cottage-home atmosphere draws people from miles around. *Ceilis* are sometimes held in the back room, and on Fridays, Saturdays and Sundays from June to September, musicians gather here to belt out tunes on fiddles, accordions and banjos. There's a relaxed attitude to the licensing laws, so relaxed in fact that the pub was closed down for a while in 1986. To find it, follow the road past the turning for the Lissadell Estate, bear right away from Maugherow church, turn left at the pub/grocery store at the crossroads and then take the second right – it's another mile straight on. Hitching is easy, because everyone will assume you're headed for *Ellen's*.

Raghly Point to Mullaghmore

A couple of miles to the west of Lissadell is **RAGHLY**, a small harbour with a lonely pier and raised beach from where there are spectacular views of the bay and surrounding mountains. On the way there you'll pass **Ardtermon Castle** (closed to the public), the seventeenth-century fortified manor house once occupied by Francis Gore-Booth, an ancestor of the Lissadell Gore-Booths. Ten years ago the place was more or less a ruin, but since then it has been well restored by its German industrialist owner – although, in the absence of documentation of the house's original appearance, the resulting garish yellow is rather more Scottish Baronial than Irish.

The next stop along the coast is sandy **Streedagh Strand** (7 buses daily from Sligo), most easily accessible by taking the main road to Grange (see below) and following the signposts from there, as roads on the Raghly Peninsula are hard to disentangle. The substantially German-inhabited colony of this whole area has earned it the nickname of "Little Bavaria", and the inflated prices of some of the chalets at Streedagh Strand have provoked a degree of antipathy from the locals. The beach itself is a fantastic stretch of sand, superb for long walks or horse riding by the waves (there are several stables in the district), and when the tide is at its lowest you can walk round to the caves at the southern end to do some fossil collecting. At the very north end of the beach is *Carraig na Spáinneach* (Spaniards' Rock), where three ships of the Spanish Armada foundered. There are numerous anonymous burial stones nearby, said to mark the mass graves of some 1100 sailors who either drowned or were butchered by the British and the locals. There's **B&B** at *Shaddan Lodge* right by the Strand (☎071/ 63350; ③), offering a wholefood menu and various alternative healing therapies – expect prices of £90–255 a week, including massage or aromatherapy.

Grange, Moneygold and Cliffony

At **GRANGE** itself there's not much apart from an old boys' bar off to the right, over the bridge, and the Sligo Crystal factory; there's a factory shop where you can buy the fantastically ornate cut glass at reduced prices. However, if you venture inland past the pub, you'll get a changing perspective of Benbulben as you approach the **Gleniff Horseshoe**, a scenic road that runs along a glen on the flank of the Dartry range and gives easy access to the top of Benbulben.

MONEYGOLD, a short way beyond Grange, offers excellent **accommodation** at the *Celtic Riding and Language Centre* (☎071/63337), in the form of hostel (①) or B&B (②), and you can also try organically produced cheeses and sample local fish and shellfish. The hostel organizes very cheap **bike rental** and **horse riding** on Streedagh Strand; and you can help work on the small farm for a week or more and earn yourself free food and accommodation. **CLIFFONY**, a couple of miles on again towards Bundoran, is remarkable for the **Creevykeel Court Tomb** (just past the village by the roadside), one of the most extensive Neolithic sites in the country, comprising two roof-less tombs within a stone court. The graves, which were originally enclosed in a barrow, probably date from between 3500 and 3000 BC, and it's easy to see in this ancient evidence of human presence a reflection of a power in the landscape that has gone on working ever since, right down to the poetry of Yeats and beyond. You can **stay** in Cliffony at Hans and Gaby Weiland's farm cottages, just outside the village. The plus is the food – the Weilands grow vegetables organically, and make totally delicious cheese, sourdough bread and cheesecake (☎071/66399; £120–140 per week for 4 people).

The Mullaghmore Peninsula

Mullaghmore headland may not be the most attractive of all the promontories north of Sligo town but it has a charm of its own and, unlike the remoter areas, offers a choice of accommodation and eating places. By now the coast is facing north, not west, and you get your first full view of the chain of Donegal's mountains stretched out ahead, with Benbulben and the Dartry range a constant presence behind you. A left turn at the Cliffony crossroads takes you onto it, past **Classiebawn Castle** (closed to the public), a construction worthy of Disneyland built by Lord Palmerston; it became the home of Lord Mountbatten shortly before he was killed by the IRA in 1979, when his boat was blown up in the bay.

MULLAGHMORE itself is a dainty place with a peaceful skiff-filled harbour and a very good beach. If you're spending some time here, there's great walking to be had along the rocky shelves of Mullaghmore Head, at the end of the village, where the ocean waves crash constantly within feet of you. Alternatively, you could explore the area on horseback: mounts can be rented from the stables on the crest of the hill. If you're wondering what all the nuns are doing in Mullaghmore, it's because the village has a convent holiday home at which they can relax after the rigours of their parishes. Non-ecclesiastical travellers can **camp** in the sand dunes, as long as they're inconspicuous. The *Beach Hotel* (☎071/66103; ⑤) offers **B&B** and good food, and knows the value of central heating on a stormy night; it also has a swimming pool. *Pier Head House* (☎071/66171; ⑤) has rooms, a bar and food, and what it rashly terms a night-club. *Eithna's* **restaurant**, decorated outside with an underwater scene in shades of vibrant turquoise, now specializes in local seafood. *Lomax Boats* rents out fishing boats (£80 a day; maximum 6 persons; rods £4 per day) and can arrange trips to Inishmurray in summer (see below). For a quiet pint, try *Annie's Bar*.

Inishmurray Island

The island of **INISHMURRAY**, about four miles offshore, has been deserted since the 1950s, but the trip out to it is noteworthy because of its ruined sixth-century monastery, an oratory – which the islanders used as a school – and the early Christian grave-stones that are some of the best preserved in the country. In addition to *Lomax Boats*, in Mullaghmore, trips are run by Mr Mulligan, *Dún Ard*, Mullaghmore (☎071/67126), and in Moneygold by Mr Christy Herrity, *Carns* (☎071/63365; £75 for maximum group of 10). The crossing takes 75 minutes, and you can spend several hours on the island.

West of Sligo town

The major sites of interest directly west of Sligo – off the Strandhill Road or R292 – are the ancient remains at the **Carrowmore Megalithic Cemetery** and, on top of Knocknarea Mountain, **Medb's Cairn**; both of which make for easy day-trips from town. The main road south and then westward from Sligo (the N59), flanked by the thrilling outlines of the **Ox Mountains** and the uninspiring coastline of western Sligo county, is scarcely an enthralling route, yet a few things crop up on the way to Mayo that are worth a mention – if you're not in a hurry, take the road running parallel to and nearer the coast.

Coney Island and Strandhill

A right turn off the Strandhill Road will lead you down to Sligo Bay, where concrete markers delineate a low-tide crossing to **Coney Island**. New York's Coney Island is said to have been named after this one by a homesick sea captain from Rosses Point, the headland opposite. There's a pub, plenty of good **birdwatching** and some tranquil sandy beaches. Back on the main road and a little further west towards the end of the headland at **STRANDHILL** (bus #285 from Sligo), there's a large, wild beach along which the sea sweeps massive boulders in winter. Sligo airport is close by, and it's a thrilling sight to see the small *Aer Lingus* planes coming in over the top of Medb's Cairn. At the end of the airstrip stands the tenth-century **Killaspugbone Church** (access across the beach), where Saint Patrick allegedly tripped on the threshold and lost his tooth. A beautiful casket in which the sacred tooth was enshrined – the *Fiacul Pádraig* – is now in the National Museum in Dublin, but the whereabouts of the tooth is a mystery. The old Strandhill village was sited here until the drifting sand forced the villagers to move a few centuries ago. In modern Strandhill village look out for *Dolly's Cottage*: sessions take place some evenings, and during the day it's a kind of folk museum (July & Aug daily 3–5pm).

If you have children in tow, *Woodville Farm* (July & Aug 2–5pm except Tues; June Sat & Sun 2–5pm; adults £2, children £1) is a useful desgination, with sheep, lambs, free-range hens, peacocks, outdoor pigs, and a woodland nature trail.

Carrowmore Megalithic Cemetery and Medb's Cairn

More excitingly, a left turn off the R292 takes you to a field studded with 45 megalithic dolmens, standing stones and stone circles: the **Carrowmore Megalithic Cemetery** (mid-June to mid-Sept daily 9.30am–6.30pm; 80p, Heritage Card). The oldest of the tombs predates Newgrange by some 700 years (and there's an unconfirmed dating of one of the tombs that suggests it may be 500 years older) – and though more than half the stones have disappeared, this is still the second-largest megalithic standing stone site in Europe after Carnac in Brittany. You can opt for the reasonably informative slide show and exhibition, but there's nothing to stop you wandering around to look at the monuments without paying the entrance fee. It's an intoxicating meander, under the eye of the big mother cairn of them all – **Medb's Cairn**, on top of Knocknarea. The easiest ascent of the mountain is along the path that meets the R292 as it skirts its southern flank (the western slopes are too difficult). The 60ft cairn on the summit is said to be the tomb of Queen Medb of Connaught, but as she was killed elsewhere it's unlikely that she's buried here; experts reckon that the 40,000 tons of rock were put here by Neolithic farmers – but it has yet to be excavated to find out why. There's a custom of taking a stone away with you which is resulting in a shrinkage of the cairn; the authorities are trying to promote an alternative tradition that says if you take a stone with you from the bottom of the mountain and put it on top of the cairn, your wish will come true....

If you want to go **horse riding**, the *Sligo Riding Centre* is right opposite the site (☎071/61353). It's a smart establishment with a bar where you can watch through a plate-glass window as nattily dressed girls put their nags through their paces in the riding school as you while the time away over a *Guinness* to endless country and western music.

You can **stay** in genteel comfort at *Primrose Grange House* (☎075/62005; ④; dinner £15), a 1723 mansion on the western slopes of Knocknarea, overlooking Ballysadare Bay.

Ballysadare and Aughris

BALLYSADARE, the first main town along the N59 and situated at the head of a beautiful bay with striking views back to Knocknarea and Benbulben, has the remnants of a

THE OX MOUNTAINS

Just after Skreen comes the turn-off for the **Ladies' Brae Scenic Route**, one of only two trails across the vast **Ox Mountains** (*Sliabh Ghamh*, stony mountain) into south Sligo. Following the course of a tumbling stream between forests of fir, the road ends not far from Coolany, a one-street village with accommodation at *The Mountain Inn* (④). Nearby is the Hungry Rock: these harsh surrroundings were the scene of many deaths during the Famine of 1845–49. **Walking** in the more remote regions of the mountains, where all you'll see are sheep and the odd turf-cutter, can be rewarding; take care, as the bogs can be treacherous. Much of the Ox range consists of surprisingly undramatic heathery slopes and flat boggy upland, but the second route across the mountains – starting with a left turning off the road just before Easky (see below) – takes you up through the gorgeous setting of **Easky Lough** and then down a dramatic descent of the southwestern face of the range into the area surrounding Tobercurry (see p.401).

seventh-century monastery and a pre-Romanesque church, neither really worth making a detour for. *The Thatch Pub*, at the very southern end of town, is an old-fashioned place where you should be able to hear a traditional tune or two (Thurs all year; open sessions Tues in summer).

About ten miles further west and just after Skeen, you can take the turning south for the route through the Ox Mountains (see above), or for an eerie sense of remoteness take the lane north down to the coast at **AUGHRIS**, a now almost completely deserted village where the road ends abruptly at a tiny harbour. There's an early monastic site and a promontory fort, and in the fields you can see remains of *booleys*, the temporary shelters built by the old nomadic herdsmen who brought their flocks to graze in these remote coastal areas, and of a village abandoned as recently as the 1950s. If you head west from the pier, there are also some cliffs that are good for walking and **birdwatching**; they start low, but rise to a height of 100ft, so it's worth persevering. The thatched *Beach Bar* (☎071/66703; ③) does **B&B**, **meals** and has traditional **music**, with an unparalleled view across to Knocknarea and Benbulben, and up to the Ox Mountains. It also has its own beach with safe swimming and sometimes allows **camping**.

Dromore West and Easky

At **DROMORE WEST**, the **Culkins Emigration Museum** (☎096/47152; June–Sept Mon–Sat 10am–5pm, Sun 1–5pm; £2) fills in some of the story behind the deserted buildings that litter the landscape hereabouts. The museum building once housed the *Shipping and Emigration Agency* run by the local draper, Daniel Culkin, which helped many local people onto the bitter road to a better life. The agency, founded in the nineteenth century, functioned right up to the 1930s.

Originally a monastic settlement, **EASKY**, about five miles northwest of Dromore West along the coast road, was a vital link in the anti-Napoleon coastal defensive chain, as two nearby Martello towers attest. These days the place is acquiring a bit of a reputation as a surfers' paradise, which means increasing numbers of tourists; it's now been designated a **heritage town**, and so, for better or worse, it will soon be cashing in on its tourist potential. There's already a spanking new surfing centre in the middle of the village and a good shower block by the shore (jetons for the shower available from the post office for 50p). At the mouth of the salmon-rich Easky river are the ruins of the fifteenth-century **Rosalee Castle**, which many of the locals are convinced is cursed (key from Mrs Mary Morrissey, above *Clerk's* shop). A few years back it was all set to be renovated with government money, and a committee was set up to steer the village into a new tourist-fed prosperity. Suddenly the chairman of the committee dropped dead, then the secretary drowned, and finally, before the project was hastily disbanded, the treasurer choked on a steakbone and was rushed to hospital. Maybe this is why the village signs read *GOD BLESS YOU* as you leave. The only **pub** of any singularity is *Sheila Sullivan's*, a talking pub for the old fellas. There's a **campsite**, *Atlantic 'n' Riverside Caravan & Camping Park* just north of the village, which also does **B&B** accommodation (☎071/49001; ②), as does the post office and, in slightly grander style, *The Old Rectory* (☎096/49181; ④), which also serves dinner. There's free camping on the tussocky land off the magical shore road – check it's acceptable to neighbours in the nearby bungalows.

A mile south of the village, beside the road, is the extraordinary **Split Rock** – a glacial erratic, ten feet high, that's said to have been thrown here by Finn McCool from the top of the Ox Mountains. Legend also has it that the rock will close on anyone who dares to go through the split three times.

Enniscrone

ENNISCRONE, on the east side of Killala Bay and the western boundary of County Sligo, is a popular, rather ramshackle, seaside resort for the Irish, with caravan sites hidden away in the sand dunes, plus the traditional golfing amenities. There's a sweeping three-mile crescent of sandy beach with ten Victorian bath-houses, built to exploit the health-giving properties of seaweed and hot sea-water. The **seaweed bathing** tradition continues at *Kilcullen's Bath House* (11am–10pm), a strapping Edwardian establishment where you can enjoy a hot sea-water bath (£5), seaweed bath (£6), or the works: a steam bath followed by a seaweed bath (£11). There's no time limit, so once you've got used to the slightly strange sensation of lying on fronds of slimy seaweed, you can lie in the enormous glazed porcelain bath in the iodine-rich brew for as long as you like before finishing off with a cold sea-water rinse.

One other thing you can't fail to notice in Enniscrone is a powerful metal sculpture of a black pig in someone's front garden on the main street (the mythical Black Pig was chased across Donegal Bay and came ashore at Enniscrone). It was supposedly commissioned by the council, then appropriated by the house's owner when the unprepossessing final result was rejected. There are numerous **B&Bs**: try *Central House* on Main Street (☎096/36234; ④) or the *Castle Arms Hotel*, also on Main Street (☎096/36280; ④), where you can get a drink and a bite to eat as well.

South Sligo

The sight worth stopping for in the village of **COLLOONEY**, five miles south of Sligo where the N4 and N17 separate (bus #247, #267, #275 or #285 from Sligo), is the **Teeling Monument** at the northern entrance to the village, built to commemorate Bartholomew Teeling, hero of the Battle of Carricknagat. The battle was fought nearby during the rebellion of 1798, when a combined Franco-Irish force – on its way from Killala in County Mayo, where the French had landed (see p.370), to Ballinamuck in County Longford – was held up by a single strategically placed English gun. Teeling charged up the hill and shot the gunner dead, turning the tide of the engagement. After their defeat at Ballinamuck the French were treated as prisoners of war, but 500 Irish troops were massacred. Irish-born Teeling, who was an officer in the French army, was later hanged in Dublin. The monument links Teeling and his fallen comrades with subsequent generations of Irish freedom fighters.

Close to Collooney is the battlemented **Markree Castle**, originally seventeenth century but with grandiose Victorian extensions, which is still the home of the Coopers – who used to be Sligo's most powerful Anglo-Irish family. It's set in impressive parklands and is now open as a **hotel** (☎071/67800; ⑦); the place also houses the excellent – though expensive – *Knockmuldowney* **restaurant**, or you can just wander in for a drink and a taste of the old high life. Comfort and gastronomic delights at a more affordable level are on offer at *Glebe House* (☎071/67787; ⑤), just outside Collooney on the other side of town. A "restaurant with rooms" rather than a guesthouse (but you don't have to stay to have dinner), *Glebe House* (open 2pm for afternoon tea; 6.30–10pm for dinner; closed Jan) is a fairly austere building filled with an assortment of heavy, Victorian-and-later furniture – the point is not so much the surroundings as the food and the freshness of the ingredients, many of which are grown in the garden outside.

Heapstown Cairn and Lough Arrow

The more appealing route south from here, to Lough Arrow, involves a turn off the N4 at Drumfin along the road that goes through the geriatric village of Riverstown. Several miles on, standing by the roadside behind a modern bungalow, is **Heapstown Cairn**, a Neolithic passage tomb as large as Medb's Cairn and traditionally the last resting place of Ailil, brother of King Niall of Tara. A lot of the cairn stones have been plundered for building material, but even in its diminished state the cairn remains impressive, best appreciated by climbing it and taking in the view from the top. What's most fascinating about the view is the relationship with the surrounding landscape: the cairn takes a perfect central position in relation to the nearby circle of hills, many with cairns on their peaks.

One option from here is to go down the eastern shore of **Lough Arrow**, whose blue waters are set with ringlets of isles and whose banks are dotted with ancient landmarks, many of them unmarked on the map. When the sun is shining there are few spots to beat it, especially if you can take a rowing boat onto the tranquil lake – keep your eye out for boats lying by the banks and then ask at a nearby house; or try *Lough Arrow Boats* (☎071/65491), which rents out fibreglass boats. The road round the southern edge of the lake goes through **BALLINAFAD**, at the back door of the Bricklieve Mountains. The road into Ballinafad from the Curlew Mountains of Roscommon gives the most stupendous view in the whole of Sligo, right up to Benbulben – it's worth backtracking up the hill to get it. **Ballinafad Castle** (left off the road at the top of the village) is a sixteenth-century building remarkable only because its huge circular towers and squat walls are of thirteenth-century design. If the charms of the area tempt you to **stay** to watch the luminous twilight descend on the lake, you've a choice between the *Rock View Hotel* (☎079/66073; ④), a down-to-earth angler's hotel halfway down the lough (much further than the signs indicate) – the owners will give plenty of advice on trout-fishing in Lough Arrow's limpid waters – and the swankier *Cromleach Lodge Country House* (☎071/65155; ⑧), which is close to the northern end of the water. Further north, outside **RIVERSTOWN**, you can stay in a graceful eighteenth-century Big House, *Coopershill* (☎071/65108; ⑦), belonging to a branch of the Coopers of Markree.

Carrowkeel and Keshcorran

The other route southwards from the Heapstown Cairn takes you along the top of Lough Allen to meet the N4. Cross at Castlebaldwin and climb the road that forks left behind *McDermot's Pub* for the Bronze Age **Carrowkeel Cemetery** – you can drive all the way up, on unmetalled roads, or walk: either way, watched over by cairns and (signposted) tumuli, the panorama is marvellous, with the whole of County Sligo spread out beneath you. Comprising fourteen cairns, a few dolmens and some fifty-odd pieces of stone foundations, the site is the most important cairn colony west of Sliabh Na Caillighe in northwest Meath. Several cruciform **passage graves** set in the cairns are still roofed, the smaller ones with great lintel stones, the larger with corbelled vaults. You can actually enter Cairn K, one of the roofed tombs: cruciform in shape, with its dry stone roof intact, it's been compared to Newgrange in County Westmeath (see p.155). Here, however, it's lit by the sun on the year's longest day.

Also of interest in the area are the caves on the hill of **Keshcorran**, the cairn-topped summit that faces Carrowkeel to the west, which you can get to by rejoining the main road across the mountains, then turning left down the hill, taking every descending turning until you reach a major road where the pub *The Traveller's Rest* stands. Take a right here towards Kesh, and beyond the *Foxes Pub* and grocery store, a fingerpost points right – after a couple of hundred yards you'll spot the line of caves cut into the forehead of the mountain. The caves have no depth at all, but the feeling of isolation is immense at this spot. According to legend, this was one of the places where the lovers Diarmuid and Gráinne lived when they fled the anger of Finn McCool, and it was here that the baby Cormac Mac Airt, later to be the greatest of all the High Kings who ruled at Tara, was reared by wolves. On the last Sunday in July, in a reflection of ancient pagan rituals, locals still gather by the caves for sessions of prayer.

Ballymote

If, instead of taking the Lough Arrow route from Collooney, you follow the N17 south-west, you could make a diversion along the R293 to the small market town of **BALLYMOTE**. Its fourteenth-century castle, built by Richard de Burgo (the "Red Earl of Ulster"), was once the strongest in Connacht but has associations with major defeats – it was O'Donnell's before he lost at the Battle of Kinsale, and it was James II's possession before he lost at the Boyne. The place has an important and ancient literary connection: it was here, in about 1400, that *The Book of Ballymote* was compiled, giving the key to the geometrical Ogham letters that are formed on many standing stones of the fourth and fifth centuries – the name comes from the townland of Ogham, outside nearby Tobercurry, which has plenty of examples of them. Ballymote makes a good centre for both **angling** and rath-spotting – the low, undramatic countryside all around is covered in ancient ring forts. The village sports a couple of nice old bars: *Sally's*, towards the east end of town, which has a dark wooden interior for serious drinking (music Sat & Sun), and *Hayden's* on the main southern street (occasional open sessions).

For **accommodation**, the *Castle Hotel* (☎017/83342; ④) offers beds and food, or enquire from John Perry at *The Corran Restaurant*. He will arrange very reasonable B&B or just a bed at the standard hostel price (☎071/83372); the restaurant is the best place to **eat**, and the proprietor acts as local information service. The most stylish **B&B** in the vicinity, however, is at *Temple House* (April–Nov; ☎071/83329; ⑤), three miles from here on the shores of the lake. Founded by the Knights Templar and expanded in 1560, this is one of the grandest and earliest Anglo-Irish houses ever built in Ireland – the bulk of the house was grandly refurbished in 1864 – on a 950-acre estate, with 97 rooms, five of which are for B&B guests, and they do a good dinner for £16. To get there take the left fork off the Collooney end of town; the house is near the N17 to Tobercurry.

Tobercurry

The district around **TOBERCURRY** – and south Sligo in general – has a reputation for **traditional music**: Michael Coleman, the greatest of Irish fiddle players, came from here, and it's also where the *Chieftains* had their roots. Today the town and the surrounding area are economically very depressed, with boarded-up houses a common sight, and scenically it's not too exciting either. Tobercurry town is a busy little market centre, usually devoid of tourists. The **tourist information office** is based in *Killoran's Traditional Restaurant*, where you can eat cheaply, although in rather more than flyblown surroundings – don't miss out on the famous fresh salmon from the River Moy. The restaurant also has a dance floor at the back, where it holds boisterous Irish evenings (June–Sept Thurs 9.30pm–12.30am). In the second week of July the town has a **music week**, featuring short courses in music and Irish dancing. For **accommoda-**

tion, there are several guesthouses and B&B's, of which the most appetizing is probably *Cawley's* (☎071/85025; ④); *Killoran's* can arrange free camping or a bed at the standard hostel rate. *Carricks* sport and fishing tackle shop, a few doors down from *Killoran's*, rents out rods, and in the *Lough Talt Inn*, a few miles up the Ballina Road, boats can be rented for trout fishing on the lake.

Gurteen and the far south

Follow the R294 ten miles or so southeast and you'll reach **GURTEEN**, once another thriving centre for traditional music, now a place with something of the scent of a ghost town. Yet some of the finest musicians in the country still live up in the hills, and from time to time they might come down to strike up a tune. *Teach Murray* has a session on Mondays, and the *R-is'n Dubh* has spontaneous music making.

Lough Gara, tucked away in the southernmost pocket of the county, is not as appealing as the map suggests it might be, having a very undramatic surrounding shoreline. **Moygara Castle**, signposted near the lake, is similarly anticlimactic, with just one of its original four towers left intact.

COUNTY LEITRIM

The **Leitrim** scenery is more distinctive than it's normally given credit for – the mountains and glens, of the north in particular, have a rugged, wide-open appeal and some great walking – but the county can't compete with Sligo for historical interest. It stretches fifty miles from County Longford to its slim two-mile coastline at-**Tullaghan** and is neatly split into north and south sections by the vast interruption of **Lough Allen**, the first lake on the River Shannon. The southern half is dominated by the presence of the **Shannon**, and the lake-peppered terrain to the east of the river, with its characteristic drumlins, or hillocks, also merits exploration. The mountains of the northern section are grouped around **Manorhamilton**, and it shares its most beautiful features – **Glencar** and **Lough Gill** – with Sligo (see pp.390–93).

Carrick-on-Shannon

The small county town of **CARRICK-ON-SHANNON**, beautifully positioned on a wide stretch of the Shannon just below Lough Key, is a major **boating** centre, and its marina is full of pleasure boats and Shannon cruisers. It also makes a good base from which to cycle round the southern loop of Leitrim or to investigate Lough Key and Lough Boderg in Roscommon, and there's good coarse fishing to be had.

Carrick's *raison d'être* as a tourist centre has recently taken a boost with the reopening of the Ballyconnel–Ballinamore Canal in the summer of 1994. The canal provides the final link in the **Shannon-Erne Waterway**, 239 navigable miles taking in stretches of still-water canal, canalized river and a sequence of lakes (see the map "The Canal System" on p.118), and ending up in Belleek in County Fermanagh. A late-comer to the canal-building boom that swept the country in the eighteenth and nineteenth centuries, the waterway was completed in 1860, and was used for only nine years before being made redundant by Ireland's growing rail network.

The single piece of historical interest the town itself has to offer is the minuscule **Costello Chapel**, at the top end of Bridge Street. Billed as the second smallest chapel in the world, it was built in 1877 by the fanatically devout businessman Edward Costello as a memorial to his wife, who died young that year. The couple's lead coffins, protected by thick slabs of glass, lie in two sunken spaces on each side of the tiny, beautifully tiled aisle. Also worth a call is **Cyril Cullen's** pebbledashed Georgian house and factory shop, *Summerhill*, on the road to St Patrick's Hospital, where he sells porcelain figures and his own distinctive knitwear designs – he breeds his own Jacob sheep for their wool. You may be lucky enough to get a chance to hear his 150-year-old harp made by J. Fall of Belfast, the first craftsman to take up harp-making after O'Carolan's death (see "Mohill", p.404). There are only two such instruments in Ireland, the other being in Pádraig Pearse's memorial house in Dublin. You might also be shown Cullen's marvellous collection of Bridget Gore-Booth paintings.

Practicalities

Carrick's **tourist office** (May–Sept; ☎078/20170) is on the quay on the Roscommon side of the river. The town boasts a number of small hotels and numerous **B&Bs**, especially on Station Road and out on the Dublin Road – try *Sunnybank*, Station Road (☎078/20988; ③), or *Attyrory Lodge* on the Dublin Road (☎078/20955; ③) – or the basic hotel, the *Mariners Reach*, on Bridge Street (☎078/20032; ③). Carrick also has one of the best independent hostels in the country, the *Town Clock Hostel* (IHH, May–Sept; ☎078/20068; ①), situated at the junction of Main and Bridge streets. **Camping** is allowed on the river bank by the bridge, just in front of *Michael Lynch's* boat rental, and you can use the washing facilities at *Clancy's* supermarket nearby.

If you're in the area on the first weekend in June, it's worth catching the energetic street-party atmosphere of the **Community and Arts Festival**. There are plenty of **pubs** in town: *Seán's Plaice* (sic) has a jovial atmosphere with noisy sing-alongs on a Sunday morning and is good for food. *Burke's Bar*, just a few doors up, has traditional music (Thurs nights). If you're looking for a place where silence is golden, then try *Armstrongs*, next door to the Costello Chapel. The *County Hotel* has traditional music sessions (Fri during July & Aug), with a small cover charge. *The Anchorage Bar*, near the bottom of Bridge Street, is where young people hang out and has music (Oct–March on Sun; rest of the year Wed).

For **food**, *Cryan's*, at the bottom of Bridge Street, offers three-course meals at reasonable prices, often to the accompaniment of traditional music. *Coffey's Pastry Case*, also in Bridge Street, has very good home bakes and is the best place for a snack lunch. For picnic provisions, *Doherty's Bakery*, on Main Street, is the place to go. *The Bookshop*, over the road from *Doherty's*, has a good selection of Irish literature and general contemporary stuff.

Michael Lynch's, on the Roscommon side of the river but before the tourist office, has **boats** for rental (£15 per day with outboard; maximum 5 people), and there are numerous companies that rent out **Shannon cruisers** (2- to 10-berth) by the week. The locks on the Shannon-Erne Waterway – there are 16 of them in all – are operated electronically with a swipe-card, so you don't need to be an expert to use the canal. For shorter **excursions**, *White Dolphin Boats* organize trips up the river leaving from the bridge on the hour (10am–5pm; £3.50 per person). Another starting point for the waterway is at **Ballinamore** (see p.406), where you can also rent boats. Rental of **bikes** and fishing tackle is available at *Geraghty's* (☎078/21316) on Main Street. **Buses** to Athlone, Boyle, Sligo, Mullingar and Dublin leave from in front of *Coffey's Pastry Case* in Bridge Street. The **train station**, ten minutes out by foot to the southwest, is on the main Dublin–Sligo line, with three trains a day in each direction (☎078/20036).

South of Carrick: Jamestown to Roosky

As with most of Leitrim, there's little of dramatic interest in the area south of Carrick, but if you're passing through, there are a couple of places where you could at least slow down a bit and enjoy the leisurely pace of life around the Shannon.

Jamestown and Drumsna

The village of **JAMESTOWN**, on the main Longford Road, is a town dating from James I's plantation of Leitrim in 1622 – the main road passes through a gate in the old estate walls. The Georgian houses and the wooded river banks create a peaceful atmosphere of planned eighteenth-century living. Jamestown makes a good centre for **fishing**; B&B and angling information can be found at *Shannonside Lodge*, next to the walls. Excavations in the summer of 1989 unearthed huge stretches of a Stone Age wall – one of the oldest artificial structures in the world – at nearby **DRUMSNA**, a single street of neat houses leading down to the river. It's been estimated that it would have taken a labour force of 30,000 men ten years to build its full length. *Taylor's Lounge*, right by the bridge, does B&B (②). A plaque on the wall records that Anthony Trollope began his novel *The MacDermots of Ballycloran* here in 1848; the MacDermots were great Catholic landowners during the eighteenth century, then were ruined by the anti-Catholic Penal Laws. Drumsna also has the *Angling Information Centre* (☎078/20694) where you can rent tackle, buy bait and gather relevant information.

Mohill and Carrigallen

To the east is **MOHILL**, a trim, busy village reached by turning off the main road south of Carrick at Drumsna or Dromod. A sculpture on the main street commemorates its most famous son – **Turlough O'Carolan** (1670–1738), the blind harpist and composer (he wrote *The Star Spangled Banner*, among other pieces). The last of the court bards, he lived by travelling round the chieftains' households playing his new compositions. He was also reputed to have been as great with the whiskey bottle as he was on the harp; it's said that on his deathbed he asked for a cup of the stuff, and finding that he hadn't the strength to drink it, touched the cup with his lip, saying that two old mates shouldn't part without a kiss. Mohill was the site of an abbey founded in the sixth century by Saint Manachan, but today its associations are entirely secular: it's a coarse fishing centre, with fifteen different choices of lake and river in a five-mile radius. For information on fishing, ring ☎078/31071.

The executive-home style advertising graphics and squeaky-clean restoration of the **Lough Rynn Estate** (mid-June to mid-Sept 10am–7pm; tours 11am & 11.30am, noon, 2pm, 3.30pm, 4pm & 4.30pm; £1.50, or maximum of £3.50 per car; indoor tours are limited to the baronial hall and not worth it) near Mohill may strike you as slightly smarmy, but don't be put off; the place offers a rare opportunity to get to grips with a way of life that's currently out of favour with historians and punters alike: the heyday of the property-owning aristocratic elite of high Victorian Ireland. The house stands on a handsome site on the shores of Lough Rynne, and was first acquired by one Nathaniel Clements, a successful Dublin banker and politician, in 1750. The Clements dynasty, Earls of Sligo, built the original Rynn Castle – an exact copy of a house in Ingestry, Staffordshire – in 1833, and in 1878 extended it to the Scottish Baronial pile you see now. By this time the house was the centre of an estate that encompassed a massive 90,000 acres, and the grounds include 1840s' farm buildings, the estate office – a picturesque building by the architect Digby Wyatt, who was also responsible for the Senate Chambers in Leinster House, Dublin – a pretty summer-house, as well as the ruins of a seventeenth-century castle and a dolmen. There's a restaurant, plus a fast-food outlet serving an unappetizing range of burgers and ice-cream, and a souvenir-shop offering the lowest order of tourist-based tat – if you come away with a feeling of being patronized by people who have never been short of a bob or two, and aren't averse to making a few more out of you, you're not the first.

The area around Mohill, rich rolling pastureland criss-crossed by hedged lanes, makes good cycling country. Further east, the terrain becomes rougher and less interesting, but **CARRIGALLEN** is a pleasant enough eighteenth-century town, with excellent fishing all around. It's at a point in Carrigallen parish that the three provinces of

Ulster, Leinster and Connacht meet, though nothing about the modest demeanour of the town suggests it. If you want to stay – and perhaps only keen anglers will – try the *Kilbracken Arms*, on the main street (☎049/39734; ④).

In Mohill itself, there's B&B **accommodation** on a grand scale at the eighteenth-century stone-built *Glebe House*, a couple of miles out of town on the Ballinamore Road (☎078/31086; ④), or at a more mundane level at *The Traveller's Rest* guesthouse in the village (☎078/31174; ③). *Fitzpatrick's* pub, near the estate, has sessions on a Tuesday night.

Dromod to Roosky

DROMOD, about five miles south of Mohill, is the home village of one of the most extraordinary characters in Leitrim, a Kerryman called **James McCarran**, whose chaotic antiques shop, housed in a corrugated iron shed on the main street, is almost as intriguing as the stories he tells. If he tries to sell you a saddle from the Battle of Hastings, think twice before shelling out. **ROOSKY**, on the Shannon a mile or so down the road, has just one attraction – *The Crews Inn*, which has sessions on Thursday nights, with *uilleann* pipes and dancing; even that is on the Roscommon side of the river.

North of Carrick

A couple of miles north of Carrick (#277 bus) is the county's namesake, **LEITRIM** village. It's a tiny one-street place with a lovely canalside setting – best appreciated from the pub on the bank. Though its name translates as "the back of the old cow's arse", **Drumshanbo**, four miles north from Leitrim, would make a decent alternative base.

Drumshanbo

DRUMSHANBO is a neat, cheerful place with an air of briskness that sits at the southern tip of Lough Allen, noted as having the best pike fishing in Europe. The **Sliabh an Iarann visitor centre** (April–Oct Mon–Sat 10am–6pm, Sun 2–6pm; £1.50) gives some interesting background on local life, including the use of the sweathouse, a sort of sauna, and the tradition of coal and iron mining, especially out towards Arigna. The mine closed in 1990.

In July the village holds a festival of music and dance – details from the **tourist office**, based at Mrs Mooney's B&B on the corner of the High Street and the Carrick Road (☎078/41013; ③). *Berry's Tavern* also has **accommodation** (☎078/41070; ③). You can **camp** for free in a field a little way down the Carrick Road, near the heated swimming pool complex (Irish dancing in the *Teach Cheoil* on Mon nights in summer; music on other summer evenings). The holiday cottages on the opposite side of the lake from the pool have a good restaurant that's a touch less pricy than the high-quality *Highbank House* on the High Street. For cheaper eating, there's a café out at the Manorhamilton end of town. The pea-green thatched *McManus* bar on the High Street has a music session every Thursday evening, but a much more interesting bar to drink in is *Conway's*, at the head of the Manorhamilton Road. There are a couple of **buses** a day in the direction of Dublin, usually at 8am and 6pm (☎078/31174). **Bike rental** is available from the garage on Convent Street, going out in the Dowra direction, or from *McGrath's Cycle Shop*, opposite the tourist office. Rowing **boats** can be rented from Mrs McGuire, who lives in the large house to the side of the holiday homes. **Riding** in the area is based at the *Moorlands Equestrian Centre* (☎078/41500).

Neither bank of Lough Allen is particularly dramatic, but the eastern route along the bottom of **Slieve Anierin** is the better bet, taking you up to the county border at Dowra. Just before the village, there's a rewarding climb up into the Iron Mountains (take right turn off by *John Ryan's* pub/grocery store on side of the road); a very rugged track for much of the way, it twists and turns to follow the run of the river that cuts between the rock faces.

Towards Ballinamore

The best move from Drumshanbo is to take the R208 south and head east along the R209 into the array of lakes that attracts most of Leitrim's tourism. This route makes a pleasant trip on a bike, as many of the lanes skirt the shores as they wind between the hills. Two of these hills have legendary names – Sheemore and Sheebeag (the hill of big fairies and the hill of the little fairies; there's a well-known Irish setdance by the same name). As with all such enchanted hills, this pair is supposed to open up on *Samhain* (Hallowe'en), when their gods and goddesses roam the land.

Sheemore lies before Keshcarrigan on the south side of Lough Scur; unfortunately it's not signposted, so you might have to question a few of the locals for directions. Topped by a cairn and a St Patrick's Cross, the hill commands the best view across Leitrim; the cairn is believed locally to be Fionn Mac Cumhaill's (Finn Mac Cool's) grave. On your way again along the south of Lough Scur you'll pass a dolmen by the roadside before reaching **Sheebeag**, which has a gorse-covered cairn but is less exciting than its bigger brother. To get there follow the road straight on rather than turning left into Keshcarrigan, and take a sharp right up the hill and continue for a mile or so.

KESHCARRIGAN is one of the places that has been revitalized by the reopening of the Shannon-Erne Waterway. *Gertie's Bar* is an amiably relaxed, child-friendly eating and drinking place, decorated with a chaotic mix of ancient beer ads and road signs. There are excellent, large portions of hearty food ranging from fresh sandwiches (£1) to chicken and chips (£3.50). *McKeown's* bar has traditional music on Friday nights. You can **stay** at *Canal View House* (☎078/42056; ④), a pristine and imposing bungalow that overlooks the waterway; it also runs a fairly sophisticated restaurant (open to non-residents, dinner £18.95). About four miles east, **FENAGH** has a few more bars and the ruins of a monastery and two churches founded in the seventh century by Saint Caillain. The key for the ruins is kept at the *Kealadaville House* **B&B** (☎078/44089; ③), a hundred yards up the Mohill Road – the place to stay for a quiet sojourn overlooking Fenagh Lough.

Ballinamore

It's not far north from Fenagh to **BALLINAMORE**, a wide-streeted former coaching town, which has a heritage and folk museum in the library building, once the courthouse, halfway down its main street. Highlight of the dull and chaotic collection seems to be the "authentic detachable shirt collar worn by executed 1916 patriot Seán MacDiarmada" – and if you don't believe it there's a photograph of the man to prove it. The library also houses the Leitrim Genealogical Centre. Today, Ballinamore acts as a centre for angling in Leitrim's lakes, and for boating on the newly opened Shannon-Erne Waterway (see p.409); canal barges can be rented from *Riverside Barge Holidays* (☎078/44122). There are plenty of **places to stay**, including *McAllister's Hotel* (☎078/44068; ④) and the more upfrontly named *Commercial and Tourist Hotel* (☎078/44675; ④), and *Mrs Gormley's* B&B (☎078/44082; ③). *Caroline's Restaurant*, at the bottom of the main street, is a nice place to **eat**; for **drinking** and listening to a bit of music, try *Reynolds* on a Thursday night.

North Leitrim

Focal point of the mountainous area north of Lough Allen is **MANORHAMILTON**, lying in the saddle of five valleys. Manorhamilton was founded on top of a strategic plateau by Sir Frederick Hamilton, a Scots colonist, during the seventeenth century; his castle was destroyed in the 1650s, but the ruins can still be visited. Today it's a handsome crossroads town, with a sense of self-importance underlined by the sturdiness of its architecture, and makes a good base for **walking** and **pot-holing** in the surrounding hills, on both sides of the border. Chief among local sights is the well-preserved megalithic tomb at **Cashel Bir**, on the slopes of Benbo. For advice on walking, pot-holing, caving, fishing and hang-gliding, as well as other local pursuits, go to the *Glens Centre*, housed in the old Methodist church in the centre of town (10am–6pm daily during summer; ☎072/55833).

Manorhamilton is well equipped with **B&Bs**, the liveliest of which is the one run by the *Central Bar* (☎072/55436; ③), which runs the local disco on Saturday nights, or try *Maguire's Bar* (☎072/55201; ③), where you can collapse after a hard day on the hills in front of the telly and enjoy a large plate of local salmon for £8.50. Sturdy bar meals can be had at around £3 from the *The Granary*, which advertises itself as a bistro and coffee shop, but is actually a straightforward bar, a few doors down from the *Central*. *Sheridan's Market Bar* has music on Thursday nights, and if you're in town on a summer Wednesday, you may catch *Siamsa Samhraidh*, a music-hall version of traditional Irish entertainment, at the *Glens Centre* (ring them for details).

Kiltyclogher

About ten miles northeast, **KILTYCLOGHER**, although trim and pretty – and a good stopover if you're walking in the high moorland country that surrounds it – has nothing to detain you after you've seen the **Seán MacDiarmada** statue. Executed in Dublin in 1916 for his part in the uprising, you can also visit the three-room cottage where Mac Diarmada was born, which is kept up as a kind of national shrine, a short way out of town and signposted off the Manorhamilton Road. There's good bar food at *Meehan's*, which also does **B&B** (☎072/54179; ②). A hostel is set to open here; ask around. Heading south, less than a mile from the village, the road passes a well-preserved **gallery grave**, dated between 2000 and 1500 BC, on a tranquil wind-blown site among the heather-covered slopes of Thur Mountain, overlooking a tiny lough; it's known locally as Prince Connell's Grave.

Rossinver to Tullaghan

North from Kiltyclogher and just outside **ROSSINVER**, at the southern end of Lough Melvin, there's a cool, leafy walk along a river that cascades through its valley in a series of waterfalls – a good outing for the baking hot days that happen sometimes even in the west of Ireland. Immediately outside the village on the Garrison Road, *Eden Plants* (☎072/54122) is one of the growing band of Irish producers of organic herbs and vegetables, and is open to visitors (Mon–Fri 2–6pm). The route on up to Kinlough, much less scenically spectacular than the country to the west, runs along the eight-mile western shore of **Lough Melvin**. The ruin of **McClancy's Castle** stands on an islet a few yards from the northern end of the lake. It was here that eight survivors from the three Spanish galleons wrecked off Streedagh Point finally found refuge.

KINLOUGH, near the tip of the lake, is a wholly unpretentious village and has a surprisingly interesting little folk museum at the Manorhamilton end. Part of the museum is the old *McCurran's Bar* (key from the grocery store across the road), where a half-bottle of *Guinness* stands fermenting on the wooden bar counter, and a *poteen* shaped like a diving bell stands by the wall. There's another more conventional room to the museum, with folk and historical knick-knacks crammed into every available space; a newspaper cutting shows De Valera on his way to the Dáil for the first session of the new Irish Free State. There are a couple of small **B&Bs**, including *Bluerock*, on the Dartry Road (☎072/41610; ③).

TULLAGHAN, a few miles away, is Leitrim's only outlet to the sea. It boasts a ninth- or tenth-century high cross, standing forlornly askew on a hummock by the roadside; today, however, it's a dreary resort on a dreary strip of coast.

travel details

Trains
Sligo to: Ballymote (3 daily; 20min); Boyle (3 daily; 40min); Carrick-on-Shannon (3 daily; 50min); Collooney (3 daily; 10min); Dublin (3 daily; 3hr 20min).

Bus Éireann
Sligo to: Belfast (1 daily; 6hr); Galway (3 daily; 3–5hr).

Private Buses
Funtrek (☎01/873 0852) operates daily services **from Sligo** Wine St car park to Carrick-on-Shannon and Dublin.

CHAPTER TWELVE

CAVAN AND MONAGHAN

Cavan and **Monaghan** sit side by side as if one were a physical imprint of the other – Monaghan all small hills, Cavan all small lakes. County Monaghan is renowned for being **drumlin** country – rashes of rounded hills that diminish as you head west into Cavan where the land breaks up into a crazy pattern of tiny **lakes**. Both landscapes have their charms, both their practical difficulties. If you're walking or cycling in either county, a compass can be very useful; although the terrain isn't inaccessible or dangerous, you should be aware that there's such a network of winding, crisscrossed roads – the minor ones often riddled with potholes – that you can very easily get lost. In Monaghan, the drumlin hills all look similar, while the myriad lakes of Cavan enforce constant twists and turns. The lakes, however, now offer a more leisurely means of travel; since the re-opening in 1994 of an old canal system, you can sail through Cavan along the **Shannon-Erne Waterway**.

Like County Donegal, Cavan and Monaghan share the peculiar identity of being historically part of **Ulster*** yet included in the Republic since Partition in 1921. Not surprisingly, Cavan and Monaghan people (Protestant and Catholic) still share a strong affinity with their Ulster neighbours. As border counties, they have also sheltered Republican activity during "The Troubles", and, despite the peace process, the communities are still largely polarized along staunchly held political lines.

Although the border has sharpened political and social definitions, there is a sense in which it has also sheltered both of these counties. You'll probably be struck by the old-fashioned feel of the countryside: while slow, rural ways are as prevalent in other Irish counties, the sharp contrast with the industrialization and development over the border makes them more striking here. Uncertainty about the future has left an unhurried rural ordinariness that constitutes much of these counties' appeal. They are not gaily painted for tourists, nor visibly quaint, and there's a dour Scottish severity in many of the villages, particularly in Monaghan – clear evidence of the Ulster planters. But as you explore, you'll find both counties have an understated and quiet charm.

ACCOMMODATION PRICES

Throughout this book, accommodation prices have been graded according to the cost per person per night in high season; with hotels and many hostels this represents half the cost of a double room, whereas with the more basic hostels it represents the cost of a single dormitory bed. The prices signified by our grades are as follows:

① Up to £6	③ £10–14	⑤ £20–26	⑦ £36–45
② £6–10	④ £14–20	⑥ £26–36	⑧ Over £45

*Confusingly, the name Ulster has come to be used to describe Northern Ireland. In fact, the ancient province of Ulster consisted of nine counties; at Partition, Monaghan, Cavan and Donegal were severed from the six counties which now form the North.

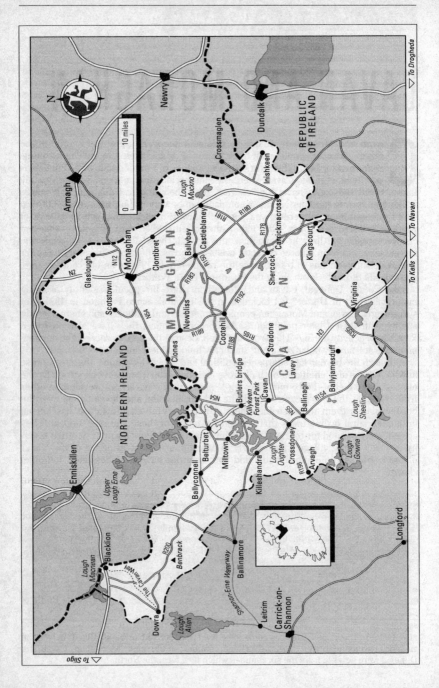

COUNTY CAVAN

Long neglected by most holiday-makers, **County Cavan** is becoming more popular, thanks to the major redevelopment of the old **Ballinamore-Ballyconnell Canal**, linking the mighty **Shannon** waterway, which serves all four provinces of the county – ending up in the southwest and boasting some great lakes – and the **Lough Erne** lake system, which flows to the northwest. The project extended the original canal and renamed it the **Shannon-Erne Waterway** (see "The Canal System" map on p.118), weaving together streams, rivers and lakes through 39 miles of wild, unspoilt countryside, free of cities and major industries. It is now possible to sail the length of the Shannon, then along the new canal, through the Erne system to Belleek, County Fermanagh, a total of 239 miles.

In former times, the region was even more water-ridden, boggy and forested than it is today. This complex of lake and bog was extremely difficult for foreign invaders to penetrate and control, and also made the land less desirable. Only the most durable relics have survived. The county is renowned for its **fishing**, and a conservative tourism is growing which neither scars the land nor disturbs the peace. Forest parks have been developed, not to encourage families to bring the children but to give fishers access to the heart of the lake complex. Everywhere, the stillness is profound.

Some history

Evidence of Neolithic peoples from as early as 6000 years ago are scattered about the region in the form of **court cairn tombs**, but they're hard to find unless you know what you're looking for. Similarly invisible are the lakes' *crannógs* – artificial islands built as early as the Stone Age, but more typically developed as secure settlements from the first century AD and now melted back into the general landscape, indistinguishable from natural islands. **The Celts** had their principal pagan shrine at **Magh Sleacht** near present-day Ballyconnell. Several Celtic stone idols bearing bold representations of the human head have been found in the lake areas of Cavan and Fermanagh, particularly potent pagan symbols. Some of them were found in circumstances suggesting that they were deliberately hidden in more recent times to deny them their power, a sign of their continuing folkloric importance. Sadly, though, none of these idols can be seen in their original setting, and most now form part of the collections of the National Museum in Dublin or the Fermanagh County Museum at Enniskillen.

When **Saint Patrick** established his seat at Armagh, he also set up a monastery at Kilnavert. Rather than crudely asserting a new dogma, the proselytizing Christians allowed pagan and folkloric traditions to continue, mingling them with the new creed. The filtering through of the new faith was fairly rapid; but more brutal invaders found the area far harder to penetrate. The network of lakes and waterways proved difficult to negotiate, and foreign invaders arrived with neither knowledge of the terrain nor the apparatus needed for conquest. The **O'Reilly** family, who dominated Cavan from the beginning of recorded history to the seventeenth century, continually blocked Anglo-Norman attempts to take control, and this explains the lack of Norman developments in the region.

Despite Elizabeth I's attempts to divide and rule by creating the **County of Cavan** (more a piece of propaganda than a sign of real political strength) and playing one Irish barony off against another, it was only after the failure of the Irish cause at the Battle of Kinsale that Cavan received the stamp of foreign invaders. Ancient Gaelic ways were crushed by the Jacobite plantation, and the county was divided up between English and Scottish settlers. Every parish was to have a Protestant church, and the new town of Virginia was built in memory of Elizabeth. As usual, the best land was given to the

English and Scottish newcomers, leaving the Irish population to face poverty and the loss of religious freedom.

The rebellion of 1641 was a direct result, and **Owen Roe O'Neill**, the Ulster Confederate leader based at Cavan, played an important part, defeating the British General Munro at Benburb to the north of the county in 1646. However, O'Neill failed to follow his victory through, and the Irish Confederates were eventually defeated. After O'Neill's death in 1649, Cromwell quickly took control of Cavan and the resulting confiscation of land and property from the Irish guaranteed the Protestant domination of the county.

Until Partition, Cavan's subsequent history was much in line with the rest of Ulster. In the eighteenth and nineteenth centuries the linen and woollen industries ensured a measure of economic growth – though Cavan was always one of the poorer parts of the province because of the difficulties of the land; and the Famine of 1845–49 brought large-scale emigration. At **Partition**, Cavan was included in the Republic, thus retaining its Irishness; but it shared the fate of Monaghan and Donegal in being torn from its historic and cultural Ulster identity.

Cavan town and Lough Oughter

CAVAN town grew up around an abbey, but nothing remains of this beyond its memory and an eighteenth-century tower beside the burial place of Owen Roe O'Neill. The town is quite subdued, with only two main streets: Main Street is the principal artery of shops and bars, while Farnham Street has an older character with some very nice stone Georgian houses, a Classical courthouse of warm sandstone and a huge Catholic cathedral, built in the 1940s, that surprisingly succeeds in confirming status and a sense of place without being overbearing.

The **tourist office** is on Farnham Street (all year Mon–Sat 9am–5pm; ☎049/31942). For **B&B**, try Mrs Anne Gaffney's *Oakdene*, 29 Cathedral Road (☎049/31698; ③); or, ten minutes' walk out of town, Mrs P. Adams' *Shandra*, Golflinks Road, Lisdaran (☎049/31183; ③). For more luxury, *Farnham Arms* on Main Street (☎049/32577; ⑤) has rooms as well as a pleasant bar and pub meals. Good for a night's supping and chatting are the *Imperial Hotel*, Main Street, and *Blessing's*, also on Main Street, two friendly bars with live music. Other useful facilities include a **laundry** called *The Laundry Basket* on Dublin Road; *McGinnity* the **travel agent**, 2 Coleman Road (☎049/31811); and *Cavan Travel*, 15 Main Street (☎049/61222). You can **rent bikes** from *Bicycle Tours* on Farnham Street (☎049/31932). Cavan town is very much the transport centre of the county, and *Bus Éireann* (☎049/31353) connects it with all major towns in the Republic and the North, and **private buses** run to Dublin.

Lough Oughter

A major focus of scenic interest in County Cavan is the complex of tiny lakes which riddle the north of the county. They're known collectively as **Lough Oughter** and form part of Upper Lough Erne. The land here is so fretted with water that its very fabric seems to be disintegrating. Contours are provided by very low, unassuming hills while the waters are edged with reeds, spindly silver birch and alder. Everything is on a small scale, but the landscape has a subtle attraction nonetheless, and the roads making their way through the labyrinthine network of lakes are quiet and empty. It makes little sense to head for a particular point in Lough Oughter – it's hard to tell when you've got there anyway – and the best plan is probably just to enjoy the gentle confusion.

The nicest of the little towns serving visitors, especially those interested in fishing, are Cavan town itself and, a few miles north, Belturbet. In between, there's also the pretty village of **BUTLERSBRIDGE**, with a notoriously enjoyable bar, the *Derragarra Inn* – touristy but serving good food throughout the day (10.30am–10.30pm). **BELTURBET** itself sits prettily on a hill beside the River Erne and is an angling and boating resort which boasts a new marina and cruiser station. For B&B, try *Mrs R. Hughes*, 8 Church Street (☎049/22358; ③).

Heading round the Lough there are a few sights of interest. Just south of **Milltown**, you'll find **Drumlane Church** and **Round Tower**. A monastery was founded here by Saint M'Aodhog in the sixth century, and Augustinians from Kells took the place over in medieval times. The church itself is plain and roofless, but its setting beside a lake, and its size in such an intimate landscape, are impressive. The earliest parts of the building are thirteenth century, but it was substantially altered in the fifteenth century, from when the carved heads outside the doorways and windows date. The round tower is eleventh century and of good, clean stonework.

Continuing south through **Killeshandra** round the west side of Lough Oughter, bear right at the Arvagh signpost, then first right – it's difficult to reach without transport – to Mrs Faris's *Pighouse Collection*, a quasi-**folk museum** at Corr House, Cornafean (open anytime, but ring ahead to check she's in; ☎049/37248; £2). In contrast to the dearth of visible history in the county as a whole, this is a massive accumulation of miscellaneous remnants of the past; three huge barns are full of dusty junk, only a small part of which, the section on domestic utensils and furniture, has so far been catalogued and labelled – the rest you rummage through and interpret for yourself. There's a vast and fascinating range of stuff which includes (for example) a fine collection of embroidered eighteenth-century waistcoats, Victorian and Edwardian evening gowns, samples of old lace and a huge collection of porcelain cheese dishes.

The Protestant cathedral of **KILMORE**, near Crossdoney on the R198 and just three miles southwest of Cavan town, is a modern structure of little interest. However, set in the wall is an impressive Romanesque doorway, removed here from a monastery that stood on Trinity Island, three miles to the west in Lough Oughter. Its deep, chunky carving is superbly intricate and repays detailed attention. Follow the narrow road that runs north from here to the hamlet of Garthrotten, and you can enter **Killykeen Forest Park**. Here **Clough Oughter** is a thirteenth-century circular tower built on a *crannóg*, the best of its kind in Ireland.

West Cavan

To the northwest of Milltown and Killeshandra, **West Cavan** sticks out like a handle, tracing the line of the border. It's quite different from the rest of the county – wilder and higher, with peat-covered hills, granite boulders and mountain streams. In this inhospitable bleakness, it has more in common with the wilds of Donegal than the more intimate Cavan lakeland.

About six miles from Belturbet is **BALLYCONNELL**, two miles west of which is the county's one **independent hostel**, the friendly *Sandville House Hostel* (March–Nov; at other times by arrangement, ring ☎049/26297; ①). Housed in a converted barn alongside a large Georgian house, the hostel is not heavily used because of its remoteness, but if you do find your way here, you're liable to stay longer than planned; they also have **bike rental** and **camping** facilities. The *Slieve Russell Hotel* (☎049/26444; ⑧), atop a hill outside town, makes a considerable contrast and seems designed to announce that its owner has made it big locally: inside it's less brash, and the dining room is the best place to eat round here, albeit expensive. **B&Bs** include Mr Mike Blower, *Rossdean*, Daisyhill (☎049/26358; ③).

Right up in the northwestern corner of the county, the **Cavan Way** is a signposted walk of seventeen miles that takes you through rugged terrain from **DOWRA** to **BLACKLION**, where it meets the southwestern end of the **Ulster Way**. Small maps of the route can be picked up in tourist offices. From the heights above Blacklion there are spectacular views over Lough MacNean and the Fermanagh lakeland, to the Sligo and Leitrim mountains in the west, and on a clear day to the heights of south Donegal. Along the route, **The Shannon Pot** is the source of Ireland's mightiest river – the Shannon – and figures heavily in Irish myth, though it's little visited.

Dowra and Blacklion themselves are tiny and remote: the former high on the young Shannon before it fills Lough Allen, the first of many lakes, the latter a border crossing point. Both have **B&Bs** which are almost certain to have space, though it's still safer to phone ahead and check. In Blacklion, try Theresa O'Dwyer's *Pinegrove* (☎072/53061; ③) or *Loughmacneann House* (☎072/53022; ④), both in Main Street; in Dowra ask at the *Hi Way Inn* (☎078/43025; ③).

COUNTY MONAGHAN

Monaghan's countryside is first and foremost drumlin country. **Drumlins** are softly rounded mounds of land left by retreating glaciers at the end of the last Ice Age, and the exceptional number of these small hills packed together in County Monaghan serves as a very good example of what textbooks call "basket of eggs" topography – a reference to the land's appearance from on high; at ground level the soil is poor and the land is broken up into small units which are difficult and uneconomic to farm. The drumlins are grass-covered, and light hedgerows stitch their way across them, marking out the fields. Initially it's a charming scene, but it soon becomes repetitive: the pathways between drumlins are pretty enough, but once you're round or over one small hill the next is much the same. Little lakes provide occasional relief and are excellent for fishing, but they're nothing like as numerous as in Cavan.

The feel of this landscape has been captured in the poetry and prose of **Patrick Kavanagh**, rated by many as Ireland's finest poet after Yeats. He was born in Inishkeen in the south of the county, and his writing evokes the poor quality of peasant life – and also something of the monotony of the rural landscape.

Particularly in the north of the county, the terrain has led to an insane criss-crossing of lanes: a compass is a good idea, as is an awareness that all available maps are unreliable. It makes for delightful walking if you're not in too much of a hurry: in these hilly areas you can wander undisturbed for miles along the labyrinth of ancient tracks and lanes – though it is advisable to avoid the border. If you know what to look for you can seek out the sites of court tombs, forts and cairns from the Bronze Age. Many of them, thanks to the underdevelopment of the land, have remained virtually untouched. The best megalithic sites in the region are the Lisnadarragh wedge tomb, **Dún Dubh**, at Tiravera, and the **Tullyrain triple ring fort** near Shantonagh.

But most of Monaghan's towns and villages have very clear origins in the seventeenth and eighteenth centuries. The influence of Scottish **planters** and English colonists is obvious in the number of planters' Gothic and Presbyterian churches, and in the planned towns and the landscaped estates developed around conveniently picturesque lakes. Stark, stern architecture reflects the character of the hard-working and hard-driving settlers who came here determined to extract prosperity from farming, and from the linen industries which they introduced. Probably the most extreme examples of such discipline are the dour, austere stone cottages of Glaslough, cold and orderly in the north of the county. Like Cavan, Monaghan's cultural identity is deeply rooted in Ulster history.

Monaghan town

You're most likely to find yourself in **MONAGHAN** town while on your way to somewhere else, but the actual fabric of the place is quite interesting as you pass through. Monaghan town epitomizes what makes this county very definitely Ulster and yet is quite distinct from Cavan. The planning of seventeenth-century settlers, the prosperity of the eighteenth-century linen industry (largely the achievement of Scots Presbyterians) and the subsequent wealth and status of the town in the following century are all very much in evidence.

The town

Three central squares are linked by a chain of lanes, a layout not, in fact, altogether typical of plantation towns. At the centre is the **Diamond** – the name given to all these Ulster "squares" – in the middle of which stands a grandiose Victorian drinking fountain, the kind of memorial strongly reminiscent of any nineteenth-century industrial British city, yet strangely out of place in rural Ireland. When it was placed here, the earlier seventeenth-century Scottish settlers' cross, with its multifaceted sundial, was shifted to Old Cross Square, where it still stands.

Alongside the Diamond is **Church Square**. Here a Classical courthouse, a solid Victorian bank and hotel and a very pretty Regency Gothic church, large and spacious, stand together, conferring a strong sense of civic dignity. The town's former importance as a British garrison town is quite clear, and a large obelisk commemorates a colonel killed in the Crimean War. Everything about the place suggests a conscious attempt at permanency, buildings placed with a view to posterity; even the rounded corners of the most mundane buildings and their boldly arched entries – both features unique to Monaghan – suggest strength and pride.

Beyond Church Square, at the top of Market Street, is a pretty, arched **Market House** built in 1792. A solid, graceful building of well-cut limestone, with finely detailed decoration of carved oak leaves and oak apples, this houses the tourist office. In the opposite direction, Dublin Street leads down to **Old Cross Square**. At number ten stands the birthplace of Monaghan's most famous son, **Charles Gavan Duffy** – a Nationalist who was instrumental in the founding of the Irish Tenant League. He was also the co-founder, along with Thomas Davis, of *The Nation*, a paper which was to disseminate politically sensitive ideas. Beyond, high on a hill out of town, **St Macartan's Catholic Cathedral** commands views over the whole town and surrounding countryside. It's a Gothic Revival building of hard grey sandstone, completed in 1892; the spire is very tall, and the interior, complete with an impressive hammer-beam roof, is spacious. As you stand on the steps looking out over the surrounding land you get a real feeling of its era – it's a most successful nineteenth-century statement of religious liberation and pride.

As well as being a busy commercial and administrative centre, Monaghan looks after the county's vigorous and sometimes violent history at the award-winning **Monaghan County Museum** on Hill Street (Tues–Sat 11am–1pm & 2–5pm; free). This has a permanent collection of archeological material, prehistoric antiquities, examples of traditional local crafts, domestic utensils and paintings, prints and watercolours from the late eighteenth century to the present day. Recent acquisitions include textiles and banners, but the museum is most proud of the **Cross of Clogher**, a processional cross dating from around 1400. Contemporary art exhibitions are also held here. The **Heritage Centre** is on Broad Road (Mon, Tues, Thurs & Fri 10am–noon & 2.30–4.30pm; Sat & Sun 2.30–4.30pm; £2) and tells the story of the religious order of Saint Louis, with an intelligent display meticulously put together by one of the sisters; you're guided through it with a cassette recording.

Practicalities

The **tourist office** is in Market House in Market Street (March–Sept Mon–Fri 9am–1pm & 2–5pm, Sat 9am–1pm; ☎047/81122). There's the usual clutch of small **hotels**, including the *Westenra Arms* on The Diamond (☎047/82298; ⑥); decent **B&Bs** include *Ashleigh House*, 37 Dublin Street (☎047/81227; ③), and *The Cedars*, Clones Road (closed Dec; ☎047/82783; ④). There's no **campsite**, but you should be able to find somewhere to pitch a tent if you ask at a farm out of town. Few of the **places to eat** are particularly inspiring, but the *Genoa Restaurant and Ice-Cream Parlour*, at 61 Dublin Street (daily noon–7.30pm, takeaway till around midnight), serves home-made pizzas, burgers and fried chicken, as well as excellent ice cream. There's also good home cooking at *Andy's Restaurant* in the Market Square, and the *Westenra Arms* offers dinner from £12.50 upwards. The *Courthouse Bar* in Church Square serves bar lunches daily (from £2.50); *Dinkin's* offers chicken, burgers and chips (Mon–Sat 9am–8.15pm, Sun 5–7.30pm), while the fast food at *Tommie's Restaurant*, 7 Glaslough Street (noon–3.30pm), includes steaks, roasts, grills, pizza and curry, to eat in or take away.

As far as **entertainment** goes, there's little beyond occasional music in **bars**. In Dublin Street, *McKenna's* has occasional rock and blues bands, and *The Shamrock Bar* has less frequent but similar music. There are a couple of local **theatre** groups that are very active: if your visit happens to coincide with a local production, it's well worth going to see them. The local **jazz festival** takes place over the first weekend in September.

Bus Éireann (☎047/82377) links Monagahan with all major towns in the Republic and with Armagh, Belfast, Derry, Omagh and Strabane in the North. **Private buses** connect with Dublin (see "Travel Details" at the end of the chapter); for longer distance transport, try *O'Hanrahan Travel* at 59 Dublin Street (☎047/81832 or ☎81133).

Around the county

Unless you're heading for the North, there are two main routes out of Monaghan: west to the pleasant town of Clones or south to Carrickmacross, the county's second town. On the latter route you'll pass first through **CASTLEBLANEY**, whose two proud broad streets hinge upon a fine Georgian courthouse at what was once the market square. Castleblaney was built by English colonists to serve the needs of a large estate, beautifully situated beside Monaghan's largest lake, **Lough Muckno**, and this is still the town's finest asset. When the English picked their spot they knew what they were about: it's a particularly attractive demesne of mixed woodlands and gentle slopes beside placid waters. The estate is now a forest park, with clearly signposted walks around beautiful grounds. The **Lough Muckno Leisure Park** contains an independent **hostel**, *The Lough Muckno Adventure Centre and Holiday Hostel* (March–Oct; ☎042/46356; ②), that attracts families and fishermen in search of peace and quiet. It offers camping facilities also. If you are looking for some water-based excitement, the *Castleblaney Waterski Club* (☎042/40752) can provide just that. **B&Bs** include Mr & Mrs Derek Wilson, *Hillview*, just outside town (☎042/46217; ③), and Mrs Coogan's *Hazelwood House*, Dundalk Road, Annahale (☎042/46009; ③). For **food**, there's *Joan's Pantry* (Mon–Sat), a delicatessen and café serving light, wholesome lunches. *Gunner Brady's* offers bar food, and there's occasional traditional music at *Corrigan's* bar.

Carrickmacross

CARRICKMACROSS is the county's second most important town, boosted in the nineteenth century by a prosperous lace-making industry, now revived for the benefit of tourists. The town has one broad main street; a planter's Gothic church stands at one end, a large Georgian house at the other. In between lies a bustling array of pubs, shops and Georgian houses. Just outside town, landscaped parkland of sumptuous oaks and beeches surrounds **Lough Fea**. Further out, some three miles down the Kingscourt Road, is the **Dún a Rí Forest Park** with more good wooded walks. The massive *Nuremore Hotel* is very expensive (☎042/61438; ⑧), but there are plenty of **B&Bs** near the centre of Carrickmacross, up the Derry Road past the *Texaco* filling station: try Mrs Hanratty's *Cloughvalley House* (☎042/61246; ③), Mrs Martin's *Nocdale*, 9 Ard Rois Avenue, Cloughvalley (☎042/61608; ③), or the *Shirley Arms* on Main Street (☎042/61209; ④). *M&S* **laundry** is on Main Street (Mon, Tues & Thurs–Sat 9am–6pm).

Iniskeen

INISKEEN, to the east of Carrickmacross, is the birthplace of **Patrick Kavanagh**, which is not, in itself, a very good reason to visit. There's a small plaque bearing some of his verse in the village, and the house he lived in is well signposted – but you can't go in and it's an entirely uninteresting building. Here, you'll find the **Patrick Kavanagh Resource Centre** (☎042/78560; £2). In a more distant past, Inishkeen was the site of a sixth-century monastic centre: scant remains of the abbey and a round tower survive. The **Folk Museum** (by arrangement only, ☎042/78102) deals with local history, folklife and the old Great Northern Railway. For **entertainment**, Daniel McNello's *Kavanagh Hide Out* has country music sessions every weekend.

Clones

Heading west from Monaghan, **CLONES** (pronounced *Clo-nez*) is a busy, friendly market town, barely half a mile from the border. Situated on top of a hill, its streets give a good perspective over the surrounding countryside. The town – as it appears today – dates from 1601 when the English took it over and started to develop it. It's very obviously an Ulster town, with large Presbyterian and Methodist churches to rival the usual Catholic and Church of Ireland offerings. The solemn and impressive **St Tiernach's Church** (Church of Ireland) gives out onto the fine Diamond, and there is some evidence of eighteenth-century prosperity in the town's handful of Georgian houses. There are also traces of Clones's earlier identity, the most impressive being the weathered, deeply carved **high cross** which stands in the Diamond. Depicted on it are Adam and Eve, Abraham's near sacrifice of Isaac, Daniel in the lion's den and, on the north side, the Adoration of the Magi, the miracle at Cana and the miracle of the loaves and fishes. Though worn, there's still a strong impression of the richness of the carving. In the sixth century Saint Tiernach founded a monastery at Clones. It became an Augustinian **abbey** in the twelfth century, and the tumbled-down traces of this can be seen in Abbey Street, along with those of a round tower. Just on the edge of town is an ancient rath (an enclosure used as a dwelling) of three concentric earthworks.

Nowadays, of course, the town's chief claim to fame is as the home of **Barry McGuigan**, the former world-champion boxer. He was closely linked to the *Lennard Arms Hotel*, which also does **B&B** (☎047/51075; ④); *Creighton's* in Fermanagh Street (☎047/51284; ④) is the other hotel option if you're looking for somewhere to stay. The newly opened **Ulster Canal Stores** offers information and exhibitions on the area's history, including lace-making and the old Erne–Belfast Canal.

Just east of Clones is the **Tyrone Guthrie Foundation** at Annamakering, **NEWBLISS**. Commemorating the famous Shakespearian director, the oversubscribed centre offers a retreat and workspace to writers, artists and composers from all over the world.

travel details

Bus Éireann

Cavan town to: Belfast (2 daily; 3hr–4hr 40min); Dublin (6 daily; 3hr).

Monaghan town to: Belfast (7 daily; 2hr); Dublin (7 daily; 2hr 15min).

Private buses

P.J. McConnon's (☎047/82020) buses **from Monaghan town to Dublin** depart Church Square twice daily (Mon–Fri 8.05am & 8.30am, Sat noon & 3pm, Sun 5.45pm & 6.30pm), return-ing from Dublin Parnell Square (Mon–Thurs 5.15pm & 6.15pm, Fri 4pm, 5pm, 5.45pm & 6.15pm, Sat 12.30pm, 5.15pm & 6.15pm, Sun 8.15pm).

Wharton's Bus (☎049/37114) runs a daily service **from Cavan town to Dublin**, outside the *Lakeland Hotel* (Mon–Sat 8am, Sun 7pm). Departs **from Dublin**, opposite the gates of the Rotunda Maternity Hospital, Parnell Square (Mon–Sat 5.45pm) and on Sun (8.30pm) from outside *Wynn's Hotel*, Abbey Street.

CHAPTER THIRTEEN

COUNTY DONEGAL

Not many people would disagree with the assertion that **County Donegal** has the richest scenery in the whole country. Second only in size to County Cork, it has a spectacular 200-mile coastline – an intoxicating run of headlands, promontories and peninsulas – rising to the highest cliffs in Europe at **Slieve League**. Inland is a terrain of glens, rivers and bogland hills, of which the best-known parts are the **Glencolumbcille Peninsula** and around **Ardara** and **Glenties** in the southern part of the county. The Glencolumbcille area attracts more visitors than any other, yet the landscape of northern Donegal is, if anything, even more satisfying, especially the **Rosguill** and **Inishowen** peninsulas and the interior region – sometimes called the **Donegal Highlands** – around **Errigal Mountain**, **Lough Beagh** and **Lough Gartan**. Other noteworthy areas are the **Rosses** and **Bloody Foreland**, which are reminiscent of the more barren stretches of Connemara and make up the strongest *Gaeltacht*, or Irish-speaking, districts in the county.

The county's original name was *Tír Chonaill*, which translates as "the land of Conal", one of the twelve sons of Niall of the Nine Hostages. Subsequent to the **Flight of the Earls** in the early seventeenth century, the English changed the name to that of their main garrison *Dún na nGall* ("the fort of the foreigner") which has a certain irony, because Donegal always eluded the grip of English power, mainly due to its wild and untillable terrain. At the time of Partition in 1922, the Protestant leader **Carson** let the county remain with the Republic, reasoning that its Catholic population would probably have voted the county and the whole of the North back into the Republic at a later stage. Hence the peculiarity of its being the most northerly piece of the island, yet belonging to the Republic, to which it's attached by just a thread of land.

Bundoran and around

BUNDORAN (*bun dobhráin*, mouth of the River Doran) is one of Ireland's liveliest seaside resorts, with three miles of blue-flag beaches; it's busy day and night with mainly Northern Irish holidaymakers and courting couples strolling around the amusement arcades, souvenir shops and pubs. The town centre is concentrated into a mile of the main street, with a tiny river and bridge separating the western part of town (known as the West End) from the East End, with its tackier atmosphere, pubs, B&Bs, eating places and golf course. As an introduction to the county of Donegal it's entirely

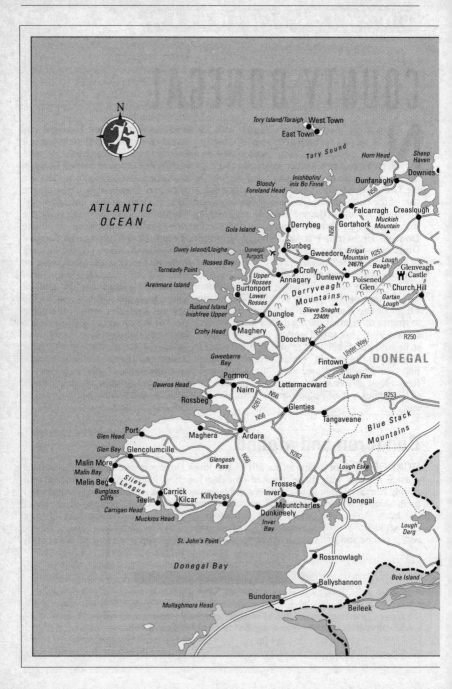

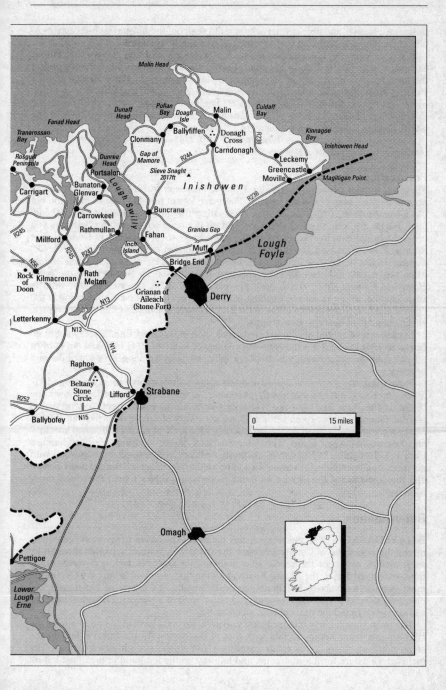

Malin Head

Dunaff
Head

Pollan
Bay

Doagh
Isle

Malin

Culdaff
Bay

Fanad Head

Tranarossan
Bay

Clonmany

Ballyfiffen

Donagh
Cross

Kinnagoe
Bay

Rosguill
Peninsula

Dunree
Head

Gap of
Mamore

R244

Carndonagh

R238

Inishowen Head

Portsalon

Slieve Snaght
2017ft

Leckemy

Carrigart

Bunaton
Glenvar

I n i s h o w e n

Greencastle
Moville

Magilligan Point

Carrowkeel

Buncrana

R238

R245

Rathmullan

Fahan

Granias Gap

*Lough
Foyle*

Millford

R247

Inch
Island

Muff

R245

N56

Bridge End

Rock
of
Doon

Kilmacrenan

Rath
Melton

Derry

Letterkenny

N13

Grianan of
Aileach
(Stone Fort)

N13

N14

Raphoe

Beltany
Stone
Circle

Strabane

R252

Lifford

Ballybofey

N15

0   15 miles

Omagh

Pettigoe

Lower
Lough
Erne

misrepresentative, and unless you really want to seek out the boisterous holiday atmosphere, Bundoran is probably best viewed from the window of a bus.

If you do stop, the chief attraction is a lovely golden-sand beach known as **Tullan Strand**, a bracing stroll along the coastal promenade away from the northern end of the town beach. The walk takes in rock formations known as the **Fairy Bridge** and the **Puffing Hole**, with the Atlantic thundering below and appetizing views across to the much more rewarding Glencolumbcille Peninsula. Along with the beach at Rossnowlagh, Tullan Strand is reckoned among the most exciting surfing spots in the world, making it one of the most dangerous for swimming.

A more recent attraction is **Waterworld** (☎072/41172; £4), a complex of heated pools with wave machine and waterslides.

Practicalities

There's a **tourist office** on the bridge (June to mid-Sept; ☎072/41350), with details of accommodation and a booking service. There are lots of **hotels**, chief of them the big old *Great Northern* (☎072/41204; ⑦), dominating the golf course right on the headland. **B&Bs** are also plentiful along and just off the main street, getting better as you cross the bridge into the West End, where many have wondrous views of Donegal Bay: *Atlantic View*, West End (☎072/41403; ④); *Glena*, almost next door (☎072/41245; ③); *Conway House*, 4 Bayview Terrace (April–Sept; ☎072/41220; ④); and *Bayview House*, Main Street (☎072/41296; ④). The cheapest place to stay in Bundoran is the basic *Homefield Holiday Hostel* (*IHH*, open all year; ☎072/41288, fax ☎41049; ②), with its large kitchen, sitting room and washing machine; to get to it, take a right turning at the church just before the bridge in the West End. Its main function is as an activity centre, so it's often full of hearty young groups.

Cycles can be rented at *Michael Goodwin's* shop in the West End. If you want to go **horse-trekking**, check out the *Stracomer Riding School* (☎072/41787), just out of town off the Ballyshannon Road, which offers fabulous pony-trekking over sandhills and beaches.

For **eating**, the *Angler's Restaurant* offers a good three-course meal for around £6. More upmarket, but still not overly expensive, is the *Fitzgerald Hotel*, just over the bridge in the West End, and the *Whistling Oyster*, on the main street, serving varied seafood dinners in a bar-room setting. There are plenty of simple cafés like the *Kitchen Bake*, in a converted chapel on the main street, for excellent cakes, coffee and snacks – an ideal stop between buses. The *Imperial Hotel* serves amazing-value bar lunches from £2. Most **pubs** in Bundoran are pretty ordinary and permanently crowded with northern holidaymakers in season. Two to try in the West End are the *Seashells Tavern* and the new *Bradog Bar*, where an intimate session involves fifteen musicians every Monday.

Ballyshannon

BALLYSHANNON, four miles on at the mouth of the River Erne, more genuinely marks the beginning of County Donegal, though it, too, is quickly passed through by most tourists eager for the scenic splendour further north. In fact, it deserves some time, especially during the **Music Festival** on the first weekend in August. One of the most popular festivals of traditional music in Ireland, it's a mix of big names and unknown talents; if you want a room, you must book in advance, although floorspace will always be found for you and your sleeping bag.

The town stands a few hundred yards upstream from a ford, at the point where the river's fresh water begins to mix with that of the ocean. All the interest lies up the steep northern slope and is easily combined in a single, straightforward stroll. The main arteries here form a wishbone, and halfway up the left-hand branch, just left off the road and past an overbearing Masonic Lodge, is the graveyard where the poet **William Allingham** (1824–89) lies: his grave is a plain white marble slab by the left side of St Anne's church. Allingham was born in Ballyshannon and, like T.S. Eliot, began work in a bank (the *Allied Irish Bank* has a bust of the poet and preserves the words scratched by him on a windowpane). He later become a poet of national significance – his verse, although usually very light, is uniquely sonorous in its descriptive lilts and rhythms:

> *Up the airy mountain*
> *Down the rushy glen,*
> *We dare not go a'hunting*
> *For fear of little men*
> *Wee folk, good folk,*
> *Trooping all together,*
> *Green jacket, red cap,*
> *And white owl's feather*
>
> *By the craggy hillside,*
> *Through the mosses bare,*
> *They have planted thorn trees*
> *For the pleasure here and there;*
> *Is any man so daring*
> *To dig one up in spite,*
> *He shall find the thornies set*
> *In his bed at night.*

From the graveyard there's a marvellous panoramic view looking down over the town and out to the surrounding hills north and south. Down at the pier you can see the backs of the tall, old warehouses lined along the river bank, their basement walls dripping with seaweed, and also the ancient isle of **Inis Saimer** just out in the river. There's only a wooden summerhouse on the island now, but it claims to have sheltered the first colonists of Ireland, around 3500 BC, offering safety from the ferocious beasts that would have roamed the forests on the mainland. The water here seems to teem with fish, and you'll find anglers still trying to catch them well into the night. Looking further out, to the mouth of the estuary, the view also takes in the white dunes of Finner, nowadays the site of a large Irish Army camp.

Practicalities

Hotel accommodation includes the *Imperial* (☎072/51147; ⑤), up the main street on the way to the churchyard. There are plenty of **B&Bs** around Ballyshannon, but few are very convenient unless you have transport to get to them. In town try *Hillcrest* (☎072/52203; ③) at the top of Castle Street by the cinema, *Mrs Matthew's* on Bishop Street (☎072/51180; ③), opposite *The Thatch Pub*, or Mrs Mullaney's *Macardle House*, 55 Assaroe View (☎072/51846; ③). Others are mostly out on the Donegal and Rossnowlagh roads: friendly *Duffy's Hostel* on the Donegal Road at the corner with Cluainbarron Road (*IHH*, March–Oct; ☎072/51535; ①) is complete with its own second-hand bookshop and camping facilities.

Embers Restaurant on Castle Street offers good seafood, pasta and vegetarian meals; while the *Ti Si Ri* Chinese **restaurant**, back over the bridge and straight ahead fifty yards, is where everyone heads after the pubs close and is much better than most Irish Chinese restaurants. There are several reasonably priced restaurants for daytime eating, including *Cúchulainn's* on Castle Street, with healthy portions of fast food; the popular *Grime's Kitchen Bake* has upstairs coffee rooms with marvellous fresh cakes and pastries. The best **pubs** in town are *Seán Óg's*, with traditional **music** every Wednesday night and rock on Saturday, *The Thatch Pub* on Bishop Street, with thatched roof and cottage-kitchen interior and traditional music most nights, and the *Green Lady*, on the bridge opposite the bus station.

As well as its August music **festival**, Ballyshannon has a number of other festivities worth looking out for. There's a **drama festival** of mainly Irish plays in the week of March 17 (St Patrick's Day); the **Allingham Festival for Writers** over a weekend at the beginning of October; and traditional **harvest fair** celebrations around the middle of September, a rural affair with crowds from the surrounding countryside. The rest of the time you can fill your evenings at the *Abbey* **cinema**, at the north end of town by the Donegal Road (following restoration, this will have several screens, a theatre and restaurant); there are Monday night Irish **dance classes** in the Market yard if you want to learn a few steps; and gaelic football every other Sunday. At Ballintra, four miles along the Donegal Road, there's **horse racing** in the open fields on the first Monday in August.

Abbey Assaroe

Back on the road, a left turn by the thatched pub at the top of the hill takes you along the Rossnowlagh Road, where a second left turn (marked by a fingerpost sign, "Fishing") takes you down to the scant remains of **Abbey Assaroe**. Founded by the Cistercians in 1184, it's pretty barren now, and Allingham's hundred-year-old description remains apt:

> *Grey, grey is Abbey Asseroe.*
> *The carven stones lie scattered in*
> *briar and nettlebed*
> *The only feet are those that come*
> *at burial of the dead.*

Following the road down past the abbey and round to the left, you'll come to a restored **mill** beside a lively little stream. This makes a pretty picture of mill-race and rotating cog wheels, and there's an **interpretative centre**, *The Watermills* (☎072/51580), with coffee and craft shop, display centre and working water wheels. There's a less obvious natural beauty to be found if you pass through the log gate next to the old bridge and go on up along the stream's left bank. Within a few minutes you'll come across two artificial **caves**. One is a small grotto known as the Catsby; the other – now around 90ft deep – is said to have once reached all the way under the abbey and run for two miles towards Rossnowlagh. The grotto was once a site for penal Masses, services that had to be held secretively during the enforcement of the penal laws during the eighteenth century – and you'll find in the Rossnowlagh museum the carved stone known as the Monk's Head that once sat above the entrance.

Back in the mill area, head up the hill again for a few yards and watch out to the left for a little track, beginning with a stone stile beside a bungalow, that runs down to the shore of the bay. Saint Patrick is said to have once stepped ashore here, and today there are several rusted metal crosses perched on small stony outcrops and a tree covered in tattered ribbon mementos. It goes without saying that there's a natural **well** that sprang up at the spot where the saint's foot touched the shore; you'll find it down by the furthest cross. Bless yourself with its water three times and your prayer for a cure will be answered.

Rossnowlagh

ROSSNOWLAGH lies on the coast away from the main Donegal Road, with a magnificent long stretch of beach raked by Atlantic surf and, to the south, good cliffs for walks. Appropriately named ("The Heavenly Cove"), it has a water-skiing, surfing and canoeing club beside the *Sand House Hotel*, which is unfortunately private, but one of the many surfing buffs will probably be able to help you out with equipment, or at least advise where else to get your hands on it.

The **Franciscan Friary** nearby has a captivating one-room museum (daily 10am–6pm) crammed with Stone Age flints, Bronze Age dagger blades, penal crosses, pistols and other local miscellany. This includes a lovely set of *uilleann* pipes with green felt bag and very handsome regulators, a fiddle that belonged to the great piper Turlough MacSuibhne and a seventeenth-century Flemish painting on glass (*The Christ of Pity*) used as a devotion plate. A mile north of Rossnowlagh towards Ballintra (itself an unappealing place) lies **Glasbolie Fort**, a huge earthen rampart 20ft high and nearly 900ft round. It's said to have been the burial place of a sixth-century High King of Ireland.

Donegal town and around

DONEGAL town is not the most exciting of places, but it is making an effort. It's not even the county capital (which is Letterkenny), and the lasting impression is one of traffic jammed around the busy triangular **Diamond** at the centre, the old market place. The only real reason to stay long in Donegal town, though, is to explore the surrounding countryside, especially in the direction of the **Blue Stack Mountains** which rise at the northern end of **Lough Eske**.

Arrival, information and accommodation

Buses stop outside the *Foodmarket* on the Diamond, with the timetables displayed in the office behind the newsagents, where luggage can also be left. One advantage of staying in Donegal is that you've plenty of choice of accommodation. There are literally dozens of B&Bs scattered around the town, but many of them are very small, so to avoid a lot of walking it's simplest to call at the **tourist office** on the Quay (July & Aug Mon–Sat 9am–1pm & 2–8pm; May, June, Sept & Oct Mon–Fri 10am–1pm & 2–5pm, Sat 10am–2pm; ☎073/21148), complete with bureau de change.

The most upmarket place to stay is the central and comfortable *Abbey Hotel* on the Diamond (☎073/21014; ⑥). A couple of **B&Bs** to try if you arrive out of hours are *Arranmore House* on Coast Road (☎073/21242; ④) and *Windermere* on Quay Street (☎073/21323; ③). The newly built *Cliffview* (☎073/21684; ②) offers hostel-style accommodation and is a short walk out the Coast Road. There are also two **hostels**, the *Donegal Town Independent Hostel* (IHH, open all year; ☎073/37057, fax ☎22030; ①), which has camping and a jovial atmosphere and lies half a mile out on the Killybegs Road, and the *An Óige Ball Hill Hostel*, about three miles out in a former coastguard station on the north side of Donegal Bay (April–Sept; ☎073/21174; ②), which also tends to be busy, but it's right on the shore. It also offers camping facilities. Swimming is safer at a second beach twenty minutes' walk away; you can **camp** nearby, and rent **horses** from Anne Carney on the Ball Hill Road (£7 per hour; pony trekking for beginners).

Guided tours (July to mid-Sept Mon–Fri 11am & 2pm; ☎073/22312; £2) of the town's historic sites are conducted in several European languages; meeting place is the Chamber of Commerce office on the Killybegs Road. **Bikes** and **fishing tackle** can be rented from *O'Doherty's* on Main Street (☎073/21119; bikes £6 per day), which is also a useful stop for supplementary information about the region. The owner is very knowledgeable and has photocopied local maps for sale (20p), marking out all the interesting sights in the surrounding countryside and also the best fishing spots in the south Donegal area; **fishing permits** are also issued here. The *Apollo* **laundry** (Mon–Sat 9am–6pm) is on Upper Main Street just past the cathedral.

The town

Just about the only thing to see in town is the well-preserved shell of **Donegal Castle**, on Tirchonaill Street by the Diamond, overlooking the River Eske (currently closed for renovation; ☎073/22405). A fine example of Jacobean architecture, it dates originally from the fifteenth century, but was substantially rebuilt by Sir Basil Brooke in the early seventeenth century. It's a fine marriage of strong defence and domestic grace – note the mullions, arches, gables and no fewer than fourteen fireplaces, over the grandest of which are carved the escutcheons of Brooke and his wife's family, the Leicesters. The castle tower on the right as you enter was originally a stronghold of the O'Donnells, who ruled Donegal between the thirteenth and sixteenth centuries before fleeing to Spain around 1600. It was then transformed by Brooke, who topped the tower with a Barbizon turret and added the mansion on the left, with the kitchens and bakery on the ground floor and living quarters on the floor above. Brooke was highly prolific in Donegal and was responsible for the overall design of the town.

In the Diamond stands an obelisk commemorating the compilers of the famed **Annals of the Four Masters**. The *Annals* were put together in Donegal Abbey, on the coast close to Bundoran, and indicate the years of research to collect all known Irish documents into a history of the land beginning in 2958 BC and ending at the time of writing, 1616 AD. The first entry dates back forty years before the Flood and relates a visit of Noah's granddaughter to Ireland. Around the Diamond there's good shopping, especially the *Four Masters* bookshop and *Magee's* department store.

Down at the **quay** a French anchor is on display, probably dating from the time when French troops were being ferried across to the aid of Wolfe Tone's rebellion in 1798. On the left bank of the River Eske, not far from here, stand the few ruined remains of a **Franciscan friary**, while on the opposite bank a woodland path known as the **Lovers' Walk** runs out alongside the bay with a nice view towards its many sandy islets and stony shoreline.

Lovingly restored old engines, railcars and carriages from the steam age are the centrepieces of the **Donegal Railway Heritage Centre** at the Old Station House (June–Sept Mon–Sat 10am–5.30pm, Sun 2–5pm; Oct–May Mon–Fri 10am–4pm; £1), and plans are afoot to rebuild part of the old railway and to operate the vintage trains.

Food, drink and entertainment

Eating places are plentiful, though it's the pubs as ever that seem to offer most choice. Alternatives include fast food at *The Harbour* opposite the tourist office (11.30am–1.30pm, Fri & Sat until 3am); *The Talk of the Town* on the Derry Road opposite the cathedral has very good value lunch specials; and the *Atlantic Café*, at the town end of the Derry Road, is good for a cheap hearty meal. The tea room in *Magee's* store on the Diamond serves light lunches, or the *Abbey Hotel* will feed you rather more substantially. *Foodland* supermarket (by which the buses congregate on the Diamond) has a great selection of cheeses, meat and fruit – the last such stock you're likely find in the county.

As for **pubs**, they're as ubiquitous as ever. The *Old Castle Bar*, next to the castle, has an excellent restaurant, plus high-quality music and dancing till 2am most nights. *Tír Chonaill*, opposite the *Ulster Bank* on the Diamond, is good for a quiet pint. The *Abbey Hotel* on the Diamond has a **disco** and dance on Sunday night (10.30pm–2am; £4; sometimes also on Fri in summer) and **Irish nights** (not for the purist; July & Aug Mon–Wed) from Monday to Wednesday in July and August. Others are mainly out on Main Street, the Derry Road: the *Star Bar* is a lively place with sing-songs and live acts, the *National Hotel* has more traditional music in the lounge at weekends, and best of all is *The Schooner*, just past the cathedral, with a nautical interior, an original nineteenth-century bar and music almost every night. In Laghy, three miles south on the Sligo Road, *Carlin's* pub has old-time dancing on Tuesday and Irish nights in summer.

If you're after souvenirs, or simply a way to fill a wet afternoon, then it might be worth heading out to the **Craft Village**, three-quarters of a mile from town on the Sligo Road. The workshops are leased to professional craftworkers whom you can see in action if you visit.

Around Donegal

Southeast of Donegal town, the corner of the county tucked into a fold in the border is replete with little lakes well stocked for fishing; the largest of these, and a place of pilgrimage, is Lough Derg. Less than five miles upriver from town is another spot of gentle natural beauty, Lough Eske; from here you can walk into the wilds of the Blue Stack Mountains, which rise up to the north.

Lough Derg

In the middle of **Lough Derg** (Red Lake) is a rocky islet known as **Station Island**, which has long served as a retreat for Catholics who feel in need of rigour and solitude to recharge their faith. Today it still thrives as a strong centre for pilgrimage (especially from June to Aug), and the island cannot be visited for any other reason – though some casual travellers and non-believers do get some sort of stimulation out of passing through this ancient ceremony, lasting a minimum three days. Participants go without sleep or food (bar black tea and toast) and walk barefoot over rocks, praying at selected points. It seems particularly popular with Irish students studying for exams – or waiting for the results. Northern Irish poet Seamus Heaney's book, *Station Island*, contains a number of poems dealing with the mystique surrounding this ritual. To get there you have to approach by the R233 from Pettigo, or a bus from Ballyshannon should drop you nearby.

Lough Eske

Lough Eske (Lake of the Fish) is no longer a particularly great fishing spot, though it is known as a place to catch char, a tasty nine-inch-long species of the salmon family. They lurk in the depths at the centre of the lake, moving out to the shallower edges around late October where they can easily be fished using worms. The sandy banks of the River Eske are also known for freshwater oysters – some of which are reputed to contain pearls – but they're a protected species so it's illegal to take them. Two or three miles along the Ballybofey Road by the lake's edge is a hotel called *Harvey's Point* (✆073/22208), owned by a Swiss millionaire; this includes the region's best **restaurant**, with an à la carte menu and seafood from £20.

The most enjoyable way to get to this area of soft beauty is to take the minor road which runs north of the river (from Donegal town, turn off Killybegs Road a little way above the hostel), though you can also take the main Derry Road (the N15) and turn off by the *Naomh Aengus* B&B. Either route will bring you to a forgotten, forested estate at the southern end of the lake with the ruins of one of the Brooke family's old fortified houses, dating from 1751, at its centre. This estate is now owned by the Forestry Commission, but they are relaxed about visits from the public. Circling the lake clockwise from here, you'll pass the western gate of the estate and then a farmyard: a hundred yards or so further on look out for a gap in the hedge on the left, where you'll find hidden a massive cauldron nearly six feet high and six feet round. This is a **Famine Pot**, manufactured in Britain and shipped over to Ireland by English landlords. It would be filled with Indian maize (a substitute porridge) and placed in a field where local people would come during the Famine and fill their own smaller pots to take home.

The Blue Stack Mountains

Carrying on along the western shore, you'll reach the point where the river flows in at the lough's northern tip. Nearby, a dirt road runs off to the left to take you into the **Blue Stack Mountains**. At the top of the pathway that leads on from the track, there's a very fine waterfall; from here, the **Ulster Way** leads by Lough Belshade (*Bél Seád*, lake with the jewel mouth). If you're intending to tramp around the mountain range, it's best to keep to the skirts of the hills, for there are many marshy patches on lower ground; be prepared for misty pockets during bad weather. If you're only making a day trek of it, then the photocopied maps from *O'Doherty's* are good enough for bringing you back safely; there's hardly any danger in the area apart from that of being caught by the descending mist. For longer and more intense trekking, enquire at *The Four Masters* bookshop or the tourist office in town about *Ordnance Survey* maps of the area.

The southern coastline

The most appealing route from Donegal town is the one which follows the north shore of the bay all the way out to Glencolumbcille, near the point. The first turning off this road will lead you down to **Holmes beach** and the *Ball Hill* hostel (see under Donegal town, p.425). At **MOUNTCHARLES**, the first place of any size on the main road, the cosy *Bosco House Hostel* (☎073/35382; ①) makes a quieter base from which to explore Donegal town, especially in mid-summer.

FROSSES, a mile or so inland off the road between Mountcharles and Inver, is a pleasant, tiny village that has traditional music every second Saturday of the month in *Frosses Hall* (open session begins 9pm). The cemetery here has the graves of two of Ireland's famous literary figures: the novelist Seamus MacManus and his wife, the very underrated poet Eithne Carberry.

The hamlet of **INVER** and its small strand, just a few hundred yards off the road, is worthwhile scenically and good for a drink (or hear traditional music on Wednesday, Fri & Sun) in the *Rising Sun* pub. Inside, this has a ceiling in the shape of the hull of a boat and stone shelves for the spirit bottles – it is also the birthplace of Thomas Nesbitt, inventor of the harpoon gun.

Dunkineely and Bruckless

At **DUNKINEELY** another deviation from the main road takes you down a long, narrow promontory to **St John's Point**, where a crumbling castle stands at the tip. As you head out, there are great views over Donegal Bay, especially back towards the narrow entry of Killybegs bay, with **Rotton Island** at its mouth. There's the *Seaview* B&B in the village, on the main road. A little further on, approaching **BRUCKLESS**, you'll spot a magical little lagoon staked out with poles for rearing mussels. Look out for a "hand-knit" sign at the top of a track that will lead you down to a dwelling where you can buy oysters (about £4 a dozen) and mussels (£1 for 2.2lbs or 1 kilo). On the other side of the lagoon you can see an eighteenth-century Georgian house, *Bruckless House* (☎073/37071; ⑤), which now offers stylish **B&B**. There's also an excellent **hostel** in Bruckless, *Gallagher's Farm Hostel*, Darney (*IHH*, open all year; ☎073/37057; ②), with camping.

Killybegs

Shortly beyond Bruckless, the road runs away from the bay, and there's a right turn which cuts off the peninsula, heading directly for Ardara. If you stick to the coast road, however, you'll round Killybegs Bay and arrive in the most successful fishing port in the country, **KILLYBEGS**, where tons of top-quality fish are hauled onto the quaysides daily. This marks the halfway point from Donegal town to Glencolumbcille and also the point where the scenery changes dramatically for the better. The mile-long approach road around the bay is idyllic, and Killybegs itself is perched on a slope, its gleaming whitewashed buildings huddled around narrow cramped streets.

In summer the place is abuzz with traffic, mostly heading down to the quay, where you can purchase fish after watching the fleet come in during the early evening. A huge **sea angling festival** takes place here in the second half of July; and you can go sea angling any time with one of six boats that go out daily. A small **town festival** takes place in early August. Picturesque though Killybegs is, it isn't exactly overflowing with interest, and most of the pubs are aimed squarely at working fishermen.

If you're staying, it's worth visiting the church at the top of the hill for a glimpse of the **McSweeney tombstone**, covered in Celtic carving. The cross standing on the hillock nearby is an ugly specimen that stands to remind one of ugly times, the penal days.

PRACTICALITIES
Accommodation in the form of B&Bs is plentiful, and you'll find rooms at the *Lone Star* pub (☎073/31518; ④) and the *Bayview Hotel* (☎073/31950; ⑥), or you could try the *Hollybush Hostel*, one mile before Killybegs on the main road (☎073/31118; ①), where you can also **camp**. The adjoining pub – favoured by local farmers and fishermen – has open sessions (Sun & sometimes Fri & Sat during summer). The hostel owner rents out fishing tackle and can arrange boats for **sea-fishing** (£80 per day, all tackle supplied; up to 10 people per boat). There's self-catering accommodation at *Glenlee Holiday Homes* (☎073/31183, from £200 a week in high season), opposite the *Spar* shop on the Kilcar Road, with bungalows overlooking the bay sleeping four to nine people.

Places to **eat** include *The Cope House Hotel*, which has a good restaurant, with daily specials for under £10 and an innovative wine list; *Melly's Café* by the harbour, with the usual cheap snack food; and the *Sail Inn* and *Lone Star*, both on the Kilcar Road, with seafood-based menus. The *Lone Star* also has ballad sessions on Friday and Saturday, as does the recently renovated *Hughies* (Thurs–Sun 10pm–1am), also on the Kilcar Road; for regular music sessions, try the *Harbour Bar* or *The Cope House Hotel*, again both on the Kilcar Road. *McGeehan's* **buses** (☎075/46150) leave from outside the *Pier Bar* for Ardara and Dublin: enquire at *Hegarty's* grocery shop by the bus stop.

Kilcar to Slieve League

The road to **KILCAR** divides just after the *Blue Haven Restaurant* (old-time Irish evening on Thurs), a few miles out of Killybegs, and once again it's best to follow the coast, with fine views all the way. In Kilcar itself, look out for *Piper's Rest Pub* which has a music session every Wednesday and occasional other entertainment. *McGeehan's* **buses** leave from outside *John Joe's* bar at 7.50am for Dublin via Killybegs and Ardara, and for Glencolumbcille at 10.50pm.

Between Kilcar and **CARRICK** there are three independent hostels: the three-storey, rather clinical *Dún Ulún House* (☎073/38137; ②), which also does B&B (③) and has en-suite facilities and TV; *Carra's Hostel*, 200 yards up the road (①) has camping; and one of the friendliest hostels in the country, the *Derrylahan Hostel*, is half a mile further on (☎073/38079; ①) – it also does camping and contains the *Glenn Liag Pony Trekking Centre*, offering rides from beginner to expert at very reasonable prices. This is an ideal base for exploring the beautiful countryside around Carrick, especially Teelin Bay and the awesome Slieve League cliffs to the west. In Carrick itself, the *Slieve League* pub is a must, and the **traditional music festival** that the pub organizes over the last weekend in October is one of the more popular and successful in the region.

CLIMBING THE SLIEVE LEAGUE

There are two routes up to the ridge of **Slieve League** (*sliabh leic*, grey mountain): a less-used back route following the homemade fingerpost pointing to Baile Mór just before Teelin, and the road route that follows the signs out of the village to Bunglass (*bunglas*, end of the cliff), which turns out to be exactly what it says, the end of the grass way above a sheer drop. These claim to be the highest marine cliffs in Europe, and standing here that seems all too likely. The sea moves so far below that the waves seem to make no noise, and the near 2000ft high face glows with mineral deposits in tones of amber, white and red. They say that on a clear day it is possible to see one-third of the whole of Ireland from the summit. A **sightseeing tour** of the cliffs from the waters below is organized from Teelin (weather permitting) by *Smith Campbell* (☎073/39079), costing £5 for two hours.

Both routes up are walkable and very enjoyable, though it's a great deal easier to drive: the less popular back route looks up continually to the ridge and is known as the *One Man's Path*; the frontal approach swings you up and round in a spectacular way to one of the most thrilling cliff scenes in the world, the **Amharc Mór**, from which the views are staggering.

If you want to make a full day of it, you can follow *One Man's Path*, which leads on to *Old Man's Path* (simply because it's a few inches wider), over the crest of the mountain and down the heather-tufted western slope. The paths are accurately named: in places they are only a few feet wide, and in wet or windy weather they can be *extremely hazardous*. On a fine day, though, it's a wonderful – if terrifying – traverse. Then make your way across towards the verdant headland village of **MALINBEG**, where there's a paradisiacal crescent-shaped golden strand enclosed by a tight rocky inlet. Malinbeg itself is a village of white bungalows, with the land around ordered into long narrow strips. Three miles offshore lies **Rathlin O'Birne Island**, a place with many folklore associations: there are occasional boats across, but nothing to see beyond some early Christian stone relics and a ruined coastguard station.

Beyond Malinbeg it's relatively easy to extend your walk through Malinmore – where the large *Glenbay* hotel serves teas – and on to Glencolumbcille. The whole distance from Teelin can be comfortably completed in six hours.

The road to **TEELIN** (*tigh linn*, house of the flowing tide) follows the west bank of the River Owenee, whose rapids and pools are good for fishing – licences are available from *Teelin Sea Angling Club* (☎073/39079). The village is Irish-speaking and rich in folklore, which has been recorded over the last half-century by Seán Ó' hEochaidh, Donegal's great folklorist. The best pub in town is the *Rusty Mackerel*, at the entrance to the trail of village buildings – it's easily noticed by its garish colour and mural painting of one of its old fisherman regulars.

Glencolumbcille and around

Approaching **GLENCOLUMBCILLE** (the Glen of St Columbcille) by road, you cross a landscape of desolate upland moor, its oily-black turf banks stitched into patches of heather and grass where not even sheep seem able to survive. After this, the rich beauty of the Glen (as it's invariably known) comes as a welcome shock. Less than forty years ago, this area was on its last legs, a typical example of rural depopulation: its new lease of life is owed to the former parish priest, Father James MacDyer, who introduced a series of collective enterprises – in knitting, agriculture and tourism – that are sending goods out of the valley and bringing visitors and new residents in.

Development has done nothing to diminish the appeal of the place, however. Its central buildings are painted in radiant colours – the village church is lavender, there's a whitewashed semi-detached estate for the newly married, one old pub is a submarine yellow and another a Mediterranean sky-blue.

Glencolumbcille village is widely known as a place of pilgrimage, a status it's held since the seventh century AD, when **Saint Columba** spent time in the valley (Columba and Columbcille/Colmcille are the same person – the latter is the name by which he was known after his conversion, and means "the dove of the church"). Every June 9 at midnight, the locals commence a barefoot circuit of the cross-inscribed slabs that stud the valley basin, finishing up with mass at 3am in the small church.

The **Folk Village**, next to the beach, usually has tourists tripping over one another on the strictly guided tours (Easter–Sept Mon–Sun hourly 10am–6pm, admission free). There's free access to the **National School** replica, which has a display of informative photographs and research projects, and a section on the American painter Rockwell Kent, who painted marvellous treatments of the area's landscapes. At **Sheebeen** house (free admission), you can try a taster of seaweed wine and other concoctions such as honey, fuchsia and elderberry (most much better than they sound) and then buy a bottle.

From behind the hostel (see below), **cliff walks** steer off around the south side of the bay above a series of jagged drops. Rising from the opposite side of the valley mouth, the promontory of **Glen Head** is surmounted by a Martello tower. On the way out you pass the ruins of **St Columbcille's Church**, with its "resting slab" where Saint Columba would have lain down exhausted from prayer. North across this headland you can climb and descend again to the forgotten little cove of Port a few miles away. Absolutely nothing happens here – although Dylan Thomas once stayed in the next valley at Glenlough, renting a cottage for several weeks and then disappearing early one morning without paying.

Practicalities

The **tourist office** (Easter–Oct daily 9am–6pm; July & Aug till 9pm; ☎073/30116) is on the main street. **B&B** accommodation is available throughout the year at Mrs Cunningham's *Brackendale*, Cashel (☎073/30038; ③), and the *Glencolumbcille Hotel*, Malinmore (☎073/30003; ⑥). The beautifully positioned *Dooey Hostel* sits above the fine shingle strand at the mouth of the valley (☎073/30130; ①); you can also **camp** here. If walking, keep on the village road as far as the Folk Village, and then take a path up to the left: in wet weather the longer route, by road, may be easier. The tea house at the Folk Village does cheapish **food** and sells watercolours as a side line. Another place to eat in the village is the *Lace House Restaurant* above the tourist office, with freshly baked bread and evening meals.

Courses in Irish, painting, archeology, hill-walking and set dancing are run from the *Oideas Gael School* (☎073/30051) in the village, which also has accommodation. Ring ahead for information and bookings.

Maghera to Crohy Head

Leaving Glencolumbcille you can either retrace your steps along the coast or take the road through the heart of the peninsula towards Ardara. This takes in the dramatic **Glengesh Pass** (*gleann géis*, glen of the swans), winding down through wild but fertile valley land. Just before reaching Ardara, a road to the left runs along the northern edge of the peninsula for five and a half miles to **MAGHERA**, with narrow **Loughross Beg Bay** on one side and steep mountains rising from the road on the other. A mile before Maghera you'll pass the transfixing **Essaranka Waterfall**, and Maghera itself (with its tea house in the village) is an entrancingly remote place, backed by an exceedingly beautiful glen and fronted by a strand that runs along to an intriguing series of caves.

One of the larger caves is said to have concealed a hundred people taking refuge from Cromwell's troops; their light was spotted from across the strand and all bar one – who hid on a high shelf – were massacred. Some of the caves are accessible only at low tide, and you'll need a torch; if you do visit, take great care to stay out of the water, as there are extremely strong currents, and tourists have drowned. Behind the village, a tiny road runs up into the glen, a former hideout of *poteen* smugglers.

Ardara

ARDARA is a pretty big town by Donegal standards, and also one of the best places to buy **Aran sweaters**, sometimes at half the price you'll find further south. *Molloy's Tweed Factory*, a mile or so out of the southern end of town, is the biggest outlet, but *Kennedy's*, at the top of the hill, is handier (its owner is also a mine of local tourist information), and all the stores are well stocked with hand-loomed knitwear and tweeds. Ardara has been declared a heritage town (one of thirty nominated by Bord Fáilte), which qualified it for a substantial EU grant; this has been used to fund the recently opened **interpretative centre** in the old Law Courts by the bridge.

For accommodation, central **B&B** is available at *Laburnum House* (☎075/41146; ③) and *Homeward Bound* (☎075/41246; ④), or for sea views a short way out of town on the Portnoo Road, try *Greenhaven House* (☎075/41129; ④) or *Bayview House* (☎075/41145; ④). Both *Woodhill House* (☎075/41112; ⑤) and the *Nesbitt Arms* (☎075/41130; ⑤) have rooms of considerably more style. There is a small **hostel**, the *Drumbarron Hostel* (☎075/41200; ②), in the middle of town on the bend. **Bike rental** is available from Don Bryne south of town (☎075/41658 or ☎41156) for £6 per day, and he also does **camping**.

The best place to **eat** is *Woodhill House*, a seventeenth-century building in a lovely setting half a mile from the centre (follow signposts off the Donegal Road); the restaurant offers an innovative menu, changed daily, well worth the £20 or so it costs. It's worth a visit even if you're not hungry as there's a bar, often with music. Less fancy meals are available at the *Nesbitt Arms*, with good bar lunches and huge platters of Irish cooking in the evening; and the *Lobster Pot*, a distinctly superior chip shop by the bridge, open till 2am or later at weekends.

Ardara is also a great place for **pubs**, dozens of which seem to be crammed into its L-shaped main street. For a quiet drink, try the ancient *Pádraig MacGiola Dé*, to the south (guaranteed to be an experience – avoid the loos), or the recently renovated *Corner House* bar at the corner of the L. For a livelier time, you shouldn't miss *Peter Oliver's*, with music (June–Sept nightly) and traditional dancing every Wednesday (£1); the publican himself is a musician, and there are fiddles, button accordion, banjo, mandolin and *bodhrán* on the wall ready to play. *Nancy's*, by the bridge, a cosy 200-year-old pub run by the same family for seven generations, is also excellent, with something happening most nights during the summer. A *McGeehan's* **bus** leaves for Dublin from outside the post office daily at 8.30am.

Dawros Head

The **Dawros Head Peninsula**, immediately north of Ardara, is much tamer than Glencolumbcille, with many tiny lakes, perfect for fishing (get a licence in Ardara), dotting a quilt of low hills. The terrain of purple heather, fields, streams and short glens makes a varied package for the enthusiastic walker. You don't get many outsiders here, but the caravan and camping sites of Portnoo and Narin are densely populated with Northern Irish tourists. As you approach Narin, just before the pastel-shaded Kilclooney church, look back to the right and you'll spot the **Kilclooney Dolmen**, probably the most elegant in the country, and just one of the many rich remains on the peninsula. The spearheaded two-and-a-half-mile-long **Narin Strand** is a wonderful beach, safe for bathing, and at low tide you can walk out to **Iniskeel Island** where there are the ruins of two twelfth-century churches with some cross-inscribed slabs.

The most worthwhile sight on the peninsula is **Doon Fort**, which occupies an entire oval-shaped islet in the middle of Lough Doon. To get there take a left out of Portnoo and then left again alongside a lake where you'll see a sign for boat rental: this leads to the farmhouse of Mr McHugh, who will row you out to the island for a small charge. The idyllic setting, rarely disturbed by visitors, makes the hassle worth it: although its walls are crumbling, the fort has been untouched for over two thousand years. The walls stand 15ft high and 12ft thick – their inner passages were used in the 1950s for storing *poteen*. Two other lakes nearby, **Lough Birrog** and **Lough Kiltoorish**, also have ruined castles, both built by later Irish chieftains, the O'Boyles. Their stones, however, have mostly been carted away for house building.

If you want to **stay** on the peninsula, *Carnaween House* in Narin offers good B&B (☎075/45122; ③); or you could rent a caravan at *Dunmore Caravan and Camping Park*, by the golf course in Narin (☎075/45121; £60–150 a week; also camping), but there's little chance of a vacancy in midsummer. *Dawros Bay Hotel*, north of Rossbeg, offers very basic accommodation at hostel rates (☎075/45252; ①) and breakfast for £3.50; it's well placed for headland walks, but the nearest grocery store is by the harbour in Portnoo. The *Lake House Hotel* in Portnoo (☎075/45123; ④) offers a great deal more comfort.

Glenties

Set at the foot of two glens, **GLENTIES** is a village of plantation grandeur, reflected in its elegant courthouse, old lodge and highland hotel. It also sports the largest **disco** in the northwest, the *Limelight*, at the north end of town (its clientele seems exclusively under sixteen), and no less than thirteen bars on its sole street. Another community attraction is a beautiful **church** at the Ardara end of town, designed by the modern Derry architect Liam McCormack; the vast sloping roof reaches down to six feet from the ground, and the rainwater drips off the thousand or so tiles into picturesque pools of water.

The **St Conall's Museum and Heritage Centre**, opposite the church in the Neoclassical courthouse (June–Sept Mon–Fri 11am–1pm & 2.30–5pm, Sat & Sun 2.30–6pm; £1), is well fitted out with items from all periods, including an interesting set of pleas submitted to the courts during the Famine and an Edison phonograph that plays *It's a Long Way to Tipperary*. The town's most famous son was **Patrick MacGill** (*Children of the Dead*, *The Rat Pit*), a navvy turned author and the inspiration for a huge **summer school** – which draws hundreds of people to exhibitions, workshops and debates – and literary festival held in his honour each year in the last week of August.

For **B&B**, try *Kelvon House* at the north end of town (☎075/51171; ③), the *Claradon*, less than a mile out on Glen Road (Easter–Oct; ☎075/51113; ③), or the family-run *Highlands Hotel* (☎075/51111; ⑤). A comfortable new **hostel**, *Campbell's Holiday Hostel* (*IHH*, March–Oct; ☎075/51491; ②), is located beside the museum. **Eating** out options are limited, but the excellent *Highlands Hotel*, very much the centre of town life, with weekend discos and a small art gallery, offers a wide range of food. There are a number of takeaways on the main street, including *Jim McGuiness's*; the *McGeehans* **buses** en route to Letterkenny and Ballybofey stop here.

Although there's little in the way of entertainment, there are plenty of places to **drink** – *Paddy's Bar*, *Wee Joe's Bar* and *McMonagle's Riverside Bar* are all good. If you want **traditional music** head for the *Glen Inn*, three miles out on the Ballybofey Road, beautifully situated by the river at the foot of the Blue Stacks; there are sessions on the last Saturday of the month at 9.30pm.

Fintown and Doochary

The inland trip north to Doochary via Fintown and then down the Gweebarra Valley to the coast at Lettermacaward is a fine scenic loop. **FINTOWN**, nine miles northeast of Glenties, is a humble roadside place set beside a lake at the foot of towering mountains. Once again, the setting has a mythical colouring – it was here that Fergoman was attacked by wild boars and cried out so piteously that his sister was driven to distraction and dived into the lake, where she drowned. There's a bar and B&B, whimsically called *Finian's Rainbow*.

DOOCHARY lies five miles northwest across a route that cuts against the grain of the hills. It's a desolate but delightful journey through moorland streaked by turf banks, where bulbous knuckles of rock force the road to duck and lunge from side to side. The village itself has a few pubs and a grocery shop. Glenveagh National Park (see p.436), is nine miles northeast, up the River Gweebarra, while five miles downstream are the headlands at Lettermacaward.

The **Dooey Point headland** makes a scenically interesting little detour if you have time at hand. The northern shore, on Traweenagh Bay, is the more gratifying, with a fine stretch of beach backed by sand dunes. Classic thatched cottages are the main characteristics. On the southern side is **Corr Strand**, fertile ground for mussels and clams, with a handy bar nearby.

The Crohy Head Peninsula

The southern approach to **Crohy Head** curls round the headland's central mountains, looking down to a rocky shelf of coastline from which plumes of spray rise like geysers. As you come round the headland to the final leg, you'll come across the three-storey *An Óige* **hostel** (Easter–Sept; ☎075/21950; ①), then the globular outline of **Aranmore Island** comes into view, lying close to the Rosses coast. The hillside below the road can be dangerous at points because of a remarkable landslip known as the *tholla brista* (broken earth), but this, and the great sea stack known as *an bríste* (the breeches), make the headland an even more dramatic experience for the walker.

The one-pub fishing village of **MAGHERY** lies at the foot of the north side of the headland. Its most unusual feature is the tall wall that runs by the abandoned mansion house at the far side of the short strand: called the Famine Wall, this windbreak was built by the villagers for the landlord, who devised the task so that he could pay them a wage as famine relief. Mrs Wallace's *Bay View House* (☎075/21672; ③) offers a couple of **B&B** rooms and meals. **Minibuses** run daily from Maghery to Dungloe and back.

The Rosses

The **Rosses**, a vast expanse of rock-strewn land and stony soil, is one of the last strong *Gaeltacht* areas. Dotted with over 120 tiny lakes, the crumply terrain stretches from Dungloe in the south to Crolly in the north. The coastal route between these two boundaries is infinitely more rewarding than the more direct inland route.

Dungloe

With its bustle of shoppers and its multitude of pubs, **DUNGLOE** is an easy place to settle into, but there's little other than impromptu entertainment to make lingering worthwhile. It's at its liveliest for the midsummer Mary From Dungloe festival, a local, more wholesome variation of the Miss World idea that provides a good pretext for general festivities and late-night drinking. Dungloe is also synonymous with the rejuvenating work of **Paddy the Cope** (1871–1966), who envisaged the salvation of these poor communities through co-operative ventures. He founded the *Templecrone Co-operative Agricultural Society* (the "Cope") in 1906, and today *Co-op* supermarkets throughout the Rosses – megastores in West Donegal terms – stand as a testament to him. Copies of his entertaining autobiography, *My Story*, are available in a local edition from the supermarket.

There are numerous **B&Bs** here – try *Mrs McCole* on Mill Road (☎075/21094; ③) or the smaller *Midway Hotel* on Main Street (☎075/21251; ③), also providing meals and a bar. *Green's Independent Holiday Hostel* (*IHH*, open all year; ☎075/21021; ②) on Carnmore Road is a newly built **hostel** and is a little sterile in appearance, but the staff are extremely helpful. For **eating**, *Doherty's Restaurant* is a good low-priced grill, and the *Riverside Bistro* offers more upmarket and reasonably priced fare. The *Tír Chonnaill* **bar** at the top end of the street is a genuine old-timers' bar with not a note of music interfering; the *Atlantic Bar* has rock music (every Sat) and traditional sounds (Fri & Sun). The *Central Bar*, in the middle of Main Street, is open during summer only, after more than twenty years in which nothing seems to have been touched – a fascinating old place. *Doherty's* **private buses** run through Fintown and Letterkenny to Derry daily in July and August.

Burtonport

Passing the smoking funnels of a kelp factory, the coastal route heads off in the direction of **BURTONPORT**, half a mile off the main road. A settlement of a handful of houses and pubs, it's the embarkation point for Aranmore Island or, if you can find someone to take you out, for the smaller islands hereabouts. With the establishment of government buildings on **Rutland Island** in the eighteenth century, this area became the first English-speaking district in the whole of Donegal. The English connection endures: until a few years ago a colony of post-hippies known as the *Screamers* ran an organic commune on another island, and their departure coincided with the arrival of three eccentric ladies from England, who live in immaculate, formal Victorian style in the white mansion at the entrance to Burtonport. Known as the "Silver Sisters", Miss Tyrrell, Miss Lucinda and their young maid are an engaging sight, doing their shopping in the village dressed in bonnets and sober black garments edged with white lace. They welcome only visitors with a serious interest in their anachronistic way of life, and not the merely curious.

The village has little to say for itself, but if you want to stay, *Mrs McGinley*, down by the pier, does year-round **B&B** (☎075/42047; ②). For **eating**, *The Lobster Pot* specializes in seafood, but is pricy – expect to pay up to £25 or more for dinner. Otherwise you'll have to make do with pies and fish and chips. Its **pubs** now look somewhat lifeless; the *Skipper Tavern* offers occasional traditional music.

Aranmore Island

It's a 25-minute journey out to **Aranmore Island**, through the straits between the nearest cluster of islands (Rutland, Inishfree, Inishcoo and Eighter), and then across a free expanse of water to the island's main village, **LEABGARROW**. *Aranmore Island Ferry Service* (8 sailings in summer, £6 return, car plus driver £18; ☎075/20532) operates a **car ferry**. At Leabgarrow, there's *An Óige* **hostel** (June–Sept; ☎075/20574; ①). The high centre ground of bogland and lakes reaches a greater altitude than anywhere else in the Rosses and has great views back to Burtonport. A few roads crisscross the island, the villages being ranged in true Rosses style round the rim of the eastern and southern sides – the western and northern shores are uninhabited and perfect for walking. Intriguingly, there are no Garda (police) on Aranmore, so you see very few cars with tax discs, and might catch sight of a ten-year-old jumping into the driving seat and setting off. The **pubs** (of which there are only six or seven) also tend to keep open into the early hours – which is helpful, as there is no other form of nightlife. The most dramatic of the several **beaches** is at the lighthouse end of the island, approached by a set of steps down the side of a perpetually crumbling cliff.

Lower Rosses and Crolly

The road up through the Lower Rosses to Gweedore passes through a wild and crazed terrain of granite boulders and stunted vegetation. **Cruit Island**, a couple of miles north of Burtonport and accessible by bridge, has beautiful beaches. A little further along the coast at **KINCASLOUGH** is the *Viking Hotel* (☎075/43295; ⑤), owned by Irish singing star and Donegal hero **Daniel O'Donnell**. Not far away is **CARRICKFINN**, which boasts a fine strand and **Donegal Airport** (direct flights from Glasgow, Birmingham and Edinburgh; ☎075/48284). Further on, in **ANNAGARY**, *Jack's* pub serves fair food, and, if you wish to spend a little more, *O'Donnell's* very pleasing restaurant in the centre of the village offers superb cuisine.

As you come down the hill into **CROLLY** (signposted "Croichsli", as this is an Irish-speaking area), look out for a sign pointing to **Leo's Tavern** – on most nights it has traditional music, and, as Leo is the father of the group Clannad and the singer/musician Enya, you might just catch them on a home visit. The large *Teach Phaidi Oig* pub has bar food, caravan, camping and laundry facilities and traditional music (Tues & Thurs in summer). For **B&B**, try *Leachrann House* (☎075/32194; ③); failing that, the postmistress in Crolly is a mine of information on accommodation in the area.

The Derryveagh Mountains and Letterkenny

The central area of north Donegal rivals any of the best bits of the Donegal coastline and, if you're travelling northwards from the south of the county, makes a good alternative to Bloody Foreland in northwest Donegal. There are a couple of routes into the mountains; at Crolly, a narrow road leads from the N56 to lovely **Lough Keel**, with its deserted village. Just as this road reaches its highest point and swings sharply right and down again to Dungloe, a little road runs straight ahead to a wonderfully situated hostel, *Screag an Iolair Mountain Centre* (☎075/48593; ②), with cosy rooms, open fires, beautiful gardens and lots of advice on walking. Nestling on the side of **Cnoc na Farragh** mountain, *Screag an Iolair* (which means "eagle's nest") provides magnificent views of mountains, lakes and, to the west, Aranmore Island. Spectacular sunsets are almost a speciality of the place, with hostellers silhouetted on the surrounding peaks as they await the magic moment.

Alternatively, you can carry on along the N56 then onto the R25 to the northern shore of Lake Nacung and into **DUNLEWY**, where an *An Óige* hostel (☎075/31180; ②) sits by Lough Dunlewy (aka Lake Nacung) at the foot of **Errigal Mountain**. Quite often the area is shrouded in mist, but on a clear day the beauty of Errigal is insurpassable, its silvery slopes resembling Hokusai's images of Mount Fuji. In the village, there's a post office, shop and *McGeady's* bar. A new tourist centre, *Ionad Cois Locha*, offers a craft shop and reasonably priced home-made food.

Glenveagh National Park

For the **Poisoned Glen** (where Lugh slew Balor of the Evil Eye – also see p.440 – thus in mythology poisoning the ground on which the Cyclopean single eye fell), turn off just below the church at the eastern end of the lough – the route continues over the bridge, and then you should follow the bank of the river deep into the gorge, always heading for the col up at the shoulder of the Derryveagh Mountains. It's not an easy tramp, for a lot of the ground is marshy, but it's the beginning of one of the finest wild walks imaginable. From the col, the views are fantastic, with the River Glenveagh flowing into Lough Beagh down below. You're now in the **Glenveagh National Park** and may well see deer hereabouts. Going straight down the hill, head for the road, which you should then follow for a short distance, before bearing down the old disused vehicle track that will take you down the barrel of the glen. The River Glenveagh writhes its way to a tiny sandy shore at the head of the lake, where rhododendrons and tall spruces grow. Waterfalls plummet down the sheer cliff sides on the other side of the lake, and **Glenveagh Castle** (May–Oct Tues–Sun 10am–6.30pm; June–Sept also Sun 10am–7.30pm; £2) now appears above the tree tops on a small rocky knoll. The grandeur of this walk into the heart of the estate is far greater than that of the routine approach via the official entrance on the north side of the lake, beautiful as that is. The castle itself, a battlemented nineteenth-century creation swathed in flower gardens, looks best from below.

The most interesting way to get from Glenveagh Park to Lough Gartan, in the next valley east, is to follow the three-mile track across the mountain bog tops (it's possible to drive), which is the only track leading off the Glenveagh Estate road. On weekdays between the beginning of September and the end of February you're forbidden to leave this road or any other recognized footpath – it's the deer-hunting season, and you may get shot.

Lough Gartan

The environs of **Lough Gartan** are one of the supreme beauties of Ireland. **Saint Columba** was born into a royal family here in 521 AD; his father was from the house of Niall of the Nine Hostages and his mother belonged to the House of Leinster. If you walk over from Glenveagh you'll pass his birthplace – take the first road right at the first house you see at the end of the mountain track, and you'll come to a colossal cross marking the spot. Close by is a slab locally known as the **Flagstone of Loneliness**, because the saint used to sleep on it, thereby giving the flagstone the miraculous power to cure the sorrows of those who lie upon it. During times of mass emigration, people used to come here the night before departure in the hope of ridding themselves of homesickness. Archeologically it's actually part of a Bronze Age gallery tomb and has over fifty cup marks cut into its surface.

Going back to the track leading downhill will bring you to a main country road, where a left turn will take you towards the remains of a church known as the **Little Oratory of St Colmcille**. It's an enchanting ruin, no larger than a modern living room, with a floor of old stone slabs with grass growing up through the cracks. To one side is the Natal Stone, where the baby Columba first opened his eyes; to this day pregnant women visit the slab praying for a safe delivery.

GLEBE HOUSE

Glebe House (Easter week & late May to early Oct daily except Fri 11am–6.30pm; £2, Heritage Card) is set in beautiful gardens on the northwest shore of the lake and is a gorgeous Regency building richly decorated inside and out. The kitchen has various **paintings** by the Tory Island group of painters (see p.439), most remarkably James Dixon's impression of Tory from the sea. A rich collection of paintings and sketches adorns other parts of the house, including international names like Kokoschka, Renoir, Braque, Picasso and Dégas. The study is decked out in original William Morris wallpaper, and there are Chinese tapestries in the morning room. It's well worth buying the guidebook and taking the tour.

HERITAGE AND OUTDOOR PURSUITS

Moving on round the northeast of the lake, in the direction of Church Hill, a right turn immediately after crossing the bridge will take you down to the modern **St Colmcille Heritage Centre** (Mon–Sat 10.30am–6.30pm, Sun 1–6.30pm), on the opposite shore from Glebe. The exhibition space is largely devoted to tracing Columba's life and the spread of the Celtic Church throughout Europe. It's not as boring as it sounds, for there are a few intriguing items – very beautiful stained glass windows of biblical scenes by Ciaran O'Conner and Ditty Kummer, and a step-by-step illustration of vellum illumination and calligraphy. The road to the heritage centre continues a little further on to the **Gartan Outdoor Pursuit Centre** (☎074/37032), where you can get involved in a range of outdoor activities; for a day it costs £18, for a weekend £60 (includes hostel-style accommodation). Continuing east from here towards Letterkenny, you ascend from the northern shore to Church Hill, with superb cross-country views as far north as the peninsulas.

The Rock of Doon and Kilmacrennan

Lying a few miles northeast of Gartan, **The Rock of Doon** and **Doon Well** are reached by taking the last right turn off the R255 just before it reaches the N56, running into Kilmacrennan; this will bring you into a rural cul de sac right next to the well. Just as you come into the area of the well, the road runs along the bottom of the large bushy outcrop that is the Rock of Doon. For centuries this was the spot where the O'Donnell kings were crowned before a great gathering of their followers. The inauguration stone on the summit is said to bear the imprint of the first Tír Chonaill king, a mark into which every successor had to place his foot as his final confirmation.

Doon, an ancient pagan healing **well**, is still a place of pilgrimage, marked out by a bush weighed down with personal effects left behind by the sick, hoping for a cure. You're meant to take off your shoes as you approach and be well intentioned before taking the water. You'll probably pick up a story or two of dramatic conversion and miracles effected by the water, which is sent to Irish emigrés all over the world.

KILMACRENNAN is a sweet-looking inland village on the road southeast to Letterkenny. The *Village Tavern* has reasonably priced pub grub.

Letterkenny

Ever since Derry was partitioned into the North, **LETTERKENNY** has been Donegal's major commercial hub – its newly refurbished centre boasts many shops, including some excellent craft outlets and three new shopping malls. Letterkenny's boast is that it is the main place for entertainment in the northwest. It has an ebullient bustle about it which, in the context of its surrounding blanket of green fields, reminds one of a typical Cork town. Although it's just at the edge of Lough Swilly, there's no water in sight, and the main visual element is the file of advertising down the main street. The only notable sight is the huge nineteenth-century **cathedral**, with its intricate stone-roped ceiling and gaelicized Stations of the Cross. Frankly, the only real reason you're likely to be here is that so much transport passes through, and it's a handy place to catch up on shopping or the business of changing money and sending mail.

The **tourist office** (July & Aug Mon–Fri 9am–1pm & 2–8pm, Sat 10am–2pm, Sun 9am–1pm & 2–5pm; Sept–June Mon–Fri 9am–1pm & 2–5pm; ☎074/21160) is on Derry Road. *Gallagher's Hotel*, very central on Upper Main Street (☎074/22066; ⑤), is the pick of the more expensive places to **stay**. B&Bs, of which there are plenty, include *Belvedere House*, Ballaghderg (☎074/23031; ③); *Covehill House*, Port Road (☎074/ 21038; ③); and *Ard na Greine*, Sentry Hill (☎074/22490; ③). There are three **hostels**: the *Rosemount Hostel*, 3 Rosemount Terrace, in a terraced house at the back of Upper Main Street (June–Nov; ☎074/21181; ①); *The Manse Hotel*, High Road (*IHH*, open all year; ☎074/25238; ①); and the newly opened *Port Hostel* (☎074/26288; ①).

Meals can be had at *Pat's On The Square*, 9 Market Square (daily 5pm–midnight; ☎074/21761), an excellent family-run **restaurant** specializing in appetizing home-made pasta and ice cream, freshly ground coffee and desserts to die for; or if you want to go more upmarket, try *The Box Tree*, Pearse Road, or *Nero's* on Port Road. Close to the heart of town, you'll find good **pub lunches** at *McGinley's* on Lower Main Street. *Bakersville*, on Church Street on the way up to the cathedral, is a good coffee shop, using all wholefood ingredients. Good-value and tasty food is available at the newly opened *Pat's Pizza*, Upper Main Street. The *O'Boyce Snack Bar* offers the cheapest, fastest and most basic food; it's handy to the bus station, down by the roundabout at the Derry side of town.

As ever there are plenty of **bars**, a few of which offer Irish music. *McGinley's* has music most nights and vegetarian food; *Downtown* also has music many nights and a disco on Wednesday; the *Cottage Bar* may also have music: all are close together on Lower Main Street. *Clanree*, about a mile out the main Derry Road, boasts a night-club and holds occasional *comhaltas* evenings. *The Brewery* on Market Square, which has a striking new brass interior, is very popular and has traditional music nights. Letterkenny also has five **nightclubs**, of which *The Golden Grill* is currently the most favoured, and is one of the largest in Ireland; there's a three-screen **cinema** nearby. Letterkenny also has two festivals: one in early July and the other in August. Finally, there's a **bureau de change** (daily 11am–6pm) and a **post office** on the main street.

The Gweedore to the Fanad Peninsula

The southwest edge of **Gweedore** district, on the coast immediately north of the Rosses, is marked by the villages of Bunbeg, Middletown and Derrybeg, their cottages sprinkled across a blanket of gorse and mountain grasses. Some buildings are grey and decaying, some are roofless or grass-covered, others are at various stages of completion. It's a dispiriting kind of landscape, and it continues like this right up the coast and round the **Bloody Foreland** to Gortahork and Falcarragh in the Cloghaneely district. It's also said to be the most densely populated rural area in Europe.

BUNBEG has a gorgeous little harbour packed with smallish trawlers – it's half a mile from the village along an enchanting rollicky road. In summer there's a regular **ferry** service to Tory Island (☎075/31991), and it's possible to negotiate a boat trip from the pier to other offshore islands such as Inishinny, Inishmaine, Inishirrer, Umfin, Inishfree, Owey and Gola. The **beach** further up the coast is approached from the road running north out of the village, by taking any track off to the left. For accommodation, there's the luxurious *Ostan Gweedore* (☎075/31177; ⑤), or *Brookvale House* (☎075/ 31149; ⑤), also pretty comfortable. *Tir na nOg* self-catering apartments at Bunbeg harbour (☎075/31232; ②) are a less expensive accommodation option. You can **eat** extremely well at *Mooney's Restaurant* (five-course dinner £12); while *Sergeant Pepper's* is a good place for kebabs and pizzas. The most popular bar in Bunbeg is *Teach Hiúdaí Beag*, which hosts a famous Monday night traditional session. The *Ostan Gweedore* holds **discos** (Wed, Fri & Sun; £2.50) and has country and western music on Wednesdays.

At Glassach, a few miles after Derrybeg, the road climbs abruptly to the **Bloody Foreland**, a grim, stony, almost barren zone, crisscrossed by stone walls. The road turns eastwards at Knockfola, hugging the side of the mountain, with the bogland and its hard-worked turfbanks stretching below towards the Atlantic. At **MEENLARAGH**, you should be able to spot the distinctive shape of Tory Island far out to sea. A road runs down to the pier, from where you can pick up the ferry to the island. In winter or stormy conditions, the ferry may be cancelled or run out of schedule. Meenlaragh has a few pubs and a grocery store, handy if you're waiting for a boat.

Tory Island

With its ruggedly indented shores pounded day and night by the ocean, **Tory Island**, though only eight miles from the mainland, is notorious for its inaccessibility. The island is completely treeless and, it's claimed, ratless, too – thanks to the intervention of Saint Columba, who arrived here in 500 AD. There's a hotel and a hostel on Tory. It has two villages – West Town and East Town; the former possesses the church, school and post office, and two of the island's three shops. The community hall is pressed into service for drinking and music.

In winter, nothing could equal the austerity and harshness of this place, and most of the island's hundred or so inhabitants decamp to the mainland for the worst months. An idiosyncratic brand of Irish is their native tongue, and it's indicative of their independence that they refer to the winter migration as "taking a visit over to Ireland". Fishing is still the staple trade, but some of the men supplement this a little through **painting**, a development which originated in a chance encounter between the English painter Derek Hill and one of the fishermen, **James Dixon**, in 1968. Dixon (now dead) had never lifted a brush before the day he told Hill that he could do a better job of painting the Tory scenery, but he went on to become the most famous of the island's school of primitive painters – Glebe House has a remarkable painting by him; see "Lough Gartan", see p.437.

It's no surprise to learn that potent legends are attached to the island. **Balor of the Evil Eye** (the Celtic god of darkness) supposedly had his residence on Tory, the remains of his castle standing on the eastern cliffs. There's also said to be a crater in the very heart of the island that none of the locals will approach after dark, for fear of incurring the god's wrath. Another superstition focuses on the **wishing stone** in the centre of the island, three circuits of which will lead to your wish being granted. It was utilized to defeat invaders by wrecking their ships – the British gunboat *Wasp*, sent to collect taxes, was caught in a sudden storm that killed all but six of its crew. The islanders have never paid tax since.

Some monastic relics from Saint Columba's time remain on Tory, the most unusual of which – now the island's emblem – is the **Tau Cross**. Its T-cross shape is of Egyptian origin, and is one of only two such monuments in the whole of Ireland. It is now relocated and set in concrete on Camusmore Pier in West Town. There are other mutilated stone crosses and some carved stones lying around, several by the remains of the round tower.

Gortahork and Falcarragh

The first town you'll come across to the east of the Bloody Foreland is nondescript **GORTAHORK**. The *Teach Bhillie* is an old men's drinking place, while the *Irish College* – up to the right after you pass *Whorskey's* on the left – has *ceilis* every night throughout July and August. The bar in *MacFadden's* hotel (☎074/35267; ③) has snack lunches and a reasonably priced Sunday carvery lunch.

FALCARRAGH is more interesting, and has more to offer by way of pubs, shops and other amenities. **Hostel** rooms are available at the large but run-down **Ballyconnel House** (☎074/35363; ②) – take the coast road at the village crossroads, and the gateposts of the estate are beside the main road where it bears left. Set in 500 acres of woodland, the house was built in the mid-seventeenth century, once belonged to one of the great landlords of the area, Sir John Olphert, and was taken over by the state in 1923. There's more regular tourist **accommodation** at the *Shamrock Lodge* independent hostel (*IHH*, open all year; ☎074/35859; ②), over the *Shamrock Pub*, and at a few B&Bs in the countryside nearby. For **eating**, *John's Café*, at the Gortahork end of town, is the best place. The *Gweedore* has **music** of varying kinds most nights in July and August and does lunches and evening meals. Also good is the *Shamrock Pub*, which serves bar meals and has traditional music and the blues on Wednesdays. *The Loft* also has live music.

Falcarragh **beach** is reached by following the coast road for a few miles – eventually the dunes will appear behind a car park. This is one of the more beautiful strands on this northwest coast, but a strong undercurrent makes it unsafe for bathing.

Leaving Falcarragh, the road to Dunfanaghy opens up a significantly milder landscape, with the green grass now beginning to outstrip the ruggedness, and the odd reed-fringed lake with swans by the roadway.

Horn Head and around

DUNFANAGHY, a resort town seven miles from Falcarragh, is the gateway to the Horn Head Peninsula. It's an aristocratically self-conscious plantation town, whose strongly Presbyterian atmosphere makes quite a contrast to anything west or south of it. The measure of the place is given by the fact that its one and only memorial was raised in honour of an agent for the estates of a nineteenth-century landlord. On the outskirts of town is the impressive **Workhouse** (Mon–Sun 9am–6pm), originally built in 1845 on the eve of the Great Famine, now restored as a local history exhibition area. There are several hotels and an art gallery (mostly soft Irish landscape impressions, supplemented by an assembly of heavily polished antique knick-knacks) just on the fringe of the west end of town. For accommodation, there are two **hotels**, *Arnold's* (☎074/36208; ⑥) and *Carrig Rua* (☎074/36133; ⑥); both also offer food. For a cheaper place to stay, try the excellent *Corcreggan Mill Cottage Hostel* (*IHH*, open all year; ☎074/36409; ②), a mile or so out on the Falcarragh Road, which also has camping and bike rental. For **eating**, *Danny Collin's* pub offers soups and pricy but delicious seafood; *Josie's* is the only fast-food outlet. *Dan Devine's* is the liveliest and cosiest **bar**, with friendly bar staff and *Roonies Nightclub*.

Horn Head is magnificent, a 600ft rock face scored by ledges on which perch countless guillemots, puffins and gulls. The best view of the cliffs, sea-stacks and caves is from the water, but the cliff road is vertiginous enough in places to give you a good look down the sheer sides. To get there take the slip road at the Falcarragh end of Dunfanaghy village; it descends to skirt the side of a beautiful inlet before rising steeply to go round the east side of the head. A spectacular vista of headlands opens up to the east – Rossguill, Fanad and Inishowen – but none can match the drama of Horn Head's cliffs, their tops clad in a thin cover of purplish heather.

Moving east again, the road follows the side of **Sheephaven Bay**; signposted turn-offs run to the popular holiday spots Portnablagh and Marble Hill Strand, the latter possessing a vast sweep of silver sand.

The Creaslough area

The sleepy village of **CREASLOUGH** stands on a slope commanding gorgeous views across the head of Sheephaven Bay. Partway down its main street is one of Liam McCormack's churches, its whitewashed whorl and backsloping table roof reflecting the thickly set **Muckish Mountain** nearby. You can see the mountain from within the church – it's usually enswirled in mist, or what's known locally as the Donegal *smir*. Creaslough (along with Falcarragh) makes the best launching pad for a climb up the mountain; from Creaslough follow the road out to Muckish Gap, down at the southern face, and from there the route ascends the grassy slopes to the flattened summit. There are pubs and grocery stores in the village, but it's otherwise fairly uninteresting and not a place you would choose for an overnight stay.

The coastal road northwards onto the Rossguill Peninsula offers a couple of worthwhile diversions. **Doe Castle**, to the left just before Lackagh Bridge, has been superbly reconstructed. The tall central keep, standing within a *bawn* and rock-cut fosse, was the original fortress of **McSwyney Doe**, whose grave slab is now fixed to its wall. The carving on the stone is faint, but its intricacy makes it historically important; the seven-speared fleur-de-lis at the top represents the close family connections with Scotland, while other carvings show a fox, cow, dolphin and eagle, as well as Celtic tracery. A walk around the battlements affords a view of the southernmost corner of Sheephaven Bay; when the tide is out the whole peaceful expanse looks like a desert, with only a slim channel of water gliding through the sandbanks. If the castle gate is padlocked, a key is kept in the cottage fifty yards back down the approach road.

Lackagh Bridge is an even better viewpoint, the curving silty shoreline lying downstream and a ginger-brown picture of rushes and heather reaching deep into the hills. Immediately after the bridge there's a turn-off to **GLEN** (two miles), a roundabout way to Carrigart that's worth taking for the scenery and the opportunity to drop in at the *Old Glen Bar*. This is a low-ceilinged place, smoky and atmospheric, with music at weekends and most other nights, too. If solitude is what you want, this is a good area to explore: apart from Lough Glen, there are several other lakelets in the district, all enclosed in a silent, rocky landscape.

The Rosguill Peninsula

CARRIGART is the back-door entrance to the extremely beautiful and very manageable **Rosguill Peninsula**. It's a beguiling village, whose **bars** define the essence of the place: *P. Logue's,* at the west end of town, is a welcoming sort of hideaway. Also note *MacGettigan's* grocers, at the eastern end of the main street, with its old-style wooden counter and shelving and a tempting array of bottles in the window. For **B&B**, try Mrs Gallagher's *Sonas* (☎074/55401; ④) or Mrs Doherty's *Hill House* (☎074/55221; ④). You can rent a **cycle** at *Charlie Coyle Cycles* (☎074/55427), based on the Creeslough Road just outside the village, in a bungalow next to the clump of fir trees. The only **bank** on the peninsula is in Carrigart (Mon–Wed & Fri 11am–2pm, Thurs 11am–1pm).

The route onto the peninsula starts by the side of the church; follow this road for a little, then fork left, and you'll be going past the rabbit-infested dunes at the back of a fantastic and usually deserted beach. The three-mile strand runs in a scimitar's curve all the way back round to the bottom of Sheephaven Bay – it's a marvellous four-hour walk to Doe Castle, though when the tide comes in, you could have to do a mile or so of the journey on the lanes.

Downings and Trá Na Rosann

At the top of the strand is **DOWNINGS**, a small and sprightly holiday centre, patronized mainly by Northern Irish tourists (especially from Belfast), with caravan sites hogging the rear end of the beach and holiday chalets creeping up the hillside behind the village. The one **pub** you should be sure to head for is the *Harbour Bar*, at the far end of the village (traditional music Tues, Thurs & Sat), which usually attracts the *Gaeltacht* crowd during the summer months. The *Fleet's Inn*, at the centre of the village, runs discos during the summer, when there are also nightly folk sessions, often lasting until 3am, at the *Beach Hotel* opposite. If you want to **stay**, the *Beach Hotel* is one possibility (☎074/55303; ④), or there are many B&Bs like Mrs McBride's *Bay Mount* (☎074/55395; ④) and Mrs Herraghty's *An Crossóg* (☎074/55498; ④).

The main street runs on round the west side of the headland to become the panoramic **Atlantic Drive**, first passing by a slip-road that runs down to the pier. Just before the pier is the only nourishing eating place on the whole peninsula – the *Coffee Shop*, great for home-made everything (10am–6pm).

If, instead of taking the left fork to Downings, you go right, you'll reach the *An Óige* **hostel** at Trá Na Rosann beach (☎074/55374; ①), perfectly placed at the northeastern corner of the headland. The management are friendly, there's virtually no curfew, and the views from the dorms are great. Fish can be bought from the fisherman who lives in the bungalow behind the hostel, and a grocery van stops by every Monday around midday. It's quite easy to **hitch** to the hostel, as everyone knows where you're heading.

At first sight, the hostel looks like an Alpine refuge out of *The Sound of Music*. One of the first things you should do on arrival is belt up the hillside immediately behind – at the summit the view is stupendous. You'll see long, narrow **Mulroy Bay** and a seemingly endless length of mountain ridges behind it. Further round there's the bombastic height of Horn Head, while closer in rises the central hump of the Rosguill Peninsula, and the **Trá Na Rosann** strand lies serene and untouched below. The remainder of the headland back towards **Mulroy Bay** stretches only as far as a caravan site and another beach at Melmore (not safe for bathing); the coastal rocks on the way harbour the odd cove and cave.

On from Trá Na Rosann beach, the route goes by the *Singing Pub* (traditional music Sat), sited on a turning up to the left. Opposite this turning and down to the right is **Mevagh Church** graveyard. It has an early Christian cross and an intriguing slab into which some cup-like cavities have been carved. And there's one gravestone that cannot but bring an appreciative smile: *Pat MacBride 1910–86, Shoemaker and Philosopher.*

The Fanad Peninsula

The **western** route onto the **Fanad Peninsula** has marvellous patches of idyllic scenery close to the Mulroy Lough and near the northwest corner, where the low-lying headland resembles the Rosses. But on the whole it's not the most inspiring of routes.

MILFORD makes for a fairly drab beginning to the western route, but an upbeat addition to the town is the very popular *Millford Inn*. **CARROWKEEL** (Kerrykeel also on maps), a little further on, offers a bit more excitement, being a popular holiday place. The *Mulroy Ballroom*, one of the few remaining 1960s' showband ballrooms (June–Aug Wed night), is on the Milford Road out of town. For **B&B**, try Mrs McGettigan's *Sea Breeze* (☎074/50110; ④). The *Rockhill Campsite Park* (☎074/50012), opposite the ballroom, provides the only basic **accommodation** in the place. The *Village Restaurant* (☎074/50062) at the northern end of the village has an expensive but wide-ranging menu.

The road north from Carrowkeel runs along the water's edge up to Ballywhoriskey, at the top of the peninsula, where the landscape becomes flatter, with dwellings spread out in the *Gaeltacht* manner. A left turn at the Fanad Drive signpost, just outside an old grey school building, will take you through hillocky and boulder-strewn terrain to a few small beaches and a pier; from here you can return to the main road to Fanad Head (see overleaf). The large **Ballyhiernan Strand**, further along towards the head, has a few caravan sites behind its grassy dunes if you're seeking a place to kip down for the night.

Rathmelton

The road crawling up the **east** side of Fanad is a much more interesting route. It starts at **RATHMELTON**, a sedate and neat little village that attracts Dublin yuppies and has been granted heritage status because of its many Georgian houses. The main part of town sits attractively on the eastern bank of the broad black flow of the River Leannan, famous for its salmon. There are some fine stone warehouses on the banks, parts of which have been converted into bars and bistros. The *House on the Brae* coffee shop sells home-baked **food** (entrance facing the river). For entertainment, try the *Bridge Bar* (Wed & Fri–Sun), when you can hear rhythm and blues, jazz or rock. If you're only passing through, *Sweeney's Tavern* is the nicest refuge for a stopover drink.

Rathmullan

Next stop north, **RATHMULLAN** looks pretty with its long row of seafront houses following the curve of the bay, but the beach itself is to be avoided, having two sewer pipes running down to the water's edge. In 1587 **Red Hugh O'Donnell** was lured onto a British merchant ship here, on the pretext of a merry drink, and ended up in Dublin jail for six years; and in 1609 it was a departure point for the **Flight of the Earls**, the event that marked the end of the Gaelic nation. It's also home to the **Rathmullen Heritage Centre** (March to mid-Sept; ☎074/58229), which provides a host of information on local accommodation and leisure activities.

The view across to Fahan on the Inishowen Peninsula is enticing (a small ferryboat operates in summer), but otherwise the only thing to delay your passing through is **Rathmullan Friary**, one of the better-preserved historical ruins in Donegal. The original part of it was built by Rory MacSweeney in 1508 and then presented to the Carmelites. George Bingham plundered it in 1595 and used it as a barracks, and in 1618 it was further adapted as a castle residence by Bishop Knox. Only the chancel area continued to serve as a church until its eventual abandonment in 1814. Today you can see traces of Gothic doorways and narrow window apertures.

On the way into Rathmullan, there's very good **eating** to be had at the *Water's Edge Restaurant*, and the comfortably old-fashioned *Pier Hotel* (☎074/58115; ④) serves excellent fresh salmon for a fraction of what you'd pay at swanky *Rathmullan House*, nearby. Sea angling can be arranged locally.

Towards Portsallon

Two miles north of Rathmullan, on the coast road, a signpost to the left indicates a little track that leads towards the tenth-century **Drumhallach cross slab**; only four and a half feet in height, it has delightful carvings of two figures sitting on the arms of the cross sucking away at their thumbs. This curiosity is linked by local folklore with Fionn MacCumhaill, who one day burned his thumb while tending to the salmon of knowledge, and immediately stuck it in his mouth – thereafter doing the same whenever he needed to be wise. The lower figures on this front face are harder to make out but are meant to represent bishops.

Back on the main route, the road climbs to give great views across to Dunree Head and the Urris range of mountains, on the Inishowen Peninsula. About seven miles north of Rathmullen is the gorgeous *Bunnaton Hostel* (☎074/50122; ①), an old coast-guard station. To get there follow the path off to the right down by the clump of fir trees. There's a small shop here, a couple of bikes for rental and great walks nearby. The hostel overlooks a small cove with a rocky beach and also has a nice view inland up the valley of **Glenvar**, which will take you across to Carrowkeel on the western side of the peninsula. Further on the road towards Portsallon is the *Knockalla Caravan and Camping Park* (☎074/59108).

Continuing north, the road rises until you're running along the clifftop approach to the most spectacular views on the peninsula at **Saldanha Head**. From here you're looking down onto the three-mile stretch of golden sand at Balinstocker Strand. The tiny village of **PORTSALLON**, on the other side of the strand, was once a great holidaying spot but is now more of a ghost resort, with its grand crenellated hotel abandoned down on the front. Just in front of it, however, is *Rita's Bar*, still thriving in its 1950s' decor, with wooden bar counter and shelves for sweets and bottled drinks. For **B&B** try Mrs Margaret Borland's *Swillyview*, Ballynashannagh.

Fanad Head

Though some stretches are forested, most of the five-mile route north from Portsallon to Fanad Head is through humpy and barren land, with clusters of granite pushing through marshy ground. By the roadside there's a **Holy Well**, decked out with a crazy collection of mementos – beads, prayer books, plastic knife and fork, a golf tee, badges, mugs, bottles, medicine bottle and so on. Before reaching the Head, there is one other curiosity worth taking in – the rock formation known as the **Great Arch**. Follow the signpost on the right of the road, then take the path down to the new house, and finally cross the fields to the rocky strand. You'll see the arch to your left, a sort of natural Arc de Triomphe with the sea crashing all around it.

Returning to the main road, you'll find that it leads straight on to **Fanad Head**, where it reaches a dramatically placed cliff-edge lighthouse and its namesake public house. The *Lighthouse Tavern* doesn't live up to its situation, serving hot toddies out of the microwave, but allegedly has wild country and western sessions (July & Aug Tues, Fri & Sun) and the views. The road from here runs on down to the low rocky coast, and a pebble beach.

The Inishowen Peninsula

Rarely sought out by tourists due to a combination of its northerly location and its proximity to the North, the **Inishowen Peninsula** is perhaps the great overlooked treasure of the Irish landscape. It's a diverse and visually exciting terrain, where the views usually encompass the waters of the loughs or the Atlantic waves. Every aspect of the land is superb – the beaches (especially Fahan, Tullagh and Pollan), the towering headland bluffs (Malin, Inishowen, Dunaff and Dunree) and the central mountain range, with **Slieve Snaght** (*sliabh sneachta*, the mountain of the snows) at the centre of it all. Its name derives from **Eoghán**, who was made First Lord of the island by his father Niall, High King of Ireland. Phases of the peninsula's history before and after Eoghán have left a legacy of fine antiquities, from the **Greenan Fort** to a host of beautiful early Christian crosses (Cloncha, Mura, Carrowmore and Cooley).

Western Inishowen

The most stimulating of all the Inishowen sights, the ancient fort known as the **Grianán of Aileach**, is a short way off the western route into the peninsula from Derry city. The turning is past Bridge End, on the south side of the Letterkenny–Derry Road, by the Liam McCormack-designed **Burt Church**, probably the most beautiful new church in all Ireland. The seating is set concentrically, under a whitewashed ceiling that sweeps up into a vortex to allow sunlight to beam down directly upon the altar; the allusions in every detail to Neolithic sepulchral architecture (especially Newgrange) are fascinating and very atmospheric.

The Grianán of Aileach (a mile up the hill from the church) was already 1700 years old when the Alexandrian geographer Ptolemy showed it on his map of Ireland in the second century, and most people today find it the most impressive of all the pre-Christian antiquities left in the country. It was said in the years after Christ to have been the base of various northern Irish chieftains. Here Saint Patrick supposedly preached in 450 AD, and baptized Eoghán, the founder of the O'Neill clan. In the twelfth century it was sacked by Brian, King of Thomond, in retribution for a raid on Clare, with the result that a large amount of its stone got carried away. What you see today owes a lot to the reconstruction by a Dr Bernard in the late nineteenth century. It's enclosed by three earthen banks, but its most stunning asset is the view across the primordial jumble of mountains and hills far away to the west and the loughs to each side of Inishowen immediately to the north.

Fahan and Buncrana

To get back towards the western coast of the peninsula from here, the safest bet is to return to Bridge End and turn onto the road to **FAHAN**. The beach at Fahan is delightful, as are its monastic ruins. The first abbot was Saint Mura (one of six saints in the one family), and what remains today from his time is the **St Mura cross slab**, a spellbinding example of early Christian stone decoration, though it's a shame that it hasn't

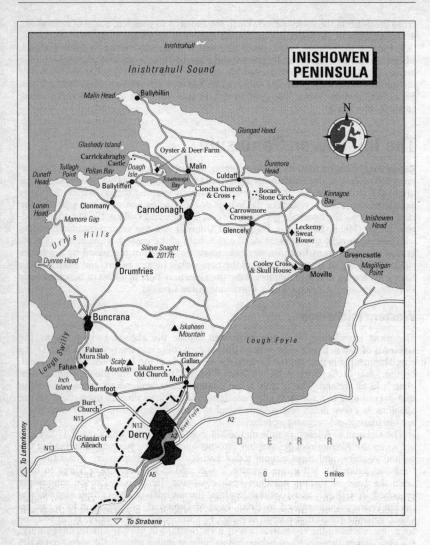

yet been cleansed of its lichen. There's said to be a rare Greek inscription on its side, but it's hard to locate. *Restaurant St Johns,* as you enter the village, offers good steaks and dinners in the £15–20 range.

The high street at **BUNCRANA**, a few miles north, is one long carnival parade of shops, each with a name saluting one or other of the local clans – Casey, McLoughlin, Hegarty, O'Doherty, Grant, McGonagle. The town is packed out during the summer, for this is the Derry people's unrivalled seaside resort. Amusement arcades are here by the dozen, as are **B&Bs**; try Mrs McCallion's *Ross-Na-Ri,* Ballymacarry (☎077/61271; ③), or Mrs McEleney's *Kincora,* Cahir O'Doherty Avenue (☎077/61174; ③). Midway between Buncrana and Carndonagh is the *Mintiagh Lodge Hostel* (☎077/61362; ①), just two miles north of Drumfries. For **eats** in Buncrana, check out the *Kebab House* on the left-hand side just as you round the corner into the main street. *Dorrians* on the main street is also a good bet for a substantial lunch. The place is crammed full of **pubs**; if you're looking for a plain and unpretentious bar try *Roddens*, and for a more upbeat venue try *O'Flaherty's*, which often has music.

The left turn that runs down to the pier at the north end of the main street will take you onto the coastal path to **Stragill Strand**, a beautiful and isolated stretch of golden sand. There's a **campsite** here, from which you can go on to get to Dunree Head by following the track away from the beach up to the main road. The view across **Lough Swilly** at this point is extremely satisfying, with the closed-in feel of a large mountain lake.

Dunree to Doagh Isle

Perched on a headland overlooking the mouth of Lough Swilly, just past the tiny village from which it takes its name, **Dunree Fort** began life as a Martello tower and was then enlarged into a fortress. It now has a museum of predictable military memorabilia (May–Sept Tues–Sat 10am–6pm, Sun noon–6pm; closed Mon except bank holidays; £2). A steepish climb going north out of the village will take you past a scattering of weatherbeaten thatched cottages before you cross a small bridge close to the **Gap of Mamore** (*madhm mór*, the great mountain pass), looking like a bite taken out of the Urris Mountains. From here the road spirals steeply downwards, an ever wider and more spectacular view of the flat foreground to Dunaff Head opening up with every bend. The mile-long **Tullagh Strand**, to the east of Dunaff Head, is a safe bathing beach, with *Tullagh Bay Caravan and Camping Site* just behind it (☎077/76289 or ☎76138). *The Rusty Nail*, by the roadside, has music at weekends and offers good-value bar food and Sunday lunch. The road from here works its way inland between the mountains to Clonmany, a village of predominantly cream-coloured terraced houses and a few grocery shops. The backdrop of mountains on all sides shields it from any thought of an outside world.

The popular holiday village of **BALLYLIFFEN** makes an earthy contrast, with a hotel at each end, a disco and several **B&Bs**. Try Mrs Sweeny's *Hillcrest* (☎077/76151; ③), or Mrs McLaughlin, *The Vartry*, at the Clonmany end (☎077/76370; ③). Its principal attraction is the beautiful **Pollan Strand**, at the northern tip of which stands the ruin of **Carrickabraghy Castle**, an O'Doherty defence built in the sixteenth century. Weathered by centuries of spray and seasalt, the stones of the tower show colours ranging from the darkest hues through oranges and reds to golden yellows. The strand itself has wonderfully wild breakers, which unfortunately make it dangerous to swim.

The castle sits on the western side of a promontory called **Doagh Isle**, which you can drive onto by a road to the east of Ballyliffen. You shouldn't miss a trip onto it, for **Trawbreaga Bay** (*trá bréige*, the treacherous strand), on the eastern side, is an exquisite piece of coastline. The mouth of the bay is bewitching – if you walk onto the beach here you'll find the sea has fashioned the rocks into myriad shapes and colours.

Carndonagh

Just before you turn into **CARNDONAGH**, coming from the Ballyliffen direction, there's a church on the corner of the turn-off. Against the church wall is the elegantly shaped and decorated seventh-century **Donagh Cross**, with two diminutive pillar stones to its right and left. The pillar stones show figures with rather large heads, while the cross depicts evil little characters jumping out of its Celtic interlacings – all of which harks back to the Druidic religion. A few other decorated stones stand by the entrance. The buildings of Carndonagh town are stacked up the hillside, near the crown of which stands the all-surveying Catholic church. The town **museum**, in the basement of the Wesleyan church, near the base of the hill as you come from the

Ballyliffen direction (July & Aug Mon–Sat 2–4pm), has many intriguing folk items. For **accommodation**, try *Radharc na Coille*, Tiernaleague, left off Church Street then on for a mile (☎077/74471; ③), or Mrs Brett's *Dunsheeny* (☎077/74292; ③) in the village. The *Sportsman's Inn*, on the Diamond, does stews and salads and has traditional music most nights throughout the year. Carndonagh has a **folk festival** in the third week of July but it's not one of the more lively ones.

East of Carndonagh: the ancient sites

Not far to the east of Carndonagh are a neighbouring set of historical remains – the Carrowmore high crosses, the Cloncha cross, the Bocan stone circle and the Temple of Deen. To get to the **Carrowmore high crosses**, take the Moville direction out of Carndonagh for four miles, then take a right forty yards after the signposted turning for Culdaff: the two plain crosses are eighty yards up the road, one on each side. These and a few meagre building stones are all that remain of the ancient monastery of Saint Chonas. For the **Cloncha cross and church**, get back to the Culdaff turning and follow it for a couple of miles until you see a small bungalow with a garden hedge of small firs – the site is behind it. This was once the most important monastic foundation in Inishowen, a status reflected in the beautiful designs carved on the cross's stem. Inside the church are a few more carved stones, the outstanding piece being a tenth-century tombstone.

For the other two sites, take a right here towards Moville and then a left uphill for fifty yards – the **Bocan stone circle** is through the first field gate on the left. Only a handful of the stones still stand, among a scrapyard of fallen ones; they were all placed here at least 3000 years ago. There's a fine vista of the surrounding ring of hills, with which the stones seem deliberately aligned. On the other side of the main road from the circle is a gallery tomb known as the **Temple of Deen** (go a little further along towards Moville and take a right up as far as the wire barrier – you'll spot it from there). It's nothing special, but it's possible that what is exposed today is only the central chamber of an immense cairn. Unfortunately, no archeological work has yet been done on either this or the stone circle. **CULDAFF** is the nearest base for all of these places, but apart from having a quaint little pier and ancient stone bridge there is little to entice you down there. For **accommodation**, try *McGrory's Guest House, Bar & Restaurant* (☎077/79104; ④) or *Culdaff House* (☎077/79103; ④).

Malin and Malin Head

Four miles north of Carndonagh is **MALIN** village, tucked picturesquely into the side of Trawbreaga Bay. A planter settlement with an overtly charming central green, it has two pubs, *McClean's* and *McGonnigle's*, as well as the *Malin Hotel* (☎077/70606; ⑤). A little way north of Malin a signpost shows the way to **Five Fingers Strand**, across the bay from Doagh Isle – it's worth the diversion for the ferocity of the breakers on the beach and the long walks on its sands. The beach hit the headlines when a large IRA cache of arms was found buried here. Back on the main road, you'll quickly come to a left turn to take you straight on for Malin Head; a more devious route is to take a left that veers off this road, and a left again at the next signpost, which brings you to the top of a hill overlooking Five Fingers Strand – one of the most captivating views of this part of the peninsula. Going downhill from here feels like a slightly less intoxicating version of the descent from the Gap of Mamore, and is decidedly more thrilling than the direct lowland road.

Malin Head, the northernmost extremity of Ireland, might not be as stupendously over-the-top as other Donegal headlands but is nevertheless excellent for windy and winding coastal walks. Look out for a large chasm in the cliffs known as Hell's Hole and the now-deserted **Inishtrahull Island** that aptly translates as the *Island of Yonder Strand*.

Eastern Inishowen

The eastern region of the peninsula from Derry to Inishowen Head and beyond is the nightclubbing circuit for the youth of Derry, and you'll see cars, buses and hitchers racing down here on Friday and Saturday nights. Favourite destinations are *Scamps* at Redcastle, *Tulmari* at Carndonagh and *Mac's Backroom* at *McGrory's*, Culdaff. Scores of new bungalows hog the slopes to capture their slice of the panorama.

The first few miles of the road entering this part of Inishowen belong to the British sector of the north of Ireland: you'll approach the army checkpoint half a mile short of the border at Culmore Point.

Muff and around

The tiny village of **MUFF**, just a few minutes' drive north of the border, is an ideal base for both Derry and the Inishowen Peninsula. The independent **hostel**, *Muff Hostel*, run by the charismatic Martin Cooke (☎077/84188; ①), is a cosy and welcoming place that also has **camping**; you get there by taking a left turn at the end of the village, just before the *Shell* petrol station. *Mrs Reddin* on the main street (☎077/84031; ③) offers a **B&B** alternative. The village itself is not quite as dead as it looks: *The Carman's Bar* has Irish music on a Wednesday, and it's possible *The Squealin' Pig* will have traditional music on a Saturday and Sunday; the pub with the toreador and flamenco mosaic outside has country and western music and dancing from Friday to Sunday. For **eats**, the town café has steaks and pies. *Lough Swilly* **buses** run six or more times a day from Derry.

The countryside immediately around Muff has several interesting megalithic remains. In the **Iskaheen** district (the hostel area), there are some standing stones not far from the sparse ruins of an old abbey that marks the spot where Eoghán, son of Niall of the Nine Hostages, died of grief for his brother Conal. To get to the more impressive of the stones from the abbey, go past the nearby St Patrick's Church for a quarter of a mile, by the garden packed with elves, and then go up into the second field behind the new-looking bungalow; from the stone you have the best view of the whole area.

Another nearby site worth seeking out is the **Ardmore Gallan** stone. Dating from the Bronze Age, it's a striking monumental stone standing all on its own in a farmer's field. It is heavily carved with symbolic forms, having forty small cup-dents and a large vertical valley down the middle of one face. To get to it, take a left off the Moville Road about half a mile out of Muff, then up the lane at the side of the red-doored house; follow the road straight up, and then take a right turn to the farmyard at the end – the stone is in the far side of the field in front of the yard.

Also to be recommended is the fourteen-mile trip across the mountains through **Gráinne's Gap** and on to Buncrana on the western side of the peninsula (see above). There are fantastic views back down onto the Foyle estuary from the gap, and the inland scenery is all trickling burns, heathery boggy slopes lined with turf banks, and rocky granite outcrops.

Moville and around

Set on a gentle hillock beside the Foyle, **MOVILLE** is a very agreeable seaside resort of the convalescent variety – one can imagine a grandfather clock ticking away in every household. It's handy for a rocky shoreline walk that you can pursue as far as Greencastle without too much difficulty, although at a few points you'll have to walk circumspectly across the bottom of a few private gardens. The village will rarely stir itself to offer anything more than even a tingle of excitement, but if want to **stay**, try *Mrs McGroarty's*, at the top end of Main Street (☎077/82091; ③), or the *Foyle Hotel* (☎077/82025; ④). The *Moville Holiday Hostel* (*IHH*, open all year; ☎077/82378, fax

☎372187; ②) also has a campsite and rents out bikes. *Rosatos*, on the Carndonagh Road, is the best place for a snack and a cosy drink. *The Prospect Bar* down by the gaudily painted Temperance Hall has folk and ballad singing (Thurs, Fri & Sat). A livelier time is to be had at the *Hair of the Dog* pub by the pier, which promises varied music every night.

There are a few historical pieces in the district, most notably the **Cooley Cross** and **Skull House**, signposted off to the left of the main road a quarter of a mile before Moville. Follow the turn-off up the steep hill for about a mile, always bearing right, and it's there – an ancient Celtic wheel-cross, guarding the entrance to a walled graveyard. There are very few examples of this kind of cross with the pierced ringhole in its head – the hole was once a pagan device used to clinch serious treaties, the hands of the opposing parties being joined in amity through it. The Skull House, in the graveyard, is in the form of the type of tomb usually kept for saints, and in this case it's probably that of **Saint Finian** (the one who argued with Columba), whose monastery this was. If you peep through the front hole you'll see some bones.

Greencastle to Kinnego Bay

Though its harbour is surprisingly ugly, **GREENCASTLE** has a pleasant view across to the extensive golden sands of Magilligan Strand on the British side of Lough Foyle. At dusk you'll see the area across the water begin to sparkle with lights like a ship at sea – these are the lights of the prison camp, just hidden behind the dunes. By the road to Stroove (see below) are the ruins of a fourteenth-century **Richard de Burgo** castle, built on a rocky knoll to guard the narrowest part of the lough. De Burgo saw it as the greatest castle-building enterprise in Donegal and hoped it would be just the job to quell the local Inishowen chieftains, the O'Donnells and the O'Dohertys. But the O'Dohertys in the end took control of the castle, until they finished up bickering among themselves and causing most of the damage seen today. It's in no great shape, with gaping breaches right round its circular enclosure making it look like a large mock-up of a stone circle, but viewed from the shore it's still an impressive sight. Next door is **Greencastle Fort**, a fortress built during the Napoleonic wars; designed as a lookout post, it unsurprisingly affords good views across the estuary. Back in the village, *The Ferryport* bar on the seafront offers meals and **B&B** as well as drinks (☎077/81296; ③), or try the *Smuggler's Rest* (☎077/81021; ③). Excellent seafood **meals** at reasonable prices can be had at *Kealy's* pub at Magilligan Strand.

At **STROOVE** (pronounced *Shroove*), the scenery jumps into a more exciting gear, with lovely clambering walks along its coastline to the lighthouse. There you'll have to return to the road to reach the small beach, from where doughtier walkers can resume the clamber as far as the cliffs of the awesome **Inishowen Head**. An easier way to the Head is to simply follow the road until it turns left, where you go straight on up the hill; a car can make it up the first couple of miles, but after that you run the risk of getting stuck in a rut. From the Head, it's a beautiful but tiring walk to **Kinnagoe Bay**. The alternative route entails going back to the main road and following it to the right turn by the thatched cottage in Stroove – this will take you over the headland through two beautiful glens, where fields set at impossible angles line the valley sides. Approached by a precipitous descent, Kinnagoe is one of the most secluded sandy beaches around, tucked between the rocky walls of headland against which the waves throw spray as delicate as lace. A plan on a roadside plaque shows where three of the Spanish Armada ships sank just off the coast; most of the ships' wreckage discovered over the last twenty years is now on view in Derry's Foyle College. The nearest **B&B** is back in Stroove, with *Mrs Gillespie* (☎077/81020; ③). The *Drunken Duck Seafood Bar* (☎077/81362), offering good **food** and fantastic views, is worth a visit.

travel details

Bus Éireann (Lellerkenny ☎074/21309)
Ballyshannon to: Bundoran (6 daily); Derry (3 daily); Donegal (4 daily); Dublin (2 daily); Rossnowlagh (1 daily); Sligo (2 daily).
Donegal to: Dublin (4 daily; 4hr).
Glencolumbcille to: Donegal town (2 daily).
Letterkenny to: Dublin (4 daily; 4hr).

Private buses
Funtrek (☎01/873 0852) operates a daily service **from Letterkenny** to Dublin.

Patrick Gallagher's (☎074/37037) operates a daily service **from Letterkenny** Market Square to the Rosguill Peninsula at 6pm, and returns from Downings on the peninsula at 10.45am every morning.

McGeehan's bus (☎075/46150) from **Glencolumbcille** to Donegal town leaves from *Biddy's Bar* at 7.30am Mon–Sun and also 3pm Sun.

Feda O'Donnell buses (☎075/48114) operate a regular service between Galway City and Crolly in the Lower Rosses, via Donegal town.

THE NORTH

O n 31 August, 1994, the IRA announced a ceasefire and a peace of sorts broke out in Northern Ireland; two months later Loyalist paramilitaries followed suit. However, the peace and the sense of optimism it brought were relatively short-lived, ending with the IRA bombing near London's Canary Wharf in February 1996. Now, while the politicians and paramilitaries are involved in the long process of talks to reach a settlement, the majority of Northern Irish people look to the future with a mixture of cautious hope – having felt the positive effects of a period of peace – and a sense of dread at the threat of a return to sectarian violence. During the ceasefire the predicted benefits of peace had started to appear – economic growth, increased employment, the return of emigrants lured back partly by the prospect of stability and partly by government incentives. Although many of the advantages of the ceasefire are still being enjoyed in the North, consolidation of these changes seems a long way off.

At the time of writing, some security measures dropped after August 1994 are once again in place, but the level of security is still much less than it was at the height of the Troubles, and the atmosphere in the North is considerably more relaxed. You'll still see armoured vehicles and heavily fortified police headquarters, but mainly in the major pressure points: parts of Belfast and Derry city, and along the border in Fermanagh and Armagh. Many of the unofficial border roads – once closed – have now been opened, making crossing into the North an easier matter. As for everyday **travel**, it is unlikely that security matters will present any problems; and as long as you use your common sense, especially in the main cities, you should have no trouble at all.

Despite the beauty of the countryside – much of which remains unspoilt – and the efforts of the tourist board, the political situation in the North since 1969 has kept tourists away. The eighteen months of the ceasefire saw the start of a turnaround, with a huge increase in the number of visitors – especially from the Republic and Britain – curious to know what this neglected corner of Ireland is like. The result has been improved tourist facilities, with plenty of new accommodation and restaurants opening up; although, of course, the current political instability has slowed down the growth in the industry and at peak times there may still be a scarcity of accommodation in the cities and some rural areas. The places that were traditionally holiday spots for Northerners, however, are well served: the **coastline of County Derry** (including the magnificent black basalt geometry of the Giant's Causeway); the green **Glens of Antrim**; and the **Mourne Mountains**, to the south of Belfast. The **Ulster Way**, which runs for over 500 miles, looping around Northern Ireland, takes in many of these scenic highlights. Unfortunately, just how efficiently maintained and signposted the Way is varies from county to county – so check with the local tourist offices before setting out. Away from the spectacular coastline, the country settles down into rolling farmland punctuated by the planned towns of the merchant companies that were entrusted with the resettlement of this region in the seventeenth century. The inland counties of **Tyrone** and **Fermanagh** are dotted with archeological sites, castles, ruined churches, raths and dolmens. Fermanagh, centred on **Lough Erne**, is a good place to head towards for watersports and fishing; scenically, **Tyrone** is duller, though it rises both physically and in terms of interest towards the wild and desolate Sperrins in the north. But to really get to grips with the history of the North you must visit its cities: **Belfast**, with its grand public buildings, was built on the profits of Victorian industry; **Derry** has just shed the security barriers and barbed wire that shrouded its medieval walled town; and the cathedral town of **Armagh**, set on seven hills, is where Saint Patrick established Christianity in Ireland.

CHAPTER FOURTEEN

BELFAST

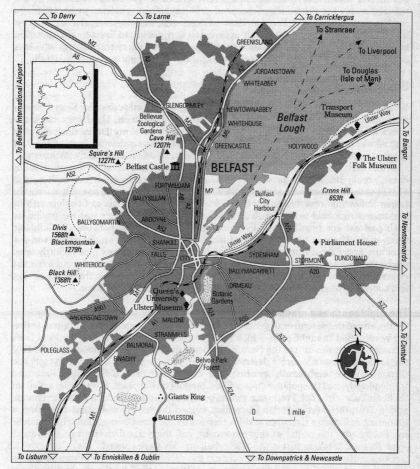

To Stranraer

GREENISLAND

To Liverpool

M2

JORDANSTOWN

To Douglas
(Isle of Man)

WHITEABBEY

GLENGORMLEY

NEWTOWNABBEY

Transport
Museum

Bellevue
Zoological
Gardens
Cave Hill
1207ft ▲

WHITEHOUSE

Belfast
Lough

Ulster Way

Squire's Hill
1227ft ▲

GREENCASTLE

HOLYWOOD

Belfast Castle 🏰

The Ulster
Folk Museum

A52

FORTWILLIAM

BELFAST

BALLYSILLAN

M7

Belfast
City
Harbour

Crons Hill
653ft ▲

ARDOYNE

Divis
1568ft ▲
Blackmountain
1279ft ▲

SHANKILL

Ulster Way

♦ Parliament House

FALLS

SYDENHAM

STORMONT

DUNDONALD

WHITEROCK

BALLYMACARRETT

A20

Black Hill
1368ft ▲

ORMEAU

Queen's
University
Ulster Museum ♥

Botanic
Gardens

ANDERSONSTOWN

MALONE

STRANMILLS

POLEGLASS

BALMORAL

FINAGHY

Belvoir Park
Forest

∴ Giants Ring

0   1 mile

BALLYLESSON

N

BELFAST, the capital of Northern Ireland, is not somewhere you can be indifferent to. A quarter of the population of the North lives in the city, and, over the years, they have grabbed more than their share of world headlines, not least on the announcement of the IRA ceasefire. The optimism engendered by the peace was perhaps most obvious here, and although the sense of relief it brought has now been dispelled, Belfast does have a different feel to it, especially at night. Gone are the constant security checks, the armoured patrols and the oppressive sense of being under surveillance. On the other hand, the tourist board tries to portray the city as some kind of Hibernian Rio – a farcical idea, but one to which the city's setting of mountains, pellucid skies and the natural harbour of **Belfast Lough** does lend some credence.

As far as what you should see goes, it's experiencing the city itself that comes top of the list. This need not take more than a couple of days, though Belfast is also an easy base from which to visit virtually anywhere else in the North. In the centre, concentrate on the glories that the industrial revolution brought: grandiose **Victorian buildings** as self-satisfied as any the British Empire created, and magnificent Victorian **pubs**. Offering a more contemporary vision, **West Belfast** is a depressed, working-class area where sectarian divisions are at their most starkly apparent. It may not sound like a tourist attraction, but it's certainly an eye-opener; and the ephemeral art of the mural painters who have claimed the district for their own gives an insight into the current temper of the North.

Some history

Belfast began its life as a cluster of forts built to guard a ford across the River Farset, a river that nowadays runs underground, beneath the High Street. The Farset and Lagan rivers form a valley that marks a geological boundary between the basaltic plateau of Antrim and the slaty hills of Down: the softer red Triassic sandstones from which their courses were eroded are responsible for the bright red colour of Belfast's brickwork.

In the early days Belfast was very slow to develop, and indeed its history as a city doesn't really begin until the seventeenth century. A Norman castle was built here in 1177, but its influence was always limited, and within 100 years or so control over the Lagan Valley had reverted firmly to the Irish, under the O'Neills of Clandeboye who had their stronghold to the south in the Castlereagh Hills. Theirs was the traditional Irish pastoral community, their livestock and families spread between the hills and valley plain. Then, in 1604, Sir Arthur Chichester, a Devonshire knight whose son was to be the first Earl of Donegall, was "planted" in the area by James I, and shortly afterwards the tiny settlement was granted a charter creating a corporate borough. By the restoration era of 1660 the town was still no more than 150 houses in five or six streets, and Carrickfergus at the mouth of the lough held the monopoly on trade.

The eighteenth and nineteenth centuries

By the end of the seventeenth century, things were looking up. French Huguenots fleeing persecution brought skills which rapidly improved the fortunes of the local linen industry, and by the turn of the century the population had reached about 2000. In 1708 the town was almost entirely destroyed by fire, but it was only a temporary setback: throughout the **eighteenth century** the cloth trade and shipbuilding expanded tremendously, and the population increased ten-fold in 100 years. It was a city noted for its liberalism – in 1784 Protestants gave generously to help build a Catholic church, and in 1791, three Presbyterian Ulstermen formed the society of **United Irishmen**, a gathering embracing Catholics and Protestants on the basis of common Irish nationality. Belfast was the centre of this movement, and thirty Presbyterian ministers in all were accused of taking part in the 1798 rebellion – six were hanged.

Despite the movement's Belfast origins, the rebellion in the North was in fact an almost complete failure, and the forces of reaction backed by the wealthy landlords quickly and ruthlessly stamped it down. Within two generations most Protestants had abandoned the Nationalist cause, and Belfast as a sectarian town was truly born. In the **nineteenth century**, Presbyterian ministers like the Reverend Henry Cooke and Hugh (Roaring) Hanna began openly to attack the Catholic Church, and the **sectarian divide** became wider and increasingly violent. In 1835, several people were sabred to death in Sandy Row, and sporadic outbreaks of violence have continued from that day on. Meanwhile, the nineteenth century saw vigorous commercial and industrial expansion. In 1888, Queen Victoria granted Belfast city status; the city fathers' gratitude to her is stamped on buildings throughout the centre. By this time the population had risen to 208,000, and, with the continued improvement in both the linen and shipbuilding industries, the population exceeded even that of Dublin by the end of the century.

The twentieth century

Although **Partition** and the creation of Northern Ireland with Belfast as its capital inevitably boosted the city's status, decline has been fairly constant over recent years. Bombing in World War II destroyed much of the city, and in the past ten years great tracts of West Belfast have been pulled down in a belated attempt to improve living conditions. Outside the centre, this is a very modern-looking place. Nowadays the city is struggling very hard for **revitalization**, and billions of pounds are being poured in from Britain and the European Union, in the hope that economic growth might bring with it some kind of more hopeful future. The linen industry, which had disappeared almost completely, is undergoing a modest revival in high-fashion clothing, and shipbuilding is also surfacing again after reaching rock bottom.

> The telephone code for Belfast is ☎01232.

Arrival, information and transport

If you **fly** into Belfast, you'll arrive either at **Belfast International Airport** – used by all international flights and most major British airlines including the *British Midland* and *British Airways* shuttles – in Aldergrove, 19 miles from the city (airport buses to Great Victoria Street bus station run Mon–Sat every 30min 6.40am–10.45pm, Sun every 60min 7.15am–10.15pm; £3.70; a taxi costs around £18), or at **Belfast City Airport**, three miles out. This has direct services with smaller operators from many British provincial airports. To get into the city catch *Citybus* #21 (Mon–Sat 6.55am–8pm every 20–30min, Sun hourly from 9.35am) to the City Hall; or take a short walk from the airport terminal to the train at Sydenham Halt for Central Station; a taxi costs around £5.

Of the **ferries** to Northern Ireland, the ninety-minute *SeaCat* Stranraer catamaran service docks in **Belfast Harbour** (a taxi from the harbour to city centre costs around £7.50). Other services are the Liverpool-to-Belfast *Norse Irish Ferries* service, and in summer, the Isle of Man-to-Belfast service run by *Isle of Man Steam Packet Company*. The rest of the ferries dock at **Larne**: *Stena Sealink*'s service from Stranraer, and *P&O*'s from Cairnryan. The port is twenty miles to the north and well connected to the city by rail and bus – *Ulsterbus* services run to Great Victoria Street bus station, and there are frequent trains to Central Station. For information about services to Larne call the **Larne Harbour Travel Centre** (☎01574/270517).

Coming in by **train** (from Larne Harbour, Dublin, Bangor, Derry, Portrush or Portadown), you'll arrive at **Central Station** on East Bridge Street, a little way east of the centre. A free rail-link bus service runs between Central and York Gate Station, to the north of the city, every ten minutes (connecting buses also run from Central Station to Donegall Place every 10min), but soon the new rail-link under construction between Central Station and Great Victoria Street will bring passengers straight into the centre. Otherwise Botanic or City Hospital Rail stations are handy if you're staying in the university area, or if you're heading north to Portstewart or Derry.

Long-distance **buses** arrive either at **Great Victoria Street** bus station, in Glengall Street behind the *Europa Hotel* (services to Armagh, Tyrone, Derry, Fermanagh and west Down – as well as for the Republic and for the airports and cross-Channel ferry terminals), or **Oxford Street** bus station (serves Antrim, east Down and east Derry). Both of these are extremely central and well served by *CityBus* services.

Information

Tourist information is available from the **tourist office**, 59 North Street (July–Aug Mon–Fri 9am–7.30pm, Sat 9am–5pm, Sun noon–4.30pm; Sept–June Mon–Sat 9am–5.15pm; ☎246609); they have lots of brochures and maps and an accommodation booking service (£1 in Belfast area, £2 elsewhere). There's also a 24-hour screen outside the office – a lifesaver if you find yourself bedless late at night. During summer, a new, friendly and extremely helpful supplementary tourist information service is on Donegall Square North (Mon–Wed 9.30am–5pm, Thurs & Fri till 8pm, Sat till 4pm). **Bord Fáilte**, supplying tourist information for the Republic, can be found at 53 Castle Street (☎327888). For a guide to entertainment in the city, the *Belfast Telegraph* has a fortnightly listings freesheet, *That's Entertainment*, and the tourist board publishes a monthly freebie, *Artslink*.

City transport

Although you can easily walk around the centre, distances to the outlying attractions can be considerable, and many of the places to stay are also some way out. Fortunately the excellent *CityBus* service (red buses) covers almost anywhere you're likely to go within Belfast, while *Ulsterbus* (blue buses) serves long-distance routes. Almost all **buses** set off from Donegall Square, right at the city centre, or the streets immediately around; you can pick up the map which outlines the main services from the tourist office or the *Citybus* kiosk in Donegall Square West (Mon–Fri 8am–5.30pm: bus information on ☎246485). The fare for city-centre journeys is 73p, and there's a zone system that comes into operation as you head further out. You can pay on board – make sure you have enough small change – but you'll save time and a little money if you buy a **multi-journey** ticket in advance (£2.30 for 4 journeys, from newsagents and other shops citywide). You push the ticket into a machine (or get the driver to do it) to cancel one journey each time you travel – two people can use the same ticket as long as it is cancelled twice. For journeys across zones, you again have to cancel the ticket twice. *Ulsterbus* also serves the routes from the city centre to the suburbs, and *Citystoppers* (red or blue buses) provides an additional service on the Falls and Lisburn roads (#523–538); late-night buses run from Shaftesbury Square along five routes on Friday and Saturday (midnight, 1am & 2am; £2).

Black taxis, which travel along set routes into West Belfast, picking up and dropping passengers anywhere along the way, can also be extremely handy, and at around £1 a journey (for each passenger) they're also cheap. The ones that operate into the Catholic areas (all of these go up the Falls Road itself) set out from the revitalized Smithfield area of Castle Street, and some of them will be prepared to give you a tour round Catholic West Belfast for about £10 an hour. Cabs servicing Protestant areas leave from North Street, slightly further north, and charge much the same. Some Belfast people are reluctant to use these cabs, believing that the money raised goes into the hands of sectarian racketeers on whichever side. **Regular taxis**, based at the main rank in Donegall Square East and other points throughout the city, charge a minimum £1.50, which rapidly starts to increase on the meter if you're going any distance. Or you can phone a minicab (try *Blue Star Cabs* ☎243118 or ☎230022), a good idea especially late at night as passing taxis tend to be en route to passenger pick-ups.

If you're **driving**, you need to be careful about where you park your car: there are still some city-centre **control zones** (clearly marked with black-and-yellow signs), although these are being phased out throughout the North. There are, however, plenty of car parks, and many city streets have pay-and-display parking in operation.

Accommodation

During the ceasefire the number of tourists visiting Belfast had almost doubled; now, although the tourism boom has waned somewhat, you may still find it difficult to find a **place to stay** at peak times – there's a particular scarcity of budget accommodation – so it's worth using the tourist office's booking service, as they'll know where the vacancies are. Another inevitable consequence of the increase in tourism is that prices are beginning to rise, but you can still find decent B&B very reasonably priced.

Nearly all the city's accommodation is south of the centre in the university area, including a high proportion of the B&Bs on Botanic Avenue, Eglantine Avenue and the Malone Road. There are dozens to choose from, all similar in facilities and price.

There is only one **campsite** in the environs of Belfast, and it is far from ideal. *Jordanstown Lough Shore Park*, some six miles north on Shore Road in Newtownabbey (☎868751), is basically a caravan site, so you need to phone ahead to organize camping and keys – the site gates are locked at 4.30pm and the maximum stay is two nights.

ACCOMMODATION PRICES

Throughout this book, accommodation prices have been graded according to the cost per person per night in high season; with hotels and many hostels this represents half the cost of a double room, whereas with the more basic hostels it represents the cost of a single dormitory bed. The prices signified by our grades are as follows:

① Up to £6	③ £10–14	⑤ £20–26	⑦ £36–45
② £6–10	④ £14–20	⑥ £26–36	⑧ Over £45

Hotels

Dukes Hotel, 65–67 University St (☎236666, fax ☎237177). Classy modern hotel, near the university, in an old building with a popular bar, smart restaurant and small gym and sauna; check for weekend reductions. ⑧.

Europa Hotel, Great Victoria St (☎327000, fax ☎327800). Much-bombed central hotel to the east of the City Hall, last refurbished in 1994 and looking very grand. The bar, with its huge windows overlooking the city's main drag, is a poseur's paradise. ⑧.

Malone Lodge, 60 Eglantine Ave (☎382409, fax ☎382706). A new hotel near Queens, with good Irish and international cuisine served in the restaurant. Check for weekend reductions. ⑥.

Wellington Park Hotel, 21 Malone Rd (☎381111, fax ☎665410). Well-known business travellers' hotel in the university area, with a bar probably best known as a cruising ground for singles. ⑧.

Bed and breakfast

Botanic Lodge Guest House, 87 Botanic Ave (☎327682). ④.

Camera House, 44 Wellington Park (☎660026). Very luxurious, and much better than many Belfast hotels. ⑤.

Eglantine Guest House, 21 Eglantine Ave (☎667585). ④.

East Sheen House, 81 Eglantine Ave (☎667149). One of the best. ④.

Liserin Guest House, 17 Eglantine Ave (☎660769). ④.

Pearl Court House, 11 Malone Rd (☎666145). ④.

Windermere Guest House, 60 Wellington Park (☎662693). ④.

Hostels and student accommodation

Arnie's Backpackers, 63 Fitzwilliam St (*IHH*; ☎242867). Independent hostel with relaxed, if cramped, friendly style; 19 beds, no private rooms. Open all year. ②.

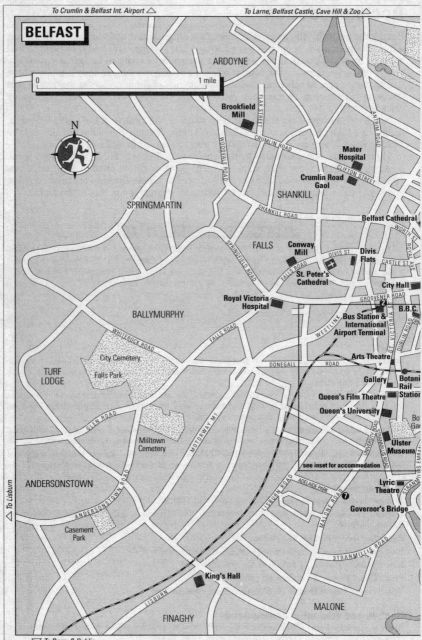

To Crumlin & Belfast Int. Airport △

To Larne, Belfast Castle, Cave Hill & Zoo △

BELFAST

ARDOYNE

0   1 mile

N

Brookfield Mill

FLAX STREET

WOODVALE ROAD

CRUMLIN ROAD

Mater Hospital

CLIFTON STREET

AN TRIM ROAD

Crumlin Road Gaol

SHANKILL

SPRINGMARTIN

SHANKILL ROAD

Belfast Cathedral

WORTH ROYAL

FALLS

Conway Mill

DIVIS ST

Divis Flats

SPRINGFIELD ROAD

CASTLE ST.

St. Peter's Cathedral

FALLS ROAD

City Hall

Royal Victoria Hospital

GROSVENER ROAD

B.B.C.

Bus Station & International Airport Terminal

BALLYMURPHY

WHITEROCK ROAD

FALLS ROAD

WESTLINK

GT VICTORIA ROAD

DUBLIN ROAD

City Cemetery

Falls Park

DONEGALL   ROAD

Arts Theatre

Gallery

Botanic Rail Station

TURF LODGE

GLEN ROAD

Queen's Film Theatre

Queen's University

Botanic Gardens

Milltown Cemetery

MOTORWAY M1

Ulster Museum

UNIVERSITY ROAD

STRANMILLIS ROAD

STRANMILLIS EMBANKMENT

see inset for accommodation

ANDERSONSTOWN

ANDERSONSTOWN ROAD

ADELAIDE PARK

LISBURN ROAD

Lyric Theatre

Governor's Bridge

△ To Lisburn

MALONE ROAD

7

Casement Park

STRANMILLIS ROAD

King's Hall

LISBURN

FINAGHY

MALONE

▽ To Derry & Dublin

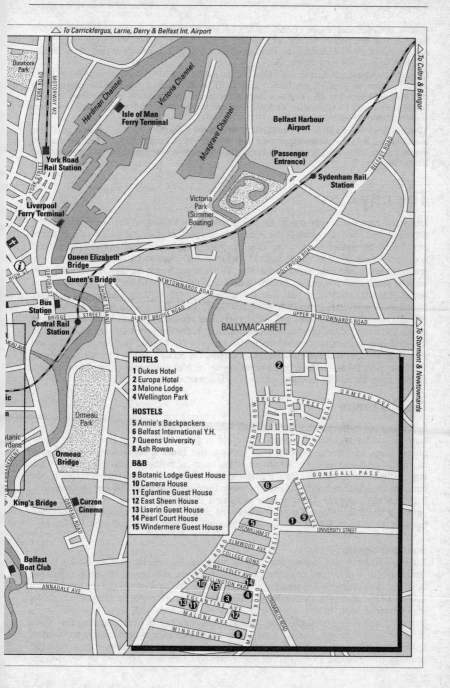

To Carrickfergus, Larne, Derry & Belfast Int. Airport

Dunmore Park

MOTORWAY M2

YORK ROAD

Herdman Channel

Victoria Channel

Isle of Man
Ferry Terminal

Musgrave Channel

Belfast Harbour
Airport

(Passenger
Entrance)

To Cultra & Bangor

BELFAST ROAD

York Road
Rail Station

YORK STREET

Liverpool
Ferry Terminal

Victoria
Park
(Summer
Boating)

Sydenham Rail
Station

HOLYWOOD ROAD

HIGH ST

OXFORD ST

Queen Elizabeth
Bridge

Queen's Bridge

NEWTOWNARDS ROAD

Bus
Station

SHORT STRAND

BRIDGE STREET

Central Rail
Station

ALBERT BRIDGE ROAD

UPPER NEWTOWNARDS ROAD

To Stormont & Newtownards

BALLYMACARRETT

MEAU AVE

Ormeau
Park

ic

otanic
rdens

Ormeau
Bridge

King's Bridge

ORMEAU ROAD

Curzon
Cinema

EMBANKMENT

HOTELS

1 Dukes Hotel
2 Europa Hotel
3 Malone Lodge
4 Wellington Park

HOSTELS

5 Annie's Backpackers
6 Belfast International Y.H.
7 Queens University
8 Ash Rowan

B&B

9 Botanic Lodge Guest House
10 Camera House
11 Eglantine Guest House
12 East Sheen House
13 Liserin Guest House
14 Pearl Court House
15 Windermere Guest House

2

BRUCE ROW

SANDY ROW

VICTORIA STREET

DUBLIN ROAD

ORMEAU AVE

DONEGALL PASS

6

BOTANIC AVENUE

1 9

UNIVERSITY STREET

5

FITZWILLIAM ST

ELMWOOD AVE

College Boat Club

Belfast
Boat Club

ANNADALE AVE

LISBURN ROAD

College Gdns

Wellesley Ave

Wellington Park

10 15

14

4

UNIVERSITY ROAD

MALONE ROAD

STRANMILLIS ROAD

13 11

Eglantine Ave

12

Malone Ave

Windsor Ave

8

Belfast International Youth Hostel, 22–32 Donegall Rd (☎315435, fax ☎439699). New 128-bed hostel just off Shaftesbury Square, with 24-hour staffing and no curfew, TV lounge, laundry and restaurant, but short on atmosphere. Booking ahead is advisable, especially at peak times. Singles and doubles available; open all year. ③.

Queen's University, contact Queen's Elms, 78 Malone Rd (☎381608). Student rooms are let out of term (mid-June to Sept). If you have a student ID these are good value (£8.50); non-students (£11.85) might be better off going to a B&B as the rooms are minuscule and you share washing facilities. Fri and Sat mornings no breakfast is served, but overnight price remains the same. Must book in advance. ②–③.

YWCA, Queen Mary's Hall, 70 Fitzwilliam St (☎240439). Take the City Hospital train stop. This old-fashioned hostel accommodates men and women, but is usually fully booked by students during college term time. Singles and doubles available; open year round except Christmas and Easter. ③.

The city

Donegall Square is very much the physical heart of Belfast: in the centre stands the City Hall, and from the sides of the square, buses and taxis set out for every part of the city. To the immediate north is the main shopping area, to the south entertainments and accommodation. Most of the grand old Victorian buildings so characteristic of the city are in the north and east, towards the river. Further out, **North Belfast** boasts Cave Hill, with its castle and zoo, while **South Belfast** has the "Golden Mile", with its pubs and entertainments, stretching out past the university, the Botanic Gardens and Ulster Museum. The River Lagan, dredged and sweet-smelling, flows down the east side of the city and offers riverside walks and an interpretative centre, the Lagan Lookout. The river is also the focus for the most radical development in the last few years, the Laganside. In the **east**, across the river beyond the great cranes of *Harland & Wolff*, lies suburbia and very little of interest apart from Stormont Castle, the former Northern Irish parliament. Working-class **West Belfast**, by contrast, seems almost a separate city in its own right, divided from the rest by the lanes of the Westlink motorway.

The city centre

Spreading out to the north from Donegall Square, Belfast's centre is fairly compact and easy to wander around. The heart of the old city can be found in the narrow atmospheric lanes of the once commercial district, the Entries, about five minutes' walk northwest of the square. On a grander scale, many of Belfast's most handsome buildings, which testify to the city's transformation during the industrial revolution, are concentrated further north and east, between the River Lagan and St Anne's Cathedral. Right by the river the latest tourist attraction is the Lagan Weir and interpretative centre. Part of an immense new development scheme, the centre explores the importance of the river to Belfast's Victorian expansion – and gives a glimpse into its future.

Donegall Square

Donegall Square – and Belfast city centre – are presided over by the **City Hall**, a handy landmark for visitors and principal departure point for city buses. It's a smug-looking building, quadrangular and squat, with bright white Portland stone; and its architecture echoes all the styles the British Empire borrowed from – turrets, saucer domes, scrolls and pinnacle pots. In the eighty-odd years since it was built, any functional civic purpose the building embodied has been secondary to its role in propagating the ethics of Presbyterian power. This is clear at the main entrance, where stands a statue of Queen Victoria, portrayed as Empress, her maternal gaze unerringly cast across the rooftops towards the Protestant Shankill area. At her feet, sculpted in bronze, are

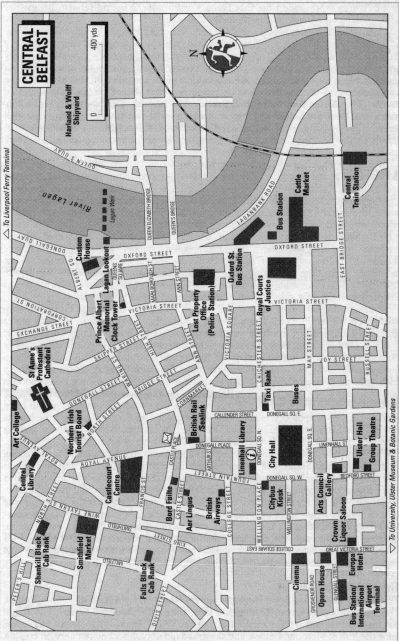

CENTRAL BELFAST

0   400 yds

N

To Liverpool Ferry Terminal

River Lagan

Lagan Weir

Harland & Wolff Shipyard

QUEEN'S QUAY

DONEGALL QUAY

ALBERT SQ.

Custom House

Lagan Lookout

OXFORD STREET

QUEENS SQUARE

MARLBOROUGH ST.

ANN STREET

QUEEN ELIZABETH BRIDGE

QUEEN'S BRIDGE

LAGANBANK ROAD

Bus Station

Cattle Market

Central Train Station

EAST BRIDGE STREET

OXFORD STREET

Oxford St. Bus Station

Royal Courts of Justice

VICTORIA SQUARE

VICTORIA STREET

Lost Property Office (Police Station)

Prince Albert Memorial Clock Tower

VICTORIA STREET

CORPORATION ST.

EXCHANGE STREET

CHICHESTER STREET

MAY STREET

JOY STREET

RUSSELL STREET

St Anne's Protestant Cathedral

DONEGALL STREET

SKIPPER STREET

WARING ST.

HIGH STREET

BRIDGE STREET

ANN ST.

CORNMARKET

Art College

ROYAL AVENUE

Northern Irish Tourist Board

NORTH STREET

British Rail /Sealink

Taxi Rank

Buses

CALLENDER STREET

DONEGALL SQ. E.

Central Library

Castlecourt Centre

WINE TAVERN ST.

NORTH ST.

ROYAL AVENUE

CASTLE PLACE

DONEGALL PLACE

ARTHUR ST.

Linenhall Library

DONEGALL SQ. N.

City Hall

DONEGALL SQ. S.

LINENHALL ST.

Ulster Hall

Group Theatre

BEDFORD STREET

Shankill Black Cab Rank

NORTH STREET

Smithfield Market

SMITHFIELD

FRANCIS ST.

Bord Fáilte

CASTLE STREET

Aer Lingus

British Airways

COLLEGE STREET

FOUNTAIN STREET

Citybus Kiosk

DONEGALL SQ. W.

Arts Council Gallery

WELLINGTON PLACE

WELLINGTON STREET

PETER'S HILL

MILLFIELD

Falls Black Cab Rank

KING STREET

DIVIS STREET

COLLEGE SQUARE EAST

Crown Liquor Saloon

GREAT VICTORIA STREET

Cinema

Opera House

GROSVENOR ROAD

GLENGALL STREET

Europa Hotel

Bus Station/ International Airport Terminal

To University, Ulster Museum & Botanic Gardens

proud figures representing the City Fathers' work ethic: a young scholar, his mother with spinning spool, and father with mallet and boat.

The City Hall does, however, offer the only real opportunity to be shown around one of Belfast's many Classical buildings, and there are 45-minute guided **tours** (July–Sept daily 10.30am & 2.30pm; rest of year Wed 10.30am; free); access is through a security entrance at the rear, opposite Linenhall Street. Inside, the **main dome**, and an unreachable whispering gallery, are 173ft above you – modelled on that of St Paul's in London; the dome has zodiac signs, both painted and in stained glass windows, around its rim. The marbled **entrance hall** itself is palatial, with staircase pillars and colonnades, and there are bronze and marble statues as well, two of which portray Frederick Robert Chichester, Earl of Belfast (1827–53): the first, upright and stalwart-looking, stands on the principal landing, while the other, Frederick reclining on his deathbed, has been hauled out of the rain into the Octagon entrance porch.

Also on the principal landing is a **mural**, executed in 1951 by John Luke, celebrating Belfast's traditional industries, now mostly dead – ropemaking, shipbuilding, weaving and spinning. Oddly though, the central position in the picture is given to the Town Crier, perhaps a reference to Belfast having the oldest continuously published newspaper in the world (*The Newsletter*, founded 1737). The tour also takes in the **robing room**, where the trick is to ask to try on one of the cloaks for a snapshot. The building's highlight is the **council chamber**, the walls wainscotted in hand-carved oak and its centre filled with councillors' pews and a visitors' gallery (open only on the first of the month), both also in oak. It's a very civilized scene (at least when the council is not in session – meetings are notoriously stormy), hung with portraits of British royalty and aristocracy; the seating puts the majority Unionists on the far side, with the rest of the parties on the near side, while the ever-present press sit in between.

At the northwest corner of Donegall Square stands the **Linenhall Library** (Mon–Wed & Fri 9.30am–5.30pm, Thurs 9.30am–8.30pm, Sat 9.30am–4pm), Belfast's oldest library, established in 1788. Irish language and reference books occupy the first floor; fiction is on the ground floor. The library contains probably the best collection of early Belfast printed books in the country. On the second floor, its "Political Collection" is a unique accumulation of over 80,000 publications dealing with every aspect of Northern Irish political life since 1966 – a range of literature that encompasses every election poster printed since then, as well as documents ranging from party political ephemera, doctoral theses sent in from all over the world, to prison letters smuggled out of Long Kesh. This radical approach is not a new departure for the Linenhall: one of the institution's librarians was Thomas Russell, executed in Downpatrick in 1803 for inciting rebellion in sympathy with Robert Emmett's 1798 uprising down south.

The library is an independent institution and you're free to examine its collection (tours daily except Sat): it has a fancy computerized catalogue, on the first floor; use is free, but a donation is welcome. There are also excellent facilities for tracing family trees, if you're interested, as well as all the daily newspapers and a good tea room.

Between the back of the City Hall and the BBC, on Alfred Street, look out for the turrets of the strange and wonderful Catholic **St Malachy's Church** (1844), the finest late-Georgian building in Belfast. The interior resembles nothing so much as an inverted wedding cake, and the fan-vaulted ceiling is modelled on that of Henry VII's chapel in Westminster Abbey. Other elaborate features are the canopied pulpit and carved marble altar – neither is original but both date from a 1926 restoration.

The commercial district

The streets leading north off Donegall Square North take you into downtown Belfast. The main shopping street, **Donegall Place**, runs from Donegall Square into **Royal Avenue** and houses familar chain-store names. Castle Place, off Donegall Place, was once the hub of Victorian Belfast, and the grand old department stores here, in creams, pinks and browns, have only recently been transformed into a flood of up-tempo shops. Mercifully, though, it's only the ground floors that have been converted, leaving the lofty grandeur of the floors above undisturbed. New structures, too, go up swiftly, but they at least tend to reflect the rhythm and sheer bulk of their nineteenth-century fore-bears. Much of this zone is pedestrianized (though buses go through), and nearly every conceivable shopping need can be supplied in this relatively small area.

The pedestrianized **Cornmarket**, marked by a cap-hooded bandstand painted red, is where the various cults gather: skinheads, punks, Mods and drunks, though most prev-alent are the religious chanteurs. This spot – or near enough to it – is where Henry Joy McCracken was hanged, after leading the Antrim rebels in the ill-fated (and in the North almost farcically unsuccessful) 1798 rebellion.

Nearby, along Ann Street, and off down any left or right turning, you're in among the narrow alleyways known as the **Entries**. There are some great old saloon **bars** down here, like *The Morning Star* in Pottinger's Entry, with its large frosted windows and Parisian café-like counter; *The Globe* in Joy's Entry; and *White's Tavern* in Winecellar Entry (off High Street), the oldest pub in the city. **Crown Entry** was where the "Society of United Irishmen" was born, led by the Protestant triumvirate of Wolfe Tone, McCracken and Samuel Nielson; Nielson printed his own newspaper in this area, the *Northern Star*, full of the French revolutionary ideals of liberty, equality and fraternity – inflammatory material which got him hounded out of town. Also in Crown Entry, Sheridan, the playwright (of *School for Scandal* fame) had his "pathetic" comic school.

Across the High Street, to the north, there used to be a similar set of Entries that ran through to Waring Street, but many of them were destroyed by bombing during World War II. Still, this end of the **High Street**, with the River Farset running underground, is the oldest part of the city, its atmosphere in places redolent of the eighteenth century. At the docks end of the High Street is the **Prince Albert Memorial Clock Tower**, built in 1867–69 and wilting slightly off the perpendicular. It's a strange memorial, especially as Prince Albert never had anything to do with Belfast, but it's a handy landmark. Beyond here are more of the grand old Classical-style buildings that stud Belfast.

The Custom House and the Lagan Lookout

North of the Albert Memorial are a series of grand edifices which grew out of a similar civic vanity as that invested in the designing of the City Hall. The recently restored **Custom House**, on Donegall Quay, is a Corinthian-style building designed – like most of the significant buildings of the period – by Charles Lanyon between 1854 and 1857, and laid out just behind the memorial in the shape of a letter E. Unfortunately, it's not open to the public, leaving you unable to verify stories of fantastic art masterpieces stored in its basements – though it is known that Anthony Trollope, the nineteenth-century novelist (and not-so-well-known inventor of the pillar box), once worked here as a surveyor's clerk.

Just beyond the Custom House on Donegall Quay is an ambitious new project – though one based on the city's prosperous industrial past – the **Laganside** development. The most obvious sign of change here, apart from the construction sites, is the new Lagan Weir which provides the city with flood protection. Millions of pounds have been pumped into dredging the river to revive the much depleted fish population – successfully it seems: there was salmon fishing on the weir's inauguration day – and to keep the water levels up. But there's much more to the project than just the weir. A housing scheme, partly completed, a vast conference and concert centre, called the Waterfront Centre, with room for over 2000 (due to be finished in late 1996), a new *Hilton* hotel, as well as the restoration of the Harbour Master's Office are all underway or already completed.

The **Lagan Lookout** (March–Sept Mon–Fri 11am–5pm, Sat noon–5pm, Sun 2–5pm; Oct–Feb Mon–Fri 11.30am–3.30pm, Sat 1–4pm, Sun 2–4.30pm; £1.50) is a small circular visitor centre which explains the weir project and explores why the river was crucial to the development of linen, shipbuilding – a glance across the Lagan to the *Harland & Wolff* shipyard confirms that the industry still survives – tobacco and ropemaking. Windows all round the centre match Belfast landmarks to explanations of their significance, and there are fascinating potted histories of local characters. **Cruises** of Belfast Lough also take off from the centre (Wed, Sat & Sun 3pm; £6, joint ticket to Lookout and cruise £7).

To St Anne's Cathedral

Walking back from Donegal Quay towards the cathedral past the Albert Clock and up Victoria Street, you'll soon hit Waring Street, where there's another of Charles Lanyon's designs, the **Belfast Banking Company** building of 1845 and now the *Northern Bank*. Originally containing eighteenth-century Assembly Rooms, the building was transformed by Lanyon into a palazzo-style remodelling of Barry's Reform Club in London. On the same street, you'll also stumble upon the **Ulster Bank** (1860), an indulgent Italianate building of rich yellow sandstone, fronted by a spate of fluted pillars and, up on the parapet, with decorated Grecian urns at the sides of an allegorical representation of war maidens. There's a surround of intricately wrought-iron railing and a few reassembled stubby but quaint Victorian street lamps, too.

The most monolithic of all these grand buildings, however, is the **Protestant Cathedral of St Anne's**, a neo-Romanesque basilica started in 1899. It's at the junction of Donegall Street and York Street, close to the beached buoys of the modern Art College. There's a glorious west door, but its overriding significance is that the body of **Lord Edward Henry Carson** is entombed underneath the nave floor. Carson (1854–1935) is a name that Ulster has never forgotten: the bodily symbol of Partition, he's seen either as the hero who saved Ulster or the villain who sabotaged the country's independence. A Dubliner of Scots-Presbyterian background, Carson took the decision in 1910 to accept the leadership of the opposition to Home Rule, which in effect inextricably allied him to the Ulster Unionist resistance movement – an association which is about the only thing for which he is remembered. Yet his personality and integrity went far deeper than this. He abhorred religious intolerance, and behind the exterior of a zealous crusader he sincerely believed that Ireland couldn't prosper without Britain and only wished that a federalist answer could have involved a united Ireland. Nonetheless, this was the same man who, as a brilliant orator at the bar, and in the role he loved the most, brought about the humiliating destruction of Oscar Wilde at his trial in 1895.

Clifton House

As it continues north, Donegall Street becomes Clifton Street, which takes its name from **Clifton House** (built 1771–74). Better known as the "Poor House", or the "Charitable Institute for the Aged and Infirm", it's in handsome Georgian style, of pedimented brick with an octagonal-based stone spire at its rear and symmetrically projecting wings to its sides. This is one of the simpler but more effective buildings that Belfast has to offer, yet was designed by an amateur architect and local paper merchant, Robert Joy, uncle of the hapless Henry Joy McCracken. The Institute was built at a time of much poverty and unrest, brought about by the Donegalls' eviction of tenants when their leases started running out – the very same Donegalls whose name is tagged to so many of Belfast's streets.

East Belfast

The Lagan Lookout (see p.465) is a good position from which to view the world's second and third largest cranes, *Goliath* and *Samson*, across the river in **East Belfast's**

Harland & Wolff shipyard. This is the city's proudest international asset: the ill-fated *Titanic* was built here, and the **shipyard** is nowadays said to possess the largest dry dock in the world – over 600yds long and 100yds wide. Unfortunately, the area is very security conscious, as its workforce has always been predominantly Protestant, and access is impossible without making a formal application.

In fact, there's virtually no reason to cross the river into **East Belfast** at all. **Van Morrison** fans might get a thrill from seeking out the many streets that feature in his songs, and there are a couple of pleasant **parks**, but few more concrete reasons to come.

Stormont, the former home of the Northern Ireland assembly, is also east of the city, off the Newtownards road (#16 or #17 bus from Donegall Square). You can't visit the house itself – which is now occupied by civil servants – but it's an impressive sight, a great white Neoclassical mansion crowning a rise in the middle of a park at the end of a magnificent long, straight drive. You can wander freely in the **grounds**, a popular place for a walk; also here, though obviously not open to the public, is **Stormont Castle**, the office of the Northern Ireland Secretary.

South Belfast

The university area occupies part of the stretch of **South Belfast** now known as "The Golden Mile", starting at the Opera House on Great Victoria Street and reaching past the university, up into the Malone, Lisburn and Stranmillis roads. It's an area in which you're likely to find yourself spending much of your time, since it's littered with eating places, pubs and bars, B&Bs and guesthouses. Dozens of restaurants have sprung up here in the last few years, the gourmet explosion said to have been triggered by the refurbishment of the grandiose, turn-of-the-century **Grand Opera House** in 1980. In December 1991, a bomb in the adjacent *Europa Hotel* cause extensive damage to the Opera House, but both establishments are now up and running again.

The Golden Mile

Among the welter of attractions on the Golden Mile is one of the greatest of Victorian **gin palaces**, the *Crown Liquor Saloon*, now a National Trust property but still open for drinking. The saloon has a glittering tiled exterior – amber, carmine, rouge, yellow, green, blue and smoke-grey – resembling a spa baths more than a serious drinking institution. The rich, High Victorian stuccowork continues inside, too: the scrolled ceiling, patterned floor and the golden-yellow and rosy-red hues led John Betjeman to describe it as his "many coloured cavern". With your drinks, grab a snug and shut the door (best to avoid the busy lunchtime and mid-evening periods): it's like sitting in a railway carriage compartment, with snatches of conversation creeping over from the neighbouring snugs. There's no let-up in decoration in here either, the mirrors painted, the oak panelling sporting flourishes of friezework (like the heraldic beasts guarding each snug entry) and the mounted gun-metal plates provided for striking matches. The push-button bell activates an indicator on a board above the bar, though it's just as much an experience to order at the bar from the white-aproned and black-bowtied staff – the bar counter a gorgeous S-curve of tile work, with exotically carved timber dividing screens.

The **Golden Mile** itself buzzes with activity in the evening, even on a weekday as long as it's in term time. As a rule, the cheaper restaurants are at the city end of Great Victoria Street, with the more expensive ones up the Stranmillis Road or in and around the skirts of the BBC in Bedford Street. There's a plethora of accommodation, too, in amongst the grid pattern of the broad, tree-lined streets surrounding the university campus, much of it in the old three-storey Victorian homes. The area also has an antiquarian **bookshop** on Dublin Road, Roma Ryan's *Books and Prints*, which has some interesting Irish material, though the prices are not giveaways by anyone's standards; and also a few second-hand bookshops, including *Bookfinders* at 47 University Road (Mon–Sat 10am–5.30pm, Thurs until 7pm).

Sandy Row

Before heading straight into the university quarter, sidestep off Great Victoria Street into **Sandy Row**, which runs parallel. A strong working-class, Protestant quarter with the tribal pavement painting to prove it, it's one of the most glaring examples of Belfast's divided worlds, wildly different from the Golden Mile's cosmopolitan sophistication, yet only yards away. In Donegall Road, off to the west, are some of the murals which characterize these sectarian areas (see under "West Belfast", p.470). Sandy Row used to be the main road south, and although hard to credit today, it was once a picturesque shoelace stretch of whitewashed cottages.

The university area

Back on the Golden Mile, and just past the southern end of Sandy Row, are three churches (Moravian, Crescent and Methodist) whose distinctive steeples frame the entrance into the **university quarter**. It's a highly characteristic area, many of the terraces leading up to the university buildings representing the final flowering of Georgian architecture in Belfast. The **Upper Crescent** is a magnificent curved Neoclassical terrace, built around 1845 but sadly neglected since, and now used mainly for office space. The **Lower Crescent**, perversely, is straight.

It's **Queen's University**, though, that's the architectural centrepiece, flanked by the most satisfying example of a Georgian terrace in Belfast, University Square, where the red brickwork has mostly been kept intact, with the exception of a few bay windows put in by the Victorians. The terrace now houses various faculty buildings. The **Union Theological College** on College Park, which was temporarily the site of the Northern Ireland assembly until Stormont was built in 1932, closes off the vista between the terrace and the university. Not surprisingly, given its Italianate lines, this is another Lanyon design, as is University College itself, built in 1849 as a mock-Tudor remodelling of Magdalen College, Oxford. Across the road from here is the Students' Union, a white 1960s design. The university **bookshop**, the *Bookshop at Queen's*, where Malone Road meets Stranmillis Road, is especially good for Irish history and politics and, oddly enough, for its collection of Beat poetry.

Botanic Gardens and Ulster Museum

Just to the side of the university are the **Botanic Gardens**, first opened in 1827 and deservedly the most popular of Belfast's gardens – compact, with walks well sheltered from the noise of surrounding traffic. Within the gardens is the **Palm House** (April–Sept Mon–Fri 10am–noon & 1–5pm, Sat & Sun 2–5pm; Oct–March closes 4pm; free), a hot-house predating the famous one at Kew Gardens in London, but very similar in style, with a white-painted framework of curvilinear ironwork and glass. It was the first of its kind in the world, another success for Lanyon who on this project worked in tandem with the Dublin iron-founder Richard Turner.

Also in the Botanic Gardens you'll find the **Ulster Museum** (Mon–Fri 10am–5pm, Sat 1–5pm, Sun 2–5pm; free but admission charged to special exhibitions; buses #69, #70 & #71), re-sited here in 1929 and expanded in 1972 with a concrete extension that matches the Portland stone surprisingly subtly. You'll need a fair bit of stamina to get round the museum, since it's a monster of a collection. Displays run from a dinosaur show through reproductions of early Irish Christian jewellery to the history of the post office in Ireland, waterwheels and steam engines, local archeological finds, Irish wildlife, rocks, fossils and minerals – the list is exhaustive and exhausting. Still, everything is well explained and well laid out, and if you're keen to know about crocodiles' digestive systems or see a 35-million-year-old mackerel, then you could happily spend a full day here – though if you have the time, the museum is much more enjoyable taken in several small doses.

The various **art collections** are excellent: try the top floor for modern work by Francis Bacon or Henry Moore and, best of all (and the one thing you won't see elsewhere), the Irish artists represented – Louis le Brocquy, Paul Henry and Belfast's own most acclaimed painter, Sir John Lavery. The museum's showpiece is the **Girona exhibition**, treasures from the Spanish Armada ships which foundered off the Giant's Causeway in 1588, salvaged by divers in the 1960s.

Further south: the river and Giant's Ring

To go beyond the university area is to head through the glades of middle-class suburbia – an area that is singularly uninteresting. However, a ten- to fifteen-minute walk south on Stranmillis Road (*struthán milis*, sweet stream), turning left onto Lockview Road, will take you back to the river and to the start of the **Lagan Towpath** – where the *Cutter's Wharf* draws thirsty crowds for Sunday lunch and jazz – from here follow the signs to the Lagan Meadows. The newly tarmacked towpath can be tramped for about eight miles south to Lisburn, passing old locks and lock-houses, rapids, woodland and marshes. The waterway opened in the late 1790s, ready to carry the newly discovered coal from Lough Neagh, but its utility declined with the advent of the railway in 1839. Today, it's been harnessed as part of the Ulster Way, for rambling and canoeing enthusiasts. Travelling south further towards the affluent Malone Road area, you'll find the internationally renowned **Mary Peters Track**, part of the Malone Playing Fields, which is just off the Upper Malone Road. Set in what amounts to a natural amphitheatre, with the Castlereagh Hills in the distance, the track, established by Olympic gold medallist Mary Peters, is on the European Grand Prix Athletics Circuit.

Less of a walk, but just as interesting, is to head a couple of miles south along the same route past the Lagan Meadows, and along the river path to Shaw's Bridge; from here take the country road, following signs to Edenderry, then along Ballysillan Road, and lastly take a right turn up Giant's Ring Road. Here, the **Giant's Ring** is a gargantuan ceremonial burial ground or meeting place, its grassy interior the size of three football pitches, contained by a twenty-foot-high circular earthen rim. You wouldn't be far wrong to think that its inwardly sloping wall would make an excellent speed-track circuit, for in the eighteenth century it was used for horse racing – six circuits making a two-mile race, with the punters jostling for position on the rampart's top. Most captivating of all is the huge dolmen left at the central hub of this cartwheel structure. As a single megalithic remain, it is immediately more impressive even than the great structures of the Irish High Kings at Tara, though here there's little information concerning its origins and usage. The ground chosen for the site, high above the surrounding lowlands (probably once marshy lake), is an impressive one: there's a powerful feeling that the great dramas and decision-making of the ancient northeast must have been played out here. If you want to do the walk in just one direction, *Ulsterbus* #22 passes below the site three times a day.

North Belfast

North Belfast's attractions amount to no more than a castle and the city's **zoo**, both out on the Antrim Road and conveniently next door to one another on the slopes of Cave Hill. In truth, though, it's **Cave Hill** itself that should be your real target.

Several paths lead up from the castle estate to the hill's summit – a rocky outcrop known as "Napoleon's Nose" – where there's an unsurpassable strategic overview of the whole city and lough. From here you can't help but appreciate the accuracy of the poet Craig Raine's aerial description of the city in his *Flying to Belfast*: like "a radio set with its back ripped off". Cave Hill was once awash with Iron Age forts, for there was flint (for weapon-making) in the chalk under the basalt hill-coverings. In 1795, Wolfe Tone, Henry Joy McCracken and other leaders of the United Irishmen stood on the top of Cave Hill and pledged "never to desist in our efforts until we have subverted the authority of England over our country and asserted our Independence".

Belfast Castle and its wooded estate are open to the public, recently upholstered and restored but, sadly, virtually empty of period accoutrements – the one exception is the recently reopened basement kitchen. It stands on the former deer park of the Third Marquis of Donegall, whose wish it was for the sandstone castle to be built here to the designs of Lanyon and his associates, in 1870. Consequently, the exterior is in the familiar Scottish Baronial style, inspired in part by the reconstruction of Balmoral Castle in Aberdeenshire in 1853: six-storey tower, a series of crow-stepped gables and conically peak-capped turrets. The most striking feature of all, however, is the serpentine Italianate stairway that leads down from the principal reception room to the garden terrace below. Upstairs a modest **visitor centre** (Mon–Sat 9am–10.30pm, Sun 9am–6pm) is best visited for a look through its remote-control camera on the roof.

Belfast Zoo

Adjoining Belfast Castle is the Bellevue Estate, the old pleasure gardens laid out by the *Belfast Street Tramway Company*, but functioning since 1934 as **Belfast Zoo** (April–Sept daily 10am–5pm; Sept–April 10am–3.30pm, Fri closed 2.30pm; buses #2, #3, #4, #5 & #6). After a fifteen-year renovation programme and an investment of £10 million the zoo is looking less like an animal prison. Set in well-landscaped parkland stretching up towards Cave Hill, the zoo offers penguins hatched out of eggs from the Falkland Islands, Malayan tapirs, sea lions, and a new bird house, where rare species have room to breed.

West Belfast

West Belfast has always been the city's working-class area. Here, in the eighteenth century, the flax and linen mills were established which in turn produced the relentless, gridded street pattern, lined with housing for the workers and their families. The overcrowded conditions were deplorable, and the sectarian riots of 1886 – the worst of the nineteenth century – inspired the creation of two separate neighbourhoods, Catholic and Protestant. In 1968 and 1969, this division was pushed to its limit when sectarian mobs and gunmen evicted over 8000 families from their homes in the city, mainly in Catholic West Belfast.

Today, however, West Belfast is no Beirut. It's as safe an urban area as any for the stranger to stroll around, and although it's principally residential, several of its sectors are worth investigating. Of most interest are the partisan **mural paintings** seen in both Catholic and Protestant areas, an ephemeral artform with new murals painted over old ones or the houses they're painted on demolished (many of the slogans and murals mentioned here may have gone by the time of your visit). As you wander the back streets, you'll be captivated (sometimes captured) by the extraordinarily open friendliness of the people, an experience that's the high point of many people's stay in Belfast: you'll not come across this openness in any other part of the city, more remarkable here given the rigours of life in West Belfast.

The busy **Westlink motorway** that effectively separates West Belfast from the rest of the city, linking motorways 1 and 2, seems innocent enough as it sweeps across the city, but there are those who see it in a more sinister light, as part of the security process. Certainly it has been handy for the police and army, allowing them to restrict east–west access to a handful of the main arteries. These points, overhead bridges and roundabouts, have acted as virtual border crossings, easily sealed and easily monitored.

The Falls

Two routes lead into the heart of the **Falls** area (known as Andersonstown): one along Grosvenor Road, the other through Divis Street. The latter is the more infamous and is also the route that carries the main injection of black taxi-cab traffic into the area (see "City transport", p.458). The taxis assemble in ranks at the end of Castle Street, in the Smithfield area; the drivers, incidentally, are said to be Republican ex-prisoners.

Smithfield itself used to have a large covered bazaar that has now been replaced by **Smithfield Retail Market** – actually a set of small shop units rather than a traditional open-air market. The area has undergone large-scale redevelopment by private developers (another shopping complex). There is a reminder of the old character of the area in Winetavern Street, with several bookshops and junky antique places.

THE FALLS ROAD

Moving on, you enter the **Falls Road** proper, which continues for a further two miles out past Milltown Cemetery (see below) and into Andersonstown. There's a life and activity along this route the like of which you'll find nowhere else in Belfast, with the possible exception of the Shankill Road – shared taxis being flagged down, the odd collection of loitering males, and children and prams being pushed through the streets. Most of the interest is concentrated in the **Lower Falls** (which is the area you've now entered), the road's left-hand side flattened and rebuilt with redbrick terraced estates of two-up and two-downs. The right side of the road is more of a hotchpotch, taking in the bright blue swimming baths (target of an IRA bomb in 1988 that killed two Catholic civilians), the DSS (the Department of Social Security, known as "the Brew") cooped up in an awning of chicken wire, a weary-looking Victorian library and a *Worshippers of Peace* convent.

By now, you'll have noticed the blockade of iron sheeting which divides the streets. Called the **"Peace Line"**, it has the Protestant working class living directly on the other side. Down one of these streets, Conway Street (by the DSS), stands the old Conway Mill, recently revitalized by a concerted community effort, spearheaded by community activist Father Des Wilson. Inside you can buy the wares of the few small businesses that operate out of here.

Further on you'll pass the redbrick buildings of the **Royal Victoria Hospital**, on the left as you head towards Andersonstown. Since the Troubles began, the Royal, as it's known locally, has been internationally acclaimed for its ability to cope with the consequences. Just beyond the Royal in a disued Presbyterian church, at 216 Falls Road, is the **Cultúrlann MacAdam O'Fiaich**, a cultural centre for Irish speakers, founded in 1991 and housing bookshop, café, school and theatre. The Irish language is thriving in Catholic areas of Belfast and throughout the North; the first Irish-speaking primary school is over twenty years old, and the first secondary school was opened in 1991. A year earlier, the *Ultach Trust* was set up, a group that aims to broaden the appeal of Irish among Unionists. Although you are unlikely to hear any Irish being spoken on the streets or in most pubs, the language has a growing presence in the city.

There's little to see beyond here, although a few hundred yards further down the Falls Road, on the left across a small rubble patch, is one of the more powerfully evocative of the murals; it commemorates the 150th anniversary of the Great Famine in Ireland.

MILLTOWN CEMETERY

Follow the road on for another mile and it'll lead to **Milltown Cemetery**, recognizable by the army encampment opposite the entrance. A peaceful place, it's significant as the main Republican burial ground in Belfast – and was also the site of grenade-throwing and shooting in 1988 at the funeral of Seán Savage, one of the IRA members (along with Mairead Farrell and Danny McCann) killed by the SAS in Gibraltar. Enter through the stone arch and you're immediately surrounded by a numbing array of Celtic and Classical crosses. If you're in search of the Republican plots, continue directly on from the entrance for about a hundred yards, then veer right, heading towards a corrugated warehouse shed just outside the perimeter of the cemetery. Along the way are two plots, marked off by a low green border fence. The nearer one holds a large memorial tablet listing the Republican casualties in the various uprisings from 1798 to the present day. The far plot contains a modern granite-block sculpture, and also the graves of Bobby Sands, Mairead Farrell, Seán Savage and others. Once you start to look, it's not difficult to spot the graves of many other victims of the Troubles, a devastatingly long list of (usually young) men and women. The M1 motorway lies below, at the bottom of the burial park: it was onto this stretch of road that Michael Stone, the Loyalist attacker, was pursued after he'd opened fire at the funeral of Seán Savage.

The Ballymurphy murals

Although the first **Republican murals** weren't painted until 1981 – in an effort to draw support for the ten prisoners who died on hunger strike in their campaign for political status – they soon became a fundamental part of the Republican propaganda campaign and an expression of the community's current cultural and political concerns, such as elections, British Army and RUC actions, community resistance and media censorship. In recent years there have been a number of new murals depicting famine scenes in commemoration of the 150th anniversary of the 1845–49 Famine.

Borrowing images and ideas, many muralists have related the Republican struggle to that of armed groups elsewhere – Nicaragua, Namibia, South Africa and Palestine. With these varied sources of reference and the Republican imagination being driven by ideas of change for the future – their slogan is *"tiocfaidh ár lá"* (our day will come) – Republican muralists have produced works of art highly regarded in the community and outside, so much so that a competition is held every year to elect the best of that year's crop. **Gerry Kelly**, known as "Macalla", who won the first prize in 1988, has been responsible for many of the best Republican murals, and you can see some fine examples of his work in an area that is known for wall painting, the **Ballymurphy Estate** up behind the Falls Road. Recently the estate has been redeveloped, and the gable ends of the new houses offer convenient new canvases for mural painters. Of Kelly's murals, one of the most impressive is a 40ft wide by 16ft high piece on the release of prisoners (carried out with the help of painter Spud Murphy). It depicts a prisoner in the foreground standing out against an image of Long Kesh, with two female prisoners on either side and the symbol of **Saoirse** (freedom) to the left. To get there, turn right off the Falls Road up Whiterock Road, passing alongside the City Cemetery wall and its slogans ("He is not your son but what if he was" and "The West has the best – Vote Sinn Féin"). Once over the brow of the hill, take the next right into Ballymurphy Road, heading towards Springhill Avenue.

Other main areas where you can find Republican murals are on the Falls Road itself, Beechmount Avenue, Donegall Road, Shaw's Road and Lenadoon Avenue in West Belfast, and New Lodge Road and Ardoyne in North Belfast.

Shankill and Crumlin roads

The Protestant areas of West Belfast receive much less attention from visitors, yet they're no less interesting – and no less deprived in terms of unrest and economic misfortune. Suffering in West Belfast operates more on a class scale than a sectarian one. For the outsider, this area is particularly rich in murals. In conception and technique the tradition of **Loyalist mural painting**, which began in Belfast in 1908, is markedly different from the Republican one. Inspired by the desire for "no surrender" and preservation of the status quo, Loyalist mural painting is certainly less dynamic and diverse, using simpler, more symmetrical images and less complex symbolism. Until the 1970s, the most common image was of King Billy on his white horse at the Battle of the Boyne; painted and repainted each July, it held pride of place in the annual celebrations. With the onset of the Troubles, many of the old certainties of Unionism were undermined, and the Loyalist mural tradition changed direction. Fewer walls were painted and in place of King Billy inanimate symbols appeared, such as flags and the Red Hand of Ulster. By the end of the 1980s, with an upsurge in Loyalist paramilitary activity the images became increasingly militaristic and continue to be so – even after the Loyalist ceasefire of 1994.

The greatest concentration of Loyalist murals are to be found on and around the Shankill Road; other areas are Sandy Row and Donegall Pass in South Belfast, and Newtownards Road and Severn Street in East Belfast. If you want to see them, you can take one of the shared cabs from the top of North Street (see "City transport", p.458).

SHANKILL ROAD

Crossing the Westlink into the **Shankill Road** (*sean chill*, the old church), a little way up on the left is a typical Ulster Volunteer Force mural, its centrepiece the outline of the six counties, without the rest of Ireland. At either side of the province stand two paramilitaries, one a 1912 Ulster Volunteer Defender in "home guard" attire, the other a contemporary Loyalist in all-black body and head gear. Accompanying them is the slogan "They fought then for the cause of Ulster. We will fight now." An alleyway on the right here will lead you into the **Shankill Estate**. Almost immediately you'll find yourself in the midst of the greatest concentration of wall paintings around (there are more in Percy Place, nearby). One mural depicts a thin William of Orange on his white horse; others show flag waving, the emotive expression of Loyalism as a creed. Slogans abound – "One faith, one Crown; Ulster Scotland, United we stand"; and there are many more which need no explanation, often executed in red, white and blue.

CRUMLIN ROAD

The **Crumlin Road** also offers several gable walls for mural musing. Most are faded, but there's a prominent set at Queen's Land Street, with a particularly unusual one in which shamrocks and the harp (traditional emblems of the Free State) are depicted alongside the red hand of Ulster. Others on the street depict the Star of David, possibly a statement of solidarity with Israel against the PLO and hence the IRA – the PLO/IRA link is tacitly acknowledged by all.

Heading back towards the city you'll pass an army encampment, set back from the road, with a tentacled iron sheeting corridor and lookout post. Further down, you pass between the courthouse and the notorious Crumlin Road jail, with their underground connecting tunnel.

Donegall Road

Other Loyalist murals can be seen along the **Donegall Road**, west off Sandy Row. As you cross the railway bridge approaching the Westlink you'll catch sight of a very large wall painting on the gable end of Roden Street; it can be seen clearly from Donegall Road itself. It bears the mottoes "Quis Separabit" and "In memory of John McMichael", with the abbreviated initials of four of the organizations under his command: the UFF, UDF, LPA and DSD. McMichael was killed in December 1987 by a bomb placed under his car. As well as being a leading member of the UDA he was responsible for forming its political wing, the Ulster Loyalist Democratic Party, and for formulating the UDA document "Common Sense". The Protestant Donegall Road ends at this intersection, and the same road continues on the other side as the Catholic Sraid Dun Na nGall – the only road in West Belfast that the communities can really be said to share.

Cafés and restaurants

In the last few years, eating out in Belfast has become a much more fashionable pursuit – restaurants are no longer unofficial late-night spots, allowing eaters (and talkers) to nurse bottles of wine into the early morning – **café society** has arrived, with a rash of chic eateries to choose from, mostly in the city centre. Although the range of cuisines is still relatively small, you'll find all the usual favourites – French, Italian, Indian and Chinese – and standards are generally good. Vegetarians or those in search of wholefood restaurants will find the choice is limited, though more restaurants now include vegetarian dishes on their menu.

There are plenty of places for daytime eating in the centre, from the new cafés to traditional pubs (many of the latter serve excellent lunches, see opposite), and along the Golden Mile; most of the city's well-established restaurants are south of the centre from the Golden Mile outwards.

Centre

Bananas, 4 Clarence St (☎501232 or ☎244844). Bright and breezy with – for Belfast – a fair-sized vegetarian menu.

Bonne Bouche, 19 Fountain St. At this breakfast place, you'll be stuffed with bacon, eggs, sausage, tomatoes, potato bread, soda bread and pancakes – all for around £3.

Café Equinox, 32 Howard St. One of the new bloom of café society hang-outs, at the back of *Equinox* interiors shop. As you'd expect, it looks good with food to match.

Café Renoir, 5 Queen St. Unpretentious self-service café with excellent and oversized wholefood dishes.

Café Roscoff, 27–29 Fountain Place. Modernist interior, gourmet coffees and, best of all, the Mediterranean breads *Roscoff's* restaurant (see opposite) is known for. A place to be seen.

Nick's Warehouse, 35 Hill St (☎439690). Atmospheric wine bar and cheap menu downstairs, chic and pricier restaurant upstairs.

Spice of Life, 62 Lower Donegall St, opposite St Anne's Cathedral (☎332744). Good vegetarian fare in what claims to be Belfast's only wholefood restaurant.

The Upper Crust, 15 Lombard St. Salad bar, guaranteed to be packed with shoppers and office workers at lunchtime.

Golden Mile and the University

Ashoka, 363 Lisburn Rd (☎660362). Excellent Indian restaurant, about £10–15 a head.

La Belle Epoque, 61 Dublin Rd (☎323244). Fancy, expensive French restaurant.

La Boheme, 103 Great Victoria St (☎240666). Cheerful bistro to try if sister restaurant, *La Belle Epoque*, is full.

Bonnie's Museum Café, 11a Stranmillis Rd (☎664714). Opposite the Ulster Museum with interesting cheapish menu in the artist Willie Conor's former studio. Good for brunch.

Bookfinders, 47 University Rd (☎328269). Second-hand bookshop serving healthy lunches in the back.

Chez Delbart, also known as *Frogities*, 10 Bradbury Place, off Great Victoria St (☎238020). Vast quantities at unbeatable prices, though you often have to queue. Serves wine or bring your own bottle (there's a shop across the road) for £1 corkage.

Friar's Bush, 159 Stranmillis Rd (☎669824). A bit of a walk, but excellent four-course meals – of the pork and cider variety – including wine for good prices.

Harvey's Pizzas, 95 Great Victoria St (☎233433). Popular pizza joint.

Manhattan, 23 Bradbury Place (☎233131). Young and trendy burger bar with live music upstairs.

The Other Place, Stranmillis Rd. Great breakfast and brunch place – large helpings and free refills.

Queen's Espresso, 17 Botanic Ave (☎325327). Good coffee and sophisticated snacks.

Rajput, 461 Lisburn Rd (☎662168). Further out, but handy to B&Bs. A good Indian restaurant at about £10 per head.

Roscoff's, 7 Lesley House, Shaftesbury Square (☎331532). Thought by some to be the best restaurant in Ireland, but expensive. Book ahead.

Saints and Scholars, 3 University St (☎325137). A cheapish and cheerful student place, with a good vegetarian menu.

Speranza, 16 Shaftesbury Square (☎230213). Massively popular Italian restaurant; three courses for under £10; expect to queue.

Students' Union Cafeteria, second and third floors of the Union building, lunchtime only. Adequate and cheap.

Sun Kee, 38 Donegall Pass (☎312016). No-frills decor, but superb adventurous Chinese restaurant. BYOB.

Villa Italia, 39 University Rd (☎328365). Queues outside are the best indicator of the quality of this cheapo Italian's menu.

Pubs, nightlife and entertainment

Belfast used to operate as a city under curfew, and unless you were a native, it was difficult to track down just where the best pubs, clubs and music were to be found. Now new bars and clubs are beginning to appear and there's a more open and vibrant atmosphere to the city at night – although remember that on Sunday nothing much happens in the city centre, and even on weekdays it empties pretty early. To tap into the pulse of the city, your best bet is to wander down the **Golden Mile**, where there is an abundance of pubs and clubs to choose from. For the latest information on what's going on in the city, the *Belfast Telegraph's* listings freesheet *That's Entertainment* and the tourist board monthly freebie *Artslink* have details of just about everything.

As always in Ireland the **pubs** are where you'll tap the heart of the city. The liveliest ones are on Great Victoria Street or down around the university, and if you start drinking at the *Crown* you can do a substantial pub crawl without moving more than about 100 yards from where you started.

The best entertainment you'll find in Belfast is **music** in the pubs. The music on offer ranges from good traditional and folk to blues, jazz and indie music. Although there is no music industry infrastructure in Northern Ireland, there are loads of good up-and-coming bands playing in the city waiting to get noticed. Classical music concerts are thin on the ground and almost entirely performed in the Ulster Hall; although this is soon set to change when the new concert hall the Waterfront Hall – part of the Laganside development – is completed in late 1996. Some of the main sessions and venues are listed below, but you should look out for posters or check the listings freebies.

Belfast's **club scene** is thriving; rave is big, so are celebrity DJs. Check *That's Entertainment* for who's on when; you'll find most clubs run different sounds on different nights. Clubs are scattered fairly evenly around the city centre; students – not surprisingly – tend to dominate those closest to the University area.

Most of the **theatres** and **cinemas** are concentrated in the south of the city; although the choice for both is relatively limited, there is enough of a range to please most tastes. Recently, the city has seen a rapid expansion in the number of **art galleries**, and there's now an interesting selection to choose from, showing the best of modern and contemporary Irish art.

Drinking: pubs and bars

The Beaten Docket, 48 Great Victoria St, just below the *Crown*. Packed with fashion-conscious youngsters upstairs and down. Very loud music.

The Botanic Inn, 23 Malone Rd, opposite the "Egg". Perhaps inevitably, known as the "Bot". Again almost entirely students, and plenty of atmosphere. The place to go before you head into *Wellington Park Hotel* next door.

The Britannic Lounge, 46 Amelia St, above the *Crown's* side entrance. Sedate, cosy and faintly exclusive (and more expensive than usual), this place even has a uniformed foyer attendant, plus some interesting *Harland & Wolff* pictures and memorabilia, including items from the *Britannic* liner itself, the sister ship of the *Titanic*.

Cratchets, 38 Lisburn Rd at the corner of Camden St, near the university. Another trendy crowd.

The Crown Liquor Saloon, 46 Great Victoria St, opposite the *Europa Hotel*. The most famous and spectacular pub in Belfast with a clientele that thinks itself intellectual (there's no music). Good repertory of Ulster food – champ, colcannon etc – and also Strangford oysters in season, usually gone by early afternoon.

The Eglantine Inn, 332 Malone Rd. Known to the students who pack it out as the "Egg". Very crowded, with a disco bar upstairs for the smart casual set.

The Empire, 42 Botanic Ave, just up from the station. Cellar bar in a former church with a boisterous beer-hall atmosphere. Good-value food.

Lavery's Gin Palace, 12 Bradbury Place. Snazzy outside but a regular pub within, with a student and local crowd. Popular, though for no apparently special reason.

Morning Star, 17 Pottinger's Entry. Fine old-fashioned bar, busy in the day, quiet at night. Other good bars in the Entries include *The Globe* (Joy's Entry), *White's Tavern* (Winecellar Entry) and the *Kitchen Bar* (Victoria Square). The latter offers great lunches – pizza on a soda bread base – and probably possesses the smallest urinal in the world.

Morrison's Spirit Grocers, 21 Bedford St, city centre. Another retro pub; go mid-afternoon to sip fruit vodkas and marvel at the hand-painted faux nicotine ceiling.

Robinson's, 38 Great Victoria St. Newish but naff theme bar spread over four floors and overshadowed by the *Crown* next door – a good bet for a seat.

Students' Union, University Rd. Basement bar and first-floor "speakeasy" with lots of heavy student drinking, but good-natured and cheap. You're really meant to be a student to drink here, but no one seems to mind.

Music: pubs and bars

The Bridge Bar, off Queen St. Live bands on Fri and Sat nights.

The Duke of York, Commercial Court (☎241062), off Donegal St. Music most nights. Northern bands on Sat.

The Elms, University Rd (☎322106). Live music/disco on Thurs–Sat nights.

Errigle Inn, 320 Ormeau Rd (☎641410). Live music on Thurs–Sun nights.

The Fly, Lower Crescent. Folk music every Thurs night, DJs on Tues, Fri & Sat; good atmosphere.

The Front Page, Donegall St, upstairs from *McElhatton's* (☎324924). Packed with journalists from the nearby *Belfast Telegraph* and *Irish News* during the day; there's live music most nights.

Katy Daly's, Ormeau Ave. Thurs folk sessions; Sat traditional.

Kelly's Cellars, 30 Bank St (☎324835). According to legend a frequent meeting place for the United Irishmen behind the doomed 1798 rebellion – Henry Joy McCracken hid under the bar counter from British soldiers. Good lunches (thumping portions of home-made Irish stew and steak pie). Folk music on Sat afternoons, blues on Sat nights.

Limelight, 17 Ormeau Ave, near the BBC. Bands on Mon, Wed & Thurs nights; also see "Clubs and discos" opposite.

The Liverpool, Donegall Quay, virtually opposite the Liverpool ferries. Small, two-roomed place with a pool table. Friendly and handy if you're waiting for the boat. Traditional sessions on Sun evenings and some Sats.

Maddens, 74 Smithfield (☎244114). Wonderful, unpretentious, atmospheric pub. Lots of locals drinking in two large rooms, one upstairs, one downstairs. Serves cheap stew and soup. Excellent traditional sessions (Mon, Wed & Sat afternoons and evenings); sometimes as many as twenty musicians with music going on upstairs and downstairs at the same time.

Pat's Bar, Prince's Dock Rd, in the north of the city by the docks, off York Rd, easiest reached by taxi (☎744524). Recently renovated in traditional style, with a choice of two bars (one large, one small) and open fires. Sessions irregular but great when they happen.

Thompson's Garage, Arthur St (☎323762). Once a garage owned by aviation freak Harry Ferguson – an addiction commemorated with a mural of an airplane in mid-flight; new local bands play most weeks in this city-centre bar.

The Warehouse, Pilot St, in the docks near *Pat's* (☎746021). No-frills bar and large venue, with music most nights, ranging from indie and jazz to traditional and folk. First class.

Other music venues

King's Hall, Balmoral (☎665225). The biggest pop and rock gigs are staged here.

Students' Union, University Rd. Officially you must show a student pass or get a Queen's student to sign you in, though pleading may work. Folk evening in the upstairs bar on Thurs. Riotous atmosphere and great fun: plenty of mock *ceili* swinging goes on because none of them knows how to do it properly.

Ulster Hall, Bedford St (☎323900). Most of the city's classical music performances are given by the Ulster Orchestra; the hall is also used for big rock and pop concerts.

Whitla Hall, Queen's University (☎245133). Stages some professional and amateur classical concerts.

Clubs and discos

Crescent Bar, Sandy Row (☎320911). In heartland of working-class Protestant area, very popular with students. Different DJs on each night, Wed–Sat.

The Edge, York St. Tiny; bills itself as the club for clubbers.

Giros, Donegall St. For Goths, try Fri nights.

Limelight, 17 Ormeau Ave. A serious dance club.

Manhattan, Bradbury Place (☎233131). Every night but Sun on three floors, a good light show and very popular but sneered at by hardcore ravers.

Sanctuary of Sound, Patterson's Place. Full-on dance music and one to dress up for; Thurs–Sat.

The Venue, Bruce St (☎321447). Hot and sweaty – but that's because of the good dance music and DJs. Relaxed crowd.

Vicos, Brunswick St. On four floors – take your pick of acid jazz, house, garage or live bands. Thurs–Sat.

Theatre

Arts Theatre, Botanic Ave (☎324936). Mostly comedy, pantomine or mainstream stuff.

Empire Bar, Botanic Ave (☎328110). Transforms into the **Comedy Club** on Tues nights with satire and killing Northern wit that will reveal more about Belfast than a volume of history. Queue early to avoid disappointment; the slaughter starts at 9pm.

Grand Opera House, Great Victoria St (☎241919). Belfast's most prestigious venue, showing many of London's West End productions.

Group Theatre, Bedford St (☎323900). Tends to be used mainly by local drama companies.

Lyric Theatre, further out on Ridgeway St (☎381081). The *Lyric* takes on more serious contemporary drama, and gave actor Liam Neeson an early platform.

Old Museum Arts Centre, College Square North (☎235053). The place to go for experimental or fringe productions.

Cinema

Mainstream cinemas showing the usual general-release movies include: the monster ten-screen *MGM* on the Dublin Rd (☎243200), the *Movie House Yorkgate* on York St (☎755000) and the *Curzon* on Ormeau Rd (☎641373).

Queen's Film Theatre, University Square Mews off Botanic Ave (☎244857). Two screens showing art-house movies and late-night shows.

Art galleries

Eakin Gallery, 237 Lisburn Rd (☎668522). A family-run terrace house gallery, which highlights Belfast's star painters.

Fenderesky Gallery, *Crescent Arts Centre*, University Rd (☎242338). Presents important Irish moderns – Barrie Cooke, Patrick Hall, Felim Egan.

One Oxford Street (☎310400). Down by the new Laganside development, the gallery shows young, mostly Northern talents.

Ormeau Baths Gallery, Ormeau Ave (☎321402). Set in what was once public baths, this is the latest – and hippest – venue on the arts scene, with four exhibition spaces spread over two floors. Hosts exhibitions of contemporary Irish and international artists' work.

Ulster Museum, Stranmillis Rd (☎381251). Has a wide-ranging collection of international – Francis Bacon and Henry Moore – and national art – Colin Middleton, Willie Conor, Basil Blackshaw and Paul Henry. Conor's old studio across the road is now *Bonnie's Café*.

Listings

Airlines *Aer Lingus*, 46 Castle St (☎245151); *British Airways* and *British Airways Express* (☎247979); *British Midland*, Suite 2, Fountain Centre (☎225151).

Airports *Belfast International Airport* (☎01849/422888); *Belfast City Airport* (☎457745).

Banks Most of the major UK banks are allied to the following Northern Irish ones (see also *Basics*, p.16), all of which have city-centre branches: *Allied Irish*, 2 Royal Ave (☎246559); *Bank of Ireland*, 54 Donegall Place (☎244744); *Northern Bank*, Donegall Square West (☎245277); *Ulster Bank Ltd*, 47 Donegall Place (☎320222). Remember that British cash cards will work in their machines.

Bike rental *McConvey Cycles*, 476 Ormeau Rd (☎238602) & Unit 10, Pottinger's Entry (☎330322); *Bike-It*, 4 Belmont Rd (☎471141).

Bookshops The Ulster Historical Foundation's bookshop, *Familia*, 12 College Square East, has an excellent selection of history, cultural studies and politics; *Bookfinders* at 47 University Rd has second-hand books; there's also *University Bookshop* on University Rd, *Waterstones* on Royal Ave and *Dillons* on Fountain St.

Buses Ring ☎333000 for long-distance *Ulsterbus* information, or there's a brilliant touch-screen computerized information service at the Great Victoria Street station with full timetables and information on places to visit and accommodation throughout Northern Ireland.

Car rental *Avis*, Belfast International Airport (☎01849/422333) and Belfast City Airport (☎452017); there are many other big names at the airports; or try *Dan Dooley*, Belfast International Airport (☎01849/452522).

Exchange As well as banks try *Thomas Cook*, 11 Donegall Place (☎550030); *American Express*, 9 North Rd; and the post offices at Castle Place, Donegall Square and Shaftesbury Square.

Ferries *Isle of Man Packet Co* (Belfast–Isle of Man) are at Donegall Quay (☎351009); *Norse Irish Ferries* (Belfast–Liverpool) are at West Bank Rd (☎779090); *P&O European Ferries* (Larne–Cairnryan) are based at Larne Harbour only (☎01574/74321); *SeaCat* (Belfast–Stranraer) are at Donegall Quay (☎01345/523523); *Stena Sealink* (Larne–Stranraer) are on Castle Lane (☎327525) and at Larne Harbour (☎01574/273616).

Festivals *Belfast International Festival at Queens* (2–3 weeks in Nov) claims to be Europe's second biggest arts festival after Edinburgh. Others are *Belfast Folk Festival* (3 days in Sept); *Orange Day* on July 12 (and marching season all around this date); *Royal Ulster Academy Annual Exhibition* (Ulster Museum, 3 weeks in Oct); and *West Belfast Féile an Phobdil* (one week at the start of Aug), a film, theatre, music and dance festival – originally a Republican event, it increasingly includes Unionist voices.

Gay The gay scene in Belfast is small and there's much travel back and forth to Dublin. The main city venues are *The Crow's Nest*, 26 Skipper St (☎325491), which caters for the older crowd, with quizzes, sing-songs or karaoke; and *The Parliament Bar*, Dunbar Link, which has events every night, but is packed on Sat, with dancing to house on table-tops. On Mon night there's classical music with food, chess and backgammon. The *Gay Counselling Service* and *Lesbian Line* is on ☎222023 (Mon–Thurs 7.30–10pm); the gay helpline is *Mensline* on ☎322023 (Mon–Wed 7.30–10pm).

Hospitals *Belfast City Hospital*, Lisburn Rd (☎329241); *Royal Victoria Hospital*, Grosvenor Rd (☎240503). ☎999 for emergency service.

Left luggage Despite the reduced level of security, there is still, unfortunately, no official place where you can leave your luggage.

Lost property Musgrave police station, Ann St (☎650222, ext 26050).

Laundry *Duds 'n' Suds*, 37 Botanic Ave (☎243956); has snack bar and giant TV screen.

Markets The *St George's Casual Retail Market* (also known as the *Variety Market*) in May St (Tues & Fri mornings) is the liveliest: the Friday food and variety-market is by far the more popular with about 200 traders taking part; on Tues it's more of a fleamarket-type affair, selling new and second-hand clothes and a variety of junk. The *Smithfield Retail Market*, at the back of the new Castle Court development on West Street/Winetavern St, is also pretty good; it operates from about 30 shop units and sells new and second-hand goods and clothes. For **antiques**, try the Sat market at *Alexander The Grates*, Donegall Pass, which sells local bits and pieces at very reasonable prices.

Police ☎999 for emergency service. Main city-centre police station is in North Queen St.

Post office General Post Office, Castle Place (Mon–Sat 9am–5.30pm).

Trains For information call Central Station (☎899411).

Travel agents *USIT*, Fountain Centre (☎324073); *American Express*, 9 North Rd; *Thomas Cook*, 11 Donegall Place (☎550030).

travel details

Trains

Belfast to: Coleraine (9 daily; 1hr 40min); Derry (7 daily; 2hr 10min); Dublin (6; 2hr 20min); Dundalk (5 daily; 1hr 20min); Larne Harbour (2 an hour; 45min); Lisburn (approx 4 an hour; 15min); Portadown (approx 2 an hour; 30min).

Ulsterbuses

Belfast: to Antrim (4–18 daily; 40min); Ballymena (2–12 daily; 50min–1hr); Cork, connecting with *Bus Éireann* (1 daily; 10hr 25min); change at Cahir for Waterford (1 daily; 10hr), at Roscrea for Limerick (1 daily; 9hr) or at Athlone for Mullingar (1 daily; 6hr 40min); Derry (hourly; 1hr 40min; also via Omagh, 4–8 daily; 2hr 55min); Dublin (3–7 daily; 2hr 55min); Enniskillen (6–8 daily; 2hr–2hr 15min); Galway, connecting with *Bus Éireann* (2 daily; 7hr 5min) via Cavan (2 daily; 2hr 40min); Monaghan (3 daily; 2hr); Newry (6–15 daily; 1hr 10min); Portadown (11–14 daily; 50–55min); Portrush (8–9 daily; 2hr 5min); Sligo (3 daily; 4hr).

CHAPTER FIFTEEN

ANTRIM AND DERRY

The northern coastline of counties **Antrim** and **Derry** is as spectacular as anything you'll find in Ireland: certainly it's the major reason to make your way north of Belfast. From most of the coastline, on good days, the Mull of Kintyre is clearly visible, and much of the predominantly Protestant population derives originally from Scotland. Unlike other parts of the North, the region has always attracted lots of tourists, and perhaps because of this, it's one of the parts where you'll feel most comfortable travelling.

Thanks to the Scottish connection, the main point of arrival to Antrim is the decidedly unlovely port of **Larne**, which marks the Irish end of the shortest crossing from Britain. The county's two main attractions are side by side: the nine **Glens of Antrim**, in the northeast corner, closest to Scotland – green fertile fingers probing inland from high cliffs – are immediately followed by the weird geometry of the **Giant's Causeway**. Along this part of the coast the **Ulster Way** offers great opportunities for short walks and long hikes, and also passes some wonderful deserted beaches. As you follow the coast road (A2) further round into County Derry, you'll come to two of the North's great seaside resorts, **Portrush** and **Portstewart**, attractive holiday spots with sandy beaches and waves perfect for surfing. But the place to head for is **Derry city**, a steep-walled town that spills over the banks of the River Foyle. It's a border town, and two-thirds of the population is Catholic; traditionally, it was the starting-point for emigrants from Donegal and around. Derry is a more alternative city than Belfast and its forward-looking city council has encouraged the arts – with great success.

Transport around the coastline, if you're not driving, can be a problem. **Buses** are infrequent – though there are summer specials to the various sights. **Hitchhiking**, though, is easy enough hereabouts. Or you can take the **train** which cuts a less interesting **inland** route through dull farming country – though you can reach either end of the coastline from Belfast, with trains to both Larne and Portstewart. But the rest of the stops along the way to Derry are at some fairly grim inland towns: **Antrim**, **Ballymena** and **Coleraine**. The other route inland is the A6 road from Antrim to Derry, passing through and near some of the counties' planters' towns, the most impressive being **Moneymore**.

If transport is somewhat scarce, then at least **accommodation** is easy, with some fine hotels, plenty of unpretentious, reasonable B&Bs – where you're generally assured of a friendly welcome and a cup of tea – a good sprinkling of hostels and an abundance of campsites. Keep in mind, though, that this is where Northerners also holiday, so accommodation may be hard to come by in July and August – you may need to book ahead.

Larne and around

Arriving by sea is always impressive, but, unfortunately, approaching **LARNE** this way – from Cairnryan or Stranraer – gives you no indication of what's to come. It's a plain, prim, boring town, whose graffitied walls proclaim untidily, in case you hadn't guessed already, that there's "No Popery Here".

Larne's **history** is tied up with its geographical convenience as a landing stage. Norse pirates used Larne Lough as a base in the tenth and eleventh centuries; Edward

AMANDA M'KITTRICK ROS

In contrast to Larne's lack of vigour is the work of the town's best-known author. **Amanda Malvina Fitzalan Anna Margaret McLelland M'Kittrick Ros** – her signature gives some indication of the embroidery of her prose style – has gone down in history as the world's worst published author. Born in 1860 in Ballynahinch, twenty miles south of Belfast, she was a true child of the Victorian era. She came to Larne as a schoolteacher and married the station master, Andrew Ros. On their tenth wedding anniversary he gave her a present that generations of fans must be grateful for – the publication of her first fantastical alliterative work, *Irene Iddlesleigh* – and a stream of feverish hyperbole followed. Take, for instance, a passage from *Helen Huddleston* about her heroine:

> *She had a swell staff of sweet-faced helpers, swathed in strategem, whose members and garments glowed with the lust of the loose, sparked with the tears of the tortured, shone with the sunlight of bribery, dimpled with the diamonds of distrust, slashed with sapphires of scandal and rubies wrested from the dainty persons of the pure ...*

Mark Twain and Aldous Huxley swooped on her work with delight and formed appreciative societies, reading circles and dining clubs dedicated to her "unintentional enormities". She became a cult figure, never, it seems, realizing what inspired such devotion. "My works", she said, "are all expressly my own – pleasingly peculiar – not a borrowed stroke in one of them." Quite. She also wrote excruciating verse.

Bruce, brother of Robert, landed here in 1315 with a force of 6000 men in his attempt to urge the Irish to overthrow the English; and in 1914 the Ulster Volunteers, opposed to the Irish Home Rule Bill, landed German arms here. History apart, though, Larne is not a place to hang around. The only real landmark is the **round tower**, at the entrance to the port, and even that's a reproduction. The other sight is the ruined sixteenth-century **Olderfleet Castle**, which cowers among the industrial wasteland of the harbour. Frankly, unless you're waiting for a ferry, the best thing about Larne is the road out.

The coast around Larne – stretching from Garron Point in the north to Black Head in the south – is of great **geological** interest, with examples of just about every rock formation and period, from the earth's original crust to raised beaches and glacial deposits. At **Curran Point** just south of the harbour, flint bands, frequently found in the chalk of this coast, provided useful material for Stone Age people, and many arrowheads and other artefacts have been found. Three-quarters of a mile out on the Antrim Coast Road north of Larne, beyond Waterloo Cottages, is a large monument to William Bald, the engineer of the road, and his stalwart workers, who blasted their way through, over and round this route in the 1830s. Here, at low tide, bands of fossil-rich Lias clay are exposed – even dinosaur remains have been discovered – and beneath the black basalt boulders, the mollusc shell, *Gryphea*, known locally as the Devil's Toenail, is common. Check at the Larne tourist office for geological tours and their useful guidebook to the rock formations of this part of the coast.

Practicalities

If you want to stay, the **tourist information office** (Easter–June Mon–Sat 9am–5pm; July–Sept Mon–Wed 9am–5pm, Thurs & Fri 9am–7.30pm, Sat 9am–6pm; Oct–Easter Mon–Sat 10am–4pm; ☎01574/260088) in Narrow Gauge Road will book B&B **accommodation** for you, and there is plenty to choose from. Close to the ferry terminal is the *Manor Guest House*, 23 Olderfleet Road (☎01574/273305; ④); for more luxury, try the upmarket Victorian *Magheramorne House Hotel* (☎01574/272272; ⑦), just south of town on the A2. There's a campsite at Curran Park caravan park near the harbour (☎01574/273797), but you are better off at Carnfunnoch Country Park on the way to

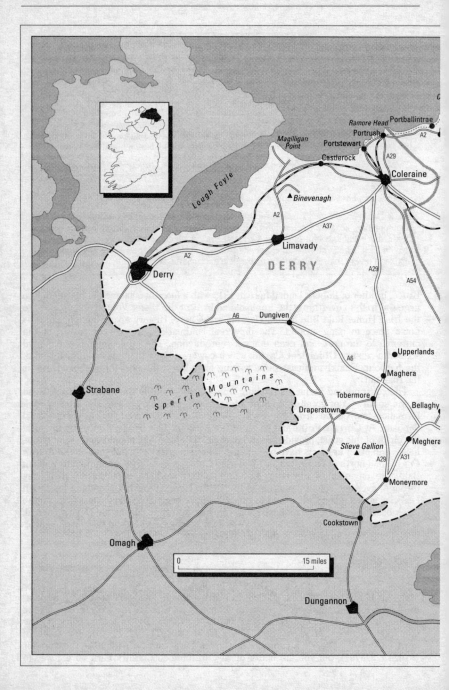

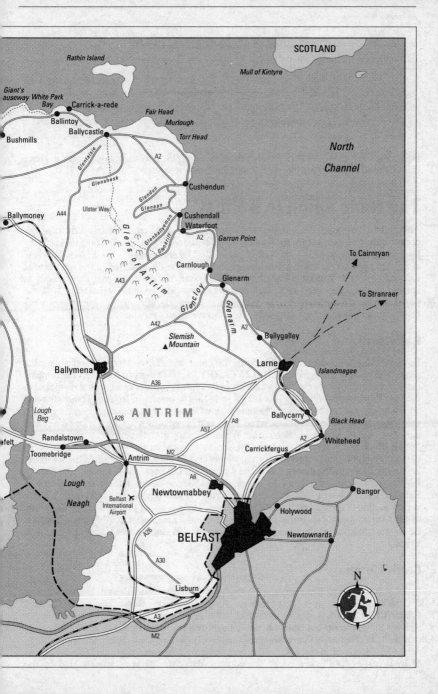

Ballygally (see p.486). **Ferry information** is on ☎01574/274321; see "Getting There from Britain" in *Basics* for more details of the crossings.

The route south to Belfast

Although all the real interest lies to the north of Larne, many people first take the opportunity to head **south to Belfast**, a quick enough option. Arriving in Larne by boat you'll see, on your left, the spit of land called **Islandmagee** – not, in fact, an island at all, but a peninsula seven miles long and two miles wide, attached to the mainland at its southern end. Tapering from high, black basalt cliffs on the east coast down to Larne Lough on the west, its history is sadly representative of these parts: in 1642 the population was massacred by the garrison at Carrickfergus, further south down the coast – some of the victims are said to have been hurled over the cliffs.

Ballycarry

Both the A2 road and rail line run down the coast from Larne towards Belfast, cutting across the neck of the peninsula. **BALLYCARRY**, just off the main road, has the remains of the first Presbyterian church to be built in Ireland, **Templecorran**, with a memorial to the first Presbyterian minister – ordained in 1613 – to preach in Ireland. The tradition is an enduring one: kerbstones are painted red, white and blue, and a gable-end carries a colourful **mural** – the first of many you'll see in this region – showing a man on a prancing horse, with the caption, "Remember William, Prince of Orange 1690".

The **church**'s graveyard contains the tombs of some of the supporters of the 1798 uprising, including that of James Burns, whose cryptic gravestone requires the following key to decipher: the numbers 1, 2, 3 and 4 represent the vowels a, e, i and o, and 5 and 6 the letter w. Another United Irishman, James Orr – better known as the Bard of Ballycarry and Ulster's answer to Robbie Burns – is also buried here, and some ringing verses in dialect are carved into his tombstone. There's also a grand Masonic memorial of 1831, which bears a patriotic poem about Ireland: "Erin, loved land! From age to age, Be thou more great, more famed and free" – not, at this stage, about Ulster or union with Britain.

Carrickfergus

Once you've turned the corner at Whitehead, you're beside Belfast Lough and fast approaching the city's conurbation. About halfway from Larne to Belfast, **CARRICKFERGUS** is an unremarkable, half-hearted sort of seaside town that's worth a visit for an afternoon but probably not somewhere you would choose to stay. The only real point of interest is **Carrickfergus Castle** (April–Sept Mon–Sat 10am–6pm, Sun 2–6pm; Oct–March Mon–Sat 10am–4pm, Sun 2–4pm; £2.70), one of the earliest and largest of Irish castles. Built on a rocky promontory above the harbour around 1180 by the

Anglo-Norman invader John de Courcy (and in continuous use until 1928), it reflects the defensive history of this entire region. In 1315 it endured a year's siege before falling to the combined forces of Robert and Edward Bruce, after which it was retaken and held by the English for most of the next three centuries. In 1760, the castle was overwhelmed by a French force and hurriedly recaptured; and in 1778, the American privateer, John Paul Jones, fought a successful battle with the British vessel *HMS Drake*, America's first naval victory. The story is that Belfast citizens – most of the Protestants were sympathetic to the American Revolution – rushed out to cheer the victors. The castle has been restored recently and peopled with alarming life-size figures plucked from various moments of its history – including King John in the garderobe. You can buy a joint ticket in the *Knight Ride Centre*, a short walk away in the Heritage Centre on Antrim Street (also the tourist office, see below) for the castle and a trip on the **Knight Ride**. A monorail journey in a huge Norman helmet through Carrickfergus history, the ride bombards you with sound, smells and sights (April–Sept Mon–Sat 10am–6pm, Sun 12–6pm; Oct–March same days till 5pm; £2.70; £4.85 joint ticket for castle and ride).

Otherwise, Carrickfergus and its environs claim plenty of **literary associations**, though not all of them are tangible: the Restoration dramatist William Congreve lived in the castle as a young child – his father was a soldier; Jonathan Swift's first sinecure was at Kilroot, just outside Carrickfergus, where, between 1694 and 1696, he wrote *The Tale of a Tub*. ICI bought the land and levelled the thatched cottage in the 1960s; they have since moved on, and the only commemoration to the writer is the **Swift Art Gallery** on the same site. Poet **Louis MacNeice** (1907–63) spent a miserable childhood here; he says sourly of the town: "The Scotch Quarter was a line of residential houses/But the Irish Quarter was a slum for the blind and halt" (*Carrickfergus*, 1937). The Protestant son of a local Home Rule cleric, he was equally repelled by Orange bigotry and the complacency found in the Republic. Although he was educated in England, where he became associated with the left-wing poets of the 1930s led by W.H. Auden, his upbringing left an indelible mark on his poetry and character. In *Valediction* (1934), he explores his ambiguous feelings towards his roots: "I can say Ireland is hooey .... But I cannot deny my past to which myself is wed/ The woven figure cannot undo its thread." The rectory on North Road – from which his mother was committed to an asylum – no longer stands. Instead the MacNeice Fold on the same spot offers sheltered accommodation and a plaque on its walls proclaims the connection. In the town centre overlooking Market Place, the **Church of St Nicholas** (the patron saint of mariners), where MacNeice's father ministered, was built by John de Courcy in 1205 – like many of the castles and historic buildings hereabouts – but extensively reworked in 1614. Some interesting features set it apart: a leper's window and a "skew", or crooked aisle, symbolizing Christ's head on the cross falling to the right.

Still, none of these claims to fame is as tenuous as that of the connection with the American president Andrew Jackson, whose parents emigrated from Carrickfergus in 1765. The **Andrew Jackson Centre** (April–May Mon–Fri 10am–4pm, Sat & Sun 2–4pm; June–Sept Mon–Fri 10am–6pm, Sat & Sun 2–6pm), two miles north of Carrickfergus on the Larne Road, isn't even their home, but a reconstruction of an eighteenth-century thatched cottage, with a little museum.

One reason to give Carrickfergus a little more time might be the **annual fair**, *Lughnasa*, which is tackily medieval – with wrestlers, archers, minstrels and people dressed up as monks – but great fun nonetheless. It's held at the beginning of August; check the dates with the **tourist office** at the *Knight Ride Centre* on Antrim Street (same hours as the *Knight Ride*; ☎01960/366455). If you do want **to stay**, *Marathon House* (☎01232/862475; ③) is an adequate B&B. This is also **golf** and **fishing** country. *Carrickfergus Golf Club* (☎01960/363713), on North Road west of the town centre, is an eighteen-hole parkland course with great views to Scotland and over the Mourne Mountains. *Whitehead Golf Club* (☎01960/353792), half a mile north of town at McCrea's Brae, also offers distracting views and a challenging course over varied terrain. If you want to go fishing, you can rent boats at Carrickfergus or fish off the rocks and piers along the coast.

The Glens of Antrim and Rathlin Island

Northwest of Larne lie the nine **Glens of Antrim**, cutting back from the sea to wild country behind. It's a curious landscape, with enormous contrasts between the neat seaside villages and the rough moorland above, and its well-defined topography gives first-time visitors the strange sensation that they know it well already.

Until the present coast road was blasted out of the cliffs in 1834, the Glens were extremely isolated, despite their proximity to the Scottish coast. They were also one of the last places in Northern Ireland where Irish was spoken. **Transport** is still a problem here. The only service to run from one end of this coast to the other is the daily Belfast–Portrush express bus (leaves Belfast in the morning and returns late afternoon; £5.20 single, £9.20 return). The Larne–Cushendall **bus** runs six times daily (Mon–Sat; £3.75 single, £6.70 return), although some services stop at Carnlough, ten miles short of Cushendall. In July and August there's an extra once-daily service in each direction; check the times with local tourist offices. **Hitching** is generally fine, though you'll hear the tale of a German woman student who was murdered on a ride north from Larne in 1988. **Cycling** is heady but strenuous, and don't rely on being able to rent a bike: one of the few places that has some is the *Ardelinas Activity Centre* (☎012667/71340) in Cushendall. One alternative means of getting about is **pony trekking**, which can be a delight in good weather. The main centre is at **Ballycastle**, at the northern extremity of the glen-fractured coast; see p.490.

Ballygally and Glenarm

Taking the road northwards out of Larne, you leave the dull suburbs behind fairly quickly, the view broadening out to take in the open sea and, beyond it, the low outline of the Scottish coast. **Carnfunnock Country Park** (daily Easter–June 8am–8pm; July–Aug 8am–9pm; Sept–June 8am–sunset; £1) is a good walking stop with a maze in the shape of Northern Ireland, a walled garden and a time garden with totally incomprehensible variations on the sun-dial. You can also camp here. The first settlement you come to is **BALLYGALLY**, with a wide, wild bay and a sandy beach embraced by hills. There's something about the sobriety of the architecture that makes it look more like Scotland, an impression heightened by the crow-stepped gables of **Ballygally Castle**, built by seventeenth-century planters. You can call in here for a drink – it's now a hotel with, they tell you, a ghost in the dungeon bar – although it's more impressive from the outside.

The southernmost of the glens, **Glenarm**, is headed by a village of the same name, which grew up around a hunting lodge built by Randal MacDonnell after Dunluce Castle, further up the coast, was abandoned. Glenarm became the major seat of the Earls of Antrim, something that might lead you to expect that **Glenarm Castle** would be worth seeing. But major rebuildings in the eighteenth and nineteenth centuries have left it a fairly horrendous compilation of styles, an unexciting amalgam of turrets and portcullises that cancel out each others' impact.

GLENARM village itself, though, is a delight and very much a taste of what's to follow, with a broad main street of colour-washed buildings leading up to an imposing gateway, the old estate entrance, which now leads into the glen itself. The lower part of the glen is blighted with Forest Service conifers, but carry on and you reach National Trust land, and far better walking. There's nowhere much to **stay** in Glenarm, but should its charm beguile you, try *Margaret's Café* on the main street (☎01574/84307; ③), which does a very reasonable B&B.

Carnlough and Waterfoot

CARNLOUGH stands at the opposite side of the next bay north of Glenarm, at the head of **Glencloy** – the "glen of hedges". The village's most striking feature is the sturdy, white limestone architecture: until the 1960s Carnlough's way of life was tied up with its limestone quarries. The centre of the village, all built in shining white stone, was constructed by the Marquess and Marchioness of Londonderry in 1854. Over the main road there's a solid stone bridge that once carried the railway, which brought the material down to the harbour; the harbour itself, with an impressive breakwater, also has a clock tower and courthouse of limestone.

Mrs McSporran, who runs the **tourist office** inside the post office on Harbour Road (July–Aug 10am–1pm & 2–4pm; Sept–June Mon–Fri 10am–1pm; ☎01574/885210) – which seems to double as the community centre – can solve any problem, accommodation or otherwise. Almost next door, the solid *Londonderry Arms Hotel* (☎01574/885255; ⑥), once owned by Winston Churchill, is a comfortable **place to stay**; you can sample the smoked salmon fished in Glenarm, or just go for a drink and admire the bizarre collection of mementos of the 1960s' steeplechaser, Arkle. Cheap B&B accommodation is thin on the ground in Carnlough, though you could try the *Bethany Christian Guesthouse* at 5 Bay Road (☎01574/885667; ③), which is full of religious paraphernalia, or the noisier rooms above the *McCauley's* pub in Bridge Street (☎01574/885669; ④). If you're **camping**, there are three small caravan sites – the *Bay View Caravan Park* (☎01574/885685), *Ruby Hill Caravan Park* (☎01574/885692) and *Whitehill Caravan Park* (☎01574/885233) – that allow tents. *Black's Pub*, on Harbour Road, is the place to head for **music**, with sessions most nights. This is also a good place to attack the **Ulster Way**, with walks up behind the village to forests and waterfalls along the Carnlough River – check at the post office/tourist office for maps and an update on the state of the paths first.

From Carnlough the road skirts round a gaunt shoulder of land to **WATERFOOT**, a short strip of houses with a cheap **inn** that comes to life in the evenings. There's also a **B&B** at *Glen Vista*, 245 Garron Road (☎012667/71439; ③). Waterfoot is the scene of the *Feis na nGleann*, one of the great competitive Irish sporting and cultural festivals, held in July.

It's **Glenariff**, though, Waterfoot's glen, that is the real attraction. Wide, lush and flat-bottomed, it's abruptly cut off by the sea, while a few miles up the glen is the **Glenariff Forest Park**, which – though it costs to enter – has a **campsite** (☎012667/58232; contact the head forester in advance) and a spectacular series of **waterfalls** skirted by a timber walkway, first built 100 years ago. You could cheat, though, and see some of the waterfalls by taking the forest park road and turning left at the *Manor Lodge* sign and stop at the restaurant.

Between Waterfoot and **Red Bay** pier, there's a series of **caves** with an odd history. The so-called "school cave" was where lessons were conducted for the children of Red Bay in the eighteenth century, a practice made necessary by the oppressive penal laws that outlawed Catholic education. And the largest of the caves, "Nanny's Cave", 40ft long, was the home of the redoubtable distiller of illicit *poteen*, Ann Murray, who died, aged 100, in 1847.

Cushendall and around

CUSHENDALL lies at the head of three of the nine Glens of Antrim, on the shores of Red Bay, and may become a busy port if a projected ferry service between Red Bay and Scotland materializes. For the moment, however, it remains delightfully understated, its charming colour-washed buildings grouped together on a spectacular shore. The red sandstone **tower** at the main crossroads was built in 1809 by one Francis Turnly, an official of the East India Company, as "a place of confinement for idlers and rioters".

Down the road on Mill Street is Cushendall's **tourist office** (July–Aug Mon–Sat 10am–1pm & 3–7.30pm, Sun 2–4.30pm; Sept–June Mon–Fri 10am–1pm & 3–5pm; ☎012667/71180), where you can check for details of **dancing and traditional music** in local pubs: *Joe McCullum's*, also on Mill Street, is worth a try, sessions usually taking place on Friday and Saturday throughout the summer.

Cushendall is probably the best base for exploring the Glens of Antrim, and accordingly it's well provided with **accommodation**. For B&B, try *Trosben Villa* (☎012667/71130; ③) or *Cullentra House* (☎012667/71762; ⑥) a mile outside town, with its wonderful views. There's a *YHANI* **youth hostel** on Layde Road (open March–Dec 23; Jan & Feb advanced bookings only ; ☎012667/71344; ②), but it's a fair step and a steep one if you're backpacking, so hitch a ride – leave town by Shore Street, go left at the fork, and look out for the youth hostel sign on the wall. The *Glenville Caravan Park* (☎012667/71520) is further up the road, and another **campsite** stands on the hill to the north of the town (☎012667/71699). You can **rent bikes** from the hostel (£6 a day).

Layde Old Church and Ossian's Grave

Beyond Cushendall, the land rises sharply and the main road swings away from the coast, which is good news for **walkers**. A clifftop path, running northwards from the beach, takes you to the calm ruins of the thirteenth-century **Layde Old Church**, recently restored, and chief burial place of the MacDonnells. It's nothing spectacular, although if you have family roots to trace in the Glens it may be worth checking out; the tourist office staff at Cushendall have just finished cataloguing the gravestones, and the results are available in their historical society booklet.

The other trip from Cushendall is to what's known as **Ossian's Grave**, on the main road to Cushendun (see below). There's a double fake involved here: Ossian, the legendary son of Fionn MacCumhaill, was the supposed author of the Ossianic Cycle of poems, translated and popularized – and largely fabricated – by James Macpherson in the 1760s. This was to give impetus to the early Romantic movement, particularly in Germany and Scandinavia. However, the tomb doesn't actually have anything to do with Ossian as it's a Neolithic court grave. All the same, standing in a sloping field above the valley, with views to Glendun, Glenaan and, in the distance, Scotland, it oozes spirit – as good a place as any to reflect on the shaky origins of the first Celtic literary revival.

Beyond the grave runs **Glenaan**, one of the smallest of the glens, soon petering out as little more than a dip of red reeds and black seams of peat between two hills of heather and cotton grass.

Cushendun to Fair Head

CUSHENDUN is an architectural oddity. On a windswept bay, it was once a fashionable resort, almost entirely designed, between 1912 and 1925, by the stylish architect of Portmerrion in Wales, Clough Williams-Ellis. However, it has nothing of the twee Italianate style that has made Portmerrion famous. Built to a commission from Ronald McNeill, the first (and last) Lord Cushendun, and his Cornish wife, Maud, Cushendun's houses are of rugged, rough-cast whitewash with slate roofs – a Cornish style which clearly weathers the Atlantic storms as efficiently here as in Cornwall. The town was home to Agnes Nesta Shakespeare Higginson (1870–1951), who crafted folksy, sentimental ballads under the far more apposite adopted name, **Moira O'Neill**. Very popular in her day, now she's better known as the mother of Mary Nesta Skrine, who has gone one better than her mother and writes under two pen names, Molly Keane and M.J. Farrell. *Good Behaviour*, written in her eighties after a thirty-year silence, is a piercingly witty novel of family life in the Big House tradition.

All of Cushendun is National Trust property, and it shows. It's a tiny and well-tended place where tourists – and everyone else – seem peculiarly out of place; but there are a tourist office (☎012667/61506) in the main street and some **places to stay**. *The Bay Hotel* is at 20 Strandview Park (☎012667/61267; ④), and there are a couple of **B&Bs** and a municipal caravan park that also allows **camping** (☎012667/61254). There's also lots of new converted **self-catering** accommodation. Best are the *Mullarts* apartments, which are located in an old church (☎012667/61221; £240 a week for 2–4 people); and *Antrim Glen's Cottages*, Old Strand House (☎012667/71378; from £280 a week for 7 people).

North from Cushendun, there's not much point in taking the main road, which runs inland, unless you have to: it traverses some impressively rough moorland, but you'll be missing some of the best of the northern coastline. Edged with fuchsia and honeysuckle, the coastal road switchbacks violently above the sea to **Torr Head**, the closest point on the Irish mainland to the Mull of Kintyre in Scotland; Protestants would row these thirteen miles to go across to church on the Scottish mainland. You can also pick up the signposted **Ulster Way** around here, although it swings inland immediately after Cushendun, joining the coast again at Murlough Bay: despite the spectacular views from the top of Carnanmore Mountain, the coastal route is generally more scenic.

That said, people will tell you that the **Ballypatrick Forest Park**, on the main road, is worth seeing. It's not, unless you're thrilled by the idea of a one-way driving route past things like fjords and even prehistoric cairns marked out like a fairground ghost train. **Camping** is allowed in the park, but check with the Forest Service in Belfast (☎01232/520100, ext 24949) before turning up.

Murlough Bay and Fair Head

Murlough Bay is probably – perhaps because of the absence of a main road – the most spectacular of all the bays along the northern coast. From the rugged clifftops, the hillside curves down to the sea in a series of wildflower meadows that soften an

---

SIR ROGER CASEMENT

A stone cross in the second car park of Murlough Bay commemorates **Sir Roger Casement**. This extraordinary figure was both a successful administrator for the British and a martyr for the Nationalist cause. Born in Dublin, he moved to Antrim to live with his guardian when both his parents died and, initially at least, espoused the Loyalist views that characterized the Anglo-Irish. There followed a brilliant diplomatic career in the Belgian Congo – where he fearlessly exposed all sorts of colonial exploitation – and Peru, which he called the "Devil's Paradise of the Amazon". He was given a knighthood in 1911. But, on his return to Ireland – influenced by his experiences abroad – he became increasingly involved with the Sinn Féin movement. Believing that Britain's involvement in World War I could give Ireland the opportunity to achieve independence, in 1916 he negotiated with Germany for military aid and arranged for a German submarine to land a shipload of arms at Banna Strand on the Kerry coast. His plans were discovered, and he was captured before the crucial Easter Rising and tried.

Seemingly determined on martyrdom, he said in the dock: "I committed high treason with my eyes open – and for a cause I love above all else. I must some day pay the penalty – I do not mind that if I have helped Ireland." However, aside from treason, the fact that Casement was a homosexual played a part in his fate; his diaries – the notorious "black diaries" – were confiscated by the British government after his arrest and circulated unofficially. The contents of these were said to be so damning that they ruined his chances of a reprieve – he was hanged. For a long time afterwards the government was suspected of forging the diaries – a suspicion bolstered by the fact that a key Casement file has never been made public – but this theory has now been discredited. The sad truth seems to be that in 1916 Casement's homosexuality was seen as compounding his treachery not only to Britain but to the ideal of British manhood, which in the midst of World War I couldn't afford to be further subverted.

otherwise harsh landscape. As much as anywhere else on the Irish coastline this is a place for just spending time and drinking it all in.

The last headland before Ballycastle is **Fair Head**, with massive cliffs rising over 600ft all the way round, and a really spectacular view across the North Channel to the Scottish islands – Islay, the Paps of Jura and, beyond them, the Mull of Kintyre; seeing the landscape makes more sense of the confusion of land ownership between Ireland and Scotland. Rathlin Island (see opposite) was hotly contested right up to the seventeenth century, while the MacDonnells owned land both here and on Kintyre. (Kintyre, incidentally, was considered dangerous enough to English interests to be settled, or "planted", with people from elsewhere in Scotland during the seventeenth century, just as Ireland was.) **Lough na Cranagh**, one of three lakes in the hinterland behind the cliffs, has an oval island that is actually a lake dwelling, a *crannóg*, with an encircling constructed parapet wall.

Ballycastle

Situated at the mouth of the two northernmost Antrim glens, Glenshesk and Glentaise, the lively market town and port of **BALLYCASTLE** divides the glens from the Causeway coast and is a base for touring in either direction. As such it has the air of a family resort and is pleasant enough, particularly if you find yourself passing through at the time of the *Fleadh Amhrán agus Rince*, the three-day music and dance **festival** in June, or the **Ould Lammas Fair** in late August. This last event is more than just a tourist promotion: Ireland's oldest fair, it dates from 1606 when the MacDonnells first obtained a charter, and has sheep and pony sales as well as the obligatory stalls and shops. You may be able to find the edible seaweed, dulse, and the tooth-breaking yellow toffee (it's so hard, you break it with a hammer) called "yellow man", delicacies that feature in a sentimental song that originates in Ballycastle:

> *Did you treat your Mary Ann*
> *To dulse and yellow man*
> *At the Ould Lammas Fair in Ballycastle-O?*

The town still has a solid, prosperous feel about it that derives from the efforts of an enlightened mid-eighteenth-century landowner, Colonel Hugh Boyd, who developed the town as an industrial centre, providing coal and iron ore mines, a tannery, brewery, soap, bleach, salt and glass works. Ballycastle's prosperity, though, really depended on its coal mines; lignite was mined at Ballintoy, on the coast a few miles further west, but that enterprise came to an abrupt end in the eighteenth century when the entire deposit caught fire, continuing to burn for several years.

Ballycastle straggles up a steep hill from the coast where, around two miles on, boats leave for Rathlin Island (see opposite). At the seafront there's a memorial to Guglielmo Marconi, the inventor of the wireless, who in 1898 made his first successful transmission between Ballycastle and Rathlin. If you're looking for a B&B, this is the place to stay, as there's a good sandy **beach** close by.

A little way out, on the main road to Cushendall, are the ruins of **Bonamargy Friary**, founded by the dominant MacQuillan family around 1500. A number of members of the rival MacDonnell family are also buried here, including the hero of Dunluce Castle, Sorley Boy MacDonnell, and his son Randal, first Earl of Antrim (see p.496). An indication of the strength of the Irish language in these parts is that the tomb of the second earl, who died in 1682, is inscribed in Irish as well as the usual English and Latin: the Irish inscription reads "Every seventh year a calamity befalls the Irish" and "Now that the Marquis has departed, it will occur every year". The **Margy river**, on which Bonamargy Friary stands, is associated with one of the great tragic stories of Irish legend, that of the Children of Lir (see p.176), whose jealous step-mother turned them into swans and forced them to spend 300 years on the Sea of Moyle (the narrow channel between Ireland and the Scottish coast). Also on this shore is **Carraig Uisneach**, the rock on which the mythical Deirdre of the Sorrows, her lover Naoise, and his brothers, the sons of Uisneach, are said by some to have come ashore after their long exile in Scotland (also see p.493).

Practicalities

If you're going to **stay** in Ballycastle, the **tourist office** in Sheskburn House on Mary Street (July & Aug Mon–Fri 9.30am–5.30pm, Sat 10am–6pm, Sun 2–6pm; Oct–June Mon–Fri 9.30am–5pm; ☎012657/62024) can point you in the right direction. If your budget is generous, the *Marine Hotel*, at the bottom of Quay Road on the waterfront (☎012657/62222; ⑧), is very comfortable. Otherwise try one of the many **B&Bs** at the harbour end of Quay Road – *Glenluce* at no. 42 (☎012657/62914; ④) or *Fragens Guest House* at no. 34 (☎012657/62168; ③). No. 62, the last house on the left, incorporates the independent *Castle Hostel* (*IHH*; open all year; ☎012657/62337; ②). On the outskirts of Ballycastle, and with stunning views, is the seventeenth-century former charter school *Drumawillan House* at Whitepark Road (☎012657/62539; ④). There are also several **caravan sites** which take tents, the nearest being *Silver Cliffs Holiday Village* (☎012657/62550), where you can also rent **self-catering** chalets (around £90 per person per week) and ready-pitched tents – it has lots of facilities including a swimming pool.

The usual range of fast **food** and tea shops can be found in town and on the front: *Donnelly's Coffee Shop* on Ann Street is excellent, and there are good bar lunches at nearby *McCarroll's* and at the *Marine Hotel*, which also has live music on Sundays and hosts *Legends* nightclub for entertainment of the karaoke kind. *Wysners*, 16 Ann Street, has a daring and inexpensive menu and is next door to the famous butcher of the same name. You'll find Ballycastle's **pubs** surprisingly lively – *McCarroll's* has traditional music on Thursdays; the *House of McDonnell*, on the main street, is young and lively; even better is the bar at the *Antrim Arms*, next door, with a magnificent range of whiskeys and a host rich in Ulster wisdom; the *Angler's Arms*, down on the seafront, is a cosy bar in which to end the evening. Finally, *Strand's* wine bar on the seafront is an unusual find in the land of pubs and pints.

There's **pony trekking** on offer in Ballycastle, too, at the *Loughareema Trekking Centre* (☎012657/62576), on the Ballyvennaght Road. **Corrymeela**, the famous centre for cross-community reconciliation (☎012657/62626), is just a few miles out of town.

Rathlin Island

Ballycastle is the departure point for rugged **Rathlin Island**, six miles and a fifty-minute boat trip offshore, and just twelve miles from the Mull of Kintyre in Scotland. **Boats** go every day (call *Iona Isle*, ☎012657/63915; or *Rathlin Venture*, ☎012657/63917; fares are £5.60 return, £4.45 single). In winter, it can get too rough for the boat to make the return trip, so it's worth making sure in advance that you find a bed on the island, as accommodation is strictly limited.

Rathlin is an impressive, cliff-ridden place, its vegetation stunted by salt winds, its barrenness seemingly in keeping with its stormy history – the islanders now take advantage of the conditions by generating their own electricity with windmills built in 1992. The island was the first place in Ireland to be raided by the Vikings, in 795 AD, and has been the scene of three bloody massacres, one by the Scots and two by the English. In 1595 the mainland MacDonnells sent their women, children and old people to Rathlin for safety from the English, but that didn't stop the invading fleet, under the Earl of Essex (whose soldiers included Sir Francis Drake), from slaughtering the entire population; Rathlin was deserted for many years afterwards.

The island's cliffs are good **birdwatching** country, particularly **Bull Point**, on the western tip. The foot of the cliff is riddled with caves, many of them accessible by boat only in the calmest of weather, and many also filled with detritus from wrecked ships, brought to the surface by storms. **Bruce's Cave**, on the northeast point of the island, below the lighthouse, is a cavern in the black basalt where, in 1306, so the story goes, the despondent Robert the Bruce retreated after being defeated by the English at Perth. Seeing a spider determinedly trying to spin a web persuaded him not to give up, so he returned to Scotland and defeated the English at Bannockburn. You can **rent a boat** to see the cave (see below), but only in calm weather.

Practicalities

There's not much in the way of **accommodation** on Rathlin: presently there's only the *Rathlin Guest House* (☎012657/63917; ③) and *Richard Branson's Activity Centre* (☎012657/63915; ③), which does hostel-style accommodation and has a **campsite**. Life on the island is simple and uncomplicated, but not entirely basic, so you'll also find a **café-pub** that does food and two shops. Rathlin is a good place for fishing, and you can **rent a boat** (☎012657/63933 or ☎63935) or get Tommy Cecil (☎012657/63915) to take you scuba diving around one of the many wrecks offshore.

The north coast and north Derry

The north coast of Antrim, west of Ballycastle, is dominated by Northern Ireland's most famous tourist attraction, the strange formation of basalt columns at the mythical **Giant's Causeway**. However, on the way to this natural wonder, around the town of **Ballintoy**, there are several attractions to divert you, not least the precarious rope bridge to **Carrick-a-rede Island**. Beyond the Causeway, you can can sample some whiskey at **Bushmills** and visit the imposing and well-preserved remains of **Dunluce Castle**, the stronghold of the local MacDonnell clan.

The coastline west of Dunluce, to **Magilligan Point**, is another major holiday spot, the twin resorts of **Portrush** and **Portstewart** filled with tourists in July and August, mainly from the rest of the North. **Castlerock**, too, gets its fair share of beach-goers, but the Inishowen Peninsula, on the other side of Lough Foyle, is now well in sight, and the beaches on the Republic side are often more exciting and less busy. From Magilligan Point, site of a high-security prison as well as a nature reserve, the coastline – overlooked by the dramatic crag of **Binevenagh** – is flat and undramatic, some of it consisting of land reclaimed from the sea to grow flax for the eighteenth-century linen trade.

Given the attractions of the coast, it's almost impossible to see why anyone would want to visit the two towns – **Coleraine** and **Limavady** – immediately inland in north Derry, though you'll pass through if you're heading for Derry city or Donegal by the most direct route.

To Ballintoy and Dunseverick Castle

As you head west from Ballycastle to Ballintoy, there are a couple of places on the way that are worth stopping for. The first of these, **Kinbane Castle**, is a decaying sixteenth-century fortification on a long white headland, built by Colla Dubh, brother of the redoubtable Sorley Boy MacDonnell. The pathway is slippery and badly eroded, but it's worth climbing up to the castle to inspect these Irish defences against the English.

Drawing level with **Carrick-a-rede Island**, not far outside Ballintoy, you'll see the **rope bridge**. Strung 80ft above the sea, between the mainland and the island, the bridge leads to a commercial salmon fishery on the southeast side of Carrick-a-rede (the name means "rock in the road": the island stands in the path of migrating salmon)

– but its main function seems to be to scare tourists, something it does very successfully. Walking its 60ft length, as the bridge leaps and bucks under you, is enough to induce giggles and screams from the hardiest of people. The bridge is up from April to September, when the salmon fishing season ends; there's a car park – always open – and a café (April–Aug daily 10am–6pm).

BALLINTOY itself has a dramatic harbour with a dark, rock-strewn strand contrasting oddly with the neat pale-stone breakwater. In the summer, it's lively with boats and visitors, but in winter it's bleak and exposed. The little white church that stands at the top of the cliff is a replacement for the one where local Protestants took refuge from Catholics in 1641, before being rescued by the Earl of Antrim. A landlord of Ballintoy in the eighteenth century was Downing Fullerton, who founded Downing College in Cambridge; the staircase and oak panelling were removed from the castle at Ballintoy when it was demolished and taken to Cambridge. In good weather you can rent boats for fishing and trips along the coast. **Sheep Island**, the bizarre rocky column standing just offshore, is home to a colony of cormorants. In the summer, **boat trips** run out from Ballintoy, past Sheep Island, to Carrick-a-rede (£1).

Continuing up the coast, **Whitepark Bay** is a delight, a mile-long sweep of white sand with a *YHANI* **youth hostel** (open all year; ☎012657/31745, fax ☎32034; ②) run by the indefatigable Norman Elder, who will organize pony trekking, canoeing, pub trips and parties. In fact, it's the sort of place where visitors arrive for an overnight stay and never move on. A footpath from Ballintoy leads past here to **PORTBRADDAN**, a hamlet that's hardly more than a few houses. The interest lies in St Gobbans, a brightly coloured bit of ecclesiastical architecture that is, supposedly, the smallest church in Ireland – twelve feet by six and a half. Needless to say, there are other contenders.

Dunseverick Castle

From here the coast path leads round a headland and through a spectacular hole in the rock and then, by degrees, up to the cliffs of **Benbane Head**, which is where the bizarre geometry of the Giant's Causeway really begins in earnest. The road almost meets the path at **Dunseverick Castle**, now no more than the ruins of a sixteenth-century gatehouse, but once capital of the old kingdom of Dalriada, which spread over north Antrim and Scotland, and the terminus of one of the five great roads that led from Tara, the ancient capital of Ireland. It was, naturally enough given its location, one of the main departure points for the great Irish colonization of Scotland that took place from the fifth century onwards, and was stormed by the Danes in the ninth and tenth centuries. Dunseverick also features in one of the great Irish love stories, the ninth-century *Longas mac n-Usnig* or "The fate of the children of Uisneach". Deirdre, the betrothed of King Conor, falls in love with his bodyguard, Naoise. Together with Naoise's two brothers – the sons of Uisneach – they flee to Scotland. Fergus, one of Conor's soldiers, believes the king has forgiven them and persuades them to return home. Landing at Dunseverick (or, some say, Ballycastle), they take the high road to Conor's court at Armagh, but the king kills the brothers and seizes Deirdre, who dashes her head against a stone and dies. And Fergus, outraged, destroys Conor's palace (though not, apparently, the king himself).

The Giant's Causeway

Ever since 1693, when the Royal Geographical Society first publicized it as one of the great wonders of the natural world, the **Giant's Causeway** has been a major tourist attraction. The highly romanticized pictures of the polygonal basalt rock formations by the Dubliner Susanna Drury, which circulated throughout Europe, did much to popularize the Causeway: two of them are on show in the Ulster Museum in Belfast, and

---

FIONN MAC CUMHAILL: THE CAUSEWAY LEGENDS

Two versions of the legend of the creation of the Causeway are current. The romantic version is the everyday story of a love affair between giants: the Ulster warrior, Fionn Mac Cumhaill (Finn McCool), became infatuated with a female giant who lived on the island of Staffa, off the Scottish coast (where the Causeway resurfaces), and built the great highway to bring his lady love to his side. This tale is recounted, alongside the scientific account, in the visitor centre's exhibition – along with some fanciful embellishments, such as an estimate of Fionn's height calculated on the basis of a large shoe-shaped stone that's known as his boot. A more robust tale has Fionn involved in a row with a Scottish giant. He built the Causeway to go over to Scotland for a punch-up, but on seeing the size of the other giant, lost his nerve and fled home. Safe in Ireland, he had his wife tuck him up in an outsize cot – when the Scots giant arrived in pursuit he saw the size of Fionn's "baby" and in turn took fright and fled, never to be heard of again.

copies are in the visitor centre at the site. Not everyone was impressed, though. William Thackeray ("I've travelled a hundred and fifty miles to see *that*?") especially disliked the tourist promotion of the Causeway, claiming in 1842 that "the traveller no sooner issues from the inn by a back door which he is informed will lead him straight to the causeway, than the guides pounce upon him". And although the Causeway is probably less overtly moneymaking now than at almost any time since the late seventeenth century, it still attracts plenty of people: there's an incongruous visitor centre (see below), and a minibus on the site rules out the necessity for any physical exertion whatsoever. But even in high season, it's easy enough to escape the crowds by taking to the cliffs.

For sheer strangeness, the Causeway can't be beaten. Made up of an estimated 37,000 black basalt columns, each a polygon – hexagons by far the most common, pentagons second, and sometimes figures with as many as ten sides – it's the result of a massive subterranean explosion, some sixty million years ago, that stretched from the Causeway to Rathlin and beyond to Islay, Staffa (where it was responsible for the formation of Fingal's Cave) and Mull in Scotland. A huge mass of molten basalt was spewed out onto the surface, and, as it cooled, it solidified into what are, essentially, crystals. Simple as the process was, it's difficult, when confronted with the very regular geometry of the basalt columns, to believe that their origin is entirely natural. The Irish folk versions of their creation (see above) are certainly more appealing.

The best way to **approach** the Giant's Causeway is undoubtedly along the cliffs, preferably on a wet and blustery day when you're scared you'll lose your footing along the muddy way. The waymarked **North Antrim Cliff Path**, cut into the cliffside alongside the black geometric configurations, runs all along this stretch of coast. **Public transport** to and from the Causeway is well organized in summer: an open-topped **bus** (the "open topper") runs in July and August four times daily between Coleraine (where the stop is opposite the train station) and Bushmills, stopping at Portstewart, Portrush, Portballintrae and the Causeway; you can flag it down anywhere along the way. If you're travelling by **train** from Belfast, the line ends at Portrush, from where you can catch either the open topper or the *Antrim Coaster* (June–Sept; £5.50, £9.70 return) from Belfast, which runs twice a day to Coleraine. There's also the #172; for more details phone ☎012657/43334.

Visiting the Causeway

The Causeway's **visitor centre** (July & Aug daily 10am–7pm, Sept–June 10.30am–5.30pm; £1) has a craft shop, coffee shop and audiovisual displays, but it's not a place to linger unless you're very cold or very wet – the real excitement is outside. There's a paying exhibition that doesn't tell you a great deal; its single interesting exhibit is one of the **trams** from the tramway that used to run between the train station in Portrush and the Causeway. Opened in 1883, it was the first electrically powered tramway in Europe, and ran on hydroelectric power generated from the River Bush. The tramway wasn't built simply for the tourists: it was thought that the area would be developed for iron mining, and the tram-owner, William Traill, planned to make his fortune. There was some concern over the possible dangers of using hydroelectricity, and Traill sought to allay fears by dropping his trousers and sitting on the live rail – it was only later that he admitted that he'd suffered a severe shock. The line was closed in 1949, although there are apparently plans to reopen it.

Resist the temptation to follow the crowds along the path straight down to the sea and the famous hexagonal blocks (and dodge the minibus that's laid on – every 15min; 80p); instead take a better route that's a round trip of roughly two miles. Follow the cinder path up behind the visitor centre and round the edge of promontories – among them **Weir's Snout** – from which you can gasp at the Causeway, and watch the eider and gannets that wheel across from Ailsa Craig, thirty miles away in Scotland. If you're in luck – and here in autumn – you may sight the Aurora Borealis bouncing in the sky northwards. A flight of 162 steps takes you down to sea level and a junction in the path, leading down to the 40ft basalt columns, known as the **Organ Pipes**. Many of the formations have names invented for them by the guides who so plagued Thackeray and his contemporaries – the Harp, for example – but at least one, **Chimney Point**, has an appearance so bizarre that it persuaded a ship of the Spanish Armada to think it was Dunluce Castle, a couple of miles further west, where they might get help from the MacDonnells: instead, the *Girona* was wrecked.

Before you reach Chimney Point, **Port-na-Spánaigh** is the place where the ship foundered in September 1588. The treasure it was carrying was recovered by divers in 1968, and some of the items are on show in the Ulster Museum in Belfast. If you are feeling energetic, you can continue along to explore these strange honeycombs, or turn back and clamber over the Causeway.

Tucked into the coastline, inaccessible from land, are some spectacular caves: Portcoon Cave, 450ft long and 40ft high; Leckilroy Cave, which you can't go into; and Runkerry Cave, an amazing 700ft long and 60ft high. Your best option, if you want to explore, is to persuade a fisherman in Portballintrae (see overleaf) or Dunseverick Harbour to take you – £40 is considered a persuasive sum.

Bushmills and Dunluce Castle

The next stop on the main road beyond the Causeway is **BUSHMILLS**, whose foremost attraction is the **Old Bushmills Distillery**, on the outskirts of town. Whiskey has been distilled here legally since 1608, making it the oldest licit distillery in the world, and it's well worth making the **tour** (July–Aug Mon–Thurs 9am–noon & 1.30–4pm, Fri 9am–4pm, Sat 10am–4pm; Sept–June Mon–Thurs 9am–noon & 1.30–3.30pm, Fri 9am–noon; £2). The great claim about Bushmills whiskey is that it's distilled three times, instead of the twice that's usual in Scotland; but perhaps the biggest surprise is just how unsubtle a business the industrial manufacture of alcohol is, despite all the lore that surrounds it. Basically, you're shown round a massive factory where an extraordinary range of (mostly unpleasant) smells assails your nostrils, making it difficult to imagine that the end product is something that will delight the taste buds. All the same, at the end of the tour you're offered a tot of the hard stuff: the best bet is the unblended malt, representative of what goes on in Bushmills itself, as the grain whiskey that goes into the blend is almost all distilled in Cork; alternatively ask for a tot of Coleraine whiskey, only a tiny amount of which is still produced. They also serve hot toddies, which may be more in order in winter. To find the distillery follow the signs from the cenotaph in the centre of town – it's barely a quarter of a mile.

Practicalities

Accommodation is mostly strung out along the Causeway Road, where for example you'll find the *Carnside Guesthouse*, 23 Causeway Road (☎012657/31337; ④), two miles east of the distillery with a Causeway view. *Ahimsa*, at 243 Whitepark Road (☎012657/31383; ③), with an organic garden and good vegetarian meals, offers inexpensive accommodation in a modernized traditional cottage. Just about the only cheap place in Bushmills itself is *Ardeevin* (③), on the road out to the distillery. The very best rooms in town are at the *Bushmills Inn*, 25 Main Street (☎012657/32339; ⑧), a former coaching **inn** with cottage-style interior complete with secret room and peat fires. Also attached is the excellent *Barony Restaurant*, with an à la carte menu and meals for around £15 – you should at least pop in for a drink in the gaslit bar while waiting for the bus (which stops outside). There's more luxury at the *Auberge de Seneirl* (☎012657/41536; ⑧), a converted nineteenth-century schoolhouse very discreetly signposted off the Coleraine Road; it's well equipped with swimming pool, sauna, jacuzzi, solarium and a **restaurant** with excellent French food. The owners aren't keen to take guests who don't want to eat there, but it can be an great place to hole up after the rigours of walking the cliffs.

A detour of a couple of miles westwards along the minor coast road from Bushmills will take you to **PORTBALLINTRAE**, a decorous little place with a friendly **hotel** if you fancy staying over: the *Bayview Hotel* (☎012657/31453; ⑦), at 2 Bayhead Road. There's good **fishing** from the tiny harbour. The bus between Bushmills and Coleraine stops here.

Dunluce Castle

A couple of miles further west, where the main road rejoins the coast, sits sixteenth-century **Dunluce Castle** (April–June & Sept Mon–Sat 10am–7pm, Sun 2–7pm; July–Aug Mon–Sat 10am–7pm, Sun 11am–7pm; Oct–March Thurs–Sat 10am–4pm, Sun 2–4pm; £1.50), easily the most impressive ruin along this entire coastline. Sited on a fine headland, high above a cave, it looks as if it only needs a roof to be perfectly habitable once again. Its history is inextricably linked with that of its original owner, **Sorley Boy MacDonnell**, whose MacDonnell clan, the so-called "Lords of the Isles", ruled northeastern Ulster from Dunluce. English incursions into the area culminated in 1584 with Sir John Perrott laying siege to Dunluce, forcing Sorley Boy ("Yellow Charles" in Irish) to leave the castle. But as soon as Perrott departed, leaving a garrison in charge, Sorley Boy hauled his men up the cliff in baskets and recaptured the castle, later repairing the damage with the proceeds of the salvaged wreckage of the *Girona*. Having made his point, Sorley Boy made his peace with the English, and his son, Randal, was created Viscount Dunluce and Earl of Antrim by James I. In 1639 Dunluce Castle paid the penalty for its precarious, if impregnable, position when the kitchen, complete with cooks and dinner, fell off the cliff during a storm. Shortly afterwards, the MacDonnells moved to more comfortable lodgings at Glenarm, and Dunluce was left empty.

However, it remains an extraordinary place. The MacDonnells' Scottish connections – Sorley Boy's son continued to own land in Kintyre – show in the gatehouse's turrets and crow-step gables; the seventeenth-century Great Hall, medieval in plan but Renaissance in style, has tapering chimneys of the Scottish style; and there's a strange touch of luxury in the loggia that faces – oddly – away from the sun.

You can see the **cave** below the castle without paying to go in. Piercing right through the promontory upon which Dunluce stands, with an opening directly under the gatehouse, it's a spectacular scramble, particularly in wild weather.

Portrush

PORTRUSH, built on the Ramore Peninsula, has sandy beaches backed by dunes, running both east and west, and everything you'd expect from a seaside resort, including summer drama staged in the Town Hall and plenty of amusement arcades. Thanks to students from the University of Ulster at Coleraine, many of whom choose to live here, it's a considerably livelier place than you might expect, even out of season. The **beach** is long and sandy: to the east, towards Dunluce, it ends in the **White Rocks**, where the weather has carved the soft limestone cliffs into strange shapes, the most famous of which is the so-called "Cathedral Cave", 180ft from end to end. On a rather different level, Portrush's newest attraction is the all-weather **Waterworld**, by the harbour, with water flumes, slides, sauna, jacuzzis, aquarium and restaurant. The former bath-house for the well-heeled patrons of the *Northern Counties Hotel* on the seafront is now the **Portrush Countryside Centre** (June–Aug; free), an exhibition and lecture centre on natural history, whose staff will happily name your rock samples or flower specimens. There is rewarding **surfing** here off West Strand and White Rocks. You **can rent** boards and gear at one of the surf shops in Portrush or further along the coast in Portstewart. Check wave status, before you hit the water, on ☎01265/824596.

The main sporting attraction, though, is the **Royal Portrush Golf Club** (☎01265/822311), which in 1993 hosted the British Amateur Championships. The North's premiere club, it boasts one nine-hole and two eighteen-hole courses, though in fact most of the coast seems to be covered in greens and putters – eighty in all – whose vistas offer a welcome distraction from your handicap. Demand is high in the summer, especially in good weather, and it's wise to book ahead. A detailed list of green fees, course lengths and standard scratch scores is available from the tourist office.

Practicalities

The very friendly and efficient **tourist office** (March–April Mon–Sat noon–5pm; May to mid-June Mon–Sat 9am–5pm; mid-June to mid-Sept daily 9am–8pm; mid-Sept to mid-Oct Mon–Sat 9am–5pm, Sun noon–5pm; mid-Oct to mid-Nov Sat & Sun only, noon–5pm; ☎01265/823333) is in the newly constructed Dunluce Centre, complete with regulation audiovisual interpretative centre, on Sandhill Road, on the western edge of town.

Accommodation ranges from the *Eglington Hotel*, near the station at 49 Eglington Street (☎01265/822371; ⑦) – not bad value for what you get – to dozens of **B&Bs**, most of them very friendly and welcoming. Try, for example, *Glenkeen Guest House*, 59 Coleraine Road (☎01265/822279; ⑤), which has won tourist board awards; the excellent *Harbour House* on Kerr Street (☎01265/822130; ⑤); *Malvern House*, 36 Mark Street (☎01265/823435; ③); or on Bath Terrace, the *Clarence* at no. 7 (☎01265/823575; ③). *Ma Cools* independent **hostel** (open all year; ☎01265/824845; ②) is nearby on Causeway View Terrace. There are also lots of **campsites** in the area – though most of them are actually fairly unattractive caravan parks that take tents; closest are the *Golf Links Hotel Caravan Park*, 140 Dunluce Road (☎01265/823539), and the municipal *Carrick Dhu Caravan Park*, 12 Ballyreagh Road (☎01265/823712).

The *Ramore Restaurant* (☎01265/824313; at least £15 a head; expensive wine) serves good **food**, or try the excellent *Rowland's Restaurant*, 92–94 Lower Main Street (☎01265/822063), which has a three-course set menu for under £10; otherwise there are plenty of cheap Chinese restaurants, fish and chip shops and the like. The *Singing Kettle* on Atlantic Avenue is an old-fashioned café. **Nightlife** is quite a serious business here. It centres on the disco at *Kelly's Hotel*, *Traks* nightclub and *Burberry's* at the *Magheraboy House Hotel*, which also has a decent modern restaurant. There are loads of convivial pubs – the nicest **bar** in town is probably the *Harbour Inn* – but if you're hoping to hear traditional music your best option is to go to Ballycastle and *McDonnell's* pub.

Portstewart and beyond

Like Portrush, **PORTSTEWART** – across the county border in Derry – is full of Victorian boarding houses. Of the two, Portstewart has always had more airs and graces: the train station is said to have been built a mile out of town (holidaymakers had to make the rest of the journey by steam tram) to stop vulgar people from coming. Certainly it's much more sedate – basically a family resort. In terms of sheer location, though, Portstewart wins hands down. Just west of the town is **Portstewart Strand**, a long sand beach firm enough to drive on – which the locals delight in doing – with some of the best **surfing** in the country. Again, it's a good place if you hit fine weather and feel like getting out your bucket and spade. The best way to take the sea air is the bracing **cliffside walk** which runs between the beach and the town, passing battlements and an imposing Gothic mansion, now a convent.

The **tourist office** (April–Sept ☎01265/832286), in the Town Hall, can help with **accommodation** bookings if you have any problems – there's slightly less choice here than in Portrush. Guesthouses doing **B&B** are mostly along the main road by the bay – or there's the *Edgewater Hotel*, 88 Strand Road (☎01265/83314; ⑥), with a breathtaking view from the lounge bar. There's also a good independent **hostel**, *Causeway Coast*, at 4 Victoria Terrace (*IHH*; open all year; ☎01265/833789; ②). The municipal **caravan park**, *Juniper Hill*, is at 70 Ballyreagh Road (☎01265/832023). *Morelli's*, on the promenade, is justly famous for its ice cream, and also serves snacks and Italian **food**. In the evenings, *Nero's* **nightclub** is the place for late-nighters, and has a pleasant pub attached.

Castlerock and Mussenden Temple

Beyond Portstewart, the coastline rears up as great cliffs once more, before settling down into monotonous flatness beyond Magilligan Point for the run into Derry. There's a long sand beach at **CASTLEROCK** (and a heated swimming pool, too) and, at the A2 crossroads a mile south of Castlerock, is **Hezlett House** (April–June & Sept Sat & Sun 1–6pm; July & Aug 1–6pm daily except Tues; £1.50), a long, low-thatched building of wood-cruck construction. It's a building method that's common in England, but enough of a rarity here to warrant preservation by the National Trust.

Further west along the A2, a pair of huge, ornate Pompeiian gates on the left mark the entry to **Mussenden Temple** (April–June & Sept Sat & Sun noon–6pm; July & Aug daily noon–6pm; grounds open all year), a domed rotunda clinging precariously to the cliff-edge. This is almost all that is left of the great estate of Frederick Harvey (1730–1803), fourth Earl of Bristol and Anglican Bishop of Derry, the enthusiastic traveller after whom all the *Hotel Bristol*s throughout Europe are named. The "Earl Bishop", as he was known, commissioned Michael Shanahan to build the temple in honour of his cousin Mrs Frideswide Mussenden, who died before it was finished. It was then used as his summer library and, with characteristic generosity and a fairly startling lack of prejudice, the Earl Bishop allowed Mass to be celebrated in the temple once a week as there was no local Catholic church. The inscription on the frieze translates, smugly, as "It is agreeable to watch, from land, someone else involved in a great struggle while winds whip up the waves out at sea."

Coleraine and Limavady

COLERAINE, designated a joint conurbation with Portrush and Portstewart, is rather unprepossessing. In fact, the best thing about Coleraine is its proximity to Portrush. A walk along the river can be pleasant, but the big pedestrianized shopping precinct in the town centre is anonymous and depressing. The one thing Coleraine does have going for it is a major campus of the University of Ulster, a bone of contention with the people of Derry, many of whom believe that the only reason the university didn't go there was because the authorities wanted it in a predominantly Protestant location.

There's a **tourist office** on Railway Road by the station (Mon–Fri 9am–5pm; ☎01265/44723), which is very helpful and will try hard to convince you of the attractions of the place. In summer there are interesting environmental **walks** (under the title *Talks and Tours*, details from the tourist office), and there's the fine *Riverside* **theatre** here, too. For upmarket country house **accommodation** try *Ardtara*, Gorteade Road, Upperlands (☎01648/44490; ⑥). B&Bs are mostly out of town; try *Alan Badger* (☎01265/31816; ③) off the road to Bushmills. The University of Ulster campus provides cheap rooms during the summer vacation (☎01265/44141; ③).

Just a mile south of Coleraine, on the eastern bank of the river, **Mountsandel** is a 200ft mound, apparently the earliest-known dwelling place in Ireland, though the recent discoveries in Boora Bog in County Offaly must run a fairly close second. The post-holes and hearths of the wooden houses that once stood here have been dated at around 7000 BC.

LIMAVADY has even less going for it than Coleraine. Still, its broad main street is recognizably Georgian. No. 51 was the home of Jane Ross, who noted down the famous *Londonderry Air* – better known as *Danny Boy* – from a travelling fiddler in 1851. **Tourist information** is available from the council offices at 7 Connell Street (☎015047/22226). At **Drenagh**, just outside Limavady (☎015047/22649; ⑤), you can experience upper-class life in a Classical Lanyon-designed mansion at *Drenagh House*. The **Roe Valley Country Park**, a couple of miles south of Limavady, preserves Ulster's first hydroelectric domestic power station, opened in 1896, with much of the original equipment intact, as well as a small weaving museum. There's a municipal **campsite** at Benone Beach (☎015047/50555), and another inland a mile from looming Binevenagh Mountain (☎015047/20742).

Derry city

DERRY lies at the foot of Lough Foyle, immediately before the border: a major crossroads where the coast road meets the faster, duller route direct from Belfast, and from where roads head on west into Donegal and the Republic, south into Tyrone. Ireland's fourth largest city, and the second largest in the North, its size makes it Belfast's sister city, but it has a markedly different atmosphere, being two-thirds Catholic. Within Ireland, Derry is highly regarded both for its characteristically caustic humour – best caught in the busier bars and at the football matches at the Brandywell – and for its musical pedigree, having produced names as diverse as Dana, Phil Coulter, The Undertones, and many less well known. This last claim to recognition is misleading, though – Derry may produce musicians, but its own music scene is largely inaccessible to outsiders.

Approached from the east in winter twilight or under a strong summer sun, the city presents a beguiling picture, with the spread of the **River Foyle** and the rise of the city's two hillsides, terraced with pastel-shaded houses from which rise the hueless stone spires of the ever-present Church Orders. This scenic appeal apart, Derry at first sight seems to have little to tempt you to stay overnight, for all the richness of its history. Yet there are things worth seeing, all of them enclosed within the seventeenth-century **walls**, themselves the most significant reminder of the city's past. And four miles or so out of the centre, across the border on the Letterkenny road, is an unmissable sight – the **Grianán of Aileach**, a stone fort that is the oldest habitation left standing in Ireland.

Outside of Ireland, the name of Derry brings to mind the troubles of recent years, difficulties with which the Bogside and the Creggan are inextricably associated. Don't be put off by this: unlike Belfast, the cutting edge of violence had receded considerably here even before the ceasefires, and a resurgence of optimism is being felt for the first time since the early 1960s. Perhaps the greatest vote of confidence in Derry's future is from the big retail chains, such as *Marks & Spencer* and *Sainsbury's*, which have recently built their first outlets in the city.

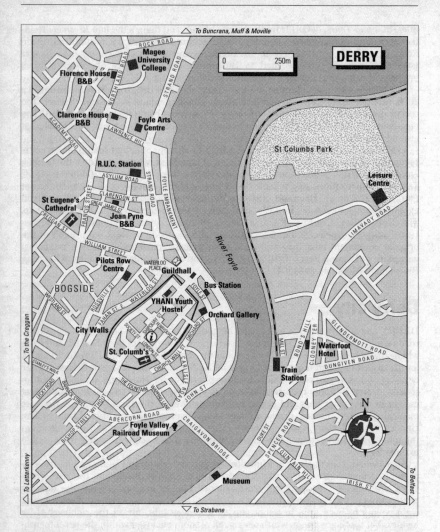

To Buncrana, Muff & Moville

DERRY

0   250m

Magee University College

Florence House B&B

Clarence House B&B

Foyle Arts Centre

ROCK ROAD

STRAND ROAD

NORTHLAND ROAD

ACADEMY ROAD

LAWRENCE HILL

R.U.C. Station

ASYLUM ROAD

CLARENDON ST

St Columbs Park

St Eugene's Cathedral

Joan Pyne B&B

CREGGAN ST

HAWKIN'S ST

GREAT JAMES ST

STRAND ROAD

FOYLE EMBANKMENT

River Foyle

Leisure Centre

LIMAVADY ROAD

WILLIAM STREET

Pilots Row Centre

BOGSIDE

To the Creggan

WATERLOO PLACE

Guildhall

Bus Station

ROSSVILLE ST

FAHAN ST

WATERLOO ST

STRAND ST

YHANI Youth Hostel

Orchard Gallery

City Walls

St. Columb's

LECKY ROAD

BERACK'S STREET

BISHOP STREET WITHOUT

STANLEY'S WALK

To Letterkenny

FOYLE ST

SHIPQUAY ST

CHURCH WAY

THE FOUNTAIN

WAPPING LANE

CARLISLE ROAD

JOHN ST

ORCHARD ST

Train Station

MILL ST

BOND'S HILL

CLOONEY TER

GLENDERMOTT ROAD

Waterfoot Hotel

DUNGIVEN ROAD

ABERCORN ROAD

Foyle Valley Railroad Museum

CRAIGAVON BRIDGE

DUKE ST

SPENCER ROAD

FOUNTAIN HILL

N

Museum

IRISH ST

To Belfast

To Strabane

Some history

Derry's original name was *Daire Calgaigh* ("oakwood of Calgach"), a warrior who led the Caledonians at the battle of the Grampians. This name remained in use until well after the coming of Saint Columba, who founded a monastery here in 546 AD; then, in the tenth century, the settlers renamed the spot *Doire Cholmcille*. As the annals of the city record, the settlement suffered frequent onslaughts, first from the Vikings, later from the Anglo-Norman barons de Courcy and Peyton. In 1566, Elizabeth I of England sent a small task force in a failed attempt to pacify such troublesome chieftains as Shane O'Neill, but at the end of the century the uprising of Hugh O'Neill, Earl of Tyrone, provoked another English invasion, this time successful. It paved the way for the first widescale "planting" of English and Scottish **settlers** in the reign of James I.

Doire became anglicized to **Derry** and then, in 1613, "London" was bestowed as a prefix after land within the newly drawn borders of the county was awarded to the Twelve Companies of the Corporation of London. Today the entrance routes to the city bear the two different names – "Welcome to Londonderry, an historic city" and "Welcome to Derry, a nuclear-free zone" – reflecting the changing sectarian majority on the city council. Indeed, the place has come to be called "Stroke City" – a reference to the tactful placating of both traditions by naming it Londonderry/Derry.

The **seventeenth century** was the most dramatic phase of the city's evolution. The city walls withstood successive sieges, the last of which (in 1688–89) played a key part in the Williamite army's final victory over the Catholic King James II at the Battle of the Boyne – the Derrymen's obduracy crucially delaying the plans of James and his ally Louis XIV. Seven thousand of the city's 30,000 inhabitants died during the fifteen-week **siege** (the longest in British history), the survivors being reduced to eating dogs, cats and rats. The suffering and heroism of those weeks still have the immediacy of recent history in the minds of Derry's citizens, who commemorate the siege through the skeleton on the city coat of arms, and the lyrical tag "maiden city", a reference to its unbreached walls.

After the siege many Derry people emigrated to America to avoid the harsh English laws, and some of their descendants – such as Daniel Boone and Davy Crockett – achieved fame there. George Farquhar (b. 1678), a Derryman who chose to stay, achieved fame as a playwright. Derry's heyday as a **seaport** came in the nineteenth century, a period in which industries such as linen production also flourished. It was a Derry weaver, William Scott, who established the world's first industrialized shirt manufacturers, cutting the shirts in Derry and sending them to the cottage women of Donegal for stitching. After **Partition**, the North–South dividing line lay right at Derry's back door, and the consequent tariffs cut off a lot of its traditional trade.

CIVIL RIGHTS

Though Derry remained relatively peaceful, its politics were among the North's most blatantly discriminatory, with the substantial Catholic majority denied its civil rights by gerrymandering which ensured that the Protestant minority maintained control of all important local institutions. On October 5, 1968, a 2000-strong **civil rights march** – demanding equality of employment and housing, and other political rights, and led by a Protestant, Ivan Cooper, and a Catholic, John Hume – came up against the batons of the Protestant police force and the B Specials. It is an event which is seen by many as the catalyst for the present phase of the Troubles: faith in the impartiality of the Royal Ulster Constabulary was destroyed once and for all, and the IRA was reborn a year or so later.

The Protestant Apprentice Boys' March, in August 1969, was a further step – the RUC attempted to storm the Bogside (from where stones were being thrown at the march), and for several days the area lay in a state of siege. The Irish prime minister, Jack Lynch, moved units of the army to the border and set up field hospitals for injured Bogsiders. In the mounting tension that ensued, British troops were for the first time widely deployed in the North, and many of the demands of the civil rights movement were forced on Stormont from Westminster. Then, on January 30, 1972, came **Bloody Sunday**. Thirteen people were shot dead when British paratroopers (who subsequently claimed that they had been shot at first) opened fire on another unarmed civil rights march.

These days, the city is controlled by the Social Democratic and Labour Party, which attempts to be scrupulously non-sectarian. In this they seem to have been successful (at least in Northern Irish terms), and they also pursue an enlightened arts policy which has succeeded in making this a lively and unexpectedly entertaining place to visit.

The telephone code for Derry is ☎01504.

Arrival, information and accommodation

Northern Ireland Railways runs about seven **trains** a day from Belfast to Derry (information on ☎42228), and there are also frequent **buses** from all parts of the North and the Republic; *Ulsterbus* (☎262261) serves all the main Northern Ireland destinations and Dublin, at frequencies ranging between twice daily to Dublin and eleven most days to Strabane; *Bus Éireann* operates a good network, connecting Derry to such as Galway and Dublin; and *Lough Swilly Bus Services* (☎262017) runs buses from across the border in north Donegal. Good roads enter the city from all directions, making it very straightforward to **hitch**. You can also **fly**: *Jersey European* and *British Airways* operate from Dublin, London, Gatwick, Glasgow and Manchester to the revamped City of Derry Airport (☎810784), seven miles out on the A2 road. A regular bus service runs from the *Ulsterbus* station, Foyle Street, to the airport. **Black taxis** run from Foyle Street and most operate in a similar way to those in Belfast, functioning like minibuses to ferry the Catholic community to and from their housing estates. For a regular taxi, call *Auto Cabs* (☎45100) or *Quick Cabs* (☎260515).

The **tourist information office** is situated in Bishop Street (July–Sept Mon–Sat 9am–8pm, Sun 10am–6pm; Oct–June Mon–Thurs 9am–5.15pm, Fri 9am–5pm; ☎267284) and also houses a **Bord Fáilte** office and a **bureau de change**. Grab a free pocket guidebook for up-to-date information. The Catholic *Derry Journal* (Tues & Fri) is good for entertainment listings.

Top-of-the-range accommodation in Derry includes *The Everglades Hotel*, Prehen Road (☎46722; ⑧), and the *Waterfoot Hotel*, 14 Clooney Terrace (☎45500; ⑧), both on the Waterside. **B&Bs** are fairly thin on the ground in the centre, but you could try the following: *Clarence House*, 15 Northland Road (☎265342; ⑤); *Florence House*, 16 Northland Road (☎268093; ③); and *Joan Pyne*, 36 Great James Street (off Strand Road; ☎269691; ④). There's a 150-bed *YHANI* **hostel** in the city centre, *Oakgrove Manor*, 4–6 Magazine Street (open all year; ☎372273, fax ☎372409; ③), which does a generous and cheap Ulster fry, **rents bikes** and acts as an unofficial tourist information centre. **Rooms** are also seasonally available at the university to the north of the centre (mid-June to mid-September; for price enquiries ring Mon–Fri on ☎265621, ext 5218).

The city

The **walls** of Derry – some of the best-preserved historical defences left standing in Europe – are the obvious point for a walkabout of the city and have recently been opened to the public after fifteen years spent wrapped in iron sheeting and barbed wire for security reasons. A mile in length and never higher than a two-storey house, the walls are reinforced by bulwarks and bastions and a parapeted earth rampart as wide as any thoroughfare. Within their circuit, the original medieval street pattern has remained, with four **gateways** – Shipquay, Butcher, Bishop and Ferryquay – surviving from the first construction, in slightly revised form.

You're more than likely to make your approach from the Guildhall Square, once the old quay. Most of the city's cannon are lined up here, between the Shipquay and Magazine gates, their noses peering out above the ramparts. A reconstruction of the medieval **O'Doherty Tower** (July–Aug Mon–Sat 10am–5pm, Sun 2–5pm; Sept–June Tues–Sat 10am–5pm, closed Sun & Mon; £2.25) is home to a prize-winning **museum** telling the city's history over the past four centuries. Tableaux and audiovisual displays supplement traditional museum exhibits in this determinedly non-sectarian gallop through time – and, as far as possible, you're supplied with the facts and left to make

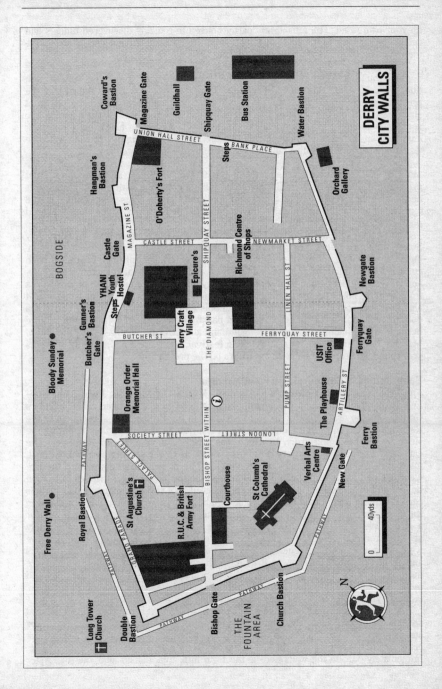

DERRY CITY WALLS

Coward's Bastion
Magazine Gate
Guildhall
Shipquay Gate
Bus Station
Water Bastion

UNION HALL STREET
BANK PLACE
Steps

Hangman's Bastion

Orchard Gallery

O'Doherty's Fort

MAGAZINE ST

SHIPQUAY STREET

BOGSIDE

Castle Gate
YHANI Youth Hostel
Steps

CASTLE STREET
NEWMARKET STREET

Epicure's
Richmond Centre of Shops

Newgate Bastion

Butcher's Gate
Gunner's Bastion

LINEN HALL ST

Bloody Sunday Memorial

Derry Craft Village
THE DIAMOND

BUTCHER ST
FERRYQUAY STREET

Ferryquay Gate

Orange Order Memorial Hall

PUMP STREET

USIT Office

The Playhouse

ARTILLERY ST

Free Derry Wall

BISHOP STREET WITHIN

SOCIETY STREET
LONDON STREET

Ferry Bastion

Royal Bastion

PALACE STREET

Courthouse

Verbal Arts Centre

New Gate

St Augustine's Church

GRAND PARADE

St Columb's Cathedral

R.U.C. & British Army Fort

Long Tower Church

Double Bastion

Church Bastion

PATHWAY

Bishop Gate

THE FOUNTAIN AREA

PATHWAY

N

40yds
0

up your own mind. The museum is partly housed in recently discovered tunnels and cellars dating back to the siege. Artefacts from the Spanish Armada wrecks are scheduled to go on show in the upper storey during 1996.

Turning left at Shipquay Gate into **Bank Place**, you follow the promenade as it doglegs round at Water Bastion, where the River Foyle once lapped the walls at high tide. On to Newgate Bastion and Ferryquay Gate, you can look across the river to the prosperous and largely Protestant Waterside. Several sculptures have been placed at strategic points on the walls by the English artist Antony Gormley, their gaping eye sockets looking out in diametrically opposite directions from a single body – a frank comment on the city's ideological split. Aesthetics aside, the figures provide welcome visual relief against the office buildings that swamp the immediate view.

Just off steeply sloping Shipquay Street as you penetrate towards the heart of the old city is **Derry Craft Village** (Mon–Sat 9.30am–5.30pm), an Inner City Trust project in a purpose-built traditional stone village complex, with shops, restaurants and a craftshop representing a range of traditional crafts. This new venture is still expanding and well worth a visit – the elegant *Boston Tea Party* coffee shop is a good place to sit and take it all in.

Abutting the city walls on London Street (from the Diamond walk down Ferryquay Street, then turn right), **The Verbal Arts Centre** is a unique project aimed at sustaining and promoting forms of communication and entertainment once central to Irish culture: legend, folklore, *seán nos* – a nasalized and unaccompanied narrative singing – and storytelling performed by a *seanachie* (storyteller). The centre commissions works from writers, hosts poetry readings and storytelling and has a resident *seanachie*. It also goes out into the community – to schools and community centres – and has a determinedly non-sectarian ethos, aided in part by its awareness of its diverse cultural heritage which includes America, Scotland and all of Ireland. Every year at the end of March it holds an international storytelling **festival**; and there are also plenty of events year-round, so drop in and check out what's on the programme.

Saint Columb's Cathedral, the Fountain area

The Protestant **Saint Columb's Cathedral** (March–Oct Mon–Sat 10am–5pm; Nov–Feb 10am–4pm; donations welcomed), built in 1633 in a style later called Planter's Gothic, was the first cathedral to be constructed in the British Isles subsequent to the Reformation. On show in the entrance porch is a cannon shell catapulted in during the siege by the besieging army, to which was attached their terms of surrender. The cathedral was used as a battery during the siege, its **tower** serving as a lookout post; today it provides the best view of the old city. The present spire dates from the late Georgian period, its lead-covered wooden predecessor having been stripped to fashion bullets and cannon shot. Inside, an open-timbered roof rests on sixteen stone corbels carved with figures of past bishops; hanging above the nave, French flags captured in the siege, and others brought back from various military expeditions, give the interior a strong sense of the British Empire. Other things to look out for are the finely sculpted reredos behind the altar, the eighteenth-century bishop's throne and the window panels showing scenes as diverse as the relief of the city on August 12, 1689 and Saint Columba's mission to Britain. In the **chapter house museum** (50p) are more relics of the siege, plus the grand kidney-shaped desk of Bishop Berkeley and mementos of Cecil Frances (1818–95), wife of Bishop Alexander and composer of the famous hymns *Once in royal David's city* and *There is a green hill far away*.

The **courthouse**, built of white sandstone from Dungiven in crude Greek Revival style, is undergoing restoration, but still shows signs of the Troubles – a security tower stands guard close to the Bishop Gate arch. The gate itself was remodelled for the first centenary of the siege and is the last of the old Derry gates to be opened to the public. Immediately outside the walls here is the **Fountain** area, named after the freshwater source that once supplied the city; take a glance at the surrounding pieces of eighteenth-century architecture, evident even in boarded-up Dean Street. Bordered by Bishop Street, Bennett Street, Abercorn Road and Hawkin Street, the Fountain area is a housing estate that sticks into the Catholic west bank like a sore thumb, with a single road entrance close to the Craigavon Bridge. Here you'll see, jammed up against the grim houses, the last remaining tower of the old Derry jail. It's of interest solely for its Union Jack kerb paintings and huge wall murals which read as direct responses to the more famous Catholic "FREE DERRY" mural in the next valley. Until recently the Fountain area had the **oldest mural** in the north. Painted in the early part of this century by Bobby Jackson, it showed the Siege of Derry and the Battle of the Boyne, and was repainted every year. In the 1970s, when the area was redeveloped, the wall was painstakingly dismantled, moved, reassembled and repainted, but it finally disintegrated in 1994. A replica was painted in 1995 on a special Bobby Jackson memorial wall. Other Loyalist murals are to be found in Fountain and in Bond Street in the Waterside.

The Bogside

Back on the walls, and continuing west, you reach the Double Bastion where the Roaring Meg cannon sits. During the siege it was said that "the noise of the discharge was more terrifying than were the contents of the charge dangerous to the enemy". In the valley below is the **Bogside**, where, at the start of the Troubles, young Catholics were caught up in an advancing disarray of army and police, who replied to bricks and petrol bombs with tear gas, rubber bullets and careering Saracen armoured cars. The area at the foot of the escarpment has been redeveloped in the form of a dual carriageway, a new estate of tenement flats and empty concrete precincts. But clinging to the opposite hillside is a classic urban landscape, with turn-of-the-century terraces of stucco facades, blue tile roofs and red chimney stacks.

Most eye-catching in this panorama is an isolated wall bearing the slogan "YOU ARE NOW ENTERING FREE DERRY". The **Free Derry Mural** was originally painted by local man John "Caker" Casey in the aftermath of the attack by Loyalists on a civil rights march in 1968. Since then the signature of the Nationalist camp in Derry has become almost a community noticeboard, marking events as disparate as Derry's win in the All-Ireland Gaelic Football Final in 1993 and the release of Republican prisoners. The rear of the wall now carries another well-known mural, with a message to the British Army that was originally a piece of wishful thinking but is now a virtual reality – *Slán Abhaile* (goodbye/safe home).

For the first two years of the Troubles the territory beyond the mural was the notorious "no go area", the undisputed preserve of the IRA. This autonomy lasted until 1972, when "Operation Motorman" was launched; the IRA men who had been in the area were warned, though, and got across the border before the invasion took place. Further across to the right of the wall stands the memorial pillar to the thirteen Catholic civilians killed on **Bloody Sunday** (January 1972) by British paratroopers. The soldiers immediately claimed they were fired upon, a claim that was later disproved, though some witnesses have come forward to report seeing IRA men there with their guns. To the right of this area once stood the Rossville flats, by far the most infamous part of the Bogside – Derry's Divis in fact. Further up the Westland Road, which runs up by the *Bogside Inn* – a former IRA stronghold, where the gunmen would set their revolvers on the bar while drinking – is a busy mural grouping the silhouetted faces of Bobby Sands, Che Guevara and Lenin.

Railway Centre

To the southeast of the walled city, the **Foyle Valley Railway Centre** on Foyle Road by Craigavon Bridge (April–Sept Tues–Sat 10am–5pm, Sun 2–6pm; Oct–March Tues–Sat 10am–5pm; free) is more interesting than it might sound and has train rides at weekends. The highlight is a short trip up the Foyle Valley on a steam train, but there are also plenty of old engines and models, plus extensive displays on the history of railways in the area, a sad tale of decline enthusiastically explained.

Eating, drinking and entertainment

Although **eating** out in the city has improved dramatically over recent years, you still won't be put out by a bewildering choice. The best food is to be found in the suburbs at *Schooners* on Prehen Road (☎311500) on the Waterside, or *Brown's* (☎45180), located in an old railway station on Victoria Road. *Piemonte Pizzeria* (☎2668228) on Clarendon Street is the best pizza place in town, while *India House*, 51–55 Carlisle Road (☎260532), is an excellent Indian with main courses around £7. Just next door is a newly opened Italian, *La Sosta* (☎374817), unlicensed at the moment, so bring a bottle along. Shipquay Street has the widest variety, including *The Gallery* (Mon–Thurs & Sat 9am–5.30pm, Fri 9am–9pm), which does very tasty and reasonably priced pizzas and home-baked food, and the new *Bewley's* – one of the much-loved chain – which is *the* place for coffee and fry. Even cheaper are *Anne's* on William Street, decorated with black-and-white photos of the Troubles in Derry, and the very sociable *Leprechaun* on the Strand. As ever, you can also get lunch in many of the pubs: the *Metro* in Bank Place, the *Linenhall* in Linenhall Street and the *Monico Lounge* opposite the main post office, for example. On the Waterside, *Brendan's* on Spencer Road is renowned for its sit-down fast food.

Bars and traditional music

What Derry lacks in restaurants, it makes up for, inevitably, in the **pubs**. For drinking and talk, the student set congregates at the *College*, *The Strand Tavern* and *Andy Cole's*, all grouped at the bottom of the Rock Road, and of course in the campus bar in Magee College grounds, where beer is cheapest. Other congenial and conversational places are *The Clarendon Bar*, 44 Strand Road; *Badgers Place*, 18 Orchard Street – for an older clientele; *McGinleys* on Foyle Street behind the bus station – a friendly bar with music at weekends; and the new *Mullins* on Sackville Street. Out past Magee College on the Culmore Road is *Da Vinci's*, one of Derry's new pubs with a restaurant and nightclub.

    Traditional music in the city is not as exciting as it once was: the venues that remain are all grouped in and around **Waterloo Street**, just outside the northern section of the walls, a mostly Catholic working-class area. The *Dungloe Bar* claims to be the most regular music-making place here (traditional on Fri & Sat; two-piece folk band on Thurs & Fri). Other sessions take place at the *Rocking Chair Pub* and the *Gweedore Bar*, which has a function room upstairs with good music and dancing, and often stays open until 1am, or try *Peadar O'Donnell's*, a recently opened pub in old style, which does set dancing. Elsewhere, the *Phoenix Bar*, on Park Avenue in the Rosemount area, has traditional music on Tuesday evenings, as does the *Pilot's Row Centre* (7.30–9.30pm), which also offers classes in Irish dancing, music and language. The *Bogside Inn* on Westland Road has music on Thursday evenings. Bear in mind, though, that the city is highly politicized, and if a hat comes round, you're advised to contribute without asking questions.

    For livelier **nightlife**, head for Shipquay Street, where the *Gluepot* and *Townsman* pubs and the cavernous *Squire's* nightclub all attract a young crowd. Another popular thing to do on Friday and Saturday nights is to cross the border, to nightclubs at Letterkenny, Redcastle and the White Strand, Buncrana.

Arts and other entertainment

Classical music thrives in the city through the Londonderry Arts Association (☎264481), with around a dozen concerts a year held in the Great Hall of Magee University College. Orchestral concerts by the Ulster Orchestra are held much less

FIELD DAY

Contrary to their reputation abroad, popular wisdom in Ireland has **Field Day Theatre Company** as a group of introverted, intellectual and very, very male academics. In Derry, locals tend to feel they give the city very little, and what is perceived as their Nationalist agenda is seen by many as limiting. Hackles rise annually at the amount of Arts Council funding Field Day is given – a new theatre site just approved is to house the company and stage their productions – given their scant output in recent years.

But it has been the publishing activities of the group – including **Seamus Heaney**, the academic **Seamus Deane**, the actor **Stephen Rea** and the playwright **Brian Friel** – who came together in 1980, that have brought the most criticism. During the 1980s, they published pamphlets that were part of a step-by-step intellectual questioning and building of identities intended to work as counterpoints to the Troubles. However, in 1991, when the much talked-about *Field Day Anthology of Irish Writing* came out, there was a storm of controversy. There were no women editors involved at all, and women were sorely misrepresented in the work. Another volume bridging the gap, and edited by some high-profile Irish women of letters, is now in preparation and due to be published in 1997.

In 1990, Brian Friel, after giving his most successful play, *Dancing at Lughnasa*, to Dublin's Abbey Theatre, left the group. Stephen Rea – who used to do Gerry Adams's voice-over on BBC TV when Sinn Féin were banned from the airwaves – is now actor/manager of the company, and with Gerry Adams now talking to anyone who'll listen, the big challenge for Field Day will be to reinvent itself successfully for the new era.

regularly in the Great Hall of the Guildhall. The Playhouse on Artillery Street is a good venue for art, dance, music and drama; however, **theatre** in Derry since the early 1980s has been associated with Field Day Theatre Company, principally directed by a set of Derrymen – for more on which see above.

The **visual arts** are also attracting a lot of international attention, thanks largely to the highly innovative contemporary art programming of the *Orchard Gallery* in Orchard Street; a visit there is a must – and watch out for the exhibitions it sometimes arranges in the *Foyle Arts Centre*, off Lawrence Hill, or at other venues around the city. The *Heritage Library*, on Bishop Street, occasionally has local artists' work on display.

Several **arts festivals** take place at regular times throughout the year, the most interesting of them being the *Foyle Film Festival* (late Oct) and the *North West Arts Festival* (early Nov). In addition, **Halloween** is traditionally an excuse for riotous celebration, with fireworks, fancy dress and partying in the streets. The tourist information office will have further details.

Listings

Automobile Association Richmond Centre (☎372323).

Banks Principally situated on Shipquay St and Waterloo Place.

Bike rental and repairs Rental at *Oak Grove Manor*, 4–6 Magazine St (☎372273) and *Eakin Bros Ltd*, Maydown (☎860601); repairs at *McClean Bros*, 108 Spencer Rd (☎43171).

Bookshop *Bookworm* on Bishop St is one of the best bookshops in the country, comprehensive and with excellent coverage of contemporary and historical Irish works.

Car rental *Hertz*, c/o *Desmond Motors*, 173 Strand Rd (☎367613).

Exchange Available from all banks; also *Bureau de Change*, 68 Strand Rd (☎367710); a kiosk in the Richmond Centre (☎260636); *Oak Grove Manor*, 4–6 Magazine St (☎372273).

Gay Counselling *Carafriend* phone-in (Thurs 7.30–10pm; ☎263120).

Health food *Life Tree*, 37 Spencer Rd (☎42865).

Hospital Accident and emergency department, Altnagelvin Hospital, Belfast Rd (☎45171); contact this number also for **dental** emergencies after working hours or at weekends.

Laundry *Foyle Dry Cleaners*, 147 Spencer Rd; *Duds n Suds*, 141 Strand Rd.

Library The Central Library, Foyle St, has a good selection on Irish studies and local history.

Market Bottom of William St every Sat.

Newspapers The Catholic *Derry Journal* (Tues & Fri) has a good run-through of what's on in the city; the Protestant local paper is the *Londonderry Sentinel* (Thurs).

Police ☎367337.

Post office Custom House Street (☎362274; Mon–Fri 9am–5.30pm, Sat 9am–12.30pm).

Travel agents *USIT*, Ferryquay St (☎371888); *Thomas Cook*, Unit 7, Quayside Centre (☎374174); *Concorde Travel*, 4 Shipquay St (☎263092).

Women's centre 24 Pump St (Mon–Fri 9.30am–5pm; ☎267672), for information and advice.

Southern Derry

South of the A6, the Derry-to-Antrim road, the landscape settles down into a pattern more familiar to the Republic: fertile farming land, rising to the **Sperrin Mountains**, punctuated by small planned towns. The pattern in the North is subtly different, though, because the grants of land here were not made to individuals but to various London guilds or companies. Consequently, there isn't the strange, late-flowering feudalism that you see in the Republic, with its repeated archetype of big house and surrounding town, but rather entirely **planned towns**, often built on green-field sites selected by professionals, who specialized in doing just that.

Dungiven

DUNGIVEN, eighteen miles east of Derry, is a fairly unremarkable town, though it does harbour one or two ruins of interest. Originally an O'Cahan stronghold, Dungiven was given to the Skinners' Company to settle in the seventeenth century. The remains of the O'Cahan fortifications are incorporated into the ruined nineteenth-century **castle**, whose battlemented outline gives Dungiven a particular flavour when approached from the south. This was the scene of the 1971 attempt to set up an independent Northern Ireland parliament.

Dungiven Priory, signposted down a footpath a little way out of the town towards Antrim, gives a taste of the pioneering life of the early plantation settlers, and of the continuity of tradition. No more than a ruin, the Augustinian priory stands on an imposing, defensible site on a bluff above the river. Founded in 1100 by the O'Cahans, it belongs to the first wave of European monastic orders which arrived in Ireland to supplant the Celtic Church. The church contains the tomb of Cooey na Gall O'Cahan, who died in 1385, rated as the finest medieval tomb in Northern Ireland: beneath the effigy are six bare-legged warriors in kilts, presumably denoting Scotsmen, who represent the O'Cahan chieftain's foreign mercenaries, from whom he derived his nickname, na Gall, or "of the foreigners". At some point, the O'Cahans added a defensive tower to the west end of the church, and later – when Dungiven was granted to the Skinners' Company, in the person of Sir Edward Doddington – this was enlarged to become a two-and-a-half storeyed defensive manor house. There's an evocative artist's impression on the site of what that building looked like.

Although the church hasn't been used since 1711, Dungiven Priory remains a religious site of sorts. The tree knotted with rags – handkerchiefs, torn-off bits of summer dresses, socks – stands over a deeply hollowed stone, originally used by the monks for milling grain, and now an object of pilgrimage for people seeking cures for physical illness.

Plantation towns

South of Dungiven, well into the Sperrin Mountains, are more of the **plantation towns** of the London companies, most of them characteristically planned around a central diamond. **DRAPERSTOWN**, unsurprisingly founded by the Drapers' Company, is essentially a junction, with well-mannered houses facing each other in a very grand street plan. Of more delaying interest, at **UPPERLANDS**, ten miles north beyond Maghera, you can get some idea of the impact of the new eighteenth-century technology on the area. You can get a taste of Victorian elegance at *Ardtara Country House* nearby (☎01648/44490; ⑤). The **Middle House Museum** here is a private textile museum owned by the Clark family: in 1740, Jackson Clark dammed the river to provide power and installed linen-finishing machinery here. If you want to look around, phone Wallace Clark (☎01648/42214 or ☎42737) in advance to arrange a guided tour.

Heading southeast, **MAGHERAFELT**, granted to the Salters' Company by James I, has another wide, sloping main street with Union Jacks fluttering everywhere. The real gem, though, is **MONEYMORE**, about five miles further south, built by the Drapers and reconstructed by them in 1817: graceful pedimented buildings face each other across a wide main street topped by an Orange Hall (plenty of red, white and blue kerbstones here). It was the first town in Ulster to have piped water – amazingly, as early as 1615. Just outside Moneymore, **Springhill** (Easter week daily 2–6pm; April–June & Sept Sat & Sun 2–6pm; July & Aug daily except Thurs 2–6pm; £2.20) is a typical example of the fortified manor houses built by the early planters. Dating from the late seventeenth century, it's a lovely bit of sober whitewashed architecture, housing a good costume collection and a delightfully overgrown garden.

Lough Neagh and Bellaghy

East of Magherafelt and Moneymore, southern Derry also gives onto the fish-rich waters of the biggest lake in Ireland, **Lough Neagh**, which has been called a huge fish factory. Tributaries flow from every point of the compass: the **Lower Bann**, which drains the lake and runs north to Lough Beg (finally reaching the sea at north of Coleraine), contains some huge trout, but the main interest for the trout angler is the *dollaghan* (best fishing mid-July to Oct). Similar to salmon – which are also common – they grow by 3lb every year and can be caught by spinning, worming and fly fishing. In fact the Ballinderry Black and the Bann Olive are famous flies derived from this region.

To fish in the lough or the river, all anglers require a rod licence (call the Foyle Fisheries Commission; ☎01504/42100); however, while this entitles you to carry a rod it doesn't mean that you can fish unless you have a permit from the owner or you're in free water. The angling clubs which control much of the water let day tickets at reasonable rates. For details of licences and permits ask at tourist offices or local tackle shops.

BELLAGHY, just east of Lough Beg, is a good place to base yourself; *Lough Beg Coach Houses* (☎01648/386235; £350 per week for up to 6 people) offers good **self-catering accommodation** with a bait-room – and extras such as wash-up and cooking services. They will also organize a ghillie and fishing for you. The area is also worth exploring for its interesting ruins – the *Coach Houses* are in the grounds of Ballyscullion House, where the remains of a palace built for the Earl Bishop, Frederick Augustus Hervey (see the Mussenden Temple on p.498), still stand. Two miles southeast on Lough Beg sits a winter-time island, the Church Island Peninsula, which is peppered with Christian relics. Besides a walled graveyard, there are the ruins of a medieval church, said to have been founded centuries before by the ubiquitous Saint Patrick, and a tower and spire added by an eccentric bishop in 1788. Now the place is a pilgrimage spot for more pagan rituals – a knee-sized dent has been worn into a large stone beside a "healing tree" decked out with ribbons and an incongruous pair of indestructible red nylon knickers.

A famous son of the area is poet **Seamus Heaney**, who was born just outside Bellaghy in 1939. He was the eldest of nine children, and his rural childhood gave him a reverence for the people, landscape and traditions of the Irish countryside that characterizes much of his poetry. Heaney, who won a scholarship to a Derry boarding school and then to Queen's University in Belfast, emerged in the 1970s as one of the most talented of a collective of Northern Irish writers known as "the Group"; in 1995, with numerous volumes of poetry to his name, he won the Nobel Prize for literature. An archive containing his original manuscripts is planned for Bellaghy (for more on his work, see pp.614 and 621).

South Antrim: Ballymena to Belfast

South Antrim is unlikely travelling country, being largely rolling and unexciting farmland, with places whose names are familiar because you've heard them so often on the news: Ballymena, Antrim and Lisburn. Still, you're likely to see something of most of these towns as the train from Belfast passes through them on the way to the northern coast.

Ballymena and Gracehill
BALLYMENA (pronounced *Ballamena*, unless you're a BBC newsreader) is a fine, upstanding, predominantly Protestant town that could have been transplanted straight from the Scottish lowlands. Indeed, most of its plantation settlers came from the southwest of Scotland, and the Ballymena accent still retains traces of Scottish lowlands speech. Like many Northern Irish towns, its prosperity derived from the linen trade, while the alleged tightfistedness of its residents earned it the soubriquet of the "Aberdeen of Ireland". There are two good Chinese restaurants in Ballymena: *Manley* on the Ballymoney Road, and *The Water Margin* on Cullybackey Road. A mile and a half west of Ballymena is **GRACEHILL**, a reminder of the curious mixture of religious oppression and tolerance that has characterized Northern Ireland's history: at the same time as Ireland's Catholics were suffering heavy penalties, the country was welcoming dissenting Protestant groups, among them the Moravians (the United Brethren), who built a model settlement at Gracehill. The elegant square survives, with separate buildings for men and women, whose main trade was making lace and clocks. Segregated in life, the sexes remained divided in death, and in the graveyard you can walk down the long path that separates the graves of the men from those of the women.

Antrim
ANTRIM, by way of contrast, is a somewhat tacky town, the sort of place that despite its recent growth – the population has trebled in the last fifteen years – isn't really given a chance by either the Troubles or the grim economics of Northern Ireland. If you've time to kill, there's a tenth-century **round tower** in Steeple Park, a mile out of town, indicating the site of an important monastery that flourished between the sixth and twelfth centuries; and a pretty, if unremarkable, eighteenth-century cottage, *Pogue's Entry*, off the main street: the tiny, neighbouring **tourist office** (June–Sept Mon–Fri 10am–5pm, Sat 10am–2pm) will let you in. **Belfast International Airport** is just four miles south of Antrim, but luckily this doesn't mean that you have to stick around – the transport links to Belfast are much better than to Antrim.

Lisburn
LISBURN, practically a suburb of Belfast, and a grimy, uninteresting sprawl of cut-price shops, is also best ignored. Again, there are few clues to its past as an important linen town. After the revocation of the Edict of Nantes in 1685, which removed French and Dutch Huguenots' freedom of worship, large numbers of them were persuaded to

come to Ulster, where they founded the linen trade. Bleach greens were set up along the banks of the River Lagan; the first of them started in 1626 at Lambeg, a mile downstream from Lisburn. The place has given its name to the big drums which appear in the Orange marches, deriving from the military drums of Prince William's army. The **museum** in Lisburn's Market Square (Tues–Sat 11am–1pm & 1.45–4.45pm; winter closed Sat) has a permanent exhibition on the development of the linen trade.

The political prison of **Long Kesh** (or the Maze), which lies to the south of Lisburn and is clearly visible from the main M1 motorway, incorporates the notorious H-blocks which were the focus of the 1981 **hunger strikes**, in which Republican inmates demanded the reinstatement of political status. The prison, erected on an old airfield soon after the Troubles began, housed hundreds of activists, Loyalist and Republican, interned without trial by the British government. Originally all inmates – convicted prisoners as well as internees – had special category status (a kind of POW status), in conjunction with the Emergency Powers legislation under which they had been convicted, but when the British government phased out internment in late 1975, special status went with it. From March 1, 1976, the prison was in the peculiar position of housing the last of these special category prisoners as well as – in the H-blocks – those convicted after this cut-off date, who were now classified, and treated, as ordinary criminals.

The IRA campaign for the reinstatement of status began in 1976 when Kevin Nugent, in refusing to wear prison clothes, initiated what became known as the "blanket protest" (quite simply, draping a blanket around himself instead of wearing prison clothes). By 1978, this had escalated into the famous "dirty protest", in which Republican prisoners refused to undertake ordinary prison duties such as emptying chamber pots, resorting instead to smearing the cells with their own excrement in order to get rid of it. In 1981, a concerted hunger strike led to the deaths of ten men, including Bobby Sands, provisional commander of the IRA men inside the prison, who had, significantly, been elected MP for Fermanagh–South Tyrone six weeks into his fast. None of this succeeded in budging the government, which steadfastly refused to back down in the face of what it believed was nothing more than moral blackmail. The motivation for the hunger strikes was made manifestly clear in a piece of contemporary graffiti that appeared in Republican areas:

> *I'll wear no convict's uniform*
> *Nor meekly serve my time*
> *That England might brand Ireland's fight*
> *Eight hundred years of crime.*

travel details

Trains
Derry to: Ballymena (6 daily; 1hr 20min); Belfast (6 daily; 2hr 20min); Coleraine (6 daily; 40min); Dublin Connolly Stn (6 daily; 2hr 20min); Portrush (6 daily; 1hr).

Ulsterbus
Derry to: Cork (1 daily; 10hr 30min); Donegal (3 daily; 1hr 30min); Dublin (5; 4hr 15min); Letterkenny/Sligo/Galway (3 daily); Limerick (1 daily; 9hr); Monaghan (2 daily; 2hr 5min); Waterford (1daily; 10hr 30min).

CHAPTER SIXTEEN

DOWN AND ARMAGH

C ounties **Down** and **Armagh** occupy the southwest corner of Northern Ireland, between Belfast and the border. It's territory where all too many of the names are familiar from the news, and certainly the border areas, especially south Armagh, have borne more than their share of the Troubles. But it's also very attractive country, especially around the coast, with a rich history which takes in **Saint Patrick** – who sailed into Strangford Lough to make his final Irish landfall in Down, founded his first bishopric at Armagh, and is buried at either Downpatrick or Armagh, depending on whose claim you choose – and the constant defence of Ulster from invasion.

Heading south from Belfast, the glowering **Mourne Mountains** dominate every view, and it's in this direction that most of the attractions lie. If you simply take the main roads in and out of Belfast – the A1 for Newry and the border or the M1 motorway west – you'll come across very little to stop for: it's in the rural areas, the mountains and coast, that the charm of this region lies. Probably the best option is to head east from Belfast around the Down shore, through the **Ards Peninsula** or along the banks of **Strangford Lough**, towards **Newcastle**, the best base for excursions on foot into the Mourne Mountains. Along the way there are plenty of little beaches, early Christian sites and fine houses to stop for. Immediately outside Belfast in this direction – easy day-trips from there – are the **Ulster Folk and Transport Museum**, one of the best in the North, and the overblown suburban resort of **Bangor**. Beyond the Mournes a fine coast road curves around to **Carlingford Lough** and the border.

Inland there's less of interest, certainly in County Down. **Armagh city**, though, is well worth some of your time for its ancient associations, cathedrals and fine Georgian streets. South Armagh has some startlingly attractive country, especially around **Slieve Gullion**, though its border position makes travelling here a less appealing proposition than it might otherwise appear.

COUNTY DOWN

In **County Down**, it's the coast and the Mourne Mountains at the southern extremity that you're heading for. The big towns in the north, **Newtownards** and **Bangor**, are not at all attractive, but beyond them the A2 road clings to the coast all the way round and inland to Newry, or lesser routes follow the shores of Strangford Lough towards

ACCOMMODATION PRICES

Throughout this book, accommodation prices have been graded according to the cost per person per night in high season; with hotels and many hostels this represents half the cost of a double room, whereas with the more basic hostels it represents the cost of a single dormitory bed. The prices signified by our grades are as follows:

① Up to £6	③ £10–14	⑤ £20–26	⑦ £36–45
② £6–10	④ £14–20	⑥ £26–36	⑧ Over £45

Downpatrick, with its associations with the arrival of Saint Patrick. There are numerous small resorts around the coast, but **Newcastle** is the biggest, and in some ways the most enjoyable. It's also the ideal place to start your exploration of the mountains.

Transport is pretty good on the main roads, with frequent buses connecting anywhere of any size, but again if you want to explore the countryside in any depth you'll need your own transport: much of Down is ideal cycling country.

East of Belfast

Heading east into County Down from Belfast, you've a choice of two routes: the A2, which heads up to Bangor and follows the coast right around the edge of the county to wind up in Newry (see p.532); or the A20 directly east to Newtownards, at the head of Strangford Lough, on the way to which you'll pass **Stormont** (p.467), four miles from the city centre.

Once you get onto the dual carriageway after Dundonald, the single interesting sight is **Scrabo Tower**, standing on a rocky, gorse-clad knoll of a hill – actually a long-extinct volcano. Getting to the tower after you've spotted it is quite a circuitous business, but follow the signs to **Scrabo Country Park** and you'll arrive in the car park just below. Up close it looks quite monstrous, like some giant rocket in its launcher, hewn out of rough black volcanic rock. It was built in 1857 as a memorial to the third Marquess of Londonderry, General Charles William Stewart-Vane, in gratitude for his efforts on behalf of his tenants during the Great Famine. The spot was originally a Bronze Age burial cairn, probably the resting place of one of the grand chieftains of the area. It's now very popular with sightseers, who come mostly for the wonderful views across Strangford Lough and the healthy, blustery weather that often curls around the side of the hill. The woodland immediately behind is country park open to the public (April–Sept Mon–Fri 9am–5pm, Sat 10am–4pm, Sun 2–6pm; Oct–March Mon–Fri 9am–5pm; free); in contrast to the tamed, prosperous countryside roundabout, Scrabo is the only piece of ground for miles around to feel at all wild. **NEWTOWNARDS**, a place strong on manufacture but unexciting for the traveller, is evenly spread out below. What you see of it from Scrabo is probably as much as you'd ever want to: if you do visit there's a ruined Dominican priory, an ancient market cross and a Scrabo stone market house (1765), now the town hall/arts centre.

The Ulster Folk and Transport Museum

The A2 towards Bangor is both more scenic and more interesting, and still within easy reach of a day-trip from Belfast. There's a lovely fifteen-mile walk between **HOLYWOOD** (pronounced *Hollywood*) and Helen's Bay, along a mildly indented estuary coast with some beautiful silvery sand beaches, especially the small crescent-shaped ones at Helen's Bay itself. The train line runs between the path and the road, with a couple of stations where you can pick up services on towards Bangor.

At Cultra station you can alight for the **Ulster Folk and Transport Museum** (April–June & Sept Mon–Fri 9.30am–5pm, Sat 10.30am–6pm, Sun noon–6pm; July–Aug Mon–Fri 10am–6pm, Sat 10am–6pm, Sun noon–6pm; Oct–March Mon–Fri 9.30am–4pm, Sat & Sun 12.30–4.30pm; £3.30; *Ulsterbus* #1 from the Oxford St terminus will also stop here), one of the most fascinating in the North. The main site is an open-air museum, still being added to, where about thirty typical buildings from all over the North – and ranging back as far as the eighteenth century – have been gathered and rebuilt, as far as possible in authentic settings and with furnishings as they would have been. The idea is that you can walk from one part of Northern Ireland to another, amid scenes typical to each: to this end traditional farms have also been created, and assorted livestock roam between the buildings. You start with a gallery

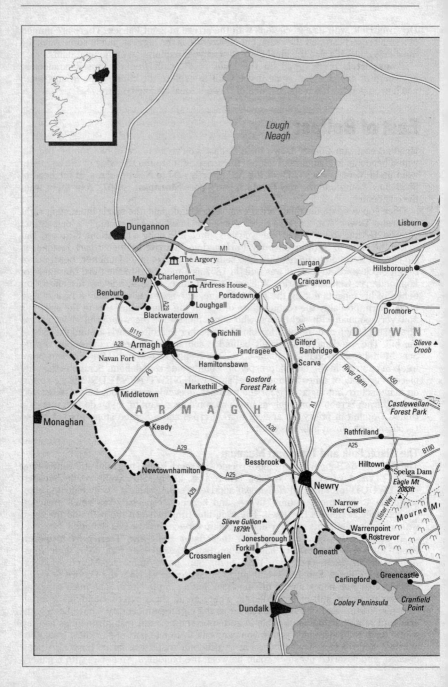

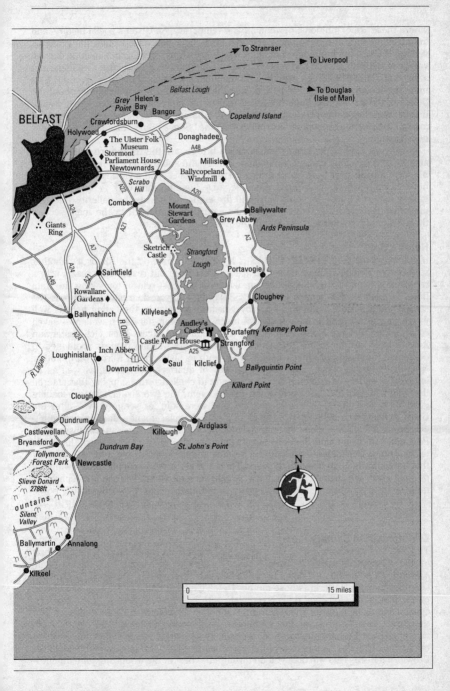

To Stranraer
To Liverpool
To Douglas (Isle of Man)

Belfast Lough

Grey Point
Helen's Bay
Bangor
BELFAST
Crawfordsburn
Holywood
Copeland Island
Donaghadee
A48
The Ulster Folk Museum
Stormont
Parliament House
Newtownards
Millisle
Ballycopeland Windmill
Scrabo Hill
A21
Comber
A20
Mount Stewart Gardens
Grey Abbey
Ballywalter
Giants Ring
A2A
A7
A21
Ards Peninsula
A2
Sketrich Castle
Strangford Lough
Saintfield
A49
A24
Portavogie
Rowallane Gardens
Cloughey
Killyleagh
Ballynahinch
R.Quoile
A7
Audley's Castle
Portaferry
Kearney Point
Castle Ward House
Strangford
A24
Inch Abbey
A25
Loughinisland
Saul
Kilclief
Ballyquintin Point
R.Lagan
Downpatrick
Killard Point
Clough
Dundrum
Killough
Ardglass
Castlewellan
Dundrum Bay
St. John's Point
Bryansford
Tollymore Forest Park
Newcastle
Slieve Donard 2788ft
N
ountains
Silent Valley
Ballymartin
Annalong
Kilkeel

0   15 miles

where there are exhibitions, permanent and temporary, on Ulster's social history, and an introduction to the buildings you'll see. From here you walk around the grounds, visiting the various buildings (not all of which are always open); they include a small village street with church and rectory, two schools, various typical farm dwellings, and a forge and other buildings used in light manufacture. Each of these is "lived in" by a member of staff, togged out in period costume and helpful with information about the building and its origins. Such historical realism is impressive – if sometimes a little disquieting: the Kilmore Church graveyard contains real tombstones donated by family members; elsewhere a replica of the Slieve Binn Mountain is under construction.

On the far side of the main road, across a bridge, are the **transport galleries** (an annexe of the Belfast transport museum), where the exhibits include every conceivable form of transport from horse-drawn carts to lifeboats and a vertical take-off plane, but especially veteran cars (and, of course, a De Lorean sports car). A road transport gallery features trams, bicycles, vans and fire engines. Outside the galleries there's a miniature railway which runs on summer Saturdays, and back in the main section there's a handy **restaurant**, located in the Education Centre.

Helen's Bay

If you're not walking, **HELEN'S BAY** is signposted a mile off the A2, or it's another stop on the Belfast–Bangor train line. It's a rather twee but restful little place, with a red-painted Scots Baronial-style station, which is the best reason for taking the train here. *Deane's on the Square* (☎01247/852841) is a tiny restaurant in what was the station waiting room. Although pricy by Northern standards, the eating here is well worth paying for, and there's a special tasting menu for starving travellers – seven courses for £37. **Grey Point Fort** (Easter–Oct noon–5pm except Tues; Oct–Easter Sun 2–5pm; free), a little to the left of the bay and on the walking path, is positioned to command the mouth of Belfast Lough, along with its sister fort at Kilroot on the other side. The fort has what you'd expect by way of quarters and stores, as well as an impressive battery of gun emplacements, ready to challenge the shipping that entered the lough during the two world wars. In the event, the two six-inch breech-loading guns were never fired except in practice, and were sold for scrap in 1957 after the Coast Artillery was disbanded. Instead an identical replacement – one six-inch gun – was brought from the prison on Spike Island in Cork harbour. The Battery Observation Post and Fire Command Post are today staffed by dressed-up mannequins, like stills taken from a war movie – though they're now staring straight into a growth of trees that have sprung up to obscure the view. There's also a selection of photos showing the original guns and their positions; but it's really as a viewpoint with an atmosphere of military history, rather than the other way round, that the fort is worth visiting nowadays. If you want to stay, there's a classy **B&B**, *Carrig-Gorm*, 27 Bridge Road (☎01247/ 853680; ④).

Crawfordsburn Country Park

The fort, and in fact the whole short stretch of coast from Helen's Bay, is actually part of the **Crawfordsburn Country Park** (Easter–Oct 9am–8pm; Oct–Easter 9am–4.45pm), an estate handed down from the Scottish Presbyterian Crawford family, then acquired by Lord Dufferin (whose mother Helen gave her name to the bay) and now in public hands. Its glens and dells are replete with beeches, cypresses, exotic conifers, cedars, the usual burst of rhododendrons and also a Californian Giant Redwood. But the park's best features are the wildflower meadow and the woodland planted with native species. Perhaps the most scenic walk (well marked) is to follow the pathway back from Grey Point to the top of the bay's beaches and turn inland by the trickle of Crawford's Burn. This will take you up through the best of the woodland, under a fine –

and still used – nineteenth-century rail viaduct, and up to a waterfall at the head of the glen. The **Park Centre** has a restaurant and a slide show on the area's chief attractions; there's also a new interactive exhibition on how to design a wildlife garden. **Helen's Tower**, which can be seen from a considerable distance, was built by Lord Dufferin in the nineteenth century to honour his mother, and as a famine relief project.

CRAWFORDSBURN village is on one of Ireland's most ancient highways, a track that ran from Holywood to Bangor Abbey (now the B20), and has a nice but twee (as with many things in this part of the world) early seventeenth-century **pub**, *The Old Inn*, which claims to be Ireland's oldest.

Bangor

BANGOR has been a popular seaside resort for Belfast people since Victorian times, today though it's pretty dull – as much a suburb of Belfast as a holiday spot – and its attractions are rather faded. But it still possesses a tawdry charm, stuck in a 1960s' time warp with all the appropriate bucket-and-spade paraphernalia – giant swan boats to paddle around a mini-lake, amusement arcades – and the presence of a semi-resident mobile Christian centre to discourage excess. There's also a 500-berth marina which makes Bangor a good place for stocking up on provisions or exploring the coast, while for the land-based the town is well equipped as a stop-off point for dinner and a stroll along the prom. Other distractions include the new **Museum of Childhood** on Central Avenue with antique dolls and teddy bears, and the **North Down Heritage Centre** (daily except Mon 10.30am–4.30pm, Sun 2–4.30pm; July–Aug open daily to 5.30pm; free), tucked away at the back of the town hall.

What history the place has, as yet another ancient monastic settlement, has entirely disappeared, and Bangor's one claim to historical fame now lies in the Ambrosian Library in Milan. This is the *Antiphonarium Benchorense*, one of the oldest known ecclesiastical manuscripts, consisting of collects, anthems and some religious poems. It came originally from the great Bangor Abbey (one of the most powerful in the country for nearly 800 years), though had it remained here it would surely have perished with the abbey's destruction.

The **tourist office** (July–Aug Mon–Fri 9am–8pm, Sat 10am–1pm, 2–8pm, Sun 2–6pm; Sept–June Mon–Thurs 9am–1pm, 2–5pm, Fri 9am–4.30pm; ☎01247/270069) is housed in an old tower on the seafront by the *Royal Hotel* and will book accommodation for you. There are scores of **B&Bs**, concentrated especially in Queen's Parade – try the *Mardee Guesthouse* (☎01247/457733; ③) – Princetown Road and Seacliff Road. The nearest **camping** is at Donaghadee, six miles south along the coast. Most of the **restaurants** are dotted along the seafront or nearby up sidestreets. *Café Brazilia* serves eleven types of espresso plus an imaginative and cheap menu; further along the esplanade *Knuttel's Restaurant* – named after and decked out in paintings by the owner himself – does a four-course dinner for £12. Other relatively inexpensive restaurants are *Stevedore* in the *Marine Court Hotel*, the *Canteen* on High Street and the *Back Street Café* on Queen's Parade. But the best food hereabouts is a few miles south in Clandeboye at *Shanks* in the *Blackwood Golf Centre* (Tues–Sat only; ☎01247/853313), with a menu in the pesto/sun-dried tomato line and a restaurant styled by Terence Conran. Traditional **music** is easy to find in Bangor: the *Windsor* pub on Quay Street most night, *Jenny Watts* for traditional sessions on Tuesday nights or, just outside town on the Clandeboye Road, the *George*.

Strangford Lough and the Ards Peninsula

The **Ards Peninsula** stretches out an arm to enclose the waters of **Strangford Lough**, with only the narrowest of openings to the sea in the south. The coast along the northern side of the peninsula south of Bangor is far from the most attractive hereabouts. Just about the only minor piece of interest is the late eighteenth-century **Ballycopeland Windmill** (April–Sept daily 10am–4pm), a mile west of Millisle. This claims to be the only working windmill in Ireland; in fact it's an historical monument which puts on tourist exhibitions. You are much better off following one of the shores of the lough, where most of the area's interest is concentrated.

Ancient annals say the lough was formed around 1650 BC by the sea sweeping in over the lands of Brena. This created a beautiful, calm inlet, the archipelago-like pieces of land along its inner arm fringed with brown and yellow bladderwrack and tangle-weed, and tenanted by a rich gathering of bird life during the warmer months and vast flocks of geese and waders in the winter. It makes a sporting haven for small boats and yachts, and several attractive stopping-off places for the land-bound make the road along the lough's western bank the most interesting route leading south from Belfast.

The lough's eastern shore

The eastern edge of Strangford Lough is not as indented as its opposite shore but betters it in having a major road (the continuation of the A20) that runs close to the water virtually all the way down. Also the scenery is delightful, and there are two places to stop off en route to Portaferry – the Mount Stewart Gardens and Grey Abbey.

Mount Stewart

The National Trust-owned **Mount Stewart House and Gardens** (April–Sept Mon–Sat 10.30am–6pm, Sun noon–5.30pm; Oct–March Sat 10.30am–6pm & Sun noon–5.30pm; £3.30 for house and gardens; £2.70 gardens; April–Sept Wed gardens free) lie five miles southeast of Newtownards. The **gardens**, part of a larger eighty-acre estate, are laid out on a grand scale. The trees and shrubs here are no more than sixty to seventy years old, but they've grown at such a remarkable rate that they look twice that. This is principally due to the microclimate, which is unusually warm and humid – the gardens get the east coast sun, causing a heavy overnight dew, and the Gulf Stream washes the shores only a stone's throw away; surprisingly for so far north, conditions here rival those of Cornwall and Devon. It was Lady Londonderry, wife of the seventh marquess, who laid out these gardens from about 1920 on, and a thorough job she made of it; among others, there are Spanish and Italian gardens, a Peace Garden and the Shamrock Garden (with a topiary harp) – well worth visiting in the blooming season.

Although the gardens are the highlight, the **house** is also worth viewing. It was once the Irish seat of the Londonderrys, one of whom, Viscount Castlereagh, was Foreign Secretary under Pitt in the late eighteenth and early nineteenth centuries and is best remembered for guiding the Act of Union into operation. Among the splendid (and occasionally eccentric) furniture inside, much of it once again the work of Lady Londonderry, is a set of 22 Empire chairs used by the delegates to the Congress of Vienna in 1815, including the Duke of Wellington and the Prince de Talleyrand; the chairs were a gift to the Viscount's brother Lord Stewart, another high-ranking diplomat of the time. The Continental connection is flaunted further in bedrooms named after various major cities; Rome, St Petersburg, Madrid, Moscow and Sebastopol (from the time of the Crimean War). One of the most notable and largest paintings in the house (and in Ireland, for that matter) is *Hambletonian* (1799) by George Stubbs, showing the celebrated thoroughbred being rubbed down after a victory at Newmarket. A little to the east of the house, the **Temple of the Winds** is a remodelling of the Athenian *Tower of Andronicus Cyrrhestes* by James "Athenian" Stuart (1713–88), one of the pioneers of Neoclassical architecture. The Temple is set on a promontory overlooking Strangford Lough, making it a great place for birdwatching.

Grey Abbey

A short diversion from Mount Stewart will take you to Carrowdore, in the middle of the peninsula, and the grave of the Ulster poet **Louis MacNeice** (see p.485). Continuing on the shore road, however, **Grey Abbey** (April–Sept Tues–Sat 10am–7pm, Sun 2–7pm; Oct–March Tues–Sat 10am–1pm & 2–4pm, Sun 2–4pm; *Ulsterbus* #10) is only a couple of miles further on: approaching from the north, take a left turn in the village of Grey Abbey. Typical of the Cistercian, or "white monks" order, of which Mellifont was the mother house in Ireland, Grey Abbey sits in remote parkland beside the fresh running water of a rivulet, a perfect example of the kind of idyllic setting the Cistercians used to seek. Even today, that setting is barely disturbed, and reason in itself to visit, with a substantial set of ruins to complete the picture.

The abbey was founded in 1193 by Affreca, daughter of the King of Man and wife of John de Courcy, as a thanksgiving for having made a safe sea-crossing during a storm. Its plans conform pretty much to the same shape as all Cistercian abbeys, with a church at one end and the living and working quarters of the monks ranged around a cloister, and its structure was realized in a very plain manner, without distracting embellishments. Grey Abbey is unusual for Ireland, though, in showing early Gothic features at a time when late Romanesque work was still common here. Among the best-preserved remains are the **west door**, much of whose carved decoration can still be made out, and the church in general. Another unusual feature is that the church is a simple hall, with no aisles around which the monks could process.

Outside the church, the guide notes on display help you to imagine the covered alleys and walks of the elongated rectangular cloister that would have been overshadowed on three sides by buildings which are now no more than stumps. These would have included the chapter house, dormitories and refectory. The village **B&Bs** are *Gordonall*, half a mile out on the Newtownards Road (☎012477/88325; ④), and *Mervue*, 28 Portaferry Road (☎012477/88619; ④); the village itself is known for its antique shops.

Portaferry

PORTAFERRY marks the bottom end of the peninsula and the only place of any real size beyond Newtownards. It's the home of the **Exploris** (April–Sept Mon–Fri 10am–5pm, Sat 11am–6pm, Sun 1–6pm; Oct–March closes 5pm; £3.25), an aquarium with some of the largest tanks around and a touch tank for the brave to stroke a stingray. But the main attraction is the marvellous **sunset** looking across the "Narrows" to Strangford. In July the **Galway Hookers Regatta** livens the place up – the traditional boats sail round from Galway to be welcomed by the *Portaferry Yacht Club*, and every pub has virtually 24-hour music sessions.

Tourist information (April–Sept) is available from a portacabin by the ferry terminal. If you're looking for somewhere to **stay**, the *Portaferry Hotel*, 10 The Strand (☎012477/28231; ⑧), is relatively luxurious and has a decent restaurant; or there's good-value B&B at the *Adairs*, 22 The Square (☎012477/28412; ③). The town also has a *YHANI* **youth hostel** called *Barholme*, 11 The Strand (open all year; ☎012477/29598; ②). A new bistro close to *Exploris* has a cheap menu, but for coffee and good cakes try the *Harlequin*, or *Café Kim* next door. The **pubs** are good at just about any time of year, with run-of-the-mill sessions at *The Fiddler's Green* most nights; better music is at the *Saltwalter Brigg*, six miles out of Portaferry, on Fridays. **Ferries** leave regularly (every 30min or so; 60p on foot, £2.50 per car) for the five-minute ride across the lips of the lough to Strangford.

The lough's western shore

Leaving Scrabo Tower on the A22, you'll pick up signs for **COMBER** – famous for its potatoes and more recently for its retro cinema (see overleaf) – and then Downpatrick,

---

TUDOR CINEMA

If you want to indulge in some classic bad movies of the 1950s, head for Comber; here Noel Spence, a B-movie addict, has built the eighty-seater **Tudor Cinema**; it's meticulously furnished to re-create the atmosphere of old-time movie going, with red-velvet seating, gold braid, footlights etc. Essentially a place for Noel and his friends to go and watch their favourite schlock movies, you can expect American favourites such as *The Blob*, *Attack of the Fifty-Foot Woman* or that tigerskin-bikini special, *The Wild Women of Wonga*. Some nights, the viewing is themed; on Sherlock Holmes evenings, for example, the audience dresses in deerstalker and pipe, and the muttering of "Elementary, my dear Watson" nearly drowns the soundtrack. Sadly a burglary in 1994 robbed Noel Spence of his vintage movie poster collection, which included the Penny Black of posters, the original bill for *War of the Worlds*. The cinema (22 Drumhirt Road; ☎01247/878589) is open three nights a week; admission is free, but donations very welcome.

---

with a turning to **Castle Espie Wildfowl and Wetland Centre** on your left (April–Sept Mon–Sat 10.30am–5pm, Sun 11.30am–6pm; Oct–April Mon–Sat 11.30am–4pm, Sun till 5pm; £2.60). Here you can learn why swans have long necks – and even adopt one. Admission earnings are ploughed back into conserving the wetlands area for the 7000 birds that visit it. The centre also has a coffee shop and art gallery. Immediately beyond Castle Espie, you'll see the excellent *Old Schoolhouse Restaurant* by the roadside, unmistakable with a fire engine lodged in its front garden; there's a fair-priced Sunday lunch (otherwise Tues–Sat 7–11pm; ☎01238/541182). From here, you can wind along the very edge of the lough, on a series of minor roads.

Travelling this scenic route is enjoyable in itself, but there are a couple of spots worth making for. First of them is **Mahee Island**, named for Saint Mochaoi, the first abbot of the island, who died tragically, burned in his cell. Heading past crumbling Mahee Castle (currently undergoing repairs) at the entrance to the island, and over the causeway, you come to the Celtic **Nendrum Monastic Site** (April–Sept Tues–Sat 10am–7pm, closed 1–1.30pm, Sun 2–7pm; 75p) a few hundred yards further on. It's a gorgeous spot, surrounded by drumlins and the lough's waterways. This was once a sizeable establishment, with church, round tower, school and living quarters all housed in a *cashel* of three concentric wards, which is itself probably even earlier. Today, the inner wall shelters the ruined church, and a reconstructed sundial uses some of the original remnants. There's an illuminating reconstruction map at the site and a helpful visitor centre.

Back on the road along the lough, follow the signs to Ardmillan, Killinchy (*Balloo House* here is an excellent restaurant, with a garden), and then Whiterock for **Sketrick Island** (which itself is not signposted). As with Mahee Island, there's a castle to guard the entrance, now no more than a shattered reminder. *Daft Eddy's Pub and Restaurant*, behind the castle, offers bar snacks as well as a more elaborate restaurant menu. An equally daft competition known as the **Hen Island race** takes place here in October, when craft constructed from oil drums and crates are ridden and paddled between Sketrick and the nearby Hen Island.

The tiny coves and inlets at the feet of little drumlins continue as far as Killyleagh, almost any of them worth exploring. The best way to do this would be to **rent a sailing boat** for a day or more, which you can do at Sketrick marina (☎01238/541400).

Killyleagh

Approaching **KILLYLEAGH**, what looks like a huge child's sandcastle comes into view, wholly out of character with the area. This began life as a John de Courcy castle in the late twelfth century, but went through a major overhaul by the Hamilton family in the nineteenth century to give it the Bavarian schloss appearance it has today. It's still a private house, and when viewed close up it's much more gaunt, with a squat mixture of high step crenellations, turrets and cones. The stone outside the castle gates commemorates the town's most famous son, Hans Sloane (1660–1753), physician to King George II and founder of both the British Museum and Kew Gardens – London's Sloane Square is named after him. Through rather more obscure connections, Prince Andrew was created Baron Killyleagh on his wedding day in 1986, the Duchess of York having some ancestors from here.

The Lecale region

Jutting around the bottom of Strangford Lough, the **Lecale Peninsula** is above all Saint Patrick's country. Ireland's patron saint was originally a Roman Briton, first carried off as a youth from somewhere near Carlisle in northern England by Irish raiders. He spent six years in slavery in Ireland before escaping home again and, at the age of thirty, decided to return to Ireland as a bishop, to spread Christianity. Christianity had actually reached Ireland a while before him, probably through traders and other slaves, and Saint Patrick was not in fact the first bishop of Ireland (then on the edge of the known world) – but he remains far and away the most famous. He arrived in Ireland this second time, according to his biographer Muirchú (also his erstwhile captor, converted), on the shores of the Lecale region, and his first Irish sermon was preached at Saul in 432. Today the region commemorates the association with sites at Struell Wells and Saul, as well as at Downpatrick town itself. The **Lecale Trail** is a thirty-mile tour of the peninsula starting in front of the Down County Museum in Downpatrick (further information and trail maps can be obtained from the tourist office); if you've had enough of Saint Patrick and his seeming connection with nearly every landmark, alternative ways of exploring the peninsula are the nature rambles and horse-riding trails also available in Downpatrick (see "Practicalities" overleaf).

Downpatrick and around

DOWNPATRICK, the county capital, is not somewhere you come for a vibrant nightlife. In modern times it seems depressed and rather lethargic, awaiting the invigorating kiss of economic revival. On the other hand its history is a rich and well-preserved one, with the major sites conveniently concentrated at one end of town, around the **Hill of Down** on which the cathedral now stands. This was once a rise of great strategic worth, fought over long before the arrival of Saint Patrick made it famous. A Celtic fort of mammoth proportions was built here and was called first *Arús Cealtchair*, then later *Dún Cealtchair* (Celtchar's fort). Celtchar was one of the Red Branch Knights, a friend of the then King of Ulster, Conor MacNessa, and, according to the *Book of the Dun Cow*, "an angry terrific hideous man with a long nose, huge ears, apple eyes, and coarse dark-grey hair". The *Dún* part of the fort's name went on to become the name of the county, as well as the town.

By the time the Norman knight **John de Courcy** made his mark here in the late twelfth century, a settlement was well established. Pushing north out of Leinster, and defeating Rory MacDonlevy, King of Ulster, de Courcy dispossessed the Augustinian canons who occupied the Hill of Down to establish his own Benedictine abbey. He flaunted as much pomp as he could to mark the occasion, and one of his festive tricks was to import what were supposedly the disinterred bodies of Saint Brigid and Saint Columba to join Saint Patrick, who was (supposedly) buried here. One of the earliest accounts of Patrick's life asserts that he's buried in a church near the sea; and since a later account admits that "where his bones are no man knows", Downpatrick's claim seems as good as any.

The site of the three graves is meant to be just to the left of the tower entrance and is marked today by a rough granite slab, put there around 1900 to cover the huge hole created by earlier pilgrims searching for the saints' bones. The cathedral built by de Courcy was destroyed in the fourteenth century, and a new abbey erected in the early sixteenth century was even more short-lived. Today's **Cathedral** (daily 9am–5pm) dates basically from the early part of this century, though it incorporates many aspects of earlier incarnations. Its most unique feature is the private box-pews, characteristic of the Regency period and the only ones remaining in use in Ireland.

Leaving the cathedral and retracing your steps a little down English Street, crowded with Georgian houses, you came to the eighteenth-century jail, which has undergone some renovation and now houses both the **Down County Museum** and the **St Patrick Heritage Centre** (July to mid-Sept daily 11am–5pm, Sat & Sun 2–5pm; mid-Sept to June closed Sun & Mon). The heritage centre occupies the gatehouse and has a video and display of illustrations telling the Saint Patrick story, principally through his own words from his autobiographical *Confessions* (the short video also provides a handy summary of what the rest of the peninsula has on offer by way of relics of the saint). The three-storey Georgian **Governor's House** (opening times variable; free), in the centre of the walled courtyard, includes a local history gallery, which has regular exhibitions. The cell block at the back of the enclosure once held the United Irishman Thomas Russell, who had already survived the 1798 uprising but was found guilty of complicity in Robert Emmett's rebellion and was duly hanged in 1803 from a sill outside the main gate of the jail.

Turn downhill between the jail and the fenced-up courthouse and you come to the **Mound of Down**, a smaller prominence half submerged in undergrowth. It's in fact 60ft high and inside its outer ditch is a horseshoe central mound of rich grass. Once a rath, or round hillfort, it was considerably altered and enlarged to create a Norman motte and bailey-style fortification, with a *bretasche* (a wooden archery tower) at the centre. Its view back onto the Hill of Down shows up clearly the attractions the Hill had for its earliest settlers; it's believed by some to be the site of the palace of the Kings of Ulster.

Practicalities

The **tourist office** is on Market Street (Mon–Fri 9am–5pm, Sat 9.30am–1pm & 2–5pm; July & Aug also 1–5pm; ☎01396/612233).

Should you want to **stay** try the *Abbey Lodge Hotel* (☎01396/614511; ⑥). The best and most central of the B&Bs is *Hillside*, 62 Scotch Street (☎01396/613134; ③); others include *Hillcrest*, 157 Strangford Road (☎01396/612583; ④), and *Havine Farm*, 51 Ballydonnell Road (☎01396/685242; ③). If you're **camping**, your best bet is to go to Castle Ward Park (see overleaf), six miles away on the A25 to Strangford. You won't find much exciting to **eat**, but you won't starve either.

The *Abbey Lodge Hotel* does a three-course Sunday lunch for around £10, and bar food on weekdays. *Hootenanny Bar* and *McGivern's Restaurant*, in a mid-eighteenth century coach house on Irish Street, offer good food. You can get vast Sunday brunches at *Harry Africa* on Market Street – a diner popular with students; while the *Arts Centre,* in the refurbished old town hall on Irish Street, definitely does the best lunches and imaginative snacks. Good **pub lunches** are easy to find: try *Brendan's Pub* on Market Street, or nearby, the newly refurbished *Rea's* pub, which has a big open fire, or *DeCourcy Arms* and *Dick's Cabin*, which are both on the Belfast Road and also popular **music** venues. There may be occasional performances in the excellent **Down Arts Centre**, which has an art gallery and performance space. A good coffee shop in the centre is *Oakley Fayre*, with the usual home-baked pastries.

Quoile Countryside Centre (☎01396/615520) on Quay Road organizes **nature rambles**, seal watches in Strangford Lough, dawn chorus walks on Quoile River, even butterfly trips; while *Tullymurray Equestrian Centre* on Ballyduggan Road takes **trail rides** to the local big houses – Tollymore, Castlewellan and Castle Ward – or along the coast with beach rides to Newcastle and Tyrella (Mon–Sat; £7.50 per hour; ☎01396/811880).

Inch Abbey

Over to the other side of the Quoile Marsh from Downpatrick lie the remains of **Inch Abbey**. Unfortunately, you can't get over to it from the town, due to the river, and it's vexing to be only a handshake away – its setting and atmosphere are among the most exquisite of all these Cistercian sites. The only access is a mile out along the Belfast Road, taking the left turn down Inch Abbey Road just before the *Abbey Lodge Hotel*. It's signposted from here down another left turning. The site (50p entrance) was once an island, and its early church was replaced by de Courcy with the Cistercian abbey. The monks were shipped over from Furness Abbey in Lancashire with the intention of establishing a strong English centre of influence – no Irish monks were ever allowed to be part of it. Not unexpectedly, little of it is now left standing, having undergone its allotted burning in 1404, with monastic life completely finished off by the mid-sixteenth century. Still, its setting, among small glacial drumlins and woodland, is picturesque; and strolling up the valley sides (now a nature reserve, created when a flood barrage downstream turned this part of the river from saltwater estuary to freshwater marshy lake) is a very pleasant way to pass time.

On the trail of Saint Patrick

About four miles west of Inch Abbey (take the B2 to Annacloy and then the first turning on the left; to get here from Downpatrick, take the Newcastle Road out past the racecourse, then look for the signpost on the right), **Loughinisland** is probably the most worthwhile of all the sites in the area that are associated with Saint Patrick, and indeed one of the most idyllically tranquil spots in County Down. It comprises a reed-fringed lake contained by ten or so little drumlin hills, one of which forms an island in the lake. Here, across a short causeway, are the ruins of three small churches, set next door to each other. The most interesting of the churches is the smallest one, **MacCartan's Chapel** (1636), which has an entrance door no taller than four or five feet. It was used by both Catholics and Protestants until they quarrelled on a wet Sunday around 1720 over which camp should remain outside during the service. The Protestants left and built their church at Seaforde instead.

Head back to Downpatrick and a couple of miles further east (take the Ardglass Road, turn left just past the hospital, then right down a narrow track into a secluded rock-faced valley) and you'll come to **Struell Wells**. The waters here were once a grand old centre for pilgrimage and their miraculous healing powers recorded as far back as medieval times. In 1744 Walter Harris described the scene at their height: "vast throngs of rich and poor resort on Midsummer Eve and the Friday before Lammas, some in the hopes of obtaining health, and others to perform penance". Mass is still said here on midsummer night, and people bring containers to carry the water home with them; but if you're not looking for health or penance, there's still the joy of spotting one of the tiny gems of Irish landscape beauty – a hideaway rocky dell with an abundance of yellow-flowering whin, its underground stream rechannelled to run through the wells' purpose-built bath houses.

The next Saint Patrick landmark is at **SAUL**, not much further from Downpatrick off the Strangford Road. Saint Patrick is said to have landed nearby, sailing up the tiny River Slaney, and it was here that he first preached, immediately converting Dichu, the lord of this territory. Dichu gave Patrick a barn as his first base (the town's name in Irish is *Sabhal*, meaning "barn"), and the saint frequently returned here to rest from his travelling missions – legend has it that he died here. Today a memorial chapel and round tower in the Celtic Revival style, built of pristine silver-grey granite in 1933 to commemorate the place as "the most ancient ecclesiastical site in the land, the cradle of Christianity", is open daily to visitors. Two cross-carved stones from between the eighth and twelfth centuries still stand in the graveyard, though there's not a trace of the medieval monastery built here by Saint Malachy in the twelfth century.

Back on the Strangford Road, a few miles further on between Saul and Raholp, **St Patrick's Shrine** sits atop Slieve Patrick, a tract of hillside much like a slalom ski-slope, with the stations of the cross marking a pathway up. The summit is no more than a twenty-minute climb and offers a commanding view of the county, a vista of the endless little bumps of this drumlin-filled territory.

Strangford and the Lecale coast

If you're coming by ferry to Lecale from the tip of the Ards Peninsula, and following the A2 round the coast, you'll arrive at tiny **STRANGFORD** village, directly opposite Portaferry. The earlier name of this inlet was Lough Cuan, but it was renamed Strangfiord by the Vikings over one thousand years ago because of the eight-knot current in the narrows. Its small harbour makes a pleasant setting for watching the to and fro of the ferry boats, and the *Lobster Pot*, on the front, has a welcome pub garden and middle-of-the-range prices for evening meals. Overlooking the village green are the *Cuan Mews* and the *Cottage Grill*, where you'll get cakes and bulging sandwiches. But there's little else, and nowhere to stay. Just on the far side of Strangford is a sixteenth-century **tower house** which can be viewed if you call to Mr Seed at 39 Castle Street for the key and – if you are lucky – an informative chat.

Immediately around Strangford are a few houses and castles worth visiting, the first of them on the road back towards Downpatrick. **Castle Ward House** (May–Aug daily except Thurs 1–6pm; April, Sept & Oct Sat & Sun 1–6pm; £2.60) is Ireland's Glyndebourne: every June three weeks of opera enliven the house and grounds, and bon viveurs flock with picnic hampers, starched napkins and candlesticks (for information call ☎01232/661090). The house, which was the eighteenth-century residence of Lord and Lady Bangor, is now owned by the National Trust. It's a positively schizophrenic building, thanks to the opposed tastes of its creators (they later split up): one half (the Lord's) is in the Classical Palladian style, the other (the Lady's) neo-Gothic, a split carried through into the design and decor of the rooms within. Outside there are pleasant gardens (open daily dawn to dusk) and preserved farm buildings. There's also a sixteenth-century tower house (Old Castle Ward) inside the grounds; the fifteenth-century **Audley's Castle** just outside on the lough shore, with superb view across the lough – though there's a better example of a tower house just south of Strangford (see below); and the Strangford **Lough Wildlife Centre** house in a restored barn (April–June & Sept Sat & Sun 2–6pm; July–Aug daily except Thurs 2–6pm). If you want to stay, you can **camp** in the grounds for £6 a night per tent. On your way back to the main coast road, **Audleystown Cairn** is marked across the fields to the right – though access isn't easy as it's in a field which usually seems full of bulls.

South along the Ardglass Road

Along the A2 south from Strangford to Ardglass, there are a number of things worth stopping for. Signposted off the road (a mile's drive and a quarter of a mile's walk) is **St Patrick's Well**, set on a wonderful rocky shore. The well is easily spotted – it looks rather like a sheep dip with concrete walls, but with a crucifix at its head. Its holy water has turned into something closer to stagnant consommé than an ever-youthful source of new life.

A mile further south, **Kilclief Castle** (April–Sept Tues–Sat 10am–7pm, Sun 2–7pm) is a well-preserved fifteenth-century tower house. One of Ireland's earliest tower houses, this was originally the home of John Cely, Bishop of Down – until he was unfrocked and thrown out for living with a married woman.

Half a mile or so before you reach Ardglass, the ruin of fifteenth-century **Ardtole Church** is well signposted just a few hundred yards off the road. It's set on the spur of a hill, which gives it a fine perspective out to sea and back across the undulating flat of Lecale. Once dedicated to Saint Nicholas, patron saint of sailors, this church was used by English fishermen until a quarrel broke out with the Irish around 1650. The story goes that the fishermen tied a sleeping Irish chief to the ground by his long hair so that he couldn't get up when he awoke. Tradition has it that Swift got the similar episode in *Gulliver's Travels* from this tale, and certainly the Ardtole region runs amok with tiny drumlins – very much like the description of the Lilliputian mountains.

Ardglass

ARDGLASS is set on the side of a lovely natural inlet. Its domestic buildings, rising steeply from the harbour (*ard glas* in Irish means "the green height"), are interspersed with seven fortified mansions, towers and turrets. These date from a vigorous English revival in the sixteenth century, when a trading company first arrived to found a colony here. The best preserved of the fortifications, and the only one open for visits, is **Jordan's Castle**, next door to the *Anchor* pub on the Low Road (April–Sept Tues–Sat 10am–7pm, Sun 2–7pm; 75p). The most elegant and highly developed of all the Down tower houses, this has recently been renovated – all whitewashed walls and massive ceiling beams – and has regular exhibitions on local history. The tall, crenellated building with white plaster trimming up on the hill was once **King's Castle**; its nineteenth-century renovation is obvious, as is modern work to turn it into a nursery. The lone ornamental-looking turret on the hilltop is **Isabella's Tower**, a nineteenth-century folly created by Aubrey de Vere Beauclerc as a gazebo for his invalid daughter.

In the nineteenth century, Ardglass was the most thriving **fishing** port in the North; and even today, as well as the prawns, herrings and whitefish brought in by the fishing fleet, there's very good rod fishing to be had off the end of the pier for codling, pollack and coalfish. Even the *Spar* supermarket on the quay is wonderfully stocked with a fantastic range of seafood (scallops, monkfish, oysters, salmon etc), enough in itself to entice a quick shopping visit. It's also sometimes possible to buy direct from fishing boats or from the cannery on the quay. The old inn, the *Commercial*, on the main street has a well – still in use; it's covered over with glass on the lounge floor. You can **eat** well at *Aldo's* popular Italian **restaurant**, which serves evening meals (Thurs–Sun 5–10pm) and Sunday lunch.

From Killough to Clough

KILLOUGH, a few miles on, is an unworldly village stretching around a much larger harbour than Ardglass, but now silted up. The A2 passes through Killough's main street: a fine avenue of sycamores with a string of picturesque cottage terraces at its southern end, making an unlikely major thoroughfare. It was the Wards of Castleward who built the harbour in the eighteenth century, and there's still a direct road running inland, virtually in a straight line, from Killough to Castleward.

From the southern end of Killough you can head out to **St John's Point** – much favoured by birdwatchers – on which lie the ruins of one of the North's best examples of a pre-Romanesque church. It's an enjoyable two-and-a-half-mile walk. The tiny west door of the tenth-century church has the distinctive sloping sides, narrowing as the doorway rises, that were a common feature of these early churches. Also still apparent are the *antae*, enclosures created by the extension of the west and east walls to give extra support to the roof. Excavations in 1977 showed up graves that extended under these walls, indicating that an even earlier church existed from the early Christian period, probably made of wood. There's a black-and-gold-striped lighthouse on the nail of the point.

From Killough, the A2 passes long, sandy beaches at Minerstown and Tyrella Strand (cars £1) – ruined by hot dog stands and cars parking on the beach – before reaching **CLOUGH**, a crossroads village between Downpatrick and Newcastle. It has a Norman motte and bailey, as pristinely preserved as a carpet of mown grass, with a poor remnant of a thirteenth-century stone keep stuck in the middle. The site, just behind a petrol station at the Belfast end of the village, has surprisingly good views considering its low-lying position – across Dundrum Bay inlet towards the Mournes and back over to Slieve Croob in central Down. It's worth taking a short detour north at Clough on the A24 to the **Seaforde Tropical Butterfly House** (April–Sept Mon–Sat 10am–5pm, Sun 2–6pm; £2). There's a flight area swarming with giant, vividly coloured butterflies, quails running underfoot and a ferocious collection of large and fast-moving insects. Best of all, though, is the overgrown walled garden, whose maze leads to a rose-covered pavilion that shelters a statue of the goddess Diana. Nearby, *Drumgooland House* on Dunnarown Road (☎01396/811956; ④) does a great **B&B** and offers riding or fishing in their own lake.

Dundrum

Although it's not officially in the Lecale region, whose inland ending is at Clough, just a few miles down the road at **DUNDRUM** you'll find some quite spectacular ruins of a large Norman **castle** (April–Oct Tues–Sat 10am–7pm, Sun 2–7pm; 75p). The town lies beside a hammer-headed tidal bay, with the ruins sitting dramatically above it; to get to them you have to take the steep turning up the hill from the village, a fifteen-minute walk. The castle has a central circular donjon (with a fine stairway in its walls), a fortified gateway and drum towers, all set upon a motte and bailey. In its time it was described as the most impenetrable fortress in the land. Some say it was a de Courcy fortress, designed for the Knights Templar; but the circular keep, a rarity in Ireland, is not at all in keeping with the other fortresses de Courcy built to defend the stretch of coast from Carlingford right up to Carrickfergus. De Courcy's successor, de Lacy, is a more likely candidate – his Welsh connections tie in with the castle's similarity to the one at Pembroke, Wales. Dundrum's **B&B** is *Mourneview House*, 16 Main Street (☎013967/51457; ③). There are also two semi-detached National Trust properties, *Murlough Cottages* on the shore of Dundrum Bay, which sleep four to six for longer periods only (☎013967/51311). Obviously, these get booked up well in advance, but you may be lucky out of season. Both the *Bay Inn* and the *Murlough Tavern* serve good meals and snacks.

Newcastle and the Mourne Mountains

Newcastle, with its lovely stretch of sandy beach, is the biggest seaside resort in Down – packed with trippers from Belfast on summer weekends – and, with Slieve Donard rising behind the town, it's by far the best base if you want to do any serious walking or climbing in the **Mourne Mountains**.

The Mournes are a relatively youthful set of granite mountains, which explains why their comparatively unweathered peaks and flanks are so rugged, forming steep sides, moraines and occasional sheer cliffs. Closer up, these give sharp, jagged outlines; but from a distance they appear much gentler, like a sleeping herd of buffalo. The wilder topography lies mostly in the east, below Newcastle, although the fine cliff of **Eagle Mountain** (2083ft), to the southwest, is wonderful if you can afford the time and effort to get there, and the tamer land above Rostrevor has views down into **Carlingford Lough** that can rival any in Ireland.

In summer at least (winters can be surprisingly harsh) there are plenty of straightforward hikes in the Mournes that require no special equipment, with obvious tracks to many of the more scenic parts. For further information, and maps, go to the Newcastle tourist office or to the youth hostel there (see p.528). There are also, of course, more serious climbs: **climbing courses** in the Mournes are run by the *Northern Ireland Mountain Centre* in Newcastle (☎013967/22158), but they must be booked at least two weeks in advance (contact *The Sports Council for Northern Ireland*, House of Sport, Upper Malone Road, Belfast; ☎01232/381222).

Newcastle

NEWCASTLE isn't exactly exciting, but it's well equipped to send you walking, pony trekking, or fishing on the river, and for the inevitable rainy day there are indoor alternatives at the Newcastle Centre and Tropicana Complex on the promenade (summer

WALKS AND HIKES IN THE MOURNES

There's little to see in Newcastle itself, but the mountains offer some beautiful walks close to the town, and, for more serious walking, plenty of good hiking routes throughout the range. The climb up **Slieve Donard**, just south of Newcastle, is the obvious first choice. Although at 2796ft it's the highest peak in the Mournes – and in all Ulster – the ascent is a relatively easy one on a well-marked trail that ends at the massive hermit cell on the summit; from here the views across the whole mountainscape are quite spectacular.

For more gentle local walking, there are several pleasant **parks**, created from the estates of old houses. The nearest is **Donard Park** on the slopes of Slieve Donard. There's a good meander along the River Glen from the town centre to the park, and if you keep following this path uphill you'll emerge on the other side and eventually come to the Saddle, a col between the two mountains of Slieve Donard and Slieve Commedagh. If you want to carry on further into the mountains from here, a good route is via **Trassey Burn** towards the **Hare's Gap**, where minerals have seeped through the rock to form precious and semi-precious stones – topaz, beryl, smoky quartz and emeralds – in the cavities of the Diamond rocks (hidden behind an obvious boulder stone on the mountainside). Around this point in spring, you might get the chance to hear the song of the Ring Ouzel, a bird which migrates from Africa to breed in these upland areas.

Two miles inland from Newcastle, along the Bryansford Road, **Tollymore Forest Park** (daily 10am–sunset; cars £2.50) is considerably bigger and better equipped than Donard, and has a **campsite** (call the ranger on ☎013967/22428). The park creeps up the northern side of the Mournes, and its picturesque trails wind through woodland and beside the river. You enter the park by one of two ornate Gothic folly gates – there are more follies in Bryansford nearby – and there's an **information centre** and café in an elaborate stone barn. **Castlewellan Forest Park** (cars £2.50) is also inland about five miles further north, outside the elegant market town of Castlewellan. The estate lies in the foothills of the Mournes, and from the highest point in the forest, Slievenaslat, you get panoramic views over the mountain range. A wonderful **arboretum**, dating originally from 1740 but much expanded since, is its outstanding feature: the sheltered south-facing slopes of its hills, between the Mournes and the Slieve Croob range, allow exotic species to flourish. There's trout fishing in its main lake and coarse fishing in the smaller lakes; there's also a café in the 1720 Queen Anne-style farmstead and courtyards, near the main entrance. The Baronial castle to which the grounds originally belonged is now the property of a Christian conference organization, and it offers a very few **cheap rooms** (☎03967/78733; ②). You can **camp** here, too (call the forest officer on ☎013967/78664). Inside the park, **Dolly's Brae** (one of the westernmost hills) is often remembered at Loyalist celebrations as the site of one of the greatest victories against Catholic uprisings.

If you are planning on more serious hiking in the Mournes, heights worth chasing include **Slieve Bingian**, beyond the Hare's Gap, and reached through the Brandy Pad passes by the Blue Lough and Lough Bingian; **Slieve Commedagh**, with its Inca-looking pillars of granite; and **Slieve Bearnagh**, up to the right of the Hare's Gap. Also, try and cross the ridge from **Slieve Meelmore** to **Slieve Muck**, the "pig mountain", descending to the shores of Lough Shannagh, where there's a beach at either end – useful for a dip, though the water's freezing. In the panorama beyond the Hare's Gap, the places not to miss are the eastern slopes of the **Cove Mountain** and **Slieve Lamagan**. If you're sticking to the roads, all you can really do is circle the outside of the range, though there is one road through the middle, from Hilltown to Kilkeel.

only), with swimming pools, water slides and playgrounds. The newest addition to the tourist menu is the *US Automobile Museum* (Easter–Sept daily 10.30am–6pm; Sept–Easter Sat & Sun 2–6pm; £2.50) on Dundrum Road, which has all the great American cars – Thunderbirds, Cadillacs, Mustangs.

The **tourist information office** is at 10–14 Central Promenade (Mon–Sat 10am–5pm, Sun 2–6pm; ☎013967/22222). There's a wide choice of **places to stay**; the best of the more upmarket **hotels** is the *Slieve Donard Hotel* on Downs Road (☎013967/23681; ⑧); the *Brook Cottage Hotel*, 58 Bryansford Road (☎013967/22204; ⑥), might be more fun at half the price. Cheaper central B&Bs include *Fountainville Guest House*, 103 Central Promenade (☎013967/22317; ③), and *Castlebridge House*, 2 Central Promenade (☎013967/23209; ③). The only *YHANI* **youth hostel** in this region is in a terraced house on the seafront at 30 Downs Road, near the bus station (open March to Dec 23, Jan & Feb advanced booking only; ☎013967/22133; ②); and you can also stay at the **YWCA/YMCA** at the *Glenada Holiday Centre*, 29 South Promenade (open all year; ☎013967/22402; ①).

Mario's Italian Restaurant on the front is the best place for evening **meals** and Sunday lunches, unless you go out of town towards Castlewellan (take the A50) and to the luxurious, but rather characterless, *Burrendale Hotel and Country Club*. The *Donard Hotel* on Main Street also does reasonable lunches. The *Pavillion* on Downs Road does everything from snacks to steaks, while the *Percy French*, also on Downs Road, offers reasonable á la carte. Otherwise there are plenty of cafés – the best is *Brambles* on the prom – and chip shops scattered among the amusement arcades. Nearby, one speciality not to miss is *Maud's Ice Cream Parlour* with its eccentric selection of home-made delights.

Out of town, three miles away, in **BRYANSFORD** village, opposite *Tollymore Forest Park* are a couple of comfortable small B&Bs: *The Cottage*, 81 Burrenreagh Road (☎01396/24698; ⑤), the restored eighteenth-century cottage and *The Briers*, 39 Middle Tollymore Road (☎01396/24347; ④). There are also eleven **caravan and camping sites** around the town – ask at the tourist information office. Nearby **riding schools** include *Castlewellan Trekking* (☎013967/71497), three miles northeast of Newcastle on the Castlewellan Road, and, for those with more experience, *Castlewellan Wood Lodge Centre* (☎013967/78947) beside the forest park (see "Walks and hikes in the Mournes", p.527).

The western slopes of the Mournes

The landward side of the Mourne Mountains is a patchwork of fields divided by dry stone walls: attractive, especially in the morning light, but with nothing of pressing interest. **HILLTOWN** has a main street extraordinarily well provided with pubs – supposedly because it was once a smugglers' hideaway, where the spoils would be divided – and it's still a crossroads where numerous roads meet. There's a pretty parish church which was founded in 1776, a Georgian market house and a monthly market; but most of the time its atmosphere is that of a ghost town. Little over a mile from Hilltown on the Newcastle Road is the handsome **Goward dolmen**, known locally as "Pat Kearney's big stone". It's well signposted off the road, though the last quarter mile of track is severely potholed.

Drumena Cashel, back in the same direction off the A25, is one of the better-preserved ring forts, or defended homesteads, in the area. It has a T-shaped underground chamber intended to give shelter from the Vikings – though this is only twelve yards long and seems better suited to its peacetime function of providing cold storage for food. The stone foundations of a few circular beehive huts (known as *clocháns*) also remain. The puzzling aspect of the *cashel* is its position below the summit of the hill:

possibly a compromise between the needs of defence and those of comfort, so there would be some shelter from the harsh winds that curl through the area.

The Mourne coastline

The A2 south along the coast from Newcastle, trailing the shore around the edge of the mountains, is a beautiful drive. Along the way, the fishing harbour towns of **Annalong** and **Kilkeel** are the best bases for **walkers** or explorers to get into the mountains.

Annalong and around

The small fishing harbour of **ANNALONG** – its name in Irish is *Áth na Long*, or "the ford of the ships" – is a pleasantly relaxed seaside town during the summer, with a stony beach and Slieve Binnion providing a grandiloquent backdrop. In the harbour, pleasure craft are tied up alongside the fishing boats and small trawlers. The only blot on the horizon is the powerful smell of herring wafting up from the harbour.

A path from the campsite just off the main road gives immediate access to an early nineteenth-century **cornmill**, still in working order and open for visits (Easter–May Sat 11am–6pm, Sun 2–6pm; June–Aug daily 11am–6pm; guided tours 2–6pm; £1.30), and to a herb garden down by the walled harbour and the beach. The village itself goes about its maritime work in its narrow streets much as it always has done, and it comes as a surprise in this out-of-the-way part of the North to find the grey harbour walls adorned with the familiar ritualized Protestant graffiti – Ulster 1690, UVF and a Union Jack flag.

There are a number of small **B&Bs** here – for example *Dromahare*, 39 Kilkeel Road (☎013967/68630; ④), and *Mrs Stevenson*, 237 Kilkeel Road (☎013967/68345; ③) – and a dreary municipal *Marine Park* **camping/caravan** site (☎013967/68736) by the harbour (summer only) that's landscaped in the shape of a shamrock; a second site, the *Annalong Caravan Park* (☎013967/68248), is on the Kilkeel Road. There's little in the way of places to eat, but right on the harbour, the *Harbour Inn* serves adequate lunches and evening **meals**, while the *Halfway House* north out of town on the A2 does pub food.

Inland a mile or so from Annalong, signposts point to the **Silent Valley** (10am–6.30pm; £2); here you'll fine Belfast and County Down's reservoir, which was begun in the 1880s and finished thirty years later. There's a car park by the lower reservoir bound by the Mourne Wall, a sturdy 22-mile-long granite boundary to the catchment area that joins the summits of fifteen mountains along its route. The views out to Slieve Binnian and Ben Crom, behind it to the west, are worth the effort of the Viewpoint Walk (starts at the car park). Less energetic, but still superb, is the half-mile Sally Lough stroll (or you can take the shuttle bus) up to the dam at Ben Crom; again the views are spectacular.

Kilkeel and Ballymartin

Continuing south, there's a good small beach just outside the hamlet of Ballymartin. Further on, **KILKEEL** – "the church of the narrows" – is a much grander version of Annalong, remarkable mainly for the even heftier stench of fish from the canneries on the harbour; the town is home to nearly a hundred trawlers. The biggest excitements here are the fish auctions that take place on the quayside when the fishing boats come home, and the annual summer **harbour festival**. The ruined "narrows" church, built in the fourteenth century, stands in the centre of Kilkeel in a ring fort. Kilkeel is a prosperous, predominantly Protestant place, but behind the village on the banks of its river memories of less happy days remain – small grave markers identify where the inmates of Kilkeel workhouse are buried. One of those buried here is the infamous **William Hare**, who murdered sixteen people in the space of a year in Edinburgh. Hare owned a lodging house and, when an old lodger died owing rent, he and his accomplice William Burke decided to sell the body to a medical school. The £7.10 they were paid spurred them on to greater efforts; however, eventually their enthusiasm raised the neighbours' suspicions and their profitable venture came to an end. Hare turned king's evidence and got his freedom, while Burke was hanged. Deciding to lie low, Hare came to Kilkeel and soon landed in the workhouse; his identity was only revealed to the locals when a Dr Reid, former medical student from Edinburgh, recognized him.

Both Kilkeel and Ballymartin have **places to stay**. In **Kilkeel** there are a couple of hotels – *Cranfield House*, 57 Cranfield Road (☎016937/62327; ④), and *Kilmorey Arms*, Greencastle Street (☎016937/62220; ⑤) – both of which serve food, and numerous B&Bs – try *Morne Abbey*, 16 Greencastle Road (☎016937/62426; ④), *Home-syde*, 7 Shandon Drive (☎016937/62676; ④), or *Heath Hall*, 160 Moyadd Road (☎016937/62612; ③). **BALLYMARTIN** has just small B&Bs such as *Mrs McCormick* at 3 Ballymartin Village (☎016937/62077; ④); *Mrs Bingham*, 6 Ballykeel Road (☎06937/62521; ④); or the award-winning establishment run by *Mrs Adair*, 30 Main Road (☎016937/63012; ④). Three miles north of Kilkeel, there's accommodation in a picturesque old farmhouse, *Ashcroft*, 12 Ballykeel Road (☎016937/62736; ③). If you're **camping** take your pick of one of the six campsites hereabouts – the best along Cranfield Point, a flat grassy piece of land jutting out at the entrance to Carlingford Lough. Try *Sandilands Caravan Park* on Cranfield Road (☎016937/63634), nearby *Shanlieve Caravan Park* (☎016937/64344) or *Cranfield Caravan Park* (☎016937/62572). Again, **restaurants** in Kilkeel are thin on the ground, but the *Fisherman* (☎016937/62130) has an extensive, but pricy, fish menu, while *Jacob Hall's*, at the other end of the price scale, does tasty fish and chips.

Carlingford Lough

The eastern shore of Carlingford Lough bordering the Mournes offers some wonderful views back to the mountains and across the lough. Driving round to Warrenpoint, though, the villages become increasingly politicized as you get nearer the border, where IRA slogans alternate with Union Jacks.

Greencastle Fort

Guarding Cranfield Point, **Greencastle Fort** (April–Sept Tues–Sat 10am–7pm, Sun 2–7pm; 75p) sits on the mouth of the lough about four miles southwest of Kilkeel, and its views alone are worth a diversion off the main route. The fort is a comparatively well-preserved Anglo-Norman edifice, with a unique rock ditch, built in the same year (1261) as Carlingford Castle on the southern side of the lough. After succumbing to several attacks from the local Magennis clan, and falling to Edward Bruce in 1316, it collapsed into complete ruin after the Cromwellian invasion and today sits forlornly next to a working farmstead, for tourist use only. It's wide open to the blustery winds that sweep up the lough, and it takes great imaginative effort to summon up warmth from the massive fireplaces and fill the large window frames. But much of the structure is its full original height, and you can climb up the corner turrets and have full run of the top storey; there's also the sandy beach below, and photographic views up the mouth of the lough.

North to Rostrevor

If you take the main road inland from Kilkeel (cutting behind Greencastle Fort), four or five miles out of Kilkeel a signpost points to the **Kilfeaghan dolmen**, a mile inland then a short walk through a couple of fields and kissing gates. This polygonal stone is enormous and could only have got here during the retreat of the glacial drift.

Further up the lough, **ROSTREVOR** sits at the point where the waters dramatically begin to narrow towards Newry; and also where the population and political climate turn more in favour of the Catholic communities of County Armagh and those of the ever-nearing border. It's a picturesque town of Victorian terraces and friendly pubs, clambering up the slopes of **Slieve Martin**. A steep forest drive leads up the mountain from the back of the town, a long and winding ascent, really only of use to motorists, though rewarded at the top with great views across to the Cooley Mountains over the border. Again there are just a few tiny **B&Bs** in town, the best of them probably *Still Waters*, 14 Killowen Road (☎016937/38743; ③). But it's worth travelling out of Rostrevor to *Forrestbrook House* on Forest Road (☎016937/38105; ③) – a vaguely French chateau-style B&B. Rostrevor also has a youth centre on Mary Street (☎016937/32284), but you need to ring ahead to organize accommodation. **Camping** is available at two caravan parks, one each in *Kilbroney Park* (☎016937/38134) and *Rostrevor Forest Park* (☎016937/38284). Big, inexpensive steaks are popular at the *Top o' the Town* (known as *Annie O's*) in Church Street; *Patrick K* on the square does more exotic – and expensive – meals. The **Fiddler's Green Festival** in August is a big, enjoyable event, attracting folk musicians from across Europe.

Warrenpoint

WARRENPOINT is equally picturesque, with a colourful esplanade of seafront housing and a spacious central square. It's a much more traditional seaside resort than Rostrevor, with plenty of good places to spend the night. For help with finding accommodation, the **tourist information office** is in the Town Hall on Church Street (year round Mon–Fri 9am–5pm; plus weekends in summer; ☎016937/52256). There are handy **boat trips** across to Omeath on the opposite side of Carlingford Lough, leaving from just in front of the *Marine Tavern* (July & Aug Mon–Sat 1–5pm, Sun 1–7pm, tides permitting; 5min).

If you want to stay, **B&Bs** include the *Lough Viero*, 10 Osbourne Promenade (☎016937/73067; ④); *Glen Rosa*, 4 Great George's Street South (☎016937/72589; ③); and *Fern Hill House*, 90 Clonallon Road (☎016937/72677; ④). For **camping**, there's *Moygannon Caravan Site* (☎016937/72589). You can dine at *Aylesforte House* on the outskirts towards Newry; or for cheaper **eating** try *Cobblers*, just off the main square, with unbelievably low-priced specials. There's also cosy **drinking** at *Molly McCabes*, at the bottom of the road that runs uphill from the square, where the old boys gather to drink bottled stout only – it can accommodate twelve people at the most. Warrenpoint also has something of a tradition of singing pubs: there's regular **ceili** dancing in St Peter's Gaelic Hall, and **traditional sessions** and discos in the *Forresters' Hall* on the seafront. *Club Charlie* (Wed & Fri) and *Chaplin's* are also good for live music (mostly rock), the *Duke of Mourne* and *Shenanigan's* on the dock have sessions most nights, while the new *Fibber Magee's* offers a mix of music. Showband fans are catered for at the *Crown Hotel*, featuring stars like veteran Joe Dolan. These days, though, Warrenpoint **discos** are the big lure – locals come from miles around: biggest are at the *Marine Tavern* (Wed, Fri & Sat 9.30pm–1.30am) and rave nights at the *Carlingford Bay Hotel* on the seafront (Thurs, Sat & Sun). You can **rent bikes** at *East Coast Adventure Centre* (☎016937/74006), which is based in a kiosk on the seafront; they will also set you up with jet skies, wind-surfing boards, canoes and all the information on local sports you could want. For **horse-riding**, try *Annett's Equestrian Centre* (☎016937/72976).

Less than a mile from Warrenpoint along the Newry Road is the ruined **Narrow Water Castle**, built in the sixteenth century to guard the entrance of the river that flows from Newry into the lough. In this serene setting, it's hard to imagine that sixteen British soldiers were blown up here by the IRA, on the same day that Lord Mountbatten was killed in Mulloughmore Bay in 1979. There are very slight remains of an earlier castle nearby, and on the other side of the road an avenue leads up to New Narrow Water Castle (a private residence but can be viewed on request; 75p).

Newry

Although **NEWRY**, astride the border of Down and Armagh, is this area's most important commercial centre, it's the least attractive proposition for a visit. Traditionally, it was the place for people from the Republic to come and shop; on market day (Thurs) you'll still find traffic at a standstill. The town here has always been a garrison, guarding the borders of Ulster at the narrow point between the mountains known as the Gap of the North, but there's no trace at all of the early fortresses that were fought over so often. Rather what you see dates mostly from the eighteenth and nineteenth centuries, when a canal (the first in the British Isles) brought ships right up from Carlingford Lough into town, and with them trade and considerable wealth. This business has gone, however, and these days Newry is probably best known from the news: the town and its immediate surroundings were repeatedly bombed by the IRA in the 1970s, and the area is still frequently a hive of helicopter and police activity. Given its central position you're highly likely to pass through Newry, and it does make a possible base for exploring Slieve Gullion and the south Armagh district, but you're unlikely to be tempted to stay.

One thing you'll notice as you wander around is that there seem to be dozens of lawyers practising here, with whole streets full of their offices. Perhaps the most interesting building in town, however, is the **Catholic Cathedral** on Hill Street, in the pedestrian precinct. Despite an unpromising exterior, the rich mosaic pattern along its walls gives an eastern feel to the interior, which also has a striking vaulted ceiling of decorative sweeping plaster arcs and vivid stained-glass windows. Nearby, there's a strange bronze totem pole by sculptor Paddy McElroy which depicts, in tortured relief, scenes from Newry's past. Not far away, the **Town Hall** is remarkable mainly because it's built on a bridge over the Clanrye river – it's half in Down, half in Armagh. The **Newry and Mourne Arts Centre**, next door at 1a Bank Parade, has a Classical facade and hosts exhibitions of local artists' work, plays and all types of music in the auditorium.

Newry's **tourist information office** is in the town hall (June–Sept Mon–Fri 9am–8pm, Sat 10am–4pm; Oct–May Mon–Fri 9am–1pm & 2–5pm; ☎01693/68877). If you want to **stay**, the *Mourne Country Hotel*, 52 Belfast Road (☎01693/67922; ⑥), is luxurious but characterless. Alternatively, there are a fair number of **B&Bs** including, a few miles east of Newry along the canal, *Ashton House*, 37 Fathom Road (☎01693/62120; ④); the more central *Hillside*, 1 Rock Road (☎01693/65484; ④); and *Millvale House*, 8 Millvale Road (☎01693/63789; ④). Plenty of places serve cheap hot **meals**: the *Ambassador* restaurant, for example, at the start of the pedestrian precinct near to the town hall, will feed you well for under £5 – worth paying for the wit of the waitress alone; or try the *Boulevard* on the same street, or in the Town Hall Square *Friar Tuck's* (fast food) and the *Island Dinner*. However, the best restaurant, *Magee's Bistro*, Dundalk Street, is fifteen miles away over the border in Carlingford (take the B79); here the cooking avoids the stodge characteristic of Newry. A good **pub** is the *Brass Monkey* on Trevor Hill; although there's little in the way of **nightlife**, you could try *Nan Rice's* on Frances Street for music, or like the locals head for the *Forrester's Hall* in Warrenpoint, or the *Independent Club* en route on the A2.

Heading south **towards Dundalk** in the Republic, you'll be struck by the multitude of petrol stations crammed in along the route to the border – people stock up here before hitting the more expensive Republic.

Southwest of Belfast: Hillsborough to Banbridge

Heading west from Belfast, the M1 motorway offers very rapid access to Armagh and Tyrone, while the A1 cuts south towards Newry. On the former route there's little to stop for until you're in County Armagh; on the latter the historic village of **HILLSBOROUGH**, just a mile off the main road, merits a quick detour. Named after Sir Arthur Hill, who built the castle in the park on the south side of town during the reign of Charles I, it hit the headlines in 1985 when the controversial **Anglo-Irish Agreement** was signed here. The main street is perhaps a bit too quaint, with a distinct rural-England ambience and a sprinkling of tea and antique shops: the real attractions of Hillsborough are its architecture and, above all, the surrounding belt of woodland.

To best appreciate these, start from the **war memorial** and head up the magnificent approach to the rather spooky parish church. Here bear to your right for the main entrance to Hillsborough's elegant **fort** (April–Sept Mon–Fri 10am–7pm; Sun 2–7pm; Oct–March Mon–Fri 10am–4pm, Sun 2–4pm; free), whose ruins you can freely inspect. Beyond this a deciduous forest opens up, set around a lake with brown and rainbow trout. Footpaths crisscross through the trees in all directions, popular with locals and day-trippers from Belfast – a circuit of the lake takes around an hour. Exiting via the car park, a driveway brings you out near the *White Gables Hotel*, beyond which you'll notice a statue on a raised column, master of all it beholds – the third Marquis of Downshire, in case you're interested.

A right turn at the end of the drive brings you back into town, with **Hillsborough Castle** on your left. Frankly, the ornate gates are the best part, but it was here that the governor of Northern Ireland used to have his official residence, and here, too, that the Anglo-Irish Agreement was signed. You'll also notice the court building in front of the main gates, and the town hall at the main street, proudly raising its Union Jack over the village. There's a campsite in Hillsborough Forest – once part of Hillsborough House and signposted off the main road.

By this time you'll be in need of **refreshment**, for which the *Plough Inn* on the square is recommended. A little further down, the *Hillside Restaurant and Wine Bar*, built in 1777, serves more substantial fare. Best of all, however, is the *Red Fox* tea shop at the bottom of the hill, through an arch and behind a boutique of the same name. When you've finished here, you'll be back where you began, at the war memorial. From here a regular *Ulsterbus* service runs to Newry and Belfast.

Banbridge

Follow the A1 south from Hillsborough and you'll pass through **BANBRIDGE** on the River Bann. A trim, mainly Protestant town, with a growing Catholic population, Banbridge sits within the linen triangle and is the departure point for the Linen Homelands Tour (April–Oct; ☎018206/23322) at the **Banbridge Gateway Tourist Information Centre**. It was also a stop on the old coach route to the Mourne Mountains, but the steep hill – now the main street – to the south of the river presented problems to the horse-drawn mail coaches. A threat to boycott the town was enough to initiate drastic action – and the result is the town's best-known feature. The wide main street was divided into three with an underpass, known to locals as "the cut", carved out in the middle to lower the hill, and the Downshire Bridge was built over the gap. The town's most famous offspring is Captain Crozier, pioneer of the Northwest Passage (the passage by sea from the Atlantic to the Pacific along the north coast of America), who was born in 1796 in a house on Church Square. The house now overlooks the Crozier Memorial, on which four polar bears gaze at the captain, who in turn gazes to the northwest. Should you want to stay the best **B&B** in the district is *Mountpleasant* (☎01762/831522; ③) on Banbridge Road, just beyond Gilford (about four miles away). This vast Georgian linen house – with castellations – sits on a grassy knoll with a fine view, and has bedrooms the size of tennis courts.

THE BRONTË HOMELAND DRIVE

The start of the **Brontë Homeland Drive** is well signposted off the A1, ten miles south of Banbridge. After that you're navigating by intuition and the odd pointer. The drive is built around a rather tenuous link – the Brontës in question are not the famous sisters or even Bramwell, but father Patrick Brontë and his parents. Nor is there any evidence that the literary daughters ever visited Ireland, though there is a story that one of the uncles took his shillelagh and headed to England to sort out a reviewer critical of *Jane Eyre*. It's more the story of local boy made good – Patrick obviously dragged himself up by his bootlaces, working in the linen works by day and reading the classics by night. With help from a local rector, he got a place to read theology at Cambridge. In 1806 he came back to preach his first sermon at Drumballyroney Church, but eventually moved to Yorkshire where he married Maria Branwell and had his six children – all of whom he outlived. There's a minuscule **interpretative centre** (March–Oct Tues–Fri 11am–5pm, Sat & Sun 2–6pm; £1), with a mock schoolroom tableau, at the end of a winding narrow drive. Little remains of Patrick's birthplace – a few feet of stone wall. And several of the other sights are specious: Knockiveagh, a hilltop stopping point, seems to be on the signposted route mainly to give you a chance to get your bearings. But if the drive doesn't yield nuggets of literary history, it does offer a route – however difficult to follow – through lovely hillocky countryside that you might not otherwise explore.

COUNTY ARMAGH

Armagh has a history as rich as any county in Ireland, especially in Armagh city, with its associations with Saint Patrick and early Christianity. The county town still has a few reminders of this, but the county as a whole is quiet and rural, with little evidence that anything of significance occurred here before this century. What has happened in recent years has hardly heightened the appeal for tourists, since the villages of south Armagh – a predominantly Catholic area – are best known for their constant appearance in news headlines. Villages like Crossmaglen, Fortkill and Newtownhamilton are overshadowed by military surveillance towers; there are fourteen in South Armagh alone. Since the end of the IRA ceasefire, daytime British army patrols are a more frequent sight, and a number of military checkpoints at border crossings have been reinstated.

From Belfast the motorway cuts across the north of the county, below **Lough Neagh**, giving easy access to the industrial towns in the north of the county: Lurgan, Craigavon and Portadown. Virtually joined now by a single strip of development, these three offer little reason to stop, and you're far better off pushing on down to Armagh city instead, pretty much at the centre of the county. If you do want to stop – and coarse anglers might be tempted by the River Bann, which teems with roach – then **Peatlands Park**, well signposted off the M1 and telling something of the social and industrial history of peat, and the nature reserve at **Oxford Island** near Craigavon offer the best excuse.

Armagh city and around

ARMAGH's small size disappoints some people, and certainly the city doesn't immediately present a greatly exciting prospect – but, rich in history at least, Armagh and its surroundings have plenty to keep you occupied for a day or two. The city offers cathedrals, museums and a planetarium set in handsome Georgian streets, while the ancient site of once-grand Navan Fort and two stately homes, Ardress and the Argory, are features of the excellent cycling country roundabout. Armagh has been the site of the Catholic primacy of all Ireland since Saint Patrick established his church here (it's also the seat of the Protestant Church of Ireland Archbishop of Armagh) and has rather

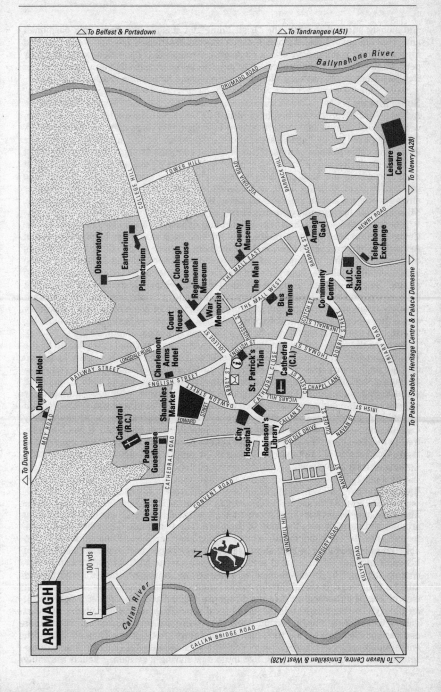

△ To Belfast & Portadown

△ To Tandrangee (A51)

Ballynahone River

DRUMADO ROAD

Leisure Centre

▷ To Newry (A28)

Telephone Exchange

Armagh Gaol

NEWRY ROAD

BARRACK HILL

TOWER HILL

COLLEGE HILL

County Museum

THE MALL EAST

R.U.C. Station

Observatory

Eartharium

Planetarium

Clonhugh Guesthouse

Regimental Museum

The Mall

Community Centre

Bus Terminus

THE MALL WEST

BARRACK ST

SCOTCH ST

LINENHALL ST

DOBBIN STREET

FRIARY ROAD

To Palace Stables, Heritage Centre & Palace Demesne ▷

War Memorial

Court House

COLLEGE ST

RUSSELL ST

St Patrick's Trian

Cathedral (C.I.)

THOMAS ST

IRISH ST

Charlemont Arms Hotel

RAILWAY STREET

LONSDALE ROAD

Drumshill Hotel

MOY ROAD

△ To Dungannon

ENGLISH STREET

ABBEY ST

DAWSON STREET

ENGLISH STREET

CATHEDRAL CLOSE

VICARS HILL

CASTLE ST

CHAPEL LANE

Shambles Market

Cathedral (R.C.)

Padua Guesthouse

CATHEDRAL ROAD

EDWARD STREET

City Hospital

Robinson's Library

CALLAN ST

CULDEE DRIVE

CULDEE ST

NAVAN ST

NURSERY ROAD

KILLYEA ROAD

Desart House

CONVENT ROAD

WINDMILL HILL

NAVAN ST

N

Callan River

0   100 yds

ARMAGH

CALLAN BRIDGE ROAD

▽ To Navan Centre, Enniskillen & West (A28)

VICTORIA ROAD

ambitiously adopted the title the "Irish Rome" for itself – like Rome, it's positioned among seven small hills. Armagh is also a thoroughly friendly city and well organized for the tourist; you can invest in a *Passport to Armagh* (£1.50), which gives you a 20-percent discount on the entrance fee to any site in the city, the Navan Centre and the Benburb Centre (obtainable from any venue and valid for any one year).

Some history

Armagh (*Ard Mhacha*, "the height of Mhacha") was first named after Queen Mhacha, wife of Nevry, who is said to have arrived in Ireland 608 years after the biblical flood. She's supposed to be buried somewhere in the side of the main hill, where the Protestant cathedral now stands. If this is true, it confirms Armagh as one of the oldest settlements in Ireland, a theory supported by the city's position on one of the most ancient roads in the land, the Moyry Pass, which once stretched from the extreme south of Ireland, through Tara, to the north. In about 300 BC, the centre of power shifted westward across the River Callan to where another queen (of the same name, Mhacha) built the legendary **Navan Fort**.

After nearly seven hundred years, the ruling dynasty at Navan was defeated by the Collas brothers, and the new rulers re-established their main base back on the hill of Armagh. A hundred years later, in 445 AD, **Saint Patrick** declared the hill the site of his primacy and first bishopric and built his cathedral here (having first converted the local chieftain, Daire, a descendant of the Collas brothers). Other churches grew up around the cathedral, and Armagh became *the* great centre of learning during the Dark Ages, the period when Ireland was known as the "Isle of Saints and Scholars". Armagh strongly challenges Downpatrick's claim to be the burial place of Saint Patrick; they argue that since the relics of Patrick's book, bell and staff are here, his body must be, too (though the burial site, somewhere on the main hill, is not identified).

Between the ninth and the eleventh centuries, the city was constantly pillaged by the **Vikings**, mainly from the Norse settlements at Lough Neagh. The Irish king who claimed final victory over the Norsemen, **Brian Boru**, is buried in Armagh cathedral. Armagh's ecclesiastical power weakened in the Middle Ages, and its history ran in line with the rest of the North for the next several hundred years, with no lengthy periods of peace until the eighteenth and nineteenth centuries, when there was a final flourish of building, much of which survives today. Modern Armagh is a predominantly Catholic city – it's strong on Gaelic sports – and, although physically it has borne up well to the Troubles (certainly in comparison to Newry and Derry), it has not avoided them. One local to fall victim to the IRA was the moderate Protestant Chairman of the Council, Charlie Armstrong.

The city

The Mall, an elegant tree-lined promenade, is as good a place as any to begin looking around, and strongly sets the tone of the place. The handsome Georgian street architecture is by the early nineteenth-century Armagh-born architect Francis Johnson, who also designed many of Dublin's best Georgian buildings; you'll come across more of his work in many of the central streets that lead off The Mall. In its late eighteenth-century heyday The Mall was used as a racecourse; nowadays there's nothing more athletic than the occasional Sunday cricket game. A former schoolhouse on the east side of The Mall houses the **County Museum** (Mon–Sat 10am–1pm & 2–5pm; free), an old-style museum with all the usual local miscellany on display plus a little art gallery tucked away on the second floor. Here there are several mystical pastels, oils and cartoon sketches by the Irish turn-of-the-century poet **George Russell** (alias AE, and a much neglected companion to Yeats); a local painter, J.B. Vallely, is also represented with a superb oil showing five musicians having a session – Vallely currently runs the town's *Armagh Pipers' Club*. There's also a permanent exhibition of stuffed wildlife, alarmingly vivid. Further along The Mall, beside the Classical courthouse and built from its leftovers, is the **Royal Irish Fusiliers Museum** (Mon–Fri 10am–1pm & 2–4pm; unreliable hours, so check with tourist office). It's pretty much as you'd expect: tons of weaponry, uniforms, medallions and regimental silverware.

The Observatory, Planetarium and Eartharium

College Hill, the road that leaves The Mall by the museum, will take you to the **Observatory** (not open to the public) and the **Planetarium** (Sept–June Mon–Fri 10am–5pm, Sat 1.30–5pm; shows daily 3pm, Sat also 2pm; July–Aug shows hourly 1am–4pm, Sat 2pm & 3pm; £3.50, £1 for exhibition hall alone; booking recommended), which are linked by a short woodland path round the back. The Observatory is an ancient one – it celebrated its second centenary in 1990 – but it's still at the forefront of astronomical research. The Planetarium was built much more recently in 1968, and its best feature is a sophisticated video projection of a multitude of skies round the world onto its hemispherical ceiling, while you sit back on reclinable seats. It also has various antique astronomical instruments from the earliest days of the Observatory on display, as well as high-tech equipment to show you the latest pictures from NASA's space telescope. There's also a new **Eartharium** (same hours as Planetarium), which – rather chillingly – allows you to zoom in on Belfast or Armagh using spy satellite pictures, or to predict the weather.

The cathedrals and around

A few minutes' walk northwest of The Mall, on a hillrise beyond the Shambles Market, the **Catholic St Patrick's Cathedral** is at first sight little different to the many other nineteenth-century Gothic Revival Catholic cathedrals across the country. But it is impressively large and airy, and inside, as befits the seat of the cardinal archbishop, every inch of wall glistens with mosaics, in colours ranging from marine- and sky-blue to terracotta pinks and oranges. Other striking pieces include the white-granite "pincer-claw" tabernacle holder, reflected in a highly polished marble floor, and a statue of the Crucifixion which looks (deliberately or otherwise) like a CND symbol. Not surprisingly, this cathedral city is known for its choral music, and the annual Charles Wood Summer School (check with the tourist office for dates) is worth catching.

Heading south (either along Dawson or English streets) you'll soon reach Cathedral Close and **St Patrick's Church of Ireland Cathedral** (April–Oct 10am–5pm, Nov–March closed 4pm; tours 11.30am & 2.30pm). This lays claim to the summit of the principal hillock, where Saint Patrick founded his first church, commanding a distinctive Armagh view across to the other hills and down over the shambles of gable walls and pitched roofing on its own slopes. The church is more spartan inside than you might expect from its noble past; there have been a string of buildings on the site, and although the core is medieval, a nineteenth-century restoration coated the thirteenth-century outer walls in a sandstone plastercast and robbed the interior of many of its ancient decorations. Just as you enter from the highly distinctive timber porch, there are a few remnants of an eleventh-century Celtic cross and a startling statue of Thomas Molyneux. Inside, high up, you should be able to sight the medieval carved heads of men, women and monsters. One other unusual feature is the tilt of the chancel, a medieval building practice meant to represent the slumping head of the dying Jesus. The **chapter house** has a small collection of stone statues (mostly gathered from elsewhere), the most noticeable of which are a *sheila-na-gig* with ass's ears – some reckon it's King Midas, but most people guess it represents one of the Queen Mhachas – and the Stone Age Tandragee Idol.

The **public library** (known locally as Robinson's), down the hill from the cathedral (Mon–Fri 9am–1pm & 2–4pm; free but donations welcomed), has a first edition of *Gulliver's Travels*, annotated by Swift himself, and an early edition of Raleigh's *History* *of the World* (1614), among many other rare tomes, as well as a collection of etchings, including some by Hogarth. The library was founded in 1771 by Archbishop Richard Robinson, who was described as converting Armagh "from mud to stone" and is responsible for almost all the older buildings in Armagh. He was obviously a magpie: the collection ranges from Roman coins – currently being catalogued – to old bells.

Walking back past the cathedral and a little way north up English Street, **St Patrick's Trian Centre**, an ambitious complex in Old Bush House and Granary Hall, offers literary and religious displays (the tourist office is also here; see below). There's a tableau of figures representing the Land of Lilliput and Jonathan Swift's connection with Armagh, and a display in an audiovisual theatre traces "The Armagh Story" and its seven eras of "belief" (April–Sept Mon–Sat 10am–7pm, Sun 1–7pm, Oct–March Mon–Sat closes 5pm, Sun 2–5pm; £3.25).

Armagh Friary

Moving south, the final piece of ecclesiastical interest, the ruins of **Armagh Friary**, lie within easy walking distance of the city centre, just off Friary Road in the grounds of the Archbishop's Palace, now the District Council offices, but with the rest of the grounds, including the stable block, converted into a heritage centre and public walks (April–Sept Mon–Sat 10am–7pm, Sun 1–7pm; Oct–March Mon–Sat 10am–5pm, Sun 2–5pm; £2.80). The stables and surrounds are frozen into tableaux of lifesize figures depicting July 23, 1776, the day on which Archbishop Robinson entertained agricultural reformer Arthur Young. This was originally a Franciscan friary, dating from around 1263; the Franciscans, known as Grey Friars because of the colour of their robes, arrived in Ireland as soon as six years after Saint Francis's death in Italy and spread their order like wildfire through the country. The ruins here are those of the church alone – and the site is an unfortunate example of how atmosphere can be destroyed when a noisy major road runs alongside.

Practicalities

The helpful **tourist information office** is in the St Patrick's Trian Centre on English Street (April–Sept Mon–Sat 9am–5pm, Sun 10am–5pm, Oct–March same hours except Sun 2–5pm; ☎01861/521800). Armagh does not offer a great deal of choice if you want to **stay**: your best bet is to ask first at the tourist office. The *Charlemont Arms Hotel* on English Street (☎01861/522028; ⑤) is central and has a reasonable restaurant; out of town on the Moy Road is *Drumsill Hotel* (☎01861/522009; ⑥). **B&Bs** are scarce, but they include two on Cathedral Road: *Desart House* at no. 99 (☎01861/522387; ④) and *Padua House* at no. 63 (☎01861/522039; ④); plus *Jill Armstrong*, Dean's Hill, College Hill (☎01861/524923; ④), and *Clonhugh House* on College Hill (☎01861/522693; ④). The nearest **camping** is *Gosford Forest Park*, seven miles along the A28 near Markethill (☎01861/551277), with fine facilities set in wooded grounds around a castle.

Many of the **pubs** will serve bar food at lunchtime, but **eating** in the evening can be more problematic. Of the pubs, one of the best is *Calvert's Tavern*, 3 Scotch Street (☎01861/524186); *Harry Hoot's*, Railway Street, has an excellent restaurant with music on the weekends; or you can always get a reasonably priced full meal at the *Drumsill Hotel*. An excellent place with healthy food is *Jodies*, upstairs at 37 Scotch Street. Other possibilities are mostly on English and Scotch streets – such as *Hester's Place* on English Street – and there's *The Wheel and Lantern* in *Lennox's* department store on Market Street; both serve good-value lunches. You can pick up picnic supplies at *Armagh Fine Foods* on Scotch Street. The best places for coffee and snacks are *The Archway*, through an arch off the east side of The Mall, and the *Pilgrim's Table* in the St Patrick's Trian Centre. The Shambles (see opposite) is a good area to pub crawl in search of **music**; weekends are best but many places have sing-songs (Tues & Thurs).

THE GAME OF BULLET

On the roads just north of Armagh city, you may be lucky enough to witness an ancient road game by the name of **Bullet**, played by local men. It's played here and in County Cork – and virtually nowhere else in the world. The game consists of throwing an iron ball (the size of a cricket ball but 28oz in weight) along about two and a half miles of winding road, and the aim is to know your road well and get the ball to the end with the least number of throws – it takes approximately twenty. Originally, cannon balls were used – or so they say.

The game draws big local crowds, and there's even some betting along the way. Oncoming cars are hastily stopped, and the crowd has to scatter as the ball hurtles along, cutting corners or clearing the heights of hedges. Roads where you're likely to catch sight of the game include Napper Road, Blackwater Town Road, Rock Road, Tassa Road, Keady Road, Newtonhamilton Road and Madden Road, usually on Sunday afternoons. The most reliable information on coming games is probably in local pubs. The "World Championship" takes place on the first Sunday in August in Armagh and the last Sunday in August in Cork: the Armagh world champion to look out for is Aiden McVeigh.

For **nightclubs**, your options are limited, but you could try the *Drumsill Hotel* on weekends.

Armagh has a big market, the **Shambles Market** (Tues & Fri) on Market Street, with a variety of stalls, but mainly clothes. Various fairs and shows take place through the summer, including a motorcycle race in May. The **Ulsterbus station** (☎01861/522266) is on the west side of The Mall, and runs regular services to Belfast.

Navan Fort

Navan Fort (open access; free) is the Irish Camelot, with the one difference that the Irish have kept better track of their ancient capital, and, in terms of its archeological importance, it is definitely worth visiting. For nearly seven hundred years this was the great seat of northern power, the rival of Tara. It was here that the Kings of Ulster ruled and that the court of the **Knights of the Red Branch**, Ireland's most prestigious order of chivalry, was based. The knights, like those of the Round Table, are historical figures who have been entirely subsumed into legend, their greatest champion the legendary defender of Ulster, **Cúchulainn**. The stories of these warriors' deeds are recited and sung in what's now known as the *Ulster Cycle*. Their dynasty was finally vanquished in 332 AD, when three brothers (the Collas), in a conquest known as the Black Pig's Dyke, destroyed Navan Fort, razing it to the ground and leaving only the earthen mounds you see today. The defeated Red Branch Knights were driven eastwards into Down and Antrim, but their glories withered away soon afterwards.

The best approach to the fort (two miles west of Armagh on the A28) is to visit the new interpretative centre first. The **Navan Centre**, cut into the land near the site (July–Aug Mon–Thurs & Sat 10am–6pm, Fri till 7pm, Sun 11am–5am; April–June & Sept Mon–Sat 10am–6pm, Sat 11am–6pm, Sun noon–6pm; Oct–March Mon–Fri 10am–5pm, Sat 11am–5pm, Sun noon–5pm; £3.95), is a circular grass-covered mound supported inside by columns, which sensitively mimics the real fort. The seventy-minute tour, which deposits you at the doors leading to the fort proper, begins with an excellent talk on the history and archeology of the site, with fascinating asides – the skull of a Barbary ape implies trade links with North Africa, the skull of a larger-than-life dog could be a genuine hound of Ulster. You then move onto an audiovisual show that replays four key myths associated with this ancient fort, including that of Cúchulainn, the hound of Ulster, and the *Táin Bó Cuailgne* (Cattle Raid of Cooley). When you reach the fort, you find an earthen mound that apart from its commanding view gives no hint of its past.

Excavation of the mound took place over a ten-year period (1961–71) and revealed a peculiar structure, apparently unique in the Celtic world. Archeologists reckon that around 100 BC the buildings that had existed since the Neolithic period were cleared, and a huge structure 108ft in diameter was constructed. An outer wall of timber surrounded five concentric rings of large posts, 275 in all, with a massive post at the very centre. This was then filled with limestone boulders – and set on fire, creating a mountain of ash that was then covered with sods of clay to make a high mound. It is anybody's guess what the purpose of the structure was – possibly a temple, or maybe a monumental funeral pyre.

The site area is defined by a massive bank with a defensive ditch. Nearby you can visit for free other ancient archeological structures: a second fort, the earliest known artificial lake and a large natural lake which has yielded incredible treasures.

Loughgall, Ardress House and the Argory

LOUGHGALL, an estate village about five miles north of Armagh along the B27 in the middle of apple orchard country, beautiful in the spring, is worth visiting mainly for its

---

THE ORANGE ORDER

The Orangeman has a very bad image of intransigence and intolerance. From inside the Orange Order, however, the view is very different. The majority of its members – and there are at least 100,000 of them in Ireland – insist that 12th July, the day of the Battle of the Boyne in 1690 and the key date in the Orange diary, is just a family celebration. It's the culmination of the marching season – when bowler-hatted and gloved Orangemen parade accompanied by fife and drum – often through hostile Catholic areas. Orangeism, they maintain, is a cultural and ethnic institution, not a political one – though in Northern Ireland, it is impossible to separate these categories. In fact, contradictions run riot in the Order: seen by outsiders as a force of bigotry, from within it is experienced as a haven of tolerance, reaching across class barriers and across the various strands of Protestantism.

Founded two hundred years ago on the spot now occupied by the Orange Museum in Loughgall, the Orange Order is the longest running political grouping in Ireland. The spark was not the Battle of the Boyne, or even anything connected with William of Orange, but a less dignified skirmish, the **Battle of the Diamond**, which took place in Dan Winter's farm near Loughgall in 1795 between the Peep O'Day boys, Protestants, and the Defenders, Catholics; neither side could claim to be the innocent party. The Defenders, in a continuation of a long-running dispute, attacked an inn. Inside the Peep O'Day boys were armed and waiting. They killed about twelve of the Defenders and in the glow of victory formed the Orange Order. Nor was the conflict over politics or even religion; it was over the linen trade and the fierce competition for the market.

Although today Orangeism is a conservative movement, at first it was affected by the same revolutionary wind that was blowing through France and America. The masonic symbol of the eye that appears occasionally on banners, collarettes and documents is still on the American dollar bill, and at the time appeared on much French Revolutionary material. In fact many of the original members were already masons, and freemasonry is the most obvious characteristic of the Order. The Orangeman must be initiated through a series of hierarchies or "degrees" – and corresponding complexities of ritual, the higher degrees involving ritual dramas in which biblical texts are re-enacted – from orange and purple to Arch Purple and the Royal Black (the latter boasts former Unionist Party leader James Molyneaux as Sovereign Grand Master).

Increasingly there are signs that the strength of the Orange Order is beginning to wane. Young Unionists are calling for the Ulster Unionist Party, for example, to cut its links with the Order, middle-class membership is falling, and Unionist politicians seem to be aware that the monoculture of Orangeism is hardly an inducement to Catholic support. Even so, the day when the marching and flag-waving become just a quaint tourist attraction is a long way away.

Orange Museum. It was just northeast of Loughgall at Diamond Hill that the Battle of the Diamond took place in 1795 and led to the foundation of the first Protestant Orange Order (see opposite). Today the little village, like many others in Armagh's rural north, is a strongly Protestant enclave. The tiny museum is sandwiched between two terraced houses at the northern end of the main street (key next door with Mrs Vallary) and includes such Orange paraphernalia as sashes, flags and the banner from the Dolly Brae victory, the first Orange Order warrant signed on a Catholic after the Battle of the Diamond, and a couple of UVF armbands. Nowadays the village is deceptively quiet – in 1988, however, it was the scene of a British army ambush in which eight IRA men died. The main street is lined with antique shops, and there's a nice tea-house parlour, *Emily's Cottage*; the *Famous Grouse Inn* on Ballyhegan Road (☎01868/891778) is rather livelier, with the best restaurant for miles and regular live music. There's B&B **accommodation** at *Lavery's*, 123 Cloreneden Road (☎01868/784218; ③).

A further five miles or so north, and only a few miles apart, are two National Trust properties worth visiting if you've more than a day in the area. **Ardress House** (April–June & Sept Sat & Sun 2–6pm; July & Aug daily except Tues 2–6pm; £2) is a seventeenth-century manor house with ornate plasterwork, a good collection of paintings, a sizeable working farmyard and wooded grounds. **The Argory** (same hours; £2.20) is a fine Neoclassical building dating back to 1824, which contains its original furniture and is still lit by an original acetylene gas plant in the stable yard.

South Armagh

South Armagh is a tiny area but a well-defined one, stretching from the border to a line drawn roughly between Newry and Monaghan. It's a completely different proposition from the more populated northern slice of the county. Today it's known to outsiders, if at all, primarily from news reports, and even locally it's often referred to as Bandit Country or The Killing Fields. Its towns, from Bessbrook through Newtownhamilton to Keady, still bear the signs of siege. These Protestant-dominated bastions have been forced into a kind of internal exile, and their Union Jack flags fly defiantly in an area where the countryside is heavily Catholic.

Slieve Gullion

Slieve Gullion (*sliabh gCuilinn*, "the mountain of Culainn"), which dominates the southeast corner of Armagh, is one of the most mysteriously beautiful mountains in the country. A store of romantic legends is attached to the mountain, especially concerning **Cúchulainn**, who took his name here after slaying the hound (*Cú*) of his chief, *Culainn*. Due south at Glendhu is where he single-handedly halted the army of Queen Maebh of Connaught, who was intent on capturing the great bull of Cooley. **Fionn Mac Cumhaill***, who founded the *Fianna*, a mythical national militia whose adventures are told in the *Fenian Cycle*, also appears in stories here. Slieve Gullion itself is surrounded by a far-flung circular rampart of smaller hills that make up what is known as the **Gullion Ring Dyke**, which rises to no more than a thousand feet and encloses some of the most beautiful countryside of these two northern counties.

A scenic way to approach the mountain is from the north, through **CAMLOUGH**, where the Tricolour flutters. As you turn off the main road to go down by the eastern slopes of Camlough Mountain, you'll see a beautiful lake, inset like a jewel into its

---

*One of the Fionn Mac Cumhaill legends refers to the little lake on the top of Slieve Gullion. A magic drinking-horn once disappeared here, near the "growth of slender twigs", and if you manage to look at the right area in the morning, having previously fasted, you'll instantly know everything that's going to happen that day.

green sides. A little further on, between Camlough Mountain and Slieve Gullion, are the **Killevy churches**. Two churches of different periods, they share the same gable wall: the west church is pre-Romanesque and one of the most important survivors of its kind in the country; the other, larger church dates from the thirteenth century. The grave of Saint Blinne, the founder of a fifth-century nunnery, is here, and there's a holy well dedicated to her a little further up the slopes of Slieve Gullion; pilgrims visit it on her feast day (the Sunday nearest July 6).

The official, tarmacked entrance up into Slieve Gullion is on the mountain's afforested southern face, after you've passed through the village of Killevy. Here there's a small forest park with a winding drive up to the summit, where various vertiginous viewpoints offer spectacular views over the Ring of Gullion and the surrounding countryside for miles around.

Jonesborough

JONESBOROUGH, east of the mountain, is the venue each Sunday for a vast **market**, with traders and customers coming from north and south of the border to buy and sell a wide range of wares (11am–5pm, up at the school). If you're around, it's well worth experiencing. Two miles south of Jonesborough is the **Pillar Stone of Kilnasaggart**, a beautifully inscribed Christian monument and one of the earliest of its kind (700 AD). Several small crosses are marked within circles on its back face, and the defaced markings on its edges are possibly *ogham* writing. It's surrounded by several other tiny stones with similar cross markings, all held within a pentagonal enclosure three fields away from the roadside, behind a farmhouse. Less than a mile west of here, on the other side of the train line, you should be able to see **Moyry Castle** on the hill. It's a timid affair and not really worth even this slight detour, but among its interesting features are several musket loopholes. It was built by Lord Mountjoy, Queen Elizabeth I's deputy, in 1601 as the defence for the Gap to the North.

Forkhill

FORKHILL is a tiny village right up by the border in the southwest foothills of Slieve Gullion, a simple, quiet and remote-looking place – but for the massive army encampment stacked upon the crown of its hill, which entirely dominates everything else in sight. To get here from Jonesborough, you have to take a long way round, back to the main Forkhill–Newry Road: the obvious and quickest route passes along unapproved border roads. The village is strong on traditional culture; O'Neill's *Welcome Inn* has a storyteller, John Campbell, and sessions most Tuesday nights (check first on ☎01693/888273). A two-day festival of *sean nós* or singing (unaccompanied by instruments) takes place in summer (check times with the *Welcome Inn*); there's a lively musical tradition both here and in Mullaghbane further north up the road – try *O'Hanlon's*. If you want to **stay** in Forkhill, there are a couple of B&Bs: *Ard Mhuire Guesthouse*, 27 Carrickasticken Road (☎01693/888316; ③), and *Green Gables*, 2 Tifferum Road (☎01693/888589; ④). Passing through Mullaghbane, you get back to the main Newry–Crossmaglen Road, on which there's a small cottage **Folk Museum**, where *Hearty's* (Sun only 2–7pm) offers good afternoon teas, a little up towards the Newry end.

Crossmaglen

CROSSMAGLEN, however, dominates the southwestern corner of Armagh. Its reputation in print looks frightening – seventeen soldiers have died in its main square alone, and it's seen by all as the centre of the storm in south Armagh. It has been a hotspot for so long largely because it's militantly Republican (note the very powerful Republican sculpture in the square) and only a couple of minutes away from the border; the army have therefore positioned one of their stronger encampments on the main square. All this said, on arrival you'll find the pubs much friendlier than you've been forewarned, and you're hardly likely to brush up against any trouble. Should you want to stay there's a tiny **B&B** at 6 Newry St (☎01693/861630; ③) and another, *Lima Country House*, at 16 Drumalt Road, Silverbridge (☎01693/861944; ③).

Darkley

There's little to lure you up the western side of Armagh except for the natural beauty of the run. Up near Keady, the small village of **DARKLEY** is, tragically, worth mentioning, because in November 1983 it was the victim of one of the most brutal attacks of the Troubles. The INLA arrived at the *Mountain Lodge Pentecostal Assembly* while a Sunday prayer meeting was in progress and shot three men who were standing outside the main door, killing them all. They fired more shots through the door, then walked round the outside of the church, shooting low through its wooden walls in the hope of killing many more. In the event, they managed only to wound a number of the congregation.

travel details

Trains

Bangor to: Belfast (4 hourly; 30min); Lisburn (4 hourly; 55min); Lurgan (hourly; 1hr 10min); Newry (6 daily; 1hr 45min); Portadown (hourly; 1hr 20min).

Ulsterbuses

Armagh to: Belfast (9 daily; 1hr 20min–2hr 20min); Cork (1 daily; 9hr); Dublin (5 daily; 3hr); Galway (1 daily; 5hr 30min); Newry (6 daily; 1hr 10min).

CHAPTER SEVENTEEN

TYRONE AND FERMANAGH

Counties Tyrone and Fermanagh form the bulk of inland Northern Ireland. Though these neighbouring counties are both predominantly rural, their characters are essentially quite different.

County Tyrone is largely dull farming country, whose chief scenic attractions are to be found in the wild and desolate **Sperrin Mountains**, to the north. It's remote country and thinly served by the local bus network; if you don't have a car it's very much a region for determined hikers and cyclists only. In the lowlands, the occasional castles, archeological sites and heritage centres are frustratingly scattered and difficult to get to – with the exception, luckily enough, of the **Ulster American Folk Park**, north of the county town of **Omagh**. Overall, it's an area where small villages dominate – none of enormous fascination, but most retaining an historical quirk or two which enliven the journey.

In contrast, **County Fermanagh** attracts plenty of visitors – chiefly for the watersports and fishing that are widely available. It has at its core the great **Lough Erne**, a huge lake complex dotted with islands and surrounded by richly beautiful countryside. Its county town of **Enniskillen** evinces a strong sense of history, while the remnants of the medieval past – along with those of the seventeenth and eighteenth centuries – are found all over the region, on islands and mainland alike. As in Tyrone, sights of interest are dispersed, and the public bus service again only serves the main routes; but the key to getting the most from Fermanagh is to get out onto the water – and this is easy enough from Enniskillen and a number of the villages that rest on the lakes' shores.

COUNTY TYRONE

Stretching from the shores of the vast Lough Neagh in the east to the border of the Republic and Donegal in the west, County Tyrone lies bang in the middle of Northern Ireland. Its northeastern limits are high in the desolate and beautiful **Sperrin Mountains**, and in the south it reaches near the lakes of County Fermanagh. It's a large and mainly featureless county, and if you are here at all the chances are you're heading elsewhere. The towns of Tyrone are not much of a draw; **Omagh** is the county's capital and is agreeable enough but with little to warrant a stop. **Cookstown** and **Dungannon** in the east, and **Strabane** on the border with Donegal, are similarly places to pass through, with minimal points of interest scattered around. It's first and foremost farming country, with little evidence of industrialization apart from the

---

ACCOMMODATION PRICES

Throughout this book, accommodation prices have been graded according to the cost per person per night in high season; with hotels and many hostels this represents half the cost of a double room, whereas with the more basic hostels it represents the cost of a single dormitory bed. The prices signified by our grades are as follows:

| ① Up to £6 | ③ £10–14 | ⑤ £20–26 | ⑦ £36–45 |
| ② £6–10 | ④ £14–20 | ⑥ £26–36 | ⑧ Over £45 |

starchily neat planters' villages that grew up with the linen industry. Perhaps the nearest the county's settlements get to being picturesque are the villages to the northwest of Omagh: Castlederg, Newtownstewart, Sion Mills and the tiny hamlets of the Sperrins.

The mountain range also offers the major scenic attractions; it's rich in **wildlife** and is an excellent target for determined, lonesome **walking**. For this, **Gortin**, a village on the **Ulster Way** footpath, is the place to head for – and the only easily accessible overnight stop in the area. Tyrone also has no shortage of archeological remains, the most remarkable being the **Beaghmore Stone Circles**, in the southeast of the Sperrins. There's little to detain the visitor in the way of sights around the county beyond the **heritage centres** that celebrate the historic connections between Ulster and the US. Of these, the **Ulster American Folk Park** near Omagh is by far the best.

The only **local transport** in the region is *Ulsterbus*, which is reliable along main routes and not as infrequent as you might expect in such a rural area; nonetheless, if this is your only way of getting around, it makes sense to pick up a timetable in a major bus station before you head off into the country. However, so scattered are the attractions of this largely empty county that you're likely to see little of the most interesting parts without a car or a bike. The one exception, of course, is in the Sperrins, where **hiking** is the best way to get around.

Some history

County Tyrone was the land of the **O'Neills**, Chiefs of Ulster, who claimed descent back to pre-history and the sons of "Niall of the Nine Hostages" and ruled from Omagh, Dungannon and Cookstown. In the sixteenth and early seventeenth centuries, cut off geographically by bog, lake and mountain, Ulster was a key centre for Gaelic resistance to English rule. When Conn O'Neill received the English title Earl of Tyrone in the mid-sixteenth century, he held to the Gaelic Brehon Laws of inheritance and chose his youngest son, Shane the Proud, as successor. The English favoured Matthew, his eldest son, but, after years of feuding, Matthew died in battle in 1558, and his son Hugh was taken to England to be educated. Meanwhile, Shane, elected The O'Neill and determined to extend his kingdom, attacked his neighbours and was promptly called to London to face Elizabeth I. The two cultures met in mutual incomprehension: the Queen sat surrounded by perfumed courtiers in silks and velvets, while O'Neill stood flanked by his wolfhounds and followers, with saffron tunic and Irish mantle. He refused "to writhe his mouth in clattering English" or attend Protestant services. After six months he returned home and continued to pursue his aims; finally he was murdered by the MacDonnells and his head sent to Dublin as a mark of their loyalty to the Crown.

But it was his nephew, **Hugh O'Neill**, who witnessed the final demise of Gaelic power in Ulster. In 1585, suitably anglicized, Hugh returned from England to Dungannon as the second Earl of Tyrone. But soon he began to "go native". English spies carried tales to London and he was proclaimed a traitor. For five years he fought off English armies, but in 1601 Gaelic forces were defeated by Lord Mountjoy at the crucial battle of Kinsale. O'Neill signed the Treaty of Mellifont (1603), which bade him adopt English laws, language and dress and give up his clan title and his land. Ulster was divided into six counties and English rule was enforced. In 1607, he led the **Flight of the Earls** out of Ireland with a retinue of Gaelic chiefs and their followers. It was the end of the old Gaelic chiefdoms and customs. Most of the *file* (bards) – respected members of every noble family and clan historians – left with their patrons. The flight ended at the Church of St Pietro in Rome. Hugh O'Neill stayed on in Rome, where romantic legend has it that he died of sadness. He is buried in St Pietro before the high altar.

With the leaders of resistance gone, the subsequent plantation of Ulster under James I (1603–25) established the hegemony of the Crown, giving control of Tyrone to the Protestant immigrants from England and Scotland. But this was certainly not the end of Gaelic insurrection, and it was again from this part of Ulster that the next serious threat to English control came. The **Great Rebellion of 1641** began in Tyrone with Phelim O'Neill's capture of Dungannon and Charlemont. The rising spread throughout the country as Catholics all over Ireland joined together to claim their religious and civic rights. The rebellion was inevitably accompanied by considerable brutality, but horror stories grew to such an extent that settlers came to believe there was a concerted plan to butcher the entire Protestant population, and the alleged scale of the violence gave Cromwell his justification for the massacre at Drogheda ten years later. Ulster remained in the hands of the planters, and it was they who introduced linen manufacture in the eighteenth century – the county's only experience of industry.

The first significant emigration from Ireland to America was that of Ulster men and women in the early eighteenth century, many of whom were of Scottish Protestant origin. Of all the immigrant communities, it was the Irish who most quickly – and profoundly – made their mark: the three first-generation American presidents were all of Ulster stock, and a further nine presidents could trace their roots here. Sit in any bar in Tyrone long enough and someone will tell you with pride that these men and women emigrated because they had ambition and vision, and that they were not, unlike later emigrants, forced out by famine and eviction.

Omagh and around

Tyrone's county town, and the most likeable place of any size, is **OMAGH** (*Ómaigh*, "seat of the chiefs" or "the virgin plain"). The golden days are gone now, though, and there's no trace of the fortress overlooking the river from which the O'Neill clan once ruled Ulster. Instead, Omagh's main street leads up to a fine Classical courthouse and the irregular twin spires of the Sacred Heart Catholic Church. It's pleasant enough, but the only reason you'll spend time here is for a breather if you're on your way to or from the west coast, or heading north into the Sperrins.

Tourism in the region is generally geared to those with cars out for scenery, and the **tourist office** on Market Street (April–Sept Mon–Sat 9am–1pm & 2–5pm; Oct–March Mon–Fri 9am–1pm & 2–5pm; ☎01662/247831) promotes a very large area. The *Silver Birches Hotel* on Gortin Road (☎01662/242520; ⑤) offers relatively luxurious **accommodation**, plus regular entertainment. But smack in the centre you'll find the *Royal Arms Hotel* on High Street (☎01662/243262; ⑥), which you'll probably return to for its good food (see below). Alternatively, several **B&Bs** are registered with the tourist office. *Mrs McCann's*, 12 Tamlaght Road (☎01662/243381; ③), is the nearest to the town centre: from the tourist office walk up the main street, take the left fork in front of the Sacred Heart up to James Street, and Tamlaght Road is the second on your right. Also near the centre is *Mrs B. Cuddihy*, 1 Georgian Villas, Hospital Road (☎01662/245354; ④); walk down the main street away from the courthouse, cross the river, and Hospital Road is to your right. For Sperrin views try *Rylands*, a comfortable farmhouse B&B, on Loughmuck Road (☎01662/242557; ③). Tyrone's only – and very new – *YHANI* **hostel**, *Glenhordial* (open all year, but book ahead for Jan & Feb; ☎01662/241973; ②), is two and a half miles north off the B48 (the hostel managers will pick you up from Omagh bus station); otherwise take the right turn at Killybrack Road, go straight through both crossroads, then right at the third tarred road. For **camping** head for the *Gortin Forest Park*, which is as pretty as is claimed but lies six miles north of Omagh up the Gortin Road (6 buses daily); better to ask a farmer if you can use a field.

The town is a good place to stop for **food**, particularly during the daytime. The *Pink Elephant* in the High Street is a local favourite, serving traditional daytime dinners in huge helpings; almost as popular is the *Libbi Eating House*. The *Royal Arms Hotel* serves excellent pub grub at midday and evening meals of a similarly high standard in its restaurant. *Woodlanders*, on Gortin Road, is a fine new restaurant and bar, with entertainment most nights. For Chinese, try *Omanni* (☎01662/247500) on Derry Road, or the *Dragon Castle* (☎01662/245208) on High Street; and for Indian, head for Campsie Road's *Taste of India* (☎01662/248342). There's no shortage of cafés and fast food either; a particularly good café is *Nichols and Shiels* in Market Street.

This is showband country and most of the **pubs and hotels** have live music at weekends. Best bet is to check the nightlife pages of the *Ulster Herald*. If you are here for an evening, *Bogan's*, in Mountjoy Road, churns out traditional Irish **music** on Fridays. The *Times* nightclub, off Main Street, draws a young crowd, and *Sally O'Brien's* on John Street has traditional, folk and country and western evenings. Occasional jazz sessions are to be found at *McElroy's* in Castle Street, though at weekends the place is generally given over to discos. *Tippler's* and *Top of the Town*, also on John Street, and the *Cellar Bar* on Bridge Street are all good music venues. The *Royal Arms Hotel* has jazz and blues sessions on a Thursday, and discos at weekends. Despite this apparently promising list of options, there is no tangible "scene" here, and what you get is very much the luck of the draw.

Omagh's *Ulsterbus* **bus depot** (☎01662/242711), for all country-wide and local connections, is just across the river in Mountjoy Road (north off the High Street). And you can **rent bikes** from *Conway Cycles* (☎01662/246195) on Old Market Place.

The Ulster American Folk Park

About five miles north of Omagh, and a short ride on the Omagh–Newtownstewart bus, is the **Ulster American Folk Park** in Camphill, the most successful of the American heritage projects dotted around the country (April–Sept Mon–Sat 11am–6.30pm, Sun 11.30am–7pm; Oct–March Mon–Fri 10.30am–5pm; public holidays 11am–7pm; £3.50). The folk park tells the story of early emigrants: the first part is a typical eighteenth-century **Ulster village**; the second shows the communities they went on to build in America. The Ulster village is reconstructed around original buildings that include cottages, a school, an austere Presbyterian meeting house and a Catholic chapel. A full-size ship depicts the gruelling voyage, forming a link with the **American settlement**. The buildings of the Irish village are modest, but the multipurpose log barns of the Pennsylvanian settlers are massive. Again the attention to authenticity is excellent and captures a sense of the ambition and hope these emigrants must have felt on their arrival in the New World. Whatever your feelings on the Ulster Presbyterian work ethic, this propagandist folk park does powerfully re-create something of the emigrants' experience. In the accompanying **museum**, which focuses on the factors leading to emigration, there's also an exhibition on the American War of Independence, the making of the Constitution, and more on the lives of the early pioneers.

The folk park makes a good afternoon out from Omagh and a good day-trip if combined with the Ulster History Park (see p.551). Bring your own picnic though, as the restaurant is surprisingly basic, or go across the road to the *Mellon Country Inn*. Here they can also provide you with walking routes and maps to take you into the **Ulster Way**, which enters the scenic Gortin area at the start of the Sperrins to the northeast.

Northwest Tyrone

Northwest Tyrone has some of the county's most attractive towns and countryside. The fastest route west – and the only feasible one if you're hitching – is the A5 through Newtownstewart, Sion Mills and Strabane. Far quieter is the route via Castlederg along minor country roads west to Castlefinn, County Donegal, which takes you through a much more remote and isolated border-crossing point; it's only really possible by car or bike.

Castlederg

The friendly village of **CASTLEDERG** sits around a spruced-up square beside the River Derg, apparently trying to ignore its police barracks bristling with barbed wire. Across the river are the ruins of a plantation castle, built in 1609 and not long after destroyed by Sir Phelim O'Neill: today it sits in picturesque innocence, as though it had nothing to do with the current state of affairs. Castlederg retains something of its traditional flavour as a staging post for travellers and watering hole for pilgrims on their way to St Patrick's Purgatory, a stony island on Lough Derg where barefoot week-end vigils, sustained on an excruciating diet of black tea, are still held. The town's bars and cafés make this a good place to stop for refuelling; and the **Castlederg Visitor Centre** on the Lower Strabane Road (☎016626/70794) will give you lots of information on local sites. One mile north of the village – off the Lurganboy Road and close to each other – two large megalithic tombs stand as memorials to the area's pre-Christian past.

Todd's Den is a cairn with a portal stone, but more impressive is the Druid's Altar – a chambered grave with two portal stones and capstones, one inscribed with *ogham* runes.

Newtownstewart

If you're taking the fastest route west from Omagh you will pass through **NEWTOWNSTEWART**, settled in rich farmland, with its **castle** – another fourteenth-century O'Neill stronghold – looking clean and lonely on a hill to the south. There is a **tourist office** just outside the village on the Omagh Road (summer Tues–Fri 11am–4pm, Sat 11am–5pm, Sun 1.30–5pm; ☎016626/62414). Newtownstewart's real draw – and its latest addition – is the gem of a **museum** that's housed in the tiny jam-packed tourist office (same hours; 90p). Local historian Billy Dunbar, himself a walking encyclopedia, donated his collection of vintage packaging, man traps, stereoscopes and war memorabilia to the museum when he could no longer navigate from one end of his house to the other. Highlights include: a *Bordalous*, or mini-chamber pot shaped like a gravy boat and used by genteel ladies, which was named after a French priest renowned for his over-long sermons; and a thrupenny bit, engraved with the *Lord's Prayer*. Behind the museum are self-catering **apartments** (☎016626/61877), should you need more time to browse, or there's a municipal **caravan** site, *Harrigan's* (☎016626/61560), just over the Strule river on the north side of Newtownstewart, but you need to arrive before 5pm.

Sion Mills

The linen industry of the eighteenth century made a big impact in Tyrone, as it did all over Ulster, but its traces are mostly faint ones – such as the disused mills along the Ballinderry River near Cookstown. **SION MILLS**, a planned linen village just two miles south of Strabane, is the glaring exception. Here simple millworkers' cottages are neatly laid out around the mill, the quaintness of the village today belying the gruesome conditions of nineteenth-century factory work. The village is now designated a conservation area, though the *Herdman's* linenworks still runs, amidst security fences and cameras. You can skirt around it on foot and down to the Mourne river, where there's good fishing. The **tourist office** at Sion Mills (summer Mon–Thurs 9am–5pm; ☎016626/58027) is geared towards the motoring traveller but can direct you to a **B&B** – otherwise *Bide-a-wee* (☎016626/59571; ④) on the main Omagh–Strabane Road (A5) is friendly and has a swimming pool.

Strabane

Grim and congested, **Strabane** seems to glower over the River Foyle. Its recent history has been troubled, which is hardly surprising: not only does the town sit right on the border, but it's a small Catholic enclave uncomfortably surrounded by largely Protestant-owned farmland.

In the eighteenth century, Strabane was an important printing and publishing centre. John Dunlap emigrated from here and went on to print the broadsheets of the American Declaration of Independence in 1776, as well as the *Pennsylvanian Packet*, America's first daily paper. All that is left in Strabane of these times is the cute, Georgian bow-windowed shopfront of *Gray's* printing shop, which is now owned by the National Trust; there's a small printing **museum** upstairs (Mon–Wed, Fri & Sat 2–5.30pm; £1.40). Sadly the shop's interior has been ripped out to provide maximum space for cards, completely destroying the scale and atmosphere the place must have once had.

One of Strabane's most famous sons is the satirical novelist Brian O'Nolan – better known as **Flann O'Brien**. Born in 1911 into an Irish-speaking household at 15 Bowling Green, he had a glittering academic career at University College Dublin. Staying in the capital, he became a civil servant. An irascible character, he was unfortunate enough to produce his best work around the time of the Second World War, when it disappeared without trace. But since his death in 1966 his absurdist novels have been republished and – much to his annoyance, no doubt – Flann O'Brien has become a cult figure (for more on his work see p.613). Another, less entertaining individual to have his roots in the area is the American president Woodrow Wilson. Head east of Strabane two miles down the Plumbridge Road and you'll find the **President Woodrow Wilson ancestral home** at the grim Republican village of **DERGALT** (open any reasonable hour – ask at the adjacent farm). The president's father, who was a printer in Strabane, lived in this small, traditional farmer's cottage. Stuffed with furniture and effects belonging to the family, it's now a target for American tourists, who dutifully meander through the hallowed rooms.

If you really can't avoid an overnight stay in Strabane, the **tourist information office** in Abercorn Square (April–Oct Mon–Fri 9am–5pm; July also Sun 2–6pm; ☎01504/883735) will help with finding accommodation; or try the central **B&B** *Thomas Casey's*, 6 Bowling Green (☎01504/884787; ③). There's a good atmospheric **pub** called *Felix's* that's alleged to have the best pint for miles, while the *Fir Trees Lodge* on Melmont Road does decent meals. The *Bonne Tasse* near the tourist office on Abercorn Square serves hearty sandwiches and snacks.

The Sperrins

The huge, undulating **Sperrin Mountains** form the northeastern limits of County Tyrone. Wild, empty and beautiful, they reach 2240ft at their highest, yet the smooth and gradually curving slopes give them a deceptively low appearance. The covering of bog and heather adds to this effect, suggesting nothing more than high, open moorland. For all this, views from the summits are panoramic, and the evenness of texture can make these mountains sumptuous when bathed in evening light. Once in the mountains, it's impossible not to catch sight of the **wildlife**. Sparrow hawks and kestrels hover above, and you might see buzzards or the far rarer hen harrier. They're attracted by rich prey in a landscape undisturbed by development – the mountains teem with assorted rodents, rabbits, stoats and badgers, even the Irish hare. One threat to this delicately balanced ecosystem has been the recent rediscovery of gold in the mountains. Their future is in the balance, but for the moment at least, the Sperrins offer a wilderness to be enjoyed.

For local sheep-farming communities, however, the underpopulation of the Sperrins is a real problem, and their traditional way of life is now slowly dying. The sparseness of the population and the lack of focal centres make it difficult for an outsider to key into this culture. For the same reason, hitching isn't easy, and walkers should bear in mind that there's a shortage of places to buy food, so thinking ahead is essential. Rely only on large villages for provisions of any sort; hamlets often have nothing.

The **Sperrin Centre** (June–Sept Mon–Fri 11am–6pm, Sat 11.30am–6pm, Sun 2–7pm; Oct–May Mon–Sat 11am–5pm, Sun 1–6pm; £1.80) lies between Cranagh and Sperrin, nine miles east of Plumbridge (see opposite), and enables you to explore the area's environmental and cultural issues without getting your feet wet. The video games and audiovisuals of this welcoming interpretative centre are quite a surprise – particularly the holographic storyteller and the quaint 3-D slideshows – and they also organize gold-panning expeditions. It's also one of the few places outside Belfast and Derry where you'll get a real cup of coffee, or even an espresso – tea is the Northern brew. The centre is tricky to get to without transport – though buses do run here from Plumbridge, and the *Sperrin Sprinter* (Tues–Thurs) also passes nearby – but worth bearing in mind for its very pleasant tearoom if you are walking in the area.

WALKING IN THE SPERRINS

The Sperrins offer good long-distance walking, without necessarily involving steep inclines. You can ramble wherever you like, but remember that – despite appearance – these are high mountains, and changeable weather makes them potentially dangerous. A map and compass are essential for serious walking. For those not equipped for the high ground, the **Glenelly** and **Owenkillen** river valleys run through the heart of this stunning countryside from Plumbridge and Gortin respectively (see below) and are particularly enjoyable for cyclists.

The official **Ulster Way** does an arduous 34-mile route – the steepish Glenelly Trail – from Dungiven up over Glenshane Mountain to Goles Forest. From Gortin a second stage of the Way takes you to the Ulster American Folk Park, a ten-mile trek. Parts of both sections of the Way are on road, however, and along some stretches signposts have disappeared or, worse, point in the wrong direction. You can pick up a guide to the Ulster Way in tourist offices (see *Basics*, p.20) or from the Sports Council of Northern Ireland (☎01232/381222), but your best bet is to ask locals about the state of the Way. For less strenuous walks the Northern Ireland Tourist Board has produced routes for fourteen mini-Ways – the longest of which is thirteen miles.

Plumbridge and Gortin

Once in the mountains, settlements are mere specks of houses, and if you're tackling the Sperrins from Tyrone, there are really only two places that'll offer you any amenities at all. And even these are comatose for much of the year.

The first, **PLUMBRIDGE**, doesn't look like it's changed much over the years, beyond encouraging the fishing fraternity to down rods and drink in its bars. Apocryphally, it gets its name from the building of the village bridge. The engineer in charge didn't have a plumb line and so, from his scaffolding, spat in the water, using his phlegm to take the perpendicular.

Nearby **GORTIN**, three and a half miles south, though greatly promoted as a tourist centre, is a one-horse town with a café and a pub. *Lenamore Lodge* on Crockanboy Road (☎016626/48426; ③) does **B&B**, and you'll find a **campsite** at *Gortin Glen Caravan Park* (☎016626/48108). The site also includes *Lislap* self-catering cottages (£270 for a 3-bed apartment per week in high season). Smaller, but far prettier, is the *Gortin Glen Forest Park* camping site opposite (☎016626/48217), a good place to stay if you're contemplating some hill-walking. A few miles south of Gortin is the **Ulster History Park** (April–Sept Mon–Sat 10.30am–6.30pm; Oct–March Mon–Fri 10.30am–5pm; last admission 1hr 30min before closing; £3), with full-scale reconstructions of buildings in Ireland from 7000 BC up to the seventeenth century. Inside there are videos and displays that serve to distract in bad weather, but far more rewarding is the interactive tour on which a guide talks you round such authentic traditional dwellings as a stinking deer-skin-covered teepee, shows you how to chip flint, explains ancient symbols and answers questions expertly, no matter how daft. Unfortunately, a recent fire destroyed the rath, but the *crannóg* and the medieval castle are particularly interesting, and a seventeenth-century settlement is soon to be completed. The **Ulster Way** passes through the village, though for now the signposting which should connect it with Goles Forest is incomplete and stops at Craignaddy (984ft), two and a half miles north. However, the signposted Way does continue to the south of Gortin through the pretty forest park, with its little loughs and wild deer, before swinging west to low farmland and the Ulster American Folk Park (see p.548).

Three and a half miles east of Gortin (on the B46 Creggan Road) is the tiny village of **Rouskey**, with the ruins of a "sweat lodge" – a sort of early sauna. After the steam treatment, the luckless invalid was plunged into the icy stream nearby. Widespread use of sweat lodges died out after the Famine years, possibly because the experience of typhoid that accompanied the Famine dealt a severe blow to people's confidence in traditional medicinal treatments, but some were still functioning up to the 1920s.

Prehistoric remains and the Beaghmore Stone Circles

County Tyrone is peppered with archeological remains, the Sperrins themselves having their fair share – including over a thousand standing stones – and the county as a whole having numerous chambered graves. The **Lough Macrory** area, just east of Mountfield on the A505 (Omagh–Cookstown Road), is particularly rich in dolmens and megaliths, though many of these are hard to find and of specialist interest only.

The uninitiated will get most out of the Bronze Age **Beaghmore Stone Circles**, in the southeast of the Sperrins; from Gortin take the B46 east onto the A505, and from here they are well signposted, just three and a half miles north off the main road. If you are coming from the opposite direction, they are also signposted all the way from Cookstown. Although most of the stones on this lonely site are no more than three feet high, the complexity of the ritual they suggest is impressive: there are seven stone circles, ten stone rows and a dozen round cairns (burial mounds, some containing cremated human remains). All of the circles stand in pairs, except for one, which is filled with over 800 upright stones, known as Dragon's Teeth. The alignments correlate to movements of sun, moon and stars. Two of the rows point to sunrise at the summer solstice; another may point to moonrise at the same period.

Back on the A505, roughly halfway between Omagh and Cookstown, **An Creagán Visitor Centre** (April–Sept daily 11am–6.30pm; Oct–March Mon–Fri 11am–4.30pm) consciously models itself on the many cairns that surround it – 44 in a five-mile radius. Circular and built from local stone, the centre stands on the land of one of the last native speakers in the district, Peadar Joe Haughey, who died in the 1950s. Staff in the centre speak Irish, and the place is actually more a cultural centre than a museum, with locals coming along to the traditional music sessions, dancing, storytelling and singing events. But An Creagán also explores the rare raised bog terrain around, with interpretative displays and signposted routes over the countryside. The farmers driven to these bogs in the eighteenth century made huge efforts to reclaim the soil; there are lime-kilns from which they treated the reclaimed land, and you can still see the potato ridges. These grassed-over Copney spade ridges – a form of cultivation that maximized production – point back to the devastating Famine of 1845–49 and the farmers' desperate attempts to survive. You can organize self-catering **accommodation** here (☎016627/61112) in the traditional *clochán* settlement – take that to mean open turf fires (supplemented, fortunately, by central heating).

Cookstown, Dungannon and around

The only places in the **east of the county** that could be described as anything more than villages are Cookstown and Dungannon. A planned planters' town, **COOKSTOWN** boasts the longest main street in Ireland, which in effect means the community now clings for dear life to the sides of a dual carriageway. There are a couple of places to eat: *The Royal Hotel*, Coagh Street, and *The Central Inn* in William Street. But the main attraction for the visitor is the *Edergole Riding School*, 70 Moneymore Road (☎016487/62924), whose one-hour to three-day treks on foot or mountain bike wind up on the slopes of Slieve Gallion to the north. The school is attached to a friendly **B&B** (④).

The **Wellbrook Beetling Mill**, three and a half miles west of Cookstown off the A505, is a National Trust-owned eighteenth-century water-powered linen mill (June–

Aug daily except Tues 2–6pm; April, May & Sept Sat, Sun & bank holidays 2–6pm; £1.40). "Beetling" is a process whereby linen is given a sheen and smoothness by hammering with wooden "beetles". The mill is very well preserved, and all the engines still work. For more ancient history, two miles south of Cookstown on the B520 is **Tullyhoge Fort**, the site of the inaugural ceremonies of the O'Neills. From the road it looks like nothing more than a copse of beech and scots pine on the top of a very gentle hill, but in fact these are very clear, comprehensible earthworks of the early Christian period – a circular outer bank with an inner oval enclosure. Ulster chiefs were crowned here from the twelfth to the seventeenth centuries, and it was in Tullyhoge forest that O'Neill tribesmen hid after the Flight of the Earls.

As you hurry through dreary **DUNGANNON**, about ten miles south of Cookstown, pause and briefly reflect on its illustrious history as the hilltop seat of the O'Neills, from which they ruled Ulster for over five centuries. Just outside the town is a **B&B** worth detouring for: *Grange Lodge* on Grange Road (☎01868/784212; ⑤) can organize riding, boating, fishing – and excellent meals (£18 extra for dinner) – in their gracious Georgian house. If you're going east to Coalisland, check out the town's new **Cornmill Heritage Centre** at Lineside (June–Sept Mon–Fri 10am–8pm, Sat 11am–6pm, Sun 2–6pm; Oct–May Mon–Fri 10am–6pm; £1.50), another monument to the Northern work ethic and the area's industrial past – especially coal. The mill itself ground to a halt in 1978 after providing employment for the town for over seventy years. Heading west by car, you might visit the **Simpson-Grant Farm**, three miles east of Ballygawley and signposted off the A4 road (April Mon–Fri 10.30am–4.30pm; May–Sept Mon–Sat 10.30am–6.30pm, Sun 12.30–7pm; 60p). Based around the nineteenth-century homestead of the maternal ancestors of President Ulysses S. Grant, it's of interest chiefly for the traditional livestock of the working farm.

Along Lough Neagh

It seems even the legendary Fionn Mac Cumhaill was unimpressed by east Tyrone's low-lying and uninspiring terrain. The tale goes that he took a massive lump of land from Ulster and hurled it across the Irish Sea. It landed and became the Isle of Man, and the hole it left behind became **Lough Neagh**. The lough's shores form the county's huge eastern boundary and provide excellent fishing and plenty of birdlife, but, beyond this, both land and lake are almost featureless. Small settlements house eel fishermen, whose catches go to the *Toome Eel Fishery* at Toomebridge (at the northern tip of the lake), the largest eel fishery in Europe.

Slight relief is to be found at **ARDBOE**, on the lough ten miles east of Cookstown, where there's a tenth-century **High Cross** heavily carved with biblical scenes. Its size is exceptional – 18ft high – and yet it lacks impact: so dull is this shore the cross stands devoid of spatial context.

Mountjoy Castle lurks behind a farm eight miles south of here on the road towards Dungannon. Built in 1602 as part of the English campaign against Hugh O'Neill, it was strategically important, but again the setting is disappointing.

COUNTY FERMANAGH

It is for the intense beauty of its lakes that Fermanagh is famous. A third of the county is water, the great **Lough Erne** complex swinging right across the region from Lower Lough Erne in the northwest to Upper Lough Erne in the southeast. Surrounding hills are wooded with oak, ash and beech, producing a scene of fresh, verdant greens in spring and rich and rusty colours in autumn. The water's rippling surface reflects whatever light there is, mirroring the palest of skies through to the ruddiest of magenta sunsets. It's a breathtaking landscape, where land and water complement one another in a fine, stately harmony.

The **Lower Lough** in winter has the character of an inland sea, dangerous waves making even the locals wary of sailing. Fabulous vistas reach across to the mostly uninhabited shores of richly wooded islands, on which are scattered early Christian ruins and evidence of earlier pagan cultures. The **Upper Lough** is quieter and less spectacular. The waterway here is a delightful muddle of little inlets and islands, where waters are shallower and shorelines reedy. Fields have shocks of bristly marsh-grasses; definitions between land and water are blurred.

The county town of **Enniskillen** sits at the point where the Upper and Lower loughs meet, long an important bridging point; it's still the only real town in Fermanagh and is a good base for exploring the region. If you've transport, there are historical tracks to cover touring Fermanagh's impressive series of **planters' castles**, while the county's two stately houses, **Florence Court** and **Castle Coole**, are both open to the public.

There are plenty of opportunities for **watersports**, and the less energetic can get out onto the lakes by renting a **boat** or taking one of the lough cruises. **Walkers** will find the countryside to be mostly gentle hills and woods, which rise to small mountains in the south and west of the county, made accessible by the **Ulster Way**. For **cyclists**, there are well-surfaced, empty roads (though routes around the Upper Lough are harder to negotiate, with little lanes often leading to nowhere but some empty reed-infested shore). Public **transport** is limited to *Ulsterbus*; although reliable enough, only the main routes from Enniskillen are served with any frequency. If you look like a foreign tourist, then **hitching** along main roads is possible during the summer months, though never easy: County Fermanagh is as friendly as anywhere in the North, but people tend to be cautious because of the border.

Some history

The region's early history was dictated by the difficulties of the Lough Erne waterways, in earlier times even more confused and forested than today. Recorded history begins with the early Christians, who slowly permeated the culture and established religious foundations. They appreciated the seclusion of the lakes, and ruins of **medieval monasteries** remain. Centres of ecclesiastical power and learning were dotted on islands in the lough, and it is likely they were visited by pilgrims on their way to St Patrick's Purgatory, the shrine on Lough Derg. More brutal invaders found the lough complex difficult to infiltrate. Neither Vikings nor **Normans** ever managed to control the region, and throughout the medieval and Tudor periods, the English similarly failed to subdue it. The surrounding land was unruly and hard to govern even for the Irish. The Maguires, who ruled the west of the kingdom of Oriel (Fermanagh, Monaghan, South Tyrone and Louth) from 1250 until 1600, were originally based at Lisnaskea, but the cattle raids of neighbouring chiefs forced them to move to Enniskillen in the early fifteenth century. The town was to become strategically crucial as the determination of the English to dominate Ireland increased during the sixteenth century. As the crossing point through the waterways it was one of only three land routes into Ulster available to the invaders, the others being over the river near Ballyshannon and the Moyry Pass between Dundalk and Newry. So Enniskillen and the Maguire castle became the main focal point of Irish resistance to the Tudors. It was taken in 1600, and in 1607, after the Flight of the Earls, the **planters** arrived.

The usurpers were obliged to build a ring of **castles** around the lough in order to maintain control: Crom, Portora, Tully, Castle Archdale, Crevenish, Caldwell and, most important of all, the old Maguire castle at Enniskillen. Given sizeable grants from the English Crown, the planters of Enniskillen built an Established church, a fort and a royal school, turning the place into a British colonial town. It became a Loyalist stronghold, which successfully defended itself against the Irish during the Great Rebellion of 1641 and against an attack by James's troops in 1689. The Loyalists of Enniskillen formed a regiment that William of Orange chose as his personal guard at the Boyne. In the late eighteenth century, Enniskillen proved to be of key military importance, with the threat of a French invasion through the northwest of Ireland. By now the town had two royal regiments – a unique phenomenon.

At **Partition**, Fermanagh became a part of the state of Northern Ireland, despite its predominantly Catholic population and despite this majority's cultural affinities with Cavan in the Republic, with whom it shares the tail end of the Lough Erne complex. In 1921, the county returned a Nationalist majority in local government elections, an undesirable state of affairs for the British. The abolition of proportional representation in 1922, and the gerrymandering which followed, ensured the subsequent Loyalist majority. With a history of such blatant injustices, a large Catholic population and a lengthy border with the Republic, Fermanagh is a nucleus of Nationalist activity and today has strong Sinn Féin sympathies. It was Fermanagh and South Tyrone that in April 1981 returned **Bobby Sands** as MP to Westminster. At the time of the election Sands was serving a fourteen-year prison sentence for possession of weapons and was leading a hunger strike for political status for IRA prisoners. His death from starvation after 66 days made him one of the most famous IRA heroes.

Enniskillen

Amid the innumerable atrocities that have scarred Northern Ireland in recent years, the name **ENNISKILLEN** has a special capacity to shock, after the IRA bomb attack on Remembrance Day 1987, which killed 11 and injured 61 people as they gathered to commemorate the dead of the two world wars. In a town of only 10,500, the bombing profoundly affected the lives of every citizen and mobilized public opinion – even among Nationalists – more strongly against the IRA; the Sinn Féin leader, Gerry Adams, admitted the Republican movement could not withstand another Enniskillen. Despite the reputation for sectarian violence earned by the bombing, Enniskillen is in reality a pleasant, conservative little town, rather relaxed and very friendly. Central to both Fermanagh and the lakes, Enniskillen is a focus for visitors and locals alike. It's the only place of any size in the county, and although you can see all that it has to offer in a day, if you're using B&Bs it makes a good base from which to explore the lakes.

The telephone code for Enniskillen is ☎01365.

Arrival, information and accommodation

The **tourist office** is housed in the Fermanagh Tourist Information Centre on Wellington Road just off Main Street (May–June Mon–Fri 9am–6pm, Sat 10am–6pm, Sun 11am–5pm; July–Aug Mon–Fri till 7pm, Sat & Sun same hrs; March, Sept & Oct Mon–Fri 9am–5pm, Sat 10am–6pm, Sun 11am–5pm; Nov–Feb Mon–Fri 9am–5pm; ☎323110). You can get fishing licences and permits here. The "Round O" jetty (☎322711 ext 230) for lough cruises is signposted off the Derrygonnelly Road to the northwest of town – see "Lough Erne" on p.558 for more boat rental details. For **bike rental**, try the *Castle Island Adventure Centre*, on Castle Island (☎324250; £9 per day) – free ferries leave (8am–midnight) from the Lakeland Forum just behind the tourist information centre. *Lochside Garages*, Tempo Road (☎324366), and *County Car*, 4 Irvinestown Road (☎322727), are two **car rental** outlets. The post office on Main Street will change money. From Enniskillen's **bus station**, next to the tourist office, you can get buses to Belfast, Dublin, Dungannon, Sligo, Derry, Omagh, and local services.

Accommodation

The tourist office has comprehensive **accommodation** lists and will book for you (£1 charge, £2 if outside Fermanagh). You could try the conveniently central, family-run *Railway Hotel*, 34 Forthill Street (☎322408; ⑥), or the *Killyhevlin Hotel* (☎323481; ⑥) on the Dublin Road (this becomes the N3 once over the border). Alternatively, **B&B** is easily found across the town's western bridges, along the A46 Derrygonnelly Road and along the A4 Sligo Road. Pick of the bunch is *Mountview*, Irvinestown Road (☎323147; ④), with TVs in all the rooms and a snooker room; or try *Lackaboy Farmhouse*, Tempo Road (☎322488; ④), or *Rossole House*, 85 Sligo Road (☎323462; ③). If you're driving, there are two country houses to sample: *Killyreagh* (☎387221; ⑥), a couple of miles south of town on the A4 in Tamlaght, and a Gothic fantasy, *Tempo Manor* (☎541450; ⑧) in Tempo, about six miles northeast on the B80. The nearest **hostel** is run by *YHANI* at *Castle Archdale* ten miles north on the B82 (it also has a campsite, see p.560). There's a handy **campsite** at the *Lakeland Canoe Centre* (☎324250) on Castle Island just offshore of Enniskillen. All the others are well out of town: *Florence Court Park* (☎348497) is off the A32, six miles south; *Blaney Caravan Park* (☎41634), eight miles to the north, off the A46, directly behind the Blaney service station, is a beautifully situated and well-equipped site.

The town

The town sits on an island like an ornamental buckle, two narrow ribbons of water passing each side, connecting the Lower and Upper lough complexes. The water loops its way around the core of the town, its glassy surface imbuing Enniskillen with a pervasive sense of calm and reflecting the mini-turrets of **Enniskillen Castle**, so making a toy image of the military presence. Rebuilt by William Cole, the man to whom the British gave Enniskillen in 1609, the castle stands on the site of the old Maguire castle, next to the island's westerly bridges. Cole's additions show obvious Scottish characteristics in the turrets corbelled out from the angles of the main wall. It houses the **Enniskillen Heritage Centre** (Mon–Fri 10am–5pm, except Mon 2–5pm; May–Sept also Sat 2–5pm & July–Aug also Sun 2–5pm; £1.50, includes museum below) and, in the keep, **The Regimental Museum of the Royal Enniskillen Fusiliers** (same times), a proud and polished display of the uniforms, flags and paraphernalia of the town's two historic regiments.

Much of Enniskillen's character comes from a wealth based on the care of a colonial presence. Evidence of British influence is widespread: on a hill to the west the stately **Portora Royal School** overlooks the town, discreetly reminding one of the continued elitism in the social order. It was founded by Charles I in 1626, though the present building dates from 1777; old boys include Oscar Wilde – the pride of the school, until his trial for homosexuality – and Samuel Beckett. Over on a hill to the east a Wellingtonian statue – **Cole's Monument** – keeps an eye on the town from a very British-style park; catch the park keeper and pay 50p to ascend to the viewing gallery for a bird's-eye view of town. Immediately below is the war memorial, scene of the bombing. The centre invites strolling: the main street undulates gently, lined with confident Victorian and Edwardian town houses, thriving shops and smart pub fronts. This street changes its name six times between the bridges at either end, running from Anne Street to East Bridge Street: lanes fall to either side down towards the water, and calmly sitting next to one another are three fine church buildings, Church of Ireland, Catholic and Methodist.

On Queen Elizabeth Road, just off the main street, the **Buttermarket** is a craft and design centre with the full range of artisans working on site. The original buildings date from 1835, and you'll find displays of art, music and drama, as well as craftwork and design. You can buy direct from the craftsworkers or from the shop attached to *Rebecca's* excellent coffee shop.

Castle Coole

Evidence of how the richest of the colonists lived is found on the outskirts of town at **Castle Coole**, the eighteenth-century home of the Earls of Belmore (June–Aug daily except Thurs 1–6pm, last tour starts at 5.15pm; April, May & Sept Sat & Sun 1–6pm; £2.50; grounds open all year, £1.50 per car). A perfect Palladian building of Portland stone, with elegant furnishings and recently restored interior of exquisite plasterwork, the castle has only been painted three times in the last 200 years. It sits in a beautiful landscaped garden, exemplifying cultivated naturalness. Castlecoole can be walked to either from the Dublin Road (signposted just opposite the *Ardhowen Theatre*) or across the golf course from the Castlecoole Road.

Eating, drinking and entertainment

Enniskillen has a handful of good cheap places to **eat**. Currently everybody's favourite is *Franco's* (daily from noon till late; ☎324424) in Queen Elizabeth Road; it has delicious pizza, pasta, seafood and satay. Around the corner on Water Street, a new Indian restaurant, *Kamal Mahal* (☎32505), does great vegetarian dishes. *Peppercorn* (☎324834), on the main street by the post office, serves huge breakfasts (£3.50) and good coffee. A lot of the bars also along the main street do decent **pub food**, particularly *The Vintage* – grilled trout and almonds – or try *Pat's Bar* for stodgier meals. Upstairs from the latter is *Melvin's Restaurant*, which offers lunches, grills and dinners. The **restaurant** (open 11am–3pm) at *The Ardhowen Theatre*, a mile out of town on the Dublin Road (☎325440), is worth visiting for its waterside setting (you can also enjoy the view from an excellent bar), should you be hungry after a traipse around Castle Coole.

Enniskillen is also well served for **cafés**, many of which do excellent inexpensive meals. Most imaginative – felafels, houmous and salads feature on the menu – is the *Barbizon* on East Bridge Street (check out the bizarre Gaudiesque seating). *Leslie's*, also on the main street, offers good ice cream, and *Johnston's Coffee Lounge* on Townhall Street is worth a try, too, for its fresh-baked patries and breads. A more formal setting can be found at *The Concorde* (☎322955) on the Tempo Road – it's best to book, as it's popular with the locals.

There's no shortage of cheerful **pubs**, and bar extensions until 1am are commonplace in summer. **Country music** is big here, and bands play in the main street at *The Crowe's Nest* most nights, at *Pat's Bar* on Sunday nights and the *Bush Bar* on Fridays. For **traditional music** try the *Bush* (Mon) or the *White Star Bar* (Thurs–Sun). *The Vintage*, on the main street, is a trendy disco bar with video jukebox and live rock and pop music at weekends. Nearby, *Blakes of the Hollow* is a traditional Victorian bar with original fittings, good traditional music sessions, a fine pint and a chatty crowd. At the west end of town, the *Tippler's Brook* is the place for a quiet drink or to play cards with local farmers in town for the night. As ever, **discos** are in the hotels, in particular Forthill Street's *Fort Lodge Hotel*, which occasionally has local bands, and *Saddlers* in the main street – which also has ostrich steak on its menu. The *Mirage* has rave nights at the Castle Entertainment Centre on Factory Road.

The hub of Enniskillen's **arts scene** is *The Ardhowen Theatre* (see above for details), which has a year-round programme of top-quality drama, film and ballet, and hosts a great range of music events – traditional Irish, jazz, opera, country, classical – as well as productions by local community groups. Check with the tourist office for dates of the Fermanagh *feis* in April – lots of traditional music, dancing, drama and crafts – the *Fleadh* in June, and the Enniskillen Festival in August.

Lough Erne

Lough Erne has had a profound effect on the history of Fermanagh. The earliest people to settle in the region lived on and around the two lakes; many of the islands here are in fact *crannógs* – early Celtic artificial islands. Its myriad connecting waterways were impenetrable to outsiders, protecting the settlers from invaders and creating an enduring cultural isolation. Evidence from stone carving suggests that Christianity was accepted far more slowly here than elsewhere: several pagan idols have been found on Christian sites, and the early Christian remains to be found on the islands show the strong influence of pagan culture. Here Christian carving has something of the stark symmetry and vacancy of expression found in pagan statues. Particularly suggestive of earlier cults is the persistence of the human head motif in stone carving – in pagan times a symbol of divinity and the most important of religious symbols.

The most popular of the Erne's ancient sites – **White Island** and **Devenish Island** – are on the **Lower Lough**, as is **Boa Island** in the far north, which is linked to the mainland by a bridge at each end. The **Upper Lough** is less rewarding, but it, too, has spots of interest which repay a leisurely dawdle. Whichever you choose, the easiest way to reach them is on one of the **cruises** or **ferries** that operate from Enniskillen, the *Castle Archdale* hostel, Belleek and surrounding villages (see below). **Renting your own boat** – again from Enniskillen, Kesh or Belleek – will cost around £45 a day, including fuel, and you should let the owner know where you're going and ask to borrow navigation charts: this lough can be dangerous, and outside the summer months, not even the locals venture out. Larger **cruisers** are generally available for a minimum of a week, though you may be lucky and find someone prepared to offer a weekend deal.

Aside from cruising the waterways and visiting the islands, there are a number of minor attractions around the loughs that are worth dropping into during your stay. Perhaps the most impressive are the series of early seventeenth-century **planters' castles** that ring the loughs.

Devenish Island and Monea and Tully castles

The easiest place to visit from Enniskillen, certainly if you don't have transport of your own, is **Devenish Island**, in the south of the Lower Lough. A monastic settlement was

---

LOUGH ERNE FERRIES AND CRUISES

To Devenish Island *Devenish Island Ferry Service* (☎01365/322711 ext 230) operates a continual service to Devenish from Trory, four miles north of Enniskillen (April–Sept Tues–Sat 10am–7pm, Sun 2–7pm; £2, includes entrance fee to tower and museum).

To White Island A boat from *Castle Archdale* hostel jetty (☎01365/322711 ext 230) in Enniskillen runs to White Island (June–Sept Tues–Sat 10am–7pm, Sun 2–7pm, less frequently during Sept; £2.25).

A two-hour **cruise** of Lough Erne, stopping at Devenish for 30min, operates from the "Round O" pier, Enniskillen (see p.555). Also leaving from the pier is the *M.V.*

Kestrel operated by *Erne Tours* (☎01365/322882), which sails around the Lower Lough, and the Upper Lough in summer (May & June Sun 2.30pm; July & Aug Mon–Fri 10.30am, 2.15pm & 4.15pm, Sun 11am, 3pm & 7.15pm – plus Tues, Thurs & Sun 7.15pm to Upper Lough Erne; first two weeks Sept Tues, Sat & Sun 2.30pm; £3). The *Harp of Erne* (call for times on ☎01365/658027; £5) also runs cruises of the Lower Lough from Belleek. A "Viking longship" runs **cruises** of the Upper Lough daily in summer from the *Share Holiday Centre* at Smith's Strand, signposted off the Lisnaskea–Derrylin Road (April–Sept Sat & Sun 11am & 3pm; £4; ☎013657/22122).

founded here by Saint Molaise in the sixth century and became so important during the early Christian period that it had 1500 novices attached to it. The foundation was plundered by Vikings in the ninth century and again in the twelfth, but continued to be an important religious centre up until the plantations. It's a delightful setting, not far from the lough shore, and the ruins are considerable, spanning the entire medieval period. Most impressive are the sturdy oratory and perfect round tower, both from the twelfth century; Saint Molaise's church, a century older; and the ruined Augustinian priory, a fifteenth-century reconstruction of an earlier abbey. The priory has a fine Gothic sacristy door decorated with birds and vines; to the south is one of Ireland's finest high crosses, with highly complex, delicate carving. Other treasures found here – such as an early eleventh-century book shrine, the *Soiscel Molaise* – are now kept in the National Museum in Dublin.

Monea Castle (free access at all times), a few miles northwest of Devenish Island off the B81, is a particularly fine ruin of a planter's castle in a beautiful setting at the end of a beech-lined lane. Built around 1618, it bears the signs of Scottish influence in its design, with similar features to the reworked Maguire castle in Enniskillen. It was destroyed by fire in the Great Rebellion of 1641 and by Jacobite armies in 1689, and was eventually abandoned in 1750 after another fire. Five miles further north, beyond Derrygonnelly, the fortified house and *bawn* of **Tully Castle** (April–Sept Tues–Sat 10am–7pm, Sun 2–7pm; 75p) sits down by the lough shore.

Castle Caldwell forest and Belleek

The **forest of Castle Caldwell**, near the northwestern extremity of Lower Lough Erne, is the main breeding site in the British Isles for the common scoter (a species of duck) and a habitat of rarities such as the hen harrier, peregrine falcon and pine marten. A commercial, state-owned forest of spruce, pine and larch, it's protected as an area of wildlife conservation. At the entrance look out for the giant stone fiddle in front of the gate lodge, the sobering memorial to Denis McCabe, a local musician who in 1770 tumbled from the Caldwells' barge while drunk, and drowned.

A couple of miles from the western edge of the lough, **BELLEEK**'s main attraction is the *Belleek Pottery* (March–June & Sept Mon–Fri 9am–6pm, Sat 10am–6pm, Sun 2–6pm; July & Aug Mon–Fri 9am–8pm, Sat 10am–6pm, Sun 11am–8pm; Oct Mon–Fri 9am–5.30pm, Sat 10am–5.30pm, Sun 2–6pm; Nov–Feb closed weekends; tours are every 20min), which offers interesting tours of the famous **pottery** and a chance to buy the rather fussy products. There's a **fiddle festival** here in summer. You can go on a **cruise** round Lough Erne (see opposite); or try the new *ExplorErne Centre* (April–Sept Mon–Fri 9am–6pm, Sat 10am–6pm, Sun 11am–5pm; £1) in the Erne Gateway, an interpretative centre that offers what's basically a day out on Lough Erne for landlubbers. A giant video wall screens an investigation of how the lake was formed and how it formed the lives of lakeside dwellers over the centuries. Tourist information is also available in the Gateway Centre (☎01365/658866). If you want **to stay**, there's B&B accommodation at Mrs Brennan's *Erneville*, Garrison Road on the outskirts of town (☎01365/658025; ③), or Moohan's *Fiddlestone*, 15–17 Main Street (☎01365/658008; ④), which combines pub and B&B. There are several places you can **rent boats**; for rowing call *Carlton Cottages* (☎01365/658181; £22 per day). **Buses** #99 and #64 run from Enniskillen (daily except Sun).

Killadeas, Irvinestown and Castle Archdale

In **KILLADEAS** churchyard, seven miles north of Enniskillen on the eastern side of the lough (take the B82), stands the **Bishop's Stone**, carved some time between the ninth and eleventh centuries. It's one of the most striking examples of the appearance of pre-Christian images in early Christian culture, having a startled pagan-style face on one side and a bishop with bell and crozier on the other. There are other interesting carved stones in the graveyard, too, including two cross slabs and a rounded pillar, possibly a pagan phallic stone. If you want to get out onto the water, *Manor House Marine* (☎013656/28100) rents out **motor boats** from £45.

A few miles north and inland, in **IRVINESTOWN**, the only site of any interest is Dr Patrick Delany's church built in 1734 – the clock tower and pinnacled battlements are all that remain. Jonathan Swift played an unlikely cupid to the rector, introducing him to court favourite and London society hostess, Mary Granville. They married and Delany later became Dean of Down; while she left a revealing record of eighteenth-century Anglo-Irish society and gossip, gathered during their visits to the Big Houses. If you want to stay in Irvinestown, there are a couple of **B&Bs** in the village: Kinnear's *Lettermoney House* (☎013656/388347; ③), on the Enniskillen–Omagh Road (A32), or Mrs Allen's *Leraine*, Kesh Road (☎013656/21627; ③); there's also dormitory accommodation available at the *Willow Pattern Complex* on the Kesh Road (☎013656/31012; ①).

To thoroughly immerse yourself in the beauty of the lough scenery, however, you could hardly do better than stay in the *Castle Archdale* **hostel** (March–Dec 23, advance bookings only in Jan & Feb; ☎013656/628118; ②), set in a forest park near Lisnarrick, around five miles west of Irvinestown. If you're relying on public transport, a bus (once a day) will drop you a mile away; otherwise take one of the buses from Enniskillen to Kesh (four daily) and hitch. It makes sense to arrive here in daylight – look out for a small sign beside a church for the turn-off from the main road. A *YHANI* hostel – but with no curfew restrictions – it's a perfect place for getting out to the lough and is a stone's throw from a large caravan park and **campsite** (☎013656/21333), which has a small supermarket and a fast-food outlet. The ferry to White Island (see below) leaves from nearby, and you can also **rent boats** and **bikes**.

White Island

Mounted on the wall of a ruined abbey, the seven early Christian carvings of **White Island** look eerily pagan. Found earlier this century, they are thought to be caryatids – carved supporting columns – from a monastic church of the ninth to eleventh centuries.

The most disconcerting statue is the lewd female figure known as a *sheila na gig*, with bulging cheeks, a big grin, open legs and arms pointing to her genitals. This could be a female fertility figure, a warning to monks of the sins of the flesh, or an expression of the demoniacal power of women, designed to ward off evil. (In the epic *Táin Bó Cuailnge*, Cúchulainn was stopped by an army of 150 women led by their female chieftain Scannlach. Their only weapon was their display of nakedness, from which the boy Cúchulainn had to avert his face.) Less equivocal figures continue left to right: a seated Christ figure holding the Gospels on his knees; a hooded figure with bell and crozier, possibly Saint Anthony; David carrying a shepherd's staff, his hand towards his mouth showing his role as author and singer; Christ the Warrior holding two griffins by the scruff of their necks; and another Christ figure with a fringe of curly hair wearing a brooch on his left shoulder and carrying a sword and shield – here he is the King of Glory at his Second Coming. There is an unfinished seventh stone and, on the far right, a carved head with a downturned mouth which is probably later than the other statues. The church of White Island also contains eleventh-century gravestones; the large earthworks round the outside date from an earlier monastery.

Boa Island and Kesh

One of the most evocative of the carvings of Lough Erne is the double-faced Janus figure of **Boa Island**, at the northern end of the Lower Lough – barely an island at all these days, as it's connected to the mainland by bridges. The place to look out for is Caldragh cemetery, poorly signposted off the A47, about a mile and a half from the eastern bridge. Follow the signs through a farm, watching out for bulls. To your left is the graveyard.

This ancient Christian burial ground of broken moss-covered tombstones, shaded by low, encircling hazel trees, has an almost druidic setting. Here you'll find the **Janus figure**, an idol of yellow stone with very bold symmetrical features. It has the phallus on one side, and a belt and crossed limbs on the other. The figure was probably an invocation of fertility and a depiction of a god-hero – the belt being a reference to the bearing of weapons. Alongside it stands the smaller "Lusty Man", so called since it was moved here from nearby Lustymore Island. This idol has only one eye fully carved, which may be to indicate blindness – Cúchulainn had a number of encounters with war goddesses, divine hags described as blind in the left eye. Across on Lusty Beg Island just off Boa, luxury log cabins with saunas (☎013656/32032; £100–200 a weekend for 2/3 twin bedrooms), canoeing, gentle walks and a restaurant make this quiet island a popular weekend retreat for Enniskillen people. A free car ferry will take you across; dial ☎0 from the telephone on the pier.

The nearest village, **KESH**, four and a half miles to the east, is a possible overnight stop, having some cheapish **B&B** accommodation. Try *Astrid Geddes*, Crevenish Road in the village (☎013656/31001; ④), or Mrs Stronge, *Roscolban House*, Enniskillen Road (☎013656/31096; ③). If you've transport there's also the option of staying in the *Ardess Craft Centre* (☎013656/31267; ⑤), housed in a fine Georgian rectory, which offers residential courses in spinning, weaving and natural dyeing (from £5 a half-day); take the Enniskillen Road out of Kesh, turn left just before the police barracks, take a hard right, then follow the road for one and a half miles.

The chief recommendation of Kesh itself is its position on the lough. You can rent **motor boats** here from Mr R.A. Graham, *Manville House* (☎013656/31668; £24 a day; £60 if he comes too and shows you the best trout spots). If you want to combine **camping** and **watersports** it makes sense to stay at the *Lakeland Caravan Park*, Boa Island Road (☎013656/31025), which offers wind-surfing, canoeing and water-skiing. Alternatively, there's the new *Erinona Boating Centre* (☎013656/32328) at Boa Island Bridgeaway over three miles from Kesh, which has a small campsite by the lake; or away from the lough shore, there's the *Clonelly Forest Campsite*, three miles north of Kesh on the A35.

Upper Lough Erne and Castle Balfour

Upper Lough Erne holds nothing like the interest of the Lower Lough, nor the scenic splendour, although it does have the best-preserved of the planters' castles nearby. The most you're really likely to do around the lough is disturb the fishers or get lost among its crazy causeways and waterways – fun on a boat, but frustrating on dry land. Should you be tempted to venture further into the maze of reed and water, a "Viking longship" runs **cruises** (see p.558) from the *Share Holiday Centre* at Smith's Strand, signposted off the Lisnaskea–Derrylin Road, where they also offer water-based activity holidays with facilities for disabled travellers, and B&B (☎013657/22122; ③). You can **rent a boat** from the National Trust **Crom Estate**, four miles west of Newtownbutler (on the A34) on the eastern shore of the lough; you can also stay here in newly renovated courtyard cottages (☎01396/881204; from £150 a week for 2–6 people). Pastimes on offer include rewarding game and coarse fishing, and there's a café and intrepretative centre; but if anything it's the place to go to enjoy some peace and quiet. If you have transport, the elegantly chiselled **gravestones** on Galoon Island, with their reliefs of skull and crossbones, hourglass and coffin, are worth a detour. *Ports House*, right by the waterside at Ports, not far from Newtownbutler, offers **B&B** (☎013657/73528; ③).

Almost five miles north of Newtownbutler, **Castle Balfour** at **LISNASKEA** shows strong Scottish characteristics in the turrets and parapets, high-pitched gables and tall chimneys. Lisnaskea itself is one of Fermanagh's few towns – and a small one at that.

Its tiny nineteenth-century cornmarket yard has an early Christian carved cross depicting Adam and Eve beneath a tree, and the library contains a diminutive but interesting **folk museum** (Mon–Wed & Fri 9.15am–5pm, Sat 9.15am–12.30pm), with displays on local Gaelic traditions and festivals, including plenty of detail on the making of *poteen*. If you're **camping**, there's a campsite within two miles of Lisnaskea at Mullynascarthy (✆013657/21640).

Western Fermanagh

The stretch of countryside on the western edge of the county offers some good walking opportunities, particularly in the hills to the south. The **Ulster Way**, which runs north from the Upper Lough and inland through this region, makes the riches of the terrain easily accessible .

The west also has two attractions that are well worth seeking out. The magnificent eighteenth-century **Florence Court**, about eight miles southwest of Enniskillen, is the most assured achievement of the colonists, built 150 years after the initial defensive planters' castles; and, if you have transport, a visit to the house can be combined with an hour or so at the **Marble Arch Caves** – the finest cave-system in Ulster. To get to the house from Enniskillen follow the A4 Sligo Road for three miles, branching off on the A32 Swanlinbar Road (there's no bus service). From here to the caves head further south along the A32 and follow the signposts (about five miles). Walkers can reach them along the **Ulster Way**, which runs four miles south from the A4 near Belcoo and past Lower Lough Macnean.

Florence Court

The magnificent **Florence Court** (July & Aug daily 1–6pm, except Tues; April–May & Sept Sat & Sun 1–6pm; £2.50; grounds open all year 10am–dusk; £1.50 per car) is a three-storey mansion built in 1764 and joined by long arcades to small pavilions. It was owned by the Coles, descendants of the planters of Enniskillen, and is notable for its – now restored – lavish Rococo plasterwork and rare furnishings. The dining-room ceiling hosts a cloud of cherubs with eagles flying out of a duck-egg blue sky. You can stay in pretty *Rose Cottage* in the Florence Court walled garden, well equipped and with two double bedrooms (✆01365/88120; from £160 per week). The *Sheelin* **restaurant** (✆01365/348232; booking essential) nearby does hearty afternoon teas and excellent dinners.

The Marble Arch Caves

Fermanagh's caves are renowned, and while some are for experts only, the most spectacular system of all – the **Marble Arch Caves** – is accessible to anyone. A tour of the system lasts around an hour and a half, beginning with a boat journey along a subterranean river, then on through brilliantly lit chambers dripping with stalactites and fragile mineral veils. **Tours** of the caves are sometimes booked out by parties, so it makes sense to ring ahead to check that your journey there will not be wasted (March–June & Sept daily 11am–4.30pm; July & Aug daily 11am–5.30pm; £4; ✆01365/348855); in a steady Irish downpour the caves can be flooded, so check weather reports. You'll need to bring warm clothing – as the temperature drops substantially – and sturdy shoes. As you leave the caves, it's worth detouring (turn right) along the **Marlbank Scenic Loop**. Spread out on either side you'll see limestone-flagged fields – much like those of the Burren in County Clare. It was 50,000 years of gentle water seepage through the limestone that deposited the calcite for the amazing stalactite growths in the caves below.

THE ULSTER WAY

In the southwest of Fermanagh, the **Ulster Way** takes you through the bog and granite heights of the **Cuilcagh Mountains** and **Ballintempo Forest**, offering fabulous views over the loughs. The Way then continues north, through the **Lough Navar Forest**, a well-groomed conifer plantation with tarmacked roads and shorter trails. Although a great deal of fir plantation walking is dark and frustrating, this forest does, at points, provide some of the most spectacular views in Fermanagh, looking over Lower Lough Erne and the mountains of Tyrone, Donegal, Leitrim and Sligo. The Lough Navar Forest also sustains a small herd of red deer, as well as wild goats, foxes, badgers, hares and red squirrels.

It is advisable to follow the signposting rather than design your own route where the Way runs close to the border with the Republic. Route sheets on the Navar Forest and Big Dog Forest trails are available from local tourist offices; and you can get a route guide for the southwest section of the Way from The Sports Council for Northern Ireland (see *Basics*, p.20).

Accommodation possibilities along the Way are limited. There are a couple of B&B places near **BELCOO**, two and a half miles west from the trail's ascent to the Ballintempo Forest: try Mrs Doherty, *Bella Vista*, Cottage Drive (☎01365/386469; ④), or Mr and Mrs Catterall, *Corralea Forest Lodge* (☎01365/386325; ④). There are a **campsite** and holiday cottages (☎01365/641673; £30 per cottage per night) in the Lough Navar Forest, five miles northwest of Derrygonnelly, off the A46. A bit further away from the route of the Way, west near the border at **GARRISON** (take the minor road from Derrygonnelly), the *Lough Melvin Holiday Centre* is a residential **outdoor pursuits** centre (☎01365/3658142; prior arrangement essential), offering caving, canoeing, windsurfing and hill-walking – prices from £5 a half-day, £55 a weekend. The centre has **hostel** accommodation open to all (①) and camping – though you should ring ahead to check on space if you want to stop here.

travel details

Ulsterbus

Strabane to: Derry (15 daily; 50min); Dublin (4 daily; 4hr 40min); Enniskillen (1 daily; 3hr); Monaghan (4 daily; 2hr 5min); Omagh (4 daily; 1hr 5min).

Enniskillen to: Armagh (1 daily; 1hr 45min); Belfast (6 daily, 2 daily in summer; 2hr 35min); Dublin (3 daily; 3hr 45min); Monaghan (2 daily; 1hr 10min).

PART THREE

THE

CONTEXTS

THE HISTORICAL FRAMEWORK

An understanding of Ireland's history is essential in order to make sense of its troubled present. In these few pages, we cannot do more than provide a brief outline of that history, in the hope that it will serve as a starting point for further reading and discussion.

EARLIEST INHABITANTS

During the last Ice Age, when most of Ireland was covered by an ice-cap, low sea-levels meant that Ireland was attached to Britain, and Britain to the European Continent. As the climate warmed (from about 13,000 BC), and the ice gradually retreated, sea-levels rose and the broad land connection between Ireland and Britain began to recede to one or more narrow land bridges. The first human inhabitants arrived over these routes, probably from Scotland, some time after 8000 BC. By about 7000 BC the land bridges were submerged and Ireland geographically isolated, while Britain remained connected to continental Europe for much longer.

The first inhabitants, **Mesolithic** (middle Stone Age) hunter-gatherers, found a densely forested land that could only be penetrated easily along its waterways, and, for the most part, they seem to have lived close to the sea, rivers and lakes (flint work from the period has been found in Antrim, Down, Louth and Dublin).

Their way of life continued undisturbed until, from about 3500 BC, **Neolithic** (late Stone Age) farmers began arriving by sea, probably from Britain. With skills in animal and crop husbandry, weaving and pottery, the new arrivals used their stone axes to clear large tracts of forest for cultivation. The hunter-gatherer and agricultural economies were, however, complimentary, and it is thought the two peoples co-existed for many centuries before the older way of life was gradually assimilated by the new.

The Neolithic people were the creators of Ireland's **megalithic remains**. There are more than 1200 such burial sites scattered throughout the country, with the greatest concentrations in the north and west. Such sites are also found all along the Atlantic seaboard of Europe, from Spain to Scandinavia – a sign of Ireland's ancestral and cultural links with the rest of Europe at this time and, in particular, with the peoples of Britain and Brittany.

The most dramatic and well-known megalithic remains in Ireland are the great **passage graves** at Knowth and Newgrange in County Meath, with their elaborate spiral engravings, cut into the stone entirely without the use of metal tools. It is thought that the function of these tombs was not purely religious or ceremonial; they were also territorial markers, which at times of population pressure staked a communal claim to the surrounding lands. Little is known of the people themselves, although their civilization was long-lasting, with thousands of years separating the earliest and the latest megalithic constructions. Only rarely have skeletons been found in the graves (in most cases only the cremated remains of bones are discovered), but what few there have been seem to indicate a short, dark, hairy race with a life expectancy of little more than 35 years.

Around 2000 BC the use of bronze spread to Ireland, though it is uncertain whether this was the result of the commercial contacts of the existing population or the migration of a new people. The next significant technological development, generally associated with the arrival of the Celts, was the introduction of iron around 700 BC.

THE CELTS

The Celts were an Indo-European group called *Keltoi* by the Greeks and *Galli* by the Romans, who spread south from central Europe into Italy and Spain and west through France and Britain. By 500 BC Celtic language and culture were dominant in Ireland, but there is no evidence of any large-scale invasion or social upheaval. It is probably more accurate to think of their arrival as a gradual and relatively peaceful process that took place over hundreds of years.

Their settlements took the form of ring forts (or raths), and they divided the island into about one hundred small **kingdoms** or *Tuatha*, each with its own king. The *Tuatha* were grouped into the Five Fifths or provinces, which were Ulster (*Ulaid*), Meath (*Midhe*), Leinster (*Laigin*), Munster (*Muma*) and Connacht (which retains its Irish spelling). In theory, the High King (*Ard R'*) ruled over all from his throne on the Hill of Tara – a place long associated with mysterious power – although only rarely did any one figure of sufficient strength emerge to lay undisputed claim to that title.

It is hard to separate the truth about the Celts from the stories they told of themselves. Theirs was an oral culture in which the immortality to be gained from being the hero of an epic tale was highly prized. With an enthusiasm for war little short of bloodthirsty, they celebrated battles decided by the single combat of great champions, guided and aided by the unpredictable whims of the gods. They also appropriated the religion and beliefs already current in Ireland; and although they had nothing to do with the building of the megaliths, the sites continued to have great symbolic significance.

The two greatest heroes of the epics, **Cúchulainn** and **Fionn Mac Cumhaill** (Finn McCool), have been tentatively identified as warrior champions of the second and third centuries, transformed by legend into semi-divinities in much the same way as King Arthur was in England.

THE COMING OF CHRISTIANITY

The **Christianization** of Ireland began as early as the fourth century AD, well before the arrival of Saint Patrick (whose existence is now the subject of some controversy). Vestiges did survive of the previous religion of the Celts, but after the collapse of the Roman Empire, Ireland assumed a position at the very forefront of European Christianity. (Also around this time

the people of Ireland took the name *Goidil* – Gaels – for themselves from the Welsh *Gwyddyl*.)

In the sixth century, the early Christian leaders successfully adapted established church organization to suit the scattered and tribal nature of Gaelic society by setting up monastic foundations. The country became a haven for religious orders, the only sources of learning at this time. The sheer impassibility of the landscape supported monastic development, and many of the great Irish monasteries, such as St Enda's on the Aran Islands, Clonmacnois in County Offaly and Clonard in County Meath, date from this period. **Ogham**, the Celtic line-based writing system seen on standing stones, was rapidly supplanted by the religious scholars, who introduced Latin. The first – and best-known – of their richly illuminated Latin manuscripts, the **Book of Kells**, can be seen in the Library of Trinity College, Dublin.

The traditional view of these times as "Dark Ages" of terror and chaos throughout Europe is not supported by events in Ireland. Although intertribal warfare was constant, the country enjoyed relative cultural and religious stability. Alongside this, well-established diplomatic and trading contact along the Atlantic seaboard encouraged the development of a strong missionary impulse in Irish Christianity. Between 500 and 800 the Irish church spread the Gospel widely across the Continent. The most prominent of the many missionaries was Saint Columba, who founded monasteries in France, Switzerland, Germany and Austria, and at Bobbio in Italy – where he died in 615.

INVASION: VIKINGS AND NORMANS

From 795, Ireland was increasingly plagued by destructive **Viking raids**, in which many of the great monasteries were plundered and burned (though many more were destoyed as a result of indigenous intertribal warfare in the eighth and ninth centuries). The instability of the period led to the development of the **round towers**, which were used as lookout posts and places of sanctuary – and which characterize early Irish architecture. The Viking raids culminated in a full-scale invasion in 914 and the subsequent founding of walled cities, usually at the mouths of rivers, such as Dublin,

Wexford, Waterford, Youghal, Cork, Bantry and Limerick. The decisive defeat of the Danes by the High King Brian Boru at the Battle of Clontarf in 1014 at least spared Ireland from becoming a Viking colony. However, the death of Brian Boru at the battle, and the subsequent divisions among his followers, meant that his victory was never consolidated by the formation of a strong unified kingdom. The Vikings that remained soon merged fully into the native Irish population.

From the time of the Norman conquest onwards, the kings of England coveted Ireland. The first of the **Anglo-Normans** to cross over to Ireland was a freelance adventurer, Richard FitzGilbert de Clare, more usually known as **Strongbow**. He came in 1169 at the invitation of Dermot MacMurrough, the exiled king of Leinster, who sought help to regain his throne. Henry II of England, however, was concerned that Strongbow might establish a threatening power base and therefore went personally to Ireland as overlord. He had earlier secured papal support and authorization over all powers – native, Norse and Norman – from, as chance would have it, the only English pope in history, Adrian IV.

In 1172, Pope Alexander III reaffirmed Henry II's lordship. This seemed to open the prospect of Anglo-Norman rule in which Gaelic tribal kingdoms would be reshaped into a feudal system on the English model, but the Irish resisted so effectively that royal authority outside the "English Pale" (an area surrounding Dublin) was little more than nominal.

THE STATUTES OF KILKENNY

By the fourteenth century, the Anglo-Norman settlers had integrated with the native Irish population to such an extent that the Crown, eager to regain control, sought to drive a permanent wedge between the natives and the colonists with the introduction of **The Statutes of Kilkenny** (1366). This legislation prohibited intermarriage with the Irish, forbade the Irish from entering walled cities, and made the adoption of Irish names, dress, customs or speech illegal. Despite these measures, Gaelic influence continued to grow until, by the end of the fifteenth century, the "Pale" had been reduced to just a narrow strip of land around the capital.

THE TUDORS AND THE STUARTS

The continued isolation of Irish politics from English and Continental influence during the fifteenth century, and England's preoccupation with the Wars of the Roses, helped Ireland's most powerful Anglo-Norman family – the **FitzGeralds** of Kildare – to establish and consolidate control of the east and southeast of the country. For the most part, their growing authority was left unchallenged by the early Tudor monarchy, whose policy towards Ireland was based mainly on considerations of economy – it was cheaper to accept Kildare's rule than establish an English deputy who would need expensive military backing; and security Irish discontent with English rule should not be allowed to take forms which might be exploited by England's foreign enemies.

THE REFORMATION

Henry VIII was able to retain his attitude of expedient caution until his break with Rome introduced several new factors. The clergy began to preach rebellion against the schismatical king, while Henry was able to reward his supporters with the spoils from the dissolution of religious houses. Convinced that his family's power was under threat, Kildare's son, Lord Offaly ("Silken Thomas"), staged an insurrection in the summer of 1534. Aid from the pope – who for the first time was seen as a potential supporter of opposition to England – was hoped for, but never came. Henry, inevitably, reacted forcibly and exchanged his policy of prudence for one of aggression. War dragged on until 1540, by which time Kildare and his supporters, their power all but crushed, were forced to submit to the Crown.

The Dublin parliament enacted legislation accepting Henry's **Act of Supremacy**, which made the king head of the Church. At least three distinct factions emerged in Ireland: the "Old English", who were loyal to the king but denied him spiritual primacy; the independent-minded and staunchly Catholic Gaelic Irish; and the new Protestants, many of whom had benefited materially by acquiring Church property. (At this stage, those "recusants" who refused to swear the oath acknowledging Henry as head of the Church were not yet subject to discrimination.) In an attempt to bind the chiefs and nobles of Ireland more closely to its authority, the Crown forced them to surrender their lands, only to return them again with the reduced status of landlords. Central to Henry's policy was the wish to rule Ireland cheaply, with least risk of foreign intervention, through Irish-born "deputies" whose loyalty was assured. But such loyalty could not be counted on, and after Henry's death the authority of the English Crown was again challenged.

ELIZABETH I AND JAMES I

During the reign of **Queen Elizabeth I** (1558–1603), a growing number of adventurers, mainly younger sons of the aristocracy, arrived from Protestant England to pillage Ireland. For the first time, the supposed moral imperative to turn the Gaelic Irish away from the papacy was used as an excuse to invade and dispossess. This justification for the suppression of Irish culture, religion and language was to be the trademark of English occupation of Ireland for many years to come.

Elizabeth's aim was to establish an English colony. This policy of **plantation** had been started, albeit unsuccessfully, some thirty years earlier during the reign of Mary I, when Laois — renamed "Queen's County" — and Offaly — "King's County" — were confiscated from their native Irish owners and given into the possession of loyal Old English. Elizabeth's first attempt, in the 1570s, to "plant" northeast Ulster, which was then the most Gaelic area of the country, failed miserably. But the colonization process, when eventually completed, was the principal instrument in subjugating the entire country.

At least three major Irish **rebellions** were prompted by Elizabeth's policies. Two, led by the Desmonds of Munster, were easily put down; the Desmond lands were confiscated and given to English settlers. The third, last, and most serious was in Ulster, and was led by **Hugh O'Neill**. O'Neill, originally a protegé of the English court (see p.546), participated in crushing the revolt of the Desmonds, and had long been groomed to become chief of Ulster. He'd always imagined the role to be that of an autonomous Gaelic chieftain; he turned against his Queen in 1595 when he began to appreciate the extent to which he would be the pawn of English Protestantism. His forces won

a major victory over the English at the battle of the Yellow Ford in 1598, but were defeated at **Kinsale** in December 1601 after failing to link up effectively with the Spanish reinforcements who had arrived there.

The Tudor conquest of Ireland was completed when O'Neill signed the **Treaty of Mellifont** in 1603, ignorant of the death of Elizabeth just a few days before. Half a million acres of land were confiscated from the native Irish, including all the estates of O'Neill and O'Donnell. English plans to redistribute the land supposedly included generous endowments to the "natives". However, an abortive and unplanned insurrection was enough to frighten them into abandoning any such idea, and English and Scottish "planters" — many of whom were ex-soldiers — were brought over to be ensconced in fortified "bawns". Chiefs such as O'Neill were still nominally landlords but, unable to accept the loss of their ancient authority, and living under constant suspicion that they were plotting against the Crown, many chose instead to leave their country as exiles. Their mass departure to continental Europe in 1607 became known as the **Flight of the Earls**.

It was at this time that the character of Ulster began to change. James VI of Scotland had just become **James I** of England, and he encouraged many Scots to emigrate the short distance to Ulster where so much newly confiscated land awaited them. There was a great deal of bitterness on the part of the dispossessed native people, and little intermarriage with the planters, so that the whole country, and above all Ulster, became divided along Catholic and Protestant lines.

CHARLES I AND THE ENGLISH CIVIL WAR

The widespread belief in England and Ireland that James's successor, **Charles I**, harboured pro-Catholic sympathies was one of the spurs for the armed rebellion in Ulster in 1641. Terrifying stories circulated in England of the torture and murder of Protestant planters, and the rebels' (bogus) claim that they were acting with Charles's blessing did much to provoke the **English Civil War**. The origins of the current situation in the six northeast counties of Ulster can in many respects be traced to the policy and events of this period.

During the Civil War, the "Old English" in Ireland allied with the native Irish in the

Confederation of Kilkenny, supporting the Royalist cause in the hope of bringing about the restoration of Catholicism. It was an uneasy alliance, characterized by inadequate leadership and personal rivalries, in which the Irish felt they had nothing to lose in pursuit of liberty, whereas the Old English lived in fear of a Protestant invasion should the forces of **Oliver Cromwell** achieve victory. The war did indeed end with the establishment of Cromwell's Protectorate and the execution of the king; and the conquest of Ireland became Cromwell's most immediate priority.

CROMWELL AND THE ACT OF SETTLEMENT

Cromwell's ruthless campaign in Ireland remains a source of great bitterness to this day. He arrived in Dublin with 12,000 men of the New Model Army in August 1649, and was soon joined by another force under General Ireton. **Drogheda** was stormed in September, and thousands, including civilians and children, were slaughtered. Cromwell continued south and quickly took Wexford and New Ross, whereupon the towns of Cork, Youghal and Kinsale in the southeast (all in the hands of Royalists) swiftly capitulated. Although Waterford held out for several months, it was not long before Cromwell's forces had overrun the entire country and broken the backbone of resistance.

By the time the struggle was over, almost two years on, one-quarter of the Catholic population was dead and those found wandering the country orphaned or dispossessed were sold into slavery in the West Indies. The **Act of Settlement** drawn up in 1652 confiscated land from the native Irish on a massive scale. All "transplantable persons" were ordered to move west of the River Shannon by May 1, 1654, on pain of death; in the famous phrase, it was a matter of indifference whether they went "to Hell or to Connacht". The mass exodus continued for months, with many of the old and sick dying on the journey. Cromwell's soldiers were paid off with gifts of appropriated land, and, remaining as settlers, constituted a permanent reminder of English injustice.

KING BILLY AND KING JAMES

Irish hopes were raised once more by the **Restoration** of Charles II in 1660. He had regained the English throne, however, only after lengthy negotiations with the Protestant parliamentarians of London and Dublin, and was in no position to give expression to any Catholic sympathies which he may have held.

Things changed only when Charles's brother James II succeeded him in 1685. He appointed a Catholic viceroy in Ireland and actually got as far as repealing the Act of Settlement. Had this had time to take effect, the land confiscated by Cromwell would have been returned to its former (Catholic) owners. However, the Whigs and the Tories in England united to invite the Protestant William of Orange to take the throne. James fled and was soon raising an army in Ireland. He was successful until 1689, when he came to lay siege to the city of **Derry** in Ulster; young trade apprentices, known thereafter as the **Apprentice Boys**, shut the gates of the city in the face of James's troops – an event still celebrated today during the annual marching season.

However, the most significant victory of Protestant over Catholic was on July 12, 1690, when William's army defeated that of James at the **Battle of the Boyne**. The repeal of the Act of Settlement was therefore never implemented – but the very idea that the Catholics still had claims to their old property which they might one day be able to reassert became established in the Protestant consciousness. As William's victory was consolidated, measures were taken to ensure irreversible Protestant control of the country.

THE PENAL LAWS TO THE ACT OF UNION

In 1641, 59 percent of the land in Ireland was owned by Catholics. In 1688 the figure was 22 percent, and by 1703 it was 14 percent. The Protestant population, about one-tenth of the total, lived in fear of an uprising by the vast majority of dispossessed and embittered Catholics. In order to keep the native Catholics in a position of powerlessness, a number of acts were passed, collectively known as the **penal laws**. Not only were Catholics forbidden to vote or join the army or navy, but it became illegal to educate a child in the Catholic faith; they could not teach, open their own schools or send their children to be educated abroad. Catholics could neither buy land nor inherit it, other than by the equal division of estates between all sons. There were vast rewards for turning Protestant; a male convert was entitled to all his brothers' inheritance, a female to her husband's property. Irish language, music and literature were banned, as was the saying of the Mass. The intention was to crush the identity of the Irish people through the suppression of their culture. However, clandestine "hedge schools" developed where outlawed Catholic teachers taught Irish language and music; Mass was said in secret, often at night in the open countryside, and although the erosion of the culture had begun, for the time being it remained strong (it wasn't until the devastating effects of the Famine that the culture went into serious decline).

GRATTAN'S PARLIAMENT

The next turning point in Irish history came in the **late eighteenth century**, when the increasingly prosperous merchant class ceased to identify its own interests exclusively with those of the British Crown. The British, in their turn, were forced to realize that the best guarantee of stability was the country's economic strength. This was an age of bourgeois revolution, and the events of the **American War of Independence** attracted much attention in Ireland. As early as 1771, Benjamin Franklin was in Dublin suggesting future transatlantic cooperation. Although the rebellion of the American colonies threatened Irish commercial interests, opposition to the war did not mean opposition to the American cause. Thus far, the bulk of Irish emigrants to the American colonies had been Ulster Presbyterians, Catholic emigration being subject to legal restrictions, and the Protestants of Ireland felt a deep sympathy with Washington's campaign. The demand for "no taxation without representation" struck an emotional chord with the parliamentarians of Henry Grattan's Patriot Party – although Ireland was not taxed directly by the British parliament, the Irish Protestants felt, increasingly, that their interests were not properly represented in the politics and policies of the British Isles as a whole.

Protestants and Catholics in Ireland made common cause to the extent that Grattan declared "the Irish Protestant could never be free till the Irish Catholic had ceased to be a slave". Its resources stretched to the limit by war, the British government was sufficiently intimidated by the thought of Irish rebellion to be in the mood for concessions. The land stipulations of the penal laws were repealed in 1778, and in 1782 **Grattan's Parliament** achieved what was felt at the time to be constitutional independence for Ireland, beyond the interference of the London parliament, although still subject to the veto of the king. In the **Renunciation Act** of 1783, the British parliament declared that the executive and judicial independence of Ireland should be "established and ascertained forever, and... at no time hereafter be questioned or questionable".

As it turned out, the independence of the Dublin parliament lasted for just eighteen years, and even those were long on dissent and short on achievement. Economic measures certainly benefited the merchants, but such issues as the extension of voting rights to Catholics – despite Grattan's personal support – were barely addressed. A major reason for its failure was the influence of the **French Revolution** in 1789.

WOLFE TONE AND THE UNITED IRISHMEN

In the 1770s, the threat of French invasion, coupled with the obvious inadequacy of the British force stationed in the country, had led to the formation throughout Ireland of bands of **Volunteers**. These were exclusively Protestant groups, at their strongest in Ulster and particularly Belfast, which rapidly acquired a political significance way beyond their role as a sort of Home Guard.

The French Revolution transformed French invasion, for Irish Nationalists of all persuasions, from a menace to be feared to a prospective means of national liberation. **United Irishmen**, led by Wolfe Tone and built on the foundations of the Protestant Volunteers but attracting, if anything, more support from Catholics, rallied to the call of Liberty, Equality and Fraternity. Tone himself was a Protestant barrister, who saw equal rights for Protestants and Catholics in Ireland as the only route to independence from England. The United Irishmen were originally disposed towards nonviolence, but for Tone the possibility of French aid was too appealing to resist. The British, and the majority of Ulster Protestants, were by contrast so alarmed by tales of the bloodshed in France that they too prepared for war; it was at this juncture that the Protestant Orange Society, later the **Orange Order**, was established (1795). Although influenced by revolutionary ideas from France, its main aim was to maintain Protestant power (for more on the Order, see p.540).

The uprising came in **1798** (see p.370); disorganized fighting broke out in different parts of the island well before the French fleet – and Tone himself – arrived, and the scattered rebels were swiftly and bloodily suppressed. Tone was sentence to be hanged, but committed suicide by cutting his own throat before his execution. The limited advances Henry Grattan had won for Catholics were withdrawn as a result of the rebellion.

THE ACT OF UNION

The destiny of Ireland during the period following the uprising was largely subject to the whim of political factions in England, ever ready to make an emotional cause célèbre of the latest developments. The rebellion of 1798 provoked Prime Minister William Pitt into support for the complete legislative union of Britain and Ireland and the dissolution of the Dublin parliament. Pitt argued that this offered the most hopeful road towards Catholic emancipation while also ensuring the perpetuation of the Protestant Ascendancy. In 1801 the **Act of Union** came into force, abolishing the 500-year-old Irish parliament and making Ireland part of the United Kingdom.

All hopes of independence seemed crushed. Ireland itself housed an utterly divided people, a minority Protestant ruling class and a politically powerless Catholic majority. **Robert Emmet**, a romantic figure in Irish history, inspired by Wolfe Tone, made one last stand for independence, and attempted a rising in 1803. His followers, however, were small in number and disorganized. The rising failed, and Emmet was executed.

DANIEL O'CONNELL

The quest for Catholic emancipation by peaceful constitutional means was the life's work of **Daniel O'Connell** (1775–1847), the lawyer who became known as "The Liberator" and whom Gladstone called "the greatest popular leader the world has ever seen". He founded the Catholic Association in 1823, which attracted a mass following in Ireland with its campaign for full political rights for Catholics. O'Connell himself was elected to the British

House of Commons as the member for Ennis, County Clare in 1828. As a Catholic, he was forbidden to take his seat in Westminster; but the moral force of his victory was such that a change in the law had to be conceded. Royal assent was given to the **Catholic Emancipation Bill** on April 13, 1829, granting voting rights to some Catholics. Stringent property qualifications, however, ensured that the Catholic vote remained a small one.

At the height of his success, O'Connell's popularity was phenomenal. He was elected Lord Mayor of (Protestant) Dublin for the year of 1841, and two years later embarked on an ambitious **campaign** for the **repeal of the Union** with England. O'Connell addressed a series of vast "monster meetings" throughout Ireland; according to the conservative estimate of *The Times*, over a million people – one-eighth of the Irish population – attended the meeting symbolically held at the Hill of Tara.

The climax of O'Connell's campaign was to be a meeting at Clontarf (where Brian Boru had defeated the Danes in the eleventh century) on October 8, 1843. All Ireland was poised and waiting, conscious of the sympathy that O'Connell's profoundly peaceful movement had won from around the world. The pacifism which had led him to say that "no political change is worth the shedding of a single drop of human blood", and his determination always to act within the law, were, however, exploited by the British. One day before the Clontarf meeting, it was declared to be an illegal gathering; and O'Connell, remarkably, obliged by calling it off. The crowds which had already gathered, and the population at large, were baffled that O'Connell backed down from direct confrontation. His moment passed, and the stage was left to those who, having seen pacifism fail to secure independence, believed that armed struggle would prove the only way forward. **The Young Ireland movement**, once aligned with O'Connell, attempted an armed uprising in 1848, but by then there was little chance of mass support. The country was already undergoing a national disaster.

THE FAMINE

The failure of the Irish potato crop from 1845 to 1849 plunged the island into appalling **famine**. Elsewhere in Europe the blight was a resolvable problem, but Irish subsistence farmers were utterly dependent on the crop. No disease affected grain, cattle, dairy produce or corn, and throughout the disaster Irish produce that could have fed the hungry continued to be exported overseas. Millions were kept alive by charitable soup kitchens, and some individual landlords were supportive to their tenants; for millions more, the only choice lay between starvation and escape.

Between 1841 and 1851, census returns suggest that 1.4 million people died in Ireland and 1.4 million emigrated to the United States and elsewhere – though the exact numbers in each case were probably higher. Many emigrants were too ill to survive the journey on what became known as "coffin ships", some drowned when overcrowded ships sank, and still more died on arrival in the United States, Canada, Britain, Australia and New Zealand.

One consequence of **mass emigration** was the creation of large Irish communities abroad, which henceforth added an international dimension to the struggle for Irish independence. Financial support from the Irish overseas became crucial to such Nationalist organizations as the Irish Republican Brotherhood, also known as the **Fenians**. Their attempted uprising in 1867 was little short of a fiasco, but they nonetheless retained a loyal following both in the States and in England (where a number of bombings were carried out in their name).

The legacy of the Famine was such that the long-standing bitterness instilled by the English connection now deepened to a new level of emotional intensity. Resentment focused on the failure of the British government to intervene, and more specifically on the **absentee English landlords** who had continued to profit while remaining indifferent to the suffering of their tenants. Such landlords had little or no contact with the realities of life on their estates; rents were far higher than most tenants could pay, and evictions became widespread.

PARNELL AND THE HOME RULE

The second half of the nineteenth century was characterized by a complex interplay of political and economic factors which contributed towards the exacerbation of religious differences. The most important of these was the struggle for land and for the rights of tenants.

A coherent nationalist movement with modest aims began to emerge, operating within British parliamentary democracy.

Charles Stuart Parnell (1846–91; see p.111), a Protestant who was elected to Westminster in 1875 and became leader of the **Home Rule Party** two years later, was the tenants' champion. He insisted that only a parliament meeting in Dublin could be responsive to the needs of the people, and to that end consistently disrupted the business of the British House of Commons.

Parnell also organized the Irish peasantry in defiance of particularly offensive landlords, adding a new word to the English language when the first such target was a Captain Boycott.

A breakthrough seemed to be approaching when Parnell won the support of the Prime Minister, Gladstone, but the **Phoenix Park murders** in Dublin in 1882 (see p.81) again hardened English opinion against the Irish. Three Home Rule Bills were defeated in the space of ten years; instead the Prevention of Crimes Act (temporarily) abolished trial by jury and increased police powers. The transparent honesty of Parnell's denials of complicity in the murders for a while served to boost his career, but public opinion finally swung against him in 1890, when he was cited in the divorce case of his colleague Captain O'Shea.

The attitude of many Irish Protestants to the agitation for Home Rule was summed up by the equation "Home Rule = Rome Rule"; such a threat was enough to unite the Anglican (broadly speaking, conservative gentry) and Presbyterian (liberal tradesmen) communities. These were certainly the people who were doing best from a modest boom in Ireland's economic fortunes, with Ulster, and specifically Belfast, having been the main beneficiary when the industrial revolution finally arrived in the country. Large-scale **industrialization**, in export industries such as shipbuilding, linen manufacture and engineering, gave the region an additional dependence on the British connection, while the fact that these industries were firmly under Protestant ownership increased social tensions.

The end of the nineteenth century saw a burst of activity aimed at the revival of interest in all aspects of Irish culture and identity. Ostensibly nonpolitical organizations such as the **Gaelic League** and the **Gaelic Athletic Association** were founded to promote Irish language, music and traditional sports, and these inevitably tended to attract the support of politically minded Nationalists. As well as those who sought to encourage the use of Irish, a body of writers, with W.B. Yeats in the forefront, embarked on an attempt to create a national literature in English.

In 1898, Arthur Griffith, a printer in Dublin, founded a newspaper called the *United Irishman*, in which he expounded the philosophy of *Sinn Féin*, meaning "We, Ourselves". His was a nonviolent and essentially capitalist vision, arguing that the Irish MPs should simply abandon Westminster and set up their own parliament in Dublin, where, with or without the permission of the British, they would be able to govern Ireland by virtue of their unassailable moral authority. Such political freedom was a prerequisite for Ireland to achieve significant economic development. Sinn Féin incorporated itself into a political party in 1905. Meanwhile, **socialist** analyses of the situation in Ireland were appearing in the *Workers' Republic*, the newspaper of **James Connolly**'s Irish Socialist Republican Party, pointing out that Ireland's frail prosperity rested on a basis of malnutrition, bad housing and social deprivation.

REACTION AND COUNTER-REACTION

In reaction to the declared intentions of Asquith's Liberal government in Britain in 1911 to see through the passage of yet another (exceptionally tame) Home Rule Bill, the Protestants of Ulster mobilized themselves under the leadership of **Sir Edward Carson**. A Dublin barrister who at first glance had little in common with the people of Ulster, a region he barely knew, his one great aim was to preserve the Union, in the face of the "nefarious conspiracy" hatched by the British government itself. To that end he declared that, should the Home Rule Bill become law, the Unionists would defy it and set up their own parliament. In preparation for that eventuality, they organized their own militia, the **Ulster Volunteers**.

James Connolly, who had spent the years from 1903 to 1910 in disillusionment in the United States, found himself on less fertile ground when he tried to convert the workers of Belfast to socialism. He was impressed, however, by the example of the Ulster

Volunteers, and the brutal police suppression of a protracted and bitter strike in Dublin, organized by James Larkin's Irish Transport Workers Union, gave him the opportunity to form the **Irish Citizen Army**. Other militant Republicans had also resolved to create an armed force in the south to parallel the Ulster Volunteers, and almost simultaneously, in November 1913, the **Irish Volunteers** came into being. The Gaelic League and Gaelic Athletic association acted as prime recruiting places, and provided such leaders as Pádraig Pearse. The movement should not, however, be seen in strictly sectarian terms; at least two of its most prominent leaders were Ulster Protestant.

REBELLION AND CIVIL WAR

The British parliament eventually passed the **Home Rule Bill** of 1912, and for a while the conditions appeared to exist for Ireland to erupt into civil war. Before this could happen, however, the outbreak of World War I dramatically altered the situation. An immediate consequence of war was that implementation of the Bill was indefinitely postponed.

For the majority of the Irish Volunteers, the primary aim of their movement was to safeguard the postwar introduction of Home Rule. Not simply to that end, but also out of loyalty to the British Crown, many of them joined the British Army. Some, however, led by Eoin MacNeill, in part supported the British war effort but were reluctant to commit too much of their strength towards defending Britain without a pledge of concrete rewards. These in turn fell under the domination of a small and secret militant faction, the revived **Irish Republican Brotherhood** (after 1916 they became the Irish Republican Army, or IRA), to whom "England's difficulty was Ireland's opportunity". They made tentative overtures for German support (and even contemplated installing a German prince as King of Ireland) but went ahead with preparations for armed insurrection regardless of whether or not they received foreign aid — indeed all but regardless of the virtual certainty of defeat.

THE EASTER RISING

The outbreak of fighting on the streets of Dublin on Easter Monday in 1916 was expected by neither the English nor the Irish Army, and was a source of bemusement to the Dubliners themselves. Republican forces swiftly took over a number of key buildings, although they missed an easy opportunity to capture the Castle itself.

The leaders of the Rising made their base in the General Post Office in O'Connell Street, and it was from there that Pádraig Pearse emerged to read the "Proclamation from The Provisional Government of the Irish Republic to the People of Ireland":

Ireland, through us, summons her children to the flag and strikes for her freedom....The Irish Republic is entitled to, and hereby claims, the allegiance of every Irishman and Irishwoman. The Republic guarantees religious and civil liberty, equal rights and equal opportunities to all its citizens... cherishing all the children of the nation equally, and oblivious of the differences carefully fostered by an alien Government, which have divided a minority from the majority in the past.

To these fine democratic sentiments Pearse in particular added a quasi-mystical emphasis on the necessity for blood sacrifice; although potential allies such as Eoin MacNeill declined to join them with so little prospect of success, these were men prepared to give their lives as inspiration to others.

So weak was the rebel position that they only held out five days; at the time of their surrender they were even less popular with the mass of the nation than when they began, as a result of the terrible physical damage Dublin had suffered.

And yet, as the leaders of the Rising were systematically and unceremoniously executed by the British – the wounded James Connolly was shot tied to a chair – sympathy did indeed grow for the Republicans and their cause. In the words of Yeats's *Easter 1916*:

... changed, changed utterly:
A terrible beauty is born.

WAR WITH BRITAIN

When the British government felt able once again to turn to Irish affairs, it found a dramatically altered situation. Sinn Féin won a resounding victory in the elections of 1918 and refused to take its seats at Westminster. Instead the newly elected MPs met in Dublin as the *Dáil Éireann (*Assembly of Ireland) and declared independence. Leadership passed to Eamonn de Valera, the sole surviving leader of

the Easter Rising, whose sentence of death had been commuted. Michael Collins, the minister of finance in the new government and its most effective military organizer, begun mobilizing the IRA for war. In January 1919, the killing of two members of the Royal Irish Constabulary (RIC), the main instrument of British power in Ireland, marked the beginning of the hostilities, which were to last for two and a half years.

The RIC experienced severe difficulties in recruiting sufficient new members (other than from Ulster). Newly demobilized British soldiers were therefore brought over from England, and by virtue of their distinctive uniforms became known as the **Black and Tans**. The Irish Republicans, fighting on home territory, were well able to hold their own in guerrilla fighting across the country, while the Black and Tans acquired an infamous reputation which endures.

The **Government of Ireland Act** of 1920 created separate parliaments for "Northern Ireland" (Derry, Antrim, Fermanagh, Down, Tyrone and Armagh) and "Southern Ireland" (the 26 counties of the present-day Republic), to remain under the nominal authority of the British Crown. Elections were held for the two bodies in 1921, but the members elected to the Southern Parliament constituted themselves instead as the **Dáil Éireann**, with De Valera as their president. With the Protestants of Ulster still firmly pledged to the Union, and the fighting at a stalemate, a negotiated settlement seemed the only way out. A truce was called in July 1921 and De Valera sent emissaries to London, including Arthur Griffith and Michael Collins, to negotiate a treaty. Lloyd George persuaded them to agree to peace terms based on the partition of the island along the terms of the Government of Ireland Act. The 26 southern counties would become not a republic but an independent nation within the Britsih Commonwealth – the Irish Free State. The northern border, Lloyd George suggested, would be so small as to preclude the North from being a viable entity, thus bringing about eventual unity. The alternative to the treaty was, he said, "immediate and terrible war".

CIVIL WAR

The **Anglo-Irish Treaty** was signed in London on December 6, 1921, and hailed by Lloyd George as "one of the greatest days in the history of the British Empire". A provisional government was formed in Ireland in January 1922, pending elections. The link with Britain had been broken at last – but not completely or cleanly enough for a militant minority in Ireland. During the negotiations, Griffith and Collins in London and De Valera in Dublin had failed to agree a clear line on an acceptable outcome. On the negotiator's return, De Valera rejected the treaty as it veered too far from the Republican ideal. He resigned from office and left the Dáil; by July he and his military supporters had plunged Ireland into a squalid and economically devastating **civil war**.

Men who had been fighting alongside each other the year before were now pitched into a bitter conflict: the "Free Staters" who supported the Treaty against the Republicans who could not. In the North, the understandably alarmed Protestant community created the Ulster Special Constabulary, including the "**B Specials**" drawn from Carson's Ulster Volunteers, ostensibly to control the rioting which persistently broke out in response to events south of the border.

De Valera and his supporters were eventually forced to capitulate in May 1923; as he put it, "military victory must be allowed to rest for the moment with those who have destroyed the Republic".

THE IRISH FREE STATE

With the death of Michael Collins and Arthur Griffith during the civil war, the leadership of the Irish Free State fell to William T. Cosgrave, and finally in the summer of 1923 the new government got on with the business of building Ireland as an independent nation. A civil service was set up, along with a police force and the hydroelectric scheme on the River Shannon, which was to lead to the establishment of the ESB (Electricity Supply Board).

Meanwhile Eamonn de Valera, still an important political force, abandoned Sinn Féin's post-civil war policy of boycotting the Dáil to form his own political party in 1926. This took the explicitly mythological name of **Fianna Fáil** (Soldiers of Destiny) and was victorious in the 1932 general election. Under de Valera other state bodies were set up, including *Coras Iompair Éireann* (road and rail transport), *Aer Lingus* (air transport) and *Bord na Mona* (peat production). In 1933 the rival

Fine Gael (Tribes of Gaels) party was founded. The recession of the 1930s was made considerably worse for Ireland by the **Economic War**. De Valera had withheld repayments to England of loans made to tenants to buy their holdings; the British responded by imposing heavy duties on Irish goods.

In 1938 a new **constitution** came into effect, which finally declared Ireland's complete independence by renouncing British sovereignty. The Free State, under the new name of **Éire**, was to be governed by a two-chamber parliament (the Dáil and the Seanad), with a president (the *Uachtarán*), and a prime minister (the *Taoiseach*).

Ireland remained officially neutral during World War II, although considerable informal help was given to the Allies. De Valera, on the other hand, was the only government leader in the world to offer his commiserations – to a Nazi German minister in Dublin – on the suicide of Adolf Hitler.

THE REPUBLIC

It took the Republic (which finally came into being in 1949) twenty years to recover from the economic stagnation brought on by the war. Vast numbers of people, disproportionately drawn from among the young and talented, moved across to fill Britain's labour shortage. Not until a break was made with the past, with the accession to the premiership in 1959 of the vigorous and expansionist **Sean Lemass**, was a sufficient level of prosperity achieved to slow down the process of chronic emigration. Foreign enterprises began investing heavily in Ireland, unemployment fell by a third, and the way was paved for the country's successful application to join the European Economic Community in 1972. The immediate benefits were enjoyed by those employed in agriculture (20 percent of the working population), although Irish fishing waters had now to be shared with other EEC members.

Ireland's and Britain's membership of the **EEC** did not, however, bring the Republic and Northern Ireland closer together. Their membership was made official on January 22, 1972; eight days later came Bloody Sunday (see p.580), and on February 2 the British Embassy in Dublin was destroyed by an angry mob.

The international recession hit Ireland very severely in the 1980s. Emigration rocketed once again and unemployment remained consistently high. Referendums on abortion in 1983 and divorce in 1986 (both remained illegal) reflected the Catholic Church's considerable influence.

CHARLES HAUGHEY

The 1987 general election, fought principally on the issues of taxation and unemployment, resulted in accession to power of the Fianna Fáil party, led by the resilient and wily **Charles Haughey**. In the summer of 1989, Mr Haughey called another election with the intention of increasing his majority. The result, however, was a Fianna Fáil/Progressive Democrat alliance, in which Haughey's hold on power always seemed tenuous.

The presidential election of 1991 yielded a surprise result when the feminist lawyer **Mary Robinson**, an independent candidate supported by Labour and Workers' parties, was elected. Some in Haughey's party (and outside) accused the *Taoiseach* of sabotaging the campaign of his own party's candidate, Brian Lenihan (an old rival), but whatever the causes of her success, there can be no doubt that the president has breathed new life into the office and into Irish politics in general: as a woman, and as a representative of causes outside the old two-party stalemate. In particular, her election gave hope to many that a new era of greater integrity and **liberalism** in politics, and perhaps some easing of positions on the intractable problems of the North, was about to dawn.

Early in 1992 Charles Haughey, whose government was weighed down by constant (though unproven) allegations of financial mismanagement and even corruption, resigned. The final straw came when Sean Doherty, speaker of the Seanad and a former minister under Haughey, claimed that he personally had delivered tapes of tapped phone calls, made by journalists unfriendly to Fianna Fáil, to Mr Haughey in 1982. Although Haughey denied any knowledge of such tapes, the threat of his coalition falling apart finally forced him to resign.

ALBERT REYNOLDS AND JOHN BRUTON

The new prime minister, **Albert Reynolds**, took over the leadership of a seemingly exhausted Fianna Fáil party. His downfall, however, less than three years later, was due

to a moral issue – as so often in Irish politics. Reynolds's years as prime minister were plagued by scandal and the powerful influence of the Church in public and political life. An early case was that of the fourteen-year-old rape victim whom the Irish High Court at first refused to allow to go to Britain to seek an abortion (see "Women in Ireland", p.582). In May 1992 came the dramatic confessions of an American woman, former lover of Dr Eamonn Casey, the Bishop of Galway, who had apparently been using church funds to bring up his teenage son. Then in 1993 it emerged that warrants from Belfast for the extradition of the paedophile priest Father Brendan Smyth had been ignored for several months. The government – under pressure from the Church – continued to cover up the scandal, but in November 1994, after questions in the Dáil, the prime minister's part in the affair came to light and he was forced to resign. It didn't help that at the same time a 68-year-old priest, Liam Cosgrave, died in a Dublin gay sauna club; this spate of clerical scandals caused disarray among Irish Catholics and would appear to have irrevocably undermined the Church's authority on moral issues.

At the time of his resignation Fianna Fáil had already been forced into coalition with the Labour Party. This continued for a month, with a new leader, Bertie A'Hearne, but further revelations about Reynolds forced the Labour leader **Dick Spring** to resign. In early 1995, a new coalition between Labour and **Fine Gael** was established without elections, and **John Bruton** became the new *Taoiseach*, with Spring as the deputy prime minister.

Today the major issue in Irish politics is the peace process in Northern Ireland (see p.581). However, for most people south of the border the power politics of that issue come second to domestic concerns – particularly the drama of the divorce referendum of 1995, which resulted in the slenderest of yes-majorities (50.3 percent; also see "Women in Ireland"), and the constant bickering over how EU funds are distributed in the battle to reduce unemployment and strengthen Ireland's standing as a modern European nation.

Despite the continuing high level of unemployment – the country suffers the Europe-wide malaise of zero employment growth – Ireland's image abroad and social reality are changing.

For one, the Irish economy is getting stronger. The Republic has one of the highest growth rates in Europe, and looks set to close the gap in gross national product per capita with the UK in the next decade. The Republic is also a conspicuously **young country**. With 28 percent of the population under the age of sixteen (the European average is 19 percent), Ireland has continued to invest strongly in education, with the result that, in world terms, it runs second only to Japan in the proportion of young workers with degrees in science and engineering.

Inevitably the youthfulness and economic success of the country have affected public debates; however, the shift towards more liberal attitudes, and Ireland's efforts to portray itself as modern and progressive, are still underpinned by hard-line conservative forces – most obviously the Church. Measures of this are the fact that abortion services remain outlawed (although information on services is legal) and the narrowness of the yes vote in the divorce referendum. In the contest between an introverted, authoritarian Ireland and a more outward-looking, liberalizing Ireland, there will be many more such battles.

NORTHERN IRELAND FROM 1921

On June 22, 1921, the new political entity of Northern Ireland came into existence with the opening of the **Northern Irish Parliament** in Belfast's City Hall. In order to understand the present situation in the North it is necessary to grasp the political background to this development. Since the settlements of the seventeenth century, the Protestant descendants of the settlers had been concentrated in the northern part of the island; they rarely intermarried with the local people or assimilated into the native culture, feeling both superior to and threatened by the Catholics, who formed the vast majority of the population of Ireland as a whole. The economically dominant group in the northern counties was essentially Protestant, and when an industrial base developed in this part of the island, the prosperity of the region was inextricably tied to the trading power of Britain. In negotiating for their exclusion from the new Irish state, Carson and the Unionist Council decided to accept just six counties of Ulster out of a possible nine, because only in this way could a safe Protestant majority be guaranteed. Thus Westminster gave political power into the hands of those whose pro-British sympathies were certain.

The Unionists were not slow to exploit their supremacy: a Protestant police force and military were set up, and "gerrymandering" (the redrawing of boundary lines in order to control the outcome of elections) was commonplace, so securing Protestant control even in areas with Catholic majorities. Thus Derry City, with a two-thirds Catholic majority, returned a two-thirds Protestant council. Nothing was done to rectify the situation for several decades. The Catholic community was to benefit from the British welfare state, but they were discriminated against in innumerable ways, most notoriously in jobs and also in housing, an area controlled by Protestant local authorities.

CIVIL RIGHTS

In 1967, inspired by the civil rights movement in America, the Northern Irish **Civil Rights Movement** was born, a nonsectarian organization demanding equality of rights for all. Massively supported by the Catholic community, the campaign led to huge protest marches, some of which were viciously attacked by Loyalist mobs. The **RUC** (Royal Ulster Constabulary) rarely intervened, and when they did take action, it was generally not to protect the Catholics. The Apprentice Boys' march of 1969 proved to be the flashpoint. This triumphal procession, commemorating the city's siege in 1689 (see p.501), annually passes through Derry's Catholic areas. The 1969 march provoked rioting that ended in the Catholic community barricading themselves in and Jack Lynch, the Irish prime minister, mobilizing Irish troops and setting up field hospitals on the border.

On August 14, British troops were sent to Derry to protect the besieged minority, and at first they were welcomed by the Catholics, who were relieved to see the troops pushing back the RUC and B Specials. Belief in the neutrality of the British army did not last long, however. Escalating violence between the two communities across the North forced the army into a more interventionist role, but confusion arose as to whether **Stormont** (the Northern Parliament) or Westminster was giving the orders. Before long the army was acting not as a protective force but as a retaliatory one, and it was clear that retaliation against the

Catholics was far harsher than measures taken against the Protestants. With the Catholics again vulnerable, the resurgent IRA quickly assumed the role of defenders of the ghetto areas of Derry and Belfast. Within a few months the **Provisional IRA**, now stronger than the less militant **Official** wing of the organization, had launched an intensive bombing and shooting campaign across the North.

At the request of Brian Faulkner, prime minister of Northern Ireland, **internment without trial** was introduced in 1971, a measure which was used as an indiscriminate weapon against the minority population. Then, on Sunday, January 30, 1972, thirteen unarmed civil rights demonstrators were shot dead by British paratroopers in Derry, an event that shocked the world and was to become known as **Bloody Sunday**. The Irish government declared February 2 a national day of mourning; on the same day an angry crowd in Dublin burned down the British Embassy. Stormont was suspended and direct rule from Westminster imposed.

POWER SHARING AND ITS AFTERMATH

In 1973 a conference was held at **Sunningdale** between representatives of the British and Irish governments and both sections of the community in Northern Ireland, a meeting that led to the creation of a power-sharing executive representing both Unionists and Nationalists. An elected executive took office in November 1973, but in May of the next year the United Ulster Unionist Council responded by organizing a massive strike which, enforced by the roadblocks of the UDA (Ulster Defence Association), crippled the power stations and other essential services run by a strongly Unionist workforce. In the same week as the strike, three car bombs planted by the UDA exploded in Dublin, without warning, at rush hour – 33 people were killed, the highest death toll since 1969. By the end of the month, the Sunningdale executive – the first ever to have Catholic representation – was disbanded, and direct rule from Westminster has continued to the present day.

Almost immediately a **bombing campaign** was launched in Britain by the IRA, aimed at destabilizing the government by provoking public revulsion. Twenty-one people were killed in a pub bombing in **Birmingham** in

1974, and in the same month seven people died in simultaneous pub bombings in Woolwich and **Guildford**. The British response was to introduce the **Prevention of Terrorism Act**, permitting lengthy detention without charge. Four people were arrested for the Guildford bombings and convicted on the basis of confessions which even at the time were thought by many people to be unreliable. After fifteen years of imprisonment, all four were released when the judiciary finally conceded, with no hint of regret for the injustice, that they were indeed innocent. Six Irish people were given life sentences for the Birmingham attack, and their convictions, too, were finally overthrown in 1991.

In 1976 Special Category Status was abolished for future prisoners in Northern Ireland (previously those arrested for offences connected with what had become known as The Troubles enjoyed the status of political prisoners), and when Republican prisoners refused to wear prison uniforms in accordance with their change in status, prisoners were locked naked in their cells in Long Kesh – the beginning of the famous **"blanket protest"** (see p.511). In 1978 Britain was found guilty by the European Court of Human Rights of "inhuman and degrading treatment" of Republican prisoners. Soon afterwards in Northern Ireland the "dirty protest" began in Long Kesh and Armagh women's prison, with Republican prisoners forcing the issue of political status by refusing to wear criminal uniform or slop out their cells. In late 1980 a hunger strike for the same demands was called off when one of the strikers was close to death. The following March a **hunger strike** was begun by **Bobby Sands**, who on April 11 was elected as MP for Fermanagh and South Tyrone. By the day of his election, nine other Republicans had joined the hunger strike. All ten died, an outcome that brought widespread condemnation of British intransigence.

THE ANGLO-IRISH AGREEMENT AND THE DOWNING STREET DECLARATION

The year 1982 saw the British government make a timid attempt to break the impasse, introducing the **Northern Ireland Assembly**, a power-sharing body with some legislative but no executive powers. It was boycotted by the Nationalists, and survived only until 1985, by which time the final stages had been reached in the negotiations over the **Anglo-Irish Agreement**. Largely drafted by John Hume, the leader of the moderate Nationalist SDLP, and signed in 1986, it instituted official cooperation between Dublin and Westminster on security and other issues, and strengthened the consultative part played by Dublin in Northern affairs. Unfortunately, the Agreement was weakened by the non-participation of the Ulster Unionists, who had not been involved in its preparation, in the processes it inaugurated.

The next major step in addressing the stalemate in the North came with the **Downing Street Declaration** of December 1993. Brokered courageously, once again, by John Hume, and issued jointly by the Irish and British premiers, Albert Reynolds and John Major, it signalled a new readiness for dialogue with all sides involved in the Troubles – including Sinn Féin and the IRA. Previously the Republican movement had been psychopaths, godfathers, crypto-fascists, and worse; now, in a remarkable volte-face, they were people who could be reasoned with. They were repeatedly assured of their place at a negotiating table if they embraced the Downing Street Declaration and if the violence stopped.

The Irish government's ban on broadcast of interviews with, or direct statements by, representatives of Sinn Féin, the IRA and other organizations associated with militant Nationalism or militant Loyalism fell due for renewal just a month after the Downing Street Declaration. This ban, which provided the inspiration for a similar, though less restrictive, prohibition in Britain, had been consistently opposed by civil liberties organizations and media professionals, and the government had it under review for months before the Downing Street Declaration. In a rare example of liberal leadership to Britain, the Irish government decided not to renew the ban, and was subsequently followed by the British government.

THE CEASEFIRE AND THE PEACE PROCESS

On August 31, 1994, the IRA declared a "complete cessation" of military activities, followed two months later by a **ceasefire** on the part of the Loyalist paramilitary groups.

However, the round of political negotiations that ensued, this time including Sinn Féin, stumbled on the issue of the decommissioning of arms. The British government insisted that the paramilitary organizations begin to surrender their weapons before all-party peace negotiations could begin in earnest, while other parties – with support from the United States – argued that decommissioning and negotiation should take place in parallel. Such was the desire for peace in the North that even the Ulster Unionists gave some indication that they might agree to the latter plan if constitutional talks were conducted through an elected assembly.

In January 1996 a report on illegal arms in Northern Ireland compiled by the US senator **George Mitchell** concluded that paramilitary groups were most unlikely to decommission arms before the start of negotiations, and instead suggested that all parties should commit themselves to six principles of democracy and non-violence. As a way of breaking the deadlock, Mitchell's suggestions had the advantage of both recognizing the political realities in the North and of committing Sinn Féin, and through it the IRA, to the democratic process for the first time, and to decommissioning arms during, rather than after, peace negotiations. Initial Sinn Féin reactions seemed favourable; but the British prime minister, John Major, responded, in answer to Unionist pressure, by making elections in Northern Ireland a precondition of all-party peace talks.

After eighteen months of ceasefire, during which Sinn Féin expressed growing impatience at what they saw as the British government's stalling tactics on all-party talks, Major's call for elections was followed on February 9 by an IRA bombing near London's Canary Wharf, in which two people were killed and many more injured. The reaction of the British and Irish governments was to cease ministerial-level negotiations with Sinn Féin until such time as the ceasefire was reinstated. At the time of going to press, peace negotiations are proceeding in Northern Ireland – with a date for all-party talks set for summer 1996 – but with Sinn Féin representatives locked out.

WOMEN IN IRELAND

No account of the role of women in Ireland can omit reference to the **Catholic Church**. Doctrinally, the Church has a curious and ambivalent position on women. It unequivocally denies them the priesthood, thereby distancing itself sharply from recent developments in the Anglican Church. In the Catholic liturgy, women are allowed only to assist the celebrant in tasks which the hierarchy glorifies, but which are, in reality, menial. Like the rest of the laity, women are denied any voice in decision- or policy-making. Simultaneously, the Catholic Church promotes the veneration of Mary, virgin mother of Christ, as a model for women, claiming that this degree of veneration elevates the status of all women. It is significant, however, that Mary is wife, mother and faithful follower, but completely asexual. This is seen as an essential aspect both of her complete sinlessness and her complete selflessness.

This role model may also reflect something of the strong position of women in traditional Irish society, which continues almost unchanged in many rural areas. For many Irishwomen, however, it is a barrier to fulfilment: not only do they have to learn to assert and enjoy their sexuality in the face of the Catholic Church's overt prohibition of sexual activity except within the bounds of marriage, but also in the face of their religion's loftiest model – an insidious pressure.

In 1986, the Irish people voted in a referendum on **divorce** legislation: of the 64 percent turnout, 63 percent voted against the legalization of divorce. In November 1995 there was another referendum on the issue, in the run-up to which every political party represented in the Dáil campaigned in favour of lifting the ban. For the Prime Minister, John Bruton, the need for the Republic to be seen as a tolerant and pluralist society gathered urgency in the context of the peace negotiations with Northern Ireland; Unionists would see reaffirmation of the ban on divorce as a reflection of the power of the Catholic Church. Given the strength of the pro-divorce campaign across all the major political parties, the "yes" vote of 50.3 percent in favour of lifting the ban was a surprisingly close-run victory. Significantly the vast majority of rural constituencies voted "no", while city dwellers in Cork and Dublin were strongly in favour. The result, however, clearly indicates that the Republic is in a state of change, and that this will, without question, redefine the status of women. How radical this change will be remains to be seen.

A 1983 referendum inserted a clause into the constitution guaranteeing the equal right of the unborn child to life. **Abortion** remains illegal in Ireland, although in practice some 4500 Irish women cross the Irish Sea every year to seek terminations in Britain. In February 1992, Irish abortion legislation was highlighted by what became known as the **X case**, in which a fourteen-year-old Dublin girl was raped by the father of her best friend and became pregnant. Planning to obtain an abortion for their daughter in England, the girl's parents reported the rape to the police, offering to provide foetal material to help in positive identification of the father. The result was a ruling by the High Court forbidding the girl to travel to Britain for an abortion. With time rapidly running out, the girl's family took the case to the Irish Supreme Court, which, amid calls for another referendum, overturned the High Court ruling. The Supreme Court ruling came as a relief to everyone, including the Church (which had refrained from using the case to take up the anti-abortion issue again), and seemed to open the road for a healthy secularization of Irish society. As a result of the X case a referendum guaranteeing women the right to travel brought a positive result, and the 1995 **Abortion Information**

Act was passed, allowing free circulation of information about legal abortions in other countries.

Contraception is easily available – at least in theory – but there is no free contraceptive. Despite the dangers of AIDS, condoms can only be bought from licensed clinics and chemists: in 1990 the Irish Family Planning Association was fined in a Dublin District Court for selling condoms in the *Virgin Megastore* in central Dublin.

The election of **Mary Robinson** as President in 1991 was an unexpected development in Irish politics. An ex-barrister and expert in European law, she is regarded as progressive and outward-looking. Before becoming President, Robinson headed the Irish single-parent association Cherish. After her appointment she continued to campaign in favour of divorce, and has made a point of drawing media attention to the activities of women's groups, supporting and legitimizing their concerns, and proving a significant role model for women across the Republic. In a country whose political life remains almost entirely dominated by men, and whose major parties, still defined by the antagonisms of the Civil War, range from centre right to far right, the presence of a liberal, female voice at the heart of Irish politics has been a welcome one.

Changes in the status of women have not yet, however, resulted in significant change in the **decision-making areas** of Irish life. Only around 12 percent of seats in the Dáil are held by women. Nor is the record any better in industry – women who succeed in the commercial world tend to make the headlines. In academic life, there are scarcely any female professors; though girls out-achieve boys in school and as college undergraduates, they are outstripped at postgraduate and research level. This issue of the dearth of female representation is often aired in the liberal media, but change is very slow: a government undertaking to fill all state appointments with women until a 40-percent target is reached is proving to be a very long-term aim. As elsewhere, women in Ireland dominate the "caring" professions – teaching, nursing and social work – and make up the bulk of the lowest-paid and temporary workers.

Women's **economic situation** remains weak: in the Republic women in manufacturing earn 40 percent less than men, and while 60 percent of civil service employees are women, only three percent are in management. Equal employment and statutory maternity leave legislation exist on both sides of the border, although in the Republic formal childcare is practically non-existent. Although politics in the North is almost as ossified as in the Republic, the situation for women there is generally a little less repressive: contraception is generally available, although abortions are difficult to obtain. The politicization brought about by the British military presence has led to a more general feminist activism, with a proliferation of women's centres.

ENVIRONMENT AND WILDLIFE

Ireland conjures up images of a romantic wild territory unscarred by human activity – a somewhat rosy picture, but with more than a little truth to it. Genuine wilderness may be scarce, but centuries of economic deprivation have ensured that most of Ireland is a rural landscape in which the only intervention has come from generations of farmers.

IRISH LANDSCAPES AND HABITATS

The topography of Ireland is fairly homogenous: there are few high mountain ranges and most of the centre of the country is covered by a flat boggy plain. And with only four degrees of latitude from north to south, it lacks extremes of weather, the enveloping Atlantic Ocean producing a mild, damp climate. Summers are rarely hot, winters rarely cold, and in parts of the west it rains on two days out of every three.

In these conditions you'd expect to find broad-leaved woodland, but intensive pressure on the landscape during the centuries leading up to the Great Famine of 1845–49 denuded the country of its original tree cover. It has been replaced mostly by a patchwork of small grass fields divided by wild untidy hedgerows – long lines of trees acting as refuges for the former woodland community of plants and animals. (In common with many islands, Ireland

has a limited number of animal species – there are no snakes, no moles and no woodpeckers, for instance.) The small population in Ireland today means that over much of the country the intensity of land use is lower than in many other European countries. Mixed farms are still more common than specialized intensive units. Visitor numbers in the countryside are still small, and it is possible to find long sandy beaches that are completely deserted even in summer.

Natural habitats such as peat bogs, dunes and wetlands still survive here, having all but disappeared elsewhere under the relentless pace of modern development. However, the pressures are growing. The great midland bogs are being rapidly stripped for fuel; mountainsides are disappearing under blankets of exotic conifers; and shoals of dead fish are becoming all too frequent a sight in Irish waterways.

THE COASTS

With over 2000 miles of shoreline and hundreds of islands, there is plenty of variety along the Irish coast. There are spectacular cliffs, especially in the west and southwest, which hold large **bird colonies**. Razorbills, guillemots, kittiwakes, shags and seven different types of gulls are among the commonest species, and a few of the larger colonies hold puffins, gannets and cormorants. After dark, some of the uninhabited islands are filled with the sounds of Manx shearwaters and storm petrels. The best time to see breeding seabirds is in early summer (May & June), but later in the year you can watch large flocks on the move by positioning yourself on a prominent headland. In the right weather conditions, some rare seabirds, such as great shearwaters, which normally feed well offshore, will come within sight of the land. Patient sea-watching from a western headland may also be rewarded with a school of **dolphins** or porpoises or the occasional **whale** feeding in the rich inshore waters.

The remoteness of the western **islands** makes them ideal habitats, and several of their deserted villages are now tenanted only by seabirds. Grey **seals** breed on island beaches and in caves during the autumn months. Due to lack of disturbance, nocturnal animals like otters can be seen here during daylight, hunting for food among rocks and pools.

Beachcombing can be a rewarding experience in the west of Ireland, where the waters of the Gulf Stream may yield up anything from tropical seeds to a massive turtle.

In some counties, notably Donegal, Mayo, Kerry and Wexford, there are extensive **sand dunes**. In summer these are clothed in a profusion of **wild flowers** such as the yellow bird's-foot trefoil and pink sea bindweed. The exotic-looking bee orchid is one of the rarities sometimes to be found in the dunes. The absence of tree cover means few breeding birds, but **cuckoos** are a special feature of Irish sand dunes, as they exploit the nests of the ubiquitous meadow pipits. The **chough**, a comparatively rare crow, breeds extensively on the south and west coasts and can be seen in large flocks feeding in sand dune systems. The low sandy coasts of the northwest, particularly where they adjoin small lakes or marshes, are populated by breeding **waders** such as dunlin and lapwing.

The low coasts, especially on the east and south, are punctuated by **estuaries**, some with vast, lonely mudflats. Despite their bare appearance, below the surface they harbour countless shellfish and other burrowing animals, attracting feeding waders and wildfowl. From October to April the estuaries are alive with the calls of curlews, redshanks, godwits, widgeon, teal and shoveler. Virtually all the pale-bellied brent geese to be seen in Europe are on Irish estuaries in winter, having travelled from their breeding grounds in northern Canada. The estuaries and inlets of the west coast are wider and sandier; at low tide herds of common seals often bask on the sand banks.

LAKELANDS AND GRASSLANDS

Travellers in the midlands and west of Ireland will encounter numerous small **lakes** and reed-fringed **marshes**. High rainfall and poor drainage ensure plentiful surface water, especially in winter, and breeding **water birds** are extremely common as a result. Every waterway has its resident pair of swans, moorhens and herons. The lakes have a unique assemblage of plants and animals, but many of these special habitats have already been drained.

Limestone grassland, a special feature of the west of Ireland, is best exemplified by the **Burren** area in north Clare. Its main attraction

is the wealth of wild flowers, which include a mixture of arctic-alpine species such as the mountain avens and Mediterranean species such as maidenhair fern – all found at or near sea level. Perhaps the most striking feature here is the large amount of bare rock, whose cracks and fissures give shelter to delicate plants.

THE BOGLANDS

Ten thousand years ago, when glaciers and ice sheets had stripped the soil from the Burren and retreated to the north, their melting ice left central Ireland covered by shallow lakes. As time went by, the lakeside vegetation grew, died and partly decomposed, in a cycle which changed these lakes to fens, and then the fens to bogs. Ireland now boasts the finest selection of **peatlands** in Europe, but it's a terrain at risk. At one time there were 850,000 acres of raised bog in the country; by 1974 there were 175,000 acres, and by 1985 that area had shrunk to just 54,000 acres. Ireland's bogs are disappearing at a rate of 8000 acres per year, and it's only recently that environmentalists have secured protection for a few of the finest.

The exploitation of the boglands has been going on for centuries. Dried peat sods have always been used for fuel; the top layer of matted vegetation was once used to insulate thatched roofs; and preserved timbers dug from the bog – some of them 5000 years old – provided stout beams for lintels. The lime-rich marl below the peat was used to fertilize the land. In World War I, sphagnum moss from the bogs was used for wound dressings, and extract of the carnivorous sundew was a traditional remedy for warts.

Because the bog preserves so well, it has provided botanists with a calendar of plant history over the past 9000 years and the archeologist with a wealth of objects: dug-out canoes, gold and silver artefacts, shoes, spears and axe heads, amber beads, wooden vessels and, of course, bodies – in an extraordinarily good state.

The best introduction to this landscape is to visit the **Peatland Interpretation Centre** in Lullymore, County Kildare; nearby is a fine expanse of **fenland** – **Pollardstown Fen**, two miles northeast of Newbridge. To see a **raised bog** of international importance, go to **Mongan Bog** in County Offaly. The bog is part of the Clonmacnois Heritage Zone, which includes one of Ireland's most important monastic sites, situated on the banks of the Shannon. Ask at the tourist office at Clonmacnois about the Shannon Callows, a wetland area of great importance to wildfowl, sadly now threatened by drainage schemes. If you are in this area in late summer and the evening is calm and fine, then go to the bridge in **Banagher** and listen for the corncrakes as they search for mates.

For the finest example of relatively undamaged **blanket bog** you must go to the **Slieve Bloom** Mountains, which straddle the counties of Laois and Offaly. The two mountain roads that divide the range rise to 1300ft, with wonderful views in every direction across the flat plains to the distant horizons of Wicklow, Galway, Roscommon and Waterford.

ENVIRONMENTAL ISSUES

Several of the areas of Ireland renowned for their rugged beauty — Kerry and the Dingle peninsula, Connemara and Donegal — are now the scene of intense **gold prospecting**. The gold finds at Croagh Patrick and Doo Lough (County Mayo) and Cornamona (County Galway) have brought an influx of mining companies. Local communities fear the economic impact of the new mines, which could damage the existing industries of farming, fishing and tourism.

The ecological consequences are a contentious issue as well. Gold mining is generally an activity of arid areas, and it is not clear how the technology will translate to an area of watery landscape with high rainfall. Local populations dependent on surface water for their water supply compound the problem. Of great concern is the risk of cyanide spillage and overflow, and long-term pollution from heavy metals released by mining and milling the ore. A coalition of concerned groups is now trying to raise the money to commission an independent environmental impact assessment (EIA).

Other environmental issues in the Republic include the **drainage of wetlands** and the consequential loss of wildfowl habitat; the **expansion of forestry**, both state and private; and the growth of the **chemical** and **pharmaceutical** industries. Over the past couple of years, attention has turned to the damage being done to the country's **waterways**. A ridiculous situation had evolved whereby it was cheaper for a farmer to empty his tanks, pollute a waterway and pay the statutory fine, than to dispose of his effluent properly. Numerous fish kills were reported, and many rivers were poisoned by effluent from silage pits and slurry tanks. A national outcry led to an increase in fines for such actions, and this, coupled with a campaign to educate the farming community to the effects of pollution, should improve the situation.

Tom Joyce and Richard Nairn

ARCHITECTURE

BEGINNINGS

Although Ireland has a rich heritage of prehistoric remains, little of it can be discussed as "architecture", as the wealth of dolmens, burial chambers and passage graves are too remote to be fully understood in terms of construction, function and use. Irish prehistoric remains do, however, attest to a highly sophisticated culture capable of astounding engineering feats. The passage grave at **Newgrange** stands within a circle of large standing stones – similar to Stonehenge but now believed to be about a thousand years older. On the shortest day of the year, December 21, a shaft of light from the rising sun penetrates the tomb. In other words, the people who constructed this tomb were sufficiently sophisticated to have possessed an annual calendar.

The Bronze Age in Ireland (c. 2000–500 BC) is remembered more for its craft and decorative artistry (jewellery, tools and pottery) than for its buildings. Little is known of domestic structures, which seem to have been constructed of wood and daub. Towards the end of this period a new type of fortified enclosure known as a hillfort began to emerge. The fortress of **Dún Aengus** on the Aran Island of Inishmore is the most impressive piece of **Iron Age** architecture, and dates possibly from the first century AD.

From the fifth century, when the island was Christianized, up to the Viking invasions of the ninth century, Ireland lived in relative peace compared with the rest of Europe. The country was divided into a series of bishoprics, which resulted in a system of scattered monasteries. As with domestic building of this period, the first churches were constructed of wood and daub, none of which has survived. The stone churches you now see when visiting early monastic sites are of a later date. **Early Christian** monastic complexes often included **round towers**, a specifically Irish phenomenon. Sometimes as high as 328ft, these towers were traditionally believed to have functioned as fortresses in times of danger, as the door was several metres off the ground. It now seems that these buildings were used as bell-towers and that the doorways were positioned high in the wall for structural purposes. One of the best-preserved towers is **Devenish**, on an island in the southeast corner of Lower Lough Erne, near Enniskillen, County Fermanagh.

FROM ROMANESQUE TO THE SEVENTEENTH CENTURY

By the twelfth century the Romanesque style, imported from England and continental Europe, had begun to have an effect on Irish ecclesiastical building. **Cormac's Chapel** in Cashel, County Tipperary, erected between 1127 and 1134, is the earliest and best surviving example of an Irish church built in the Romanesque style, although very much a miniature version of its counterparts elsewhere. It was not until this century that Irish church builders stopped using the simple box design in favour of the basilica style, characterized by a nave, side aisles and a round apse at the eastern end. The religious orders such as the Cistercians, Augustinians and Benedictines did much to propagate this change in taste. Monastic settlements such as the one at **Boyle**, County Roscommon, are very European in their layout of a cloister surrounded by church, chapter house and dormitories. A wing of government called the Board of Works is the body now responsible for most of the country's early and medieval remains; although chronically underfunded, it has achieved some major restorations.

By the end of the twelfth century much of Ireland had been brought under the control of the Normans. The **Anglo-Normans,** as they came to be known, introduced to Ireland the mighty **stone castle** of the European tradition.

Good examples of the genre survive throughout the country, for example at **Trim** in County Meath and **Athenry** in County Galway. The Anglo-Normans also introduced the Gothic style to Ireland. In Dublin, both **St Patrick's** and **Christchurch** are good examples of the Early Gothic style.

Fortified dwellings of the fifteenth and sixteenth centuries tended to be smaller than their earlier prototypes. A good **sixteenth-century** example is **Dunguaire**, County Galway, which has been restored and is now open to the public. **Bunratty Castle**, which dates from the middle of the fifteenth century, has also been fully restored and can be visited by the public.

Rothe House, in Kilkenny town, was erected in 1594 and is one of the very few examples of domestic architecture to survive from the period before 1600. It's now open as a museum. Nearly all domestic architecture of the **seventeenth century** has some provision for defence, reflecting the political unrest resulting from a succession of land confiscations, plantations of English settlers and religious suppression. While tower houses were still the favoured domestic building type, towards the end of the century a small number of unfortified, purely domestic houses were built. **Beaulieu**, County Louth, is the best surviving example of this type. Built in red brick, Beaulieu reflects the influence of Dutch prototypes popular in England at this time.

At about the same period, the **vernacular thatched cottage** came into being. These dwellings were usually built of clay with only one or two rooms in total. Windows were small, and whitewash was used both inside and out. As a type it is perfectly suited to the damp Irish climate. Its simple, humble design did, however, reflect a repressive social system based on the rights of the landlord. Often viewed as picturesque by tourists, the thatched cottage has fallen into disuse during the latter half of this century because of these unpleasant connotations.

THE EIGHTEENTH CENTURY

In the 1680s the **Royal Hospital at Kilmainham**, Dublin, was built. Modelled on Les Invalides in Paris, the hospital catered for retired soldiers and consists of ranges around four sides of a courtyard. It is the first great Classical building in Ireland; recently fully restored, it now houses the Irish Museum of Modern Art.

The eighteenth century in Ireland produced an unparalleled spate of building, both public and domestic. The Ascendancy, having consolidated their claim to the lands granted to them in the previous century, began to build unfortified dwellings. A parliament independent of, but subject to, Westminster sat in Dublin, the city often subsequently referred to as the second capital of the Empire. It is still possible to get some idea of the great prosperity and confidence which emanated from this parliament by simply walking round Dublin and looking at the many splendid public buildings and elegant squares. This prosperity and confidence, however, was based on a repressive regime weighted very much in favour of the Protestant Ascendancy. The penal laws, as they were known, sought to prevent Catholics from holding public office, owning property and practising their religion.

In the first half of the century, the **Palladian style** (derived from the work of the sixteenth-century Italian architect Andrea Palladio) was favoured by the Irish ruling classes, as it was by the aristocracy in England. The great **Parliament House** in Dublin (now the *Bank of Ireland*) was built to a design by Sir Edward Lovett Pearce between 1729 and 1739. It is the earliest large-scale Palladian public building in all Ireland or England, and the model, a century later, for the British Museum building in London. Palladianism was also the style favoured for country house architecture in the first half of the century. As a style it was extremely adaptable, producing, on the one hand, splendid houses that bear comparison with any in Europe, such as **Castletown**, County Kildare, or **Russborough**, County Wicklow; and on the other, simpler houses built as much for utility as for ostentation, such as **Hazelwood**, County Sligo, and **Ledwithstown**, County Longford.

Towards the end of the century the **Neoclassical style**, based on Roman and Greek prototypes, became popular. **Marino Casino** just outside Dublin was built by Sir William Chambers for Lord Charlemont during the 1760s. Intended as a country villa, the Casino is one of the most refined architectural creations in the city and is well worth a visit.

Castlecoole, County Fermanagh, is arguably the finest Neoclassical house in Ireland. Designed by James Wyatt, it is now owned by the British National Trust and has recently been lavishly, if controversially, restored – the National Trust's new colour scheme involves a shade that the previous owner, who still lives there, calls "Germolene pink".

Much of Ireland's **Georgian** architecture has disappeared. Thirty years ago Dublin was still one of the most perfectly intact eighteenth-century cities in Europe; today much has been lost (for more on this see opposite). This century has witnessed a decline in the fortunes of the **Anglo-Irish Ascendancy** with the consequent selling-off of estates and **Big Houses**, many of which are now in ruin. Because of their unsavoury associations, many of these houses were destroyed by the people who for so long had been held in check by a political system completely identified with the houses. The Anglo-Irish, and their estates and mansions, were viewed as alien to the country, and since independence in 1922 much has been done to erase their trace. Happily, this situation is now changing and the Anglo-Irish heritage is beginning to be seen as something inherently Irish. A good example of this change can be seen at **Strokestown**, County Roscommon, where an outstanding Palladian house is being carefully restored by a small local garage business. The house is now open to the public.

Surviving eighteenth-century church architecture is not all that common. Rarest of all are eighteenth-century Catholic churches, a notable survivor being the **South Parish Church** in Cork, built in 1766.

THE NINETEENTH CENTURY

In spite of the Act of Union (1801), which dissolved Ireland's independent government, building work flourished throughout the nineteenth century. An increasing number of Irish-born architects enjoyed patronage although, as in the previous century, many English architects also enjoyed considerable Irish practices. The Anglo-Irish Ascendancy, perhaps feeling further isolated from their English contemporaries after Dublin ceased to be a centre of power, embarked on vast building programmes. In 1860, **Temple House**, County Sligo, originally a modest, late-Georgian residence, was turned into an enormous 100-room mansion which is now being run as a guest house.

Throughout the century, and in line with developments in England, the revival of styles as diverse as Gothic, Tudor, Greek and Oriental enjoyed great popularity. Much public architecture was undertaken throughout the country, such as jails, courthouses and buildings to accommodate the fast-developing railway system. With the advent of Catholic emancipation in 1829, church architecture flourished. Although predating emancipation, the **Pro-Cathedral** in Dublin is worth mentioning. Catholic church design usually took as its inspiration Baroque French or Italian models; in the Pro-Cathedral a graceful but severe Greek Revival influence is evident, a style more often associated with large-scale public building. The Victorian period, characterized by an unrestrained eclecticism, flourished all over the country and is particularly evident in much urban public and suburban building.

The **Celtic Revival** was also reflected in architecture, particularly church architecture. Hiberno-Romanesque was the style favoured, and its influence can be seen in **Spiddal Church**, County Galway, and **St Honan's Chapel**, University College Cork.

THE PRESENT

A history of Ireland's twentieth-century architecture is as much about what has been lost as what was built. Any postcolonial country necessarily inherits a complicated relation to its past, and buildings are one of the most tangible reminders of past eras. After Independence in 1922, the country went into a dormancy from which it only began to emerge in the last three decades. The great public buildings of the colonizer continued, unproblematically, to function as intended under the new order. Country house architecture fared badly with only a few hundred period houses left intact (see opposite), and Dublin's elaborate Georgian squares and domestic architecture have been vandalized as much by central government as by the property developers. The eminent English architectural historian Sir John Summerson was employed by the Electricity Supply Board in the 1960s to justify the demolition of a range of Georgian houses on Fitzwilliam Square, Dublin. Sir John said he believed that the interjection of some modern buildings would greatly relieve the monotony of red brick!

With the economic boom of the 1960s, it was inevitable that little attention would be paid to past traditions. Systematic and effective legislation preserving buildings and monuments presupposes a buoyant economy and a sort of uncomplicated approach to the past which hadn't developed. Similarly, modernism had little real effect in Ireland (literature apart), and the conservative complexion of Irish society until fairly recently meant that the manifestation of progressive tendencies in the applied or fine arts was rare. What took place did so without any debate or planning.

This is not to say that nothing notable was built between 1922 and 1960. The dominant influence during this period was **Art Deco**. While a restrained use of the style was invoked to good effect in the construction of institutions such as hospitals, it barely disguised their sombre debt to the workhouses of the mid-nineteenth century.

The relative prosperity of the last three decades has seen a move away from vernacular prototypes, the thatched cottage or isolated two-storey farmhouse, to the more comfortable and easily maintained **bungalow**. Unfortunately, in the absence of strict planning regulations, unchecked bungalow construction has marred the landscape from Kerry to Donegal. Will time ever reconcile them with their environment? In the same way, Dublin is littered with endless examples of retarded modernist building. One of the worst examples of this trend is the **Civic Offices** at Wood Quay. Commonly known as the "bunkers", these offensive structures are doubly horrible in that they were constructed on the most important early Viking archeological site in Europe before it was fully excavated. **Busáras**, the central bus station, is one of a handful of modern Dublin buildings which embraces modernity successfully. The station includes a theatre, an indication perhaps of the relative benevolence of the 1960s. A particularly good example of a juxtaposition of old and modern

buildings can be seen at **New Square** in Trinity College, Dublin.

In the past ten years, the large-scale influx of European funding to Ireland has initiated a building boom similar to that experienced in the country during the eighteenth century. The economic recovery of the country lies, it is officially believed, in the area of tourism, particularly cultural tourism. Almost every county now has its own heritage or interpretative centre. While existing buildings are, for the most part, converted to accommodate these attractions, several new buildings have been constructed. The Office of Public Works are at the forefront of this trend. Several large-scale **interpretative centres** have already been completed by them, including **Dunquin**, County Kerry, and **Ceíde Fields**, County Mayo. Others already initiated include one for the Burren and one to interpret Newgrange, County Meath. Some of these centres have attracted huge criticism because of their siting in environmentally sensitive areas. The standard of architecture of these new buildings is varied, in many cases falling prey to the worst excesses of postmodern magpie architecture.

The marketing of the past in the service of economic recovery has touched every country town. Fake timber shopfronts abound, creating an illusory but gentler version of the past, which has more to do with cultural stereotypes than with the grim realities of the subsistence of the majority of Irish people in the last century. Dublin too has been affected. The inner-city area, known as **Temple Bar**, is presently being developed as Dublin's answer to Paris's Left Bank or London's Covent Garden. The streets have been cobbled and pedestrianized, street sculpture installed, and several cultural institutions have or will be established here. After many centuries on the periphery of Europe, central Dublin will soon look like any other modern European city. Do Irish people run the risk of becoming tourists in their own country?

Luke Dodd

THE ART OF IRELAND

THE STONE, BRONZE AND IRON AGES

Sunrise at the time of the winter solstice on the passage grave at **Newgrange** illuminates the deep recesses of a burial chamber some 6000 years old. At this tomb can be seen the dawn of Irish art. The simple and poorly understood motifs consist of whorls and spirals, zig-zags and rectangles which are cut into the stone in and around this great mound. The most impressive is the decorated entrance stone to the tumulus which is repeated again within. While these are the most impressive survivors of an obviously highly sophisticated culture, the sites have also yielded stone balls and beads as well as some poor contemporary pottery.

The **Bronze Age** in Ireland began around 2000 BC and lasted about 1500 years. Some decorative work is found on stone but the most striking pieces are in the applied arts of gold. The Gleninsheen gorget and the gold-plated lead pendant from the central Bog of Allen are perhaps the finest examples – both can be seen in the National Museum in Dublin. Much surviving bronze work consists of axe heads and the like which, like most prehistoric art from this country, are abstractly decorated.

From the **Iron Age**, with its great fortresses of Dún Aengus on Inishmore and the Grianán of Aileach in Donegal, are a number of fine exam-

ples of carving in stone. These are scattered around the country and take a bit of a hike to get to, but are well worth the effort. Two conjoined figures carved back-to-back at **Boa Island** in County Fermanagh, and the **Tandragee Idol**, which is now in the cathedral in Armagh, are among the best examples of figurative stone art from this period. Another is the three-faced stone in the National Museum. At about this time Celtic linear designs of flowing tendrils typical of the **La Tène** style of Celtic art were becoming more common in Ireland. They can be seen on the well-known **Turoe stone** in County Galway (see p.340). If you only have time to spend in Dublin, then good examples of this style can be seen in the National Museum, where you should look at the **Somerset box lid** (also from Galway) and the so-called **Petrie Crown** in bronze. A fine gold torc or neck ornament in this manner was unearthed in 1896 in Broighter, County Derry, as part of a hoard which included a small but extraordinary model of a boat.

EARLY CHRISTIAN ART

In Ireland, the early Christian era (432–1170 AD) is often described as the **Golden Age**. It reached its pinnacle with justifiably famous manuscripts such as the **Book of Kells.** Although these illuminated texts may be the best known, however, there are other wonderful artefacts – especially those in metal – and the magnificent **High Crosses** will take you to some of the most beautiful parts of the country.

ILLUMINATED MANUSCRIPTS

The first of the surviving books, **the Cathach** (pronounced *Kohok*), from the early seventh century, is a book of psalms that is now in the Royal Irish Academy. The decorative features are confined to the first letters of the paragraphs of Latin text and consist of scrolls and animals. These motifs set the style for the greater books.

The Book of Durrow, written about the same time, is the first of the really great illuminated manuscripts and, together with the Book of Kells, is kept in the Long Room in Trinity College, Dublin. In this book of the Four Gospels the three major stylistic components of spirals, animals and interlacing bands which are typical of the great books can be seen. The last of these, like the dots which surround some of the initial letters in the Cathach, may provide a stylistic link with Coptic or other Middle Eastern sources. Some of the pages, called carpet pages, are given over entirely to ornament or to a depiction of the saint whose gospel follows.

For about 150 years other books were written; some, such as the **Book of Dimma** (also at Trinity College), are in a smaller pocket format designed to be carried around. Similar manuscripts can be found in museums and libraries abroad, reflecting the travels of many of the monks of the period. Saint Columba, for example, spread the Gospels and founded monasteries around Britain and Europe.

But without a doubt the culmination of this art form in Ireland was the **Book of Kells**. This magnificent manuscript, also a copy of the Four Gospels in Latin, is a perfect synthesis of all the motifs and styles which had either been imported or developed locally and which had been used in previous books. Completed about the year 800, it takes its name from the Columban monastery at Kells, County Meath, where it was kept for many years although its precise origin is still a matter of conjecture. If you can see the contemporary Book of St Gall (Library of St Gall), the Book of Lichfield (Lichfield Cathedral) or the Book of Lindisfarne (British Library), which are stylistically similar, then these should whet your appetite. Words without illustrations will do this book no justice and you should really try to see it for yourself.

METALWORK AND JEWELLERY

The style of the books is echoed in metalwork, the most impressive examples of which are the **Ardagh and Derrynaflan chalices**. Some 20cm in height, they are similar in shape, with a rounded cup and a conical base. The ninth-century Derrynaflan Chalice has neither medallions on the bowl nor engravings and is technically less fine than the Ardagh Chalice, which is a century older. But not all was holy art. The bronze **Tara Brooch**, covered with gold and decorated with amber, glass and fine metalwork (c. 700), is perhaps the finest piece of secular metalwork of the period, and clearly related in design to the religious pieces.

As metalworking continued, influences from Romanesque and Viking styles became apparent. The **Crucifixion Plaque** from County Offaly and the magnificent **Cross of Cong** show these influences best. The Cross was made around 1123 and originally contained a chip from the True Cross, pieces of which were in demand as relics. The pope presented one to Turlough O'Connor, then King of Connacht, who had the Cross made as a shrine. It is made of wood covered with gilt bronze, and the arms are decorated with fine gold filigree. There is a central bronze boss into which is set a polished crystal.

HIGH CROSSES

This cross is a useful point at which to introduce another great, but also relatively short-lived, genre of Irish art, the **High Crosses**, which began in this period.

It is in **Ahenny**, County Tipperary, that the prototypes are to be found. The pyramidal base of these massive decorated crosses is surmounted by a cross, the arms of which are joined by a circle. This is the standard format for most subsequent crosses. The figures on the bases are, however, dissimilar to the more native design on the uprights.

The Ahenny crosses, although similar in style, predate the **Scriptural Crosses**, the best of which rank with the finest artistic endeavours on this island. One of the earliest is at **Moone**, County Kildare. The setting is, perhaps, not as picturesque as that of some of the others but the long, narrowly proportioned cross with its almost naive flat figures depicting biblical scenes has an instantly appealing charm.

More striking examples are to be found at the beautiful locations of **Clonmacnois**, County Offaly, and at **Monasterboice**, County Louth, where, in spite of a thousand years of the inclemencies of Irish weather, Eve still tempts Adam, Cain slays Abel and the Magi come to see the newborn Saviour. Others can be seen in **Kells**, County Meath, and also in the north at **Donaghmore** and **Arboe** in County Tyrone. Many of these crosses were carved from local sandstone which has, sadly, perished or faded, but the granite **Castledermot Crosses**, in County Carlow, have done better than many and are also worth a look.

Although production of the scriptural crosses ceased early in the tenth century, crosses were still carved in stone almost two hundred years later. The later style is very different as can be seen in **Dysert O'Dea**, County Clare, where the biblical panels have been replaced by large figures on the shaft and the characteristic circle no longer links the arms of the cross.

NORMAN AND MEDIEVAL ART

From the twelfth to the sixteenth centuries, the church remained the premier focus and patron of the arts. The earliest of the stone figure carvings in the period following the Norman invasion of Ireland were of bishops; some of these can be seen at the great Norman cathedrals of **St Patrick** and **Christchurch** in Dublin. Not to be outdone, some Norman knights also had effigies carved of themselves – that of **Strongbow** in Christchurch is one of the best.

There are fine cloister carvings, probably from around 1400, in the important Cistercian monastery at **Jerpoint**, near Thomastown, County Kilkenny. This was the work of the nearby Callan carvers, who were also responsible for the tomb of Piers Fitz Oge Butler in **Kilcooly Abbey**, County Tipperary. The beautiful black marble effigies of Piers Butler and Lady Margaret Fitzgerald, his countess, can be seen in **St Canices Cathedral**, Kilkenny.

The Kilcorban Madonna (thirteenth century) and Saint Catherine carvings in the **Diocesan Museum, Loughrea**, the Saint Molaise of Inishmurray and God the Father from Fethard, County Tipperary, both in the **National Museum**, are worth a look but few other figures in wood have survived. The misericords in **St Mary's Cathedral, Limerick**, are perhaps the finest carvings still extant from this period. While in Limerick try also to see the crosier and mitre in **St John's Cathedral**, as these are the finest religious artefacts of the Middle Ages in Ireland – unfortunately they may not currently be on public view.

Protective shrines or casings in metalwork have survived from the first millennium, and some of these were reworked in medieval style. **The Cathach Shrine**, for example, has work dating from about 1050, but the most impressive panels are possibly fifteenth century. This, the **Breac Maodhóg** (pronounced *Brack Mwee-ogue*) and the **Domhnach Airgid** (*Dow-nock Arriggid*) shrines can be seen in the National Museum.

All are lavishly decorated with bronze or silver gilt illustrations of the Crucifixion, the saints or other religious themes.

SEVENTEENTH- TO NINETEENTH-CENTURY ART

Despite traces of frescoes in the Middle Ages and some portraits from the late sixteenth and seventeenth centuries, Irish painting really only developed from the eighteenth century onwards – the time of Swift and Berkeley. Portraiture in a Neoclassical style became very popular and landscape painting developed alongside this.

Garrett Morphey (1680–1716) may have been the first Irish-born painter and portraitist of stature, but the Antwerp-trained **James Latham** (1696–1747) was more important. His grand subjects, with elegant robes and modestly bejewelled women, were the best portraits of the day. The Englishman Stephen Slaughter, who also worked in Ireland at about this time, produced similarly magnificent pictures of lavishly costumed subjects. **Nathaniel Hone** (1718–84), ancestor of the later Nathaniel Hone and Evie Hone, was a painter of children and a miniaturist of note. His most famous work, *The Conjurer*, is now in the National Gallery, Dublin. This was a satire of Joshua Reynolds's derivative approaches from Old Masters, and was rejected for exhibition by the Royal Academy in London in 1775. Not to be bullied, Hone apparently went off to hold a one-man show instead.

When the Dublin Society's Drawing Schools were founded around 1740 many artists such as **Robert Healy** received training in black-and-white chalk techniques. His work and that of the pastellist **Hugh Hamilton** can be seen in the National Gallery. Hamilton also achieved distinction as a painter in the Neoclassical mode which came into vogue later in the eighteenth century, much of it inspired by antique sculpture. In 1782, **James Barry** (1741–1806) of Cork became Professor of Painting at London's Royal Academy. His *Self Portrait* and *Adam and Eve* in the National Gallery are typical of this style. In yet another example of Anglo-Irish discord he was sacked in 1795 because of altercations with his colleagues, and died in poverty at the age of 65.

The earlier landscapists of the eighteenth century, such as **Robert Carver** and **George**

Barrett (1732–84), were often romantic in flavour, but there was also a Classical school which owes much to the Frenchman Claude Lorraine: both **Thomas Roberts** and **William Ashford** painted in this style. The green and brown foreground, green middle-distance and the lighter, blue background, often with Gothic-style ruins in the distance, are characteristic. Glimpses of contemporary Dublin architecture can be seen in the work of topographical paint-ers such as **James Malton**, whose *Views of Dublin* was drawn in 1790–91.

APPLIED ARTS

Classical and Rococo styles were also seen in the applied arts in the eighteenth century, particularly in stuccowork. **Powerscourt Town House** in Dublin, now an imaginatively designed shopping centre, has a magnificent ceiling by **Michael Stapleton** and staircase by **James McCullagh** and **Michael Reynolds**, which have been decorated with motifs of urns, scrolls and heads. The rich Baroque ceiling of the **Chapel** in the Rotunda Hospital by **Bartholomew Cramillion** is unlike anything else in the country. Life-size figures by the **Francini brothers** and detailed birds and musical instruments by **Robert West** decorate **Newman House** at 85/86 St Stephen's Green.

The extraordinary beauty of these make it all the more poignant that heartless town "planners" and "developers" have allowed the wanton destruction or neglect of many equally fine interiors in Ireland's principal city.

The eighteenth century was also noted for heavy, deep-cut glasswork and for high-quality silverware – some of which, such as three-legged sugar bowls, were made in characteris-tically Irish shapes. Sculpture in Classical and Neoclassical styles can be seen on a number of buildings such as the **Custom House**, **the City Hall** and the **Casino in Marino**, Dublin.

THE NINETEENTH CENTURY

James Arthur O'Connor's (1792–1841) *Homeward Bound* and **Edwin Hayes**'s seascape *The Emigrant Ship* reflect the persis-tence of Classical and Romantic painting into the nineteenth century. **George Petrie**, also distinguished as an antiquarian and music collector, produced many topographical pictures to illustrate travel books which became quite

fashionable for a time. Portraiture continued although the style, less promising than a hundred years before, was sometimes a little sentimental and sweet, as in **Richard Rothwell**'s *The Young Mother's Pastime*.

Daniel Maclise (1808–70), born in Cork, was noted for genre scenes such as *Merry Christmas in the Baron's Hall* and also composed numerous historical works. Filled with sometimes overpowering detail, his *Marriage of Eva and Strongbow*, like **Frederick Burton**'s touching medieval *Meeting on the Turret Stair*, depicts a life of earlier centuries.

The bust, in Classical style, of Mrs Prendergast by **John Foley** (1818–74) shows one aspect of **sculpture** from the Victorian period. He was also responsible for major public monuments to Henry Grattan, Oliver Goldsmith and Edmund Burke now in College Green. There is some fine stuccowork from this time such as in the Hall of Ballyfin House, County Laois, by **Richard Morrison**.

IMPRESSIONISM AND THE TWENTIETH CENTURY

Continental painting of the French Realists influenced the late nineteenth-century landsca-pist **Nathaniel Hone**, the great-grandnephew of his namesake; **Walter Osborne** also shows the mark of the Realist Jules Bastien Lepage. Osborne, however, is better known for more Impressionistic work, such as *Tea in the Garden*, and for his depiction of the grime of the poorer areas of Dublin, as in his *St Patrick's Close*. He was also much in demand as a portraitist. The influence of post-Impressionists can be seen in **Roderic O'Conor**'s *Ferme de Lezaver*, and his *Field of Corn* in the Ulster Museum is reminiscent of Cezanne and even Van Gogh.

William Orpen, a prodigious draughtsman, began at the Metropolitan School of Art at the age of eleven but spent much of his profes-sional life in England. While an instructor at the school he painted some wonderful coastal scenes with figures near Howth. There are some studies dating from just before the 1916 Rising that illustrate dormant feelings for the country which he left. The early period of **John Lavery** of Belfast, like Osborne, shows the influence of Lepage, but in the 1920s he became involved in Irish political life by portraying many of the leading figures of the day, including Carson and Collins. Lady Lavery, his wife, was depicted on Irish paper money until 1976, when the design was changed in favour of motifs of figures from Irish cultural history.

The beginning of the twentieth century in Ireland was an awakening time for poet, playwright and patriot. It is odd that this period, seminal in literary, theatrical and political affairs, never gave birth to a true national school of painting. Social scenes and landscapes were, however, depicted by many, including **Jack B. Yeats** (1871–1957), the brother of W.B. Yeats, **William Conor**, **Seán Keating** and **Paul Henry**. The early social paintings of Yeats, also a fine portraitist, have great character in a strong, rugged style, although his later period was wilder and more expressionistic. Henry's western landscapes of mountains and lakes with their large, flat areas of purple and blue are now almost a formula but are no less beautiful for that. However, his paintings steadfastly ignored events like the food riots of 1910, which happened in his village, preferring to produce a romantic or even utopian view of the Irish landscape.

Abstract art arrived relatively late in Ireland, and the Cubists **Mainie Jellett** and **Evie Hone** were among the most important. Interestingly, early modernism's masculinist avant garde was given little credence in Ireland, leaving space for women like Jellet and Hone to be the main proponents of Irish modernism – as has been recently recognized. Evie Hone was best known as a distinguished member of a school for stained glass – *An Túr Gloine* – founded by the painter Sarah Purser, and her best works include windows in the chapel at Eton College in England, CIE headquarters in O'Connell Street in Dublin, and at St Stanislais College in Tullabeg, County Offaly.

The late **Séamus Murphy** of Cork was a noted stonemason, and active sculptors include **Clíona Cussen** and **Oisín Kelly**, whose *Children of Lir* in Parnell Square, inspired by the Celtic legend, is one of a number of public monuments placed around the capital by the Dublin Corporation. The tradition of religious artwork has been continued by **Imogen Stuart** and **Niall O'Neill**. Abstract painting is represented by **Louis le Brocquy**, among others, and an interesting school of primitives has emerged on the Irish-speaking Tory Island off the coast of Donegal.

Over the past 25 years, partly due to government patronage introduced under Charles Haughey, the visual arts – traditionally never very strong in Ireland – have flourished, with the North running to keep pace. Dublin's Irish Museum of Modern Art (IMMA; opened in 1991), the Douglas Hyde Gallery and commercial galleries like the Kerlin and Green on Red ensure that a steady stream of high-quality contemporary Irish art is constantly on show, including work by artists such as James Coleman, Alice Maher, Shane Cullen and Dorothy Cross. This is backed up around the country by numerous local art centres and galleries such as the Triskell, Cork, and the Model Art Centre, Sligo. In the North, the Orchard Gallery in Derry has a long history of top-quality exhibitions, and the newly opened Ormeau Baths Gallery in Belfast plans an equally strong contemporary Northern Irish programme. Other names to watch out for include John Carson, Brian Connolly, Rita Duffy, Philip Napier and Louise Walsh.

All this activity, underpinned by serious debate in the pages of *Circa* (published in both Dublin and Belfast), augurs well for the future of the visual arts in what remains primarily a literary culture.

Killian Robinson

THE IRISH IN FILM

The current international profile of film-making in Ireland is higher than it has ever been before. Due to financial incentives for foreign filmmakers the level of activity in the country has soared since 1993; the most notable of the recent foreign productions was Mel Gibson's *Braveheart* in 1994. Increased government funding for indigenous filmmakers has spawned a thriving film community, catapulted onto the world stage over the past five years thanks largely to the activities and successes of directors Neil Jordan and Jim Sheridan.

The Irish have always been conscious of the stereotypical images of Irishness in foreign, particularly, American pictures: the country a pastoral idyll, its people a good-humoured mix of priests and nuns, firey redheads and hard-drinking and -fighting men. More recently, however, films made in and about Ireland have started to explore broader themes, reflecting the changing state of Irish society and giving the world a very different image of Irishness: urban, diverse and outward looking.

THE SILENT ERA

The first film was screened in Ireland in 1896; however, it took until 1909 for the first permanent cinema, part owned by James Joyce, to open in Dublin, and until 1910 for film production to begin in earnest – when the Kalem Film Company arrived from the US. Over the next four years its output was prolific, and besides portraying images of Ireland to the first and second generations of the initial great Irish diaspora, it generated interest in and provided training on feature-film production in Ireland. This bore fruit in 1916 when the **Film Company of Ireland** was established. With the twin issues of land ownership and Nationalism occupying the social and political agenda, it was no surprise that the FCI should choose similar subject matter for its films. *Knocknagow* (1917) was a sprawling epic – similar in scale to Griffiths' *Birth of a Nation* – and was effectively a call to arms. Willy Reilly and his *Colleen Bawn* (1920) dealt with the land question once more and also with the more delicate issue of Catholic/Protestant relations.

Another notable film of the silent era was *Irish Destiny* (1925), a well-received portrayal of the events of 1920–22 during the Anglo-Irish War of Independence and the civil war. In the US, Irish directors such as Herbert Brenon and Rex Ingram (whose *The Four Horsemen of the Apocalypse* remains a masterpiece of cinema) were demonstrating their capabilities on generally acclaimed features.

THE 1930s TO THE 1960s

The year 1929 saw the arrival of "**talkies**" in Ireland – with an account of the Irish Catholic Emancipation centenary celebrations – and a drop in the previously high levels of European films on Irish screens. Two protectionist film societies were set up around this time to combat the increased saturation of Irish cinema by British and American pictures; there was widespread concern at the usurping of the Irish language by the "foreign" tongue. Verbal, and in some cases physical, attacks on such films as *Smiling Irish Eyes* and the adaptation of Sean O'Casey's *Juno and the Paycock*, which were perceived in Ireland to be parodying the Irish, were not uncommon. Throughout the 1930s there were calls for state support for an indigenous film industry, but the absence of private investment, production facilities and experienced personnel rendered such a venture too risky. Consequently from the 1930s right up to the late 1960s, the most potent celluloid images of the Irish – images that still hold strong today – were created by Americans.

FORD, FLAHERTY AND DOCUMENTARIES

In the 1930s, Anglo-Irish affairs – already occupying much of Irish literature and playwriting – dominated films made about Ireland, most famously in the work of director **John Ford**. The US-born son of Irish parents, Ford is best remembered for his vast, sweeping westerns. However, ever aware of his roots, he directed a number of silent films aimed at Irish America, as the titles *Mother Machree* and *The Shamrock Handicap* bear out. He also adapted two works of major Irish literary figures: Liam O'Flaherty's civil war novel *The Informer* (1935) and Sean O'Casey's play *The Plough and the Stars* (1936), dealing with the 1916 Rising.

The film for which he is most fondly remembered in Ireland, however, is his 1952 classic **The Quiet Man**. Undoubtedly the pinnacle of Hollywood Irishness, this romantic comedy stars **John Wayne** as a prize fighter who has hung up his gloves and returned to the *auld sod* from the States. Featuring language and characterization that gave rise to the stage-Irish term "Oirish", the film largely concerns itself with Wayne's courtship of the feisty **Maureen O'Hara** and the hostility he encounters from her pugilist brother. With a devoted following, the picture appears with alarming regularity on Irish top-ten lists of films. Moreover, the tradition is still going strong; listen to the painful accents of Tom Cruise in Ron Howard's 1991 "epic" *Far and Away* or Mia Farrow in *Widow's Peak* (1992), and it's clear that even today the stage-Irish accent is mistaken for the real thing in Hollywood.

One of the most impressive films made about and shot in Ireland in the 1930s was American **Robert Flaherty**'s *Man of Aran* (1934), portraying the lives and culture of the Aran Islanders. The director had received international acclaim for his previous anthropological film *Nanook of the North* (1921), about the Eskimo peoples of Newfoundland; however, while *Man of Aran* purported to be a documentary, the film in fact portrayed a way of life that had disappeared from the islands decades before. Although in 1934, Flaherty also made the first Irish-language film – a documentary short, *Oidhche Sheanchais* – it was *Man of Aran* that brought the staged lifestyles of the island community to worldwide audiences. It also brought lasting, justified recognition to

Flaherty as a filmmaker: the whale-hunting sequence, though anachronistic, still possesses the power to impress and excite audiences over sixty years on.

From 1948 up until the establishment of the national television service (RTE) in 1961, there was a great deal of activity in government-supported **documentary filmmaking**, initially arising from ministers' use of the medium to promote their departments. Besides shorts, this period produced two feature documentaries on the emergence of the modern state: *Mise Éire* (*I am Ireland;* 1959) and *Saoirse?* (*Freedom?;* 1961), both directed by George Morrison. These films dealt with the still dominant theme in Irish filmmaking – and in the nation's consciousness: the events from 1916 to 1922. *Mise Éire* explored the Nationalist struggle up to 1918, while *Saoirse?* took up the story from 1918 to the civil war. **Gael Linn**, an organization promoting Irish language and culture, had a prolific output of documentaries during these years, most notably by Morrison, Colm O'Laoghaire and Louis Marcus.

Yet the vast majority of feature films produced in Ireland during the postwar period – among others Carol Reed's *Odd Man Out* (1947) starring James Mason, *Shake Hands With the Devil* (1959) starring Cagney, and John Huston's *Moby Dick* (1956) starring Gregory Peck – were by foreign directors and generally with foreign cast and crew. In those pictures not directly concerned with an Irish subject, the countryside lent a backdrop to a film that could have been shot anywhere.

THE ARDMORE STUDIOS

From 1958 onwards, however, the main attraction for foreign productions was the existence of a national film studios complex at **Ardmore** in Bray, County Wicklow. Set up by the far-sighted then-Minister for Industry and Commerce, Sean Lemass, the studios were geared more towards employment and export value than cultural benefit. Besides providing sound stages for studio shooting, Ardmore was to function as a base for foreign productions, which could make use of location shooting – being only twelve miles from Dublin city and perched at the edge of some of the most spectacular and wild scenery in the country. The studios not only proved successful in bringing in foreigners, it also provided the basic infrastructure – along with RTE – for the subsequent development of Ireland's indigenous filmmaking culture.

EMERGING DIRECTORS AND EARLY SUCCESSES

The late 1960s and early 1970s saw the emergence of a group of **young filmmakers**, some of whom had worked with RTE, where they learned their trade, primarily as cameramen. It was this group – in particular Cathal Black, Joe Comerford, Kieran Hickey, Thaddeus O'Sullivan and Bob Quinn – who broke with the traditional perception of Ireland and the Irish as a pastoral nation, and began instead to show the flawed, more urban-oriented society that was developing. The very nature of Irish society was being questioned in literature, music and politics; film was the next medium to follow.

Joe Comerford's *Withdrawal* (1974) dealt with both mental illness and drug addiction in an uncharacteristically raw manner, and for the first time on Irish screens. Four years later he made *Down the Corner*, which is now recognized as the first urban working-class film shot in Ireland by an Irish director. *Black's Our Boys* (1981) turned out to be another iconoclastic milestone, which, through a combination of documentary and drama, highlighted the inequities of the Christian Brothers' schools in Ireland – "The Brothers" were renowned for their insensitivity and the outbursts of savage brutishness they inflicted on pupils. *Our Boys* was deemed so subversive that it was not broadcast on RTE – one of the backers – until nearly ten years after its completion. **Thaddeus O'Sullivan's** *On a Paving Stone Mounted* (1978) dealt with what had re-emerged to haunt yet another generation: emigration. His tale of the lives of the Irish in London is significant not just for the subject matter but also for the improvisational scope given to the actors.

The availability from 1977 of film funding from the Arts Council was the first overt financial state support for indigenous filmmakers, enabling a number of features to go into production. However, just as the momentum generated by the filmmakers themselves and propelled further by the establishment of the **Irish Film Board** (*Bord Scannán na hÉireann*) in 1980 had begun to gather pace, the Board was suddenly axed in 1987.

In its stead, and as a sop to the film industry, the then-*Taoiseach* Charles Haughey introduced a provision in the 1987 Finance Act, which has since proved of immeasurable value. **Section 35**, an enabling provision for the raising of finance in Ireland for feature films, continues to attract numerous foreign production companies and accounts in large part for the industry's current success.

NEIL JORDAN AND JIM SHERIDAN

Artistically, it has been the work of two directors, Neil Jordan and Jim Sheridan, that has brought Ireland's indigenous filmmaking to the world's attention. In the 1990s, they have received not only international box-office and critical success for their films, but also Academy Awards: Jordan for the script of *The Crying Game* (1992) and Daniel Day-Lewis and Brenda Fricker for best actor and best supporting actress in Sheridan's *My Left Foot* (1990).

Neil Jordan, originally a well-regarded author, had his first entry into film as the screenwriter of Joe Comerford's *Traveller* (1978), Ireland's first "road movie" of sorts, which concerned itself with two under-represented aspects of modern Irish society: the travelling community and the North of Ireland. Over the years, however, Jordan's success has lain more with lower-budget independent films than his forays with major studio pictures (such as *We're No Angels* and *High Spirits*).

The best of his work – stylized films full of surreal touches – includes his acclaimed first feature *Angel* (1981; US title *Danny Boy*), which also takes as its setting the North and which deals with the moral quandaries encountered by a saxophone player Danny (played by Stephen Rea) when, after witnessing the murder of a deaf mute girl, he stumbles from one situation to another, inadvertently leaving a trail of death behind him. Jordan also received considerable box-office and critical success with the tragic love affair *Mona Lisa* (1986), starring Bob Hoskins and Cathy Tyson. After two disastrous studio pictures, Jordan returned to form with *The Miracle* (1990), a beautiful coming-of-age story of a young boy and the relationships he tries to forge with a girl and his estranged mother. His latest film, a biopic of the Irish revolutionary and visionary Michael Collins, stars

Liam Neeson as *The Big Fellow* (due to be released in Britain in autumn 1996).

Jim Sheridan was a theatre director in New York and Dublin before he decided to try directing his first feature in 1989. The end result – *My Left Foot,* the story of the disabled Dublin writer Christy Brown – was a resounding success, and Sheridan went on the next year to direct *The Field*, adapted from John B. Keane's play about the influence of the land over mens' lives, and featuring a towering, Oscar-nominated performance by Richard Harris. Sheridan's finest film to date, however, has been *In the Name of the Father* (1993), for which he himself and three members of his cast (Day-Lewis again, Pete Postlethwaite and Emma Thompson) received Oscar nominations. Based on Gerry Conlon's book, it tells the powerful story of Conlon's time in prison, wrongly jailed for a pub bombing in Birmingham in 1974. The film was attacked for combining elements of two stories – the Guildford Four and the Birmingham Six – to come up with a more "dramatic" composite. However, these allegations appear churlish when viewed in the light of the end result on screen.

In 1993, the day after Neil Jordan won his Oscar, the Irish Film Board was re-established by the visionary Minister for Arts Culture and the *Gaeltacht*, Michael D. Higgins. It has since facilitated the making of feature films by many first-time Irish feature directors, including women such as Trish McAdam (*Snakes and Ladders*) and Mary McGuckian (*Words Upon the Window Pane* and *This Is the Sea*) – going some way to redress the previous dearth of female filmmakers. Other more established directors who have benefited are Pat O'Connor (*Circle of Friends*) and Cathal Black (*Korea*). The re-introduction of the Board, the government's commitment to increasing the level of independent productions on RTE and the continued foreign interest in filmmaking in Ireland, all seem set to assure the industry of further successes. Although it will clearly never be on a par with that of the US industry, filmmaking is now a integral part of modern Ireland's efforts to promote itself both economically and culturally. And with its young *auteurs* keen to express the changing reality of contemporary Irish life, the celluloid notion of the "Oirish" is finally beginning to fade from the screen.

Paul Power

IRISH SOUL

Alan Parker's engaging film "The Commitments" centred on the activities of a young Dublin soul band. Soul bands in the James Brown mode are thin on the ground in Ireland, much less Dublin city, but soul musicians . . . that's another story.

Nothing, it would seem, connects the young urbanites of *The Commitments* to native Irish traditional music culture, but Irish soul singer Van Morrison thinks otherwise. He identifies, rather loosely, "soul" as the essence of Irish and Scottish traditional music.

Native-grown Irish "soul" thrives in the cities, towns and rural fastnesses of the country. Kept alive by a combination of historical, political, and cultural forces, Irish traditional music remains today one of the richest music cultures in the western world. From an exclusively rural pre-industrial base, traditional music culture set down roots not only in the cities and towns of Ireland but also among the large immigrant Irish communities in Britain, North America, and Australia. Mass communications media and international travel have ensured that these dispersed musical communities are linked by an extensive network of festivals, competitions, concerts and informal comings and goings. Long after much traditional music in the industrialized west has ceased to exist in any meaningful way, Irish music continues to represent itself, not as a museum piece but as a living and breathing bridge between the past and the future.

Argument rages as to the authenticity of the current manifestations of traditional music. Some see innovation as the death knell of the tradition; others see renewal and reinterpretation as the only way forward. Time will tell.

COME DANCE WITH ME IN IRELAND

Most of the instrumental music the visitor will hear in Ireland is **dance music**. Originally played in kitchens, barns and at crossroads, for weddings, wakes and seasonal celebrations, it was for centuries the recreational and social expression of Irish people, and nowadays it evokes the same response as it did then – get up on your feet! A vital feature of the music is the demands it makes on the listener to get actively involved. Nothing cripples traditional music faster than polite applause from a seated audience, and in some ways the division between performer and audience is an artificial one that works against the fullest expression of the music. In the loose and convivial setting of the pub session, where a more satisfying range of responses may be employed, enjoyment can get more physical with toe tapping, finger drumming and shoulder shrugging, and of course dancing.

The melody of any dance tune is but bare bones to a traditional musician; it's dependent on performance for flesh, blood and soul. Ornamentation, decoration and embellishments are the way in which the performer breathes life into the music. It's a kind of controlled extemporization in which the player re-creates the tune with every performance. Technical mastery is only half the story, for the skill with which musicians decorate a tune is the measure of their creative powers, and often even accomplished players will play the *settings* of established master players.

Nearly all Irish tunes conform to the same basic structure: two eight-bar sections or *strains*, each of which is played twice to make a 32-bar whole, which is then repeated from the top. In a session one tune is followed without any appreciable break by another couple, and after a brief pause for refreshment the musicians break into another selection of two or three tunes.

The majority of dance tunes are **reels and jigs**, but every musician must be able to play

DANCE TUNES

Until well on into this century the house dance or crossroads dance was the most popular form of entertainment in rural Irish communities. The dances were either group dances now known as "sets", based on quadrilles where two sets of two couples danced facing each other, or solo dances performed by the best dancers in the locality. Rural depopulation, church interference, the commercial dance halls, the radio and the record-player nearly killed the custom off, but over the last ten years the country has witnessed a quite phenomenal revival in "set dancing". The crossroads dances have not reappeared, but increasingly pub venues are making space available for dancers.

The dance tunes are the jigs, reels and hornpipes known to every traditional player. Not every player can play for dancers though, or wants to. In dancing, the dancer and not the piper calls the tune, and playing for dancers requires special skills. The beat must be rock steady, the tunes are played at a slower tempo than is usual in a session, and the player is restrained from excessive improvisation and personal expression. Nonetheless, the recent set-dancing craze has involved more people than ever in an active relationship with traditional music. Sets can be got up with as few as four people (the "half set"), and it's now possible to find set-dancing sessions in pubs all around the country. Anyone who knows the steps is welcome to join in, and if you don't it's always possible to turn up at a local set-dancing class and learn from scratch.

hornpipes, polkas, slides, mazurkas, *scottiches*, and highlands. At the last survey in 1985 the number of jigs, reels and hornpipes in the national repertoire stood at over 6000. Although formal classes exist, the tradition is an oral one, with tunes being handed on from player to player in performance, and the repertoire is constantly changing as new tunes are added and others shed. And the arena in which this takes place is the session.

THE SESSION: MUSIC AND CRACK

The session is the life-blood of traditional music, and with the session goes the associated notion of *crack*. Crack is hard to define and impossible to plan for, and when it happens is obscurely described as being "ninety" or "mighty", as in "there was a mighty session last night in X's and the crack was only ninety". Music, conversation, drink and people combine in mysterious fashion to produce good, or even great, crack.

As a rule sessions take place in **pubs**, the temples of Irish traditional music culture. Many pubs and bars hold pay-on-entrance sessions or gigs (after which a "real" session might happen), but they also cater for musicians who need a place to meet and play informally. In this case the pub owner is usually into the music and not just out to make a fast punt. Under this arrangement the musicians are not paid, but neither are they under any obligation to play, or even to turn up. It's possible to arrive at a pub known for its sessions only to find that on this particular night no one is in playing mood. The venues of sessions are as changeable as their personnel, and situations can change overnight. A change of ownership, a row, or too many crowds can force the musicians out to other meeting places. Nevertheless, summertime is a good time for sessions, particularly in the west of Ireland, and a few enquiries locally will usually yield the necessary intelligence.

At first sight sessions may seem to be rambling, disorganized affairs, but they have an underlying order and etiquette. Musicians generally commandeer a corner of the pub which is then sacred to them. They also reserve the right to invite selected nonplaying friends to join them there. The session is not open to all comers, although it might look that way, and it's not done simply to join in with no form of introduction. More than one session has been abruptly terminated in full flight by the insensitive or inebriated ignoramus insisting on singing *Danny Boy* or banging away inexpertly on the *bodhrán* (Irish frame drum) in the mistaken belief that his or her attentions are welcome. The newcomer will wait to be asked to play, and may well refuse if they consider the other musicians to be of a lower standard than themselves.

Good traditional sessions can feature group playing, solo playing, singing in Irish and English or any combination of these: it all depends on who's in the company and where their musical bias lies. Singers may gang up and keep the musicians from playing or vice versa. The **all-inclusive session** often occurs at festivals during the summer when large numbers of musicians congregate in one place. These can be unforgettable occasions when it seems the music just couldn't get any better and all its treasures are on display.

Originally all this music was unaccompanied and a single fiddler, piper, flute-, whistle- or accordion-player played for the dancers. The single decorated melody line was the norm in playing as in singing, and the music had no rhythmic or harmonic accompaniment. Nowadays there are few traditional musicians who play exclusively solo and unaccompanied, but all good players can and will play solo on occasion. However, western ears are now attuned to playing and singing with a chordal backing, and over the past fifty years this has inevitably found its way into traditional playing and singing.

AIRS AND GROUPS

The instrumental repertoire is, as already described, mainly made up of dance tunes. But there is also a group of instrumental pieces known as *Fonn Mall* – "slow airs" – played without accompaniment and usually to hushed attention. Most of them are laments or the melodies of songs, some of which are of such great age that the words have been lost. The **uilleann pipes** (see instruments box on p.605) are particularly well suited to the performance of airs, as their plaintive tone and ability to perform complex ornaments cleanly allows them to approach the style of *sean nós* singers (see p.604).

Playing airs offers the musician challenging expressive possibilities. Just listen to the great "box" (accordion) player **Tony MacMahon** play *Port na bPucai* (*The Ghosts' Tune*), a haunting and exquisite air supposedly taught to fishermen in the Blasket Sound by fairy musicians at the dead of night. Or listen to **Davy Spillane**, one of the country's younger pipers, reworking the conventions of the slow air in his own composition *Equinox*, which incorporates electric guitar and low whistle. To listen to a solo player, whatever their instrument, is to get close to something old and fundamental in the tradition.

Playing in **groups** or with accompaniment is a prominent feature of traditional music performance today. Most concerts that charge for

JOHNNY DORAN: LAST OF THE TRAVELLING PIPERS

One of the greatest *uilleann* pipers of all time was **Johnny Doran**, who worked as a travelling piper throughout Ireland during the 1930s and '40s, until his untimely death, aged 42. He has had a huge influence over almost every subsequent Irish piper, including all the great modern players such as Davy Spillane, Finbar Furey, and ex-Bothey Band piper Paddy Keenan.

Doran was born into a piping family and grew up in the village of Rathnew, County Wicklow. He moved with his family to Dublin and in his early twenties embarked on the life of a travelling piper, setting out each spring in a horse-drawn caravan to play at crossroad dances, fairs, races and football matches. It was that caravan that caused his death, crushing him after a wall collapsed on its roof; Johnny was left crippled and died two years later, in 1950.

Doran was recognized as one of the greats in his lifetime, and his arrival in a village was treated as a considerable honour. As one writer of the time put it, he was "a man of tremendous personal charisma and capable of sending out a musical pulse which utterly captivated the listener". Although Doran never made a commercial recording, he played on a handful of 78s made by the Comhairle Bhéaloideas Éireann (Irish Folklore Commission) and reissued by them on a cassette, *The Bunch of Keys*.

What's special about Doran's playing is the rhythmic backing that supports the melody. His rhythms are continually varied and masterfully accentuated, and the two recorded versions he left of *Rakish Paddy* reveal the truth that traditional musicians never play the same thing twice. *The Bunch of Keys* also includes recordings of reels, jigs, hornpipes and airs, all played with astonishing virtuosity. As an outdoor player, he played in a legato or open-pipe style, although as the music historian Brendan Breathnach observed, his style was essentially personal: "It always strikes me he was playing for himself, in response to some innner urge or feeling, and he went over and over the tune until he got the whole thing out of his system."

CLANCYS AND DUBLINERS

Singing folk songs to instrumental accompaniment became universally popular in Ireland in the 1960s with the triumphal return from America of **The Clancy Brothers**. The Clancys had taken New York's Carnegie Hall and the networked Ed Sullivan Show by storm, and they were welcomed home to Ireland as conquering heroes. Their heady blend of rousing ballads accompanied by guitar, harmonica, and five-string banjo revitalized a genre of folk song that had been all but scrapped. Hundreds of sound-alike ballad groups decked out in a motley selection of ganseys – The Clancys' hallmark was the Aran sweater – sprang up.

The ballad group fashion eventually petered out, but it had laid the foundations for a revival of interest in popular folk singing that has remained strong. Another great group of this era, one still going strong, is **The Dubliners**. As well as fielding two unique singers, Luke Kelly (who died in 1984) and Ronnie Drew, they boasted two fine instrumentalists: banjoist Barney McKenna and fiddler John Sheehan. Moreover the Dubliners were resolutely urban and their repertoire and approach to performance was gritty, energetic and bawdy. Songwriter Elvis Costello once remarked of North London Irish folk-punk band The Pogues that their music was "the promise of a good time", and this was ever so of the Dubliners.

No surprise then to see the two bands coming together to record one of the best-known and most raucous of folk songs, *The Irish Rover*. This deadly combination produced an explosive single which is crack on vinyl.

entry feature at least two musicians playing together, and frequently more plus a singer or two. One of the most exciting exponents of this style is the band **De Dannan**, which in its heyday featured three women singers who have now all gone on to solo careers in commercial rock: Mary Black, Dolores Keane, and Maura O'Connell. When they were in full song, driven by the band's virtuoso instrumentalists, it was physically impossible for the audience to stay seated as the crack topped the ninety mark. De Dannan carries on the tradition today with two remaining original members, Alec Finn and Frankie Gavin.

Ireland's best-known traditional band, **The Chieftains**, carry on the virtuoso tradition, too. This group was the spearhead of the 1960s' revival of Irish traditional music – indeed, the revival is largely down to the efforts of the group's founder, composer and arranger, **Seán Ó Riada**. Living in the *Gaeltacht* (Irish-speaking area) of Cuil Aodha, renowned for its singers and passionate devotion to music, Ó Riada hit on the idea of ensemble music-making using traditional instruments like the pipes, fiddle and whistle. It was a brilliantly obvious innovation and, over the past three decades, The Chieftains have developed the concept of ensemble playing to the point where it has become universally accepted and adopted. In addition Ó Riada brought his genius for interpretation to bear on choral, liturgical and orchestral music. The choir he founded in the 1960s is still going strong and can be heard every Sunday in the church in Cuil Aodha as well as at sessions and concerts.

A recent newcomer to the ensemble scene is **Sharon Shannon**. Playing furiously energetic dance music, Shannon is a mesmerizing accordion player who can also turn her hand to the fiddle. Having spent a few years playing with **Mike Scott and the Waterboys**, she recently went on the road with her own band. Her first solo album mixed well-known and much- played tunes like *The Silver Spire* and *O'Keefes* with cajun, Swedish, North American, and new material in traditional style. In contrast **Altan**, another bright young band, originally led by fiddler Mairéad Ní Mhaonaigh and flautist Frankie Kennedy (he died in 1995), concentrate on bringing to light little-known traditional material.

These and a handful of other bands are full-time professionals, but much group playing is organized on an ad hoc basis. Many traditional musicians have day jobs and use music to supplement their income. Others seldom if ever get paid for playing. From time to time small tours which cover the traditional music circuit around the country are organized. The line-up depends on who's available and willing to travel at the time.

SEAN NOS AND THE VOCAL TRADITION

It's the **songs in the Irish language** that are at the heart of the music of Ireland, and of these the most important belong to a tradition known as **sean nós**, literally "in the old style". An unaccompanied singing form of great beauty and complexity, it is thought to derive in part from the bardic tradition which died out in the seventeenth century with the demise of the old Gaelic order. It makes great demands on both singer and listener. The former requires the skill to vary the interpretation of each verse by means of subtle changes in tempo, ornamentation, timbre and stress, while the latter needs to possess the knowledge and discrimination to fully appreciate the singer's efforts. To the untutored ear it can easily "sound all the same", with its slightly nasal tone and unemotional manner of performance, but perseverance will lead to great rewards.

Different areas have slightly differing *sean nós* styles: the songs of Connemara, for example, have elaborate melodies that lie within a small vocal range, whereas those from Munster are simpler but have a wider range. The *sean nós* repertoire is made up of long songs which have an allusive and delicate poetic style.

There is a more recent tradition of Irish-language singing which resembles the English-language style. These songs include lullabies, ballads, drinking songs, love songs and nonsense songs.

The majority of Irish people today are English speakers, and much unaccompanied song is in that language. The repertoire, constantly being revised and renewed, contains imported Scottish and English ballads like *Barbara Allen* or *Mattie Groves*, as well as native **compositions in English**: love songs, carols, emigration songs, and rebel songs. There are plenty of singers around to sustain this tradition, and they can frequently be heard at concerts or in the singers' clubs which are a feature of big cities like Dublin and Cork.

In addition the tradition of **informal singing**, especially in pubs, is still widely found in Ireland, despite the gutting of lovely old bars and the abominable karaoke. This kind of music-making blurs the distinction between performer and listener in a most satisfying way. It isn't so much that everybody sings, although there can be group singing; it's more that the absence of artificiality and the spontaneity of the event involves everybody present.

Even younger singers like **Mary Black** or **Liam Ó Maonlai** are accomplished unaccompanied singers. Ó Maonlai in particular is a proficient *sean nós* singer and is as much at home at a traditional session in the west Kerry *Gaeltacht* as at a stadium gig with his pop band, The Hot House Flowers.

SHAMROCK AND ROLL

Since the 1960s Ireland has had an indigenous rock scene which owes little or nothing to traditional music. Indeed it can be difficult to identify anything recognizably Irish – either musical or lyrical – in much Irish rock. Ballad singing, the Irish language, and traditional music in general were associated with values considered narrowly nationalistic and repressive by young people who looked to America and Britain as exemplars of cultural freedom. Both Bono of U2 and Philip Chevron of The Pogues speak of having Irish culture forced down their throats when young and rejecting it, although both have revised their opinions in the meantime and drawn on the ballad tradition in their own work.

While the rock'n'roll revolution was taking place in the 1960s and '70s, however, a revival of interest in traditional music and singing was also happening. Ireland is a small country so it was inevitable that a certain amount of **crossover** took place, although the traffic was mostly in one direction, as rock musicians raided the storehouse of Irishry to lend a Celtic air to their songs.

The most influential figures in blending rock with traditional music, from the 1970s on, have been *bouzouki* and keyboard player **Donal Lunny** and singer **Christy Moore,** the founders of **Planxty**, a band which really changed the way young Irish people looked on the old folk repertoire. Their arrangements of old airs and tunes, and Liam O'Flynn's wonderful *uilleann* piping, opened a lot of ears and inspired a lot of the new Celtic groups of the last two decades.

In 1981 Lunny and Moore made a more radical attempt to fuse traditional and rock music with the launching of **Moving Hearts**. Their objective was to bring traditional music up-to-date by drawing on all the apparatus of rock,

INSTRUMENTS AND PLAYERS

We've included mention of the best instrumentalists on the Irish music scene in this round-up of traditional instruments. If you get the chance to see any of them at the festivals, don't miss it.

The harp

There are mentions of harp playing in Ireland from as early as the eighth century. Indeed, in Irish legend the harp is credited with magical powers and it has become symbolic of the island (as well as of *Guinness*). The old Irish harpers were a musical elite, as court musicians to the Gaelic aristocracy, and had a close acquaintance with the court music of Baroque Europe; the hundred or so surviving tunes by the greatest of eighteenth-century harpers, **O'Carolan**, clearly reflect his regard for the Italian composer Corelli.

The harp these players used was metal-stringed and played with the fingernails. Today's harpers play (with their fingertips) a chromatic, gut-string version, which one of its best exponents, **Maire Ni Chathaisaigh**, describes as "neo-Irish". Maire has been notably successful in adapting dance music for the harp, drawing on her knowledge of and love for the piping tradition to breathe life and passion into her music.

Be warned that there is also a bland, anodyne type of twee Irish music played on a gut-strung instrument, often as accompaniment to ersatz medieval banquets held at tourist locations around the country. About as traditional as green beer, it should be given a wide berth.

Uilleann pipes

"Seven years learning, seven years practising, and seven years playing" is reputedly what it takes to master the *uilleann* (pronounced *illun*) pipes. Perhaps the world's most technically sophisticated bagpipe, it is highly temperamental and difficult to master. The melody is played on a nine-holed chanter with a two-octave range blown by the air from a bag squeezed under the left arm, itself fed by a bellows squeezed under the right elbow. As well as the usual set of drones, the *uilleann* pipes are marked by their possession of a set of regulators, which can be switched on and off to provide chords. In the hands of a master they can provide a sensitive backing for slow airs and an excitingly rhythmic springboard for dance music.

The pipes arrived in Ireland in the early eighteenth century and reached their present form in the 1890s. Taken up by members of the gentry, who became known as "gentlemen pipers", they were also beloved of the Irish tinkers or travellers,

and two different styles evolved: the restrained and delicate **parlour style** exemplified by the late **Seamus Ennis**, and the **traveller style** which, designed as it was to coax money from the pockets of visitors to country fairs, is highly ornamented and even showy.

Some of the most acclaimed musicians of recent years have been pipers: **Seamus Ennis**, **Willie Clancy**, and travellers **Johnny** and **Felix Doran**, all alas now dead. Today **Liam O'Flynn** is regarded as one of the country's foremost practitioners and has pushed forward the possibilities for piping through his association with classical composer Shaun Davey and with the band Planxty. Other contemporary pipers include **Finbar Furey** and **Davy Spillane**, who learned much of his technique from travelling pipers.

The bodhrán

The *bodhrán* is an instrument much in evidence at traditional sessions, and a recent addition to the dance music line-up. It is not universally welcome, partly because it looks like an easy way into playing – and it isn't. The great piper Seamus Ennis, when asked how a *bodhrán* should be played, replied "with a penknife". The *bodhrán* is a frame drum usually made of goatskin and originally associated with "wren boys" or mummers who went out revelling and playing music on Wrens Day (Dec 26). It looks like a large tambourine without jingles and can be played with a small wooden stick or with the back of the hand.

When played well by the likes of famed Galway musician **Johnny "Ringo" MacDonagh**, **Donal Lunny**, **Mel Mercier**, or **Tommy Hayes**, the *bodhrán* sounds wonderful, a sympathetic support to the running rhythms of traditional music. Since it was introduced into mainstream traditional music in the 1960s by the great innovator **Sean Ó Riada**, it has developed by leaps and bounds, and new techniques are constantly being invented. Many traditional ensembles now regard it as de rigueur.

Flutes and whistles

It's the **wooden flute** of a simple type that is used in Irish music, played mostly in a fairly low register with a quiet and confidential tone which means that it's not heard at its best in pub sessions. Played solo by such musicians as **Matt Malloy** or **Desi Wilson**, its clear flow of notes displays a gentler side to the rushing melodies of jigs and reels.

While anyone can get a note, though not necessarily the right one, out of its little cousin the **tin**

continued overleaf

whistle, it can take a long time to develop an embouchure capable of producing a beautiful flute tone, and so piper Finbar Furey has introduced the **low whistle**, which takes the place of the flute when there is no proper flute player around. In the right hands, those of **Packie Byrne** or **Mary Bergin**, for example, the whistle itself is no mean instrument, but it's also suitable for the beginner. If you're interested, make sure you get a D-whistle, as most Irish music is in this key.

Fiddles

The fiddle is popular all over Ireland, and each area has its own particular characteristics: Donegal breeds fiddlers with a smooth melodic approach but lively bowing techniques, whereas the Sligo style, exemplified in the playing of the great **Michael Coleman**, is more elaborate and flamboyant.

The bouzouki

At first sight it might seem odd to include the bouzouki on a list of traditional Irish instruments. Nevertheless, its light but piercing tone makes it eminently suitable both for melodies and providing a restrained chordal backing within an ensemble, and since its introduction to the island by **Johnny Moynihan**, in the late 1960s, and subsequent popularization by **Donal Lunny**, it has taken firm root. In the process it has lost much of its original Greek form, and with its flat back the Irish bouzouki is really closer to a member of the mandolin family. Along with other string instruments like the guitar and banjo, which provide supporting harmonies in a "folky" idiom, bouzoukis crop up at sessions all over the country, and some of the best accompanists are bouzouki players.

---

yet without compromising the folk element. It was a tall order, but they came as close as any Irish band has ever done. The line-up included two pipers, saxophone, bass and lead guitars, electric bouzouki, drums and percussion. Their gigs were memorable events, feasts of exciting music that seemed both familiar and new at the same time. Unfortunately the band was too large to survive financially and folded in 1984. Since then there have been a few reunions which have played to crowds of fans old and new. Their 1985 album, *The Storm*, released after their break-up, is a landmark in its pioneering use of rock and jazz idioms to rethink the harmonic and rhythmic foundations of Irish music.

Davy Spillane, one of the pipers with Moving Hearts, continues the exploration. He tours and records with a rock line-up and worked with Van Morrison on his album *A Sense of Wonder* while still with the Hearts. More recently, he collaborated with Elvis Costello on *Spike the Beloved Entertainer* and with the Senegalese singer Baaba Maal.

Other groups working in the borderlands of rock include **Altan**, **Four Men and a Dog**, **Alias Ron Kavana** and **Déanta**, each of whom maintains a traditional core repertoire, using rock mainly for its image and sound. "Traditional music with balls" is how the Four Men describe their likeably unclassifiable mix, which is one of the most danceable sounds on

the circuit today. They have some great players, too, including Conor Keane on accordion and veteran guitarist Artie McGlynn, whose career takes in the Clancys, Planxty and a spell with top '80s band Patrick Street. Ron Kavana, who is responsible for the recent series of trad reissues on the GlobeStyle Irish label, has a somewhat different approach, combining Irish material and instruments (including pipes) with African and Latin rhythms, and an energetic delivery hailing back to his R&B days.

Clannad are another band who have moved with grace between the trad and pop worlds, and have had a fair amount of success in film music, fusing Irish tradition into an atmospheric sound. Their former singer, **Enya**, has moved further into the rock sphere, with a kind of Gaelic new wave sound.

Most recently – and with huge success, both in Ireland and Britain – **The Saw Doctors** have broken into the pop mainstream with a string of hit songs about Irish village life. The band, a mix of young and old musicians, using fiddles and accordions and other trad instruments, are from the west of Ireland, and their music owes much to their roots there. It also owes a good deal to the showband tradition of Irish pub bands from the 1960s on. Showbands have a pretty dreadful history but the good Doctors could just be the one great exception. Time will tell.

Less obvious, perhaps, is the influence of *sean nós* on Irish rock singers. That voice, primitive and complex at the same time, is as much a part of the Irish tradition as any array of instruments, and it can be heard in the best of the music by **Sinead O'Connor**, **Van Morrison**, **Dolores Ó Riordan** of The Cranberries, and, not least, in the The Pogues' singer, **Shane McGowan**.

The Pogues, a band of London Irish who emerged in the early 1980s playing a chaotic set of "Oirish" standards and rebel songs, deserve special mention in any feature on Irish music. Originally known as Pogue Mahone ("kiss my arse" in Irish), they were iconoclasts to the core, bringing a punk energy to the Irish ballad. They were also blessed with one of the finest Irish songwriters of recent years, Shane McGowan, who captured the casualties and condition of Irish exile in London in a series of superb new ballads.

The Pogues, said fan and producer Elvis Costello, "saved folk from the folkies". Perhaps. Certainly they helped bring a new audience, and a new generation of musicians, back to look at its roots. However, my guess is that the "rock meets traditional" path is a bit of a cul-de-sac, and that what's to be gained and explored, by and large, has been. In its place is something a lot more exciting and broad – the World Music scene. This global ocean is the perfect place for traditional music to flow, picking up and shedding influences along the way, in sessions and at festivals. And the Irish are in poll position to inhabit the world stage in traditional music.

Nuala O'Connor

IRISH LITERATURE

Samuel Beckett, in an interesting turn of phrase, maintained that Irish writers had been "buggered into existence by the English army and the Roman pope". Oscar Wilde sighed to Yeats that "we Irish have done nothing, but we are the greatest talkers since the Greeks". Despite recurrent attempts to keep them separate, politics, religion and literature in Ireland have always been inextricably linked, sometimes in a futile effort to escape from each other. And the suppression of the Irish language did give rise to a fresh and vital use of colloquial English that managed to retain the musical rhythms of the dying tongue. But it's a more complex story than that, and any outline of Ireland's vast canon of very different literatures has to go back a long way.

THE GAELS

Irish writing first appeared in the fifth century AD when monastic settlers brought Classical culture into contact with a Gaelic civilization that had a long and sophisticated oral tradition. Faced with the resistance of the pagan bards, the newcomers set about incorporating the Celtic sagas into the comparatively young system of Christian belief. These ancient tales told of war and famine, madness and love, death and magical rebirth — story sequences from deep in the folk memory. One of the earliest of these, the *Táin Bó Cuailnge*, deals with a rumpus between **Cúchulainn**, a prototypical Celtic superman, and the mighty Queen Medb, over the theft of a prize bull.

Later Irish artists made much of the early tales, sometimes with less than proper reverence; in Beckett's novel *Murphy*, for instance, a character attempts suicide by banging his head repeatedly against the buttocks of the statue of Cúchulainn, which still adorns the lobby of Dublin's GPO. New versions still appear from time to time, Seamus Heaney's translation of the mythical wanderings of the mad king *Sweeney Astray* being particularly brilliant.

Fairy tales from this Celtic era reveal a world of witches, imps and banshees, all jolly-ing around in a Manichaean struggle with the forces of love, wisdom and goodness — which, refreshingly, do not always triumph. Check out Kevin Danaher's *Folk Tales of the Irish Countryside* for full-blooded retellings.

In the eighth century **Fionn Mac Cumhaill** toppled Cúchulainn from the top of the folk hero charts, and stories of his exploits with his posse, the Fianna, began to appear. Fionn was a more disturbing and sophisticated figure, and his antics can be read in various modern translations.

A LITERATURE OF RESISTANCE

The first of many incursions from England took place in the twelfth century, when gangs of Norman adventurers invaded at the invitation of an Irish king. But it wasn't until five centuries later that the English presence found its way into the literature, when the excesses of English rule began finally to provoke an early literature of resistance.

The high point of this Irish-language tradition is the long poem from 1773 by **Eibhlín Dhubh Ní Chonaill** (1748–1800), *Caoineadh Airt Uí Laoghaire* (in English, *A Lament for Art O'Leary*). A traditional *caoineadh* or lament infused with a new political awareness, it deals with the execution of the poet's lover, who had refused to sell his prized white horse to the local redcoat and was therefore hunted down and killed. Even in translation it has a sparse and chilling beauty.

Other marvellous laments include the anonymous *Donal Óg*, Lady Gregory's translation of which was included with cheeky but effective licence in the 1985 John Huston film of Joyce's short story, *The Dead*. But the early written tradition wasn't all tears, and some pieces harked back to a pre-Christian earthiness. One such text from the later Irish-language era is **Brian Merriman**'s satirical *aisling* (vision poem), *Cúirt an Mheán Oíche* (*The Midnight Court*), a trenchant attack on the sexual inadequacy of the Irish male. One translation which preserves the raunch of the original is by Frank O'Connor, in *Kings, Lords and Commons*.

Despite persecution the Irish language persisted well into the last century, and Seán Ó Tuama and Thomas Kinsella's book of translations, *An Duanaire: Poems of the Dispossessed*, records the voices of those marginalized by foreign rule and famine. But thanks to the ineptitude of successive Irish governments, the Irish language is now in an advanced state of decay, with people having to be subsidized to remain in the *Gaeltachts* (Irish-speaking areas). Despite occasional revivals, contemporary Irish-language literature has been almost completely wiped out. Urban Irish schoolchildren are forced into reading **Peig Sayers** (1873–1958), a miserable native of the Blaskets whose sentences usually start with "God between us and all harm" or "Ah sure, life, what can you do?" Arguably the finest of modern Irish-language writers is **Pádraig Ó Conaire** (1883–1928), whose statue stands in Eyre Square, Galway. His *Scothscéalta* reads like Maupassant, capturing the stark cruelty of the Irish landscape and the petty malices of rural life. But unless you want to know about turf cutting, hill farming and getting up at five in the morning to milk your one mangy cow, recent Irish-language literature is generally unrewarding.

THE START OF A LITERARY TRADITION

Between the 1690s and the 1720s the hated penal laws were passed, denying Catholics rights to property, education, political activity and religious practice. British misrule created widespread poverty which devastated the countryside and ravaged the population. It's in this period that **Anglo-Irish literature** began.

One of the most prominent of the early pamphleteers and agitators was **John Toland** (1670–1722), whom the authorities gave the dubious distinction of being the first Irish writer to have his work publicly burned. But the first big-league player arrived in the angry little shape of **Jonathan Swift** (1667–1745), Dean of St Patrick's Cathedral, Dublin. Swift was a cantankerous but basically compassionate man who used his pen to expose viciousness, hypocrisy and corruption whenever he saw it, which in eighteenth-century Dublin was pretty often. In one of his 75 pamphlets he proposed that the children of the poor should be cooked to feed the rich, thereby getting rid of poverty and increasing affluence. His masterpiece is *Gulliver's Travels* (1726), a satire as terrifying now as it ever was. Following a life of unrequited love he died a bitter man, and in his will he left an endowment to build Dublin's first lunatic asylum, adding in a pithy codicil that if

he'd had enough money he would have arranged for a 20ft-high wall to be built around the entire island. He is buried in the vault of St Patrick's, where, as his epitaph says, "Savage indignation can rend his heart no more."

The elegant prose of **Edmund Burke** (1729–97) – graduate of Trinity College, philosopher, journalist and MP – argued for order in all things, decrying the French Revolution for its destruction of humanity's basic need for faith. He is a complex and difficult figure, and his ideas are claimed in Ireland both by the civil-liberties-trampling Right and by elements of the progressive Left.

1780–1880: THE CELTIC REVIVAL

Towards the end of the eighteenth century, a Europe-wide vogue for all things Celtic prompted a renaissance in Irish music and literature. This period also saw the birth of that misty, ineffable Celtic spirit, which was to influence Yeats a century later. A couple of important books appeared, including **Joseph Cooper Walker**'s *Historical Memoirs of the Irish Bards* (1786) and **Edward Bunting**'s *General Collection of Irish Music* (1796).

Dublin at the time of the Act of Union with Britain (1801) had long been a truly European city, frequently visited by French, German and Italian composers. Indeed, Handel's *Messiah* was first performed in Dublin's Fishamble Street. One Irish composer and writer who thrived under the European influence was the harpist **Turlough O'Carolan** (1670–1738), who met and traded riffs with the Italian composer Geminiani.

At the turn of the century a series of Irish harp festivals began, their purpose being to recover the rapidly disappearing ancient music. With their evocation of the bardic tradition they became a focus not just for nifty fingerwork but for political agitation. The harpers continued into the nineteenth century until **Thomas Moore** (1779–1852) finally stole many of their traditional airs, wrote words for them, published them as *Moore's Irish Melodies* and made a lot of money.

The concomitant literary revival entailed a resurrection of the Irish language too, and although few went so far as to learn it, it became a vague symbol of an heroic literary past that implied a fundamentally Nationalist world view. **John Mitchell**'s Fenian movement, provoked by Britain's callous response to the Famine, was at least as influenced by the Celtic Revival as it was by the new revolutionary ideas being imported all the time from Europe. Particularly in their impact on Yeats, the Fenians were to provide a bridge between the heroic past and the demands of modernism. One of their supporters, **James Clarence Mangan** (1803–49), inaugurated in *My Dark Rosaleen* the image of suffering Ireland as a brutalized woman, awaiting defence by a heroic man. In a country where visual and literary imagery of the Virgin Mary is ubiquitous, the symbolism escaped nobody.

THE NINETEENTH-CENTURY NOVEL

The unease generated among the aristocracy by the growth of Irish Nationalism and the Fenian Rebellion of 1848 found expression in novels showing the peasantry plotting away in their cottages against their masters up in the mansion – the "Big House" sub-genre of Anglo-Irish writing, represented by such writers as **Lady Morgan** (1775–1859). Typically, such a book will involve an evil-smelling Irish hoodlum inheriting the mansion and either turning it into a barn or burning it to the ground. *Castle Rackrent* by **Maria Edgeworth** (1776–1849) is one of the few good Big House novels, its craftily resourceful narrator telling the story of the great family's demise with a subtle glee.

The Irish fought back, appropriating the well-made novel for themselves. **Gerald Griffin** (1803–40), **John Banim** (1798–1842), **William Carleton** (1794–1869) and **Charles Lever** (1806–72) emerged as the voice of the new middle class, protesting at the stereotyping of the Irish as savages, and demanding political and economic rights.

This period also sees the entry of the Anglo-Irish into the crisis that would haunt them until their complete demise in the 1920s, as they struggled between the specifically "Anglo" and "Irish" sides of their identity. This kind of angst can be found running throughout the work of **Sir Samuel Ferguson** (1810–86), **Standish O'Grady** (1846–1928), and **Douglas Hyde** (1860–1949), the founder of the Gaelic League (1893) who went on to become Ireland's first president in 1937.

The writing of **E.O. Sommerville** (1858–1949) and **(Violet) Martin Ross** (1861–1915) – cousins and increasingly impoverished daughters of the Ascendancy – is typical of nineteenth-century Anglo-Irish confusion. Their work, such as *Some Recollections and Further Experiences of an Irish RM* (1899) and the powerful novel *The Real Charlotte* (1894), is imbued with a genuine love of Ireland and the ways of the Irish peasantry, yet occasionally there's a chilling sense of things not being quite right. Previously marginalized in the tradition, the peasants now seem to keep intruding, sneaking into the upstairs rooms, interrupting their betters, conspiring behind the bushes in the well-kept gardens. And we see them, in ominous prophecy of things to come, wielding ploughshares and scythes which slowly begin, in the grey light of Galway which the two genteel old ladies capture so well, to look like weapons.

Meanwhile **Bram Stoker** (1847–1912) was busily writing his way into the history books with a novel that would enter modern popular culture in all its forms, from the movies to the comic book. *Dracula* is a wonderful novel, more of a psychological Gothic thriller than a schlock horror bloodbath, and its concerns – the nature of the soul versus the bestial allure of the body, for instance – are curiously Irish. But even this had its political implications. With its pseudo-folkloric style and its pitting of the noble peasants against the aristocratic monster debauching away in his castle, its symbolism is inescapably revolutionary and romantic.

THE STORY OF THE STAGE IRISHMAN

It's one of the delicious twists of fate which seem to beset Irish literary history that the country's most important early dramatist only took up writing by mistake. One evening a young Derry actor named **George Farquhar** was playing a bit part in the duel scene of Dryden's *Indian Emperor* at the Dublin *Smock Alley* theatre when, in a moment of tragic enthusiasm, he accidentally stabbed a fellow actor, almost killing him. Understandably shaken, Farquhar gave up the stage for good and went off to London to write plays instead.

Farquhar (1677–1707) is often credited, if that is the word, with the invention of the stage Irishman, the descendants of whom can still be seen on many of the programmes euphemistically referred to as "situation comedies" on British television. Effusive in his own way, but basically sly, stupid and violent, this stock character stumbled through the dramas of **Steele** (1672–1729), **Chaigneau** (1709–81), **Goldsmith** (1728–74) and **Sheridan** (1751–1816), tugging his forelock, bumping into the furniture and going "bejayzus" at every available moment. In fact Irish stereotypes had existed in the British tradition for many centuries before these dramatists had at least the good sense to make some money out of them. The stage Irishman was brought to his ultimate idiocy by **Dion Boucicault** (1820–90), whose leprechaunic characters seemed to have staggered straight out of the Big House novel and onto the London stage. Boucicault, however, has undergone something of a revival in recent years, with a few clever critics arguing that his unstable and unpredictable dramas were subversive attacks against the version of colonial reality imposed upon Ireland in the nineteenth century.

Boucicault's chum, **George Bernard Shaw** (1856–1950), turned out to be the kind of stage Irishman the English couldn't patronize out of existence. A radical socialist and feminist, he championed all kinds of cranky causes and some very admirable ones, and lived long enough to be a founder member of CND. His cerebral and often polemical plays – of which *Saint Joan* is perhaps the best – have remained a mainstay of theatre repertoire.

Yet even Shaw paled in comparison to the ultimate king of the one-line put-down, **Oscar Wilde** (1856–1900). After a brilliant career at Oxford – during which he lost both his virginity and his Irish accent – Wilde went on to set literary London alight, creating the smiling resentment that would finally destroy him. In *The Picture of Dorian Gray* he expanded on the Gothic tradition of Stoker and Sheridan Le Fanu (1814–73) to explore the fundamental duality of the romantic hero. But it was in his satirical plays, particularly *The Importance of Being Earnest*, that he was at his most acerbic. A brilliant and gentle man, he poured scorn on his critics, openly espoused home rule for Ireland and lived with consummate style until the debacle of his affair with Lord Alfred Douglas. This self-obsessed bimbo persuaded Wilde into a foolish libel action against his thuggish father, the Marquess of Queensbury, which Wilde lost. Immediately afterwards he was arrested for homosexuality, publicly disgraced and privately condemned by his many fair-weather friends. He served two years in prison where he wrote his finest works, *The Ballad of Reading Gaol* and *De Profundis*. In early 1900 Ireland's greatest, and saddest, comedian died alone and distraught in Paris. "I will never live into the new century", he declared. "The English would just not allow it."

IRISH MODERNISM: POETRY AND DRAMA

Shortly before Wilde's death, the myth of the fallen hero had entered the vocabulary of Irish literature with the demise of Charles Stuart Parnell, Protestant hero of the Irish Nationalist community. Savaged from the pulpit and the editorial page for his adulterous involvement with Kitty O'Shea, Parnell had resigned in disgrace, defended by only a few lonely voices in the literary world. He died shortly afterwards, and Irish constitutional politics died with him.

The changed atmosphere of Irish life is caught in the work of **J.M. Synge** (1871–1909) and **George Moore** (1852–1933), who wrestled to accommodate a tradition they now saw rapidly slipping into the hands of the priests. Synge's *The Playboy of the Western World*, with its parricidal hero, is the last and perhaps the most brilliant attempt at a fundamentally English view of Irish peasant life, and was greeted by riots when it opened at *The Abbey*. His friend George Moore identified Catholicism as a life-denying and authoritarian creed, and his extraordinary volume *The Untilled Field* in many ways anticipates much later writers.

Meanwhile the separatist Sinn Féin party made great advances, and in 1916, led by the poet **Pádraig Pearse** (1879–1916) and **James Connolly** (1868–1916), an important socialist figure and powerful writer, there was an armed insurrection in Dublin. It was crushed savagely. Connolly and all the other leaders were court-martialled and shot, thereby becoming heroes overnight, and leading Yeats to observe that everything had been "changed utterly" and that "a terrible beauty" had been born.

William Butler Yeats (1865–1939) is one of the most written-about but most elusive characters in Irish literature. A Protestant aristocrat who argued for Irish independence, he helped found the world's first national theatre, *The Abbey*, before the nation even existed. He wrote early lyrical ballads about gossamer fairies and stunning sunsets until, stricken with desire for the beautiful Maude Gonne, he began reaming out some of the century's greatest works of unrequited love. Much of the work of his middle period lambasts the Dublin middle class for its money-grabbing complacency – *September 1913* is well worth a read if white-lipped rage is your thing. The late period is more problematic, producing a series of spare, lucid but complex meditations on the artist's task, but also some dodgy marching songs for the fascist Blueshirt movement.

Until the 1920s Yeats kept up a friendship with **Sean O'Casey** (1884–1964), who was that rarest of things, a working-class Irish writer. The Dublin slums in which he was born were later immortalized in his trilogy, *Shadow of a Gunman*, *Juno and the Paycock* and *The Plough and the Stars*. As with Synge, O'Casey's first nights were occasions for rioting and were usually attended by more policemen than punters. Indeed one night, in one of the more unusual moments in Irish literary history, Yeats had to lead the coppers' charge into the stalls to break up the fracas. Later he harangued the audience, screeching that the very fact they had broken up his play meant that O'Casey was a genius, and that "this was his apotheosis". O'Casey's journal records that while he smiled nervously and twiddled his thumbs backstage he couldn't wait to get home so that he could look up the word "apotheosis" in the dictionary. He is currently the subject of a misplaced revisionism which condemns his plays as sentimental and preachy.

IRISH MODERNISM: FICTION

As the tide of history turned towards Nationalism and Republicanism, and Yeats wondered glumly whether the tradition would die with the aristocracy, one of the seminal figures of literary modernism was emerging in Dublin. While still a student at the new University College – established in 1908 as a college for Catholic middle-class youth along lines suggested by Cardinal John Henry Newman – **James Joyce** (1882–1941) set himself against the world of politics and religion, and announced that he would become, in his own phrase, "a high priest of art". His subsequent career was to be the epitome of obsessive dedication.

Dubliners, his first book, continued where George Moore had left off, evoking the city as a deathly place, its citizens quietly atrophying in a state of emotional paralysis. *A Portrait of the Artist as a Young Man* is largely autobiographical and deals with Stephen Dedalus's decision to leave Ireland, criticizing the country as a priest-ridden and superstitious dump. After ten years of trying to get it published, Joyce finally had the bad luck to get it printed in 1916, the year of the Easter Rising. Perhaps understandably, lack of patriotism was not fashionable. Joyce was condemned by just about everyone who mattered and quite a few people who didn't.

His next novel, *Ulysses*, came out in 1922, another flashpoint in Irish history, as the new Irish government turned its guns on its former supporters. Modelled on Homer's *Odyssey*, the book follows Stephen Dedalus and Leopold Bloom through one day and one night of Dublin life, recording their experiences with a relish and precision that repulsed the critics, including Virginia Woolf and D.H. Lawrence. The book was widely banned and its self-exiled author was condemned as a pornographer. *Ulysses* is a kaleidoscope of narrative techniques; Joyce's last work, the vast *Finnegan's Wake*, is the only true polyglot novel, a bewitching – and often impenetrable – stew of languages, representing the history of the world as dreamed by its hero, Humphrey Chimpden Earwicker (alias "Here Comes Everybody", "Haveth Childers Everywhere" etc). Critics of different persuasions see it as either the pinnacle of literary modernism or the greatest folly in the history of the novel.

The other great Irish modernist, **Samuel Beckett** (1906–89), emigrated to Paris and became Joyce's secretary in 1932. One writer has remarked that while Joyce tried to include everything in his work Beckett tried to leave everything out, and that's a pretty good summary. Beckett is bleak, pared down, exploring the fundamental paradox of the futility of speech and yet its absolute necessity. A modernist in his devotion to verbal precision, Beckett is on the other hand a dominant figure in what has been termed the postmodern "literature of exhaustion". As he said shortly before his death – "I have never been on my way anywhere, but simply on my way." Despite his reputation for terseness, Beckett was a prolific writer – the best places to start are the trilogy of novels (*Molloy*, *Malone Dies* and *The Unnamable*), and the play *Waiting for Godot*.

The absurdity of **Flann O'Brien** (1912–66) goes a little easier on the desperation. His comic vision of Purgatory, *The Third Policeman*, includes the famous molecular theory, which proposes that excessive riding of a bicycle can lead to the mixing of the molecules of rider and machine – hence a character who is half-man, half-bike. O'Brien's other great book, *At Swim-Two-Birds*, is a weird mélange of mythology and pastiche that plays around with the notion that fictional characters might have a life independent of their creators. Under one of his several pseudonyms, Myles Na Gopaleen (Myles of the Little Horses), he wrote a daily column for the *Irish Times* for many years, and his hilarious journalism is collected in *The Best of Myles* and *Myles Away from Dublin*.

Traditional fiction continued, of course – for instance, **Brinsley MacNamara** (1890–1963) devastatingly portrayed small-town life in *The Valley of the Squinting Windows*. But many writers had moved away from social observation and into a kind of modernist fantasy that had its roots way back in the Celtic twilight. **James Stephens** (1882–1950), a writer with an unjustly insignificant international reputation, used absurdity as a route to high lyricism. His *The Crock of Gold* is a profoundly moving fantasy on the Irish mythological tradition, part fairy story and part post-Joycean satire – in a sense, a precursor of "Magic Realism".

POSTWAR LITERATURE

Ireland in the late 1940s and 1950s suffered severe economic recession and another wave of emigration began. Added to this, the people had in 1937 passed a constitution – still operational today – which enshrined the Catholic Church's teachings in the laws of the land. Intolerance and xenophobia were bolstered by an economic war against Britain and a campaign of state censorship which was truly Stalinist in its vigour. Books which had never been read were snipped, shredded and scorched by committees of pious civil servants.

No history of postwar Irish literature would be complete without at least a mention of *The Bell*, a highly influential but now defunct literary magazine. In its two runs, between 1940 and 1948 and 1950 and 1954, it was a forum for writers like **Frank O'Connor** (1903–1966), **Seán Ó Faoláin** (1900–91) and **Liam O'Flaherty** (1897–1984), all of whom were veterans of the Independence War, and all of whom became outstanding short-story writers. They chronicled the raging betrayal they felt at state censorship and social intolerance – O'Connor's *Guests of the Nation* is perhaps the most eloquent epitaph for Ireland's revolutionary generation, a terrifying tale of the execution of two British soldiers by the IRA that influenced Brendan Behan's *The Hostage* enormously. *The Bell* also opened its pages to writers like **Peadar O'Donnell** (1893–1985), a radical socialist who, only six months before he died, publicly burned his honorary degree from the National University of Ireland on the occasion of a similar honour being conferred on Ronald Reagan.

In an infamous speech President Eamonn de Valera envisaged a new rural Ireland full of "comely maidens dancing at the crossroads and the laughter of athletic youths". But writers such as **Denis Devlin** (1908–59), **Francis Stuart** (1902–90), **Mary Lavin** (b. 1912) and **Brian Moore** (b. 1921) took up the fight for truth against propaganda. Their youths and maidens didn't dance. They were too busy packing their bags, or wandering in bewilderment across the desolate pages of an Ireland that had failed to live up to its possibilities. In their poetry **Austin Clarke** (1896–1974) and **Thomas Kinsella** (b. 1928) mourned the passing of hope into despair and fragmentation.

Patrick Kavanagh (1906–67) was an exception to all the rules. His poetry is almost entirely parochial, celebrating what he called "the spirit-shocking wonder of a black slanting Ulster hill", and his contemplative celebrations of the ordinary made him perhaps Ireland's best-loved poet. But as time went on, the harshness of reality began to press in on his work. His long poem *The Great Hunger* portrays rural Ireland – the same Ireland he had formerly extolled – as physically barren, with the blasted landscape an incisive metaphor for sexual repression. Its publication was widely condemned and the writer was even questioned by the police, an event he discussed with customary venom in his own shortlived journal, *Kavanagh's Weekly*.

The forces of reaction were again about to wage war on Irish literature. O'Casey's anti-clerical play *The Drums of Father Ned* was produced in Dublin in 1955 and received aggressive reviews. Three years later there was a proposal to revive it for the new Dublin Theatre Festival. The Catholic Archbishop of Dublin, John Charles McQuaid, insisted that the plans be dropped, and when the trade unions stepped into the fray on his behalf, he succeeded. The year before, the young director Alan Simpson had been arrested and his entire cast threatened with imprisonment for indecency following the first night in Dublin of Tennessee Williams's play *The Rose Tattoo*. The important novelist **John McGahern** (b. 1935) lost his teaching job in a Catholic school in 1966 following the publication of his second book, *The Dark*, which was immediately banned. It's a marvellous novel, dealing tenderly with adolescence and clerical celibacy.

A more celebrated literary victim – in this case a self-destructive one – was **Brendan Behan**, who died in 1964, only six years after the publication of his first book, *Borstal Boy*. He spent the last years of his life as a minor celebrity, reciting his books into tape recorders in Dublin pubs, drunk and surrounded by equally drunk admirers, some of whom sobered up for long enough to try and save him from becoming the victim of his own myth.

CONTEMPORARY WRITING

It was only in the 1970s that the post-revolutionary climate of repression began to lift, and a sophisticated and largely progressive generation began having their works published. **Seamus Heaney** (b.1939) is the leading light of an unofficial group of Northern Irish poets who combine a sophistication of technique with a self-conscious political commitment. In 1995 Heaney became Ireland's fourth Nobel literary laureate (after Yeats, Shaw and Beckett), and if his latest work doesn't have quite the same fire as the early collections (such as *Death of a Naturalist*, *North* and *Station Island*), he continues to explore the classic Yeatsian dilemma between commitment and aloofness in compelling ways, even as he looks to shrug off the influence of the earlier poet. Heaney's poetical-cum-critical deliberations on his racial and literary lineage

have also earned him a place as personal advisor to President Mary Robinson; while the fact that he is recognized internationally has added fuel to those who like to pay lip-service to the country's wonderful literary heritage – but usually only to the extent that it can be converted into tourist revenue.

John Banville (b.1945) is another writer who prefers to remain at a tangent to the national identity, taking Ireland (when he writes of it at all) as the means rather than the end of his artistic vision. His first book, *Long Lankin*, appeared in 1970, a precocious debut that has been followed by a string of extraordinarily inventive novels.

The *Irish Writers' Co Op* produced novelists such as **Desmond Hogan** (b.1951), **Ronan Sheehan** (b.1953) and **Neil Jordan** (b.1951), the last of whom has gone on to major international success as a film director (see "The Irish in Film", pp.596–99). Jordan's work (much like Banville's), is located firmly within the counter-tradition of the novel coming out of Joyce, which in its turn owed something to the fantastic narratives of the sagas and to the rejection of the traditional novel form – what Joyce saw as its built-in British view of the world. The 1970s also saw the establishment of courageous publishing companies founded by writers, of which Peter Fallon's Gallery, Dermot Bolger's Raven Arts Press, and Steve McDonogh's Brandon are still going from strength to strength.

At the end of the decade **Paul Durcan** (b.1944) emerged as the inheritor of Kavanagh's mantle. He is a quirkily witty and profoundly religious poet, whose work encompasses social issues such as IRA bombings and Ireland's prohibition, until recently, of divorce and continuing ban on abortion, but always addresses them in personal terms.

Other important poets include **Padraic Fiacc** (b.1924), **Richard Murphy** (b.1927), **Michael Hartnett** (b.1934), **Brendan Kennelly** (b.1936), and **Derek Mahon** (b.1941). **Michael Longley** (b.1939) seems doomed always to be cited as the husband of the major revisionist critic Edna Longley, although his poetry is innovative and striking. Two poets having close relations with the US, **Paul Muldoon** (b.1951), born in Mayo but now living in New York, and **John Montague** (b.1929), born in Brooklyn of Irish parents but brought up in Tyrone, explore the relations between different poetic traditions on the island. Even more recently, **Christopher Nolan** (b.1965), a severely disabled writer, has proved to be an amazing talent, employing a rich language reminiscent of Dylan Thomas. His first book of poetry, *Damburst of Dreams*, received great acclaim, and he later won the Whitbread Prize for his autobiographical novel *Under the Eye of the Clock*.

Perhaps the most exciting contemporary verse is been written by minor women writers who, in the absence of civic or political opportunities, have turned to poetry to express their experiences of modern Ireland. Up and down the country poetry groups and workshops turn out collections that deal with the realities of being an Irish daughter, wife, mother, or girlfriend. In this they receive support from established poets such as **Eiléan Ní Chuilleanáin** (b.1942), **Eavan Boland** (b.1944), and **Medbh McGuckian** (b.1950). Boland, especially, has explored the complexities of modern Irish female experience in particularly enabling ways.

Drama has undergone a resurgence too, with Galway's *Druid Theatre* doing groundbreaking reinterpretations of Irish classics under the guidance of its brilliant director Garry Hynes. Roddy Doyle and Paul Mercier's Passion Machine theatre company offers plays about urban working-class experience in the manner of Stephen Berkoff or John Godber. Two other young companies whose work is political and challenging, if more international in scope, are Co-Motion and Rough Magic.

Without doubt, the most successful theatre company and cultural initiative on the island in recent times has been **Field Day**, a Northern-based team founded by Seamus Deane (b.1940), Tom Paulin (b.1949), Brian Friel (b.1929), Seamus Heaney and actor Stephen Rea. As well as being established poets, Deane and Paulin are also insightful critics who from their locations in England and the US continue to do battle with all comers over the rights to Irish literary history. Friel, who turned from short-story writing to the theatre in the 1960s, provided Field Day with their greatest successes, in particular his play about the suppression of the Irish language, *Translations* (1980). However, after giving his best-received work, *Dancing at Lughnasa* (1990), to Dublin's Abbey Theatre, he left the group.

In addition to producing plays the company publishes an excellent series of short cultural and critical essays, perhaps attempting to revive the radical pamphleteering culture of the early eighteenth century. Their most ambitious project was the commissioning and publication in 1991 of the *Field Day Anthology of Irish Writing*, a massive three-volume attempt to encapsulate some of the grandeur of the country's literary heritage. The project ran into trouble, however, when it was seen that women were grossly under-represented at both editorial and authorial levels. A "girls-only" fourth volume is due for publication in 1997, and it is already haunted by accusations of tokenism (for more on *Field Day* see p.507).

Any list of Ireland's innovative theatre writers must include **Tom Murphy** (b.1936) and **Thomas Kilroy** (b.1934), but in the opinion of many the most important dramatist to emerge in the last few decades is **Frank McGuinness** (b.1953). His play *Observe the Sons of Ulster Marching Towards the Somme*, staged in Dublin as talks began on the Anglo-Irish agreement, focuses on the participation of a group of Northern Loyalists in the battle of the Somme. Its imagery exploits the symbolism of the whole Irish tradition, permitting a range of readings, in which the Somme represents the current situation in the North, or the battlefield of the Boyne, or the slaughters of the early sagas. It was his 1987 piece, *Carthaginians*, a play set in his native Derry, which thrust him into the major league of Irish writers. The play found a vocabulary in which to explore ancient Irish themes – the nature of political allegiance, death and resurrection, the relationship between Britain, Ireland and the North, sexuality, religion – in a way that seems to sum up the whole tradition while simultaneously threatening to demolish it. His work provides, if not some hope of unifying the various strands of Ireland's long cultural histories, at least an analysis of what divides them.

The Irish stage has produced few first-rate dramatists in recent years; as McGuinness himself has argued in a recent provocative article, "although the current generation of young Irish playwrights and gifted poets – Paula Meehan, Ciaran Carson, Pat Roran and Cathal O'Searcaigh among others – have continued to appear, it is in the pages of contemporary Irish fiction that the most exciting work is to be found". Over the past decade, writers like Hugo Hamilton, Anne Enright, Eoin McNamee, Ferdia McAnna, Ronan Bennett, Michael O'Loughlin, Glenn Patterson and Robert MacLiam Wilson have begun to turn the accepted version of Irish literary tradition on its head. **Dermot Bolger** (b.1959), as well as being a gifted poet and playwright, has produced hard-hitting yet lyrical novels of contemporary Dublin. **Colm Toibín** (b.1955) has written two deceptively understated novels of Irish experience at home and abroad in *The South* (1990) and *The Heather Blazing* (1992). *The Butcher Boy* (1992) by **Patrick McCabe** (b.1955) won numerous awards as well as being shortlisted for the prestigious Booker Prize, and the grisly comedy of that novel reappeared in even grimmer form in *The Dead School* (1995). Younger writers such as **Joseph O'Connor** (b.1963) and **Emma Donoghue** (b.1969) are typical inasmuch as they work in a number of genres besides the novel. Their writing responds to the new Ireland of sex and drugs and rock 'n' roll in which they grew up, with Donoghue producing in her debut novel *Stir-fry* (1994) perhaps the first happy lesbian love story in Irish fiction.

Without doubt, the most successful of the new generation of novelists has been **Roddy Doyle** (b.1958), a writer who, along with Bolger and others, disdains the critical title of "Northside realist" (referring to the North Side of the River Liffey where most of their work is set). The first two novels of The Barrytown Trilogy, *The Commitments* (1987) and *The Snapper* (1990), have been made into successful films, and after just missing out with the third, *The Van* (1991), Doyle snapped up the Booker Prize in 1993 for *Paddy Clarke Ha Ha Ha*. Doyle's fiction makes deceptively easy reading, while the enormous sales figures for his books must compensate somewhat for the criticism that he merely reproduces modern urban variations on the stage Irishman.

In the work of these novelists, gone are the hackneyed themes of the traditional canon: the Catholic Church, the lure of the land, the repression of sexuality. Gone too is the Joycean aesthetic project to forge the "uncreated conscience" of the Irish race. These writers have nothing in common except a faith in language, a facility for storytelling and a palpable unease with received cultural notions of Irishness, which frequently have much more to do with tourism than art. Irish novels and short stories are beginning to anatomize social change rather than conservatism. Recent anthologies, like Dermot Bolger's Picador Book of *Contemporary Irish Fiction* and Colm Toibín's Irish edition of Bloomsbury's annual review *Soho Square*, reveal an Ireland populated by women as well as men, Protestants as well as Catholics, fervent atheists as well as true believers, gays as well as straights, people who feel British as well as people who feel Irish. People in Ireland may not know exactly who or what they are supposed to be anymore, but a brave and committed generation of new writers is helping dissipate the fear of difference.

Joe O'Connor

BOOKS

Most of the books listed below are in print and in paperback – those that are out of print (o/p) should be easy to track down in second-hand bookshops. Publishers follow each title; first the UK publisher, then the US. Only one publisher is listed if the UK and US publishers are the same. Where books are published in only one of these countries, UK or US precedes the publisher's name.

HISTORY AND POLITICS

John Ardagh, *Ireland and the Irish: Portrait of a Changing Society* (Penguin). Comprehensive and lively, this is an excellent anatomy of Irish society and its efforts to come to terms with the modern world.

Jonathan Bardon, *A History of Ulster* (Blackstaff/Dufour). A comprehensive account from early settlements to the current Troubles.

J.C. Beckett, *The Making of Modern Ireland 1603–1923* (Faber/Trafalgar, o/p). Concise and elegant, this is probably the best introduction to the complexities of Irish history.

David Beresford, *Ten Men Dead* (Grafton/Grove-Atlantic, o/p). Revelatory account of the 1981 hunger strike, using the prison correspondence as its basic material; a powerful refutation of the demonologies of the British press.

Peter Beresford Ellis, *Hell or Connaught* and *The Boyne Water* (Blackstaff/Dufour). Vivid popular histories of Cromwell's rampage and the pivotal Battle of the Boyne.

Terence Brown, *Ireland: A Social and Cultural History 1922–1985* (Fontana/Cornell University Press). Brilliantly perceptive survey of writers' responses to the dog's breakfast made of post-revolutionary Ireland by its leaders.

Tim Pat Coogan, *The Troubles: Ireland's Ordeal 1966–1995 and the Search for Peace* (UK Hutchinson). The former *Irish Press* editor's popular-history writing has many followers. His earlier books on two icons of modern Ireland, *Michael Collins* (UK Arrow) and *De Valera: Long Fellow, Long Shadow* (Arrow/HarperCollins), are essential reading.

Liz Curtis, *Ireland: the Propaganda War* (Pluto/InBook). An unanswerable indictment of the truth-bending of the British media.

Seán Duignan, *One Spin on the Merry-go-round* (UK Blackwater). Government press officer's memoirs, well spiced with insider anecdote, of a turbulent period serving *Taoiseach* Albert Reynolds.

Michael Farrell, *Arming the Protestants: The Formation of the Ulster Special Constabulary and the Royal Ulster Constabulary, 1920–1927* (Pluto/Longwood, o/p). Farrell is a fine journalist and veteran of Northern Ireland's civil rights campaigns. In *Northern Ireland: The Orange State* (Pluto/InBook) he argues, as the title implies, from a Republican standpoint; it's an occasionally tendentious but extremely persuasive political account of the development of Northern Ireland.

Garret FitzGerald, *All in a Life* (UK Gill & Macmillan). The first former *Taoiseach* to write his memoirs has produced an extraordinary book, characteristically frank, and full of detail on the working of government.

Roy Foster, *Modern Ireland 1600–1972* (Penguin). Superb and provocative new book, generally reckoned to be unrivalled in its scholarship and acuity, although it has been criticized for what some feel to be an excessive sympathy towards the Anglo-Irish. Not recommended for beginners.

Gemma Hussey, *Ireland Today: Anatomy of a Changing State* (Penguin). A well-regarded and invaluable source of information on Ireland's changing identity by this ex-government minister.

Robert Kee, *The Green Flag* (Penguin; 3 vols). Scrupulous history of Irish Nationalism from the first plantations to the creation of the Free State. Masterful as narrative and as analysis.

J.J. Lee, *Ireland 1912–1985: Politics and Society* (Cambridge University Press). Stunning new history, that is most provocative and readable in its lengthy final part devoted to the Ireland of today.

F.S.L. Lyons, *Ireland Since the Famine* (UK Fontana). The most complete overview of recent Irish history; either iconoclastic or revisionist, depending on your point of view.

T.W. Moody and F.X. Martin, *The Course of Irish History* (UK Mercier). Shows its age a bit, but still very good on early Irish history.

Conor Cruise O'Brien, *Ancestral Voices: Religion and Nationalism in Ireland* (Poolbeg/ University of Chicago Press); *On the Eve of the Millennium: the Future of Democracy through an Age of Unreason* (Free Press). Essays by the sometimes apocalyptic, always readable and stimulating commentator and former government minister.

Cecil Woodham Smith, *The Great Hunger* (Penguin). Definitive, harrowing history of the Famine.

A.T.Q. Stewart, *The Narrow Ground* (Gregg Revivals/Ashgate). A Unionist overview of the history of the North from 1609 to the 1960s, providing an essential background to the current situation.

Kevin Toolis, *Rebel Hearts: Journeys within the IRA's Soul* (UK Picador). Highly acclaimed and topical account of what makes the IRA tick by this journalist and screenwriter.

GAELIC TALES AND MUSIC

Brendan Behan, *An Giall*; in English, *The Hostage* (Eyre Methuen/Grove-Atlantic). Behan's play is better in Irish, but still pretty good in English. The best work from an overrated writer.

Breandán Breathnach, *Folk Music and Dances of Ireland* (Mercier/Dufour). All the diddley-eye you could want, and in one volume.

Kevin Danaher, *Folk Tales of the Irish Countryside* (US David White Co, o/p). The best volume on fairy and folk tales, recorded with a civil servant's meticulousness and a novelist's literary style.

Myles Dillon, (ed), *Irish Sagas* (Mercier, o/p/ Irish Books & Media o/p). An excellent examination of Cúchulainn, Fionn Mac Cumhaill etc, in literary and socio-psychological terms.

Seamus Heaney, *Buile Suibhne*; in English, *Sweeney Astray* (Faber o/p/Farrar, Straus & Giroux). A modern translation of the ancient Irish saga of the mad king Sweeney.

Thomas Moore, *Irish Melodies*, edited by Seán Ó Faoláin (US Scholarly Resources). All the pret- tied-up tunes Moore stole from the harpers, along with lyrics of mind-numbingly perfect rhythm. Moore is an important historical figure, who expressed the Nationalism of the emerging middle class and brought revolution into the parlour.

Pádraig Ó Conaire, *Finest Stories* (Poolbeg/ Dufour). Ó Conaire's dispassionate eye roams over the cruelties of peasant life.

Tomás Ó Criomhtháin, (sometimes Thomas O'Crohan), *An tOileánach*; in English, *The Islandman* (Oxford University Press). Similar to Ó Conaire but non-fiction and, if possible, even more raw.

Seán Ó Tuama and Thomas Kinsella, *An Duanaire: Poems of the Dispossessed* (Dolmen/ University of Pennsylvania, o/p). Excellent translations of stark Irish-language poems on famine and death. See also Kinsella's translation of one of the earliest sagas, the *Táin Bó Cuailnge* (Baile Átha Cliath, o/p/University of Pennsylvania, o/p).

George Petrie, *The Native Music of Ireland* (Gregg International Books, o/p). One of the most important cultural documents in Irish history.

Mark J. Prendergast, *Irish Rock: History, Roots and Perspectives* (The O'Brien Press, o/p). The only decent book on Irish rock music.

Peig Sayers, *An Old Woman's Reflections* (Oxford University Press). Unfortunately, Sayers's complacent acceptance of her own powerlessness is still held up as an example to Irish schoolchildren. Still, in spite of itself, a frightening insight into the eradication of the Irish language through emigration, poverty and political failure. A funny deconstruction of the Sayers style is Flann O'Brien's *An Beál Bocht*; in English, *The Poor Mouth* (Paladin/Dalkey Archive).

William Butler Yeats, *Fairy and Folk Tales of Ireland* (Colin Smythe/Random House). Yeats gets all misty eyed about an Ireland that never existed.

FICTION

John Banville, *Birchwood* (Minerva/Norton, o/p); *The Newton Letter* (Minerva/Warner); *The Book of Evidence* (Mandarin/Warner); *Ghosts* (Mandarin/Random House); *Athena* (Minerva/ Random House). Five novels from the most important Irish novelist since McGahern, including his 1989 Booker Prize nomination, a sleazy tale of a weird Dublin murder.

Leland Bardwell, *The House* (Brandon Books, o/p/Longwood o/p); *There We Have Been* (Attic/InBook). Quirky, bleak prose, often dealing with domestic violence, male cruelty, drink and poverty; but funny too, in a black way.

Samuel Beckett, *Molloy/Malone Dies/The Unnamable* (Calder/Riverrun). A wonderful trilogy of breakdown and glum humour.

Brendan Behan, *Borstal Boy* (UK Arrow). Behan's gutsy *roman à clef* about his early life in the IRA and in jail.

Dermot Bolger, *The Journey Home* (Penguin). Dublin unforgettably imagined as both heaven and hell. *A Second Life* (Penguin) is an assured novel about a man who, miraculously given a second chance at life, sets out to find out the truth about his adoption.

Elizabeth Bowen, *The Death of the Heart* (Penguin). Finely tuned tale of the anguish of unrequited love; generally rated as the masterpiece of this obliquely stylish writer.

Clare Boylan, *Concerning Virgins* (Penguin, o/p). Thirteen short stories from an emerging star of contemporary fiction, her first book since the novel *Nail on the Head* (Hamish Hamilton, o/p/Viking, o/p).

Emma Donoghue, *Stir-fry* (Penguin/Warner). Well-wrought love story from young Irish lesbian writer.

Roddy Doyle, *Paddy Clarke Ha Ha Ha* (Minerva/Penguin). Hilarious and deeply moving novel of Dublin family strife that won the Booker Prize in 1993. The earlier trilogy, *The Commitments* (Minerva/Random House), *The Snapper* (Minerva/Penguin), *The Van* (Minerva/Penguin), lighter and funnier, made Doyle's reputation.

Maria Edgeworth, *Castle Rackrent* (Penguin/ Oxford University Press). Best of the "Big House" books, in which Edgeworth displays a subversively subtle sympathy with her peasant narrator. Would have shocked her fellow aristos if they'd been able to figure it out.

Anne Enright, *The Portable Virgin* (Minerva/ Butterworth-Heinemann). Highly original stories of life on the outside.

Hugo Hamilton, *The Love Test* (UK Faber). Irish-German novelist's thriller set on both sides of the Berlin Wall, before and after its fall, combines excitement with a tender portrait of a disintegrating marriage. *Dublin Where the Palm Trees Grow* (UK Faber) is a fine collection of stories set with equal assurance in Berlin and middle-class Dublin.

Dermot Healy, *A Goat's Song* (Flamingo/ Penguin). Dark and deep novel which convincingly weaves a study of obsessive love into a fresh view of the Northern conflict.

Aidan Higgins, *Asylum and Other Stories* (Calder/Riverrun, o/p); *Langrishe, Go Down* (Minerva/Riverrun, o/p); *Lions of the Grunewald* (UK Minerva). The most European of Irish writers, whose later works play with language in a mordantly humorous and deeply personal way.

Desmond Hogan, *The Ikon Maker* (Faber/ George Braziller, o/p). Impressive, impressionistic first novel from one of Ireland's most lyrical prose writers, about angst-ridden adolescence in the 1970s, before Ireland was hip. *A Farewell to Prague* (UK Faber) is an intense, episodic, autobiographical novel that wanders lonely through the new Europe.

Neil Jordan, *Night in Tunisia* (Vintage/ Random House). Film director Jordan first made his name with this impressive collection, which prefigures treatments and themes of his films. His most recent novel, *Sunrise with Sea Monster* (UK Vintage), is a delicate, powerful study in love and betrayal set in neutral Ireland during World War II.

James Joyce, *Dubliners* (Penguin); *Portrait of the Artist as a Young Man* (Penguin); *Ulysses* (Penguin/Random House); *Finnegan's Wake* (Faber/Penguin). No novel written in English this century can match the linguistic verve of *Ulysses*, Joyce's monumental evocation of 24 hours in the life of Dublin. From the time of its completion until shortly before his death – a period of sixteen years – he laboured at *Finnegan's Wake*, a dream-language recapitulation of the cycles of world history. Though indigestible as a whole, it contains passages of incomparable lyricism and wit – try the "Anna Livia Plurabelle" section, and you could be hooked.

Molly Keane, *Good Behaviour* (Abacus/Knopf, o/p). Highly successful comic reworking of the "Big House" novel.

Benedict Kiely, *God's Own Country: Selected Stories 1963–1993* (UK Minerva). A good introduction to the quirky fiction of a veteran novelist and travel writer.

Mary Lavin, *In a Café* (UK Country House). New collection of previously published stories by one of the great short-story writers, in the Chekhov tradition. Earlier books include *The House in the Clew* (Joseph, o/p/Viking, o/p) and *Stories* (Constable/Viking, o/p).

Bernard MacLaverty, *Cal* (Penguin/Norton); *Lamb* (UK Penguin). Both novels of love beset by crisis; the first deals with an unwilling IRA man and the widow of one of his victims. *Lamb* is the disturbing tale of a Christian Brother who absconds from a borstal with a young boy.

Eugene McCabe, *Death and Nightingales* (UK Minerva). Powerfully relevant novel of love, land and violence, set in late-nineteenth-century Ireland.

Patrick McCabe, *The Butcher Boy* (Picador/Doubleday); *The Dead School* (Pan/Dell). Scary, disturbing, but funny tales of Irish small-town life.

John McGahern, *The Dark* (Faber/Viking, o/p); *The Barracks* (UK Faber); *Amongst Women* (Faber/Penguin); *Collected Stories* (Faber/Random House). *The Barracks* is classic McGahern; stark, murderous and not a spare adjective in sight. *Amongst Women* is an excellent tale of an old Republican and the oppression of rural and family life.

Eoin McNamee, *Resurrection Man* (Picador/Warner). Beautifully written psychological thriller set in war-torn Belfast.

Deirdre Madden, *Hidden Symptoms* (Faber/Grove-Atlantic, o/p); *The Birds of the Innocent Wood* (Faber, o/p in the US); *Remembering Light and Stone* (Faber); and *Nothing is Black* (Faber). Evocatively grim novels of life in the North.

Aidan Mathews, *Lipstick on the Host* (Minerva/Harcourt Brace). Delicate stories of breathtaking skill.

Brian Moore, *The Lonely Passion of Judith Hearne* (Paladin/Little Brown). Moore's early novels are rooted in the landscape of his native Belfast; this was his first, a poignant tale of emotional blight and the possibilities of late redemption by love.

Mary Morrissy, *A Lazy Eye* (Vintage/Simon & Schuster); *Mother of Pearl* (Cape/Simon & Schuster). Impressive stories and a novel by rising star in the new generation of writers.

Christopher Nolan, *Under the Eye of the Clock* (Weidenfeld, o/p/St Martin's, o/p).

Extraordinary and explosive fiction debut; largely autobiographical story of a handicapped boy's celebration of the power of language.

Edna O'Brien, *Johnnie I Hardly Knew You* (Weidenfeld/Avon Books, o/p); *The Country Girls* (Penguin/NAL-Dutton). Sensitively wrought novels from a top-class writer sometimes accused, unjustly, of wavering too much towards Mills and Boon.

Flann O'Brien, *The Third Policeman* (Penguin/NAL-Dutton). O'Brien's masterpiece of the ominously absurd and fiendishly humorous. *At Swim-Two-Birds* (Penguin/NAL-Dutton) is a complicated and hilarious blend of Gaelic fable and surrealism; essential reading. Also see "Other Non-Fiction", p.623, under Myles na Gopaleen.

Frank O'Connor, *Guests of the Nation* (US Dufour). The best Irish political fiction this century.

Joseph O'Connor, *True Believers* (Flamingo/Trafalgar, o/p); *Cowboys and Indians* (Flamingo/Trafalgar, o/p). Life on the peripheries in London and Dublin: love and loss, madness and redemption; *Desperadoes* (Flamingo) is a love story stretching from 1950s' Dublin to modern Nicaragua.

Peadar O'Donnell, *Islanders* (Mercier/Dufour). Evocative, mesmerizing prose from important Republican figure.

Julia O'Faolain, *No Country for Young Men* (US Carroll & Graf). Spanning four generations, this ambitious novel traces the personal repercussions of the civil war.

Seán Ó Faoláin, *Bird Alone* (US Oxford University Press, o/p); *Collected Stories* (Constable/Little Brown). A master of the short-story form and the juiciness of rural dialect.

Liam O'Flaherty, *The Pedlar's Revenge and Other Stories* (Wolfhound/Dufour). Best of the postwar generation of former IRA men turned writers.

Glenn Patterson, *Burning Your Own* (UK Minerva). Distinctive young Northern writer gives Protestant child's-eye view of late 1960s' Northern Ireland just about to explode.

E.O. Somerville and (Violet) Martin Ross, *Some Recollections and Further Experiences of an Irish RM* (UK Dent). The needle pushes the begorra factor a little too heavily here and there, but Somerville and Ross write with witty flair and are very significant for what they reveal, accidentally, about a dying class.

James Stephens, *The Crock of Gold* (US Irish Books & Media); *The Charwoman's Daughter* (Gill & Macmillan, o/p/North Books). Two fabulous masterpieces from the country's most underrated genius.

Bram Stoker, *Dracula* (Penguin/Oxford University Press). Stoker woke up after a nightmare brought on by a hefty lobster supper, and proceeded to write his way into the nightmares of the twentieth century.

Francis Stuart, *Redemption* and *The Pillar of Cloud* (both New Island Books/Flat Iron, o/p); *Black List Section H* (Lilliput/Irish Book Centre, o/p). Once a protégé of Yeats, Stuart has consistently maintained a stance of opposition, in his life and his art. *Black List*, his masterpiece, depicts the life of an Irishman in wartime Germany.

Jonathan Swift, *Gulliver's Travels* (Penguin/Oxford University Press); *The Tale of a Tub and Other Stories* (Oxford University Press). Surrealism and satire from the only writer in the English language with as sharp a pen as Voltaire.

Colm Tóibín, *The South* (Picador/Viking, o/p). A woman turns her back on Ireland for Spain and returns thirty years later to resolve her life, and to die. *The Heather Blazing* (Picador/Penguin) is a powerfully understated novel of personal and political loss.

William Trevor, *Stories* (Penguin). Five of Trevor's short-story collections in one volume, revealing more about Ireland than many a turgid sociological thesis. Often desperately moving, Trevor is one of the true giants of Irish fiction. *Reading Turgenev* (Penguin), a sensitive account of an unhappy marriage, was shortlisted for the 1991 Booker Prize.

Oscar Wilde, *The Picture of Dorian Gray* (Penguin/Oxford University Press). Wilde's exploration of moral schizophrenia. A debauched socialite maintains his youthful good looks, while his portrait in the attic slowly disintegrates into a vision of evil.

POETRY

Eavan Boland, *The Journey* (Carcanet, o/p). Thoughtful, spare and elegant verse from one of Ireland's most significant poets.

Pat Boran, *The Unwound Clock* (UK Dedalus). Wry insightful poems of contemporary Irish life.

Austin Clarke, *Selected Poems* (Dolmen/Penguin). Clarke's tender work evokes the same stark grandeur as the paintings of Jack Yeats.

Denis Devlin, *Collected Poems* (US Wake Forest). Pre-eminent Irish poet of the 1930s, owing allegiance to a European modern tradition rather than the prevailing Yeatsian.

Paul Durcan, *A Snail in My Prime* (Harvill/Penguin); *O Westport in the Light of Asia Minor* (UK Harvill); *The Berlin Wall Café* (Harvill/Dufour). Ireland's most popular and readable poet. *Berlin Wall* is a lament for a broken marriage, recounted with agonizing honesty, dignity and, ultimately, forgiveness.

Padraic Fiacc, *Missa Terribilis* (Blackstaff, o/p). Fiacc's work is informed by the political and social tribalisms of Northern Ireland, and explores personal relationships in these contexts.

Seamus Heaney, *Death of a Naturalist* (Faber); *Selected Poems*, *Station Island* and *Seeing Things* (Faber/Farrar Straus & Giroux). The most important Irish poet since Yeats. His poems are immediate and passionate, even when dealing with intellectual problems and radical social divisions. *The Redress of Poetry* (Faber, o/p/Farrar, Straus & Giroux) is an example of his energetic prose, consisting of the lectures he gave while Professor of Poetry at Oxford from 1989 to 1994.

Patrick Kavanagh, *Collected Poems* (Martin Brien & O'Keefe/Flat Iron). Joyfully mystic exploration of the rural countryside and the lives of its inhabitants by Ireland's most popular poet. See also his autobiographical novel, *Tarry Flynn* (Penguin/Proscenium).

Brendan Kennelly, *Cromwell* (Bloodaxe/Dufour). Speculative meditation on the role of the conqueror in Irish history. *Poetry My Arse* (UK Bloodaxe) is an epic poem which "sinks its teeth into the pants of poetry itself".

Thomas Kinsella, *Poems: 1956–1973* (US Wake Forest). See also his translations from the Irish (see p.618, with Seán Ó Tuama) and his first-rate anthology *The Oxford Book of Irish Verse* (Oxford University Press).

Shane MacGowan, *Poguetry* (Faber, o/p in the UK). Rock-solid debut by the former Pogues' bardperson. Not for Yeats fans.

Louis MacNeice, *Collected Poems* (Faber). Good chum of Auden, Spender and the rest of the "1930s' generation", Carrickfergus-born MacNeice achieves a fruitier texture and an even more detached tone.

Derek Mahon, *Selected Poems* (Penguin); *The Hudson Letter* (Gallery/Wake Forest). One of the more considerable Irish poets, a Northern contemporary of Heaney. See also his Penguin (UK) *Book of Contemporary Irish Poetry* (ed. with Peter Fallon).

Medbh McGuckian, *Venus in the Rain* (UK Gallery). Trawling the subconscious for their imagery, McGuckian's sensuous and elusive poems are highly demanding and equally rewarding.

Paula Meehan, *The Man who was Marked by Winter* (Gallery/Paul & Co). Memorable work, often concerned with women's lives, issues of family, gender and sexuality.

John Montague, *Collected Poems* (Gallery/Wake Forest). Terse poetry concerned with history, community and social decay. See also his anthology, *The Faber Book of Irish Verse*.

Eileán Ní Chuilleanáin, *The Rose Geranium* (UK Gallery). A promising and constantly surprising young poet. Joint editor of *Cyphers*, a good Dublin literary magazine.

Nuala Ní Dhomhnaill, *Selected Poems* (UK New Island Books) is in Irish and English. Haunting translations of her modern erotic verse by the fine poet Michael Hartnett are included in *Raven Introductions 3* (UK Colin Smythe) and in Frank Ormsby's anthology (see below).

Frank Ormsby, (ed), *The Long Embrace: Twentieth Century Irish Love Poems* (Blackstaff, o/p/Faber, o/p). Excellent anthology with major chunks from the work of almost every important twentieth-century Irish poet from Yeats to the present day. See also his *Poets from the North of Ireland* anthology (Blackstaff/Dufour).

Tom Paulin, *Fivemiletown* and *The Strange Museum* (Faber, o/p in the US); *Walking a Line* (Faber). Often called "dry" both in praise and accusation, Paulin's work reverberates with thoughtful political commitment and a sophisticated irony.

Oscar Wilde, *The Ballad of Reading Gaol* (Dover). The great comedian achieves his greatest success, in tragedy.

William Butler Yeats, *The Poems* (Papermac/Cassel). They're all here, poems of rhapsody, love, revolution and eventual rage at a disconnected and failed Ireland "fumbling in the greasy till."

DRAMA

Samuel Beckett, *Complete Dramatic Works* (UK Faber); *Collected Shorter Plays* and *Waiting for Godot* (Faber/Grove-Atlantic). Bleak hilarity from the laureate of the void. All essential for swanning around Dublin coffee shops.

Brendan Behan, *The Complete Plays* (Eyre Methuen/Grove-Atlantic). Flashes of brilliance from a writer destroyed by alcoholism. His *The Quare Fellow* takes up where Wilde's *Ballad of Reading Gaol* leaves off.

George Farquhar, *The Recruiting Officer* (Oxford University Press). The usual helping of cross-dressing and mistaken identity, yet this goes beyond the implications of most restoration comedy, even flirting with feminism before finally marrying everyone off in the last scene.

Brian Friel, *Dancing at Lughnasa* (Faber). Family drama by Derry playwright examines the coexistence of Catholicism and paganism in Irish society, and the tension between them. *Plays* (UK Faber) contains six of his greatest works; also available is *Selected Plays* (US Catholic University of America Press).

Oliver Goldsmith, *She Stoops to Conquer* (Nick Hern Books/Norton). Sparky dialogue, with a more English sheen than Farquhar. Included in the same volume is Goldsmith's novel *The Vicar of Wakefield* (Penguin/Oxford University Press), an affecting celebration of simple virtue.

Augusta, Lady Gregory, *Collected Plays* (Colin Smythe/Dufour). The Anglo-Irish writer who understood most about the cadences of the Irish language. This gives not only her translations, but her original drama, an authenticity lacking in the work of others.

Frank McGuinness *Plays* (UK Faber). Observe the *Sons of Ulster Marching towards the Somme* and four other major works by one of Ireland's most important playwrights.

Tom Murphy, *Famine*, *The Patriot Game*, *The Blue Macushla* and *The Gigli Concert* (Methuen/Heineman). Along with Friel and McGuinness, Murphy is one of the three outstanding contemporary Irish playwrights.

Sean O'Casey, *Three Plays* (Pan/St Martin's). Contains his powerful Dublin trilogy, *Juno and the Paycock, Shadow of a Gunman* and *The Plough and the Stars*, set against the backdrop of the civil war.

John Millington Synge, *The Complete Plays* (Eyre Methuen/Random House). Lots of begorras and mavourneens and other dialogue kindly invented for the Irish peasantry by Synge; but *The Playboy of the Western World* is a brilliant and unique work, greeted in Dublin by riots, threats and moral outrage.

Oscar Wilde, *Complete Works* (HarperCollins). Bittersweet satire, subversive one-liners and profound existentialist philosophy all masquerading as well-made, drawing-room farce.

William Butler Yeats, *Collected Plays* (Papermac/Simon & Schuster). Long-haired hunky Celts and gorgeous princesses, as Yeats inaugurates the Finian's Rainbow school of Irish History. Stick to the poems.

OTHER NON-FICTION

A.M. Brady and Brian Cleeve, (eds), *Biographical Dictionary of Irish Writers* (Lilliput, o/p/St Martin's Press, o/p). Succinct entries on all the greats, better used as a magical mystery tour through the lost byways of Irish literature.

Seamus Deane, *Short History of Irish Literature* (Hutchinson, o/p/University of Notre Dame Press, o/p). Deane brings a poet's sensitivity to a massive and sometimes unwieldy tradition, with skill and a profound sense of sociopolitical context.

Katie Donovan & Brendan Kennelly, (eds) *Dublines* (Bloodaxe/Dufour). A lively anthology of Dublin writing – history, fiction, poetry and song – compiled by two poets of different generations.

Richard Ellmann, *James Joyce* (Oxford University Press); *Oscar Wilde* (Penguin/Random House). Ellman's *Joyce* is a major literary work in itself, a massive and brilliant book. His *Oscar Wilde* is at least its equal, an eloquent corrective to the image of Wilde as an intellectual mayfly.

Field Day Pamphlets, especially: **Seamus Deane**, *Heroic Styles: The Tradition of an Idea* (o/p); **Declan Kiberd**, *Anglo-Irish Attitudes* (o/p); **Michael Farrell**, *Apparatus of Repression in Ireland* (o/p); and **Seamus Heaney**, *An Open Letter* (o/p). Other pamphlets by Robert McCartney (a Northern Unionist lawyer), Tom Paulin and other leading lights of the Irish cultural scene. *The Field Day Anthology of Irish Writing* (Field Day/Norton; general editor Seamus Deane) is a book to visit rather than buy: running to more than 4000 pages (in three volumes), and covering everything from early Celtic literature to the present, it costs £150. This insanely ambitious project aims to examine the nature of Irish writing – emphatically not just literature: as well as plays, poems and novels, it includes political speeches, pamphlets, analyses and essays; a fine record of a primarily literary culture.

Myles na Gopaleen, (aka Flann O'Brien), *The Best of Myles* (UK Paladin). Priceless extracts from a daily humorous newspaper column by O'Brien's alter ego.

Michael Holroyd, *The Search for Love; The Pursuit of Power; The Lure of Fantasy, 1918–50* (Penguin/Random House). Holroyd's three-part biography of Shaw has been unfairly slammed by the critics, but is actually a pretty successful stab at understanding one of the most difficult and complex authors of the whole Anglo-Irish canon.

Joss Lynam, (ed.), *Best Irish Walks* (Moorland/NTC). Seventy-six walks through some of the most beautiful and remote parts of the country.

Brenda Maddox, *Nora: A Biography of Nora Joyce* (Minerva/Fawcett). Eminently readable story of the funny, irreverent and formidable Nora Barnacle and her life with James Joyce – an interesting complement to Ellmann's Joyce biography.

Sally and John McKenna, *Bridgestone Food Guide* (UK Estragon). The best in an almost non-existent field of Irish food writing. The same authors' smaller guides, to restaurants and places to stay, are also popular.

T. Augustine Martin, *Anglo-Irish Literature* (Irish Department of Foreign Affairs/Irish Books & Media, o/p). Readable scholarship and precise insight from the country's foremost Yeatsian scholar.

Joseph O'Connor, *The Secret World of the Irish Male* (Minerva/Heineman). Best-selling collection of the novelist's newspaper columns; frequently very funny.

Tim Robinson, *The Stones of Aran: Pilgrimage* (Penguin/Viking, o/p). Treats the largest of the Aran Islands to a scrutiny of Proustian detail. *The Stones of Aran: Labyrinth* (Lilliput/Viking, o/p) completes the project, to form a uniquely challenging travel book.

Colm Tóibín, *The Sign of the Cross: Travels in Catholic Europe* (Vintage/McKay). Novelist Tóibín uses his journalistic skills to find the old-time religion in Ireland and elsewhere. *Bad Blood* (UK Vintage) is a perceptive account of a journey along the line that divides Northern Ireland from the rest of the island.

Brendan Walsh, *Irish Cycling Guide* (Moorland/Irish Books & Media). This is a grand tour of the country, in 36 stages, taking the roads with least traffic.

John Waters, *Jiving at the Crossroads* (Blackstaff/Dufour). Curiously engaging autobiography which traces a fascination with Fianna Fáil politics through the formative years of a western youth in the 1970s and 1980s.

Robert Welch (ed.), *Oxford Companion to Irish Literature* (Oxford University Press). This encyclopedic tour through who's who and what they've written fills a long-standing need.

LANGUAGE

Irish is a Celtic language, evolved from a linguistic base of which ancient Gaulish is the sole written record.

The Celtic settlement of Ireland probably began in the seventh century BC; the later migration of Irish tribes to the Isle of Man and to Scotland established Irish-speaking kingdoms in those areas. With the rise of Rome the Celtic languages survived only in the peripheral western areas – today, Celtic languages are limited to parts of Scotland, Wales and Brittany in addition to Ireland. Cornish, another Celtic derivative, died out in the eighteenth century, and this century Manx ceased to be a community language. In Ireland a succession of invaders speaking Norse, French and English were assimilated into the population, with a resulting cross-fertilization of languages. The first Anglo-Norman aristocracy became thoroughly Gaelicized, and even as late as 1578, the Lord Chancellor could report that "all English, and most part with delight, even in Dublin, speak Irish and greatly are spotted in manners, habit and conditions with Irish stains".

This situation soon changed, however. The Tudor and Stuart wars, Cromwell's campaign, the Orange invasion and the subsequent penal laws resulted in the virtual elimination of the Irish aristocratic and learned classes and replaced them with English-speaking landowning middle classes.

Immediately after independence in 1921, Irish was installed as the first national language and steps were taken to revive it as a community tongue. It's now estimated that in the designated Irish-speaking (*Gaeltacht*) areas – in counties Donegal, Galway and north Mayo, and in counties Kerry, Cork and Waterford – there are around 66,000 speakers of the language, which is 77 percent of the *Gaeltacht* population. The use of Irish is widespread in Irish society, on public notices and documents, on television and radio, and in newspapers, books and magazines. Irish has been compulsory in Irish schools since independence, and until recently a qualification in Irish was required for university matriculation and for entrance to the civil service.

Yet figures show that only 30 percent of the population is competent in the language, and that the native speaker category is still declining, paralleling the population decline in the *Gaeltacht* areas. Only half of Irish children are introduced to the language before they attend school. The modernization of Irish society is accelerating the decline of the native tongue, which has become associated with an economic status lower than that implied by the use of the international English language. The new social structures being introduced to these are threatening the existence of the tightly knit family communities on which the survival of Irish as a living language depends.

PHRASEBOOKS AND PRIMERS

Teach Yourself Irish, Miles Dillon/Donncha Ó Cróinín (Hodder, o/p/NTC). Archaic teaching methods; student needs to be a saint; southern dialects favoured.

Learning Irish, Mícheál Ó Siadháil (Yale University Press). Modern guide to language through speaking. Cassettes available. Strong on grammar; Connacht dialect preferred.

AN IRISH GLOSSARY

BAWN A castle enclosure or castlefold.

BODHRÁN (pronounced *bore-run*) A hand-held, shallow, goatskin drum.

B-SPECIALS Auxiliary police force of the Stormont government; disbanded in 1971.

CASHEL A kind of rath (see below), distinguished by a circular outer stone wall instead of earthern ramparts.

CLOCHÁN A beehive-shaped, weather-proof hut built of tightly fitted stone without mortar. *Clocháns* date from the early Christian period.

"THE CRACK" Good conversation, a good time, often accompanying drinking. "What's the crack?" means "what's the gossip?"

CRANNÓG Celtic lake or swamp dating from the Bronze Age.

CURRACH/CURRAGH Small fishing vessel used off the west coast; traditionally made of leather stretched over a light wood frame, modern *currachs* are of tar-coated canvas.

THE DÁIL Lower house of the Irish parliament.

DOLMEN (or "portal tomb") A chamber formed by standing stones that support a massive capstone. The capstone often slopes to form the entrance of the chamber. Dates from the Copper Age (2000–1750 BC).

DRUMLIN Small, oval, hummocky hill formed from the detritus of a retreating glacier.

DUP Democratic Unionist Party. A Loyalist political party founded by Ian Paisley and Desmond Boal (Shankill MP) in 1971. The party appeals to the hard-line Loyalist section of the Protestant community, staunchly defends the Union with Britain, and is typified by intense hostility towards Catholicism.

ÉIRE Irish name for Ireland, but officially indicates the 26 counties.

FIANNA FÁIL The largest and most successful of Ireland's two main political parties since Independence. Essentially a conservative party, it has its origins in the Republican faction of Sinn Féin, and fought against pro-Treaty forces in the civil war. During the 1930s, the party did much to assert Ireland's separateness from Britain, and has always claimed a united Ireland.

FINE GAEL Ireland's second largest political party, Fine Gael sprang from the pro-Treaty faction of Sinn Féin which formed the first Free State government in 1921. Since that time it has not been able to gain a strong majority, and periods in office have been in coalitions – as at present with the Labour Party. It advocates more liberal policies than Fianna Fáil in terms of social welfare, but in fact there is very little to distinguish the two main parties.

FIR Men (sign on men's public toilets).

GALLERY GRAVE A simple burial chamber of squared stones, generally found under a long mound.

GARDAÍ The police force of the Republic of Ireland.

INLA Irish National Liberation Army. Extreme splinter group of the IRA.

IRA Irish Republican Army.

LOYALIST A person loyal to the British Crown, usually a Northern Irish Protestant.

MARTELLO TOWER Circular coastal tower used for defence.

MNÁ Women (sign on women's public toilets).

MOTTE A circular mound, flat on top, which the Normans used as a fortification.

NATIONALISTS Those who wish to see a united Ireland.

THE NORTH Term referring to Northern Ireland used by most people, except Loyalists.

OGHAM (rhyming with *poem*) The earliest form of writing used by the Irish (fourth to seventh centuries), and found on the edge of standing stones. Employing a twenty-character alphabet derived from Latin, the letters were represented by varying strokes and notches, and read from the bottom upwards.

ORANGE ORDER A Loyalist Protestant organization, found throughout Northern Ireland, which promotes the Union with Britain. The name comes from William of Orange ("King Billy"), the Protestant king who defeated the Catholic James II at the Battle of the Boyne (1690) and at the Battle of Aughrim (1691). Most Unionist MPs are Orangemen, and outside of Northern Ireland, Orange Lodges (branches) are found amongst Loyalist expats. Also see p.540.

OUP Official Unionist Party, the largest elected Protestant party.

PASSAGE GRAVE A megalithic tomb from the Neolithic period. A simple corridor of large, square, vertical stones lead to a burial chamber, and the whole tomb is covered with earth. The stones are decorated with simple patterns: double spirals, triangles, zigzag lines, and the sun symbol.

POTEEN/POITÍN (pronounced *potcheen*) Highly alcoholic (and often toxic) and illegal spirit distilled from potatoes.

RATH or RINGFORT A farmstead dating from the first millennium AD. A circular timber enclosure banked by earth and surrounded by a ditch formed the outer walls, within which roofed dwellings were built and, in times of danger, cattle were herded. Today raths are visible as circular earthworks.

REPUBLICAN An Irish Nationalist.

ROUND TOWER Narrow, tall (65–110ft) and circular tower, tapering to a conical roof. Built from the ninth century onwards, they are unique to Ireland. They are found on the sites of early monasteries, and served to call the monks to prayer. The entrance is usually a doorway 10–15ft above the ground, which was reached by a wooden or rope ladder that could be pulled up for safety.

RUC Royal Ulster Constabulary. Northern Ireland's regular, but armed, police force.

SDLP Social Democratic and Labour Party. A moderate Nationalist party in the North.

SOUTERRAIN Underground passage that served as a hiding place in times of danger; also used to store food and valuables.

TAOISEACH Irish prime minister.

TD *Teachta Dála*. Member of the Irish parliament.

TRICOLOUR The green, white and orange flag of the Republic.

THE TWENTY-SIX COUNTIES The Republic of Ireland (Éire).

UDA Ulster Defence Association. A legal Protestant paramilitary organization, the largest in Northern Ireland.

UDF Ulster Defence Force. Illegal paramilitary Protestant organization.

UDR Ulster Defence Regiment. A regular regiment of the British army recruited in Northern Ireland.

UFF Ulster Freedom Fighters. Another illegal Protestant paramilitary faction.

UNIONISTS Those (predominantly Protestant) who wish to keep Northern Ireland in union with the rest of the United Kingdom.

UVF Ulster Volunteer Force. Yet another illegal Protestant paramilitary organization.

INDEX

THANKS

Thanks to all the readers whose letters were an enormous help in the production of this fourth edition: Jim & Francie Bainbridge, Fineschi Antonio, Gwyn Williams, Angela Quinn, Tony Hegarty, Louise Mullen, Richard & Elizabeth Smith, John Dougill, Peter Pilsner, Linda Morgan, Cathleen Dore, Gavin Reeve, Melissa McHugh, Alison Houtheusen, Deidre Madden, Thomas Heneghan, Eleno Joriath, D.A. Elden, Clare D'Arcy, Peter Smith, Annelise Crean, C. McBride, Marcus Metz, Sean Fitzgerald, Conor McCabe, Steve Pearson, Karen Wellen, Barry Humphries, David Griffiths, Grace Meenan, Mrs W.J.R. McKay, Blair O'Connor, Ridolfo Michele, Heather Smith, Laura Coles, Michael Jeeves, G. Bennett, Dave Lee, William O'Toole, Michal Havlíl, Maurice Carroll, Mary Finucane, Frances Lambert, Mika Sam, Mrs P.S. Holt, Lucy Goulding, Hannah Brown, Julie Reed, Paul Crimes, Jonathan Dalton, Barbara Bisanti, Ruth & Malcolm Ridge, Jasmina Vanrintel, Mike & Kathryn Bieber, Charlotte Argyle, Mrs J. Kingston, Frank O'Dwyer, Frances Getz, Claus Dahl, Mark Real, Eva Woloshyn, Klaas Tjoelker, Victoria Lee, Bill Kerr, Janet Smith, Ian Paul, Phil Booth, Jason Hayes, Mary Mulvihill, Michael Thomas, Helen Rigby, Janet Mearns, Peter Ogunremi, Dr J.G. Manners, Maura Sheeran, Nancy Golding, Ms J. Stokes & Ms K. Milsom, Leilah Rawle, Maureen Birmingham.

HELP US UPDATE

We've endeavoured to make this guide as up-to-date as possible, but it's inevitable that some of the information will become inaccurate between now and the preparation of the next edition. Readers' updates and suggestions are very welcome – please mark letters "Rough Guide Ireland Update" and send to:

Rough Guides, 1 Mercer Street, London WC2H 9QJ
  or
Rough Guides, 375 Hudson Street, 9th Floor, New York NY10014
  or
Ireland@roughtravl.co.uk

direct orders from

Amsterdam	1-85828-086-9	£7.99	US$13.95	CAN$16.99
Andalucia	1-85828-094-X	8.99	14.95	18.99
Australia	1-85828-141-5	12.99	19.95	25.99
Bali	1-85828-134-2	8.99	14.95	19.99
Barcelona	1-85828-106-7	8.99	13.95	17.99
Berlin	1-85828-129-6	8.99	14.95	19.99
Brazil	1-85828-102-4	9.99	15.95	19.99
Britain	1-85828-126-1	8.99	14.95	19.99
Brittany & Normandy	1-85828-126-1	8.99	14.95	19.99
Bulgaria	1-85828-183-0	9.99	16.95	22.99
California	1-85828-090-7	9.99	14.95	19.99
Canada	1-85828-130-X	10.99	14.95	19.99
Corsica	1-85828-089-3	8.99	14.95	18.99
Costa Rica	1-85828-136-9	9.99	15.95	21.99
Crete	1-85828-132-6	8.99	14.95	18.99
Cyprus	1-85828-032-X	8.99	13.95	17.99
Czech & Slovak Republics	1-85828-121-0	9.99	16.95	22.99
Egypt	1-85828-075-3	10.99	17.95	21.99
Europe	1-85828-159-8	14.99	19.95	25.99
England	1-85828-160-1	10.99	17.95	23.99
First Time Europe	1-85828-210-1	7.99	9.95	12.99
Florida	1-85828-074-5	8.99	14.95	18.99
France	1-85828-124-5	10.99	16.95	21.99
Germany	1-85828-128-8	11.99	17.95	23.99
Goa	1-85828-156-3	8.99	14.95	19.99
Greece	1-85828-131-8	9.99	16.95	20.99
Greek Islands	1-85828-163-6	8.99	14.95	19.99
Guatemala	1-85828-045-1	9.99	14.95	19.99
Hawaii: Big Island	1-85828-158-X	8.99	12.95	16.99
Holland, Belgium & Luxembourg	1-85828-087-7	9.99	15.95	20.99
Hong Kong	1-85828-066-4	8.99	13.95	17.99
Hungary	1-85828-123-7	8.99	14.95	19.99
India	1-85828-104-0	13.99	22.95	28.99
Ireland	1-85828-095-8	9.99	16.95	20.99
Italy	1-85828-167-9	12.99	19.95	25.99
Kenya	1-85828-043-5	9.99	15.95	20.99
London	1-85828-117-2	8.99	12.95	16.99
Mallorca & Menorca	1-85828-165-2	8.99	14.95	19.99
Malaysia, Singapore & Brunei	1-85828-103-2	9.99	16.95	20.99
Mexico	1-85828-044-3	10.99	16.95	22.99
Morocco	1-85828-040-0	9.99	16.95	21.99
Moscow	1-85828-118-0	8.99	14.95	19.99
Nepal	1-85828-046-X	8.99	13.95	17.99

New York	1-85828-171-7	9.99	15.95	21.99
Pacific Northwest	1-85828-092-3	9.99	14.95	19.99
Paris	1-85828-125-3	7.99	13.95	16.99
Poland	1-85828-168-7	10.99	17.95	23.99
Portugal	1-85828-180-6	9.99	16.95	22.99
Prague	1-85828-122-9	8.99	14.95	19.99
Provence	1-85828-127-X	9.99	16.95	22.99
Pyrenees	1-85828-093-1	8.99	15.95	19.99
Romania	1-85828-097-4	9.99	15.95	21.99
San Francisco	1-85828-082-6	8.99	13.95	17.99
Scandinavia	1-85828-039-7	10.99	16.99	21.99
Scotland	1-85828-166-0	9.99	16.95	22.99
Sicily	1-85828-178-4	9.99	16.95	22.99
Singapore	1-85828-135-0	8.99	14.95	19.99
Spain	1-85828-081-8	9.99	16.95	20.99
St Petersburg	1-85828-133-4	8.99	14.95	19.99
Thailand	1-85828-140-7	10.99	17.95	24.99
Tunisia	1-85828-139-3	10.99	17.95	24.99
Turkey	1-85828-088-5	9.99	16.95	20.99
Tuscany & Umbria	1-85828-091-5	8.99	15.95	19.99
USA	1-85828-161-X	14.99	19.95	25.99
Venice	1-85828-170-9	8.99	14.95	19.99
Wales	1-85828-096-6	8.99	14.95	18.99
West Africa	1-85828-101-6	15.99	24.95	34.99
More Women Travel	1-85828-098-2	9.99	14.95	19.99
Zimbabwe & Botswana	1-85828-041-9	10.99	16.95	21.99

Phrasebooks

Czech	1-85828-148-2	3.50	5.00	7.00
French	1-85828-144-X	3.50	5.00	7.00
German	1-85828-146-6	3.50	5.00	7.00
Greek	1-85828-145-8	3.50	5.00	7.00
Italian	1-85828-143-1	3.50	5.00	7.00
Mexican	1-85828-176-8	3.50	5.00	7.00
Portuguese	1-85828-175-X	3.50	5.00	7.00
Polish	1-85828-174-1	3.50	5.00	7.00
Spanish	1-85828-147-4	3.50	5.00	7.00
Thai	1-85828-177-6	3.50	5.00	7.00
Turkish	1-85828-173-3	3.50	5.00	7.00
Vietnamese	1-85828-172-5	3.50	5.00	7.00

Reference

Classical Music	1-85828-113x	12.99	19.95	25.99
Internet	1-85828-198-9	5.00	8.00	10.00
World Music	1-85828-017-6	16.99	22.95	29.99
Jazz	1-85828-137-7	16.99	24.95	34.99

ROUGH GUIDE TO IRISH MUSIC
ON CD AND CASSETTE!

Irish Music is one of the strongest living musical traditions Europe and its popularity is increasing both at home and abroad. So wherever you are planning to visit in Ireland check out the perfect musical companion to your travels – the ROUGH GUIDE TO IRISH MUSIC

Compiled by the WORLD MUSIC NETWORK from top Irish record labels, and featuring leading artists in a striking mix of musical styles from modern Irish dance through to the traditional fiddle music of Galway, the ROUGH GUIDE TO IRISH MUSIC is a journey to the musical heart of Ireland

And it's over 60 minutes long and mid-price!

ALSO AVAILABLE:

ROUGH GUIDE TO WORLD MUSIC CD & CASSETTE
contains over 70 minutes of the music from around the world, culled from the top world music labels

ROUGH GUIDE TO SCOTTISH MUSIC CD & CASSETTE
is the ideal introduction to the music of Scotland featuring top artists including Capercaille, Wolfstone, Iron Horse, Tannahill Weavers, Dick Gaughan and many more

ABOUT THE WORLD MUSIC NETWORK

The world Music Network is an international information and direct sales network linking all those working in world music with you, the audience. It is free to join and you will be sent information on new and classic releases, live shows and details of special offers and competitions.
To join please fill in the form below, ticking the relevant box

Please send me:
- ☐ copy(ies) of the Rough Guide To Irish Music   ☐ CD (£9.99 each)   ☐ Cassette (£6.99 each)
- ☐ copy(ies) of the Rough Guide To Scottish Music   ☐ CD (£9.99 each)   ☐ Cassette (£6.99 each)
- ☐ copy(ies) of the Rough Guide To World Music   ☐ CD (£9.99 each)   ☐ Cassette (£6.99 each)

Prices include UK postage and packing. Overseas customers add £1.00 per CD or Cassette.

☐ Please debit my Visa/Access card number

Signature: .... expiry date: ....
Credit Card sales also available via phone: (0)171 486 6720 (UK) and fax: (0)171 486 6721 (UK)
or
I enclose payment for £..........
- ☐ UK cheque or postal order made payable to World Music Network
- ☐ International Money Order drawn in sterling (£) on a British Bank; payable to World Music Network

☐ I would like to join the World Music Network. Please send me future catalogues and live/media information, without obligation to purchase.

Name...
Address..
....
Country... Postal Code...

Please send your completed form to: **World Music Network, PO Box 3633, London NW1 6HQ**

PHOTOCOPY THIS PAGE IF YOU DO NOT WISH TO DAMAGE YOUR BOOK!

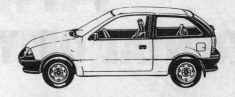